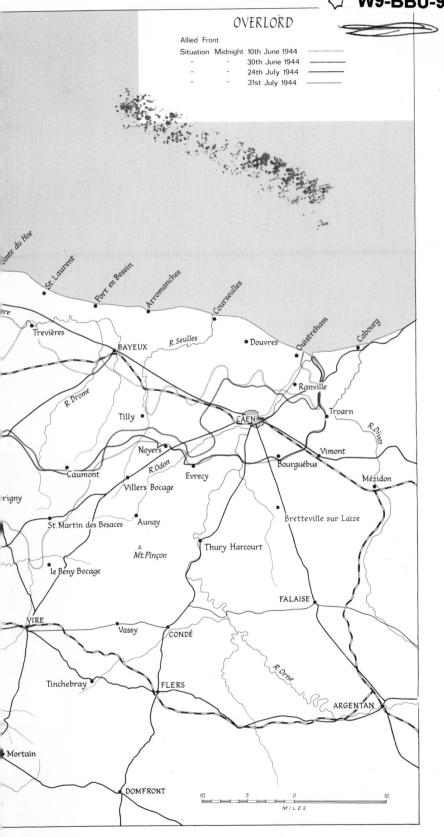

OVERLORD

Allied Front

Situation Midnight 10th June 1944
"   "   30th June 1944
"   "   24th July 1944
"   "   31st July 1944

Pointe du Hoe
St. Laurent
Port en Bessin
Arromanches
Courseulles
Trevières
BAYEUX
R.Seulles
Douvres
Ouistreham
Cabourg
R.Drome
Ranville
Tilly
CAEN
Troarn
R.Dives
Noyers
Vimont
Caumont
R.Odon
Evrecy
Bourguébus
Mézidon
Villers Bocage
rigny
St.Martin des Besaces
Aunay
Bretteville sur Laize
△
Mt.Pinçon
Thury Harcourt
le Beny Bocage
FALAISE
VIRE
Vassy
CONDÉ
R.Orne
Tinchebray
FLERS
ARGENTAN
Mortain
DOMFRONT

10   5   0   10
MILES

BRITISH INTELLIGENCE
IN THE SECOND
WORLD WAR

ITS INFLUENCE ON STRATEGY
AND OPERATIONS

VOLUME THREE
PART II

The authors of this, as of other official histories
of the Second World War, have been given free access
to official documents. They alone are responsible
for the statements made and the views expressed.

BRITISH INTELLIGENCE IN THE SECOND WORLD WAR

Its Influence on Strategy
and Operations

VOLUME THREE

PART II

by

F. H. HINSLEY
Master of St John's College and Emeritus
Professor of the History of International Relations
in the University of Cambridge

with

E. E. THOMAS
C. A. G. SIMKINS
C. F. G. RANSOM

CAMBRIDGE UNIVERSITY PRESS
NEW YORK

Burgess
D
810
.S7
H49

c.1

v.3,
pt.2

Printed in the United Kingdom for
Her Majesty's Stationery Office

Dd 239475 C80 12/87

Published in the USA by the
Syndicate of Cambridge University Press
32 East 57th Street, New York, NY10022, USA

ISBN 0 521 351960

CONTENTS

PART XIII:
OVERLORD

PART XIV:
THE LAND FRONTS IN THE
SECOND HALF OF 1944

PART XV:
THE OTHER FRONTS IN THE
SECOND HALF OF 1944

PART XVI:
THE DEFEAT OF GERMANY

APPENDICES

PREFACE

W E THINK it will be helpful if we repeat here the conditions under which we have worked as we stated them in the prefaces to all our previous volumes.

In carrying out our brief, which was to produce an account of the influence of British intelligence on strategy and operations during the Second World War, we have encountered two problems of presentation. The first was how to furnish the strategic and operational context without retelling the history of the war in all its detail; we trust we have arrived at a satisfactory solution to it. The second arose because different meanings are given to the term intelligence. The value and the justification of intelligence depend on the use that is made of its findings; and this has been our central concern. But its findings depend on the prior acquisition, interpretation and evaluation of information; and judgment about its influence on those who used it requires an understanding of these complex activities. We have tried to provide this understanding without being too much diverted by the problems and techniques associated with the provision of intelligence. Some readers will feel that we have strayed too far down the arid paths of organisation and methods. Others, to whom such subjects are fascinating in themselves, will wish that we had said more about them.

It is from no wish to disarm such criticisms that we venture to point to the novel and exceptional character of our work. No considered account of the relationship between intelligence and strategic and operational decisions has hitherto been possible, for no such account could be drawn up except by authors having unrestricted access to intelligence records as well as to other archives. In relation to the British records for the Second World War and the inter-war years, we have been granted this freedom as a special measure. No restriction has been placed on us while carrying out our research. On the contrary, in obtaining access to archives and in consulting members of the war-time intelligence community we have received full co-operation and prompt assistance from the Historical Section of the Cabinet Office and the appropriate government departments. Some members of the war-time community may feel that we might have made our consultation more extensive; we have confined it to points on which we needed to supplement or clarify the evidence of the surviving archives. As for the archives, we set out to see all; and if any have escaped our scrutiny we are satisfied that over-sight on our part is the sole explanation.

In preparing the results of our research for publication we have been governed by a ruling that calls for a brief explanation. On 12 January 1978, in a written reply to a parliamentary question, the Secretary of State for Foreign Affairs advised war-time intelligence staff on the limited extent to which they were absolved from their undertakings of reticence in the light of recent changes of policy with regard to the release of war-time records. He drew a distinction between the records of the Service intelligence directorates, which will be placed with other departmental archives in the Public Record Office, and 'other information, including details of the methods by which this material was obtained'. He explained that this other information 'remains subject to the undertakings and to the Official Secrets Act and may not be disclosed'. And he concluded with a reference to this History: 'if it is published, the principles governing the extent of permitted disclosure embodied in the guidance above will apply in relation to the Official History'. This statement has not prevented us from incorporating in the published History the results of our work on records which are not to be opened. The records in question are the domestic records of some of the intelligence-collecting bodies. We have been required to restrict our use of them only to the extent that secrecy about intelligence techniques and with respect to individuals remains essential.

The need to apply this restriction to the published History has at no point impeded our analysis of the state of intelligence and of its impact, and it has in no way affected our conclusions. It has, however, dictated the system that we have adopted when giving references to our sources. Government departments, inter-governmental bodies and operational commands – the recipients, assessors and users of intelligence – have presented no difficulty; to their intelligence files, as to their other records, we have always supplied precise references. This applies not only to documents already opened in the Public Record Office, and those to be opened after a stated period of extended closure, but also to individual files and papers which, though they may not be available for public research for a considerable time to come, nevertheless fall into categories of war-time records whose eventual opening in the Record Office may be expected. But it would have served no useful purpose to give precise references to the domestic files of the intelligence-collecting bodies, which are unlikely ever to be opened in the Public Record Office. We have been permitted – indeed encouraged – to make use of these files in our text and we have done so on a generous scale, but in their case our text must be accepted as being the only evidence of their contents that can be made public. This course may demand from our readers more trust than historians have the right to expect, but we believe they will agree that it is preferable to the alternative, which was to have incorporated no evidence for which we could not quote sources.

The above limitations have arisen from the need for security. We turn now to others which have been imposed on us by the scale on which we have worked. The first of these is that not merely when security has required it but throughout the book – in the many cases where security is no longer at stake and where readers may regret our reticence – we have cast our account in impersonal terms and refrained from naming individuals. We have done so because for our purposes it has generally sufficed to refer to the organisations to which individuals belonged; the exceptions are a few activities which were so specialised or were carried out by such small staffs, and thus became so closely associated with individuals, that it has been convenient sometimes to use names. In addition, however, we must admit to a feeling for the appropriateness of Flaubert's recipe for the perfect realistic novel: *pas de monstres, et pas de héros.* The performance of the war-time intelligence community, its shortcomings no less than its successes, rested not only on the activities of a large number of organisations but also, within each organisation, on the work of many individuals. To have identified all would have been impossible in a book of this canvas; to have given prominence to only a few would have been unjust to the many more who were equally deserving of mention.

As for the organisations, it has been impossible to deal at equal length with all. In some cases we have had to be content with a bare sketch because they kept or retained few records. With others we have dealt briefly because most of their work falls outside our subject. This applies to those responsible for counter-intelligence, security and the use of intelligence for deception purposes; like the intelligence activities of the enemy, we have investigated them in these volumes only to the extent that they contributed to what the British authorities knew about the enemy's conduct of the war. Lack of space has restricted what we have been able to say about intelligence in the field – about the work that was carried out, often in hazardous conditions, by Service intelligence officers with fighting units and by the people who were responsible in the field for signal intelligence, for reporting to the SIS and SOE, for examining enemy equipment and for undertaking photographic interpretation, POW examination and many similar tasks. As for the contribution of the many men and women who carried out essential routine work at establishments in the United Kingdom and overseas – who undertook the continuous manning of intercept stations or of cryptanalytic machinery, the maintenance of PR aircraft and their cameras, the preparation of target information for the RAF or of topographical information for all three Services, the monitoring of foreign newspapers, broadcasts and intercepted mail, and the endless indexing, typing, teleprinting, cyphering and transmitting of the intelligence output – only occasional references to it have been possible in an account which sets out to reconstruct the influence of intelligence on the major decisions, the chief operations and the general course of the war.

Even at this last level there are unavoidable omissions. The most important of these is that we have not attempted to cover the war in the Far East; when this was so much the concern of the United States, it is not possible to provide an adequate account on the basis of the British archives alone. A second derives from the fact that while the archives are generally adequate for reconstructing the influence of intelligence in Whitehall, there is practically no record of how and to what extent intelligence influenced the individual decisions of the operational commands. It has usually been possible to reconstruct what intelligence they had at their disposal at any time. What they made of it under operational conditions, and in circumstances in which it was inevitably incomplete, is on all but a few occasions a matter for surmise. And this is one matter which, after stating the facts to the best of our ability, we have left to the judgment of our readers and to the attention of those who will themselves wish to follow up our research by work in the voluminous records which are being made available to the public.

That room remains for further research is something that goes without saying. Even on issues and episodes for which we have set out to supply the fullest possible accounts, the public records will yield interpretations that differ from those we have offered. At the opposite extreme there are particular undertakings and individual operations to which we have not even referred. In our attempt to write a co-ordinated yet compact history we have necessarily proceeded not only with a broad brush but also with a selective hand, and we shall be content if we have provided an adequate framework and a reliable perspective for other historians as well as for the general reader.

□

In sending this final volume to press we wish once again to express our deep sense of gratitude to Miss Eve Streatfeild. As well as sharing in the research, she has from the beginning to the end of the project greatly lightened our load by carrying out the bulk of the administrative and editorial work with great skill and patience. We wish also to thank Mrs Joan Murray and Mr H J C Dryden CBE for the valuable assistance we have derived from their knowledge of the British effort against enemy cyphers, and Sir Michael Perrin CBE, FRSC for his assistance with the section on intelligence relating to German nuclear research.

ABBREVIATIONS

AAI	Allied Armies Italy
AAPIU	Army Air Photographic Interpretation Unit
ACAS(I)	Assistant Chief of Air Staff (Intelligence)
ACIU	Allied Central Interpretation Unit
ACV	Armoured Combat Vehicle
ADGB	Air Defence of Great Britain
ADI (K)	Assistant Director of Intelligence (Prisoners of War)
ADI (Ph)	Assistant Director of Intelligence (Photographic)
ADI (Sc)	Assistant Director of Intelligence (Science)

(at the Air Ministry)

AEAF	Allied Expeditionary Air Force
AFHQ	Allied Force Headquarters
AFV	Armoured Fighting Vehicle
AI	Air Intelligence (Branch of the Air Ministry)
ANCXF	Allied Naval Commander Expeditionary Force
APIS	Army Photographic Interpretation Section
ASI	Air Scientific Intelligence
ASV	Anti-Surface Vessel Radar
'C'	also CSS: Head of the Secret Service
CAS	Chief of the Air Staff
CCS	Combined Chiefs of Staff (Anglo-US)
CD	Coastal Defence
CIC	Combined Intelligence Committee (Anglo-US)
CIGS	Chief of the Imperial General Staff
CIS	Combined Intelligence Section (at GHQ Home Forces)
CIU	Central Interpretation Unit
CNS	Chief of Naval Staff (First Sea Lord)
COS	Chiefs of Staff (British)
COSSAC	Chief of Staff to the Supreme Commander (Designate)
CSDIC	Combined Services Detailed Interrogation Centre
CSS	Chief of the Secret Service, also 'C'
CSTC	Combined Strategic Targets Committee
DF	Direction Finding
DMI	Director of Military Intelligence
DMO	Director of Military Operations
DNI	Director of Naval Intelligence
DTA	Directorate of Tube Alloys
ETOUSA	European Theatre of Operations United States Army
FHO	Fremde Heere Ost
FHW	Fremde Heere West

OKH's intelligence branches

Flivos	Fliegerverbindungsoffiziere
FUSAG	Notional 1st US Army Group
GAF	German Air Force
GC and CS	Government Code and Cypher School
HDU	Home Defence Unit
ISTD	Inter-Services Topographical Department
JIC	Joint Intelligence Sub-Committee (of the COS)
JIS	Joint Intelligence Staff
JPRC	Joint Photographic Reconnaissance Committee (Anglo-US)
JPS	Joint Planning Staff (of the COS)
KdK	Kommando der Kleinkampfverbände
LCT	Landing Craft Tank
LST	Landing Ships Tank
MAAF	Mediterranean Allied Air Forces
MEW	Ministry of Economic Warfare
MI	Military Intelligence (Branch of the War Office)
MIRS	Military Intelligence Research Section (Anglo-American)
NIB	Noise Investigation Bureau
NID	Naval Intelligence Division
OIC	Operational Intelligence Centre (Admiralty)
OKH	Oberkommando des Heeres (High Command of the German Army)
OKL	Oberkommando der Luftwaffe (High Command of the GAF)
OKM	Oberkommando der Kriegsmarine (High Command of the German Navy)
OKW	Oberkommando der Wehrmacht (High Command of the German Armed Forces)
OSS	Office of Strategic Services (US)
PG	Panzer grenadier
PIU	Photographic Interpretation Unit
PR	Photographic Reconnaissance
PRU	Photographic Reconnaissance Unit
PWE	Political Warfare Executive
Pzkw	Panzerkampfwagen
RAE	Royal Aircraft Establishment
R/T	Radio Telephony

SACMED	Supreme Allied Commander Mediterranean
SCU	Special Communications Unit
SD	Sicherheitsdienst
SHAEF	Supreme Headquarters Allied Expeditionary Force
SIGINT	Signals Intelligence – the general term for the processes of interception, analysis and decryption and the intelligence they produced
SIS	Special or Secret Intelligence Service
SLU	Special Liaison Unit
SOE	Special Operations Executive
TA	Traffic Analysis – the study of wireless communication networks and procedure signals, call-signs, low-grade codes and plain language, together with DF (see above)
TAF	Tactical Air Force
TDS	Theatre Documents Section
TIC	Theatre Intelligence Section
TRE	Telecommunications Research Establishment
USSTAF	US Strategic Air Force
VCAS	Vice-Chief of the Air Staff
VCIGS	Vice-Chief of the Imperial General Staff
VCNS	Vice-Chief of the Naval Staff
VG	Volksgrenadier
W/T	Wireless Telegraphy
Y	The interception, analysis and decryption of wireless traffic in low and medium-grade codes and cyphers. The term 'low-grade' refers to the degree of security provided by a code or cypher and does not imply that the traffic in it was either unimportant or easy to break and interpret

LIST OF MAPS

PART XIII

Overlord

CHAPTER 43

The Initial Plan and its Revision
July 1943 – January 1944

A T THE Casablanca conference in January 1943 the western Allies accepted that a large-scale cross-Channel invasion would be impracticable before the spring of 1944 unless Germany showed signs of collapsing under the strain of strategic bombing and of reverses on the Russian and Mediterranean fronts. They provided for this eventuality, however, by agreeing to assemble the largest possible force in the United Kingdom for what was later to be called Operation *Rankin*, and they also ordered that the possibility of seizing a bridgehead by 1 August 1943, for later exploitation, should be examined. At the same time, they decided to appoint a Chief of Staff to the Supreme Allied Commander Designate (COSSAC) to be responsible with an independent US-British staff for 'the control, planning and training of cross-Channel operations'.[1]*

In the next few weeks the JIC expressed the view that, in the changed situation brought about by Germany's defeat at Stalingrad, the prospects of seizing a bridgehead, and even of carrying out Operation *Rankin*, might well become favourable in 1943. The JIC's view attracted support from the Joint Planners and led to discussions which were terminated only when the Chiefs of Staff ruled that a bridgehead operation in 1943 would be impracticable. The JIC rested its arguments on the calculation that in certain circumstances the number of German divisions in France, which had been estimated at 40 on the eve of the Casablanca conference,[2] might drop by July or August 1943 to 22, of which at most six would be first-class.[3] In the event, Sigint was to show that while the number of divisions in France did drop steeply after Stalingrad, the Germans had restored it to 42, including 21 good quality offensive divisions, by July 1943,[4] and that they were also delaying their summer offensive in Russia until they learned what

---

* See Volume II, pp 13, 115–116, Volume III Part 1, pp 3, 44–45.

1. Howard, *Grand Strategy*, Vol IV (1972), pp 245, 254, 272, 274–275.
2. WO 208/3573, MI 14 Weekly Intelligence Summary for the CIGS, 4 January 1943.
3. JIC(43)100(o) of 9 March, 171 of 28 April.
4. WO 208/3573 of 5 July 1943.

the Allies would do after the fall of Tunisia.[5]* For the Chiefs of Staff, however, the reliability or otherwise of the JIC's forecast was not the issue; the operation was impracticable for lack of Allied troops and assault craft.† By giving priority to the Battle of the Atlantic at the Casablanca conference, the Allies had held back the production of assault craft in favour of the building of anti-submarine vessels, and the struggle with the U-boats had reduced the planned transfer of US troops and equipment to the UK.[6]‡

Together with drafting difficulties, this episode delayed until the end of April 1943 the completion of COSSAC's directive from the Combined Chiefs of Staff. The directive omitted the requirement that he should examine the possibility of an operation to secure a bridgehead in 1943. Instead, the Combined Chiefs of Staff instructed him that his first commitment was to carry out in 1943 an amphibious feint, in order to bring on an air battle for the purpose of attrition, and to prepare 'an elaborate camouflage and deception scheme extending over the whole of the summer with a view to pinning the enemy in the West and keeping alive the expectation of large-scale cross-Channel operations in 1943'. His other tasks were to prepare for a return to the Continent at any time in the event of German disintegration with whatever forces were available, and to plan a full-scale assault against the Continent as early as possible in 1944.[7]

In carrying out the first of these assignments (code-named *Cockade*) COSSAC's staff co-operated with the deception authorities in London from the beginning of May. Making use of double agents, W/T deception and dummy invasion equipment to produce exaggerated German estimates of the strength of Allied forces in south-eastern England, they planned three operations. The first (*Starkey*) was a feigned attack with fourteen divisions to establish a bridgehead either side of Boulogne. After three weeks, when it might be assumed that all German reserves had been drawn in against it, *Starkey* was to be followed by the notional sailing of two US Army Corps against Brittany (Operation *Wadham*). The descent on Brittany was then to be called off and

---

* See below, p 9 et seq, for intelligence on the German Army's order of battle.
† See Volume III Part 1, p 3 et seq.
‡ The defeat of the U-boats from May 1943 released capacity which allowed the Allies to restore priority to these programmes, and also to embark on the construction of the Mulberry harbours; but not in time to prevent the shortages of assault shipping from generating fierce Anglo-American controversy about Allied strategy until the spring of 1944.

5. ibid, 14 June 1943.
6. Ellis, *Victory in the West*, Vol I (1962), pp 9, 28, 85; Ehrman, *Grand Strategy*, Vol V (1956), p 4.
7. CAB 106/969, *History of COSSAC 1943–1944*, pp 2–4.

replaced by the notional sailing of five divisions from Scotland against Stavanger (Operation *Tindall*). The plans for Operation *Starkey* involved an actual concentration of landing craft in south-east England; and the actual embarkation of troops and sailing of landing craft and other vessels to within ten miles of the French coast in the second week of September were preceded by small naval raids, RAF attacks against targets in and behind the bridgehead landing area, and (as was duly reported to Germany by the double agents) the suspension of coastal convoys and the imposition of security restrictions in East Anglia and Kent.[8]

Operation *Starkey* elicited little visible response from the Germans.[9] By 6 September the GAF Enigma had shown that they were undertaking precautionary measures including emergency minelaying in the *Starkey* area and later decrypts established that they had also carried out a special GAF reconnaissance and provided for the C-in-C West to obtain Abwehr reports about England direct from Madrid.[10] But by noon on 9 September, when they had sighted some of the *Starkey* forces, it had emerged from naval and air Enigma decrypts that while they were on special alert in view of the Italian capitulation, and because the weather was favourable for landings, they were not committing their forces until they had excluded the possibility of a large-scale ruse. The *Wadham* and *Tindall* deceptions, implemented on only a limited scale, produced even less enemy reaction.[11]*

No comfort could be drawn from this evidence by those who had thought it possible that Germany might disintegrate before the Allies were ready to carry out a full-scale invasion. Planning for this eventuality (Operation *Rankin*) proceeded alongside the *Cockade* measures from July 1943, when COSSAC was told that it was his most urgent task. The basic *Rankin* plan was drawn up in time to be approved by the Quebec conference in mid-August. It provided for action in three different contingencies, defined by the extent to which Germany could be seen to be disintegrating. In the first the Allies would be making a landing in France against continuing opposition; in the second, against crumbling resist-

---

* The German archives confirm that OKW was satisfied that the Allies had committed themselves to Mediterranean operations and was unimpressed by the deception. C-in-C West, however, regarded *Starkey* as a serious rehearsal.[12]

8. ibid, p 13 et seq; Howard, *Strategic Deception* (forthcoming), Chapter 5; CAB 44/242, *Operation 'Overlord'*, Chapter 1, p 27.
9. CAB 106/969, pp 20–21; Cruickshank, *Deception in World War II* (1979), pp 72, 219.
10. WO 208/4311, MI 14 Appreciation of 4 October 1943.
11. CAB 106/969, pp 20–21; Howard, *Strategic Deception*, Chapter 5.
12. Howard, *Strategic Deception*, Chapter 5.

ance, they would be seizing bridgeheads in France and Norway from which to complete Germany's military defeat; and in the third they would be occupying unopposed the Jutland peninsula and areas of north Germany in preparation for enforcing Germany's surrender and rehabilitating the liberated countries. It was recognised from the outset that action under the first of these contingencies could not be contemplated before January 1944 for lack of adequate Allied forces, but until the autumn of 1943 detailed planning went forward in the hope that at least the second contingency might materialise. In the summer COSSAC believed it 'possible that Germany would retire before the threat of invasion offered by *Cockade*', so that instead of turning back when they neared the French coast, as planned, the *Starkey* forces might be able to go forward with an actual landing, and in September the Chiefs of Staff instructed the JIC to alert COSSAC if intelligence indicated that conditions were becoming favourable for Operation *Rankin*.* By the end of 1943, however, COSSAC had accepted that '*Cockade* had failed to shake Germany' and that the 'likelihood of *Rankin* conditions developing in Europe prior to the implementation of *Overlord* was becoming more and more remote'. From January 1944, when the Combined Intelligence Committee on the instructions of the Combined Chiefs of Staff began to issue regular assessments of the prospects for *Rankin*,† COSSAC continued to update the plans drawn up for the second and third of the *Rankin* contingencies, but those which had been made for the first contingency, a landing against opposition, were merged with the preparations for Operation *Overlord*.[13]

Together with the *Rankin* plan, COSSAC's outline plan for *Overlord* was submitted to the Quebec conference in August 1943. At the Washington conference in the previous May the Combined Chiefs of Staff had already fixed the target date, 1 May 1944, and specified what troops and landing craft would be available; nine divisions for the assault phase and a further twenty divisions to be moved into the lodgement area. Working within these limits the outline plan concluded that the descent should be made in Normandy; and it proposed that the initial assault by three seaborne divisions and one airborne division should be made against the least heavily defended sector – the Caen sector between the rivers Dives and Vire – after comparing its advantages and disadvantages with those of the Pas de Calais and the Cotentin peninsula in the light of a mass of intelligence about the defences

---

* See Volume III Part 1, pp 44–45.
† ibid, p 45.

13. CAB 106/969, pp 22–27.

and the topography of the whole of the French coast and its hinterland.* But the chief feature of the plan was COSSAC's insistence that certain pre-conditions must be fulfilled if the operation was to have a reasonable chance of succeeding.

The first pre-condition was that the Allies should have greatly reduced the enemy's fighter strength, which was known to be on the increase.† Until they had done this it would be impossible to set a date for the assault; and it would thereafter be essential to prevent the arrival of air reinforcements from other theatres and to destroy the airfields and fighter control sites in the Caen sector and – in view of the importance of achieving tactical surprise – in other sectors also.[14] Tactical surprise was the second pre-requisite. Indeed, if the enemy, with prior knowledge of Allied plans, was able to move his ground, sea and air forces to the landing area there would be no chance of penetrating inland. There would thus be a special call for deception measures and the highest degree of security.[15] Even if the deception succeeded, however, the Germans would still have time to bring in some reserves. The crucial battle would be that with the Panzer divisions, and its outcome would depend on the extent to which the Allies could reduce and delay the arrival of reinforcements in the Caen area by air interdiction and by diversionary operations, perhaps in the south of France. It would also depend on the number and quality of the German divisions deployed in France and the Low Countries on D-day. And as these things could not be predicted twelve months in advance, the plan laid down a third pre-condition:

'On the target date, if the operation is to have a reasonable chance of success . . . , the German reserves in France and the Low Countries, excluding divisions holding the coast, and GAF and training divisions, should not exceed . . . twelve full-strength, first-quality divisions. In addition the Germans should not be able to transfer more than fifteen first-quality divisions from Russia or elsewhere during the first two months. Moreover, on the target date the divisions in reserve should be so located that the number the Germans could deploy in the Caen area to support the divisions holding the coast should not exceed three on D-day, five by D+2 or nine by D+9.'

It further specified that one of the three divisions on D-day could be armoured and that the two additional divisions by D+2 might be armoured or otherwise.[16] A further pre-condition was that 'the

---

* See below, p 11 et seq.
† See Volume III Part 1, pp 62, 294–295.

14. CAB 80/72, COS(43)416(o) of 30 July, pp v, vi, 8.
15. ibid, pp viii, 9, 14.
16. ibid, pp vi, viii, 8–9, 24–25.

state of the defences in the Caen sector and the strength of the defensive troops holding it should remain approximately as it is to-day'.[17]

It may seem remarkable that COSSAC should have presumed that, as the target date approached, the intelligence authorities would be able to establish whether or not such precise requirements as those applying to the German ground resistance were being met. To the Americans and the Russians, indeed, it was incredible; they suspected that the British were preparing the way for a demand that *Overlord* should be cancelled or deferred.* Nor can it be disputed that in the inter-Allied discussions the British produced arguments that may have seemed to give colour to this suspicion. But these arguments did not question the ability of the intelligence authorities to discern whether or not COSSAC's conditions were being met; they accepted it and did so with justification as we shall see. What they questioned was whether COSSAC's conditions would be fulfilled unless certain steps were taken – a very different thing.

On 3 August the Joint Planners advised the Chiefs of Staff that COSSAC had over-estimated the extent of the land opposition the assault forces could accept; even if his pre-conditions were fulfilled, the assault would have a very narrow margin of superiority, and it was 'not to be contemplated' if, by failure to solve the beach maintenance problems, the margin could not be guaranteed. On 4 August the Chiefs of Staff shared this anxiety and agreed with the Joint Planners that, as interdiction bombing was unlikely to be effective in reducing the scale of the opposition

---

* COSSAC's US deputy had to reassure Washington that the purpose in laying down precise figures for the number of German divisions was not to establish that the operation should be cancelled if the number was exceeded, but only to emphasise that in that case everything must be done to limit the excess by air interdiction and other means.[18] In October 1943 Voroshilov asked Mr Eden in Moscow what would happen if the Germans had 13 or 14 first-class divisions in France, rather than 12, and brought in 16 or 17 from Russia, rather than 15; and he also enquired how the British could expect to estimate in advance the number the Germans would bring in from other fronts. To the first question Mr Eden replied that the numbers were a rough guide – a division here or there would be of no consequence. To the second he replied that 'we are constantly and accurately informed of the whereabouts of all German first-quality divisions'; he added that the Germans were unlikely to exceed the number specified by COSSAC if they were fully stretched in Russia and Italy and that Allied bombing would disrupt the German communications.[19] At the Tehran conference in November 1943 Stalin returned to these questions and the Prime Minister again emphasised the importance of the conditions for success laid down by COSSAC.[20]

17. ibid, p 8.
18. Harrison, *Cross-Channel Attack* (Washington 1951), p 77.
19. CAB 121/390, SIC file D/France/6/11, Secretary of State to Prime Minister, 29 October 1943.
20. Ehrman, op cit, Vol V, p 57 (n); Churchill, *The Second World War*, Vol V (1953), p 328.

in the early stages, they must press for its reduction by diversionary measures – more pressure in Italy; a landing in the south of France – as well as for an increase in the forces allotted to *Overlord*.[21] At the Quebec conference the Prime Minister argued both for a greater Allied effort in Italy and for an increase in the forces allocated to the assault phase of *Overlord*, and did so in the knowledge that either of these courses would require postponement of the invasion; he also argued that plans should be prepared for a landing in Norway in case the decision to launch *Overlord* had later to be reconsidered.[22] He returned to this argument in a cable to the President in October when, worried lest 'by landing in north-west Europe we might be giving the enemy the opportunity to inflict on us a military disaster greater than that of Dunkirk', Whitehall was re-examining the relation of the Mediterranean theatre to *Overlord*. 'All this', he told the President, 'shows the need for the greatest care and foresight in our arrangements, the most accurate timing between the two theatres, and the need to gather the greatest possible forces for both operations, particularly *Overlord*'.[23] But this message went on to say that 'I do not doubt our ability in the conditions laid down to get ashore and deploy'; and in this statement he was repeating what he had said at Quebec. He had there subjected his approval of the outline plan to the fulfilment of COSSAC's pre-conditions, and had made it plain that the decision to launch the operation would have to be reviewed only 'if it developed that the German ground and air fighter strength proved to be greater than that on which the success of the plan had been premissed.'[24]

It has been suggested that the Anglo-American controversy about the *Overlord* plan which set in at the Quebec conference reflected conflict between the American preference for 'a settled plan' and the British 'dependence on opportunity', and that this difference of outlook was intensified by the fact that the Americans had had 'no equivalent' of the experience the British had derived over two years from 'complete information on the European war'.[25] However that may be, the conference was informed that the number of German divisions in France had risen to 44 and that Germany's fighter output was still rising,[26] and

---

21. CAB 121/390, JP(43)290 of 3 August, COS(43)180th (o) Meeting, 4 August.
22. Howard, *Grand Strategy*, Vol IV, pp 567, 571; Ellis, op cit, Vol I, pp 17, 19; Harrison, op cit, pp 91–98.
23. CAB 121/128, SIC file A/Policy/ME/3, COS(43)639(o) of 19 October, COS(43)254th (o) Meeting, 19 October; Churchill, op cit, Vol V, p 278.
24. Howard, op cit, Vol IV, p 571.
25. Harrison, op cit, pp 90, 95.
26. CAB 121/413, SIC file D/Germany/1 Vol II, CCS/300/1 of 7 August 1943.

it is not unreasonable to suppose that it was on this account that the Americans made some concession to the British view. They rejected any increase in the size of the force allocated to *Overlord* and any postponement of the target date, but the outline plan was approved on the understanding that the case for a diversionary landing in the south of France would be examined and that some limited flexibility in the allocation of forces between *Overlord* and the Mediterranean might be justifiable.*

At the end of November 1943, at the Cairo conference, the British argued that a diversionary landing in the south of France (*Anvil*) should be cancelled in favour of a more vigorous prosecution of the Italian campaign and action in the eastern Mediterranean. The Americans were disposed to agree until the discussions with the Russians at Tehran persuaded both of the western Allies that *Overlord* and *Anvil* must be carried out in May 1944 and that 'nothing must be undertaken in any other part of the world which hazards the success of these two operations'. The planning for *Overlord* and the Anglo-American debate about the relation of *Overlord* to operations in the Mediterranean thereupon entered a new stage. Early in December the Combined Chiefs of Staff agreed to do everything practicable to increase the strength of *Overlord*, to consider providing additional resources for *Anvil* should they be called for, and to make every effort to provide essential additional landing craft for the European theatre.† Later in December AFHQ requested that the *Anvil* force, earlier set at two divisions, should be raised to three divisions. And in January 1944, when General Eisenhower arrived at SHAEF to take up the post of Supreme Allied Commander, he recommended that the *Overlord* seaborne assault should be increased from three to five divisions and its front widened, and that the operation should be postponed.‡

□

The outline plan for *Overlord* which was now to be revised had inaugurated the 'purposeful' stage of planning for a cross-Channel invasion. A comprehensive plan for Operation *Roundup*§ had been completed as long ago as December 1941. During the first half of 1942 Operation *Sledgehammer* and other alternatives to *Roundup* had been actively discussed until they were abandoned in favour of the decision to carry out Operation *Torch* and the raid on

---

* See Volume III Part 1, pp 10–11.

† See Volume III Part 1, pp 16–18.   ‡ See Volume III Part 1, p 24.

§ *Roundup* was the plan for a cross-Channel invasion in 1943, *Sledgehammer* the plan to take advantage of a possible decline in German strength to make a quick return to the Continent in 1942. See Volume II, pp 13, 89.

Dieppe.* A revised *Roundup* plan had been completed in September 1942. Between November 1942 and April 1943 the Combined Commanders Group had undertaken two further studies, the second of which culminated in a plan for a large-scale invasion operation code-named *Skyscraper*.[27] None of these earlier plans had been related to a target date or to the availability of forces or to the actual strategic situation. But if they were hypothetical, they had been based on progressively more exhaustive intelligence about the topography and the defences of the entire French coast; and it was thanks to this that COSSAC, who took them over in a file 'some inches thick',[28] was able to complete the task of converting them into a definite project as soon as the end of July 1943.

The need for a specialised organisation to be responsible for collecting and collating this intelligence, and for disseminating it to planners and commands, had been recognised at an early stage in the planning for Operation *Roundup*. By October 1941 the staff of GS Int GHQ Home Forces, which had been studying the French coast throughout the period of the German invasion threat, was moved to Norfolk House and given responsibility for intelligence on this subject in the area up to 30 miles inland between Den Helder and the Loire, in connection with Allied cross-Channel invasion plans. The new body collected its information from all sources on defences and installations of potential military usefulness, but depended on the Service intelligence branches for intelligence on enemy armed forces and on the ISTD for topographical intelligence. Early in 1942, by which time it had been joined by the NID staff which worked on the fortifications of the Channel coast, it had been renamed the Combined Intelligence Section (CIS) of GHQ Home Forces. In the summer of 1942 some of CIS's staff had been temporarily diverted to assist in the planning of Operation *Torch* under AFHQ. But its responsibility for collating and disseminating the intelligence required for the planning of cross-Channel operations had remained unaffected, as it did when COSSAC began to set up a staff of his own in Norfolk House early in 1943.[29]†

---

* See Volume II, pp 100–102.

† See Volume II, pp 12–13 and, for the subsequent relations of the CIS to COSSAC and SHAEF, Appendix 1.

27. CAB 44/242, pp 7, 8, 15; Butler, *Grand Strategy*, Vol III Part 2 (1964), pp 619, 626, 629–630, 633.

28. CAB 106/969, p 2.

29. Mockler-Ferryman, *Military Intelligence Organisation*, pp 9, 125, 135; C Morgan, *NID History 1939–1942*, pp 54–55, 60; ADM 223/287, Gonin report on *Overlord* and 'The Part played by NID in Operation *Neptune*'; Harrison, op cit, pp 49–50.

The scope and quality of CIS's work is clear in the weekly *Martian* reports in which, in a form which facilitated rapid dissemination and easy updating, it issued its intelligence from the spring of 1942 without interruption to June 1944.* Its value to the planners may be judged from the following summary of the *Skyscraper* plan drawn up by the Combined Commanders Group on the basis of intelligence provided mainly by the CIS:†

'Their planners had summarised among other things an exhaustive collection of information on the nature of the whole seaboard from Holland to the Bay of Biscay. In this they had examined the respective advantages and demerits of every beach on which a landing might be made, of every port which might be captured and every locality from which operations could then be developed. In each case they took into account the sea approaches, the prevailing winds and tides; the nature of the beaches, their exits, hinterlands and possible inundations; the prospect of an early seizure of one or more major ports; the availability of airfields or land suitable for their early construction; the volume of fighter protection that could be afforded from British airfields in the opening phase; the enemy's coastal and beach defences, and the strength of the troops holding them; the location of enemy naval forces and minefields; the nature and strength of the naval support required; and finally, the capacity of the assault area for a build-up of forces to compete with the enemy's reserves. Taking all these into consideration the Combined Commanders agreed that the most favourable place for a large-scale landing was the Caen sector of Normandy provided that the eastern beaches of the Cotentin peninsula were included in the assault area so as to facilitate the early capture of Cherbourg. They regarded this condition as essential.'[30]

Using the same exhaustive intelligence for his outline plan, COSSAC agreed with the Combined Commanders in selecting the Caen-Cotentin area in preference to all others within the range of Allied fighters, including the Pas de Calais. The Pas de Calais had the strategic advantage of being nearest to Germany and so placed that a successful Allied advance from there would outflank all enemy forces to the south; it also had considerable tactical advantages. It was indeed for these reasons that the Germans from the outset regarded it as the most threatened part of the coast. But COSSAC found that the beach exits there would limit

---

* See Appendix 2.

† Some of the information was provided by other sources. For example, information about the winds and tides was provided by the Service meteorological branches and the Hydrographer of the Navy; intelligence about airfields and airfield sites came from the Air Intelligence Branch; port capacities were calculated by the Transportation Branch of the War Office from port data provided by intelligence. But most of the information came from the CIS.

30.   Ellis, op cit, Vol I, p 15.

the initial assault to two divisions; that the beaches were not sheltered from prevailing wind; that the terrain in the hinterland was unsuitable for the build-up of a large follow-up force; that the coastal defences, more formidable than those of any other sector of the French coast, would have to be reduced by protracted preliminary bombardment by air and sea, which would alert the enemy; and that in view of its communications inland, and their relation to enemy dispositions, it was the area most favourable for counter-attacks by the German Army and Air Force.[31] On logistic grounds, moreover, as well as in the light of topography and of what was known about Germany's defences, it had serious disadvantages. The nearest major ports, Antwerp and Le Havre, were too far away from the United Kingdom and difficult of approach, while the embarkation ports in the Dover area were inadequate for the assembly of the necessary Allied shipping.[32] The Allies would avoid these disadvantages by striking in the Caen-Cotentin area, where the beaches were much more favourable for landing men and equipment and were the least heavily defended part of the French coast. In that area, however, the outline plan set aside the proviso laid down by the Combined Commanders and recommended that the assault should be concentrated against the Caen sector, rather than being distributed between the Caen sector and the Cotentin beaches.[33]

This recommendation was prompted only in part by the limit that had been placed on the size of the assault force; the plan recognised that the capacity of the Caen beaches and their exits was in any case sufficient only for a three-division assault. More important, a minute re-examination of the intelligence about the topography and defences of the Caen-Cotentin area led to the conclusion that a single landing was better than two and that the Caen sector was preferable to the Cotentin beaches; the defences were less heavy and the topography more favourable to the Allies for a variety of tactical reasons. It was noted, moreover, that the Germans had fixed the boundary between their two armies in northern France, Seventh and Fifteenth Armies, along the river Dives just east of Caen. COSSAC's recommendation made it essential that the Allies should seize Caen – the important bottleneck for communications – on D-day[34] and even then it carried the disadvantage that the Allies would take longer to capture the major port of Cherbourg. But he judged that the

---

31. CAB 80/72, COS(43)416(o) of 30 July, Appendix C; Ehrman, op cit, Vol V, pp 54–55; F Morgan, *Overture to Overlord* (1950), pp 138–139.
32. CAB 106/969, p 27; Ellis, op cit, Vol I, pp 15–16.
33. CAB 80/72, COS(43)416(o) of 30 July, Appendices, B, D, R and V.
34. ibid, p 21.

above considerations more than off-set these drawbacks.

At the same time the outline plan emphasised that the Germans would probably appreciate that, before the landings could be consolidated by the capture of Cherbourg or Le Havre, the Allied forces would have to undertake a hazardous flank march during which they could be destroyed by the Panzer reserves.[35] Together with the consideration that the longer the delay in capturing and restoring a port, the greater the difficulty of maintaining the invasion forces across the beaches, it was this threat that chiefly made the British authorities anxious about the viability of the plan before the Quebec conference. It was on the same account that, the Americans having vetoed any increase of the *Overlord* forces, the approval of the outline plan at the Quebec conference was followed by months in which British representations – and Anglo-American differences – were focused on the scale on which Allied effort should be devoted to diversionary operations.*

By the autumn of 1943, however, as preparations for *Overlord* entered a new stage with the appointment of C-in-C 21st Army Group, who was to command all the Allied land forces until a bridgehead was consolidated, the Allied Naval Commander of the Expeditionary Force (ANCXF) and C-in-C Allied Expeditionary Air Force to be jointly responsible for detailed force-planning for the invasion, it was coming to be accepted that diversionary operations, however ambitious, would not meet the fundamental difficulties. These were being emphasised by the fact that intelligence pointed to a continual intensification of the enemy's fixed defences and to an apparent determination on his part to raise the number of his divisions in France well above the limits specified by COSSAC.

It was chiefly on account of these developments that the Combined Chiefs of Staff resolved in December to do all in their power to increase the strength of *Overlord* and that, in January 1944, it was finally accepted that the outline plan must be revised.

□

Germany began to give serious attention to her western defences in March 1942. Hitler appointed von Rundstedt C-in-C West to command in France at the beginning of that month, and at the end of the month, in Führer Directive No 40, he placed Rundstedt and the Commander in Denmark under OKW, leaving OKH to supervise the eastern front. In Directive No 40 Hitler also

---

* See above, pp 9–10, and below, p 316 ff.

35. ibid, Appendix R, para 12.

laid down the tactical doctrine that was to govern planning for the defence of the European coastline for more than a year. It was to be expected that the Allies would attempt small raids as well as larger-scale landings, and make them with other than strictly military objectives; they might therefore sometimes achieve surprise. But any penetration was to be immediately sealed off and if possible the Allies were to be defeated before consolidating ashore. In the defence programme priority was thus to be given to fortifying the areas most likely to be attacked, with special attention to preventing the landing of tanks on open beaches. At the same time, strongpoints were to be developed which could hold out to the last if the Allies got ashore.[36]

Until July 1942 the Germans ruled out the risk of a serious invasion in the belief that the Allies lacked the necessary shipping space. On 9 July, however, Hitler concluded that landings were likely to be made in the near future in an attempt to stave off the defeat of Russia, and decided to send two SS divisions to the west immediately.* His judgment seemed to be vindicated by the raid on Dieppe on 19 August, regarded by the Germans as a first attempt to establish a bridgehead, and by two deception operations (Operation *Solo* against Norway and Operation *Overthrow* in the Channel), carried out in October with a view to diverting Germany's attention from Operation *Torch*. In September, reflecting that however serious the threat to Norway might be, the Allies would have to attempt to invade France, Hitler elaborated and accelerated the programme for an Atlantic wall; the threat from naval and air bombardment must be countered by casemating all important defence works in concrete to create 'an impervious defence ring' comprising 15,000 strongpoints, manned by 300,000 men, which must be completed by May 1943.[37] On 5 October Hitler brought the defences of the whole of the French coast to a state of readiness, designating Cherbourg as the most threatened area. On 12 October C-in-C West's staff expected attacks at any time in different places, most probably in Normandy and on the north coast of Brittany.[38]

From high-grade Sigint the Allies received no news of Directive No 40, and little intelligence about the effect on the German defence preparations of the subsequent alarms. In the spring of

---

* These were the Leibstandarte Adolf Hitler and Das Reich, both motorised divisions (see Volume II, pp 700–701).

36. Butler, op cit, Vol III Part 2, p 643; Harrison, op cit, pp 132 et seq, 459–463.
37. Harrison, op cit, p 137.
38. Howard, *Strategic Deception*, Chapter 4; Butler, op cit, Vol III Part 2, p 643.

1942 they had several indications from Enigma that the Germans were nervous about attacks on Norway and Denmark. In April, and again in June, Japanese diplomatic decrypts informed them that Ribbentrop had told the Japanese Ambassador that the Allies were making extensive preparations to establish a second front. By the end of April they had learned of von Rundstedt's appointment, which MI 14 took to be a sign of German 'disquiet'.[39] From such signs they could conclude nothing beyond the fact that the enemy was at last beginning to give serious attention to his western defences. But they were able to watch the general development of the German defences with the aid of other sources – PR and photographic interpretation, which provided 80 per cent of the information on the subject, and SIS agents and refugees, who supplied increasingly valuable reports.[40]

In March 1943 MI 14 summarised what had been disclosed by these sources up to the time of the drafting of the *Overlord* outline plan. There had been no defensive works, as distinct from such offensive developments as the batteries at Cap Gris Nez, before April 1941. In April 1941 the first signs of defensive activity, involving beach wire and pill boxes, had been detected on the more vulnerable beaches in the vicinity of ports; none of it was formidable and it was clearly directed against the danger of small raids. Between then and October 1941 the Germans had made rapid progress with the construction of elaborate concrete defences between the Hook of Holland and Cherbourg and on the Channel Islands. From May 1942 the system had been re-organised around a limited number of strongpoints; incorporating elaborate concrete shelters for personnel and weapons and providing all-round defences, these had been started following a tour of inspection by von Rundstedt and their construction was pushed on with great speed. Artificial anti-tank obstacles had been detected for the first time in June 1942; and from August 1942, following the Dieppe raid, the Germans had begun to thicken the defences in some areas, erecting anti-tank obstacles at beach exits, laying minefields on land, preparing for port demolition and burying cables for radar warning, gun control and other communications. From January 1943 the area affected by these preparations had been steadily extended. The thickening of anti-tank defences was especially marked from the Pas de Calais to Den Helder; but the construction of a limited number of formidable strongpoints elsewhere was also being pushed forward with the greatest possible speed, and every port from Holland to

---

39. WO 208/3573 of 20 April 1942.
40. F Morgan, op cit, p 86; AIR 41/7, *Photographic Reconnaissance*, Vol II, pp 141–142.

Spain was already heavily protected by artillery of all calibres.[41]*

At the end of March, in a comprehensive survey of every type of defence work yet observed, the CIS gave prominence to the spread of beach and land minefields, which had recently become less difficult to detect as a result of improvements in the technique of vertical PR.[42] This apart, no new development in the form or method of the enemy's defences had been detected by June 1943, though MI 14 then noted that the strengthening of the fortifications was proceeding at a 'hectic' pace, and an Enigma decrypt mentioned that Hitler had ordered the inspection of all anti-tank defences by a special staff.[43] In the autumn, however, agents' reports prompted a re-examination of photographs of a part of the east coast of the Cotentin peninsula, which now disclosed a line of metal tripods, three to four feet high, a short distance below the water line. Careful PR detected no underwater obstacles in other areas until February 1944, but it was then discovered that they were being strewn thickly along the beaches of Belgium and northern France in such a way as to obstruct tanks and landing craft. Meanwhile, the resort to other new defence measures had been detected since the autumn. Over and above the preparations the Germans were making for the demolition of ports and quays, they had begun to install flame-throwers, to casemate coastal batteries and other gun positions with six feet of reinforced concrete, to prepare inundations and to construct a second defence line several miles inland. At the beginning of December 1943 all this work was proceeding rapidly except in relation to the inland defence line.[44] Evidence for this line was found only in Holland, but an anxious watch for its extension to Normandy was kept without result; we now know that its extension was planned, but that lack of resources delayed its progress and that Rommel cancelled it in April 1944.[45]

On the remainder of the German programme a great deal of confirmatory and additional intelligence was obtained before the end of 1943. It came from documents captured in Italy from

---

* MI 14 noted that the greater part of the artillery on the coast was non-divisional; its density did not fluctuate with the coming and going of divisions. This was correct. The coastal defence (CD) batteries were manned by GHQ troops and were supplemented by naval batteries.

41. WO 208/4308, MI 14 Appreciation of 8 March 1943, Appendix on 'Defences of the French Coast'.
42. WO 219/1936, Martian Report No 40 of 27 March 1943.
43. WO 208/4309, MI 14 Appreciation of 6 June 1943; Dir/C Archive, 3627 of 22 June, CX/MSS/2774/T3.
44. WO 219/1937, Martian Reports Nos 74 and 75 of 1 and 21 December 1943; AIR 41/7, p 144; Harrison, op cit, p 177.
45. Harrison, op cit, pp 156, 163.

divisions recently transferred from France;[46] from plans of the Atlantic wall, stolen from time to time by agents from the Todt Organisation;[47] and from decrypts of signals from the Japanese Military Attaché in Berlin. In November he sent a 32-part report to Tokyo on his tour of the defences; eleven of the parts were decrypted by the end of the year, the remainder at long intervals up to June 1944. They gave a detailed and extremely valuable account of the numbers and sites of every element in the coast defence system, from the heaviest CD battery down to grenade throwers, with comments showing how 'enormously' the system had been improved since an earlier visit in February 1943.[48]* But neither Sigint nor any other source disclosed that on 3 November Hitler had issued for the second time a general directive (No 51) on the threat of Allied invasion. It had stated that the threat was now greater than that in the past and could be expected to materialise 'not later than the spring, and perhaps earlier'. 'Unless all indications are misleading', the Pas de Calais which covered the V-weapon sites was the most endangered stretch, but there were some grounds for anxiety about Denmark.[50]† To meet the threat the maximum emplacement of coastal artillery, fixed anti-tank weapons, dug-in tanks, mines and other obstructions was to take place along endangered parts of the coast. In addition the

---

* It has been claimed that the cypher of the Japanese MA had recently been broken again after a considerable interval in consequence of its capture by the OSS from the Japanese embassy in Lisbon.[49] In fact, though there were problems in the latter half of 1943 for GC and CS and its counterpart in Washington, who by agreement were each working on the JMA cypher, these had not ever lasted long and had been solved cryptanalytically. In May 1944 cryptanalysis of the cypher was threatened again when a new conversion square was introduced by the Japanese and it was this crisis that was surmounted, after a couple of months delay, by judicious use of an agent. Decrypts had shown that the Japanese MA in Tangier had not received the new square and had asked Tokyo to arrange for it to be telegraphed to him from Madrid. Between Madrid and Tangier telegraphic communication was by land-line and therefore could not be intercepted. But GC and CS considered that five gaps in its Madrid register of serial numbers probably covered the wanted telegrams and decided to use 'a certain source' which had on occasions supplied copies of cypher telegrams passing through the Tangier Post Office. From this source it received four of the five telegrams in July 1944. There is no clue as to the source, which could have been either OSS or the SIS.

† In August a sabotage campaign, fostered by SOE, had led to German demands that saboteurs should be tried by German courts under German law. The Danish government resisted these demands and the Germans seized complete control, reinforcing the garrison in Denmark by two or three divisions.[51]

46. WO 219/2004, History of SHAEF Documents Centre, p 2.
47. Haswell, *The Intelligence and Deception of the D-day Landings* (1979), p 80.
48. JMA 3724 to 3742, 3790 and 3800 of 16–22 December 1943.
49. Lewin, *The American Magic*, (New York 1982), p 11.
50. Ellis, op cit, Vol I, p 55; Harrison, op cit, pp 148 et seq.
51. WO 208/4310, MI 14 Appreciation of 29 August 1943.

directive had inaugurated a programme to raise the number and quality of the divisions kept in France.*

□

MI 14's ability to assess the fluctuating strength of the German Army in France and the Low Countries, and to follow the changes in its order of battle there, depended on the state of its knowledge about the organisation, the chain of command, the deployment, the logistic and support systems, and the condition of the German Army as a whole. The Army was a huge and complex structure and the task of acquiring comprehensive information about it, and of keeping that information up to date, was always to be more difficult than that of keeping abreast of the strength and order of battle of the Air Force or the Navy. Apart from the Ersatzheer (the Home Army or Training Army) and apart from the Waffen SS and the GAF field divisions, which supplied an increasing proportion of the field forces from 1942, it came to comprise over 300 divisions and many non-divisional units, notably the special-ised units of the GHQ pool which supplied up to a third of each field division in battle conditions. Its armies, corps, divisions and non-divisional units were frequently re-distributed between the various theatres. New formations were always being created. The divisions and the non-divisional units fell into different categories according to function and composition, and varied in quality. For estimates of strength in any one theatre at any time, and forecasts of likely changes to it, continuous and detailed studies of the total capacity of the Army was the essential basis.

Before the spring of 1943 it was not easy to achieve accuracy in these studies, and still less easy to do so without considerable delay. Enigma and Army Y threw a steady light on operations and orders of battle in north Africa and on some sectors of the Russian front, but about the Army as a whole and about its order of battle in theatres where it was not engaged in active operations – and especially western Europe, where it used land-lines for its communications – Sigint still provided only fitful intelligence. MI 14 had thus to rely mainly on the other sources, all of which left much to be desired. Captured documents, however reliable, were as yet obtained only at long intervals. The monitoring of the German Press and radio occasionally produced information of great value mainly on the Army's organisation. The Russians reported more frequently than before on the identities and

* For the text of the directive see Harrison, op cit, Appendix D.

locations of German divisions, but the hope that they would regularly exchange order of battle intelligence had not been fulfilled by January 1943.[52] Reports from agents and attachés were in contrast received in great numbers, either from the SIS, SOE and the embassies or through the exiled governments in London and the British Army Staff in Washington; but they varied greatly in quality and were often fragmentary and inconsistent with each other, and, like the no less voluminous POW interrogations, they could not be relied on until they had been checked against established facts and found to be compatible with them. In the quality of the intelligence they provided, all these sources steadily improved from early in 1943, as we shall see. Until then MI 14's appreciations reflected its dependence on weighing up incomplete and conflicting evidence; many, perhaps most, of the conclusions it circulated were supported by painstaking analyses that were sometimes as much as thirty pages in length.*

Even so, its standards were rigorous, and when allowance has been made for all the difficulties, its conclusions already revealed a remarkable familiarity with the organisation and composition of the German Army. In September 1942 an 'Order of Battle of the German Army' produced by the US War Department identified 382 active divisions as against 234 accepted by MI 14.[53] The disparity led to a series of discussions in which MI 14 was able to convince the American order of battle experts that their estimate was far too high. It based its arguments on its understanding of the system Germany used for numbering her divisions and their component units – an understanding which was providing effective guidance through the maze of conflicting evidence, as may be judged from the fact that the German records show that the number of active divisions had been 233 in July.[54]† On the other hand, the discussions persuaded MI 14 that its own total of 297 identified divisions of all types under-estimated potential German strength by omitting formations not classified as divisions and taking no account of divisions known to be forming. In December, as the basis for the regular exchange of views on future changes in the order of battle, a first 'agreed combined estimate' set the

---

* See Appendix 3 for examples.

† MI 14's appreciations show that the identification and whereabouts of a division often rested on the ability of an agent to give the divisional emblem or the number of a component unit. Conversely, its understanding of the numbering system enabled MI to detect and correct errors in agents' reports.

52. WO 208/4308 of 25 January 1943.
53. Mockler-Ferryman, op cit, p 66.
54. Müller-Hillebrand, *Das Heer 1933–45*, Vol III (1969), pp 287–288.

strength of the German Army on 1 November 1942 at 325 divisions – 278 operational divisions (of which 257 had been identified) and 47 administrative divisions.[55]

The 'agreed combined estimate' attempted a break-down of the distribution of the divisions among the different theatres. But MI 14 was well aware that their distribution had for some months been subject not only to changes dictated by the enemy's operational needs, but also to regular fluctuations arising from his adoption of a new system for the refurbishing of existing divisions and the training of new ones. Designed to make optimum use of his available forces as they became increasingly stretched, the new system had been introduced at the end of 1941; when Germany began sending her tired and depleted divisions for rest and re-organisation in France, where she also based newly formed or re-constituted divisions before deploying them to the active fronts; together, these divisions would reinforce the permanent garrison in the event of invasion. She maintained this system down to the end of 1943; but the regular 'roulement' of divisions was interrupted in the spring of 1942 by her preparations for an eastern offensive, for which she took divisions from France but released none from Russia, and again during the invasion alarms in the west in the summer of 1942 and the autumn of 1943, when she suspended the despatch of divisions out of France and brought additional forces in.

As early as February 1942 MI 14 did not hesitate to conclude from what it had learned of the first of these interruptions that the German Army was fully extended in the sense that it had no strategic reserve of combat-ready divisions in Germany; it was having to replace losses on the eastern front with divisions taken from other fronts and with new formations as they completed their training.[56] This had indeed been the case since December 1941.[57] And by the autumn of 1942 it was clear that as well as having no combat divisions in Germany, the field Army was no longer able to garrison the occupied countries; captured documents and agents' reports revealed that the Ersatzheer was undergoing a radical re-organisation, re-grouping its training depots in Germany and converting its infantry training divisions into what the Germans called 'Reserve' divisions which undertook garrison and defence duties in France and other areas while completing their training.[58] By February 1943 MI 14 had identified thirteen such divisions, some of which had taken part in the

---

55. JIC(42)491(0) of 19 December.
56. WO 208/3573 of 2 March 1942, quoting an appreciation of 26 February.
57. Müller-Hillebrand, op cit, Vol III, pp 27, 30.
58. WO 208/3573 of 7 December.

occupation of Vichy France in November 1942 and now held sectors of the Riviera coast, and was assuming that the number would rise to twenty.[59] This re-organisation had in fact begun in the autumn of 1942 and there were 18 Reserve divisions by the spring, of which about ten were to be kept in France.[60]

Meanwhile, although as yet it detected the movements and locations of German formations with some delay, MI 14 was acquiring a good deal of accurate intelligence about Germany's response to her first serious alarm about the threat of a cross-Channel invasion. At the end of September 1942, when Germany's anxiety was at a peak, MI 14 calculated that she had raised the permanent garrison in France to three Panzer divisions, two SS motorised divisions and 25 infantry divisions – a total of 30 operational divisions, of which it identified all but two of the infantry divisions – and had brought in four training divisions. The German records show that the number of operational divisions was actually 28, two infantry divisions less; all but two of MI 14's identifications were correct, but it had failed to identify three newly created field divisions and one newly created lines of communication division (Sicherungsdivision).* In the same appreciation MI 14 listed the location of the divisions and their subordination to the different armies and corps, and showed a considerable knowledge of the command arrangements in France. It had discovered that, as another of her anti-invasion measures, Germany had set up five new Army Corps there, including LXXXI Corps as the left-hand corps of Fifteenth Army which commanded from the Scheldt to Seine Bay and LXXXIV Corps on the right hand of Seventh Army (Normandy and Brittany); that the boundary between those two Armies lay just east of Caen; and that First Army (which commanded from the Loire to the Spanish border) had transferred three divisions of its permanent garrison to Fifteenth Army and one to Seventh Army.[61]

Between November 1942 and January 1943 the Germans moved divisions away from France in large numbers, mainly to Russia but also to Tunisia. MI 14 received no firm evidence of the moves until 15 January 1943, when an 'unusually reliable' agent reported that 18 divisions were leaving for Russia; nor was it until the end of that month that high-grade Sigint revealed that three which had till recently been in France were in action on the Russian front. By 10 February, however, further Ultra from the

---

* See Appendix 4.

59. WO 208/4308 of 2 February 1943.
60. Müller-Hillebrand, op cit, Vol III, pp 71–72.
61. MI 14 Appreciation of 28 September 1942.

eastern front and information supplied by the Russian General Staff and by agents in France had established most of the facts, and on 21 February MI 14 issued an almost completely accurate list of the movements and of the formations involved in them.* On MI 14's evidence up to 10 February, nine first-quality and eight second-quality divisions had gone to Russia and two first-quality divisions to Tunisia by the end of January. By 22 February it was clear that although, as a result of the return from Russia of 1st Panzer Division and the arrival of several Reserve divisions, 30 divisions remained in France and the Low Countries, only two or three less than in the previous November, the number of first-quality divisions there had dropped from 12 to 6 or 7, of which three were below normal strength and only 1st Panzer Division and one other were in 'fighting trim'. Four second-quality offensive divisions and nine defensive and ten training divisions made up the total.[62]

Reports were then coming in, however, of many train movements into France of less than divisional size. MI 14 judged from them that new recruits were arriving in large numbers from Germany, as well as battered divisions from Russia, and it expected the battered divisions to lose their identities as they were incorporated into new divisions.[63] It had heard from 'a reliable source' in December that Hitler was determined to create new divisions, 'rather than bolstering up the old'[64], and had concluded that Germany could not maintain the number of her divisions, let alone increase it, without reducing their strength and quality.[65] Some evidence to this effect was obtained in January, when POW from 334th Infantry Division, recently arrived in Tunisia, reported that it was one of five newly formed 'economy' field divisions with two regiments, instead of three, and limited artillery, reconnaissance and anti-tank elements, and was made up from 'a mixture of recruits and convalescents from all over Germany.'[66] More such evidence came in at the beginning of March; captured documents and POW disclosed that five 'defensive' divisions consisting of only two regiments had been forming in France since the autumn of 1942.[67] On 8 March MI concluded that, though Germany might form other 'economy' divisions

---

* See Appendix 4.

62. WO 208/4308 of 30 January and 10, 21 and 22 February 1943.
63. ibid, of 21 February 1943.
64. MI 14 Appreciation of 3 December 1942.
65. MI 14 Appreciations of 8 and 13 December 1942; WO 208/4308 of 15 January 1943.
66. WO 208/4308 of 21 January 1943.
67. ibid, of 28 February and 3 March 1943.

during the remainder of 1943 instead of bringing existing divisions up to strength, she would probably be unable to increase her total number of divisions.[68] It had already satisfied itself in February that she had lost ten divisions at Stalingrad in addition to the twenty which had capitulated in the city.[69]

This conclusion represented MI's position in what had become a vigorous debate, both in Whitehall and between Whitehall and Washington, about forward projections of the size of the German Army based on what was known of the overall manpower situation in Germany and on estimates of her past and future casualties. Hitler had resisted any substantial civilian comb-out until January 1943, but had then placed the economy for the first time on a total war footing and given highest priority to the provision of men for the Army. The outcome was that by the replacement of men by women and foreigners in the economy, the introduction of foreigners into the Army, and the relaxation of the age and medical standards of recruits, nearly 2 million men were released to the Army during 1943, and that the Army was able to raise its manpower from 5.8 million in mid-1942 to 6.55 million in mid-1943 and to avoid any serious reduction by mid-1944, when it stood at 6.51 million.[70] In March 1943 MI believed that the size of the Army would drop from the present 6.0 million men to 5.2 million by the end of 1943, whereas the US authorities contended that it was 7.0 million and would remain at that figure.[71] MI was initially supported by MEW, which believed there was little scope for a further comb-out of men from the civilian community.* But MEW revised its calculations during April; it had discovered that a drastic comb-out was taking place to produce a million men, and now estimated that as a result of further measures the Army's total intake in 1943 might be as much as 1½ million.[72]

This revision prompted the JIS on behalf of the JIC to challenge MI's picture of a declining German Army. Using lower estimates than MI's of Germany's likely casualties in 1943, it also interpreted what MI took to be evidence that the Army was 'plugging holes' as being evidence of a determination to increase the size of the Army. The evidence included the fact that Germany was registering the 1897–1900 age group and the 1926 class (17 year olds) and

---

* See Volume II, p 139.

68. ibid, of 8 March 1943.
69. ibid, of 6 and 7 February 1943.
70. Müller-Hillebrand, op cit, Vol III, pp 173, 254.
71. WO 208/4308 of 5, 8 and 9 March, MI 14 Review of German forces in France and the Low Countries of 12 March 1943.
72. JIC(43)171 of 25 April.

recruiting 16 year olds for Flak duties; that POW captured in Tunisia included men of low medical standard; that Volksdeutsche and non-Germans, and also women, were being introduced into the Army; and that the Army was suffering from a shortage of officers and NCOs.[73] MI 14 strongly resisted this argument; on 16 May it insisted that if the JIS was correct 'we must conclude that after 3 years of war Germany can take Stalingrad and North Africa in her stride and yet bring the army up to nearly what it was in July 1942' – and that that was impossible.[74] It was still resisting on 4 June even though it had by then accepted after further discussion with the US authorities that the total strength of the Army at the end of 1943 would be 6.32 million.[75]

By the end of June MI had been induced to change its ground by intelligence to the effect that Germany was reconstituting the divisions destroyed in Stalingrad, as Hitler had publicly avowed she would, as well as forming new divisions. In March, when an Enigma decrypt disclosed that small elements of 14th and 24th Panzer Divisions, both from Stalingrad, were moving by train to C-in-C West's Command, MI was still assuming that these troops would be incorporated into new formations.[76] But at the beginning of May it learned that one Stalingrad division had already re-formed and that eight more were re-forming, and at the beginning of June it admitted that the number known to be re-forming had risen to eighteen, 'seven more than we were willing to accept', and that with astonishing rapidity two had already become operational.[77]* By then, moreover, it had learned a good deal about the creation of GAF field divisions and the expansion of the Waffen SS.

In September 1942 the GAF Enigma had disclosed that Hitler had ordered the GAF to release trained men to the Army, but this intelligence was soon overtaken by further decrypts showing that he had decided, instead, to allow the GAF to create its own divisions. By the end of 1942 MI knew that 15 such divisions were forming, and by 31 January 1943 it had identified 20 and was referring to them as 'a separate army'.[78] By 3 May the number had

---

* Enigma decrypts had disclosed at the end of May that 16th Panzer Division, the third Stalingrad Panzer formation, and 29th Motorised Division were in Italy. For their roles in the fighting there see Volume III, Part 1, Chapters 31 and 34.

73. WO 208/4309 of 3 May 1943.
74. ibid, Minute by MI 14 Colonel of 16 May 1943.
75. ibid, Appreciations of 25 May and 4 June 1943.
76. WO 208/4308, 12 and 13 March 1943; WO 208/3573 of 8 and 22 March 1943.
77. WO 208/4309 of 3 May and 7 June 1943.
78. JIC(42)491(o) of 19 December; WO 208/4308, Appreciation of 31 January 1943.

risen to 21, and although none of them had yet been detected in France, MI had identified a GAF Field Corps there. It had also discovered that the divisions were not all destined, as it had originally thought, for garrison and defence duties; some of them were organised for mobile warfare and were 'potentially of great value'.[79] It was not until October 1943, however, by which time captured documents had established that the GAF divisions were being incorporated into the Army, that MI included them in its order of battle estimates.[80]

The expansion of the Waffen SS, hitherto the military arm of the Nazi Party, had meanwhile constituted a more serious development, not least because so many of its new divisions were Panzer divisions. The expansion had begun with the re-organisation of the original SS motorised divisions (the Adolf Hitler, Das Reich and the Totenkopf Divisions) as 1st, 2nd and 3rd SS Panzer Divisions in December 1942.* That two more such divisions, later identified as 9th and 10th SS Panzer Divisions, were forming in France had been reported in January.[82] By 13 June 1943 MI had identified a total of six SS Panzer Divisions, and believed that another was being formed, and had also identified one SS motorised division and one SS cavalry division.[83]

In the second half of June, accepting that the Army would take in 1½ million men in 1943, MI concluded that this would be sufficient to replace casualties, to re-form the 20 Stalingrad divisions and to provide for the four new SS divisions; but it still believed that Germany would be unable to bring other battered divisions up to strength or to form further new divisions, or, indeed, to avoid weakening existing divisions.[84]

Early in July, the JIC having asked it to reconsider its earlier conclusion that the German Army had no central strategic reserve, MI 14 drew up a report in which it again admitted that it had been mistaken in believing there was no scope for further comb-out from German industry, and thus in forecasting a drastic decline in army strength and the cannibalisation of divisions. But it empha-

---

* The expansion of the Waffen SS was made possible by the allocation to it of national servicemen; it had previously relied on volunteers. In December 1942, it totalled 230,000 men. It was 430,000 strong in July 1943, 600,000 by July 1944 and 830,000 by the end of the war.[81]

79. WO 208/4308 of 19, 23 and 24 March; WO 208/4309 of 27 March, 4 April, 2 and 5 May 1943.
80. WO 208/4311, Report of 16 November 1943 on German order of battle.
81. Müller-Hillebrand, op cit, Vol III, p 254.
82. WO 208/4308 of 29 and 30 January 1943.
83. WO 208/4309 of 15 June 1943.
84. ibid, of 4 June 1943.

sised that the number of German divisions was less important than their quality and the way in which they were being deployed. The number of divisions identified was 324, almost the same as in October 1942 (325). In an army of 324 divisions, of which 230 were offensive, one would expect a strategic reserve. It was clear, however, that the new divisions had been created at the expense of existing ones. The Russian General Staff had recently reported that the divisions on the eastern front were on average only 60 per cent of full strength in men and equipment. High-grade Sigint had disclosed that, of the three Stalingrad divisions that had so far gone to Italy, 16th Panzer Division had 12,000 men, as compared with an establishment strength of 16,000, and that 29th PG Division* had had to be given some 600 vehicles as a matter of urgency to render it 50 per cent mobile. The broad picture painted by order of battle intelligence was of 'divisions being re-formed and sent to operational theatres against time, largely composed of new men and with a shortage of vital equipment'; furthermore, divisions were being withdrawn hastily from less threatened to more threatened areas. It was inconceivable that Germany would take such risks if she had a reserve; she was being forced to keep all her resources on the outside ring.[85]

In a memorandum to the CIGS on the preparation of this report MI 14 noted that the German Army might now have between 6½ and 6¾ million men. It added that the figure was highly speculative, and enlarged on the futility of mathematical calculations and the theoretical approach. When the quality and the distribution of the German divisions were so important, 'one is thrown back on the Order of Battle to provide the best possible answer'.[86] By then, however, disputes about the reliability of manpower and casualty calculations as a basis for assessing the strength of the German Army had subsided, whereas recent weeks had brought an increase in the volume and the quality of order of battle intelligence that was to continue without a break to the end of the war.

At the beginning of 1943 a large consignment of documents, including promotion and appointments lists and files of the Allgemeine Heeresmitteilungen (the equivalent of Army Council Instructions), had been captured from the HQ of 90th Light Division in Tunisia.[87] The first important haul for a long time, this was soon followed by many others. By May 1943 documents were

---

* In May the German motorised divisions were re-named Panzer Grenadier divisions.

85. WO 208/4310 of 8 July 1943.
86. ibid, Memo of DMI to the CIGS of 8 July 1943.
87. WO 208/4308 of 21 and 23 January 1943.

being captured so frequently, and were casting so much light on all aspects of the German Army, that a new research group, the Anglo-American Military Intelligence Research Section (MIRS), was set up to exploit them, thus enabling MI 14 itself to concentrate on studying the enemy's current deployments.[88]* On the current order of battle, too, intelligence was improving rapidly. POW were being taken in larger numbers. The volume of reports from agents, which still provided the bulk of the evidence on the identification and location of the German formations in the west, greatly increased, the disruption of Bertrand's organisation at the end of 1942, following the German occupation of Vichy France,† being more than off-set as the SIS, SOE, other French organisations and the Polish network expanded their activities in France and the Low Countries; by the spring of 1944 MI would be receiving reports from that area alone at the rate of 150 a day.[89] The reports were being received with less delay. At the beginning of 1943 the time-lag between the date of a German troop movement and MI's receipt of the news of it by courier was 'at least a month',[90] but from the middle of the year more and more reports were sent by W/T or by the pigeon service (code-name *Columba*) which MI 14 described as being 'amazingly current'.[91]‡

Agents reporting on troop movements by rail and on the location of enemy formations could generally be relied on even before 1943. On other matters – the enemy's organisation and chain of command; the identification of his formations, which was usually derived from divisional emblems; the quality and state of training of the divisions – their claims, though increasing in accuracy, had still to be treated with caution until they were

---

* Called the Combined Order of Battle Group until June 1943, MIRS was also responsible for briefing Commands in the field on what to look for and for ensuring that captures got back to London or Washington without delay. Initially small, with a still smaller sub-section in Washington, it was by the end of the war employing 80 people, two-thirds of them American.

† As we have seen in earlier volumes Bertrand's reports from agents throughout France had been a valuable source of information. He was able to resume this service after an interval.

‡ From the middle of 1943, the two main French networks, one Gaullist and the other non-Gaullist, had 2,000 agents each and 40 W/T sets between them. They built up from that date a comprehensive system for reporting German rail movements of the kind that had previously existed only in Belgium. In 1942 the Belgian network had been exceptional in that it was already tapping the telephone cables of the State Railways and the teleprinter links between the German and Belgian authorities and, with agents at most of the main traffic centres, reporting by W/T the date, size and route of most troop movements.[92]

88. Mockler-Ferryman, op cit, p 28.
89. Johnson, *The Secret War* (1978), pp 321–323.
90. WO 208/4308 of 23 January 1943.
91. WO 208/4310 of 31 August and 9 September 1943.
92. MI 14 Appreciation of 4 October 1942.

confirmed by other sources.[93] But the process of checking them was facilitated by the increase of evidence from other sources. Over and above the greater flow of captured documents and POW interrogations, documents stolen by the underground networks themselves were now reaching London regularly. Still more important, because its evidence was more recent, not to say current, Sigint was making an ever-growing contribution to MI's familiarity with the German order of battle in all theatres including, indirectly, France. From the summer of 1943 Enigma and Army Y provided all but exhaustive intelligence about the formations engaged in Sicily, Italy and the Balkans, while the intelligence obtained from the Enigma and the Fish traffic about those on the Russian fronts was steadily expanding. These developments substantially improved MI's understanding of the situation in the west, though the Enigma and Fish keys in use in that area were not to be broken before the spring of 1944.*

One feature was established beyond doubt as the order of battle intelligence improved: Germany continued to create new divisions. By the end of July it was known that 51 had been formed since October 1942, all but one of them before the beginning of 1943. They included a further SS Panzer division (the Hitler Jugend, later to become 12th SS Panzer Division). By the end of August a total of thirteen SS Panzer divisions had been identified, two of them still forming and the remainder already on active fronts, and it was clear that they were being given preferential treatment; they had three battalions of tanks, whereas the Army's Panzer divisions had only two, and they were among the first divisions to receive Tiger tanks.[94]† By the same date documents acquired by the Polish SIS had established that all twenty Stalingrad divisions had been re-formed without using up all the Army's available manpower.[95] In October, when the War Office, the US War Department and the main operational commands held another order of battle conference to review the strength of the German Army in terms of manpower and number of divisions, the number of divisions was estimated to be 328 (of which 316 were identified) but it was accepted that together with the GHQ pool – not used up, as had previously been thought, with the

---

* For further details of the Sigint preparations and performance before D-day see Appendix 6.

† Evidence about the SS divisions was being obtained primarily from the SS Enigma keys, so much so that in the autumn of 1943 GC and CS appointed one of its staff to be SS Adviser on the decrypts about SS front-line troops.

93. WO 208/4310 of 31 August 1943.
94. ibid, of 23 June, 12 and 21 July, 23 and 25 August 1943.
95. ibid, of 10 August 1943.

reconstitution of the Stalingrad divisions – the available man-power would permit the formation of still more divisions.[96]

The conference agreed, however, that further divisions could be created only at the expense of reducing either the establishment strength or the actual strength, or both, of existing divisions. By that time it was known that Germany had formed more two-regiment divisions, and since there was already some difficulty in distinguishing between those formed as defensive (static) divisions and those intended for the offensive role – the more so as some defensive divisions had three regiments – it seemed possible that as one way of finding additional divisions she would turn her remaining three-regiment divisions into two-regiment divisions, as she had done towards the end of the First World War. Meanwhile, research on captured documents had arrived at the establishment strengths of many combat divisions and of the units of the GHQ pool, and it was known that in many divisions the actual strength was well below establishment; high-grade Sigint had disclosed that in some of the divisions in Italy the short-fall was between 15 and 40 per cent. As it was known that recruits were being taken more and more from civilian prisoners, foreigners* and the elderly, and that the Air Force and the Navy were giving up men to the Army, it could also be assumed that the divisions had declined in quality as well as in actual strengths. These conclusions should be

---

* MIRS produced a comprehensive report on the foreigners, based almost entirely on captured documents, on 12 June 1943 and another, still more complete, on 1 January 1944. Leaving aside men of German origin from the occupied countries (Volksdeutsche), who were conscripted from 1942, three categories of foreigners were taken into the German Army. The first were 'Nordic' volunteers; recruited by the SS from the autumn of 1940, they were in 1943 formed into four non-German 'Nordic' SS divisions – Dutch, Flemish, Norwegian and Danish. The second, recruited by the Army and the SS from June 1941, were foreigners from western Europe and the Balkans, who volunteered to serve against Bolshevism; they included the Spanish division and three Croat divisions on the Russian front, but also served as individuals in German Army divisions. The Germans sent neither of these categories to western Europe.

The third category, by far the largest, consisted of non-Germans from the Baltic states, the Ukraine and most of the Russian minority racial groups, who on being taken prisoner by the Germans volunteered for service against Soviet Russia from the autumn of 1941. Some of the non-Germans served as auxiliaries attached to German divisions, but from May 1942 the majority were organised, on ethnic lines, into artillery, infantry and pioneer battalions and cavalry squadrons, the units generally known as Osttruppen.

The troops in the third category were chiefly used in the Balkans, Italy and western Europe for garrison and line of communication duties, but by the end of 1943, when there were some 250,000 auxiliaries and 370,000 men in the Osttruppen, they were beginning to relieve German troops in the coastal defence formations in the less vulnerable sectors. They had been formed into four regiments and several battalions and were supplying the third regiment of some German divisions in the west under German officers and NCOs.[97]

96. WO 208/4311, Appreciation of 16 November 1943.
97. WO 208/4310, MIRS Report of 12 June 1943; WO 208/4312, MIRS Report of 1 January 1944.

considered in the light of the re-organisation that was being carried out in the German Army. Early in October 1943 OKW had ordered that all the infantry divisions on the eastern front should be reduced from an establishment strength of between 15,000 and 17,000 to one of 10,708 (plus 2,065 foreign auxiliaries). On 27 November, realising that Germany's heavy losses in Russia called for further measures, Hitler ordered the Army to find another one million men from its own resources by reducing the establishment strength of all divisions outside Russia, including the Panzer and Panzer Grenadier divisions, to 12,769 men. As a result of these decisions the Germans were able to form 24 more Army divisions, 3 GAF divisions and 13 more SS divisions in the first half of 1944.[98]

Some information about the reduction of the divisional establishment strength was obtained from documents captured in the Mediterranean – though these were not received until January 1944.[99] In the meantime, towards the end of October 1943, 21st Army Group attempted a more precise estimate of the strength and quality of the divisions in the west. It estimated that as compared with a standard divisional strength of some 16,000 men, the average strength of the GAF field divisions was 8,000, of the Reserve divisions 15,000, of the original defensive divisions (the 700-series) 10,000 and of the offensive infantry divisions in the 300-series 12,000. All the divisions were relying to a considerable extent on inferior non-German equipment. They normally included up to 25 per cent of disaffected foreigners. The appreciation recognised that these deficiencies were partly explained by the static role of the divisions – they were usually rectified before a division was transferred to an active front – and the fact that the Germans were not expecting an imminent invasion. Even so, practically all the withdrawals had been divisional troops, and had included all the best formations, and there were good grounds for believing that since May the strength of the Army in the west had declined by some twenty per cent (200,000 men).[100]

This assessment may be compared with statements drawn up at the time by C-in-C West and his Chief of Staff, General Blumentritt, for the High Command. In September 1943 Blumentritt pointed out that although the defensive divisions in the west had been increased from 22 to 27 in the past year, the increase was largely nullified by reduction of most of the divisions to two regiments; the offensive divisions had meanwhile declined

---

98. Müller-Hillebrand, op cit, Vol III, pp 134–138.

99. WO 208/4312, Appreciation of 15 January 1944.

100. Extracts circulated as NID LC Report No 870 of 23 October 1943 (in ADM 223/119).

only slightly in numbers to six armoured or motorised and seven infantry, of which three were new formations, but their mobility had declined very substantially. In October von Rundstedt himself reported that 17 of the 23 defensive divisions on the coast between the Scheldt and Spain were fit for defence but of little or no offensive value, many being armed with captured weapons and having battalions of foreigners, and that five were only partially fit for defence. He urged that while the quality of the defensive divisions must be improved, a 'rigid defence' of the long stretch of coast for any considerable length of time would be impossible. Defence must be based on a general mobile reserve. But of his notional strength of 23 mobile reserve divisions, eleven were still being formed and two had not yet arrived.[101]

Whitehall learned nothing from any source of these German assessments or of the response that Hitler was to make to them in Directive No 51. In November, however, it received two decrypts about Germany's preparations and expectations in the west; each was the first of several of its kind and they marked the point at which high-grade Sigint began to throw direct light on these subjects.* The first was a telegram from the Japanese Ambassador in Berlin following a tour of the defences in October. It was a comprehensive account, Blumentritt having briefed him on the parts of France he did not visit. It listed the number of divisions by type under each of C-in-C West's subordinate commanders, and the forces held by the Military Administrations of France and Belgium, and described the relationship between the divisional commanders, fortress troops and the naval commands. It described the organisation of the Ersatzheer in France, adding that three Reserve Panzer divisions were to be sent from Germany, two parachute divisions from Italy and a number of infantry divisions from other fronts, and that a number of field divisions were to be formed from the Reserve (Training) divisions. It gave 1.4 million as the total strength of German Service personnel in France (all Services). As for Germany's expectations and intentions, the Ambassador said that 'the Straits area is given first place in the German Army's fortification scheme and troop dispositions, Normandy and Brittany coming next in importance', though some mobile forces were held in reserve near the Pyrenees in case the Allies landed in the Iberian peninsula; her policy was to destroy the Allies on the beaches, but if they got ashore they would be attacked by mobile forces and flanking fire from batteries and

---

* Compare the inaccurate claims made in F W Winterbotham, *The Ultra Secret* (1974), pp 149–150.

101. Ellis, op cit, Vol I pp 54–55; Harrison, op cit, p 142.

strong points.* The second decrypt was obtained from GAF Enigma traffic. While adding little to Allied knowledge, it was an appreciation from von Rundstedt himself. Issued on 15 November, it pointed out that while there were no indications of an imminent attack, and while the movement of landing craft from the Mediterranean back to the United Kingdom was still not heavy, German air reconnaissance was hardly possible on account of the weather and the strong Allied defences; and it added that as 'it is certain that the enemy is methodically and on the largest scale proceeding with his preparations to attack', German counter-measures must be pushed forward with 'the utmost exertion of all forces'.[103]

A fortnight earlier, on 3 November, Hitler had responded to C-in-C West's earlier representations by issuing Directive No 51. The directive ordered a further strengthening of the coastal defences.† But it also inaugurated a programme for raising the number and quality of the C-in-C's divisions, laying down a series of measures for improving the equipment and the mobility of the divisions, particularly those forming the mobile reserve, over the next three months and decreeing that no units stationed in the west or in Denmark, including such Panzer, assault gun and anti-tank units as might be sent there to complete their training, were henceforth to be transferred without the Führer's permission.[104] As already noted, the directive was not mentioned by Sigint or any other source, but MI 14 did not fail to detect that with only occasional exceptions divisions ceased to be withdrawn from November 1943, while the number kept in the west was steadily raised by the creation of new formations and the arrival of divisions brought in from Russia for re-fitting. Its estimate of the number rose from 37 in October 1943 to 44 on 10 January 1944, when the actual number was 48, and from that date, such was its expectation of further arrivals, its weekly estimate for the CIGS always compared the latest estimate with the previous one.[105]

Most of the newly formed divisions identified by MI were infantry, but they included 12th SS Panzer Division (Hitler Jugend), 17th SS PG Division and three Panzer Reserve (Training)

---

* For MI 14's report on this decrypt see Appendix 5. The Prime Minister asked that the decrypt should be shown to the President.[102]
† See above, p 18.

102. Dir/C Archive, 8 December 1943.
103. CX/MSS/T7/7; WO 208/4311 of 5 December 1943.
104. Harrison, op cit, Appendix D.
105. WO 208/3573 of 10 January 1944; WO 208/4311 of 2 October 1943; Müller-Hillebrand, op cit, Vol III, pp 213–215.

divisions, the first such divisions to be stationed in France.[106] By the end of November 1943, moreover, MI had noted that whereas no Panzer division had been transferred out of France in recent weeks, four had gone to Russia from other fronts – 1st Panzer Division from Greece, 16th Panzer and 1st SS Panzer Divisions from Italy and 25th Panzer Division from Norway.[107]

The JIC summed up at the beginning of January 1944 in an estimate of the scale of the German opposition to Operations *Overlord* and *Anvil*, assuming as was then intended that they would take place in May and be synchronised with a Russian offensive.[108] It was impossible to predict the total size of the air forces Germany would have in the west on D-day, not to speak of the extent to which she would deploy them against the landings. But the JIC's guess at the total size put it considerably higher than COSSAC's outline plan had done (2,530 aircraft as compared with 1,740, including 975 single-engined fighters as compared with 655) and its guess at the scale of the attack that could be made against the embarkation ports, convoys and beaches on D-day itself was the huge figure of 1,750 sorties.* But it emphasised that the GAF would be heavily handicapped by inexperienced crews and shortage of crews and replacement aircraft, and it realised that the impact of the Allied air offensive on the GAF in the coming months, which again could not be predicted, might well transform the situation. The scale of the opposition on land was less difficult to assess, and it remained within the upper limit which COSSAC's outline plan had regarded as acceptable.† Germany now had some forty divisions of varying strength and quality in France and the Low Countries. She would raise the number to about 45, but could spare no more from other theatres and had no reserves. About 12 of the 45 would be offensive, and these would be brought up to strength before the weather conditions became favourable for invasion. In the two months following D-day she might bring in ten additional divisions from fronts other than the Russian and, dependent on conditions there, five divisions from the Russian fronts; but in the first three or four weeks she would be unable to commit these reinforcements because she would be unable to rule out follow-up landings by the Allies on the French south coast and elsewhere. In these circumstances, subject to the delays that might

---

* See Volume II p 522 for the disturbing increase in estimates of German fighter strength in the autumn of 1943.

† See above, p 7.

106. WO 208/4311 of 22 November and 25 December 1943.
107. ADM 223/119 of 29 November 1943, quoting MI 14.
108. JIC(43)524, issued 2 January 1944.

be imposed on her by interdiction and the resistance forces, the build-up against the *Overlord* beaches would be as follows:

Time	Type of Division	Number
By D-day evening	One SS, one Infantry	2
D + 2	Two Panzer, One Panzer Grenadier, Two SS, One Infantry (plus elements of two defensive)	6 plus
D + 7	Two Panzer, two Panzer Grenadier, two SS, two Infantry, One defensive (plus elements of two defensive)	9 plus

When this estimate was drawn up the *Overlord* plan envisaged that the landings would be confined to the Caen sector, but the conviction that COSSAC had accepted too small a margin of Allied superiority had become so overwhelming that the *Overlord* plan was about to be revised.

□

Commenting on 'the marked increase in available armoured and motorised divisions in the west since 1 November', COSSAC's intelligence staff on 17 December 1943 emphasised the importance COSSAC had always attached to the need for action by the Allied air forces and SOE to reduce the German capacity for a quick counter-attack.[109] By then, however, the Combined Chiefs of Staff had already set in train the revision of the COSSAC plan by resolving early in December to do everything practicable to increase the strength of the *Overlord* forces.* By the end of December Generals Eisenhower and Montgomery had seen the COSSAC plan, and Eisenhower had instructed his Chief of Staff, General Bedell Smith, and Montgomery to discuss its revision with the naval and air commanders in London before his own arrival in England in the middle of January.[110]

By the middle of January a new plan had been outlined, Montgomery proposing an increase in the front from 25 to nearly 50 miles, an additional beach being taken in on the left wing and the right wing being extended to the eastern shore of the Cotentin peninsula. The seaborne assault force was increased to five divisions, and the rate of reinforcement and supply accelerated. None of COSSAC's principal staff officers entirely agreed with Montgomery's proposals – they questioned the soundness of

---

* See above, p 10.

109. WO 219/1837, COSSAC Intelligence Report of 17 December 1943.
110. Ellis, op cit, Vol I, p 32.

extending the front to the Cotentin instead of increasing the weight of attack in the original assault area – and when the planners came to work on them they, too, raised serious doubts that by reducing the weight of the assault on Caen they might jeopardise the prospects of capturing the town on D-day. Indeed, they prepared an alternative plan for a four-divisional assault on the Caen sector only, pointing out that little would be gained if the Cotentin landings succeeded and the Caen landings failed. But this plan in its turn involved serious risks in that it did not permit the rapid post-assault rate of build-up that had come to be regarded as of overwhelming importance. In the end, only the Montgomery plan was submitted for approval. Eisenhower approved it on 21 January and at once obtained the concurrence of the Combined Chiefs of Staff.[111]

It was easier to change the plan than to find the extra resources. COSSAC's staff, which had itself concluded during December that the *Overlord* force and rate of build-up must be increased,[112] suggested on 6 January that they should be found by reducing Operation *Anvil* to a threat. On 8 January the JIC advised that the threat of a landing would be enough to tie down till D-day the forces the Germans had in the south of France: it knew from Sigint that although they were keeping a close watch on the movement of landing craft back to the United Kingdom, they were assuming that enough remained in the Mediterranean to lift four divisions, and it believed that in view of their lack of intelligence they would be unable to discount the danger of a landing.[113]* The Joint Planners examined these representations, together with the JIC's recent estimates of the scale of opposition to the landings,† on 12 January. Although the estimate of the threat from the air had been increased they felt confident that the Allies would maintain air superiority. But they remained anxious about the estimated land opposition. 'According to the latest estimate by the JIC the enemy land opposition throughout *Overlord* is unlikely to be less, and in the earlier stages may exceed,

---

* Although the Germans continued to get some information about shipping movements from Spain, the Spanish government had by this time closed down the German ship-watching organisation in the Gibraltar area (see Volume II, Appendix 15). We shall see that Enigma showed that the Germans continued to expect an attack on southern France down to D-day, and sometimes thought it more imminent than a cross-Channel landing. They kept six defensive divisions in the south and between one and three offensive divisions (see Volume III, Part I, p 27).

† See above, pp 34–35.

111.   ibid, p 32; Harrison, op cit, pp 165–166, 182; CAB 44/42, pp 59–60; D'Este, *Decision in Normandy* (1983), pp 65–68.
112.   Ehrman, op cit, Vol V, pp 233–234.
113.   JIC(44)10 of 8 January.

the maximum which COSSAC reported he was willing to encounter. . . . We cannot afford to fail in *Overlord*. On the latest JIC forecast . . . , which quite rightly takes no account of possible spectacular development on the Russian front, success is doubtful, and there is a considerable risk that when the target date arrives the operation would have to be postponed for a considerable time.' The Joint Planners accordingly supported the argument for an increased assault force and rate of build-up, and proposed that, to permit its enlargement, *Overlord* should be postponed by a month. They also supported the reduction of *Anvil* to a threat: a landing in the south of France would not affect the course of the battle during the critical days of the main invasion, and a landing there with only two divisions might even fail to get ashore if the Germans continued to stiffen the defences of the limited number of suitable beaches.[114]

The recommendations were welcomed by the British Chiefs of Staff, who in any case preferred that *Anvil* should be sacrificed to assist the Allied advance in mainland Italy, but were opposed by the US Joint Chiefs; they insisted on retaining *Anvil* and were not persuaded that, though it had to be enlarged, *Overlord* need be postponed. Nor was it until the last week of February that a further round in the long-standing Anglo-American controversy about the relation of *Anvil* to the Italian campaign and to *Overlord* was settled by another compromise.[115]*

The dispute about *Anvil* did not delay the completion of revised plans for *Overlord*, but the work ran into considerable difficulties as a result of the decision to accelerate the capture of Cherbourg by landing an additional division on the eastern shore of the Cotentin peninsula. COSSAC's plan had rejected a landing there, and accepted delay in capturing Cherbourg, on topographic grounds. The landing had to be made north of the floodable marshland of the valley of the river Douve, which ran almost the whole length of the base of the peninsula, but the coast north of the Douve was itself backed by a floodable area traversed by only a few causeways. The discovery at the end of December 1943 that this area had been flooded had confirmed COSSAC's staff in the belief that it was out of the question to attempt a landing there,[116]

---

* See Volume III Part I, pp 24–27. SACMED was directed to give overriding priority to the campaign in Italy over all other Mediterranean operations. But so far as possible without prejudice to that campaign he was to prepare for alternative amphibious operations with the object of contributing to *Overlord* by containing the maximum enemy forces. Among these alternatives *Anvil* had priority.

114. CAB 121/390, JP(44)4 (Final) of 12 January.
115. Ehrman, op cit, Vol V, pp 231–242.
116. D'Este, op cit, p 154.

and they continued to resist the proposal after the revised plan had been approved by Eisenhower.[117] At the end of January the impasse was resolved by the decision to drop a US airborne division behind the beach to secure the causeways. Although the knowledge that there were two German divisions in the Cotentin continued to fuel misgivings – misgivings which eventually led to the decision to drop a second US airborne division in the narrow gap between the Douve valley and the west coast of the peninsula – the Army, Navy and Air Commanders of the expedition issued the revised over-all plan on 1 February.

The revised over-all plan was entitled the Initial Joint Plan for *Neptune*, *Neptune* being the code-name for the first phase of *Overlord* in which the assault force crossed the Channel and got ashore. It laid down the framework within which the subordinate commanders drew up their detailed force-plans; there were in all nine of these, of which those of the naval command, of Second British Army and of First US Army were issued before the end of February. It directed the Navy to land the initial assault forces, five divisions with some additions, on D-day and the maximum number of follow-up troops by D+3, setting the target at some nine divisions by that date and twenty divisions by D+14. It stipulated that seven hours before the first landings one US airborne division (later increased to two, as already noted) would drop behind the Cotentin beach (*Utah*) and one British airborne division on the Dives estuary to seize the bridges across the river Orne and so protect the bridgehead's eastern flank. It set out the tasks allotted to the assault forces. Those landed on the newly added eastern-most beach (*Sword*) were to take Caen, a distance of twelve miles, occupy airfields to the south-east of Caen and join the two British divisions landed on the *Gold* and *Juno* beaches, which would be advancing to the Bayeux-Caen road, in providing flank protection to the US forces to the west of them; most of the German mobile divisions lay to the east of Caen. The US troops landed on the *Omaha* beach would advance to the line St Lo-Périers-Lessay while those landed in the Cotentin drove against Cherbourg; they should have joined forces and be advancing into Brittany by D+20, when they would be reinforced by the arrival of Third US Army under General Patton.[118]

In part because the Russians had been assured that the assault would be delivered in May, the Initial Joint Plan gave 31 May as D-day. But D-day depended on the Plan's decisions about H-hour,

117. Harrison, op cit, p 182.
118. Ehrman, op cit, Vol V, pp 273–284; Harrison, op cit, pp 173–174, 180–188; CAB 44/242, p 70.

which it settled with reference to light and tide conditions. In the Mediterranean the Allies had made their landings under cover of darkness. For *Overlord* the advantages of landing by night were off-set by several considerations. Some light was imperative for the preliminary bombardments which were an essential feature of the Plan. It was also essential if the nearly simultaneous landing of so large a force, which in view of the formidable nature of the defences called for meticulous instructions to every unit involved, was to be effectively co-ordinated. Given the distance between the embarkation ports and the beaches, moreover, daylight landings reduced the danger of detection during the passage, which would take place at night. Above all, the tide, enormous in Normandy, had to be taken at a point which limited the ground the troops would have to cover across the exposed beaches. These considerations determined the choice of H-hour: approximately half-flood on the main beaches in a period when, while the time would vary from beach to beach with the difference in the tide and the optimum ratio of tide to beach gradient, half-flood occurred some 40 minutes after nautical twilight following a night when the moonlight had been sufficient for accurate landings by the airborne troops. If these conditions were to be fulfilled D-day would be on 5, 6 or 7 June, weather permitting.

Eisenhower received his directive from the CCS on 12 February. His instructions were 'to undertake operations aimed at the heart of Germany and the destruction of her armed forces'. He was to aim at 'the month of May' but to be prepared 'at any time to take advantage of favourable circumstances . . . to effect re-entry to the Continent'.[119]

---

119. Ellis, op cit, Vol I p 39.

CHAPTER 44

Intelligence on German Appreciations and Preparations from February 1944 to D-Day

I N ADDITION to raising the strength of the initial assault and the rate of build-up to provide a safer margin of superiority over the expected scale of enemy opposition, the Initial Joint Plan had allowed for exceptionally heavy losses, particularly in landing craft, and had done all that was practicable to increase the naval and air support. In the knowledge that the enemy had fortified the coast to an unprecedented extent, the detailed force-plans had taken account of the hydrographic and topographic conditions in the landing areas, including such details as the gradients, the exits and the weight-bearing qualities of every beach, and of a mass of intelligence about the location and arc of fire of the active defences, from the heaviest batteries to machine-gun nests, and the nature and location of the extensive minefields behind the beaches. They had sought, indeed, to produce 'the perfect plan' for each sector of the assault – one which in the light of long study of a fifty-mile stretch of coast settled in advance where, and with what air support, every Allied assault craft would land and every ship in the bombarding force would take up station.[1]

Once completed, such plans would be reconsidered only if intelligence called for revised estimates of the form and scale of the enemy's resistance. But they had been drawn up so far in advance that for many weeks the Allies could not exclude the possibility that, either because it was becoming apparent that the enemy had discerned the size and destination of the landings, or was for other reasons altering his plans for countering them, *Overlord* would have to be re-fashioned, or even postponed or abandoned.

In the event no further serious revision was made; the Initial Joint Plan was 'substantially that which was put into operation', and few changes were made to force-plans.[2] That this was so was

---

1. ADM 223/287, SO(I) to ANCXF, 'Notes on *Round-up* and *Overlord*', pp 7, 16.
2. CAB 44/242, *Operation 'Overlord'*, p 71.

due in the first instance to the fact that, as we shall see, order of battle intelligence showed that the Allied estimate of the scale of opposition to the landings continued to be reasonably accurate. But that estimate had rested on the supposition that the landings would gain surprise; and it was no less important that the Allies succeeded in keeping secret throughout those weeks the time, the destination and the scale of the assault. In view of the scope of their preparations and the number of people involved in them, this was to say the least a considerable achievement, and one which down to the final days of waiting and D-day itself, when only the poor weather still concealed their design, rested on various efforts and precautions.

The Initial Joint Plan, like COSSAC's outline plan, regarded surprise as a pre-requisite for the success of *Overlord*; it repeated COSSAC's requirement that in the preliminary air offensive and in all reconnaissance operations targets should be covered along the whole length of the Belgian and French coasts, notably in the Pas de Calais and in Normandy but with at least two sorties in the Pas de Calais for every one in Normandy. Over and above the security precautions that were in any case in force in Whitehall and throughout the country, additional precautions, some of them severe and controversial, were introduced in the spring of 1944, the opposition of the Prime Minister and the civil departments being overcome by urgings from SHAEF and MI 5.* SHAEF insisted that *Overlord* would have small chance of success if the enemy obtained so much as 48 hours' notice of the plans and that a longer period of notice would spell 'certain defeat'. MI 5 argued that although there was as yet 'no single uncontrolled agent in the UK', the Germans might introduce 'a large influx' of new agents, some of which might escape detection.[4]

Neither these measures nor the Allied deception plan, to which we will come, would have sufficed to keep the enemy guessing if he had been blessed with reasonably good intelligence. Far from

---

* In February a ban was imposed on Press speculation about the second front. From 1 April all unauthorised travel to and from a coastal zone from The Wash to Land's End and an area around the Firth of Forth was forbidden, other communications to and from those areas were considerably restricted and travel to and from Ireland was suspended. On 6 April all normal leave was stopped for British forces in the United Kingdom, and limits were placed on the movements of Allied troops there. As for communications between Britain and overseas, it was decided on 16 April to ban all travel to and from the United Kingdom by Allied and neutral diplomats (other than those of the Dominions, the US and the USSR), to prohibit the receipt or despatch of all messages, and to forbid the use of cyphers.[3]

3. Hinsley and Simkins, *Security and Counter-Intelligence*, (forthcoming); Ehrman, *Grand Strategy*, Vol V (1956), pp 316–317; Cruickshank, *Deception in World War II* (1979), pp 172–175.
4. Hinsley and Simkins, op cit.

having good intelligence, however, Germany in the weeks before D-day lacked any source of reliable information. All German agents in the United Kingdom were controlled by the British; and while the reports that the Germans received from uncontrolled agents in Lisbon, Stockholm and other capitals were occasionally uncomfortably close to the mark, their accurate reports were but a few among many that were wildly inaccurate.* There is no evidence that the Germans derived any benefit from such breaches of security as were suspected at the time.† So complete was the Allied control of the air, and also Germany's lack of adequate aircraft, that the GAF was virtually unable to carry out overland reconnaissance in southern England; it succeeded in obtaining some coverage of shipping off the south coast, but its offshore operations were also insufficiently regular to provide the basis for good reconnaissance.[9]‡ Above all, the Allies had good reasons for

---

* Two trusted German agents, one in Lisbon and one in Stockholm, who were outside the Double-Cross net caused anxiety. Both were judged to be frauds in the sense that they had no genuine sources of information in the United Kingdom (although there was a residue of doubt regarding the Stockholm agent), but it was feared that they might nevertheless hit on the truth and be believed.[5] In the event they did no damage to *Overlord*, though at the last minute the Lisbon agent reported that the Cherbourg peninsula was the target (see below, p 61).

Between November 1943 and February 1944 there was a major penetration of the British embassy in Ankara – the *Cicero* case. A considerable amount of material, some of which dealt with the Allied attempt to bring Turkey into the war and was highly classified, was photographed by the Ambassador's valet and transmitted to Berlin. The existence of a leak from the embassy became known to the Allies in January 1944, but neither investigation in the embassy nor such diplomatic and Sicherheitsdienst traffic from Ankara as was decrypted disclosed the source, which was not identified until after the war. The mythology of the case has greatly exaggerated the damage which was done. The Allied aim to draw Turkey into the war was widely known and it is unlikely that the leakage had more than a marginal influence on the course of events. The compromised material did not reveal the plans for *Overlord* as has often been claimed. There were passing references to *Overlord* in the documents, but they cannot have done more than indicate to the Germans that this was the code-name for an Allied amphibious operation in the west, probably the major invasion. After very full investigation the heads of the SIS and MI 5 agreed that the Allies had escaped the 'appalling national disaster' which might have accrued from the enemy's penetration of a key embassy.[6]

† Several possible cases were reported from March and brought to the attention of the Prime Minister. But the anxiety they caused proved to be exaggerated, few being of more than local significance though, just before D-day, anxiety was revived by a Columbia Radio broadcast.[7] This last incident was referred to in letters between 21st Army Group and SHAEF on 4 and 5 June.[8] For other examples see Haswell, *The Intelligence and Deception of the D-day Landings* (1979), pp 155, 157, 159; and Roskill, *The War at Sea*, Vol III Part 2, (1961) p 38.

‡ Not more than 32 overland reconnaissance flights by the GAF were recorded in daytime in the first six months of 1944, and by no means all of those were over southern England. Flights in that area were recorded on only two days in January; there were none in February

5. ibid.
6. ibid.
7. ibid.
8. WO 219/5104.
9. AIR 41/23, *The Liberation of North-West Europe*, Vol III, p 35.

being confident that the Germans were decrypting no Allied signals.* In all these directions, moreover, they enjoyed the double advantage of knowing not only that the enemy was poorly served but also that their own intelligence was so comprehensive and so prompt that it was unlikely that any substantial change in German appreciations and dispositions would escape their attention.

That the Allies could rely on intelligence at least to this extent was due to the fact that PR, agents and reports from the Resistance – the non-Sigint sources whose contribution to knowledge of Germany's defences and order of battle continued to increase† – were being supplemented more and more by Sigint. Benefiting from the expansion of Sigint resources and from the fact that, though still on a limited scale, the GAF and the German Army were at last using wireless in western Europe, GC and CS and the Y services were now making sufficient progress against the enemy's communications in that theatre to ensure that, if he did take steps or make changes that had not been allowed for, they would get some evidence about them. In particular, most of the new Enigma keys of the German Air Force were broken soon after they were introduced, from February 1944, and although little progress was made against the new Army keys that were identified, the Fish link between C-in-C West and Berlin was broken in March. As had long been the case, moreover, the naval Enigma keys in the west were being read without interruption.‡

□

In addition to giving the Allies some assurance that, should any occur, untoward changes in German expectations and preparations would not go undetected, these Sigint developments enabled them to undertake a deception programme which had reasonable

---

and March. Between 26 April and 9 May the Germans increased their reconnaissance effort. SHAEF's intelligence summary for the week ending 3 May noted that there had been daily reconnaissance of the western Channel with landfall over the coast in the Plymouth–Dartmouth and Sidmouth–Southampton areas, and possibly brief coverage over Eastbourne and Dover. Its summary for 10 May reported that the sorties had slightly decreased and that overland coverage was thought to have been obtained only at high levels in the Falmouth and Dover areas. The only recorded overland flight in daylight in the first week of June was over Margate on 7 June. The number of successful flights over coastal waters was obviously larger, but it was clear that they were much less frequent over the Channel than over Scotland and the Orkneys and Shetlands – not least because from mid-April to D-day ADGB maintained daily standing Spitfire patrols far out into the Channel along the whole of the south coast.[10]

* See Volume II, Appendix 1.
† See above, pp 16, 28.
‡ See Appendix 6(i).

10.   AIR 41/49, *The Air Defence of Great Britain*, Vol V, p 88; WO 219/1919, SHAEF Weekly Intelligence Summaries, Nos 7 and 8 of 6 and 13 May 1944.

prospects of prolonging the enemy's uncertainty about Allied intentions. Such a programme would have been impracticable if Sigint had not provided detailed information about Germany's measures and frequent confirmation that her own intelligence was in a poor state, and this was recognised in January 1944 when, as part of the Allied preparations for *Overlord*, arrangements were made for the deception authorities to receive from GC and CS without delay all decrypts that might have a bearing on their work.

At the Tehran conference the Combined Chiefs of Staff ordered that a general strategic deception plan should be drawn up for 1944 and the Russians agreed that a Russian deception scheme including a simulated attack on northern Finland should be concerted with this plan; the Russians accepted detailed proposals two months later.[11] Designed to draw the attention of the Germans away from *Overlord* altogether, and also from *Anvil*, the Anglo-US plan (code-name *Bodyguard*) was put into force in January 1944. Its object was to impress the Germans with three arguments. The Allies would need 50 divisions for a cross-Channel invasion, and because of the difficulty of assembling and training so large a force and providing adequate landing craft, the invasion would not take place till late in the summer, if then. In view of this delay, the Allies would, secondly, direct their main effort against the Balkans, though there would also be landings on both sides of Italy and, in the spring, an attack on northern Norway in conjunction with the Russians, who would not launch their main offensive before the end of June. Thirdly, the Allies hoped that strategic bombing would meanwhile bring about Germany's collapse; the priority they were giving to bringing to England from America the ground personnel and other resources demanded by the Allied air offensive was one reason why they were encountering difficulties in mounting the invasion.[12] In choosing to emphasise these themes the deception authorities were without doubt guided by the decrypt of a telegram from the Japanese Ambassador in Berlin early in November 1943. This had reported that while the withdrawal of Allied landing craft from the Mediterranean was leading the Germans to believe that the next major landing would be in France, not Italy or the Balkans, they still had some doubt as to whether the Allies would embark on 'so hazardous a venture' as a cross-Channel invasion, for which they would require 50 divisions.

By January 1944, however, the hope that the Germans could be influenced by deception measures based on such arguments had

---

11.   Howard, *Strategic Deception* (forthcoming), Chapter 6.
12.   ibid.

been undermined. The evidence about their defence preparations and the increase of the strength of their Army in France had put it beyond doubt that they expected the main effort of the western Allies in 1944 to be a cross-Channel invasion; and this evidence had been reinforced by decrypts disclosing their response to General Eisenhower's appointment as Supreme Allied Commander and their decision to appoint Rommel to a command in the west. In an appreciation decrypted at the end of December 1943 OKH's intelligence branch (Fremde Heere West – Foreign Armies West) had taken the news of Eisenhower's appointment to be proof of 'the manifest decision of the enemy command to concentrate the main effort in the England area'; operations made in the Mediterranean to coincide with the large-scale attack from England would aim at tying down German troops rather than at forcing strategic decisions.[13] A few days later, when Whitehall had already heard the rumour that Rommel was to replace von Rundstedt as C-in-C West, the decrypt of a signal sent by the Japanese Military Attaché in Vichy on 13 December disclosed that Rommel was to command under C-in-C West 'all forces held in reserve for the counter-offensive', and that a further four divisions were to be allotted to him. This signal added that a single armoured HQ of Army Group strength was also being set up under the C-in-C, and that a force composed of 9 infantry brigades, 6 mechanised brigades and other units was being assembled under Hitler's direct control in Germany.[14]* A further message from the Attaché at the end of February, decrypted at the end of March, named Rommel's command – Army Group B – and stated that it controlled the offensive forces in the Netherlands Command and in Fifteenth and Seventeenth Armies.[16]†

Before the end of December further decrypts had emphasised the need to complement the *Bodyguard* plan with deception measures specifically designed to deflect German attention from Normandy to other western sectors. On 16 December the decrypt of an appreciation by C-in-C West, dated 14 December, had

---

* Rommel was appointed C-in-C Army Group B on 31 December 1943. At that time OKW intended to reinforce the west by the transfer of some 7 divisions and other units from Norway, Denmark, Italy and the Balkans in readiness for invasion, but in March it decided that C-in-C West would not receive emergency reinforcements until the Allied landing intentions had been clearly established.[15]

† For subsequent intelligence on the armoured Army Group HQ and Army Group B see below, pp 66–68.

13. WO 208/3573 MI 14 Weekly Summary for the CIGS, 6 January 1944; CX/MSS/T50/43.
14. JMA 3867; WO 219/1937, Martian Report No 75 of 21 December 1943.
15. Harrison, *Cross-Channel Attack* (Washington DC 1951), pp 231–233.
16. AWL 1702 of 21 March 1944.

disclosed that German Y was continually detecting landing exercises in the Portsmouth–Plymouth area.[17] On the same day this salutary warning against W/T activity which might well focus the enemy's attention on Normandy and Brittany was reinforced by the decrypt of a telegram from the Japanese Ambassador in Berlin reporting on a recent interview with Ribbentrop. Ribbentrop had said that there was little doubt that the Allies had agreed that a second front in the west should coincide with a big Russian offensive; the Germans were uncertain where the landings would be, but Belgium and the narrows between England and France seemed the most likely area. The Ambassador had suggested that in view of the difficulty of landing in that area the western Allies might well fulfil their promise to the USSR by opening their attack in the Normandy peninsula or Brittany, allowing a decision about the main landing in the narrows to depend on the progress of their preliminary operations. Ribbentrop had agreed that this was quite possible, adding in a reference to the V-weapons that Germany had plans not only for crushing any invasion but also for destroying England. At the end of December, as MI 14 noted on 6 January, an appreciation from OKM was decrypted; it associated concentrations of shipping in the Scottish anchorages and the Bristol Channel with 'the great landing planned against western Europe' and assumed on the part of the Allies 'a high degree of readiness'.[18]

In January 1944, in the wake of this intelligence, SHAEF's deception staff began to draw up in conjunction with the London Controlling Section and MI 5 a more elaborate version of the original COSSAC plan for concentrating German attention on the Pas de Calais.* The new plan (code-name *Fortitude*) was approved on 23 February. Simulating a threat both to Scandinavia and to the Pas de Calais, it was also divided into two chronological parts. Up to D-day the aim was to persuade the Germans that the main invasion across the Channel would take place only after attacks had been made in Norway in conjunction with the Russians; it was being prepared so as to enable the Allies to take advantage of any weakening of Germany that might result from these attacks and

---

* The original deception plan for *Overlord* was drafted by COSSAC's staff in September 1943 and provisionally approved by the Chiefs of Staff in November. It sought to divert the enemy's attention from the Caen sector, and to pin down his forces before and after the landings, by simulating a threat against the Pas de Calais, visual deception (dummies), W/T deception and double agents being used to indicate the assembly of a force of six divisions in eastern and south-eastern England and 'discrete display' in that area being accompanied by total concealment of the actual preparations that were being made in the Southern and Western Commands.

17. Dir/C Archive, 5183 of 16 December 1943; CX/MSS/T33/79.
18. WO 208/3573 of 6 January 1944.

from strategic bombing. After D-day the real landings in Normandy would be portrayed as being only a feint to draw off German reserves while the main attack was launched with six assault divisions against the Pas de Calais with the object of consolidating a bridgehead with 50 divisions ultimately embracing Antwerp and Brussels. When this other assault had been made, shipping would be available for operations against Norway.[19] In the Mediterranean the deception measures continued to conform to plan *Zeppelin*, a part of Operation *Bodyguard*. This sought to exaggerate the amount of Allied assault shipping in the Mediterranean and to convince the Germans that, although the Allies were considering a landing in the south of France, they might not carry it out because of their larger intentions in the Balkans.[20]*

The feasibility of *Fortitude* rested heavily on the knowledge that, as was obvious from the priority given to the defences there, and as was to be confirmed by Sigint, the Germans were convinced that the Pas de Calais was the most likely invasion area. They were so on grounds of inherent strategic probability,† and also in the belief that the Allies must invade there in order to eliminate the V-weapons bases for which they were showing so much concern and in which Germany was investing so much hope. Had it been otherwise, no amount of deception would have tied their attention to the Pas de Calais; and as deception succeeds in proportion as it ministers to expectations, we may suppose that, had it been otherwise, the deception programme would have been different. As it was, however, the German fixation on the Pas de Calais was increasingly moderated as D-day approached by another German conviction – the belief that the strength of the Allied forces in the United Kingdom was far greater than was in fact the case.

The Allied deception authorities had been using false W/T and double agents since 1942 to give the Germans an inflated picture of Allied military strength in the United Kingdom and the Mediterranean. From the beginning of 1944 they learned from Sigint that the Germans were themselves building up this picture by attaching particular significance to their identification of 1st US Army Group (FUSAG) in the United Kingdom. A decrypt of 10 January disclosed that FUSAG, 'not previously established by Traffic Analysis', was among the units they had identified in plain language signals, and that First US Army, 'last established on 1

---

* For further details of Operation *Zeppelin* see below, p 289 fn*.
† See above, p 12.

19. Howard, op cit, Chapter 6; CAB 44/242, p 186 et seq.
20. Howard, op cit, Chapters 5 and 7.

November in the United States', had also been identified.[21] On 12 March and 29 April decrypts revealed that Foreign Armies West had heard that General Patton had arrived in England and was apparently commanding one or two Armies.[22] On 14 May, in a signal decrypted on 20 May, the Japanese Military Attaché reported that the Germans had concluded that FUSAG had evolved out of First US Army and were associating it with Patton's 'return to Britain'.[23] We need not doubt that these decrypts inspired *Fortitude South*, the extension of *Fortitude* which the deception authorities prepared in April with the object of persuading the enemy that FUSAG was waiting in southern and south-eastern England to invade the Pas de Calais under Patton's command after the landings in Normandy.* And we shall see in due course that on D-day and for some time afterwards the Germans were severely impeded in the deployment of their armoured reserves by the fact that, as a result of their exaggerated estimates of the size of the invasion forces, and particularly of their fear of FUSAG, they could not exclude the threat of a follow-up invasion.† In the run-up to D-day, on the other hand, the more they reflected on the supposed vast scale of the armies available for invasion, the more they were disposed to believe that the Allies need not restrict the invasion to the Pas de Calais and might indeed land, either simultaneously or even initially, elsewhere.

These were the circumstances in which the Chiefs of Staff authorised the implementation of *Fortitude South*, which was formally brought into force on 18 May[24] at a time when, as we shall see, the Germans were exhibiting a disturbing propensity to conclude that the first and perhaps the main landings would be made in Normandy.

□

The decrypts which enabled the deception authorities to monitor changes of emphasis in Germany's expectations, and to

---

* FUSAG was eminently suitable for its fictional task. It was a formation which had actually set up a skeleton HQ in the UK in October 1943, when the intention was that it should assume command under SHAEF of the two – later three – American armies in France after the consolidation of the lodgement area. In the event this responsibility was allotted to 12th US Army Group.

† See Chapter 46.

21. CX/MSS/T75/29.
22. DEFE 3/152, VL 9732 of 29 March; DEFE 3/38, KV 773 of 12 April 1944.
23. BAY/KV 150 of 20 May.
24. CAB 44/242, p 189.

adjust the deception programme accordingly, were part of the steady increase in Sigint relating to western Europe which, coinciding with Germany's growing conviction that 1944 would bring the opening of the second front, took place from the beginning of that year.*

On 30 January a naval Enigma decrypt circulated an order of the day in which Hitler stated that the Anzio landings were the first step 'in the invasion of Europe planned for 1944'; while the mass of the invasion troops remained in readiness in England, the Allies would carry out such operations at as great a distance as possible from the main base with a view to tying down strong German forces and gaining experience.[25] The Japanese Ambassador telegraphed that in an interview on 22 January Hitler had said that the Allies could hardly abandon their plans to attack in the west, given the threat to the United Kingdom from his reprisal weapons, and had added that while invasion across the Channel was the most effective action the Allies could take, they might think it too hazardous and decide to land in the less heavily defended area around Bordeaux or even in Portugal.[26] When this telegram was decrypted, early in February, it had already emerged from naval decrypts of 29 January that, following a false GAF sighting of between 200 and 300 landing craft about 100 miles off the Gironde estuary, U-boats from as far away as Rockall had been ordered to proceed to Biscay at full speed, regardless of the danger from Allied aircraft and mines.[27] Later in February Sigint showed the Navy and the GAF carrying out elaborate anti-invasion exercises between the Gironde and the Spanish frontier, and also over the Loire estuary and the Brest and Cherbourg peninsulas.[28]

A naval Enigma decrypt of 27 February emphasised the vulnerability of the south coast of France to Allied invasion.[29] According to the decrypt of a telegram from the Japanese Ambassador in Vichy the Germans remained anxious as to that area in the first week of March; they suspected that in view of the set-backs the Allies had encountered in Italy, they might risk a large-scale landing there in the near future.[30] On 21 March the

---

* The increase was not confined to German sources. Such was their number and importance that from 30 March the Japanese diplomatic decrypts were included in a separate series of signals, the BAY series, among the intelligence transmitted from GC to CS to the *Overlord* and Mediterranean Commands.

25. DEFE 3/134, VL 5160 of 30 January.
26. AWLs 1472 and 1494 of 8 and 11 February.
27. ADM 223/171, OIC SI 842 of 30 January.
28. Air Sunset 146 of 19 February; AWL 1535 of 19 February; ADM 223/318, Coastal Defence Report No 4 of 5 March.
29. DEFE 3/143, VL 7247 of 27 February.
30. AWL 1626 of 7 March.

decrypt of a signal sent by the Japanese Military Attaché in Vichy at the end of February reported that the Germans were sending four infantry divisions and two armoured divisions to Avignon, Montpellier, Toulouse and Bordeaux.[31] On 1 April, in a signal reporting on his recent tour of the defences in the area which was decrypted on 4 April, the Attaché added that of the two corps defending the coast east and west of Marseilles with three divisions each, the western one was being strengthened by a fourth division in the belief that the Allied attack was most likely to come between Narbonne and Sète.[32]*

By the time these decrypts were obtained the Allies had agreed, on 21 March, that Operation *Anvil* should not be timed to coincide with Operation *Overlord*.† They had also received by then intelligence indicating at least for the present that the Germans had come to the conclusion that the attack in the south of France would be concerted with the larger invasion, and that the larger invasion was not imminent. The decrypt in the middle of February of a circular telegram sent by the German Foreign Ministry had revealed that the Abwehr had learned in Stockholm that the second front had been postponed till June, partly on account of disagreements between the Allied Expeditionary Air Force and the British and US strategic bomber forces.[36] In a telegram decrypted on 23 February the Japanese Minister in Berne had quoted a German intelligence authority as saying that the main invasion was not expected in March and that the preparations for a secondary landing in the south of France by the Americans from Corsica would take between two and four months to complete.[37] On 29 February the decrypt of a telegram from the Japanese Ambassador in Berlin had reported the views of the German Ministry of Foreign Affairs. It estimated that between 75 and 85

---

* It has been said that the Germans used the Japanese embassy in Vichy to spread false information about their dispositions.[33] It will be seen from these and subsequent decrypts from this source that, if this is true, the deception did not find its way into the reports made to Tokyo. For Allied intelligence on the transfer of two newly-formed infantry divisions and 9th SS Panzer Division to the south of France and of 2nd SS Panzer Division to Bordeaux, see below pp 72–73. The move of 272nd Infantry Division from Lyons to Perpignan had been disclosed by Enigma decrypts by 28 March.[34]

† No doubt because he would have preferred that *Anvil* should be cancelled altogether, except as a threat, the Prime Minister asked on 4 April that the decrypts should be shown to General Eisenhower with his compliments.[35]

31. AWL 1702 of 21 March.
32. BAY/KV 15 of 7 April.
33. Hastings, *Overlord* (1984), p 67.
34. DEFE 3/152, VL 9644 of 28 March; AWL 1775 of 1 April.
35. Dir/C Archive, 6175 of 4 April.
36. AWL 1532 of 18 February.
37. AWL 1558 of 25 February; WO 208/3573 of 7 March 1944.

divisions had been assembled in Britain but judged that the second front was being postponed; air reconnaissance had suggested that the Allies had enough shipping for a landing but not for bringing up supplies.[38] Summing up on 1 March the JIC had concluded that 'Germany . . . expects that the main attack will be made against the coastline facing the English Channel or possibly against Brittany, probably in conjunction with diversionary landings in the west and south of France. . . . The Germans probably appreciate that the Allies will not be ready to undertake large-scale operations from the United Kingdom within the next two or even three months unless there is a substantial weakening of the German forces in France and the Low Countries'.[39]* In the middle of March the decrypt of a telegram from the Japanese embassy in Madrid had quoted the Spanish authorities as believing that the second front would not be opened before April; the Allies had not yet completed the concentration of their assault forces in England or assembled enough landing craft in north Africa and, as the Germans were moving high quality troops from the west to Russia, the Allies would wait until the west had been weakened by these transfers.[41]

From other decrypts it was clear, however, that the German operational commands were not relaxing their vigilance. On 23 February a GAF Enigma decrypt had stressed that Allied preparations were well advanced: W/T activity had indicated that some bombers had been withdrawn for use in airborne landings and that airfields in the south-west were heavily occupied with transport aircraft and gliders, while other evidence, presumably air reconnaissance, showed that Bristol was 'particularly heavily occupied' with shipping.[42] On 5 March an OKM appreciation assessed the results of air reconnaissance over the Scottish anchorages: between four and six divisions were assembled, and as there was sufficient shipping on the east coast to transport them, the Allies might be considering an operation to prevent the withdrawal of further German forces from the north. This

---

* The JIC was relying on monthly analyses of Germany's appreciations of Allied intentions prepared by MI 14 and NID 12 and based not only on decrypts but also on intelligence derived from other sources – the European Press and radio, Allied diplomatic reports, the SIS and SOE. NID 12's analysis of 8 February had noted that the Germans knew from experience that 'they cannot rely on their Intelligence Service to warn them of impending attacks . . .' MI 14's first analysis was issued on 5 February.[40]

38. AWL 1589 of 1 March.
39. CAB 121/413, SIC file D/Germany/2, Vol 2, JIC(44)66(o) of 1 March, paras 7 and 8.
40. WO 208/3573 of 5 February 1944.
41. AWL 1670 of 16 March.
42. DEFE 3/141, VL 6878 of 23 February.

appreciation was not decrypted until 22 March.[43] It was followed by an appreciation from C-in-C West of 21 March. Decrypted on 6 April, this said that the Allied preparations were 'as good as complete', all information indicating that the jumping-off base would be 'the occupied west coast'; he was bringing 21st Panzer Division to Brittany to strengthen the defensive grouping behind his west coast front.* The C-in-C went on to say that agents had reported that the invasion had been postponed for a time, and he himself believed that the recent increase in Allied air attacks on communications behind the Channel front did not mean that the main attack was imminent since it must be expected that they would become still more intensive and continuous before that point was reached. He added that agents had also reported the completion of invasion preparations in north Africa, so that an undertaking against the south coast of France had always to be allowed for.[44] C-in-C West's conclusion that the invasion was not imminent was echoed in another decrypt of 6 April, that of a signal in the recently broken cypher of the Japanese Naval Attaché in Berlin.† He reported that the authorities there were inclined to believe that the second front would be opened after the period of mud on the eastern front, and thus in June or July.[45]

The evidence in C-in-C West's appreciation that the Allies had not succeeded in concealing the threat to western France might have been thought disturbing – the more so as it was reinforced by the decrypt on 19 March of a telegram from the Japanese Ambassador to the effect that the Germans did not now believe that the Allies would make an organised attack on the Dutch coast.[46]‡ But on 9 April 21st Army Group, while accepting that the enemy had reduced his estimate of the risk to the Low Countries and the Mediterranean coast, believed that he still expected 'an assault anywhere from the Pas de Calais to the Bay of Biscay';[47] and reassurance to this effect was soon obtained from decrypts of other appreciations. These appreciations, moreover, by no means accepted that the invasion had been deferred. An appreciation by

---

* For this movement and that of 3rd Parachute Division to Brittany see below p 75.

† See Appendix 6(i).

‡ This decrypt was followed by evidence that the Germans were reducing their armoured cover for the Low Countries by moving 2nd Panzer Division from Cambrai to Amiens and 12th SS Panzer Division from Antwerp to Evreux. See below pp 75–76.

43. DEFE 3/150, VL 9126 of 22 March.
44. DEFE 3/36, KV 353 of 6 April.
45. SJA 20 of 6 April.
46. AWL 1683 of 19 March.
47. WO 205/532, 21st Army Group Weekly Review of 9 April 1944.

Foreign Armies West dated 20 March, and decrypted on 12 April, read as follows:

'Numerous items of information about the alleged postponement of the invasion or its complete abandonment in favour of intensified air warfare and small-scale local landings ... are a planned cover for the actual intentions. Such reports are refuted by, *inter alia*, reports from numerous sources of troop movements throughout England which show a considerable increase on previous months. Similar indications are given by the great intensification of the signals traffic of the agents' and resistance organisation in France; this has increased by about 70 per cent as against January and February. Continuing observation of enemy air attacks, agents' activities and agents' wireless networks in the occupied areas of the west unanimously and clearly show concentrations in the areas Pas de Calais, Paris, Tours, Loire estuary and the south coast of France'.[48]

In another appreciation of 23 March, also decrypted by 12 April, Foreign Armies West repeated that General Patton had arrived in England and was possibly commanding two US Armies, and that operations against the south of France were to be expected, though not at once.[49] On 13 April the decrypt of another Army appreciation, dated 6 April, reported that the disposition of the Allied Air Forces, the move of Command HQs from London to Portsmouth and the co-ordination of British and American W/T all pointed to 'a further step in the concluding phase of invasion preparations.'.[50]

These German appreciations were followed on 15 and 27 April by decrypts of signals from the Japanese Naval Attaché in Berlin. The first, the account of an interview on 4 April with Admiral Meisel, Chief of the Naval Operational Staff, reported as follows. The Allies had completed their preparations and had concentrated their main force in southern England; taking the weather into account, they were more likely to move in May–July than in April, but they might choose April from the wish to co-ordinate the invasion with the Russian offensive in the south. Although it was so heavily defended, northern France remained the most likely place as it gave the Allies the shortest distance; but there would probably be a pincer movement from the Mediterranean and Biscay and fairly strong commando operations to cut sea communications in Norway, and possibly a landing in Greece to secure air bases. There was, however, no information on which to base a reliable forecast. Asked about the possibility that the Allies might desist from invasion and rely on intensified air attack while

---

48. DEFE 3/38, KV 773 of 12 April.
49. ibid.
50. ibid, KVs 848 and 965 of 13 and 14 April.

the invasion threat tied down large German forces, Meisel replied that they were bound to invade; they would wish to forestall Soviet penetration of central Europe, and the British could not withstand a long war of attrition.[51] A second decrypt, received on 27 April and reporting an interview on 13 April, disclosed that Meisel had by then concluded that the second front would start soon, possibly within four weeks. Although he could not wholly exclude the possibility that the Allies were conducting a deception prog-ramme, he believed that all the evidence – the concentration of troops and shipping in southern England; an increase in daylight air raids in France, and of Allied espionage activity there; the fact that severe restrictions had been imposed on the civilian popula-tion in the United Kingdom and could not be maintained for very long – pointed to that conclusion. The evidence included the interrogation of captured agents, and articles taken from them, which suggested that the Allies would mount 'a direct second front' without diversionary operations in the Mediterranean and Norway, and that the landings would take place in northern France. There were still no firm indications of the Allied plans: since 'thorough' GAF reconnaissance had observed no concentra-tion of landing craft on the south-east or southern coast of England, it was concluded that the concentration was in the west coast ports, but they were difficult to reconnoitre.[52] In a third signal, decrypted on 27 April and reporting yet another interview with Meisel on 17 April, the Attaché enlarged on the reasons for the change in the Navy's opinion: the extension of Allied bombing to communications and airfields; the establishment of a security zone in the UK and the prohibition of inward and outward mail; the news that war correspondents had been attached to invasion forces; evidence of landing exercises; statements by British political leaders.[53]

Naval, air and army decrypts had meanwhile disclosed that the Germans had indeed concluded that the invasion was imminent. The naval Enigma decrypts of 20 April included a proclamation from Dönitz to all ranks to the effect that a large-scale landing in western France was to be expected at any time.[54] On 24 April the GAF Enigma disclosed that Luftflotte 3 was instituting procedures for the interrogation of POW taken from the invasion forces.[55] On 27 April an army decrypt revealed that Hitler had

---

51. SJA 54 of 15 April.
52. BAY/KVs 59 and 67 of 27 and 29 April.
53. BAY/KV 60 of 27 April.
54. DEFE 3/408, ZTPG 232340 of 20 April.
55. DEFE 3/42, KV 1867 of 24 April.

cancelled all leave in C-in-C West's command from 26 April.[56] On 29 April the decrypt of a telegram from the Japanese Ambassador disclosed that the Ministry of Foreign Affairs in Berlin was taking the threat seriously on 24 April; it had informed him that if the threat did not materialise that week the landings would have to be postponed for several weeks, but that it had believed for some days that they would be attempted in the near future.

From 18 April, and especially from 26 April, there was a marked increase in day and night reconnaissance by the GAF between Dover and Land's End, in Scotland and over Scapa Flow; it lasted until the alarm subsided, and was accompanied on the south coast by minelaying and bombing raids on ports.[57]* Among the Enigma decrypts reporting on this activity, which showed that a number of Me 410s had been brought in for reconnaissance,[58] two disclosed that on 25 April and 8 May no penetration overland had been achieved and several offshore sorties had had to be broken off; but one gave details of a large concentration of warships and assault shipping in Plymouth and noted that such good cover had not been obtained since August 1943, and others recorded that assault shipping had been detected.[59]

E-boat activity off the south coast also increased. It included a successful attack at 0220 on 28 April on Exercise *Tiger*, a trial landing by Force U on Slapton Sands in the south-west of Lyme Bay. They sank two LSTs (large ships carrying tank landing craft) and damaged a third. This was a serious set-back for the Allies in view of the shortage of landing craft; and the loss of life – some 700 men, many of them engineers – was greater than that incurred by Force U in the landings on *Utah* beach.[60] As was invariably the case with E-boat operations, Sigint gave no warning of the attack. A signal disclosing that nine E-boats were to leave Cherbourg at 2200/27 April for operations to the westward was not decrypted till late 28 April. Other signals decrypted after the event revealed that the E-boats had caused alarm in the German naval commands by sighting Allied landing craft about 20 miles from Slapton Sands on an easterly course, but that Senior Officer E-boats had by 0347 on 28 April appreciated that as the landing craft had turned north, and as the E-boats had been in the area

---

* See above pp 43–44 fn‡ and, for the FX raid on Plymouth at the end of April, Volume III Part 1, p 326.

56. DEFE 3/43, KV 2161 of 27 April.
57. AWL 1942 of 1 May; WO 219/1918, Nos 5 of 22 April, 6 of 29 April; WO 219/1919, No 8 of 13 May 1944.
58. AWL 1931 of 29 April.
59. CX/MSS/T166/105.
60. ADM 234/366, BR 1736(42) (1), p 65; Harrison, op cit, p 270.

west of a line Portland–Casquets since 2300 on 27 April without sighting large Allied formations, no major Allied landing attempt need be assumed.[61]*

The Chiefs of Staff expressed some anxiety on 2 May about the Sigint evidence on the results of the German air and E-boat reconnaissance.[62] Their anxiety was justified by the receipt on 14 May of the decrypt of a situation report of 8 May from C-in-C West, which gave this assessment of the results obtained: 'Although visual and photo reconnaissance has not been able to cover the whole of the English south coast, it is clear from observed concentrations of assault shipping in the Portsmouth–Southampton area that a special build-up (Schwerpunkt) is being formed there.'[63]†

By the early days of May the alarm was over, as was soon confirmed by the Japanese diplomatic decrypts from Berlin. On 6 May, in a telegram decrypted on 11 May, the Ambassador disclosed that the favourable period late April to early May having passed, there was a strong body of opinion that the invasion would now be postponed for two or three weeks.[67] On 9 May, in a telegram decrypted on 13 May, he added that Dönitz had told him that, although domestic and international pressures would still compel the Allies to invade in 1944, they would not do so 'for some time'; they probably realised that Germany's 'somewhat precipitate withdrawal' on the eastern front reflected the transfer of some of her finest troops to the west and were thus being forced to increase the scale of their invasion measures.[68] But even before these signals were decrypted, it was the turn of the Allies to be alarmed

---

* This belies the claim in the official history (see Ellis, *Victory in the West*, Vol I, (1962) p 33) that the Germans did not associate the Allied activity with invasion preparations.

† On 19 May the decrypt of a signal of 11 May from the Japanese Naval Mission in Berlin said that GAF PR of a week before had detected, in addition to many landing craft at south coast ports, 'a floodable sort of pontoon which could be sunk for use as landing piers'.[64] The mission had previously speculated that the Allies might have developed some unconventional device to make them independent of a major port during the early stages of the invasion,[65] but does not appear to have realised that the floodable pontoons were that device (Mulberry). Nor did it link the pontoons with the fact which had been reported in a decrypt of 27 April – that the Germans had got wind of the Allied development of a submarine pipeline (Pluto).[66]

61. ADM 223/117, Ultra signal 2001/28 April; DEFE 3/44, KV 2273 of 28 April; ADM 223/172, OIC SI 903 of 29 April; ADM 223/287, Use of Special Intelligence during Operation *Neptune*, (USION) pp 41–43.
62. CAB 121/394, SIC file D/France/6/12, COS(44)142nd(o) Meeting, 2 May.
63. DEFE 3/155, KV 3763 of 14 May.
64. BAY/KV 146 of 19 May.
65. BAY/KV 123 of 13 May.
66. BAY/KV 64 of 27 April.
67. BAY/KV 106 of 11 May.
68. BAY/KV 121 of 13 May.

by intelligence to the effect that the Germans might have discerned where they intended to land.

This intelligence, more disturbing than C-in-C West's reference in March to the threat to Brittany,* or than the decrypts in April and early May in which the enemy had noted the movements of Allied Command HQs to Portsmouth and the concentration of Allied shipping in the Portsmouth–Southampton area,† came in a signal from Luftflotte 3. Sent on 8 May and decrypted the same day, it reported that the main effort of Allied fighter activity during 7 May had 'consisted unmistakeably of attacks . . . on the course of the Seine between Mantes and Le Havre', and went on to say: 'From this the view of Luftflotte 3, already often expressed, that landing is planned in the area Le Havre–Cherbourg, is confirmed once more'.[69] Its receipt coincided with the decryption of signals from the Japanese Naval Attaché in which he reported that, on a tour he had made of northern France between 20 and 24 April, he had learned that the German commands, particularly the Navy, believed on topographic and strategic grounds that the landings would centre on Boulogne, with the main force to the east, but also that diversionary landings with detached forces were quite probable in the Le Havre–Cherbourg area, on the Dutch coast and on the west coast of Denmark.‡

The Attaché's report, referring back to the third week of April, did nothing to reduce the anxiety aroused by Luftflotte 3's appreciation of 8 May. Nor could GC and CS offer any reassurance; asked to check the translation of the appreciation to see whether the text could mean 'diversionary landing' or 'landings', it found that the context favoured the interpretation of 'landing' to mean 'main landing'.[70] Between 9 and 14 May the anxiety expressed itself in agitated exchanges between the Prime Minister and 'C' and the CIGS. 'C' could only say that the Air Force's appreciation might not be in accord with that of the Army or with the views held in Berlin. The CIGS replied to the Prime Minister in similar terms: 'We have no evidence that C-in-C West accepts the views of the Luftflotte 3. Nor have we any indication

---

* See above, p 53.

† See above, pp 54, 57.

‡ For these decrypts see Appendix 7. Earlier decrypts having established the dates on which the Attaché was to make this tour, steps were taken to ensure that a complete and uncorrupt text of his report was intercepted by alerting the Y stations at Freetown, Mauritius, Abbotabad and Brisbane. Although the Attaché sent his report to Tokyo in thirteen signals by three different routes, a good text of all thirteen signals was received at GC and CS by the evening of 6 May.

69. DEFE 3/47, KV 3242 of 9 May; DEFE 3/153, KV 3281 of 9 May.
70. DEFE 3/153, KV 3281 of 9 May.

from Most Secret Sources that he yet appreciates we shall land in an area more closely defined than somewhere between Belgium and Brittany. The dispositions of the German forces in France and the Low Countries support this. I understand that SCAEF has arranged that his air forces shall try to direct Luftflotte 3's attention to some other area'. To this minute the Prime Minister replied that 'the greatest care must be taken . . . [to] confuse the Luftwaffe's outlook'.[71]

The CIGS's minute, issued on 13 May, took advantage of the decryption that evening of an appreciation by the C-in-C West.* Like that of Luftflotte 3, it had been made on 8 May, and it went some way towards providing relief in Whitehall. Its main conclusions were:

1.   On the basis of the amount of invasion shipping observed, the Allies would probably employ 20 divisions, and possibly more, in the first wave; in addition they would use strong air-landing forces with the object of forming a bridgehead.

2.   Although the whole Channel front from the Scheldt to the tip of Brittany was under threat, the most threatened sector appeared to be 'roughly from Boulogne as far as Normandy inclusive'.

3.   Given the importance to the Allies of capturing Le Havre and Cherbourg, Normandy and perhaps also Brittany were likely areas for the strong airborne attacks.

4.   Defence in the most threatened sector had been strengthened by 'the bringing up of 2nd Parachute Division and 7th Werfer Brigade and by elements which had already arrived of 91st Air Landing Division and of Panzer Lehr Division'.† In addition Normandy was being strengthened 'also in the interior against air landings by special measures . . .'‡

The C-in-C's acceptance that the Allies might land anywhere between Belgium and Brittany was echoed in signals from the Japanese Naval Attaché in Berlin. In a signal decrypted on 13 May

---

* See Appendix 8.

† See below pp 76, 77, 79–80, for the intelligence received about these troop movements to Normandy.

‡ These perhaps included the move of 21st Panzer Division to Caen, for which see below pp 80–81. Although the C-in-C did not mention 21st Panzer's move in this appreciation, it was then in train, and it was directed against airborne troops as well as against seaborne attack. On D-day 21st Panzer was in fact the chief threat to the British airborne troops.

71.   Dir/C Archive, 6444, 6460, 6475 and 6483 of 9 to 14 May 1944.

he stated that if the Allies wanted swift landing operations they would probably choose Biscay and the Mediterranean, but that if indeed the landings were to be made in northern France, he personally agreed with the assessment, given to him during his tour, that the main force would attack east of Boulogne, with diversionary landings probable between Le Havre and Cherbourg and elsewhere.[72] On the same day the decrypt of a separate signal from him disclosed that Meisel had told him that while a landing on the west coast of France could not be ruled out, Biscay was less likely than the north coast of France if only because the landing craft observed in the Portsmouth area were 'unsuitable for long-distance operations'.[73] It remained disturbing, even so, that C-in-C West had singled out the sector from Boulogne to Normandy inclusive as the most threatened sector and had stressed the fact that Normandy was being reinforced, and Allied anxiety again increased when, between 14 and 27 May, Sigint disclosed that its reinforcement included the transfer of 21st Panzer Division to Caen and the strengthening of the German forces in the Cotentin peninsula in a manoeuvre that was more purposeful and greater in scale than any the Germans had so far carried out. This came just in time for the American Commands to make last minute changes in their plan for the airborne landings behind the Cotentin peninsula.*

Some post-war commentators have argued that this development was due to the fact that Hitler had firmly concluded during April that the invasion would come in Normandy.[75]† The JIC was at the time briefly inclined to take a similar view. On 22 May the first of three weekly reports it issued on 'German Appreciation of Allied Intentions Regarding Overlord' stated that:

'The main assault is expected against the northern coast of France from Boulogne to Cherbourg inclusive. Although the German High Command will, until our assault takes place, reckon with the possibility that it will come across the narrow Straits of Dover to the Pas de Calais area, there is some evidence that the Le Havre–Cherbourg area, including as it does

---

* See below, pp 80–82 and Appendix 9 for further details. From Chequers late on 28 May the Prime Minister requested by telephone that the latest report on enemy movements in the *Overlord* area should be sent to him.[74]

† It has also been claimed that Milch, the Inspector General of the GAF, reached the same conclusion after considering the pattern of the Allied preliminary air offensive.[76]

72. BAY/KV 113 of 13 May.
73. BAY/KV 120 of 13 May.
74. CAB 121/394 Record of telephone message.
75. Winterbotham, *The Ultra Secret* (1974), pp 154–156.
76. Irving, *The Rise and Fall of the Luftwaffe* (1973), p 278.

those two first class ports, is regarded as a likely, and perhaps even the main, point of assault.'[77]

A week later it reiterated this warning in somewhat more emphatic terms:

'The recent trend of movement of German land forces towards the Cherbourg area tends to support the view that the Le Havre–Cherbourg area is regarded as a likely, and perhaps even the main, point of assault.'[78]

Further evidence in support of this conclusion was provided in the decrypt of a report from a German agent in Lisbon – probably available in London on 1 June – to the effect that 'the plan of attack favoured by the Allies was an assault on La Manche [Cherbourg] peninsula'.[79]

The decrypt on 1 June of the Japanese Ambassador's telegram reporting an interview which Hitler had granted him on 27 May quoted Hitler as saying that the Allies had completed their preparations; that they had assembled 80 divisions, eight of which had combat experience and were 'very good troops'; that after diversionary operations in Norway, Denmark, south-west France and on the French Mediterranean coast, they would establish a bridgehead in Normandy or Brittany; and that after seeing how things went, they would embark on establishing a real second front in the Straits.[80]

It was no doubt with mixed feelings that the authorities scrutinised this decrypt, which was the first diplomatic decrypt to be sent to the *Overlord* Commands by GC and CS with maximum priority. It indicated that neither the Allied deception programme nor the enemy's shortage of good intelligence had prevented the Germans from appreciating that the Allies would probably deliver not merely diversionary landings but even their initial main assault in Normandy, and that it was on this account that the defence forces in Normandy, hitherto comparatively weak, had recently been strengthened. On the other hand, it reiterated the assumption, adopted in Germany from the outset on grounds of inherent military probability, that wherever the initial landings might come, the Allies would direct their major effort against the Pas de Calais; and to this extent it indicated that, if only because the deception plan had led him to exaggerate the scale of the Allied preparations, the enemy remained far from certain of the place of the coming invasion.

---

77. CAB 121/394, JIC(44)214(o) of 22 May.
78. ibid, JIC(44)221(o) of 29 May.
79. Hinsley and Simkins, op cit.
80. BAY/KV 179 of 1 June.

By 1 June such recent evidence as was obtained from decrypts had favoured the conclusion that of the two hypotheses prompted by Hitler's remarks, the second deserved the greater weight. On 27 May another appreciation from Luftflotte 3 was decrypted; it differed little from that of 8 May, stating that the pattern of Allied air attacks on the Seine bridges during 27 May had 'reinforced the views already expressed by Luftflotte 3 as to the probable Allied intentions against the Dieppe and the Seine Bay areas', but at least it was still concerned about the threat to both sides of the Seine.[81] By 30 May, however, the Enigma decrypts had disclosed that the GAF had introduced contingency measures on 28 May against landings in Italy and the French Riviera. 'These measures', commented the Air Ministry, 'reflect not firm intentions but rather German indecision. The GAF has no clear view as to the direction of the next Allied threat . . . even if northern France continues to be the first priority . . .'[82] Since the beginning of May Sigint had referred to the existence of similar contingency plans in the Aegean, the western Mediterranean, Denmark and Norway,[83] as also to anti-invasion preparations and exercises in sectors of northern France other than Normandy,[84] and to actual short-lived alerts in several western areas.[85] It would have been easy to place too much reliance on this evidence as proof that the Germans remained radically unsure of the main thrust of the Allied plan. But there was no mistaking the significance of another GAF decrypt of 30 May. It disclosed that the GAF had been planning since 30 April to lay defensive minefields and that it was now making final preparations for laying them from Ostend to the Garonne. As AI noted, this was the first Sigint reference to defensive sea mining from the air since Operation *Starkey* in September 1943.[86]*

It was on this evidence, and also on the negative evidence that there had been no Sigint references since 28 May to further German troop deployments affecting Normandy, that on 3 June, in its final assessment of the German appreciation of Allied

---

* These minefields were to cause more Allied shipping losses from D-day than any other form of attack at sea.

81. DEFE 3/161, KV 5446 of 27 May.
82. AWL 2118 of 30 May (Air Sunset 177).
83. DEFE 3/153, KV 3498; DEFE 3/155, KVs 3884 and 3924; DEFE 3/160, KV 5186; DEFE 3/163, KV 5813, dated 11 to 30 May.
84. DEFE 3/153, KV 3434; DEFE 3/154, KVs 3552 and 3582; DEFE 3/156, KVs 4153 and 4230; DEFE 3/157, KVs 4301, 4423 and 4477; DEFE 3/158, KVs 4559 and 4728, dated 10 to 21 May.
85. DEFE 3/153, KV 3256; DEFE 3/154, KV 3687; DEFE 3/155, KV 3918; DEFE 3/163, KV 5956, dated 9 May to 1 June.
86. DEFE 3/163, KV 5762 of 30 May.

intentions, the JIC ignored the Japanese Ambassador's interview with Hitler and reached a more relaxed conclusion than that of 29 May. On the positive side the JIC emphasised the preparations that were being made for defensive minelaying by air along the whole of the north and west coasts of France, and it also noted that defensive sea-minelaying had continued in areas from the Belgian coast round to the Gironde. It summed up as follows:

'There has been no intelligence during the last week to suggest that the enemy has accurately assessed the area in which our main assault is to be made. He appears to expect several landings between the Pas de Calais and Cherbourg.'[87]

As for German expectations of the timing of the assault, the JIC repeated the assessment it had given on 19 May: 'the enemy considers Allied preparations sufficiently advanced to permit of operations at any time now'. Since the German recovery from the major alarm at the end of April there had been few explicit Sigint references to this subject. But these assumed that, as the Allies had completed their preparations, they might attack at any time. C-in-C West's appreciation of 8 May, decrypted on 13 May,* had noted that although agents were reporting a plethora of landing dates, mainly pointing to the middle of May, the invasion was bound to be heralded by ceaseless air attacks, and that 'this stage cannot yet be recognised'. It had allowed, however, that the landings might come as soon as the favourable weather, 'a series of days of continuous fine weather', set in. On 19 May, in a telegram decrypted on 23 May, the Japanese embassy had reported that the German Foreign Ministry had informed it that the invasion was 'not far off'; for this reason, and also because other landings were expected in southern France and Dalmatia, Germany would not fall into the trap of diverting troops from France against the Allied offensive in Italy.[88]†

There were no further changes in the intelligence picture before MI 14 issued its final assessment of German expectations

---

* See Appendix 8.

† It has been suggested that one other decrypt, of 29 May, indicated that C-in-C West did not expect the invasion in the first ten days of June.[89] It was a request for a fuel reserve to be made available for construction work to which the C-in-C added the statement that 'recourse would only be had to this reserve if after the first ten days of June the situation could be reviewed as a whole'.[90] But if this statement meant anything it could only have been a further indication that the C-in-C remained of the opinion that the landings would come at any time.

87.   CAB 121/394, JIC(44)232(0) of 3 June.
88.   BAY/KV 167 of 23 May.
89.   Lewin, *Ultra goes to War* (1978), pp 313–314; Bennett, *Ultra in the West* (1979), pp 51–52.
90.   DEFE 3/162, KV 5689 of 29 May.

on 5 June. This concluded that the enemy expected the invasion 'at any time now', though it noted that he had not yet instituted the U-boat patrols he had planned for the western approaches to the Channel and the Bay of Biscay.* It believed that he still thought the most threatened area was from Boulogne as far as Normandy inclusive, but noted that he was still carrying out defensive minelaying from the Belgian coast to the Gironde, that he was still over-estimating the size of the Allied force and that he was still reckoning with the possibility of diversionary operations against the Biscay coast and Norway and with the probability of amphibious attacks against the south of France and in the Gulf of Genoa.[91] In the light of the known dispositions of the German infantry, SHAEF agreed with this assessment; it added that 'the enemy sees the greatest threat to one or more of four groups of ports – Pas de Calais, Le Havre, Cherbourg, Brest'.[92]

As we now know, the Germans did not believe in the few days before D-day that the landings were imminent, and they remained uncertain of their destination. On 1 June, in an appreciation that was not decrypted till 11 June, Foreign Armies West believed that the period from 12 June onwards must be considered the new danger period.[93] In an appreciation of 5 June that was not decrypted, C-in-C West similarly concluded that 'as yet there is no immediate prospect of the invasion', and he had this to say about the areas of the threat:[94]

'The main front between the Scheldt and Normandy is still the most probable place of attack. Its possible extension along the north coast of Brittany, including Brest, is not excluded. *Where* within this entire sector the enemy will attempt a landing is still obscure. Concentration of enemy air attacks on the coastal fortifications between Dunkirk and Dieppe, and on the Seine–Oise bridges, in conjunction with the paralysing of supply services and of the southern flank between Rouen and Paris (inclusive) might be indicative of the main front of a major landing intended by the enemy. However, the cessation of traffic across the Seine would equally affect troop movements required in the case of an enemy attack on the western part of the Baie de la Seine, Normandy and the North coast of Brittany. As yet there is no immediate prospect of the invasion.'

On the same day Army Group B, in another report that was not

---

* See below, pp 97–98.

91. WO 208/3573 of 5 June 1944.
92. CAB 44/243, *Operation 'Overlord'*, p 40.
93. DEFE 3/170, KV 7502 of 11 June.
94. AL 1623, OB West Lagerbeurteilung 4 January – 11 July 1944, held in the Imperial War Museum and quoted in Ellis, *Victory in the West*, Vol 1 (1962), p 129.

decrypted, considered that the concentration of the Allied air attacks between Dunkirk and Dieppe pointed to 'the previously assumed focal point of the major landing' – the Pas de Calais.[95]

□

Closely connected with Germany's uncertainty as to when, where and on what scale the Allied attack would come was her uncertainty as to how best to oppose it. Should she give priority to defeating it on the beaches or hold back her offensive divisions with a view to destroying the assault forces by counter-attack after they had landed?* The intelligence sources revealed that the German commanders themselves remained divided on the subject.

The COSSAC plan had assumed that because the enemy had to defend so long a coast-line, he would group his mobile reserves methodically, so that they could move at high speed against the weakest or most accessible point of the bridgehead, but would delay the counter-attack until he had determined the scope of the assault, and that he would be unable to do this before D+2 on account of the risks of Allied landings elsewhere. This remained the assumption when the COSSAC plan was revised; as the JIC concluded on 1 March, the enemy 'cannot rely on being able to defeat us on the beaches. He must plan to conserve and concentrate so as first to prevent the enlargement of the main bridgehead and then to counter-attack to drive us into the sea'.[96] At the beginning of February, indeed, it had received some support from the decrypt of the Japanese Ambassador's telegram reporting on his interview with Hitler on 22 January: Hitler had said that while everything would be done to prevent the enlargement of any bridgehead, it was impossible to repulse every landing at the water's edge.[97] On 18 February, however, another Japanese decrypt – that of a telegram from the Ambassador in Vichy about an interview with Abetz, the Military Governor in France – had disclosed that the Germans were divided as to whether to aim to drive an invasion force back into the sea as soon as possible or to allow it to land and then surround and destroy it.

---

* It is of interest that at no stage did the Allied intelligence authorities believe that Germany would resort to the use of gas against the invasion. For a full discussion of the intelligence on chemical warfare see below, p 573ff.

95. AL 1562/1. Geschichte OBW, Part 1, item 47, held in the Imperial War Museum and quoted in Ellis, op cit, Vol 1, p 129.
96. WO 219/1837, General Morgan to ACOS-G2 SHAEF, 4 January 1944; CAB 121/413, JIC(44)66(o) of 1 March.
97. AWLs 1472 and 1494 of 8 and 11 February.

Abetz had said that he preferred the former course as being less likely to encourage the resistance forces in France, but that the decision lay with the military authorities.[98]

A month later the decrypt of a signal by the Japanese Military Attaché in Vichy revealed that the decision had gone as Abetz had wished. The Attaché had been informed by Rundstedt's Chief of Staff on 17 February that the primary object of the defences in Holland, Belgium and France was to enable the Germans 'to hold firmly on to the coast'. Their strategic aim was to destroy the Allies at sea and on the beaches. If they failed in that, they would try to destroy them as close to the coast as possible; there was to be no question of luring them inland.[99] He expanded on this report in a further signal on 28 February, decrypted on 27 March. Headed 'German Army's New Defence Policy in Holland, Belgium and France', this explained that up to January the German plan had been primarily to hold the coast but, if the situation demanded it, to allow the Allies to penetrate a certain distance before launching a counter-offensive. Following Rommel's appointment, to command Army Group B,* however, it had been decided to hold the coast 'absolutely'. As a result, there had been changes in troop dispositions. Previously the large number of infantry and armoured divisions which were to come under Rommel's command for the counter-offensive had been held back as a reserve at Rundstedt's disposal. Now, all the infantry divisions of the general reserve were allotted to the various Armies and only the armoured forces (nine divisions under General Geyr von Schweppenburg) remained at Rundstedt's disposal. The change had been made because experience in the Mediterranean had shown that the Allies did not move quickly and boldly after consolidating their bridgeheads, and generally sought to use air superiority to control the rear of the defending forces; moreover, there were great political disadvantages in letting the Allies advance inland.[100]

These decrypts coincided with the first Enigma references to the existence in France of Army Group B and the armoured command – Panzer Gruppe West. Enigma decrypts established on 11 and 18 March that the HQ of Panzer Gruppe West was at Paris and confirmed on 19 and 21 March that Rommel commanded Army Group B, which appeared from Traffic Analysis to have its HQ at St Quentin.[101] Together with existing information about

---

* See above, p 46, for the intelligence on this appointment.

98.   AWL 1550 of 23 February.
99.   AWL 1702 of 21 March.
100. AWL 1738 of 27 March.
101. DEFE 3/146, VL 8188 of 11 March; DEFE 3/149, VLs 8758 and 8846 of 18 and 19 March; DEFE 3/150, VL 9037 of 21 March.

the chain of command, they suggested that Army Group B, with Fifteenth and Seventh Armies, and Panzer Gruppe West were each directly subordinate to C-in-C West, who himself also commanded Army Group D with First and Nineteenth Armies. But they left some uncertainty as to whether and to what extent Rommel was under Rundstedt.[102]

As it happened, the decisions reported by the Attaché had not prevented continuing disagreement between Rundstedt and Rommel. In pursuit of the policy of destroying the invasion on the beaches, Rommel requested in March that all armoured and motorised units and all GHQ artillery should be placed directly under his command; but Rundstedt protested and towards the end of March a compromise was reached. Three of the armoured divisions (2nd Panzer, 21st Panzer and the newly constituted 116th Panzer) were assigned to Rommel and four (1st SS Panzer – Adolf Hitler – 12th SS Panzer, 17th SS PG and Panzer Lehr) were kept as a central mobile reserve under the direct control of OKW. In May the remaining three – the newly constituted 9th Panzer and 11th Panzer and 2nd SS Panzer (Das Reich) – were to be placed under Army Group G in southern France.[103]

The Allies learned nothing about these differences. But they had all along believed that the enemy would be forced to compromise between the need to limit the bridgehead and the need to reserve formations for a counter-attack, and, alerted by the decrypts of the signals from the Japanese Attaché in Vichy, they inferred that the Germans were having difficulty in reaching a compromise. Thus General Montgomery noted on 7 April, during a presentation of his intentions, that Rommel 'is a determined Commander and will hurl his armour into the battle. But according to what we know of the chain of command the armoured divisions are being kept directly under Rundstedt, and delay may be caused before they are released to Rommel . . . quarrels may arise between the two of them'.[104]

An indication that the Germans reached some compromise about their mobile reserves followed at the end of April. A decrypt then disclosed that four of the armoured divisions in the west had been placed in OKW Reserve, to be employed only with OKW's permission.* But this left it uncertain whether the remainder were under Rundstedt or Rommel, as did decrypts early in May of signals from the Japanese Naval Attaché in Berlin about his tour

---

* See below, p 79.

102. WO 208/3573 of 27 March 1944.
103. Harrison, op cit, pp 239, 247–249, 252, 254, 256–257, 262–263.
104. CAB 44/242, p 160.

of northern France. He stated that Rommel had been especially appointed by Hitler to lead an assault army, but that if the Allies invaded in several places their divided forces would be destroyed by Rommel in the north and by Rundstedt elsewhere.*

It was not easy to reconcile this statement with the evidence of the Japanese Attaché in Vichy, to the effect that the armoured forces were to be under Panzer Gruppe West at Rundstedt's disposal, or with the more recent decision to place four of the armoured divisions in OKW reserve. Nor was the situation clarified by the disclosure in a decrypt of 8 May that a new Army Group G had been set up under General Blaskowitz, GOC First Army, to command First and Nineteenth Armies in the south and south-west.[105]

In the absence of any further direct intelligence about the chain of command MI 14 concluded on 5 June that Rommel (Army Group B), Blaskowitz (Army Group G) and von Schweppenburg (Panzer Gruppe West) were all directly subordinated to von Rundstedt (C-in-C West and GOC Army Group D). It also concluded that while Panzer Gruppe West would assume an operational role if an additional Army Staff became necessary, it remained mainly administrative for the present.[106] These conclusions were substantially correct.

Within this framework German disagreements about the use of the mobile divisions had continued during May. Rommel, convinced that it would be difficult to manoeuvre the armoured formations under Allied air attack, had pressed that the four divisions in OKW reserve be moved closer to the coast; Rundstedt had resisted.[107] The Allies learned nothing of these further exchanges but from order of battle intelligence they knew the locations of the reserve divisions and they had detected no movement by them. At the same time, however, they had known since April from this intelligence that infantry divisions which had been inland were being moved closer to the seaboard throughout Rommel's command.[108]

□

---

* See Appendix 7.

105. DEFE 3/47, KV 3205 of 8 May.
106. WO 208/3573 of 5 June 1944.
107. Harrison, op cit, p 257.
108. WO 219/1836, Nos 8, 10, 11, 12 of 3, 16, 23, 30 April; WO 219/1919, No 4 of 15 April; CAB 121/394, CCS 454/5 of 15 April; JIC(44)176(o) of 30 April.

The evidence that the Germans were moving divisions closer to the coast was part of an increasing amount of intelligence about the strength and deployment of the German Army in the west. In the end, as we shall see, it enabled the Allies to make an all but totally accurate assessment of the German order of battle in the *Overlord* area on D-day, but in the meantime it did nothing to reduce their anxieties. It showed that against the general background of an increasing total number of divisions in the west the Germans were bringing in additional armour, were up-grading more divisions to field status and, in particular, were concerned to reinforce the Normandy area.

For the purpose of the Initial Joint Plan the probable strength of the German Army in the west on D-day was set at a higher level than that which the COSSAC plan had regarded as tolerable. It was assumed, on the other hand, that the enemy's ability to bring in reinforcements in the two months after D-day would be less than COSSAC had been prepared to accept. The projections were set out in a JIC paper of 1 March. There would be between 16 and 20 'offensive divisions' (seven of them infantry) and between 39 and 35 'defensive divisions'. A high proportion of the 'offensive divisions' would be at or near full strength, but they would vary in quality. The 'defensive divisions' would probably be well below first-class divisions in quality. Although it did not attempt to assess what the quality would be, the JIC explained that 'an estimate of the opposition to *Overlord* in terms of number of divisions is misleading'. As for reinforcements after D-day, Germany might bring in eight first-quality divisions from other fronts than the Russian in the first two months, and the possibility could not be excluded that five would be switched from the huge number on the Russian front; but this possibility was unlikely to materialise if, as promised, Russia had begun her offensive.[109]

These estimates diverged from statements made in recent decrypts of Japanese telegrams; if only for that reason they had been much discussed between MI 14, SHAEF and 21st Army Group before they were issued. A decrypt available on 4 February contained a telegram from the Japanese Ambassador in Berlin reporting that Hitler had told him on 22 January that there were 61 divisions in France and the Low Countries. Thirty of them were 'mobile reserve' divisions. Not all of the reserve divisions were first class, but they included as many armoured formations as possible – in particular, four SS divisions and the Hermann Göring Division – and he was attaching great importance to raising their mobility. Hitler had added that to avoid reducing the forces in the

---

109. CAB 121/413, JIC(44)66(0) Final (Revised) of 1 March.

west he would yield ground on the eastern front if necessary.[110] These figures were not inconsistent with those obtained from two signals from the Japanese Military Attaché in Vichy. The first, dated 9 December 1943 but not fully decrypted till mid-February, had given details of the distribution of Rundstedt's divisions in Holland, Belgium and France; they numbered 31 coastal and 23 'mobile reserve' divisions, including a parachute division east of Paris, and there were also three infantry training divisions, one armoured training division and a newly formed mounted cavalry division.[111] The second, dated 18 February and issued to the Commands on 23 February, had stated that these forces had been increased by nine divisions and now totalled over sixty.[112] Such numbers were considerably in excess of MI 14's estimate of the number of divisions available at the beginning of February: a total of 49 of which not more than 15 were offensive and three were Panzer training divisions that were probably to some extent mobile.[113]

In two letters to 'C' on 5 February the DDMI had attempted to account for the discrepancy. The fact that the Hermann Göring Division was known to be in Italy might suggest that the number of divisions given by Hitler might represent the number Germany aimed to have by the summer. Alternatively, in view of his remarks about mobility, and the fact that agents were reporting that cars and lorries were being commandeered and PR was reporting that motor transport shelters were being constructed along main roads, the possibility could not be excluded that she had, or would have, a reserve of motor transport sufficient to enable her to move some of the static divisions to the battle area. Neither of these explanations was reassuring, and the DDMI had added that the CIGS was particularly anxious that unexpected mobility on the part of the so-called defensive divisions might constitute a serious threat to the success of *Overlord*.* 'C' had submitted the letters to the Prime Minister with the text of the decrypt of the Japanese Ambassador's telegram. The Prime Minister had underlined the words 'serious threat'.[115] On 14 February Major-General Hollis,

---

* Anxiety on this score had been aroused at the end of January when the Enigma disclosed that 715th Infantry Division was moving to Italy and ground reports indicated that it had been hastily motorised before leaving Lyons. By the end of February it was known that it had moved in commandeered French buses.[114]

110. AWLs 1472 and 1494 of 8 and 11 February.
111. AWL 1551 of 23 February.
112. AWL 1550 of 23 February.
113. WO 208/3573 of 5 February 1944.
114. DEFE 3/133, VL 4979 of 27 January; WO 208/3573, of 24 and 31 January; WO 219/1836, No 3 of 27 February 1944.
115. Dir/C Archive, 5595 of 5 February, Letters from DDMI to 'C', DO/Inf 592 and 593 of 5 February 1944.

head of the Chiefs of Staff Secretariat, had testified to the continuing anxiety by requesting the JIC to consider the extent to which COSSAC's pre-conditions for the success of *Overlord* were likely to be met: these were that the Allies should have complete air superiority; that the Germans should not have more than twelve full-strength first-quality mobile divisions with which to counter-attack; that the number of first-quality divisions they could transfer from other fronts in the first sixty days should not exceed fifteen. General Hollis's minute had concluded: 'Before long we shall have to review the position in the above three respects and ultimately take a decision whether . . . we can go ahead or not.'[116]

On 7 March, uncertain whether the discussion preceding the paper of 1 March had taken account of COSSAC's pre-conditions, Hollis again wrote to the JIC. 'I may be quite wrong, and probably the matter is under constant review, but if it is not so, I suggest the time will soon come when enquiries will be made as to how we stand.' The JIC's Secretary replied:

'The conditions precedent to *Overlord* have been much in our minds . . . and you may be sure that the question is not being overlooked. The position briefly is as follows:
   Condition (a) has already been achieved and . . . is being daily intensified.
   Condition (b) is not so good. The present position is that there are in France and the Low Countries the equivalent of some 16 full-strength, first-quality mobile divisions. General Eisenhower's staff is of course aware of this. They have not, as far as I know, ever in so many words stated that they are prepared to meet the increased scale of defence. By implication, however, they have done so. I think the argument is that we have in the new *Neptune* plan widened the area of assault and increased the number of invading forces and thus, to some extent, compensated what the Germans have done.
   As regards Condition (c) all is well. The JIC in a very conservative estimate have stated that a minimum of 8 first-quality divisions could be transferred from other fronts during the first two months of operations. . . . It is highly unlikely that this figure . . . could be achieved.'[117]

General Hollis expressed himself as entirely satisfied, and in the next two weeks intelligence indicated that the projections in the paper of 1 March could be scaled down. By 20 March MI 14's total count of divisions in the west had risen to 55, and the number of these that were thought to be 'offensive' was fourteen.[118] Agents

116. CAB 121/394, Minute from Hollis to Secretary of JIC, 14 February 1944.
117. CAB 121/390, SIC file D/France/6/11, COS 308/4 and JS/44/178 of 7 March 1944.
118. WO 208/3573 of 20 March 1944.

had reported the arrival of 2nd Panzer Division at Amiens from Russia and of 2nd SS Panzer Division at Bordeaux, which had brought the number of Panzer and PG divisions to nine;[119] Enigma had disclosed that 3rd Parachute Division was being set up in France with cadre from 1st Parachute Division in Italy;[120] and on 24 February the decrypt of an OKH circular signal of 22 February disclosing that 349th, 352nd and 353rd Infantry Divisions were being set up in France had brought the number of three–regiment divisions there to four at a time when the fact that a division of that type (362nd) was being used to counter-attack at Anzio had led to the conclusion that such divisions must be rated as offensive.[121]* By 22 March, on the other hand, Sigint had suggested that 21st Panzer Division was leaving Mantes possibly, as MI believed, for Italy or Russia,[123] and MI had removed it from the order of battle. It had also removed 2nd Panzer Division and two others (10th Panzer and 164th PG Divisions)† for lack of firm evidence of their existence. This reduced the number of offensive divisions from fourteen to ten.

On 22 March the JIC's next periodical review concluded that it was doubtful whether the number of offensive divisions available on D-day would reach even the lower estimate of sixteen given in the paper of 1 March. Of the ten offensive divisions still in the east, the JIC now believed that only seven would be able to reach the bridgehead by D+10, that these would be the equivalent of only five full-strength divisions, and that from the Reserve Panzer Divisions and independent GHQ tank battalions and Corps troops Germany would be able to provide only the equivalent of two further full-strength divisions. It added that in view of the situation in the east, which made it unlikely that she could bring in any battle-worthy divisions from Russia in the two months after D-day, she might have to reduce her present strength in France despite her reluctance to withdraw any first-class divisions.[124]

Early in April it did indeed emerge that three of the offensive divisions, two of them the best in France, had been transferred to

---

* It was known by now that infantry divisions set up in 1944 – the so-called '1944' divisions – had fewer men but greater fire-power than earlier divisions, mainly as a result of a high ratio of automatic weapons.[122]

† These had fought well in Tunisia and MI 14 had hitherto assumed that, like 21st Panzer, they would have been reconstituted.

119. ibid, 27 and 28 February, 6 March; DEFE 3/144, VL 7657 of 2 March; AWL 1614 of 5 March.
120. DEFE 3/145, VL 7992 of 8 March; DEFE 3/146, VL 8174 of 11 March.
121. DEFE 3/141, VL 6997 of 24 February; WO 219/1836, of 5 March 1944.
122. WO 219/1942, Martian Report No 91 of 12 April 1944.
123. DEFE 3/149, VL 8953 of 20 March; WO 219/1836, of 26 March 1944.
124. CAB 121/394, JIC(44)113 of 22 March 1944.

Russia. By the middle of March agents' reports and the low-grade traffic intercepted by Army Y in England had established that as well as sending 2nd SS Panzer Division to Bordeaux, the enemy had transferred 9th SS Panzer Division from Amiens and two newly formed infantry divisions to the south of France;[125] but between 7 and 9 April Enigma decrypts disclosed that II SS Panzer Corps comprising 9th and 10th SS Panzer Divisions (10th SS Panzer from Lisieux) was at Lwow en route to assist First Panzer Army, which was encircled in Galicia, and that 349th Infantry Division, known to have been at Lille since January, was also on the Russian front.[126]* On 6 April, however, the decrypt of a C-in-C West appreciation disclosed that the three Reserve Panzer Divisions in the west (155th, 179th and 273rd) were being reconstituted as full Panzer Divisions.[128] 21st Army Group regarded this as 'a desperate improvisation', but MI 14 accepted that they would be fully offensive by D-day.[129] By 10 April, moreover, it had on further consideration restored 21st Panzer Division and added 2nd Panzer, of whose presence it had hitherto been sceptical, to the order of battle in France. Its estimate of the number of offensive divisions in France at that time was accordingly eleven: five Panzer Divisions (2nd and 21st and the three Reserve Panzer Divisions); three SS Divisions (2nd and 12th SS Panzer and 17th SS PG); 3rd Parachute Division; and 2 three-regiment infantry divisions (352nd and 353rd). Though it had no doubt that, subject to her difficulties on the eastern front, Germany would bring the number back to 55, MI's estimate of the total number of divisions in the west then stood at 50 identified and two unidentified.[130]

Early in April, after further Anglo-US order of battle consultations, the German divisions were re-classified. Panzer and Panzer Grenadier divisions were placed in one category and the infantry divisions were divided into those capable of full service in mobile

---

* These were the first divisions, apart from 715th Infantry, to leave France since the beginning of the year. The crisis in Russia had already led to the withdrawal of 214th Infantry Division from Norway, which was reported by agents and followed by PR in February, and of 361st Division from Denmark in March; this move was detected by 27 March.[127]

125. WO 208/3573 of 21 and 28 February, 6 and 13 March; WO 219/1939, Martian Report No 84 of 23 February; WO 219/1940, No 8606 8 March; AWL 1614 of 5 March.
126. AWL 1691 of 20 March; DEFE 3/36, KV 485 of 8 April; WO 219/1836, Nos 9 and 10 of 9 and 16 April 1944.
127. WO 208/3573 of 27 March 1944.
128. DEFE 3/36, KV 353 of 6 April; AWL 1837 of 11 April.
129. WO 205/532 of 23 April 1944.
130. WO 208/3573 of 10 April 1944.

operations (Field divisions), those capable only of defensive fighting (Static divisions) and an intermediate category of Limited Employment (LE) divisions.* In the middle of April it was estimated that there were ten Field divisions in the west, 33 Limited Employment divisions, including ten Reserve (training) Infantry divisions, and no Static divisions. Although it was thought that many of them were of recent formation, at an early stage of training, this represented an increase of seven Field divisions since January. It was known from captured documents, moreover, that five of the divisions still classed as Limited Employment (271st, 272nd, 275th, 276th and 277th Infantry) were to be organised on an offensive War Establishment. And it was believed that further infantry divisions were forming in France, probably of a new type with numbers below 100 and having only six battalions; Sigint had recently reported that one such division – 84th Division – had arrived in Rouen from Poland.[132]

By this time, as we have seen, it had been observed that some Field divisions were being moved closer to the coast and even into coastal sectors.† By 20 March there was already 'an extraordinary assemblage' of divisions in the Pas de Calais,[133] and the process was then detected in Brittany and Normandy. On 2 April it was

---

* The new classification, as issued as an appendix to a report by the CIC of 17 May,[131] was as follows:

'1. *Classification of German divisions* – A new system of classifying German divisions has been adopted, as it was found that the terms "offensive" and "defensive" were too rigid. Furthermore, the old system equated highly mobile divisions of great striking power, such as panzer divisions, with less mobile infantry divisions, much of whose transport is horse-drawn. Under the new system German divisions are classified into the following categories:–

    (a) *Panzer and panzer grenadier divisions*, including SS panzer and SS panzer grenadier divisions and also the Hermann Göring Panzer Division. Panzer and panzer grenadier divisions have been merged into one category, because each contains armour and is capable of great mobility.

    (b) *Field divisions*, including all other divisions intended for full service with the field armies in mobile operations, ie, the better-class infantry divisions, and all parachute, light and mountain divisions, and also SS divisions which have no armour.

    (c) L.E. (limited employment) divisions, including divisions intended for special purposes, such as occupation duties and training recruits; ie, the less mobile infantry divisions, L. of C. divisions, GAF infantry divisions, training divisions (panzer or infantry) and divisions composed of foreigners.

    (d) *Static divisions*, including divisions that are only capable of defensive fighting in the sectors which they were formed to hold; ie, coastal divisions in Norway, fortress divisions in South-Eastern Europe, and frontier guard divisions in Central Europe.'

† See above p 68.

131. CAB 121/394, CCS 454/6 of 17 May 1944.
132. WO 219/1836, No 8 of 2 April; DEFE 3/35, KV 156 of 3 April; AWL 1837 of 11 April; WO 219/1919, No 4 of 15 April; WO 208/3573 of 10 and 24 April 1944.
133. WO 219/1836, No 2 of 20 March 1944.

noted that the infantry divisions that had previously been inland 'lie close behind the northern seaboard, six in Flanders, Artois and Picardy, two in Normandy and one in Finisterre'.[134] By 15 April it was known that 353rd Infantry Division had moved up to the coast in Brittany, and on 17 April 243rd Infantry Division, classified as LE but believed, correctly, to have been made partly mobile, was firmly identified at the base of the Cotentin peninsula.[135]*

This 'striking reinforcement of the coastal zone'[136] was accompanied by the discovery that 21st Panzer Division had been transferred from Mantes to Rennes, that 12th SS Panzer Division had moved from Antwerp to Evreux, the area vacated by 10th SS Panzer Division's transfer to Russia, and that 3rd Parachute Division was in a 'lay-back' position inland of Brest. On 6 April a high-grade decrypt stated that C-in-C West had brought 21st Panzer Division to Brittany; by 9 April agents had located it at Rennes; and by 19 April they had provided full details of its position, sixty miles across, in the Rennes area.[137] At the end of March the Enigma had disclosed that it had more than the normal one regiment of tanks.[138] That 12th SS Panzer was moving from Antwerp was reported by agents in the first week of April and confirmed by an Enigma reference to its Field Post Number on 18 April;† by 22 April it had been located in a wide area round Evreux.[139] Agents reported in the middle of April that 3rd Parachute Division had been in Brittany since mid-March.[140] As for the other formations included among the offensive divisions on 10 April – 2nd Panzer, the three Panzer Reserve divisions, 2nd SS Panzer and 17th SS PG – the following was learned about them by the end of the month.

2nd Panzer Division remained under close scrutiny by PR and

---

* 352nd Division also moved from St Lo to the *Omaha* beach, but this move was not detected, see below, p 150 and Appendix 14(ii).

† Field Post Numbers, which were referred to by many of the intelligence sources – by agents, POW and the German Press and radio as well as by Sigint – were of great importance in the reconstruction of the order of battle of the German armed forces, and particularly the Army, for the information they provided on locations and identifications. MI, MIRS and GC and CS collaborated in the work of associating the Field Post Numbers themselves with their respective units and formations, keeping a common register and exchanging solutions.

134. ibid, No 8 of 2 April 1944.
135. ibid, No 10 of 16 April; WO 219/1919, No 4 of 15 April; WO 208/3573 of 17 April 1944.
136. WO 219/1836, No 8 of 2 April 1944.
137. DEFE 3/36, KV 353 of 6 April; WO 219/1836, No 9 of 9 April; WO 219/1941, Martian Report No 92 of 19 April 1944.
138. AWL 1780 of 2 April 1944.
139. WO 219/1836, No 9 of 9 April; DEFE 3/40, KV 1333 of 18 April; WO 219/1919, No 5 of 22 April 1944.
140. WO 219/1836, No 10 of 16 April 1944; AWL 1876 of 18 April.

agents at Amiens, where it had been since arriving from Russia in January in a depleted state; but the observation of train movements indicated that it might have received one or two of its heavy tank battalions, and a decrypt of 20 April reported that it was receiving new equipment, including self-propelled artillery.[141] The same decrypt mentioned that 2nd SS Panzer Division was being re-equipped, and agents had reported by mid-April that it had moved from Bordeaux to Toulouse.[142] Beyond confirmation that it had not yet moved, and some evidence that its training was well advanced, nothing had been heard of 17th SS PG Division since February, when it was south of Tours.[143] But a good deal had been learned about the Reserve Panzer divisions. By mid-April, agents had located 155th at Nîmes, 179th in the Mantes area and 273rd near Bordeaux, and had reported that they were taking part in formation exercises and that Panther tanks had been sighted in their vicinity.[144] On 25 and 28 April decrypts of signals from C-in-C West disclosed that 9th Panzer Division was arriving to be merged with 155th into a new 9th Panzer Division, that 16th PG was arriving to be merged with 179th into a new 116th Panzer Division, and that a new Panzer division was also to be formed out of 273rd.[145]* On the strength of an agent's report that notice boards for 9th Panzer, 16th PG and 10th PG Divisions had been seen at Vienna's main railway station it was assumed that the third division would be 10th PG until a further decrypt of 7 May revealed that 11th Panzer Division was returning from Russia to Bordeaux to form a new 11th Panzer Division with 273rd.[147]†

Over and above this intelligence a decrypt of 12 April had referred to 2nd Parachute Division, then in Russia, and to two previously unidentified divisions – 5th Parachute Division and 91st Air Landing Division – as 'a reserve for any theatre of war'; and this implication that at least one more parachute division might arrive in the west was strengthened by a decrypt which had disclosed on 7 April that II Parachute Corps was moving from

---

* When 9th Panzer Division arrived from Russia Ultra disclosed that it came in only eight trains, viz with only 10 per cent of its normal strength.[146]

† In the event the remnants of both 11th Panzer and 10th PG were amalgamated with 273rd to form a new 11th Panzer Division.[148]

141. WO 219/1836, Nos 11 and 12 of 23 and 30 April 1944; DEFE 3/41, KV 1538 of 20 April.
142. WO 219/1919, No 4 of 15 April 1944.
143. DEFE 3/142, VL 7001 of 24 February; WO 219/1836, No 8 of 2 April 1944.
144. AWL 1837 of 11 April; WO 219/1836, Nos 9 and 10 of 9 and 16 April 1944.
145. DEFE 3/43, KV 2012 of 25 April; DEFE 3/44, KV 2295 of 28 April.
146. DEFE 3/47, KV 3183 of 8 May.
147. ibid, KV 3070 of 7 May; WO 219/1836, No 13 of 7 May 1944.
148. Müller-Hillebrand, *Das Heer*, Vol III (1969), p 308.

Ghent to Melun.[149] And by the end of the month it was recognised that III Flak Korps, which Sigint had identified in the west in February, constituted a formidable addition to enemy strength; in a paper issued on 30 April the JIC estimated that it might use some 300 heavy guns and 1,000 light guns in a dual purpose role.*

In this paper, summarising the latest intelligence on the German Army's order of battle, the JIC advised that the number of divisions opposing *Overlord*, then 53, would have risen to 55 by D-day. There would be 8 Panzer or PG, 14 Field and 33 LE; the enemy would also have III Flak Korps and independent artillery units and tank battalions. Four of the 8 Panzer-type (2nd Panzer, 21st Panzer, 12th SS Panzer and 17th SS PG) were first class and likely to be up to strength; but 2nd SS Panzer was unlikely to be up to strength, and the three Reserve Panzer divisions would not be complete and would hardly be the equivalent of two good divisions. No Panzer or PG division in a battle-worthy condition was likely to be transferred to the west before D-day, though the Hermann Göring Division was a possible exception. As for the Field divisions, 3rd Parachute Division would be up to strength and eleven infantry divisions would have the equipment and transport to make them capable of fighting in the front line; but only two (352nd and 353rd) were likely to be in an advanced stage of training, manning and equipment by D-day. To them should be added 5th Parachute Division and 91st Air Landing Division, though they needed several further weeks of training. It was unlikely that more than one or two other Field divisions would be created. The 33 LE divisions included ten Reserve (training) divisions and four GAF divisions; some of these might be up-graded to Field divisions, but no new LE divisions would be created. Assuming that the Panzer, PG and the three most powerful infantry-type divisions retained their present dispositions,† the JIC after some disagreement with the Washington JIC and much discussion with SHAEF and 21st Army Group, and with the warning that the calculation must be 'largely conjectural and becomes increasingly speculative in the later stages', gave the following assessment of the German rate of build-up from D-day:

---

* This was a large over-estimate, but III Flak Korps was to play an important part throughout the fighting in Normandy.

† As given in the JIC paper, these were 12th SS Panzer (Evreux), 21st Panzer (Rennes), 17th SS PG (Thouars, south of Tours), 2nd Panzer (Amiens), 2nd SS Panzer (Toulouse), 273rd Reserve Panzer (Libourne, near Bordeaux), 179th Reserve Panzer (Mantes), 155th Reserve Panzer (Nimes), 3rd Parachute (Brest), 352nd Infantry (St Lo), 353rd Infantry (Brittany).

149. DEFE 3/36, KV 456 of 7 April; DEFE 3/38, KV 828 of 12 April.

D-day morning:	Three LE divisions plus Flak and artillery.
D-day evening to D+1:	Two Panzer divisions, one Field division, four LE divisions.
D+1 to D+2:	Four Panzer divisions, seven Field divisions, four LE divisions.
D+3 to D+7:	Seven Panzer divisions, seven Field divisions, four LE divisions.

The JIC believed that the only transfers from other theatres after D-day would be two divisions from Italy by about D+20 and two from Scandinavia by about D+25.[150]

At least in relation to the identity and location of the armoured divisions, the accuracy of the intelligence in this paper was confirmed in striking fashion on 2 May, when the decrypt of a Fish signal of the middle of April gave the time-table for a tour by Guderian, Inspector General of Panzer Troops. It disclosed that he was to inspect 2nd Panzer Division at Amiens on 28 April, 12th SS Panzer at Evreux on 29 April, 21st Panzer at Rennes on 1 May, 17th SS PG at Thouars on 2 May, 273rd Reserve Panzer (10th Panzer) at Libourne on 3 May, 2nd SS Panzer at Montauban on 4 May, 155th Reserve Panzer (9th Panzer) at Nîmes on 6 May and 179th Reserve Panzer (116th Panzer) at Paris/Melun on 8 May.[151]*
But by the beginning of May other decrypts were undermining the assumption that there would be no further increase in the offensive divisions and no change in their dispositions.

The most valuable of these, an order from Jodl of 26 April, was

---

* The decrypt also disclosed that he was to inspect at Mailly on 24 and 25 April Abteilung 654 (known to be a heavy anti-tank battalion), an unidentified non-divisional battalion and the Panzer regiments of the following divisions: Grossdeutschland Panzer, 3rd SS Panzer. These divisions were known to be in Russia, but regiments from Russia were often at Mailly for the purpose of converting to Panther tanks. Although it had long been known that Mailly was one of the two most important armoured depots in the west, it is probably safe to assume that the decrypt prompted the heavy raid by Bomber Command on Mailly on 3 May; Mailly had become an important target with the approach of D-day, especially as the JIC had concluded during April that the detached battalions refitting there would be used for the crash conversion of the Reserve Panzer divisions or in operations against the Allied landings.[152] In a signal of 8 May, decrypted on 14 May, C-in-C West reported that the raid had caused much damage to buildings and heavy casualties, but that damage to material had been 'relatively light owing to dispersal'.[153] It had been carried out by 362 bombers, of which 42 were lost.[154]

150. CAB 121/394, JIC(44)176 of 30 April; CCS 454/5 of 16 April 1944.
151. DEFE 3/45, KV 2624 of 2 May.
152. CAB 121/394, JIC(44)176 of 30 April; AWL 1904 of 24 April.
153. DEFE 3/155, KV 3763 of 14 May.
154. Webster and Frankland, *The Strategic Air Offensive against Germany*, Vol III (1961), pp 137, 156.

decrypted on 29 April. It specified that certain formations had been set up as an OKW reserve which was to be moved and employed only with OKW's permission:[155]

1.	West	I SS Panzer Corps with 1st and 12th SS Panzer, 17th SS PG Division and Panzer Lehr Division 'when brought up'.*
2.	Italy	Hermann Göring Division.
3.	South-East	42nd Jäger Division and 1st Mountain Division 'when brought up'.
4.	Hungary	16th and 18th SS PG Divisions and 8th SS Cavalry Division.
5.	Denmark	20th GAF Field Division.
6.	Home Area	Parachute Regiment 6, coupled with air transport space earmarked for 91st Air Landing Division and Werfer (ie. multi-barrelled mortar) Brigades 7 and 8.†

This decrypt gave a firm indication that 1st SS Panzer Division and Panzer Lehr were to be brought into the west. It suggested that reinforcements for the west from the OKW reserve might also be drawn from the Hermann Göring Division; possibly from Parachute Regiment 6, the two Werfer Brigades and 91st Air Landing Division (as an infantry division); and from the five divisions in the south-east and Hungary if they were not needed for Russia.[159] It gave no clue as to when the reinforcements would arrive. But it was not long before Sigint rectified this omission. On 8 May the decrypt of a signal from C-in-C West dated 4 May disclosed the recent arrival in France of Panzer Lehr, and ground reports subsequently added that it had arrived via Orléans and was located at Chartres.[160] The same decrypt announced that 91st

---

* Ultra had first identified Panzer Lehr at the end of March, reporting its arrival in Hungary.[156] It was thought, correctly, to be an assemblage of high-quality instructional units. It had remained in Budapest throughout April but the decrypts had continued to refer to it as being associated with C-in-C West.[157]

† A further decrypt of 5 May disclosed that Hitler had ordered the immediate transfer of Werfer Brigade 7 to C-in-C West.[158]

155. DEFE 3/44, KV 2388 of 29 April.
156. DEFE 3/765, VL 9838 of 30 March; WO 219/1836, No 8 of 2 April; WO 219/1919, No 3 of 8 April 1944.
157. eg DEFE 3/43, KV 2189 of 27 April.
158. DEFE 3/46, KV 2873 of 5 May.
159. AWL 1949 of 2 May.
160. DEFE 3/47, KV 3183 of 8 May; AWL 2019 of 15 May; WO 205/532, of 14 May 1944.

Infantry Division had arrived in 'the west coast area'; and on 15 May Sigint located the division at Redon, between St Nazaire and Rennes.[161] The presence in the west of 1st SS Panzer Division (Leibstandarte Adolf Hitler), was finally confirmed on 20 May, when Sigint located it in Belgium.[162]*

No less disturbing than the evidence of these arrivals was the discovery that the Germans were re-disposing their forces in the west to strengthen their position in the *Overlord* area. The decrypt about Guderian's tour had placed 21st Panzer at Rennes in the middle of April.† By then, however, reports of train movements were suggesting that a smallish division was moving from Caen to the St Malo area and being replaced by an armoured formation.[169] On 15 May a decrypt identified the small division as 77th Infantry, a new Field division which had been forming south of Caen, and confirmed recent ground reports that it had been replaced in the Caen area by 21st Panzer Division.[170] As the decrypt stated only that the remaining elements of the division had arrived, without giving its new area, MI 14 and SHAEF hesitated before finally accepting on 21 May that it was in the Caen area.[171] 21st Army

---

* The delay in finally accepting the arrival of 1st SS Panzer provides a good illustration of the complex nature of order of battle intelligence. There were rumours of its arrival in April[163] and, as noted above, it was included in OKW Reserve for the west in the decrypt of 29 April. By 1 May the decrypts had suggested it might be arriving by disclosing that I SS Panzer Corps, to which it was subordinate, was moving with its Corps troops, including its Tiger tank battalion, SS Panzer Abteilung 101, from Brussels to (possibly) Alençon;[164] but in mid-April the Russians had reported that the division was still on the eastern front and there was still no evidence of a large-scale train movement.[165] Decrypts of 3 and 5 May disclosing that elements of the division were at the SS Panzer depot at Tournhout near Antwerp persuaded 21st Army Group that the whole division had arrived,[166] but MI 14 remained sceptical as late as 15 May: the Russians had reported that most of the division was still on the eastern front on 2 May, and though agents had now reported train movements through Holland during April, these movements did not appear to be on a sufficient scale.[167] On 22 May MI 14 accepted that the division had been transferred, but believed it was well below strength.[168]

† See above, p 78.

161. DEFE 3/47, KV 3183 of 8 May; DEFE 3/155, KV 3892 of 15 May.
162. DEFE 3/158, KV 4608 of 20 May.
163. WO 205/532, of 25 April 1944.
164. ibid, of 30 April; DEFE 3/42, KV 1891 of 24 April; DEFE 3/43, KV 2012 of 25 April; AWL 1939 of 1 May.
165. AWL 1948 of 2 May.
166. DEFE 3/45, KV 2700 of 3 May; DEFE 3/46, KV 2960 of 5 May; WO 205/532, of 7 May 1944.
167. WO 208/3573 of 15 May 1944; AWL 2020 of 15 May.
168. AWL 2058 of 22 May.
169. WO 219/1836 of 7 May 1944.
170. ibid of 14 May; DEFE 3/155, KV 3892 of 15 May; AWLs 2019 and 2020 of 15 May.
171. WO 219/1842, Martian Report No 96 of 17 May; WO 219/1836, No 9 of 20 May; WO 208/3573 of 22 May 1944.

Group had no reservations; as early as 14 May, indeed, it had concluded on the basis of reports of tracks and tank carriers that 'the division is now close to Caen with its tanks apparently east of the Orne. The exact area of the division and its dispositions are not known, but on any reckoning it now lies but a short run from the eastern beaches of the *Neptune* area'.[172]

In the same report 21st Army Group had noted that there was evidence for 'a drastic redisposition of enemy armour. . . . The Pas de Calais and the mouth of the Seine were stiff with infantry, while it is to the area between the Seine and the Loire that his armour has been coming'. This appreciation was much influenced by the fact that, over and above the information about 21st Panzer, 'a good report' received on 10 May had stated that 17th SS PG was moving from Thouars to Rennes and that 1st SS Panzer was leaving Antwerp to replace 17th SS PG at Thouars.[173] Not till 24 and 25 May did a further agent's report and (in the case of 17th SS PG) a decrypt prove that this 'good report' had been inaccurate.[174] By 15 May, however, there was some evidence that 5th Parachute Division had replaced 21st Panzer at Rennes;[175] several decrypts had reported the setting-up of this division in April and had located it at Nancy[176] and in the first week of May another decrypt disclosed that elements of 4th Parachute Division from Italy were to be sent – presumably as cadres – to strengthen 5th Parachute Division forming at Rennes.[177] On 26 May the presence of 5th Parachute in the Rennes area was mentioned in the decrypt of a signal reporting the arrival of reinforcements for the Cotentin peninsula.[178]

Ground reports of train movements had indicated by 21 May that some reinforcement of the Cotentin was taking place. We have already seen that, coming on top of the re-disposition of 21st Panzer and the location of Panzer Lehr, this news prompted the JIC on 22 May to wonder whether the enemy had concluded that the Le Havre–Cherbourg area would be 'a likely, and perhaps the main point of assault'.* It was followed by decrypts issued on 24, 25 and 27 May of Fish signals, dating from the middle of the month, which reported the completion of a considerable reinforcement of the Cotentin and gave exceptionally full details of

---

* See above, p 61.

172. WO 219/1836, of 14 May 1944.
173. WO 219/1942, Martian Report No 95 of 10 May 1944, No 96 of 17 May.
174. ibid, No 97 of 24 May; DEFE 3/160, KV 5189 of 25 May.
175. WO 208/3573 of 15 May 1944.
176. DEFE 3/40, KV 1339 of 18 April.
177. DEFE 3/47, KV 3184 of 8 May.
178. DEFE 3/161, KV 5320 of 26 May.

the locations, boundaries and subordinations of the formations involved.[179]*

□

These disclosures, together with evidence from Sigint and the other sources that some divisions were still being up-graded and new ones formed in the west, required frequent upward revisions during May of the estimates of the total number of divisions available under C-in-C West's command. At the end of April, when the JIC had estimated that *Overlord* would be opposed by 55 divisions – 8 Panzer and PG; 14 Field and 33 LE – it had believed that the enemy would maintain C-in-C West's strength at that level, and that, if forced to transfer divisions to Russia, he would replace them with newly-formed or battered divisions.[180] By 13 May the number of divisions already identified had risen to 56 and the JIC had raised its estimate for D-day to 60. It had also revised its estimate of the number that could be transferred to France in the two months after D-day. On 30 April it had believed that these would be limited to two from Scandinavia and two from Italy; on 13 May, though continuing to insist that no divisions would be released from Russia, it thought that one or two could arrive from Denmark, two or three from Norway, and two from Italy and, possibly, two from the Balkans and a few newly-formed divisions from Germany and Poland. Nor did it exclude the prospect that should the situation become critical on the eastern or the western fronts, Germany might withdraw in Italy and the Balkans to enable her to release a further four divisions from each of these theatres. To account for this last revision the JIC referred to the lull on the eastern front, to Germany's improved position in Hungary and Romania and to the probability that with the start of the Allied offensive against the *Gustav* line in Italy she would down-grade the threat of an Allied landing in the eastern Mediterranean.[181]

On 16 May the Chiefs of Staff believed that the number of additional divisions Germany might bring in by D+60 would not exceed thirteen. And as for the number she would have available by D-day, the CIGS was satisfied that when allowance was made for 'the revised method of assessing and classifying German

---

* See Appendix 9 for these details and for the effects of this intelligence on US First Army's operational plans.

179.   WO 205/532 of 21 May; DEFE 3/160, KVs 5081 and 5158 of 24 and 25 May; DEFE 3/161, KV 5416 of 27 May; WO 208/3573 of 29 May 1944.
180.   CAB 121/394, JIC(44)176 of 30 April.
181.   ibid, JIC(44)198 of 13 May.

strengths, it appeared that enemy opposition to *Overlord* fell within the limits previously agreed as being the maximum under which the operation could be launched'. In order to reassure themselves on this score, however, the Chiefs of Staff asked that the latest estimate of the scale of opposition should be assessed on the old classification, in terms of full-strength, first-quality divisions.[182] This was done by MI 14, which relied on a considerable amount of recent intelligence, much of it provided by Fish decrypts and giving detailed strength returns,* to work out that the offensive divisions (that is, the Panzer and PG divisions, of which ten had now been located, and those of the Field divisions that were not holding coastal sectors) were the equivalent of between twelve and sixteen full-strength, first-quality divisions.

On 20 May MI 14's re-evaluation was incorporated into a draft minute for the Prime Minister. On 23 May this draft was approved by the Chiefs of Staff who, briefed by the DMO, added a further paragraph (paragraph 10) before forwarding it with the suggestion that the Prime Minister might send it to Stalin once the date of D-day had been fixed.[183] The relevant paragraphs read as follows:

'Land Forces

7. We estimate that, on the target date of OVERLORD, the Germans will have six to seven full-strength, first-quality divisions in reserve in France and the Low Countries. They will also have in reserve some eleven to fourteen offensive divisions of rather lower quality, roughly equivalent to some six to nine full-strength, first-quality divisions. Instead of twelve full-strength, first-quality divisions in reserve, as stipulated by COSSAC, there will thus be a total of seventeen to twenty-one offensive divisions which will be the equivalent of some twelve to sixteen full-strength first-quality divisions.

8. During the first two months it is unlikely that the Germans will be able to transfer any divisions from the Russian front to the West, but they may make available, from elsewhere, for use against OVERLORD, some five to seven divisions of varying strength and quality. Dependent on the course of events on the Russian and Italian fronts, and at the cost of major withdrawals in the Mediterranean theatre, a further six divisions, at the most, might also be brought against OVERLORD. This represents a maximum of thirteen divisions which might be brought against

---

* See Appendix 10 (i).

182.   ibid, COS(44)158th(o) Meeting of 16 May.
183.   ibid, COS(44)167th(o) Meeting of 23 May.

OVERLORD, as compared with the maximum of fifteen which COSSAC considered acceptable.

9. In the following table we compare the build-up in equivalent full-strength, first-quality divisions, which, according to COSSAC's conditions, should not be exceeded, with that which we now believe the Germans might achieve. Our estimate makes no allowance for interference by air or airborne attack or by sabotage.

	German build-up	
Time	*Maximum build-up acceptable to COSSAC*	*Present Estimate*
By D Day	3	3
D+2	5	6–7
D+8	9	11–14

10. It should be noted, however, that since COSSAC laid down his conditions in his appreciation of 30 July 1943, the OVER-LORD Plan has been revised with the object of increasing the breadth and weight of the initial assault, ensuring the earlier capture of a deep water port, and improving the rate of our build-up. These factors, together with the reduction in the likely rate of German reinforcements against OVERLORD in the first two months of the operation, should in some measure compensate for the present increase in German opposition during the initial stage of the operation.'*

These conclusions may be compared with those of the review by the Combined Intelligence Committee for the Combined Chiefs of Staff of 'Conditions in Europe', issued on 17 May, and based on intelligence up to 10 May. This accepted the JIC's estimate that there would be 60 divisions in the west on D-day, but set a slightly higher estimate of the enemy's rate of build-up: his main counter-attack would be made about D+7 with seven Panzer and PG and seven Field divisions.[184]

The JIC's final report in the series entitled 'Periodic Review of Conditions in Europe and the Scale of Opposition to *Overlord*' followed on 25 May.[185] The number of divisions located in the

---

* See Appendix 10 (ii, iii and iv) for MI 14's reassessment, for the full text of the memorandum and for the DMO's brief. There is no record that the memorandum was sent to Moscow. The memorandum referred to the exchanges on 20 October 1943 (see above, p 8) at the Moscow conference, when Marshal Voroshilov had enquired what the Allies would do if Germany had more than twelve good divisions in France and the Low Countries and had been told that, as the estimate of twelve was an approximation, it might be thought that the invasion had a reasonable prospect of success against thirteen or fourteen good divisions.

184. ibid, CIC 454/6 of 17 May 1944.
185. ibid, JIC(44)215(o) of 25 May.

west was then 59 – 10 Panzer and PG, 14 Field, 34 LE and one unidentified but probably LE – as compared with 53 on 30 April. The JIC believed that the number might be raised to 62 by D-day, as compared with its estimate of 55 on 30 April, by the arrival of one armoured and two Field divisions.* As for the enemy build-up against the landings, the JIC thought the Allies would encounter three LE divisions, elements of 21st Panzer Division and one Field Division (352nd Infantry) in the forenoon of D-day but that they would be joined by last light by the whole of 21st Panzer Division, elements of a second armoured division (12th SS Panzer), one Field Division (91st Infantry) and three more LE divisions; and that D+1 would see the arrival of two other armoured formations (Panzer Lehr and 17th SS PG). Between D+7 and D+25, the period in which the enemy was most likely to attempt a large-scale counter-attack, the Germans would be able to assemble ten or eleven Panzer and PG divisions, between eleven and thirteen Field divisions and eight LE divisions. But the forces actually available would have been reduced by battle casualties since D-day, by air attack and sabotage against the movement of mobile divisions and by the difficulty of bringing non-mobile divisions up to the bridgehead; and the damage already done to rail communications was such that the LE divisions and most of the Field divisions would be wholly dependent on improvised road transport.

The strength of the counter-attack would also depend on the quality of the divisions, and the JIC paper offered an assessment of the state of every division.† But it noted that the available intelligence was variable in extent and reliability, and uncertainty on this subject continued to be a major source of anxiety down to D-day. On 30 May the CIGS asked whether further information about the quality of the listed divisions could be provided so that it could be compared with the original limits laid down by COSSAC. The DMI pointed out that although it was known that some of the Field divisions were recently converted training divisions, very much under strength, and that some of the Panzer and PG divisions had been re-formed from battered formations and were not yet operational, the state of individual divisions could not be assessed with any greater precision.[186]

---

* As for the possible further increase from 59 to 62, the paper in fact chose to add three from a list of seven divisions which might arrive before D-day (see Appendix 10 (v)). This probably indicates an anxiety to err on the safe side, if at all, since MI 14 did not normally agree to the inclusion in such estimates of divisions of which it was uncertain. On the other hand, it is a tribute to the accuracy of its work that, as we shall see, it was able to eliminate four of the seven before D-day and that two of the remainder moved to Normandy soon after.

† See Appendix 10 (vi).

186. ibid, COS(44)175th(o) Meeting, 30 May.

Estimating the scale on which reinforcements might reach the west in the two months after D-day, the JIC's final paper repeated the assessment it had made on 13 May. Between five and seven divisions might be sent from Scandinavia, Italy and the Balkans, and possibly a few newly-formed divisions from Germany and Poland. Should the situation become critical for Germany in Russia or the west, she might find a further seven for either or both of these fronts by withdrawing in Italy and the Balkans; but no battle-worthy divisions would be transferred to the west from Russia. The paper added that not even battered divisions would be transferred from Russia if Russia went over to the offensive concurrently with *Overlord.**

Additions to Allied intelligence about the Army order of battle were still being made in the few days before D-day. By 28 May Sigint had reported that the Hermann Göring Division was moving from Leghorn to the Italian front, thus establishing that it would not appear in France in the early stages of *Overlord*.[189] On 29 May MI 14 tentatively placed II Parachute Corps at Rennes, a decrypt of 26 May having reported that it was moving forward from Melun.[190] On 5 June reference in decrypts to Field Post numbers disclosed that XLVII Panzer Corps was being brought in from Russia, and associated it with the reinforcements recently sent to the Cotentin.[191] These and other less important disclosures† were either too late or too tentative to be included in the order of battle lists and maps that were issued to the Allied forces but they enabled MI 14 and 21st Army Group to arrive at final

---

* In the absence of any hint from the Russians, uncertainty as to when they would carry out their promised offensive added to Whitehall's anxieties. In a search for clues MI 14 had scrutinised the Sigint, particularly the decrypts of signals in the German Y Service key (Mustard). Its report, issued on 25 May, found that while the Germans were reporting Russian preparations for an offensive, it was not possible on their evidence to forecast the date.[187] By 18 June, however, the Russians had advised the Allies that following a first attack in one sector about the middle of June their operations would develop at the end of June into a general offensive.[188]

† These included the news that 245th Infantry Division had arrived in France;[192] the fact that 156th, 171st and 191st Reserve Divisions on the coast in the Pas de Calais had been converted to Field Divisions (47th, 48th and 49th Infantry Divisions);[193] and confirmation that the division which had recently moved to St Malo was 77th Infantry Division.[194]

187. WO 208/4312, Report of 25 May 1944 on 'The Russian Plan for Summer 1944'.
188. WO 208/3573 of 18 June 1944.
189. WO 205/532 of 28 May 1944.
190. DEFE 3/161, KV 5320 of 26 May; WO 208/3573 of 29 May 1944.
191. DEFE 3/166, KV 6506 of 5 June.
192. DEFE 3/161, KV 5359 of 27 May.
193. WO 208/3573 of 29 May; AWL 2106 of 29 May.
194. AWL 2178 of 5 June.

estimates of the number, identification and location of the enemy's land forces on D-day that were remarkably close to the facts.

On 4 June 21st Army Group's assessment of the total number of divisions in the west was 59 identified plus two (245th Infantry and 6th Parachute) unconfirmed. On 5 June MI 14, which believed that 6th Parachute was still forming in central France, gave the total as 60, of which two were unidentified; and it was soon to emerge that the two unidentified were already among the 58 identified.* These estimates may be compared with the figure derived from German records. This is 60, but it may be amended to 58 because it includes two divisions (2nd Parachute and 19th Panzer) which, though about to leave for the west, did not do so before D-day. As for the locations, comparison of the German and Allied maps show that the Allied estimates were almost equally accurate.[196]† As we shall see, however, the intelligence on the location of two formations that were to play a critical role on D-day – 21st Panzer and 352nd Infantry – was either insufficiently precise or not spelled out with sufficient emphasis when relayed to the Commands.

□

In his signals reporting on his tour of northern France, decrypted early in May, the Japanese Naval Attaché repeated that as it was Rommel's policy to destroy the Allies 'near the coast, most of all on the beaches', the strengthening of the coastal defences, like the movement of troops to the coastal sector, had been 'particularly noticeable since he had taken command.'‡ The details given in his report filled some gaps in Allied knowledge of the enemy's coast defence preparations but were chiefly valuable for confirming what the Allies had learned since February, the month in which they detected that the Germans were adopting new measures, notably the laying of underwater obstacles and the erection of obstacles against airborne landings, as well as intensify-

---

* 245th Infantry, which MI 14 had located at St Lo, had in fact gone to Dieppe, where MI 14 had located an unidentified division.[195] It thus appeared on maps for a time both as 245th in western Normandy and as an unidentified division at Dieppe. The other unidentified division was later to be identified as 189th Reserve, which already appeared in the identified list of 5 June.

† See maps facing p 101.

‡ See above, pp 67–68 and Appendix 7.

195.   AWL 2106 of 29 May; WO 208/3573 of 29 May; WO 205/532 of 4 June 1944.

196.   WO 205/532 of 4 June; WO 208/3573 of 5 June 1944; Müller-Hillebrand, op cit, Vol III, p 144.

ing the construction of fixed defences, the inundation of coastal areas and defensive sea-minelaying.

In a Press interview in February Rundstedt stated that, together with a wide mined belt, lines of underwater obstacles on the beaches would create great difficulties for the Allies in the initial phase of a landing.[197] From 20 February PR detected such obstacles, which had previously been noted in small numbers only at Quinéville,* on many beaches, beginning with those in the *Neptune* assault area but eventually including practically every good beach in France and Belgium.[198] They were not yet being laid lower than about 100 yards below the high-water mark, but in view of the necessity of landing below them, the danger that they would be extended down to the low-water line created prolonged anxiety about the time set for H-hour. On 6 May General Eisenhower described the underwater obstacles as 'one of the worst problems of these days'.[199] Nor was it until 8 May that, in the light of PR showing the precise positions of the obstacles laid by then, the Allies felt able to take the difficult decision to stand by their original intention to land at half-flood on the day when that came at forty minutes after nautical twilight (that is 5 June with postponement acceptable to 6 and 7 June).[200]

We now know that only lack of time and shortage of manpower and materials prevented the Germans from extending these obstacles down to the low-water line, as they planned to do.[201] Even so, the fact that it was imperative to remove or destroy in advance of the first assault wave those they were laying necessitated the training of large numbers of Royal Engineers and naval personnel and the provision of special craft and equipment. For these purposes, moreover, it was not enough to pin-point the location of the obstacles. This could be done by the vertical photography flights of the normal PR squadrons which had previously carried out other essential work, including the photographing of every beach at every stage of the tide to provide the basis for the all-important need to estimate the beach gradients. It was essential, also, to determine the nature of the obstacles. The decrypt of a signal from the Japanese Military Attaché in Vichy provided some technical details about them on 21 March.[202] But

---

* See above, p 17.

197. WO 205/532, No 2 of 20 February 1944.
198. WO 219/1939, Martian Report No 84 of 21 February; WO 219/1940, ibid, No 85 of 1 March; ADM 223/120, NID UC Report No 434 of 26 February 1944.
199. Harrison, op cit, p 177n.
200. CAB 44/242, p 262, quoting ANCXF Report Vol 1, p 9.
201. Harrison, op cit, pp 264–265.
202. AWL 1706 of 22 March.

more information was needed – a continuous watch, indeed, as was illustrated at the end of April when a bombing attack on coastal batteries detonated a series of mines which, it emerged, had been attached to stakes set between the obstacles.[203] It was obtained by Lightnings of the USAAF which, flying daily until D-day along the lines of obstacles at zero feet, took oblique photographs with a new moving camera. Low-level oblique photography, an outstandingly important development in PR which also proved invaluable for coverage of the other fixed defences and of the V-weapons sites, was supplemented by the physical examinations carried out by the Combined Operations Pilotage Parties.[204]

At the turn of 1943–1944 Combined Operations Pilotage Parties (COPP) carried out small reconnaissance operations off the French coast. To conceal the intended landing area these parties worked in the Dover Straits and the Channel Islands as well as on the Normandy coast. Some parties remained offshore to investigate the tides, but the most remarkable work was carried out by men landed from the midget submarine X-20 whose main task was to investigate patches of soft peat and clay mentioned by a French guidebook as occurring on certain beaches but who also brought back information about beach gradients, inundations and defences. The intelligence brought back by this party led to experiments off the Norfolk coast, where similar conditions obtained, and the devising of counter-measures.[205] In May 1944, in Operation *Tarbrush*, four similar landings were made in the Pas de Calais with the object of investigating outer beach obstacles and, in particular, the types of mine attached to them.

Inundations and obstacles against airborne landings presented further problems. The inundations were under PR observation from the beginning of 1944, and an enormous effort was devoted to plotting them as they were extended in the Low Countries and northern France, even though only those behind Courseulles and around the river Dives and those at the base of the Cotentin peninsula and on its east coast directly affected the *Overlord* plans.[206] As a final coastal defence measure Rommel ordered the staking of all fields suitable for glider landings. This was at the

---

203. WO 219/1836, No 12 of 30 April; WO 219/1942, Martian Report No 94 of 3 May 1944.
204. Saunders, *The RAF 1939–1945*, Vol III (1954), p 93; Ellis, op cit, Vol I, p 116; De Guingand, *Operation Victory* (1947), p 366; Haswell, *The Intelligence and Deception of the D-day Landings* (1979), p 93; CAB 44/242, pp 165–166; AIR 41/7, *Photographic Reconnaissance*, Vol II, p 144.
205. Roskill, *The War at Sea*, Vol III Part 2 (1961), pp 11–12; McLachlan, *Room 39* (1968), pp 331–332; De Guingand, op cit, p 366; Haswell, op cit, pp 93–94.
206. CAB 44/242, p 209: D'Este, *Decision in Normandy*, (1983) p 154.

time of the heightened fear of airborne landings which produced in May the reinforcement of the Cotentin by additional ground forces to deal with this threat.* The work was started in Brittany and Normandy, areas which the Germans judged to be favourable for diversionary and subsidiary landings, and was soon detected.[207] On 30 April 21st Army Group observed that, in the wake of Rommel's tour of Seventh Army's area, fields suitable for airborne landings up to ten miles inland were rapidly being staked and wired.[208] On 7 May it noted that Rommel had publicly drawn attention to the need for fending off airborne landings.[209] In his important appreciation of the following day, decrypted on 13 May,† C-in-C West stated that the development of field works and outer beach obstacles, and the staking of ground against air landings, were being driven forward with all available labour. The importance the Germans were attaching to such defence was confirmed by a decrypt of 31 May in which Luftflotte 3 issued instructions for repelling airborne landings.[210]

The Allies could do little to circumvent or mitigate the hazards created by this last-minute development. For at least one airborne landing made subsequent to the seaborne assault – that of 6th Airlanding Brigade at St Aubin on the afternoon of D-day – plans were made for Royal Engineers to cut the posts beforehand, but this proved impossible and in the event the gliders either sheared off the poles or lost their wings in landing.[211]

As well as having to be assembled and assessed for the operational and intelligence staffs by the Theatre Intelligence Section (TIS), which gave particular attention to the underwater obstacles in daily reports issued from the spring of 1944, information on the coastal defences had to be reproduced on charts, maps and coastal silhouettes by mid-April for distribution to the troops and ships. This labour was undertaken by the ISTD with assistance from the Hydrographer of the Navy; it used up large resources, including one million photographs, and as Germany's preparations showed no sign of slowing down, it had to be reinforced by a procedure for issuing amendments right up to D-day.[212] A final report on the fixed defences for the Combined Chiefs of Staffs, issued on 17 May, pointed out that while their

---

* See Appendix 9.
† See Appendix 8.

207. Harrison, op cit, p 250.
208. WO 205/532, of 30 April 1944.
209. ibid, of 7 May 1944.
210. DEFE 3/163, KV 5956 of 1 June.
211. D'Este, op cit, p 136.
212. Ellis, op cit, Vol 1, p 176; ADM 223/287, Gonin report on *Overlord*.

pattern was settled, detailed additions and improvements were still being made.[213]

□

Concurrently with the intensification of work on the coastal and beach defences the German Navy made a start with an extended programme of defensive minelaying.[214] Largely with the assistance of Sigint, though not without much tedious analysis of it by the OIC and GC and CS, the programme was reconstructed in considerable detail – a fact which proved to be of crucial importance for the success of the landings.

Much of the defensive mining was carried out in deep waters. General evidence about it was derived from Enigma decrypts disclosing that minelaying sorties were taking place or, more frequently, from decrypts which were less explicit but showed that naval units known to be equipped for minelaying had taken an undue length of time to complete a voyage. The interpretation of such decrypts was often assisted by PR. More specific information as to where mines had been laid was provided by decrypts announcing that a swept channel had been closed or diverted. The usefulness of these decrypts depended entirely on the fact that the positions of the swept channels had been identified by means of the patient study of information gleaned from Enigma and other sources since the early stages of the war. 'By July 1943 an inshore route had been established from Cherbourg to Dunkirk, and by the beginning of 1944 the inner and outer swept channels were known . . . with a fair degree of accuracy . . .'[215] It was on the strength of the previous study and the arrival of new evidence that the OIC was able on 21 February to give the first warning that the German torpedo-boats had begun laying a major barrage in the Seine Bay, or to the eastward of it, at the end of January, and that the enemy had since established a safety margin to seaward of the inner swept channel between Le Havre and Cherbourg, routeing all traffic through this channel and confining minesweeping in the Bay to the channel.[216] Between the end of February and 24 May a further 22 possible minelaying sorties by torpedo-boats, E-boats and minesweepers from Cherbourg, Le Havre and St Malo were detected.[217]*

---

* See 'Use of Special Intelligence during Operation *Neptune*' (in ADM 223/287) for a detailed account of all that was learned from Sigint about German operations in the Channel area from January to September 1944. See Volume III Part 1, p 287 for operations by British destroyers and MTBs against these sorties in association with their attacks on German convoys.

213. CAB 121/394, CCS 454/6 of 17 May 1944, Appendix D.
214. ADM 223/267, USION, p 3.   215. ibid, p 13.
216. ibid, p 4.   217. ibid, p 4.

A second type of defensive activity, inshore minelaying and the laying of underwater obstacles by R-boats, converted landing craft and minesweeping trawlers, was also first detected in February. It was kept under observation with the aid of PR, R/T intercepts at the coastal Y stations, Enigma decrypts, and decrypts of a form of German W/T traffic first intercepted in October 1943. Called 'PP', it consisted of easily decoded ship-to-ship signals of a tactical nature and was heard from most parts of the coast from Flushing to Bordeaux. The PP traffic disclosed in mid-March that an experimental barrage had been laid off Ouistreham. But inshore operations were only occasionally detected in the Seine Bay before April.[218]

In the first week of April the OIC believed that except for the Ouistreham barrage none of the inshore or offshore mining had taken place in the Seine Bay south of 49° 30′ N (roughly on the line from Le Havre to Marcouf). But it had found it difficult to distinguish between inshore minelaying and the laying of underwater obstacles from ships, and it recognised that intelligence about the offshore lays remained scanty.[219] The intelligence situation was soon to change.

By the end of April a general upsurge of inshore activity was known from PP and R/T traffic to have included two complex operations by specially assembled groups of LCT IIIs (heavily armed landing craft) on the banks south of St Vaast (the Banc de la Rade, the Banc de St Marcouf and the Banc du Cardonnet) at the northern end of what the Allies knew as *Utah* beach, across the 'boat-lane' selected for the approach of the assault force. Enigma decrypts provided unusually full details of the position of the minefield laid in these operations; they were issued to Ultra recipients by the OIC on 1 May.[220]*

Some of these decrypts formed part of a series of Offizier Enigma signals addressed to all holders of the keyword Schranke (barrage). Between 19 and 30 April, as well as confirming the closure area of the Cardonnet bank, they gave details in terms of

---

* These were the only inshore mines laid in the Seine Bay. Captain Heinz Bonatz, head of the B-Dienst, has explained that though Rommel pressed for more inshore mining, the naval authorities believed the beaches there were adequately protected by sandbanks and reefs.[221] The decision to make an exception for the area of St Vaast was presumably associated with the other measures taken to strengthen the defences in the Cotentin (see Appendix 9) but there is no evidence that the location was decided by anything but topographic and operational calculations.

218. ibid, pp 25, 49–68.
219. ADM 223/172, OIC SI 908 of 8 April 1944.
220. ibid, OIC SI 935 of 30 April; ADM 223/193, Ultra signal 1105/1 May; ADM 223/287, USION, pp 58–59.
221. Heinz Bonatz, *Seekrieg im Äther* (Herford, 1981), p 353.

the German naval grid of closed areas between Boulogne and Dieppe, off Flushing, off L'Abervrach in Brittany and west of Fécamp; reported the diversions from the swept channel brought about by inshore mining between St Valery-sur-Somme and Dieppe; and disclosed that an 'alarm barrage' had been established north of the Cotentin.[222] Another Schranke message was of even greater importance. Decrypted on 17 May, it announced the closing of two adjacent areas together measuring roughly 12 miles by 7, and gave their boundaries; they were in the middle of the Seine Bay, half-way between Barfleur and Antifer.[223]

Within these closed areas the limits of the actual minefield remained uncertain, but information about the southern limit of the field in the Seine Bay, which was invaluable in that it enabled the Allies to extend the sea-room available for the boat-lowering area to be used by the assault forces, was obtained a fortnight before D-day. An Offizier signal of 19 May, decrypted on 20 May, contained the news that the torpedo-boats in Cherbourg were ordered to proceed to Le Havre in order to lay two flanking minefields. In the light of this warning and of subsequent air reconnaissance, Allied aircraft and MTBs engaged on 23 May a force of torpedo-boats, minesweepers and E-boats a few miles south of the assumed northern limit of mine-free water, 49° 30′ N. It seems probable that the interception succeeded because the OIC had hoped for some such opportunity and made preparations for it. The Germans lost one torpedo-boat and one minesweeper, while one torpedo-boat, one minesweeper and one R-boat were damaged. Their defensive mining effort was thus irreparably crippled; no further minelaying was attempted in the *Neptune* area before D-day.[224] Still more important, a flood of PP signals specified the points through which the damaged ships and their rescuers were to manoeuvre. This enabled the OIC to establish, and to promulgate on 31 May, the exact limits of mine-free water in the Seine Bay and the vicinity of Le Havre.[225]

Meanwhile, on 14 May, an Enigma decrypt had provided further intelligence of great value about the minelaying in shallow waters. It disclosed that the mine being used was the KMA, of which it gave details, and that it was a ground-mine laid in water between 3.5 and 5 metres deep. With this information the OIC

222. ADM 223/172, OIC SI 935 of 30 April.
223. ADM 223/287, USION, pp 4, 26, 71; ADM 223/195, Ultra signal 1459/31 May. See also ADM 223/172, OIC SI 948 of 9 May.
224. Roskill, op cit, Vol III Part 1 (1960), p 291; Beesly, *Very Special Intelligence* (1977), p 231.
225. ADM 223/287, USION, pp 4, 25–26; ADM 223/195, Ultra signal 1459/31 May.

was able, after reviewing the Enigma and PR evidence on the enemy's inshore activity since February, to distinguish the mining from the laying of beach obstacles and to conclude that KMA mines had been laid at various specified locations between Den Helder and Bayonne. This appreciation, together with an assessment of the KMA's characteristics, was drawn up by the OIC and the Admiralty's Directorate of Torpedoes and Mining, and issued to Ultra recipients between 16 May and 1 June.[226] None of the locations mentioned in the appreciation was in the Seine Bay. This correct conclusion was adopted by ANCXF in his final operational orders. They stated that inshore of the German coastal channel, in which the Allied boat-lowering positions were to be sited, there was no evidence that ground-minelaying had taken place.[227]

The orders added, however, that ground-minelaying in shallow water off the beaches by aircraft, and possibly E-boats, was to be expected as soon as the enemy became aware of Allied intentions. As we have already noted, a decrypt of 30 May disclosed that he was making final preparations to carry out such minelaying, the first by the GAF since September 1943, from Ostend to the Garonne.*

□

Unlike the intelligence the Allies obtained about Germany's minelaying, the mining they themselves carried out in the weeks before D-day made little if any contribution to the success of *Overlord*. The large-scale mining that was undertaken with a view to D-day was mainly concerned to seal off the anchorages and convoy routes from intervention by the German Navy. But in the event during the assault phase the beaches were approached only by minor vessels and, as was confirmed by post-war research, the mining did not greatly limit their freedom of movement in the areas adjacent to the beaches.[228] The German main units did not leave the Baltic and the U-boats achieved no successes before mid-June.†

The official history of the war at sea has recognised that there was a risk that the surface units of the German Fleet from the pocket-battleships downwards 'might all be used on forays into the

---

* See above p 62 and, for the operational consequences of the GAF effort, below pp 151 fn*, 165ff.

† See below, p 160.

226. ADM 223/287, USION, p 71; ADM 223/194, Ultra signals 1839/16 May, 1634/18 May; ADM 223/195, Ultra signal 1854/1 June.
227. CAB 44/242, pp 248–249.
228. BR 1736(56)(1), pp 403–404.

eastern approaches to the Channel if the enemy was really determined to stake everything on interrupting the invasion convoys'. It has nevertheless criticised the NID for exaggerating this threat by assuming that all the ships – the entire fleet except for *Tirpitz* and *Gneisenau* – were fit for operations.[229]* The NID did indeed take the view on 5 May that 'all main units except *Tirpitz* and *Gneisenau* are fully effective'.[230] On 10 May, moreover, on the OIC's advice, a paper which was drawn up by the British and US JICs and issued a week later as a CIC appreciation, allowed that they might all intervene against *Overlord*. The pocket-battleships *Scheer* and *Lützow* and the 8″ cruisers *Hipper* and *Prinz Eugen* would not be used directly against the assault except as a desperate measure, but they might be moved to north Norway to threaten a break-out into the Atlantic and thus divert some of the Allied forces covering and supporting the invasion. The four light cruisers (*Leipzig*, *Köln*, *Nürnberg* and *Emden*) might make sorties into the North Sea to attack convoys off the east coast. The paper conceded, however, that whether or not the ships were so used would depend on how badly they were needed in the Baltic against the Russian advances.[231]

The OIC did not modify this appreciation until 30 May, when, presumably on the strength of the regular PR of the Baltic bases that was maintained up to D-day, it reported that *Hipper* and *Köln*, now believed to be refitting, would not be effective for another four weeks.[232] But it came as no surprise to the OIC that, in the event, none of the ships left the Baltic. In relation to the light cruisers, though not in relation to the threat of a break-out into the Atlantic by the other ships, the appreciation of 10 May was clearly no more than a worst-case hypothesis. The OIC no doubt felt that it must assume the worst, as it felt that it must maintain the PR watch, in view of the fact that the other intelligence sources might not give advance information on the enemy's intentions about the use of his surface ships.

With regard to the use of the U-boat fleet, the OIC assumed from the outset that the Germans would use the U-boats against the landings and the follow-up convoys regardless of losses; and it would naturally have done so even if the Enigma had not disclosed

---

* The NID appreciated early in May that *Tirpitz* would not be operational before July; thereafter, despite the lack of conclusive evidence and the failure of two further attempts to attack her in May, it stood by this appreciation (See Volume III Part 1, pp 273 ff). It was known from PR that *Gneisenau* was lying dismantled in Gdynia.

229.   Roskill, op cit, Vol III Part 2, pp 10, 11fn.
230.   ADM 223/120, NID UC 480 of 5 May 1944.
231.   CAB 121/394, CCS 454/6 of 17 May 1944.
232.   ADM 223/172, OIC SI 967 of 30 May.

the reaction of the U-boat Command to the invasion alarm in Biscay in January 1944.* As events were to show, the OIC also exaggerated the number of U-boats that would be committed in the western Channel and the approaches to it. On 1 March it believed that some 75 500-ton U-boats would have been committed there by D+4 or D+5.[233] By 30 April it had advised the JIC that ten to twelve 500-ton U-boats might enter the western Channel in advance of the invasion, of which one or two might be stationed off the south coast or north Cornwall; that a total of 90 such boats would be assembled in Biscay by D-day; and that other 500-ton U-boats would then be pulled in from the Atlantic (50 by D+2 and 65 by D+5).[234]†

The fact that the occasional U-boat was patrolling close to the south coast had emerged from Sigint at the end of February, though not before the destroyer *Warwick* was sunk by a U-boat off the north Cornish coast on 20 February.‡ In a decrypt of 23 February the U-boat was told that it could either stay in the area or operate towards the North Channel, between Scotland and Ireland, and was informed that two U-boats would be patrolling north of the North Channel in the next new moon period.[236] On 7 March another decrypt had revealed that a U-boat was en route to the Minches; it was told that no U-boat had operated there for two years.[237] And in April analysis of U-boat movements as revealed in Enigma decrypts established that the enemy was holding back the departure of 500-ton U-boats to the Atlantic in order to accumulate them as an anti-invasion force.

For weeks before D-day this policy on the part of the U-boat Command, together with the decision to strengthen the Arctic and Mediterranean flotillas, produced a drastic fall in the U-boat effort in the north Atlantic, which had already been greatly reduced by the losses incurred in the enemy's attempts to renew the offensive against the convoy routes.§ The fact that the Allies were aware of

---

* See above p 50.

† It emerged from later appreciations that the OIC allowed that this further reinforcement might include up to three 740-ton U-boats.

‡ It has been claimed that *Warwick* was sent to these waters because intelligence had indicated the enemy intention to send a U-boat there. No such intimation came from Sigint. Possibly there was confusion with Sigint's disclosure in mid-January that a quite separate U-boat had been ordered to operate off the coast of Northern Ireland.[235]

§ See Volume III Part 1, p 236 et seq.

233. CAB 121/394, JIC(44)66 of 1 March.
234. ibid, JIC(44)176(o) of 30 April.
235. Roskill, op cit, Vol III Part 1, p 293; Naval Headlines of 15 January.
236. ADM 223/190, Ultra signal 1547/23 February.
237. ADM 223/191, Ultra signal 1625/7 March.

this was an enormous strategic asset, enabling them to re-organise the convoy system (convoys of more than 100 ships were sailing from mid-April) and transfer destroyers and other escort vessels to meet the huge demand for naval support that was created by the enlargement of the *Overlord* assault area.[238] In fact, ten U-boats were formed into a group in south Norway (*Gruppe Mitte*) in February and their number was raised to 22 by the end of March. On 22 March fifteen were held back in Biscay (*Gruppe Landwirt*); early in April they were reinforced by six which had just entered the Atlantic from the Baltic, and from the middle of April all 500-ton U-boats in Biscay ports were held back apart from the few sent to patrol off the British coast.[239] On 9 April the OIC noted that since 22 March no 500-ton U-boat had left Biscay, where 17 of them had been in port for longer than their normal turn-round period, and that six which had recently entered the Atlantic from the Baltic on their first cruise were proceeding direct to Biscay; and it estimated that 65 500-ton U-boats would be available in Biscay by mid-May.[240] On 8 May, however, it believed the number in Biscay to be only 43, and it was then that it also reported for the first time 'a tendency' for 500-ton U-boats to be held back in south Norway.[241]

In its next appreciation, the JIC paper of 10 May drawn up for discussion with the US JIC before being issued by the CIC on 17 May, the OIC repeated the forecast made at the end of April: 90 boats would be available in Biscay by D-day, and would be joined by 50 from the Atlantic by D+2, by 65 by D+5.[242] Within a few days of its release, however, decrypts received on 19 and 20 May threw a flood of light on the actual plans of the U-boat Command.

In one of them, which clearly would not have been transmitted by W/T but for the disruption by Allied bombing of the enemy's land-lines, Captain U-boats West informed Naval Gruppe West of his anti-invasion intentions. It stated that an unspecified number of U-boats were to sail at intervals, but that if any had not sailed before the Allied D-day, and if the Channel appeared to be the theatre most threatened, all U-boats at Brest and Lorient, plus seven from St Nazaire and five from La Pallice, would sail on the evening of D-day and the remainder on the evening of the following day. They would be disposed as follows:

(1)   an unspecified number, all but one equipped with *Schnor*-

---

238.   Roskill, op cit, Vol III Part 2, p 10.
239.   ADM 234/68, pp 55–56, 67.
240.   ADM 223/172, OIC SI 910 of 9 April.
241.   ibid, OIC SI 944 of 8 May.
242.   CAB 121/394, CCS 454/6 of 17 May.

*chel**, in the coastal area between the Scillies and a point east of Start Point;

(2) four non-*Schnorchel* boats from Brest in waiting positions in the north Biscay area with a view to possible employment in the Channel as a second wave;

(3) all other non-*Schnorchel* boats in Brest in waiting positions about 150 miles south-west of Brest;

(4) an unspecified number of *Schnorchel* boats from Lorient in the coastal area between the Scillies and Trevose Head;

(5) an unspecified number of non-*Schnorchel* boats from Lorient to a waiting area in central Biscay.

Together with the seven boats from St Nazaire and the five from La Pallice, those sent to waiting positions in Biscay would dispose themselves evenly in a 45-mile wide strip of which the centre line was joined by a point 150 miles west of St Nazaire and a point off the Spanish coast, 30 miles west of Bilbao. The message added that these non-*Schnorchel* boats would not be very effective for reconnaissance as they would be surfaced only at night.[243]†

The other decrypts of 19 and 20 May disclosed that three 500-ton U-boats had been ordered from Brest into the Channel, the first leaving on the evening of 18 May and the other two on the evening of 20 May.[245] The signal gave no indication of their destination, and it was at first assumed that they were to patrol off the English south coast. By 26 May, however, further decrypts had revealed that the number of U-boats, now named *Gruppe Dragoner*, had risen to five, that one had returned to port with defects, that another had been attacked and forced back and that the remaining three had patrolled as far east as St Malo until recalled on 25 May. These decrypts indicated that one of the objectives of the sortie had been to test the effectiveness of the *Schnorchel* in coastal waters under air attack in advance of the planned incursion of U-boats into the Channel to operate against the invasion.[246]

---

* See Volume III Part 1, pp 241–242, for the evidence leading to the identification of *Schnorchel* as a ventilation trunk in February 1944.

† A summary of this decrypt was sent to the Prime Minister, who asked the First Sea Lord for comments and a short note on 'our own counter-measures'.[244] For the First Sea Lord's reply see Appendix 11.

243. Naval Headlines 1052 of 21 May; ADM 223/88, Colpoys, *Admiralty Use of Special Intelligence in Naval Operations*, p 295.
244. Dir/C Archive, 6548 of 21 May 1944.
245. ADM 223/172, OIC SI 956 of 19 May.
246. Naval Headlines 1051, 1052, 1056, 1057 of 20 to 26 May; ADM 223/172, OIC SI 960 of 22 May; US Department of Defense, *Allied Communication Intelligence and the Battle of the Atlantic*, Vol II, pp 195–196.

This intelligence left several questions unsettled. The numbers of U-boats involved in the signal from Captain U-boats West could only be guessed at. A chart submitted to the Prime Minister by the First Sea Lord estimated that in Biscay something over 34 non-*Schnorchel* boats and an unknown but far smaller number of *Schnorchel* boats were probably fit for operations. The extent to which they would be reinforced before D-day, particularly from the accumulation of U-boats in south Norway, could not be foreseen. It was clear from Sigint that some of these U-boats from south Norway, whose numbers were also unknown, were already leaving; on 5 June the OIC was to report that between 33 and 37 had sailed, their destination unknown, since the middle of May.[247]* On 25 May the final appreciation issued by the JIC gave the OIC's estimates on these two points. It stated that 45 500-ton U-boats had been located in Biscay ports by 20 May, but that they would be reinforced by D-day by a further 25 boats, making 70 in all. In addition the enemy might move ten or more 500-ton U-boats from the Atlantic to the western and central Channel. From D-day other U-boats would follow into the western and central Channel, some from among the 70 Biscay boats and others from the eastern north Atlantic, to the number of 45 by D+2, 60 by D+5.[250]

It also remained uncertain to what extent the U-boats concentrated in Biscay would be used to attack the initial Allied landings or to harass the follow-up convoys in the western and south-western approaches to the Channel. On this account, as well as on security grounds, the arrangements already made for intensive anti-submarine measures throughout the vast area of the approaches were retained. But steps were taken to ensure that those measures were heavily concentrated against the patrol and waiting positions specified in the Enigma decrypts, and in order to ensure that maximum use was made of any further Sigint, a U-boat plot was set up for C-in-C Plymouth under an officer from the OIC's U-boat Tracking Room.[251]

---

* Decrypts of 1 and 14 May associated some of them with an operation code-named *Wallenstein*.[248] Earlier Sigint references to this operation had suggested that it might be a general plan for defence against invasion of southern Norway and the Baltic entrances, but those references had been few and obscure. It is now known that some of them went to reinforce the Arctic flotilla and others went to the Atlantic. No less than 22 of them were sighted by Coastal Command, which, with the help of Sigint, sank 7 and forced 4 to return to port.[249]

247. ADM 223/172, OIC SI 973 of 5 June.
248. DEFE 3/413, ZTPG 23755; DEFE 3/730, ZTPGU 25126, 25133, 25189.
249. Roskill, op cit, Vol III Part 1, pp 260–262, Part 2, pp 20–21.
250. JIC(44)215(o) of 25 May.
251. ADM 223/88, pp 294–295; Handling of Naval Special Intelligence, pp 38, 51; Beesly, op cit, p 242.

No further Sigint about the U-boats in Biscay was obtained before D-day; nor did air reconnaissance detect any sign that any of them had sailed.[252] In these last few days, however, the decrypt of a signal from the head of the Japanese Naval Mission in Berlin enabled the Admiralty to discount, however belatedly, the threat from 'small . . . high-speed submarines or submersibles . . . within the Channel itself'. This threat had first been mentioned in those terms in the JIC's appreciation for the CIC of 10 April.[253] By 30 April the OIC had advised the JIC that while such craft might be a threat in the eastern Channel and the southern North Sea, there was no evidence that any were yet operational.[254] The JIC appreciation of 10 May had contained no such hesitation. It had stated that some twenty 250 to 300-ton U-boats and an uncertain number of submersibles of unknown characteristics 'will be based on ports in the Low Countries and the eastern Channel' for offensive operations.[255] The final JIC assessment of the scale of opposition to *Overlord*, issued on 25 May, was hardly less emphatic: 'Offensive operations in the eastern half of the Channel and the southern North Sea are likely to be carried out by the small type of U-boats (of 250–300 tons) and small submersible craft'.[256]

The 250 to 300-ton U-boats were the Type XXIII boats, which had at last been observed under construction in the third week of April.* The submersibles were the W-boats, now distinguishable from the Type XXIIIs; the threat from them as a specific anti-invasion weapon had been discerned at the end of February. The threat from both had thereafter continued to be a source of grave and growing anxiety. An *ad hoc* NID *Overlord* Committee had singled out the W-boat training centre as a priority target. Measures against W-boats had been rehearsed in the final Allied exercise, Operation *Fabius*, early in May. Torpedo tubes had been replaced by depth-charges in some of the MTBs in the Channel Commands. Although the OIC regularly advised the Commands that there was as yet no evidence from W/T traffic that the new type of U-boat was operational, the Commands had received and distributed frequent reports of suspicious sightings and tracks, especially after the circulation of the appreciation of 10 May. Nor were such reports to cease after 30 May when, to the great relief of the Admiralty, the decrypt of Admiral Abe's signal disclosed that

---

* See Volume III Part 1, p 244.

252. ADM 223/172, OIC SI 973 of 5 June; AIR 41/23, p 240.
253. CAB 121/394, CCS 454/4 of 10 April 1944.
254. ibid, JIC(44)176(0) of 30 April.
255. ibid, CCS 454/6 of 17 May 1944.
256. JIC(44)215(0) of 25 May.

the Germans had not yet completed their experiments with U-boats using a form of closed-cycle engine for underwater propulsion.* But Traffic Analysis at the last minute revealed that HQ Small Battle Units (KdK) had established communications with Le Havre similar to those which existed with its bases in the Mediterranean: NID thought that this pointed to the possibility of KdK-type operations in the Channel and so informed SHAEF.

---

* See Volume III Part 1, pp 243–245 and its Appendix 11.

CHAPTER 45

The Preliminary Air Operations

THE FIRST and fundamental contribution of the Allied air forces to *Overlord* was the establishment of air superiority over France, itself the consequence of the defeat of the German fighter forces over Germany. As we now know, this defeat was accomplished by 1 April 1944, the date set at the Casablanca conference for the climax of the strategic air offensive against Germany's morale and economy and especially against her aircraft production and her fighter aircraft (Operation *Pointblank*) and the beginning of the phase in which the Allied air forces would operate in direct preparation for the invasion.[1]* But if the Allies were thereafter confident that, in terms of the resistance to be expected on and after D-day from the GAF, they could proceed with the invasion, they still could not measure the scale of that resistance. In November 1943, when the continuing increase in German fighters was causing grave anxiety, the newly appointed AOC-in-C of the Allied Expeditionary Air Force (Air Chief Marshal Leigh-Mallory) expected to have to fight a major air battle over the beaches. 'We shall not have fought our main battle for air superiority before the *Overlord* battle begins . . . I would not . . . be prepared to recommend commencement of *Overlord* unless I was certain of the favourable outcome of the air battle'.[2] From the spring of 1944 it was clear that the battle would be won, but it remained impossible to foresee that the forces nominally available to the GAF in the west would in fact be incapable of making a serious challenge.[3]

The Air Ministry's estimates of the GAF's nominal first-line strength at D-day rose steadily as the date approached. On 22 February it had predicted that it would have 1,450 aircraft immediately available, making possible some 1,750 sorties on D-day. On 1 March, following the heavy casualties inflicted on the German fighters in 'Big Week',† it revised this number of aircraft downwards to 850 (including 350 long-range bombers and 300

---

* See Volume III Part 1, Chapter 37.
† For 'Big Week' see Volume III Part 1, pp 317, 320–321.

1. Craven and Cate, *The USAAF in World War II*, Vol III (1951), pp 7–8; Webster and Frankland, *The Strategic Air Offensive against Germany*, (1961) Vol II, p 209, Vol III, pp 132–133.
2. AIR 41/66, *The Liberation of North-West Europe*, Vol I, p 121.
3. AIR 41/24, *The Liberation of North-West Europe*, Vol III, pp 14, 33, 59, 61; Harrison, *Cross Channel Attack* (Washington DC 1951), p 180.

single-engined fighters) and had believed that the decline would continue.[4] On 30 April, on the other hand, it noted that the GAF was managing to maintain its front-line strength to a surprising degree, and it guessed that on D-day there would be a total of 1,950 aircraft in the west (from Norway to the south of France, including northern Germany), of which 750 would be immediately available (including 400 bombers and 180 single-engined fighters) and a further 450 would arrive by D+4.[5] On 25 May, in its contribution to the last regular review by the JIC before D-day, it again raised the estimated figures. The total available in the west might be 2,350; 900 of them would be immediately available (including 500 bombers and 220 single-engined fighters), to be followed by 230 immediate reinforcements by D+1, by 300 further reinforcements by D+4 and also by 170 fighters from Germany and Austria, making a total of 1,600 aircraft. With serviceability at 65 per cent there might be 1,100–1,250 sorties on D-day.[6]* In a final estimate issued on 5 June AI gave the total aircraft immediately available to Luftflotte 3 (France and the Low Countries) at the end of May as 1,015 (including 435 long-range bombers, 435 fighters and 55 close-support fighter-bombers).[7]

As it happened, these rising projections were not seriously astray, and AI's final estimates were reasonably accurate. The actual nominal strength of Luftflotte 3 at the end of May was 891 aircraft (including 425 fighters of all types, 402 bombers and anti-shipping aircraft) and it rose to some 1,300 by D+10.[8] AI knew from a variety of sources – agents, PR of airfields, the GAF's low-grade communications and high-grade Sigint – that there had been a slight increase in actual strength in the west during May.[9] By 7 May the Enigma had disclosed the reception areas to which, on the receipt of a given code-word, fighters and ground-attack aircraft would be transferred from Italy, and on 19 May it gave full details of the steps being taken to stock these areas with bombs, fuel and ammunition.[10]† By 30 May the Enigma had

---

* These estimates were based on comprehensive calculations for which see Appendix 12.
† Other decrypts showed that similar preparations were being made for the reinforcement in emergency of Norway, Denmark and Finland.[11]

4. JIC(44)66(o) (Final) and (Final Revise) of 22 February and 1 March.
5. JIC(44)176(o) of 30 April.
6. JIC(44)215(o) of 25 May.
7. Air Sunset 179 of 5 June 1944.
8. Ellis, *Victory in the West*, Vol I (1962), p 567; Wynn and Young, *Prelude to Overlord* (1983), pp 29, 54.
9. Air Sunset 177 of 30 May.
10. Air Sunsets 169 and 174 of 19 May; AWL 1846 of 12 April.
11. eg DEFE 3/138, VL 6085 of 12 February; DEFE 3/141, VL 6862 of 22 February; DEFE 3/149, VL 8773 of 18 March.

identified ten Gruppen of single-engined fighters in Germany (a total of 280 aircraft) as being due for transfer to the west.[12] On 5 June it disclosed that anti-shipping units which had been training in the Baltic had moved to southern France, raising the number of such aircraft there from 180 to 240, and that a further 50 were still re-equipping in Germany.[13]

AI attributed the increasing establishment strength largely to the fact that the GAF was deliberately conserving its forces and pursuing an intensive repairs programme. It knew from high-grade Sigint that the conservation policy was chiefly due to the shortage of pilots.* As early as February decrypts had disclosed that the GAF was preparing to use aircraft from flying schools and training units in case of emergency.[14] Notwithstanding the German decision to move Fliegerkorps II from Italy to northern France and to provide it with a 'ground-attack Fliegerführer' and a staff officer for close support – a further important indication of the seriousness of Germany's anti-invasion preparations which was obtained from high-grade decrypts early in February –[15] there was also evidence of a shortage of close-support aircraft from decrypts showing that fighters were being fitted with bomb racks and trained in the use of rocket projectiles.[16] Further Enigma references to these plans for converting fighters for ground-attack operations were obtained by 7 May, when AI estimated that some 175 fighters were involved.[17] No less significant was the absence of any evidence for plans to make transfers from the Russian front, which was tying down a huge force of fighter-bombers and ground-attack aircraft.[18] It was known from other decrypts, as well as from POW and actual performance,† that the potentially formidable anti-shipping force had been seriously weakened, as had the bomber arm, by the GAF's concentration on the development of its fighter force. The GAF had suspended the use of the FX and Hs 293 in the Mediterranean and decrypts showed that desperate efforts were being made to equip as many aircraft as possible with these weapons, including the ageing FW 200s.[19] The torpedo units were sustaining heavy losses in operations

---

* Volume III, Part 1, p 318.
† See Volume III, Part 1, p 326 for the failure of the FX units in what was clearly meant to be a major raid on Plymouth on 29–30 April.

12. Air Sunset 177 of 30 May.
13. Air Sunsets 168 and 179 of 5 May and 5 June.
14. Air Sunset 146 of 18 February.
15. Air Sunset 142 of 6 February.
16. AWL 1535 of 19 February.
17. Air Sunset 168 of 5 May.
18. Air Sunsets 163 and 172 of 15 April and 11 May.
19. Air Sunset 173 of 16 May; AWL 2029 of 16 May.

against convoys in the Mediterranean which decrypts were attributing to the inexperience of new crews.[20]

On the strength of such intelligence AI did not fail to stress at regular intervals that its projections of the nominal strength of the GAF in the west on D-day were a poor guide to what its actual strength would be. But its inability to gauge the scale of the resistance the GAF would offer was not the least of the uncertainties confronting the Allied air forces after they had turned their attention to the operations they were to carry out in preparation for *Overlord*.

□

The largest of these operations, and the most controversial, was the offensive directed to the disruption of communications throughout north-western Europe with a view to delaying the enemy's reinforcement of the bridgehead, and in particular to preventing him from massing his Panzer formations for a counter-attack during the first crucial days of the assault. The project encountered widespread opposition on the ground that the French rail and road system was too dense for air power to be effective against it – a view which had been expressed by the Prime Minister and the CAS as early as October 1943.[21] There was a prolonged reluctance to accept the unavoidable consequence of heavy French civilian casualties. The danger that the bombing would betray the whereabouts of the landing area was another difficulty, and yet another was the enormous cost of the diversionary operations that would be needed if that danger was to be avoided. But the planning, and eventually the implementation, of the offensive took place with mounting urgency as successive estimates of the scale of the opposition to be encountered from the German Army increased the anxiety of the Allied commanders that the enemy might have 'superior strength at the moment of assault'.[22]

An initial plan, drawn up by 21st Army Group in January 1944, was rejected by the AOC-in-C. It called for a concentrated bombing effort close to D-day, which he could not guarantee in the event of bad weather and pressure from other last-minute commitments. Its suggested targets – bridges and tunnels – were judged to be unsuitable for air attack in that they called for precision and enormous quantities of bombs; experience had

---

20. eg DEFE 3/155, KV 3921 of 15 May.
21. CAB 121/390, SIC file D/France/6/11, vol 1, COS(43) 245th (o) Meeting, 19 October.
22. Ehrman, *Grand Strategy*, Vol VI (1956), p 357; AIR 41/66, pp 14, 115, 141.

shown, moreover, that the Germans were quick to repair them or find alternative routes. In its place, HQ Allied Expeditionary Air Force developed what came to be known as the Transportation Plan. Based on analysis of the bombing carried out in Sicily and Italy, this aimed at deadening the nerve centres of the railway system to such an extent that they would be unable to bear the extra strain that was called for when the emergency arose. In its final form it had two phases. In the initial strategic or attritional phase railway control centres, repair and servicing depots and their concentration of locomotives and rolling stock, and selected power stations, would be attacked repeatedly with the object of slowing traffic and limiting it to fewer lines, and thus forcing it on to the roads. In the tactical or interdiction phase, from shortly before D-day and as part of the systematic last-minute bombing of many other targets, there would be intensive operations against all rail movements and against such junctions, cuttings and bridges,* and also such road centres, as were related to the known locations and probable approach routes of the German reserve formations.[23]†

HQ AEAF hoped to implement the plan from the beginning of March, but Bomber Command and the US Strategic Air Force opposed any diversion of their forces from Operation *Pointblank*. Indeed, they objected to the plan as such. Its targets were too small for the heavy bombers, which had no experience in precision bombing; its objective was too limited to justify the effort that would need to be expended; by reducing the strategic air offensive and giving the GAF the opportunity to recover, it would undermine the objective of winning air superiority by D-day, whereas the gaining of that objective might itself bring about the collapse of Germany and render *Overlord* unnecessary. Nor were the strategic air commanders alone in objecting to the plan.

The JIC, asked to estimate what number of trains a day Germany would have to run after D-day to maintain all her three Services in Normandy, reported on 18 March in terms which

---

* Bridges were included at a late stage in the development of the plan as a result of intelligence which countered the earlier belief that they were poor targets. (See below, pp 111–112.) They proved to be the most worthwhile of all the tactical targets.

† Sabotage by the Resistance and the SOE for this stage had been planned since the end of 1943. It proved to be of great value as bad weather largely frustrated the air forces on and immediately after D-day. The Resistance implemented two basic plans from D-day, one for road cutting and one for rail cutting. Both contributed to a severe reduction of the enemy's mobility behind the beachhead front. 26 trunk lines were cut on D-day, including the main lines between Avranches and St Lo, St Lo and Cherbourg and St Lo and Caen.[24]

23. Harrison, op cit, p 217 et seq; AIR 41/66, pp 142, 144, 153; Rostow, *Pre-Invasion Bombing Strategy* (University of Texas 1981), p 13.

24. JIC(43)52nd(o) Meeting, 19 October; Harrison, op cit, pp 202–206. See also MRD Foot, *SOE in France* (1968).

discouraged optimism about the effects of the Transportation Plan. It assumed that Germany had already made all her dispositions, that her coastal defence programme was close to completion and that she would be able to substitute road for rail movements without great difficulty; and it asserted that she would be able to manage with as few as 80 trains a day, perhaps with less over a limited period if she accepted a drastic limitation of stocks, without impairing her ability to oppose *Overlord*. At about the same time a group composed of the logistics and organisation section of AI(A1 3(e)), the MEW, the Director of Transportation in the War Office and the Enemy Objectives Unit which carried out in the US embassy work similar to that of MEW, expressed the view that only one-fifth of the French rail system was used for military traffic (AEAF believed that the proportion was two-thirds), that some 500 rail centres would have to be demolished before the system was seriously damaged and that, bearing in mind Germany's impressive ability to improvise and the fact that her counter-attack would be delivered over a limited area, the effort required to achieve this outcome would not be justified. The advocates of the Plan (Tedder, the Deputy Supreme Commander; Leigh-Mallory; Professor Zuckerman) retorted that these criticisms betrayed an ignorance of railway operations and, in the case of the JIC report, which they dismissed as 'special pleading based on unsound assumptions', what they judged to be ridiculously low estimates of the enemy's needs in the light of their own experience of actual operations in the Mediterranean. But they could only oppose one set of convictions with another. Differences of judgment about the feasibility and the effectiveness of attrition bombing arose from applying different interpretations of the results obtained by bombing in Sicily and Italy to the same body of intelligence about the state of the European railway system.[25]

If intelligence had thus far given no decisive lead, the situation was not altered when, following a directive on 4 March, Bomber Command carried out a trial series of attacks in moonlight against selected targets which included six marshalling yards. The attacks were unexpectedly successful – they were something of a landmark in establishing Bomber Command's ability to hit precision targets in night raids.[26] But the PR evidence of their results was duly given different interpretations. SHAEF was impressed by the fact that as late as 26 March the Germans had made no attempt to begin repairs on the heavy installations; 21st

---

25. JIC(44)106(o) of 18 March; AIR 41/66, pp 148–151, 159(n); Craven and Cate, op cit, Vol III, pp 76–78; Ehrman, op cit, Vol V (1956), p 294 et seq.
26. Webster and Frankland, op cit, Vol III, (1961) pp 27–28.

Army Group, which had no faith in the effectiveness of attrition bombing, was struck by the fact that the yards were already working again by the beginning of April.[27] There followed several references to the raids in high-grade decrypts. A decrypt of 31 March commented that 'despite the importance of the targets', the attacks had not been followed up.[28] A decrypt of 6 April, much delayed, reported considerable damage to the locomotive depot and to locomotives at Trappes on 6–7 March.[29] On the same day the decrypt of the situation report issued by C-in-C West on 21 March listed all the centres so far attacked by Bomber Command and said that the raids had caused severe damage to locomotives and rolling stock.[30] This evidence no doubt encouraged the advocates of the Transportation Plan. But it did not influence the outcome of the debate. The decision to adopt the plan in principle had been taken on 25 March at a meeting attended by the CAS, General Eisenhower, the *Overlord* air commanders, the commanders of the Allied Strategic Air Forces, the MEW, the War Office and the JIS.

The meeting considered two alternatives: the Transportation Plan, under which the chief objective of the strategic air forces would be the destruction of specific railway targets; and a programme put forward by General Spaatz under which the strategic air forces would carry out intensive bombing of Germany's refineries and synthetic oil plants, of which 14 produced 80 per cent of Germany's synthetic fuel, and other selected targets of crucial industrial importance, such as rubber production plants, over a period of fifteen days of fine weather before undertaking a brief and massive interdiction campaign in support of *Overlord*. The objectives of the attack on oil and industry would be further to reduce the GAF by forcing it to fight, and to produce such a fuel famine and such damage to the economy as might of themselves bring about Germany's collapse. As between these alternatives the issue was settled by the intervention of MEW, which insisted that an oil offensive would make little or no contribution to the crucial assault phase of *Overlord*; Germany had built up considerable fuel reserves in the west, and the attack on her oil industry would not affect output for four or five months. But the decision to go forward with the Transportation Plan did not represent a meeting of minds. The Plan was severely criticised at the meeting, not least

---

27. WO 219/5165, SHAEF Weekly Intelligence Summary of 26 March; WO 205/532, 21st Army Group Weekly *Neptune* Review of 2 April.
28. DEFE 3/765, VL 9911 of 31 March.
29. DEFE 3/36, KV 328 of 6 April.
30. ibid, KV 353 of 6 April.

by the JIS; its supporters argued only that it did not seek the complete stoppage of rail traffic and that it would be justified in that it was bound to achieve some reduction of military movements, however slight. The meeting adopted it *faute de mieux* and because it was imperative to avoid further delay.[31]

The policy having been settled in principle, direction of the strategic air forces passed to the Supreme Allied Commander on 14 April. But the directive issued to them on 15 April gave only second priority to attacks on rail centres; their first priority was for the present to remain the defeat of the GAF, and in particular the reduction of its fighter arm, by means of attacks on German industry.[32] Apart from the fact that the extent of US Eighth Air Force's victory over the German fighters was as yet unclear, these terms reflected the resistance of General Spaatz, who interpreted them as authorising the continuation of Operation *Pointblank* and, indeed, the beginning of attacks on oil plants.* They also reflected the insistence of the Prime Minister on obtaining the approval of the War Cabinet for the offensive against rail targets – or at any rate for the attack on those 12 out of a total of 74 which the Transportation Plan had so far allocated to Bomber Command.

The War Cabinet, led by the Prime Minister and advised by Lord Cherwell, was not convinced that the offensive would be so effective as to outweigh the moral and political disadvantage that would follow from its unavoidable consequences in terms of casualties to civilians in the occupied countries. Throughout April it would consent only to the step-by-step implementation of the plan in selective raids, carried out on such of the targets as offered the least risk of casualties, with a view to measuring French and Belgian reactions and to comparing the damage caused with the casualties inflicted. It was not until the beginning of the first week of May, when the AEAF had in fact been implementing the Transportation Plan for three weeks and the number of targets attacked by its aircraft and Bomber Command had risen to 32, when Leigh-Mallory had called on US Eighth Air Force to begin its full participation and when a final decision could be deferred no longer, that the War Cabinet assented to the continuation and extension of the bombing. It did so with the greatest reluctance and on the understanding that SHAEF would do its utmost to keep the level of civilian casualties below a total of 10,000 deaths.[33]

---

* See below, Chapter 54.

31.　AIR 41/66, p 53; Craven and Cate, op cit, Vol III, pp 76–78; Webster and Frankland, op cit, Vol III, pp 32–33; Ehrman, op cit, Vol V, p 297.

32.　Webster and Frankland, op cit, Vol III, pp 22–24; Craven and Cate, op cit, Vol III, p 75; Ellis, op cit, Vol 1, p 98.

33.　Webster and Frankland, op cit, Vol III, pp 34–38; AIR 41/66, pp 156, 158, 160, 164–172; Ehrman, op cit, Vol V, pp 298–304.

Evidence of the damage done by the April raids, as of the civilian casualties they were causing, had been inconclusive. Except for three high-grade decrypts, the only sources of information were agents, PR and statements in the French, Belgian and German newspapers.* The assessment of SHAEF's air intelligence staff on 29 April was that the raids had been highly successful; the locomotive servicing centres at La Chapelle, Charleroi/St Martin, Laon, Aachen and Paris/Juvisy had been made almost useless and much rolling stock had been destroyed.[37] The JIC was more cautious in a review of 1 May. Although at least twelve targets were so badly damaged that they would not need to be attacked again for several weeks, only French and Belgian traffic was being restricted. German troop and supply trains were still moving without serious delay; the Germans were only now beginning to establish Flak at rail centres and they had not yet brought in fighter units; they were resourceful in carrying out repairs. All in all, the Allies would probably have to repeat their attacks more frequently than they had allowed for.[38] On 3 May 21st Army Group was even more unimpressed. It demanded attacks on the Seine bridges as being far more likely to have decisive effects than 'pin-pricking on rail communications'.[39]

The insistence of the authors of the Transportation Plan that bridges were unsuitable targets, too expensive to attack and too easy to repair, had withstood the defeat of their views at the hands of the tactical air commanders in Italy. It had withstood, also, pressure from Air Intelligence.[40] The destruction of bridges had become a major objective of the Allied air offensive in Italy by March, and the results, as reported by PR and high-grade Sigint, had been not unimpressive.[41]† In February and March AI 3(e) had carried out two analyses of the effects of attacks on bridges in the light of this evidence, and in April, after discussing its conclusions with AFHQ and GC and CS, it had joined 21st Army

---

* In a decrypt available on 15 April OKW reported its intention to send a rail engineering battalion to France in the event of invasion.[34] A decrypt of 21 April disclosed that in the raid on Aachen the main station had been destroyed and all rail traffic stopped indefinitely.[35] In a message dated 21 April, decrypted on 25 April, C-in-C West gave the number of deaths caused by the raid on La Chapelle rail centre near Paris as provisionally 200 German and 268 French.[36]

† See Volume III, Part 1, p 199.

34. DEFE 3/39, KV 1062 of 15 April.
35. DEFE 3/41, KV 1558 of 21 April.
36. DEFE 3/43, KV 2013 of 25 April.
37. WO 219/1918, SHAEF Weekly Intelligence Summary of 29 April.
38. JIC(44)177(0) of 1 May; Craven and Cate, op cit, Vol III, pp 153–154.
39. Craven and Cate, op cit, Vol III, p 157.
40. AIR 41/24, pp 28, 171.
41. ibid, p 376.

Group and the US Enemy Objectives Unit in calling for attacks on the bridges over the Seine and the Loire.[42] Under the growing pressure experimental attacks on bridges in France by aircraft of the tactical air forces (2nd TAF and US Ninth Air Force) were carried out in April, but were indecisive. On 7 May, however, further attacks by eight of US Ninth Air Force's fighter-bombers achieved spectacular success against four Seine bridges.[43]

The bridges were at once added to the targets in the Transportation Plan. But they were not attacked again for more than a fortnight. The raids of 7 May were followed on 9 May by the decrypts which disclosed that they had led Luftflotte 3 to conclude that the Allies planned to make their landings in the area between Le Havre and Cherbourg.* We may take it that it was on this account that on 10 May HQ AEAF ordered attacks on the bridges over the Albert Canal and banned further attacks on the bridges over the Seine until all the Belgian bridges were down. The ban was not lifted until 24 May.[44] In lifting it the Allies took a calculated risk, but attacks on the Seine could point to the intention to land on either side of it. On 27 May the decrypt of a message from Luftflotte 3 disclosed that it believed that attacks on the Seine bridges on 26 May reinforced its 'previously expressed opinion' as to where the Allies would land, indicating uncertainty as to whether the landings would come north or south of the Seine by adding that they would probably be in the Dieppe–Seine Bay area.† By D-day expensive low-level attacks in the face of heavy Flak, which were repeated when PR detected that repairs were nearing completion, had ensured that all 24 Seine bridges between Rouen and the sea had been made impassable and that 12 others over major waterways in France and Germany were blocked.[45] For security reasons, attacks on the Loire bridges were deferred till after D-day.

The offensive against the rail network, which had begun in earnest early in May, had meanwhile given rise to a large and ever-growing number of references in high-grade decrypts. Most of them were reports of the damage done in individual raids, but they included several general assessments. A decrypt of 6 May which outlined the GAF's plans for bringing in reinforcements from Italy emphasised that, in view of the possible breakdown of

---

* See above, p 58.
† See above, p 62.

42.   The Use of Ultra to AI 3(e), p 2; AWL 1797 of 4 April.
43.   Craven and Cate, op cit, Vol III, p 158; Rostow, op cit, p 64.
44.   AIR 41/24, p 25; Craven and Cate, op cit, Vol III, p 158.
45.   Craven and Cate, op cit, Vol III, p 159; Ellis, op cit, Vol 1, p 102; Harrison, op cit, pp 229–230.

the railway network, units must be prepared to complete their movements by road.[46] A message from Keitel on 1 May, decrypted on 6 May, stated that OKW's requirements for the repair of railway damage were not being met and instructed C-in-C West and the military commanders in France and Belgium to ensure that the necessary measures were carried out.[47] C-in-C West's appreciation of 8 May, decrypted on 14 May,* reported that, while attacks in the past week on pin-point targets (rail bridges, viaducts and embankments) had had no lasting effects, the systematic destruction of the railways had already brought about the interruption of supplies and troop movements. An appreciation by Luftflotte 3, made on 17 May and decrypted on 18 May, noted that whereas the Allies should have been making thrusts along the railway routes and disrupting repairs at rail centres already heavily damaged, their activity had been slight in the past few days; they were possibly holding back deliberately. The appreciation added that the preparation for a large-scale landing would call for another series of attacks lasting several days to disrupt rail junctions.[48] In a message of 10 May, decrypted on 26 May, C-in-C West advised Berlin that the locomotive situation had become so serious that it had become essential to draft labour into the repair shops and that, as the civilian work-force was not responding, consideration should be given to using POW.[49] A decrypt of 27 May reported that heavy damage had been done in attacks carried out the previous day by US Fifteenth Air Force from Mediterranean bases on the Var viaduct near Nice and to all the railway installations and Rhône bridges at Lyons; it noted that the consequences were particularly severe for supply to the Bordeaux area.[50] On 27 May, in a message decrypted on 29 May, C-in-C West reported that extensive disturbance to the coast defence construction programme and interruption of the most important supply lines in many places had resulted in a considerable increase in fuel consumption.[51]

On 1 June the Deputy Supreme Commander quoted some of these decrypts in a report he submitted to the Prime Minister in response to several requests for information about the level of civilian casualties. It pointed out that all the operations against targets in the occupied territories, and not only the attacks on the

---

* See above, p 59 and Appendix 8.

46. DEFE 3/46, KV 2983 of 6 May.
47. DEFE 3/47, KVs 3015 and 3037 of 6 May.
48. DEFE 3/157, KV 4281 of 18 May.
49. DEFE 3/161, KV 5314 of 26 May.
50. DEFE 3/161, KV 5446 of 27 May.
51. DEFE 3/162, KV 5689 of 29 May.

rail networks, had inevitably resulted in civilian casualties, and that it had been impossible to obtain reliable figures for the total casualties caused. The number associated with the attacks on rail centres by the reports of the German and Vichy controlled Press, the only comprehensive source, was 10,776, and this was probably exaggerated. As against this, it set the fact that the Resistance had reported that the attacks had caused 3,300 German casualties and the fact that the attacks were known to have seriously dislocated all communications in northern France and Belgium. However, since the object of the Transportation Plan had not been specifically to disrupt rail communications – since it had been aimed at so deadening the whole system as to delay the concentration and reinforcement of the German forces in the *Neptune* area and weaken their fighting power in the subsequent campaign – it conceded that the ultimate test was still to come.[52]

The opponents of the Transportation Plan were unimpressed by the Enigma decrypts. The decrypts showed that the bombing was causing the Germans considerable problems but, as Cherwell wrote in a minute for the Prime Minister on Tedder's report, 'we have never denied that dislocation would be caused. The whole question is whether it will be sufficient to hamper appreciably military movements – which remains to be seen. I still believe the attacks on bridges will be far more effective for this purpose and that the attacks on purely military targets will have given a better yield . . .'[53] On the strength of the PR evidence and the reports from the Resistance and SOE networks SHAEF had concluded on 20 May that the Plan had failed to restrict the enemy's ability to move up reinforcements or to maintain his forces; he still had three times the number of railway lines he needed, four times the amount of rolling stock, eight times the number of locomotives, ten times the number of servicing facilities.[54] 21st Army Group was no less scathing on 4 June. Of the 13 main lines running into the *Neptune* area not more than six at any one time had been cut in the strategic phase of the bombing. Even though the tactical phase of actual interdiction had benefited from the reduction in the flexibility of the rail system brought about by the attrition bombing, the Germans were still left with a line capacity into the area of at least 250 trains a day, which would easily cover the required traffic, and with an ample margin of wagons, locomotives and locomotive servicing facilities for his essential peak military and supply movements. The not inconsiderable general weakening of the system would lead to some delays – perhaps 6 to 12

---

52.   CAB 82/43/1(2),D/SAC/TS.100 of 1 June.
53.   ibid, Cherwell minute to the Prime Minister, 2 June.
54.   Harrison, op cit, p 224; Craven and Cate, op cit, Vol III, p 161.

hours for a division moving from the French–Belgian frontier to the Seine area, less for the divisions in the south and south-west of France. The greatest delays would result from the extraordinarily successful attacks on the Seine rail bridges and on the Grand Ceinture junctions in Paris. The attacks on the Seine road bridges had also been an outstanding success.[55] The JIC's assessment of the effects of the offensive, issued on 3 June, was more even-handed. It accepted that the Germans were continuing to make troop movements by rail even through the heavily damaged areas, but felt that the damage was 'causing them anxiety as to whether, when such movements have to be made on a large scale and urgently, they will be able to move . . . with the speed that operations may demand'. Moreover, the effects of the preliminary strategic bombing could not be assessed separately from those of tactical bombing on or after D-day.[56]*

□

As D-day approached, and the Transportation Plan entered its tactical phase, the Allied air forces implemented plans prepared over a period for attacks on other targets, notably airfields within range of the beachhead, coastal batteries and the enemy's coast-watching and early warning radar sites.

The AEAF was in January 1944 already attacking airfields in operations, complementary to *Pointblank*, which aimed at tying down German fighters and destroying them on the ground. In that month, however, a plan related directly to *Overlord* was drawn up. It was to take place in two stages. In the first, starting on D-21, attacks would be directed against airfield installations that were

---

* Controversy as to the relative effects of the attrition bombing and of the tactical or interdiction bombing continued after D-day; and it still continues. SHAEF changed its pre-D-day views some months later, concluding that the attrition had been more effective than interdiction. The US Strategic Bombing Survey after the war took the opposite view. An independent US Air Force investigation after the war concluded that the attrition programme had been unnecessary. The official US Army historian believes it was of decisive importance.[57] The post-war RAF narrative quoted from a German Air Ministry report dated 13 June 1944. This said: 'the raids carried out in recent weeks have caused the breakdown of all main lines; the coastal defences have been cut off from the supply bases in the interior, thus producing a situation which threatens to have serious consequences. Although even the transportation of essential supplies for the civilian population have been completely stopped for the time being and only the most vital military traffic is moved, large scale strategic movement of German troops by rail is practically impossible at the present time and must remain so while attacks are maintained at their present intensity'.[58]

55. WO 205/532, Weekly *Neptune* Review of 4 June.
56. JIC(44)228(o) of 3 June.
57. Craven and Cate, op cit, Vol III, pp 160–163; Harrison, op cit, p 224 et seq; Pogue, *The Supreme Command* (Washington DC 1954), p 132.
58. AIR 41/56, *The RAF in the Bombing Offensive against Germany*, Vol VI, p 257.

not easy to repair, with the object of dislocating the maintenance, repair and administrative structure. They would be followed by attacks delivered as near as possible to H-hour on runways, aircraft control centres and GAF HQs.[59] It depended closely on the work of AI's airfield section (AI 2(b)). Set up in 1941, and a wholly integrated Anglo-American organisation since 1943, this sifted intelligence from all sources on the location, characteristics, operational capacity and inter-relationship of all enemy airfields and issued analyses at all levels down to the descriptive details needed by bomb aimers.[60] For the first draft 25 airfields within 110 miles of Caen, together with their satellite or advanced landing strips, were selected from the list prepared by AI 2(b).

By the beginning of May the Germans had started to withdraw their fighters and bombers to more distant bases in response to the continued attacks on airfields that the Allies were carrying out partly in support of *Pointblank* and partly as intruder operations against the bombers which were attacking London and the invasion ports. On 6 May, however, following earlier references to preparations for GAF moves to the west in the event of emergency, high-grade Sigint finally disclosed the GAF's plans for delaying the bringing up of reinforcements for the invasion area till the last moment, and for sending them to reception airfields before deploying them to more forward bases. The reception areas were not all specified, but some were in the vicinity of Paris, Brussels and Marseilles.[61] At the same time, decrypts established that the GAF intended to double the anti-shipping force in the south of France.* Since the enemy's reinforcement plans indicated that deserted airfields close to the invasion area could not be left unattacked, the plan's targets were altered on 7 May in the light of surveillance by PR and agents of the state of the deserted airfields, as well as to take account of the Sigint evidence. The new list consisted of the 41 main airfields constituting an immediate threat to the beachhead: 22 within 130 miles of Caen, of which the majority were in the Paris area and thus able to be attacked without betraying that the Allies would land in Normandy rather than the Pas de Calais; 12 in the Pas de Calais; 7 in Brittany. In addition 59 bomber and anti-shipping bases in northern and southern France, the Low Countries and Germany were selected for attack; they included the reception areas near Marseilles and Brussels. By the same date more intelligence had been obtained

---

* See above p 105.

59. AIR 41/66, p 121.
60. *Air Ministry Intelligence*, pp 213–215.
61. DEFE 3/46, KVs 2983 and 2985 of 6 May; AWL 1973 of 7 May; Air Sunset 169 of 7 May. See also, eg DEFE 3/151, VL 9471 of 26 March.

about the control centres which were to be attacked just before D-day; previously AI 2(b) had located only the main control centre of Jagdkorps II at Chantilly, but by early May RAF Y had identified four Jagdführer control centres.[62]

The first stage of the plan was implemented from 11 May. The targets for each day were chosen at HQ AEAF in the light of AI 2(b)'s latest information on the results of the attacks, on the enemy's efforts to avoid and repair damage and on the strengths and locations of the German formations. PR and RAF Y were the principal sources for evidence of the results of the raids. RAF Y provided information about strengths and locations.[63] Enigma identified the GAF units, and also yielded information about the damage inflicted and about German defence measures. A decrypt of 14 May disclosed that Göring had ordered the Todt Organisation to take what steps were necessary to deceive the Allies into attacking airfields that were no longer used, or only occasionally used.[64] Jagdkorps II's proposals for keeping satellite landing grounds serviceable in the face of the Allied attacks were decrypted on 16 May.[65] Many decrypts reported on the results of the raids – so many that while all were sent to AI 2(b), GC and CS had to announce on 29 May that it could no longer summarise all of them for despatch to the *Overlord* Commands.[66]

By the end of May 34 airfields in the main list of targets had been attacked in 90 raids, mainly by the US air forces, and 14 other operational bases had been bombed.* It was estimated that only four of the 34 had been so severely damaged that no further attack was called for; 14 of them were placed in a second category on which a further attack might be necessary. But AOC-in-C AEAF then decided that it was safe to suspend or greatly reduce the attacks in order to concentrate on the tactical targets in the Transportation Plan. He did so in the belief that any attack the GAF might make against the landings could be countered and that it was more important to impede the approach of the German armoured divisions. He was bitterly reproached on 3 June for

---

* Two of these were attacked from the Mediterranean by US Fifteenth Air Force. In addition the Mediterranean authorities were asked on 24 May to attack airfields in the Piacenza area, to which it was known that a large part of the German fighter-bomber force in Italy had been withdrawn, possibly for transfer to the west. In raids carried out on 25 May the Mediterranean air forces destroyed or damaged 18 FW 190s on these airfields. None of the FW 190s from Italy reached France.[67]

62. AIR 41/66, pp 126(n), 127–128; Craven and Cate, op cit, Vol III, p 165.
63. AIR 41/66, p 33; *Air Ministry Intelligence*, pp 79, 223–224.
64. DEFE 3/155, KV 3863 of 14 May.
65. DEFE 3/156, KV 4057 of 16 May.
66. DEFE 3/162, KV 5562 of 29 May.
67. Air Sunset 177 of 30 May; AWL 2082 of 24 May.

changing his priorities by Tedder and the Commander of the US Strategic Air Forces, who argued that the threat from the GAF was greater than that from the Panzer divisions.[68]

□

As with bridges in the Transportation Plan, so with the German coastal batteries, there was a division of opinion as to whether they were suitable targets for air attack. In January 1944 21st Army Group requested that the air forces should eliminate some 12 to 16 of the batteries that covered the landing areas. The air authorities regarded them as unprofitable targets – small, heavily defended and calling for special forms of attack and a heavy weight of bombs. They argued that the attack on them should be left until the general air and naval bombardment of the coastal defences that was to take place immediately before H-hour and all the more so because on security grounds an earlier offensive could not be limited to those in Normandy. They maintained this position until March. But in that month PR detected that the number of batteries covering the assault area had risen to 49, some of which were already casemated, and that the German case-mating programme, which had already been completed in the Pas de Calais and the Dieppe area, was being extended to a further eight of these 49. On receipt of this evidence 21st Army Group, supported by the ANCXF, pressed for immediate destruction of the eight and for bombing to take place against other open-site large-calibre batteries as soon as PR observed that the enemy was starting to case-mate them.[69]

The offensive began on 10 April with an attack by 219 medium bombers of US Ninth Air Force on the long-range battery at Le Grand Clos which covered Le Havre and the approaches to the British assault beaches. It continued with attacks on all the other priority targets; all eight of these had been bombed by the end of April, together with 16 in the area between the Seine and Dunkirk which were attacked in accordance with the security requirements that two had to be attacked elsewhere for every battery attacked in the assault area.[70]* The results were judged to be sufficiently satisfactory to justify continuation of the attacks – PR indicated

---

* It was in these attacks that Operation *Fortitude*, hitherto implemented only passively through double agents and visual and W/T deception, was for the first time actively supported by actual Allied operations.[71]

68.   Ellis, op cit, Vol 1, p 96; Craven and Cate, op cit, Vol III, pp 165–166; AIR 41/56, pp 41, 44–46; AIR 41/66, pp 128–129.
69.   AIR 41/66, pp 132, 135–136; AIR 41/56, pp 47–48.
70.   AIR 41/66, p 134.
71.   ibid, p 134.

that five of the eight in the *Overlord* area had been damaged and at ten of the others at least one gun had been damaged* – and Bomber Command carried out the first raids with heavy bombers on the nights of 7 and 8 May. It carried out a further 30 raids on batteries by the end of the month; they were supplemented by raids by US Eighth Air Force from 25 May; and medium-bomber attacks also continued. The prolongation of the campaign and its costliness to the Allied air forces testify both to the difficulty of the targets and to the significance attached to them.[73]

On 26 May HQ AEAF estimated that the eight priority targets had all been considerably damaged, but that at other batteries only 18 of the 51 guns attacked in the assault area, and 26 out of 101 attacked in other areas, had been partially damaged. On 31 May 21st Army Group accepted that five batteries in the *Overlord* area had been completely destroyed and six others so badly damaged that they were unlikely to be effective on D-day. It expressed itself satisfied with these results, in that it was 'not hoping for destruction of guns but reduction in efficiency . . . and delay in building of casemates'; but it nevertheless requested continued attacks on a further five batteries as a matter of urgency. The campaign was accordingly intensified in the last few days before D-day, and on 4 June AEAF reported that 21 of the batteries covering the assault area had been damaged. On the night of 5–6 June Bomber Command devoted a large part of its total effort to renewed bombing of the ten most formidable batteries overlooking the assault area.[74]†

On D-day only four large batteries were active in the entire invasion area, but it is not possible to say to what extent this success was due to the bombing campaign and to what extent it was also due to the last-minute naval bombardment.[75]

☐

The neutralisation of the German radar chain called for close

---

* PR was the only source of information on the results of the raids. Agents were unable to report from the coastal zone. Only three decrypts were available on the subject. One on 6 May disclosed that some damage had been done to the Le Havre battery in April. A situation report from C-in-C West for the period 1–7 May, decrypted on 14 May, stated that only slight damage had been done to batteries. A decrypt of 22 May reporting a coast-defence radar out of order added that damage at other sites in Calvados and the Pas de Calais had been slight.[72]

† See below, Chapter 46.

72. DEFE 3/47, KV 3018 of 6 May; DEFE 3/155, KV 3763 of 14 May; DEFE 3/159, KV 4811 of 22 May.
73. AIR 41/66, pp 134–139; AIR 41/24, p 30; Craven and Cate, op cit, Vol III, pp 168–169.
74. AIR 41/66, p 139; AIR 41/56, p 48; Craven and Cate, op cit, Vol III, p 170.
75. AIR 41/66, p 140; Craven and Cate, op cit, Vol III, p 170.

co-ordination between the air offensive and a jamming programme. The chain consisted of so large a number of stations,
most of which housed installations of two or three different types,
that only those that were unsuitable for jamming, or were of the
greatest importance, could be selected for air attack when the
Allied air forces were faced with so many other commitments.[76]

Like the preparation of the jamming programme, the selection
of the sites that were to be bombed rested on a very considerable
knowledge of the location and the functions of the installations.
This knowledge had been built up over many months by the Noise
Investigation Bureau (NIB) and the Telecommunications Research Establishment (TRE), on the basis of intercepts of the
enemy's radar transmissions, and by the staff of ADI (Sc) in
collaboration with the CIU on the basis of PR, POW interrogation,
captured equipment and documents and the low-grade Sigint of
all three Services.[77] The efforts of these two groups, the signals
and the intelligence authorities, had been brought closer together
from early in 1944, when a chain of high-accuracy equipment
specially designed by TRE and capable of DFing radar transmissions from France to the nearest quarter of a degree was deployed
along the south and south-east coasts. Any new bearing recorded
by the chain (code-name *Ping Pong*) was immediately followed up
by PR from that date.[78]

The results of this research, which was available in the form of
an index of enemy radar stations, arranged by type and location
and accompanied by maps, diagrams and close-up photographs,
may be judged from the fact that, of the 120 installations at 47
stations between Calais and Cherbourg, all had been located by
D-day and only six had been mis-identified – the mis-identification
arising chiefly from confusion by the *Ping Pong* stations of the
transmissions of the large coast-watching radar (*Seetakt*) with those
of the modified *Freya* radars used for aircraft reporting.[79]*

To supervise the bombing offensive, SHAEF set up at HQ
AEAF on 15 May a Radio Counter-Measures Staff under the
direction of the Air Ministry's Director General of Signals. Its tasks
were to direct the noise-watching agencies (the *Ping Pong* chain,
the ship-borne and airborne interception programme of the Navy
and the RAF and six of the south coast HDUs);† to decide with the

---

* For these and the other German radars see Volumes II and III Part 1.
† See Volume I, p 180 for the HDUs.

76.   AIR 41/24, p 31.
77.   AIR 41/7, *Photographic Reconnaissance*, Vol II, p 145; *Air Ministry Intelligence*,
      pp 96, 324; Jones, *Most Secret War* (1978), p 400.
78.   Price, *Instruments of Darkness* (1967), p 200.
79.   *Air Ministry Intelligence*, pp 301–302, 325.

advice of the NIB and the intelligence authorities which installations were to be bombed and which were to be dealt with by jamming; and to make daily recommendations on the bombing of targets in the light of the results of previous attacks.[80] By bringing about not only closer collaboration between the radio countermeasure authorities and the intelligence agencies, but also, unusually, co-operation between the Royal Navy's anti-radar organisation and the other radio counter-measures authorities, this staff proved to be a highly effective steering committee.

Bombing began on 10 May with raids on the enemy's long-range *Wassermann* and *Mammut* radars following an experimental raid on a *Wassermann* near Ostend. These were selected for attack because their narrow beam made it difficult to jam them, and they were attacked first because they could be least easily repaired. The offensive was extended a week later to installations used for night-fighter control and the control of coastal guns.[81] Five installations thought to be German jamming stations were also bombed; it was known from high-grade Sigint that the Germans had captured 'Gee', the British radio navigational system on which the assault forces would be heavily dependent for precision in making their land-falls, and were therefore in a position to jam it.*

The evidence for the effects of the raids came mainly from the noise-watching stations and from PR, which took low-level oblique photographs after each raid and kept a close watch for signs of repairs and replacements. But naval and RAF Y intercepts, the reports of pilots and the photographs taken by their camera guns also made a valuable contribution.[83] As was the case with the other preliminary air offensives, high-grade Sigint provided no conclusive evidence. Only two decrypts referred to the radar targets; a report from Luftflotte 3 decrypted on 21 May, stating that 'the increased Allied attack on GAF and naval radar was particularly

---

* For 'Gee' see Volume III, Part 1, p 576. On the strength of intercepts of German jamming the NIB initially believed that it was carried out from some 23 separate sites. But following the identification, with assistance from high-grade decrypts, of a jamming station at Mont Couple near Boulogne, which had 90 transmitting arrays extending over a considerable area, and intensive search by the CIU for sites with a similar lay-out, or sites which were otherwise inexplicable, only four other such stations had been located. Beginning with a highly accurate precision attack on the Mont Couple site by Bomber Command, all five were bombed on the recommendation of ADI (Sc). One of the sites turned out to be the GAF Y interception station at Urville-Hague, near Cherbourg, for which see Chapter 46, p 127 below. There was no German interference with 'Gee' on D-day.[82]

80.   AIR 41/24, p 31; Jones, op cit, p 402.
81.   AIR 41/56, p 45; AIR 41/7, p 145; Jones, op cit, pp 403–404.
82.   Jones, op cit, p 410; *Air Ministry Intelligence*, pp 325–326.
83.   AIR 41/7, p 145; Jones, op cit, p 405; *Air Ministry Intelligence*, p 96; *The handling of naval Special Intelligence*, p 108.

worthy of note', and a report decrypted on 22 May to the effect that the radar at La Pernelle overlooking the approach to the beaches on the Cotentin was out of order.[84]

By 3 June the evidence had confirmed that only 14 of the 42 sites selected for air attack had been destroyed.* It was then decided that the heavy bombers of Bomber Command and US Eighth Air Force should join the rocket-firing aircraft of the AEAF which had so far borne the brunt of the offensive, and that in the remaining time available the offensive should be concentrated against the twelve most important sites that were still operational. In the three days before D-day all 39 installations at these twelve sites were bombed.[86]

The low and, as it turned out, over-pessimistic assessment of the effects of the bombing had meanwhile put a premium on the success of the jamming programme that was to be put into force during the passage of the Allied convoys and the assault on the beaches. In preparation for this programme – the largest jamming operation ever devised – the counter-measures authorities established the radio characteristics and frequency spread of every radar station from Ostend to Brest, and supplemented the existing jamming organisation by distributing 200 jamming transistors to the Royal Navy ships that were to accompany the assault forces and by mounting in two heavy bomber squadrons a battery of 'Mandrel' jammers capable of forming a screen 200 miles long behind which the German radars would be unable to detect any movement.[87]†

In the event, according to American assessments, the bombing had reduced the effectiveness of the German radar chain in the

---

* The total list from which the 42 were chosen was not that of the 47 between Calais and Cherbourg to which we have already referred, but that of the 66 main stations and the numerous radars controlling coastal batteries and Flak which constituted the German radar chain from Dunkirk to Brest. Two targets outside the *Neptune* area had to be attacked for every target attacked inside it. However, some stations in the Pas de Calais area were deliberately not attacked so that they might detect the electronic deception to simulate the approach of convoys in the eastern Channel that was planned for the night before D-day.[85] For these see Chapter 46.

† For 'Mandrel' see Volume III, Part 1, pp 308, 556. Experiments in mounting an airborne 'Mandrel' screen had been made at the end of 1942 with the object of jamming the early warning *Freya* radars. The *Freyas* had then been modified, and while 'Mandrel' had been re-designed to counter the new frequencies, no further use of the 'Mandrel' system was made before D-day lest the Germans anticipate the probable neutralisation of *Freya* in the Channel.

84.   DEFE 3/158, KV 4690 of 21 May; DEFE 3/159, KV 4811 of 22 May.
85.   AIR 41/24, p 131; Ellis, op cit, Vol 1, p 160; Saunders and Richards, *The RAF 1939–1945*, Vol III (1954), p 109.
86.   AIR 41/56, p 45; Craven and Cate, op cit, Vol III, p 173.
87.   Price, op cit, pp 111, 209–210, 223; Webster and Frankland, op cit, Vol III, p 150.

invasion area to 18 per cent, and with the introduction of the jamming measures during the crossing of the Channel this figure was reduced to five per cent.[88] It appears that only about half a dozen of the stations in the area that had survived the air offensive escaped the jamming.[89] And it is clear that their reports were insufficient to give early warning: as we shall now see, the first radar reports, from coastal radar stations, did not reach the German authorities till 0200 on D-day and the enemy remained confused as to what was happening for some hours after they were made.

88.   Craven and Cate, op cit, Vol III, p 172.
89.   *Air Ministry Intelligence*, p 325.

CHAPTER 46

The Assault

A T 0430 on 4 June Eisenhower postponed the landings for 24 hours, to 6 June: on 3 June the forecasts had predicted for 5 June weather which might permit landings from surface craft but would forbid air operations, including airborne landings. On the evening of 4 June the meteorological officers at SHAEF forecast a break in the weather for the assault area; it would last over the morning of 6 June, but not beyond, and while producing conditions 'barely tolerable' for the assault forces, would permit in conditions of 'considerable cloudiness' the heavy bombing of coastal defence batteries planned for the early hours of D-day and, probably, the air spotting required for the naval bombardments.[1] A further postponement beyond 6 June would have entailed postponement for at least a fortnight and other grave disadvantages, including the danger that the enemy would be alerted to Allied intentions. On the other hand, in conditions that were more typical of December than of June, a decision there and then in favour of 6 June carried with it the risk of condemning the expedition to failure. Eisenhower decided for 6 June.

SHAEF's weather forecasts were derived primarily from reports sent in by US and British ships from pre-determined positions in the Atlantic.[2] There is no substance in the claim that the decrypts of German meteorological reports contributed significantly to their accuracy.[3] On the contrary, the German meteorological service, crippled by the loss of its outlying stations in Greenland, Spitzbergen, Iceland and Jan Mayen* and reduced to dependence on reports from a mere two or three U-boats in the Atlantic† and daily meteorological flights to the west of Ireland, was unable to provide the forecast of the short-lived break in the bad weather

---

* See Volume II, Appendix 7; Volume III Part 1, Appendix 12.
† The U-boat weather patrols were instituted on 31 December 1943, when Sigint disclosed that weather-reporting zones in the central North Atlantic had been assigned to three U-boats. Between then and D-day 29 U-boats were rotated through the patrols; their reports were regularly decrypted. By the beginning of May the transmission of weather reports was the main function of U-boats in the North Atlantic.[4]

1. Harrison, *Cross-Channel Attack* (Washington DC 1951), p 272.
2. CAB 106/976, SHAEF Report of 22 June 1944, 'Meteorological Implications in the Selection of the Day for the Allied Invasion of France', p 21.
3. Lewin, *Ultra goes to War* (1978), pp 294–295.
4. US Department of Defense, *Allied Communication Intelligence and the Battle of the Atlantic*, Vol II, pp 193–194; ADM 223/172, OIC SI 944 of 8 May 1944.

that enabled Eisenhower to make his decision. Had it been otherwise, moreover, it must be regarded as highly improbable that the Germans would have been influenced by such a forecast. As C-in-C West had stated in his appreciation of 8 May, their basic assumption was that the Allies would attempt to land when they were sure of 'a series of days of continuous fine weather'.*

It was on this account that, although the Allies had had to plan on the assumption that in normal weather the enemy would know by H−12 hours that the expedition had sailed, and would be sure of its destination by H−4,[5] the landings achieved tactical surprise. During 5 June, when the whole expedition was at sea – five assault forces carried by some 6,500 vessels, including 4,250 landing craft, in some 75 convoys, each five miles long – and when one of the Allied minesweeping flotillas was in sight of the French coast for the last three hours of daylight,[1] only five German aircraft flew over the Channel on routine sorties that were easily evaded, and the only aircraft detected by Allied radar during the night of 5–6 June were over the Pas de Calais.[6] The German Navy, which cancelled the naval patrols and minelaying operations scheduled for that night, made no change in its dispositions in the Channel ports, of which precise details were issued to the Allied naval commands on the evening of 5 June,[7] Rommel had gone to Germany for a few days on 5 June, and several other senior German officers – GOC Seventh Army and his divisional commanders; GOC I SS Panzer Corps; and, though there is some doubt in this case, GOC 21st Panzer Division – were absent from their posts on the night of 5–6 June.[8]

Put off his guard by the weather, the enemy was not alerted, as he might well have been, by unusual last-minute W/T activity on the part of the Allies. Their decision to postpone the operation necessitated an unwelcome amount of signalling, since many of the convoys had already set out and one was half way across before it could be turned back, but it appears to have gone unnoticed.†

---

* See above, p 63, and Appendix 8.

† This is possibly explained by the fact that two of the principal German intercept stations had been destroyed by air attack. The main naval station at Château Terlinden near Bruges had been located by POW and PR at the instigation of GC and CS, which recommended that it should be eliminated ten days before D-day. The Enigma signal reporting attacks on it on

5. WO 219/1835, SHAEF Appreciation of 9 May 1944; CAB 44/243, *Operation 'Overlord'*, p 40; ADM 234/366, BR 1736(42)(1), p 83.

6. Ellis, *Victory in the West*, Vol I (1962), p 130; CAB 44/243, pp 41–42; ADM 234/366, p 87

7. Roskill, *The War at Sea*, Vol III Part 2 (1961), p 42; ADM 223/195, Ultra Signal 1821/5 June 1944.

8. Ellis, op cit, Vol I, p 198; Harrison, op cit, pp 77–79, 275; D'Este, *Decision in Normandy* (1983), p 111.

The SOE's arrangements for instructing the French Resistance to begin the planned programme of sabotage necessitated the transmission of an operational signal at intervals throughout 5 June. Late in the evening, at 2215, this unusual development was brought to the notice of the German Service authorities. Fifteenth Army took it to be a warning that invasion would follow within 48 hours, but Seventh Army and the naval authorities took no action and C-in-C West's HQ doubted whether Fifteenth Army's deduction was justified.[11]* It was not until he got the first news of the Allied airborne landings that the enemy brought his forces to the highest state of readiness.

6th Airborne Division landed north-east of Caen at 0020 on 6 June and 101st and 82nd US Airborne Divisions began their drops in the Cotentin about 0200. These operations were accompanied by the dropping of dummy parachutists and the simulation of shipping movements in other areas.† At about 0200 Fifteenth Army asked Army Group B to have 12th SS Panzer Division

---

28–29 May was decrypted on 5 June.[9] The GAF station at Urville-Hague near Cherbourg was bombed on the night of 3–4 June; it had not been identified as an intercept station, but was known to be an important installation of a special character.[10]

* The operational signal had been preceded by signals relayed by the BBC during the first three days of June alerting the Resistance to stand by for orders. The Sicherheitsdienst, which had got wind of the alerting system, issued a warning that invasion 'could be considered possible in the next fortnight'; but the Service authorities took no action as, unlike the operational order transmitted on 5 June, such preliminary alerts had been issued previously on several occasions.

† Two sets of diversionary operations were carried out with the airborne landings. The first was the dropping of dummy parachutists to the accompaniment of 'Window' and noise from soon after midnight at places along a wide arc inland from the bridgehead from west of St Lo to east of Le Havre. The second, carried out by Bomber Command in conjunction with motor launches, used electronic deception to simulate the movement of a large convoy towards beaches between Le Havre and Dieppe and the approach of shipping to the coast in the Pas de Calais, while motor launches operating off Cap Barfleur were intended to create a similar threat in the Cherbourg area. Of the dummy parachute drops. that at Marigny drew 915 Infantry Regiment, the third regiment of 352nd Infantry Division, as far as the Carentan–Isigny area from its position in reserve near Bayeux, thus providing some relief to the troops landing on the *Gold* and *Omaha* beaches.[12] As will be seen in Appendix 13, the simulated shipping threat off the Pas de Calais produced a search by night-fighters off Boulogne, these being the only German aircraft detected by Allied radar during the crossing, and an E-boat sortie; and the simulated threat in the Cherbourg area also produced a German reaction.

9. DEFE 3/166, KV 6519 of 5 June 1944.
10. AIR 41/24, *The Liberation of North-West Europe*, Vol III, p 32; Jones, *Most Secret War* (1978). pp 410, 412.
11. Ellis, op cit, Vol I, p 198; Harrison, op cit, pp 275–276; Foot, *SOE in France* (1968), p 388; Haswell, *The Intelligence and Deception of the D-day Landings* (1979), pp 172–173; Hinsley and Simkins, *Security and Counter-Intelligence*, (forthcoming).
12. Ellis, op cit, Vol I, pp 159–160, 211; Harrison, op cit, pp 275(n), 321; Haswell, op cit, pp 176–177; Jones, op cit, pp 406, 409; AIR 41/24, pp 109, 124.

brought up from Rouen to the Caen area. At 0215 Fifteenth and
Seventh Armies ordered the highest state of readiness, as did
Naval Gruppe West; but at 0300 the naval authorities, C-in-C
West, AOC-in-C Luftflotte 3 (Sperrle) and the Chief of Staff at
Army Group B (Speidel) still believed they were faced only with a
diversionary operation preceding an invasion in the Pas de Calais.
Not till 0400 did C-in-C West, persuaded by further reports that
the airborne landings were on such a scale that they would be
supported by a sea assault in the Seine Bay whatever the Allies
planned to do elsewhere, order 12th SS Panzer Division to move at
once towards Caen and Panzer Lehr Division to prepare to move.
At 0500 he ordered Army Group B to release 21st Panzer Division
to Seventh Army for a counter-attack on the airborne forces
north-east of Caen. By 0515 Seventh Army had concluded from
the airborne landings and the location by radar of sea targets off
the Cotentin and along the whole of the Calvados coast that 'a
large-scale enemy assault' was in progress. But further delays
followed. 21st Panzer Division did not receive the 0500 order till
0700.* At 0730 Jodl for OKW permitted 12th SS Panzer to move
as far as Lisieux but otherwise refused to approve von Rundstedt's
orders to 12th SS Panzer and Panzer Lehr until Hitler had been
consulted. Hitler was asleep till mid-day, and did not consent to
the movement of the divisions till the afternoon.[14]

Meanwhile Naval Gruppe West had concluded by 0320 that a
major operation was in progress. At 0320, following reports at
0215 of radar echoes from shipping off the Cotentin, where the
assault forces were anchoring off the *Utah* and *Omaha* beaches
between 0230 and 0300, and of the detection at 0309 of ten large
vessels north of Port-en-Bessin, it brought the U-boats in Biscay
ports to immediate readiness, and issued the following orders: the
8th Destroyer Flotilla to move from Royan to Brest; the 5th
Torpedo-Boat Flo..lla from Le Havre to carry out reconnaissance
in the area Port-en-Bessin and Grandcamp; the 5th and 9th
E-Boat Flotillas from Cherbourg to patrol off Cape de la Hague
and Barfleur respectively.[15]

If only because the airborne landings necessarily alerted the
enemy, the Allied assault forces could at no time after midnight on

---

* According to some accounts the division manned its tanks at 0200 on learning of 6th
Airborne's parachute landing, but in the absence of its GOC and of Rommel it had not
received the 0500 order when the GOC decided on his own initiative to start about 0730.[13]

13. Hastings, *Overlord: D-day and the Battle for Normandy* (1984), p 79.
14. Ellis, op cit, Vol I, pp 198–200; Harrison, op cit, pp 278, 332–333; D'Este,
     op cit, pp 111–112, 138.
15. Ellis, op cit, Vol I, p 199; Harrison, op cit, p 301; Roskill, op cit, Vol III Part
     2, pp 16, 42; ADM 234/366, pp 86–87.

5–6 June be sure that they would escape attack before reaching the beaches. From the naval Enigma, however, they received a full and prompt account of the German Navy's reactions, as distinct from those of the Army and the Air Force. The first reports of parachutists, intercepted from just before midnight on 5 June, were relayed to them from 0132 on 6 June. From 0338 they were informed of most of the orders issued by Naval Gruppe West. The first news of positive action by the German Navy, an order to the 5th Torpedo-Boat Flotilla at 0348 to leave Le Havre and attack landing boats off Port-en-Bessin and Grandcamp, near the Vire estuary, was transmitted to them at 0420.*

In this sortie the torpedo-boats in fact encountered the eastern-most bombardment force, which received no 'Headache' warning of their approach, and sank the Norwegian destroyer *Svenner*.[16] They attacked between 0515 and 0530, before the force had received the Sigint warning. But the fact that only 32 minutes had elapsed between the transmission of the German order and the despatch of the decrypt to the Commands by the Admiralty at 0420 illustrates the speed with which, thanks to the decision to intercept the naval traffic within the perimeter of Bletchley Park, the naval Enigma decrypts were being processed.† Throughout the assault phase the average time-lag between the interception of the German signals and the delivery of the decrypts to the OIC was to be 30 minutes during those large parts of each day in which the Enigma keys were being decrypted currently.[17]

□

The Allied naval bombardment began about 0530, immediately after the completion of overnight air attacks on the ten most formidable batteries. While the big warships concentrated on the batteries, destroyers, venturing in as far as depth allowed, attacked the beach defences and smaller gun positions.[18] From dawn until ten minutes before the first troops landed the attack on the beach defences was continued by an enormous force of heavy bombers and was completed by guns and rockets mounted on landing craft, some specially designed, which drenched them for the final five minutes.[19] Although the Allied air offensive had already done much in the weeks before D-day to retard the development of the

---

* See Appendix 13(i) for the decrypts relayed to the assault forces during the crossing.
† See Appendix 6.

16. Ellis, op cit, Vol 1, p 163; ADM 234/366, pp 87–88.
17. Information from Sir Harry Hinsley.
18. CAB 44/242, *Operation 'Overlord'*, p 320; CAB 44/245, *Operation 'Overlord'*, p 282; AIR 41/24, p 39; Ellis, op cit, Vol 1, pp 102, 165.
19. Ellis, op cit, Vol I, pp 167–168; Harrison, op cit, pp 301, 303.

enemy's coastal batteries, and especially the programme for casemating them,[20] it was still essential to neutralise the defences if the assault troops were to get ashore, and this objective the combined air and naval bombardment – the largest ever planned – very largely achieved. The bombardment was not marked by great accuracy; the naval gunfire scored few direct hits and the bombing of the beaches, carried out in overcast conditions, was only 'partly successful'. It also turned out that there were some unavoidable deficiencies in the intelligence on which the planning of the attacks had absolutely depended. Perhaps the most important was that the Allies had not detected that the principal enemy gun positions on the beaches had been constructed to give enfilading fire; they could not fire to seaward but neither were they seriously damaged by off-shore bombardment. Had this been known the naval fire plan would have been differently framed.[21] Another arose from the fact that although most of the batteries had been correctly plotted, and their characteristics correctly assessed, some of the more formidable had either been moved and their original sites preserved as decoys, or else the number and calibre of their guns had been over-estimated.[22]* But these deficiencies were to cause serious problems only when troops had got ashore. The sheer weight of the barrage so far succeeded in suppressing the guns and demoralising the defenders that during the run-in to the beaches there was 'little reaction on the part of the enemy'.[26]

The run in, timed to be completed at varying H-hours between

---

* Of those batteries which were of such importance that special measures were taken to eliminate them, the easternmost, at Merville-Sallenelles east of the Orne, was believed to mount four 150 mm guns which, with a range of 15,000 yards, would threaten the whole of the *Sword* beach; it had indeed been so designed. But when captured by a battalion of 6th Airborne Division, for the loss of 66 men, it was found to house only old French 75 mm guns.[23] A second, at Pointe du Hoe a short distance west of *Omaha* beach, covered the *Omaha* and *Utah* beaches and the western end of *Gold* beach with six 155 mm guns. It was heavily bombed before D-day and heavily bombed and shelled on D-day, but in addition a force of US commandos was detailed to capture it. They did so with heavy casualties, only to find that its guns had been removed and replaced with telegraph poles; the guns were later found unguarded a mile or so inland.[24] At the southern end of *Utah* beach at St Martin de Varreville a third battery, thought to be equally formidable, was captured by a force of US paratroopers; they found that in consequence of earlier bombing, its guns had been removed.[25]

20. CAB 44/242, pp 357–358; Richards, *The RAF 1939–1945*, Vol II, (1954), p 110; AIR 41/24, pp 29–30.
21. Ellis, op cit, Vol 1, p 174; ADM 234/366, p 98; CAB 44/243, p 95.
22. CAB 44/242, pp 355–356.
23. CAB 44/244, *Operation 'Overlord'*, pp 203–208, Ellis, op cit, Vol I, p 158; Haswell, op cit, pp 180–181; Hastings, op cit, p 74.
24. Harrison, op cit, p 322; Haswell, op cit, pp 179–180.
25. Harrison, op cit, p 280 fn – 281.
26. Ellis, op cit, Vol I, p 167; Harrison, op cit, p 301; Roskill, op cit, Vol III Part 2, p 52.

0630 and 0755 at the five beaches, took place in weather that was worse than had been forecast, with steeper seas and stronger winds. Many of the smaller landing craft foundered during the crossing. On some of the beaches it was difficult to locate the pre-arranged landing places. Still more serious, the stiff on-shore wind had so raised the level of the tide that the underwater obstacles were already under water when the first landing craft arrived. Grievous casualties followed from the fact that it proved impossible to carry out the prepared operations for removing the obstacles, as also from the fact that the beaches were now being raked by enfilading fire which delayed the opening of beach exits and compounded the congestion as men and vehicles were landed in an increasingly restricted area.[27]

Heavy though they were, the casualties incurred on D-day were far smaller than had been expected. The British authorities had feared that British and Canadian casualties might rise to 30 per cent of all men landed; the actual figure was 3 per cent.[28]* By the end of the day 75,215 British and Canadian troops and 57,500 American had been landed from the sea, and 23,000 Allied troops had landed by air, and the casualties amounted to 3,000 British and Canadian seaborne troops, 1,300 British airborne troops and a total, seaborne and airborne, of 6,000 US troops.[30] ANCXF's Report and the subsequent Naval Staff study attributed this remarkable success in breaching the Atlantic wall at so little cost in large measure to the excellence of the intelligence on the defences and the topography of the invasion area, and particularly to the work of the TIS and the ISTD in processing it for the use of the Allied Commands.[31]

Among the operational factors which contributed to the success, the most important were the equally remarkable fact that the Allies achieved tactical surprise and their control of the sea and the air. With regard to the former Eisenhower recorded that it 'accounted to some extent for the low order of active opposition on most of the beaches.'[32] As for the importance of the air supremacy, he stated when postponing the operation on 4 June that '*Overlord* is going in on a very slim margin of ground superiority and only Allied superiority in the air makes it a sound operation of war. If the air cannot operate, the landings should

---

* The Prime Minister had feared that 20,000 British and Canadian troops would be lost.[29]

27. Ellis, op cit, Vol I, pp 174, 181–182, 186, 195–219.
28. Letter from Commander JWR Thompson, *The Times* of 16 June 1984.
29. Gilbert, *Winston S Churchill*, Vol VII (1986), p 981.
30. Ellis, op cit, Vol I, p 194; ADM 234/366, p 91; CAB 44/244, p 355.
31. ANCXF Report, Vol I, p 51, quoted in ADM 234/366, p 25.
32. Eisenhower, *Crusade in Europe* (1948), p 278.

not be risked.'[33] He had, of course, made preparations for one of
the assault forces to be re-formed at short notice in case he should
have to order another landing to relieve a precarious situation in
the Normandy bridgehead, and had ready a draft telegram
informing the Chiefs of Staff that he had decided to order a total
re-embarkation because 'the venture has been overtaken by
misfortune amounting to disaster.'[34] We need not doubt that if not
even the lesser of these misfortunes came close to materialising, it
was largely due to the combination of air power with tactical
surprise.

But the achievement of tactical surprise was, as we have seen,
wholly due to the adverse weather; and in its turn the adverse
weather went far to reduce the ability of the Allies to exploit either
the advantages of surprise or the offensive benefits they might
have derived from air power in the critical period following the
landings. By creating confusion on the beaches, and delay in
getting away from them, it seriously hampered the Allied plans for
rapid thrusts inland. While fighters could operate defensively in
the overcast weather that prevailed till the afternoon, the heavy
bombers were severely handicapped in implementing 'carefully
laid plans to stop enemy movement by demolishing towns to block
main roads'. 500 bombers which set out to attack eight key road
centres had to return without bombing.[35] Armed fighter-bomber
patrols were substituted, and inflicted some delay to the approach
of the German armoured formations. And while the fighter-
bombers provided useful sightings of these formations, intelligence on their movements was impaired by the fact that the poor
weather almost eliminated the work of the PR squadrons on
D-day.[36] Although they were greatly accentuated, as we shall now
see, by shortcomings in Allied knowledge of the dispositions of the
German Army – notably by uncertainty concerning the deployment of 21st Panzer Division and 352nd Infantry Division – it was
these two consequences of the unseasonable weather which
prevented any of the assault forces from gaining its D-day
objectives and which, in particular, frustrated the Allies in their
central purpose, the rapid capture of Caen.

□

For obvious reasons, the capture of Caen on D-day had been

33. Harrison, op cit, p 272.
34. CAB 44/242, p 220; ADM 234/366, p 62; Strong, *Intelligence at the Top*
     (1968), p 138.
35. AIR 41/24, pp 70(n), 71.
36. ibid, p 70(n).

regarded throughout the planning of *Overlord* as crucial to the entire operation. Caen and the open ground to the south-east commanded the main routes by which the bulk of the enemy's mobile reserves – six of the ten Panzer-type divisions in the west – would have to approach the bridgehead. The seizure of these objectives would give the Allies control of the crossings of the Orne and the Odon, and access to the only open country in which they could use the British armoured divisions to maximum effect. By enabling them to establish forward airfields, it would also increase their power to prevent the German reserve divisions from reaching the bridgehead, and thus among other things enable the Allied forces to get through the difficult *bocage* country.[37] After the event the planners would have accepted, as commentators have subsequently concluded, that 'rapid seizure of the Caen-Falaise plain would not only have eliminated the dreadful battles of attrition, but might well have shortened the campaign . . .'[38]

The force allotted to the Caen sector was I British Corps comprising 3rd British Division, landing on *Sword* beach, and 3rd Canadian Division landing on *Juno* beach, together with various supporting units. Its D-day tasks were to establish a line ten miles inland along the Bayeux-Caen road from Putot-en-Bessin to Caen and, on taking Caen, to cross the river Orne and make a junction with 6th Airborne Division. 6th Airborne Division's task was to guard the eastern flank of the assault from enemy interference by seizing the area north of a line from the outskirts of Caen to the river Dives, capturing the bridges across the Orne and the Caen canal (the Bénouville-Ramville bridges known together as the Pegasus bridge), demolishing bridges across the Dives and capturing the Merville battery. These lines being gained, I Corps was to carry out rigorous patrolling and push forward its armour with a view to breaking up the first German counter-attacks, which were expected towards evening, and to ensuring that 'the advance could be resumed against a weakened and improperly organised enemy.'[39]

I Corps recognised that success in achieving these objectives would call for 'great speed and boldness' in pushing forward from the beaches with strong armoured support. It does not appear to have allowed for the contingency that its plans would prove to be over-ambitious. It accepted, indeed, that if the Allies failed to take Caen on D-day, or at the latest on D+1, the most they could hope to do was to mask the town for three or four days until the

---

37. Eisenhower, op cit, p 282; letter from Eisenhower to Montgomery, 23 May 1944 (in Eisenhower Papers, Vol VII, pp 1068–1069).

38. eg D'Este, op cit, p 485.

39. CAB 44/244, pp 143–145, 169 et seq, 296.

follow-up divisions – 51st Division and 4th Armoured Division –
were able to resume the attack on it. At the same time, however, I
Corps must have reflected that unless the air forces could succeed
in stopping them, it would not in these circumstances have the
resources to keep enemy reinforcements away from Caen for that
length of time; for it had been advised that the Germans would
have brought a total of thirteen divisions up to the beachhead by
D+2, and that these would include six or seven armoured
divisions by D+4 at the latest.[40] In the event, we shall see that the
failure to take the town by the end of D+1 forced General
Montgomery to conclude that it could not be taken by direct
assault.

A number of factors have been singled out as contributing to the
failure. The adverse weather and the unexpectedly high water
caused congestion on the beaches and delay in opening up the
beach exits. Sea-sickness among the troops, another consequence
of the weather, combined with relief at penetrating the Atlantic
wall to produce some loss of momentum after the break-out from
the beaches. Some commentators have concluded, moreover, that
as compared with the Germans, the Allied troops were lacking in
professionalism and aggressiveness. However that may be, it
certainly emerged that while the Allies incurred far fewer
casualties on the *Sword* and *Juno* beaches than they had expected,
they had under-estimated the fighting quality and the capacity to
resist of the enemy forces they would meet inland; the stubborn-
ness with which the Germans clung to some of their strongpoints
did much to hold up and dilute the British armoured thrusts. But
though such misfortunes and mistakes proved to be critical on
D-day, they all stemmed from defective analysis at the planning
stage. The *Overlord* plan courted failure to gain its central objective
either by making insufficient allowances when defining the
objective for the difficulties of mounting a co-ordinated all-arms
attack with infantry, armour and artillery following a long sea
crossing or, alternatively, by allotting to the Caen sector less of the
available assault forces than were required to ensure that the
objective was achieved. The official historian has concluded that
'the operations . . . had made a good start but had subsequently
developed too slowly for the main (and perhaps over-ambitious)
object to be *fully* realised – namely, the capture of Bayeux and the
road to Caen, the seizure of Caen itself and the safeguarding of
the Allies' left flank with a bridgehead east of the Orne . . . Caen is
eight miles from the coast . . . and Bayeux six or seven. There was
no possibility of taking them that day unless the advance was made

---

40. Ellis, op cit, Vol I, p 228; WO 171/129, 21st Army Group Intelligence
    Summary, 9 June 1944.

as rapidly as possible . . .'[41] It would be more to the point to say that there was no possibility of taking them unless all went according to plan in a plan which had left no margin for contingencies.

The COSSAC planners had expressed serious forebodings on this score in January when the COSSAC plan was revised and the assault area greatly extended.* It may well be that by necessitating an increase in the scale of the assault forces, the revision left the Allied commanders with no choice but to overlook these forebodings – that they could not both extend the assault frontage and increase the forces allotted to the Caen sector. To pronounce on such an issue would be out of place in an account of the contribution made by intelligence to the planning of *Overlord*. For whatever reasons the forebodings were originally set aside, however, we have to ask why the planners continued to suppress them even when intelligence disclosed during May that the Germans were reinforcing Normandy and, in particular, had transferred 21st Panzer Division to the Caen area. As we have seen, this intelligence was received in time to permit changes to be made to the plans for the American airborne operations in the Cotentin.† There is no indication in the surviving evidence that it prompted any consideration of the need to revise and strengthen the British plans for the capture of Caen.

The explanation may well lie partly in the settled conviction of the commanders that there was still no scope, and now no time, for any major revision; when the intelligence was received ANCXF had already decreed that he would accept no more alterations in the plans for lifting the assault forces to France.[42] If this was their view, it would account for the fact that they put their anxieties aside and proceeded in the further conviction that, given the necessary boldness and speed, the existing plan would suffice despite 21st Panzer's arrival in the Caen area. Except in terms of this further conviction, moreover, it is difficult to explain why, despite strong warnings from the intelligence authorities, they so proceeded without bargaining for the possibility that 21st Panzer might be widely deployed around Caen.

If their difficulties are to be fully understood it has to be added that whereas Sigint gave precise details about the deployment of the Contentin reinforcements, it was unfortunately silent as to that of 21st Panzer, as was every other source until late on D−1.‡ Had

---

* See above, pp 35–36.
† See above, p 60, and Appendix 9.
‡ See Appendix 14(i) for the intelligence on 21st Panzer Division.

41. Ellis, op cit, Vol I, pp 212–213.
42. ADM 234/366, p 69.

it been otherwise, there would at least have been time to make tactical changes to I Corps's plans, and it may be accepted that such changes would have been made even though I Corps itself was not a recipient of Ultra. As it was, the intelligence authorities had done all that could be expected to sound the alert. On 22 May I Corps was advised that there would be up to 540 German tanks in its D-day area, 300 (a gross exaggeration) with 21st Panzer, 160 with 12th SS Panzer and 80 others scattered throughout I SS Panzer Corps; and it had been specifically warned to expect immediate local counter-attacks by reserves and tanks of 21st Panzer near the coast and an armoured counter-attack on its left flank by 12th SS Panzer in the evening.[43] But it is clear from their contemporary orders and their later testimony that I Corps's commanders continued down to D-day to believe that all or most of 21st Panzer's units lay with its tanks some 30 miles south-east of Caen, and would counter-attack as a whole division, and were confident that the speed of their advance and the ability of the Allied air forces to delay the enemy's approach would enable them to reach Caen before 21st Panzer arrived.[44] As it happened, they encountered greater opposition than they had allowed for, 3rd British Division in particular becoming involved in more tasks than it could hope to accomplish, and the most important single reason was that 21st Panzer Division had been widely dispersed. Only its tanks had been kept to the rear, a few miles north-east of Falaise. Its anti-tank guns with a battalion of its 192 Regiment of lorried infantry had been deployed on the Périers ridge, three miles inland from 3rd Division's beach, with a battalion of field guns to the south of the ridge at Beauville. The rest of its artillery had been placed on high ground fifteen miles south-east of Caen. Its anti-aircraft guns had been deployed around the town. One battalion from each of its grenadier regiments had been stationed on each side of the Orne, 125 PG Regiment's to the east and 192 PG Regiment's to the west.[45]

It was the opposition of these battalions on the Orne to 6th Airborne Division which administered the first upset to the Allied plans. 6th Airborne's operational plan had had to be revised following the discovery in the middle of April that the Germans

---

43. WO 285/3, Second Army Planning and Intelligence Summary of 22 May, quoted in D'Este, op cit, p 123; Ellis, op cit, Vol I, pp 167, 171; CAB 44/243, p 74; Terraine, *The Right of the Line* (1985), p 639.

44. D'Este, op cit, pp 124 (n), 128, 129 (for the testimony of the commanders of 3rd British Division and Brigades 9 and 85, and the War Diary of Canadian Armoured Brigade 2); Ellis, op cit, Vol I, p 302 and CAB 44/244, p 306 (for 3rd Division's orders and its expectation of reaching Caen before 21st Panzer Division counter-attacked).

45. Ellis, op cit, Vol I, p 201.

were erecting obstacles against air landings in its area. It had originally intended to land 6 Air Landing Brigade and a parachute brigade soon after 0001 on D-day. In the event, two parachute brigades were landed in the first wave to clear the obstacles before the Air Landing Brigade arrived with the heavier equipment in gliders in the evening. The first wave achieved complete surprise; the decrypt of a signal from the Japanese Naval Attaché in Berlin later disclosed that the Germans had been astonished that large numbers of gliders should land in high winds and all but total cloud cover.[46] And thanks to the intense study that had been made in advance of the obstacles, the terrain, the bridges and the defences, especially the Flak, it was largely successful in gaining its objectives, seizing the Pegasus bridge intact and demolishing four bridges across the Dives. From 0500, however, subjected to frequent and severe attacks from 125 and 192 PG Regiments and 736 Regiment of 716th Infantry Division, and handicapped by the lack of the heavy equipment, the parachute brigades were penned into a constricted bridgehead around the Pegasus bridge, where they took heavy losses. Although they held on to the bridge, and thus delayed the D-day counter-attack by 21st Panzer's tanks by forcing them to go through Caen,* they were unable to prevent the enemy from moving through Troarn to secure a strong footing in the bridgehead which 6th Airborne Division had hoped to establish by the end of D-day. In the evening the unexpectedly strong enemy pressure forced 6 Air Landing Brigade to make its landings half to the east and half to the west of the Orne.[47]

These developments reduced I Corps's prospects of gaining Caen. But I Corps's anxiety about the fragility of the position of the parachute brigades was compounded by equally serious difficulties on 3rd British Division's front, as may be judged from the fact that 3rd Division, which was to have relieved the brigades at the bridges at noon, did not do so until midnight, and then with troops intended for the capture of Caen. And these difficulties, though they partly arose because 3rd Division's advance inland was delayed, also resulted mainly from the unforeseen presence in forward positions of non-armoured elements of 21st Panzer.

It was known that the entire coast in I Corps's sector was held by three battalions of 736 Regiment of 716th Infantry Division and it was believed that as this Regiment, like 716th Infantry as a whole, was so greatly over-extended, it would provide little opposition.

---

* See below, pp 139–140.

46. SJA 296 of 13 June 1944.
47. CAB 44/244, pp 170, 178–179, 191, 198, 217–218.

This proved to be correct. On *Sword* beach, as elsewhere, the landings encountered enfilading fire, but within 15 minutes of H-hour at 0730 it was suppressed by the prompt arrival of the DD (amphibian) tanks, and 736 Regiment was quickly pushed back, some of its units, particularly those comprising foreigners, surrendering without offering resistance. But if the landings incurred comparatively few casualties, they were followed by delays and severe congestion on the beaches, the high water making it impossible to begin clearing the beach obstacles until the tide receded in the afternoon.[48] When it moved inland, moreover, 3rd Division's plans foundered on the unexpectedly strong opposition put up by the Germans.

In accordance with these plans, 8 Brigade, landing at H-hour, was to clear the beaches and the coastal areas and then relieve 6th Airborne Division, capture the La Brèche strongpoint and the batteries at Lion-sur-Mer and Ouistreham, capture Périers and establish a firm base on the ridge, and destroy two other strongpoints near Colville, two miles inland on the road to Caen (*Morris* and *Hillman*). 185 Brigade, landing 2½ hours later and starting inland at 1125, supported by the tanks of the Staffordshire Yeomanry – one of the three regiments of 27 Armoured Brigade – was to take Caen, secure a bridgehead south of the Orne some seven miles south of Caen and deny the enemy reconnaissance of the area south-east of Caen. 9 Brigade was to land at 1300, advance on the right along the boundary with 3rd Canadian Divison to Carpiquet and be ready to attack Caen from the west if 185 Brigade failed to penetrate the northern defences. If all went well, 27 Armoured Brigade, landing in support of 3rd Division, was to make a rapid armoured thrust to seize the high ground astride the Caen–Falaise road.[49]

In the event, while 8 Brigade landed on time and quickly overcame most of the beach defences, it was occupied for the rest of the day in suppressing batteries and strongpoints; La Brèche was taken at 1000 and *Morris* at 1300, but those at Ouistreham did not fall till the evening, when Lion was still holding out, and *Hillman*, a formidable complex of trenches, pill-boxes, and shelters which turned out to be the HQ of 736 Regiment, held out till 2000 against violent attacks that were supported by tanks from the Staffordshire Yeomanry and the rest of 27 Armoured Brigade which should have been supporting 185 Brigade's drive to Caen.*

---

* It has been argued that the intelligence authorities had under-estimated the size and strength of the *Hillman* position.[50] In fact, although they had not known that it was the HQ of

48. Ellis, op cit, Vol I, pp 184–186, 195; ADM 234/366, p 103.
49. CAB 44/244, pp 144, 295–298, 314–315, 337–340; D'Este, op cit, p 146.
50. D'Este, op cit, pp 130, 133.

185 Brigade's advance was further jeopardised by the congestion on the beaches. Although its infantry assembled punctually, its vehicles and heavy weapons and the Yeomanry's supporting tanks were so delayed that, after much heart-searching, it was ordered to start on foot without them. It was still without them when it encountered the artillery of 21st Panzer on the Périers ridge. Following up, the Yeomanry lost seven tanks in the ensuing engagement, detached one squadron to deal with *Hillman* and were persuaded – perhaps by an unfounded report that enemy tanks had been seen advancing north from Caen – to station another on the height of the ridge. They were held up later by anti-tank obstacles so that the support for 185 Brigade's advancing column was reduced to less than ten tanks.[52]

Although 185 Brigade's leading infantry (2nd Battalion of the King's Shropshire Light Infantry) had meanwhile had to detach one company to deal wtih 21st Panzer's artillery on the ridge, its two remaining companies reached Biéville by 1600. But 185 Brigade's remaining infantry (2nd Battalion Warwickshire Regiment and 1st Battalion Norfolk Regiment) were held up by congestion around the *Hillman* strongpoint until, at about 1500, they were ordered to by-pass it on the east. The Norfolks lost 150 men to *Hillman's* direct fire in this manoeuvre before assaulting 21st Panzer's field gun position at Beauville; still without their heavy weapons, they were unable to take it until 1900 and were unable to advance further that day. The Warwicks, ordered to advance on Caen through St Aubin d'Arquenay, were forced by opposition from 21st Panzer's PG regiments to halt for the night five miles short of Caen, where they finally relieved the paratroop garrison at the western end of Pegasus bridge.[53]

The Shropshires with one company and the Yeomanry with one troop (three tanks) had meanwhile begun to move forward from Biéville towards Caen when their reconnaissance units reported German tanks advancing from the town. They were the tanks of 21st Panzer. Delayed in their start from the Falaise area till about 0730,* their move had been detected by Army Y by 0830, they had been sighted from the air several times from 1000, and Y had located them half way between Falaise and Caen between 1000

---

736 Regiment, they had established, no doubt from PR, that *Hillman* was an extensive and formidable area containing shelters, pill-boxes and trenches, and 3rd Division should have been aware of this as the position was shown as such in a contemporary diagram.[51] The problem with the strongpoints was that while some surrendered quickly and others held out fanatically, there was no way of predicting how they would respond when attacked.

* See above, p 137.

51. CAB 44/244, pp 314, 346.
52. Ellis, op cit, Vol I, pp 201–202; CAB 44/244, pp 344–345.
53. CAB 44/244, pp 346, 349–350, 353–354.

and 1030. They had then been delayed by air attacks from which, however, they suffered no great damage. The sightings had so far indicated, correctly, that they were making for 6th Airborne Division's area east of the Orne, but between 1300 and 1500 Y had disclosed that 21st Panzer's reconnaissance unit was active west and north-west of Caen, air reconnaissance had detected some 150 tanks approaching Caen and striking north-west, and a POW captured on the Périers ridge had reported that the division's tanks were west of the Orne. Its tanks, accompanied by two of its PG battalions, had in fact been ordered to switch the direction of their attack at noon, Seventh Army appreciating that the Allied penetration from *Sword* beach was the crucial threat, but had again been delayed by finding that the Pegasus bridge was in British hands. At 1630 Second British Army was warned by its intelligence staff that 21st Panzer would be fully committed before the evening. In fact, it began its attack at 1630, through the two-mile gap which still separated 3rd British from 3rd Canadian Divisions.[54]

At Biéville the Staffordshire Yeomanry, recalling the squadron which was assaulting *Hillman*, and the Shropshires, which had fortunately been joined by their heavy weapons and anti-tank guns and by 7 Field Regiment RA, checked 21st Panzer's attack with help from the Yeomanry squadron which had been left on the Périers ridge, inflicting heavy tank losses on the Germans. In all on D-day 21st Panzer lost 50 of its 127 tanks. German tanks and infantry in small numbers pushed on, reaching the German positions that were still holding out at Lion at about 1900. But at 2100, when part of the large glider fleet of 6 Air Landing Brigade began to land at St Aubin d'Arquenay, they withdrew from the corridor they had threatened to establish to the coast and fell back to a defence line already formed by other elements of 21st Panzer in front of Caen.[55]

If 21st Panzer failed in its counter-attack, the arrival of its tanks finally destroyed all possibility that 3rd Division would reach Caen. Advancing with one company of the Shropshires, a troop of tanks and a few field guns, 185 Brigade encountered fierce fire from 21st Panzer two miles south of Biéville and, fearing renewed tank attacks, was forced to return there after heavy casualties.[56] 3rd Division's 9 Brigade, which had meanwhile landed at 1600, three hours late on account of the beach congestion, was given new orders at 1730, again as a result of 21st Panzer's incursion and

54. CAB 44/245, pp 437, 442–444; Ellis, op cit, Vol I, pp 201–204; Harrison, op cit, p 332; Hastings, op cit, p 112.
55. Ellis, op cit, Vol I, p 205; D'Este, op cit, p 140.
56. CAB 44/244, p 352.

anxiety about the position of the parachute brigades beyond the Orne; instead of taking Caen from the west, the task originally envisaged for it if 185 Brigade was held up, it was directed to cover the Orne bridges against attack from the west, and it spent the night of D-day on the high ground near St Aubin d'Arquenay.[57] Nor could I Corps make further progress towards Caen on the following day.

185 Brigade, advancing in greater strength on D+1, was driven back with heavy casualties after a day-long battle with 21st Panzer to a line between three and four miles from the centre of Caen, and was held there for the next month by a strong German salient running from the Caen canal through Biéville to the west of Carpiquet. 9 Brigade, resuming its advance towards Carpiquet, was stopped before Cambes by part of 21st Panzer's 192 PG Regiment and remnants of 716th Infantry. This force, together with advance elements of 12th SS Panzer, also frustrated 9 Canadian Brigade's attempt to reach Carpiquet on D+1.* Although the two Allied sectors linked up that day, the German front for the next month continued on a line running just south of Cambes, which was taken by 9 Brigade with heavy losses on D+3. East of the Orne 6th Airborne Division attacked on D+1, and again on 9 June, in an attempt to extend its bridgehead; it made little progress and was hard put to it to hold its ground against German attacks.

In the operations around 6th Airborne's bridgehead the Allies derived some advantage from Sigint. During 7 June Army Y disclosed that in their attempts to dislodge the parachute brigades the Germans were forming a Battle Group Luck (named after the CO of 125 PG Regiment) consisting of battalions from 711th and 346th Infantry Divisions and a company of tanks and other elements from 21st Panzer Division.[58] It was on the strength of this Y evidence that, when Battle Group Luck put in a strong two-pronged attack against the eastern front of the airborne bridgehead on 8 June, it was repulsed by the pre-arranged defensive fire of 3rd Division's guns from across the Orne.[59] Army Y, which had helped to track the arrival of 21st Panzer's tanks on D-day, identified and helped PR to locate most of the other enemy

---

* See below, p 144.

57. ibid, pp 257, 354, 359; ADM 234/366, p 104; Ellis, op cit, Vol I, p 206; D'Este, op cit, p 142.

58. *History of Sigint in the Field*, pp 171–172; WO 285/3, Intelligence Summary of 7 June; WO 171/129 Intelligence Summary of 7 June 1944.

59. Ellis, op cit, Vol I, p 227; WO 285/3, Intelligence Summary of 8 June; WO 171/129, Daily Intelligence Summaries of 8 and 9 June 1944.

divisions that were approaching the bridgehead.* But the Allies otherwise derived little advantage from Sigint during these early ground operations. On I Corps's sector before 8 June, as elsewhere, high-grade decrypts were limited to those of the German Navy and the GAF.† They divulged nothing of value on D-day beyond reports to the effect that 'the focal point of Allied landings was Orne – Port-en-Bessin, especially east of Arromanches', that 'powerful counter-measures' were in progress in that sector and that while no landings had yet taken place in the Seine-Somme area and the Pas de Calais, further landings were to be expected.[61]‡

On the evening of D+1 the Allies recognised that they could no longer hope to take Caen by frontal assault, and they attributed this failure, and the failure to take or destroy the Orne and the Odon bridges, to the 'particularly strong opposition' of 21st Panzer and its PG regiments. 'The difference in quality between units of 352nd Infantry Division, and to an even greater extent 716th Infantry Division, on the one hand and that of 21st Panzer is not surprising, but it has been fully illustrated in the last few days.'[63] At the same time, however, they could still hope that although the chief consequence of the failure was that the enemy would be able to array his Panzer divisions in a line running westwards from Caen and contain the bridgehead within the difficult *bocage*, the length of their front, the constant pressure the Allies were keeping up on all sectors and the limited scale of the enemy's reserves, factors which were forcing him to commit his armoured divisions 'piecemeal', would prevent him from organis-

---

* Army Y, which in any case declined in volume after 7 June, was not free from error. On 7 June and 8 June it created alarm by wrongly identifying a battle group of 12th SS Panzer east of the Orne. On 7 June it identified 346th Infantry as 363rd Infantry. It is a tribute to the accuracy of Allied order of battle intelligence that after 21st Army Group had referred to the appearance of 363rd as 'the first of the surprises of this battle', the error was rectified by POW on 8 June. MI 14 had known that 711th was on the extreme left wing of Fifteenth Army and that 346th was near Le Havre. It did not know, however, that 346th was partly mobile, and only on 8 June was it realised that a battle group from the division had been ferried across the Seine overnight on 6–7 June. An Enigma signal decrypted on 7 June had requested extra Flak protection for the Seine ferry at Quillebeuf and for bridge repairs at Elbeuf, but there is no evidence that this was taken as pointing to the transfer of reinforcements across the river.[60]

† For the sources of high-grade Sigint after D-day see Appendix 15(i).

‡ Decrypts of German signals issued on D-day to the effect that an air strike (which did not take place but which was evidently planned in preparation for 21st Panzer's armoured counter-attack) was intended at 1300 against British armour at Périers, and on D+1 to the effect that the counter-attack had failed, were not available till 8 June.[62]

60. WO 285/3, of 7 and 8 June; WO 171/129, of 7 and 8 June; DEFE 3/167, KV 6822 of 7 June; Ellis, op cit, Vol I, p 216.
61. DEFE 3/166, KVs 6634, 6635, 6651 of 6 June.
62. DEFE 3/167, KVs 6850, 6854 of 8 June.
63. WO 285/3, of 7 June.

ing a concerted attack against what was known from Sigint to be regarded as his most threatened sector – his right flank between the Dives and Bayeux.[64]

□

On the evening of D-day, after holding up the release of 12th SS Panzer and Panzer Lehr till the afternoon, OKW had put I SS Panzer Corps in charge of the sector from Bayeux to the Orne, with 12th SS Panzer, Panzer Lehr, 21st Panzer and the regiments of 716th Infantry Division under command, and had ordered an immediate attack by all available forces to liquidate the bridge-head, but had been advised by C-in-C West that as 12th SS Panzer would not be ready till 7 June and Panzer Lehr till 8 June, 21st Panzer was attacking on its own. On 7 June I SS Panzer Corps hoped to carry out a two-divisional counter-attack that evening with 12th SS Panzer and Panzer Lehr from Caen north-westward to the sea, but was forced to postpone it to 8 June when air attacks delayed the arrival of these divisions. On 8 June, by which time Panzer Gruppe West had been put in command of it, the counter-attack (this time with all three divisions) was again postponed, in part because Panzer Gruppe West's move from Paris was delayed till 9 June by air attack* but mainly because it had been necessary to commit 12th SS Panzer and Panzer Lehr against 3rd Canadian and 50th British Divisions.[65]

The D-day objectives of 3rd Canadian Division from *Juno* beach, which complemented those of the remainder of I Corps on its left, complemented on its right those of 50th British Division and 8 Armoured Brigade (of XXX Corps) from *Gold* beach. 3rd Division was to secure the Caen-Bayeux road from Carpiquet westward to the left wing of 50th Division's advance. 50th Division was to advance east and south-east of Bayeux to the Caen-Bayeux railway, to link up with the Canadians; to take Bayeux and advance west and south-west beyond it to the river Drôme, to link up with V US Corps; to advance south of the town to the river Aure; and to move westwards along the coast through Arro-manches to Port-en-Bessin, where it would again join up with V Corps. The approaches to Bayeux from Caen were, exceptionally for Normandy, good tank country through which the Germans might be expected to counter-attack, and their capture was

---

* The attack on Panzer Gruppe West, in which it lost much of its wireless equipment, was a chance attack not based on prior air sighting or other intelligence.

64. WO 171/129, of 7 June.
65. Ellis, op cit, Vol I, pp 216, 238–239; Harrison, op cit, pp 334, 348.

regarded as vital. Striking south through this area XXX Corps was also to make an armoured thrust with 8 Armoured Brigade in an attempt to reach Villers-Bocage by last light.[66] This would complement similar thrusts by I Corps to the east, one by 2 Canadian Armoured Brigade towards Evrecy and one by 27 Armoured Brigade,* and a subsidiary thrust from *Juno* beach by the armoured cars of the Inns of Court Regiment which was to destroy crossings over the Orne and bridges over the Odon south-west of Caen. All these thrusts aimed at holding off the approaching enemy armour. In fact, none of them materialised.

The *Juno* and *Gold* assaults both fell behind schedule. Heavy surf held up the clearance of underwater obstacles and delayed the arrival of the amphibious tanks; lacking their protection, the landings were further handicapped by the enfilading fire of the enemy's gun positions.† At *Gold* beach, particularly, the resistance was unexpectedly heavy; it had been assumed that the immediate defences would be limited to one inferior battalion of 716th Infantry, but 50th Division encountered three battalions of which one (from 352nd Infantry) held out at Le Hamel, a strongpoint at the western end, until 1600, inflicting heavy damage on vehicles and assault craft.[67]‡

3rd Canadian Division was all ashore by 1400. By night-fall it was two miles short of the Caen-Bayeux road.[68] Its 9 Brigade set out on D-day to reach Caen through Carpiquet and by night-fall was five miles from Carpiquet. But it was stopped on D+1 by fire from 21st Panzer Division and direct confrontation with advance elements of 12th SS Panzer. Early the following day elements of 12th SS Panzer attacked the Canadians further west, at Putot. After heavy fighting all day the outcome was stalemate with both sides holding their original positions on the Caen-Bayeux road.[69]

50th Division with 8 Armoured Brigade fared similarly in their advance from *Gold* beach. As early as 1000 the collapse of one of 716th Infantry's battalions (441st Ost Battalion of 726 Regiment) at Mont Fleury opened up the road to Bayeux. But 50th Division, starting late from the beaches and unaware of this collapse and also of the fact that the Germans were evacuating Bayeux, halted at night-fall two miles short of Bayeux;[70] it was rendered cautious

---

* See above, p 138.
† See above, p 130.
‡ See Appendix 14(ii) for intelligence about 352nd Infantry Division before D-day.

66. CAB 44/242, p 176; CAB 44/243, pp 45, 81; D'Este, op cit, p 81.
67. Ellis, op cit, Vol I, pp 178–183, 210, 213; CAB 44/243 pp 89, 135, 140–141; AIR 41/24, p 78.
68. Ellis, op cit, Vol I, pp 207–209.
69. ibid, p 229, Harrison, op cit, p 348.
70. Hastings, op cit, p 126.

by stiff opposition from 915 Regiment of 352nd Infantry, which had arrived back in the Bayeux area in the evening from its dash towards the Carentan area.* 50th Division's infantry took Bayeux early on D+1 and by the end of that day it had reached all its D-day objectives except Port-en-Bessin. But 8 Armoured Brigade had started even later – it had not been able to land till D+1 – and on the morning of 8 June it was attacked near Loucelles by 12th SS Panzer. By night-fall, after confused fighting throughout that day, its advance had been stopped two miles north of Tilly-sur-Seulles. Early on 9 June, reinforced by two brigades of 50th Division, it advanced to the river opposite Tilly, but was unable to cross; opposed by the elements of 12th SS Panzer and Panzer Lehr Divisions, the British force held on in a salient.[71]

The appearance of 12th SS Panzer and Panzer Lehr can have caused no surprise. XXX Corps had been advised to expect 12th SS Panzer to reach the battle area sometime after mid-day on D-day, either through Lisieux or Argentan or both, and, in addition, that 17th SS PG Division might arrive very late on D-day and an unidentified Panzer division in the Orléans area (viz Panzer Lehr) on D+1.[72] Early on D-day movements were sighted from 12th SS Panzer's concentration area near Dreux, and in the afternoon the division was detected moving towards Lisieux by air reconnaissance and Army Y. The bulk of the division was held back by the threat of air attacks and, after reaching Lisieux, by OKW's temporary ban on its further advance.† But elements were detected on the move by 1600 and were seen approaching Caen at 1945. 21st Army Group believed that evening that it might reach the battle area that night; Second Army that it would not be committed in strength before noon on 7 June.[73] Early on 7 June air reconnaissance established that at least part of the division was using the axis Dreux-Argentan and Y reported (wrongly) that elements of it were east of the Orne. But that evening, following the success of 12th SS Panzer's forward elements in stopping 9 Canadian Brigade, 21st Army Group did not expect the bulk of the division to reach the front before night-fall.[74] Panzer Lehr's movement from the Orléans-Chartres area was also sighted on the afternoon of D-day. That night and throughout the following day

---

* See above, p 127 fn†.

† See above, p 128.

71. WO 285/3, of 7 June; WO 171/129, of 8 June; Ellis, op cit, Vol I, pp 217, 231.

72. CAB 44/243, pp 21, 73–75.

73. CAB 44/245, pp 437, 442–445; WO 285/3, of 6 June; WO 171/129, of 6 June.

74. AIR 41/24, p 151; WO 285/3, of 7 June; WO 171/129, of 8 June.

it was heavily attacked from the air and engaged by naval gunfire, and its non-armoured elements suffered considerable casualties as it advanced by several roads through Alençon and Domfront to an assembly area near Thury-Harcourt, 15 miles south-west of Caen. Thus delayed, its arrival there was not complete till noon on 8 June.[75] That evening 21st Army Group and Second Army believed it had reached the front but were uncertain where it was; Army Y had DFd it south of Bayeux, but they suspected it might be to the south-west in the Forêt de Cerisy.[76]*

Panzer Lehr thus reached the front in time to join 12th SS Panzer in halting 8 Armoured Brigade's delayed thrust to Villers-Bocage on 8 and 9 June and also in spoiling on 10 June the attempt by XXX Corps's follow-up forces to envelop Caen from the west. On 9 June 8 Armoured Brigade took POW from Panzer Lehr and Y located its HQ at Hottot.[77] On the strength of this intelligence, which was subsequently confirmed by an Enigma decrypt, Hottot was bombarded at extreme range by HMS *Nelson* on 10 June.[78] As we shall see, however, Panzer Lehr was by then sufficiently established to hold the attack delivered by 7th Armoured Division through 50th Division's front on 10 June. 7th Armoured Division and 49th Division, XXX Corps's follow-up forces, had themselves been delayed by the loss of landing craft at *Gold* beach and the continuing bad weather; they should have landed in the evening of D+1 and gone into action on 9 June.[79]†

---

* There is considerable discrepancy in the operational histories as to the reasons for the delayed arrival of these two divisions. Ellis (p 206) says that 'it seems very unlikely that either . . . could have intervened in the battle on D-day seeing that the former had to come from the south of Rouen (over 70 miles away) and the latter from south-west of Chartres (over 100 miles) and that both went by road under constant air attack . . . It was the fact that the Germans were taken by surprise and that movement was delayed by Allied air attack as much as by Hitler's delay . . .' Harrison (p 333) points out that part of 12th SS Panzer, which was in any case spread over the wide area Berney-Dreux-Evreux-Laigle, was under way from 0400, that if it had not been halted by OKW at Lisieux till 0430 it would have been able to advance for about 8 hours in overcast conditions which would have held off air attacks. It is arguable that, but for this halt, it could have reached the front on D-day since it was trained to move fast by road and the pre-D-day Allied air attacks on communciations had concentrated mainly on rail centres; D'Este (p 149) accordingly believes that 'nothing less than a stroke of good fortune kept it [12th SS Panzer] from being a major threat on D-day.' It seems highly unlikely, however, that Panzer Lehr could have reached the front on D-day even if it had not been held up by OKW. The overcast conditions lifted from mid-day and, having farther to go, Panzer Lehr was more vulnerable than 12th SS Panzer to air attack.

† High-grade Sigint provided no intelligence of value to the *Juno* and *Gold* forces before 9 June. Two naval situation reports on the fighting on *Gold* beach were decrypted on D-day,

---

75. AIR 41/24, pp 150, 152; D'Este, op cit, pp 76, 91, 154.
76. WO 285/3, of 8 June; WO 171/129, of 8 June; *History of Sigint in the Field*, p 172.
77. *History of Sigint in the Field*, p 172; WO 285/3, of 9 June.
78. *History of Sigint in the Field*, p 172; WO 171/129, of 10 June; Ellis, op cit, Vol I, p 250; DEFE 3/169, KV 7451 of 10 June.
79. Ellis, op cit, Vol I, p 264; CAB 44/242, p 254; D'Este, op cit, p 165 fn 1.

But, as we have noted, Panzer Lehr's delayed arrival had already frustrated the enemy's intention to make a counter-attack from Caen to the sea on 7 June, and the advance of 3rd Canadian Division and 50th British Division had again prevented him from making this attack on 8 June.

On the enemy's intentions for the counter-attack, and on the deferment of his plans, no precise intelligence was obtained. A decrypt available late on 8 June disclosed that by 1400 on 7 June Panzer Gruppe West had been given an operational command, but provided no details.[84] On 8 June Army Y indicated that I SS Panzer Corps was in command of the armour in the Caen-Bayeux sector.[85] Decrypts during 9 June confirmed the presence of I SS Panzer Corps and indicated that 12th SS Panzer and 21st Panzer Divisions were subordinated to it, but left its involvement with Panzer Gruppe West unclear.[86] But two other decrypts might well have reassured the Allies that the pressure they were maintaining along the whole of the front was frustrating plans for a counter-attack by forcing the enemy to commit his reserves piecemeal. The first of these decrypts – the first to be obtained since D-day from the new Flivo key (Ocelot) – disclosed that at 0800 on 7 June 12th SS Panzer and Panzer Lehr Divisions were under orders to attack to the north-west or the north-east from an unspecified starting area.[87] When it became available, however, at 0718 on 8 June, Panzer Lehr was known to be under air attack between Alençon and Domfront. Early on 9 June a message of 8 June was decrypted reporting that 21st Panzer and 12th SS Panzer were to continue on 8 June the attack they had already begun;[88] but no concerted counter-attack had materialised.

On the evening of 8 June Second Army believed that the 'expected counter-attack in force . . . cannot now be long delayed', given that Panzer Lehr was now available and that 1st SS Panzer Division was expected soon from Belgium, and 2nd Tactical Air

one of them announcing that the Allies had made a penetration at Arromanches.[80] Early on 7 June decrypts disclosed that orders had been given in the afternoon of D-day for the evacuation of the GAF base at Carpiquet[81] but on 8 June a decrypt showed that those orders had been cancelled on 7 June and that the base was still in use.[82] The only reference to the fighting inland was given in the Flivo message of 8 June which added that the Germans were forming a blocking position running through Loucelles westward to Bayeux.[83]

80.   DEFE 3/166, KVs 6622, 6634 of 6 June.
81.   ibid, KVs 6655, 6721 of 7 June.
82.   DEFE 3/167, KV 6952 of 8 June.
83.   ibid, KV 6893 of 8 June.
84.   DEFE 3/168, KV 7002 of 8 June.
85.   WO 171/129 of 8 June.
86.   DEFE 3/168 KVs 7035, 7105 of 9 June.
87.   DEFE 3/168, KV 6893 of 8 June.
88.   DEFE 3/168, KV 7051 of 9 June.

Force still expected a major counter-attack from the direction of Caen now that 12th SS Panzer, Panzer Lehr and 21st Panzer Divisions were all in the line.[89] Twenty-four hours later, however, Second Army noted that the enemy 'still hesitates . . . four days after the start of the Invasion . . .' while 21st Army Group, though still expecting the counter-attack, was sure that it was becoming harder and harder for the enemy to mount it because he was still responding piecemeal to the pressure the Allies were exerting throughout their long front.[90]

Another development referred to in 21st Army Group's summary of 9 June must have contributed to the growing confidence of the Allied intelligence staffs: the discovery from captured documents and Sigint that they had over-estimated German tank strengths. At the end of D-day, as 21st Panzer was believed to have some 300 tanks (four battalions) and as only half that number had been detected in the Caen sector, Second Army had concluded that it must have 'more armour in reserve'. But by 8 June the number of tanks counted in the Caen-Bayeux sector was still not more than 150; and since it knew that those of 12th SS Panzer and Panzer Lehr had not yet arrived, Second Army had begun to suspect that 21st Panzer's strength had been exaggerated. This suspicion was confirmed on 9 June by a captured document which showed that the division had only two battalions and that they did not have Panthers.* 21st Army Group, noting this discovery in its intelligence summary of 9 June, also announced that '12th SS Panzer possibly has fewer tanks than we allowed it, but we still know nothing of Panzer Lehr'.[91] It was here relying on GC and CS's interpretation of a tank return on 25 May, the first to be received since D-day. Decrypted on 5 June, it used *pro forma* which GC and CS was unable to solve until late on 7 June.† But the tentative (and as it later emerged, largely accurate) solution which was then sent to the Commands showed that whereas before D-day 12th SS Panzer had been credited with 'over 200 tanks and a high proportion of Panthers', and whereas its appearance at the front had been accompanied by reports that it had some Tiger tanks, the division had in fact had on 25 May only 85 Pzkw IV and 29 Pzkw V (Panthers) – and no Tigers.[92]

---

* See Appendix 14(i).
  † For this return see Appendix 10(i). It also gave tank figures for 1st SS Panzer, 2nd SS Panzer and 9th Panzer Divisions, for which see below, pp 181, 187, 202, and strengths for Panzer Abteilung 205, for some heavy anti-tank Abteilungen and for several infantry divisions.

89. WO 285/3, of 8 June: AIR 41/24, p 154.
90. WO 285/3, of 9 June; WO 171/129, of 9 June.
91. WO 285/3, of 6 and 8 June; WO 171/129, of 9 June.
92. WO 171/129, of 28 May; DEFE 3/166, KV 6705 of 7 June; AWL 2222 of 8 June.

On 8 and 9 June, when these appreciations were being made, Panzer Gruppe West was still planning to attack with 21st Panzer, Panzer Lehr and 12th SS Panzer and the remnants of 716th Infantry, but on 10 June the enemy finally abandoned his hopes of a decisive counter-attack and bent all his efforts to soldifying his defence.[93] A serious gap had by then been opened up on Panzer Gruppe West's left by the advance of 1st US Division from *Omaha* beach.

□

On 8 June 50th British Division's westwards thrust along the coast through Arromanches had made contact with 1st US Division which on 8 June gained the high ground west of Port-en-Bessin, its D-day objective, after recovering from its initial set-backs on the *Omaha* beaches.

At *Omaha* V US Corps's D-day objectives had been to take Isigny and Carentan and establish a bridgehead up the Isigny-Bayeux road, five miles inland, from the Vire to the boundary with Second British Army, a distance of fifteen miles. In the event the assault force was pinned down on the beaches during most of the forenoon, and by the end of D-day it held only a tenuous beachhead, five miles long and a mile and a half deep, and had lost 2,800 killed, missing or wounded out of nearly 35,000 men landed. As late as 1600 a German naval situation report appreciated that the landing had failed. This report, decrypted later on D-day, was the only reference available from Sigint to the *Omaha* fighting; it stated that the attack between Port-en-Bessin and Vire had been cleaned up except for a pocket of resistance at St Pierre (that is, the Pointe du Hoe, where US Rangers had seized the battery).[94]

V Corps's difficulties were chiefly brought about by the fact that at *Omaha*, the only beach overlooked by cliffs and the one with the strongest coast defences, the assault force suffered most heavily from all the consequences of bad weather.[95] They were compounded by the fact that, as on *Gold* beach, the enemy was on the coast in unexpected strength. When V Corps had recovered from its initial set-backs, and began to open up the beach exits, it took POW who established that it was being opposed by two regiments

93. Harrison, op cit, p 374.
94. DEFE 3/166, KV 6651 of 2101/6 June.
95. Ellis, op cit, Vol I, pp 190–192, 215; Harrison, op cit, pp 302, 309, 313, 317, 319, 330; Hastings, op cit, p 88; ADM 234/366, pp 57, 95; CAB 44/245, pp 395–396, 402, 404–406.

of 352nd Infantry Division, on 716th's left.[96]*

Fortunately for V Corps – for its two divisions were by then exhausted and lacking most of their equipment – the regiments of 352nd Infantry were committed piecemeal instead of in a concentrated counter-attack.[97] V Corps was thus able to begin its advance during D+1, 29th Division thrusting westward towards Isigny and 1st Division eastwards. But there remained considerable anxiety that the Germans would counter-attack with 12th SS Panzer Division before 1st Division could join up with 50th British Division's advance westward from *Gold* beach.[98]

This anxiety stemmed from the fact that on the morning of D+1 PR had detected trains arriving at Vire and Lison and heavy road movements, including tanks, from St Lo towards Bayeux. In the afternoon, when POW were taken south of Bayeux from 12th SS Panzer Division, and Y had located elements of the division inaccurately in the same area, it was concluded that part of the division had arrived in the Forêt de Cerisy and might attack at any time; and heavy raids on the Forêt by Bomber Command were hastily organised.[99] But no counter-attack developed. By the morning of 8 June 12th SS Panzer was contacted and firmly identified between Carpiquet and Bayeux.[100]† 1st US Division, pushing forward against 726 Regiment of 716th Infantry and elements of 352nd Infantry, reached the high ground west of Port-en-Bessin and made contact with 50th Division later on 8 June.

During the night of 8–9 June the Germans withdrew 716th Infantry and the remnants of 352nd's western flank to a line south of Bayeux. On 9 June V Corps extended its advance, 1st Division pushing towards the St Lo-Bayeux road and 2nd Division (newly arrived) attacking against 352nd's centre towards the Forêt de Cerisy. Heavy fighting on that day ended in a second enforced withdrawal of 716th and 352nd Divisions and opened up a ten-mile gap in the German line, from Berigny to Panzer Lehr Division's position at Longraye. As the Germans realised, unless

---

* For the Allied failure to detect before D-day that 716th had narrowed its sector to let 352nd take over on its left, see Appendix 14(ii).

† The POW had been taken from its reconnaissance unit, which during the morning of D+1 had surveyed the gap between 21st Panzer in the Caen area and 352nd Infantry's eastern boundary south-east of Bayeux, while the division itself had swung north to the Caen front after reaching Evrecy. The rail and road movements towards Bayeux detected in the morning seem to have been rear elements of 915 Regiment.[101]

96. WO 171/129, of 6 June.
97. CAB 44/245, p 420.
98. Harrison, op cit, p 337.
99. WO 171/129, of 7 June; AIR 41/24, pp 83, 197.
100. WO 285/3, of 8 June; WO 171/129, of 8 June.
101. Harrison, op cit, pp 321, 330, 334, 348.

the Allies were prevented from advancing through this gap to the high ground beyond Caumont, they would be able either to turn east and out-flank Caen or to drive towards Avranches, thus out-flanking 352nd Division and the German forces in the Cotentin; or worse still, to do both.[102]

29th US Division's thrust to Isigny had meanwhile become all the more essential for the junction of V Corps with VII US Corps in that VII Corps, landing at *Utah*, had also failed to achieve its D-day objectives.

At *Utah*, where the bombardments and the landing had been least handicapped by the weather, the assault force had met little opposition; it had suffered only 200 casualties, though it had lost four destroyers and two minesweepers, the largest naval casualties incurred during Operation *Neptune*, on an enemy minefield across the Cardonnet Bank.* 4th US Division had thus crossed the causeways and linked up with the 101st US Airborne Division according to plan, but by the end of D-day 101st Division had failed to link up with 82nd US Airborne Division at Sainte Mère Eglise and 82nd Division had failed to secure a bridgehead across the Merderet in preparation for the westward advance across the peninsula. 101st Division had also failed to secure its other objective, a bridgehead over the Douve to facilitate the junction of VII Corps and V Corps. 82nd Division had been held up by 91st Infantry Division and 100th Panzer Ersatz Battalion. 101st Division had been held up by 91st Infantry and 6 Regiment, which had been brought up from twenty miles away on the morning of D-day to hold Carentan as a wedge between the *Utah* and *Omaha* forces.[104]

On the other hand, the Germans in the Cotentin were slow to organise counter-attacks. Surprised by the arrival of airborne troops in territory strongly held by their own forces, they had also been impeded by an unfounded report of a further airborne descent on the west coast of the peninsula near Coutances. On the morning of 7 June this report, which had prompted the Navy to order preparations for demolitions at Granville, St Malo and

---

* Advance intelligence on this minefield, which was to damage a further 25 vessels in the next ten days, had been sent to Ultra recipients on 1 May (see above, p 92) but the Senior Officer of the Western Task Force, an Ultra recipient, appears to have overlooked it.[103] The reason for the oversight may lie in the fact that the minefield was not referred to in the final assessments of enemy minelaying in the Seine Bay issued by the OIC and ANCXF at the end of May and the beginning of June (see above, p 94).

102. Harrison, op cit, pp 370–371.
103. ADM 223/193, Ultra signal 1105/1 May; ADM 223/287, Use of Special Intelligence during Operation *Neptune* (USION), p 59; ADM 234/366, pp 29, 92 fn; CAB 44/245, p 391; Roskill, op cit, Vol III Part 2, p 55.
104. Harrison, op cit, ibid, pp 286–289.

Brest, persuaded Rommel to order II Parachute Corps to make
for the south-west of the Cotentin with 17th SS PG Division from
Poitiers, 3rd Parachute Division from Brest and 77th Infantry
Division from St Malo. During 7 June 4th US Division was able to
link up with 82nd Airborne, beleagered at Sainte Mère Eglise, in
time to repulse a counter-attack delivered by elements of 91st,
709th and 243rd Infantry Divisions and another of the independent battalions which had reinforced the Cotentin in May (Seventh
Army Sturmabteilung).[105]

High-grade Sigint, though slightly more plentiful than from the
Omaha sector, provided only a retrospective commentary on these
developments. A naval situation report decrypted on D-day
appreciated that there was as yet no sign of Allied activity at St
Malo or on the west side of the Cotentin.[106] On 7 and 8 June,
however, naval Enigma decrypts disclosed that demolition preparations had been ordered at Granville, St Malo and Brest following
the report of airborne landings at Coutances.[107] The German
intention to counter-attack at Sainte Mère Eglise was reported in
the first Ocelot message to be decrypted; intercepted on the
morning of 7 June, this was not decrypted until 24 hours later, by
which time the naval decrypts had reported first that the town had
been recaptured and then that it had had to be abandoned to the
Americans.[108]

Following the failure of the counter-attack, elements of 709th,
91st and 243rd Divisions under the command of GOC 243rd
began forming a line from Quinéville to Montebourg to block the
threat to Cherbourg, with southern outposts around the coastal
batteries at Azeville and Marcouf. This emerged from the decrypts
during 8 June.[109] Reports of heavy fighting in front of this line,
together with evidence that the Germans were anxious about their
ability to hold it during 9 June, were decrypted on 9 and 10 June.
They included the disclosure that at 1020 on 10 June von
Rundstedt had ordered the destruction of Cherbourg insofar as it
was not essential for the Navy's operations.[110] But in the event,
with the formations already disposed in the Cotentin and with
77th Infantry Division – detached from II Parachute Corps and
ordered up the west coast to Valognes on 9 June, as was disclosed
by a decrypt on 11 June[111] – the Germans managed to delay the

---

105.   ibid, pp 341–344, 349, 395–396(n).
106.   DEFE 3/166, KV 6622 of 6 June.
107.   DEFE 3/167, KVs 6762, 6909 of 7 and 8 June.
108.   ibid, KVs 6881, 6882, 6893 of 8 June.
109.   ibid, KVs 6881, 6915, 6921, 6944 of 8 June.
110.   DEFE 3/168, KVs 7040, 7236 of 9 and 10 June; DEFE 3/169, KV 7387 of 10
       June.
111.   DEFE 3/169, KV 7480 of 11 June.

American advance westward from Sainte Mère Eglise for several days and to hold up the American thrust to Cherbourg till the third week of June.

In order to ensure their junction, V and VII Corps had meanwhile been ordered on 7 June to give priority to the capture of Isigny and Carentan. V Corps's thrust with 29th Division against the left flank of 352nd Infantry Division took Isigny on the night of 8–9 June; 101st Airborne Division's attack from the north forced 6 Parachute Regiment to fall back on Carentan on 8 June. At Carentan, however, 6 Parachute Regiment was to hold out till 11 June, the US forces barely winning the race for time against the arrival of those which Rommel had ordered up from the west and south-west.[112]

Of these reinforcements, a battle group of 275th Infantry from St Nazaire and elements of 265th Infantry from Lorient had been ordered to Normandy by rail and road respectively on D-day. II Parachute Corps, 17th SS PG Division and an advanced group of 3rd Parachute Division were all moving up by 7 June, when Rommel directed them to the west coast of the Cotentin. On 8 June he re-directed them to the Balleroy area to fill the gap that was opening up with 1st US Division's advance against 716th Infantry and the western flank of 352nd Infantry near Bayeux. On 9 June, deciding that the threat to Carentan was more serious than the Balleroy gap, he left only the reconnaissance battalion of 17th SS PG to watch the gap but otherwise re-directed these formations, ordering 17th SS PG to Carentan, 3rd Parachute to the area between Balleroy and St Lo and II Parachute Corps to St Lo. On the same day he ordered a battle group of 353rd Infantry from Brest to join II Parachute Corps near St Lo.[113]

These movements were all delayed by Allied air attacks and rail disruptions carried out by the Resistance. 275th Division's battle group was attacked by air while it was entraining at St Nazaire. During 8 June, 1,100 heavy bombers and 1,500 fighter-bombers raided the rail centres between Brittany, the Loire and Normandy, and also the Loire bridges which 17th SS PG had still to cross, and on the night of 8–9 June another 1,000 sorties were flown against the same targets. Although the weather prevented all flying on 9 June, 17th SS PG was unable to reach the Carentan area till 11 June and the battle groups of 275th and 265th Infantry Divisions did not arrive till 14 June.[114] But though the Allies were aware that the movements had begun and were able to delay them by attacking the lines of communication, they remained for some

112. Harrison, op cit, pp 381–383.
113. ibid, pp 370–371.
114. ibid, pp 360, 371, 378, 379, 382; AIR 41/24, pp 83–85.

time uncertain as to where these reinforcements would be committed. As well as being far from complete, their intelligence was confused by uncertainty on the part of the enemy.

It was presumably on the strength of agents' reports that 275th Infantry had been attacked while entraining near St Nazaire. PR detected train movements from 17th SS PG's area on 7 June, and subsequent sightings on that day included train arrivals at Villedieu which suggested that it was making for western Normandy.[115] The first Sigint about the movements of 17th SS PG was obtained on 8 June from signals made on 7 June. The earliest included it, together with 1st SS Panzer and Panzer Lehr Divisions, an unidentified SS Panzer division and 10 Panzer Brigade, in a list of code-names for armoured formations which were to operate under Seventh Army.[116]* A second signal reported at 1230 that it was subordinated to Seventh Army and was moving to Villedieu.[117] A third signal stated that at 1400 on 7 June it was subordinated to Panzer Gruppe West and was moving north.[118] By the evening of 8 June air sightings had made it plain that it was moving to western Normandy, and 21st Army Group and Second Army believed that evening that it was making for the St Lo area and would come in on the left of 352nd Division to block the American advance.[119] On the evening of 9 June, however, the force of the Ultra evidence was strengthened in First US Army's mind by 'a curious multiplication of rumours from prisoners and civilians that there were large enemy concentrations in the Forêt de Cerisy',[120] and by the belief that enemy resistance in the Drôme corridor was a delaying action pending the arrival of armoured counter-attack forces.[121] First Army concluded on the evening of 9 June that 'an armoured or a motorised division' might well be lurking in the forest.[122] On 10 June, moreover, 1st US Division took POW from 17th SS PG's reconnaissance unit on the right of 352nd Division near Balleroy, where Rommel had left it, and on the strength of this evidence, together with the erroneous belief that the division had tanks,† concluded that on 11

---

* See below, p 180 fn*.

† Sigint had disclosed before D-day that 17th SS PG had an assault gun battalion but no tanks.[123] V Corps was not an Ultra recipient.

115.   WO 171/129, of 7 June.
116.   DEFE 3/167, KV 6933 of 8 June.
117.   ibid, KV 6958 of 8 June.
118.   DEFE 3/168, KV 7002 of 8 June.
119.   WO 285/3, of 8 June; WO 171/129, of 8 June.
120.   Harrison, op cit, p 371.
121.   ibid, p 372.
122.   ibid, p 372.
123.   DEFE 3/160, KV 5097 of 25 May.

June 17th SS PG would counter-attack from the Forêt de Cerisy. It even suggested that 17th SS PG might be joined by 1st SS Panzer and 11th Panzer Divisions, which had been reported on 8 June as preparing to move, in a heavy counter-attack on its front.[124] These fears were not to be finally dispersed by further Sigint till 10 June, when a decrypt reported that 17th SS PG and 3rd Parachute Division had arrived in the St Lo area with II Parachute Corps the previous evening.[125] This decrypt did not entirely clear up the confusion in that the bulk of 17th SS PG was in fact still widely dispersed between the Loire and Normandy and that 3rd Parachute Division – and only its advance group – was still struggling across the base of the Cotentin peninsula. It was disturbing, moreover, in that it associated these two formations for the first time with II Parachute Corps: other decrypts on 8 and 9 June had disclosed only that the naval authorities in Brittany were to provide lorry transport for 3rd Parachute Division and that II Parachute Corps with 77th Infantry Division and other unspecified formations had been ordered to 'the exposed west coast' – a destination which had been inexplicable in the absence of any firm indication that the order was connected with the false alarm about airborne landings at Coutances.[126] But it at least enabled the Allied authorities to conclude firmly that, while some of 17th SS PG had been sent to Balleroy to watch the gap, the bulk of it was to be used with the remainder of the German force to counter the American threat at Carentan.[127] This was confirmed by the decryption on 11 June of a message in which on 9 June an unspecified authority had stated that Balleroy was too far to the south-east for the assembly of II Parachute Corps; the main task was to prevent the Allied forces from linking up south of the mouth of the Vire.[128]

□

In the assault phase – those first days in which the landings might have been repelled, or at least so disrupted as to produce a decisive effect on the subsequent battle on land – the Germans were unable to intervene more than marginally at sea. For immediate action they could call only on the enfeebled bomber and anti-shipping forces of the GAF and on limited naval forces – on only limited naval surface forces, indeed, for they were unable

---

124. Harrison, op cit, pp 371–372; WO 171/129, of 8 June.
125. DEFE 3/169, KV 7311 of 10 June.
126. DEFE 3/168, KVs 7003, 7105, 7112 of 8 and 9 June; WO 285/3 of 10 June.
127. WO 285/3, of 10 June; WO 171/129, of 10 June.
128. DEFE 3/170, KV 7548 of 11 June.

to commit the U-boat fleet in the critical period on account of the formidable scale of the Allied defences and the absence of warning as to where and when the Allies would invade. Whatever hopes the Germans placed on these resources, the Japanese were quick to appreciate that they were unlikely to have much effect. A decrypt of 12 June contained the Ambassador's view that the U-boats were unable to deal with Allied warships and the E-boats were too weak for good results.[129] On 18 June a further decrypt revealed that the head of the Japanese Naval Mission was of the opinion that little could be expected of either the U-boats or E-boats.[130] And from a decrypt of 13 July the Allies learnt that in the Ambassador's opinion German attempts to arrest the Allied build-up by air and naval attack had been frustrated by the Allies' 'sharp look-out'.[131]

At midnight on 5–6 June the U-boats in Home Waters were disposed as follows:

Gruppe Mitte with 22 non-*Schnorchel* boats was at short notice in south Norway;
Gruppe Landwirt with 36 or 37 U-boats comprised eight *Schnorchel* and nine non-*Schnorchel* boats at Brest and 19 others (only one of which was equipped with *Schnorchel*) distributed between St Nazaire, Lorient and La Pallice;
En route from Norway to the Atlantic, ten non-*Schnorchel* and seven *Schnorchel* boats; of these, unknown to the U-boat Command, five had been sunk and one damaged.[132]

Alerted at 0305 on 6 June, the U-boat Command at once ordered five of the U-boats on passage to make for Biscay on the surface at high speed, ordered the remainder of those on passage first to halt and then to form a patrol off south Norway until further notice, and at noon sent the eight *Schnorchel* boats from Brest to the central Channel north of Cherbourg, where they were expected to arrive in four or five days. Despite its reluctance to send non-*Schnorchel* boats into the danger area, it also ordered the nine in Brest to sail at high speed on the surface to the area between the Lizard and Hartland Point. The remaining *Landwirt* boats were ordered to establish an anti-invasion patrol on a line north-westward from Bayonne. All but one of the *Landwirt* boats had sailed by the end of D-day. *Gruppe Mitte* remained in harbour.[133]

---

129. BAY/KV 198 of 12 June.
130. BAY/KV 218 of 18 June.
131. BAY/XL 36 of 13 July.
132. ADM 234/68, BR 305(3), *The U-boat War in the Atlantic* Vol 3, pp 67–68; Roskill, op cit, Vol III Part 2, p 56.
133. ADM 234/68, p 68.

These decisions were in large measure disclosed by Sigint during D-day, but the decrypts gave no details of the departure times or whereabouts of the U-boats.* The omission was not serious. Dense anti-submarine patrols were in force from before D-day in expectation of an exodus of U-boats from Biscay. Five U-boats were sighted outward-bound by Coastal Command aircraft as early as 1850 on D-day, and aircraft sighted 14 U-boats, all but two off Ushant, during the night of 6–7 June. In eight air attacks that night two U-boats were sunk and six forced to return to port with damage. On 7 June, as a result of the intensity of the air attacks, the U-boat Command allowed all U-boats to proceed to their stations submerged. Although this reduced the number of sightings, non-*Schnorchel* boats still had to surface for re-charging. Three more were sunk on the night of 7–8 June and others forced to return.[134]

During 7 June the OIC concluded on the basis of its knowledge of the number that had sailed and of indications as to the number that had been sunk or damaged – indications which included decrypt evidence that three were returning damaged to Brest early on 7 June[135] – that although two were probably still making for the Scillies, the U-boats presented little threat to the convoys off the south coast.[136] The two escort groups stationed there on the strength of the Sigint received before D-day were accordingly transferred to the Ushant area.[137] At the time it was not known how many U-boats were making for the Channel from Biscay or to Biscay from the Atlantic. But by 1400 on 8 June decrypts had established that six or seven were moving into the Channel and that four in the Atlantic had been ordered to proceed not to Biscay, but to the area between the Scillies and the Lizard.[138] The Allied escort groups and the surface and air anti-submarine patrols were then re-disposed on the assumption that the former had been proceeding at between 2.5 and 2.75 knots and that the boats from the Atlantic had been south of Ireland by midday.[139] Other decrypts of 8 June gave the precise positions of the U-boats, then numbering 19, which had established an anti-invasion patrol line in Biscay,[140] and disclosed that 11 U-boats from south Norway had been ordered on 7 June to establish an anti-invasion patrol

* See Appendix 13(ii).

134. ibid, p 68; Roskill, op cit, Vol III Part 2, p 57; ADM 234/366, p 112.
135. ADM 223/195, Ultra signal 1929/7 June.
136. ibid, Ultra signals 1640 and 2031/7 June.
137. ADM 234/366, p 135.
138. ADM 223/195, Ultra signal 1400/8 June.
139. ADM 234/366, p 135.
140. ADM 223/195, Ultra signals 1400 and 1528/8 June.

line south of Bergen, to continue the line of six boats already on patrol between Trondheim and Bergen.[141] There was no reference to the formation of an anti-invasion patrol line by the Arctic flotilla.

On 9 June it emerged that one U-boat from the patrol line north of Bergen had been ordered to the North Channel and that one of the U-boats in the Atlantic had been ordered to Cape Wrath; both were *Schnorchel* boats and they were told that their objective was to tie down British forces.[142] Signals decrypted on the same day warning that three German destroyers would be operating to the south of 'the Channel operational area', and subsequently shifting the operational area to the south of the Isle of Wight, were addressed to six U-boats.[143] Other decrypts of 9 June revealed that four U-boats additional to those already identified had been ordered in from the Atlantic and that four of the eleven U-boats on patrol south of Bergen had been ordered into the Atlantic.[144] The OIC assumed that all these boats were destined for the Channel.

Decrypts of 10 June revealed that, following the engagement with the German destroyers,* the U-boat operational area in the Channel had been extended to the French coast as far south as Barfleur; that one of the U-boats ordered from the Atlantic to the Scillies–Lizard area had been directed to join the group proceeding into the Channel; that a *Schnorchel* U-boat which had been forced back to La Pallice was sailing for the Channel on that day.[145] Although these decrypts allotted precise patrol areas near the Allied convoy lanes to each U-boat, the actual positions of the U-boats remained unknown. Allied anti-submarine patrols and escort groups were redisposed on 10 June in the belief that they could now have reached the line Portland–Cap de la Hague or the convoy routes off the north Cornish coast and in the area Scillies–Lizard.[146]

On 12 June the OIC summed up the intelligence received since D-day. Leaving aside those which were patrolling off Norway and those sent in to the Atlantic whose destination was as yet unknown, 35 U-boats had sailed against *Overlord* on D-day and three since. Eight of them were moving towards the Channel – six *Schnorchels*

---

* See below, pp 161–162.

141. ibid, Ultra signal 1919/8 June.
142. ADM 223/196, Ultra signal 1817/9 June.
143. ibid, Ultra signals 0526 and 1334/9 June.
144. ibid, Ultra signals 1436 and 1836/9 June.
145. ibid, Ultra signals 2122 and 2233/10 June.
146. ADM 234/366, p 136.

from Brest and two that were then south of Ireland.* Of nine
non-*Schnorchels* from Brest, some of which had made for the
Scillies–Lizard area, all but two had returned with damage or
casualties.† Nineteen had sailed from ports south of Brest for the
patrol line in Biscay. Two had been sent to the North Channel and
Cape Wrath. It was to be expected that more would be sent to the
Channel as soon as fears for south Norway declined[149] Late on 12
June Sigint revealed that two further 500-ton U-boats had been
ordered to proceed from the Faroes–Iceland passage to Biscay at
high speed,[150] and that another had left Brest for the Channel.[151]

There had so far been no firm reports of attacks by U-boats in
the Channel, though reports of torpedoes fired at frigates and
destroyers and sightings of *Schnorchels* had been received, and no
U-boat had made a signal. But the OIC assumed on 12 June that
some of them, by now addressed as *Gruppe Holzbein*, had reached
the operational area; one of the Gruppe's number had reported
an attack by Allied destroyers and was thought to be returning to
base.[152] On 14 June, however, it became apparent that they had
made less ground than had been expected: decrypts disclosed, to
the complete surprise of the OIC, that another of them had
arrived in St Peter Port in Guernsey the previous day, expecting to
leave again in the evening of 14 June, and that two others had
been instructed to give Ushant a wide berth and approach the
operational area through the northern part of the Channel.[153]
Later on 14 June decrypts gave details of the routes to be followed
by these two boats when entering the Channel, and by four others
from the Atlantic; disclosed that the U-boat Command had
recommended in the light of a report from the U-boat in St Peter
Port‡ that boats entering the Channel from Biscay should be
routed well clear of Ushant and ordered to return if they found no

---

* Compare the German record, that eight *Schnorchels* had sailed from Brest on D-day,[147]
and the official British historian's account, which gives the number as nine.[148] The
discrepancy is partly accounted for by the Sigint evidence that an additional *Schnorchel* sailed
to the Channel from La Pallice.

† These two had also been sunk on 9 and 10 June, but Sigint had not yet established this.

‡ This report, decrypted on 15 June, stated that the U-boat had left Brest at 1600 on 6
June and had been almost continuously hunted and depth-charged from 0915 on 8 June; it
concluded that the *Schnorchel* could not be used by day owing to the density of air cover and
the danger of hydrophone detection, and that charging in the operational area would be very
difficult.[154]

---

147. ADM 234/68, p 68.
148. Roskill, op cit, Vol III Part 2, p 56.
149. ADM 223/172, OIC SI 976 of 12 June.
150. ADM 223/196, Ultra signals 1401/11 June, 1350/12 June.
151. ibid, Ultra signal 1350/12 June.
152. ibid, Ultra signal 1334/13 June; Naval Headlines of 13 June.
153. ADM 223/196 Ultra signals 1351 and 1615/14 June.
154. ibid, Ultra signal 1703/15 June.

prospects of success;[155] and reported that a second U-boat was putting in to St Peter Port. Early on 15 June Sigint reported the departure of the U-boat from St Peter Port and the arrival there of the second.[156]

The first U-boat successes in the Channel followed on 15 June. The frigate HMS *Blackwood* was torpedoed and sunk off Cap de la Hague and an American LST was sunk off Barfleur.[157]

Throughout their passage into the Channel accurate plotting of the individual U-boats had been impossible and even their numbers had been obscure. Even now it is not possible to give an entirely accurate account of how they fared, for the U-boat Command was itself uncertain as to their movements, but it is clear that nine *Schnorchel* boats from Biscay had been trying to reach the *Overlord* convoy lanes, of which one had been sunk on 10 June and two others forced to return damaged to Brest. Of the remaining six, one had turned back with defects after a week, one had entered St Peter Port with empty batteries on 13 June, the third had arrived there on 15 June, subsequently returning to Brest, the fourth sank HMS *Blackwood* but was so damaged in the counter-attack that she went back to Brest, and the fifth was to be sunk on 18 June. Only the sixth reached her intended patrol position south of the Isle of Wight; she arrived on 15 June, sank an LST and attacked, but missed, two US battleships, but was so continuously harried by Allied patrols that she withdrew to Brest after three days.[158] We shall see that no further U-boat was to reach the Channel until 25 June and that although the U-boat Command persisted with its campaign there throughout July, there were never more than four U-boats in the area.

A decrypt of 14 June had meanwhile disclosed that only two U-boats, arrived from the Atlantic, were still present off Cornwall, and that they had been ordered to withdraw if the state of the defences or the lack of shipping precluded attacks.[159] This was followed on 15 June by the sinking of the frigate HMS *Mourne* off Lands End, but it was impossible to tell whether the U-boat had come from the Atlantic or, as the OIC believed, from Biscay.[160]

As for the U-boats on patrol in Biscay itself, decrypts of 9 June had revealed that on the previous evening, in consequence of a GAF sighting of an 'invasion convoy' 120 miles west of Brest, ten of them had been ordered to attack and that, when the scare had subsided, all 19 had been moved to specified positions in a new

---

155. ibid, Ultra signals 1947, 2220 and 2251/14 June.
156. ibid, Ultra signal 0649/15 June.
157. ibid, Ultra signals 1415/15 June, 1357/16 June; Roskill, op cit, Vol III Part 2, p 58.
158. Ellis, op cit, Vol 1, pp 242, 289.
159. ADM 223/196, Ultra signal 2220/14 June.
160. ibid, Ultra signal 1415/15 June.

patrol line on the fifth fathom line, where they could lie on the bottom for long periods and thus shorten their re-charging time.[161] As they had been since D-day, they were still attacked from the air almost every night until 13 June, when they were recalled to their bases; this news emerged from a decrypt on 14 June.[162] They remained in port, as was known from PR. As is now known, this was partly as a precaution against Allied landings in Biscay,* but mainly because the U-boat Command had concluded that to sail them anywhere until they had been equipped with *Schnorchel* would 'only result in further heavy losses'.[164] As early as 11 June Sigint had disclosed that it had decided to sail no further non-*Schnorchel* boats, but to sail all *Schnorchel* boats as fast as possible.[165]

Like the U-boats, and for the same reasons, the main units in the Baltic would have arrived too late for decisive intervention had the enemy decided to commit them and had they arrived at all.† In their absence, the large modern destroyers in the Biscay ports were the only surface force in a position to make a serious challenge to the invasion convoys, and the only other ships capable of offensive action other than minelaying were the torpedo-boats and E-boats based in the Channel.

The enemy made a determined attempt to bring the destroyers to bear. As the Allies knew from Sigint and PR, two of them, Z23 and Z37, were undergoing refit or repair, and the other three (Z24, Z32 and the ex-Dutch ZH1) were operational in the Gironde. At 0621 on D-day, as the OIC was able to inform the Commands within just over an hour, a decrypt disclosed that these three had been ordered to prepare to transfer to Brest, and by 0850 a further decrypt had added that they were likely to leave Royan at 1230.[166] They were seen by air reconnaissance as they left the Gironde and in the early evening decrypts gave their course and speed.[167] As a result of this intelligence the destroyers were attacked by Beaufighters 40 miles south-west of St Nazaire, though Allied destroyer sweeps failed to make contact.[168] In a

---

* The German anxiety about landings in Biscay appears to have owed nothing to Allied deception. A plan to suggest that landings were intended in Biscay (Operation *Ironside*) was put into effect too late to have any influence.[163]

† See below, p 286, for the watch that was kept on the Baltic units.

161. ibid, Ultra signal 1148/9 June.
162. ibid, Ultra signal 1251/14 June.
163. Howard, *Strategic Deception* (forthcoming), Chapter 6.
164. ADM 234/68, p 69.
165. Naval Headlines of 11 June.
166. ADM 223/195, Ultra signals 0728 and 0850/6 June.
167. ibid, Ultra signals 1700 and 1840/6 June.
168. ADM 234/366, p 112; ADM 223/287, USION, pp 103–104.

signal sent at 2026 and decrypted by 2312 they reported that they had sustained slight damage; a further damage report from Brest, disclosing that Z32 would be available 'at reduced war readiness' from 1200 on 8 June, was decrypted on 8 June.[169]

Further decrypts of 8 June gave advance notice that, accompanied by torpedo-boat T24 (a small destroyer), they would leave Brest for Cherbourg at 1830, arriving at 0500 the following morning.[170] In the evening of 8 June decrypts gave their detailed route and intended speed, and disclosed that they would make an offensive sweep against south-bound shipping north of Cherbourg before entering the port.[171] On the strength of this prompt intelligence they were shadowed from 2245 by aircraft of Coastal Command which assisted 10th Destroyer Flotilla, reinforced and concentrated north-east of Ushant, to make contact at 0130 on 9 June. HMS *Tartar* was badly damaged in the action which followed, but ZH1 was sunk, Z32 was driven ashore and totally wrecked, and Z24 was badly damaged.[172] Z24 and T24 escaped to Brest; a report on the action giving details of the extensive damage to Z24 was decrypted in the afternoon on 9 June.[173]

The action of 9 June put an end to the danger from the destroyers and reduced the threat from surface ships to that coming from the torpedo-boats and the E-boats based in the Channel.* The OIC estimated from Sigint and PR on the eve of D-day and during the next 24 hours that there were 15 E-boats (probably not more than 12 operational) at Cherbourg, 15 at Boulogne and 12 at Ijmuiden, and five torpedo-boats at Le Havre.[175]† Of the torpedo-boats, two were in dock, but the

---

* Sigint disclosed that one or two subsequent attempts to sail T24 to Cherbourg were abandoned in face of Allied preparations to intercept. Z24 and T24 then went to the Gironde, where they were sunk in an air attack at the end of August. On 13 June a decrypt disclosed that Z23's repairs were a month off completion;[174] neither the Z23 nor Z37 became operational.

† Given that serviceability and disposition could change so rapidly, these were not bad estimates. The actual deployment was: Cherbourg: 5th E-boat Flotilla, 7 boats operational and 7 non-operational; 9th E-boat Flotilla, 7 boats operational. Boulogne: 4th E-boat Flotilla, 8 boats operational. Ostend: 2nd E-boat Flotilla, 5 boats operational and 2 on passage from Ijmuiden. Ijmuiden: 12 E-boats. Le Havre: 5 torpedo-boats.[176]

169. ADM 223/195, Ultra signals 2312/6 June, 1225/8 June.
170. ibid, Ultra signals 1230 and 1405/8 June.
171. ibid, Ultra signals 1911 and 2017/8 June; ADM 223/196, Ultra signal 2310/8 June.
172. ADM 234/366, p 133; ADM 223/287, USION, pp 106–107; Roskill, op cit, Vol III Part 2, p 57.
173. ADM 223/196, Ultra signal 1558/9 June.
174. ibid, Ultra signal 1158/13 June.
175. ADM 223/195, Ultra signals 1821/5 June, 0025 and 0200/7 June; ADM 223/172, OIC SI 967 of 30 May.
176. ADM 234/366, p 110(n).

remaining three and all available E-boats carried out minelaying operations and torpedo attacks every night. The casualties they inflicted by direct attack were not severe – some 20 Allied ships sunk or damaged in the first week, mostly small, over and above what they achieved by mining – and their operations did not seriously threaten the Allied build-up.* But they were six times more active in the week after D-day than they had been before, and they were a continued source of anxiety – so much so, that ANCXF called for an exceptional raid by heavy bombers on their forward base at Le Havre on the night of 14 June.

It can scarcely be claimed that they would have scored more successes and created still greater anxiety if high-grade Sigint had not been providing good intelligence about their operations. The naval Enigma regularly reported the strengths of the flotillas in operational boats, thus providing a valuable check on Allied claims that E-boats had been sunk or damaged. It also disclosed the extent to which the enemy was making up for losses and damage by bringing in reinforcements from further east. On most days decrypts gave advance notice of E-boat and torpedo-boat intentions for the coming night, stating which flotilla would be operating from which port and with how many boats, whether they were undertaking torpedo or mining operations or both, and to which port and at what time they would return. This had not been a feature of E-boat operations before the invasion and was no doubt due to the disruption of German land-line communications. From time to time this intelligence prompted the re-disposal of the Allied surface patrols and, particularly when the enemy was returning to port, the launching of air attack. But against such mobile and fast-moving vessels it can have been of little operational value to unindoctrinated Allied crews who in any case expected nightly attacks against the western and eastern 'Walls' – standing patrols of destroyers, frigates and MTBs which protected the point of convergence for convoys (the Spout) and the convoy channels to the anchorages in the Seine Bay.†

---

* Apart from sinking the destroyer *Svenner* early on D-day, the torpedo-boats achieved no recorded successes in their torpedo attacks. For a contemporary estimate of the total losses due to E-boat and torpedo-boat action, and of their own casualties, see Appendix 16.

† To give but three examples. On the night of 6–7 June the patrols off Barfleur were strengthened after the receipt of the news that 14 E-boats from Cherbourg would operate against the US assault area. The E-boats ran into the patrols but sank an LCT; they lost two of their number on a minefield while returning to port.[177] On the night of 7–8 June the patrols were again redeployed in the light of a decrypt reporting that 11 E-boats from Cherbourg had just left to operate in the Marcouf-Barfleur area; they sank two LCTs and damaged another, and their penetration into the Spout was such that the OIC was surprised that they

177. ADM 223/195, Ultra signal 0030/8 June; ADM 223/287 USION, pp 116–117.

The activities of the E-boats reached a climax on the night of 10–11 June with minelaying and attacks on convoys by 12 from Le Havre and 11 – all available boats, including some that were barely serviceable – from Cherbourg; and they were scarcely less determined, though using fewer boats, on the night of 11–12 June. Their successes were so considerable, including the sinking of *Mulberry* components in convoys, and the penetration of the *Utah* anchorage and the sinking of the US destroyer *Nelson*, that on 12 June the Allied authorities decreed that *Mulberry* convoys must make the latter part of the crossing in daylight.[180] But the strain on the E-boats was also beginning to tell. On 11 June one decrypt disclosed that of the 15 boats at Cherbourg only six were operational; in another the 9th E-boat Flotilla reported that it was proving 'extremely difficult' to break through north of Barfleur and that 'drastic measures would be necessary against the patrol line if further operations from Cherbourg were intended'.[181]

As a result of these operations, and of a further decline in activity during the nights of 12–13 June, there was an unusually large concentration of E-boats in the forward base at Le Havre by 13 June. A decrypt revealed that 15 were operational there on the evening of 12 June.[182] Most of them arrived from Cherbourg and Boulogne, and PR, flown 'by 14 June' in preparation for the raid by Bomber Command, no doubt showed that they were still there on 13 June. In fact, by a stroke of good luck for the Allies, they were still there on 14 June, E-boat operations having been cancelled on the night of 13–14 June on account of bad weather.[183] The raid, which included 22 Tallboy bombs for attack on the E-boat shelters, was delivered that evening, before the customary departure time, by 228 aircraft, and 116 aircraft made a follow-up raid 3 hours later, together the largest daylight operation Bomber Command had ever carried out. It destroyed nine E-boats, seriously damaged two and damaged one other, leaving only one conditionally able to proceed. It also sank three of

---

did not sink more.[178] On the nights of 8–9 June, again as a result of advance notice, Allied forces were specially disposed off Cherbourg, but the E-boats evaded the patrols and sank two LSTs in attacks on two convoys.[179]

178. ADM 223/195, Ultra signal 0030/8 June; ADM 223/287 USION, p 119; ADM 234/366, p 132.
179. ADM 223/195, Ultra 1317 and 1952/8 June; ADM 223/267, USION, p 123; ADM 234/366, p 133.
180. ADM 223/287, USION, pp 128–130; ADM 234/366, pp 129, 134; Roskill, op cit, Vol III Part 2, p 61.
181. ADM 223/196, Ultra signal 1649/11 June; ADM 223/287, USION, p 133.
182. ADM 223/196, Ultra signal 1852/12 June.
183. ADM 223/287, USION, pp 137–138.

the five torpedo-boats and damaged another, and sank or damaged several R-boats and other smaller vessels. A raid by 297 aircraft struck Boulogne on the night of 15 June; some 26 smaller vessels were sunk but no damage was done to the eight E-boats present.[184] Detailed reports on the destruction achieved by the raids were decrypted on 15 and 17 June.[185]

The German Naval Command assessed the raid on Le Havre as 'a catastrophe' and believed that as a result of it 'the naval situation in the Seine Bay had [been] completely altered'.[186] And it is, indeed, true that until 25 June, when two broke through to the eastern Channel, the E-boats left at Cherbourg were to be largely occupied in transferring to St Malo, and in transporting ammunition from there to Cherbourg, and that until July those based in Boulogne were to be used mainly for minelaying. But the greatest threat to shipping in the assault area in the first ten days after D-day had in fact arisen from enemy mining of the anchorages; and far from declining after 14 June, this menace continued to grow. In part this was because, as Sigint had foretold,* the mining was carried out by the GAF as well as by the Navy – and by other ships as well as, if also mainly, by the torpedo-boats and E-boats.† But it was also due to a development which had not been wholly foreseen. From D-day or soon after – the date has not been exactly determined – the Germans used two new types of pressure-operated mine (*Oyster*), one the acoustic *Oyster* which could be swept only in favourable weather, and the other the magnetic *Oyster* which defied all known methods of sweeping and could be destroyed only by counter-mining.[188]

No advance warning of the existence of the *Oyster* mines had been obtained from Sigint or any other source. The Admiralty was no doubt on the look-out for evidence of their use – it had itself developed mines on similar principles – and suspicions appear to

---

* See above, p 62.

† Unlike the GAF, which confined itself to the mining of anchorages, the Navy carried out other mining operations – laying alarm barrages with moored mines and sowing KMA (shallow water) mines in Brittany, the Cotentin and the Pas de Calais to protect the German shipping lanes and guard against further Allied landings, and mining ports and harbours such as Cherbourg, Le Havre, Rouen and Boulogne against further use by the Allies. It took the Allies three months to clear Cherbourg completetly. It would have taken much longer without the extensive intelligence about the location and types of mine used in these operations which was obtained from Sigint, captured documents and POW.[187]

184. ADM 234/366, p 129; Roskill, op cit, Vol III Part 2, p 55; Ellis, op cit, Vol 1, p 243.
185. ADM 223/196, Ultra signals 1001 and 1637/15 June, 1036/17 June; ADM 223/287, USION, pp 140–141.
186. Quoted in Ellis, op cit, Vol 1, p 243.
187. ADM 223/287, pp 208–220.
188. Roskill, op cit, Vol III Part 2, pp 54, 122; Ellis, op cit, Vol 1, p 244.

have arisen from mid-June, when spontaneous detonations were
reported in waters previously swept for mines. As late as 21 June,
however, when 44 Allied ships had been sunk or damaged by
mines, 33 of them in the week after D-day, the OIC thought it a
'reasonable prediction' that the losses would continue to decline 'as
more minefields were swept'.* It must have been shortly before
this that parts of one of the mines were recovered on *Sword* beach
and flown back to HMS *Vernon*, for on 26 June the NID recorded
the discovery of two new types of mine and on 27 June the
Admiralty informed all ships of their properties and of the
counter-measures to be adopted.[190] The first Sigint reference to
the mines, a decrypt ordering Senior Officer E-boats to lay DM 1
mines near Le Havre, followed on 30 June.[191]†

Minelaying with the *Oyster* mine had meanwhile emerged as the
most effective weapon of the GAF. Its limited activity on D-day
had come as 'a distinct surprise after all the estimates of the GAF
menace to the assault force'.[193] From 1500 on D-day it had carried
out small and ineffective tip-and-run raids against the anchorages;
after dark it had carried out torpedo and bombing attacks with a
total of 175 aircraft, of which only 40 had reached the targets, and
damaged three ships and sunk one LST for the loss of 12
aircraft.[194] Nightly raids on this scale on the next few nights
achieved equally limited success. On about 10 June, however, the
long-range bombers of Fliegerkorps IX turned to minelaying, and
on 16 June a decrypt disclosed that the GAF had decided that the
scale of minelaying by five Geschwader of Fliegerkorps IX should
be increased.[195] From then until mid-July, when they were
diverted to support the Army, and again for a few days early in
August, when they carried out what were virtually the last
anti-shipping operations by the GAF, the long-range bombers
devoted their entire effort to minelaying; and their operations,
greatly exceeding those of the E-boats in scale and frequency,
proved no less difficult to counter.

---

* See Appendix 16, para 4(i). By no means all these losses were due to the *Oyster* mines. In
the *Utah* sector, where they were particularly severe, four destroyers and two minesweepers
being sunk and 25 other ships damaged in the first ten days, most if not all of the casualties
were caused by the minefield previously laid on the Cardonnet bank.[189] (See above, p 151).

† It has been claimed that the OIC noticed a reference to a new type of mine, given the
prefix D (Druck = pressure) in a decrypt 'shortly after D-day'.[192] We have found no such
reference before that of 30 June.

189. ADM 234/366, p 130(n).
190. ibid, p 411; Admiralty General Message 274A of 27 June.
191. ADM 223/198, Ultra signal 1300/30 June.
192. Beesly, *Very Special Intelligence* (1977), p 232.
193. AIR 41/24, p 73.
194. ibid, pp 73-74.
195. DEFE 3/173, KV 8252 of 16 June; ADM 223/287, USION, pp 154-155.

The Enigma and RAF Y usually gave two or three hours' notice of the time of their attacks and of their general target area. But since the aircraft flew too low to be detected by radar, and usually operated singly, intelligence was of little assistance in intercepting them. Regular Allied air attacks were made on their bases, and these no doubt did something to reduce the frequency of their incursions, but Allied minesweeping in the anchorages and on the cross-Channel routes failed for some time to keep pace with them. In his Report of Proceedings ANCXF stated that 'by 24 June casualties due to enemy mining were becoming serious. . . Special measures were taken to reduce all traffic and the speed at which it proceeded within the assault area'.[196] On 6 July it was estimated that of some 600 *Oyster* mines laid, less than a dozen had been destroyed, and during July and early August the number of Allied ships sunk or damaged by mines still averaged four per week.[197]

In nine out of an estimated total of 27 minelaying sorties carried out by aircraft between 28 June and 7 August GAF Enigma decrypts showed that out of 1,060 mines laid, 440 were magnetic *Oyster*, 270 acoustic *Oyster* and 350 non-*Oyster*.[198] It has subsequently been calculated that during June and July the bombers laid between 3,000 and 4,000 mines.[199] The naval Enigma decrypts showed that E-boats laid mines, including 50 *Oyster* mines, in the Seine Bay on three nights during this period.[200]

The success of the GAF's bombers in delaying the Allied rate of build-up by mining operations stood in sharp contrast to the ineffectiveness of its specialised anti-shipping units. The anti-shipping units of Fliegerkorps X with the FX and Hs 293 bombs and of Fliegerdivision 2 with torpedo aircraft had from the outset had little success. An attack on the night of 7 June, preceded by decrypts ordering reconnaissance in the Seine Bay which emphasised that the exact location of heavy naval units was of special importance,[201] had been a conspicuous failure; and a decrypt of 10 June analysing the operation attributed it to the inexperience of the aircrew.[202] Serviceability was also particularly low in the anti-shipping force; Sigint had shown that three torpedo-bomber Gruppen in southern France had only 32 aircraft available for operations on the night of 7–8 June.[203] Decrypts disclosed

---

196. Quoted in ADM 223/287, USION, p 219.
197. ADM 223/172, OIC SI 1054 of 18 August; Roskill, op cit, Vol III Part 2, p 122.
198. ADM 223/172, OIC SI 1054 of 18 August.
199. AIR 41/10, *The Rise and Fall of the German Air Force*, p 331.
200. ADM 223/172, OIC SI 1054 of 18 August.
201. DEFE 3/167, KVs 6788 and 6801 of 7 June.
202. DEFE 3/168, KV 7221 of 10 June.
203. Air Sunset 182 of 8 June.

Fliegerkorps X's intention to operate with FX bombs on the nights of 11 and 14 June.[204] In a signal of 14 June, decrypted on 15 June, Fliegerkorps X stated that the sinking of battleships was of decisive importance and ordered immediate preparations for a daylight operation with FX bombs under fighter cover.[205] On 16 June a signal from KG 100 requested fighter cover and stated that the best time for the attack was the first half-hour from sunrise.[206] That evening the Allies delivered a successful pre-emptive attack on Mérignac.[207]* During the next few days the decrypts disclosed abortive attempts to remount the operation.[209] Thereafter the anti-shipping units remained largely inactive until Sigint disclosed on 8 July that II and III/KG 6 and KG 40 had been ordered to transfer their He 177s and FW 200s from south-west France to Norway.[210] As well as reflecting the almost total failure of the anti-shipping units, the transfer, which was soon followed by the disbandment of Fliegerkorps X, was due to the growing fuel shortage.[211] About 100 torpedo-carrying Ju 88s of Fliegerdivision 2 remained in France until Operation *Dragoon*, but they were rarely active and they had no success before then being withdrawn to Germany.[212]

It was left to Fliegerkorps IX to make the last attempt to attack the Allied battleships off Normandy; and it did so with yet another new weapon. On 22 July orders of 18 July to IV/KG 101 at St Dizier to carry out a *Mistel* attack on a French battleship off the Orne estuary were decrypted.[213] The code-word *Mistel* had not previously been encountered by the intelligence authorities, but they inferred from other clues that it stood for a composite aircraft in which a crew-less twin-engined fighter loaded with explosives was slung to the under-side of a single-engined fighter.†

---

* The Prime Minister having expressed anxiety about these decrypts, he was assured by the CAS on 17 June that the danger was likely to be reduced by the success of the recent attacks on the key bases, Mérignac, Bordeaux and Orleans/Bricy and by the inexperience of the German aircrew. The CAS noted that the GAF had not carried out an FX operation since the ineffective attack on Plymouth on 29–30 April.[208]

† An agent and an escaped POW had reported in the spring of 1944 that they had seen a pick-a-back aircraft, and shortly afterwards 27 such aircraft were photographed by PR at an

204. DEFE 3/170, KV 7570 of 11 June; DEFE 3/172, KV 8057 of 14 June.
205. DEFE 3/172, KV 8164 of 15 June.
206. DEFE 3/173, KV 8360 of 16 June.
207. ibid, KV 8266 of 16 June.
208. Dir/C Archive, 6819 of 17 June.
209. DEFE 3/173, KV 8308 of 16 June; DEFE 3/174, KVs 8542 and 8724 of 17 and 19 June.
210. DEFE 3/53, XL 1282 of 8 July; Air Sunset 205 of 9 July.
211. AIR 41/24, p 334.
212. ibid, p 336.
213. DEFE 3/60, XL 3119 of 22 July.

The attack followed but it was unsuccessful, as were a few others that were made in the Channel before Fliegerkorps IX withdrew with the German Army into Holland and Belgium after the Falaise battle.

---

airfield near Prague.[214] Further evidence had been supplied on 17 May by the decrypt of a Japanese signal from Berlin which described the make-up of the new weapon and explained that it flew on the three engines until the lower aircraft was released against the target.[215] The Admiralty had issued these details in an Ultra signal to the Commands on 19 May.[216] In June another agent had linked the composite aircraft with St Dizier.

214. *Air Ministry Intelligence*, pp 43, 371.
215. SJA 168 of 17 May.
216. ADM 223/194, Ultra signal 1814/19 May.

CHAPTER 47

The Battle of Normandy

B Y THE evening of 9 June the Allied front was continuous from east of the Orne to the Vire at Isigny and the junction of V US with VII US Corps, across the Vire estuary, was imminent.[1]* The Allies had by then encountered seven enemy infantry divisions – 711th, 346th, 716th, 352nd, 91st, 243rd and 709th – three Panzer Divisions – 21st, 12th SS (*Hitler Jugend*) and Panzer Lehr – and a Parachute Regiment. These were disposed as follows:

Orne bridgehead (viz, east of the Orne): 711th, elements of 716th, 346th battle group, 21st Panzer battle group

Orne to Drôme: 716th, 21st Panzer, 12th SS Panzer, Panzer Lehr

Drôme to Vire: 352nd

Cotentin: 709th, 91st, 243rd and Parachute Regiment 6.[2]

Of the infantry divisions, all except 346th and 91st had been holding coastal sectors in the area of the assault. A battle group of 346th had been brought west from Le Havre and ferried across the Seine after dark on D-day. 91st Division in Seventh Army Reserve in the Cotentin had been subordinated to LXXXIV Corps as early as 0235 on D-day on news of the airborne landings. Parachute Regiment 6 had been brought up from Carentan. 21st Panzer had been in Army Group B Reserve in the Caen area; it had been given to LXXXIV Corps at 0700 on D-day, and was in action by the afternoon in the Orne bridgehead and north of Caen. 12th SS Panzer, south-west of Rouen, and Panzer Lehr, near Chartres, had been in OKW Reserve; they had at first been held back by Hitler, but 12th SS Panzer had joined in the fighting on 7 June and Panzer Lehr on 9 June.[3]

Other reinforcements were moving, or were under orders to move, to the battlefield. 275th Infantry Division from St Nazaire and a battle group of 265th Infantry Divison from Lorient had been put in motion towards Bayeux and St Lo by rail and road

---

* See map facing p 225, and front end paper.

1. Ellis, *Victory in the West*, Vol I (1962), p 247.
2. ibid, p 248 map.
3. ibid, pp 200, 206.

respectively on the afternoon of D-day.[4] 77th Infantry Division and 3rd Parachute Division from Brittany and 17th SS PG Division from OKW Reserve south of the Loire had been ordered up on 7 June. 2nd Panzer Division from Army Group B Reserve near Amiens, 2nd SS Panzer Division (Das Reich) from Toulouse under Army Group G, 1st SS Panzer Division (Adolf Hitler) from OKW Reserve in Belgium, together with Werfer Brigade 8 and some artillery units had been ordered up on 8 June.[5] The enemy had redefined Command responsibilities to take account of the large reinforcements that had reached the front or were moving there. LXXXI Corps under Fifteenth Army was to destroy the Orne bridgehead.[6] Under Seventh Army Geyr von Schweppenburg's Panzer Gruppe West was to take charge between the Orne and the Vire, where 21st Panzer, 716th, 12th SS Panzer and Panzer Lehr were subordinated to I SS Panzer Corps.[7] LXXXIV Corps was to be responsible for the Cotentin. II Parachute Corps was to command 77th Infantry, 17th SS PG and 3rd Parachute Divisions and was itself subordinated to LXXXIV Corps.[8]

Because of the strong resistance offered by the Germans north of Caen, General Montgomery decided on 8 June 'not to have a lot of casualties by butting up against the place', and his orders on 9 June were directed to outflanking and encircling it. I British Corps would pass 51st Division into the Orne bridgehead to attack southwards towards Cagny, six miles south-east of Caen. To the west XXX British Corps would launch 7th Armoured Division southwards through Villers-Bocage and Noyers, and then across the Odon to high ground above Evrecy. US V Corps would meanwhile capture Caumont and make a firm junction with VII US Corps, which would taken Carentan and drive west to cut the Cotentin peninsula and isolate Cherbourg.[9]

The Germans had been preparing to make a further attempt to counter-attack north of Caen with all available forces under Panzer Gruppe West since 8 June. They abandoned it in the afternoon of 10 June, about an hour before Panzer Gruppe West was destroyed by an Allied air raid, but they attacked in the Orne bridgehead on that day. There was fierce fighting around the perimeter during the next ten days. The British attack towards Cagny, launched on 13 June, met strong resistance from a battle

---

4. ibid, p 216.
5. ibid, p 237.
6. ibid, p 227.
7. ibid, p 238.
8. ibid, p 238.
9. ibid, p 247; D'Este, *Decision in Normandy* (1983), p 164, quoting Montgomery's letter to the Military Secretary, War Office, 8 June 1944.

group of 21st Panzer Division and was broken off the same day. During the next few days the bridgehead front continued active, but with neither side gaining any significant advantage.[10]

7th Armoured Division attacked on 10 June with the road from Bayeux to Tilly-sur-Seulles as its main axis of advance. Strongly opposed by Panzer Lehr Division, it make little progress that day, or on 11 June, but V US Corps on its right was nearing Caumont without meeting serious opposition and appeared to have found a soft spot in the German defences.[11] On 12 June General Dempsey, in command of Second British Army, ordered XXX Corps to switch 7th Armoured Division west of the Aure to push southward to the Caumont neighbourhood and seize Villers-Bocage from the west. General Dempsey felt that, if this manoeuvre was carried out with drive and speed, there was a chance of a breakthrough before the front congealed.[12] At first all went well. The leading elements of the division entered Villers-Bocage from the west early on 13 June and moved out along the Caen road towards Point 213.[13] But they were stopped that afternoon by a mixed force of tanks and infantry, cut off and overwhelmed. Meanwhile the road from Caumont through Tracy-Bocage was threatened by attacks at several points by infantry identified as belonging to 2nd Panzer Division, newly arriving at the front. Attempts to drive the Germans from the Tilly-Balleroy road failed. On 14 June 7th Armoured Division withdrew from Tracy-Bocage to the Caumont area.[14]

West of the Seulles XXX Corps had therefore come to a standstill. East of the river it had made slow progress. The first attempt to take Cristot, and an attack to clear up the Mue valley, failed on 11 June. But in further stiff fighting the enemy was driven from Cristot and Tilly-sur-Seulles, and pushed south to the outskirts of Hottot.[15]

General Dempsey had been right in sensing that there was a soft spot in the German line south of Bayeux. 352nd Infantry Division had found its position on the coast untenable. During the night of 9–10 June it was withdrawn to the river Elle, between Berigny and Airel, thus opening a gap 10 miles wide from Berigny eastwards across the Aure to Longraye near Tilly-sur-Seulles where Panzer Lehr was established. The enemy's first plan was to fill this gap with II Parachute Corps (less 77th Infantry Division which had

10.   Ellis, op cit, Vol 1, pp 250, 261.
11.   ibid, pp 251, 252.
12.   WO 285/9 (Dempsey Papers), entry for 12 June 1944.
13.   Ellis, op cit, Vol I, p 254, 256 with map.
14.   ibid, p 256.
15.   ibid, p 253.

been ordered to Valognes in the Cotentin). But by the evening of 9 June the bulk of 3rd Parachute Division had only reached Brecy, east of Avranches, and part of 17th SS PG Division was in the same area; only advance elements had reached the gap at Balleroy. Moreover, Rommel now considered that weakness in the Carentan area was more dangerous than the gap on the right of LXXXIV Corps. II Parachute Corps was therefore diverted to block the sector between Carentan and St Lo, and 353rd Division was ordered from Brittany to St Lo, where it would come under II Parachute Corps. Only reconnaissance elements of 17th SS PG Division were left in the vicinity of Balleroy to hold the gap until the arrival of XLVII Panzer Corps with 2nd Panzer Division, which had begun its move from Amiens on the night of 9–10 June.[16]

On the afternoon of 10 June an air attack destroyed Panzer Gruppe West; seventeen officers, including the Chief of Staff, were killed, the GOC was wounded and all its communications were smashed. I SS Panzer Corps took over its duties while it went back to Paris to be reconstituted. On the same day von Rundstedt ordered the demolition of all Cherbourg harbour installations that were not indispensable for German naval operations. For, in the US sector, progress had meanwhile been made on both sides of the Vire estuary. V US Corps was in Balleroy on 10 June. On 12 June it was in the outskirts of Caumont and made a firm junction with VII Corps which completed the capture of Carentan that day. XIX US Corps was now inserted between V and VII Corps. During the next few days V and XIX Corps exerted pressure towards St Lo against stiffening resistance which brought them to a standstill on 18 June about five miles from the town.[17] Meanwhile VII Corps repulsed a counter-attack on Carentan on 13 June and next day attacked westwards from its bridgehead over the Merderet. It took St Sauveur le Vicomte on 16 June, reached the west coast of the Cotentin on 18 June and began its advance north to capture Cherbourg. Its rear was guarded by VIII US Corps, brought in to hold a line facing south from Carentan to the west coast.[18]

On 11 June, following the disaster to Panzer Gruppe West, von Rundstedt and Rommel met and agreed to report independently, but in the same sense, to Hitler. They emphasised that the German forces between the Orne and the Vire must remain on the defensive until reinforcements had arrived to release the striking

---

16. Harrison. *Cross-Channel Attack* (Washington DC, 1951) pp 370–373 and map XVII.
17. ibid, pp 361–365, 376–383; Ellis, op cit, Vol I, pp 256, 257.
18. Harrison, op cit, p 403 et seq and map XXII; Ellis, op cit, Vol I, pp 261, 262.

power of the armoured divisions. They noted the inhibiting effect of Allied air supremacy, which prevented any major movement by day, and of Allied naval gunfire, which made any advance into the zone dominated by fire from the sea impossible.[19] Hitler at once ordered the transfer of II SS Panzer Corps, consisting of 9th and 10th SS Panzer Divisions, to Normandy from the eastern front, contrary to the JIC's expectations before D-day.* He directed that the Allies between the Orne and the Vire must be destroyed piece by piece: as a start, the Orne bridgehead was to be eliminated.

Hitler issued a further directive on 16 June. Von Rundstedt was to concentrate his forces, taking the risk of weakening all fronts except that of Fifteenth Army. An Infantry Corps, LXXXVI, was to be brought up from First Army. 12th SS Panzer, Panzer Lehr and 2nd Panzer Divisions were to be relieved in the front line by infantry divisions from Holland, Fifteenth Army and Nineteenth Army. Fifteenth Army would get two new divisions from Norway and Denmark. A massive armoured counter-attack was to be prepared, using the three Panzer divisions withdrawn from the line and four more which were on their way to the battle area (2nd SS Panzer from southern France, 1st SS Panzer from Belgium and 9th and 10th SS Panzer Divisions from the east).[20]

On 17 June, meeting the two Field Marshals at Soissons, Hitler insisted on a rigid defence of every inch of ground. His determination on this point had already been illustrated by his reaction to developments in the Cotentin. Rommel and Seventh Army had decided that as the peninsula was in danger of being cut in two the German forces should also be divided. Gruppe von Schlieben, comprising 70th, 243rd and 91st Divisions, would fall back on Cherbourg and Gruppe Hellmich, with 77th Division and all troops south and west of the Merderet, would man a defence line north of La Haye du Puits. As 77th Division was in the Montebourg sector, orders would have to be given in time to allow it to disengage. On 16 June Hitler forbade a planned withdrawal of Gruppe von Schlieben on Cherbourg, and modification of this order on 17 June, permitting withdrawal under pressure, came too late to enable the bulk of 77th Division to get through to the south.[21]

Meanwhile the movement of reinforcements ordered forward after the landings had been seriously delayed by Allied air power, which was making movement by day hazardous and disrupting railway communications, and, in the case of 2nd SS Panzer

---

* See above pp 77, 82, 86.

19. Ellis, op cit, Vol I, pp 258, 259.
20. ibid, pp 258, 259.
21. Harrison, op cit, pp 412–414.

Division, by the Maquis. By 17 June battle groups of 265th, 275th and 353rd Divisions had reached the front and XLVII Panzer Corps had been brought up to take command of 2nd Panzer and 2nd SS Panzer Divisions; but 2nd Panzer Division was still short of its armoured regiment and 2nd SS Panzer had not yet arrived.[22]

□

Between D-day and 8 June the naval and GAF Sigint had shown the Germans to be anxious lest the Normandy landings be followed by landings elsewhere. In a message of 6 June, decrypted that evening, Naval Gruppe West had announced that although the invasion of Normandy was recognisable as a major operation, all units were to be prepared for surprise attacks in further areas.[23] GAF reconnaissance orders decrypted on the evening of 7 June had contained the warning that Allied landings for a thrust towards Belgium were to be expected.[24] Naval and air warnings of possible landings in Norway, near Lorient and on the west coast of the Cotentin had been decrypted on 7 and 8 June.[25]

In the week beginning on 9 June Sigint continued to produce references to the threat of follow-up landings. In a message of 8 June, decrypted on 10 June, Luftflotte 3 reported that C-in-C West had ordered a state of emergency in view of the possibility of landings outside the bridgehead and of Allied reinforcements by air.[26] An appreciation issued by Admiral Atlantic on 9 June, which was decrypted on 10 June, suggested that the hesitant and slow progress of Allied land operations in the Cotentin and Seine Bay might indicate 'an intended second landing at another point'.[27] On 11 June the decrypts included one of a signal in which Panzer Gruppe West referred to certain reports indicating that the Allies were planning a landing on the Belgian coast that night,[28] and another of a warning of 10 June from Admiral Channel Coast, on the basis of the interception of a British transmission, that a landing at a place unknown was expected that day.[29] Orders to GAF reconnaissance units, decrypted on 10, 11, 12 and 14 June, directed attention to the Dutch-Belgian coast; strong troop concentrations had been observed in English east coast

---

22. Ellis, op cit, Vol I, p 262.
23. DEFE 3/166, KV 6635 of 1850/6 June 1944.
24. DEFE 3/167, KV 6834 of 2151/7 June.
25. DEFE 3/166, KV 6724 of 7 June; DEFE 3/167, KVs 6863, 6918 of 8 June.
26. DEFE 3/169, KV 7305 of 10 June.
27. ibid, KV 7312 of 10 June.
28. DEFE 3/170, KV 7535 of 11 June.
29. DEFE 3/169, KV 7331 of 11 June.

harbours.[30] Orders for the night 14–15, 15, and night 15–16 June required photographic reconnaissance of English east coast harbours south of Hull, and security patrols both sides of the Straits of Dover and from the Dutch coast to the Dogger Bank – an Allied landing on the west coast of Denmark was said to be planned.[31] Similar orders were decrypted during the next three days.[32] On 16 June Naval Gruppe West saw strong indications (jamming of radar, shipping concentrations and Allied air activity) of invasion operations against Holland and Belgium during the night 16–17 June.[33]

Several telegrams from the Japanese embassies in Berlin and Vichy, decrypted between 9 and 22 June, provided further evidence of German anxiety. The Vichy embassy sent telegrams on 7, 11 and 13 June reporting that landings were probable in the south of France and in the Boulogne-Calais area, where the Germans believed that the 'violent bombing' of airfields and other targets was preparatory to a landing.[34] From Berlin there were telegrams on 7 June reporting that naval activity in the Straits of Dover might point to landings in that area, others on 12 June reporting special precautions at St Malo and Calais, and one on 15 June reporting that special precautions were being taken between Dieppe and Boulogne.[35]

The *Overlord* intelligence staffs regarded these decrypts as in large measure explaining why the German build-up was taking place more slowly than they had expected. They had appreciated before D-day that the Germans would take the decision to commit themselves to Normandy by D+2 and that twelve further divisions would be rushed there between D+3 and D+6: 3rd and 5th Parachute Divisions and 77th Infantry Division from Brittany; 11th Panzer and 2nd SS Panzer Divisions from the south of France; 1st SS and 2nd Panzer Divisions, 84th, 85th, 326th and 331st Infantry Divisions* and 19th GAF Division from beyond the

---

* These divisions and 19th GAF Field Division were thought to be likely to be transferred to Normandy, with the armour which was in OKW and Army Group B Reserve behind Fifteenth Army, because they occupied a lay-back position behind the eleven static or coastal divisions of Fifteenth Army which were massed in the concrete defences between the Seine and the Scheldt. Contrary to what is assumed in some exaggerated accounts of the influence of the *Fortitude* deception, the Allies did not envisage and the Germans did not contemplate

30. ibid, KVs 7381, 7431 of 10 and 11 June; DEFE 3/170, KV 7595 of 12 June; DEFE 3/171, KV 7962 of 14 June.
31. DEFE 3/172, KVs 8088, 8139, 8232 of 14 and 15 June; DEFE 3/173, KV 8270 of 16 June.
32. DEFE 3/173, KVs 8415, 8472 of 17 June; DEFE 3/174, KV 8567 of 17 June.
33. DEFE 3/173, KV 8427 of 17 June.
34. BAY/KVs 190, 207, 208 of 9, 15 and 16 June.
35. BAY/KVs 194, 198, 222 of 11, 12 and 19 June.

Seine. On the evening of 9 June 21st Army Group believed that while the Germans had probably by then decided to reinforce Normandy, the build-up was likely to be smaller and slower than expected because 'the enemy has tied his hands strategically by his fear of future landings'. Three Panzer divisions (1st SS Panzer, 11th and 116th Panzer) might be expected by D+6 and possibly four infantry divisions; but the infantry from the Pas de Calais was likely to be delayed not only by the German anxiety for that sector but also by the difficulty of reaching Normandy, and 2nd SS Panzer and 2nd Panzer were also likely to arrive later than D+6.[36] 21st Army Group's appreciation underwent little change in the next two days. Its intelligence summary on the evening of 11 June repeated that whereas it had been expected that the enemy would after D+2 adjudge the assault on Normandy to be the over-riding menace, and would have brought up eleven divisions* between D+3 and D+6, the evidence was that only five would have arrived, none of them from east of the Seine; and it again attributed the short-fall to the fear of further landings, especially in the Pas de Calais, and the damage to communications, in particular the destruction of the Seine bridges.[37]

The decrypts referring to the enemy's anxiety about further landings were used as evidence not only of the effectiveness of the Allied deception programme, but also of the importance of maintaining it by every possible means. On 7 June, despite heavy commitments in other directions, the Air C-in-C ordered the continuation of the bombing of *Fortitude* targets and this was reaffirmed by Tedder two days later.[38] On 11 June, in support of a

---

the transfer of the static divisions, or even of the three field divisions (47th, 48th and 49th) which were known to have been formed out of reserve infantry divisions just before D-day (see above, p 86 fn†); the latter were judged by the Allies to be static, like the coastal divisions. Even the lay-back or so-called mobile infantry divisions were largely dependent for transport on horse-drawn vehicles and bicycles, and though the Allied intelligence authorities suspected this, they appear to have under-estimated in their assessments before D-day the difficulty the Germans would have encountered if they had decided to move them to Normandy under Allied air attack and with communications disrupted and all the Seine bridges down.

These considerations do not reflect on the effectiveness of *Fortitude*, but they greatly qualify a widespread misconception as to what the Allies hoped from *Fortitude* and as to what it actually achieved. Thus: '. . . how valuable it was that Fifteenth Army was thus held in idleness . . .' (Ellis, *Victory in the West*, Vol 1 (1962) p 323). '*Fortitude* imprisoned the whole of Fifteenth Army in the Pas de Calais . . .' (Hastings, *Overlord* (1964) p 221). '. . . the whole of Fifteenth Army was neutralised.' (Lewin, *Ultra Goes to War* (1978) p 32). 'One double-agent report prevented the whole of Fifteenth Army from being moved to Normandy . . .' (Calvocoressi, *Top Secret Ultra* (1980) p 97).

  * It was 11 instead of 12 because, as the summary reported, it was now known, presumably from agents' reports, that 19th GAF Division had left Belgium for Italy.

36. WO 171/129, 21st Army Group Intelligence Summary No 127 of 9 June.
37. ibid, No 129 of 11 June.
38. AIR 41/24, *The Liberation of North-West Europe*, Vol III, pp 74, 85–86.

plea that the suspension of diplomatic privileges imposed in the spring should not be relaxed until 21 June, Eisenhower's Chief of Staff submitted a selection of the decrypts to the Foreign Office, which was objecting to the prolongation of the suspension after D-day. He argued that when it was 'imperative that the enemy receive no scrap of information which might indicate to him the true nature of our plans . . . the mere lifting of the ban . . . will indicate . . . that no further landings are to be contemplated'.[39] On the same day MI 14 advised the CIGS that the continuation of the Allied cover plan should be given full support. It believed, more optimistically than 21st Army Group, that 'at about D+6 or 7 he [the enemy] may realise that no major attack on the Pas de Calais-Belgian Coast is intended for the time being,' and that the date on which he took this decision would depend a great deal on the successful continuation of the deception.[40]

Thus far, although high-grade Sigint had begun to make its contribution during 8 and 9 June,* it had thrown little light on the progress of the enemy's build-up. On the morning of 10 June the decrypts of signals sent the previous evening had located Panzer Gruppe West at La Caine[41] and the HQ of I SS Panzer Corps near Tourville,[42] and had prompted Allied air attacks later on 10 June. Two raids on the Panzer Corps HQ produced no result but the attack on Panzer Gruppe West put it out of action.[43]† In other signals which were sent on 9 June but not decrypted till 11 June, Panzer Gruppe West had reported that it would assume command as soon as communications were established, and had requested that it should be given only general instructions and entrusted with their execution, and had been instructed to attack north-wards, concentrating its forces as much as possible and screening on the left.[45] But apart from confirming on 10 June the transfer of II Parachute Corps with 17th SS PG and 3rd Parachute Divisions to the St Lo area,‡ the decrypts provided no precise information

---

* See above, pp 146–147, 154.

† The results of the attack on Panzer Gruppe West were reported in a decrypt of 12 June: all communications had been destroyed; its Chief of Staff and the head of its operational and intelligence staffs had been killed and its CO slightly wounded; I SS Panzer Corps had taken over its command responsibilities.[44]

‡ See above, pp 153–155.

39. CAB 121/394, SIC file D/France/6/12, Letter from General Bedell Smith to Mr Eden, 11 June 1944.
40. WO 208/3573, MI 14 Weekly Summary for the CIGS, 11 June.
41. DEFE 3/168, KV 7225 of 10 June.
42. ibid, KV 7203 of 10 June.
43. Harrison, op cit, p 373; AIR 41/24, p 87.
44. DEFE 3/170, KV 7681 of 12 June.
45. DEFE 3/169, KV 7435 of 11 June; DEFE 3/170, KV 7506 of 11 June.

about the movements of the reinforcements before 11 June. Until then, the Allied assessments depended entirely on agents, PR, Army Y and contacts with the enemy; and the evidence of these sources had been less than conclusive.

On D-day air reconnaissance had detected rail loading activity in 2nd Panzer's and 1st SS Panzer's areas as well as in those of 12th SS Panzer, 17th SS PG and Panzer Lehr.[46] On the evening of 8 June 21st Army Group had believed that, as agents had by then reported heavy loading in Belgium, 1st SS Panzer was likely to be the next armoured formation to arrive after 12th SS Panzer, Panzer Lehr and 17th SS PG, and that it would be followed by 2nd SS Panzer from Toulouse. It had also noted that there were signs that 11th Panzer might be leaving the Bordeaux area, but had concluded that 2nd Panzer would wait for a while astride the Somme in view of German anxiety about the threat to the Pas de Calais.[47]* On 9 June 21st Army Group's intelligence summary had believed that three Panzer divisions would arrive by D+6, probably 1st SS Panzer from Belgium, 11th Panzer from Bordeaux, where rail activity was reported, and 116th Panzer from Mantes, of which, however, nothing had yet been learned. It had added that reports of railway activity in 2nd Panzer's area remained inconclusive.[49] On 10 June, when air reconnaissance detected heavy movements from Paris through Dreux, 21st Army Group and Second Army had associated them with 1st SS Panzer, though Second Army had noted that 'other candidates' were 2nd Panzer, 116th Panzer or the balance of I SS Panzer Corps, and that the enemy was 'counting on I SS Panzer Corps's tank battalion' as well as on his Panzer divisions.[50]†

The first Sigint references to these movements were in keeping

---

* Support for this conclusion, as for the expectation with regard to 1st SS Panzer and 2nd SS Panzer, was probably found in the decrypt of 8 June informing Seventh Army of new cover names for armoured units: this had listed 1st SS Panzer, 17th SS PG, Panzer Lehr, an unspecified SS Panzer division (clearly 2nd SS) and Panzer Brigade 10, but had omitted 2nd Panzer as well as the two divisions which were already in the line (21st Panzer and 12th SS Panzer).[48]

† 21st Army Group found support for its conclusion in a decrypt of 10 June which disclosed that 19th Panzer Division had arrived in Holland on 2 June in a battered condition from Russia; it thought its arrival might have been intended to make up for the departure of 1st SS Panzer. A further decrypt of 13 June reported that its equipment was inadequate even against air landings.[51]

46. WO 171/129, No 124 of 6 June.
47. ibid, No 126 of 8 June.
48. DEFE 3/167, KV 6933 of 8 June.
49. Wo 171/129, No 127 of 9 June; Ellis, op cit, Vol 1, p 120 map.
50. WO 171/129, No 128 of 10 June; WO 219/1920, SHAEF Intelligence Summary for week ending 10 June; WO 285/3, Second Army Intelligence Summary No 7 of 10 June.
51. DEFE 3/169, KV 7270 of 10 June; DEFE 3/171, KV 7767 OF 13 June.

with Allied expectations. Issued on 11 June, they confirmed that 2nd SS Panzer was on the move and reported that its main loading base was Perigueux.[52] Decrypts issued on 12 June added that it was to move to Poitiers that day and that it was expecting to have to carry out limited operations against guerrillas until its rear elements were brought up.[53] When estimating on the evening of 11 June that the enemy's build-up would by D+6 be some six divisions less than had been expected, 21st Army Group still included 2nd SS Panzer in this figure in view of the fact that it was unlikely to be in effective action before D+8; but it also included the two ex-Panzer training divisions (11th and 116th Panzer), of which there was still no sign, three or four of the infantry divisions which had been expected (83rd, 85th, 326th and 331st) but which were still on the wrong side of the Seine, and 2nd Panzer. With regard to 2nd Panzer, 'it shows no sign of movement: it is delayed by the threat to the Pas de Calais and must in any event take a circuitous route from the Somme'.[54] MI 14 on 11 June reached a similar conclusion: 1st SS Panzer was moving up, leaving 2nd Panzer and 116th Panzer to guard the Pas de Calais, but 2nd Panzer might leave Amiens within a week if the *Fortitude* deception measures were relaxed.[55] It was thus with some surprise that on the evening of 12 June the Allied authorities learned from the decrypt of a signal from the Flivo of XLVII Panzer Corps that 2nd Panzer had been due to move to an assembly area 20 km south of Falaise, about 35 miles from the battlefield, during the night of 11–12 June.[56]

In view of the fact that air reconnaissance had indicated that only one division had moved through Paris, this disclosure involved only the substitution of 2nd Panzer for 1st SS Panzer, a substitution which 21st Army Group effected by announcing in its intelligence summary for 12 June that reports of tank movements indicated that 1st SS Panzer might be replacing 2nd Panzer astride the Somme in order to release the fitter division for Normandy, and that 2nd Panzer might arrive on 14 June.[57]* Thus the real

---

* The tank return of 25 May, not available till 11 June (see Appendix 10(i)) had given 1st SS Panzer Division 45 Pzkw IV and 41 Pzkw V (Panther) tanks. In another return of 19 May, which was not interpreted for the Commands till 11 June, it had 45 Pzkw IVs and 39 Pzkw Vs; it had a shortage of motor transport and heavy weapons and was said to be 'not ready for operations' and in need of 6 weeks' training.

52. DEFE 3/169, KV 7415 of 11 June; DEFE 3/170, KV 7458 of 11 June; WO 171/129, No 129 of 11 June.
53. DEFE 3/170, KV 7638, 7645 of 12 June.
54. WO 171/129, No 129 of 11 June.
55. WO 208/3573, MI 14 Weekly Summary for the CIGS, 11 June.
56. DEFE 3/170, KV 7707 of 12 June.
57. WO 171/129, No 130 of 12 June.

surprise was not, as is commonly said,[58] the appearance of advanced elements of the division, but the fact that the Allies encountered them on the afternoon of 13 June near Villers-Bocage; as General Montgomery told the CIGS the following day, 21st Army Group had expected it to go into action against I Corps in the Caen sector.[59] Decrypts disclosing that it had established communication with Panzer Lehr in XXX Corps area on the evening of 12 June were issued on 13 June after its troops had been identified.[60]

The Germans in fact ordered 2nd Panzer forward on 7 June and released 1st SS Panzer from OKW Reserve on 8 June. But the two divisions had not begun to move to Normandy until 9 June, when 116th Panzer was also ordered to release one regiment. Thus except for the remainder of 116th Panzer, which was newly formed and far from ready,* all the armour that had been kept back behind Fifteenth Army was being sent into the Normandy battle on D+3, much as the Allies had predicted, notwithstanding the continuing German fear of a second landing. On the morning of 10 June however, 1st SS Panzer had been stopped following the receipt by the Germans on the previous evening of two warnings that the Allies were intending to carry out another major invasion, probably in the Pas de Calais. The first warning had come from an uncontrolled Abwehr agent in Stockholm and the second, from one of the double-cross agents, had been sent as part of the *Fortitude* deception programme, which had been intensified since 8 June. It appears to have been this coincidence which impressed the enemy at a time when he was acutely torn between his fear of a further landing and his anxiety to gain a decision in Normandy before a further landing took place.[61] 1st SS Panzer was not to move to Normandy until, on 16 June, Hitler ordered von Rundstedt to take the risk of weakening all his fronts except that of Fifteenth Army and prepare a massive armoured counter-attack.†

---

* For the state of 116th Panzer Division, as disclosed in a decrypt of 25 May, see Appendix 10(i). On this evidence the Allied estimate before D-day was that it needed nearly three months to reach operational readiness. As we shall see, between 11 and 25 June decrypts disclosed that it was regularly on the move between the Seine and the Somme. Later decrypts were to show that the other newly upgraded Panzer divisions (9th and 11th Panzer) were equally unready.

† By then, on the evidence of high-grade Sigint, the Germans were hesitating about the likelihood of an early second landing. As early as 11 June an appreciation by Fremde Heere

58. Ellis, op cit, Vol 1, p 261; D'Este, op cit, p 178.
59. Ellis, op cit, Vol 1, p 261.
60. DEFE 3/171, KVs 7861, 7863 of 13 June.
61. Ellis, op cit, Vol 1, pp 237–238; Harrison, op cit, p 373; Howard, *Strategic Deception* (forthcoming), Chapter 9.

2nd Panzer Division, continuing its movement by road through Paris, had meanwhile been directed not to the Caen sector, where Panzer Gruppe West had abandoned the attempt to counter-attack on 10 June, but to the gap in the Caumont – Balleroy sector. Its reconnaissance battalion, moving by train and only by night, had reached the gap on the night of 12 June.[65] But the set-back to 7th Armoured Division at Villers-Bocage on 13 June was administered not by 2nd Panzer's infantry, but by one of the two Tiger tank companies of Heavy Panzer Abteilung 101. In April high-grade Sigint had identified Panzer Abteilung 101 as part of the Corps troops of I SS Panzer Corps, and shown that it was receiving Tigers and Panthers from Panzer Brigade 10, a staff formation.[66] In the middle of May agents had located it at Gournay, near Beauvais, 50 km north-west of Mantes, and Sigint had located its twin, Panzer Abteilung 102, in Belgium, and the Allied order of battle experts had then believed that between them these two units controlled all the heavy tanks in the west except for a GHQ Tiger battalion near Bordeaux.[67] On 2 June a decrypt had located I SS Panzer Corps HQ at Mantes.[68] The decrypt of 8 June allotting cover names to armoured formations which included Panzer Brigade 10* had been a strong indication that the Allies would encounter Panzer Abteilung 101, and they were certainly on the look-out for it. Later that day 21st Army Group and Second Army had concluded on the basis of sightings and Y reports of movements east of Caen in the past two days that I SS Panzer Corps troops, including Abteilung 101, were moving from

---

West, which was decrypted on 16 June, noted that, as Normandy appeared to be the employment area for the whole of Montgomery's Army Group, and also the unloading area for the strong US reserves that were to be transported direct to Cherbourg, FUSAG might be destined for the Somme-Seine sector; but it added that this was speculation in the absence of firm evidence from captured documents, the Abwehr or 'sure source'.[62] A telegram from the Japanese embassy in Berlin, decrypted on 18 June, quoted a German appreciation obtained on 13 June: further landings were not improbable given that some 18 Allied divisions still stood ready in the Portsmouth area and some 30 were available in south-east England, but there were indications that the main strategy of the Allies would be to extend and strengthen their present bridgehead. The Japanese Ambassador repeated this assessment on 16 June in a telegram decrypted on 20 June.[63] On 19 June, however, in a telegram decrypted on 22 June, he referred to the German fears that Patton's Army Group might land in the Dieppe-Boulogne area.[64] See also p 201 below.

* See above, p 180 fn*.

62. DEFE 3/173, KV 8251 of 16 June.
63. BAY/KVs 218, 224 of 18 and 20 June.
64. BAY/KV 230 of 22 June.
65. Hastings, *Overlord: D–day and the Battle for Normandy* (1984), p 170.
66. DEFE 3/41, KV 1512 of 20 April; DEFE 3/42, KV 1891 of 24 April.
67. WO 205/532, Weekly *Neptune* Reviews of 14 and 28 May; DEFE 3/155, KV 3988 of 15 May.
68. DEFE 3/164, KV 6131 of 22 June.

Gournay to, probably, the Falaise area.[69] But except that a decrypt had located I SS Panzer Corps's HQ just south of Tourville early on 10 June,[70] and that on the evening of 10 June Second Army had surmised that the tank movements sighted near Dreux might be the balance of I SS Panzer Corps's troops, rather than or as well as 1st SS Panzer Division, and expected them to include Panzer Abteilung 101,* no further indications were obtained of the approach of the Abteilung to Villers-Bocage, where it arrived during 12 June. It had in fact left Gournay on 7 June and had suffered severely from air attack near Versailles on 8 June, but had thereafter moved only by night.[71]

Sigint disclosures about the enemy's formations became more frequent from 13 June. Decrypts of 13 and 14 June reported that 2nd SS Panzer had been marching to Tours on 12 June and that it had urgently requested fuel to be sent to Châtellerault on 13 June.[72] Decrypts of 12 and 14 June showed that 116th Panzer had been under command of LXXXI Corps, had been placed under LXVII Corps and was moving to an area south of the Somme.[73] There was still no reference to 1st SS Panzer, but agents reported on 13 June that it had moved to Ghent.[74] Early on 14 June Sigint gave the location of 2nd Panzer, less its armoured regiment, and confirmed its subordination to LXXXIV Corps; it had closed the gap between I SS Panzer Corps and LXXXIV Corps, and had Panzer Lehr on its right and 3rd Parachute Division on its left.[75]

The enemy had intended to fill this gap with II Parachute Corps until he was forced to divert that Corps against the American advance in the Carentan sector. Sigint became plentiful on 12 June in that sector, where it contributed significantly to the frustration of a counter-attack delivered by 17th SS PG on 13 June. A Flivo signal giving the order of battle of LXXXIV Corps at 1000 on 12 June was decrypted within a few hours. The right group comprised II Parachute Corps, 3rd Parachute and 352nd Infantry Divisions, Parachute Regiment 6, 17th SS PG Division and (in the first reference to this formation) a battle group of 275th Infantry Division. The left group comprised 91st, 77th, 709th and 243rd Divisions under the GOC 91st Division.[76]

---

* See above, p 180.

69. WO 285/3, Intelligence Summary of 8 June; WO 171/129, No 126 of 8 June.
70. DEFE 3/168, KV 7203 of 10 June; AIR 41/24, p 87.
71. Hastings, op cit, p 132.
72. DEFE 3/171, KVs 7795, 7798 of 13 June, 7978 of 14 June.
73. DEFE 3/170, KV 7593 of 12 June; DEFE 3/171, KV 7982 of 14 June.
74. WO 171/129, No 131 of 13 June.
75. DEFE 3/171, KV 7973 of 14 June.
76. DEFE 3/170, KV 7678 of 12 June.

Another decrypt of a Flivo signal reported that GOC LXXXIV Corps (General Marcks) had been killed.[77] Decrypts issued on 12 June added that elements of 3rd Parachute had been in action at 1300 that day, and that they were to join the right wing of 352nd Infantry on both sides of the St Lo-Bayeux road and operate defensively until full fighting efficiency was achieved.[78]* The news that 17th SS PG was assembling south and south-west of Carentan for mobile operations was obtained from the decrypt of another signal issued on 11 June.[80] It was overtaken by Flivo signals of 12 June which, decrypted with little delay, enabled GC and CS to issue at 1101 the warning that 17th SS PG was to counter-attack that day to recapture Carentan. At 1316 GC and CS added that LXXXIV Corps had urgently requested air support for preparatory bombing and for ground attack from H-hour, which would probably be 1500. Signals decrypted later in the day disclosed that communications difficulties had prevented the redirection of GAF formations and that the attack had been postponed until the morning of 13 June. At midnight on 12–13 June GC and CS signalled 17th SS PG's latest intentions, together with requests for preliminary air attacks at 0230 and attacks from 0320 in front of the attacking spearheads.[81] There can be little doubt that these timely decrypts helped the US forces to repulse this counter-attack.†

Decrypts of 14 June disclosed that battle groups of 275th and 265th Infantry Divisions had been approaching the battlefield on 10 June,[83] and that II Parachute Corps intended to use its remaining reserves for a counter-attack to eliminate a penetration east of the Douve but was doubtful of success because of the slow arrival of reinforcements.[84] A decrypt of 16 June showed that this

---

* No further Sigint was obtained on this obstinately contested sector till 18 June, when it disclosed that LXXXIV Corps was anxious about 352nd Infantry's sector because of the division's poor fighting strength, and mentioned the employment of a battle group of 353rd Infantry Division.[79] See below p 187 fn*.

† See above p 174. It is recorded by the official US historian that on 12 June General Bradley heard of a German concentration south-east of Carentan but that an armoured task force assembled to meet that threat was diverted before the counter-attack came in on 13 June from the south-west.[82]

77. ibid, KV 7743 of 12 June.
78. ibid, KV 7591 of 12 June.
79. DEFE 3/174, KVs 8602, 8606 of 18 June.
80. DEFE 3/170, KV 7591 of 11 June.
81. ibid, KVs 7662, 7671, 7693, 7713, 7738 of 12 June.
82. Harrison, op cit, pp 364–365; Bradley, *A Soldier's Story* (1951), p 293; Bennett, *Ultra in the West* (1979), p 78.
83. DEFE 3/171, KV 7987 of 14 June.
84. DEFE 3/172, KV 8008 of 14 June.

attack was still being contemplated late on 15 June.[85] On 17 June decrypts reported that 2nd SS Panzer had been at Champsecret on 15 June under the command of XLVII Panzer Corps with 2nd Panzer Division.[86] The next references to 2nd SS Panzer were received on 18 June; it had left XLVII Panzer Corps on 17 June and LXXXIV Corps reported that it was assembling south of St Lo on the morning of 18 June.[87]

Three decrypts of 16 June had meanwhile reflected the enemy's growing difficulties in the Cotentin. The earliest disclosed in the afternoon that he intended to regroup his forces under Hellmich in the south and von Schlieben in the north.[88] In the evening a signal made at 1230 reported that the situation was becoming critical and that Battle Group von Schlieben was preparing to withdraw into Fortress Cherbourg, and another made at 1530 stated that an Allied attack towards St Sauveur le Vicomte had broken through on a front of five kilometres.[89]

On 17 June Sigint established that 1st SS Panzer Division was still in Belgium on the evening of 16 June and that 116th Panzer was then in Fifteenth Army Reserve under LXVII Corps.[90] From 17 June, however, the decrypts began to reflect the developments inaugurated by Hitler's directive of the previous day.* On 17 June they reported that 16th GAF Field Division was being withdrawn from its coastal sector in Holland and that 6th Parachute Division from eastern France had arrived in Amiens,[91] and on 18 June that 363rd Infantry Division, from Denmark, was moving to a billeting area near Bruges.[92] On 17 June they revealed that since 15 June preparations had been going forward for the transfer from Bordeaux of the Corps Staff of LXXXVI Corps and an unspecified infantry division.[93]† This last information was amplified on 18 June when the decrypt of a signal of the previous day reported that LXXXVI Corps was being put into the line to take over the sector between the Seine and the Orne; the Seine would be its right boundary with LXXXI Corps, and also Seventh Army's right boundary with Fifteenth Army, and its left boundary with I SS

---

* See above, p 182.

† This was presumably 276th Division. See Ellis, op cit Vol I, map p 120.

85. DEFE 3/173, KV 8303 of 16 June.
86. ibid, KVs 8271, 8376 of 16 June.
87. DEFE 3/174, KVs 8593, 8707 of 18 June.
88. DEFE 3/173, KV 8324 of 16 June.
89. ibid, KV 8389 of 16 June.
90. ibid, KV 8484 of 17 June; DEFE 3/174, KV 8527 of 17 June.
91. DEFE 3/173, KVs 8456, 8476, 8484 of 17 June; DEFE 3/174, KV 8527 of 17 June.
92. DEFE 3/174, KV 8703 of 18 June.
93. DEFE 3/175, KV 8499 of 17 June.

Panzer Corps would be the Orne from Caen.[94] Additional information had been received from other sources by the evening of 18 June. The Resistance had reported that two infantry divisions might be coming up from the southern Biscay coast. Reports of train movements indicated that two divisions might have been brought up from Germany. Allied troops had made contact in the St Lo area with elements of 353rd Infantry Division.[95]*

In its intelligence summary of 15 June 21st Army Group reviewed the state of the German build-up. It had been expected that the Germans would assemble 25 divisions by D+10, including nine Panzer and PG divisions. The actual number was six armoured divisions, one parachute division and elements of eleven infantry divisions – some of the latter being only brigade groups.† The summary attributed the short-fall to the effects of Allied air power and the extent to which the Germans had continued to fear further landings, particularly in the Pas de Calais.[97] The Army Group's summary of 18 June, issued on the day on which VII US Corps reached the west coast of the Cotentin and began its advance on Cherbourg, reflected the knowledge that reinforcements were coming in now from Holland, Denmark and Bordeaux, and probably from Germany. It noted that as the Germans must be resigned to the loss of Cherbourg, they might be reconsidering their appreciation of Allied intentions and reviewing their own order of battle. But it did not expect them to 'sell out' of the Seine-Somme area.[98]

□

On 18 June Montgomery issued a new directive requiring Second British Army to take Caen by a pincer attack while First US

---

* The move of this division from Brittany appears to have gone unnoticed by any of the intelligence sources until late on 18 June, when the decrypt of an Enigma signal of 17 June disclosed that a battle group of 353rd Division was at the front.[96]

† On the strength of earlier order of battle intelligence and of battlefield contacts the summary assessed the armoured content of the opposition as being the equivalent of four divisions, not six, and the infantry divisions as being the equivalent in strength to about nine divisions. It said that 17th SS PG was largely made up of youths and Romanians; that Panzer Lehr and 3rd Parachute Divisions were not as formidable as had been expected; and that, of the infantry divisions, 716th and 709th were of indifferent quality; 352nd, though it had fought well, was reduced to a skeleton. For what was known about 2nd SS Panzer Division's tank strength see Appendix 10(i).

94. DEFE 3/174, KV 8680 of 18 June.
95. WO 171/129, No 133 of 18 June.
96. DEFE 3/174, KV 8602 of 18 June.
97. WO 171/129, No 132 of 15 June.
98. ibid, No 133 of 18 June.

Army pressed on with the capture of Cherbourg. It was originally intended that the main British attack (Operation *Epsom*) should be made on 22 June from the Orne bridgehead by VIII Corps which was just landing, preceded by a supporting operation by XXX Corps which would begin on 18 June. This decision had to be changed because, following the failure to take Caen, the success of the determined German efforts to seal off the British forces meant that there was inadequate room in the bridgehead. A directive on 19 June scaled down operations from the bridgehead to such as could be mounted by I Corps with the troops already there. Beginning on 22 June the right flank of Second Army was to swing south-eastwards through Aunay-sur-Odon and Evrecy towards the bridges over the Orne between Thury Harcourt and Amaye-sur-Orne. VIII Corps was switched to the western wing of the pincer movement and was to attack across the Odon on 23 June, on the general thrust line St Mauvieu-Esquay-Amaye-sur-Orne, to establish itself south-east of Caen in the area Bourguébus-Vimont-Bretteville-sur-Laize.[99]*

On 19 June a storm began in the Channel, the like of which had not been known for over forty years. It lasted three days and compelled the postponement of Operation *Epsom* and the subsidiary attacks; I Corps's advance was now to take place on 23 June, to be followed by XXX Corps's attack on 25 June and VIII Corps's on 26 June.[102] The storm also delayed the build-up of XIX US and VIII Corps. But VII US Corps continued to advance northwards, and by 20 June it was facing the landward defences of Cherbourg. It began the attack on the town on 22 June and entered it on 25 June. The Fortress Commander surrendered next day, although

---

* It has been claimed that 'Montgomery's decision to switch VIII Corps from the Orne to the Odon was largely influenced by the flow of intercepted signals provided by Ultra, particularly those revealing the movements of 1 SS Panzer Division to replace 716 Division and [of] II SS Panzer Corps, thus making it imperative for the new offensive to begin before their arrival further strengthened the German defence of Caen'.[100] The decision was taken on 18 June, as may be seen from Dempsey's diary entry for that day: 'Saw C-in-C at my HQ, I told him that I had come to the conclusion that an attack by VIII Corps from the bridgehead . . . is too risky. The bridgehead is too small to form up satisfactorily . . . I will therefore put VIII Corps in between XXX Corps and I Corps'.[101] But while it need not be doubted that Montgomery was anxious to attack before the Germans could strengthen their line, we shall see (below, p 191) that the decrypt containing the report of the withdrawal of 716th Division and the movement of large forces in the opposite direction was not available till 20 June, that the fact that 1st SS Panzer Division had moved from Belgium was not finally established till 20 June, and that the decrypts confirming that II SS Panzer Corps with 9th and 10th SS Panzer Divisions were arriving were not obtained till 24 June.

99. Ellis, op cit, Vol I, p 271: WO 285/2, 21st Army Group Directives.
100. D'Este, op cit, p 237.
101. WO 285/9, entry for 18 June.
102. Ellis, op cit, Vol I, pp 272–274.

resistance in outlying positions lasted till the end of the month.[103]*

Meanwhile, while Second Army had temporarily lost the initiative following the failure to take Caen by assault or envelopment, there was no lack of intelligence about either the order of battle in the German front line or the continuation of the German build-up in the interval before the opening of Operation *Epsom*.

Of the tactical dispositions, the chief adjustments to the front had occurred on the enemy's left wing, where he had to respond to the American breakthrough to the west coast of the Cotentin. A message sent at 1400 on 19 June, and signalled from GC and CS to the Commands five hours later, revealed that LXXXIV Corps had been relieved of responsibility for the sector east of the Vire held by II Parachute Corps, and that a battle group under the GOC 91st Division (General König) had taken command from the Prairie Marécageuses to Portbail.[104] At 0534 on 20 June GC and CS confirmed that II Parachute Corps had been subordinated directly to Seventh Army from 1200 on 19 June.[105]

Early on 21 June GC and CS signalled to the Commands decrypts of two messages which had passed late on 18 June. The first referred to the stationing of 2nd SS Panzer Division in the area of Torigny-sur-Vire as Seventh Army Reserve and the movement forward to Périers under LXXXIV Corps of 353rd Division.[106]† According to the second message II Parachute Corps held the sector between the Drôme and the Vire, with XLVII Panzer Corps on its right and LXXXIV Corps on its left. Its task was to keep open the Vire crossings at Torigny and St Lo. Its right wing was to press forward to conform with the progress of an attack being made by XLVII Panzer Corps. LXXXIV Corps was operating between the Vire and the west coast of the Cotentin. It was to hold the existing defence line between the Vire and the Prairie Marécageuses while establishing a defensive front from the Prairie Marécageuses to the west coast at Portbail. Its task was to prevent an Allied thrust towards Périers and La Haye du Puits from east and north.[107] At 2146 on 21 June GC and CS signalled the decrypt of a Flivo message sent at midday on 20 June which disclosed the detailed lay-out of LXXXIV Corps. Its right

---

* See Appendix 17 for the Enigma decrypts covering the German retreat to Cherbourg and the Allied capture of the town.

† See above, p 187.

103. ibid, pp 286–289.
104. DEFE 3/175, KV 8835 of 19 June.
105. ibid, KB 8883 of 20 June.
106. DEFE 3/176, KV 9009 of 21 June.
107. ibid, KV 9073 of 21 June.

boundary with II Parachute Corps was from Airel south along the Vire before bending west. The sector between the Vire and Prairie Marécageuses was held by 17th SS PG Division, a battle group of 275th Division and Parachute Regiment 6. Gruppe König with the remnants of 91st, 243rd and 77th Divisions and 353rd Division was responsible from the Prairie Marécageuses to the coast. 353rd Division was moving up and was partly committed already.[108] A decrypt signalled by GC and CS on 23 June showed that II Parachute Corps and LXXXIV Corps had agreed that an Allied thrust from north-east of St Lo across the Vire to the Coutances area would out-flank LXXXIV Corps's northward facing front and it was therefore necessary to strengthen the defence north of St Lo by all available means.[109]

II Parachute Corps held the sector between the Vire and the Drôme with 3rd Parachute Division and the remnants of 352nd Infantry Division under command. A signal issued by GC and CS at 0901 on 24 June showed that elements of 353rd Division and a battle group of 266th Division were also in the sector.[110]

XLVII Panzer Corps (commanding 2nd Panzer Division) was on the right of II Parachute Corps with I SS Panzer Corps on its right. On 20 June it broke off the attack, to which II Parachute Corps had been told to conform, because 'continuation impossible owing to Allied strength'.[111] XLVII Panzer Corps's boundary with I SS Panzer Corps on the evening of 21 June was given in the decrypt of a Flivo message signalled by GC and CS the next day.[112] A new boundary, extending XLVII Panzer Corps's sector north-east approximately to Villers-Bocage, was given in a message from 2nd Panzer Division's Flivo, sent at midday on 22 June and signalled by GC and CS to the Commands that evening.[113]

A message from I SS Panzer Corps in the evening of 18 June, signalled by GC and CS the next day, said that the extension of the Corps's sector was not possible until 21st Panzer Division was available.[114] (21st Panzer was then attacking east of the Orne.) A signal from GC and CS on 21 June gave the Orne as I SS Panzer Corps's right boundary on the previous day.[115] The boundary of the sectors held on 22 June by 21st Panzer, 12th SS Panzer and Panzer Lehr Divisions under I SS Panzer Corps were given in a

---

108. ibid, KV 9075 of 21 June.
109. DEFE 3/177, KV 9313 of 23 June.
110. ibid, KV 9374 of 24 June.
111. DEFE 3/176, KV 9073 of 21 June.
112. ibid, KV 9120 of 22 June.
113. ibid, KV 9241 of 22 June.
114. DEFE 3/175, KV 8791 of 19 June.
115. DEFE 3/176, KV 9058 of 21 June.

signal from GC and CS very early on 23 June.[116] SS Standarten-führer Kurt Meyer's appointment on 15 June to command 12th SS Panzer Division was known from high-grade Sigint on 21 June.[117]

A signal from GC and CS at 2033 on 22 June reported that LXXXVI Corps had taken over the Seine-Orne sector by 0600 on 20 June.[118] Information of 21 June, signalled by GC and CS in the afternoon of 24 June, gave the Seine as the new boundary between Seventh and Fifteenth Armies, and the Orne as the boundary between LXXXVI Corps and I SS Panzer Corps.[119] Information from a message sent very early on 25 June, signalled by GC and CS at 1010 that morning, listed 711st Infantry Division, 346th Infantry Division and Battle Group Luck (of 21st Panzer Division) as subordinated to LXXXVI Corps, with 16th GAF Field Division being brought up. The Seine and the Orne were the Corps boundaries. The boundaries of 711th and 346th Divisions were also given.[120]

As for the continuation of the German build-up, local sources had reported by 20 June that 1st SS Panzer Division had finally left Belgium by rail between 17 and 19 June. On 20 June, when the decrypt of a signal of the previous day disclosed that on reaching its assembly area it would be subordinated to I SS Panzer Corps, which had its HQ at Baron, 21st Army Group expected it to reach the front on 21 June with (on the strength of a decrypt of a signal from C-in-C West of 25 May) about 100 tanks.[121] A decrypt on the evening of 21 June confirmed that it was moving up and was under I SS Panzer Corps.[122] On 20 June 276th Infantry and 16th GAF Field Divisions, whose departure from Bordeaux and the Dutch coast respectively had already been reported by the Enigma,* were believed to be arriving, as was 48th Infantry, which was reported, incorrectly, to have left Belgium on 16 and 17 June.[123] On the other hand, a decrypt of the morning of 20 June disclosed that remnants of 716th Infantry were being withdrawn and railed from Le Mans to First Army; it was to proceed to Le Mans by lorry and on foot at night, using side roads from Argentan because of the movement of 'large formations' in the

---

* See above, p 186.

116. ibid, KV 9241 of 23 June.
117. ibid, KV 9060 of 21 June.
118. ibid, KV 9205 of 22 June.
119. DEFE 3/177, KV 9393 of 24 June.
120. ibid, KV 9491 of 25 June.
121. WO 171/129, No 134 of 20 June; DEFE 3/175, KV 8881 of 20 June.
122. DEFE 3/176, KV 9058 of 21 June.
123. WO 171/129, No 134 of 20 June.

opposite direction.[124] 21st Army Group believed that one or two other divisions, notably 352nd Infantry, were so weakened that they might be withdrawn.[125]

Decrypts issued on 21 June reported that Seventh Army had 2nd SS Panzer Division in reserve in the area Torigny-sur-Vire – Canisy – Tessy-sur-Vire on 18 June and that 353rd Infantry, less elements already committed, was to be brought forward to Périers as LXXXIV Corps Reserve.[126] On 22 and 23 June, the Enigma established that 116th Panzer still showed no signs of moving from Fifteenth Army's area.[127] 21st Army Group placed 1st SS Panzer north of Thury Harcourt as I SS Panzer Corps Reserve on 23 June. It was then expecting the early arrival not only of 16th GAF from Holland and 276th Infantry from Bayonne, but also of 277th Infantry from Narbonne; PR had detected railway activity in its area as well as in that of 276th Infantry, and a ground source had reported that it was due to move on 21 June. It also noted on 23 June reports of movement into the Nancy area of a formation from Germany, possibly 10th SS Panzer returning from Russia, and evidence of other movements from Germany, possibly of one or two training formations coming forward to release 'better stuff' for Normandy.[128]

This information was confirmed and amplified by high-grade Sigint during 24 June. A signal from GC and CS at 0645 revealed that 27 trains of II SS Panzer Corps and 9th SS Panzer Division had arrived in C-in-C West's area by 18 June, 21 of them at Nancy.[129] This was followed at 1015 by a signal carrying an important budget of information dated 21 June. Seventy-eight trains of II SS Panzer Corps and 9th SS Panzer Division had reached C-in-C West's area, of which 62 had unloaded at Nancy and ten at Dreux, west of Paris. The assembly area for the elements which had arrived was Laigle-Nogent le Rotrou-Alençon.* Another 62 trains carrying 10th SS Panzer Division had also arrived: 47 of them had unloaded in the Saarbrücken – Nancy area and 15 at Dreux. The main body of 353rd Division was level with St Lo. Two trains of 276th Division had unloaded at Le Mans and nine south of Angers; personnel were on the march to the

---

* A GAF decrypt on 24 June disclosed that air cover was bring promised that morning to protect Army deployment on the line Alençon-Nogent le Rotrou-Chartres.[130]

124. DEFE 3/175, KV 8885 of 20 June.
125. WO 171/129, No 134 of 20 June.
126. DEFE 3/176, KV 9009 of 21 June.
127. ibid, KV 9125 of 22 June; DEFE 3/177, KV 9337 of 23 June.
128. WO 171/129, No 135 of 23 June.
129. DEFE 3/177, KV 9364 of 24 June.
130. ibid, KV 9365 of 24 June.

area Domfront – Flers; there were three trains in Tours and six more on the way. A battle group of 266th Infantry Division had arrived south-east of Avranches and four trains of 16th GAF Field Division had unloaded west of Paris.[131] Decrypts of further signals of 24 June, issued by GC and CS at 1453, dealt with 277th Infantry Division. The elements of the Division unloaded so far comprised two Grenadier Regiments (less one battalion each), four batteries and an Engineer Company. This third bulletin from GC and CS added that there was a heavy artillery unit with three batteries in the area south of Lisieux, the remainder being 35 kilometres north-west of Le Mans, and that other heavy artillery units, 1192, 1193, 1194 and 1198, were assembling round Tours, Angers and Thouars.[132]

21st Army Group's intelligence summary for 24 June noted the infantry reserves drawn from Brittany, Holland and southern France and the strategic reinforcement in the shape of II SS Panzer Corps with 9th and 10th SS Panzer Divisions. It thought that the Corps would probably be joined by a Panther battalion and a Tiger battalion and be deployed according to need in the 'Panzer cockpit', between Caumont and Caen, and in the St Lo area, where a strong Allied drive would endanger the troops of LXXXIV Corps at the base of the peninsula.[133]

Early on 25 June high-grade Sigint added information from the decrypt of a report from C-in-C West of 18 June: Werfer Brigade 9 had arrived south-west of Paris; all trains of 1st SS Panzer Division's Panther unit had left; 34 trains of 363rd Division and 12 trains with elements of 6th Parachute Division had arrived in Fifteenth Army's area; and 276th Division's sector (in the Bayonne area) had been taken over by an *ad hoc* regiment.[134] At 1010 a very prompt decrypt which gave LXXXVI Corps's order of battle early on 25 June, revealed that 16th GAF Field Division was being brought up to the Corps.[135] A signal from GC and CS in the afternoon indicated that a battle group of 11th Panzer Division near Bordeaux might have been on the move on 22 June.[136]

Enigma decrypts covered the adjustments the enemy made to his tactical dispositions between 18 and 23 June as fully as it covered the movements of his reinforcements – so fully, as we shall now see, that when Operation *Epsom* was launched the only major uncertainty about the German order of battle concerned the

131. ibid, KV 9378 of 24 June.
132. ibid, KV 9395 of 24 June.
133. WO 171/129, No 136 of 24 June.
134. DEFE 3/177, KV 9473 of 25 June.
135. ibid, KV 9491 of 25 June.
136. DEFE 3/178, KV 9537 of 25 June.

precise whereabouts of 1st SS Panzer Division and of II SS Panzer Corps with 9th and 10th SS Panzer Divisions. 21st Army Group's intelligence summary of 26 June noted that 1st SS Panzer Division had not been committed piecemeal, but had been assembling with the van of 9th and 10th SS Panzer Divisions south of the road Argentan – Dreux 'in the concealment of the *bocage*, yet faithfully reported, north-west of the Orleans gap . . .'. It suggested that Rommel might use this 'formidable reserve' for his long-delayed counter-attack and added that 'a normally good source'* had given 27 June as the day chosen for it.[137] In the event, as we shall see, 1st SS Panzer Division and II SS Panzer Corps attacked the Odon salient on the afternoon of 29 June.†

□

On 23 June I Corps attacked in the Orne bridgehead where it captured and held St Honorine la Chardonnerette. XXX Corps followed on 25 June. Its task was to protect the right flank of VIII Corps by first seizing the line Rauray-Vendes-Juvigny, and then exploiting south to the Noyers area. It made some progress on the right towards Vendes, but Fontenay le Pesnil was only cleared during the night and the spur north of Rauray was still in German hands when VIII Corps attacked on 26 June from the front held by 3rd Canadian Division between Bronay and Bretteville l'Orgueilleuse. VIII Corps's task was to force the crossings of the Odon and the Orne and establish itself on high ground north-east of Bretteville-sur-Laize commanding the roads to Caen from the south. As its advance progressed I Corps would support its eastern flank by capturing Carpiquet. VIII Corps met strong resistance on the line St Mauvieu-La Gaule-Cheux-Le Haut du Bosq. The advance resumed on 27 June: no progress was made towards Grainville, but the capture of Colleville, Tourville and Mondrainville opened the way for leading elements of 11th Armoured Division to cross the bridge over the Odon near Tourmauville and advance to the lower slopes of Hill 112.[138]

On 28 June VIII Corps held the Tourmauville bridgehead and captured another bridge near Gavrus, but the road between Gavrus and Le Valtru remained in German hands. VIII Corps now held a salient five miles deep but less than two miles wide which was threatened on both sides. XXX Corps captured Rauray

---

* We have found no clue to the source of this information.
† See below, p 195 ff.

137. WO 171/129, No 137 of 26 June.
138. Ellis, op cit, pp 274–280.

on 27 June, but had lost Brettevillette, and an attack by I Corps aimed at Carpiquet had been brought to a standstill north of Epron. Prisoners had been taken from 2nd Panzer and 1st and 2nd SS Panzer Divisions. II SS Panzer Corps with 9th and 10th SS Panzer Divisions was believed to be approaching. It was therefore decided to await the counter-attacks which appeared to be building up. These began during the afternoon of 29 June towards Cheux and Le Valtru, and south of the Odon in the Baron area. Elements of both 9th and 10th SS Panzer Divisions were identified. VIII Corps withdrew that night from its advanced positions in the Baron area and at Hill 112 and was disposed in strength to hold the rest of the salient. After a quiet day on 30 June the German counter-attacks were renewed on 1 July, first south and then north of the Odon. They were met by very strong artillery concentrations and were finally repulsed. Their failure marked the end of the *Epsom* battle.[139]

Intelligence as a whole performed reasonably well during the *Epsom* battle. Except that DF consistently supplied valuable locations, Army Y was now in the doldrums; information from VHF was so far negligible despite intensive search and low-grade MF was pretty well confined to 21st Panzer Division's Reconnaissance Battalion.[140] But high-grade Sigint continued to come in large volume and without much delay.

XXX Corps's attack on 25 June was reflected in reports from 12th SS Panzer and Panzer Lehr Divisions on the same day and signalled by GC and CS at 1519 on 26 June. 12th SS Panzer reported 'drum fire' and Allied reinforcements at the point of penetration. Panzer Lehr had sustained heavy losses in the early morning. After hours of barrage fire, which had flattened the main defence line, the Allies had broken through in the Fontenay sector.[141]

The afternoon and evening of 26 June brought German reactions after VIII Corps's attack that morning. At 1754 GC and CS signalled that I SS Panzer Corps thought the main threat lay to the south of Le Mesnil Patry and wanted German fighters to counter continuous low-level attacks by Allied aircraft.[142] A signal from GC and CS at 2038 carried a suggestion by an unknown authority that Allied reinforcement of the Orne bridgehead indicated that in the event of success west of Caen the Allies intended to by-pass the town east of the Orne.[143] Jagdkorps II's

---

139. Ibid, pp 281–285.
140. *History of Sigint in the Field*, p 173.
141. DEFE 3/178, KV 9619 of 26 June.
142. ibid, KV 9692 of 26 June.
143. ibid, KV 9710 of 26 June.

intentions for 27 June – the protection of German movements and support of the defensive battle with the main effort in the area of Panzer Lehr and 12th SS Panzer Divisions – were signalled by GC and CS at 2248.[144] The decrypt of a situation report made at 1430, evidently by I SS Panzer Corps, was signalled at 2335; there was heavy fighting at an Allied penetration east of Juvigny and the front line was approximately St Mauvieu-Cheux-Tessel Bretteville-Vendes-centre of Juvigny. Single Allied tanks had reached the railway near Granville. The Allies had made a penetration north-west of Hottot. The extension of the battle to the whole Corps area seemed probable.[145] But as we have seen,* the Allies were expecting a long delayed counter-attack from the three Panzer divisions concealed in the *bocage*.

At 0601 on 27 June GC and CS signalled a situation report made at 2230 the previous evening. This spoke of heavy fighting in which Allied armoured thrusts had reached the railway near Mouen and gave the German front line as running from north-west of Carpiquet via Château Marcelet, the railway north of Mouen, Noyers and Vendes to Juvigny.[146] At 1345 GC and CS signalled the decrypt of a message, thought to be from the Flivo with 10th SS Panzer Division, stating that at 0800 that morning the Division was 'moving up, duration of march 4 to 5 days'.[147] At 1536 GC and CS reported the position of Panzer Lehr's battle headquarters at 1115 that morning.[148] Signals at 1738 and 1755 carried reports made at 1130 by 12th SS Panzer Division on the Allied attack and its own front line.[149] Signals at 1914 and 1923 gave Jagdkorps II's intention to protect German movements during the night 27–28 June and to support operations in the Tilly area on 28 June.[150] Second Army's intelligence summary reported that a battalion of tanks from 2nd Panzer Division and reconnaissance elements from 21st Panzer Division had joined in the battle. The latter were identified by Army Y. But 1st SS Panzer Division was still not in evidence and uncertainty about the whereabouts of 9th and 10th SS Panzer Divisions continued in spite of air reconnaissance.[151]

---

* See above, p 194.

144. ibid, KV 9726 of 26 June.
145. ibid, KV 9735 of 26 June.
146. DEFE 3/179, KV 9771 of 27 June.
147. ibid, KV 9806 of 27 June.
148. ibid, KV 9826 of 27 June.
149. ibid, KVs 9839 and 9840 of 27 June.
150. ibid, KVs 9844 and 9846 of 27 June.
151. WO 285/3, No 234 of 27 June; WO 171/129, No 138 of 28 June, Part II, Appendix X.

Intelligence from I Corps's front north of Caen was signalled by GC and CS very early on 28 June. This was the decrypt of a report made by 21st Panzer Division at 1900 the previous evening about operations in the area of Château le Londel; it had repulsed five attacks and there were heavy losses on both sides.[152] In another report at 0900 on 28 June, signalled by GC and CS at 1301, 21st Panzer Division asked for fighter cover over the battle at the critical point in the Epron area.[153] In a message at 1100, signalled by GC and CS at 1436, JK II told 21st Panzer that on Seventh Army's orders its efforts had to be concentrated elsewhere.[154]

An emergency signal from GC and CS at 1340 on 28 June reported that 12th SS Panzer Division had intended at 0400 that morning to regain the defence line along the railway.[155] At 2058 GC and CS issued the decrypt of a message from the Flivo with 10th SS Panzer Division stating that at 1130 the Division was moving and that his station would re-open at 0430 on 29 June.[156] Jagdkorps II's operational intentions for 29 June were signalled by GC and CS at 2111.[157] During the day Second Army identified both PG regiments of 2nd SS Panzer Division in the Tessel Bretteville area, and 2nd Panzer Division's Panther tanks in the Vendes area. The presence of infantry belonging to 1st SS Panzer Division in the Gavrus area was established in the evening.[158]

At 0435 on 29 June GC and CS reported that LXXXVI Corps considered that the assembly of tanks at Escoville and Ste Honorine in the Orne bridgehead and heavy traffic over the Orne bridge (at Bénouville) indicated an attack south or possibly east.[159] This was followed by the information at 0728 that at 2100 on 28 June LXXXVI Corps was subordinated to Panzer Gruppe West,* that 21st Panzer Division was under LXXXVI Corps and that the latter's western boundary ran from Luc-sur-Mer, through Epron and west of Caen.[161] At 1335 GC and CS informed the Commands of a message at 0500 that morning in which 9th SS Panzer Division's Flivo reported that it was moving to attack that morning.

---

* A decrypt of 2 July was to confirm that Panzer Gruppe West was again operational; it had assumed command on 29 June under Seventh Army of LXXXVI, I and II SS Panzer and XLVII Panzer Corps.[160]

152. DEFE 3/179, KV 9884 of 28 June.
153. ibid, KV 9918 of 28 June.
154. ibid, KV 9928 of 28 June.
155. ibid, KV 9923 of 28 June.
156. ibid, KV 9973 of 28 June.
157. ibid, KV 9975 of 28 June.
158. WO 285/3, No 24 of 28 June.
159. DEFE 3/48, XL 27 of 29 June.
160. DEFE 3/49, XL 426 of 2 July.
161. DEFE 3/48, XL 44 of 29 June.

At 0900 the attack had been postponed.[162] A signal from GC and CS at 1432 reported that Panzer Lehr had been put under XLVII Panzer Corps,[163] and another at 1704 listed 1st, 9th, 10th and 12th SS Panzer Divisions as subordinated to I SS Panzer Corps from noon.[164] However, the decrypt of a message from the Flivo with Panzer Lehr at 1230, signalled by GC and CS at 2106, while confirming that the division had been under XLVII Panzer Corps from 2000 on 28 June, gave its right-hand neighbour as II SS Panzer Corps.[165] At 2344 GC and CS signalled information that at 1000 II SS Panzer Corps had moved up across the line Bougy-Brettevillette.[166] 21st Army Group's intelligence summary for the day declared that the need to contain the British salient had spoilt Rommel's plan for a large-scale attack. First it had drawn in infantry of 2nd SS Panzer Division and tanks of 2nd Panzer Division, and then infantry of 1st SS Panzer Division. Finally Rommel had impatiently rushed the Panzer divisions from the east into battle.[167]*

During 29 June GC and CS reported that GAF intentions included the destruction of the Orne bridge at Bénouville, and just before midnight that the Flivo with LXXXVI Corps was requesting this urgently as an Allied attack from the bridgehead was expected.[169]

At 0546 on 30 June GC and CS reported that according to JK II at 1630 on 29 June Allied fighter-bomber attacks had considerably delayed the bringing up of strong forces.[170] At 0655 GC and CS signalled that orders by 5th Jagd Division for 30 June stated that every available aircraft was to be used to support the Army in operations at 0430, 0830, 1230 and 1700.[171] Another signal at 1244 reported that 5th Jagd Division had told unit commanders that the Army was heavily engaged and needed full fighter support. They were to stake all to reach the battle with strong

---

* In the afternoon of 29 June a German officer was taken prisoner carrying plans of the counter-attack for which he was reconnoitring. In the counter-attack, which began at about 1800, tanks and infantry attacked astride the Noyers-Cheux road and a few tanks managed to reach Cheux before being knocked out. The rest of the attacking troops were driven back, the situation was restored and the holding troops re-organised.[168]

162. ibid, XL 70 of 29 June.
163. ibid, Xl 77 of 29 June.
164. ibid, XL 102 of 29 June.
165. ibid, XL 128 of 29 June.
166. ibid, XL 151 of 29 June.
167. WO 171/129, No 139 of 29 June.
168. Ellis, op cit, Vol I, p 283; D'Este, op cit, p 242.
169. DEFE 3/48, XLs 9 and 123 of 29 June.
170. ibid, XL 175 of 30 June.
171. ibid, Xl 176 of 30 June.

forces and direct their main effort against fighter-bombers and in aircraft-spotting for artillery.[172] Information that 10th SS Panzer Division intended to attack at Baron at mid-day and that 9th SS Panzer Division intended to attack towards Cheux that night was signalled at 1651 and 1612.[173] (The latter's attack did not take place and a signal the next day revealed that this was because its regimental and divisional staffs had been partly put out of action by artillery and bombing.)[174] At 1714 GC and CS informed the Commands that according to the Flivo with Panzer Lehr that morning the Division was to be gradually relieved by 276th Infantry Division.[175] The decrypt of a request by 9th SS Panzer Division for air support at first light in the area Cheux-Marcelet and north thereof was signalled by GC and CS at 1949.[176]

In signals at 1534 and 2159 on 1 July GC and CS informed the Commands that 12th SS Panzer Division's Panzer Regiment had been relieved by the Panzer Regiment of 10th SS Panzer Division, and that the relief of Panzer Lehr Division by 276th Infantry Division was continuing.[177] During the day GC and CS also reported that Panzer Lehr was intercepting the W/T reports made by Allied reconnaissance units – these showed an almost complete coverage of the battle and assembly area between Caen and Villers-Bocage, constantly giving targets for Allied artillery and bombing[178] – and that on 29 June Panzer Gruppe West had told GOC Flak Korps III that on 28 June his batteries had played an important part in blocking the deep penetration in 12th SS Panzer Division's sector and stopping a tank breakthrough to the Orne. They had suffered and inflicted considerable losses.[179]

□

On 24 June, advised that the massive armoured counter-attack on the bridgehead which he ordered on 17 June could not begin till 5 July, Hitler had asked Rundstedt to consider carrying out in the next few days an attack against the rear of the US forces investing Cherbourg. Rundstedt had refused after conferring with Rommel: all the approaching reinforcements might be needed to destroy the offensive the Allies were preparing around

---

172. ibid, XL 198 of 30 June.
173. ibid, XLs 227 and 229 of 30 June.
174. DEFE 3/49, XL 362 of 1 July.
175. DEFE 3/48, XL 230 of 30 June.
176. ibid, XL 249 of 30 June.
177. DEFE 3/49, XLs 362 and 411 of 1 July.
178. ibid, XL 378 of 1 July.
179. ibid, XL 368 of 1 July.

and to the west of Caen. On 27 June, the day on which VIII Corps crossed the Odon, Rundstedt had submitted that his forces west of the Vire might soon be encircled unless he and Rommel were given a free hand to make extensive adjustments to the front, thus questioning Hitler's insistence that every inch of ground must be rigidly defended pending the counter-attack. On 29 June, in a conference at Berchtesgaden, Hitler had agreed with Rundstedt and Rommel that an attack on the Americans was not possible until the British thrust through Baron to the Orne had been stopped. Returning to learn that Panzer Gruppe West and Seventh Army were advocating the immediate evacuation of Caen and withdrawal to a line beyond the range of naval guns, the two Commanders had endorsed these recommendations and had requested freedom to act on them, but Hitler had insisted that there was to be no withdrawal. He dismissed Rundstedt on 2 July and Schweppenburg on 4 July, replacing them with Field Marshal Kluge and General Eberbach.

On 8 July he issued a new directive. It forecast further Allied landings between the Seine and the Somme and on the French Mediterranean coast, allowed that a surprise attack on one of the Brittany ports was possible and recognised that 'the present relative strengths of the opposing forces, and the fact that the majority of all our mobile formations are already committed, preclude for the time being any major offensive aimed at the destruction of the enemy in the bridgehead.' But it insisted that, 'Nevertheless in no circumstances may the bridgehead be allowed to increase in size . . . otherwise our forces would prove inadequate to contain it and the enemy will break out into the interior of France where we do not possess any comparable tactical mobility with which to oppose him'.[180]

The directive was followed by a message issued for promulgation to all officers. On every front the keynote of the fighting must be to gain time, which would enable Germany to bring about an equilibrium of forces particularly in the air. Fighter production was highly satisfactory. Heavy tanks, assault guns and the development of the flying bomb, the long-range rocket and new types of U-boat afforded great hope. A few months might be decisive. Every square kilometre must be defended tenaciously.

Except that the message to all officers was decrypted on 11 July,[181] the Allies learned nothing of these exchanges. But decrypts had disclosed by 4 July that the Germans still feared landings between the Seine and the Somme and on the French

---

180.   Ellis, op cit, Vol I, pp 295–297, 319–322.
181.   DEFE 3/54, XL 1589 of 11 July.

Mediterranean coast and, possibly, a surprise attack to capture one of the large Brittany ports – the threats to which Hitler drew attention in his directive.

In telegrams decrypted on 23 June the Japanese embassy in Berlin had reported that on the basis of POW remarks and captured documents OKW believed that Patton had 23 divisions, and that this was one reason why the Germans had 'so far refrained from pouring their reserves into Normandy'; for their own part, the Japanese believed that the fact that the Allies were continuing to develop the Normandy bridgehead might soon force the Germans to commit their resources on the assumption that the present invasion represented the main Allied effort.[182] These decrypts were followed by an appreciation by FHW dated 22 June: over and above 21st Army Group's formations – between 22 and 24 divisions in Normandy and between 10 and 12 in reserve – FUSAG had some 28 large formations in south-east England; the employment of FUSAG in Brittany was unlikely; but a *coup de main* to seize Brest could not be ruled out.[183]

On 26 June GC and CS issued the decrypt of a signal from the Japanese Naval Mission about an interview with Meisel on 19 June. Meisel had believed that further large-scale landings were no longer likely in the immediate future as the Allies had used 60 per cent of their airborne strength in Normandy, though such landings, possibly between Calais and Le Havre and in the south of France, were undoubtedly being planned. In these circumstances Germany was now trying to get a large proportion of her reserves – though not all of them – into Normandy, but was being gravely handicapped by Allied air and naval bombardment. He had added that Germany had failed in her original intention to destroy the Allies at the water's edge, and that it was difficult to foresee the future.[184] On 22 June, in a telegram decrypted on 28 June, the Japanese Ambassador had reported that, while many voices were raised in favour of a quick counter-offensive in Normandy, the German High Command still felt that the main task was to meet the main body which the Allies had not yet landed;[185] and on 24 June, in another telegram also decrypted on 28 June, he had given it as his personal view that since Patton was waiting to land, it would be dangerous for Germany to put strong reserves into Normandy.[186] In this telegram he had added that it was uncertain whether the Allies would make their further

---

182. BAY/KVs 231 and 232 of 23 June.
183. DEFE 3/48, XL 103 of 29 June.
184. BAY/KV 243 of 26 June.
185. BAY/KV 244 of 28 June.
186. BAY/KV 248 of 28 June.

landing soon, in conjunction with a renewed offensive in Normandy, or defer it until Cherbourg was in use and the bridgehead had been extended to the high ground round Le Havre, and that the Germans felt the former course very likely; in either case they were determined to counter with a general offensive even though this would require sacrifices on other fronts.

Three decrypts had been issued on 1 July. The first, a circular sent out on 27 June by the German Ministry of Foreign Affairs, announced that the Allies had been unable to carry out their promise to Russia to attack with a second invasion army, but that, though postponed, a further landing was still to be expected.[187] The second was another telegram from the Japanese embassy dated 27 June to the effect that Patton's army was expected to land in the near future, probably in the area from the beachhead to Le Havre.[188] The third was a C-in-C West appreciation of 26 June: the C-in-C believed that beyond their immediate objective in Normandy the Allies probably intended to use FUSAG in successive waves for landings on both sides of the Somme, with the object of capturing Le Havre and developing in conjunction with 21st Army Group a pincer movement against Paris on both sides of the Seine, and also to use between 12 and 14 divisions in north Africa for landings on the Mediterranean coast. He went on to express grave anxiety. The reserves behind Fifteenth Army were likely to be inadequate for defence against the strong airborne landings that were to be expected, and the mobile reserves there were insufficient for a massive counter-attack. In the south Nineteenth Army's reserves consisted only of 9th Panzer Division, which was not yet fully mobile, and Assault Brigade 341; in the event of a landing there the fact that the French forces had proved themselves in Italy might exert great psychological effect on the Resistance movement, which was increasing its activities. In the event of German reverses it had to be faced that the revolt which had been prepared might well break out.[189]

In a signal of 2 July, decrypted the same day, C-in-C West had ordered the greatest alarm readiness and reinforced patrols during the next few days. There had been a remarkable increase of traffic on the French and Belgian wireless networks, and French and British signals to parachutists in France revealed advance warnings of a landing similar to those that had been intercepted before D-day; there was no clue as to where landing might be made.[190] This decrypt was followed on 4 July by the

---

187. BAY/XL 4 of 1 July.
188. BAY/XL 7 of 1 July.
189. DEFE 3/48, XL 242 of 30 June; DEFE 3/49, XL 356 of 1 July.
190. DEFE 3/50, XL 502 of 2 July.

decrypt of an appreciation of 30 June in which Fremde Heere West expected the capture of Cherbourg to release landing craft for operations by Patton's Army Group. When and where the Army Group would be used remained unclear. The Allies were carrying out a war of nerves to tie down German forces on the Mediterranean coast; they would attack there when they recognised that the war of nerves was not succeeding. The Franco-Belgian Resistance organisations expected new Allied landings about 6 July, but FHW believed the second half of July to be 'more probable'.[191]

□

On 30 June General Montgomery issued a new directive. Second British Army was to hold the main enemy forces between Caen and Villers-Bocage, and 'develop operations for the capture of Caen . . . the sooner the better'. First US Army was to begin an offensive southwards on 3 July and then, pivoting on its left at Caumont, to swing eastwards to the general line Caumont-Vire-Mortain-Fougères. When the base of the Cotentin peninsula was reached, near Avranches, VIII US Corps on the right would turn westwards into Brittany. General Bradley would direct a strong right wing in a wide sweep south of the *bocage* country to secure successively the line Laval-Mayenne and Le Mans-Alençon.[192]

On 1 and 4 July German assessments of 21st Army Group's immediate objectives were obtained from the decrypts of the general appreciations issued by C-in-C West on 26 June and Fremde Heere West on 30 June. The C-in-C had expected the Allies to extend their bridgehead south-east from the Tilly area, to strengthen the Orne bridgehead as a pivot for operations to the east or south-east between the Orne and the Seine, and to attack the German front in the south of the Cotentin when the US divisions operating against Cherbourg became available; in this last sector they would seek to destroy the German forces north of the line Périers-Lessay and thrust to Coutances.[193] FHW had expected First Army to attack from the St Lo area, to cut off German forces west of Carentan, and then to advance south in the direction of Avranches-Domfront, its task being to protect the southern flank of the Army Group while Second Army sought a decision south of the Seine by thrusting eastwards.[194]

Decrypts in the first few days of July disclosed the progress to

---

191. ibid, XL 687 of 4 July.
192. Ellis op cit, Vol I, p 309.
193. DEFE 3/48, XL 242 of 30 June; DEFE 3/49, XL 356 of 1 July.
194. DEFE 3/50, XL 687 of 4 July.

the front up to 23 June of 16th GAF Field Division, 1st, 9th and 10th SS Panzer Divisions, II SS Panzer Corps with its Heavy Panzer Abteilung 102, 276th and 277th Infantry Divisions and four artillery units.[195] All these formations were already known to be arriving except Heavy Panzer Abteilung 102, now mentioned for the first time. A decrypt of 28 June had disclosed that Parachute Regiment 15 was being brought up from 5th Parachute Division in Brittany to be Army Group Reserve north of Périers; a decrypt of 2 July gave the locations of its battalions on 29 June.[196] Signals of 29 June, decrypted on 1 July, disclosed that 271st and 272nd Infantry Divisions were being transferred with utmost despatch to Army Group B from Army Group G, 271st to be stationed between the Seine and the Somme and 272nd south of the Seine on Panzer Gruppe West's right wing. In return for them Army Group G was to receive 716th Infantry Division, originally intended for First Army, and 352nd Infantry Division as soon as it was relieved.[197]

□

Between 3 and 18 July the Allies suffered heavy casualties in return for inconsiderable gains; but they knew from the close watch they were able to keep on the enemy's conduct of the battle that their attacks had tied down three armoured divisions (1st and 10th SS Panzer and 2nd Panzer) and elements of a fourth (9th SS Panzer), thus frustrating his attempt to deliver a counter-attack, and also that he had been forced to commit two others (Panzer Lehr and 2nd SS Panzer) against the US threat to St Lo.

Operations for the capture of Caen in pursuance of Montgomery's directive of 30 June began on 4 July with an attack on Carpiquet village and airfield. The former was captured; the latter was not and a further attempt was postponed until Caen itself was attacked on 8 July. As a prelude to the attack on Caen the rearward defences were bombed by the Strategic Air Force in the evening of 7 July. In fierce fighting on 8 and 9 July I Corps reached the Orne at Caen and the Odon above the junction of the two rivers.[198]

Meanwhile First US Army began an offensive to secure the line St Lo-Marigny-Coutances. On 3 July VIII Corps attacked southwards towards La Haye du Puits. On the next day VII Corps entered the battle in the Carentan sector aiming at Périers. On 7

---

195. DEFE 3/49, XLs 393 and 488 of 1 and 2 July.
196. DEFE 3/179, KV 9878 of 28 June; DEFE 3/49, XL 426 of 2 July.
197. DEFE 3/49, XLs 328, 332, 348 and 349 of 1 July.
198. Ellis, op cit, Vol I, pp 311–316.

July XIX Corps made assault crossings of the Vire and the Vire-Taute canal, and on 9 July thrust east of the Vire directly towards St Lo. LXXXIV Corps and II Parachute Corps resisted stubbornly, but by 5 July the position had become sufficiently threatening to make the Germans move Panzer Lehr, which had been relieved on the front held by XLVII Panzer Corps by 276th Infantry Division, to the west of St Lo, and 2nd SS Panzer Division from Army Reserve towards Périers.[199]

After a conference with his Army Commanders on 10 July Montgomery issued another directive. His broad policy continued to be to draw the main enemy forces into the battle on the east flank so that affairs on the western flank might proceed the easier. Second British Army was to operate strongly southwards with its left flank on the Orne to secure the general line Thury Harcourt-Mont Pinçon-Le Bény Bocage. It was to retain the ability to operate with a Corps of three armoured divisions east of the Orne in the general area between Caen and Falaise, and it was to be prepared to take over the sector from Caumont to the river Drôme from First US Army at 24 hours' notice. First US Army was to pivot on its left and swing south and east to the general line Le Bény Bocage-Vire-Mortain-Fougères. On reaching Avranches VIII Corps was to turn west into Brittany, directed on Rennes and St Malo. Plans were to be made for a wide sweep south of the *bocage* country to Laval-Mayenne and Le Mans-Alençon successively. Third US Army was to be ready to take control of operations on the extreme western flank and would have the task of clearing the whole of the Brittany peninsula.[200]

Between 10 and 12 July a battle was fought by Second Army to expand the bridgehead south of the Odon by the capture of Eterville, Maltot and Hill 112. Eterville and half of Hill 112 were captured, but little ground was gained and casualties were heavy.[201]

When the *Epsom* attacks ended the dispositions of the German armoured divisions in the line were, from right to left, 21st Panzer with elements both sides of the Orne, 12th SS Panzer in the Caen sector, 9th and 10th SS Panzer facing the Odon salient, Panzer Lehr in the Noyers sector and 2nd Panzer in the Caumont sector. 2nd SS Panzer was Army Group Reserve west of the Vire. 1st SS Panzer had also reached the front, and elements had been identified around Gavrus in the Odon salient, but its precise whereabouts remained uncertain.

21st Army Group's intelligence summary for 1 July noted that

---

199. ibid, pp 318, 319.
200. ibid, p 327; WO 285/2 (Dempsey Papers).
201. Ellis, op cit, p 317.

although 21st Panzer Division had sent elements to the Odon salient it was still heavily involved east of the Orne, where, according to POW information of uncertain reliability, one of its PG regiments was being relieved by 16th GAF Field Division.[202] The summary for 3 July said that the exact layout of 21st Panzer was no longer clear. The reinforced PG regiment east of the Orne was being relieved by elements of 16th GAF Field Division, while other elements had been identified opposite the Odon salient. It was some measure of the success of Operation *Epsom* that the enemy layout had become 'so messy'.[203] Very early on 5 July GC and CS signalled a new location for 21st Panzer,[204] and 21st Army Group's intelligence summary that day described the Division as 'wholly in reserve' having been relieved by 16th GAF Field Division.[205] But on 7th July Second Army thought that the relief was still in progress. Y had placed units formerly in the Colombelles area at Argences, and a headquarters, which had been in Caen, near Troarn.[206] The attack on Caen on 8 July encountered elements of 21st Panzer Division backing up 16th GAF Field Division north of the town.[207] On 10 July prisoners taken by Second Army 'confirmed the impression' that the relief of 21st Panzer Division had not been completed and that only part of it was in reserve.[208] At 0417 on 10 July GC and CS signalled that by 2100 the previous evening 16th GAF Field Division was subordinated to 21st Panzer Division east of the Orne.[209] Another GC and CS signal in the evening gave 21st Panzer's sector from Colombelles north-east of Caen on the right via Giberville, Le Mesnil-Frémental and Le Poirier to the southern exit from Caen.[210] On the next day 21st Army Group commented that the enemy 'had been trying to have it both ways: not to yield ground, yet to have armour in reserve'. But 'every time a Panzer Division gets relief it is back in the battle to plug a hole somewhere else'. 21st Panzer Division was one of four armoured divisions partially in reserve which had been dragged back into the fighting.[211]* On 13 July 21st Panzer's PG regiments were in the front line east and

---

* The others were 1st SS, Panzer Lehr and 2nd SS. See below, pp 207–210.

202. WO 171/131, 21st Army Group Intelligence Summary No 140 of 1 July.
203. ibid, No 141 of 3 July.
204. DEFE 3/51, XL 832 of 5 July.
205. WO 171/131 No 142 of 5 July.
206. WO 285/3, No 33 of 7 July.
207. WO 171/131, No 143 of 8 July.
208. WO 285/3, No 36 of 10 July.
209. DEFE 3/53, XL 1455 of 10 July.
210. DEFE 3/54, XL 1518 of 10 July.
211. WO 171/131, No 144 of 11 July.

south of Caen while its tanks were thought to be in reserve around Vimont.[212]

At the end of June 12th SS Panzer Division, which had borne the initial brunt of *Epsom*, held the sector west and south of Caen including Carpiquet village and airfield. In a message early on 3 July its Flivo quoted the intelligence view that a new attack was coming south-west of Caen.[213] Its intention at 2100 that evening, reported by GC and CS at 0125 on 4 July, was to hold its line.[214] Early next morning a penetration was admitted and further attacks were expected north-west of Carpiquet airfield.[215] In the evening GC and CS signalled a report that the Division had regained a key position for the defence of Caen, but that Carpiquet was still in Allied hands,[216] and at 2352 that the Division's intention for 6 July was to hold and develop its position.[217] 21st Army Group thought that elements of 1st SS Panzer Division had come in on its left in the area of Verson.[218] Around midnight on 9–10 July high-grade Sigint reported that part of 1st SS Panzer had come into the line south-west of Caen and that this Division, with elements of 12th SS Panzer, was occupying the new main defence line.[219] At 0912 on 10 July GC and CS signalled that, while elements of 12th SS Panzer were still fighting north of Caen, Flak was being moved to protect the assembly of the Division north of Falaise.[220] On 11 July the high-grade Sigint reported that the Division was being withdrawn for the time being and that by 1015 most of it was out of the line.[221] On 13 July 21st Army Group's intelligence summary referred to the withdrawal of the Division in order to sort itself out, and on 16 July the summary noted that it was the only formation uncommitted.[222] On 17 July high-grade Sigint reported that 12th SS Panzer was moving that day to the area Lisieux-Cambremer-Pont L'Evèque and required air cover.[223]

Elements of 1st SS Panzer Division had been contacted on 28 June near Gavrus in the Odon salient, but the Division continued to be elusive. On 3 and 4 July its whereabouts were unknown to

---

212. ibid, No 145 of 13 July.
213. DEFE 3/50, XL 599 of 3 July.
214. ibid, XL 648 of 4 July.
215. DEFE 3/51, XL 831 of 5 July.
216. ibid, XL 869 of 5 July.
217. ibid, XL 893 of 5 July.
218. WO 171/131, No 142 of 5 July.
219. DEFE 3/53, XLs 1437 and 1452 of 9 and 10 July.
220. ibid, XL 1471 of 10 July.
221. DEFE 3/54, XLs 1639 and 1657 of 11 July.
222. WO 171/131, Nos 145 and 146 of 13 and 16 July.
223. DEFE 3/57, XL 2383 of 17 July.

21st Army Group and Second Army.[224] On 5 July elements were thought to be on 12th SS Panzer's left in the Verson area.[225] The next evening high-grade Sigint reported its battle headquarters south of Caen, its assembly area, and that W/T silence had been ordered until contact was made with the Allies.[226] On 8 July 21st Army Group was still doubtful where the Division was, but on 9 July high-grade Sigint reported that it had occupied the main defence line from the east bank of the Orne to the confluence of the Orne and the Odon, and thence west through Louvigny.[227] On 11 July 21st Army Group noted with satisfaction that the Division had been dragged in to the battle south of Caen.[228] However, at 1514 on 15 July an emergency signal from GC and CS reported a message from its Flivo that morning stating that 272nd Infantry Division (arriving from the south of France) would be taking over next morning. 1st SS Panzer Division would stay close behind the front as Corps Reserve.[229] High-grade Sigint duly reported that by the evening of 16 July 272nd had taken over in the main defence line,[230] but what 21st Army group called 'the magnetic attraction of the Odon salient' drew elements of 1st SS Panzer Division again into the battle a little further west at Esquay, where prisoners were taken.[231]

In the *Epsom* battle II SS Panzer Corps with 9th and 10th SS Panzer Divisions had been committed against the Odon salient, 9th SS north of the river and 10th SS south of it. On 5 July 21st Army Group's intelligence summary placed them west and south of the salient, probably with 102nd Tiger Battalion in support.[232] At 0754 on 11 July GC and CS reported that, according to II SS Panzer Corps late the previous evening, 9th SS Panzer was being relieved by 277th Infantry Division,[233] and confirmation of the relief came from high-grade Sigint the next day.[234] Meanwhile, the same source had shown that 9th SS Panzer was being brought in south of the Odon to help 10th SS Panzer and 12th SS Panzer Divisions to repulse Second Army's attempt to extend the salient south-west towards the Orne.[235] A Flivo message sent at 0400 on

---

224. WO 171/131, No 141 of 3 July; WO 285/3, No 30 of 4 July.
225. WO 171/131, No 142 of 5 July.
226. DEFE 3/51, XL 999 of 6 July.
227. WO 171/131, No 143 of 8 July; DEFE 3/53, XL 1437 of 9 July.
228. WO 171/131, No 144 of 11 July.
229. DEFE 3/56, XL 2161 of 15 July.
230. DEFE 3/57, XL 2416 of 17 July.
231. WO 171/131, No 146 of 16 July.
232. ibid, No 142 of 5 July.
233. DEFE 3/54, XL 1583 of 11 July.
234. ibid, XL 1644 of 12 July.
235. ibid, XL 1568 of 11 July; DEFE 3/55, XL 1753 of 12 July.

13 July, the decrypt of which was issued in the evening, reported that 9th and 10th SS Panzer Divisions were expecting a large-scale Allied attack in both their sectors.[236] Elements of both Divisions were located by Y, and 21st Army Group's summary noted that 9th SS Panzer had been relieved by 277th Infantry Division, but had had to come back on 10th SS Panzer Division's right in the Maltot area.[237] At midday on 15 July 9th SS Panzer was again out of the fighting for the time being, according to its Flivo,[238] but another decrypt disclosed that by 1700 the next day it had been committed near Gavrus to stem the Allied thrust towards Noyers and Bougy.[239]

On 30 June high-grade Sigint had disclosed that Panzer Lehr, then under XLVII Panzer Corps, was to be relieved by the newly arrived 276th Infantry Division.[240] A Flivo message at 1200 on 5 July, signalled by GC and CS that evening, announced that 276th had taken over, but that a Panzer battalion and part of an anti-tank battalion of Panzer Lehr had remained in the sector under 276th Division; the main body of Panzer Lehr was in XLVII Panzer Corps Reserve to support either 276th or 2nd Panzer Division.[241] Decrypts on the next day confirmed Panzer Lehr's role and placed it in the area of Aunay;[242] but at 0654 on 8 July GC and CS signalled information from XLVII Panzer Corps's Flivo at 2300 the previous evening that the Division was transferring to the area west of St Lo. Elements had already started and the staff would move during the night 8–9 July.[243] Another Flivo message, sent at 1600 on 8 July and signalled to the Commands the same evening, gave the destination.[244] In its new sector the Division was at once fully occupied in resisting First US Army's drive against St Lo.

2nd Panzer Division in the Caumont sector under XLVII Panzer Corps sent help to its right-hand neighbour, Panzer Lehr, during the *Epsom* battle. During the first half of July its sector was comparatively quiet and intelligence sources had hardly anything to say about it.

2nd SS Panzer Division, in Army Reserve on the western flank, had also contributed units to stem the *Epsom* offensive. High-grade

---

236. DEFE 3/55, XL 1864 of 13 July.
237. WO 171/131, No 145 of 13 July.
238. DEFE 3/56, XL 2162 of 15 July.
239. DEFE 3/57, XL 2354 of 16 July.
240. DEFE 3/48, XL 230 of 30 June.
241. DEFE 3/51, XL 858 of 5 July.
242. DEFE 3/52, XLs 1005 and 1092 of 6 July.
243. ibid, XL 1196 of 8 July.
244. DEFE 3/53, XL 1283 of 8 July.

Sigint indicated that it was still in Army Reserve on 4 July,[245] but disclosed on 6 July that it had been subordinated to LXXXIV Corps.[246] During the next few days it was actively engaged all along the Corps front.[247] High-grade Sigint reported its reversion to Army Reserve on 10 July,[248] but the respite was brief, high-grade Sigint reporting two days later that it was assuming command both sides of the Carentan-Périers road.[249]

□

The news that 2nd SS Panzer and Panzer Lehr were being committed on the western flank was part of the very full intelligence disclosed by high-grade Sigint relating to the offensive opened by First US Army on 3 July.

On 2 and 3 July decrypts had given the order of battle of LXXXIV Corps as, from right to left, 17th SS PG, 77th, 91st (battle groups) and 243rd Divisions with 353rd Division in reserve, had located the Corps and divisional battle headquarters,[250] and had included a warning from II Parachute Corps of 1 July that even the best troops would be unable to stand up to the losses caused by the American artillery fire, which was continuously controlled by spotting aircraft.[251] II Parachute Corps's weekly report on the fighting value of its Parachute formations, made on 2 July and decrypted on 4 July, had placed them all in Category II (fit for limited offensive operations).[252] A report from C-in-C West of 30 June on the situation in this sector was also decrypted on 4 July: as the remnants of 352nd Division were completely exhausted and 3rd Parachute Division was no longer able to withstand a strong attack, there was a danger of a breakthrough into the flank of LXXXIV Corps, on II Parachute Corps's left, and he had therefore put a Panzer battalion of 2nd SS Panzer Division under II Parachute Corps for operations north of St Lo.[253]

The situation report issued by LXXXIV Corps on the evening of the first day of the offensive was decrypted on the morning of 4 July. It announced that the front had collapsed north-east of La Haye du Puits but that the breakthrough had been held by

---

245. DEFE 3/50, XL 723 of 4 July.
246. DEFE 3/52, XL 1023 of 6 July.
247. ibid, XL 1137 of 7 July; DEFE 3/53, XLs 1289, 1365 and 1468 of 9 and 10 July.
248. DEFE 3/53, XL 1468 of 10 July; DEFE 3/54, XL 1511 of 10 July.
249. DEFE 3/54, XL 1717 of 12 July.
250. DEFE 3/50, XLs 509 and 557 of 2 and 3 July.
251. ibid, XL 597 of 3 July.
252. ibid, XL 680 of 4 July.
253. ibid, XL 644 of 4 July.

committing a battalion of 353rd Division; for the time being all penetrations had been mopped up, or blocked, but the forces still holding out, and the reserves which had been committed, were worn out by the overwhelming US artillery fire. Much weakened by heavy losses the German troops would be in a bad way if the attacks continued.[254] Another decrypt of a message of 2200 on 3 July, signalled by GC and CS at 1346 on 4 July, reported LXXXIV Corps's intended defence line and disclosed that the battle group of 77th Division would take over control of sector and troops from the battle group of 91st Division, and that the rest of 353rd Division would be committed between 77th Division's battle group and 243rd Division.[255] A penetration in 243rd Division's sector, which the German forces were too weak to clear up, was reported in a message at 1100 on 4 July signalled by GC and CS at 1704 that evening.[256] That afternoon, in another signal decrypted the same evening, LXXXIV Corps insisted that GAF support was essential if the main defence line was to be held, particularly to deal with the spotting aircraft which directed fire on every movement and on artillery positions.[257]

A Flivo report on the battle up to 2100 on 4 July, signalled by GC and CS at 1703 on 5 July, was less alarmist, but nevertheless reported penetrations in the sectors of 77th and 243rd Divisions.[258] A message at 1500 on 5 July, signalled by GC and CS at 2154, disclosed that Parachute Regiment 15 and an artillery unit, both from 5th Parachute Division, had been subordinated to 77th Division and 17th SS PG Division respectively. Parachute Regiment 15 was to be deployed in depth on the left wing of 77th Divisions's battle group.[259] LXXXIV Corps's situation report at 1400 on 5 July, signalled by GC and CS soon after midnight, spoke of heavy fighting and high casualties.[260]

At 2255 on 6 July GC and CS informed the Commands that 2nd SS Panzer Division (which high-grade Sigint had placed in Army Reserve two days earlier)[261] had been subordinated to LXXXIV Corps by 0930 that morning, and was to co-operate with 77th Division's battle group and 353rd Division.[262] Information to the effect that at 1530 on 6 July a counter-attack was being prepared in 353rd Divisions's sector, where Parachute Regiment 15 was

---

254. ibid, XLs 639 and 686 of 4 July.
255. ibid, XL 697 of 4 July.
256. ibid, XL 711 of 4 July.
257. ibid, XL 742 of 4 July.
258. DEFE 3/51, XL 850 of 5 July.
259. ibid, XL 881 of 5 July.
260. ibid, XL 899 of 6 July.
261. DEFE 3/50, XL 723 of 4 July.
262. DEFE 3/52, XL 1027 of 6 July.

joining up with that Division to reoccupy the main defence line, and that 243rd Division had had considerable losses, was signalled by GC and CS very early on 7 July.[263] So too was information that (exceptionally) JK II's main effort on 6 July had been in the Lessay area where extremely strong Allied fighter activity had led to costly combats.[264]

The decrypt of a message from Panzer Lehr's Flivo at 2300 on 7 July announcing that the Division was transferring to the area west of St Lo, some elements being already on the way, was signalled by GC and CS at 0654 on 8 July.[265] Another Flivo message sent at 1600 giving the destination of the divisional staff was signalled at 2226.[266]

A decrypt of 8 July reporting that battle groups of 2nd SS Panzer Division were to attack penetrations in 17th SS PG's sector was available very early on 9 July.[267] A report that an attack by 17th SS PG Division's Panzer regiment had been halted with heavy losses was signalled by GC and CS in the evening.[268] Information that, even when there was little fighting, casualties in 3rd Parachute Division from artillery and mortars were up to a hundred dead daily was decrypted on 8 July.[269] Decrypts of reports on 8 July by LXXXIV Corps of Allied penetration at La Haye du Puits were signalled by GC and CS at 0928 and 1534 on 9 July.[270]

A message sent on the evening of 9 July and decrypted at 0022 on 10 July reported that Panzer Lehr was subordinated to LXXXIV Corps and gave its boundaries with II Parachute Corps on its right and 17th SS PG Division on its left.[271] Another decrypt signalled at 0426 disclosed that Panzer Lehr intended to attack the Allied bridgehead south of the Vire, probably that evening.[272] This intended attack was also reported by the Flivo with LXXXIV Corps in a message at 0215 on 10 July, signalled by GC and CS at 1403.[273] An emergency signal to the Commands at 1537 contained a report from Panzer Lehr at 1100 that its regiments were on the line Pont Hébert-Le Hommet-La Haye and that its intention was

---

263. ibid, XL 1043 of 7 July.
264. ibid, XL 1035 of 7 July.
265. ibid, XL 1196 of 8 July.
266. DEFE 3/53, XL 1283 of 8 July.
267. ibid, XL 1289 of 9 July.
268. ibid, XL 1416 of 9 July.
269. ibid, XL 1243 of 8 July.
270. ibid, XLs 1328 and 1383 of 9 July.
271. ibid, XL 1447 of 10 July.
272. ibid, XL 1456 of 10 July.
273. ibid, XL 1492 of 10 July.

to attack the Allied bridgehead south of the Vire-Taute canal at dusk.[274]

In a message of 2000 on 9 July, available at 0757 on 10 July, 2nd SS Panzer Division's Flivo reported that the Division was operating battle groups at all focal points of LXXXIV Corps's front, but that elements of the Division would be assembled during the night 9–10 July in the Périers sector at the disposal of Seventh Army.[275] Confirmation that by 1230 on 10 July 2nd SS Panzer (less elements operating) had left LXXXIV Corps and was in Army Reserve round Périers was signalled at 1511 the same day.[276] The Flivo claimed that the Division's battle groups had played a decisive part in preventing a breakthrough on LXXXIV Corps's front.[277]

Panzer Lehr's counter-attack had meanwhile been delayed until dawn on 1 July. It then ran into trouble, as was disclosed by decrypts at 1754 and 2044.[278]* 21st Army Group's intelligence summary for that day noted that the German left wing as being steadily forced back; 2nd SS Panzer Division had been committed in two sectors and Army Y had identified elements of Panzer Lehr west of St Lo.[281] At 1308 on 12 July GC and CS signalled that LXXXIV Corps's intention at 0838 that morning had been for Panzer Lehr to be on the defensive for the time being and for 2nd SS Panzer Division to take command both sides of the Carentan-Périers road.[282] 21st Army Group's intelligence summary for 13 July noted that Panzer Lehr had been hard hit and that 2nd SS Panzer Division had had to return to the battle.[283] Decrypts on 14 July reported that Panzer Lehr had had heavy losses in an Allied thrust on 12 July, as had 3rd Parachute Division on 13 July, when it had repulsed numerous attempts to break through to St Lo.[284]

A report by II Parachute Corps timed 2130 on 11 July was signalled at 1244 on 12 July; the Corps was trying to hold a new main defence line by scraping together the last reserves, but after

---

* In a message decrypted on 12 July the Flivo with LXXXIV Corps thought that Panzer Lehr had run into a concentration under XIX US Corps forming up for a breakthrough to the south.[279] It seems that this surmise was correct and that the repulse suffered by Panzer Lehr was not attributable to the warnings from high-grade Sigint.[280]

274. DEFE 3/54, XL 1502 of 10 July.
275. DEFE 3/53, XL 1468 of 10 July.
276. DEFE 3/54, XL 1511 of 10 July.
277. ibid, XL 1594 of 11 July.
278. ibid, XLs 1638, 1641 and 1661 of 11 July.
279. DEFE 3/55, XL 1756 of 12 July.
280. Blumenson, *Breakout and Pursuit* (Washington DC 1961), pp 134–138.
281. WO 171/131, No 144 of 11 July.
282. DEFE 3/54, XL 1717 of 12 July.
283. WO 171/131, No 145 of 13 July.
284. DEFE 3/55, XLs 1952 and 1956 of 14 July.

their heavy losses the troops would be unable to prevent Allied attempts on the same scale to break through to St Lo.[285] Two days later a decrypt described how Parachute Regiments 5 and 9 had been overrun, shot to pieces at their posts, by vastly superior forces.[286]

The decrypts of two messages early on 14 July from the Flivo with LXXXIV Corps were signalled by GC and CS in the evening. The first showed that Regiments 13 and 14 of 5th Parachute Division from Brittany were joining the battle. Parachute Regiment 13 was under 17th SS PG Division and a battalion of Parachute Regiment 14 was operating with Panzer Lehr.[287] In the second message the Flivo reported that successful defence could no longer be guaranteed. There had been high officer casualties and units were no longer standing their ground against extraordinarily heavy artillery fire and air attack.[288] Twenty-four hours later II Parachute Corps thought that a major attack in the area of 3rd Parachute Division to capture St Lo must be expected the next day. Because of the daily casualties strength was sinking to the point where even the bravest troops could not prevent a breakthrough.[289]

Decrypts on 17 and 18 July reported repeated withdrawals by Panzer Lehr which exposed II Parachute Corps's left flank.[290] On 17 July JK II was preparing to shift more effort into the area of penetration at St Lo, where II Parachute Corps was resisting desperately.[291] Reviewing its situation early on 18 July II Parachute Corps reported that at several points the Allies had thrust through units which were exhausted and severely reduced in numbers, and which had fought for weeks without relief.[292] The decrypt of this message was signalled by GC and CS at 0454 on 19 July, the day on which First US Army captured St Lo.

□

On 15 July, having approved on 12 July proposals for an offensive east of the Orne (Operation *Goodwood*), Montgomery issued an instruction defining the objects of the operation and the tasks of the four Corps that would take part. The final plan called

---

285. DEFE 3/54, XL 1713 of 12 July.
286. DEFE 3/55, XL 1948 of 14 July.
287. DEFE 3/56, XL 2028 of 14 July.
288. ibid, XL 2030 of 14 July.
289. ibid, XL 2201 of 15 July; DEFE 3/57, XL 2256 of 16 July.
290. DEFE 3/57, XLs 2377 and 2497 of 17 and 18 July.
291. ibid, XL 2375 of 17 July.
292. DEFE 3/58, XL 2659 of 19 July.

for preliminary operations by XII and XXX Corps between Caen and Tilly-sur-Seulles, one purpose of which was to persuade the Germans that Second Army intended to break out across the Orne between Caen and Amaye-sur-Orne. XII Corps was to secure a firm base on the Bougy-Evrecy road with a view to a subsequent advance towards Aunay-sur-Odon or Thury Harcourt; XXX Corps was to secure the Noyers area and be prepared to exploit the high ground east of Villers-Bocage; I Corps was to capture and hold the area Bures-St Pair-Emiéville-Touffreville. On 18 July, after a massive attack by the Strategic Air Force, VIII Corps with three armoured divisions would seize the area Bourguébus-Vimont-Bretteville-sur-Laize, and II Canadian Corps would establish a firm bridgehead on the general line Fleury-sur-Orne-Cormelles-Mondeville.[293] It was hoped that First US Army would begin a new offensive (Operation *Cobra*) on 19 July from a start-line west of St Lo. But as German resistance delayed the capture of St Lo till 19 July, *Cobra* had to be postponed.

When the preliminary operations for *Goodwood* began on the night of 15–16 July it was known that the Germans expected a major attack by Second Army. Signals to that effect from 21st Panzer Division, 10th SS Panzer Division and LXXXVI Corps were decrypted on 13 and 14 July.[294] There is no evidence, however, for the suggestion that they expected the attack to come in the *Goodwood* sector.[295]* On the contrary, the plan for the preliminary operations exploited the knowledge that the enemy continued to believe, as he had believed up to the beginning of July,† that the offensive was to be co-ordinated with a further Allied landing between the Seine and the Somme. In a signal of 7 July, which was decrypted on 9 July, the Japanese Naval Mission in Berlin had again reported that there were 30 divisions in England waiting to land between Le Havre and Calais.[296] On 12 July the decrypt of a telegram from the Japanese Ambassador in Berlin reporting German views on 6 July had disclosed that while some authorities were impatient for a general counter-attack in Normandy, von Kluge preferred to wait until the Allies renewed their attempts to enlarge their bridgehead; moreover, he thought it essential to wait until he knew what they intended to do with the

---

* The suggestion is based on a misinterpretation of the decrypt of 16 July of a message from Field Marshal Sperrle (see below, p 216).

† See above p 200.

293. Ellis, op cit, Vol 1, pp 331–332, 336.
294. DEFE 3/55, XLs 1927 and 1951 of 14 July; DEFE 3/56, XLs 2099, 2107 and 2129 of 15 July.
295. D'Este, op cit, p 368.
296. BAY/XL 29 of 9 July.

main forces they had reserved in England, which would probably land near the Straits.[297] On 10 July, in a telegram decrypted on 13 July, the Japanese Ambassador added that the Germans believed that the withdrawal of Allied airborne forces from the bridgehead pointed to a landing in the area Calais-Le Havre, for which the next suitable dates were 18 to 20 July.[298] Another of his telegrams, decrypted on 15 July, repeated that the Germans appeared to think that Patton's army would be used to cross the Straits of Dover and cut off their forces in Normandy. The Germans would probably counter-attack only after ascertaining what the Allies intended to do with Patton's forces.[299]*

On 16 July it became clear that the preliminary operations were succeeding in their object of deceiving the Germans. Some of the evidence came from Army Y, which indicated that they were taking the fighting round Evrecy to be part of the main offensive.[301] More conclusively, Field Marshal Sperrle, AOC-in-C Luftflotte 3, stated in an Enigma message, the decrypt of which was signalled by GC and CS at 1036, that Allied concentrations observed in the Caen-Tilly area made it probable that the offensive would be launched from there about the night of 17–18 July; as its success would be crucial for the future course of the war, it must be stopped, and as a further Allied landing was also expected north of the Seine or elsewhere, it was imperative to avoid delay in submitting reconnaissance reports.[302] During the rest of 16 July Sperrle's general directive was followed by the decrypts of numerous signals giving detailed orders for reconnaissance sorties and for spoiling attacks on shipping, on airfields and on tank and troop concentrations west of Caen. JK II's instructions cancelled the resting of two Gruppen, required that every pilot and aircraft that could be got ready must be used against the Allied troop and tank concentrations from 17 July,

---

* This decrypt was sent to Eisenhower on 16 July, on the instructions of the Prime Minister who added a note saying: '1 have a feeling, which the attached Boniface stimulates, that a part of the Patton Army Group might do more good by remaining in England than by coming immediately into the *Overlord* bridgehead. You have no doubt deeply weighed this. Uncertainty is a terror to the Germans. The forces in Britain are a dominant preoccupation of the Huns. The question must be considered whether, once they know where these are going or have gone, they will not feel free to liberate greater forces than those which we now menace simultaneously at so many points. This idea has been with me for some little time and when we next meet perhaps you will tell me whether there is any sense in it. At any rate everything should be done to exaggerate the forces remaining in Britain'.[300]

297. BAY/XL 33 of 12 July.
298. BAY/XL 34 of 13 July.
299. BAY/XL 44 of 15 July.
300. Dir/C Archive, 7177 of 16 July.
301. WO 171/131, No 147 of 20 July.
302. DEFE 3/56, XL 2287 of 16 July.

brought JG 27 to two hours notice for observation of the concentrations, and gave the screening of German artillery in the Evrecy area as the principal task for 17 July.[303] Fliegerkorps IX announced that its heavy formations would attack targets west of Caen at 2100 and 0200, and that FW 190s and Me 410s would make harrassing attacks north of Caen at 2100 and again at dawn.[304] Fliegerkorps X ordered KG 100 to hold all its units equipped with Hs and FX radio-controlled missiles and bombs ready for attacks on warships off the Orne from that evening in view of Allied concentrations for a big offensive.[305]

The *Goodwood* offensive itself, launched on 18 July, achieved tactical surprise.[306] This was indicated early on 18 July by a decrypt which disclosed that JK II's main effort that day would again be made west of the Orne;[307] nor was it till the late afternoon of 18 July that – without any warning from Sigint – Luftflotte 3's operations were re-directed east of the Orne.[308] Thereafter, however, the Germans having revised their appreciation of Second Army's intentions in the light of VIII Corps's advance, the operation achieved results that were disappointing in relation to the high hopes with which it had been launched. This has prompted not only the suggestion that the Germans expected it in the *Goodwood* sector but also the argument that it suffered from inadequate intelligence about the enemy's defences.[309] With regard to the resources Germany commanded – as distinct from their precise dispositions, for which the only source of intelligence was Allied reconnaissance – this argument is not well-founded. The information that Sigint had supplied was very nearly correct about the infantry and armour she had in the line east of the Orne, as also about the heavy concentration of anti-tank artilllery she had assembled there.*

In the event, VIII Corps's advance was stopped at Cagny and the Bourguébus ridge and was counter-attacked in the afternoon of 18 July between Cagny and Emiéville by 21st Panzer Division, Panzer Abteilung 503 and battle groups of 1st SS Panzer. Von Kluge asked for the return of 12th SS Panzer from reserve near Lisieux in the afternoon and, early in the evening, for permission

---

* See Appendix 18.

303. DEFE 3/57, XLs 2264, 2274, 2353 and 2375 of 16 July.
304. ibid, XLs 2327 and 2355 of 16 July.
305. ibid, XL 2300 of 16 July.
306. Ellis, op cit, Vol 1, p 334; Blumenson, op cit, p 192; WO 285/2, Notes on Second Army operations 16–18 July.
307. DEFE 3/58, XL 2502 of 18 July.
308. Cabinet Office Historical Section, EDS II 4/iii, s 102.
309. Bennett, op cit, pp 100, 108; D'Este, op cit, pp 367, 368, 376–378.

to move 116th Panzer to the battlefield from north of the Seine; and at 1700 he ordered Panzer Gruppe West to regain the Caen-Troarn road.[310] His signals were not decrypted; but it was known from the Enigma by 1900 that fighter protection had been requested for 1630 to cover the arrival of a battle group of 12th SS Panzer,[311] and by 2200 that 1st SS Panzer was moving to clear the Caen-Cagny road and then intending to advance to the line Manneville-Mondeville.[312] At 0246 on 19 July 12th SS Panzer's destination was indicated by a decrypt informing it that Allied tanks and troop carriers had been sighted north and west of Cagny.[313] About 0900 on 19 July the main body of 12th SS Panzer took over the defences at Cagny.[314]

VIII Corps was unable during 19 July to drive the Germans out of Bourguébus; but Panzer Gruppe West delayed the counter-attack till the arrrival of 116th Panzer, which was ordered to accept losses in moving up by road, and at 2230 it instructed XLVII Panzer Corps and II SS Panzer Corps to send battle groups to reinforce I SS Panzer Corps east of the Orne.[315] These decisions were not disclosed in Enigma decrypts, but during 21 July it was learned from Army Y that elements from 2nd Panzer and 9th and 10th SS Panzer Divisions had been sent east of the Orne.[316]

On 20 July VIII Corps occupied Bourguébus and Frénouville, but could make no progress towards Vimont. I Corps had by then failed to capture Troarn and Emiéville. II Canadian Corps, which had entered Caen across the Orne and the Odon on 18 July and reached Fleury-sur-Orne on 19 July, attacked the Verrières ridge, which was defended by 272nd Infantry Division with support from 1st SS Panzer and a battle group of 2nd Panzer. Hard fighting there during 20 and 21 July left the Canadians holding the line of the road from Hubert Folie to St André-sur-Orne, and northwards along the Caen road, on the evening of 21 July, when Montgomery signalled the end of *Goodwood* by ordering that the new positions gained on the eastern flank should be firmly held and further improved while the US forces advanced into the Cherbourg and Brittany peninsulas.[317]

□

---

310. Ellis, op cit, Vol 1, pp 340–344, 346; EDS II 4/iii, s 96, 102, 103, 104.
311. DEFE 3/58, XL 2604 of 18 July.
312. ibid, XLs 2623 and 2628 of 18 July.
313. ibid, XL 2648 of 19 July.
314. Ellis, op cit, Vol 1, p 351.
315. ibid; EDS II 4/iii, s 104.
316. WO 171/131, Nos 147 and 148 of 20 and 23 July; WO 285/3, No 47 of 21 July; *History of Sigint in the Field*, pp 171–173.
317. Ellis, op cit, pp 347–350.

Throughout the battle for Normandy Sigint provided prompt and comprehensive intelligence on the activities of the German Air Force. Over and above the fact that the Allies usually received advance warning of its reconnaissance intentions and its operational orders from the Enigma and the interception of its tactical communications*, high-grade decrypts gave a full account of its order of battle – the arrival of its reinforcements, the locations and strengths of its formations, the serviceability of its airfields – and threw much light on the difficulties it progressively encountered as a result of Allied command of the air and its own manpower and fuel shortages.

The GAF provided no close support for the Army during the first three days of *Overlord* largely as a result of the dislocation caused by Allied air attacks on its airfields, transit depots, air parks and communications.[319] Sigint disclosed on the evening of D-day that it had brought into force at 0930 Operation *Emergency West*, its plans for the transfer of reinforcements to the invasion theatre from areas as far away as Austria and Hungary.[320] Decrypts of other signals issued on D-day had disclosed early on 7 June that one day-fighter Gruppe was being brought up to each of seven airfields in (probably) northern France and Belgium and five airfields in (probably) central France.[321] A decrypt issued at 0813 on 7 June gave the locations of eight Gruppen on the evening of D-day.[322] Decrypts issued on 9 June reported the arrival and location on 8 June of six more Gruppen[323] and the dispositions of another eleven Gruppen on 9 June.[324]

On the basis of these decrypts and of much tactical Sigint the Air Ministry estimated on 8 June the reinforcements which had been brought into France and the Netherlands since D-day: 300

---

* The following are but a few examples of the early warning obtained from the Enigma. Fliegerkorps II's plans for 13 June – operations north of Caen and at Bayeux against tanks and shipping – were signalled to the Allied Commands at 2312 on 12 June. Luftflotte 3's orders to Jagdkorps II for free-lance patrols over the beachhead on 13 June, with the main effort against Allied fighter-bombers, and for an escorted operation to supply the Douvres strong point, were signalled at 0502 on 13 June. The information that Fliegerkorps X planned to attack heavy units off the Orne at dark on 14 June, and that aircraft of Fliegerkorps IX would be flying in and out over the Vire estuary between 0015 and 0100 and 0200 and 0245 on 15 June, was signalled at 1810 on 14 June.[318]

318.   DEFE 3/171, KVs 7755 of 12 June, 7791 of 13 June; DEFE 3/172, KV 8058 of 14 June.
319.   Ellis, op cit, Vol 1, p 569; AIR 41/24, p 330.
320.   DEFE 3/166, KV 6647 of 6 June; Ellis, op cit, Vol 1, p 567; Bennett, op cit, p 73.
321.   DEFE 3/166, KVs 6675 and 6712 of 7 June.
322.   ibid, KV 6735 of 7 June.
323.   DEFE 3/168, KV 7133 of 9 June.
324.   ibid, KV 7138 of 9 June.

single-engined fighters, approximately 70 per cent of which were based west and 30 per cent north-east of the Seine; 30 night-fighters; 50–60 torpedo-bombers; and 25–30 radio-controlled bombers. The total forces available in France and the Netherlands were thought to comprise 1,430 aircraft: 340 long-range bombers; 55 fighter-bombers; 520 single-engined fighters; 420 twin-engined fighters; 95 reconnaissance aircraft*. The enemy's close-support effort was rising steadily. He intended to use some of his single-engined fighters as fighter-bombers fitted with 21 cm rocket projectors. The long-range bomber effort, however, was likely to be much less than had been expected. The bomber Gruppen were much below establishment and serviceability was below 60 per cent.[326]

On 12 June the Air Ministry estimated that total strength had risen to 1,615 aircraft, but noted that there was ample evidence of weakness in many close-support units. Recent strength returns of ten fighter and fighter-bomber Gruppen, nominally comprising 300 aircraft, indicated an actual strength of 240 aircraft with serviceability about 50 per cent. The scale of effort per fighter Gruppe (nominally of 30 aircraft) did not exceed ten aircraft per mission, and of fighter-bombers only five aircraft per mission. Fighter and fighter-bomber strength had passed its peak and reinforcements would do no more than maintain strength at around the present figures.[327]

On 10 June high-grade decrypts revealed that Fliegerkorps II, the specialised close-support HQ, had complained that operations were seriously hampered by inadequate communications, most land-lines having been interrupted, and that on 9 June, after very heavy bombing for two nights at Flers, Condé, Argentan and Ecouche, men were showing signs of nervous exhaustion.[328] On 14 June the Air Ministry noted that, due in large part to Allied attacks on airfields, fighter strength and serviceability remained low. Most recent evidence for 14 fighter and fighter-bomber

---

* This was a considerable over-estimate. As we have seen (above, p 104) Luftflotte 3's front-line strength was 891 aircraft on D-day and it had been reinforced with some 300 fighters, 90 bombers and 45 torpedo-bombers by D+10. AI had set the D-day figure too high, and its estimates after D-day were unable to take account of the heavy losses inflicted on the reinforcements as they flew in. Guided by the Sigint about the GAF's reinforcement plans, the Allied tactical air forces took a heavy toll in flank attacks on the long flight routes used by the reinforcements and their transport aircraft, and also in raids on the airfields that had been got ready for them. Moreover, much of the manpower of the units had to come by rail and was heavily delayed. Luftflotte 3's total strength was 1,100 aircraft at the end of the first week, and this was to be the highest figure it reached.[325]

325. AIR 41/24, pp 48–49; Ellis, op cit, Vol 1, pp 567, 569.
326. Air Sunset 182 of 8 June.
327. Air Sunset 184 of 10 June.
328. DEFE 3/169, KVs 7371 and 7383 of 10 June, 7497 of 11 June.

Gruppen indicated a strength of 275 aircraft, or 65 per cent of establishment.[329] (The actual strength of ground-attack aircraft and fighter-bombers had fallen to 130 aircraft on 12 June). By then, moreover, Sigint had disclosed a significant change in GAF policy. Decrypts had confirmed by 8 June that the enemy intended to use some of his single-engined fighters as fighter-bombers equipped with bomb racks and 21 cm rocket projectors for ground attack, and this had been repeated in a decrypt of 12 June which went on to emphasise that bombing was the primary task and the shooting down of aircraft only secondary.[330] On 13 June, however, a decrypt revealed that this policy had been reversed by Luftflotte 3 on 12 June at the instance of Berlin: all fighter Gruppen were to be re-equipped as fighters; until further notice the task of fighters was to clear the skies over the battlefield, and they would use only aircraft armament in attacks on ground targets; and the operations of all fighters would be controlled by Jagdkorps II.[331] The reversal of policy was no doubt a response to the situation reported by C-in-C West on 9 June, in a signal decrypted on 14 June, which complained that the operations of thousands of Allied bombers and fighter-bombers were stifling German tank attacks and severely harrassing all movements.[332] A message decrypted on 15 June reported that the situation was similar on the front held by LXXXIV Corps; total Allied air supremacy made movement near the front impossible by day while even at night Allied aircraft were lighting the roads in the St Lo area with flares and attacking single vehicles.[333] A decrypt of 16 June confirmed that fighter units hitherto controlled by Flieger-korps II had been subordinated to Jagdkorps II to protect roads against low-level Allied attacks.[334]

On 16 June the Air Ministry estimated that the bomber force, with a strength rising to 400 aircraft, had maintained an average of about 130 sorties per night, of which about 45 had been by anti-shipping units. Further bomber reinforcements of up to 100 aircraft were expected from Italy and Germany. After reinforcements of some 450 aircraft the estimated fighter strength of 500 single-engined fighters was an increase of 250 over that on D-day. There had been heavy wastage in the air and on the ground under Allied bombing. The average daily fighter effort had ranged between 250 and 300 sorties.[335]

---

329. Air Sunset 187 of 14 June.
330. DEFE 3/170, KV 7634 of 12 June.
331. Air Sunset 186 of 13 June; DEFE 3/171, KV 7815 of 12 June.
332. DEFE 3/171, KV 7998 of 14 June.
333. DEFE 3/172, KV 8240 of 15 June.
334. DEFE 3/173, KV 8399 of 16 June.
335. Air Sunset 189 of 16 June.

On 16 June the decrypt of an appreciation of 14 June by Fliegerkorps IX noted that heavy anti-aircraft fire had been first encountered over the Orne estuary during the night of 9–10 June and that the subsequent development of the Allied defences had forced its bombers to approach at great heights. This increased the difficulty of target location even on clear nights: on dark nights targets could not be found. The possibility of successful attacks on shore targets was therefore limited. Bomber operations against Allied shipping, either by direct attack or by mining, offered better prospects.[336] This appreciation foreshadowed the increase in the mining operations by Fliegerkorps IX which, as we have seen, caused the Allies more worry and losses than any other form of attack.*

By 17 June it was known that fighter operations in the Cotentin were being controlled by AOC Fighters Brittany, with four Gruppen comprising some 90 aircraft; in the Caen-Bayeux area Jagdkorps II controlled elements of some thirteen Gruppen with an estimated strength of 315 aircraft. Strength returns available by 18 June gave continued indications of the strained fighter position. The actual strength of I and III/JG2, for example, was 24 aircraft with only nine serviceable. AI noted, however, that some recovery of fighter strength might be expected in the next two or three weeks, since the GAF was re-organising the replacement system and since the negligible current wastage in Italy and on the eastern front would permit maximum allocation of aircraft to France.[337] Since D-day the Allied bombing of the airfields around Paris and on the replacement routes in France had forced the enemy to move his main transit depots to the Rhineland, and this had resulted in serious delays in bringing up replacements for the losses suffered in France.[338] By the end of June the GAF had indeed overcome this handicap; it had also brought forward some of the few remaining units kept back for the defence of the Reich. In July the number of single-engined fighters available for the defence of Germany was down to 370 from 700 on D-day, while 425 were available in France and 475 were tied down on the Russian and Balkan fronts.[339] At the beginning of July Sigint disclosed that Fliegerkorps II's experienced commander, General Bülowius, had returned to the battle front and taken command of JK II.[340]

---

* See above, pp 62, 165 ff.

336. DEFE 3/173, KV 8252 of 16 June.
337. Air Sunset 190 of 17 June.
338. Air 41/24, p 332.
339. Air 41/10. *The Rise and Fall of the German Air Force*, pp 332–333.
340. DEFE 3/49, XL 463 of 2 July.

On 15 July AI noted that there had been a marked recuperation in the close-support forces and on 16 July it estimated that the number of single-engined fighters had increased in the past week from 435 to 520 aircraft; it believed this force would be capable of exceeding the previous maximum effort of 600 sorties a day delivered on 30 June at the end of the *Epsom* battle.[341] The extent to which its estimates were based on high-grade Sigint is indicated by the fact that there were some three dozen decrypts giving the locations and strengths of single-engined fighter units in the few days before the opening of the *Goodwood* and *Cobra* offensives.

Sigint had meanwhile provided continuing evidence of the stranglehold on movement imposed by the Allied air forces. In a decrypt obtained on 21 June Luftflotte 3 was asked to order that lorries should only approach battle headquarters and supply establishments, especially ammunition issuing stations, at night. Motor cycles and cars travelling singly by day should only proceed after searching the sky. These precautions were necessary because lively Allied reconnaissance activity was quickly followed by bombing.[342] In a decrypt available on 22 June 21st Panzer Division enquired about German fighter patrols over supply roads in daylight since 50 per cent of supplies had been lost through Allied air attacks.[343] An extract from an OKW circular of 24 June, signalled by GC and CS on 27 June, referred to experiences gained during approach marches by units going into the battle area. Because of Allied air superiority precautionary measures had been ordered. Only energetic and circumspect leaders were capable of getting their columns forward. Bad weather was often not properly utilised for getting on with the march. This applied mainly to supply columns but also, sometimes, to fighting troops. Alterations in rail or road route because of bombing caused confusion: individuals must be told their destination. Newly arriving units must be met and guided by officers conversant with the situation.[344]*

During July it became evident that the shortage of manpower in

---

* Several Japanese diplomatic decrypts contained information on this subject. In a signal of 15 June, decrypted on 18 June, the Naval Mission in Berlin noted that skilful use of Allied air superiority was hampering movement and preventing the concentration of the German forces and that the outlook had some disturbing features.[345] From the decrypt of 22 June of his telegram of 19 June it was known that the Ambassador had reported that Allied air superiority, while not preventing comparatively easy movement of infantry, was causing considerable losses of tanks and guns; therefore there had for the present been only infantry counter-attacks and the position was fluctuating.[346] A third – a signal from the Naval Mission

341. Air Sunsets 207 and 208 of 15 and 16 July.
342. DEFE 3/176, KV 9005 of 21 June.
343. ibid, KV 9114 of 22 June.
344. DEFE 3/179, KV 9793 of 27 June.
345. BAY/KV 218 of 18 June.
346. BAY/KV 230 of 22 June.

the GAF was reaching critical proportions. On 11 July GC and CS decrypted an order by Göring on 5 July designed to reduce the intolerable losses of unit commanders and officers in fighter and close-support operations. Unit commanders, officers qualified for command and officers with other special qualifications, such as adjutants and technical officers, were only to fly when this was warranted by the importance of the operation and the number of aircraft employed (45 in the case of Geschwaderkommodore.) No crew except that of a unit commander was to comprise more than one officer, and unit commanders should only fly on reconnaissance or night-fighter operations if their importance, or the maintenance of the officer's own efficiency, made this requisite.[348] A decrypt on 13 July showed that personnel were being transferred from the bomber to the fighter arm, and evidence accumulated that the former was being run down.[349]

Sigint references to fuel shortages in the GAF had been frequent since D-day, when a decrypt had given the general warning that the Allied air offensive against oil production plants had made it necessary to break into OKW's strategic reserve and impose restrictions on consumption throughout the armed forces.[350]* From the beginning of July such references multiplied and became more insistent. Decrypts of 2 and 8 July disclosed that acute difficulty over the supply of aviation fuel had restricted crew training; that motor transport fuel was also very short, and that Sperrle had ordered the ruthless prohibition of all journeys not operationally necessary.[351] An order by Göring on 6 July, decrypted on 9 July, spoke of deep inroads into the supply of aviation spirit making drastic economy absolutely essential. Liaison travel and communication flights must be drastically reduced and transport flights limited strictly to operational requirements and supply of the fighting forces. Safe storage and constant control of aviation fuel was indispensable. Stocks of aviation fuel were being depleted because of the shortage of MT fuel; accordingly no aircraft fuel was to be released for travelling purposes, except in operational areas where extreme emergency might justify it, and then only with permission of the AOC-in-C of the relevant Luftflotte. Transgressors would be liable to court martial.[352]

---

on 19 June decrypted on 26 June – reported that the Army's greatest difficulty was the Allied air and naval bombardment of German reserves and supplies in the rear.[347]

  * See below pp 502–503.

347. BAY/KV 243 of 26 June.
348. DEFE 3/54, XL 1671 of 11 July.
349. DEFE 3/55, XLs 1827 and 1873 of 13 July; Air Sunset 209 of 21 July.
350. DEFE 3/166, KV 6673 of 6 June.
351. DEFE 3/49, XLs 445 and 478 of 2 July; DEFE 3/53, XL 1260 of 8 July.
352. DEFE 3/53, XL 1438 of 9 July.

CHAPTER 48

The Allied Break-out and the German Withdrawal from the South of France

ONTGOMERY's directive of 21 July, which marked the end of Operation *Goodwood*, made First Canadian Army operational with responsibility for the left flank from the sea to the Caen-Mézidon railway. It had I British Corps under command and its task was to push the enemy back to the east side of the river Dives. Second British Army was ordered to operate intensively to secure a line running westward from St Sylvain to Cauvicourt-Gouvix-Evrecy-Noyers and Caumont where it was to take over the left divisional sector of First US Army. After gaining this line Second Army's front to the east of the Orne was to be kept as active as possible in order to make the enemy believe that the Allies contemplated a major advance towards Falaise and Argentan, and induce him to build up his strength east of the Orne so that 'our affairs on the western flank can proceed with greater speed'. On the western flank First US Army's immediate task was to secure the whole of the Cherbourg peninsula as far as its base in the Avranches area, pivoting on its left to the general line Vire-Mortain-Fougères. The right-hand Corps was then to turn westward into Brittany. The remainder of the Army was to prepare plans for a wide sweep by its right wing south of the *bocage* with the lines Laval-Mayenne and then Le Mans-Alençon as successive objectives. Third US Army was to be brought up to control operations on the western flank with the task of clearing the whole of the Brittany peninsula. 12th Army Group would be formed to command First and Third US Armies.[1]

The Germans expected that Second Army would resume its offensive east of the Orne. They brought 9th SS Panzer Division, which had been relieved in the Evrecy sector by 277th Infantry Division, across the Orne into the woods west of Bretteville-sur-Laize; moved 2nd Panzer Division, which was relieved in the Caumont sector by 326th Infantry Division from Fifteenth Army, in the same direction; assembled 116th Panzer Division, also from Fifteenth Army, in the area of St Sylvain; reinforced their anti-tank artillery; and began to bring 271st Infantry Division, which had come up to Fifteenth Army from the south at the

---

1. WO 285/2, Dempsey Papers.

beginning of July, into the line just west of the Orne.[2] On the western flank the US offensive, which had opened on 3 July and finally captured St Lo on 19 July, had put Seventh Army under great pressure. To sustain the front 2nd SS Panzer Division had been brought in from Army Reserve; Panzer Lehr Division had been moved from XLVII Panzer Corps to the west of St Lo; and 5th Parachute Division and the remainder of 275th Infantry Division had come from Brittany. The commanders of both Corps under Seventh Army (II Parachute and LXXXIV) expected the US offensive to be resumed, and feared that they would be unable to withstand it, but no further reinforcements were provided.*

On 25 July, when Second Army resumed its attack and First US Army launched Operation *Cobra*, which had originally been intended to accompany *Goodwood*, the German order of battle was as follows:[3]

Panzer Gruppe West
Coast to Caen-Mézidon railway (approx): LXXXVI Corps
    711th Infantry, 346th Infantry, 21st Panzer.
Caen-Mézidon railway (approx) to river Orne: I SS Panzer Corps
    12th SS Panzer, 1st SS Panzer, 272nd Infantry.
    In reserve: 116th Panzer, 9th SS Panzer, 2nd Panzer (moving).
River Orne to river Odon: II SS Panzer Corps
    10th SS Panzer (with 271st Infantry under command), 277th Infantry.
River Odon to river Drôme: XLVII Panzer Corps
    276th Infantry, 326th Infantry.

Seventh Army
River Drôme to river Vire: II Parachute Corps
    3rd Parachute, 352nd Infantry.
River Vire to West Coast: LXXXIV Corps
    Panzer Lehr, 5th Parachute, 17th SS PG, 2nd SS Panzer, 91st Infantry (elements), 243rd Infantry (elements).
    In reserve: 353rd Infantry, 275th Infantry (elements).

Except for the moves of 326th Infantry and 116th Panzer Divisions, which were not identified until they reached the battlefield,† intelligence had been kept well abreast of the enemy's expectations and the alterations in his order of battle by

---

* See above, p 210ff.

† In its intelligence summary for 23 July, 21st Army Group referred to a report of troops

2. Ellis, *Victory in the West*, Vol 1 (1962), p 378; WO 208/4316, MI 14 Weekly Summaries for the CIGS, 23 and 30 July 1944.
3. Ellis, op cit, Vol 1, Map p 378.

high-grade Sigint. Several decrypts confirmed that, as was hoped, he was expecting a resumption of the offensive east of the Orne. Early on 22 July Luftflotte 3 and Flak Korps III were aware of Allied concentrations south-east of Caen, which were thought to include 800–1,000 tanks, and expected a major attack when the weather permitted air operations.[6] 12th SS Panzer Division was expecting to be attacked on 23 July,[7] and that evening 21st Panzer Division, noting that Allied tank concentrations were being continuously reinforced, expected an attack south-east from a line Banneville-Cagny when the weather lifted.[8] In a message sent at 1930 on 24 July, and decrypted at 0121 on 25 July, I SS Panzer Corps noted that the Allies were digging-in, but thought this was cover for the intended attack.[9] From 22 to 25 July inclusive JK II concentrated its main effort south-east of Caen and Fliegerkorps IX planned night operations against troops in the Caen area.[10]

Elements of 9th SS Panzer Division and 2nd Panzer Division were identified east of the Orne on 21 July.[11] A decrypt signalled to the Commands at 0613 on 23 July gave the location of 9th SS Panzer's battle headquarters[12] and another at 1338 confirmed that at 0830 that morning it was occupying a new sector.[13] (No details were given.) A decrypt signalled at 1954 on 23 July revealed that 2nd Panzer Division was moving to the Moulines area east of the Orne,[14] and another at 1759 on 24 July that the Division's Flivo was on the move.[15] Signals decrypted on 21 and 23 July indicated that the anti-tank artillery east of the Orne was being further strengthened.[16] By 20 July 21st Army Group had learnt from deserters that 271st Division was approaching from north of the

---

entraining at stations in the Pas de Calais.[4] This proved to be 326th Infantry Division which was not identified until it was met in the Caumont sector on 25 July.[5] For 116th Panzer Division see below, pp 230, 234, 235.

4. WO 171/131, 21st Army Group Intelligence Summary No 148 Part III of 23 July.
5. ibid, No 149 of 25 July.
6. DEFE 3/60, XL 3102 of 22 July.
7. ibid, XL 3153 of 23 July.
8. DEFE 3/63, XL 3273 of 24 July.
9. ibid, XL 3377 of 25 July.
10. DEFE 3/59, XL 2988 of 21 July; DEFE 3/60, XLs 3132 and 3139 of 23 July; DEFE 3/61, XLs 3271 of 24 July, 3379 of 25 July.
11. WO 285/3, Second Army Intelligence Summary No 47 of 21 July.
12. DEFE 3/60, XL 3149 of 23 July.
13. ibid, XL 3175 of 23 July.
14. ibid, XL 3213 of 23 July.
15. DEFE 3/61, XL 3336 of 24 July.
16. DEFE 3/59, XL 2923 of 21 July; DEFE 3/60, XL 3146 of 23 July.

Seine.[17] A delayed decrypt signalled to the Commands on 23 July included information that substantial elements of 271st Infantry Division had been ferried across the river,[18] and decrypts on 24 and 25 July disclosed that the Division was on the right of 10th SS Panzer Division and temporarily under its command.[19]

On the western flank the enemy's order of battle showed fewer changes. A decrypt of 20 July confirmed that 5th Parachute Division was subordinated to LXXXVI Corps,[20] and another on 22 July showed that it had become responsible for a sector on the left of 17th SS PG Division.[21] By 23 July 21st Army Group knew from battlefield identifications that the remainder of 275th Infantry Division had reached the front from Brittany.[22] At 1324 on 23 July GC and CS signalled that LXXXIV Corps intended to withdraw 353rd Infantry Division into reserve.[23] A decrypt of 24 July disclosed that the previous day 5th Parachute Division had taken over a sector between Marigny and La Vallée with Panzer Lehr on its right and 17th SS PG on its left.[24] Finally the order of battle of LXXXIV Corps as at 1800 on 24 July was neatly laid out in a decrypt at 0448 on the first day of Operation *Cobra*.[25]

The Allies also knew from decrypts of 14 and 21 July that both LXXXIV Corps and II Parachute Corps had been seriously shaken by the American offensive, and were uneasy about their ability to continue a successful defence.[26] In messages decrypted on 22, 24 and 25 July Meindl, GOC II Parachute Corps, emphasised the steadily shrinking fighting power of the Parachute units, and was given permission to use cadre personnel from a training regiment to fill the gaps in his front line units.[27] A message late on 22 July from the Flivo with Seventh Army, decrypted at 0818 the next morning, requested an urgent reconnaissance of powerful new US forces with tanks, presumed to belong to Third US Army, which had appeared in front of the sector held by 17th SS PG Division.[28]

□

---

17. WO 171/131, No 147 Part II of 20 July.
18. DEFE 3/60, XL 3131 of 23 July.
19. DEFE 3/61, XLs 3332 of 24 July, 3417 of 25 July.
20. DEFE 3/59, XL 2823 of 20 July.
21. DEFE 3/60, XL 3056 of 22 July.
22. WO 171/131, No 148 Part II of 23 July.
23. DEFE 3/60, XL 3173 of 23 July.
24. DEFE 3/61, XL 3307 of 24 July.
25. ibid, XL 3399 of 25 July.
26. DEFE 3/56, XL 2030 of 14 July; DEFE 3/59, XL 2986 of 21 July.
27. DEFE 3/59, XL 3000 of 22 July; DEFE 3/61, XLs 3252 and 3311 of 24 July, 3375 of 25 July.
28. DEFE 3/60, XL 3155 of 23 July.

On 25 July II Canadian Corps under Second Army attacked southward down each side of the Caen-Falaise road. Little progress was made against strongly held German positions and the attack was broken off after a day of 'bloody and abortive' fighting.[29]

First US Army's offensive began the same day and fared better.* VII US Corps crossed the St Lo-Lessay road towards Marigny and St Giles and captured both places the next day. 27 July brought a decisive advance. On the left XIX US Corps almost reached Tessy-sur-Vire; VII US Corps in the centre was nearly half way to Villedieu and further to the right was within two miles of Coutances. VIII US Corps, advancing in the coastal sector, captured Coutances on 29 July. Avranches was entered on 30 July and on 31 July a bridgehead was secured embracing crossings over the Sienne, the Sée and the Sélune rivers. The enemy had been forced back to a line from Torigny to Tessy and Percy, with only scattered and crumbling defences to the south where the way to open country was almost clear.[31]

Montgomery had meanwhile issued new instructions on 27 July. Noting that German forces east of the Orne were so strong that large-scale operations were unlikely to succeed and that the enemy's six Panzer and SS divisions facing Second Army were all to the east of Noyers, he ordered Second Army to mount a new strong offensive with not less than six divisions on its right wing from the general area of Caumont. The initial objective would be the area St Martin des Besaces-Le Bény Bocage-Forêt l'Evêque. On its left wing Second Army was to conduct operations so as to keep the strong enemy forces in the Caen sector pinned down. First Canadian Army was to extend its sector westward to the Orne.[32]

Second Army's new offensive began on 30 July. On the left XXX Corps was held up by 276th Infantry Division well short of its first objectives – Amaye-sur-Seulles and Point 361 at the western end of the Mont Pinçon ridge. On the right VIII Corps made better progress against 326th Infantry Division, and by nightfall had opened a gap between 326th Division and II Parachute Corps which exposed the latter's right flank. On 31 July XXX Corps

---

* Bad weather on 24 July caused a postponement of twenty-four hours. Part of the preliminary strike was made because not all the bombing forces were warned of the postponement in time. This led LXXXIV Corps to believe that the offensive had begun and had been smashed by the German artillery, with great expenditure of ammunition.[30]

29. Ellis, op cit, Vol I, pp 378, 379.
30. DEFE 3/61, XL 3491 of 25 July.
31. Ellis, op cit, Vol 1, pp 381–383.
32. ibid, p 386; WO 285/2.

made progress towards the western end of the Bois du Homme. VIII Corps held firm against counter-attacks, cleared St Martin des Besaces, pushed through the Forêt l'Evêque and seized a bridge over the Souleuvre river west of Le Bény Bocage. Contact was made with the Americans south of the Forêt l'Evêque.[33]

Von Kluge's first reaction to the US offensive was to order on 26 July that 2nd Panzer Division should be ready to move westwards if the situation deteriorated. During the next few days he ordered the transfer of both 2nd Panzer and 116th Panzer Divisions from Panzer Gruppe West to Seventh Army, together with XLVII Panzer Corps, which was to assume command of these divisions and of the remnants of Panzer Lehr and 352nd Divisions. With these forces XLVII Panzer Corps came into the line on the left of II Parachute Corps and on the flank of the US breakthrough. LXXIV Corps from Brittany took over command in the Caumont sector from XLVII Panzer Corps. On 29 July 21st Panzer Division was withdrawn from LXXXVI Corps sector into Panzer Gruppe West Reserve, and the next day it was ordered to move at once to join LXXIV Corps now threatened by Second Army's advance. On 31 July 84th Infantry Division, which was crossing the Seine into the sector facing First Canadian Army was re-directed to Seventh Army; 89th Infantry Division, also on the way from Fifteenth Army, was to join Panzer Gruppe West. The latter was ordered to move II SS Panzer Corps with 9th and 10th SS Panzer Divisions and Corps troops to join 21st Panzer Division on its left wing: 10th SS Panzer Division was to hold the British thrust towards Amaye-sur-Odon; 9th SS Panzer Division was to gain a line from Le Bény Bocage-Le Tourneur and link up with II Parachute Corps at Carville.[34]

□

Sigint provided a good account of the enemy's reactions on Second Army's front, and even fuller coverage of his worsening situation in the face of First US Army's advance.

On Second Army's front a decrypt of 25 July showed that 272nd Infantry Division was being withdrawn to rest and being replaced in the line by 9th SS Panzer Division.[35] A decrypt forwarded to the Commands by emergency signal at 2108 on 25 July disclosed that 9th SS Panzer would attack Verrières at 2130;[36] but on 26 July a decrypt reported that the attack had failed because of Allied

---

33. Ellis, op cit, Vol 1, pp 389–394.
34. ibid, pp 384, 385, 395.
35. DEFE 3/62, XL 3589 of 26 July.
36. ibid, XL 3630 of 25 July.

artillery fire.[37] During 27 July Army Y located 9th SS Panzer's battle HQ in the Forêt de Cinglais;[38] high-grade Sigint disclosed on 29 July that its GOC had been wounded in an air attack on the HQ.[39] At 2214 on 28 July it emerged that 21st Panzer Division was leaving LXXXVI Corps and being replaced by 272nd Infantry;[40] 272nd's return to the front line in 21st Panzer's former sector was confirmed by decrypts on 29 and 30 July[41] and a decrypt on the morning of 30 July reported that 21st Panzer was in Panzer Gruppe West's Reserve in the Moulines area.[42] Army Y followed 2nd Panzer's move westward during 28 July.[43] 21st Army Group's intelligence summary for that day considered that 363rd Infantry Division would arrive soon – the Resistance had reported that it was leaving the Ghent area by train on 18 July – and that it might be accompanied by 11th Panzer Division, elements of which had been located north of the Loire by ground reports and photographic reconnaissance.[44] Decrypts at 1104 and 1315 on 29 July disclosed the unexpected arrival of LXXIV Corps from Brittany.[45] Reports from LXXXIV Corps and its two subordinated divisions (272nd and 326th Infantry) on the first day of Second Army's offensive in the Caumont sectors, 30 July, were decrypted in the evening.[46] The further development of this offensive was reflected in decrypts on 31 July which disclosed at 1423 that 21st Panzer had entered the line on the left of 326th Infantry and, at 1850, that retreating elements of 326th's left wing had been subordinated to a battle group under II Parachute Corps.[47] A signal at 1700 from 326th's Flivo, giving the line to which the rest of the division was withdrawing, was decrypted at 2230.[48]

First US Army's attack was heralded by a message from Panzer Lehr at 1000 on 25 July, signalled at 0427 the next morning. The tremendous air bombardment to which the Division had been subjected was reported phlegmatically, but it was presumed to be the prelude to an attempted Allied breakthrough in the sector and GAF help was urgently requested.[49] A decrypt at 1456 on 26 July

---

37.   ibid, XL 3757 of 26 July.
38.   WO 285/3, No 53 of 27 July.
39.   DEFE 3/63, XL 3960 of 29 July.
40.   ibid, XL 3817 of 28 July.
41.   ibid, XL 3945 of 29 July; DEFE 3/64, XL 4012 of 30 July.
42.   DEFE 3/64, XL 4045 of 30 July.
43.   WO 285/3, No 54 of 28 July.
44.   WO 171/131, No 150 of 28 July.
45.   DEFE 3/63, XL 3928 and 3935 of 29 July.
46.   DEFE 3/64, XL 4105 of 30 July.
47.   ibid, XLs 4179 and 4197 of 31 July.
48.   ibid, XL 4241 of 31 July.
49.   DEFE 3/62, XL 3527 of 26 July.

furnished a report at 0700 by the Flivo with LXXXIV Corps on the situation at 2200 on 25 July. German losses had been high. The situation had deteriorated and the Corps had committed its reserve with the intention of regaining its main defence line.[50] Decrypts of messages from 2nd SS Panzer Division gave the information that its GOC had been wounded on 24 July and that the Division had used up its Flak 88 mm ammunition by the evening of 25 July.[51] But JK II's orders for 26 July, decrypted at 0814 that morning, still placed its main effort in the Caen sector,[52] and the same was true of Fliegerkorps IX's intentions for the night 26–27 July and JK II's for 27 July.[53]

Several decrypts from LXXXIV Corps on 27 July reflected a worsening situation. Early that morning it was withdrawing its centre and left and intending to form a new defence front and regain contact with its right-hand neighbour (II Parachute Corps).[54] The latter was taking up a new main defence line.[55] LXXXIV Corps was finding movement by road impossible because of the intensive fighter-bomber activity.[56] A decrypt at 1630 showed that Fliegerkorps IX had switched its heavy bombers to the west for the night 27–28 July,[57] and decrypts at 0431 and 0504 on 28 July showed that JK II was concentrating all its units on the area of penetration south-west of St Lo and had told them that, in view of the severity of the fighting, they must try in all circumstances to reach the battle area with all available forces.[58]

A decrypt at 0148 on 28 July disclosed that the HQ of LVIII Panzer Corps was transferring to Seventh Army from the Toulouse area.[59] (The fact that this HQ was moving had been revealed by a decrypt on 20 July asking for air cover for six days.)[60] A statement by LXXXIV Corps at 1500 on 27 July that it was taking up a new blocking position with the forces withdrawn from its northern front was decrypted at 1119 on 28 July,[61] but in messages early that morning, decrypted at 1438 and 1725, its Flivo quoted Panzer Lehr's report that the Division had no forces fit for battle and that remnants were collecting in the Percy area, and the

---

50. ibid, XL 3566 of 26 July.
51. ibid, XLs 3534 and 3568 of 26 July.
52. ibid, XL 3541 of 26 July.
53. ibid, XLs 3642 and 3648 of 26 July.
54. ibid, XLs 3682 and 3717 of 27 July.
55. ibid, XL 3685 of 27 July.
56. ibid, XL 3747 of 27 July.
57. ibid, XL 3702 of 27 July.
58. DEFE 3/63, XLs 3774 and 3777 of 28 July.
59. ibid, XL 3763 of 28 July.
60. DEFE 3/59, XL 2773 of 20 July.
61. DEFE 3/63, XL 3798 of 28 July.

Corps admitted that it had no communication with its right wing and did not know where the front line was.[62] In response to a request for fighter cover in the Coutances area LXXXIV Corps was told that all GAF forces would be operating in its sector when the weather permitted.[63] A decrypt at 1749 disclosed targets in the St Lo area which were to be attacked during the night by Fliegerkorps IX's bombers.[64]

A report by II Parachute Corps was signalled to the Commands around midday on 29 July: late on 27 July its fighting strength was 3,440, it had no reserves whatsoever and it would be unable to resist serious pressure.[65] This was followed at 1254 by information that at 0630 that morning the Corps was withdrawing to a new main defence line, where its left flank would make a junction with XLVII Panzer Corps.[66] GC and CS commented that there was no other evidence that XLVII Panzer Corps had transferred from the right of II Parachute Corps to its left, but this evidence was quickly forthcoming: the decrypt of a message giving 2nd Panzer Division's front at 1930 on 28 July showed that 3rd Parachute Division (which belonged to II Parachute Corps) was its neighbour on the right.[67]

A decrypt signalled at 1742 on 29 July disclosed that Flieger-korps IX's heavy bombers would concentrate on targets south of St Lo during the night 29–30 July,[68] and another at 2139 that all JK II's units were to operate in the area of penetration south of St Lo on 30 July. Rocket-firing Gruppen were to be ready to attack with fighter escorts.[69]

At 0017 and 0404 on 30 July GC and CS signalled decrypts of messages sent out the previous evening by 2nd SS Panzer and 2nd Panzer Divisions. The former gave the blocking position it was trying to hold in the area Montabot-Percy-Sourdeval and asked most urgently for fighter cover;[70] the latter complained that its troops had been bombed by 60 German aircraft.[71] A message of 29 July from Fliegerkorps IX was also decrypted on 30 July: it told its units that only by extreme effort could the gap caused by the US breakthrough be closed and strategic Allied successes be

---

62. ibid, XLs 3815 and 3832 of 28 July.
63. ibid, XL 3882 of 28 July.
64. ibid, XL 3835 of 28 July.
65. ibid, XL 3933 of 29 July.
66. ibid, Xl 3934 of 29 July.
67. ibid, XL 3943 of 29 July.
68. ibid, XL 3966 of 29 July. See also ibid, XL 3990 of 29 July.
69. ibid, XL 3996 of 29 July.
70. DEFE 3/64, XL 4010 of 30 July.
71. ibid, XL 4019 of 30 July.

prevented.[72] An emergency signal sent to the Commands at 1552 gave the information that by 1000 that morning 2nd Panzer Division with 352nd Division under command, and 116th Panzer Division with an unspecified formation, were subordinated to XLVII Panzer Corps.[73] A GAF message at noon, decrypted at 1840, said that a defence line was being constructed from Percy to the west coast.[74] 2nd SS Panzer Division claimed that some of its elements had forced their way through to the south but had suffered heavy losses in air attacks.[75] XLVII Panzer Corps's line as at 1015 on 30 July was given in a decrypt of 1244 on 31 July, which also disclosed that at that time it had no firm contact with its left-hand neighbour, 2nd SS Panzer Division, in the Percy area.[76] A decrypt at 1333 gave the information that on 28 July the staff of 275th Infantry Division had ceased to function and the troops had been subordinated to 17th SS PG Division.[77] Another at 2137 reported that Panzer Lehr was being withdrawn from the front and transferring to the south-east of Vire.[78] Just before midnight on 31 July GC and CS signalled the decrypt of orders from Seventh Army given at 0001 on 29 July to the newly arriving 363rd Infantry Division, placing it under command of XLVII Panzer Corps.[79]

A decrypt at 1903 gave a target south of St Lo which was to be attacked during the night by Fliegerkorps IX,[80] and another decrypt at 2143 showed that JK II would be making its main effort south-west of St Lo on 31 July.[81]

A decrypt at 0749 on 31 July contained a review by Luftflotte 3 at 1000 on 30 July of the situation on both fronts. Operations by the Allies on Panzer Gruppe West's front, which had begun early that morning, were thought to be holding attacks. On Seventh Army's front the breakthrough crisis was not yet ended. There was strong pressure against the new main defence line east of the Vire: attacks by XLVII Panzer Corps had been checked, and although contact had been made with II Parachute Corps, an unbroken front had not been established yet. 116th Panzer Division had lost heavily to Allied air attacks during its move west.[82]

72. ibid, XL 4068 of 30 July.
73. ibid, XL 4067 of 30 July.
74. ibid, XL 4085 of 30 July.
75. ibid, XL 4079 of 30 July.
76. ibid, XL 4166 of 31 July.
77. ibid, XL 4172 of 31 July.
78. ibid, XL 4233 of 31 July.
79. ibid, XL 4248 of 31 July.
80. ibid, XL 4088 of 31 July.
81. ibid, XL 4116 of 30 July.
82. ibid, XL 4152 of 31 July.

Decrypts at 1926 and 2234 showed that both Fliegerkorps IX and JK II would continue their efforts to support the western flank.[83]

21st Army Group's intelligence summary for 31 July noted that the appearance on the Vire front of 116th Panzer Division had come as 'a surprise'. Although movement across the Seine during the previous week, and across the front from Alençon towards Vire on 29 July, had been spotted and heavily attacked, it was not known that 116th Panzer Division was involved. The summary referred to slightly conflicting reports about 11th Panzer Division, but still thought that it would soon arrive on the battlefield. It also noted that 9th Panzer Division, moving up the Rhône valley, had been met by a tank battalion coming down from the armoured depot at Mailly, and that this presumably meant that the Division would not come further north than Lyons.[84]

□

12th US Army Group, comprising First and Third US Armies, became operational on 1 August. General Bradley ordered First US Army to drive south and seize the zone Mortain-Vire, and Third US Army to seize the area Rennes-Fougères and then to turn west into Brittany. Two days later First US Army had captured Juvigny and Mortain and it was clear that between Mortain and the Loire there was no continuous front but only disjointed opposition at various points. Accordingly, on 3 August, after consultation with Montgomery, Bradley ordered First US Army to secure the Mayenne-Domfront area and prepare for further action eastwards, and Third US Army to clear Brittany and secure its ports with minimum forces while the rest of the Army cleared the country southwards to the Loire and prepared for further action towards the east and south-east. By 6 August Rennes was in American hands, the Brittany ports were about to be invested, and Mayenne and Laval had been captured. But on First US Army's left a stubborn defence was still being maintained. Vire was not taken until 6–7 August: Sourdeval and the westward bulge of rugged country round Gathémo were still in enemy hands.[85]

On Second Army's front VIII Corps resumed its advance on 3 August, when armoured forces broke through to Perrier and Estry; during the next few days, while infantry cleared the ground which had been overrun, the armour held firm against counter-

83. ibid, XLs 4204 and 4242 of 31 July.
84. WO 171/131, No 151 of 31 July.
85. Ellis, op cit, Vol 1, pp 403, 404, 412.

attacks by II SS Panzer Corps which came into the line on the left of LXXIV Corps. XXX Corps made less progress; Amaye-sur-Seulles and Jurques were captured, but no progress was made towards Aunay-sur-Odon.[86]

Although, on 1 August, all the forces available to von Kluge in Normandy were committed, an armoured division and six infantry divisions were on the way to the front. 9th Panzer Division from the south was approaching the Loire. 363rd Infantry Division was already arriving in Seventh Army's sector; 89th Infantry Division had crossed the Seine and 331st Infantry Division was crossing the river; 84th and 85th Infantry Divisions were moving towards Falaise from the Pas de Calais; and 708th Infantry Division from the Biscay coast was crossing the Loire near Angers. Early on 1 August von Kluge asked permission to move 2nd Parachute Division from Brest, and to bring 319th Infantry Division from the Channel Islands, in order to deny the Americans entry into Brittany. Permission was given to use 2nd Parachute Division, but Hitler refused to evacute the Channel Islands. By midday on 1 August US troops were already fanning out beyond Pontaubault. Von Kluge ordered XXV Corps to conduct the defence of Brittany in a campaign which developed quite separately from the battle in Normandy. XXV Corps disposed of 2nd Parachute Division, 343rd Infantry Division, elements of 265th and 266th Infantry Divisions which had not been committed in the Cotentin, survivors from 77th and 91st Infantry Divisions, Flak and coastal artillery units and naval and Air Force personnel. On 2 August von Kluge ordered First Army to extend its control northwards from the Biscay coast to the Loire and to hold bridgeheads on the north bank at crossings between Nantes and Orléans, and LXXXI Corps to hurry from Rouen to command 708th Infantry and 9th Panzer Divisions on Seventh Army's left flank between Domfront and Alençon.[87]

Early on 3 August von Kluge received new orders from Hitler. The front between the Orne and the Vire was to be held mainly by infantry divisions on a new main defence line Thury Harcourt-Vire-Fontenermont. The armoured formations hitherto employed there were to be released and moved complete to the left wing, where they were to drive through to Avranches and make contact with the west coast. Von Kluge immediately issued orders for Panzer Gruppe West to withdraw to the new main defence line. Using 84th and 363rd Infantry Divisions, Seventh Army was to release the battle groups formed by the surviving elements of

---

86. ibid, pp 401, 402.
87. Blumenson, *Breakout and Pursuit* (Washington DC 1961), pp 391, 392, 421, 422.

2nd SS Panzer and 17th SS PG Divisions. Panzer Gruppe West was to assemble 1st SS Panzer Division and another unspecified Panzer division north of Falaise. Seventh Army was to prepare an armoured attack on both sides of Sourdeval to annihilate the Allies between Mortain and Avranches and re-establish the Cotentin front. XLVII Panzer Corps was to conduct the attack. LXXXI Corps HQ would also probably be available. On 4 August von Kluge and Hausser, commanding Seventh Army, agreed that the attack would not be launched before the night 6–7 August.[88]

Panzer Gruppe West began its withdrawal during the night 3–4 August. XII Corps on Second Army's left and XXX Corps in the centre followed up. By night-fall on 5 August XII Corps had reached the west bank of the Orne between Grimbosq and Thury Harcourt, and on 6 August it established a bridgehead at Brieux which it held during the next two days against counter-attacks involving a battle group of 12th SS Panzer Division. XXX Corps occupied Aunay-sur-Odon, captured Ondefontaine on 5 August, and Mont Pinçon on 6–7 August. Meanwhile on Second Army's right VIII Corps was having to fight hard to keep its positions at Perrier. Estry was firmly held by 9th SS Panzer Division and on the night of 6 August 10th SS Panzer Division, brought from the Aunay front, made a strong but unsuccessful attack on the Perrier position.[89]

On 4 August Montgomery ordered First Canadian Army to prepare a heavy attack from the Caen sector towards Falaise, to be launched as early as possible and not later than 8 August. Two days later he reviewed the operational situation in a new directive and announced his intention to destroy the enemy forces in the area bounded from the sea to Paris by the Seine, then southwards to Orléans and from Orléans westward along the Loire to the sea. To this end First Canadian Army was to attack towards Falaise, beginning on the night of 7–8 August, and advance eastwards to the Seine on the axis Lisieux-Rouen. Second Army was to advance eastwards, through Argentan, Laigle, Dreux and Evreux to the Seine below Mantes, and be prepared to force crossings between Mantes and Les Andelys. 12th US Army Group was to move on a broad front with its main weight on its southern flank, which was to swing eastwards and then north-eastwards towards Paris. An airborne force would be landed in the Chartres area to block the Paris-Orléans gap.[90]

The German counter-offensive to re-establish the Cotentin front began soon after midnight on 6–7 August. 116th Panzer

---

88. Ellis, op cit, Vol 1, pp 405, 406.
89. ibid, pp 409, 410.
90. ibid, p 407; WO 285/2.

Division, which was being relieved by 84th Infantry Division, was to attack north of the river Sée. On its left 2nd Panzer Division was to send one column along the south bank of the Sée and another (reinforced by a tank battalion of 1st SS Panzer Division) to capture St Barthélemy and Juvigny. 2nd SS Panzer Division was to capture Mortain and push on westwards. The remainder of 1st SS Panzer Division was to follow up the attack towards Juvigny in order to exploit success and re-capture Avranches. 116th Panzer Division failed to start. 2nd Panzer Division's right-hand column was stopped as it approached Le Mesnil Adelée. Its left-hand column overran St Barthélemy but was held up on the road to Juvigny, as was 1st SS Panzer Division following up. 2nd SS Panzer Division captured Mortain and fanned out towards St Hilaire, Chèvreville, Fontenay and Le Bazoge. But around mid-day on 7 August the advance had been checked in all sectors; it had been favoured by the weather, and when that lifted in the afternoon the Germans were subjected to devastating Allied air attacks and pinned to the ground they had gained. American reinforcements were quickly available, and that evening General Montgomery told the CIGS that he had 'no anxiety whatever' for the security of the sector.[91]

□

As we shall now see, intelligence gave accurate and timely warning of all the decisions and movements made by the Germans in the first week of August. It was largely because the Allied break-out from Normandy was accompanied by 'a spectacular rise' in the number obtained from France that the volume of Army Enigma decrypts was larger in August than in any previous month of the war; nor was it exceeded in any subsequent month before March 1945. A similar increase in the German Army's low-grade traffic improved Army Y's coverage of the locations of the German units.[92] Ground sources and aerial reconnaissance continued to supplement Sigint by providing information about the bringing up of enemy reinforcements. A large proportion of the Sigint was of a tactical nature, quickly overtaken by events in what had become a fast-moving battle. But it was so comprehensive that there can be little doubt that the Allied Commands derived great benefit from it; and it would in particular be surprising if it did not influence their decision to bring to bear the whole weight of US Ninth Air Force and 2nd Tactical Air Force to stop XLVII Panzer Corps's counter-attack towards Avranches.

---

91.   Ellis, op cit, Vol 1, pp 413–416.
92.   *History of Sigint in the Field*, p 184.

We deal first with the intelligence received from the front held by Panzer Gruppe West which was re-named Fifth Panzer Army on 6 August. A decrypt signalled early on 1 August gave the boundaries of the sector held by 326th Infantry Division the previous evening, when the Division had the Reconnaissance Abteilung of 21st Panzer Division on its left.[93] A decrypt at 0818 on 2 August reported that 10th SS Panzer's Reconnaissance Abteilung had arrived to support 276th Division.[94] An emergency signal from GC and CS at 1408 on 2 August reported that, according to 21st Panzer Division, II SS Panzer Corps had been brought into the line during the night 1–2 August between LXXIV Corps* and II Parachute Corps in order to stabilise the situation. 21st Panzer Division was under command of II SS Panzer Corps and had 10th SS Panzer Division on its right and 9th SS Panzer Division on its left.[95] A decrypt at 2014 gave 9th SS Panzer Division's front line at 1400 that afternoon: its task was to throw the Allies back to the Souleuvre river.[96]

A report late on 1 August by the Flivo with 326th Infantry Division that its GOC had been killed was decrypted on 3 August.[97] Decrypts that evening referred to penetration by Allied armour in the area Le Bény Bocage, and appreciated that a breakthrough to the Falaise-Vire road was intended.[98] Reporting the move west of II SS Panzer Corps to meet the threat north-east of Vire and the parlous state of the enemy on his left flank, 21st Army Group's intelligence summary considered that he was losing control of the battle. Only if large reinforcements were quickly available could he hope to stabilise the situation, but there were no large forces available and no forces quickly available. It had become apparent that 11th Panzer Division was after all not coming north of the Loire. An infantry division might come from the Bordeaux area. Either 9th Panzer Division or an infantry division was probably coming up from Dijon. Three divisions were thought to be on the way from north of the Seine. These reinforcements would not be enough.[99]

Decrypts on 4 August showed 326th Infantry Division, 9th and 10th SS Panzer Divisions and 277th and 276th Infantry Divisions

---

* 21st Panzer's message said LXXXIV Corps: GC and CS commented that this must be a mistake and that LXXIV was intended.

93.   DEFE 3/65. XL 4260 of 1 August.
94.   ibid, XL 4413 of 2 August.
95.   ibid, XL 4437 of 2 August.
96.   ibid, XL 4475 of 2 August.
97.   DEFE 3/112, XL 4590 of 3 August.
98.   ibid, XLs 4605 and 4611 of 3 August.
99.   WO 171/132, No 152 of 3 August.

all carrying out planned withdrawals.[100] The Flivo with 10th SS Panzer Division was particularly explicit, reporting at 0800 that the former main defence line was still occupied by rearguards; the Division would hold two positions until its right-hand neighbour had withdrawn and it would then withdraw itself.[101] An emergency signal sent out by GC and CS at 1612 reported that 12th SS Panzer Division was being relieved by 272nd Infantry Division.[102] A decrypt just after midnight confirmed that the relief had taken place.[103] Other decrypts during the day indicated that 1st SS Panzer Division was to move shortly, but that its position was unchanged at 1900 that evening.[104]

JK II's orders for 5 August, signalled at 0303, called for operations in the area Pontaubault–St Hilaire–Pontorson. The area around Avranches which was strongly protected by Allied anti-aircraft batteries was to be avoided. Two Gruppen daily were to be rested in turn on 5, 6, 7, 8 and 9 August.[105] Early on 5 August GC and CS decrypted a report by JK II the previous morning that the main defence line between Thury Harcourt and the Vire was being withdrawn.[106] At 1040 an emergency signal to the Commands carried a message of 0530 from the Flivo with 1st SS Panzer Division reporting that the Division had begun to pull out from the line during the night.[107] Later decrypts that day revealed that its sector was being taken over by 89th Infantry Division and that it would assemble north of Falaise.[108] 272nd Infantry Division also reported its front line in the new sector which it had taken over from 12th SS Panzer Division.[109] A decrypt at 2031 revealed that at 1500 that afternoon 9th SS Panzer Division and its neighbour (3rd Parachute Division) were intending to attack west of Chênedolle:[110] another decrypt signalled at 2331 reported that the attack had been abandoned because of Allied artillery fire but would be renewed next day.[111]*

---

* GOC II Parachute Corps referred to this operation in his day report, decrypted late on 6 August; serious losses had reduced the fighting strength of 3rd Parachute Division to about

100. DEFE 3/112, XLs 4635, 4682, 4688 and 4692 of 4 August.
101. ibid, XL 4682 of 4 August.
102. ibid, XL 4685 of 4 August.
103. DEFE 3/113, XL 4743 of 5 August.
104. DEFE 3/112, XLs 4630, 4670 and 4684 of 4 August; DEFE 3/113, XL 4744 of 5 August.
105. DEFE 3/113, XL 4759 of 5 August.
106. ibid, XL 4764 of 5 August.
107. ibid, XL 4795 of 5 August.
108. ibid, XLs 4833 and 4873 of 5 August.
109. ibid, XL 4864 of 5 August.
110. ibid, XL 4854 of 5 August.
111. ibid, XL 4877 of 5 August.

There was no advance warning of the attack by 10th SS Panzer Division on the Perrier position on the night of 6 August. A message sent at 1800 and signalled at 2314, said that the Division was being used briefly to deal with penetration between 3rd Parachute Division and 9th SS Panzer Division.[115] Another message at 2000, signalled at 0233 on 7 August, reported that the attack had been stopped by Allied artillery.[116] At 0530 on 7 August the Division said that the attack had been finally broken off. The old main defence line had been restored. The Division had had considerable losses.[117]

21st Army Group's intelligence summary of 6 August appreciated that Panzer Gruppe West was making an orderly withdrawal towards the Orne with a strong hinge in I SS Panzer Corps south and south-east of Caen.[118] The summary went on to say that liberation of Brittany was being rapidly accomplished. The enemy's southern flank was exposed, but it was still too strong to be described as open. 84th, 89th and 708th Infantry Divisions had joined the battle and 9th Panzer Division was certainly on the way from Seventh Army's front.

On 7 August Army Y gave timely warning of preparations to counter-attack XII Corps's bridgehead east of the Orne with two battle groups drawn largely from infantry and tanks of 12th SS Panzer Division. The counter-attack began that evening. A decrypt signalled at 0432 on 8 August warned that it was to be renewed that morning. It was repulsed in hard fighting by 59th (Staffordshire) Division, whose GOC acknowledged how valuable the Y information had been.[119]

The following intelligence had meanwhile come in from Seventh Army's front. Decrypts on 1 August and in the small hours of 2 August reflected the crisis caused by the gap which had been torn in Seventh Army's left wing. On 31 July LXXXIV Corps admitted that the area south and east of Avranches was open.[120]

1,200.[112] On 1 August he had reported it as about 1,500.[113] On 6 August a delayed decrypt brought a report made by C-in-C West on 18 July on German casualties from D-day to 16 July. These amounted to 100,000 men including 2,760 officers. Counting drafts already announced only 12 per cent of the losses could be replaced.[114]

112. DEFE 3/114, XL 5011 of 6 August.
113. DEFE 3/112, XL 4662 of 4 August.
114. DEFE 3/113, XL 4989 of 6 August.
115. DEFE 3/114, XL 5023 of 6 August.
116. ibid, XL 5039 of 7 August.
117. ibid, XL 5093 of 7 August.
118. WO 171/132, No 153 of 6 August.
119. DEFE 3/114, XL 5184 of 8 August; WO 285/3, Nos 64 and 65 of 7 and 8 August; Letter of 7 January 1983 from Major Skillen to the authors.
120. DEFE 3/65, XL 4376 of 2 August.

That night reinforcements were being brought up to join a battle group of 116th Panzer and elements of 91st Infantry Division in an attempt to close the gap.[121] In the afternoon of 1 August Allied tank spearheads were threatening Rennes.[122] The airfield there was to be partially destroyed and the airfields at Lorient, Vannes and Gael totally destroyed.[123] In a message timed 1600 on 1 August 13th Flak Division reported that save for defence by isolated elements the Army's left flank was open. The main body was flooding back. 13th Flak Division knew of no available reserves. In co-operation with Seventh Army it had assembled Flak Regiment 87 to protect Mortain, but without any infantry support.[124] At 2100 the bringing up of fuel and ammunition to Flak elements employed in a ground role to block Allied penetration into Brittany was called a matter of life and death.[125]

A decrypt signalled at 1347 on 2 August revealed that Hitler had approved the move of 2nd Parachute Division from Brittany to the Normandy operational area, but had ruled against bringing 319th Infantry Division over from the Channel Islands.[126] A decrypt signalled at 1044 giving the Vire as the boundary between II Parachute Corps and XLVII Panzer Corps,[127] and another at 1541 giving 116th Panzer Division's front,[128] were helpful in keeping track of Seventh Army's order of battle. 116th Panzer's task was to counter-attack towards Avranches.[129] Panzer Lehr's Flivo reported at midday that it had only one battle group still in the front line, near Villedieu.[130] Survivors of 243rd Infantry Division's battle group had reached outposts of LXXXIV Corps on 29 July: the Staff had been on foot.[131]

In a message sent at 0715 on 2 August, decrypted at 0301 on 3 August, LXXXIV Corps's Flivo referred to re-grouping and listed 353rd Infantry Division, 116th Panzer Division and 275th Infantry Division as subordinated. The Corps's right-hand boundary was at Gathémo, the left was open.[132] A decrypt signalled at 0534 gave the GAF's view of the land situation at 1730 the previous evening. A new defence front was being constructed under strong Allied

---

121. ibid, XL 4338 of 1 August.
122. ibid, XL 4342 of 1 August.
123. ibid, XL 4375 of 2 August.
124. ibid, XL 4385 of 2 August.
125. ibid, XL 4408 of 2 August.
126. ibid, XL 4434 of 2 August.
127. ibid, XL 4422 of 2 August.
128. ibid, XL 4439 of 2 August.
129. ibid, XL 4459 of 2 August.
130. ibid, XL 4376 of 2 August.
131. ibid, XL 4396 of 2 August.
132. DEFE 3/112, XL 4517 of 3 August.

pressure on the general line Villedieu-Le Mesnil Adelée-Reffuveille (on the flank of the breakthrough). In the area St Hilaire-Fougères-Rennes the task of the German troops was to hold up the Allies until reinforcements arrived. The weak covering forces between Rennes and Dinan were being strengthened. The Allies were pouring strong forces through the Avranches-Pontaubault defile.[133] In a message sent at 1600, and signalled to the Commands at 2255, JK II said that the Army's main intention was to delay the Allied advance from Avranches by all available means.[134] The GAF's operations were in line with this appreciation. Decrypts reported that JK II was committing all its resources on 2 and 3 August to prevent further breakthrough south or south-east.[135] Warning that Fliegerkorps IX intended to make a concentrated attack on Avranches during the night of 2–3 August was given at 2103 on 2 August.[136] An emergency signal to the Commands at 1705 on 3 August warned that six Do 217s were to attack the bridges at Pontaubault and Pontorson between 2010 and 2030 that evening.[137] JK II ordered road strafing throughout the night 3–4 August, telling unit commanding officers to impress on their crews the unqualified necessity for these unusual operations because of the gravity of the situation.[138]

Orders by Seventh Army in the evening of 2 August, signalled by GC and CS at 0217 on 4 August, directed II Parachute Corps to make a junction on its right with Panzer Gruppe West and on its left with XLVII Panzer Corps. The latter was to withdraw during the night of 2–3 August, and in the process pull out the main body of 2nd Panzer Division from the front and assemble it east of the Forêt de la Sever for operations on the Army's left wing.[139] Decrypts signalled at 0604 and 0649 on 4 August showed that on 2 August 353rd, 2nd Panzer and 352nd* Divisions were being supplied by XLVII Panzer Corps, which was also supplying 116th Panzer Division on behalf of its left-hand neighbour, and that the

---

* 352nd Infantry had been virtually destroyed. In a message decrypted on 1 August the Division suggested withdrawing Staff, signals and other survivors from 2nd Panzer Division to form cadres for new units.[140] A decrypt late on 4 August reported that the remaining elements of the Division were moving to an area south-east of Alençon.[141]

133. ibid, XL 4536 of 3 August.
134. ibid, XL 4617 of 3 August.
135. DEFE 3/65, XLs 4375 and 4429 of 2 August; DEFE 3/112, XL 4537 of 3 August.
136. DEFE 3/65, XL 4481 of 2 August.
137. DEFE 3/112, XL 4595 of 3 August.
138. ibid, XL 4626 of 4 August.
139. ibid, XL 4625 of 4 August.
140. DEFE 3/65, XL 4323 of 1 August.
141. DEFE 3/112, XL 4715 of 4 August.

elements of 2nd SS Panzer and 17th SS PG Divisions, which had been merged under the former, were also subordinated to XLVII Panzer Corps.[142] The locations of the battle HQs of XLVII Panzer Corps and 2nd Panzer Division in the morning of 4 August were given in a decrypt signalled at 1557.[143] Another, signalled at 2122, reported that early that morning 2nd Panzer Division had a northern and a southern battle group. The northern group had 3rd Parachute Division on its right and 2nd SS Panzer Division on its left. The southern group had Panzer Lehr on its right and 116th Panzer Division on its left.[144] A decrypt signalled at 2245 contained an extract from the day report of 3 August by an unspecified Corps. The supply situation in respect of ammunition was strained. In respect of fuel it was serious in view of a new Army order.[145] From a reference to 2nd SS Panzer and 353rd Infantry Divisions it could be deduced that the report was by XLVII Panzer Corps, and with benefit of hindsight we can see that the new Army order concerned the counter-attack ordered by Hitler.

A Flivo message of 0600 on 5 August, giving the order of battle of LXXXIV Corps as 363rd and 353rd Infantry Divisions and 116th Panzer Division was decrypted by 1047.[146] Another message, decrypted soon after midday, revealed that the Corps was taking over a sector from XLVII Panzer Corps, its left-hand neighbour, and had II Parachute Corps on its right.[147] An emergency signal sent out by GC and CS at 1052 announced that 2nd SS Panzer Division was being withdrawn from the front line west of Vire to an assembly area.[148] A decrypt signalled at 1221 disclosed that the Flivo who was known to have been with LXXXI Corps at the end of July was reporting that morning at a location 12 kilometres east of Alençon.[149] Confirmation that LXXXI Corps was on the move from Rouen was received on 6 August.[150] 84th Infantry Division was identified in the Mortain area during 5 August.[151] A decrypt signalled at 1905 carried an appreciation by the Parachute Army on 2 August that in respect of time, space and strength 84th, 363rd, 708th, 2nd Parachute and 9th Panzer

---

142. ibid, XLs 4638 and 4639 of 4 August.
143. ibid, XL 4683 of 4 August.
144. ibid, XL 4721 of 4 August.
145. ibid, XL 4738 of 4 August.
146. DEFE 3/113, XL 4795 of 5 August.
147. ibid, XL 4805 of 5 August.
148. ibid, XL 4799 of 5 August.
149. ibid, XL 4804 of 5 August.
150. DEFE 3/114, XL 5006 of 6 August.
151. WO 285/3, No 62 of 5 August.

Divisions, which were coming up, were still not adequate to seal off the Allied penetration.[152]

A decrypt signalled at 0313 on 5 August reported that JK II was again committing all its effort to road strafing in the general area Pontaubault–St Hilaire–Fougères–Pontorson. (The area around Avranches protected by Allied anti-aircraft was to be avoided.)[153] Warning that Fliegerkorps X intended to make dusk and moonlight attacks on the Pontorson bridges, and that Fliegerkorps IX intended to attack St Hilaire and Mortain between 2153 and 2255, was given in decrypts signalled at 1701 and 1921.[154]

A request by LXXXIV Corps at 2000 on 5 August for continuous fighter cover over 84th Infantry Division, which was relieving 116th Panzer Division during the night 5–6 August, was the subject of an emergency signal to the Commands at 0004 on 6 August.[155]* JK II's reply, decrypted at 0613, was that support in this manner was impossible as it would require the employment of about 1,000 aircraft, but that it intended to operate on 6 August over the southern part of the area.[157] A decrypt signalled at 0212 disclosed that both Flak regiments in the western sector were being transferred to an unspecified wing of Seventh Army, while both regiments in the eastern sector were being shifted towards the centre, or left half, of Panzer Gruppe West's front.[158] The day report for 4 August decrypted by 0145, submitted to Seventh Army by an unspecified Corps, stated that its supply situation was nowhere near assured having regard to the tactical intentions. Ammunition and fuel were needed immediately.[159] A flurry of decrypts sent out from 1912 onwards revealed what these tactical intentions were. At 1400 on 6 August 2nd SS Panzer Division asked for fighter protection over its attack in the area St Clement–St Hilaire, and for day-fighters over the same area on 7 August.[160] In an emergency signal at 1948 GC and CS warned that at 1330 that afternoon 116th Panzer, 2nd Panzer, 1st SS Panzer and 2nd SS Panzer Divisions (reading from right to left) were

---

* In its summary for the CIGS for the week ending 6 August MI 14 pointed out that the enemy had managed to withdraw four Panzer divisions (12th SS, 1st SS, 10th SS and Panzer Lehr) from the line and a fifth (116th Panzer) was due to be withdrawn during the night 5–6 August. He would probably use them to prevent his left flank being turned.[156]

152. DEFE 3/113, XL 4847 of 5 August.
153. ibid, XL 4759 of 5 August.
154. ibid, XLs 4835 and 4851 of 5 August.
155. ibid, XL 4881 of 6 August.
156. WO 208/4316, MI 14 summary for the CIGS, 6 August.
157. DEFE 3/113, XL 4917 of 6 August.
158. ibid, XL 4887 of 6 August.
159. ibid, XL 4920 of 6 August.
160. ibid, XL 4991 of 6 August.

subordinated to XLVII Panzer Corps for an attack westward.[161] Another emergency signal sent out at 2001 reported that 2nd SS Panzer was to attack Mortain and then St Hilaire. The latter would be bombarded until midnight.[162] The decrypt of JK II's affirmative reply to 2nd SS Panzer's request for support was signalled at 2140.[163]

At 0011 on 7 August another emergency signal from GC and CS reported JK II's statement that Seventh Army would attack west from the Sourdeval-Mortain area in the evening of 6 August with elements of five Panzer divisions. The Brécy-Montigny road was the first objective.[164] The decrypt of orders for 7 August, signalled at 0135, disclosed arrangements for liaison with the Panzer divisions and emphasised that success of the attack would be decisive for clearing up the situation in Brittany.[165] An incomplete message in the afternoon of 6 August (probably from XLVII Panzer Corps), signalled to the Commands at 0429 on 7 August, mentioned Avranches and said that the objective was to cut off the Allies, who had broken through to the south, from their supply base and make junction with the coast.[166] An emergency signal sent to the Commands at 1723 reported that two hours earlier 2nd SS Panzer Division was still intending to capture St Hilaire,[167] but another decrypt, signalled at 1918, confirmed that XLVII Panzer Corps's offensive had stalled. 1st SS Panzer Division's Flivo had reported at 1245 that the Army's attack had been brought to a standstill by extremely strong fighter-bomber activity. Screening of the air over the area St Barthélemy–Juvigny–Romagny was urgently required. The GAF had replied that its very strong fighter effort had failed to reach the target area because of continuous air battles which went on right back to its take-off points.[168]

A decrypt signalled early on 7 August reported orders to 708th Division (en route from the Biscay coast) to collect ammunition, and indicated that it was, or would be, subordinated to LXXXI Corps (en route from Rouen).[169]

□

---

161. ibid, XL 4997 of 6 August.
162. ibid, XL 4999 of 6 August.
163. DEFE 3/114, XL 5012 of 6 August.
164. ibid, XL 5027 of 6 August.
165. ibid, XL 5029 of 6 August.
166. ibid, XL 6063 of 7 August.
167. ibid, XL 5119 of 7 August.
168. ibid, XL 5125 of 7 August.
169. ibid, XL 5028 of 7 August.

Decrypts in the first few days of August had meanwhile shown that XXV Corps had been made responsible for Brittany and that steps were being taken to mobilise naval and Flak personnel to assist the Army.[170]

Early on 5 August GC and CS decrypted an announcement by C-in-C West that Hitler had approved giving up field installations in Brittany in order to provide forces for the fortresses, but only in cases of absolute necessity. All fortress-type installations were to be defended. Small harbours might be destroyed in agreement with the naval authorities.[171]

Orders late on 4 August from XXV Corps to 265th Infantry Division were decrypted by 1004 on 5 August. The Allied approach to the fortress (St Nazaire) was to be resisted as far from it as practicable so that the attack on it was delayed as long as possible.[172] Decrypts signalled at 1054 and 1424 carried XXV Corps's report of its intention at 0100 that morning. The Allies had not yet made contact with 2nd Parachute Division holding a defence line outside Brest. Elsewhere forces employed in blocking positions would fight their way back to the fortresses by sectors under Allied pressure. Forces in the coastal sectors would be drawn into the fortresses. Since the evening of 3 August 'terrorists' had gone into action supported by the population. Numerous attacks had been made on marching troops and movements were only possible in fairly strong battle groups. Most telephone communications were interrupted.[173] According to a decrypt signalled at 2128 the population of Brest was still quiet late on 2 August: part of it was being evacuated and part was leaving voluntarily. There were demonstrations in several other places.[174]

In a message decrypted by 0317 on 6 August Naval Gruppe West quoted C-in-C West's opinion that St Nazaire, Nantes and Angers were not in immediate danger as strong German forces had crossed the Loire northwards and sufficient forces had been thrown in to protect the Loire crossings.[175] The extension of First Army's responsibilities north of the Loire was confirmed by a decrypt signalled at 0408.[176] A successful attack on the submarine pens at Brest was reported in a decrypt signalled at 0510, which added that the Gendarmes Maritimes and the workers at the

170. DEFE 3/65, XLs 4271, 4319 and 4373 of 1 August, 4386 and 4390 of 2 August; DEFE 3/113, XL 4774 of 5 August.
171. DEFE 3/113, XL 4783 of 5 August.
172. ibid, XL 4789 of 5 August.
173. ibid, XLs 4798 and 4811 of 5 August.
174. ibid, XL 4860 of 5 August.
175. ibid, XL 4891 of 6 August.
176. ibid, XL 4900 of 6 August.

arsenal were on strike.[177] Further particulars of the damage sustained were given in another decrypt.[178] According to a report by XXV Corps at 1900 on 5 August, decrypted by 0605 on 6 August, 353rd and 266th Divisions were under pressure east of Brest. It was doubtful whether the latter, which included three Ost battalions of little fighting value and limited mobility, would get back into the fortress.[179] Orders by von Kluge to XXV Corps about demolitions were decrypted in the afternoon of 6 August. Von Kluge complained that demolitions were often premature because the Allies were over-rated.[180]

The decrypt of XXV Corps's situation report at 0900 on 6 August was signalled at 1551. 265th Division was holding a line covering St Nazaire. Its forces in the Lorient sector were in contact with the Allies at Vannes. No reports had been received from 343rd or 266th Divisions. The battle group of 77th Division was subordinated to the Fortress Commander at St Malo.[181] The latter reported that his outpost positions had been overrun that morning.[182]

In a message to Army Group B, which was decrypted on 6 August, XXV Corps submitted that the Corps staff should not transfer from Lorient to Brest because this would cause communications problems with the east which would make command difficult; the command in Lorient would be inadequate; and it was doubtful whether the move could be accomplished.[183] However, a later message, decrypted on 7 August, informed the Fortress Commander Brest that XXV Corps (30 officers and 300 men) was transferring there during the night 6–7 August.[184] In the event this move was not made. XXV Corps stayed in Lorient, where it was soon isolated.[185]

XXV Corps's situation report at 0730 on 7 August was decrypted that afternoon. 343rd Division had moved its battle HQ into the fortress. 266th was trying to fight its way back. Fighting had begun in the fortress area defended by 2nd Parachute Division.[186] Three long decrypts from several sources about the

---

177. ibid, XL 4907 of 6 August.
178. ibid, XL 4931 of 6 August.
179. ibid, XL 4912 of 6 August.
180. ibid, XL 4964 of 6 August.
181. ibid, XL 4969 of 6 August.
182. DEFE 3/114, XL 5016 of 6 August.
183. DEFE 3/113, XL 4925 of 6 August.
184. DEFE 3/114, XL 5075 of 7 August.
185. Blumenson, op cit, p 343.
186. DEFE 3/114, XLs 5102 and 5112 of 7 August.

situation in Brittany were sent to the Commands in the afternoon and evening of 7 August.[187]

□

On the night 7–8 August First Canadian Army opened the attack in the Caen sector towards Falaise called for by Montgomery's directive of 4 August* (Operation *Totalize*). During the next three days, in heavy fighting, a substantial advance was made on both sides of the Caen-Falaise road, compelling the enemy to reinforce his front with 85th Infantry Division from Fifteenth Army, but by 11 August it was clear that another full-scale attack would have to be mounted in order to break through to Falaise. Meanwhile Second Army's XII Corps had repulsed a determined counter-attack on its bridgehead east of the Orne in the Forêt de Grimbosq and west of the river had pressed forward to Thury Harcourt. Further west between the Orne and the Vire XXX Corps and VIII Corps had made little progress.[188]

Although on 7 August Hitler ordered the renewal of the counter-attack in the Mortain sector towards Avranches it made no further progress. First US Army set about eliminating the salient which had been created, capturing St Barthélemy and Mortain on 11 August. Third US Army continued its sweep west and south. Le Mans was captured on 8 August when General Bradley, with the approval of Montgomery and Eisenhower, turned the American spearhead (XV US Corps) northwards towards Alençon to meet the Canadians attacking southwards towards Falaise.[189]

On 9 August Hitler issued new orders for a surprise attack, at a time to be decided by him, from the Domfront area, first south-westwards, later north-westwards, by an armoured force under General Eberbach. It would be supported, and its southern flank would be protected, by a new group to be formed south-east of Domfront under LXXXI Corps. For this group, and to man a covering line on the Loire, First Army with its Army troops was to be brought up, as were 48th Infantry and 6th Parachute Divisions from Fifteenth Army and 338th Infantry Division from Nineteenth Army, to be followed by another infantry division from Fifteenth Army later. Seventh Army was permitted to

---

* See above, p 237.

187. ibid, XLs 5118, 5143 and 5148 of 7 August.
188. Ellis, op cit, Vol 1, pp 419–425.
189. ibid, p 425.

shorten its line in order to secure the release of necessary forces for Eberbach.[190]

On 11 August Montgomery issued a directive modifying 'for the present' the full plan outlined on 6 August* in order to concentrate on closing the gap behind the enemy forces 'so that we can possibly destroy them where they are now'. First Canadian Army and Second Army were to capture Falaise as the 'first priority and a vital one', after which First Canadian Army was to secure Argentan. 12th US Army Group was to swing its right flank forward to Alençon and then to the general line Sées-Carrouges (about 12 miles south of Argentan). If it appeared 'likely that the enemy may escape us here', the full plan given in the directive of 6 August would be executed. In a significant passage Montgomery stated that: 'The enemy force that will require to be watched carefully is the main concentration of armour now in the Mortain area: it is a formidable force and must be well looked after'.[191]

On the same day that Montgomery issued this directive von Kluge recognised the increasing risk of envelopment and began to extract armoured divisions to meet the northward thrust by XV US Corps which threatened to overwhelm 9th Panzer and 708th Infantry Divisions. That evening Hitler endorsed von Kluge's action, ordering an armoured attack under Eberbach to eliminate this threat in place of the previously planned attack from Domfront.[192]

On 12 August II Canadian Corps and XII Corps resumed their advance towards Falaise. By 14 August II Canadian Corps was about six miles from Falaise at Claire Tizon, and XII Corps some seven miles from the town athwart the Thury Harcourt road.[193]

XV US Corps captured Alençon and Sées on 12 August and was directed on Argentan. But XLVII Panzer Corps with 116th Panzer Division got there first and took control of what remained of 9th Panzer and 708th Infantry Divisions. On 13 August, when 1st SS Panzer and 2nd Panzer Divisions began to arrive, the American advance on Argentan was halted at Ecouché.[194]

Important decisions were taken on 13 and 14 August, one on each side. On the Allied side General Bradley halted the advance northwards of XV US Corps, which already had elements well beyond the Carrouges-Sées line named by Montgomery. Next day he ordered Third US Army to direct part of the Corps eastwards

---

* See above, p 237.

190. ibid, pp 425–426.
191. WO 285/2.
192. Ellis, op cit, Vol 1, pp 426–427.
193. ibid, p 427.
194. Blumenson, op cit, pp 502–503.

to the Seine in accordance with the plan laid down in Montgomery's directive of 6 August.* On the German side on 13 August von Kluge asked permission to withdraw Seventh Army to a line astride Flers, reinforcing Eberbach with all available armour. Very early the next morning he received Hitler's reply giving permission to shorten the line west of Flers, but only under Allied pressure, and naming armoured divisions to be given to Eberbach for the attack on XV US Corps in the Alençon-Carrouges area. Von Kluge accordingly ordered withdrawal in two nights to a shorter line roughly through Flers. During the withdrawal Fifth Panzer Army was to disengage II SS Panzer Corps with 9th SS and 21st Panzer Divisions and transfer them to Eberbach. However, 21st Panzer Division had to be diverted to Falaise where I SS Panzer Corps was in great difficulty.[195]

On 14 August First Canadian Army renewed its main attack southwards with orders to envelope Falaise, which was to be taken by Second Army (Operation *Tractable*). As soon as Falaise was secured, First Canadian Army was to exploit to Trun. Progress was made, but by nightfall on 15 August the Allies were still two or three miles short of Falaise. North-east of the town, however, the Polish Armoured Division (under II Canadian Corps) crossed the river Dives at Jort and set out for Trun, and on its left I Corps began driving the German LXXXVI Corps across the river, opening a gap between it and I SS Panzer Corps. On the southern flank 10th SS Panzer Division was unable to disengage, and from Briouze through Rânes and Ecouché to the east of Argentan Panzer Gruppe Eberbach, with 1st SS Panzer and 2nd and 116th Panzer Divisions in the line, was under heavy pressure. 2nd SS Panzer Division was assembled north-east of Argentan, but 9th SS Panzer Division was still west of the Orne.[196]

For most of 15 August von Kluge, who had set out early to visit Hausser and Eberbach, was 'missing'. He had been caught in an Allied air attack, which knocked out his radio, and delayed by traffic congestion. In his absence Blumentritt, his Chief of Staff,

---

* These decisions have been criticised. The first decision, as we shall see, seems, however, fully justified in the light of the knowledge that Eberbach's armour, which had been singled out by Montgomery for special care, was arriving on the southern flank (see below, pp 256, 258). Indeed, Bradley has said that he preferred a solid shoulder at Argentan to a broken neck at Falaise. His order to Third Army on the next day seems somewhat inconsistent with the first decision. Bradley has attributed it partly to his belief that the German forces were already 'sluicing back' through the gap. This belief did not correspond with the facts or with the available intelligence (see below, pp 260–261). It was certainly not held by Montgomery's intelligence staff although he himself told the CIGS on 14 August that in his opinion a good many of the enemy had managed to pass eastward out of the ring (see below, p 261).

195. Ellis, op cit, Vol 1, p 429; Blumenson, op cit, pp 516–517.
196. Ellis, op cit, Vol 1, pp 430–431, 434.

warned Jodl that the situation was grave. Hitler, who was undergoing 'the worst day of his life' with the crisis on the western front, the Allied landing in the south of France* and his suspicion that von Kluge was secretly contacting the Allies, placed Hausser in temporary command and consulted Kesselring and Model about a possible successor to von Kluge as C-in-C West.[197]

Very early on 16 August von Kluge reported in the strongest terms that a large-scale counter-offensive to restore the situation was out of the question. There were not enough tanks, and the shortage of fuel was a decisive fact. Seventh Army must be evacuated while the gap between Falaise and Argentan was still open. In reply to his request for an order to this effect Hitler authorised withdrawal in two stages behind the Orne and the Dives. Contact was to be established with LXXXI Corps at Gacé. Falaise was to be held as the northern bastion and Eberbach was to attack south-east to enlarge the mouth of the pocket. During the day, Montgomery ordered First Canadian Army to seize Trun as quickly as possible and asked Bradley to push north-east from Argentan and make a junction with the Canadians at Chambois, four miles south-east of Trun.[198]

Falaise was captured during the night 16–17 August while the Germans began to withdraw from the west end of the pocket in good order. The order of battle of Fifth Panzer Army and Seventh Army on 17 August was approximately as follows:

Fifth Panzer Army
Cabourg-St Pierre-sur-Dives: LXXXVI Corps
    711th, 346th, 272nd Infantry Divisions.
St Pierre-sur-Dives-Orne; I SS Panzer Corps
    85th Infantry, 12th SS Panzer, 21st Panzer, 89th and 271st Infantry Divisions.
Orne–Condé-sur-Noireau: LXXIV Corps
    277th, 276th, 326th Infantry Divisions.

Seventh Army
Condé–Flers: II Parachute Corps
    3rd Parachute, 363rd, 331st (elements) Infantry Divisions.
Flers–Briouze: LXXXIV Corps
    353rd, 84th, 243rd (elements), 275th (elements) Infantry, 10th SS Panzer Divisions.
Briouze–Argentan–Gacé: Panzer Gruppe Eberbach, including

---

* See below, p 273 et seq.

197. Blumenson, op cit, pp 519–520.
198. Ellis, op cit, Vol 1, pp 432, 433–439.

LVII Panzer Corps, XLVII Panzer Corps and II SS Panzer Corps (arriving)
708th Infantry (elements), 2nd Panzer, 1st SS Panzer, 116th Panzer, 9th Panzer (elements), 2nd SS Panzer, 17th SS PG (elements) and 9th SS Panzer (arriving).

East of Panzer Gruppe Eberbach LXXXI Corps with improvised forces (battle groups of 331st and 334th Infantry and 6th Parachute Divisions, and 17th GAF Division) was stretched along a 70-mile front from Gacé to Rambouillet.[199]

On 17 August the Allies followed up the German withdrawal at the western end of the pocket. By night-fall enemy rearguards were still 12 to 15 miles west of the Falaise–Argentan road, but a great deal of traffic had been moving eastward through Chambois and Trun to the neighbourhood of Vimoutiers. This included II SS Panzer Corps, which had been ordered into Army Group Reserve with 9th SS Panzer, and 2nd SS Panzer Division. The latter was withdrawn that evening from Le Bourg–St Léonard, some four miles south of Chambois, where, with 116th Panzer Division, it had checked the American advance. During the day, Montgomery gave orders to First Canadian Army that the Polish Armoured Division was to push on to Chambois as quickly as possible regardless of cost. On the German side Field Marshal Model took over command from von Kluge in the evening.[200]

The Canadians captured Trun on 18 August and pressed on to the neighbourhood of St Lambert. Polish elements reached Coudehard. The American attack towards Chambois was halted about three miles short of the objective. A loose encirclement was nearly complete and very late that day II SS Panzer Corps was ordered to restore contact with Seventh Army by attacking towards Trun. During 18 and 19 August the Germans resumed their withdrawal towards the Falaise–Argentan road.[201]

On 19 August the Canadians got into St Lambert but could only hold half the village. Further left they crossed the Trun–Vimoutiers road at Hordouseaux, but could not reach the Poles in the neighbourhood of Coudehard. In the evening a Polish group fought their way into Chambois, where they met the Americans who had arrived just before them. Intensive Allied air attacks prevented II SS Panzer Corps counter-attacking from Vimoutiers.

Despite these advances the encirclement remained incomplete. Early on 20 August a determined attempt to break out, led by II Parachute Corps south of Trun and XLVII Panzer Corps near

199. ibid, pp 439–440.
200. ibid, pp 441–442.
201. ibid, p 442.

Chambois, was assisted by II SS Panzer Corps's belated counter-attack and was partially successful. It was not until 21 August that the gap was finally closed in strength. Thanks to the partial exodus which began some days before the climax of the battle and the determination of the troops which led the break-out, a sizable number of men escaped from the pocket. But a comparatively small proportion of these were combat troops and the average combat strength of the divisions was no more than a few hundred men. The Germans lost some 10,000 killed, 50,000 prisoners (among them the Generals commanding LXXXIV Corps and 84th and 276th Infantry Divisions) and a huge quantity of material, including tanks, artillery, vehicles, horses and radio equipment. They had suffered a devastating defeat.[202] According to Luftflotte 3 in a message decrypted on 22 August, 40–50 per cent of Seventh Army and Fifth Panzer Army had broken out of the pocket, but there had been exceptionally high losses of material.[203] On 27 August MI 14 considered that six infantry field divisions had been destroyed – 84th, 271st, 276th, 277th, 353rd and 363rd.[204]

□

Even more so than in the earlier stages of the Normandy fighting, the intelligence obtained from Sigint was prompt and copious between 8 and 21 August. Viewing it with hindsight, when it presents a coherent picture, there may be some danger of over-rating its value to the commanders who received it piecemeal while the battle was being fought. Even when allowance has been made for this, however, the fact remains that all the enemy's major decisions were disclosed with little delay. In particular, orders for the renewed attack towards Avranches by strengthened forces from the Domfront area issued at 1800 on 9 August were decrypted by 0349 the next morning, and detailed information about the forces involved followed during the day. Indications that the armour under Eberbach was being redeployed to meet the threat of envelopment were received late on 11 August and confirmed on 12 and 13 August. Von Kluge's urgent advice, very early on 16 August, that the Armies must be evacuated while the Falaise–Argentan gap remained open was known that evening, as was Army Group B's order for withdrawal which stemmed from it. The creation of an Army Group Reserve of two armoured divisions under II SS Panzer Corps was known on 18 August.

---

200. ibid, pp 441–442.
201. ibid, p 442.
202. ibid, pp 442–446; Blumenson, op cit, pp 538–539, 542–558.
203. DEFE 3/123, XL 7470 of 22 August.
204. WO 208/4316, MI 14 Weekly Summary for the CIGS, 27 August.

Orders for 8 August by JK II, decrypted in the small hours of the morning, indicated that the Germans intended to continue their counter-attack towards Avranches.[205] JK II ordered its forces to concentrate in order to avoid the needless losses suffered by small formations.[206] The decrypt of General Hausser's order, at 2000 on 7 August, that XLVII Panzer Corps's attack was to be continued with all forces so far as the situation allowed, and the decisive breakthrough to Avranches achieved, was signalled at 1801 on 8 August.[207] In fact the situation that day had not allowed the attack to continue. A complaint by 2nd SS Panzer Division at 1100 that fighter-bombers were stopping all movement was decrypted by 2214,[208] and JK II's report that strong Allied fighter screening had forced vigorous air battles and ruthless operation with losses by 0340 on 9 August.[209] A decrypt signalled at 2024 on 8 August gave Brécy, Avranches and St Hilaire as Fliegerkorps IX's targets for the night.[210] Another signalled at 2053 reported that JK II would again be supporting the Army in the Mortain area on 9 August.[211]

A report by I SS Panzer Corps at 1430 on 8 August on the massive bombing which accompanied First Canadian Army's attack towards Falaise was decrypted by 0241 on 9 August; it stated that casualties had been relatively light.[212] Army Y reported that 276th Infantry Division had been thrown into confusion by XII Corps's attack west of the Orne, and had wanted to put part of 21st Panzer Division's reconnaissance battalion, which had been monitoring the battle, into the fighting. GOC 21st Panzer Division had intervened to veto this proposal.[213] A report by JK II in the evening of 8 August was decrypted by 1323 on 9 August. According to this a defence line, echeloned to the rear, was being constructed from Domfront through Mayenne and Sille. Allied reconnaissance forces were driving on boldly from Laval. Allied movements and behaviour showed them to be very fully informed of the German situation and state of forces.[214] A decrypt signalled at 1722 reported that 2nd SS Panzer Division had been transferred from XLVII Panzer Corps to the newly arrived LVIII Panzer

205. DEFE 3/114, XL 5164 of 8 August.
206. ibid, XL 5175 of 8 August.
207. ibid, XL 5248 of 8 August.
208. DEFE 3/115, XL 5285 of 8 August.
209. ibid, XL 5318 of 9 August.
210. ibid, XL 5264 of 8 August.
211. ibid, XL 5269 of 8 August.
212. ibid, XL 5310 of 9 August.
213. WO 285/3, No 66 of 9 August.
214. DEFE 3/115, XL 5356 of 9 August.

Corps.[215] A decrypt later in the evening indicated that a battle group of 11th Panzer Division was moving north from Blois towards Chartres.[216] During the day tactical air reconnaissance reported considerable movement in and around Falaise, mostly in an easterly direction.[217]

The next day, 10 August, Sigint provided information in advance about the armoured attack to be mounted under Eberbach. An emergency signal from GC and CS at 0349 summarised orders issued at 1800 the previous evening to Seventh Army and General Eberbach. After re-grouping and bringing up decisive offensive weapons, a Panzer Gruppe under Eberbach (with von Kluge's son as Chief of Staff) was to launch an attack from the southern wing of Seventh Army to reach the sea at Avranches by a bold and unhesitating thrust from the area Mortain–Domfront. To ensure unity of supply and command the Panzer Gruppe would be subordinated to Seventh Army. The likely date for the attack was 11 August, but there might be a postponement at short notice.[218] Another emergency signal two hours later disclosed that 9th Panzer Division's Panther battalion, a Werfer Brigade and medium artillery Abteilung 992 were to be brought up to Eberbach.[219] A third emergency signal at 1304 disclosed that 10th SS Panzer Division was moving west to the area between Mortain and Domfront,[220] and a fourth emergency signal at 1436 listed the formations under Panzer Gruppe Eberbach as XLVII Panzer Corps with 2nd and 116th Panzer, 1st, 2nd and 10th SS Panzer Divisions, the main body of 9th Panzer Division with its Panther Abteilung, Werfer Brigades 8 and 9 and medium artillery Abteilung 992. Sepp Dietrich was to take over command of Fifth Panzer Army as Eberbach's deputy.[221] A decrypt signalled at 1041 gave the location of Panzer Gruppe Eberbach's headquarters at 0700 that morning.[222]

Further information about the western sector was supplied by high-grade Sigint during the day. A situation report by LXXXIV Corps at 1700 on 9 August, admitting penetration in the sectors of 363rd and 353rd Divisions, was decrypted by 0407,[223] and information that these divisions intended to counter-attack at daybreak to regain their main defence line was signalled by GC

---

215. ibid, XL 5396 of 9 August.
216. ibid, XL 5438 of 9 August.
217. WO 285/3, No 66 of 9 August.
218. DEFE 3/115, XL 5461 of 10 August.
219. ibid, XL 5470 of 10 August.
220. DEFE 3/116, XL 5502 of 10 August.
221. ibid, XL 5516 of 10 August.
222. DEFE 3/115, XL 5492 of 10 August.
223. ibid, XL 5463 of 10 August.

and CS at 0954.[224] From the eastern flank a decrypt signalled at 0415 on 10 August gave I SS Panzer Corps's line at 2130 the previous evening and mentioned a 'newly committed formation',[225] and another signalled at 0726, gave the boundary between I SS Panzer Corps and LXXXVI Corps.[226] Yet another, signalled at 1039, disclosed that on 8 August 12th SS Panzer Division had had 34 Pzkw IV and 20 Pzkw V tanks serviceable.[227]

Other decrypts of 10 August dealt with the movements of German reinforcements. 331st Infantry Division, less the battle group which had already reached Seventh Army's front, would be halted in the Gacé area;[228] 6th Parachute Division was to be brought up from the Paris area and subordinated to Seventh Army;[229] 49th Infantry Division (also from Fifteenth Army) was to be brought up to Seventh Army in the Argentan area;[230] First Army was handing over to LXIV Corps at Bordeaux and transferring to Fontainebleau.[231] A decrypt signalled at 2314 gave Fliegerkorps IX's targets for the night as Juvigny and Brécy.[232] Ultra also disclosed that OKW had ordered the immediate development of a rearward position and that comprehensive and draconian measures were to be employed to push it ahead. One section of the position was along the Marne from Dormans to Vitry le François, towards the Marne–Saône Canal. It could be inferred that the line would probably continue northwards along the Somme, and that east of Paris the Germans would use the Seine and its tributaries running south as delaying positions and then withdraw to the Somme-Marne line.[233]*

Second Army's intelligence summary for 10 August noted that 85th Infantry Division had been identified on I SS Panzer Corps's front and 331st Infantry Division south of Vire. The summary took particular note of the activities of 21st Panzer Division's reconnaissance battalion, which had had patrols on all parts of the front; one with 12th SS Panzer east of the Orne, another with

---

* This appreciation was confirmed by the decrypt on 16 August of a message ordering the most rapid possible provision of manpower to develop the Somme–Marne–Saône–Jura position.[234]

224. ibid, XL 5489 of 10 August.
225. ibid, XL 5464 of 10 August.
226. ibid, XL 5481 of 10 August.
227. ibid, XL 5490 of 10 August.
228. ibid, XL 5457 of 10 August.
229. DEFE 3/116, XL 5525 of 10 August.
230. ibid, XL 5577 of 10 August.
231. ibid, XL 5540 of 10 August.
232. ibid, XL 5588 of 10 August.
233. ibid, XLs 5501 and 5533 of 10 August; WO 208/4316, Weekly Summary for the CIGS, 13 August.
234. DEFE 3/119, XL 6450 of 16 August.

276th and 277th Divisions west of the river, a third in the Mortain area, a fourth as far south as Le Mans. The report centre was 20 miles south of Falaise, near Rânes, where a conference summoned for 1800 that evening had been attacked by the RAF, but weather had obscured the results.[235]

A decrypt signalled at 0934 on 11 August gave the right and left boundaries the previous evening of the front held by I SS Panzer Corps with 85th, 89th and 271st Infantry Divisions in line and 12th SS Panzer Division in Corps Reserve.[236] The sector boundaries of the infantry divisions at 1900 on 11 August were given in a decrypt signalled at 2340.[237] The decrypt of a report by I SS Panzer Corps on 10 August to the effect that shortage of ammunition would be felt at any moment and shortage of fuel by 12 August was also signalled.[238]

For the western flank on 11 August Sigint provided the day reports by XLVII Panzer Corps for 9 and 10 August. That for 9 August included 2nd Panzer, 116th Panzer and 2nd SS Panzer Divisions.[239] On 10 August 2nd Panzer and 2nd SS Panzer were no longer subordinated: the Corps was supplying 1st SS Panzer Division, but its subordination was not clear.[240] Two decrypts late in the evening gave strong indications that the armour was being redeployed. At 2128 GC and CS reported in an emergency signal that at 1300 Panzer Gruppe Eberbach was moving to a location 20 kilometres north-east of Alençon.[241] A decrypt signalled at 2328 disclosed that 116th Panzer was being withdrawn from the line during the day.[242] Fliegerkorps IX gave Juvigny and troops in the Vire area as targets.[243] JK II intended to support the Army and force through a reconnaissance in the area Mamers–Alençon–Le Mans.[244]

Second Army's intelligence summary for 11 August suggested that the layout of Fifth Panzer Army and Seventh Army, which had been subject to 'change and decay', was as follows:

Sea to St Sylvain: LXXXVI Corps
     711th, 346th and 272th Infantry Divisions.

---

235. WO 285/3, No 67 of 10 August.
236. DEFE 3/116, XL 5643 of 11 August.
237. ibid, XL 5730 of 11 August.
238. ibid, XL 5691 of 11 August.
239. ibid, XL 5668 of 11 August.
240. ibid, XL 5687 of 11 August.
241. ibid, XL 5720 of 11 August.
242. ibid, XL 5728 of 11 August.
243. ibid, XL 5710 of 11 August.
244. ibid, XL 5737 of 11 August.

St Sylvain to Thury Harcourt: I SS Panzer Corps
  85th, 89th and 271st Infantry Divisions and 12th SS Panzer
  Division.
Thury Harcourt to Chênedolle: LXXIV Corps
  276th, 277th and 316th Infantry Divisions,
  II SS Panzer Corps,
  9th SS and 21st Panzer Divisions.
Chênedolle to Vire: II Parachute Corps*
  3rd and 5th Parachute Divisions (amalgamated).

Area south of Vire: Two Corps Headquarters (XLVII Panzer†
and LXXXIV) had been identified and there must be others
commanding six Panzer Divisions (1st, 2nd and 10th SS, 2nd, 9th
and 116th Panzer) with elements of Panzer Lehr and possibly a
battle group of 11th Panzer Division and five Infantry Divisions
(84th, 353rd, 363rd, 331st, 708th).[247]

Major changes in German dispositions were reported in the
afternoon and evening of 12 August by air reconnaissance[248] and
by decrypts. A decrypt signalled at 1536 disclosed that XLVII
Panzer Corps had begun a withdrawal movement at 2100 on 11
August and that the whole of 116th Panzer Division was moving
towards Alençon.[249] A message at mid-day on 12 August stating
that XLVII Panzer Corps was moving from its sector for other
employment was signalled at 1637.[250] And this was followed at
1904 by the decrypt of a message from XLVII Panzer Corps at
0800 the previous day stating that its new battle headquarters was
to be 1 kilometre south of Vieux Pont (5 kilometres south of
Ecouché) from 0300 on 13 August, and that fuel was urgently
needed for the transfer of 2nd Panzer and 116th Panzer
Divisions.[251] Information that LVIII Panzer Corps had taken over

---

* A decrypt signalled around midnight on 10–11 August disclosed II Parachute Corps's
weekly return for 6 August which assessed the fighting value of its subordinated formations.
3rd Parachute Division, with two medium strength, six weak and five exhausted battalions
was Category III; the remnants of Panzer Lehr and Panzer Reconnaissance Abteilung 12
were 'barely IV'.[245] The German Army used four categories in its assessment of a division's
fighting value: I fully suitable for any offensive task, II suitable for limited offensive
employment, III fully suitable for defensive employment, IV conditionally suitable for
defensive employment.

† Another decrypt, also signalled around midnight on 10–11 August, supplied a return by
XLVII Panzer Corps giving the actual strength in weapons (machine guns, mortars and
artillery) of 2nd Panzer, 116th Panzer and 2nd SS Panzer Divisions on 7 August.[246]

245. ibid, XL 5601 of 11 August.
246. ibid, XL 5600 of 11 August.
247. WO 285/3, No 68 of 11 August.
248. ibid, No 69 of 12 August.
249. DEFE 3/117, XL 5845 of 12 August.
250. ibid, XL 5849 of 12 August.
251. ibid, XL 5860 of 12 August.

XLVII Panzer Corps's former sector was signalled at 1943.[252] The motive for this redeployment emerged very clearly from a decrypt signalled at 2212; a message from C-in-C West at 0430 on 11 August had appreciated that the Allies were trying to envelop Fifth Panzer Army and Seventh Army from two sides and intending to advance north rapidly from Le Mans, and that the weak forces of LXXXI Corps would be unable to hold up the Allied spearheads.[253] JK II's orders for 13 August, decrypted by 2143 on 12 August and 0234 on 13 August, reflected this appreciation. The area north of Le Mans was described as the critical point and all means were to be used to prevent further Allied advances.[254]

An emergency signal from GC and CS at 1030 on 13 August reported that the Flivo with Army Group B had stated on 11 August that there was to be a withdrawal in an area including Mortain in order to free armoured forces to attack XV US Corps's thrust towards Alençon. The Allies were attempting a double out-flanking movement. Elements of 9th Panzer Division, 331st Infantry Division and Parachute Regiment 6 had been scraped together to hold this thrust. German movements for concentration against it would begin during 11–12 August.[255] Other decrypts received during 13 August indicated that withdrawal on the western flank was in progress.[256] Second Army's intelligence summary for the day commented that an orderly retreat according to plan was in full swing, but that, especially as 21st Panzer's reconnaissance patrols had fallen silent, information about the extent of the retreat and the enemy's order of march in the Mayenne sector was scanty. 116th Panzer Division appeared to have moved first and fastest. Tactical reconnaissance had observed movement eastward in the sector facing Second Army.[257] In a telegram at 2235 General Montgomery told the CIGS that there had been considerable enemy movement, but that in his view only administrative echelons had passed through the Falaise–Argentan gap. His intelligence staff thought that the fighting parts of five German Corps were still west of the Falaise–Argentan road.[258] Decrypts signalled in the evening disclosed that Sées and the Sées–Alençon roads were Fliegerkorps IX's targets for that night, and that on 14 August JK II would be supporting the Army in the

252. ibid, XL 5866 of 12 August.
253. ibid, XL 5898 of 12 August.
254. ibid, XLs 5896 and 5937 of 12 and 13 August.
255. ibid, XL 5993 of 13 August.
256. DEFE 3/118, XLs 6001, 6020 and 6117 of 13 August.
257. WO 285/3, No 70 of 13 August.
258. CAB 121/370, SIC file D/France/6/1 vol 1, 21st Army Group to War Office, M/90 of 13 August.

area Mortagne–Alençon–Le Mans–Nogent le Rotrou.[259]

Decrypts early on 14 August disclosed that 338th and 48th Infantry Divisions, from Nineteenth and Fifteenth Armies respectively, were being brought up to First Army,[260] while other decrypts showed that the enemy wanted to withdraw the remnants of Panzer Lehr, 352nd and 275th Infantry Divisions for rest and refit.[261] Regarding the redeployment of the armour, in a message at 0900, signalled at 1752, the Flivo with 2nd Panzer reported that the Division had moved to Carrouges during 12–13 August; it had found the Allies further north than had been supposed and the German troops in some confusion.[262] A message at 1300 from XLVII Panzer Corps, decrypted by 1924, reported that a covering line had been established in the area south-west of Ecouché. Near Rânes fighting was in progress with Allied reconnaissance elements which had broken through.[263] It is claimed that DF and low-grade enemy traffic enabled the Army Y authorities to produce a statement on 14 August showing the location of almost every important unit in the Falaise pocket.[264] But that evening Second Army thought that, while the enemy order of battle east of the Orne and facing Second Army west of the Orne was reasonably clear, the remainder was extremely confused. Tactical reconnaissance had observed scattered movements on a reduced scale west of the Falaise–Argentan gap.[265] 21st Army Group's intelligence summary appreciated that not much of the German armour had yet made its way out.[266] In a telegram to the CIGS at 2240 Montgomery said: 'There is no (repeat no) doubt that a good many enemy are still inside ring. It is my opinion that a good many enemy have managed to pass eastward out of ring'.[267]

On 15 August, when JK II was again to support the Army on the southern flank,[268] a decrypt signalled at 0234 reported that, at 2130 the previous evening, 116th Panzer and 708th Infantry Divisions were subordinated to XLVII Panzer Corps, and 'the remaining elements' of 9th Panzer to 1st SS Panzer Division.[269] Another decrypt signalled at 0420 disclosed that 344th Infantry Division and 17th GAF Division (both from Fifteenth Army),

259. DEFE 3/118, XLs 6049 and 6091 of 13 August.
260. ibid, XLs 6137 and 6138 of 14 August.
261. ibid, XLs 6102, 6139 and 6165 of 14 August.
262. ibid, XL 6215 of 14 August.
263. ibid, XL 6225 of 14 August.
264. *History of Sigint in the Field*, p 184.
265. WO 285/3, No 71 of 14 August.
266. WO 171/132, No 155 of 14 August.
267. CAB 121/370, 21st Army Group to War Office, M/93 of 14 August.
268. DEFE 3/119, XL 6262 of 15 August.
269. ibid, XL 6286 of 15 August.

formerly intended for Seventh Army, had become Army Group Reserve.[270] Around breakfast time the pace quickened. A decrypt signalled at 0739 disclosed that at 1100 on 14 August Seventh Army had reported Eberbach's view that the situation could not be cleared up by an attack and had asked permission to withdraw its front and the left wing of Fifth Panzer Army to the line Falaise–Argentan under the protection of Eberbach. It requested that II SS Panzer Corps should be sent ahead with orders to attack from east of Argentan towards the south. The message added that the situation regarding fuel and ammunition was decisive.[271] This request was amplified in three decrypts available between 0830 and 0900. Seventh Army asked that in the event of its proposal being accepted Panzer Gruppe Eberbach, II SS Panzer Corps and LXXIV Corps should be subordinated to it; 9th SS Panzer Division should be transferred from II SS Panzer Corps to Panzer Gruppe Eberbach; and withdrawal lines for the nights 14–15 and 15–16 August should be approved.[272]*

A decrypt signalled at 1001 on 15 August reported a message from Eberbach at 1605 on 14 August with information that two battle groups of 2nd SS Panzer Division should reach Baillieu (north of Argentan) during the night, and that 2nd Panzer Division was to capture Ecouché the next morning (15 August).[274] In another message, decrypted by 1128, Eberbach declared his intention, if von Kluge approved, to place 2nd SS Panzer Division north-west of Argentan in view of Allied pressure from the Falaise direction.[275] An emergency signal from GC and CS at 1201 reported that, in a message at 1710 on 14 August, Eberbach had announced that XLVII Panzer Corps would attack the Allied flank on 15 August from the area of Vieux Pont. 116th Panzer Division would join in the attack from the right wing. 2nd SS Panzer Division would thrust north of Argentan into the flank of the Allies advancing on Trun.[276] Simultaneously, Army Group B was telling von Kluge at Fifth Panzer Army HQ that, according to

---

* These decrypts, while highly informative about the views of enemy field commanders, were potentially misleading, being indicative of what might be happening, not what actually was happening. In his telegram to the CIGS at 2230 of 15 August, Montgomery, perhaps influenced by these decrypts, said that it was now quite clear that the enemy had decided to pull out from west of the Falaise–Argentan road and was making a full scale withdrawal to get out of the pocket.[273] In fact Hitler did not sanction withdrawal from the pocket until 16 August.

270. ibid, XL 6294 of 15 August.
271. ibid, XL 6312 of 15 August.
272. ibid, XLs 6322, 6324 and 6325 of 15 August.
273. CAB 121/370, 21st Army Group to War Office, M/94 of 15 August.
274. DEFE 3/119, XL 6330 of 15 August.
275. ibid, XL 6337 of 15 August.
276. ibid, XL 6342 of 15 August.

Eberbach at 1400, no attack was possible unless his fuel and ammunition were replenished.[277] The large-scale attack forecast did not develop on 15 August. Supply difficulties may have been partly responsible. A message at 0800, decrypted by 1702, from the Flivo with 1st SS Panzer Division (which was subordinated to XLVII Panzer Corps) reported that very strong Allied air attacks were preventing a tank thrust by the division and urgently requested fighter protection in the area Rânes–Vieux Pont.[278]

In a message at 1200 on 15 August, signalled at 1634, XLVII Panzer Corps stated that it now had only 2nd Panzer and 1st SS Panzer Divisions subordinated, the latter with 9th Panzer under command. 708th Infantry Division was under Seventh Army; Panzer Lehr and 116th Panzer were directly under Eberbach.[279] A decrypt signalled at 1710 disclosed that II SS Panzer Corps, at the western end of the pocket, had been pulling back that morning according to plan and that 9th SS Panzer Division had been extricated from the front line.[280] On the northern flank of the pocket, the decrypt of a message at 1045 from I SS Panzer Corps was available by 1924; it emphasised the urgent need for GAF cover for withdrawal movements, which had to be made by day as well as by night.[281]

A decrypt signalled at 2217 on 15 August contained orders by von Kluge early on 13 August which nevertheless had some continuing relevance. Seventh Army was to withdraw during the night 13–14 August; 10th SS Panzer Division was to be got out of the line at all costs and sent to Eberbach in the Rânes area; and Seventh Army was to be responsible for defence against the Allies attacking from the Mayenne area.[282] Four other decrypts of 15 August were mainly of historical interest. These were: a message from Hausser on 12 August arguing at length in favour of consolidating the front on the line Falaise–Flers–Domfront as a base for an eventual attack west when the situation on Seventh Army's deep flank had been cleared up by Panzer Gruppe Eberbach;[283] von Kluge's reply on 13 August that Hitler had ruled that the proposed withdrawal would yield too much ground without compelling reason;[284] and two decrypts giving Hitler's orders on 9 August for the attack from the Domfront area by

---

277. ibid, XL 6333 of 15 August.
278. ibid, XL 6399 of 15 August.
279. ibid, XL 6423 of 15 August.
280. ibid, XL 6401 of 15 August.
281. ibid, XL 6423 of 15 August.
282. ibid, XL 6449 of 15 August.
283. ibid, XL 6334 of 15 August.
284. ibid, XL 6344 of 15 August.

Panzer Gruppe Eberbach supported by LXXXI Corps.[285] These orders had been substantially disclosed in decrypts available on 10 August, but the delayed decrypts added the information that to build up a covering line on the Loire, and to form an attack group, the following forces could be brought up: First Army with Army troops, LXXXI Corps, 48th Infantry and 6th Parachute Divisions from Fifteenth Army, and 338th Division from Nineteenth Army. Another infantry division could be brought up from Fifteenth Army when it had received three static divisions (26th, 64th and 58th). Hitler had reserved his decision on the employment of 11th Panzer Division.*

Rather surprisingly, Fliegerkorps IX ordered mining operations for the night 15–16 August.[287] JK II's forces were to screen the Army on 16 August in the area Laigle–Falaise–Alençon–Mortagne.[288]

Messages of 15 August from II SS Panzer Corps were decrypted early on 16 August; the Corps was making a withdrawal east of Condé-sur-Noireau and 21st Panzer Division was coming out of the line.[289] A decrypt signalled at 0713 on 16 August disclosed that the previous evening GOC Flak Korps III had drawn C-in-C West's immediate attention to the extremely serious situation both sides of Falaise, where resistance was not far from collapse with incalculable consequences. At the expense of defence against intolerable Allied air assault additional Flak batteries had been diverted to an anti-tank role on the northern flank.[290] Emergency signals from GC and CS at 1105 and 1114 covered messages from Seventh Army in the afternoon of 15 August. The first, which was incomplete, reported that its available covering forces were too weak; the battle strength of 708th Infantry Division was 60 men; Panzer Reconnaissance Abteilung 9 was immobile at present; Seventh Army requested that LVIII Panzer Corps and 10th SS Panzer Division be left to conduct a mobile battle on the southern wing. The second reported increased pressure on 10th SS Panzer Division; if it could be got out of the line it would be held ready for mobile battle in the Briouze area under LVIII Panzer Corps.[291] Another emergency signal from GC and CS at 1608 warned that at 1030 that morning 9th SS Panzer Division was intending to close

---

* Decrypts of 13 and 14 August showed that Hitler had decided that 11th Panzer was to stay with Nineteenth Army.[286]

285.   ibid, XLs 6435 and 6459 of 15 August.
286.   DEFE 3/117, XL 5956 of 13 August; DEFE 3/118, XL 6162 of 14 August.
287.   DEFE 3/119, XL 6426 of 15 August.
288.   ibid, XL 6447 of 15 August.
289.   ibid, XL 6470 of 16 August; DEFE 3/120, XL 6513 of 16 August.
290.   DEFE 3/119, XL 6495 of 16 August.
291.   DEFE 3/120, XLs 6521 and 6522 of 16 August.

the gap in the front near Ecouché, and added that on the previous evening Eberbach had asked that II SS Panzer Corps HQ should be moved immediately to the area north of Argentan.[292] A decrypt signalled at 1844 carried a message sent the previous afternoon in which a headquarters, probably XLVII Panzer Corps, appreciated that, owing to the bottle neck, losses of men, morale and material were uncommonly high. Supply difficulties were increasing, as were tank losses because of lack of fuel.[293]

High-grade Sigint's most important contribution that day was still to come – the decrypt of von Kluge's urgent recommendation that the pocket must be evacuated. In an emergency signal at 2042 GC and CS reported a message sent very early on 16 August by an unspecified authority. Discussion with Eberbach and Hausser had confirmed the view already given* that the total tank forces available were insufficient for a large-scale offensive to restore the situation in the area of the Army Group. Fuel shortage was a decisive factor. The position on the extreme south wing had deteriorated further. Strong Allied attacks had compelled XLVII Panzer Corps to take up a switch position with its right wing at Rânes. 9th SS Panzer Division would have to clear up a penetration north-west of Ecouché. 2nd SS Panzer Division must counter-attack to halt the advance on Trun.[294] Another decrypt signalled at 0211 on 17 August confirmed that the originating authority was von Kluge, and completed his message. The situation at the bottle neck was still such that orderly evacuation was possible to a certain degree, but if there was any hesitation the development of the Army Group's situation could not be foreseen. It was imperative that the west bulge be evacuated without delay through the narrow channel still open. The message had concluded, 'I request corresponding order'.[295] Meanwhile, in another emergency signal sent at 2048 on 16 August, GC and CS had reported an order by Army Group B at 1630 that afternoon for a general withdrawal to the line of the Orne in two to three nights, beginning 16–17 August.[296]

The intended attack on Ecouché was reported by Army Y[297] as well as by Ultra. With the assistance of the enemy's reconnaissance traffic, the former was also able to establish that 12th SS Panzer Division was east and south-east of Thury Harcourt and that 1st

---

* Cf p 262.

292. ibid, XL 6570 of 16 August.
293. ibid, XL 6588 of 16 August.
294. ibid, XL 6605 of 16 August.
295. ibid, XL 6648 of 17 August.
296. ibid, XL 6607 of 16 August.
297. *History of Sigint in the Field*, p 184.

SS Panzer and 2nd Panzer Divisions were sharing a defensive front immediately north of Rânes, with 9th SS Panzer Division behind them.[298] In the evening of 16 August Second Army thought that 116th Panzer Division was engaged at the eastern end and 10th SS Panzer Division at the western end of the southern flank, and that 2nd SS Panzer and 21st Panzer Divisions might be finding their way out of the pocket. Tactical reconnaissance had seen scattered movement in the battle area, all of it in an easterly direction.[299] In his telegram to the CIGS, despatched at 2245, Montgomery said that there were good grounds for thinking that there were six Panzer and SS divisions inside the pocket.[300]

Decrypts signalled early on 17 August disclosed that LXXXVI Corps, on the German right flank, had made an urgent request the previous evening for a reconnaissance of its sector;[301] that Luftflotte 3 had ordered the main bomber force to lay mines in the Seine Bay during the night 16–17 August;[302] and that on 17 August JK II was to screen the Army in the Falaise–Argentan sector and attack Allied spearheads in the area Rambouillet–Dreux–Chartres.[303]

An emergency signal sent by GC and CS at 1018 on 17 August reported that, according to Naval Gruppe West at 0300 that morning, the Orne front was being withdrawn to the Dives. The situation of Seventh Army and Fifth Panzer Army was serious.[304] An order by Seventh Army that one of the Orne bridges was to be used for supplies going west and the other two for the withdrawing of formations was decrypted by 2003.[305] A list of the Seine ferries in operation was decrypted by 2334.[306]

A message from Eberbach at midday on 16 August, signalled at 2144 on 17 August, included the information that II SS Panzer Corps had taken command of 2nd SS Panzer and 116th Panzer Divisions. 9th SS Panzer Division, less one reinforced battalion which was helping 2nd Panzer and 1st SS Panzer Divisions, was assembling north of Ecouché at the disposal of the Panzer Gruppe.[307]

Army Y reported that 21st Panzer Division's supply column had

---

298. WO 285/3, No 73 of 16 August.
299. ibid.
300. CAB 121/370, 21st Army Group to War Office, M/97 of 16 August.
301. DEFE 3/120, XL 6661 of 17 August.
302. ibid, XL 6692 of 17 August.
303. ibid, XL 6707 of 17 August.
304. ibid, XL 6722 of 17 August.
305. DEFE 3/121, XL 6791 of 17 August.
306. ibid, XL 6809 of 17 August.
307. ibid, XL 6803 of 17 August.

been severely mauled by air attack while withdrawing towards Trun. Air reports during the afternoon and evening spoke of major movements eastward with the roads congested in places. Explosions suggested that the Orne bridges were being blown by the enemy.[308] General Montgomery told the CIGS that the best part of five Panzer divisions and a good mass of infantry were in the pocket but that if a major break-out was attempted elements would get through.[309]

A decrypt signalled at 0043 on 18 August indicated that on the previous day 21st Panzer Division had been operating in three battle groups under other divisions on the northern flank of the pocket between Falaise and Morteaux.[310] Another, signalled at 0319, disclosed that around mid-day on 17 August 9th SS Panzer Division was temporarily in Corps Reserve, and that three hours later it was being transferred.[311] In the early hours of 18 August an officer deserter from 9th SS Panzer Division gave valuable information, including routes to be taken by 1st, 9th and 10th SS Panzer Divisions and 3rd Parachute Division. This resulted in massive air attacks on large concentrations of enemy vehicles.[312]

An emergency signal sent out by GC and CS at 0916 on 18 August reported that at 2100 the previous evening II SS Panzer Corps had been ordered to make a concentric attack to clear up the situation resulting from an Allied penetration north-west of Trun, which had created a gap in the German front.[313] Another emergency signal at 1122 reported that, according to von Kluge at 1630 on 17 August, the situation both sides of Falaise necessitated the quickest possible withdrawal across the Orne.[314] This was followed by a decrypt disclosing that in view of an order by Army Group B Hausser had asked Fifth Panzer Army's agreement that I SS Panzer and LXXIV Corps should be subordinated to him so as to obtain unity of command in the withdrawal.[315] The replacement of von Kluge by Field Marshal Model in the evening of 17 August was disclosed by a decrypt signalled at 1534 on 18 August.[316]

Decrypts signalled to the Commands at 1731 and 1824 on 18 August, belated but still informative, showed that on 16 August von Kluge had told Eberbach to place two divisions under II SS

---

308. WO 285/3, No 74 of 17 August.
309. CAB 121/130, 21st Army Group to War Office, M/98 of 17 August.
310. DEFE 3/121, XL 6815 of 18 August.
311. ibid, XL 6835 of 18 August.
312. WO 285/3, No 75 of 18 August.
313. DEFE 3/121, XL 6896 of 18 August.
314. ibid, XL 6905 of 18 August.
315. ibid, XL 6906 of 18 August.
316. ibid, XL 6929 of 18 August.

Panzer Corps in the Vimoutiers area as Army Group Reserve, and had ordered that two divisions from Seventh Army were to be brought up to Fifth Panzer Army with all speed in the direction of Falaise.[317] Messages from II SS Panzer Corps and 2nd SS Panzer Division in the early afternoon of 18 August, decrypted by 2017 and 2112 respectively, reported that GAF protection had been requested against ceaseless Allied air attacks which were preventing almost all movement by day. 'Panzer Groups', including 2nd SS and 9th SS Panzer Divisions, were directed on Trun.[318] A decrypt signalled at 2058 on 18 August gave the positions at various times on 18 August of I SS Panzer Corps; LXXXVI Corps and 272nd Infantry Division; 326th Infantry Division; and 277th Infantry Division.[319] JK II's intentions for 19 August were unchanged: to screen the Army in the Falaise–Argentan sector.[320] Tactical reconnaissance reported very heavy movement astride the Falaise–Argentan road, and on all roads north-east and south-east of Vimoutiers.[321] On the night of 18 August Montgomery told the CIGS that the east end of the pocket was closed against any large-scale movements.[322]

In the final stage of the battle on 19 and 20 August the intelligence authorities had little to add. A decrypt signalled at 1919 on 19 August gave bombing targets suggested by Fifth Panzer Army for the night 19–20 August, and a dropping zone for supplies to XLVII Panzer Corps. It also disclosed that during the night Fliegerkorps IX was to drop fuel supplies north-west of Argentan for 10th SS Panzer Division.[323] An emergency signal sent by GC and CS a few minutes earlier reported that II SS Panzer Corps had asked for fighter protection from first light on 20 August in the Trun–Vimoutiers area over a decisive attack.[324] A decrypt at 0449 on 20 August reported that, according to Army Group B on 19 August, Trun was to be attacked at all costs. Fuel for II SS Panzer Corps in the Vimoutiers area was to be assured. I SS Panzer Corps had been told that an attack to recapture Trun would be made early on 20 August with three battalions and 20 tanks.[325]

□

Throughout the battle, as has been shown, high-grade Sigint

---

317. ibid, XLs 6938 and 6941 of 18 August.
318. ibid, XLs 6952 and 6955 of 18 August.
319. ibid, XL 6953 of 18 August.
320. ibid, XLs 6951 and 6956 of 18 August.
321. WO 285/3, No 75 of 18 August.
322. CAB 121/370, 21st Army Group to War Office, M/100 of 18 August.
323. DEFE 3/122, XL 7092 of 19 August.
324. ibid, XL 7099 of 19 August.
325. ibid, XL 7153 of 20 August.

regularly gave advance warning of the efforts made by JK II's light forces and, from time to time, by the bombers of Fliegerkorps IX, to assist the Army in what, as the decrypts made abundantly clear,[326] the GAF recognised was a grave crisis. Its operations, which were concentrated in the Caen sector to begin with, were switched to the western flank in the closing days of July in a vain attempt to check the American breakthrough and, later, to support the German counter-attack towards Avranches. By 11 August the threat of envelopment posed by the advance of Third US Army towards Alençon was clearly recognised and JK II's efforts were concentrated on reconnaissance and support of the crumbling defences. In the closing stages of the battle JK II strove to cover the withdrawal of the Army and keep open the Falaise–Argentan gap. Some of Fliegerkorps IX's effort was, surprisingly, dissipated on a resumption of mining operations in the Seine Bay. In the event the GAF's influence on the battle was almost negligible, while the cost to the light forces of JK II was very severe.

At the start of the battle Allied intelligence which, as had been the case since D-day, enjoyed (and, during the battle, continued to enjoy) comprehensive knowledge of the identity, locations and strengths of the units involved, appreciated that as a result of the cautious policy followed in July except for a few days before and during Operation *Goodwood*, JK II disposed of some 500 single-engined fighters.* The strength of Fliegerkorps IX in northern France and Belgium, which until just before *Goodwood* had devoted most of its effort to mining operations, was put at around 210 aircraft.[327]

By the end of July sorties by the light forces, which had averaged 350–400 in the first three days of the battle, were already falling. Bomber attacks on targets south of St Lo had proved ineffective.[328] On 5 August the Air Ministry appreciated that, while the urgency of the situation was fully recognised, the scale of the close-support effort was only 200–250 sorties a day. This was due to the strain of continuous operations, the not inconsiderable losses† and the fact that withdrawal of the fighter units eastward to

---

* The order of battle comprised five Geschwader HQ (JG 1, JG 2, JG 3, JG 26, JG 27) and thirteen Gruppen (I, II, III/JG 1; II, III/JG 2; II, III/JG 3; I, III/JG 26; I, IV/JG 27; I/JG 5; III/JG 54).

† For example on 31 July.[329]

326. DEFE 3/64, XL 4088 of 30 July; DEFE 3/65, XL 4429 of 2 August; DEFE 3/112, XL 4626 of 4 August; DEFE 3/114, XL 5029 of 7 August as examples.

327. Air Sunset 212 of 27 July.

328. Air Sunset 213 of 31 July.

329. DEFE 3/65, XL 4283 of 1 August.

the Paris area[330] meant that on the western flank they were operating at extreme range.[331]

JK II flew 225 sorties on 6 August,[332] but its support for the counter-attack towards Avranches on 7 August proved totally ineffective.[333] JK II claimed that its strong fighter effort did not get through to the target area because of the continuous Allied air interception.[334] In the light of the Sigint the Air Ministry thought that this was only part of the explanation. One Geschwader, which had been moved from Angers to east of Paris around 4 August,[335] had been unable to operate and another Geschwader had been resting.[336] The result had been that JK II had probably not had more than 110 aircraft actually serviceable, and these had made perhaps 150 sorties.[337] A decrypt on 10 August disclosing that on 8 August JK II had 102 aircraft operational at first light tended to confirm this estimate.[338] However, 244 sorties had been flown on 8 August; two aircraft had been lost and ten were missing.[339]

Orders on 8 August for the transfer of units from the Chartres–Dreux area to airfields east of the Seine in the Romilly–Paris area were decrypted the next day.[340] A decrypt signalled on 10 August disclosed orders for the withdrawal of four fighter Gruppen* for rest and refit and their replacement from Germany.[341]† The Air Ministry appreciated that, if the intended programme of reliefs were fully implemented, the close-support forces would again comprise some 500 aircraft, but that because of the shortage of crews with operational experience JK II's fighting value would not be commensurate with its front-line strength.[342]

The difficulties JK II was encountering from the overwhelmingly powerful Allied air forces were illustrated by decrypts disclosing that on 11 August, when it had flown 95 sorties, JK II had been unable to carry through an urgent, escorted, reconnaissance of the

---

* I/JG 5, II/JG 3, I, IV/JG 27.

† By II/JG 11, I/JG 2, II/JG 26, III/JG 27.

330. ibid, XL 4443 of 2 August; DEFE 3/112, XLs 4503 and 4617 of 2 and 3 August.
331. Air Sunset 215 of 5 August.
332. DEFE 3/115, XL 5288 of 8 August.
333.·· Air Sunset 218 of 8 August.
334. DEFE 3/114, XL 5125 of 7 August.
335. DEFE 3/113, XLs 4761 and 4832 of 5 August.
336. DEFE 3/114, XL 5027 of 7 August.
337. Air Sunset 218 of 8 August.
338. DEFE 3/116, XL 5503 of 10 August.
339. ibid.
340. DEFE 3/115, XL 5344 of 9 August.
341. DEFE 3/116, XL 5521 of 10 August.
342. Air Sunsets 219 and 220 of 10 and 12 August.

area north of Le Mans because of numerous combats on the approach flight.[343]

Decrypts on 10 and 12 August emphasised the increasing impact of fuel shortages on the GAF's operational capability. In the first Luftflotte 3 countermanded JK II's orders for road strafing during the night of 10–11 August because it would be too dark: for reasons of fuel economy night-fighter operations were only to be undertaken when there were adequate prospects of success.[344]* The second decrypt revealed Luftflotte 3 passing on orders from Berlin for a considerably greater reduction of flying because of further damage to fuel production. Henceforth, only defensive fighter operations were permitted without restriction; reconnaissance was to be undertaken only when essential for the general conduct of operations and for security; bomber and ground-attack aircraft were only to be employed on decisive operations.[346]

Decrypts on 13 and 15 August disclosed orders that newly arrived Gruppen were to be carefully introduced to operations around and east of Paris, combat only being accepted from an absolutely superior position, and that training was to be completed by night-fall on 15 August.[347] The Air Ministry appreciated on 15 August that close-support sorties had been averaging about 100 a day and revised downwards its estimate of JK II's likely strength to about 375 aircraft.[348] On the next day, when high-grade Sigint had reported further planned withdrawals† and replacements,[349]‡ and operations orders stipulating that battle formations must be made up in such a way that there was an experienced Gruppe providing top cover,[350] the Air Ministry appreciated that the GAF had suffered a crippling defeat. The close-support forces operating in France since D-day had been virtually eliminated by overwhelming Allied air superiority and replaced by second-rate material.[351]

---

* It is of interest that during the last week of the battle the night-fighters were to be at readiness to combat Allied air landing and parachute operations especially in the area east of Paris.[345]

† I, II/JG 1, III/JG 2.

‡ I/JG 11, II/JG 53.

343. DEFE 3/117, XL 5772 of 12 August; DEFE 3/118, XL 6065 of 13 August.
344. DEFE 3/116, XL 5574 of 10 August.
345. DEFE 3/118, XL 6079 of 13 August; DEFE 3/119, XL 6253 of 14 August;
     DEFE 3/120, XL 6702 of 17 August; DEFE 3/121, XL 6951 of 18 August.
346. DEFE 3/117, XL 5773 of 12 August.
347. DEFE 3/118, XL 6091 of 13 August; DEFE 3/119, XL 6262 of 15 August.
348. Air Sunset 222 of 15 August.
349. DEFE 3/119, XLs 6493 and 6494 of 16 August.
350. ibid, XL 6469 of 16 August.
351. Air Sunset 223 of 16 August.

Decrypts on 17 August disclosed orders for the withdrawal of two more fighter Gruppen* and for the destruction of airfields in the Paris area.[352] Decrypts on the next day disclosed that a Geschwader HQ (JG 1) and 5th Jagd Division, formerly in control of fighter operations west of the Seine, were being withdrawn from operations and replaced by JG 27 and 4th Jagd Division respectively,[353] and that Luftflotte 3 had moved to Rheims.[354] Other decrypts on 18 August disclosed that JK II had flown 374 sorties on 15 August,[355] and that on 16 August 203 aircraft had made 297 sorties; three aircraft had been lost and 14 were missing. The operational serviceability of one of the newly arrived Gruppen had fallen away completely because of inexperience.[356]

Decrypts on 19 August showed that JK II had had 149 aircraft serviceable the previous day. Its fighting strength had declined because of heavy and costly battles on 17 August and the transfer of units. On 18 August it had been greatly hampered by Allied operations over its airfields and an Allied fighter screen along the Seine. Two Geschwader alone had 22 aircraft missing. Total losses known were five aircraft, but another 27 had not reported back.[357]

A long decrypt signalled in the afternoon of 19 August covered an order of 18 August by JK II.[358] GC and CS commented that this order, and other recent orders, derived from what appeared to be a comprehensive plan dated 13 August for the redistribution of fighter units. Another Geschwader HQ and two more fighter Gruppen were being withdrawn for rest and refit† but two Geschwader HQ and five more Gruppen‡ were being brought up from Germany on 20 August. As a result of these and other recent moves there would be sixteen fighter Gruppen distributed as follows:

St Quentin area:	Stab JG 53 with I/JG 4, II/JG 53
Champfleury–Vertus area:	Stab JG 76 with III/JG 3, I, III/JG 76
Creil area:	Stab JG 2 with I, II/JG 2, I/JG 11, III/JG 27

---

* IV/JG 27, III/JG 54.

† JG 3, II/JG 2 and II/JG 3.

† JG 53, JG 76, I/JG 4, II/JG 6, I, III/JG 76, I/JG 77.

352. DEFE 3/120, XLs 6621 and 6725 of 17 August.
353. DEFE 3/121, XLs 6844 and 6852 of 18 August.
354. ibid, XL 6847 of 18 August.
355. ibid, XL 6851 of 18 August.
356. ibid, XL 6826 of 18 August.
357. DEFE 3/122, XLs 7016 and 7031 of 19 August.
358. ibid, XL 7052 of 19 August.

Juvincourt–Laon area: Stab JG 27 with II/JG II, III/JG 1,
                          II/JG (?)6, I/JG 77
Beauvais area: Stab JG 26 with I, II, III/JG 26.

Orders by Luftflotte 3 for the conduct of operations covering the
Army's withdrawal were also decrypted. The main effort was to be
made in defence of the Seine crossings, particularly in the greater
Paris area.[359]

□

In the morning of 15 August, when the situation of Army
Group B was already desperate and von Kluge was 'lost' in the
pocket, Seventh US Army landed east of Toulon in the area
Fréjus–St Tropez (Operation *Dragoon*). Its task was to capture
Toulon and Marseilles and exploit towards Lyons and Vichy.[360] It
was opposed by Army Group G's Nineteenth Army with seven
relatively low-grade infantry divisions and 11th Panzer Division.
From west to east these forces were disposed as follows:

IV GAF Field Corps
716th Infantry Division   Perpignan
198th Infantry Division   Narbonne
189th (Reserve) Infantry Division   Montpellier

LXXXV Corps
338th Infantry Division (less one   Arles
  regiment)
244th Infantry Division   Marseilles

LXII Corps
242nd Infantry Division   Toulon–river Argens
148th (Reserve) Infantry Division   River Argens–Italian
                                     frontier
157th (Reserve) Infantry Division   Grenoble area

11th Panzer Division was being re-deployed from west to east of
the Rhône. Because all the bridges had been destroyed by Allied
bombing, movement had to be by ferry and had hardly begun.[361]
   The GAF forces immediately available consisted of 65 serviceable aircraft (45 torpedo-bombers, 15 FX and/or Hs bombers and
5 single-engine fighters).[362] High-grade Sigint disclosed that a
fighter Gruppe was being brought in from Italy,[363] but that the

---

359. ibid, XL 7071 of 19 August.
360. Jackson, *The Mediterranean and Middle East*, Vol VI Part 2 (1987), p 185.
361. ibid, pp 189, 190.
362. Air Sunset 221 of 13 August.
363. DEFE 3/120, XL 6512 of 16 August.

move of two fighter Gruppen from northern France had been turned down by Berlin.[364] On 18 August the Air Ministry described GAF operations in southern France as 'too insignificant for comment'.[365]

The beachhead was quickly secured and developed. High-grade Sigint disclosed on 16 August that the movement of ground forces to oppose the landings was being hampered by the destruction of the Rhône bridges.[366] This was confirmed by Army Group G appreciations of 16 and 17 August, decrypted on 18 August. In his report on 16 August General Blaskowitz, in command of Army Group G, said that against the main landing at St Tropez the Germans, who had given up their motorised anti-tank weapons, were unable to offer adequate resistance. A decisive factor was the destruction of the Rhône bridges. Reserves had to be ferried across and came into action in driblets. On 17 August he said that the German counter-attack lacked striking power because of the destruction of the bridges.[367]

At 1408 on 17 August GC and CS despatched an emergency signal with the decrypt of a message sent at 0940 that morning in which Naval Gruppe West informed Admiral Atlantic of orders from OKW. All troops and authorities of all branches of the armed forces in the area of Army Group G, west of a line Orléans–Clermont Ferrand–Montpellier, except those required for the defence of fortresses and the fighting troops of Nineteenth Army, were to transfer behind the line Seine–Yonne–Canal de Bourgogne beginning immediately.[368] Twenty-four hours later another emergency signal from GC and CS disclosed orders from Hitler to C-in-C West at 1730 on 17 August. As the development of the situation with Army Group B created the threat that Nineteenth Army would be cut off within the foreseeable future, Army Group G, except for forces remaining in Toulon and Marseilles, was to disengage from the Allies and gain contact with the south wing of Army Group B. The development of an intermediate line Sens–Dijon–Swiss frontier was to begin at once. The main body of 11th Panzer Division was to stay in the Rhône valley to protect the area against airborne forces and later to become the rearguard of Nineteenth Army. LXII Corps with 148th and 157th Reserve Divisions was to withdraw, when pressed, into the Franco–Italian Alpine position, meanwhile protecting the east flank of Nineteenth Army, and was subordinated to C-in-C

---

364. Air Sunset 223 of 16 August.
365. Air Sunset 224 of 18 August.
366. DEFE 3/120, XLs 6635 and 6600 at 16 August.
367. DEFE 3/121, XLs 6934 and 6950 of 18 August.
368. ibid, XL 6753 of 17 August.

South-West. The latter was to assume responsibility immediately for the defence of the Alpine position from the Swiss frontier to the Ligurian Sea. Fortresses were to be held to the last man – Marseilles and Toulon by a division each.[369]

Decrypts signalled on 20, 21 and 22 August reflected the implementation of Hitler's orders. C-in-C West designated the fortresses in Army Group G's area as La Pallice, La Rochelle, areas north and south of the Gironde, Sète, Marseilles and Toulon.[370] Army Group G told LXIV Corps (which had taken over from First Army from the Loire southwards to Bayonne and had 16th Infantry Division and 159th Reserve Division subordinated)* to evacuate its area to the general area of Dijon, except for elements left to defend fortresses. Parts of 159th Reserve Division south of the Gironde were to be withdrawn through the Garonne valley. The covering forces on the Loire were to be withdrawn last.[372] Army Group G reported to C-in-C West that LXIV Corps would withdraw via Bourges, except for elements using the Garonne valley which would join up with IV GAF Field Corps and reach Avignon on 23 August.[373] LXIV Corps told C-in-C West that the movement of 100,000 men, including civilians with 2,000 women, would not reach Moulins (on the river Allier) before 12 September.[374] C-in-C South-West issued instructions to 148th Reserve Division to defend the area round Grasse as long as possible and then withdraw via Nice to Mentone.[375]

Nineteenth Army left 242nd and most of 244th Divisions to hold Toulon and Marseilles (both fell on 28 August) and withdrew in two groups up the Rhône valley: LXXXV Corps with 11th Panzer Division, the truncated 338th Infantry Division, 198th Infantry Division and elements of 244th Infantry Division on the east, and IV GAF Field Corps on the west of the river with 716th Infantry Division, 189th Infantry Division and elements of 159th Infantry Division (from LXIV Corps).[376]† But it was seriously

---

* 16th Infantry Division was an amalgamation of 158th Reserve Division and the remnants of 16th GAF Field Division.[371]

† All Reserve Divisions in France and the Low Countries had been transferred to the Field Army as infantry divisions. MI 14 categorised 189th and 159th as LE Divisions.[377]

369. ibid, XL 6919 of 18 August.
370. DEFE 3/123, XL 7294 of 21 August.
371. Blumenson, op cit, p 561.
372. DEFE 3/122, XL 7171 of 20 August.
373. ibid, XL 7168 of 20 August.
374. DEFE 3/123, XL 7448 of 22 August.
375. DEFE 3/122, XL 7198 of 20 August.
376. Jackson, op cit, Vol VI Part 2, pp 196, 198.
377. WO 208/4316, MI 14 Weekly Summary for the CIGS, 20 August.

hampered by guerrilla attacks and a bold attempt by Seventh US Army to cut its lines of retreat.

In the light of the decrypts disclosing the German orders for the withdrawal and of the success of a thrust towards Grenoble from Nice by an armoured task force and 36th US Division, Seventh US Army turned this spearhead westward along the Drôme valley. By late on 20 August the forward US troops were within effective artillery range of the roads on both sides of the Rhône at Montelimar.[378] German attempts to clear the block began on 23 August; a decrypt signalled by GC and CS at 0268 warned that 11th Panzer Division would attack that day.[379] The major effort, however, was made on 25 August. Decrypts available that morning disclosed that Nineteenth Army had ordered 198th Infantry Division to be brought up speedily to open the Rhône gorge and had announced that it would try to break through that day with the reinforced 148th Infantry Division and 11th Panzer Division.[380] The attack was partially successful, and Nineteenth Army's intentions for 26 August, decrypted before mid-day, were to continue the attack and pass 338th Infantry Division through the gap.[381] But the withdrawal soon encountered further difficulties: decrypts of 1 and 3 September disclosed that 198th and 338th Divisions had been surrounded while crossing the Drôme and had fought their way out heroically with heavy losses. 198th Division had escaped with 1,050–1,200 men and 29 guns, 338th Division with 1,100 men and 10 guns.[382]

The German position at Lyons had by then become untenable. Decrypts of 25 and 26 August had disclosed that IV GAF Field Corps was making a forced march to the city and that 11th Panzer Division was to be despatched there as soon as the Montelimar gap was cleared.[383] A message of 30 August, signalled by GC and CS the following day, had ordered IV GAF Field Corps to hold a bridgehead until all troops were out of Lyons.[384] Early on 2 September a report from Nineteenth Army, decrypted in the evening, announced that the city was to be evacuated that night, and that LXXXV Corps and IV GAF Field Corps were to continue their withdrawal northwards.[385]

---

378. Jackson, op cit, Vol VI Part 2, pp 196, 198–199.
379. DEFE 3/124, XL 7578 of 23 August.
380. DEFE 3/125, XLs 7815 and 7830 of 25 August.
381. DEFE 3/125, XL 7979 of 26 August.
382. DEFE 3/220, XL 8788, of 1 September; DEFE 3/221, XL 9039 of 3 September.
383. DEFE 3/125, XL 7858 of 25 August; DEFE 3/125, XLs 7956 and 7979 of 26 August.
384. DEFE 3/128, XL 8742 of 31 August.
385. DEFE 3/220, XL 8992 of 2 September.

As we shall see, decrypts received since 25 August had meanwhile reflected grave anxiety on the part of the German High Command that Nineteenth Army from the Rhône valley and LXIV Corps from south-west France would fail to make contact with First Army in time to fill the gap on the left wing of the line that was being hastily formed across northern France.

PART XIV

The Land Fronts in
the Second Half of 1944

CHAPTER 49

The Soviet Offensives and the German Withdrawal from Greece and in Yugoslavia

BEFORE THE Russians embarked on their summer offensive in 1944 they advised the western Allies that following a first attack in one sector about the middle of June, their operations would develop at the end of June and during July into a general offensive. At that time MI 14 believed the Russians were strong enough to take the offensive in any sector and that they would attack on several sectors in quick succession.[1] It estimated that against some 300 Russian divisions the Germans disposed of 197 field divisions, leaving aside twelve in Hungary and the Balkans; that many of them were well below strength; and that they were distributed as follows: twelve in Finland, 41 under Army Group North on the Baltic front from the Gulf of Finland to the river Dvina, 55 under Army Group Centre on the White Russian front from the Dvina to the Dnieper at the Bug, 43 under Army Group North Ukraine from the Dnieper to the Czech and Romanian borders, and 46 under Army Group South Ukraine which commanded the Romanian front.[2] The actual German strength in field divisions was 189, 164 facing the Russian armies and 25 in the Balkans.[3]

After attacking from the Leningrad front on 10 June and capturing Viborg by 20 June, the Russians on 22 June opened a major offensive against the northern sector of the central front with Minsk as their objective. They took Minsk on 3 July after inflicting on Germany a defeat of Stalingrad proportions. On 4 July they crossed the Polish frontier north of Minsk and, striking towards the Baltic states, took Vilna on 13 July and were close to the East Prussian border by 16 July. After a visit to the Minsk front between 6 and 9 July the head of the British Military Mission reported that Army Group Centre had lost some 28 divisions,

---

1. WO 208/4312, MI 14 Appreciations File of 4 June 1944; WO 208/3573, MI 14 Weekly Summary for the CIGS, 5 June.
2. WO 208/3573, 18 June.
3. Seaton, *The Russo-German War 1941–45* (1971), p 458, quoting Müller-Hillebrand, *Das Heer 1933–1945*, Vol 3 (1969), Table 62.

including most of Fourth Army and part of Ninth Army, in the battle for Minsk, and that cases of panic and refusal to obey orders were occurring among the German forces.[4]* On 6 July MI 14's résumé for the Chiefs of Staff noted that the speed of the Russian advance, some 15 miles a day, compared favourably with that achieved by the Germans in July 1941, before the Russians had organised their resistance to the German invasion.[6] On 9 July MI 14 forecast that, while the Russians would pause to consolidate this first advance after taking Vilna and Dvinsk, the Germans would soon be in grave danger further north unless they at once withdrew Sixteenth and Eighteenth Armies of Army Group North from Latvia and Estonia.[7]

The Germans delayed this withdrawal too long, as MI 14 observed on 16 July.[8] On that day the Russians opened a second offensive which, pushing northwards from Lake Peipus, was 20 miles south of Riga on 1 August. By the middle of July it was clear that the Germans were not going to withdraw from the Baltic states. In the first half of August, as decrypts disclosed, they carried out partially successful counter-attacks with the two Panzer Corps of Third Panzer Army, brought up from the central front, and attempted to reinforce that Army with two Panzer divisions from Army Group South Ukraine in Romania, but were forced to begin the evacuation of Estonia and Latvia in the middle of August.[9] Many naval Enigma decrypts illustrated the Navy's difficulties in keeping the retreating armies supplied via Riga, where the Germans held out till October.[10]

In mid-July, simultaneously with the opening of the offensive

---

* As indicated by this visit, the Soviet authorities were unusually forthcoming in supplying information during the early stages of their offensive. They did not respond, however, to requests for detailed accounts comparable to those they were receiving about the progress of *Overlord*. By August they had returned to their accustomed reticence – though they reported in detail on the progress of the fighting to the 'Tolstoy' conference in Moscow in mid-October.[5] But the western Allies kept in touch with the operations on the eastern fronts through the intelligence they obtained from the Enigma and Fish decrypts. For the state of the high-grade Sigint from the eastern front and the Balkans after the middle of 1944 see Appendix 15(iii).

4. CAB 121/464, SIC file D/Russia/4, BMM telegram 1563 of 9 July.
5. Ehrman, *Grand Strategy*, Vol V (1956), pp 367–368; CAB 121/464, COS(44)209th(o) Meeting, 26 June, BMM telegram 1563 of 9 July, WARX telegram to Moscow 64651 of 13 July; CAB 121/466, SIC file D/Russia/5, Vol 1, COS(44)212th(o) Meeting, 27 June; CAB 121/160, SIC file A/Strategy/15, COS(44)915(o) of 26 October, pp 12–13 (Minutes of 1st Military Meeting, 14 October).
6. CAB 80/44, COS(44)125 of 6 July (Résumé No 253).
7. WO 208/4316, MI 14 Weekly Summary for the CIGS, 9 July.
8. ibid, 16 July.
9. Seaton, op cit, p 457; Erickson, *The Road to Berlin* (1983), p 307 et seq.
10. eg DEFE 3/112, XL 4543 of 3 August; DEFE 3/115, XL 4505 of 9 August.

against Army Group North, the Russians had advanced on the Lwow sector of the front held by Army Group North Ukraine. Lwow had fallen on 27 July, and by the first week of August the Russians had reached the Vistula to the north and were close to the Czechoslovak border in the south. By then, moreover, they had resumed the offensive against Army Group Centre, and by 31 July the left wing of this offensive, advancing from Lublin, was 15 miles from Warsaw. The progress of the Russian forces, as recorded in Soviet communiqués, was confirmed by high-grade decrypts.[11] On 3 August MI 14 reported them to be 12 miles from Warsaw, with spearheads probably closer, and to be firmly established on the east bank of the Vistula and preparing bridgeheads across it.[12] On the same day GC and CS decrypted a telegram to Tokyo from the Japanese Ambassador in Berlin; the German authorities had informed him on 31 July that they would not put up a desperate defence to save Warsaw.[13] A decrypt on the previous day had contained a GAF appreciation that the Russians intended to strengthen their bridgeheads rather than make new attempts to cross the Vistula but that a *coup de main* could not be ruled out.[14]

The intelligence available in Whitehall threw no light, however, on the planning of the Warsaw rising, which was ordered by the General commanding the Polish Home Army on 1 August, or on the inability or the failure of the Russians to give assistance to it. Whitehall had known of long-term Polish plans for a national uprising since October 1942, but it had long been clear that, for operational reasons, the western Allies could not send in supplies on any appreciable scale. In the spring of 1944, when more became known of the quality of the Polish resistance movement, the possibility of relating its activities to Allied strategy and future operations was examined by the JIC; it concluded that the choice of the right moment for an uprising necessitated close collaboration between the Polish and Russian authorities which was most unlikely to be achieved.[15] But, helpless to overcome the difficulties in sending large-scale assistance, the Combined Chiefs of Staff did not impose a ban on a rising, the decision for which they left specifically to the Polish commander on the spot.[16] The Polish

---

11. WO 208/4316 of 23 and 30 July; CAB 80/44. COS(44)137 of 27 July (Résumé No 256); Dir/C Archive 7226 of 27 July, 7256 of 30 July; CX/MSS/T257/110, T260/104.

12. CAB 80/44, COS(44)139 of 3 August (Résumé No 257).

13. BAY/XL 84 of 4 August.

14. Dir/C Archive, 7283 of 2 August; CX/MSS/T263/53.

15. CAB 121/309, SIC file B/Special Operations/4/1, Vol 1, JIC(44)204(o) of 18 May.

16. Ehrman, op cit, Vol V, p 371.

Government-in-exile also gave him full powers of decision and, on 29 July, told British authorities in London that all was ready and awaited his final order to act.[17] As for the Soviet lack of support for the rising, the explanation offered by Stalin to the Polish Prime Minister in Moscow in the middle of August, that his forces had suffered an unexpected setback outside Warsaw,[18] was accepted in Whitehall at the time. In the first week of September MI 14 was unable to decide whether Russia had mounted a major effort to encircle Warsaw, and been rebuffed, or had confined herself to local attacks there while she prepared for another major offensive.[19]* The Russians entered the Praga suburb of Warsaw on the east bank of the Vistula on 14 September after four days of heavy fighting.[20]

On the same day the Russians resumed their thrust towards Riga in the attempt to cut off Army Group North from East Prussia. Their advance was halted a few miles south of Riga on 16 September, but when they broke through further north, near Tartu in Estonia, on 17 September Hitler grudgingly admitted that the whole of Army Group North must pull back to a shorter line, running from the Gulf of Finland to the west Dvina, from which it would be able to send stronger contingents to Courland and western Lithuania. Third Panzer Army was transferred to Army Group North, extending its frontage down to Memel and the East Prussia frontier. The Russians thereupon changed the direction of their main thrust from north to west. They suspended the attempt to advance towards Riga on 24 September and their next offensive, attacking Third Panzer Army in a bid to reach Memel and cut off Courland, was opened on 5 October. By 10 October this offensive had reached the Lithuanian coast and the outskirts of Memel. By mid-October it had forced Third Panzer Army southwards into East Prussia, where the Germans stabilised a front on the line of the Niemen, and had cut off the rest of Army Group North in Courland. The offensive was supported by renewed attacks in Latvia; Riga fell on 13 October. But Memel held out till January and in Courland, which Hitler refused to evacuate, the Germans succeeded in maintaining a bridgehead until the end of the war.[21]

---

* For fuller accounts of these developments see Ehrman, *Grand Strategy*, Vol V (1956), pp 370–372; Woodward, *British Foreign Policy in the Second World War*, Vol III (1971), Chapter XXXIX: Erickson, *The Road to Berlin* (1983), p 247 et seq.

17. CAB 121/309, COS(44)670(o) of 29 July, 677(o) of 31 July.
18. CAB 121/310, SIC file B/Special Operations/4/1, Vol II, Clasp telegram No 54 of 15 August.
19. WO 208/4313, MI 14 Appreciations File of 3 September.
20. Erickson, op cit, pp 287–288.
21. ibid, pp 411–422 Seaton, op cit, pp 522–523, 525–526.

The resumption of the Russian attacks on 14 September was reported in a naval Enigma message decrypted on 16 September.[22] Naval decrypts on 24 September reported the withdrawal of the German forces in Estonia, culminating in the mining and destruction of Tallinn on 22 September.[23] A GAF Enigma message of 27 September, decrypted on 3 October, contained Luftflotte 1's instructions for reconnaissance; it stressed that the capitulation of Finland and the German retreat would enable the Russians to build up on the boundary between Army Group North and Army Group Centre for a thrust into East Prussia, and to withdraw strong forces to other sectors.[24] During the first two weeks of October the increasing threat to Riga and Memel was reflected in Fish and naval Enigma decrypts, as was the German effort to hold on in the Sworbe peninsula on the island of Oesel (Saare Maa), a strategic position covering the Irben Straits on the Gulf of Riga.[25] Decrypts of 17 and 20 October reported that the defence line in the Memel area was holding on 14 October, but that heavy Russian landings on Sworbe had begun on 19 October.[26] A GAF message of 14 October, which was not decrypted until 23 October, disclosed that Luftflotte 6 was unable to give adequate fighter protection to the Navy; it was expecting a Russian threat into East Prussia and had to conserve its fuel.[27]

Naval operations in support of the Army were carried out by the Second Battle Group, main units with destroyers and a torpedo-boat flotilla, and could be followed in the naval Enigma decrypts.[28] It sailed with the *Prinz Eugen* and the *Lützow* from Gdynia on 11 October to carry out bombardments in the Memel area but was forced to break off on the following day for lack of fighter protection.[29] On 23 October it returned to the Memel area with fighter protection, and on 24 October, with the *Hipper* and the *Lützow*, it carried out a brief bombardment in support of the Army on the Sworbe peninsula, Hitler having ordered that the peninsula should be held as a fortress and the naval authorities regarding its

---

22. DEFE 3/225, HP 347 of 16 September.
23. DEFE 3/229, HPs 1069, 1074 and 1080 of 24 September; Naval Headlines of 24 September.
24. Dir/C Archive, 7725 of 3 October; CX/MSS/T326/75.
25. eg DEFE 3/233, HP 2108 of 4 October; DEFE 3/235, HP 2638 of 8 October; DEFE 3/236, HPs 2855 of 10 October, 2950 of 11 October; DEFE 3/237, HP 3245 of 13 October; Naval Headlines of 9–11 October, 14 October, 18 and 19 October; Dir/C Archive, PROC 8630 (Summary of 15 October).
26. DEFE 3/239, HP 3592 of 17 October; DEFE 3/240, HP 3991 of 20 October.
27. DEFE 3/242, HP 4261 of 23 October.
28. eg DEFE 3/225, HP 132 of 14 September; DEFE 3/229, HP 1156 of 25 September; Naval Headlines 14 September.
29. DEFE 3/238, HP 3484 of 16 October; DEFE 3/240. HPs 2501 of 16 October, 3592 of 17 October.

retention as essential for the eventual evacuation of the Army from Courland.[30] Decrypts between 30 October and 1 November disclosed that plans to resume the bombardment were postponed on 28 October and 31 October and then cancelled.[31] Following further Russian landings, the Battle Group returned to Sworbe in mid-November, and from 19 November, when Hitler ordered that at least one heavy cruiser must be operating there at all times, it kept up the bombardments until the peninsula was evacuated on the night of 23–24 November.[32] In a message of 29 November, decrypted on 1 December, Admiral Eastern Baltic complained that no air reconnaissance had been flown during November despite his urgent requests for it.[33]

The naval Enigma showed in even greater detail the effort to keep the Army supplied and, in the absence of regular army and GAF decrypts, was the chief source of information about the Army's withdrawals. On 5 November, in the light of the decrypts and what was known from Russian reports, MI 14 believed that some 30 divisions had been cut off in Memel and Courland.[34] On 22 November the SIS, which had received earlier information about the deterioration of morale in Eighteenth Army, reported that both Sixteenth and Eighteenth Armies were being re-organised, officers of the rank of major and above being replaced by officers who were members of the Nazi party or from the SS.[35]*

□

The Russian offensive on the Romanian front had meanwhile begun on 20 August. It had not been expected in Whitehall. For some time past Enigma decrypts had shown that the Germans were aware that the Russians had been withdrawing forces from that front, and that they themselves had withdrawn most of their armoured formations.[36] From Axis diplomatic decrypts, on the other hand, it had emerged that the German withdrawals were arousing the disquiet of the Romanian government, and it can

---

*   These reports were in the series referred to in Volume III Part 1, p 305 and fn.

30.   DEFE 3/239, HP 3706 of 18 October; DEFE 3/240, HP 3991 of 20 October; DEFE 3/242, HP 4435 of 25 October; DEFE 3/472, ZTPG 296055; Naval Headlines of 17 and 18 October, 20 October, 25 and 26 October.
31.   DEFE 3/300, HPs 5003 of 30 October, 5167 of 31 October; DEFE 3/301, HP 5264 of 1 November; Naval Headlines of 30 October.
32.   Naval Headlines 16 November, 19–23 November, 25 November.
33.   DEFE 3/313, HP 8331 of 1 December.
34.   WO 208/4317, MI 14 Weekly Summary for the CIGS, 5 November.
35.   Dir/C Archive, No 232 of 27 September, 471 of 22 November.
36.   as examples, DEFE 3/59, XL 2776 of 20 July; DEFE 3/61, XL 3500 of 26 July; DEFE 3/114, XL 5132 of 7 August.

have caused no surprise that the first few days of Russian successes produced general disintegration in Romania and throughout the Balkans. On 23 August the King dismissed the Romanian government and two days later the new government declared war on Germany. On 26 August the Bulgarian government announced its withdrawal from the war – it had never declared war on Russia – and the Hungarian government fell on 29 August. The Russians took Galats on 28 August and Ploesti on 30 August, and entered Bucharest the next day. Ignoring the Bulgarian announcement, the Russians entered Bulgaria unopposed on 8 September; Bulgaria capitulated on 9 September.

To begin with, the Germans hoped to keep the loyalty of some at least of what remained of the Romanian forces; this was revealed in high-grade messages between Jodl, Keitel and Himmler of 23 and 26 August, which were decrypted on 3 September.[37] Between 25 and 28 August, however, other decrypts disclosed that they were unable to move troops by rail, all stations being in Romanian hands, or send reinforcements to the capital by air, and that they had abandoned an airborne operation to relieve Ploesti in view of the strength of the Romanian anti-aircraft defences.[38] And by 2 September further decrypts had established that most of the Romanian Army had gone over to the Russians by the end of August, when the Germans estimated that, of its front-line strength of 20 divisions and 5 brigades, 14 divisions and 1 brigade had been destroyed by the Russians in the previous fighting.[39] As for the fate of the German divisions, the JIC knew by 28 August that of those in eastern Romania and Moldavia – between 22 and 25 in all – some 10 or 12 were surrounded by the Russians at Kishinev and that 5 or 6 in the Galats–Braila area had failed to prevent the Russians from forcing the Galats gap; it was probable that only 7 would be able to withdraw to the Carpathians.[40]

Bulgaria's withdrawal from the war was accompanied by preparations for the withdrawal of her forces from Yugoslavia and Greece, where they had been guarding the German lines of communication. German messages expressing anxiety at this prospect were decrypted by 23 August and a further message indicating that the Bulgarians were concentrating for their withdrawal from Serbia was decrypted on 1 September.[41] It

---

37. CX/MSS/T287/57, T288/75; DEFE 3/221, XL 9086 of 3 September.
38. DEFE 3/125, XLs 7814 of 25 August, 7965 and 8000 of 26 August; DEFE 3/126, XL 8234 of 28 August: Air Sunset 228 of 28 August.
39. DEFE 3/128, XL 8623 of 30 August; DEFE 3/220, XL 8975 of 2 September; WO 208/4316 of 3 September.
40. JIC(44)379(o) of 28 August.
41. DEFE 3/124, XL 7641 of 23 August; DEFE 3/220, XL 8887 of 1 September; WO 208/4316 of 27 August, 3 September.

seemed obvious, as the JIC observed on 28 August, that in part to fill the gap left by the Bulgarians, and in part to provide necessary reinforcements for a defence line from the Carpathians to Salonika, German withdrawals from the outlying Balkans should follow. But the JIC was not convinced that Germany would depart from her policy of evacuating territory only under direct military pressure; Hitler might continue to insist that retreats were delayed beyond the point at which withdrawal was possible.[42] And on 5 September it considered that if indeed she had intended to withdraw in good order in the Balkans, she had again acted too late. It did not know 'how fast, how far, and in what direction' the Russians would advance into the Balkans, but the probability was that they would make straight for Belgrade in order to make contact with Tito and cut off the Belgrade–Salonika railway, the main line of retreat for the German forces in Greece.[43]

□

Until the beginning of August, far from withdrawing troops from Greece, Germany had continued to contemplate the re-inforcement of the Greek islands. The threat to her from the Greek guerrillas, though still limited by the political rivalries of the two main guerrilla forces, ELAS and EDES, had increased from June 1944 – a development of which the Allies were aware from the reports of the British liaison officers with the guerrilla organisations,[44] but also from high-grade Sigint. Army and naval Enigma decrypts in June and July had shown that the Germans were undertaking large-scale anti-guerrilla operations in the Peloponnese,[45] were complaining of serious guerrilla interference with coastal shipping off the north coast of Euboea,[46] and were fearful that the start of an EDES offensive in Epirus would lead to increasing sabotage throughout Greece.[47] Down to the last week of August decrypts were still reporting operations against guerrilla shipping off Euboea and the Peloponnese and against guerrilla bands in the Peloponnese.[48] These preoccupations prevented any German withdrawals. At the same time, Sigint had made it clear

---

42. JIC(44)379(o) of 28 August.
43. JIC(44)395(o) of 5 September.
44. CAB 80/44, COS(44)112 of 12 June (Résumé No 251).
45. DEFE 3/179, KV 9775 of 26 June; DEFE 3/669, ZTPGMs 86678, 86687; Naval Headlines of 28 June.
46. DEFE 3/52, XL 1103 of 7 July.
47. DEFE 3/54, XL 1575 of 11 July.
48. DEFE 3/669, ZTPGMs 86678, 86687; Naval Headlines 1146 of 23 August; DEFE 3/126, XLs 8018 and 8027 of 26 August; DEFE 3/670, ZTPGM 87079; Naval Headlines of 26 and 27 August.

that the Germans were unable to exclude the possibility of Allied landings in the eastern Mediterranean and Albania. Decrypts expressing anxiety on this score before and after D-day in Normandy were frequent until the end of July, when the Germans concluded that the Allied build-up in the Mediterranean had been in preparation for the landings in the south of France.[49]* Other decrypts showed that they were still planning to despatch additional troops to the Greek islands at Hitler's insistence. On 8 and 9 July GC and CS had decrypted Hitler's order of 15 June that two regimental groups be sent to serve as a tactical reserve in Crete, together with a protest from C-in-C South-East; he thought the transfer virtually impossible in view of the air situation and transport difficulties, and urged that the troops would be better employed in Serbia.[51] In the middle of August naval Enigma decrypts had disclosed that at the beginning of the month the Germans were preparing to transfer 1,000 men to Lemnos from Salonika.[52] But, as we now know, the German decision to retreat followed on 26 August.

The C-in-C South-East was instructed on that day to withdraw from the Aegean and southern Greece. Early in September, by which time he had been told to evacuate, also, some of the Dalmatian islands, he was ordered to evacuate the Aegean and Ionian islands and the Peloponnese, but to hold the mainland for the time being.[53] These orders were not decrypted, but Sigint disclosed from 26 August that the Germans were discussing a withdrawal. In a message of 24 August, decrypted on 26 August, Admiral Aegean's liaison officer with Army Group F informed him that the supply of the islands was to continue until the Cs-in-C of Army Groups E and F returned from a visit to Hitler's HQ; and

---

* Up to D-day Allied deception was seeking to suggest that as the Allies were not yet ready to invade north-west Europe, their main effort would be made in the Balkans, and Operation *Zeppelin*, representing a threat to Crete and the Peloponnese and to Istria and the Dalmatian coast, was supplemented in May by Operation *Turpitude*, which put it about that the seizure of Rhodes was to be followed by an assault on Salonika and a thrust up the Struma to link with the Russians. It cannot be said that these plans persuaded the Germans that major Allied operations were intended, but they perhaps helped to discourage the Germans from withdrawing their forces by playing on their natural expectation that small-scale landings would be attempted.[50]

49.   DEFE 3/169, KV 7279 of 10 June; DEFE 3/170, KV 7502 of 11 June; DEFE 3/173, KV 8251 of 16 June; DEFE 3/179, KV 9967 of 28 June; DEFE 3/50, XL 689 of 4 July; DEFE 3/64, XL 4192 of 31 July; Naval Headlines of 12 June.

50.   Howard, *Strategic Deception*, (forthcoming) Chapter 7.

51.   DEFE 3/52, XL 1229 of 8 July; DEFE 3/53, XLs 1305 of 9 July, 1475 of 10 July.

52.   DEFE 3/668, ZTPGMs 85544 and 85547; Naval Headlines of 15 August.

53.   Ehrman, *Grand Strategy*, Vol VI (1956), p 43; Jackson, *The Mediterranean and Middle East*, Vol VI Part 2 (1987) pp 319–321.

another signal of 24 August from the Sea Defence Commandant South Peloponnese, advising what forces should be withdrawn from his area and concentrated for the defence of Attica, was decrypted on 27 August.[54] Between 27 and 31 August the Enigma disclosed that a battle group was to be withdrawn from Crete.[55] Admiral Aegean's instructions to Sea Defence Commandants for withdrawal from the islands, an operation which he defined as 'transfer, not evacuation', were decrypted on 31 August.[56]

Sigint covered the withdrawal in detail. Decrypts of 8 and 9 September disclosed that the Peloponnese was to be evacuated by 15 September, excluding Corinth, and listed the order of withdrawal from the islands – the Ionian islands first, then Crete and the Dodecanese, next Lesbos and Chios as soon as possible, finally the Cyclades. They distinguished, however, between evacuation and thinning-out. Only fighting men with their equipment were to participate in the thinning-out; coastal defence troops were to fight to the last cartridge until evacuation was ordered.[57] On 13 September it emerged that C-in-C South-East had ordered that the Ionian islands were to be held until the Peloponnese had been evacuated,[58] but other decrypts had shown by then that the evacuation of Cephalonia and Zante began on 9 September following the landing of a small British party on Cephalonia.[59] Thereafter there was a flood of Sigint about the withdrawal from the Peloponnese and the Ionian islands, where the evacuation of Corfu was ordered on 24 September and completed on the night of 9–10 October[60] and Patras was abandoned on 4 October.[61] Decrypts from the Aegean between 11 and 21 September had meanwhile disclosed that, while the whole of 22nd Infantry Division was to be withdrawn from Crete, the western end of the island was to be held as a fortress;[62] that troops were being

---

54. DEFE 3/125, XL 7992 of 26 August; DEFE 3/126, XL 8119 of 27 August; Dir/C Archive, 7472 of 27 August.
55. DEFE 3/126, XL 8205 of 27 August; DEFE 3/127, XL 8284 of 28 August; DEFE 3/128, XL 8702 of 31 August; Naval Headlines of 29 August.
56. DEFE 3/128, XL 8689 of 31 August; Naval Headlines 1155 of 1 September.
57. DEFE 3/222, XL 9471 of 8 September; DEFE 3/223, XLs 9537 and 9606 of 9 September; Naval Headlines of 9 and 10 September.
58. DEFE 3/224, XL 9951 of 13 September.
59. DEFE 3/223, XLs 9530 of 9 September, 9726 and 9744 of 10 and 11 September; Naval Headlines of 10 and 12 September.
60. DEFE 3/229, HP 1120 of 25 September; DEFE 3/235, HPs 2525 and 2621 of 7 and 8 October; Naval Headlines of 8 and 9 October.
61. DEFE 3/226, HP 485 of 18 September; DEFE 3/231, HPs 1687 and 1708 of 20 September; DEFE 3/232, HP 1937 of 2 October; DEFE 3/233, HPs 2011, 2017, 2029, 2120 of 3 October, 2154 of 4 October, 2158 of 5 October; Naval Headlines of 29 September, 4 October, 5 October.
62. DEFE 3/223, XL 9750 of 11 September; DEFE 3/224, XL 9877 of 12 September; Naval Headlines of 12 September.

withdrawn from Samos, Cos, Rhodes and Scarpanto;[63] that Paros, Milos and Syros were being retained temporarily as bases for transports.[64] Plans for turning Rhodes and Leros into fortresses were decrypted on 15 October.[65]

Withdrawal from the mainland was by then in full swing. By 10 September decrypts had revealed that 1st Mountain, 4th SS Police PG and 11th GAF Field Divisions were transferring from anti-guerrilla operations in Greece, Macedonia and Serbia to replace the Bulgarian divisions which had hitherto defended the Belgrade–Nis–Skoplje–Salonika railway.[66] By 13 September they added that 117th Jäger Division was moving from the Peloponnese to central or northern Greece, that 22nd Infantry Division was moving from Crete to the Struma sector in Thrace, and that 104th Jäger Division was on Hitler's orders leaving Epirus for the Pindus heights to defend the main route to Salonika.[67] By 6 October 41st Fortress Division, the remaining formation in the Peloponnese, had been located at Thebes on 28 September.[68] Decrypts reported the evacuation of the Piraeus on 9 October, of Athens on 14 October, of Chalkis and Volos on 16 and 18 October.[69] Early in October, following the evacuation of Corfu, it emerged from Sigint that XXI and XXII Mountain Corps were abandoning a third of Albania and withdrawing to the line Durazzo–Elbasan–Kastoria–Metsovo; and on 18 October a decrypt showed that XXI Corps's line ran from Valona to Lake Ochrid along the Albanian frontier.[70]

Much of the Sigint was derived from naval and GAF Enigma, and was decrypted and signalled to the Mediterranean Commands with little delay. And although that part of it which dealt with individual air and shipping movements – a large part – normally arrived too late to influence particular Allied operations, it nevertheless afforded the Commands a detailed account of the

---

63. DEFE 3/223, XL 9297 of 10 September; DEFE 3/224, XL 9951 of 12 September.
64. DEFE 3/225, HP 71 of 13 September; DEFE 3/228, HP 777 of 21 September; Naval Headlines of 22 September.
65. DEFE 3/238, HP 3436 of 15 October.
66. DEFE 3/222, XLs 9307 of 6 September, 9404 of 7 September; WO 208/4316 of 10 September.
67. DEFE 3/222, XL 9352 of 6 September; DEFE 3/224, XL 9951 of 13 September; DEFE 3/225, HP 27 of 13 September.
68. DEFE 3/234, HP 2422 of 6 October.
69. DEFE 3/236, HP 2792 of 9 October; DEFE 3/238, HPs 3337 and 3367 of 14 October, 3400 of 15 October; DEFE 3/239, HP 3720 of 18 October; DEFE 3/240, HPs 3837, 3851 and 3895 of 19 October; DEFE 3/676, ZTPGM 83439; Naval Headlines of 10 and 11 October, 16 October, 20 October.
70. DEFE 3/234, HPs 2330 and 2331 of 5 October; DEFE 3/239, HP 3707 of 18 October; WO 208/4317 of 15 October.

enemy's situation when, from 9 September, they opened their naval and air attack against the evacuation of the islands. Until 11 September the evacuation proceeded within the framework of Germany's regular convoy system; one decrypt obtained that day was a report from Admiral Aegean of 4 September to the effect that Allied reaction remained 'unexpectedly quiet'.[71] But another decrypt of 11 September disclosed that, alarmed by Allied air attacks and mining, he had ordered the Sea Defence Commandants to stop all other tasks and use every available ship for the withdrawal.[72] It was known by then that as the withdrawal of all German aircraft from the islands had been ordered on 6 September, and most of the few fighter aircraft in Greece had moved to Yugoslavia to meet the threat of a Russian advance,[73] the enemy's ability to protect his convoys was, as the JIS put it, 'practically negligible'.[74] And from the time when warships joined in the Allied offensive, sinking a convoy of small ships between Crete and Santorini on the night of 12–13 September and working north of Crete from 15 September for the first time since May 1941, a succession of decrypts reported on the increasing seriousness of the shipping situation, the damage that was being inflicted on ports, and the progressively severe restrictions the Germans were forced to place on the sea routes that could be used.[75] By the end of September they were having to route the bulk of the shipping along the east coast to Salonika.[76]

The efforts to evacuate the islands were brought to an end by 27 October. A few days later the decrypt of a report on the German Navy's contribution to them disclosed that it had employed 52 merchant vessels in all and that, of those of medium and large tonnage, 29 had been sunk; in addition, the Navy had lost 5 torpedo-boats, the mine-layer *Drache*, one R-boat and three anti-submarine craft.[77] The 29 merchant vessels no doubt included the four available large war transport (KT) ships, valuable for their heavy-loading gear; the fact that these had been sunk or damaged beyond repair between 14 and 20 September had been

71. DEFE 3/223, XLs 9748 and 9750 of 11 September.
72. DEFE 3/672, ZTPGM 89535.
73. Air Sunset 235 of 12 September.
74. CAB 121/419, SIC file D/Germany/4, JS/O/3 of 10 September.
75. eg DEFE 3/229, HP 1115 of 25 September; DEFE 3/232, HP 1784 of 1 October; DEFE 3/233, HP 2142 of 4 October; DEFE 3/234, HP 2427 of 6 October; DEFE 3/235, HP 2647 of 8 October; DEFE 3/236, HP 2760 of 9 October; DEFE 3/237, HPs 3053, 3090 and 3109 of 12 October; DEFE 3/238, HPs 3263, 3335 and 3367 of 14 October.
76. Roskill, *The War at Sea*, Vol III Part 2(1961), pp 114–115; Jackson, op cit, Vol VI Part 2 pp 329–333.
77. DEFE 3/303, HP 5753 of 6 November.

disclosed by decrypts at the time.[78] Of the torpedo-boats, three were Italian. From 9 September decrypts had disclosed the intention to transfer the boats from Pola and, following their arrival in the Piraeus on 24 September, Sigint reported the destruction of all three between 6 and 16 October.[79] The destruction by air attack of the *Drache* on 22 September followed the disclosure in the Enigma that she was to take the German garrison from Samos on that day; it was reported in decrypts of 23 September.[80] The sinking of the last German torpedo-boat on 19 October was disclosed by a decrypt on 23 October.[81] In the last few days of October the Enigma reported the dissolution of Admiral Aegean's command, together with the scuttling of all ships remaining in Salonika and the German destruction of the harbour.[82]

As well as recording its losses, the Navy's report on the evacuation claimed that it had brought over 37,000 men, 400 guns and 2,000 vehicles off the islands between 23 August and 27 October, and that only 380 men had been lost at sea.[83] The GAF's estimate of its contribution to the evacuation from the islands and mainland Greece was decrypted on 12 November; it claimed that between 1 September and 31 October it had transported 40,298 men and 1,266 tons of equipment.[84] German estimates – available later – showed that in all 67,000 men were brought off the islands

---

78. DEFE 3/225, HP 205 of 15 September; DEFE 3/226, HP 442 of 17 September; DEFE 3/228, HP 860 of 22 September; DEFE 3/229, HP 1099 of 25 September; DEFE 3/673, ZTPGMs 90450, 90507; Naval Headlines of 20 September.

79. DEFE 3/223, XL 9568 of 9 September; DEFE 3/224, XL 9890 of 12 September; DEFE 3/225, HPs 84 of 14 September, 200 of 15 September; DEFE 3/228, HPs 797 of 21 September, 831, 836 and 840 of 22 September, 934 and 947 of 23 September; DEFE 3/229, HPs 1053, 1063 and 1066 of 24 September, 1130 and 1165 of 25 September; DEFE 3/231, HPs 1583 of 29 September; DEFE 3/234, HP 2377 of 6 October; DEFE 3/235, HP 2624 and 2647 of 8 October, 2739 of 9 October; DEFE 3/236, HPs 2754 and 2816 of 9 October, 2852 of 10 October; DEFE 3/237, HPs 3005 of 10 October, 3043 of 11 October, 3096 of 12 October, 3160 and 3170 of 13 October; DEFE 3/239, HPs 3506 of 16 October, 3576 of 18 October; Naval Headlines 10 and 11 September, 13 September, 23–25 September, 7 October, 9 October, 17 October.

80. DEFE 3/228, HPs 817 of 22 September, 931 and 948 of 23 September; Naval Headlines of 24 September.

81. DEFE 3/241, HP 4233 of 23 October. See also DEFE 3/242, HP 4361 of 24 October; Naval Headlines of 25 October.

82. DEFE 3/224, HP 4804 of 28 October; Naval Headlines of 29 and 30 October.

83. DEFE 3/303, HP 5753 of 6 November.

84. DEFE 3/305, HP 6430 of 12 November.

by sea and air, and that 28,000 tons of supplies were withdrawn by sea and 1,000 tons by air.[85]

The Germans carried out their evacuation of mainland Greece to the accompaniment of increasing guerrilla activity and mounting tension between the rival guerrilla movements. The British War Cabinet had foreseen these developments when, in August, in the hope of averting civil war, it approved plans for sending an enlarged British army contingent and an air contingent to mainland Greece as the Germans withdrew. Under an earlier plan (Operation *Noah's Ark*), drawn up with a view to hastening Germany's withdrawal by supporting guerrilla activity, British irregular forces began to arrive in the Dodecanese and the Peloponnese and to land on the Adriatic coast from 9 September. The enlarged plan (Operation *Manna*), which called for negotiations with the Greek government and the leaders of the main guerrilla movements, and which also depended on detailed information about the German withdrawal, was not put into effect till the second week of October.[86]* The many decrypts signalled to the Commands during this period added little to the information the British authorities were receiving about the activities of the guerrillas and the progress of the German withdrawal from the SOE liaison missions and the Greeks themselves. But there were some which indicated that the Germans expected British forces to follow up their own retreat as closely as possible with a view to preventing a guerrilla take-over. A decrypt of 27 September revealed that Fremde Heere Ost, on the look-out for evidence that British forces would be sent in to control the resistance factions, had found none by 15 September, but on 3 October the C-in-C South-East concluded from the British occupation of Patras and the concentration of Allied warships south of Attica that the British would intervene in the struggle for power at any time.[87] His message was not decrypted till 14 October, the day on which British forces entered Athens as the Germans left. A decrypt of 7 November reported that the last of the German rearguards had crossed out of Greece into Macedonia on 2 and 3 November.[88]

□

---

* For the details of the British operations see Jackson, *The Mediterranean and Middle East*, Vol 6, Part 2 (1987).

85. Jackson, op cit, Vol VI Part 2, p 333.
86. Ehrman, op cit, Vol V, pp 368–369, 384–387; Vol VI, p 45; Woodward, *British Foreign Policy in the Second World War*, Vol III (1971), pp 410–411, 576.
87. DEFE 3/230, HP 1360 of 27 September; DEFE 3/238, HP 3352 of 14 October.
88. DEFE 3/303, HP 5804 of 7 November.

The collapse of Romania and Bulgaria had meanwhile forced the Germans in Yugoslavia to abandon concentrated operations against the Partisans, to turn round their front so as to face east and to pull back their forces from the Dalmatian coast in an effort to build up a defence line against a Russian advance.

The German drive against the Partisans early in June had soon petered out. By July the Partisans had regained the initiative. Reports from the SOE liaison missions in July revealed that, following the defection of Djuric from the Cetniks in June, the Partisans had begun to establish themselves in Serbia in clashes with Cetnik forces and were presenting an increasing threat to German communications in Montenegro.[89] In a message of 19 July, decrypted early in August, the Commander of Second Panzer Army had supported his request for permission to use 1st Mountain Division against the Partisans in Montenegro by drawing attention to the fact that the increased supply of Allied material and personnel from Italy, the arrival of more Allied missions, the 'W/T picture' and the adoption by the guerrillas of 'strict modern conduct of operations with employment of general staff' all pointed to the growing danger in that area.[90] But British plans for disrupting the German lines of communication by co-ordinating the operations of the Partisans with attacks by the Balkan Air Force and Land Forces Adriatic, two new commands set up at Bari in July, were thwarted until the end of August by mounting distrust between Tito and the Royal Yugoslav Government and by British suspicions, fuelled by reports of fighting between Partisans and Cetniks in Serbia, that Tito was primarily concerned to use his forces and the increased scale of Allied supplies to consolidate his control in Yugoslavia.*

---

* Evidence about the relations between the Germans and the Cetniks followed the news of Djuric's defection. On 17 June the decrypt of an OKH appreciation of Allied intentions in Yugoslavia indicated that the Germans were not entirely confident of Mihailovic's loyalty,[91] as did a telegram from the Japanese Ambassador in Berlin, decrypted at the end of August, to the effect that Mihailovic was maintaining a superficial co-operation with Germany but would betray her when the chance arose. Reports received from the British liaison officers in Yugoslavia in August spoke of open Cetnik co-operation with the Germans, and in particular of the presence of Mihailovic at a staff conference with the German Command at Ruma on 13 August.[92] A decrypt of 6 September disclosed that Hitler had decided that his forces would continue to work with 'hitherto reliable' Cetnik formations in Serbia, but that they were to be used only in local operations under German control.[93] Decrypts available by 16

89.   Ehrman, op cit, Vol V, p 385; Jackson, op cit, Vol VI Part 2, p 212; CAB 101/126, p 136; CAB 121/532, SIC file F/Balkans/4 Vol 2, Bari to FO no 150 of 15 June 1944 for example. For an account of the Partisan situation in Serbia in mid-July by Colonel Deakin see CAB 121/532.
90.   DEFE 3/113, XL 4763 of 5 August.
91.   DEFE 3/173, KV 8488 of 17 June.
92.   CAB 121/532, Bari to Caserta No 59 of 7 August, No 113 of 23 August.
93.   DEFE 3/222, XL 9304 of 6 September.

These difficulties were only partly overcome in discussions between SACMED and the Prime Minister and Tito at Caserta during August, but Tito then agreed to participate in a sustained offensive against German communications throughout Yugoslavia.[98] This offensive (Operation *Ratweek*) took place in the first half of September and encountered little opposition from the GAF; most of this had been withdrawn to Hungary and Slovakia to face the Soviet advances, and what little remained was severely handicapped by attacks on airfields by the Mediterranean Allied Strategic Air Force. Sigint and PR guided the attacks on airfields, which were particularly effective in the Belgrade area and on the Bulgarian frontier.[99] The communications targets attacked by the Strategic Air Force and the Balkan Air Force were selected in the light of PR and of information provided by the Partisans via RAF liaison officers at the main Partisan HQs.[100] Reports on the attacks were obtained from several Enigma decrypts; one disclosed that as a result of attacks on 3 September the Metkovic–Ploca railway would be out of action for a week.[101] The results of the offensive, as estimated at Bari in mid-September, were that over and above the destruction of road bridges, river ferries, rolling stock and motor transport, rail traffic would be impossible on the main lines to Greece and Albania for two months, between Belgrade and Ljubljana for two weeks and for a week between Dalmatia and the Sava valley.[102] The effects of the disruption on German move-

---

September disclosed that V Mountain Corps was to maintain contact with the Cetniks through Mihailovic's representative, Bacevic, and that Mihailovic was in touch with the roving German diplomatic representative in the Balkans.[94] In a message of 15 September, decrypted on 27 September, Fremde Heere Ost believed that Mihailovic was co-operating with the German-controlled Nedic government.[95] In a message of 9 September, on the other hand, decrypted on 13 September, the Sea Defence Commandant Dalmatia reported that Cetniks and Ustashi were for the first time uniting with the Partisans; a complete Ustashi brigade had gone over to Tito.[96] Other decrypts disclosing Cetnik opposition to the Germans and Ustashi defections were received late in September and early in October.[97] See also below, pp 300–301, fn*.

94. DEFE 3/573, CX/MSS/C 334 of 16 September; Dir/C Archive, 7642 of 24 September.
95. DEFE 3/230, HP 1380 of 27 September.
96. DEFE 3/224, XL 9975 of 13 September.
97. DEFE 3/229, HP 1204 of 25 September; DEFE 3/232, HPs 1755, 1759 and 1949 of 1 and 2 October.
98. Ehrman, op cit, Vol V, pp 387–388; Woodward, op cit, Vol III, p 330 et seq; Jackson, op cit, Vol VI, Part 2, p 202; CAB 101/126, pp 136A–137; CAB 101/228, p 15.
99. Ehrman, op cit, Vol V, pp 43–44; Jackson, op cit, Vol VI Part 2, pp 316–318; CAB 101/228, pp 24–28.
100. Jackson, op cit, Vol VI Part 2, p 316.
101. DEFE 3/221, XL 9194 of 5 September; DEFE 3/223, XL 9695 of 10 September; DEFE 3/224, XL 9832 of 11 September.
102. CAB 121/532, Bari to Caserta No 626 of 13 September.

ments were indeed severe for the rest of September, and were never to be entirely overcome.[103]

Operation *Ratweek* coincided with the early stages of the withdrawal of German forces in Greece and Yugoslavia and their redeployment in an effort to build up a defence line against the Russians from the Bulgarian frontier to Turnu Severin on the Romanian border. We have seen* that by 10 September the decrypts had revealed that the Germans were transferring 1st Mountain Division, 11th GAF Field Division and 4th SS Police PG Division from Greece to replace the Bulgarian divisions which had hitherto defended the Belgrade–Salonika railway. On 9 September the decrypt of a message of 7 September disclosed the warning to Admiral Adriatic that the Army intended 'the continuous evacuation or partial evacuation' of the Dalmatian islands;[104] and on 18 September another warning to the naval authorities was decrypted: Second Panzer Army would have to abandon remote strongpoints on the south Dalmatian coast because it had to supply reinforcements against the Russian threat and replace demoralised Croatian troops on its supply routes.[105]

The Army's withdrawal from the southern Dalmatian coast was completed by the end of September. Messages ordering the evacuation of the islands of Korcula and Mljet and the western part of the Peljesac peninsula on 8 September, of Brac on 9 September and of the eastern part of Hvar and the small islands Supetar and Sumartin on 12 September were decrypted between 10 and 14 September.[106] Decrypts reporting the completion of the evacuation of Mljet, Supetar, Brac and Korcula, in some cases in the face of Allied opposition, followed on 14 and 16 September.[107] Parties of British troops and Partisans had been landing on Hvar and Brac and parts of the mainland since 6 September; Hvar was already in their hands when the Enigma reported the completion of the German evacuation on 22 September.[108] By 25 September further decrypts had reported the withdrawal from the island of Solta on 23 September and from the Peljesac peninsula on the

---

* Above, p 291.

103.   Ehrman, op cit, Vol VI, p 44.
104.   DEFE 3/223, XL 9616 of 9 September; Naval Headlines of 11 September.
105.   DEFE 3/226, HP 490 of 18 September.
106.   DEFE 3/223, XL 9652 of 10 September; DEFE 3/224, XL 9933 of 12 September; DEFE 3/225, HP 112 of 14 September; Naval Headlines of 13 September, 16 September.
107.   DEFE 3/225, HPs 112, 116 and 164 of 14 September; DEFE 3/226, HPs 357 and 369 of 16 September; Naval Headlines of 16 September.
108.   DEFE 3/228, HPs 833 and 848 of 22 September.

following day.[109] On 25 September, as was disclosed by a decrypt of 29 September, the Partisans seized the coast between Peljesac and Omis, south of Split.[110] In messages decrypted at the end of the month the naval authorities recognised that the Army had abandoned the defence of the southern Dalmatian coast to naval units with inadequate artillery, but nevertheless issued instructions to the effect that in accordance with army policy the Navy was to hold out to the last man.[111]

The Russians had meanwhile begun their advance into Yugoslavia from Turnu Severin on 22 September. By the beginning of October, accompanied by strong Partisan forces, they were pouring across the Danube north and east of Belgrade. On 8 October they reached the river Morava, cutting the main railway to Belgrade from the south, and advanced northwards to reach the capital on 14 October.[112]

The threat to Belgrade was revealed by decrypts of 5 October onwards. On 5 and 6 October they disclosed that C-in-C South-East had moved his HQ from the city to Vukovar, to the north-east, and that the HQ of GAF South-East was to withdraw as soon as possible.[113] In another message decrypted on 6 October the naval authorities warned that withdrawals ordered by the Army to meet the Russian thrust north of Belgrade would mean abandoning the coast between Sibenik and Split and leaving only one battalion to defend each of those important harbours.[114] On 10 and 11 October it emerged that, to counter the Russian threat to Belgrade and its communications from the south, C-in-C South-East, with Hitler's approval, had withdrawn Second Panzer Army's two remaining German divisions (118th Jäger and 264th Infantry) and ordered Second Panzer Army to pull back from the coast, withdrawing all equipment by 21 October.[115] Decrypts on 11 and 12 October showed that the Russians had crossed the river Tisa at several places north of Belgrade and that 117th Jäger Division had encountered them at a bridgehead only 17 miles to the south-east.[116] Between 16 and 18 October they disclosed the entry of Russian tanks into the city on 14 October and the failure

---

109. ibid, HPs 912 of 23 September, 1013 of 24 September, 1199 of 25 September; Naval Headlines of 25 September.
110. DEFE 3/231, HP 1534 of 29 September.
111. DEFE 3/231, HPs 1534 and 1635 of 29 September.
112. Ehrman, op cit, Vol VI, p 42; CAB 101/228, p 37; CAB 80/45, COS(44)197 of 5 October (Résumé No 266).
113. DEFE 3/234, HPs 2252 of 5 October, 2358 of 6 October.
114. ibid, HP 2440 of 6 October.
115. DEFE 3/236, HPs 2875 and 2943 of 10 and 11 October; DEFE 3/237, HP 3051 of 11 October; Naval Headlines of 12 October.
116. DEFE 3/237, HPs 3035 of 11 October, 3086 of 12 October.

of the German reinforcements to reach it in time to support the garrison.[117] For the final defence of Belgrade the Germans mustered only five infantry battalions, over and above police and SS forces and local defence units, and they surrendered to Russian and Partisan generals on 20 October.[118] Nis had meanwhile fallen to a combined attack by Russian, Bulgarian and Partisan forces on 15 October; a decrypt available on that day gave the GAF order of 12 October for the evacuation of the city and the destruction of the airfield.[119]

With the fall of Nis and Belgrade the Germans concentrated their forces in the centre of Yugoslavia and confined themselves to protecting the retreat route to Istria and Italy and keeping open the main lines of communication to the south. C-in-C South-East's detailed orders of 9 October for the withdrawal of Second Panzer Army to a line in the mountains running from the coast east of Fiume to Mostar and Gacko were decrypted on 18 October.[120] They specified that the army and naval batteries on the coast were to provide tactical and moral support by fighting to the end, the destruction of batteries being forbidden so long as they could hold out. But naval protests that the policy of retaining strongpoints on the coast was misguided had already been decrypted on 11, 12 and 13 October,[121] and plans for evacuation of the remaining islands, to be followed by withdrawal first from the Split and Zara sectors and then from the area between Biograd and Sibenik, were decrypted on 17 October.[122] In a decrypt of 20 October OKW approved the C-in-C's request that the strongpoints should be abandoned when the Army had completed its withdrawal.[123]

By the end of October Second Panzer Army had completed its withdrawal and established contact with Army Group E in the south, thus enabling the Germans to form a front of sorts, and Germany was preoccupied with the task of withdrawing her remaining forces from further south to form the strongest possible defence line from the head of the Adriatic across northern Yugoslavia and south-west Hungary.[124] Throughout November, though it generated a mass of intelligence from high-grade Sigint, Allied air reconnaissance and reports from the

---

117. DEFE 3/239, HPs 3541 and 3566 of 16 October, 3673 of 17 October.
118. Ehrman, op cit, Vol VI, pp 45–46; CAB 101/228, pp 36–37.
119. DEFE 3/238, HP 3539 of 15 October.
120. DEFE 3/240, HP 3776 of 18 October.
121. DEFE 3/237, HPs 3026 of 11 October, 3136 of 12 October, 3152 of 13 October.
122. DEFE 3/239, HP 3615 of 17 October; Naval Headlines 1203 of 18 October.
123. DEFE 3/240, HP 3965 of 20 October.
124. Ehrman, op cit, Vol VI, p 46; CAB 101/228, p 37; Cabinet Office Historical Section, EDS/Apprec/19, Chapter 2, p 23.

liaison officers with the Partisans, the withdrawal proceeded without much interruption except on the coast – where the Partisans, following up Second Panzer Army's retreat, seized all the main ports south of Fiume with assistance from Allied naval and air attacks on the enemy's coast defences and shipping movements[125] – and on the escape route of XXI Mountain Corps.

Sigint reported losses of and damage to enemy small craft in Allied naval and air attacks on a number of occasions during October and early in November, but it is rarely possible to show that it was directly instrumental in obtaining the Allied successes. The main exception was the sinking of the ex-Italian torpedo-boat, TA 20, and two escorting corvettes by British destroyers in inshore waters between Fiume and Zara on the night of 1–2 November. The decrypt of a message of 31 October disclosing that these ships were to leave Fiume was sent to the Commands at 0247 on 1 November; a decrypt signalled after the engagement showed that they had left at 1500 on 1 November.[126] But many naval decrypts giving information about the demolitions and the minelaying operations carried out by the Germans during their withdrawal were of great value to the Allied clearance and minesweeping programme that followed the withdrawal.[127] The German intention to close down Admiral Adriatic's command was mentioned in the naval decrypts in the middle of November; its dissolution, and the incorporation of its few remaining forces with those in the western Mediterranean under a single command, Naval Chief Command South, was reported by Sigint early in the new year.[128]

XXI Mountain Corps, with 181st and 299th Infantry Divisions and two Fortress Brigades, was cut off in Albania when guerrilla activity prevented it from joining the main body of Army Group E as that crossed out of Greece into Yugoslavia in the middle of October. Army Group E arranged for the Corps to break out to the north-east via Prijepolje with assistance from a relieving operation by 22nd Infantry Division. The plan succeeded. The Corps's withdrawal was held up at the river Tara for a fortnight by Partisan attacks, which were assisted by a small British artillery contingent,* by Allied air raids and by atrocious weather. But the

---

* The British force (Floydforce) landed at Dubrovnik at the end of October in response to Tito's request for field artillery. Messages decrypted from 5 November disclosed that the

125. eg CAB 80/46, COS(44)228 of 9 November (Résumé No 271).
126. DEFE 3/300, HP 5189 of 1 November; DEFE 3/301, HP 5320 of 2 November.
127. Roskill, op cit, Vol III Part 2, pp 110–111, 113.
128. DEFE 3/305, HP 6445, of 12 November; Naval Headlines of 13 November; DEFE 3/325, BT 1342 of 5 January 1945.

Corps crossed out of Albania in the middle of December and withdrew into the German lines in the Sarajevo salient at Visegrad on 19 January.[134]*

These lines, which the Germans had succeeded in stabilising by the end of November, ran inland of the coast from Fiume to Mostar, thence to Sarajevo, and thence northwards to the Danube at Vukovar, north-east of Belgrade. As Sigint disclosed, C-in-C South-East held the front with Second Panzer Army and Army Groups E and F until the beginning of December. When, with a motley collection of battle groups surviving from the fighting in Serbia, Second Panzer Army was then transferred to Army Group South in Hungary to strengthen the front south of Lake Balaton,† its two Corps (XV Mountain Corps and V SS Mountain Corps) and the largely Croatian formations that were all that remained to

---

Germans had at once learned from POW and agents of the arrival of British artillery specialists.[129] It operated under the orders of the local Partisan commander against 181st Infantry Division near Kotor between 9 and 21 November, but the Partisans, distrustful on account of the unexpectedly large size of the force and of their suspicions about British intentions with regard to Mihailovic's forces and confident that they could prevent the withdrawal of XXI Mountain Corps without assistance, then ordered it back into reserve at Dubrovnik. From 14 to 24 December, at the request of the Partisans, it was again in action against XXI Mountain Corps's retreating forces at Podgorica and Danilovgrad, but its intervention had been unduly delayed and its operations were still hampered, so it felt, by the fact that the Partisans continued to put political considerations before military requirements. It was not used again before its return to Italy in mid-January.[130]

There were no grounds for the Partisans' suspicions that the Allies might seek to make contact with Mihailovic after his final dismissal by the Royal Yugoslav Government following Tito's discussions with the British authorities in August. It was known from a decrypt of 19 November that he had provided Second Panzer Army with a list of his local leaders on 2 November, but that Second Panzer Army had dismissed the Cetniks as 'almost devoid of military importance'.[131] In a decrypt of 9 November, however, Army Group E, reporting on discussions with a delegate from Mihailovic's HQ, had remarked on the 'vacillating' attitude of the Cetniks and expressed anxiety that they might turn against the Germans; the Army Group advised continued negotiations with them, and help on a limited scale, to keep them neutral at least until its forces had completed their withdrawal to the Sarajevo–Mostar area.[132] Thereafter Sigint showed that the Cetniks continued to maintain contact with the Germans and collaborate with them in military operations until April 1945, when it was referring to a 'Serbian Volunteer Force'.[133]

* See Appendix 19 for a selection of the decrypts covering the escape of XXI Mountain Corps; this will serve to illustrate the scale on which Sigint was available during the German withdrawal in Yugoslavia.

† See below, p 304.

129. DEFE 3/302, HP 5682 of 5 November; DEFE 3/304, HP 6098 of 9 November; DEFE 3/305, HP 6420 of 11 November; CX/MSS/ROB 10 of 17 November (item 15), 16 of 25 November (item 14).
130. CAB 101/126, pp 142–147; CAB 101/228, pp 57–61, 65–69, 71, 72.
131. DEFE 3/308, HP 7071 of 19 November.
132. DEFE 3/303, HP 5992 of 9 November.
133. DEFE 3/556, KO 445 of 14 April 1945.
134. CAB 101/228, pp 62–63, 68–69; EDS/Apprec/19, Chapter 4, pp 28–33, Chapter 6, pp 3, 29–31.

them were subordinated to Army Group E.[135] But the Germans were to hold their front throughout the winter, the Russians having switched their forces to the north for their offensive in Hungary.

□

In Hungary by the third week of October the Russians were threatening Csap (Cop) in the north-east, had reached the Danube to the south of Budapest, and were forcing the German and Hungarian armies into a long and increasingly narrow salient in Transylvania.[136]

In this salient – the Szekler tip – Germany's Army Group South (formerly Army Group South Ukraine) had Eighth Army in the north-east with three German and three Hungarian divisions and Sixth Army in the south with four German and six Hungarian divisions. Sixth Army had only precarious contact with the German forces in Yugoslavia. Eighth Army had First Hungarian Army on its left; this formed part of Army Group A (formerly Army Group North Ukraine) which was itself under attack from the Russian armies and, following an uprising in Czechoslovakia in August, from Slovak forces. Second Hungarian Army was at Cluj on the south-eastern edge of the salient and Third Hungarian Army was forming on the western flank. The Hungarians were unreliable allies; desertions had been widespread since the Regent had announced Hungary's withdrawal from the war in the middle of October and the Germans had replaced him with a puppet government.[137]

MI knew from Enigma and Fish decrypts that the Germans had been reinforcing Army Group South from the end of September, mainly from Army Group A in the central sector but also with formations from Yugoslavia. By 1 October it had information from a Hungarian General Staff Mission – given during talks with the Allies in Italy – that the Germans intended to defend southern Hungary by holding the line of the river Tisa.[138] And by 8 October, when MI 14 noted that the Army Group had received five Panzer divisions and four PG divisions from Army Group A,

---

135. DEFE 3/309, HP 4760 of 22 November; DEFE 3/314, HP 8645 of 5 December.

136. Ehrman, op cit, Vol VI, p 42; Seaton, op cit, p 489 et seq; CAB 80/45, COS(44)175 of 7 September, 183 of 14 September, 190 of 28 September, 197 of 5 October, 206 of 12 October (Résumés Nos 262, 263, 265–267); CAB 80/46, COS(44)215 of 19 October, 221 of 26 October (Résumés Nos 268, 269).

137. Seaton, op cit, pp 490–495.

138. WO 208/4316 of 1 October.

including 1st, 23rd and 24th Panzer Divisions, and 4th SS Police PG Division from the Belgrade area,[139] it seemed clear from the decrypt evidence that the Germans hoped to stem the Russian drive at the river Tisa after first counter-attacking in an effort to extricate their forces from the salient.[140] The intention to counter-attack was confirmed by GAF Enigma decrypts during the battle for Debrecen from 12 October,[141] and in a message decrypted on 18 October Luftflotte 4 hoped that the expected arrival of 24th Panzer Division would bring a 'decisive turn in the battle'.[142]

Attacking west of Cluj in the middle of October, the Russians had taken Debrecen and Nyiregyhaza by 22 October, cutting off Eighth Army.[143] The German counter-attack took place between 23 and 29 October; it recaptured Nyiregyhaza and enabled Eighth Army to withdraw to the west bank of the Tisa. But the Russians were already across the Tisa further to the south, where their advance was not halted until it was within a few miles of Budapest, and on 11 November they attacked from the north-east, driving Eighth Army and the left flank of Sixth Army back to the Matra Hills by the end of the month.[144] Among many other decrypts obtained during this phase, one of 29 October revealed that the Germans expected a major attack on Budapest from the south-west on 23 October;[145] one of 5 November ordered Sixth Army with Panzer reinforcements to smash the Russian thrust and establish contact with the forces of C-in-C South-East, beginning on 29 October;[146] one of 8 November disclosed that the development of positions on the Tisa had been abandoned by Army Group South on 28 October;[147] and one of 16 November gave Army Group South's appreciation on 7 November that the Russians were massing for the advance on Budapest on both sides of the Danube to the south, in the east and in the north-east.[148] By 19 November it was clear from other decrypts that the Germans had prevented a major Russian penetration east and north-east of the capital only by concentrating most of Army Group South's

---

139. DEFE 3/229, HP 1097 of 24 September: DEFE 3/231, HP 1524 of 29 September; DEFE 3/232, HP 1882 of 2 October; DEFE 3/236, HP 2388 of 6 October.
140. WO 208/4317 of 8 October.
141. eg DEFE 3/237, HP 3105 of 12 October.
142. DEFE 3/240, HP 3758 of 18 October.
143. Seaton, op cit, pp 492–494.
144. ibid, pp 494–495; Ehrman, op cit, Vol VI, p 82.
145. DEFE 3/244, HP 4880 of 29 October; WO 208/4317 of 29 October.
146. DEFE 3/302, HP 5626 of 5 November.
147. DEFE 3/303, HP 5966 of 8 November.
148. DEFE 3/307, HP 6769 of 16 November.

forces there, and that a division was being brought up from Istria in an attempt to maintain contact between Army Group South and the northern forces of C-in-C South-East and strengthen the defences to the south of the city.[149]* On 26 November MI 14 reported that the Germans had developed a strong delaying position between Lake Balaton and Ercsi (Erd) to counter the encirclement of Budapest from the south-west; and in the first week of December decrypts gave details of this position in the sector south of the lake where it was held by Second Panzer Army, brought in from Yugoslavia.[150]

The Russians resumed their advance in the middle of December, and by the end of the month, against desperate German resistance, their armies had reached Esztergom from the north and the south-west and completed the encirclement of Budapest.[151] That they had succeeded in doing so was confirmed by the decryption on 3 January of a message from Army Group South dated 27 December,[152] but other decrypts had made it plain by 28 December that despite bringing up 3rd Panzer Division from East Prussia, 6th Panzer Division from Warsaw and 8th Panzer Division from Cracow – reports of these transfers were decrypted on 22 and 24 December[153] – the Germans had failed to stem the tide.[154]

In an attempt to relieve the capital the Germans ordered further reinforcements to the Budapest front in the shape of IV SS Panzer Corps with 3rd and 5th SS Panzer Divisions from Army Group Centre. The Corps re-took Esztergom on 5 January and then, putting the Russians off balance near Balaton, got to within twelve miles of the city before its advance was stopped towards the end of the month.[155] Whitehall received its first news of the counter-attacks in the first week of January from a Russian communiqué which announced that elements of six Panzer divisions, including 3rd and 5th SS Panzer Divisions, were involved; MI 14 commented that the presence of these divisions, if confirmed, would mean that half of the Panzer divisions on the

---

* See below, pp 351, 355–356.

149. WO 208/4317 of 19 November; as examples DEFE 3/305, HPs 6476 of 13 November; DEFE 3/306, HP 6559 of 14 November; DEFE 3/307, HPs 6789 and 6815 of 16 November, 6994 and 6999 of 18 November.
150. WO 208/4317 of 26 November; DEFE 3/313, HP 8458 of 3 December; DEFE 3/314, HPs 8528 and 8594 of 4 December, 8671 and 8678 of 5 December, 8710 of 6 December.
151. Seaton, op cit, pp 495–500.
152. DEFE 3/324, BT 1119 of 3 January 1945.
153. DEFE 3/320, BTs 119 of 22 December, 248 of 24 December.
154. CAB 80/46, COS(44)255 of 28 December (Résumé No 278).
155. Seaton, op cit, pp 500–501; Ehrman, op cit, Vol VI, p 83.

eastern front were in Hungary.[156] A decrypt signalled by GC and CS on 11 January reported that 5th SS Panzer Division had been arriving on 31 December.[157] The arrival of IV SS Panzer Corps was foreshadowed in a decrypt of 8 January and this was followed on 16 January by a decrypt containing promises from Himmler himself that the city would be relieved.[158] On 28 January MI 14 knew that the Germans were still trying to break through to Budapest 'despite the obvious need for armour on the central sector'.[159]

It had long been obvious that should they fail to relieve the city, the Germans would hold it as a fortress for as long as possible. Hitler's order of 30 November insisting on the defence of the city, and stating that 'an evacuation . . . without fighting does not come into question even in the case of an unfavourable development of the situation', was decrypted on 17 December.[160] But it was equally obvious that the resources did not exist for a prolonged defence. At the end of December the German force cut off in the city consisted of 8th and 22nd SS Cavalry Divisions, a battle group of 60th PG Division and elements of 13th Panzer Division.[161] MI 14 estimated the garrison at between two and three German divisions and some Hungarian formations.[162] During November decrypts had established that IX SS Mountain Corps was moving from Yugoslavia to take command in Budapest;[163] in a message decrypted on 4 January it reported that its strength was 25,667 (of which 19,661 were Germans) plus 10,542 wounded, and that its battle strength was 15,149.[164]

By 28 December, as was disclosed by a situation report from Army Group South decrypted on 4 January, deep Russian penetrations had forced the garrison to fall back to an inner defence ring on the city perimeter.[165] In a message of 8 January, decrypted on 11 January, GOC Waffen SS in Hungary, who was commanding the garrison, reported that the supply situation was 'extremely critical'.[166] On 17 January (decrypted on 19 January)

---

156. WO 208/4317 of 7 January 1945.
157. DEFE 3/327, BT 1954 of 11 January.
158. DEFE 3/326, BT 1650 of 8 January, amended in DEFE 3/327, BT 1939 of 11 January; DEFE 3/330, BT 2511 of 16 January.
159. WO 208/4317 of 28 January.
160. DEFE 3/318, HP 9622 of 17 December.
161. Seaton, op cit, p 500.
162. WO 208/4317 of 31 December.
163. DEFE 3/306, HP 6558 of 13 November; DEFE 3/311, HP 8000 of 27 November; DEFE 3/316, HP 9113 of 11 December.
164. CX/MSS/444 para E5.
165. DEFE 3/324, HP 1095, of 4 January.
166. CX/MSS/426, para E14.

he reported that it had been impossible to construct a defence line and that house-to-house fighting was in progress in parts of the city.[167] His increasingly desperate situation reports included a message to Himmler of 29 January (decrypted on 31 January): the defences were at 'the last ditch. . . . If Gille [IV SS Panzer Corps] does not arrive almost at once, he will come too late. We are at our last gasp. . . .'[168] His last message, sent out on 8 February and decrypted three days later, reported desertions by Hungarian troops and the fact that the supply of the garrison by air had failed for several days.[169] On 11 February the Germans still able to fight or walk, some 16,000, tried to break out to the north-west; about 12 miles out of the city they were all but totally destroyed. The Russians announced the capture of Budapest on 13 February.[170]

167. DEFE 3/331, BT 2793 of 19 January; Dir/C Archive, 8547 of 31 January, Boniface Summary for the Foreign Office.
168. DEFE 3/503, BT 3813 of 31 January; Dir/C Archive, 8547 of 31 January, Boniface to FO.
169. CX/MSS/458 para E4.
170. Seaton, op cit, p 501.

CHAPTER 50

The Advance to Florence and the Gothic Line Battles

AS SOON as his forces had reached Rome on 4 June 1944 General Alexander ordered an advance with all possible speed by Eighth Army on the general area Florence–Bibbiena–Arezzo and by Fifth US Army on the general area Pisa–Lucca–Pistoia. As the Germans retreated Fourteenth Army's position west of the Tiber became critical, and Kesselring, the C-in-C South-West, prevented its collapse only by bringing up reinforcements from the rear (162nd, 20th GAF Field and 356th Divisions) and transferring XIV Panzer Corps HQ and 26th Panzer and 29th and 90th Panzer Grenadier Divisions from Tenth Army. Tenth Army, under less pressure, withdrew in comparatively good order.[1]

During their advance the Allies were well supplied with tactical intelligence. Army Y, derived principally from the enemy's divisional VHF links, gave notice of every nightly pull-back by the German divisions and provided detailed information about the positions to which they were withdrawing.[2] Enigma decrypts, plentiful as ever, fully reflected the decisions of the enemy's higher formations and threw much light on the condition of his armies and the measures he was taking to reinforce them.

A return of 12 May, signalled to the Commands on 15 May, had shown that when Operation *Diadem* (the Allied advance on Rome) began the German armoured forces in Italy were at peak strength with 405 tanks, of which 311 were serviceable, 238 assault guns (168 serviceable), 255 Italian assault guns (182 serviceable) and 737 heavy anti-tank guns (697 serviceable).[3] Decrypts between 31 May and 3 June, covering the period up to 30 May but omitting some important formations, reflected the severe losses that had been suffered.[4] Thus 26th Panzer Division had lost 28 Pzkw tanks out of 76 and 15th PG Division 14 out of 40. Heavy Panzer Abteilung 508 had lost 17 out of 48 Tigers (Pzkw VI). 90th PG Division had lost 13 out of 42 assault guns and 3rd PG Division 19

---

1. Cabinet Office Historical Section, EDS/Appreciation/18, Chapters 1 and 2.
2. *History of Sigint in the Field*, p 129.
3. DEFE 3/155, KV 3971 of 15 May 1944.
4. DEFE 3/163, KV 5875 of 31 May; DEFE 3/164, KV 6195 of 1 June; DEFE 3/165, KV 6289 of 3 June.

out of 44. Among infantry divisions which had been specially hard hit, 71st had lost 34 out of 40 anti-tank guns, 94th had lost 26 out of 29, and 715th had lost 38 out of 39.

In a long message of 5 June, signalled by GC and CS on 8 and 9 June, C-in-C South-West assessed the state of his divisions. By 2 June they had reported 38,024 personnel killed, wounded or missing; but this figure would continue to rise. Losses of material were even more difficult to establish. In the last few days reports of losses were almost entirely lacking, but quite a considerable increase must be expected especially in Fourteenth Army. On the basis of reported figures, and taking account of operations in progress, the C-in-C's signal went on to assess the fighting value of his divisions in infantry battle strengths, artillery and heavy anti-tank guns as a percentage of their strengths at the start of the battle. Apart from 278th and 356th Divisions, which were shown as complete, the figures were startling. 4th Parachute Division was the only one credited with 50 per cent in all three categories. The infantry battle strengths of 1st Parachute, 44th Infantry, 15th PG, 71st Infantry, 26th Panzer, 114th Jäger, 94th Infantry, 3rd PG, 362nd Infantry, 715th Infantry, 90th PG and 29th PG Divisions were all assessed at 20 per cent or less.[5] A decrypt on 17 June showed an unspecified division in Fourteenth Army reporting that all its battalions were exhausted and not serviceable for any battle tasks.[6] Another contained an incomplete strength return in which 26th Panzer Division reported itself very weak: I/PG Regiment 9 was 192 strong; II/PGR 9 had been temporarily disbanded; I/PGR 67 was 318 strong and II/PGR 67 was 226 strong; the Panzer Reconnaissance Abteilung comprised only 89 all ranks.[7] In a telegram of 19 June to the Prime Minister and the CIGS, holding out the prospect of 'a great victory which has unlimited possibilities', Alexander referred to these decrypts which showed the enemy's extreme weakness in men and material.[8]*

From the beginning of June high-grade Sigint showed that some losses were being made good. Orders of 2 June for unloading and despatching tanks arriving in Florence were signalled on 5 June;[9] decrypts of 11 and 16 June referred to tanks en route to I/Panzer

---

* This telegram was part of the exchanges which took place in the effort to persuade the US Chiefs of Staff to give to the Italian front priority over Operation *Anvil*, see below, p 316ff.

5. DEFE 3/167, KV 6885 of 8 June; DEFE 3/168, KV 7032 of 9 June.
6. DEFE 3/174, KV 8546 of 17 June.
7. ibid, KV 8570 of 17 August.
8. CAB 121/396, SIC file D/France/6/14, PM's Personal Telegram T 1322/4 of 19 June.
9. DEFE 3/165, KVs 6429 and 6446 of 5 June.

Regiment 4;[10] and Heavy Panzer Abteilung 504 (which had 42 Tigers) was brought in from France. C-in-C South-West's return of armoured fighting vehicles for 23 June, signalled on 29 June, showed 159 tanks serviceable out of 319; 109 assault guns out of 185; 43 Italian assault guns out of 100; and 326 heavy anti-tank guns out of 400.[11] The order for the movement of Heavy Panzer Abteilung 504 from France, dated 2 June, was signalled on 10 June.[12] A message from C-in-C South-West reporting the arrival on 19 June of trains bringing 34th Infantry from the Russian front was signalled on 22 June.[13] A message of 12 June from the C-in-C, signalled on 13 June, stated that 715th Infantry Division, which earlier decrypts had shown to be under orders to transfer to France, would stay with his Army Group C to rest and refit in the Ravenna area.[14] Decrypts of orders of 20 June from OKH for re-forming this division and refitting 65th Division were available on 23 and 24 June; the Infantry Division Wildflecken was to be brought from Germany for 715th Division, and the Infantry Division Ostpreussen (less one regiment) for 65th Division, and the C-in-C was to report the probable dates of readiness for employment of both the re-formed divisions by 5 July.[15] A decrypt of 30 June stated the C-in-C's requirements for re-equipping 94th and 305th Infantry Divisions. Their deficiency in personnel, excluding officers, was 6,045, and large quantities of weapons, signal equipment and motor transport were needed. Army Group C was unable to meet these deficiencies except at the expense of other divisions. This incomplete message also contained a reference to the recent allocation of three more battalions of replacement drafts (Marsch battalions) and elements which were no longer needed for re-equipping 715th Division.[16]

Kesselring's re-disposition of his forces was well covered in high-grade Sigint. The forward movement of 20th GAF Field and 162nd Infantry Divisions to the Orbetello area behind the German right wing was disclosed by decrypts of 2 and 6 June.[17] Decrypts on 7 June revealed that LXXVI Panzer Corps was now under Tenth Army, that the Tiber was the boundary between Fourteenth and Tenth Armies and that the latter had been ordered on 5 June to withdraw by stages to the *Caesar* line, shifting its main

---

10. DEFE 3/170, KV 7577 of 11 June; DEFE 3/173, KV 8344 of 16 June.
11. DEFE 3/48, XL 30 of 29 June.
12. DEFE 3/169, KV 7284 of 10 June.
13. DEFE 3/176, KV 9100 of 22 June.
14. DEFE 3/171, KV 7933 of 13 June.
15. DEFE 3/177, KVs 9314 of 23 June, 9407 of 24 June.
16. DEFE 3/48, XL 234 of 30 June.
17. DEFE 3/164, KV 6170 of 2 June; DEFE 3/166, KV 6648 of 6 June.

effort behind its right wing.[18] At midnight on 8 June GC and CS signalled an order issued by Kesselring late on 6 June; as no bridging equipment was available at Orte, 26th Panzer Division must by using detours move as quickly as possible to the area south-west of Orvieto, while a reinforced battalion must cross to the west bank of the Tiber, near Orte, if necessary without vehicles, and establish contact 'with neighbour'.[19] Decrypts on 8 and 9 June showed that Fourteenth Army commanded a Battle Group Göritz as well as I Parachute Corps, which had been joined by 356th Infantry Division from Genoa.[20] Other decrypts on 9 June referred to 29th PG Division being withdrawn from the front line and to its movements being hampered by traffic and fuel difficulties.[21] On 11 June it was learnt that two days earlier Battle Group Göritz had comprised 20th GAF Field, 65th and 162nd Infantry Divisions.[22] By 17 June decrypts had disclosed that Heavy Panzer Abteilung 504, recently arrived from France, had been placed under Fourteenth Army in the Grosseto area.[23]

The extent to which Fourteenth Army had been reinforced by formations from Tenth Army became apparent from decrypts available on 13, 14 and 15 June. A decrypt on 13 June disclosed that 29th PG Division was north-west of Lake Bolsena on 12 June and that 90th PG Division's battle headquarters was also west of the Tiber near Acquapendente.[24] Later decrypts that day revealed that 26th Panzer Division was coming into I Parachute Corps's front line between 3rd PG and 4th Parachute Divisions[25] and that Kesselring had given orders for 29th PG Division to be moved north of Grosseto with all speed.[26] On 14 June a decrypt revealed a message addressed to XIV Panzer Corps care of Fourteenth Army[27] and others on 15 June showed clearly that this experienced HQ was now commanding Fourteenth Army's right wing.[28] Its intention late on 14 June was to withdraw to a line from Castiglione della Pescaya–north of Grosseto (which was captured on 15 June)–Istia.[29] Its left-hand neighbour was 29th PG Division under I Parachute Corps, which also commanded 26th Panzer, 4th

---

18. DEFE 3/166, KV 6696 of 7 June; DEFE 3/167, KV 6847 of 7 June.
19. DEFE 3/168, KV 7025 of 8 June.
20. DEFE 3/167, KV 6920 of 8 June; DEFE 3/168, KV 7087 of 9 June.
21. DEFE 3/168, KVs 7089 and 7126 of 9 June.
22. DEFE 3/169, KV 7493 of 11 June.
23. DEFE 3/171, KV 7964 of 14 June; DEFE 3/173, KV 8412 of 17 June.
24. DEFE 3/171, KV 7843 of 13 June.
25. ibid, KV 7902 of 13 June.
26. ibid, KV 7935 of 13 June.
27. DEFE 3/172, KV 8079 of 14 June.
28. ibid, KVs 8143, 8149 and 8180 of 15 June.
29. ibid, KV 8149 of 15 June.

Parachute and 356th Infantry Divisions.[30] A message from Kesselring on 15 June saying that the right wing of Fourteenth Army had been taken over by XIV Panzer Corps commanding 90th PG, 20th GAF Field, 162nd and 65th Infantry Divisions (the last of which was being withdrawn for rest and refitting) was decrypted early on 17 June.[31]

Decrypts referring to the withdrawal of Fourteenth Army into the *Albert* line followed on 20 and 21 June,[32] by which time the Allies had learned from high-grade Sigint that this line ran from Castiglione della Pescaya on the west coast to the east coast south of Ancona through Grosseto, Lake Trasimeno and Gualdo Tadino; that Kesselring had strict instructions from Hitler to hold it; and that he had grave doubts about his ability to do so.

□

At the beginning of June, in view of the heavy defeat of their armies, Kesselring and his Commanders, von Vietinghoff of Tenth Army and Lemelsen who took over Fourteenth Army from von Mackensen on 7 June, envisaged a steady withdrawal into the Pisa–Rimini line running through the Apennines – the *Gothic* line as the Germans called it until mid-June.[33] Hitler thought differently. His customary reluctance to surrender territory was heightened by uncertainty about Allied Mediterranean strategy and his view that Italy was a bastion for the Balkans. Moreover, he had a poor opinion of the defensive qualities of the *Gothic* line. Throughout June he was insisting that Kesselring must not simply adopt delaying tactics back to the *Gothic* line, but must stand and fight with the intention of bringing the Allies to a halt as far south as possible. And because the flanks of a line of resistance, when it had been established, would be threatened by Allied amphibious capabilities, steps had been taken to defend the Ligurian coast in particular, pending clarification of Allied intentions.[34]

On 3 June Jodl told Kesselring that Hitler had agreed that the centre of Army Group C should be withdrawn with all speed to the *Caesar* line, but had ordered that the reconstruction of the front north of Rome was to be attempted as far south as in any way possible. On 6 June General Warlimont, Jodl's deputy at OKW, was sent to look at the *Gothic* line and to meet Kesselring and his Commanders. It was expected that his report would provide a

---

30. ibid, KV 8215 of 15 June.
31. DEFE 3/173, KV 8467 of 17 June.
32. DEFE 3/175, KVs 8874 and 8880 of 20 June, 8971 and 8979 of 21 June.
33. EDS/Appreciation/18, Chapters 1 and 2.
34. ibid.

basis for further decisions.* On 9 June Kesselring issued a
directive which envisaged a staged withdrawal to the *Gothic* line.
On the following day, however, he was again told by OKW that on
the Führer's orders he was not to pursue delaying tactics back to
the *Gothic* line but to stand firm on a line as far as possible to the
south, the course of which was to be reported to OKW. 19th GAF
Field Division, which was arriving in Italy from Belgium, was to be
held in reserve on the Ligurian coast. On 12 June the C-in-C was
ordered to reinforce the Genoa–Leghorn sector. Two days later a
directive was sent to him which had been signed by Hitler
personally. The text opened by stating that the Apennines from
La Spezia to Pesaro represented the last obstacle which could
prevent the enemy from breaking into the Po valley, a development which would have immeasurable military and political
consequences. At present, however, the Apennine line did not
offer security against attacks by superior forces and it would take
many months of intensive work to achieve this. The operations of
Army Group C must be geared to gaining this time. It must
therefore go over to defence on a line Piombino–Lake
Trasimeno–Civitanova or, if possible, on a line even further south,
Orbetello–Spoleto–Rieti–River Tronto–Adriatic. After a categoric
order that Elba was to be held and not evacuated (as Kesselring
had intended) Hitler declared that any erroneous idea entertained
by officers and men of Army Group C regarding the existence of a
fortified defence system in the Apennines must be eradicated. On
15 June he hammered home this point by decreeing that as the
name *Gothic* line was liable to create 'false impressions' it was to be
changed to *Green* line.[35]†

The most southerly line indicated by Hitler being already
impracticable, on 14 June Kesselring ordered his armies to bring
the Allies 'conclusively' to a halt on the *Albert* line. Allied advances
quickly threatened to breach the western coastal sector of this line
and on 18 June Fourteenth Army was instructed to prepare a
switch-line, *Anton*, running eastwards from the coast at Follonica.
Reporting his plans, Kesselring asked if he could see Hitler in
order to justify his conduct of operations and to discuss future
possibilities. He was told that this visit must be postponed for a few
days. In consequence on 18 June he sent Jodl an account of his
conduct of the campaign since the fall of Rome which could be
presented to the Führer 'to correct certain inaccuracies'. Kesselring pleaded that only the use of delaying tactics had made it

---

* The expectation was not fulfilled.

† See further below, pp 323, 333, 336ff.

35. ibid, Chapter 1.

possible to rally and to some extent re-organise the battered formations of Tenth and Fourteenth Armies. The armies had been ordered to stand on the *Albert* line and he would do everything in his power to ensure its defence, but he was 'concerned' for its prospects. He was convinced of the necessity to defend Italy as far south of the Apennines as possible, and was 'doubly bound' thereto by the Führer's orders, but he wanted to be sure that he had the latter's confidence.[36]

On 19 June Hitler allowed the evacuation of Elba after three days fighting. By 21 June Fourteenth Army had occupied the *Anton* line with XIV Panzer Corps and part of the *Albert* line with I Parachute Corps. Tenth Army's LXXVI Panzer Corps and LI Mountain Corps were still forward of the *Albert* line west of Lake Trasimeno and in the Adriatic sector.[37]

Until high-grade Sigint began to disclose the substance of these German exchanges, which it did from 9 June, the Allied assessment of Kesselring's situation and intentions was the same as that made by Kesselring himself. The intelligence summaries issued by AFHQ on 7 June[38] and Allied Armies Italy (AAI) on 8 June[39] both appreciated that the Germans had little choice but to withdraw to the Pisa–Rimini line. The former noted that, as had been revealed by decrypts between 29 May and 7 June, the divisions brought in as reinforcements (16th SS PG, 19th and 20th GAF Field and 42nd Jäger Divisions) were not being brought forward. 16th SS PG Division was to be positioned partly for coast defence of the Carrara–Leghorn sector and partly as a mobile reserve; 19th GAF Division was to be put on coastal defence south of Leghorn; 20th GAF Division would be in Army Group Reserve in the area Civitavecchia–Orbetello; and 42nd Jäger Division was relieving 356th Infantry Division around Genoa, the latter moving to an operational area. Finally, 162nd Infantry Division was being withdrawn from coast defence and brought forward east of Orbetello.[40] Nor did the decrypts available on 7 and 8 June call for a re-assessment; they dealt with the strengthening of the Apennine line. A message of 5 June from Warlimont asking C-in-C South-West that details of meeting place and route should await him at Florence was signalled by GC and CS on 7 June.[41] The programme for his visit covering 6–10 June was signalled the next

36. ibid.
37. ibid.
38. WO 204/969, AFHQ Intelligence Summary No 93 of 7 June.
39. WO 170/66, AAI Intelligence Summary No 48 of 8 June.
40. DEFE 3/162, KV 5685 of 29 May; DEFE 3/163, KVs 5861 and 5944 of 31 May; DEFE 3/164, KVs 6109, 6157 and 6170 of 2 June; DEFE 3/165, KV 6428 of 5 June; DEFE 3/166, KV 6556 of 6 June, 6700 and 6728 of 7 June.
41. DEFE 3/167, KV 6786 of 7 June.

day; he was to inspect the Apennine line north of Florence, meet Kesselring, visit Fourteenth and Tenth Armies, and inspect the eastern sector of the Apennine position or the coastal plain.[42] Other decrypts on 8 June revealed that the Mountain Jäger School, Mittenwald, was to be sent to Florence for use as a defence garrison in the Apennine position;[43] and that OKH had asked Kesselring how many mines he required for the Apennine position, bearing in mind that Hitler had ordered large-scale mining.[44]

On 9 June, however, GC and CS signalled the message of 3 June in which Jodl informed Kesselring that Hitler had ordered him to withdraw the centre of Army Group C with all speed to the *Caesar* line and to reconstruct the front north of Rome as far south as in any way possible.[45] On 10 June two decrypts contained orders of the previous day by Kesselring to his armies to withdraw to a line from Orbetello through Terni and Rieti, Tenth Army gradually wheeling its left wing to the line Aquilla–Gran Casso–Pescara. Armee Abteilung von Zangen was to bring up the artillery of 356th and 162nd Divisions as soon as possible after the divisions and prepare a deep defence zone between the coast and the Orvieto–Siena road; the preparations were to be chiefly against tanks and to be heaviest in the Grosseto area where the rearward battalions of 162nd Division were to form a protective garrison.[46] Other decrypts on 10 June contained news of Lemelsen's appointment to command Fourteenth Army[47] and an order from Keitel that battalions of civilian workers were to be set up in the area of the Apennine position.[48] A decrypt of 11 June disclosed that according to von Zangen the line of the foremost blocking positions ran from Castiglione della Pescaya on the west coast along the north bank of the river Bruna to Grosseto and Istia, thence via the south bank of the Ombrone eastwards to Arcidosso, Monte Amiata and Radicofani.[49]

AFHQ's intelligence summary issued three days later appreciated that the Germans intended to make a stand on the general line Trevi–Lake Trasimeno–Grosseto, and that this was presumably because of a pressing need to improve the defences of the final Pisa–Rimini line.[50] The German intention to stand on the

---

42.   ibid, KV 6956 of 8 June.
43.   ibid, KV 6900 of 8 June.
44.   DEFE 3/168, KV 7009 of 8 June.
45.   ibid, KV 7169 of 9 June.
46.   DEFE 3/169, KVs 7307 and 7373 of 10 June.
47.   ibid, KV 7338 of 10 June.
48.   ibid, KV 7434 of 10 June.
49.   DEFE 3/170, KV 7572 of 11 June.
50.   WO 204/969, No 94 of 14 June.

Trasimene line was forecast in Eighth Army's intelligence summary of 17 June and AAI's of 21 June. Both attributed the information to an operations order captured from 334th Infantry Division and to statements allegedly made by one of Kesselring's senior staff officers to his Italian doctor.[51]

The next information about Hitler's intervention was available on 19 June from decrypts referring to Elba. The decrypt on 16 June of a message from the German naval command in Italy had revealed that on the previous day Kesselring had instructed Fourteenth Army to discontinue transport to Elba.[52] On 19 June, however, by which time the Allies had invaded Elba and the last defenders were being evacuated, GC and CS signalled a message of 18 June in which Kesselring told the naval authorities that the defence of Elba to the uttermost was of decisive importance to the whole conduct of the war on the southern front.[53] Hitler had insisted on this in his directive of 14 June. No other part of that directive was to appear in the decrypts for some days, but on 20 June an incomplete message was available which, as we can now see, was part of the appreciation which Kesselring had submitted on 18 June for presentation to the Führer. Beginning with an incomplete sentence reading '... still allows of conduct of operations at all', the decrypt went on to say that 114th Jäger, the strongest division, had eight battalions, of which three were weak and one exhausted; it had 12 heavy anti-tank guns and 36 light guns, was 80 per cent mobile and had a fighting value between categories II and III.* 94th Infantry Division was the weakest division with three weak battalions, no heavy anti-tank guns, 16 light guns, 60 per cent mobility and fighting value category IV. The other divisions taken together were about halfway between the strongest and the weakest. Kesselring was convinced of the need to hold as far south-west of the Apennines (ie the *Gothic* line) as possible. Doubly anxious to do so because of Hitler's order, he had initiated all possible measures to accomplish this. But the Führer's confidence was a prerequisite for success in directing the next phase of the battle.[54]†

It was not until 27 June that a summary of Hitler's directive

---

* For the definition of these categories see above, p 259fn*.

† A copy of this decrypt was passed to the Prime Minister by 'C' who marked it 'important'.[55]

51. WO 170/202, Eighth Army Intelligence Summary of 17 June; WO 170/66, No 50 of 21 June.
52. DEFE 3/173, KV 8322 of 16 June.
53. DEFE 3/175, KV 8804 of 19 June.
54. ibid, KV 8867 of 20 June.
55. Dir/C Archive, 6840 of 20 June.

became available in the decrypt of a message of 17 June to the naval authorities in Elba.[56] The decrypt disclosed that Hitler had ordered that the Apennine position was to be held as a final blocking line since Allied entry into the Po valley would have incalculable military and political consequences, but was at the same time insisting that in large parts of the position nothing had so far been done in the way of defence works. The misconception in the minds of commanders and men that there was a fortified Apennine position should therefore be eradicated once and for all. C-in-C South-West must conduct his operations to gain time until adequate development of the Apennine position was achieved – a task which would take months. In consequence Hitler had ordered that the armies should go over to the defensive in the *Albert* line. Elba must not be evacuated as this would endanger the coastal flank. At this point there was a gap in the message. It went on to say that possession of efficient harbours such as Leghorn and Ancona* would provide the Allies with springboards for landings to outflank the Apennine position and concluded by stating that on 17 June Hitler had again ordered that Elba was to be held at all costs.

□

The evidence available from Sigint about the state of the enemy's forces and the nature of his intentions encouraged the British authorities to persist in a renewed attempt, on which they had embarked after the fall of Rome, to persuade the Americans to abandon Operation *Anvil* (plans for landings in the south of France) in favour of an all-out campaign in Italy.

The latest directive Alexander had received from SACMED (General Wilson), on 22 May, had informed him that his operations would have over-riding priority until he captured Rome, but that SACMED had been ordered to mount an amphibious operation which might be in close support of Alexander's advance or in areas outside his responsibility, and had warned him that if that operation were to be Operation *Anvil*, he might be called on to release one US division by 17 June, one French division by 24 June and a second US division by 27 June; in addition, an experienced US Corps headquarters would be required.[57] On 8 June Alexander recommended to SACMED and

---

* German plans for sabotage and assault boat operations in these and other ports were to appear in decrypts in July, see Appendix 20.

56. DEFE 3/179, KV 9843 of 27 June.
57. CAB 106/609, Alexander's Despatch, *The Allied Armies in Italy*, p 24.

the CIGS that his armies should attack the Pisa–Rimini line in August and carry the offensive into the Po valley in order to form a base for operations into either France or Austria. He noted that this plan would be practicable only if the forces and the administrative backing at his disposal were left intact.[58] The US Chiefs of Staff being then in England, Alexander's proposal and other options were discussed by the Combined Chiefs of Staff at meetings on 11 and 13 June. Partly because they thought that the Germans might choose to economise forces by making a voluntary withdrawal to the Alps, so that an offensive in Italy would strike a vacuum, the US Chiefs were unwilling to give priority to an advance into the Po valley. Accordingly on 14 June the CCS told SACMED and Eisenhower that the over-riding necessity was to apply all Allied forces in the manner best calculated to assist *Overlord*; the destruction of the German forces south of the Pisa–Rimini line must be completed but the final choice among the courses of action then open to the Allies could not be made yet.[59]

During the next fortnight Alexander, Wilson, the British Chiefs of Staff and the Prime Minister argued strenuously, in favour of Alexander's proposal, that high-grade Sigint left little doubt that the Germans intended to stand on the Pisa–Rimini line and that the condition of Kesselring's armies was such that they would be unable to resist an all-out offensive unless given substantial reinforcements at the expense of other vital theatres. This argument accorded with the assessment of German intentions and capabilities with regard to the Pisa–Rimini defences that was made by the JIC(AFHQ) on 15 June and circulated in Whitehall on 20 June.[60] JIC(AFHQ) considered that Germany's withdrawal to the Pisa–Rimini line had become a military necessity and that the defeats the enemy had suffered had resulted in the destruction of the forces, perhaps five divisions, which could have been made available for operations in other theatres if he had made a voluntary withdrawal earlier. Nothing could now be withdrawn from Italy unless he decided to abandon virtually the whole country. There was no indication of such an intention, but every sign that he proposed to stand on the Pisa–Rimini line. This was a defensive position of considerable natural strength which had been partly fortified. Withdrawal beyond this line might compromise the defence of southern France, lead to an Allied advance to the Austrian frontier and open the gateway to Yugoslavia, whereas by holding it the enemy would deny the Allies airfields in the Po valley which would bring important targets in east

---

58. Ehrman, *Grand Strategy*, Vol V (1956), pp 266, 365; CAB 106/609, p 30.
59. Ehrman, op cit, Vol V, p 346.
60. JIC(44)267(o) of 20 June (JIC(AF)24/44 of 15 June).

Germany, Poland and Czechoslovakia within bomber range. By the time the enemy reached the Pisa–Rimini line he would probably be some four to six divisions short of the forces needed to man it. He might scrape together five infantry divisions from other theatres and, assuming that the battle in France had not taken a critical turn meanwhile and the Russians had not broken into the Balkans, he might well move these into Italy by mid-July when the Allies should reach the Pisa–Rimini line.

In a final memorandum on the subject to the US Chiefs of Staff, dated 28 June, the British Chiefs argued that the decrypt of 27 June giving the gist of Hitler's directive completely vindicated their conclusion that it would be a grave strategic error not to take advantage of the opportunity of destroying the German forces presently in Italy and drawing further reserves to this front. A brief which accompanied their memorandum listed points which the British Joint Staff Mission in Washington should make if asked why the Chiefs of Staff had become so decidedly pro-Italy and anti-*Anvil*. These included: '(c) Hitler's and Kesselring's policy to fight south of Apennines (d) most importantly of all "Boniface" [ie the decrypt of 27 June] having turned a matter of opinion into a matter of fact.'[61]

The US Chiefs of Staff, however, had already put in train the withdrawals of which Alexander had been advised in May. VI US Corps was withdrawn on 14 June, 3rd and 36th US Divisions on 17 and 27 June, a French division on 17 June and another on 1 July.[62] They believed that the forces left to Alexander would be adequate for successful action against all enemy forces then in Italy or likely to be brought there. And they had been advised by Eisenhower that the Allied forces in Italy did not directly threaten any area vital to the Germans, who therefore had the initiative in deciding whether or not to withdraw out of Italy, and that he and his Commanders were convinced of the transcendent importance of *Anvil*, which provided the most direct route to northern France and another major port for deploying reinforcements from the United States. Despite a final appeal from the Prime Minister to the President, they therefore stood firm for *Anvil*. On 2 July SACMED was instructed to launch *Anvil* at the earliest possible date and to use all available Mediterranean resources not required for *Anvil* to carry out his existing directive regarding operations in Italy. On 5 July a new directive from SACMED informed Alexander that priority for all resources in the Mediterranean theatre was given to *Anvil* to the extent necessary to complete a build-up of ten divisions in the south of France. He would lose

---

61. Ehrman, op cit, Vol V, p 353; CAB 121/396, COS(W)134 of 28 June.
62. CAB 106/609, p 25.

three US divisions and four French divisions together with their necessary Corps, Army and Service troops. His task continued to be the destruction of the German forces in Italy. To this end he was to advance to the Apennines and secure the area Ravenna–Bologna–Modena. Thereafter he was to advance north of the Po and secure the line Venice–Padua–Verona–Brescia.[63]

□

The battle known to the British as the battle of the Trasimene line had meanwhile occupied the last ten days of June. By 26 June Fourteenth Army's front was dangerously eroded and on 28 June Lemelsen reported that the physical and moral stamina of his troops was noticeably reduced and only a concerted disengagement could save his army from possible disintegration. Von Vietinghoff's defensive battle had been more successful, but Fourteenth Army's retreat was endangering his own forces.[64]

When the battle began the German front ran from Civitanova on the Adriatic coast–River Chienti–exclusive Assisi–Lake Trasimeno–Lake Chiusi–Montalcino–north of Grosseto–coast west of Follonica. Tenth Army, in command from the Adriatic to Montepulciano, had LI Mountain Corps (with 278th and 71st Infantry, 5th Mountain and 114th Jäger Divisions) holding the coastal sector and eastern Apennines, and LXXVI Panzer Corps (with 44th and 305th Infantry, 15th PG, 334th Infantry, 1st Parachute and the Hermann Göring Divisions) from east of Lake Trasimeno to the junction with I Parachute Corps which commanded 356th Infantry, 4th Parachute, 26th Panzer and 29th PG Divisions on Fourteenth Army's left wing. XIV Panzer Corps (with 90th PG, 20th GAF, 3rd PG and 162nd Infantry Divisions) was on I Parachute Corps's right and LXXV Corps with 19th GAF Field and 16th SS PG Divisions was guarding the west coast behind XIV Panzer Corps.

Eighth Army attacked on both sides of Lake Trasimeno and met stiff resistance from LXXVI Panzer Corps. West of the lake there was fierce fighting for Chiusi which changed hands several times before it was finally evacuated by the Germans on 26 June. East of the lake Eighth Army's X Corps made little progress against 15th PG Division and on 26 June the Germans were able to transfer this division to strengthen their forces on the western side. Hard fighting continued with the Germans giving ground slowly. At the end of the month LXXVI Panzer Corps was preparing reluctantly

---

63. ibid, pp 38–39; Ehrman, op cit, Vol V, pp 353–357, 358.
64. EDS/Appreciation/18, Chapter 1.

to withdraw from the lake to a position south of Arezzo in order to conform with the movements of Fourteenth Army. The latter had fared much less well. By the evening of 22 June XIV Panzer Corps's front had been penetrated north of Roccastrada, and 162nd Division was near the end of its tether. On 23 June there was another penetration on the boundary between 20th GAF Field and 3rd PG Divisions and the latter lost touch with its right-hand neighbour, 162nd Division. On 24 June Fifth US Army outflanked Follonica and pressed on towards Piombino which fell on 25 June. The same day I Parachute Corps's front was deeply penetrated by the French Expeditionary Corps south and west of Montalcino. On 26 June Kesselring agreed that Fourteenth Army must withdraw and that LXXVI Panzer Corps could prepare to fall back to the north end of Lake Trasimeno. During the last few days of the month Fourteenth Army's right wing was pushed back towards Cecina and its left towards Siena.[65]

While the battle was in progress the comparative stability of Tenth Army's front and the developing crisis on Fourteenth Army's were reflected by high-grade Sigint. During the fighting between Lake Trasimeno and Chiusi LXXVI Panzer Corps reported in a message on the afternoon of 24 June, signalled by GC and CS early next morning, that the Allies had penetrated its main defence zone with high losses on both sides;[66] another message from LXXVI Panzer Corps at 0700 on 25 June stated that penetrations in the sector held by 334th Infantry Division had compelled the commitment of the Hermann Göring Division's reserves.[67] This decrypt, signalled at 0551 on 26 June, followed closely on another which disclosed that 15th PG Division had started to move from east to west during the night.[68] A decrypt signalled late on 27 June showed that it was to take over 334th Infantry Division's sector west of the lake on 28 June, handing over its own sector to its left-hand neighbour, 305th Division.[69] Later decrypts mentioned that the hand-over to 305th Division had been completed at 1700 on 27 June and part of 334th Division's sector had been taken over by 1500 on 28 June.[70] LXXVI Panzer Corps's withdrawal to a new general line during the night 28–29 June was reported in a message signalled at 1000 on 29 June;[71] another on 30 June showed that the Corps was

65. ibid, Chapter 2; CAB 106/609, pp 32–36.
66. DEFE 3/177, KV 9483 of 25 June.
67. DEFE 3/178, KV 9621 of 26 June.
68. ibid, KV 9604 of 26 June.
69. DEFE 3/179, KV 9863 of 27 June.
70. ibid, KV 9904 of 28 June; DEFE 3/48, XL 51 of 29 June.
71. DEFE 3/48, XL 59 of 29 June.

withdrawing together with the rest of the German front but was not under pressure.[72]

Decrypts from Fourteenth Army's front were more numerous and revealed the strain it was under. In a message of 2030 on 23 June, signalled soon after mid-day on 24 June, XIV Panzer Corps doubted whether the exhausted troops of 162nd Infantry Division on its right flank could hold the main defence line unless reinforcements were quickly forthcoming.[73] At 1500 on 24 June 3rd PG Division reported that it was out of touch with its right and left-hand neighbours (162nd Infantry and 20th GAF Field Divisions). It was still out of contact on its right flank at 1930, when there was apparently a gap without a single German soldier.[74] The decrypt of this message was signalled by GC and CS at 0403 on 25 June and was quickly followed by another of a message from 90th PG Division on the afternoon of 24 June reporting that it was carrying out a laborious withdrawal and would then be out of petrol.[75] Also on 24 June XIV Panzer Corps appreciated that the Allies had recognised the weakness of 162nd Division, which would not be able to withstand a heavy attack. This message, too, was signalled on 25 June.[76] Decrypts on 26 June disclosed that 26th Panzer Division in I Parachute Corps's sector of the *Albert* line had handed over command to 4th Parachute Division,[77] and they also included an incomplete message of 23 June about plans for relieving 162nd Division with an unspecified formation and for moving the Infantry Lehr Regiment to the Leghorn area, where it would be subordinated tactically to 65th Infantry Division in Army Group Reserve and its refitting speeded up by all possible means.[78] Messages from GAF liaison officers (Flivos) of 26 June, signalled to the Commands by GC and CS late on 27 June, reported strong Allied attacks on 3rd PG Division in the Montieri sector, and that 162nd Division's right flank was threatened.[79] Another decrypt reported that in heavy defensive fighting on 25 June II/Regiment 956 under 3rd PG Division had lost some 200 out of 300 men and that the Division's Battle Group Grosser had lost 35 out of 124 men in a counter-attack.[80] Decrypts signalled on 28 June of messages of 27 June mentioned that 162nd Division had established contact with 19th GAF Field Division, which had

72. ibid, XL 156 of 30 June.
73. DEFE 3/177, KV 9393 of 24 June.
74. ibid, KV 9472 of 25 June.
75. ibid, KV 9475 of 25 June.
76. DEFE 3/178, KV 9577 of 25 June.
77. ibid, KV 9617 of 26 June.
78. ibid, KV 9651 of 26 June.
79. DEFE 3/179, KV 9862 of 27 June.
80. ibid, KV 9869 of 27 June.

come under command of XIV Panzer Corps but had lost contact with its left-hand neighbour,[81] while command of 90th PG Division on XIV Panzer Corps's left had been transferred to I Parachute Corps which was threatened by the penetration of XIV Panzer Corps's left wing.[82]

A decrypt signalled at 0559 on 29 June reported that 26th Panzer Division had taken over from 162nd Division at about mid-day on 28 June.[83] Orders for a withdrawal by XIV Panzer Corps during the night 28–29 June were signalled by GC and CS at 0801 on 29 June.[84] A decrypt in the afternoon revealed that the GOC of 19th Field Division had been replaced.[85] XIV Panzer Corps's intention to make a further withdrawal beginning at 2000 on 29 June, leaving strong rearguards, was known early on 30 June.[86] A decrypt signalled at mid-day on 30 June gave the order of battle of LXXV Corps from 1800 on 29 June as 16th SS PG, 19th GAF Field and 65th Infantry Divisions (the last named in tactical reserve).[87] A report by XIV Panzer Corps at 1400 on 30 June that the battle strength of 20th GAF Field and 3rd PG Divisions was 430 men was signalled by GC and CS at 1114 on 1 July.[88]

The continuing pressure on Fourteenth Army's right wing was reflected in a message at 1000 on 1 July (signalled very early on 2 July) reporting penetration by Allied infantry and tanks at Cecina, where isolated strongpoints in 16th SS PG Division's main defence line were still holding out and a counter-attack by the last small reserves and the few serviceable anti-tank guns and Tigers was in progress.[89] Another message of 2230 on 1 July (passed on by GC and CS at 0721 on 2 July) spoke of unceasing Allied attacks on 26th Panzer Division; the last reserves had been thrown in and in bitter, fluctuating fighting the Allies had made one small penetration.[90]

□

On 1 July Kesselring reported to OKW, for the attention of the Führer, that the defensive battle enjoined on his Army Group C in

81. ibid, KV 9904 of 28 June.
82. ibid, KV 9925 of 28 June.
83. DEFE 3/48, XL 38 of 29 June.
84. ibid, XL 47 of 29 June.
85. ibid, XL 93 of 29 June.
86. ibid, XL 172 of 30 June.
87. ibid, XL 199 of 30 June.
88. DEFE 3/49, XL 331 of 1 July.
89. ibid, XL 434 of 2 July.
90. ibid, XL 457 of 2 July.

June had led to heavy casualties in men and equipment. As further weakening could jeopardise retention of the *Green* line, he proposed to revert to delaying tactics while the armies withdrew to a new line – *Heinrich* – north of the Arno, where they would stand until the *Green* line was fully consolidated. He informed Lemelsen and von Vietinghoff of his action, and told them that the *Heinrich* line (Pisa–north bank of the Arno to Remole–Subbiano–Senigallia) would probably have to be held for some four to six weeks. No date was given for its occupation and numerous intermediate lines were indicated, the first of which – *Georg* – screened Volterra and Arezzo.[91]

On 3 July Kesselring was granted the audience with the Führer which he had requested in June. Hitler repeated the familiar injunction to fight tooth and nail for every inch of central Italy. Abandonment of territory on the Adriatic flank brought the Allies nearer to the vital Balkans; if the *Green* line were broken Army Group C would be unable to hold the Po valley and Istria and the south-eastern Reich would be in danger; time was a prerequisite on all fronts while German war production was being boosted and V-weapons prepared.[92]

The directive which followed this meeting, issued on 5 July, began by reiterating Hitler's earlier instructions. Army Group C must continue to defend central Italy as far south as possible while protecting the Ligurian and Adriatic coasts, and Istria, against outflanking landings. Time must be gained for the maximum consolidation of the *Green* line, 'the last bulwark in front of the plains of upper Italy', from which the Allies must be kept at a distance by stubborn resistance which would deny them Leghorn and Ancona. But it then made significant concessions to Kesselring by allowing that defence south of the *Green* line could be offered in 'suitable terrain' and that, when a breakthrough seemed inevitable, he could permit retreat from the threatened sector to the next line of resistance, leaving rearguards to contest the intervening areas. The directive announced that two Italian divisions forming in the Reich would be transferred to Italy during July; apart from these no fresh formations could be sent for the time being, but C-in-C South-West's divisions were to be kept up to strength and mobile by the allocation of Marsch battalions, heavy weapons and towing equipment.[93]

Kesselring was instructed to report his plans and on 8 July he informed OKW that he would hold his present front as long as possible. When the *Heinrich* line was reached it would be

91. EDS/Appreciation/18, Chapter 3, pp 14, 15.
92. ibid, pp 15, 16.
93. ibid, p 17.

defended. The Italian divisions would be assigned to coast defence in the Genoa area. The Rimini–Ravenna coastal strip would be defended by 715th Infantry Division, supported by 162nd and 94th Infantry Divisions which would be refitted there. Reinforcements were needed in Istria, which could only be defended on a makeshift basis. OKW raised no objection and on 11 July Kesselring issued a directive to his armies. It began by saying that they must continue to resist as far south as possible, but went on to tell Fourteenth Army that it could make a fighting withdrawal on its right wing, holding Leghorn as long as possible and keeping it under artillery fire after evacuation, while Tenth Army was to stand as far south of the *Green* line as it could manage and establish defensive strongpoints to prevent the capture or by-passing of Ancona, or a breakthrough up the Tiber valley to San Sepolcro.[94] To this extent (and thanks partly to the pressure of developments on other fronts) Kesselring had obtained the freedom of action which he had been denied in June. And during July, except for the removal of the Hermann Göring Division to the eastern front and orders from Hitler regarding the defence of Florence, he was to suffer little interference. His restoration to favour was marked by the award of diamonds for his Knight's Cross, to receive which he paid his next visit to Hitler's headquarters on 19 July. As neither he himself nor any of his senior commanders was implicated in the attempted coup next day, this was not followed by any command upheavals in Italy.[95]

When and how the Allies intended to employ their uncommitted resources in the Mediterranean Kesselring was unable to decide. On 10 July he instructed his armies to make plans to counter landings in either the Genoa or Rimini–Ravenna areas, but did not then envisage landings on a 'strategic' scale. By the end of the month his assessment of Allied preparations and resources had led him to conclude that he must be prepared for a major assault on the *Green* line accompanied by landing operations on the Ligurian coast. The latter might be 'decision-seeking' (if the Allies decided to make Italy the primary target) or diversionary (if France was chosen). Moreover, a landing on a smaller scale on the Rimini–Ravenna strip could not be excluded in as much as a frontal assault on the *Green* line was a formidable undertaking and the Allies might decide to attempt to outflank it on the Adriatic wing. Holding these views he was trying to build up mobile forces around 90th PG Division, which was assembling in the Modena area, to deal with any invasion; had moved 1st Parachute Division to the Adriatic flank and brought 98th Infantry Division from

94. ibid, p 17; Chapter 4, p 13.
95. ibid, Chapter 3, pp 1, 17.

Istria to help in the defence of the Rimini–Ravenna sector; and had decided that the headquarters of LXXVI Panzer Corps and LI Mountain Corps should change places early in August.[96]

With the battle drawing closer to the *Green* line Kesselring made Tenth and Fourteenth Armies responsible from 5 July for the consolidation of the sectors they would occupy with the southern bank of the Po as their rear tactical boundary. Armee Abteilung von Zangen in consequence reverted to its original status as LXXXVII Corps, only to be rechristened Armee Abteilung Ligurien towards the end of the month as the forerunner of a new Army of Liguria under the command of Marshal Graziani.[97]

For their part, the Allies learned less from Sigint about these high level exchanges and decisions than they had done about those that had taken place during June. Kesselring's report of 1 July, OKW's directive to him of 5 July and his own directive of 11 July to his armies were not decrypted. But a decrypt signalled by GC and CS on 11 July referred to his audience with Hitler on 3 July and repeated the Führer's exhortation to defend every square kilometre tenaciously so as to gain time while production was boosted and the new weapons were brought into service.[98]* And other decrypts recorded not only the removal of the Hermann Göring Division to the eastern front in the middle of the month† but also the arrival of reinforcements in Italy.

The intention to send 34th Infantry Division from Russia and most of the Ostpreussen Division from Germany had been disclosed in June.‡ On 3 July a decrypt confirmed that 34th Division and thirteen trains bringing the Ostpreussen had arrived by 29 July.[100] The reversion of Armee Abteilung von Zangen to Corps status was revealed as early as 7 July and also the location of its battle headquarters at Novi Ligure.[101] A decrypt of 16 July, evidently from this headquarters, described at length the intended composition and layout of the Army of Liguria under Marshal

---

* It emerged from other decrypts that this exhortation had been issued to all commanders in all theatres. A message sent out by the German naval authorities on 10 July in Offizier signals stressed the 'certain expectation' of fresh successes by new types of U-boats, the effects of which would be felt in a foreseeable period. The demand was therefore; 'Fight, defend, hold out'.[99] For the intelligence on the new U-boats see Chapter 53.

† See below, p 329.

‡ See above, p 309.

96. ibid, Chapter 3, pp 6–8, 38.
97. ibid, pp 17, 21.
98. DEFE 3/54, XL 1589 of 11 July.
99. Dir/C Archive, 7045 and 7053 of 10 and 11 July; DEFE 3/440, ZTPG 262228.
100. DEFE 3/50, XL 565 of 3 July.
101. DEFE 3/52, XL 1145 of 7 July.

Graziani: Corps Abteilung Lieb, responsible from the French frontier to Arezzano, would include 34th Infantry Division and the Italian San Marco Division; 42nd Jäger Division would cover the Genoa sector; and the Alpini Monte Rosa Division and Fortress Brigade 135 the sector from Portofino to Levanto. The Army's battle headquarters would remain for the time being at Novi Ligure, where Graziani intended to go on his return from Germany.[102] This intelligence was supplemented by a signal from the Japanese Naval Attaché in Berlin, decrypted on 21 July, which reported that four Italian divisions were being trained in Germany and would be on the Italian front by the autumn.[103] On 26 July, however, AFHQ's intelligence summary mentioned that the Italian San Marco Division had arrived from Germany and that another Italian division was expected, while on 2 August AAI's intelligence summary reported that the Monte Rosa Division was arriving in Liguria and AFHQ commented that the Littorio and Italia Divisions might also come.[104]* A message available on 5 August from Corps Witthöft (on the Adriatic coast) reported that 98th Infantry Division (which had been refitting in Croatia) had relieved 94th Infantry Division.[105]

□

At the beginning of July Fourteenth Army's right flank was under heavy pressure. Cecina and Saline, fiercely defended by 16th SS PG and 26th Panzer Divisions, were captured on 3 July. The French entered Siena on the same day. Volterra fell on 8 July, Rosignano on 9 July, and Poggibonsi (to the French) on 14 July. Leghorn was captured on 19 July. LXXV Corps and most of XIV Panzer Corps (less 90th PG Division which was taken into Army Group Reserve) withdrew to the north bank of the Arno. I Parachute Corps remained south of the river covering Florence.[106]

On Tenth Army's front LXXVI Panzer Corps withdrew into the *Georg* line covering Arezzo. Probing by XIII Corps of Eighth Army met strong resistance and on 9 July Alexander decided to

---

* The information about the arrival of the Italian divisions cannot be traced in the Enigma or Japanese diplomatic decrypts; it could have come from Army Y or through the SIS and SOE.

102. DEFE 3/56, XL 2241 of 16 July.
103. BAY/XL 55 of 23 July.
104. WO 204/969, Nos 100 of 26 July, 101 of 2 August; WO 170/68, No 56 of 2 August.
105. DEFE 3/112, XL 4750 of 5 August.
106. EDS/Appreciation/18, Chapter 4; CAB 106/609, p 39 et seq.

bring forward 2nd New Zealand Division for a full scale assault. Meanwhile an offensive by the Polish Corps on the Adriatic wing had captured Osimo on 6 July and Filottrano on 9 July, but no breakthrough was achieved and the Germans were in fact more concerned about the progress made by X Corps up the Tiber valley towards Citta di Castello. The loss of Monte Favalto at the junction between LI Mountain Corps and LXXVI Panzer Corps during the night 11–12 July compelled the latter to take its left wing back to Monte Lignano. On 15 July XIII Corps captured Monte Lignano, the corner-stone for the defence of Arezzo, from 15th PG Division; LXXVI Panzer Corps withdrew north of Arezzo in order to avoid a general encounter in country favouring the preponderant Allied armour and to facilitate the relief of the Hermann Göring Division by 715th Infantry Division. On 17 July the Allies renewed their offensive towards Ancona and broke through the defences of 278th Infantry Division in several places. The port was captured on 18 July. On 19 July the Poles crossed the Esino river and Kesselring ordered the move of 1st Parachute Division from LXXVI Panzer Corps to support his left wing.[107]

For the rest of the month attention was focused on the battle for Florence. During Kesselring's visit to Hitler's headquarters on 19 July the Führer gave orders that I Parachute Corps (29th PG, 4th Parachute and 356th Infantry Divisions) was to hold a defence line (*Paula*) ten to twelve kilometres south of Florence for as long as possible. Heavy fighting forward of the *Paula* line between 4th Parachute Division and the New Zealanders developed on 23 July. By 27 July the Germans had retreated into the *Paula* line. After several days of stubborn resistance they withdrew across the river on the night of 3–4 August and the Allies entered Florence the following day.[108]

Throughout their advance from the beginning of July to the capture of Florence the Allies continued to obtain good tactical intelligence. Army Y followed the activities of practically every German formation, mainly through the interception of their VHF links.[109] Fortunately some of Y's contributions during this period are identifiable from contemporary intelligence summaries, which illustrate the character of the assistance provided. Thus AAI's intelligence summary of 6 July[110] noted that on 29 June 26th Panzer Division was on the river Cecina covering the approaches to Volterra with Grenadier Regiments 1027 and 314 and PG Regiment 9 holding defined sectors. It was supported by some of

---

107. EDS/Appreciation/18, Chapter 4; CAB 106/609, pp 41–42.
108. EDS/Appreciation/18, Chapter 4; CAB 106/609, p 44 et seq.
109. *History of Sigint in the Field*, pp 129, 130.
110. WO 170/67, No 52 of 6 July.

the artillery of 162nd Division (which it had earlier relieved) and by 764th Battery. 26th Reconnaissance Battalion was in divisional reserve with two Pzkw IVs and two Pzkw VIs under command. The fighting strength of 26th Panzer Division's Tank Regiment was less than 100 all ranks. On 1 July the GOC of 2nd Company of Parachute Regiment 4 was complaining about a 5-kilometre gap between his company and the Hermann Göring Division on his right. Respective strengths of II and III Battalions of Grenadier Regiment 134, which had made a successful counter-attack in 44th Division's sector, had been 150 and 120 men. AAI's next intelligence summary on 12 July remarked that LXXVI Panzer Corps showed no signs of giving up the dominating ground on which it stood; on 5 July 1st Parachute Division was preparing to stay several days and on 6 July it asked for more entrenching tools to be sent forward.[111] The intelligence summary of 19 July referred to the greatly increased arrival of drafts.[112] At the end of the month Army Y was able to keep track of the locations of the formations engaged in the battle for Florence.[113] The relief of the Hermann Göring Division by 715th Infantry Division in LXXVI Panzer Corps's sector, and the removal of 1st Parachute Division from LXXVI Panzer Corps to support the Adriatic flank, were also detected by Y but seem to have been disclosed earlier by the Enigma.

The Enigma also gave a full account of the fortunes of LXXV Corps and XIV Panzer Corps on Fourteenth Army's right wing, the decrypts disclosing changes of position,[114] the withdrawal of 19th GAF Field Division from the front line,[115] the failure to carry out a counter-attack on the left wing of Battle Group Crisolli (formed from elements of 20th GAF Field and 3rd PG Divisions) because of extraordinarily high German casualties,[116] the transfer of 20th GAF Field Division from XIV Panzer Corps to LXXV Corps on 11 July,[117] the return of 3rd PG and 65th Infantry Divisions to the front line,[118] and the withdrawal of 90th PG

---

111. ibid, No 53 of 12 July.
112. ibid, No 54 of 19 July.
113. *History of Sigint in the Field*, p 130; WO 170/68, No 56 of 2 August.
114. DEFE 3/50, XLs 535 and 556 of 3 July, 659 of 4 July; DEFE 3/51, XL 950 of 6 July; DEFE 3/52, XLs 1110 of 7 July, 1197 and 1198 of 8 July; DEFE 3/54, XL 1564 of 11 July; DEFE 3/55, XLs 1797, 1804 and 1833 of 13 July; DEFE 3/56, XL 2017 of 14 July; DEFE 3/57, XL 2490 of 17 July; DEFE 3/58, XL 2533 of 18 July; DEFE 3/59, XL 2907 of 21 July; DEFE 3/60, XL 3036 of 22 July.
115. DEFE 3/51, XL 940 of 6 July; DEFE 3/52, XL 1046 of 7 July.
116. DEFE 3/50, XL 729 of 4 July; DEFE 3/52, XL 1178 of 8 July.
117. DEFE 3/55, XL 1884 of 13 July.
118. DEFE 3/55, XL 1884 of 13 July; DEFE 3/58, XLs 2526 of 18 July, 2669 of 19 July; DEFE 3/59, XL 2887 of 21 July.

Division on 20 July.[119] On Tenth Army's front decrypts signalled on 5 July disclosed the withdrawal of LXXVI Panzer Corps to the *Georg* line,[120] and on the Adriatic flank decrypts between 2 and 9 July reflected what the Germans considered to be a satisfactory performance by 278th Infantry Division against the Poles.[121] The failure with high casualties on 10 July of a counter-attack in the Tiber valley by 44th Infantry Division was reported in a decrypt the following day.[122] A decrypt signalled at 0357 on 13 July disclosed that 715th Infantry Division was moving south from the Cesena area to join LXXVI Corps.[123] Information that the Hermann Göring Division was to be withdrawn from C-in-C South-West's theatre in the near future came 24 hours later,[124] and a decrypt of 15 July indicated East Prussia as its destination.[125] The next day brought the decrypt of an order that it was to hand over command to 715th Infantry Division at 0600 on 17 July;[126] confirmation that the hand-over had been completed was signalled by GC and CS at 1631 on 17 July.[127]*

When the battle for Ancona was renewed on 17 July 278th Infantry Division was thrown back in disorder, leaving substantial elements virtually cut off. A message from LI Mountain Corps at 1100 on 18 July, available 24 hours later, reported that withdrawal movements were much hampered by air attacks and that it was not yet possible to see whether the German forces would succeed in breaking through from the area south of Ancona.[130] In the event

---

* Later decrypts reported the progress of the move.[128] C-in-C South-West had warned on 13 July that it might be delayed by the destruction of the Po bridges. The Allied air forces carried out a sustained attack on the bridges from 12 July; its results, which were not overwhelming, were reported in several decrypts.[129]

119. DEFE 3/59, XL 2887 of 21 July.
120. DEFE 3/51, XLs 766, 778, 789 and 795 of 5 July.
121. DEFE 3/49, XLs 305 of 1 July, 476 of 2 July; DEFE 3/50, XLs 553 of 3 July, 698 of 4 July; DEFE 3/52, XL 1046 and 1067 of 7 July; DEFE 3/53, XL 1331 of 9 July.
122. DEFE 3/54, XL 1582 of 11 July.
123. DEFE 3/55, XL 1796 of 13 July.
124. DEFE 3/55, XL 1963 of 14 July.
125. DEFE 3/56, XL 2167 of 15 July.
126. DEFE 3/57, XL 2286 of 16 July.
127. ibid, XL 2456 of 17 July.
128. DEFE 3/59, XLs 2765 of 20 July, 2912 of 21 July; DEFE 3/60, XLs 3052, 3090 and 3110 of 22 July.
129. DEFE 3/55, XL 1943 of 14 July; DEFE 3/56, XLs 2020 of 14 July, 2187 of 15 July; DEFE 3/57, XLs 2281 of 16 July, 2429 of 17 July; DEFE 3/59, XLs 2783 and 2808 of 20 July; DEFE 3/60, XLs 3052 and 3105 of 22 July; DEFE 3/61, XL 3285 of 24 July; DEFE 3/62, XL 3690 of 27 July; DEFE 3/63, XL 3906 of 29 July; DEFE 3/112, XL 4580 of 3 August.
130. DEFE 3/58, XL 2669 of 19 July.

they did succeed, as was recorded in messages available on 20 July.[131] But 278th Infantry Division had been severely battered. In a message at 2200 on 19 July, signalled by GC and CS the next day, LI Mountain Corps said that the Division had suffered 1,000 casualties, mostly dead, in the last three days and had lost many heavy weapons during its retreat because the horses had been shot up by aircraft.[132] Timely notice was given by high-grade Sigint of 1st Parachute Division's move to the Adriatic flank. A message of 1845 on 19 July reporting that the Division was to be taken out of its present sector next evening was signalled by GC and CS at 0937 on 20 July,[133] followed two hours later by another message which reported that according to its Flivo the Division would probably operate on the Adriatic.[134] A decrypt sent out at 0859 on 21 July stated that the Division's left-hand regiment would be relieved during the night by its neighbour, 334th Infantry Division, and sent to Cattolica (south-east of Rimini).[135] A decrypt confirming the completion of this relief was signalled at 0805 on 22 July,[136] but on 25 July a decrypt showed that on 24 July the remainder of the Division was still in its old sector.[137] A decrypt signalled at 2103 on 27 July reported that, except for one battalion which was to stay another 24 hours, it was to pull out the previous evening and transfer to Cattolica as Army Reserve.[138]

Messages signalled on 24 July reflected the severe fighting forward of the *Paula* line the previous day. The Flivo with 4th Parachute Division reported that II/11 and II/12 Battalions had suffered considerable losses.[139] At 1630 I Parachute Corps was expecting that strong Allied attacks would continue next day to force a breakthrough towards Florence. It reported that 4th Parachute Division and the right wing of 356th Infantry Division had been attacked by the New Zealand Division, which had made insignificant territorial gains and incurred very heavy losses.[140] German losses had also been high. A situation report by Luftflotte 2 late on 27 July, signalled early on 29 July, reported the withdrawal of the main defence line south of Florence.[141] Decrypts referring to I Parachute Corps's withdrawal into the

---

131.   DEFE 3/59, XLs 2785 and 2836 of 20 July.
132.   ibid, XL 2864 of 20 July.
133.   ibid, XL 2787 of 20 July.
134.   ibid, XL 2795 of 20 July.
135.   ibid, XL 2908 of 21 July.
136.   DEFE 3/60, XL 3042 of 22 July.
137.   DEFE 3/61, XL 3391 of 25 July.
138.   DEFE 3/62, XL 3738 of 27 July.
139.   DEFE 3/61, XL 3272 of 24 July.
140.   ibid, XL 3282 of 24 July.
141.   DEFE 3/63, XL 3887 of 29 July.

Paula line on 27 July, and giving its location, were available on 31 July,[142] but the best information about the enemy forces during the fighting on this position seems to have been provided by Army Y, which detected the extension eastwards on 27 July of XIV Panzer Corps's front to enable 29th PG Division to concentrate against the assault by the New Zealand Division on the right wing of the *Paula* line.[143]

□

High-grade Sigint supplied several reports during July on the battle-worthiness of the enemy's formations.

A decrypt on 30 June gave the requirements in personnel and weapons for the re-equipment of 94th and 305th Infantry Divisions;[144] another on 28 July reported that 305th Division was still 750 men under strength on 18 July.[145] In a message of 1 July, decrypted on 4 July, I Parachute Corps announced that in view of the weakness of the divisions under its command (90th PG, 29th PG, 4th Parachute and 356th Infantry) these would be designated battle groups named after their commanders.[146] The same decrypt contained the information that 20th GAF Field and 3rd PG Divisions (reduced according to an earlier message to a battle strength of 430 men)[147] had been combined under the commanding officer of the former as Battle Group Crisolli. However, AAI's intelligence summary of 19 July referred to the greatly increased arrival of drafts for Kesselring's more battered formations – presumably detected by Y.[148] As already mentioned,* a decrypt signalled on 20 July disclosed the heavy casualties suffered by 278th Infantry Division in the battle for Ancona. Another signalled on 26 July, put the casualties sustained by 1st Parachute Division between 1 April and 20 July as some 95 officers and 3,996 other ranks killed, wounded, missing or sick.[149] Another, signalled on the next day, contained the information that 3,260 replacement personnel for this division were being sent forward in batches.[150] A decrypt available on 29 July contained OKH's agreement that

---

* Above, p 330.

142. DEFE 3/64, XLs 4130, 4147, 4155 and 4208 of 31 July.
143. WO 170/68, No 56 of 2 August.
144. DEFE 3/48, XL 234 of 30 June.
145. DEFE 3/63, XL 3769 of 28 July.
146. DEFE 3/50, XL 729 of 4 July.
147. DEFE 3/49, XL 331 of 1 July.
148. WO 170/67, No 54 of 19 July.
149. DEFE 3/60, XL 3609 of 26 July.
150. ibid, XL 3697 of 27 July.

the Grenadier Lehr Brigade should be reduced to two battalions.[151] According to a decrypt signalled on 31 July 42nd Jäger Division was short of 63 officers and 362 NCOs on 20 July; its state of training was variable and it was conditionally ready for defence (Category IV).[152]

On 12 July GC and CS signalled to the Commands the decrypt of a long message of 30 June from Kesselring to Jodl. To off-set the huge Allied material superiority, particularly in tanks and artillery, the German forces needed a very high degree of mobility, but mobility was absolutely inadequate. Time and again heavy anti-tank guns had had to be blown up because of lack of traction which had also prevented the timely formation of adequate anti-tank defences at certain points. To make his artillery, anti-tank guns and Flak adequately mobile Kesselring needed approximately (an extra) 700 assorted tractors. An increased supply would be of decisive importance and was essential. Before the battle (ie Operation *Diadem*, the battle for Rome) began supplies of tanks and assault guns were satisfactory and replacements during the battle were adequate. The usual number were knocked out in action but extraordinarily high losses were caused by inability to tow them away and by lack of spare parts. These deficiencies affected both the fighting power of the units and the morale of the crews. Increased allocation of spares and tractors was actually more urgent than new tanks and would enable more tanks to be kept in action than could be supplied by the home base.[153]*

An incomplete return of Kesselring's armoured fighting vehicles on 11 July, issued on 13 July and decrypted on 25 July, showed 145 tanks serviceable out of 262.[154] On 28 July GC and CS signalled the decrypt of an order of 18 July to the Hermann Göring Division on the disposal of its AFVs. Seventeen Pzkw IVs and nine light assault guns were allocated to 15th PG Division; seventeen Pzkw IVs to 26th Panzer Division; six Pzkw IIIs to Armee Panzer Abteilung 208; and two heavy self-propelled anti-tank guns to 1st Parachute Division.[155] Another decrypt signalled the same day recorded the receipt on 18 July from a new allocation of 23 Pzkw IVs for 29th PG Division and 11 Pzkw IVs for 26th Panzer Division.[156] For whatever reason – alteration in

---

* See above, p 323, for the response made in Hitler's directive of 5 July to this request for towing equipment.

151. DEFE 3/63, XL 3918 of 29 July.
152. DEFE 3/64, XL 4142 of 31 July.
153. DEFE 3/54, XL 1688 of 12 July.
154. DEFE 3/61, XL 3384 of 25 July.
155. DEFE 3/63, XL 3778 of 28 July.
156. ibid, XL 3841 of 28 July.

allocations or battle losses – it proved impossible to reconcile these figures with those in the C-in-C's AFV return for 30 July, decrypted on 8 and 12 August, which showed 136 tanks serviceable out of a total of 163. Of the serviceable tanks, 100 were with Tenth and Fourteenth Armies and 36 with the Army of Liguria. Between them Tenth and Fourteenth Armies also had serviceable 83 assault guns, 96 Italian assault guns, and 320 heavy anti-tank guns.[157]

□

The objective of the Allies after the capture of Florence was to drive the Germans out of the *Gothic* line, the system of strong-points connected by a continuous line of positions running through the northern Apennines from the Magra river on the west coast to Pescara on the Adriatic,* and exploit to the general line of the Po. The final plans for this next stage of their offensive were drawn up in the first week of August. Eighth Army was to transfer to the Adriatic wing and roll up the enemy's left. When he had weakened his centre to meet Eighth Army's attack, Fifth US Army, strengthened by XIII British Corps, was to advance along the axis Florence–Bologna.[160]

In the lull before the start of the offensive (Operation *Olive*) on 25 August high-grade Sigint furnished comprehensive intelligence on changes in the German order of battle. On 9 and 10 August decrypts disclosed that Kesselring had strengthened his left wing by switching LXXVI Panzer Corps to LI Mountain Corps's sector on the Adriatic.[161] On 10, 11 and 12 August it emerged that XIV Panzer Corps was assuming command of LXXV Corps's sector and of 16th SS PG and 20th GAF Field Divisions on Fourteenth Army's right wing, and that LXXV Corps HQ and Corps troops were joining the Army of Liguria in the area

---

* We have seen above (p 312) that Hitler had changed the name of the *Gothic* line to the *Green* line. The Allies knew of the change from Sigint, but continued to call it the *Gothic* line, the name given to it in documents they captured in June.[158] They kept the development of the line under close PR surveillance, the value of which was proved when they broke through the line on the Adriatic. An investigation then carried out by the Army Air Photographic Interpretation Unit (AAPIU) showed that 95 per cent of the installations had been detected and 75 per cent correctly identified; the omissions and mistakes were largely due to the fact that the Germans had constructed and camouflaged new works in between PR sorties.[159]

157. DEFE 3/114, XL 5185 of 8 August; DEFE 3/117, XL 5797 of 12 August.
158. WO 204/969, No 95 of 19 June; WO 170/66, No 49 of 15 June.
159. WO 204/8233, Technical Summary by HQ II Polish Corps of 5 December 1944.
160. CAB 106/610, Alexander's Despatch, *The Allied Armies in Italy*, pp 2, 4–8.
161. DEFE 3/115, XLs 5435 of 9 August, 5482 of 10 August; DEFE 3/116, XL 5593 of 10 August.

north of Genoa.[162] A decrypt signalled on 17 August reported that
LXXV Corps had taken over command of 42nd Jäger and the
Monte Rosa Divisions.[163] Several others disclosed the German
response to the Allied landings in the south of France (Operation
Anvil, re-named *Dragoon*) which had taken place on the night of
14–15 August. On 16 August it was known that Corps Abteilung
Lieb (commanding 34th Infantry and the San Marco Divisions)
had been ordered to send strong elements to the French frontier
to protect the flank of the Army of Liguria.[164] Orders issued by
Hitler on 17 August were signalled on 18 August.[165] They
specified that to prevent Nineteenth Army from being cut off,
Army Group G was to disengage in the south of France and make
contact with the southern wing of Army Group B. Nineteenth
Army's LXII Corps with 148th (Reserve) and 157th (Reserve)
Divisions was to withdraw into the Franco–Italian Alpine position
when pressed. 148th Division was to keep contact with C-in-C
South-West's forces defending the coast; 157th Division was to
protect the eastern flank of Nineteenth Army's rearguards. LXII
Corps and both divisions were subordinated with immediate effect
to C-in-C South-West who was made responsible for the defence
of the Franco–Italian Alpine position from the Swiss frontier to
the Ligurian Sea. Over the next fortnight (during which the
Alpine front occupied a good deal of Kesselring's attention)[166]
numerous decrypts reflected the implementation of these orders
in considerable detail.[167]

Further decrypts had meanwhile revealed the repercussions of
Operation *Dragoon* on the main Italian front. By 22 August it was
known that 15th PG and 3rd PG Divisions were being transferred
to France, their sectors in the line being taken over by 65th and
305th Infantry Divisions,[168] and that 90th PG Division, which had
been taken out of the line in July, had been committed to the
Franco–Italian frontier.[169] On 23 August it emerged that 5th
Mountain Division was also being withdrawn, its sector being taken

162.   DEFE 3/115, XL 5475 of 10 August; DEFE 3/116, XL 5705 of 11 August;
       DEFE 3/117, XL 5752 of 12 August.
163.   DEFE 3/121, XL 6797 of 17 August.
164.   DEFE 3/120, XL 6601 of 16 August.
165.   DEFE 3/121, XL 6919 of 18 August.
166.   EDS/Appreciation/18, Chapter 5, pp 21–22.
167.   DEFE 3/122, XLs 7198, 7201, 7246 of 22 August; DEFE 3/123, XL 7453 of
       22 August; DEFE 3/124, XL 7513 of 22 August; DEFE 3/125, XLs 7821,
       7827 and 7828 of 25 August; DEFE 3/127, XLs 8447 and 8456 of 29
       August; DEFE 3/128, XLs 8510 of 30 August, 8721 and 8738 of 31 August.
168.   DEFE 3/118, XLs 6260 and 6307 of 15 August; DEFE 3/121, XL 6836 of 18
       August; DEFE 3/122, XL 7236 of 20 August; DEFE 3/123, XLs 7479 and
       7493 of 22 August; DEFE 3/124, XL 7506 of 22 August.
169.   DEFE 3/122, XL 7198 of 20 August; DEFE 3/124, XL 7513 of 22 August.

over by 278th Infantry Division;[170] and it was correctly appreciated that 5th Mountain was relieving 90th PG and that 278th's sector was being taken over by 1st Parachute Division.

On the eve of Operation *Olive* the Allies knew that, before account was taken of the last of these items of intelligence, Army Group C's divisions – 26 German and 2 Italian – were disposed as follows:[171]

Tenth Army
LXXVI Panzer Corps (Adriatic to San Sepolcro):
    278th Infantry, 71st Infantry and 5th Mountain in the line. 1st Parachute, 162nd (Turcoman) in Corps Reserve.
LI Mountain Corps (San Sepolcro to Pontassieve):
    114th Jäger, 44th, 305th, 334th and 715th Infantry.
Army Reserve:
    98th Infantry near Bologna.

Fourteenth Army
I Parachute Corps (Pontassieve to Empoli):
    356th Infantry, 4th Parachute, 29th PG.
XIV Panzer Corps (Empoli to West Coast):
    362nd Infantry, 26th Panzer, 65th Infantry, 16th SS PG.
Army Reserve:
    20th GAF Field near Viareggio.

Army of Liguria
Corps Abteilung Lieb:
    42nd Jäger, 34th Infantry and the Italian San Marco and Monte Rosa Divisions.
LXXV Corps (on the French frontier):
    90th, 148th (Reserve), 157th (Reserve).

Also under Army Group
    94th Infantry recuperating in the Udine area. 237th Infantry newly arrived on the Adriatic coast.*

□

Eighth Army, attacking with II Polish Corps, I Canadian Corps and V British Corps, advanced rapidly from the Metauro river

---

* The arrival of elements of this division on the Adriatic coast had been reported in a decrypt of 20 August.[172]

170. DEFE 3/124, XL 7585 of 23 August.
171. CAB 106/610, pp 10–11, Map 2 and Appendix A; WO 204/970, No 104 of
      30 August.
172. DEFE 3/123, XL 7281 of 20 August.

against an enemy who was already carrying out a voluntary withdrawal. On 31 August Eighth Army crossed the Foglia and reached the *Gothic* line. Kesselring was slow to appreciate the scale of the Allied offensive; although 26th Panzer subordinated to Tenth Army on 27 August it could not be committed without Army Group approval. On 28 August, however, the Germans having captured an order of the day issued by General Leese, Kesselring learned that Eighth Army had been brought across Italy for an 'all out push' to the plains of the Po, and the first reinforcements from 26th Panzer and 98th Infantry Divisions were now fully committed; the movement of Mountain Regiment 100 to join 5th Mountain Division in the north-west was reversed; and Fourteenth Army was instructed to hasten the transfer of 29th PG to Tenth Army in exchange for 334th Infantry Division, and to release 20th GAF Field Division which would be replaced by 42nd Jäger Division.* Eighth Army's advance continued, the Canadians crossing the Conca river on 2 September, and on 3 September 1st Parachute Division evacuated Cattolica. The first elements of 29th PG began to arrive the next day and on 5 September Eighth Army's advance was brought to a temporary halt on the Coriano ridge by 1st Parachute Division (with elements of 162nd Turcoman), 26th Panzer, 29th PG, 98th and 71st Infantry Divisions and Mountain Regiment 100. On 6 September Kesselring decided that 356th Infantry Division should move to Tenth Army from I Parachute Corps, that Mountain Regiment 100 should rejoin 5th Mountain Division, and that 90th PG should become Army Group Reserve on the Po.[173]

Although the Germans brought a new field cypher into force on almost all links down to company and troop level on 1 September, as part of a general drive to improve their communications security,[174] Army Y again performed well during the *Gothic* line battles. A steady flow of plain language on VHF during active operations from nearly every enemy formation engaged provided most of the intelligence, only 29th PG and 114th Jäger Divisions maintaining a consistently high standard of communications security.[175] Army Y was thus able to provide a detailed day to day account of operations and keep track of the numerous changes in the enemy's order of battle. The arrival in the line of 26th Panzer

---

* 20th GAF Field Division was originally destined for Trieste, OKW having told Kesselring that provision against an attack on Istria should take precedence over all other tasks, but had to be diverted to LXXVI Panzer Corps.

173. EDS/Appreciation/18, Chapter 5; EDS/Appreciation/19, Field Study No 1; CAB 106/610, pp 13–15.
174. *History of Sigint in the Field*, p 138.
175. ibid, p 138.

Division was disclosed on 30 August by one of its regimental links, and on 4 September Army Y established the presence on Eighth Army's front of elements of 29th PG Division.[176]

High-grade Sigint had already disclosed on 27 August that 26th Panzer was moving to a new area.[177] Decrypts sent out on 25, 27, 28 and 29 August referred to adjustments in the sectors held by 29th PG and 334th Divisions,[178] and early on 31 August GC and CS signalled that the former was being relieved by 334th Infantry.[179] In a decrypt of 4 September LXXVI Panzer Corps referred to a blocking position held by 26th Panzer and stated that the Corps intended to hold its line with 98th Infantry Division echeloned in depth and that a regiment of 29th PG was to be employed.[180] A decrypt on 5 September confirmed that 334th had taken over from 29th PG that morning.[181] The move of 20th GAF and its replacement by 42nd Jäger Division from Liguria was disclosed by decrypts of 1, 7 and 11 September,[182] and the withdrawal of 356th Division from I Parachute Corps was referred to in decrypts of 10 and 12 September.[183] Another decrypt of 12 September disclosed that a new division – 232nd Infantry – was arriving in the Genoa area and that the Schlesien Division was also en route, presumably to be used like the Ostpreussen and Wildflecken Divisions earlier in the summer to rehabilitate battle-scarred formations.[184]

While battle raged on LXXVI Panzer Corps's front LI Mountain Corps on its right withdrew into the *Gothic* line without being unduly pressed. Fourteenth Army also withdrew along its whole front. In the central sector, where Fifth Army's attack was to be made by II US and XIII British Corps, I Parachute Corps halted temporarily on the line of hills immediately north of Florence, but a further withdrawal beginning on 8 September took it back to positions just forward of the *Gothic* line covering Il Giogo and La Futa passes. Knowing that the enemy had committed 26th Panzer and 29th PG Divisions on the Adriatic front and had further weakened the centre by withdrawing 356th Division from I

---

176. ibid, p 140.
177. DEFE 3/126, XL 8156 of 27 August.
178. DEFE 3/125, XL 7914 of 25 August; DEFE 3/126, XLs 8122 of 27 August, 8247 of 28 August; DEFE 3/127, XL 8404 of 29 August.
179. DEFE 3/128, XL 8666 of 31 August.
180. DEFE 3/221, XL 9109 of 4 September.
181. ibid, XL 9236 of 5 September.
182. DEFE 3/220, XL 8898 of 1 September; DEFE 3/222, XL 9396 of 7 September; DEFE 3/224, XL 9793 of 11 September.
183. DEFE 3/223, XL 9710 of 10 September; DEFE 3/224, XL 9875 of 12 September.
184. DEFE 3/224, XL 9852 of 12 September.

Parachute Corps, Alexander decided to launch Fifth Army's offensive on 10 September.* Two days later Eighth Army, reinforced by 2nd New Zealand Division and 3rd Greek Mountain Brigade, renewed the assault on the Coriano ridge. This began a fierce battle lasting ten days in which both sides incurred heavy casualties. The Germans brought up further reinforcements – 356th Infantry Division, elements of 20th GAF, and finally a battle group of 90th PG Division which had arrived from the north-west – but on 20–21 September they were compelled to withdraw to the north bank of the river Marecchia and the Allies entered Rimini. Further advances were made which by the end of the month had brought Eighth Army almost to the Fiumicino river, but an early break in the weather had reinforced the natural obstacles and assisted the enemy to maintain a stubborn resistance.[185]

The arrival on Eighth Army's front of 356th Division and the severe mauling it received were noted by Army Y, which also reported on 13 September that contact was being established between 29th PG and 20th GAF's reconnaissance unit.[186] The appearance of a battle group of 90th PG caused no surprise, although the plentiful information about its movements from high-grade Sigint had been somewhat confusing. A decrypt signalled on 31 August had confirmed the expectation that it was to be relieved on the Franco–Italian frontier under LXXV Corps by 5th Mountain Division,[187] and in another decrypt its Flivo had said that it was interested in the exact front line in the Adriatic sector.[188] A message decrypted on the next day said that one of its units was moving by rail.[189] However, messages from LXXV Corps and the Division's Flivo on 4 and 5 September showed that part of it, at least, was still in the north-west.[190] In a message of 6 September, decrypted on 12 September,[191] C-in-C South-West reported the departure of three trains with 90th PG Division. On 14 September the decrypt of a message from its Flivo said that the Division would hand over its sector to 5th Mountain Division on 13 September, but elements still in action would remain. The divisional staff was moving to the Ferrara area.[192] AAI's intelligence summary of 13 September described the position of 90th

---

* See below, p 340.

185.   CAB 106/610, pp 15–18; EDS/Appreciation/19, Field Study No 1.
186.   WO 170/69, Nos 61 and 62 of 13 and 22 September.
187.   DEFE 3/128, XL 8721 of 31 August.
188.   ibid, XL 8740 of 31 August.
189.   DEFE 3/220, XL 8821 of 1 September.
190.   DEFE 3/221, XLs 9122 of 4 September, 9155 of 5 September.
191.   DEFE 3/224, XL 9952 of 12 September.
192.   DEFE 3/225, HP 104 of 14 September.

PG as confusing; a battle group might be moving to the east flank.[193] A decrypt of 25 September placed 90th PG in the line between 26th Panzer and 278th Infantry Divisions and listed the units under its command.[194]

Further information on the enemy's order of battle, and on the shifts to which he was sometimes put, was obtained from some high-grade decrypts of weekly reports on the state of Tenth Army's divisions; they gave details about units attached to a division from other divisions, and stated which of its units were detached elsewhere. Decrypts on 25 and 28 September contained the report for 11 September;[195] the report for 25 September occurred in decrypts on 1 and 2 October;[196] and decrypts on 9 and 10 October gave an incomplete report for 3 October.[197] As for the state of the divisions, the pro-forma used covered the battalions under command of a division and their condition; the division's holding of heavy anti-tank guns, assault guns and (where applicable) tanks; its artillery; the mobility of its horse-drawn and motorised elements; and an assessment of its fighting efficiency on the scale from I to IV.* In the return for 11 September the highest rated divisions were 29th PG (II) and 114th Jäger (II–III); 715th, 305th, 447th, 278th and 98th Infantry Divisions, 1st Parachute Division and 26th Panzer Divisions were rated III and 71st Infantry Division IV. On 25 September 90th PG was rated II so far as its own units were concerned, but the attached elements of 5th Mountain Division (which had suffered heavily on the Coriano ridge) were rated IV; 114th Jäger was unchanged at II–III but 29th PG was now III; 715th, 305th, 278th, Infantry, 26th Panzer and 1st Parachute were still rated III; 356th and 20th GAF, brought from Fourteenth Army and severely mauled, were rated

---

* For the definition of these categories see above, p 259fn*. The following are examples from Tenth Army's weekly reports:

715th Infantry 11 September — 7 Bns (2 medium, 5 average); 1 Field Ersatz Bn (strong); 26 heavy A/T guns; 18 light; 8 medium barrels artillery; mobility, horse-drawn 90%, motorised 65%; fighting efficiency III.

90th PG 25 September — 2 Bns (medium) 3 Bns (average); 2 Bns subordinated to 5th Mountain Division; of bns (medium) subordinated from 5th Mountain Division, 3 Bns (exhausted), 1 Field Ersatz (strong); 15 heavy A/T guns; 28 Assault guns; 6 tanks (Pzkw IV) 11 light; 4 medium barrels artillery subordinated from 5th Mountain; 25 light, 8 medium barrels artillery subordinated from 98th Infantry; mobility, motorised 70%; fighting efficiency II [but] elements of 5th Mountain IV.

193. WO 170/69, No 61 of 13 September.
194. DEFE 3/229, HP 1140 of 25 September.
195. ibid, HP 1200 of 25 September; DEFE 3/230, HP 1490 of 28 September.
196. DEFE 3/232, HPs 1839 and 1842 of 1 October, 1957 of 2 October.
197. DEFE 3/235, HP 2714 of 9 October; DEFE 3/236, HPs 2825 and 2868 of 10 October.

IV and so was 98th Infantry Division. In the incomplete return for 3 October the highest rating was II–III for an unidentified division; 90th PG was down to III.

□

Fifth US Army's attack of 10 September had meanwhile fallen on I Parachute Corps, which had 4th Parachute and 334th Infantry Divisions under command, and its capture of the important position of Monte Calvi on 12 September produced a crisis in the German centre. During the next few days contact between 4th Parachute Division on Fourteenth Army's left and 715th Infantry Division on Tenth Army's right was lost, regained and lost again. Fifth Army captured Il Giogo pass on 17 September and Firenzuola and La Futa pass on 21 September, and its advance through this gap in the *Gothic* line towards the Via Emilia threatened to cut Tenth Army's life-line. By 22 September neither LI Mountain Corps on Tenth Army's right nor I Parachute Corps on Fourteenth Army's left was in control of the situation despite urgent steps to restore it.[198]

On 11 September 362nd Infantry Division on XIV Panzer Corps's left was told to extend its sector eastwards and was subordinated to I Parachute Corps. On 15–16 September 16th SS PG Division was ordered to side-step left and come in between 65th and 362nd Infantry Divisions so as to enable the latter to shift eastwards to assist 4th Parachute Division, while on Tenth Army's front a regiment of 44th Infantry Division was moved to the right wing of LI Mountain Corps to buttress 715th Division. On 18 September 362nd Division was ordered to hand over its sector to 334th Division and 16th SS PG and take post on I Parachute Corps's left flank. Attempts to re-establish contact between Tenth and Fourteenth Armies were in vain and on 22 September the remainder of 44th Division was placed astride the Firenzuola–Imola road with orders to hold Monte La Fine and close the gap between the armies. On 23 September 44th Division was subordinated to Fourteenth Army in order to achieve unity of control at the vital point, but on 24 September the Allies were on Monte La Fine.

To meet what was now a very serious threat Kesselring ordered that 334th Division, which had distinguished itself by stout resistance between La Futa and Vernio, should be relieved by 16th SS PG and brought into the line between 362nd and 44th Divisions. On the other side of the gap 98th Infantry Division, which had been refitted after losing heavily on Eighth Army's front, was to be re-committed, a reinforced regimental group

---

198. CAB 106/610, pp 18, 19; EDS/Appreciation/19, Field Study No 2.

making an accelerated move to LI Mountain Corps's right flank. Despite these decisions the situation continued critical. Emergency reinforcements were scraped together for I Parachute Corps – a GAF guard battalion for 4th Parachute Division; Mountain Regiment 100 with the reconnaissance battalion and a battery of artillery; the reconnaissance battalions of 42nd Jäger and 65th Infantry Divisions; and elements of GHQ's Panzer Abteilung 216 – and Kesselring announced that 94th Infantry Division, which had been recuperating near Udine, would be moved south; he postponed deciding which army it would join. In the last days of the month Fifth Army's impetus slackened and bad weather came to the help of the enemy, who at last succeeded in re-establishing firm contact between his two armies.[199]

During Fifth Army's advance, as on Eighth Army's front, high-grade decrypts and Army Y threw valuable light on the enemy's situation. In a message on 14 September, signalled by GC and CS very early the next morning, I Parachute Corps appreciated that the Allied attack was not a feint but an offensive designed to break through to Bologna, adding that 362nd Division had been subordinated to the Corps from 0800 on 14 September.[200] The strain on 4th Parachute Division, which had so far borne the brunt of the battle, was reflected in a decrypt of 16 September; its daily loss was about 150 men and the last divisional reserves had been committed.[201] A decrypt signalled at 0709 on 19 September disclosed that the main body of 362nd Division was to reach a position between La Futa and Firenzuola on 18 September.[202] Army Y reported the arrival of units of this division on 4th Parachute Division's left on 19 September, and on 21 September it revealed that units of 44th Division had come to help 715th Division on LI Mountain Corps's right wing.[203] A decrypt of 22 September gave 362nd Division's defence line and its left boundary as that of Fourteenth Army.[204]

Kesselring's reaction to the Allied threat to his centre emerged from two decrypts signalled on 23 September. Orders issued on 20 September by one of his senior staff officers accepted that a gradual withdrawal was necessary on Tenth Army's right wing and Fourteenth Army's left. The threatened flanks of the armies were to be strengthened and Tenth Army was enjoined to keep close contact with Fourteenth Army. 98th Infantry Division, which was

---

199. EDS/Appreciation/19, Chapter 1 and Field Study No 2.
200. DEFE 3/225, HP 207 of 15 September.
201. DEFE 3/226, HP 370 of 16 September.
202. DEFE 3/227, HP 581 of 19 September.
203. WO 170/69, No 62 of 22 September.
204. DEFE 3/228, HP 900 of 22 September.

resting, might have to be re-committed at short notice.[205] An order of 21 September (which was only partly decrypted) instructed Fourteenth Army to draw as much as possible from 65th Division to reinforce the Army's left wing. The gap was to be filled by elements of 232nd Division, which in turn were to be replaced from 148th Division.[206]

A message from I Parachute Corps on 24 September (signalled by GC and CS the next day) spoke of heavy attacks on 334th Division: the troops were very exhausted and the losses suffered meant that only strongpoints could be manned; there had been heavy fighting on the front of an unspecified division which had come under command that morning.[207] A decrypt of 26 September gave I Parachute Corps's order of battle on 25 September as (from right to left) 16th SS PG, 334th Infantry, 4th Parachute, 363nd Infantry and a newly arrived division; this proved to be 44th Infantry.[208] AAI's intelligence summary of 29 September noted that the whole of this division had moved to the Imola–Firenzuola axis,[209] and a decrypt of 30 September confirmed that it had been under I Parachute Corps since 24 September.[210] A decrypt of 28 September disclosed that 94th Infantry Division was leaving GOC Adriatic's command, which was receiving the battered 71st Infantry Division.[211] Decrypts of 24, 29 and 30 September gave some particulars of the heavy casualties suffered by 4th Parachute Division, which on 27 September was reported to be short of 231 officers and 5,233 other ranks.[212]

□

On 22 and 23 September, when the Germans were under the severest strain, GC and CS decrypted two messages of 21 September from C-in-C South-West's Chief of Staff referring to movement *Herbstnebel*.[213] The first complained that gross violations of security had been frequent during preparatory work on the movement; the greatest secrecy was to be observed in future reference to it. The second ordered that in the event of *Herbstnebel* no undestroyed river crossing equipment of any kind was to be left

---

205. ibid, HP 919 of 23 September.
206. DEFE 3/229, HP 1005 of 23 September.
207. ibid, HP 1139 of 25 September.
208. DEFE 3/230, HP 1267 of 26 September.
209. WO 170/69, No 63 of 29 September.
210. DEFE 3/231, HP 1741 of 30 September.
211. DEFE 3/230, HP 1443 of 28 September.
212. DEFE 3/229, HP 1009 of 24 September; DEFE 3/231, HPs 1568 of 29 September, 1741 of 30 September.
213. DEFE 3/228, HPs 894 of 22 September, 993 of 23 September.

for the Allies, above all on the Po. All equipment which could be transported was to be taken away for use on future water obstacles and officers were to be posted at every crossing who would be responsible for seeing that no such equipment remained undestroyed on the Allied side of the river. From the fact that the contingency plan for a withdrawal was being mentioned in the Enigma the Allies naturally deduced that the German preparations for it were far advanced – and all the more so because a Japanese diplomatic decrypt had indicated in the first week of September that Hitler had decided on a pull-back. The Japanese Ambassador in Berlin, in a telegram covering interviews held with Hitler and Ribbentrop on 4 September, had represented Hitler as saying that although the present line in Italy had been under construction for about a year, and could be held, he intended to retire on the mountainous region of the Alps which could be held with small forces while he strengthened the decisive battle areas. AFHQ received a summary of the Japanese decrypt on 11 September,[214] and it had noted that OKW must be aware that there were cogent reasons for withdrawing to a defensive line in north-eastern Italy.[215]

On 25 September, following the receipt of the *Herbstnebel* decrypts, AFHQ's intelligence summary took the view that the enemy could not re-establish himself on the line of the Apennines now that Rimini was in Allied hands, the Allies had solid bridgeheads over the Marecchia and the *Gothic* line was broken in the centre on both the Futa and the Firenzuola axes; it added that he appeared to be thinning out on the Franco–Italian border and this would be an essential preliminary to a general withdrawal.[216]

In a signal to London on 1 October AFHQ again appreciated that the situation called for a German withdrawal, but also noted that Kesselring had been given discretion when to effect it.[217] There is no record of the further intelligence on which this claim was based; whatever it was, the claim was premature. Withdrawal had indeed been seriously considered by Hitler; its technical aspects had been examined by Kesselring's subordinate commands; his Chief of Staff had discussed it at the Führer's headquarters on 23 September; and on 27 September Kesselring had requested permission to begin movement *Herbstnebel*. But permission had been refused and the refusal was formally confirmed on 5 October; for 'political, economic and military

214. BAY/XL 151 of 11 September.
215. WO 204/970, No 106 of 11 September.
216. ibid, No 108 of 25 September.
217. GAD/PK 141 of 1 October.

reasons', the Apennine position was to be held indefinitely.[218] On 6 October Hitler's order was communicated to all ranks and also, it seems via Army Y, to the Allied authorities.[219]

□

The Allied armies were then resuming the offensive against the German line, which was now held (from left to right) as follows:[220]

Tenth Army

GOC Venetian Coast: 162nd (Turcoman).

LXXVI Panzer Corps; 1st Parachute, 29th Panzer (with elements of 20th GAF), 90th PG, 278th Infantry, 114th Jäger.

LI Mountain Corps: 356th Infantry, 305th Infantry, 715th Infantry, 98th Infantry (arriving).

Fourteenth Army

I Parachute Corps: 44th Infantry, 334th Infantry, 362nd Infantry, 4th Parachute, 16th SS PG.

XIV Panzer Corps: 65th Infantry, 232nd Infantry (arriving), 42nd Jäger, Fortress Brigade 135, 94th Infantry (en route from Udine).

On Eighth Army's front atrocious weather paralysed movement in the coastal plain, but on the higher ground V Corps made progress in the Savio valley. Monte Farneto was captured on 7 October and the German Command moved 29th PG Division from north of the Via Emilia to counter the threat. But it was not left there long. On 12 October it was ordered to transfer to the central front to stem Fifth Army's offensive towards Bologna. 90th PG followed a few days later. The loss of these divisions obliged LXXVI Panzer Corps to yield ground. On 19 October AAI appreciated that the enemy would not make a serious stand before the Savio defences were reached. That day Eighth Army entered Cesena and secured a bridgehead over the Savio.[221]

The removal of 90th PG left 114th Jäger Division (which had exchanged places with 356th Infantry Division at the end of September) holding the vital sector astride the Via Emilia. To strengthen his defences the enemy decided to switch 114th Jäger with 1st Parachute Division from his left wing; the latter division had had a comparatively quiet fortnight and had received a large

---

218. EDS/Appreciation/19, Chapters 1 and 2.
219. WO 204/970, No 110 of 9 October; WO 170/70, No 64 of 12 October.
220. EDS/Appreciation/19, Chapter 3, pp 2, 3, 14 and 15.
221. CAB 106/610, pp 27, 28; WO 170/70, No 65 of 19 October; EDS/Appreciation/19, Chapter 2, p 29, Chapter 3, p 14.

draft of reinforcements. The change-over was carried out between 20 and 23 October. But on the central front Bologna and the Via Emilia were now under imminent threat from Fifth Army. On 24 October 1st Parachute Division was ordered to the central front and LXXVI Panzer Corps was authorised to withdraw to the river Ronco. Eighth Army followed up and obtained a bridgehead at Meldola, and another (which was subsequently lost) at Forlimpopoli.[222]

At the end of September the Germans had re-established contact between Fourteenth and Tenth Armies and were making desperate, but finally unsuccessful, attempts to regain Monte Battaglia on the Imola axis. XIII Corps, reinforced by 78th Division, now took over this sector from II US Corps, which concentrated its effort on Route 65, the direct road to Bologna. Monghidoro was captured on 2 October and Loiano on 5 October. By 10 October II US Corps was threatening Livergnano and captured it on 15 October.[223]

The German Command found various expedients to thicken up against the threatened breakthrough. 334th Infantry Division had been switched to I Parachute Corps's eastern flank at the end of September. On 3 October 98th Infantry Division, which had been re-committed on Tenth Army's right, was transferred to I Parachute Corps. On 5 October 94th Infantry Division, which had been refitted in the Udine area, began to relieve 65th Infantry Division and the latter to transfer from XIV Panzer Corps to I Parachute Corps. On 12 October 29th PG Division was ordered to the assistance of I Parachute Corps. By the middle of October 232nd Infantry Division had been relieved in the Genoa area by 148th (Reserve) Division and brought down to XIV Panzer Corps, where it released 94th Infantry Division to reinforce I Parachute Corps.[224]

Fifth Army's offensive continued. On 16 October the Allies made a deep penetration west of Route 65 and after a break-through next day on 98th Infantry Division's front they were only 11 kilometres from the Via Emilia. Monte Grande was captured on 20 October, La Costa on 22 October and Monte Belmonte and Monte Spaduro on 23 October. On 24 October Fifth Army reached Vedriano, 7 kms south of the Via Emilia. Here it was held by 90th PG Division and the remnants of 98th Infantry Division, the enemy having taken drastic measures to meet the emergency. On 17 October Kesselring had ordered 90th PG Division to the

---

222. CAB 106/610, p 28; EDS/Appreciation/19, Chapter 2, pp 33, 37–38.
223. CAB 106/610, pp 24–25; EDS/Appreciation/19, Chapter 3, pp 5–14.
224. EDS/Appreciation/19, Chapter 2, pp 27–28, Chapter 3, pp 6–14.

central sector and told OKW that in order to hold Bologna he would have to withdraw on the Adriatic flank. During the next two days he had decided to subordinate I Parachute Corps to Tenth Army and to bring XIV Panzer Corps HQ from his western flank to take over from LI Mountain Corps. On 23 October Kesselring was seriously injured in a road accident. On 24 October von Vietinghoff was appointed Deputy C-in-C South-West. 1st Parachute Division was ordered to the central front and LXXVI Panzer Corps was authorised to withdraw to the Ronco. On 27 October XIV Panzer Corps was placed in command of the sector south and south-east of Bologna and took over all I Parachute Corps's divisions except 16th SS, 4th Parachute and 94th Infantry, while surrendering 305th and 715th Infantry to LXXVI Panzer Corps.[225]

Although the extension of the German communications security precautions to the Enigma links was now delaying the production of high-grade Sigint,* high-grade decrypts, together with Army Y, continued to provide adequate and generally timely intelligence about the enemy's conduct of the October fighting.

On Eighth Army's front a report by 29th PG Division on 8 October that it was withdrawing from the line was signalled to the Commands very early the next day and Army Y reported on 9 and 10 October that it was reappearing south of Cesena between 114th Jäger and 356th Infantry Divisions.[226] 29th PG Division's subsequent move west was also followed by Army Y which on 14 October established that all three battalions of PG Regiment 71 had arrived in the central sector and that divisional HQ had left Eighth Army's front.[227] A decrypt of 16 October referred to 29th PG's sector (on the Savio) having been taken over by 278th Infantry and 114th Jäger Divisions.[228] Several decrypts between 21 and 24 October dealt with the switching of 1st Parachute and 114th Jäger Divisions.[229] In a signal sent at 0457 on 25 October, the decrypt of a message of 1430 on 24 October disclosed that 1st Parachute was to pull out during the night 24–25 October and assemble in the Imola area under command of LI Mountain Corps.[230] LXXVI Panzer Corps's withdrawal to the Ronco river

---

* See Appendix 15.

225. CAB 106/610, pp 25–26; EDS/Appreciation/19, Chapter 2, pp 30–31, 34–38, Chapter 3, pp 22–32, 43–59, 70.
226. DEFE 3/235, HP 2726 of 9 October; WO 170/70, No 64 of 12 October.
227. WO 170/70, No 65 of 19 October.
228. DEFE 3/239, HP 3538 of 16 October.
229. DEFE 3/241, HP 4085 of 21 October; DEFE 3/242, HPs 4323 and 4324 of 23 October, 4349 and 4370 of 24 October.
230. DEFE 3/242, HP 4441 of 25 October.

consequent on the transfer of strength to the centre was indicated by Army Y intercepts from 26th Panzer Division on 26 October.[231] Decrypts of 24, 30 and 31 October showed that on Tenth Army's extreme left wing 114th Jäger and 162nd (Turcoman) were under command of GOC Venetian Coast.[232]

On the central front the transfer of 334th Infantry Division to Fourteenth Army's left wing and occupation of its former sector by 16th SS PG Division were referred to in a message of 27 September.[233] The decrypt of this was not available until 3 October, but information that 94th Infantry Division had taken over from 65th Infantry Division late on 5 October was signalled by GC and CS early the next morning.[234] Flivo messages of 8 October (signalled on 9 October) referred to leftward shifts of 16th SS PG and 94th Infantry Divisions.[235] A message on 8 October by 4th Parachute Division to the effect that its main line was inadequately manned and that it had no reserves to counter the danger of a breakthrough was signalled on 10 October.[236] A decrypt of 11 October disclosed that 232nd Infantry Division was being relieved in the Genoa area by 148th (Reserve) Division;[237] information that 232nd Division had taken over 94th sector was signalled by GC and CS at midnight on 14 October;[238] and on 16 October it was known from decrypts that 94th Division had partly relieved 16th SS PG,[239] which in turn (as was revealed on 18 October) had taken over a sector from 4th Parachute Division.[240] The presence of elements of 90th PG Division on the central front was established by Army Y on 18 October.[241] Decrypts signalled on that day confirmed that 29th PG Division had been under the command of I Parachute Corps for two days, with 65th Infantry on its right and 362nd Infantry on its left. It was under pressure along the whole front and had repelled nine attacks.[242] A Flivo message on 21 October available the next day said that 29th PG had extended its sector, bringing another regiment into the line.[243]

---

231. WO 170/70, No 66 of 26 October.
232. DEFE 3/242, HP 4349 of 24 October; DEFE 3/300, HPs 5021 of 30 October, 5085 of 31 October.
233. DEFE 3/233, HP 2091 of 3 October.
234. DEFE 3/234, HP 2367 of 6 October.
235. DEFE 3/235, HP 2750 of 9 October.
236. DEFE 3/236, HP 2870 of 10 October.
237. ibid, HP 2978 of 11 October.
238. DEFE 3/238, HP 3364 of 14 October.
239. ibid, HP 3476 of 16 October; DEFE 3/239, HP 3538 of 16 October.
240. DEFE 3/239, HP 3723 of 18 October.
241. WO 170/70, No 65 of 19 October.
242. DEFE 3/239, HPs 3713 and 3718 of 18 October.
243. DEFE 3/241, HP 4146 of 22 October.

High-grade Sigint provided valuable if incomplete coverage of the very important Command re-organisation made by the enemy as the battle reached its climax. Information that the HQs of XIV Panzer and LI Mountain Corps were being switched was signalled early on 25 October.[244] Decrypts of 27, 29 and 30 October disclosed that XIV Panzer Corps had given up 305th Infantry Division to LXXVI Panzer Corps and, having taken over three divisions from I Parachute Corps, was in command (from right to left) of 65th Infantry, 29th PG, 362nd Infantry, 90th PG, 1st Parachute and 334th Infantry Divisions, while I Parachute Corps was left with only three divisions – 94th Infantry, 16th SS PG and 4th Parachute.[245] A decrypt signalled on 29 October revealed that Fourteenth Army was to be subordinated to the Army of Liguria and to take over command of Corps Lombardy.[246]

Miscellaneous order of battle information included the re-designation of Corps Witthöft as GOC Venetian Coast (10 September);[247] the substitution of Corps Lombardy for Corps Abteilung Lieb (15 September);[248] and the conversion of GOC Adriatic Coast into XCVII Corps (11 October).[249] A message of 2 October, signalled on 13 October, indicated that 44th Infantry Division was to be withdrawn from the line and transferred to GOC Adriatic:[250] the transfer was delayed by the crisis on the central front, but a signal by XCVII Corps giving the Division's billeting area was decrypted on 22 October.[251] A decrypt of 18 October revealed that 148th (Reserve) Division had been up-graded to an infantry field division;[252] 157th (Reserve) Division became a Mountain Jäger Division.[253] A decrypt of 24 October stated that an advance detachment of the Littorio Division was en route to the Army of Liguria and that the main body would follow at the end of the month[254] – a reinforcement of doubtful value in the light of a decrypt signalled on 16 October showing that there had been 1,099 deserters from the Monte Rosa Division up to 21

---

244. DEFE 3/242, HP 4446 of 25 October.
245. DEFE 3/243, HP 4661 of 27 October; DEFE 3/244, HPs 4895 and 4991 of 29 and 30 October.
246. DEFE 3/244, HP 4876 of 29 October.
247. DEFE 3/223, XL 9701 of 10 September.
248. DEFE 3/225, HP 204 of 15 September.
249. DEFE 3/236, HP 2983 of 11 October.
250. DEFE 3/237, HP 3153 of 13 October.
251. DEFE 3/241, HP 4174 of 22 October.
252. DEFE 3/240, HP 3753 of 18 October.
253. WO 170/70, No 66 of 26 October.
254. DEFE 3/242, HP 4372 of 24 October.

September and 1,825 from the San Marco Division up to 10 October.[255]*

□

After their failure to take Bologna in the fierce fighting of 10–23 October the Allies decided to continue their offensive until the middle of December, Eighth Army maintaining its advance while Fifth Army recuperated on the defensive before making a final attempt to take Bologna about the end of November.[257] They were not yet excluding the possibility that the enemy would be compelled to withdraw by the pressure of events on other fronts. At the beginning of November AFHQ commented on 'the surprising immunity' of the Italian theatre from the German withdrawals to meet more pressing needs elsewhere.[258] On 8 November the JIC(AF), while recognising that the enemy had overcome his immediate problems and could prolong his resistance south of the Po if he chose, thought it reasonable to expect him to withdraw sometime in the winter; a pull-back to the line he was preparing on the Adige would release some twelve divisions for Hungary, where they were desperately needed.[259] By the end of November, however, Eighth Army's advance having reached the Lamone river but the Germans having given no signs of intending a voluntary general withdrawal, this prospect had been abandoned. The JIC(AF) accepted on 25 November that the Germans would fight south of the Po as long as they could hold Bologna,[260] and in his operations order of 28 November General Alexander appreciated that they would continue a fighting withdrawal with their left wing to a defence line connecting their

---

* Decrypts of telegrams from the Japanese Naval Mission in Berlin and the Japanese Ambassador to Italy (then in Venice) referred from time to time to the Italian divisions. In August they had reported that the Monte Rosa and San Marco Divisions had arrived in Italy during July, for use chiefly against Italian guerrillas, and would soon be followed by the Italia and the Littorio Divisions. During September they had reported the imminent arrival of these last two divisions and had noted that since August the Monte Rosa and San Marco Divisions had been defending the Ligurian coast as part of a mixed German–Italian Army Corps under Graziani. A telegram of 20 October (which was not decrypted until 16 November) explained that the Italia and Littorio Divisions were still in Germany, delayed by German distrust, and another of 4 November (decrypted on 17 November) said that parts of them had at last left Germany after Mussolini had brought pressure to bear on Hitler.[256]

255. DEFE 3/239, HP 3523 of 16 October.
256. BAY/XL 92 of 8 August; SJA 631 of 16 August; BAY/XL 159 of 13 September); BAY/HP 32 of 4 October (SJAs 919 and 920 of 27 September); BAY/HPs 99 and 100 of 17 and 18 November.
257. CAB 106/610, p 31.
258. WO 204/970, No 114 of 6 November.
259. JIC(44)469(o) of 15 November (JIC(AF)/33/44 of 8 November).
260. JIC(44)489(o) of 30 November (JIC(AF)/36/44 of 25 November).

positions south-east of Bologna with Lake Commachi on the Adriatic coast where they would give battle with the available resources to retain Bologna.[261]

The operations order of 28 November instructed Eighth Army to drive the enemy west of the Santerno, secure bridgeheads and thrust along the general axis Imola–Budrio, while Fifth Army was to be ready to advance on Bologna at three days' notice from 7 December. On 2 December the Combined Chiefs of Staff ordered SACMED to secure the general line Ravenna–Bologna–La Spezia, and thereafter to conduct operations to contain Kesselring's armies.[262] But Eighth Army's advance was impeded by bad weather; it took Ravenna on 4 December and Faenza on 16 December, but had reached only the general line of the river Serio by Christmas, when Imola and the Santerno river, 'necessary springboards for the co-ordinated assault on Bologna by both Armies', still lay well behind the German lines.[263] By then, moreover, the Allies had been alerted to the possibility of an enemy counter-attack on their western flank,* and they were taking extensive precautions against it, which, by unbalancing Fifth Army, contributed to the final postponement of the assault on Bologna to the spring of 1945.[264]

At the beginning of November, following the desperate measures adopted by Army Group C against the threat to its centre in the October fighting, the German front was held (from left to right) as follows:[265]

Tenth Army

GOC Venetian Coast: 114th Jäger, 162nd (Turcoman).

LXXVI Panzer Corps: 26th Panzer (with elements of 20th GAF), 278th, 356th, 305th, 715th Infantry.

XIV Panzer Corps: 334th, 98th, 1st Parachute, 90th PG, 362nd Infantry, 29th PG, 65th Infantry.

I Parachute Corps: 94th Infantry, 16th SS PG, 4th Parachute.

Fourteenth Army (under Army of Liguria)

LI Mountain Corps: 42nd Jäger (moving to XIV Panzer), 232nd Infantry, Monte Rosa, 148th Infantry (elements), Fortress Brigade 135.

Corps Lombardy (north-western coastal section, Chiavari–Imperia

---

* See below p 357ff.

261. CAB 106/610, Appendix B-2.
262. Ehrman, op cit, Vol VI (1956), p 56.
263. CAB 106/610, p 38; Fisher, *Cassino to the Alps* (Washington DC 1977), p 411.
264. Fisher, op cit, pp 406–410.
265. EDS/Appreciation/19, Chapter 3, Appendix 1.

and the hinterland): 148th Infantry (elements), San Marco, Littorio.

LXXV Corps (under Army of Liguria) covering the Franco–Italian frontier: 34th Infantry, 5th Mountain, 157th Mountain.

XCVII Corps (north-east Italy and Istria): 71st Infantry, 44th Infantry (en route), 237th Infantry, 188th Reserve Mountain.

Von Vietinghoff, acting C-in-C South-West since Kesselring's accident,* was in no doubt that the Allies would resume their offensive and that the Bologna front was the vital sector. Throughout November he struggled to keep his reserves in hand for this sector at the price of withdrawals on the Adriatic flank in front of Eighth Army which were accepted only with great reluctance by OKW.[270] After losing Forli to Eighth Army's advance on 9 November he contented himself with a switch between 26th Panzer Division, which moved west to cover Route 9, the Via Emilia main Parma–Bologna–Rimini highway, and the shaken 356th Infantry Division. Ordered in the middle of the month to stand firm on the Montone river and to find another division to reinforce the Adriatic front, he suggested that this should be either 157th Mountain Division from north-west Italy or 71st Infantry Division from Istria (whence 44th Infantry Division was already leaving for Hungary). Hitler sanctioned the move of 157th Mountain; but 71st Division followed 44th to Hungary and 710th, a static division, was ordered to Istria from Norway. At von Vietinghoff's request the Venetian Coast command was upgraded to become LXXIII Corps responsible for Tenth Army's left wing.[271]

When Eighth Army attacked west of Forli on 21 November C-in-C South-West appreciated that this was the prelude to the resumption of the attack on Bologna and did not move his reserves. After hard fighting 26th Panzer Division withdrew behind the Marzeno river on 23–24 November, still covering

---

* The appointment of von Vietinghoff as acting C-in-C and of Lemelsen as acting GOC Tenth Army was revealed by high-grade Sigint on 11 November,[266] and the fact that Kesselring was reported to have been wounded was mentioned in AFHQ's intelligence summary of 13 November.[267] On 17 November the decrypt of a telegram from the Japanese Ambassador in Venice disclosed that Kesselring had been injured in a car accident at the end of October.[268] On 11 December AFHQ's intelligence summary quoted a prisoner of war to the effect that Kesselring was still in hospital and that von Vietinghoff was probably acting for him.[269]

266. DEFE 3/305, HP 6255 of 11 November.
267. WO 204/970, No 115 of 13 November.
268. BAY/HP 100 of 18 November.
269. WO 204/970, No 119 of 11 December.
270. EDS/Appreciation/19, Chapter 4.
271. ibid, Chapters 4 and 5.

Faenza. A week later the Canadian Corps attacked the front held by 114th Jäger and 356th Infantry Divisions south and west of Ravenna. On 2 December the C-in-C asked, and two days later was given, permission to withdraw behind Ravenna. But his suggestion that the left wing of Tenth Army should be withdrawn to the *Genghis Khan* position, running from Lake Comacchio along the Reno and the Idice to south of Bologna, was turned down. To withstand Eighth Army's pressure he was obliged over the next fortnight to reinforce his left wing with 90th PG (brought in south-west of Faenza from Army Group Reserve), 98th Infantry from XIV Panzer Corps (placed between 114th Jäger and 356th Infantry Division) and 29th PG (replaced in XIV Panzer Corps by 362nd Infantry from reserve and sent to relieve 26th Panzer Division on Route 9).

The supply of Sigint declined significantly from the beginning of November. While VHF continued to provide a stream of tactical information in plain language during operations, Army Y from the German W/T frequencies was greatly reduced by the introduction of improved security measures* which made it difficult to identify the enemy's formations.[272] On the Army Enigma links, where these same precautions were already delaying the sorting and decrypting of high-grade Sigint at GC and CS, still greater problems arose in mid-November when the German Army brought into force modifications to the Enigma machine. Henceforth GC and CS depended heavily on Bream – the non-morse Fish teleprinter link between C-in-C South-West and OKH – for high-grade Army Sigint relating to the Italian front. Bream was decrypted with a delay of a week or even more, but it carried high-level intelligence of the greatest importance and, with occasional help from GAF and naval Enigma decrypts, it kept the Allies well informed about the enemy's general military situation and his order of battle.†

Partly, no doubt, because of the delicacy of the source and the absence of collateral information from prisoners or captured documents, and partly because delays in decryption led to uncertainty as to whether these measures remained in force, the switch between LI Mountain and XIV Panzer Corps's HQs, the concentration of forces under XIV Panzer Corps on the Bologna

---

* See Appendix 15.

† See Appendix 15(ii). On the Italian front the most serious result of this set-back was that the Army-Air liaison key (Puma) became unreadable except on isolated occasions. Puma, hitherto broken regularly and currently, had produced a high proportion of the total GC and CS output of military intelligence in the Italian theatre, providing a daily survey of the battle and continually locating German divisions and disclosing their intentions.

272. *History of Sigint in the Field*, pp 140–142.

sector and the subordination of Fourteenth Army to the Army of Liguria, all of which had been revealed by high-grade Sigint at the end of October,* were not mentioned in intelligence summaries for several weeks. The order of battle maps accompanying AFHQ's summaries continued to show LI Mountain Corps under Tenth Army and XIV Panzer Corps and I Parachute Corps under Fourteenth Army, and to credit I Parachute Corps with the bulk of the forces in the Bologna sector. A message sent on 24 October by the Flivo with I Parachute Corps indicating that the Corps might have been subordinated to Tenth Army was signalled on 16 November[273] and on 19 November a return by Tenth Army's Quartermaster listed I Parachute Corps, XIV Panzer Corps, LXXVI Panzer Corps and GOC Venetian Coast.[274] But it was not until 4 December that AFHQ suggested that Fourteenth Army 'has now little if any connection with the Bologna front'.[275] A week later (when high-grade Sigint had disclosed that LXXIII Corps was in command of Tenth Army's left wing) AFHQ said that it was now fairly clear that Tenth Army was directing the whole of the main battle with four corps under command.[276] These were shown on the order of battle map as LXXIII, LXXVI, LI and I Parachute Corps. AFHQ continued: 'it seems strange that LI Mountain Corps should still find itself in AOK 10 and that the more experienced XIV Panzer Corps should retain the relatively unimportant western sector, but there is no direct evidence to show that they have exchanged responsibilities'. The switch over of the Corps HQs was first shown on the order of battle map with the summary for the week ending 26 December, which mentioned documentary evidence establishing that LXXVI Panzer Corps had XIV Panzer Corps on its right and the new LXXIII Corps on its left, but XIV Panzer Corps's sector and its subordinated formations were both shown incorrectly.[277]†

It was clear from high-grade Sigint that C-in-C South-West was in no doubt about Allied intentions. An appreciation of 8 November, decrypted on 12 November, looked for the resumption of large-scale attacks south of Bologna and south and

---

* See above, p 348.

† These errors were repeated in Alexander's account of the German order of battle in mid-December in his report to the Combined Chiefs of Staff.[278]

273. DEFE 3/307, HP 6852 of 16 November.
274. DEFE 3/308, HP 7118 of 19 November.
275. WO 204/970, No 118 of 4 December.
276. ibid, No 119 of 11 December.
277. ibid, No 121 of 26 December.
278. CAB 106/750, Alexander's Report to the CCS covering operations December 1944–May 1945, p 17.

south-east of Forli.[279] A decrypt signalled on 25 November revealed that on 20 November C-in-C South-West considered that changes in the Allied order of battle confirmed that the Americans were building-up south of Bologna; XIII British Corps would support them and would also thrust towards Imola while Eighth Army was able to sustain its offensive along and south-west of Route 9.[280] Reporting two days later that a large-scale attack had begun south-east of Faenza, the C-in-C added that the assault on Bologna must be imminent.[281] That was decrypted on 26 November. On 29 November his appreciation of 25 November was signalled to the Commands by GC and CS. He appreciated that there might be a pause for re-grouping in the attack on Faenza; the attraction of German reserves was an important object of the Allied offensive along Route 9 and he expected an offensive in the Bologna sector.[282]

By 30 October it was known from high-grade Sigint that XIV Panzer Corps was in command of 65th Infantry, 29th PG, 362nd Infantry, 90th PG, 1st Parachute, 98th and 334th Infantry Divisions.* A message from the Corps's Flivo on 1 November signalled very early the next morning added 42nd Jäger Division to the list;[283] decrypts of 30 and 31 October and 5 November showed that its place on Fourteenth Army's front was being filled by the Italian Monte Rosa Division and elements of 148th Infantry Division.[284] The Monte Rosa Division was to be replaced for anti-guerrilla operations south of Piacenza by the Littorio Division en route from the Reich.[285] In a message of 2 November, signalled by GC and CS on 3 November, the Flivo with XIV Panzer Corps disclosed that 362nd Infantry Division had taken over from 90th PG, which had been withdrawn to rest and refit.[286] Decrypts of 7, 9 and 10 November showed that 362nd was in turn relieved by 42nd Jäger and that XIV Panzer Corps's front was held (from right to left) by 65th Infantry, 29th PG, 42nd Jäger, 1st Parachute, 98th and 334th Infantry Divisions.[287]

On Eighth Army's front the switch between 356th Infantry and

---

* See above, p 350.

279. DEFE 3/305, HP 6407 of 12 November.
280. DEFE 3/310, HP 7739 of 25 November.
281. DEFE 3/311, HP 7864 of 26 November.
282. DEFE 3/312, HP 8164 of 29 November.
283. DEFE 3/301, HP 5312 of 2 November.
284. DEFE 3/300, HPs 5065 and 5139 of 30 and 31 October; DEFE 3/302, HP 5655 of 5 November.
285. DEFE 3/302, HP 5677 of 5 November.
286. DEFE 3/301, HP 5398 of 3 November.
287. DEFE 3/303, HPs 5824 and 5851 of 7 November; DEFE 3/304, HPs 6065 and 6163 of 9 and 10 November.

26th Panzer, bringing the latter on to Route 9 after the loss of Forli, was quickly revealed by a decrypt – signalled at 0205 on 9 November – of a message of 1600 on 8 November in which the Flivo with 356th Division said that sectors were to be exchanged on 9–10 November.[288] Another message from the Flivo at 1000 on 12 November, available early the next morning, reported that the exchange had been completed.[289]

Hitler's order that 44th Infantry Division should transfer to the area of Budapest to rest and refit and thereafter to be employed on the extreme right of Army Group South, so as to ensure contact with the left wing of Army Group F on the Danube, was transmitted by OKW in a message of 7 November signalled by GC and CS on 13 November.[290] The despatch of trains carrying the division was reported in decrypts of 15 and 21 November.[291] A message of 22 November reporting that all 60 trains had been handed over was signalled on 26 November.[292] A naval message on 17 November stated that 157th Mountain Division would be relieved by the Littorio Division and moved to 'GOC Adria' and that 162nd (Turcoman) Division would go to the Piacenza area from Tenth Army.[293] This statement seems to have been premature so far as the move of 157th Mountain Division was concerned since a message from C-in-C South-West on 18 November (decrypted on 23 November) discussed whether 71st Infantry Division should be brought to Bologna from Istria, and suggested that the alternative of moving 157th Division was ruled out because the Littorio Division would then have to be equipped for mountain warfare and the relief of 157th would take a long time because of the weather conditions.[294] In the event, as recorded above, 157th Division was relieved by the Littorio Division and brought down to the southern front and 71st Division followed 44th to Hungary. A message of 22 November, signalled to the Commands on 26 November, said that all the Littorio Division's trains had been taken over and that one train out of 36 for 157th Mountain Division had left.[295] Another message of 25 November, signalled on 29 November, said that 26 of the Littorio trains had reached their destination while six of 157th Division's trains had

288. DEFE 3/304, HP 6046 of 9 November.
289. DEFE 3/305, HP 6478 of 13 November.
290. ibid, HP 6476 of 13 November.
291. DEFE 3/306, HP 6710 of 15 November; DEFE 3/309, HP 7308 of 21 November.
292. DEFE 3/311, HP 7849 of 26 November.
293. DEFE 3/307, HP 6900 of 17 November.
294. DEFE 3/310, HP 7577 of 23 November.
295. DEFE 3/311, HP 7849 of 26 November.

left.[296] This message also gave the first indication that 71st Division was on the move, and a decrypt the next day disclosed that it was following 44th Division to Hungary;[297] both were in action there by the end of the month, as shown by a decrypt signalled on 2 December.[298] A C-in-C message of 3 December, decrypted on 7 December, recorded that 20 trains carrying 157th Division had left and ten had arrived, and that a train with advance personnel of the Italia Division (which had been forming in the Reich) had been taken over.[299] The moves of 157th, the Littorio and Italia Divisions were again chronicled in a message of 6 December, signalled on 9 December.[300] This also mentioned that two trains carrying 710th Division (known to have been located in Norway at the end of November but to be moving) had been taken over. The decrypt of an order of 2 December that this Division was to join C-in-C South-West as Army Group Reserve in the area Padua–Treviso was signalled on 12 December.[301] A decrypt of 31 December reported that 27 trains with the Division had been taken over and 18 had arrived.[302]

In his message of 18 November quoted above* the C-in-C said that he intended to put 90th PG (then in reserve) under LXXVI Panzer Corps, but that for the present nothing more could be spared for LXXVI Panzer Corps because of the obscure situation in the Bologna sector. However 90th PG did not move until early December: Army Y reported on 4 December that it was showing signs of life and from 8 December it came into the line between 305th Infantry and 26th Panzer Divisions.[303] LXXIII Corps, formerly GOC Venetian Coast on Tenth Army's left wing, first appeared in high-grade Sigint on 7 and 8 December with 114th Jäger and 356th Infantry Divisions under command.[304] The transfer of 98th Infantry and 29th PG Divisions to LXXIII and LXXVI Panzer Corps respectively was also known to Allied intelligence on 19 December,[305] presumably from Army Y and/or battlefield identifications. A Flivo message of 17 December about the relief of 26th Panzer by 29th PG was not decrypted until 26

---

* See p 355.

296. DEFE 3/312, HP 8144 of 29 November.
297. DEFE 3/313, HP 8290 of 30 November.
298. ibid, HP 8424 of 2 December.
299. DEFE 3/315, HP 8807 of 7 November.
300. ibid, HPs 8966 and 8967 of 9 December.
301. DEFE 3/317, HP 9255 of 12 December.
302. DEFE 3/323, BT 838 of 31 December.
303. WO 170/71, Nos 72 and 73 of 5 and 12 December.
304. DEFE 3/315, HPs 8780 and 8869 of 7 and 8 December.
305. WO 204/970, No 120 of 19 December; WO 170/71, No 74 of 19 December.

December,[306] and a message of 19 December stating that 26th Panzer and 305th Infantry Divisions had been withdrawn for rest and refit not until 27 December.[307]

Information dated 16 December that 16th SS PG Division was to be withdrawn from its sector (under I Parachute Corps) into Army Group Reserve by 19 December was signalled by GC and CS on the latter date.[308] Decrypts on 28 and 31 December and 4 January revealed that this division had joined LXXIII Corps where it had relieved 98th Infantry Division, which came under command of LXXVI Panzer Corps on 30 December.[309] The decrypt of 31 December also announced the arrival of 157th Mountain Division in Tenth Army.

□

Meanwhile, between 26 and 28 December, Fourteenth Army had carried out a successful local attack (Operation *Wintergewitter*) with LI Mountain Corps in the Serchio valley, where Fifth US Army's front was held by inexperienced troops. Perhaps because OKW was not consulted – indeed, it subsequently disapproved of the operation on the ground that it had alerted the Allies to the vulnerability of a sector that might have been suitable for a later strategic counter-offensive[310] – high-grade Sigint gave no clear warning of attack. But on 10 December GC and CS decrypted a telegram in which the Japanese Ambassador to the Italian government, then at Brescia, reported that Mussolini had urged on Hitler the argument that an attack on the weakly-held western sector of the Allied front in Italy by two Italian and two German divisions would, by advancing to the Arno and cutting off Eighth Army, give the Axis a much-needed military success.[311]* On this evidence, which received some support in the middle of December from PR reports that roads and bridges on the western sector had been repaired,[313] the Allied Command accepted that an attack was a serious possibility, the more so because the German counter-offensive in the Ardennes had recently come as an unpleasant

---

* On his copy of this decrypt the Prime Minister minuted: 'Make sure General Alexander sees this at my desire.'[312]

306. DEFE 3/321, BT 427 of 26 December.
307. ibid, BT 468 of 27 December.
308. DEFE 3/319, HP 9854 of 19 December.
309. DEFE 3/322, BT 607 of 28 December; DEFE 3/323, BT 838 of 31 December; DEFE 3/324, BT 1215 of 4 January.
310. EDS/Appreciation/19, Chapter 6.
311. BAY/HP 130 of 13 December.
312. Dir/C Archive, 8175 of 10 December.
313. Fisher, op cit, pp 406, 407; WO 204/970, No 121 of 26 December.

surprise. On 22 December the JIC(AF) drew attention to the Ardennes analogy after noting that, although there was 'little or no indication that the German Command itself is considering an operation of this kind', the Italian Command in north-west Italy, which now had four divisions in the field, might feel that given some German support there was a chance for a cheap counter-attack to cut the supply route Leghorn–Pisa–Florence and if possible regain the Arno valley. The enemy's dispositions, the JIC(AF) thought, would enable him to assemble a force of roughly five divisions (16th SS PG,* elements or the whole of 148th Infantry, Monte Rosa, Italia and elements of 232nd Infantry) and he would probably bring in 15–20 additional fighter-bombers; a counter-offensive with roughly five divisions was 'a capability within the enemy's present resources although there is no firm evidence that he actually intends to attack'.[316]

It must be reckoned a tribute to the strength of the shock administered by the Ardennes offensive that a similar desperate move was thought possible in Italy despite what high-grade Sigint had disclosed about the fighting efficiency of the divisions that were expected to be involved. The weekly report of 20 November on the state of Tenth Army's divisions was sent out to the Commands on 25 and 27 November.[317] The highest rating for fighting efficiency allotted was III for 94th Infantry, 16th SS PG, 4th Parachute, 65th Infantry, 29th PG, 42nd Jäger, 1st Parachute, 98th Infantry, 715th and 305th Infantry, 26th Panzer, 114th Jäger and 90th PG; 356th and 278th Infantry were rated III–IV; and 362nd Infantry as IV. 26th Panzer had 47 serviceable Pzkw IV tanks and 29th PG had 28. I Panzer Regiment 4 (under XIV Panzer Corps) had 23 serviceable Panthers, and Panzer Abteilung 504 (under LXXVI Panzer Corps) had 19 Tigers. A similar report by Fourteenth Army was signalled on 1 December.[318] The San Marco and Monte Rosa Divisions were fit only for anti-guerrilla operations; an unidentified division (presumably 162nd Turco-man) and 148th Infantry Division were rated IV; 232nd Infantry Division was rated III.

These decrypts were but two among several which threw light

---

* Alexander later recorded that POW from 16th SS PG claimed that it was being moved to the western sector to take part in an attack.[314] In fact it was sent to LXXIII Corps's sector, where it arrived in time to oppose Eighth Army's attacks in the first week of January.[315]

314. CAB 106/750, p 22.
315. EDS/Appreciation/19, Chapter 6.
316. JIC(44)519(o) of 31 December (JIC(AF)/39/44 of 22 December).
317. DEFE 3/310, HP 7738 of 25 November; DEFE 3/311, HP 7962 of 27 November.
318. DEFE 3/313, HPs 8309 and 8352 of 1 December.

on the condition of the German armies at the end of the year, as the Allied offensive drew to a close. In messages decrypted on 1 and 10 December C-in-C South-West proposed that 20th GAF Division, which was of 'mediocre fighting value', should be dissolved and redistributed, some of it to 155th Field Training Division[319] (a new division which the C-in-C had recently been told to set up out of his own resources).[320] In a decrypt signalled on 27 December OKH stated that the disbandment of 20th GAF was to be completed by 15 January.[321] A decrypt of 16 November gave the establishment of a Parachute division as 17,571 and the actual combined strength of 1st and 4th Parachute Divisions as 32,962, but noted that as the latter figure included 4,400 wounded, sick and missing, there was a short-fall of 6,580.[322] A decrypt of 31 December gave the ration strength in men and horses of Army Group C on 20 December, a total of 1,084,649 men and 125,557 horses.[323] (On 25 May 1944 the corresponding figures had been 995,122 and 76,500.) On 10 December, for the first time since 5 August with the exception of two partial decrypts,[324] GC and CS decrypted one of C-in-C South-West's regular returns of AFVs. Although this return, dated 6 December, was still incomplete for Fourteenth Army,[325] decrypts signalled on 27 and 28 December brought a complete return for 20 December.[326] Compared with the position at the end of July, the C-in-C then had 241 tanks of all types (213 serviceable) as against 263 (136 serviceable); 251 assault guns (219 serviceable) as against 192 (83 serviceable); 148 Italian assault guns (133 serviceable) as against 167 (96 serviceable); and 507 heavy anti-tank guns (446 serviceable) as against 498 (466 serviceable). The 56 Pzkw III tanks were all in XCVII Corps in the north-east. The 117 Pzkw IVs (118 on 30 July) were all in Tenth Army – 68 (60 serviceable) with 26th Panzer, 44 (43) with 29th PG, 2 (2) with 90th PG and 3 (3) with 16th SS PG. The 32 (23) Panthers of I Panzer Regiment 4 and the 36 Tigers shared between Panzer Abteilungen 504 and 508 were also under Tenth Army. The number of Tigers had fallen from 60 on 30 July but all 36 were now serviceable compared with only 22 at the earlier date.

Operation *Wintergewitter*, a short-lived diversion, was followed in the first week of January 1945 by attacks by Eighth Army; they

319. ibid, HP 8311 of 1 December; DEFE 3/316, HP 9068 of 10 December.
320. DEFE 3/305, HP 6382 of 12 November.
321. DEFE 3/321, BT 471 of 27 December.
322. DEFE 3/307, HP 6804 of 16 November.
323. DEFE 3/323, BT 821 of 31 December.
324. CX/MSS/T290/13, T323/51.
325. DEFE 3/316, HP 9046 of 10 December.
326. DEFE 3/322, BTs 518 of 27 December, 569 and 576 of 28 December.

eliminated German bridgeheads over the Senio and brought Eighth Army to the southern shore of Lake Comacchio. The enemy's reaction to the attacks, which marked the end of the Allied offensive, was reflected in high-grade decrypts. Messages of 3 and 4 January, signalled by GC and CS on 6 January, reported that 278th Infantry Division had been pushed back over the river in costly fighting and that the Allies had made a deep penetration in the sector held by 114th Jäger Division, where a counter-attack involving 16th SS PG Division had been organised after some confusion.[327] AFHQ thought the counter-attack was 'badly managed'.[328] A message at 1300 on 4 January from the Flivo with 42nd Jäger (then under XIV Panzer Corps) saying that the Division was moving to the Adriatic coastal sector was signalled by GC and CS at 1756 on 5 January;[329] a decrypt the next day showed that it was being replaced by 305th Infantry Division, which had been resting out of the line.[330] Decrypts signalled on 7 and 8 January revealed that important adjustments were being made in the responsibilities of the Army Corps under Tenth Army; the HQs of XIV Panzer and I Parachute Corps were being switched and LXXVI Panzer Corps was shifting eastward to include the sector formerly commanded by LXXIII Corps.[331] According to the naval liaison officer with Tenth Army, its order of battle at 1900 on 6 January was (from right to left): XIV Panzer Corps commanding 94th Infantry, 4th Parachute, 65th, 362nd and 305th Infantry Divisions; I Parachute Corps commanding 1st Parachute, 334th and 715th Infantry, 90th PG and 29th PG Divisions; LXXVI Panzer Corps commanding 278th and 356th Infantry, 16th SS PG and 42nd Jäger Divisions; LXXIII Corps with 114th Jäger Division and miscellaneous coast watching units. 157th Mountain, 98th Infantry and 26th Panzer Divisions were in reserve.[332]

□

In the last four months of 1944, throughout the Allied advance, the German Air Force played a negligible part in the fighting. Even before the Allies had reached Florence its operations had been severely restricted. With all long-range bombers withdrawn from Italy after the Normandy landings, its strength was down to

---

327. DEFE 3/325, BTs 1400 and 1458 of 6 January 1945.
328. WO 204/971, No 1 of 9 January.
329. DEFE 3/325, BT 1343 of 5 January.
330. ibid, BT 1466 of 6 January.
331. DEFE 3/326, BTs 1602 of 7 January, 1674 of 8 January.
332. ibid, BT 1674 of 8 January.

50 single-engined fighters, 35 miscellaneous reconnaissance air-craft and 40 Ju 87 night-harassing bombers.[333] By the third week in July, as the Enigma disclosed, these had been forced to withdraw from the land battle by low serviceability, fuel shortage, the strength of the Allied defences and the fact that the main task of the GAF was reconnaissance against out-flanking landings.[334] Decrypts of signals from the Japanese Naval Mission in Berlin in the last week of July showed that the GAF was admitting this to the Japanese authorities.[335] During September and October the GAF Command* attempted small ground-attack operations by night in front of LXXVI Panzer Corps; but it was by then reduced to a total of some 70 aircraft and its attacks, to which the Allies were normally alerted by Enigma decrypts, were continually frustrated by bad weather.[338] A decrypt signalled on 4 November disclosed that on account of bad weather and the fuel situation ground attacks would be possible only in isolated cases,[339] and during the next two months reconnaissance by day and night over the Adriatic and the Ligurian Sea continued to be the Command's chief occupation.[340] But messages announcing its intention to carry out night ground attacks were decrypted on six days in

---

* The Enigma showed that its name was changed in September from GAF General, Central Italy, to GAF General, Italy, and then to GAF General, Upper Italy,[336] but it later emerged that the second of these changes was not implemented.[337]

333. AIR 41/10, *The Rise and Fall of the German Air Force*, p 385.
334. DEFE 3/59, XL 2802 of 20 July.
335. BAY/XLs 64 of 28 July, 77 of 31 July.
336. DEFE 3/224, XL 9856 of 11 September; DEFE 3/225, HP 43 of 13 September; DEFE 3/231, HP 1748 of 30 September.
337. DEFE 3/309, HP 7456 of 22 November.
338. DEFE 3/126, XL 8216 of 27 August; DEFE 3/127, XLs 8332 and 8460 of 28 and 29 August; DEFE 3/220, XLs 8777 of 31 August, 8902 of 1 September; DEFE 3/221, XL 9240 of 8 September; DEFE 3/224, XL 9862 of 12 September; DEFE 3/229, HP 1163 of 24 September; DEFE 3/230, HPs 1297 of 26 September, 1310 of 27 September, 1440 and 1445 of 28 September; DEFE 3/234, HPs 2109 of 4 October, 2355 of 6 October; DEFE 3/236, HP 2935 of 10 October; DEFE 3/241, HP 4138 of 22 October; DEFE 3/243, HPs 4562 of 26 October, 4654 of 27 October; DEFE 3/244, HPs 4753 of 27 October, 4869 of 28 October.
339. DEFE 3/301, HP 5497 of 4 November.
340. eg DEFE 3/301, HP 5593 of 5 November; DEFE 3/302, HPs 5801 and 5887 of 6 and 7 November; DEFE 3/305, HP 6363 of 12 November; DEFE 3/307, HP 6909 of 17 November; DEFE 3/308, HP 7159 of 19 November; DEFE 3/309, HP 7490 of 22 November; DEFE 3/311, HPs 7802 and 7889 of 25 and 26 November; DEFE 3/314, HP 8562 of 4 December; DEFE 3/316, HPs 9087 and 9238 of 12 December; DEFE 3/317, HP 9344 of 13 December; DEFE 3/318, HP 9663 of 17 December; DEFE 3/319, HPs 9837 and 9956 of 19 and 20 December; DEFE 3/321, BTs 342 and 421 of 25 and 26 December; DEFE 3/322, BT 508 of 27 December.

November and eight in December, about half of which were signalled by GC and CS in time to provide warning of the attack.[341]

The Allied air forces, in contrast, provided continuous close support to the ground forces and in addition, from the first week of November, carried out a major bombing offensive against the railway system into and throughout northern Italy. High-grade Sigint supplied some intelligence on the effects, direct and indirect, of the raids and it was all the more useful in that PR, the other major source of information, was often impeded by bad weather. A decrypt signalled on 9 November reported that the Brenner line between Innsbruck and Verona had been breached in several places on 6 November.[342] In a message on 8 November, signalled by GC and CS on 17 November, C-in-C South-West reported widespread damage to bridges and railway tracks by bombing and guerrillas,* and expressed the fear that if the weather remained good the continuation of the air offensive would, in view of inadequate stocks, put the whole supply situation under severe strain, especially as regards light and medium howitzer ammunition.[343] On 21 November the decrypt of a message from Tenth Army on 17 November disclosed that the fuel situation was extremely strained; some divisions had fallen below half a consumption unit and necessary tactical moves were impossible.[344] AAI's intelligence summary suggested on 22 November that the enemy's fuel and ammunition supplies had probably been seriously depleted,[345] but by the end of the month it was felt that as the restriction of the air effort by unfavourable weather had eased the railway situation, the enemy's supply position had probably improved.[346] The AAI intelligence summary of 12 December described the enemy's line of communications as 'somewhat precarious', but saw nothing to indicate that he was not getting enough for his current needs.[347]

---

* For decrypts of German reports on the activities of the Partisans see Appendix 21.

341. DEFE 3/301, HP 5556 of 4 November; DEFE 3/302, HPs 5637 and 5654 of 5 November; DEFE 3/305, HPs 6349 of 11 November, 6363 of 12 November; DEFE 3/309, HP 7490 of 22 November; DEFE 3/312, HP 8118 of 28 November; DEFE 3/313, HP 8447 of 3 December; DEFE 3/320, BTs 103 of 22 December, 174 of 23 December; DEFE 3/321, BTs 272 of 24 December, 342 of 25 December, 421 of 26 December; DEFE 3/322, BTs 508 of 27 December, 620 of 29 December.
342. DEFE 3/304, HP 6071 of 9 November.
343. DEFE 3/307, HP 6869 of 17 November.
344. DEFE 3/309, HP 7355 of 21 November.
345. WO 170/71, No 70 of 22 November.
346. ibid, No 71 of 28 November.
347. ibid, No 73 of 12 December.

Most of the Allied air effort in December was concentrated on the Brenner route between Trento and Bolzano, but a very heavy attack was made on Innsbruck on 15 December by the strategic bombers.[348] A GAF Enigma decrypt of 16 December revealed that the line was still cut in both directions and would probably re-open the following evening.[349] Another of 19 December carried a request that railway Flak units should be brought up to meet the rising scale of attacks on traffic installations in south Germany, including Innsbruck and Salzburg.[350] In the last few days of the month the strategic bombers joined in renewed attacks on the Brenner and north-eastern lines.[351] A message signalled by GC and CS on 2 January reported that the Brenner line had been buried in debris after attacks on 27, 28 and 29 December.[352]

348. AIR 41/58, *The Italian Campaign*, Vol II, pp 139, 140.
349. DEFE 3/318, HP 9595 of 16 December.
350. DEFE 3/319, HP 9803 of 19 December.
351. AIR 41/58, p 140.
352. DEFE 3/324, BT 1038 of 2 January 1945.

CHAPTER 51

The Check in the West

O N 5 JUNE the JIC had assessed Germany's capacity to resist on the assumption that *Overlord* went according to plan. It would not estimate precisely when her resistance would collapse, but 'viewing the picture as a whole . . . and making full allowance for the efficiency of the German military machine and of Nazi control of the Home Front, we believe that . . . Germany's defeat should occur before 1945'.[1] The CIC's assessment in a paper of 12 June, to which the JIC had contributed, had been less precise but scarcely less optimistic. 'A formal surrender by the Nazi regime is unlikely in any case. It is apparent, however, that Germany cannot long maintain her land and air forces in the face of further heavy attrition. If the cross-Channel operation succeeds in effecting a secure lodgement on the continent and the Red Army succeeds in piercing or even threatening to pierce the Niemen–Bug–Carpathians–Danube delta line, it is quite possible that high German military authorities will seek to end the conflict before the then inevitable collapse of military resistance actually occurs'.[2]

A month later, by which time the Germans had failed to prevent a Russian breakthrough north of the Pripet marshes and to stem the Allied build-up in Normandy, and had been thrown out of their defensive positions south of Rome, the JIC had been still more emphatic. 'All the elements for a collapse . . . already exist . . . when collapse comes it is likely to develop with startling rapidity'. With the Nazi party in control of some of the higher positions in the Services, and in the absence of organised civilian opposition, it was unlikely that the enemy would seek an armistice before the collapse came. 'It is impossible . . . to predict how long this unprecedented state of affairs can last since ordinary standards cannot be applied. It is, however, equally difficult to see how Germany can . . . prolong the struggle beyond December'.[3]

Later in July the excitement aroused by the attempt to assassinate Hitler was quickly dampened by the news that the attempt had failed.* But decrypts of Japanese diplomatic mes-

---

* See Appendix 22.

1. CAB 121/413, SIC file D/Germany/1, Vol 2, JIC(44)235(o) of 5 June.
2. CAB 88/59, CIC 47/D of 12 June (JIC(44)272 of 22 June).
3. CAB 121/413, JIC(44)302(o) of 14 July.

sages from Berlin stressed that, while the Nazi regime had easily re-asserted its authority, Germany's deteriorating military situation was producing widespread demoralisation. At the end of July the head of the Japanese Naval Mission reported that the German leaders were not contemplating surrender, but he noted that the strategic situation was so unfavourable that the Service chiefs had begun to turn their minds to the possibility of driving a wedge between Russia and the western Allies; the plotters had pinned their hopes on an accommodation with the west, but the Air Force was favouring a Russo–German peace.[4] Early in August he expressed admiration for the handling of the aftermath of the July plot, the maintenance of services in the face of constant air raids and the high morale of the younger troops and the SS.[5] He also noted, however, that there was evidence of demoralisation on the eastern front – 'a scandal unparalleled in the annals of the German Army'* – and that while the bombing of cities was having no military effect, the Allied oil offensive was achieving 'catastrophic results', so that 'oil is Germany's problem'.[6]† The Japanese Ambassador reported in similar terms in a telegram decrypted on 29 July: the Germans had failed in their strategy of routing the western invasion before reinforcing the eastern front; they would now have to concentrate on stabilising the eastern front; but they had no clear idea of the prospects there, Soviet advances having been more rapid than they had expected, and 'the same may be said of the war as a whole'.[7] And on 17 August Admiral Abe submitted another gloomy appreciation. Decrypted on 19 August, this declared that the set-backs of the Army on all fronts were beginning to 'wear a different aspect from all previous defeats'; that civilian morale had been shaken by the plot, the ceaseless air raids and the failure of the V 1 offensive, as well as by the Army's defeats; and that while he and his colleagues were encouraging them to prolong the war, 'I regret to say it is hard to see what the Germans can do that will suffice to bridge the yawning gap between the material and military strength of themselves and their opponents'.[8]

The conclusions that were being drawn in London corresponded closely with these Japanese assessments; here, too, a distinction was drawn between the poor prospects for the collapse

---

* See above, p 286.
† See Chapter 54 for the oil offensive.

4. BAY/XL 77 of 30 July 1944.
5. BAY/XL 91 of 8 August.
6. ibid; BAY/XL 95 of 12 August.
7. BAY/XL 71 of 29 July.
8. BAY/XL 114 of 21 August.

of the regime and the brightening prospects for Germany's military defeat. On 10 August the JIC ruled out the possibility of another coup, at least until Hitler was dead or Himmler's control of the country broke down, and thus expected that Germany's military defeat would be accompanied by a state of disorganisation, with no central authority capable of negotiating her capitulation.[9] It still believed, however, as it reported on 14 August, that her military defeat would come before the end of 1944, even though it was evident that her leaders were determined to prolong the war through the winter in the hope that improved fighter defences, the further dispersal of industry and increased production of the new weapons – rockets, U-boats, midget craft and mines – would enable them to retrieve the situation.[10] On 27 August the CIC's review concurred: 'the German strategic situation has deteriorated to such a degree that no recovery is now possible . . . unmistakeable signs of the imminence of collapse are unlikely to be apparent until the end of resistance is close at hand, but . . . we consider that organised resistance is unlikely to continue beyond 1 December 1944 and that it may end even sooner'.[11]

On 5 September the JIC noted the 'further catastrophic disasters' the German Army had incurred on every front and concluded that 'the process of final military defeat leading to the cessation of organised resistance has begun'. The task of forecasting was 'complicated by the fact that Hitler is increasingly out of touch with all reality'. Hitherto determined not to give ground, he might by now have realised that his only hope of prolonging the war was to withdraw his troops from outlying areas. 'Even if he has so changed his strategy, however, he has left it too late.' 'Whatever action Hitler may now take, it will be too late to affect the issue in the West, where organised German resistance will gradually disintegrate under our attack, although it is impossible to predict the rate at which this will take place. . . .'[12]

SHAEF and 21st Army Group agreed with these assessments. On 25 July 21st Army Group believed that 'the revolt of the military Junta, even if it is quelled which is far from certain, will have ineradicable consequences. . . . The almost unanimous outburst of venom [against Hitler] amongst senior captives is a fair mirror of the feelings . . . of many German soldiers inside the Reich. . . . It will take more than the blandishments of Goebbels

9. CAB 121/419, SIC file D/Germany/4, JIC(44)349 of 10 August.
10. CAB 121/413, JIC(44)354(o) of 14 August.
11. CAB 121/419, CCS 660 (CIC 47/4 of 27 August).
12. CAB 121/413, JIC(44)395(o) of 5 September, quoted extensively in Ehrman, *Grand Strategy*, Vol V (1956) pp 399–401.

and the blackmail of Himmler to replace the faith that is dead'[13].

By the middle of August the Commands had accepted that the revolt had been quelled, and that neither Germany's civilian population nor her armed forces were yet ready to give in;[14] but their confidence remained high. SHAEF commented on 19 August: 'Two things are certain. The enemy has lost the war and the defeat of Seventh Army and Panzer Gruppe West will hasten the end. One thing is uncertain. Would it have been more profitable for the Allies if Hitler's bomb had been a better and bigger one? Or ought the Allies to feel grateful that he has lived to continue his strategic blunders'.[15] A week later it was euphoric. 'The August battles have done it; have brought the end of the war in Europe in sight, almost within reach.'[16] 21st Army Group echoed these sentiments on 27 August. After estimating the enemy's losses in the Battle of Normandy – 400,000 men with 1,300 tanks and 3,500 guns; twenty senior commanders killed or captured; twenty-five divisions eliminated and a further twenty savagely mauled – it concluded that 'it seems perhaps not altogether a pity that the bomb failed'.[17]

It is easy to understand this optimism when we take into account the intelligence assessments of the state of the German Army in the west. On 2 September SHAEF noted that the enemy had no coherent order of battle and no strategy outside the West Wall, his armies having been reduced to a number of fugitive battle groups.[18] MI 14 agreed on 3 September that in terms of her minimum requirements for garrisoning the *Siegfried* line Germany was 'bankrupt'; on 10 September it estimated that Germany's fighting strength was down to about 18 divisions of which 5½ were isolated in Brittany, the Channel Islands, Flanders and the Channel ports.[19] SHAEF estimated on 9 September that, after allowing for reinforcements and the recovery of troops cut off in Belgium and southern France, Germany might soon have some 15 divisions, including four Panzer divisions, for the defence of the West Wall; the total might rise to 20 by the end of the month, but this would be inadequate for holding the Wall even if supplemented by many oddments and large amounts of Flak.[20]

The War Cabinet and the Chiefs of Staff did not dissent. On 4

---

13. WO 171/131, 21st Army Group Intelligence Summary No 149 of 25 July.
14. eg WO 219/1922, SHAEF Intelligence Summary No 21 of 12 August.
15. ibid, No 22 of 19 August.
16. ibid, No 23 of 26 August.
17. WO 171/132, No 158 of 27 August.
18. WO 219/1923, No 24 of 2 September.
19. WO 208/4316, MI 14 Weekly Summaries for the CIGS, 3 and 10 September.
20. WO 219/1923, No 25 of 9 September.

September, for planning purposes, the Cabinet accepted 31 December as the date for the end of the war in Europe.[21] On 8 September the CIGS informed the Prime Minister that while they were not ignoring the possibility that Germany would prolong her resistance into the winter, the Chiefs of Staff were inclined to share the JIC's belief that she could not survive for long.[22] But the Prime Minister was by no means convinced. On 8 September he argued that 'it is at least as likely that Hitler will be fighting on 1 January as it is that he will collapse before then. If he does collapse before then the reasons will be political rather than military'. The western Allies had still not secured a major port other than Cherbourg and their advances into Germany could well be delayed by the enemy's evident determination to hang on to the Channel ports and defend the Scheldt. This might give him time to withdraw his forces from the Baltic states and Italy and concentrate them on the *Siegfried* line; and the 'fortifying and consolidating effect of a stand on the frontier of her native soil should not be underestimated'.[23]

The force of some of these arguments became apparent in the next few weeks when the momentum of the Allied advance was checked by Germany's retention of the Scheldt, her defeat of the Allied attempt to establish a bridgehead at Arnhem and her increasing resistance to the American armies on the Rhine and the Moselle.

□

On 20 August, as the battle of the Falaise pocket was ending, Montgomery issued a new directive. By then I Corps on 21st Army Group's left flank had taken Troarn and Houlgate, reached the Touques river south-west of Pont L'Evêque, was approaching Lisieux and had taken Livarot. US forces had reached the Seine at Mantes Gassicourt and First US Army was swinging north to cut off the withdrawal of Seventh Army and 5th Panzer Army in the area Lisieux–Elbeuf.[24] Montgomery stated that his intention was to complete the destruction of the enemy in north-west France and then to advance northwards, with a view to the eventual destruction of the enemy in north-east France. The eventual boundary between the Army Groups would be the line Argentan–

21. Ehrman *Grand Strategy*, Vol VI (1956), p 615.
22. CAB 121/159, SIC file A/Strategy/14, COS(44)875(o) of 9 October, pp 104, 105 (COS(o) 3rd and 4th Meetings, 8 September).
23. ibid, pp 109–110 (COS(o) 5th Meeting, 9 September Annex I), quoted in Ehrman, op cit, Vol V, pp 401–402.
24. Ellis, *Victory in the West*, Vol I (1962), pp 448, 449.

Dreux–Mantes Gassicourt–Amiens–Ghent–Antwerp. Second British Army was to cross the Seine between Mantes Gassicourt and Louviers and First Canadian Army in the neighbourhood of Rouen. Second Army was to cross the Somme between Amiens and the sea and clear the Pas de Calais while First Canadian Army cleared Le Havre peninsula. 12th US Army Group was to advance to the general line Orléans–Troyes–Rheims–Amiens and be prepared to advance north-eastwards towards Brussels and Aachen and, perhaps, due east towards the Saar.[25]

To oppose this advance the German order of battle from right to left comprised LXXXVI Corps, the elements of Seventh Army and Fifth Panzer Army which had escaped from the pocket; LXXXI Corps, which with inadequate forces had been given the difficult task of screening the south flank of Seventh Army and Fifth Panzer Army between Gacé and Paris; the Paris garrison under von Choltitz; and First Army which, with parts of two divisions and miscellaneous units, was responsible for the defence of the upper Seine covering the Paris–Orléans gap. On 21 August Fifth Panzer Army was put in charge of the whole front from the Channel to the junction with First Army. North of the Seine and in the Low Countries there remained considerable German forces which had not yet been sucked into the battle. On 23 August 21st Army Group listed nine divisions as possible reinforcements. None of them was armoured.[26] 21st Army Group's intelligence summary for 23 August commented that the enemy's rapid withdrawal, leaving no firm line of contact along which to establish identifications and boundaries, and the very disordered state of the enemy's formations, made it very difficult to give an accurate plan of his dispositions facing the Army Group. On its right was LXXXVI Corps with 711th, 346th, 272nd and the remnants of 85th Infantry Divisions and armoured battle groups under 21st Panzer Division. Next was II SS Panzer Corps with 89th Infantry and 9th SS Panzer Divisions, and then LXXXI Corps with elements of 331st and 334th Infantry, 17th GAF Field, 6th Parachute and 9th and 116th Panzer Divisions. The remainder of the armour which had escaped from the pocket was under I SS Panzer Corps immediately west of the Seine. 18th GAF Field and 49th Infantry Divisions had also been identified east of the Seine and north of Paris.[27] Much of this information had been provided by a decrypt of 22 August.[28]

---

25. ibid, p 450.
26. WO 171/132, No 157 of 23 August; Ellis, op cit, Vol I, p 451; Blumenson, *Breakout and Pursuit* (Washington DC 1961), pp 532, 566, 577, 583, 592, 593.
27. WO 171/132, No 157 of 23 August.
28. DEFE 3/123, XL 7457 of 22 August.

First US Army spearheads secured Louviers and Elbeuf on 25 August. Here they were relieved by XII Corps and II Canadian Corps and turned back south towards Paris. 21st Army Group closed up towards the Seine against an orderly German withdrawal. Second Army's XXX Corps established a bridgehead on 25 and 26 August and XII Corps another one on 27 August. Lower down the river First Canadian Army was delayed by strong German resistance north-west of Elbeuf. Paris was liberated on 25 August, with its bridges intact. South-west of the city Third US Army secured bridgeheads between Sens and Moulins and occupied Troyes on 26 August. In the south Nineteenth Army's withdrawal up the Rhône valley was seriously hampered by guerrilla attacks and a bold attempt by Seventh US Army to cut its evacuation routes.[29]*

Meanwhile high-grade Sigint had thrown further light on Hitler's response to the crisis facing his armies in France. An order circulated by OKW on 19 August and signalled to the Commands by GC and CS the next day directed that the line Dijon–Lyons–Aix les Bains was to be held as long as possible. Bordeaux town and harbour might only be given up under heavy pressure. First Army was to stay west of the Seine and its reinforcement was to be speeded up, even at the expense of Fifth Panzer Army if necessary.[30] The decrypt of orders by C-in-C West on 20 August for the reinforcement of First Army was signalled on 21 August.[31] Decrypts of 24 August disclosed the instructions which Hitler had given in a directive four days earlier for the conduct of operations by C-in-C West and C-in-C South-West. C-in-C West was told that his most important task was to hold a bridgehead west and south of Paris to prevent an Allied thrust between the Seine and the Loire towards Dijon. Fifth Panzer Army and Seventh Army were to re-organise behind the river Touques, the armour being shifted to the southern flank. If it proved impossible to stand in front of the Seine then, with the exception of the bridgehead south-west of Paris, all forces west and south-west of a line Seine–Yonne–Bourgogne Canal–Dijon–Dôle–Switzerland were to be withdrawn behind this line. Fifth Panzer Army was to ensure that Seventh Army got safely across the Seine and was to prevent the Allies crossing the river below Paris. The city was to be held at all costs, even if this meant its destruction.† First Army was to be reinforced

---

* See above, pp 275–277.

† The decrypt on 25 August of an order by Hitler at 0900 on 23 August reiterated this instruction. The defence of Paris and its bridgehead was of decisive military and political

29. Ellis, op cit, Vol 1, pp 453–458; Blumenson, op cit, pp 583–589.
30. DEFE 3/122, XL 7201 of 20 August.
31. DEFE 3/123, XL 7261 of 21 August.

as soon as possible by the forces from south-west France: meanwhile it was to cover their withdrawal, and Nineteenth Army's, and maintain contact with the south wing of Fifth Panzer Army. Nineteenth Army, led by its fighting elements, was to make a junction with Army Group B in good time north-west of Dijon, its withdrawal being co-ordinated with developments on the southern wing of Army Group B. Any forces that were cut off were to join C-in-C South-West via the Mt Cenis and Little St Bernard passes.[33]

Hitler's long directive of 20 August to C-in-C West and C-in-C South-West ended with a promise that orders would be issued about bringing up personnel and material to C-in-C West. The most important reinforcements proved to be 15th PG and 3rd PG Divisions from Italy. The withdrawal of 15th PG from the line in Italy had been disclosed by high-grade Sigint on 15 August.[34] and a decrypt of 20 August showed that the division was destined for C-in-C West.[35] Orders on 21 August for 3rd PG to move to Châlons-sur-Marne, east of Paris, were decrypted the next day.[36] Decrypts of 21, 24 and 25 August disclosed that two SS Grenadier Divisions (26th and 27th) were being brought up to First Army for incorporation in 17th SS PG Division;* two LE divisions (59th and 64th) were being moved to the Channel coast; two SS Grenadier Divisions (29th and 30th) were being brought up west of Paris; and Panzer Brigades 106 and 109, three Volksgrenadier (VG) Divisions (553rd, 36th and 563rd), two shadow divisions and other miscellaneous detachments were moving on various dates towards the western frontier of the Reich.[38]† The intended transfer to First Army of 47th and 49th Infantry Divisions from Fifteenth

---

importance. Their loss would tear open the whole coastal front and deprive Germany of the base for the V-weapons. History showed that the loss of Paris meant the loss of all France. The sharpest measures must be taken against the first sign of insurrection, eg public execution of the ringleaders. Demolition of the Seine bridges must be prepared. Never or only as a heap of rubble must Paris fall into Allied hands.[32]

* A decrypt signalled on 19 August had disclosed that both these divisions, and 352nd Infantry Division, were being sent to First Army for rest and refit.[37]

† On 27 August MI 14 assessed the SS Grenadier Divisions as weak and low grade. The Volksgrenadier divisions were expected to be three-regiment, six-battalion LE divisions.[39] By 12 September it had been learnt from captured documents that a series of Panzer Brigades was being set up and that a brigade comprised a lorried infantry battalion, a tank battalion

---

32. DEFE/125, XL 7820 of 25 August.
33. ibid, XLs 7753 and 7793 of 24 August.
34. DEFE 3/119, XL 6260 of 15 August.
35. DEFE 3/122, XL 7236 of 20 August.
36. DEFE 3/123, XL 7479 of 22 August.
37. DEFE 3/122, XL 7122 of 19 August.
38. DEFE 3/123, XL 7261 of 21 August; DEFE 3/125, XLs 7757 of 24 August, 7802 and 7818 of 25 August.
39. WO 208/4316 of 27 August.

Army and of XLVII Panzer Corps HQ from Fifth Panzer Army was also disclosed by high-grade Sigint.[41]

On 24 August Eisenhower told Montgomery that the task of 21st Army Group was to operate north-eastwards, west of a line Amiens–Lille, to destroy the enemy's forces, seize the Pas de Calais and airfields in Belgium, get a secure base at Antwerp and, eventually, advance eastwards to the Ruhr. 12th US Army Group would be directed to thrust its left wing forward with its principal mission for the moment to support 21st Army Group to attain its objectives. It would also be told to clear up Brittany and build up strength to advance towards Metz. Montgomery issued a corresponding directive on 26 August. First Canadian Army was to secure Dieppe and Le Havre and clear the coastal belt as far as Bruges. Second Army was to secure the area Amiens–St Pol–Arras, make an armoured dash for Amiens and be prepared to advance through north-east France into Belgium. 12th US Army Group had selected First US Army to support 21st Army Group and it would advance north-east to establish itself in the general area Brussels–Maastricht–Liège–Namur–Charleroi. Montgomery's directive said nothing about Third US Army, but Bradley ordered it to advance to the line Troyes–Châlons-sur-Marne–Rheims, and to be prepared to advance rapidly to seize Rhine crossings from Mannheim to Koblenz.[42]

On 29 August Second Army's XXX Corps broke out from its bridgehead over the Seine at Vernon. Two days later Amiens was captured. Brussels was liberated on 3 September and Antwerp was taken the next day with its port almost intact. On the left of XXX Corps, XII Corps crossed the Somme at Picquigny and Longpré on 1 September and by 4 September was about 25 miles from Ghent. By then First Canadian Army had taken Dieppe and St Valéry and invested Le Havre, and its leading elements were approaching Boulogne and St Omer. On Second Army's right First US Army crossed the Somme on 1 September and on 3 September was in Tournai. Further east its right flank crossed the Aisne between Soissons and Compiègne on 1 September and liberated Laon and Rethel. It was then turned northwards through Avesnes and Maubeuge and on 3 and 4 September coralled a large number of retreating Germans in a pocket south-east of Mons. Third US Army attacking eastwards took Châlons sur Marne (29 August), Rheims and St Dizier (31 August)

---

with 11 assault guns and 33 tanks (Pzkw IV or Panthers), an engineer company, a supply company and a workshop.[40]

40. WO 171/133, No 159 of 12 September.
41. DEFE 3/123, XL 7261 of 21 August; DEFE 3/125, XL 7964 of 26 August.
42. Ellis, op cit, Vol 1, pp 462, 464, 465.

and, pressing on, had established bridgeheads across the Meuse at Verdun, St Mihiel and Commercy by 1 September when it ran out of fuel.

The speed of these spectacular advances, which outpaced all the sources of detailed tactical intelligence (high-grade Sigint, Army Y, POW interrogation and captured documents), and the disintegration of the German forces made the maintenance of an accurate enemy order of battle virtually impossible, particularly in the north-western sector. On 2 September Second Army saw no sign of any order creeping into the enemy camps and considered that identifications were meaningless.[43] 21st Army Group issued no intelligence summary between 28 August and 12 September. However, high-grade Sigint continued to provide a few valuable insights.

Decrypts signalled to the Commands on 27 August disclosed orders on 25 August to Fifth Panzer Army to withdraw the German forces to the Seine and develop the defences on the river. The armour which had escaped from the pocket was to be formed into two tactical reserve corps stationed north-east of Rouen and in the Beauvais area. Seventh Army was to withdraw the remnants of eleven divisions (84th, 89th, 263rd, 276th, 277th, 708th, 272nd, 273rd, 343rd and 326th Infantry Divisions and 5th Parachute Division) and the army troops behind the Somme to the area Flixécourt–St Quentin for rest and refit and was to employ all available manpower on building defences. The staff of II Parachute Corps was to refit at Nancy under First Parachute Army.[44] Other decrypts signalled on 31 August showed that C-in-C West had intended to hold a defence line running from Dieppe to the Marne Canal by way of Beauvais–Creil–Senlis–Soissons–Aisne–Vesle–south of Rheims–Marne. This was to be commanded from the sea to a line Arras–Flixécourt–Neufchatel by Fifteenth Army, thence by Seventh Army to the river Oise. Fifth Panzer Army with LVIII Panzer, I SS Panzer and II SS Panzer Corps and 347th Division (being brought up from Holland) was to be responsible for the Aisne sector eastwards to a junction with First Army on a line Rethel–Rheims–Melun. Fifth Panzer Army had been ordered to close the gaps in its sector by an offensive conduct of operations.[45] A decrypt signalled on 2 September covered orders by C-in-C West for 9th Panzer, 21st Panzer, Panzer Lehr, 3rd PG and 15th PG Divisions to refit in the area St Avold–Saarbrücken, 2nd Panzer and 116th Panzer

43. WO 285/3, Second Army Intelligence Summary No 90 of 2 September.
44. DEFE 3/126, XLs 8098 and 8105 of 27 August: see also DEFE 3/221, XL 9080 of 3 September.
45. DEFE 3/128, XLs 8647 and 8654 of 31 August.

Divisions to refit south of Liège and 1st, 2nd, 9th, 10th and 12th SS Panzer Divisions to refit north of Namur–St Trond.[46] A decrypt signalled the following day disclosed orders of 28 August for the despatch of all personnel of 276th, 277th, 326th, 363rd and 708th Infantry Divisions to refitting areas in the Reich and Denmark, and the disbandment of 243rd Infantry and 5th Parachute Divisions, the remnants of the latter being incorporated in 3rd Parachute Division which was to refit at Nancy.[47]

High-grade Sigint was most informative about the situation on the German left wing. A decrypt signalled on 30 August showed that 3rd PG Division was subordinated to First Army,[48] and a decrypt of 31 August that a counter-attack by both 3rd and 15th PG Divisions under XLVII Panzer Corps had been attempted the previous day in the area Bar le Duc–St Dizier.[49] Decrypts signalled on 1 September reported First Army's vain efforts on 31 August to prevent Third US Army's advance across the Meuse with XLVII Panzer and LXXX Corps, 3rd and 15th PG, 17th SS PG and elements of Panzer Lehr Divisions.[50] Orders to First Army from Army Group B to employ XLVII Panzer Corps to eliminate Allied bridgeheads over the Meuse, and to develop a defence line on the Moselle between Thionville and Nancy, using 559th and 553rd Grenadier Divisions, were also decrypted on 1 September, when First Army was told that it would be given Panzer Brigade 105 and possibly Panzer Brigade 106.[51] In messages on 2 September, decrypted the next day, First Army reported that the two Grenadier Divisions had been brought up.[52] A message from Blumentritt, C-in-C West's Chief of Staff, on 3 September, signalled by GC and CS on 5 September, drew attention to the importance of the West Wall on the German–Luxembourg, German–French frontier between Trier and Merzig. An Allied thrust towards Trier would tear open the West Wall before it was ready for defence.[53]

On First Army's left there was a gap which the German High Command hoped to plug with Army Group G, using the forces withdrawing under LXIV Corps from south-west France, and under Nineteenth Army up the Rhône valley. An exhortation from Blaskowitz on 23 August calling for the speediest possible withdrawal of Nineteenth Army in view of the situation south-east

---

46. DEFE 3/220, XL 8994 of 2 September.
47. DEFE 3/221, XL 9030 of 3 September.
48. DEFE 3/128, XL 8556 of 30 August.
49. ibid, XL 8701 of 31 August.
50. DEFE 3/220, XLs 8802 and 8809 of 1 September.
51. ibid, XLs 8810, 8874 of 1 September.
52. ibid, XL 9000 of 3 September; DEFE 3/221, XL 9023 of 3 September.
53. ibid, XL 9174 of 5 September.

of Paris was decrypted on 25 August.[54] In a message to OKW on 25 August, signalled by GC and CS on 28 August, summarising the withdrawal situation of Army Group G, Blumentritt said that C-in-C West and the Army Group were alive to the danger of the Allies reaching Dijon first, and of Nineteenth Army being outstripped and surrounded from the mountains east of the Rhône. The blocking of the Rhône valley near Lyons had to be prevented at all costs and battle groups of 198th Infantry and 11th Panzer Divisions must be despatched to Lyons as quickly as possible. Mobile elements of LXIV Corps were to be sent ahead in effective fighting strengths. Movement with improvised motor transport and horse-drawn vehicles could not compete with the speed of the fully mechanised Allies. The German workmen and the women with LXIV Corps had to be protected in constant fighting with terrorists, and the oppressive heat was imposing a great strain on people unaccustomed to marching.[55] A message from C-in-C West on 28 August, decrypted the next day, said that Army Group G's task was to hold a blocking line Dijon–Dôle–Swiss frontier west of Geneva. To assist it, besides Sicherungs units and Ost battalions in the area, 553rd Grenadier Division* was being brought up and subordinated to the Army Group, while 21st Panzer Division was being transferred to the Langres area to refit and as C-in-C West Reserve.[56]

The decrypt of an appreciation by Blaskowitz of Army Group G's situation on 1 September was signalled on 4 September. A rallying position with weak covering forces had been established running from Chaumont (on the Marne)–Châtillon-sur-Seine–Montbard–Saulieu–Autun–Châlons-sur-Sâone–Dôle–Swiss frontier. Advance elements of 16th Infantry Division had reached the rallying position and were being put in on the line Châtillon–Montbard. 159th (Reserve) Division was moving towards Vesoul, but would not arrive there before 10 September. The rest of LXIV Corps was expected to cross the Loire on 9 September. This must be expedited if possible. Nineteenth Army was making a fighting withdrawal north of Lyons. The Army Group was making every effort to collect men and material to bring Nineteenth Army up to strength on arrival in the Dijon area. Nineteenth Army had to co-ordinate its movement with those of LXIV Corps, which would be subordinated to it after arrival at Dijon. The danger point for the Army was its northern flank. The situation along the Swiss

---

* Diverted on 1 September to First Army. See above, p 375.

54. DEFE 3/125, XL 7915 of 25 August.
55. DEFE 3/126, XL 8240 of 28 August.
56. DEFE 3/127, XL 8412 of 29 August.

frontier was obscure, but was not an imminent threat. Frontal Allied pressure against Nineteenth Army could be borne.[57]

This appreciation was closely followed by the decrypt on 4 September of a message to Jodl on 2 September in which Blumentritt argued that the gap between Lunéville and Belfort could not be closed until elements of Army Group G were available. The main body of LXIV Corps would not cross the Loire before 9 September and only mobile elements would be over the Canal de Bourgogne by 8 September. The main body of Nineteenth Army would not reach Dijon before 12 September; even that depended on the development of the situation and the condition of the troops would be very doubtful. C-in-C West therefore renewed his request for the bringing up of three infantry divisions to close the gap. As the Allied forces consisted of armoured and motorised divisions plentifully supplied with tanks, the divisions brought up must be adequately equipped with anti-tank weapons. The allocation of Panzer brigades was specially desired.[58]

□

On 1 September General Eisenhower took personal command of the ground forces. The next day he allocated fuel to keep both First and Third US Armies mobile and ordered both towards the Rhine. First Army (Hodges) was to advance eastward towards Koblenz and Cologne and send one corps through the Ardennes to cover the gap between it and Third Army (Patton), which was to advance towards Mannheim and Frankfurt. On 3 September Montgomery agreed with Dempsey, Bradley and Hodges that Second Army would resume its advance on 6 September and seize the Rhine bridges between Wesel and Arnhem, airborne troops being used to capture the main bridges in advance of the ground troops (Operation *Comet*). On 4 September Eisenhower issued a directive. The northern group of armies and part of the central group (21st Army Group and First US Army) were to secure Antwerp, breach the *Siegfried* line and capture the Ruhr. The central group of armies was to capture Brest, protect the southern flank, occupy the *Siegfried* line covering the Saar and seize Frankfurt. He thus reaffirmed the 'broad front' strategy, recommended by the SHAEF planners, which he had approved on 27 May, but which had been challenged by Montgomery as the end of

---

57. DEFE 3/221, XL 9089 of 4 September.
58. ibid, XL 9104 of 4 September.

the Battle of Normandy came in sight.[59]* To the extent that intelligence influenced Eisenhower's decision, the enemy's sensitivity about his left wing, disclosed by high-grade Sigint, would have tended to support it.

Although on 3 September ANXCF alerted SHAEF and 21st Army Group to the fact that the capture of Antwerp would be of little value without the seizure of the Scheldt estuary,[60] Eisenhower's directive placed no special emphasis on this objective and, as we shall now see, it was not in the forefront of Montgomery's mind. Almost at once, however, high-grade Sigint made it abundantly clear that the Germans were attaching very great importance to the defence of the estuary, both as an escape route for Fifteenth Army on their right wing and as a means of denying the Allies the use of Antwerp. A decrypt signalled on 5 September disclosed that in the evening of 3 September Army Group B had been informed of Hitler's orders that, in view of the Allied breakthrough to Antwerp, it was of decisive importance for the conduct of future operations to hold the fortresses of Boulogne, the Calais defence area and Dunkirk, Walcheren Island with Flushing harbour, a bridgehead round Antwerp and the Albert Canal position to Maastricht.[61] Decrypts signalled earlier in the day contained orders which evidently reflected Hitler's directive. GOC Netherlands was told to leave only covering forces on the coast, except in fortresses, and prepare flank protection on the general line of the Albert Canal. Fifteenth Army was to withdraw to the general line Heyst–Namur and put in 70th Infantry Division to hold a rallying position both sides of Ghent.[62] Elements of Fifteenth Army were to break through to Louvain–Hasselt and other elements with the Army staff towards Breda via Flushing. The Albert Canal and Louvain were to be held.[63] Decrypts signalled early on 6 September gave fuller information about Hitler's directive of 3 September for the future conduct of operations. The fortresses were to be stocked up with ammunition by Fifteenth Army, and with supplies from the countryside. Their population was to be ruthlessly evacuated. First Parachute Army was subordinated to Army Group B for the defence of the Albert Canal between Brussels and Maastricht.[64]

---

* See further below, p 380.

59. Blumenson, op cit, pp 684, 686; Ellis, op cit, Vol I, pp 82, 83; Vol II (1968), pp 7, 9.
60. Ellis, op cit, Vol II, pp 5, 6.
61. DEFE 3/221, XL 9219 of 5 September.
62. ibid, XL 9162 of 5 September.
63. ibid, XL 9192 of 5 September.
64. ibid, XLs 9247 and 9248 of 6 September.

A decrypt of 6 September disclosed that the Navy had ferried a GAF division and several smaller groups across the Scheldt from Breskens and Terneuzen, and that a survey preparatory to ferrying larger army units had shown that landing points on South Beveland were intact.[65] On 7 September the decrypts included orders from Naval Commander West for the defence of Walcheren as essential for the defence of the Scheldt, together with a veto on giving up any battery south of the estuary;[66] orders to the effect that Fifteenth Army was to make a fighting withdrawal to the line Zeebrugge–Bruges–Ghent and then redistribute its forces to exploit the serviceable crossings to Flushing and South Beveland;[67] and orders that morning by Hitler to Fifteenth Army that if Antwerp could not be recaptured the harbour must be made unusable by the Allies for a long time: the mouth of the Scheldt must be barred by adequate occupation, including infantry, and by obstinate defence of the islands of Walcheren and Schouwen and the batteries south and west of Breskens.[68] A message from C-in-C West, signalled by GC and CS early on 8 September, stated that Hitler had given 'strictest instructions' for blocking the west Scheldt by all conceivable means. A bridgehead was to be formed round the batteries on the south bank and surrounded by a belt of water and bog created by ruthless inundation.[69] This was closely followed by a decrypt containing plans for minelaying on the night 8–9 September.[70]

High-grade Sigint continued to provide prompt and copious evidence about the evacuation of Fifteenth Army across the river. On 8 September, for example, naval decrypts disclosed the locations and availability of ferry services from Breskens and Terneuzen to Flushing and other points for the night 7–8 September and estimated that so far 25,000 men, 350 vehicles and 50 tons of equipment had been ferried across.[71] On 10 September it was known from decrypts that Fifteenth Army's LXXXVI Corps, commanding 59th, 70th and 712th Infantry Divisions, intended that day to hold its main defence line, running north-east from Bruges to some two miles from the western Scheldt, and to ferry forces across at Terneuzen.[72] A message signalled to the Commands on 12 September referred to ferrying

---

65. DEFE 3/222, XL 9308 of 6 September.
66. ibid, XL 9381 of 7 September.
67. ibid, XLs 9370 and 9376 of 7 September.
68. ibid, XL 9409 of 7 September.
69. ibid, XL 9440 of 8 September.
70. DEFE 3/223, XL 9502 of 8 September.
71. DEFE 3/222, XL 9466 of 8 September.
72. DEFE 3/223, XLs 9708 and 9713 of 10 September.

being impeded by Allied air activity.[73] In its intelligence summary
for 12 September 21st Army Group appreciated that Germany
had realised that the best defence of the Rhine was to impede the
supplies of the troops advancing to cross it, and that the enemy
intended 'to hold out as long as possible astride the approaches to
Antwerp, without which the installations of the port, though little
damaged, can be of no service to us'.[74]

The British Chiefs of Staff were quick to recognise the
implications of Hitler's orders of 3 September. On 7 September, at
a meeting in Quebec before the opening of the 'Octagon'
conference, they discussed the necessity of reducing the defences
of the Scheldt, but agreed that it was unnecessary to bring this
matter to the attention of SHAEF and its Commands as they must
clearly have recognised its importance.[75] Since the break-out in
Normandy, however, SHAEF and its Commands had been deep in
controversy as a result of Montgomery's demand that rather than
advance into Germany on two axes north and south of the
Ardennes, as planned, the Allies should concentrate on a single
thrust under a single command. On 4 September Montgomery
pressed his case once more in a telegram to the Supreme
Commander, calling for 'one really powerful and full-blooded
thrust' towards Berlin via the Ruhr.[76] Eisenhower stood firm on
his broad front strategy, but agreed to give Montgomery's
northern thrust temporary priority. On 12 September he placed
First Allied Airborne Army at Montgomery's disposal to help seize
a bridgehead across the Rhine at Arnhem and conceded emergency arrangements for supplying 21st Army Group (at the
expense of Third US Army).[77] On the same day, at the instigation
of the British Chiefs of Staff, who may have been influenced by
the continuing flow of Sigint about the Scheldt and disturbed at
receiving no evidence that it was having an impact on Command
plans, the Combined Chiefs decided to draw Eisenhower's
attention to the importance of neutralising the defence of the
Scheldt, preferably by air attack, 'in view of the apparent massing
of German forces on the islands guarding the port of Antwerp'.[78]
In a separate telegram to Montgomery the CIGS doubted whether
bombing would be adequate and brought up the possibility of

---

73. DEFE 3/224, XL 9907 of 12 September.
74. WO 171/132, No 159 of 12 September.
75. CAB 121/159, COS(44)875(o), pp 99–100 (COS(o) 2nd Meeting, 7
    September).
76. Ellis, op cit, Vol II, p 16.
77. ibid, pp 21–24.
78. CAB 121/159, loc cit p 130 (COS(o) 10th Meeting, 12 September), p 12
    (CCS 172nd Meeting, 12 September).

airborne operations to secure Walcheren.[79] Montgomery at once advised the CIGS that he intended to 'launch airborne operations to secure the Antwerp approaches' and Eisenhower at once reassured the Combined Chiefs that he attached importance to the early opening of Antwerp.[80]*

On 13 September Eisenhower issued a directive in which, after emphasising the fragility of the supply position, he stated that the general plan was to secure bridgeheads over the Rhine and then concentrate for a final drive into Germany. During this time the northern group of armies must secure the approaches to Antwerp or Rotterdam, so that one of these ports could provide maintenance for the drive into Germany, and the central group of armies must open up Brest.[82] On the same day he wrote to Montgomery detailing the emergency supply arrangements which he was willing to make for a limited time 'to enable you to cross the Rhine and capture the approaches to Antwerp' and, after referring to plans under discussion for opening the Scheldt estuary, concluded: 'In any event I consider that the use of Antwerp for future operations is so important . . . that I am prepared to go a long way to make the operation a success'.[83]

In his own directive, issued on 14 September, Montgomery stated that 'the real objective' was the Ruhr. He added that 'on the way to it we want the ports of Antwerp and Rotterdam'. In that part of the directive which addressed the clearing of the ports he instructed First Canadian Army to devote its 'whole energies' to Antwerp after capturing Boulogne and Calais.[84] It is recorded that he had nevertheless emphasised to General Crerar that the use of Antwerp had become 'probably' more important than Boulogne and Calais. But it is also recorded that he had concluded on 9 September after 'careful consideration' that he could advance on Berlin with the use of Dieppe, Boulogne, Dunkirk and Calais, together with 3,000 tons of cargo per day through Le Havre, and that he could reach the Münster triangle with one good Pas de Calais port, an airlift of 1,000 tons per day and additional motor transport.[85] He was later to admit that he had made 'a bad mistake'. 'I underestimated the difficulties of opening up the

---

* The CCS's final report to the President and Prime Minister, dated 16 September, referred to the necessity of opening up the north-west ports, particularly Antwerp and Rotterdam, before the bad weather set in.[81]

79. ibid, p 131 (COS(o) 11th Meeting, 12 September).
80. ibid, pp 133, 147 (COS(o) 12th and 16th Meetings, 13 and 15 September).
81. ibid, p 78 (CCS 680/2 (Oct) of 16 September).
82. Ellis, op cit, Vol II, p 25.
83. ibid, p 23.
84. ibid, pp 26, 27.
85. Stacey, *The Victory Campaign* (Ottawa 1960), pp 310, 358–359.

approaches to Antwerp. I reckoned the Canadian Army could do it *while* we were going for the Ruhr. I was wrong.[86]

□

Montgomery's directive for the advance to Arnhem (Operation *Market Garden*) was issued on 14 September. 101st US Airborne Division was to seize bridges at Eindhoven, Zon and Veghel. 82nd US Airborne Division was to take the bridges at Grave and Nijmegen. 1st British Airborne Division was to take the bridge at Arnhem. XXX Corps was to advance from its bridgehead over the Meuse–Escaut Canal, which it had established on 10 September, to link up with the airborne divisions and establish a bridgehead at Arnhem, 65 miles from its starting point, by D+3 or D+4.[87] These were ambitious plans, the more so as it had become apparent while they were being drawn up that the Germans were no longer retreating in this sector, and were making efforts to stabilise a front.

An order from Hitler was decrypted on 6 September subordinating First Parachute Army, hitherto a training command, to Army Group B and making it responsible under General Student for the defence of the Albert Canal between Brussels and Maastricht. It was to command all Parachute Army formations from the Reich, including 3rd, 5th and 6th Parachute Divisions which were to be brought up to strength by 1st GAF Training Division; LXXXVIII Corps with 719th and 344th Infantry Divisions; battle groups from the Netherlands formed from SS training units and Training Regiment Göring; and ten Flak battalions equipped with heavy anti-tank guns and short-range weapons.[88] Subsequent decrypts gave details of the deployment of some of these formations.[89] By 9 September Second Army had identified on the Albert Canal elements of 136th, 119th, 347th and 176th Infantry Divisions, two companies of Parachute Regiment 2, GAF Regiments 51 and 53 and Parachute Regiment 6, and had noted that strong resistance was preventing its enlargement of the bridgeheads over the Canal.[90] It was known that some of these formations were among those that had

---

86. Ellis, op cit, Vol II, p 95.
87. Ellis, op cit, Vol II, p 29; CAB 44/254, *Operation "Market Garden" and the Action at Arnhem*, p 63; CAB 106/972, I Airborne Corps's Report on Allied Operations in Holland September–October 1944, para 10.
88. DEFE 3/221, XLs 9247 and 9248 of 6 September.
89. eg DEFE 3/223, XL 9599 of 9 September; DEFE 3/225, HPs 38 and 180 of 13 and 14 September; DEFE 3/226, HP 294 of 16 September.
90. WO 285/3, Nos 96 and 97 of 8 and 9 September.

withdrawn across the Scheldt.[91] South of the Scheldt the Germans were still putting up strong resistance. But the decrypts showed that the withdrawal of Fifteenth Army was steadily continuing.[92] On 17 September MI 14, in the light of evidence from reconnaissance and decrypts, calculated that 70,000 men had been ferried across by that morning.[93]

It was no doubt in the light of these developments that, as General Dempsey noted in his diary on 10 September, the decision was taken to expand the earlier plan for an airborne operation (Operation *Comet*) by raising the number of airborne divisions to three 'because of increasing German strength . . . in the Arnhem–Nijmegen area'.[94] It must be assumed, moreover, that this decision took some account of the knowledge at the high level of command that high-grade Sigint had referred to the presence in Holland of Panzer divisions. A decrypt signalled by GC and CS on 5 September had reported that those elements of 2nd and 116th Panzer Divisions and 9th and 10th SS Panzer Divisions that were not still operating were to rest and refit in the area Venlo–Arnhem–s'Hertogenbosch.[95] A decrypt of 6 September had disclosed that II SS Panzer Corps was to be subordinated to Army Group B and to move to Eindhoven to supervise the refit of 2nd and 116th Panzer, 9th SS Panzer and Heavy Assault Gun Abteilung 217.[96]*

By 12 September, however, 2nd and 116th Panzer Divisions had been identified on Seventh Army's front;[98] and 21st Army Group's intelligence summary of that date was clearly not disposed to regard 9th and 10th SS Panzer Divisions, which had not reappeared in the decrypts and had not been located, as constituting a threat that called for further revision of the *Market Garden* plans. It noted that what was left of them was no longer in the line and might have found its way into Holland, but did not

---

* Low-grade was limited at this stage. Its only contribution as to what opposition might be met was DF bearings on a call-sign suspected of belonging to 10th SS Panzer Division.[97]

91. WO 171/132, No 159 of 12 September.
92. DEFE 3/222, XL 9466 of 8 September; DEFE 3/223, XL 9502 of 8 September; DEFE 3/225, HPs 189 and 228 of 14 September; DEFE 3/226, HPs 316, 362 of 16 September; Naval Headlines 1162, 1163, 1164 of 8–10 September, 1169 of 15 September, 1171 of 17 September; WO 208/4316 of 10 September.
93. WO 208/4316 of 17 September; DEFE 3/226, HP 491 of 18 September.
94. WO 285/9, Entry for 10 September.
95. DEFE 3/221, XL 9188 of 5 September.
96. ibid, XL 9245 of 6 September.
97. *History of Sigint in the Field*, p 196.
98. WO 171/132, No 159 of 12 September.

believe that much of them was left.[99] Second Army had used the Sigint references to the refit of Panzer formations in its summary of 6 September, attributing them to POW, but had dismissed them as 'wishful thinking'. 'There can either be rest and refit or defence of the West Wall and Holland. There cannot be both.'[100]* Its summary of 13 September reported that elements of 9th and 10th SS Panzer had been 'seen in small pockets', but thought they were in no condition to operate as a division.[101] Presumably from Second Army – they were not themselves Ultra recipients – I Airborne Corps and XXX Corps had learned that 'one broken Panzer Division' had been sent to the Arnhem area for refit and that the presence of II SS Panzer Corps was suspected.[102] But XXX Corps's G2 subsequently recalled that as the planning of *Market Garden* progressed the feeling grew that either the evidence for the presence of the division was weak or that the division was not fit for action.[103]

In the few days before the operation was launched, on 17 September, this feeling was challenged in some quarters. The US Army archives record that on 16 September Eisenhower's Chief of Staff visited 21st Army Group to convey a warning based on recent indications that there was German armour in the *Market Garden* area, and that the warning was not taken seriously.[104] As recorded in SHAEF's intelligence summary of 16 September, these indications were to the effect that '9 SS Panzer Division, and with it presumably 10, has been reported as withdrawing altogether to the Arnhem area of Holland to be equipped with new tanks from Cleves'.[105] According to one post-war account, this intelligence had been received by 14 September from the Dutch Resistance, which had located 9th SS Panzer between Arnhem and Apeldoorn; it had also reported that Field Marshal Model was at an HQ at Oosterbeek, four miles from Arnhem.[106] According to the same account the G2 of I Airborne Corps claimed that he received similar information from the Dutch Resistance via Second Army and Dutch liaison officers at the Corps's HQ, and was sufficiently anxious by 12 September to request air reconnaissance of the Arnhem area; taking place on 15 September, this

---

* Perhaps this meant that they would have no time to rest or would have to rest further to the rear.

99. ibid.
100. WO 285/3, No 94 of 6 September.
101. WO 285/4, No 101 of 13 September.
102. CAB 44/254, p 65.
103. ibid, p 30.
104. MacDonald, *The Siegfried Line Campaign* (Washington DC, 1963), p 122.
105. WO 219/1924, No 26 of 16 September.
106. Ryan, *A Bridge Too Far* (1974) pp 99; 107–109, 111.

convinced him of the presence of German armour, but it did not impress the Corps Commander.[107]

With regard to this account it may be noted that Sigint had pointed to the presence of an Army Group B HQ at Oosterbeek on 15 September; a decrypt despatched to SHAEF, 21st Army Group and Second Army on that day disclosed that the Flivo attached to Army Group B had arrived there the previous day.[108] There is a discrepancy between the account and the Air Ministry's post-war narrative which records that there was no reconnaissance of Arnhem on 15 September, when the weather was bad. But it adds that in sorties on 12 and 16 September, employing only eight aircraft in all, nothing significant was detected, and observes that 'a greater effort should surely have been made'.[109] The fact that the PR effort was so limited provides further testimony to the euphoria with which 21st Army Group and I Airborne Corps, as briefed by Second Army, responded to the interventions from SHAEF and I Airborne Corps's G2. They clearly felt that the warnings added nothing to their existing intelligence and called for no revision of their latest estimate of the strength of the German opposition.*

This estimate was given in the Instructions for Operation *Market Garden* drawn up by I Airborne Corps on 13 September. The instructions reflected Second Army appreciations of 11 and 12 September. On 11 September Second Army reported that the enemy had contrived to put into action a large number of men who had at times fought very tenaciously; on 12 September it noted the incompetence of the resistance, the troops being untrained, but emphasised its 'fanatical spirit'; 'we are up against a different type of opponent who is fighting hard because he wants to'.[111] I Airborne Corps instructions read:

'The enemy is fighting determinedly along the general lines of Albert and Escaut canals from inclusive Antwerp to inclusive Maastricht. His line is held by the remnants of some good divisions, including Parachute divisions, and by new arrivals from Holland. They are fighting well but have very few reserves. The total armoured strength is probably not more than 50–100 tanks, mostly Mark IV. There is every sign of the enemy strengthening the defences of the river and canal lines through Arnhem

---

* XXX Corps Commander later claimed that he had no idea that 9th and 10th SS Panzer Divisions were in the area; he added that XXX Corps would have defeated them easily, but they were too heavily armed for the lightly equipped airborne troops.[110]

107. ibid, pp 85–87, 109–110.
108. DEFE 3/225, HP 220 of 15 September.
109. AIR 41/67, *The Liberation of North-West Europe*, Vol IV, p 147.
110. Horrocks, *Corps Commander* (1977), p 100.
111. WO 285/3, Nos 99 and 100 of 11 and 12 September.

and Nijmegen, especially with Flak, but the troops manning them are not numerous and many are of low categories . . .'[112]*

To this may be added extracts from I Airborne Corps's subsequent report:

'It was considered that once the crust of resistance had been broken, the German Army would be unable to concentrate any other troops in sufficient strength to stop the break-through. It was not expected that any outside force larger than a brigade group, with very few tanks and guns, could be concentrated against the airborne troops before relief by the ground forces . . . Thus the general picture, before the operations started, was that the flight and landings would be hazardous, that the capture intact of the bridge objectives was more a matter of surprise and confusion than hard fighting, that the advance of the ground forces would be very swift if the airborne operations were successful, and that in these circumstances the considerable dispersion of the airborne forces was acceptable . . .'[114]

It was known from Sigint that the Germans appreciated that the Allies probably intended a thrust to Arnhem and might carry out airborne landings. Decrypts signalled to the Commands on 13 September disclosed that on 10 September Luftflotte 3 had intended reconnaissance to find out whether the Allies were preparing a thrust to Aachen or a thrust against First Parachute Army and Arnhem, and that on 13 September its orders included reconnaissance to establish whether there were gliders in the area of The Wash.[115] On 14 September the decrypt of an assessment issued on 11 September drew attention to Abwehr reports of arms-drops in the Apeldoorn–Zwolle areas and mentioned the danger of landings.[116] The decrypt of an assessment of 9 September, signalled on 15 September, believed that the probable intention of Second Army's XXX Corps was to thrust to Arnhem and that there might be an operation west of Nijmegen and Wesel to surround German forces in western Holland.[117]

The airborne landings on 17 September nevertheless achieved tactical surprise;[118] in a report of 1 October, decrypted on 4

---

* XXX Corps's final orders of 16 September noted that the German front was held by 'mostly airborne formations under General Student'. They added: 'additional troops arriving from Germany, every day, mostly consisting of young paratroopers, highly indoctrinated, therefore very brave, while the NCOs are the best and most experienced in the German Army'.[113]

112. CAB 106/972, Operation Instruction No 1, para 1.
113. Horrocks, op cit, p 98.
114. CAB 106/972, paras 9, 22, 25.
115. DEFE 3/224, XL 9986 of 13 September; DEFE 3/227, HP 9 of 13 September.
116. DEFE 3/225, HP 175 of 14 September.
117. ibid, HP 242 of 15 September.
118. MacDonald, op cit, pp 135–136; Stacey, op cit, p 314; Ryan, op cit, p 107 fn.

October, von Rundstedt attributed this to the fact that the preparatory bombing did not appreciably exceed the normal level of Allied air activity, and that, in particular, the attacks on the Flak near Arnhem were thought to be aimed at the destruction of the bridges.[119] The US airborne divisions thus obtained early successes, 101st taking Zon and Veghel on 17 September and Eindhoven the following day and 82nd taking the Grave bridge, a bridge on the Maas–Waal Canal and important high ground in the Nijmegen area.[120] As luck would have it, however, at the time of the landings Model was at the Oosterbeek HQ, in a position to organise the prompt resistance which frustrated 1st British Airborne Division at Arnhem and delayed the Allied advance further south.*

The forces at Model's disposal were four divisional battle groups of First Parachute Army on the Meuse–Escaut Canal, Fifteenth Army's 59th Infantry Division, which was already in transit in First Parachute Army's sector, and 9th and 10th SS Panzer Divisions. 9th SS Panzer mustered one company of Panthers, an armoured infantry regiment, an artillery battalion, two assault gun batteries and its reconnaissance battalion. 10th SS Panzer probably had an amoured infantry regiment, two artillery battalions and a reconnaissance battalion.[122] At the news of the landings 9th SS Panzer was ordered to reconnoitre towards Arnhem and Nijmegen, to occupy Arnhem and the bridge and defeat the Allied troops west of the town, and 10th SS Panzer, some of which had begun to move towards Germany, was ordered to re-group and march on Nijmegen. Later in the afternoon II SS Panzer Corps sent a battalion of 9th SS Panzer Division to the south across the Arnhem bridge before 1st Airborne Division had taken it. 10th SS Panzer, arriving later, had to cross by ferry; but it arrived at Nijmegen in time to stop the first US attempt to take the bridge there.[123] At the same time Model ordered Student, reinforced by 59th Infantry Division from Fifteenth Army and Panzer Brigade 107, which had

---

* The claim that the *Market Garden* plan had been betrayed on 15 September by a member of the Dutch Resistance, and that his treachery accounted for the presence of the two SS Panzer Divisions near Arnhem, was refuted by US and Canadian official histories and a Dutch Parliamentary Commission of Inquiry on the grounds that these divisions had already been moved into the area; and Student denied that he received any such warning. The Dutch official history of the Resistance subsequently concluded that a member of the Resistance warned the Abwehr in Holland on 15 September that an airborne operation was imminent, but that he was disbelieved.[121]

119. DEFE 3/233, HP 2188 of 4 October.
120. Ellis, op cit, Vol II, p 34. For an extended account of the US operations see MacDonald, op cit, p 143 et seq.
121. MacDonald, op cit, p 136 fn 57; Stacey, op cit, p 313 fn*; Ryan, op cit, p 107 fn; Letters to *The Times* 18 December 1980 and 10 January 1981.
122. MacDonald, op cit, p 143.
123. ibid, pp 142–143, 164.

been en route to Aachen, to contain the Allied ground offensive
from the Meuse–Escaut Canal and destroy the airborne force at
Eindhoven; sent 406th Landesschützen Division and other
makeshift troops (Corps Feldt) from Wehrkreis VI to hold the
high ground at Nijmegen and help to hold the bridges; and
ordered a hastily assembled collection of defence and training
battalions (Division von Tettau) to attack from the north and
north-west against Arnhem, where 16th SS PG Training and
Research Battalion was also available.[124]*

XXX Corps, which did not reach Veghel till 19 September,
joined 101st Airborne Division in routing 59th Infantry at Best on
that day. Its efforts to take the Nijmegen bridge in conjunction
with 82nd Airborne did not succeed, however, until 20 September.
Its medium artillery was supporting 1st Airborne Division at
Arnhem from 21 September, but its efforts to reach Arnhem in
strength were then held up by the attack from Panzer Brigade 107
towards Zon and a concerted drive by Panzer Brigade 107 and
59th Infantry Division to cut the road north of Veghel. These
counter-attacks were spent by 23 September, with heavy losses to
the Panzer Brigade; but II Parachute Corps had meanwhile
contained the Americans at Nijmegen and II SS Panzer Corps had
stepped up its operations at Arnhem. At Arnhem, moreover, the
plan to reinforce 1st Airborne by the Polish Parachute Brigade
had gone awry. The Brigade's drop had been reduced by bad
weather and had had to be made south of the Rhine at Driel. Some
of the Brigade managed to cross the river on 23 September and
troops from XXX Corps's 43rd Infantry Division crossed on 24
September. But it was clear by then that there was no prospect of
consolidating a bridgehead. The evacuation of 1st Airborne
Division was ordered on 25 September and took place that
night.[126]

Once the operation had begun the Allied forces received no
great advantage from intelligence. The information that Germany
was bringing in further reinforcements was obtained from
high-grade Sigint on 21 September; a decrypt then disclosed that

---

* There are conflicting opinions as to whether a copy of the *Market Garden* operational
plan, which had been captured from one of the US Airborne Divisions, had reached Model
when he gave these orders. The official US history believes his orders were based on the
document. Other accounts argue either that it had not reached him or that he thought it was
a plant.[125]

124. ibid, p 142; Ellis, op cit, Vol II, p 45.
125. MacDonald, op cit, pp 141, 142; Ellis, op cit, Vol II, pp 45, 46; Ryan, op cit,
       pp 191, 214–215.
126. Ellis, op cit, Vol II, pp 26–45; MacDonald, op cit, pp 153, 182, 188–192,
       197; Horrocks, op cit, p 111; CAB 44/254, p 60.

on the previous day Hitler had ordered the transfer of XII SS Corps from the eastern front to Army Group B, where it was to command 180th and 190th Infantry Divisions, brought in from the Reich.[127] Another message bearing on the enemy's response to the offensive was issued by OKW on 19 September, but was not decrypted till 24 September. It stated that as the situation in Holland demanded the employment of all available forces, Hitler had ordered the immediate formation of battle groups from elements east of the Rhine belonging to 1st, 2nd, 9th and 12th SS Panzer Divisions.[128] These decrypts apart, high-grade Sigint yielded only tactical intelligence and the decrypts, which were obtained too late to be put to operational use, added little to the information that had already been obtained from Army Y and POW. These sources, together with the Dutch Resistance, provided a fair amount of intelligence in some sectors; it appears to have given advance notice of the German counter-attack on XXX Corps at Veghel.*

On 26 September GC and CS signalled orders of the previous day in which Model reorganised his Command. All forces to the west of the Allied corridor were placed under GOC Fifteenth Army. East of the corridor First Parachute Army was to assume command of II SS Panzer Corps, II Parachute Corps, LXXXVI Corps, Corps Feldt† and XII SS Corps.[129]

□

With the failure to establish a bridgehead at Arnhem the Allied hopes that Germany might be defeated before the winter set in were finally dispelled, for First US Army had already been checked at Aachen and in the Ardennes and Third US Army at Metz.

Eisenhower's plan of manoeuvre was that while the northern group of armies seized the bridgehead at Arnhem, Third US Army would carry out a limited advance to seize bridgeheads over the Moselle, to prevent the enemy from transferring troops to the north, and First US Army would capture Bonn and Cologne, establish a deep bridgehead over the Rhine and then advance eastward round the south face of the Ruhr.[130]

---

* See Appendix 23.
† For the identification of Corps Feldt by Y and POW see Appendix 23.

127. DEFE 3/228, HP 752 of 21 September.
128. DEFE 3/229, HP 1017 of 24 September.
129. ibid, HP 1221 of 26 September.
130. Ellis, op cit, Vol II, p 26, 27.

First Army began its attack on the *Siegfried* line on 12
September. On its right wing V US Corps made breaches towards
Bitburg and north of Prüm but both penetrations had been
blocked by 17 September. VII US Corps attacked south-east of
Aachen, achieving some success initially, but German reinforcements arrived and on 18 September the Corps was ordered to
consolidate. On First Army's left wing XIX Corps was to attack the
line north of Aachen; it took Maastricht on 14 September and by
18 September had reached Sittard and was threatening Geilenkirchen, but its advance was then postponed by unfavourable
weather, shortage of ammunition, the arrival of enemy reinforcements and anxiety about a gap that was developing between First
Army's left wing and Second Army. On 22 September the attack
was postponed indefinitely.[131] Third US Army had meanwhile
continued to press hard on the Moselle, but had made little
progress; German resistance, sustained by armoured and infantry
reinforcements, had proved very stubborn.[132]

The fact was that, by the time the US armies renewed their
advance, the enemy's defence was consolidating under von
Rundstedt who had been reinstated as C-in-C West on 6
September. On his left wing the fighting elements of Nineteenth
Army and LXIV Corps had escaped encirclement in the south and
passed Dijon, Army Groups B and G had managed to join up, and
the German armies were fighting along the whole front with
renewed resolution in a recovery which the Germans were later to
call the 'Miracle of the West'.

To the east of Fifteenth Army (Channel ports and Walcheren)
and First Parachute Army (Albert Canal) the line was held from
right to left by Seventh Army (Maastricht to Libramont, north-east
of Sedan), First Army (Libramont to exclusive Lunéville),
Nineteenth Army (Lunéville to the Swiss border south of
Belfort).[133] On 12 September, the day First US Army began the
attack on the *Siegfried* line, a decrypt showed that an order of 8
September had been signed by von Rundstedt as C-in-C West; the
order was to the effect that the Allies were in no circumstances to
be allowed to pass through the west position and the West Wall.[134]
A naval situation report decrypted on 13 September claimed that
some 150,000 men were at work on the western fortifications.[135]
On 12 September 21st Army Group's intelligence summary noted
the weakness of Seventh Army's front from Aachen to Luxem-

---

131. MacDonald, op cit, Chapters IV, VI and p 250.
132. Blumenson, op cit, p 700; Ellis, op cit, Vol II, pp 74, 75.
133. WO 208/4316 of 10 September.
134. DEFE 3/224, XL 9943 of 12 September.
135. DEFE 3/225, HP 20 of 13 September.

bourg, where (except that Panzer Brigade 105 had been sent there) only battered divisions had been identified, as compared with the Moselle front, where more substantial forces faced Third US Army.[136] On 15 September a decrypt disclosed that Seventh Army had received an important reinforcement in the Aachen area: Hitler had ordered 12th Infantry Division to be brought up by battle groups beginning on 13 September, with the Assault Gun Abteilung in the first battle group.[137] On 16 September SHAEF's intelligence summary reported that Seventh Army had been reinforced in the Aachen area and had delayed Allied progress considerably, and this despite the fact that the enemy had given highest priority to the area between Nancy and Metz: the fighting there had been very heavy and several new formations had been identified.[138]

Decrypts had revealed that the enemy was attaching special importance to his left wing. One reported that on Hitler's orders Panzer brigades were to be allotted to Army Group G rather than to First Parachute Army; another disclosed the telegram in which the Japanese Ambassador reported that Hitler was concentrating troops in the Nancy area for attacks on the American columns, which did not form a continuous front.[139] A directive on 9 September, decrypted on 12 September, from Army Group G (which had now taken command of First Army) described its sector as the key part of the western front.[140] A decrypt of 6 September had disclosed that Fifth Panzer Army and LVIII Panzer Corps were being withdrawn to Koblenz for refit, Seventh Army taking over their sector.[141] On 13 September orders issued by Army Group G on the previous day were decrypted; they subordinated XLVII Panzer Corps, LVIII Panzer Corps, 21st Panzer Division and Panzer Brigades 111, 112 and 113 to Fifth Panzer Army, which was to entrust XLVII Panzer Corps with mobile operations in the Nancy–Chaumont–Langres–Remiremont area in co-operation with Nineteenth Army.[142] In the next few days several decrypts reported on German counter-attacks south of Epinal.[143] A situation report by First Army on 16 September, signalled the next day, referred to heavy Allied forces

---

136. WO 171/132, No 159 of 12 September.
137. DEFE 3/225, HP 236 of 15 September.
138. WO 219/1924, No 26 of 16 September.
139. DEFE 3/221, XL 9247 of 6 September; BAY/XL 151 of 11 September.
140. DEFE 3/223, XL 9582 of 9 September; DEFE 3/224, XL 9884 of 12 September.
141. DEFE 3/221, XLs 9245, 9249 of 6 September.
142. DEFE 3/225, HP 15 of 13 September.
143. ibid, HPs 32 of 13 September, 225 and 237 of 15 September; DEFE 3/226, HPs 293 of 16 September, 384 of 17 September.

in the Nancy area and to German counter-attacks on the Pont à Mousson bridgehead and in the Bitburg area.[144]

☐

The German recovery was quickly reflected in the decrypts of telegrams from the Japanese embassy in Berlin. On 11 September one had shown that the representative of the Japanese Ministry of the Interior believed that it was only a matter of time before Germany collapsed and that the war might be over before the end of the year.[145] But early in October others disclosed that the same authority no longer saw any signs of internal collapse and that the Ambassador believed that because the lull in the fighting had strengthened the will to fight to the end, 'the progress [of the Allies] would not be so simple', and that the war would carry over 'till next year'.[146] A change of tone had by then been registered by the Allied intelligence summaries. SHAEF had remained optimistic on 16 September: 'the enemy is momentarily fighting better on his own soil. How long this rejuvenation . . . in the West is likely to last is difficult to say. Probably only . . . as long as the Siegfried Line [is not] . . . breached in force . . .'[147] On 27 September, however, 21st Army Group admitted that 'with the Allies still adjusting their maintenance . . . the enemy has gained a respite of which he has taken fuller advantage than it was supposed he might manage',[148] and on 30 September SHAEF agreed that the Germans had fared better than might have been expected.[149] On 27 September, in its regular review of the effects of the bombing offensive, which found no evidence that the bombing was producing a collapse of civilian morale, the JIC noted that morale was rallying in the Army as the fighting approached the frontiers of the Reich.[150] Nor was it long before Sigint disclosed that the enemy planned a sizeable counter-attack on the Allied salient at Nijmegen.

During the battle of Arnhem, and for a few days afterwards, the Germans had made strenuous efforts to pinch off the salient at Nijmegen by cutting its supply line. When these failed Allied intelligence had thought that the enemy would stand on the defensive with the aim of preventing exploitation by the Allies north of the Waal and the extension of their bridgehead eastwards

---

144. DEFE 3/226, HP 397 of 17 September.
145. BAY/XL 155 of 11 September.
146. BAY/HPs 34 and 35 of 4 October, 42 of 7 October, 44 of 10 October.
147. WO 219/1924, No 26 of 16 September.
148. WO 171/133, No 162 of 27 September.
149. WO 219/1924, No 28 of 30 September.
150. CAB 121/419, JIC(44)417(0) of 27 September.

across the Meuse in the Venlo area.[151] However, it became clear from decrypts of 28 and 29 September that a serious offensive was in the offing. A message from Army Group B on 28 September requested a bombing operation on Nijmegen town and roads to it during the night 28–29 September.[152] A decrypt signalled to the Commands at 1052 on 29 September disclosed that Army Group B's Chief Quartermaster urgently required additional ammunition and fuel for offensive operations involving numerous motorised troops, including two Panzer divisions.[153] Decrypts signalled in the evening disclosed that at 0800 on 29 September Army Group B had asked for attacks by strong bomber forces against Nijmegen on the nights 29–30 September and 30 September–1 October, and had suggested that as the attack was on Hitler's orders it might be possible to bring in Fliegerkorps IX.[154]* Meanwhile Army Y had obtained indications that elements of 116th Panzer Division were south-east of Emmerich, and further evidence that the Division was in the vicinity was provided by the same source on 30 September.[155] On 1 October attacks were made in some strength on the bridgehead north of the Waal and it was established from prisoners and Army Y that, along with elements of 116th Panzer and 10th SS Panzer Divisions, units of 9th Panzer had taken part and that 9th SS Panzer had been close at hand.[156] Both 116th Panzer and 9th Panzer Divisions had come from south of Aachen. On 2 October elements of 1st SS Panzer Division and Panzer Brigade 108 were identified in an attack from the Reichswald against the eastern flanks of the salient.[157] On 3 October a decrypt disclosed that by 1 October new reporting centres had been established in the sector of First Parachute Army for Panzer Brigades 107 and 108, 9th Panzer Division (with Panzer Brigade 105) and 116th Panzer Division.[158] During the next few days enemy pressure was directed against the western flank of the salient by the newly arrived 363rd VG Division.

On 8 October 21st Army Group appreciated that although there were all the signs of a serious counter-attack from the enemy's bridgehead at Arnhem by II SS Panzer Corps, which controlled 116th and 9th Panzer Divisions, Panzer Brigade 105 and 9th and

---

* For the KdK's attempted attacks at Nijmegen see below, p 460.

151. WO 285/4, No 114 of 26 September; WO 171/133, No 162 of 27 September.
152. DEFE 3/230, HP 1484 of 28 September.
153. DEFE 3/231, HP 1559 of 29 September.
154. ibid, HPs 1637 and 1639 of 29 September.
155. WO 285/4, Nos 117 and 118 of 29 and 30 September.
156. ibid, Nos 119 and 120 of 1 and 2 October.
157. ibid, No 121 of 3 October.
158. DEFE 3/233, HP 2082 of 3 October.

10th SS Panzer Divisions, it looked as though the ineffectual attacks which had been broken up by the Allied artillery and air forces represented the enemy's best efforts.[159] This appreciation proved to be correct. It was not long before Allied intelligence had evidence that First US Army's offensive towards Aachen, which had been renewed at the beginning of October, was drawing the German armour to the Aachen sector. A decrypt of 9 October revealed that I SS Panzer Corps HQ was moving to Jülich the next day.[160] Second Army reported on 10 October that Panzer Brigade 108 had moved from the Reichswald to Aachen and on 11 October that there was evidence from Army Y that 116th Panzer Division, which had not been identified on Second Army's front for three days, had almost certainly gone the same way.[161] A decrypt of 12 October disclosed that on the previous day C-in-C West had subordinated I SS Panzer Corps, with 3rd PG and 116th Panzer Divisions, to Army Group B, which was to try to put the divisions into battle as a unit, but had stipulated that I SS Panzer Corps was to be released to Sixth Panzer Army by 20 October at the latest.[162]* Later on 12 October high-grade Sigint reported that I SS Panzer Corps had taken over its new sector, north-east from Aachen, by 0800 that morning, with 116th Panzer, 3rd PG, 183rd and 49th Infantry Divisions under command.[163] Elements of 1st SS Panzer Division were also encountered in the Aachen sector on 12 October.[164]

These reinforcements failed to prevent the capture of Aachen, which was virtually surrounded by 16 October and taken on 21 October. But they were sufficient to bring First US Army's offensive to a halt after the capture of Aachen. On the Moselle Third US Army had meanwhile fought a hard and ultimately unsuccessful battle for Metz.[165]

□

In these operations the Allies were increasingly handicapped by the fact that their supply position was deteriorating. Boulogne, the first port to fall in the Pas de Calais, had been taken on 23 September, and Calais, Le Havre and Brest were captured by the

---

* For the formation of Sixth Panzer Army see below, pp 403, 405–406.

159. WO 171/133, No 163 of 8 October.
160. DEFE 3/236, HP 2815 of 9 October.
161. WO 285/4, Nos 128 and 129 of 10 and 11 October.
162. DEFE 3/237, HP 3102 of 12 October.
163. ibid, HP 3123 of 12 October.
164. WO 285/4, No 130 of 12 October.
165. Ellis, op cit, Vol II, pp 160–162.

end of the month. But the possibility that the Scheldt would soon be cleared had quite disappeared. A naval decrypt of 24 September had disclosed that the evacuation of Fifteenth Army was nearly complete: 82,000 men, 530 guns, 4,600 vehicles, 4,000 horses and much valuable equipment had been ferried over.[166] First Canadian Army had by then cleared all the country south of the estuary except the Breskens pocket behind the Leopold Canal. But in the Breskens pocket, as in Walcheren, German garrisons were firmly dug in, and east of Antwerp the Canadians were held up at the Antwerp–Turnhout Canal by three divisions, two of them from among those that had crossed the Scheldt.[167] Sigint had disclosed on 20 September that Breskens had been declared a fortress on Hitler's orders; on 25 September it had referred to Fortress Walcheren.[168] 21st Army Group had recognised on 23 September that the Germans had no intention of withdrawing from these positions.[169]

On 22 September Eisenhower had insisted that priority should be given to operations for freeing the approaches to Antwerp, its use being indispensable for the drive into Germany; and on 29 September he informed the Combined Chiefs that he had ordered 21st Army Group to make a major effort to reduce Walcheren and South Beveland as a matter of urgency. But Montgomery was then facing German attacks on Nijmegen and hoping to destroy the German bridgehead west of the Maas as a preliminary to a thrust to the Rhine. On 25 September he ordered First Canadian Army to continue its operations to secure Boulogne, Calais and Antwerp while Second Army attacked with all available strength from the Nijmegen area against the north-west corner of the Ruhr and took any opportunity to seize a Rhine bridgehead. It was not till the effort to clear the enemy from the west bank of the Maas had been frustrated that in the middle of October, following a conference at SHAEF on 4 October at which his argument that he could take the Ruhr without the use of Antwerp was vigorously disputed, he gave absolute priority to the clearance of the Scheldt by ordering Second Army to employ all its offensive power in a westward drive to assist First Canadian Army.[170]

---

166. DEFE 3/229, HP 1019 of 24 September; WO 208/4316 of 24 September.
167. Ehrman, op cit, Vol VI, p 31; Ellis, op cit, Vol II, pp 69–70; Stacey, op cit, p 366.
168. DEFE 3/227, HP 723 of 20 September; DEFE 3/229, HP 1137 of 25 September; Naval Headlines 1175 of 21 September; WO 208/4316 of 24 September.
169. WO 171/133, No 161 of 23 September.
170. Stacey, op cit, pp 317, 319, 379, 387, 389; Ellis, op cit, Vol II, pp 78–81, 83–85, 94; Ehrman, op cit, Vol V, pp 528–529; Vol VI, pp 30–31; Roskill, *The War at Sea*, Vol III Part 2 (1961), pp 145–146.

It can have caused no surprise that First Canadian Army had meanwhile encountered stiff resistance before reaching the approaches to South Beveland on 10 October. Orders from Jodl and GOC Fifteenth Army of 3 and 7 October, insisting that the defence of the approaches to Antwerp were decisive for the further conduct of the war,[171] were not decrypted, but as MI 14 noted on 8 October there was no doubt that the enemy would hold out to the bitter end.[172] Not until the end of October, moreover, after further hard fighting which drew in Fifteenth Army's last reserves and included a German spoiling attack on Second Army's flank in the Venlo area from 27 October, were the Breskens pocket and South Beveland finally cleared. And not until 8 November, after British Army and Royal Marine commandos had assaulted Walcheren on 1 November and taken Flushing on 4 November, was all resistance brought to an end. Allied mine-sweeping in the Scheldt had begun by then, but it was not till 28 November that the first convoy entered Antwerp, 84 days after the capture of the city.[173]

In the course of these operations high-grade Sigint provided a good deal of detailed intelligence. Much of it related to the measures the Germans took to mine the Scheldt and to foul its harbours before giving them up to Allied attack. But the decrypts also covered the composition and the state of the forces defending the estuary. By 27 September 21st Army Group knew that only two divisions were involved, 64th Infantry in the Breskens pocket and 70th Infantry at Flushing, and that even scantier forces held North and South Beveland.[174] By 8 October decrypts had disclosed that only one regiment of 70th Infantry remained on Walcheren, the other two having been withdrawn to strengthen the line north of Antwerp.[175] On 2 October a naval decrypt questioned whether Walcheren was tenable as a fortress in view of the Army withdrawals; instead of the three divisions with Flak that had been promised, it was held by only one and a half divisions without Flak.[176] A decrypt of 13 October revealed that 64th Infantry had been classified as a limited offensive division on 1 October.[177] On 31 October, in the decrypt of a message dated 17 October, 64th Infantry was stated to be now capable only of limited defence and 70th Infantry was classified as fully

---

171. Stacey, op cit, pp 381, 387, Ellis, op cit, Vol II, p 101 fn.
172. WO 208/4317, MI 14 Weekly Summary for the CIGS, 8 October.
173. Stacey, op cit, pp 369–385; Ellis, op cit, Vol II, pp 100 et seq, 141, 159; Roskill, op cit, Vol III Part 2, p 147 et seq.
174. WO 171/133, No 162 of 27 September.
175. DEFE 3/231, HP 1743 of 30 September; WO 171/133, No 163 of 8 October.
176. DEFE 3/232, HP 1913 of 2 October; WO 208/4317 of 8 October.
177. DEFE 3/237, HP 3171 of 13 October.

defensive.[178] Decrypts during the second half of October showed that 64th Infantry was being supplied by convoys of KdK craft running from Flushing to the Cadzand area.[179] They also showed that the attempt to evacuate the remains of the division through Cadzand were frustrated by the speed of the final Canadian advance.[180]

The German spoiling attack in the Venlo sector on 27 October fell on 7th US Armoured Division, which was temporarily under command of Second Army's VIII Corps. It achieved tactical surprise[181] despite the knowledge from a decrypt on 25 October that Army Group B wanted close air support for a limited attack and had called a conference at the battle HQ of LXXXVI Corps (which was responsible for the Venlo sector).[182] Second Army's intelligence summary for 25 October reported that its front facing east had been generally quiet but that it was difficult to forecast what the enemy would do, the complete absence of air reconnaissance because of the weather being a severe handicap.[183] The summary for 26 October again reported a generally quiet front to the east and added that tactical reconnaissance had been largely abortive because of the weather.[184] Very short warning was provided by a decrypt signalled by GC and CS to the Commands with high priority at 2154 on 26 October disclosing that on the next day JK II intended to provide a fighter screen and support for the Army in the Venlo area[185] and by an emergency signal from GC and CS at 0134 on 27 October reporting that I/KG 51 had been ordered to attack Eindhoven that day in support of a German tank attack in the area.[186]

Thereafter high-grade Sigint provided useful information about the attacking forces engaged and their intentions. At 1526 on 27 October GC and CS signalled a claim by 9th Panzer Division to have penetrated to Meijel.[187] An emergency signal at 0108 on 28 October gave JK II's intention for the day as support of the

---

178. DEFE 3/300, HP 5094 of 31 October.
179. eg DEFE 3/239, HPs 3619 of 17 October, 3705 of 18 October; DEFE 3/241, HP 4182 of 22 October; DEFE 3/243, HP 4676 of 27 October; DEFE 3/244, HP 4904 of 29 October; Naval Headlines 1201 and 1202 of 17 and 18 October, 1207 of 23 October.
180. DEFE 3/300, HPs 5019, 5080 of 30 October, 5084 of 31 October, 5215, 5228 of 1 November; Naval Headlines 1215 and 1216 of 31 October and 1 November.
181. MacDonald, op cit, p 243; Ellis, op cit, Vol II, p 139.
182. DEFE 3/242, HP 4462 of 25 October.
183. WO 285/4, No 143 of 25 October.
184. ibid, No 144 of 26 October.
185. DEFE 3/243, HP 4631 of 26 October.
186. ibid, HP 4646 of 27 October.
187. ibid, HP 4704 of 27 October.

further attack by XLVII Panzer Corps in the Venlo area.[188]*
Another emergency signal at 0256 reported that I and III/KG 51
were to support the attack by bombing Allied concentrations.[190]
JK II's original intention for 29 October was to continue to
support XLVII Panzer Corps's attack; this had to be altered to
defence of the Reich from which, however, JK II was released at
1130 on 29 October.[191] A decrypt signalled at 1521 on 29 October
reported that Liessel had been taken that morning by 15th PG
Division.[192] The decrypt of a message of 27 October from Army
Group B, signalled at 2140 on 29 October, stated that the attack by
9th Panzer Division under XLVII Panzer Corps was designed to
tie down the Allies and relieve Fifteenth Army, and that 15th PG
Division was held ready to exploit success.[193] A decrypt signalled
at 1644 on 31 October reported that by 0800 that morning 9th
Panzer Division had gone over to defence,[194] and Army Group B's
situation report for 31 October, decrypted the next day, con-
firmed that the attack had been called off after drawing 15th
British Infantry Division and 4th Armoured Brigade away from
Fifteenth Army's front.[195] A message from 9th Panzer Division's
Flivo at midday on 1 November, reporting that the offensive had
been completed and that the Division was leaving the area, was
signalled by GC and CS in the evening.[196] A message from the
Flivo with XLVII Panzer Corps on 2 November stating that the
Corps was being withdrawn from operations for special employ-
ment was decrypted the next day.[197]

The decision to go forward with commando operations against
Walcheren was deferred pending confirmation that preliminary
bombing, carried out between 3 and 17 October, had breached the
dykes and flooded the interior of the island. On 22 October, when
PR confirmed that it had done so, the date of the operation was
fixed for 1 November.[198] From 4 October the regular PR reports
had been supplemented by Enigma decrypts which disclosed the

---

* A decrypt of 15 October had indicated that XLVII Panzer Corps might be moving north
and this was confirmed in a decrypt of 17 October.[189]

188. DEFE 3/244, HP 4759 of 28 October.
189. DEFE 3/238, HP 3464 of 15 October; DEFE 3/239, HP 3676 of 17 October.
190. DEFE 3/244, HP 4765 of 28 October.
191. ibid, HPs 4878 and 4932 of 29 October.
192. ibid, HP 4928 of 29 October.
193. ibid, HP 4957 of 29 October.
194. DEFE 3/300, HP 5155 of 31 October.
195. ibid, HP 5223 of 1 November.
196. DEFE 3/301, HP 5265 of 1 November.
197. ibid, HP 5397 of 3 November.
198. Roskill, op cit, Vol III Part 2, p 148; WO 171/133, APIS reports on PR
      sorties.

state of the flooding at West Kapelle, Flushing and Veere and gave details of the enforced move of battle HQs and batteries, of damage to guns and of the shortage of transport and labour for repairs.[199] Decrypts of 20 October disclosed that the whole of Walcheren was flooded except for the north and east, and that, as a result of the flooding, elements of 70th Infantry Division were being moved to South Beveland.[200] On 26 October the decrypt of a naval situation report of the previous day that disclosed three-quarters of the island was under water and warned that withdrawals from 70th Infantry had left only one battalion to defend Flushing and removed all defence forces from the north and west of the island.[201]

The second phase of the bombing of Walcheren, carried out in the few days before the assault, was directed against the coastal and anti-aircraft batteries at West Kapelle and Flushing, the sites of the two seaborne landings. It appears that they nevertheless remained formidable;[202] but the air target lists of the time indicate that intelligence about their strength and locations was 'in general excellent'.[203] Their locations were no doubt known from PR but naval decrypts in October reported on the state and serviceability of one of the coastal batteries and one of the Flak batteries.[204]

---

199. DEFE 3/233, HPs 2128 of 4 October, 2234 of 5 October; DEFE 3/236, HP 2971 of 11 October; DEFE 3/237, HPs 3181 and 3209 of 13 October; DEFE 3/239, HP 3608 of 17 October; DEFE 3/242, HP 4362 of 24 October.
200. DEFE 3/240, HPs 3958, 3988, 3996 of 20 October.
201. DEFE 3/243, HP 4559 of 26 October.
202. Roskill, op cit, Vol III Part 2, pp 147, 149–150.
203. Stacey, op cit, pp 407, 410.
204. DEFE 3/243, HP 4559 of 26 October; DEFE 3/244, HP 4858 of 28 October.

CHAPTER 52

The Allied Autumn Offensives and the German Counter-Attack

G ENERAL EISENHOWER'S plan for the autumn offensive, defined in directives at the end of October and the beginning of November, was to make the main effort in the north, defeat the enemy west of the Rhine, secure bridgeheads, seize the Rhine and then advance deep into Germany. The central group of armies north of the Ardennes was to advance to the Rhine and gain bridgeheads south of Cologne. Concurrently the northern group of armies, after clearing the approaches to Antwerp, would drive the enemy across the Meuse and advance to the Rhine. Subsidiary operations, timed so as best to support this main effort, would be conducted to destroy the enemy in the Saar and secure crossings over the Rhine which could be used as and when required. On the extreme right flank in the south 6th US Army Group would also act aggressively to overwhelm the enemy west of the Rhine.[1]

On 2 November First US Army's V Corps, which was slowly fighting its way through the Hürtgen Forest towards the Roer, renewed its efforts with an attack to capture Schmidt and the high ground overlooking the upper Roer. This was checked by a vigorous German counter-attack. Hard fighting continued in the Hürtgen Forest. On the left Montgomery's armies had to re-group after the Scheldt operation; First Canadian Army assumed responsibility from the sea to the Reichswald Forest, while Second British Army extended its right flank southwards towards Geilenkirchen, taking over some front from the Americans.

Third US Army's subsidiary operations to clear the Saar began on 8 November north and south of Metz against First Army. 6th Army Group's offensive against Nineteenth Army began on 13 November with drives by Seventh US Army towards Blamont and by First French Army on Belfort. Second British Army's offensive to clear the enemy from the west of the Meuse began on 14 November. Ninth and First US Armies began the main Allied offensive on 16 November, their first objectives being to advance to the Roer between Linnich and Jülich and seize bridgeheads

---

1. Ellis, *Victory in the West*, Vol II (1968), pp 157, 158.

from which the offensive could continue towards Cologne and Bonn.[2]

□

In the early part of November, before these offensives began, high-grade decrypts brought to a head Allied speculation about Germany's intentions. They came from the Japanese diplomatic cyphers as well as from those of the German Services.

In the first of a series of telegrams from the Japanese embassy in Berlin, the decrypt of which was sent to the Commands by GC and CS on 24 August, the Ambassador had reported that the Foreign Ministry had informed him on 21 August that no large-scale German offensive would be possible for about two months, but that by then 'the recent very thorough mobilisation' would have made it possible to form 100 to 125 divisions and an air force, primarily fighters, capable of standing up to the western Allies. He had added that it was not yet known to what line the German armies would meanwhile withdraw, but that the loss of territory was not important and the line would be decided with due regard to 'the coming offensive'.[3] In a second, the decrypt on 31 August of a signal of 23 August, the Naval Attaché had repeated that Germany was mobilising for an offensive which, according to the Chief of Staff of the Home Army, would come by about November or December.[4] A third, from the Ambassador on 4 September, had been decrypted on 10 September. In this he had reported on an interview with Hitler and had quoted him as saying that when 1 million new troops now being formed were ready, together with units withdrawn from other fronts, and as soon as the replenishment of the air force was concluded, the intention was to undertake a great offensive in the west 'probably from November onwards'.[5] In a signal of 20 September, decrypted on 26 September, the Naval Attaché reported that on a recent visit to the GAF HQ in East Prussia he had been told that the crisis on the western front would be surmounted by the Army and the counter-attack resumed.[6]* On 26 September, decrypted on 4

---

* Asked to comment on this by the Prime Minister the AOC-in-C Bomber Command criticised Japanese gullibility and did not believe that there would be a German attack in the west.[7]

2. ibid, pp 158, 160, 163.
3. BAY/XL 119 of 24 August 1944.
4. BAY/XL 128 of 31 August.
5. BAY/XL 152 of 10 September.
6. BAY/HP 25 of 28 September; SJA 918 of 26 September.
7. Cabinet Office file 82/43/1 Part 1, ATH/DO of 30 September.

October, another telegram from the Ambassador had stated that despite the 'unexpected mistakes' Germany had made in the west, she was now preparing to make a decision by force the basis for the future conduct of the war.[8]

At the end of September Sigint had disclosed that 1st, 2nd, 9th and 12th SS Panzer Divisions, Heavy SS Panzer Abteilungen 501, 502 and 503 and the Corps troops of I SS Panzer Corps were to withdraw east of the Rhine for rest and refitting and to be subordinated to Sixth Panzer Army, which was being set up under Sepp Dietrich.[9] Orders decrypted by 7 October had added Panzer Lehr Division to this list and had required I SS Panzer Corps and its Corps troops to be withdrawn from operations and despatched to Sixth Panzer Army at once.[10] Decrypts of 9, 11 and 12 October had revealed that First US Army's advance had obliged the enemy to bring I SS Panzer Corps into the front at Aachen, but had insisted that it must be with Sixth Panzer Army by 20 October at the latest.[11] Meanwhile, a decrypt of 2 October had revealed that Hitler had stated that there was to be 'no second position' behind the West Wall;[12] and this policy had been re-affirmed in a later message which stated that, although he had sanctioned the development of a position between the Ems and the Rhine, this was not to be at the expense of the development of the Ijssel position and the extension of the West Wall north of Arnhem.[13] By 22 October Sigint had established that Sixth Panzer Army and its subordinated units were OKW Reserve; that delays in getting its divisions out of the line had prompted orders to the effect that battle groups of 2nd and 9th SS Panzer Divisions were to be pulled out by 22 October and those of 1st SS and 12th SS Panzer and Panzer Lehr Divisions as soon as possible; that I SS Panzer Corps was to be withdrawn as a matter of priority; and that the programme for completing establishments in tanks and other weapons for the SS Panzer divisions and probably three Army Panzer Divisions* would extend into November.[15]† A message

---

* The wording of the German signal was ambiguous and at first was rendered as '3 Pz Division' by GC and CS. On reflection GC and CS thought there was 'a good possibility that it really meant "three Pz Divisions".'[14]

† The tank establishment intended for the SS Panzer divisions, which was markedly lower

8. BAY/HP 35 of 4 October.
9. DEFE 3/230, HP 1378 of 27 September.
10. DEFE 3/234, HPs 2274 of 5 October, 2483 of 7 October.
11. DEFE 2/236, HP 2815 of 9 October; DEFE 3/237, HPs 3018 of 11 October, 3102 and 3123 of 12 October.
12. DEFE 3/232, HP 1891 of 2 October.
13. DEFE 3/235, HP 2675 of 8 October.
14. DEFE 3/241, HP 4086 of 21 October.
15. DEFE 3/239, HPs 3621 and 3678 of 17 October, 3693 of 18 October, 3935 of 20 October.

decrypted on 18 October had disclosed that the order for the rest and refit of the armoured divisions had emanated from Hitler.[17] Messages of 18 and 22 October, decrypted on 24 October, had referred to the withdrawal from the line of I SS Panzer Corps, of battle groups of 1st, 2nd and 12th SS Panzer Divisions, of Panzer Lehr Division and of the remainder of 9th SS Panzer Division, all of which were to report to centres in Westphalia, and had also mentioned that the withdrawal of 11th Panzer Division from the front in the south was being delayed by lack of loading space.[18]

Sigint and ground sources had also indicated that three Parachute divisions were out of the line and in the Terborg area under First Parachute Army HQ.[19] Further evidence that 3rd, 5th and 6th Parachute Divisions were refitting in Holland was obtained from a decrypt on 28 October.[20]

Sigint received between 18 October and 12 November had disclosed other changes in the enemy's order of battle. At the beginning of October it was known that the front from the mouth of the Scheldt to Trier was held by Army Group B with Fifteenth Army, First Parachute Army and Seventh Army, and that Army Group G held it from Trier to Switzerland with First Army, Fifth Panzer Army and Nineteenth Army.[21] Decrypts available on 18 October had disclosed that Fifth Panzer Army was moving with all speed from the Nancy area to Army Group B, and a decrypt of 27 October had reported that it had taken over the sector between Roermond and Stolberg.[22] Between 4 and 12 November it had emerged from Sigint that a new Army Group H, thought to comprise Fifteenth Army and First Parachute Army, had been set up under Student, previously GOC of First Parachute Army.[23] In addition to this information about the re-disposition of the armies, it was learnt from decrypts up to 12 November that LVIII Panzer

---

than the former standard for armoured divisions, was reported to be one Abteilung consisting of four Companies, two of them equipped with 14 Pzkw IVs each, and two with 14 Pzkw Vs each. There would also be 4 ACVs, bringing the total to 60 tanks. It was hoped to provide each division with another Abteilung by subordinating a Tiger Abteilung with 35–45 tanks, from Corps or Army troops.[16]

16. ibid, HP 3693 of 18 October; WO 208/4317, MI 14 Weekly Summary for the CIGS, 22 October.
17. DEFE 3/239, HP 3693 of 18 October.
18. DEFE 3/242, HPs 4341, 4342, 4357, 4405 and 4417 of 24 October.
19. WO 219/1925, SHAEF Weekly Intelligence Summary No 31 of 22 October.
20. DEFE 3/244, HP 4761 of 28 October.
21. WO 171/133, 21st Army Group Intelligence Summary No 163 of 8 October.
22. DEFE 3/239, HPs 3734 and 3822 of 18 October; DEFE 3/243, HP 4672 of 27 October.
23. DEFE 3/302, HP 5519 of 4 November; DEFE 3/304, HP 6077 of 9 November; DEFE 3/305, HPs 6261 and 6345 of 11 November, 6350 of 12 November.

Corps under First Army was being relieved and that XLVII Panzer Corps, which had directed the Meijel offensive, was being withdrawn for special employment under Army Group B north of the Moselle;[24]* that 2nd SS Panzer Division in Seventh Army was being relieved by a newly identified division (18th VG Division);[27] and that 11th Panzer Division had gone into reserve under First Army, being relieved by 361st VG Division from Holland.[28] On 1 and 7 November decrypts had disclosed that the GAF had been ordered to transfer motor transport capable of cross-country performance to First Parachute Army.[29]

By that time, Sigint had provided evidence of extensive troop movements towards the front. A message from First Parachute Army of 5 November, decrypted on 6 November, ordered those of its formations that were not at the front to observe wireless silence.[30] It was followed by ground reports to the effect that refitted Parachute divisions had moved off in buses.[31] Requests from Army Group B for air cover for important troop unloadings at places from 25 miles north-east of Aachen to south of Trier, together with the corresponding orders from JK II, were decrypted between 3 and 11 November;[32] on 12 November MI 14 estimated that these movements involved perhaps two more divisions.[33] On 12 and 13 November decrypts provided important information about Sixth Panzer Army.† It was being moved by rail to the west of the Rhine on a tight schedule which could be maintained only if all formations were despatched promptly; 2nd

---

* These two Panzer Corps were shown as unlocated, as was Fifth Panzer Army, in SHAEF's order of battle map on 12 November.[25] Sigint made only one further reference to LVIII Panzer Corps before the Ardennes offensive – in a message of 22 November (decrypted on 25 November), no location given.[26]

† At the end of October some decrypts had referred to it as Sixth SS Panzer Army, and thereafter it was sometimes so called by the German and the Allied intelligence authorities. But in almost all official German records it continued to be Sixth Panzer Army (see Pogue, *The Supreme Command* (Washington 1954) pp 359–360).

24. DEFE 3/301, HPs 5368 of 2 November, 5397 and 5467 of 3 November.
25. WO 219/1926, No 34 of 12 November.
26. CX/MSS/T378/77.
27. DEFE 3/242, HP 4357 of 24 October; DEFE 3/243, HP 4505 of 26 October.
28. DEFE 3/244, HP 4786 of 28 October; DEFE 3/302, HPs 5742 and 5886 of 7 November.
29. DEFE 3/301, HP 5278 of 1 November; DEFE 3/303, HP 5896 of 7 November.
30. DEFE 3/303, HP 5744 of 6 November.
31. WO 219/1926, No 34 of 12 November.
32. DEFE 3/301, HPs 5437 and 5484 of 3 and 4 November; DEFE 3/302, HPs 5599 and 5676 of 5 November, 5690 of 6 November; DEFE 3/303, HP 5820 of 7 November; DEFE 3/304, HPs 6042 and 6165 of 9 and 10 November; DEFE 3/305, HP 6256 of 11 November.
33. WO 208/4317, MI 14 Weekly Summary for the CIGS, 12 November.

and 12th SS Panzer and Panzer Lehr Divisions had either begun to entrain or would do so shortly, but were behind schedule.[34]

Decrypts of 27 and 28 October had meanwhile provided startling information about measures being taken by the GAF. A decrypt of 27 October had disclosed that Luftgau VI (stretching from the Dutch–Belgian border approximately to the line Hanover–Kassel) was preparing to stock up eleven airfields north of Aachen with fuel and ammunition in connection with the switch of a large force of day-fighters to close-support operations in 'a sudden project' (Schlagartiger Einsatz) under JK I and 3rd Jagd Division in the first few days of November.[35] Decrypts on 28 October had included a request from one of the airfields for ammunition for three operations by 53 FW 190s and orders by JK I for spoof wireless traffic in the first days of November during bad weather and during 'operational attack'.[36]*

□

The Allied authorities recognised by the end of September that the enemy had recovered his morale and succeeded in consolidating his defences,[37] and they knew from decrypts and other sources that he was making a supreme effort to mobilise new divisions; thus, MI 14 reported on 24 September that 30 Volksgrenadier divisions were being formed expressly for the defence of the Reich, and that 30 more were to follow.[38]† But they were undecided and by no means unanimous in their views as to the

---

* In the signal relaying this decrypt to the Commands GC and CS had pointed out that 'operational attack' was its translation of 'Scharfer Einsatz', and that the German words translated as 'sudden project' in the first decrypt could be translated as 'lightning blow'.

† Since reporting the formation of Volksgrenadier divisions at the end of August (see above, pp 372–373 and fn†) MI 14 and SHAEF had continued to note in their intelligence summaries the movement of these divisions out of Germany to the west. By the end of November enough was known about the composition of the VG divisions for SHAEF to include a special item on their chain of command, personnel strengths and weapons. Features common to all the VG divisions, which distinguished them from previous infantry divisions, were the inclusion of young, but experienced naval troops, as well as some GAF personnel and new, young call-ups; innovations in equipment and organisation such as the concentration of heavy weapons under higher control, all anti-tank guns, for example, coming under divisional command; the fall in strength to about 10,500 per division against 12,700 in the 1944 class and 17,000 in the 1940–43 class of division. The main lack was in training. VG divisions were designed tactically for a relatively static role, being brought up in order to relieve Panzer-type divisions for reserve and counter-attack.[39]

34. DEFE 3/305, HPs 6372 and 6377 of 12 November, 6477 of 13 November.
35. DEFE 3/243, HP 4687 of 27 October.
36. ibid, HP 4731 of 28 October; DEFE 3/244, HP 4844 of 28 October.
37. WO 285/3, Second Army Intelligence Summaries Nos 97, 99 and 100 of 9, 11 and 12 September; WO 219/1924, No 26 of 16 September.
38. WO 208/4316, MI 14 Weekly Summary for the CIGS, 24 September.
39. WO 219/1926, No 36 of 26 November.

significance for his intentions and capabilities of the evidence about Sixth Panzer Army and the GAF's preparations.

On 27 September 21st Army Group had no doubt that the Allies continued to hold the initiative: 'We can dictate to him where his reinforcements must go'.[40] On 15 October MI 14 had believed that, although the new mobile reserve of Sixth Panzer Army was being created 'to meet the emergency of an Allied break-through', it would have to be dissipated in local counter-attacks.[41] On 22 October, noting signs of re-grouping between Army Groups B and G and forecasting the appearance of a new Army Group, it had appreciated that Germany was making use of the probability that the Allied offensive would be delayed by supply difficulties for some weeks; but it had still doubted whether she would be able to prevent an armoured reserve from being frittered away under Allied pressure.[42] To begin with SHAEF had shared these views. On 3 October it believed that 'Hitler's projected November offensive tends to fade into the distance'.[43]* On 15 October its widely distributed intelligence summary stated that, in view of the last-ditch nature of Germany's resistance, Hitler must have concluded that he had no alternative but to hold the West Wall; but it noted that his main preoccupation was to build up a reserve of crack troops as 'a fire brigade'.[44] On 19 October, however, it allowed for the possibility of a German offensive: 'Hitler wants a November offensive. Possibility not excluded of Sixth Pz with I and II SS Corps plus three Para divisions (also refitting) putting in spoiling attack in North before we start large-scale offensive action. Such action however depends entirely on enemy's ability to retain his front. . . . This unlikely unless more infantry arrive.'[45]

On 22 October, on the other hand, its intelligence summary noted that 'the general picture remains unchanged – unbroken determination to hold the West Wall (despite the loss of Aachen and the Vosges) and to deny base ports to the Allies, assiduous efforts to build up a reserve of Pz and Parachute troops by November, lack of hope of reinforcements before November and of anything really substantial even then. Meanwhile to fight back wherever the Allies strike, and reinforce wherever they strike in

---

* SHAEF sent this assessment, and others to which we refer throughout this chapter, in the Ruby series used in the interchange of views about high-grade intelligence which was carried on the SCU/SLU link.

40. WO 171/133, No 162 of 27 September.
41. WO 208/4317 of 15 October.
42. ibid, of 22 October.
43. RUBY/SH 32 of 3 October.
44. WO 219/1924, No 30 of 15 October.
45. RUBY/SH 66 of 19 October.

force, with a growing conviction that the really essential sector is in the north, opposite the Ruhr'.[46] At this juncture AI intervened with its appreciation of the GAF decrypts of 27 and 28 October. AI had no doubt that they were more consonant with a German plan for a spoiling attack than with preparations for a counter-attack.[47]

Before reaching this conclusion, AI pointed out that there was other evidence that Hitler had long entertained the project of a November offensive: this was clearly a reference to the Japanese diplomatic decrypts. It also rested its conclusion on the knowledge that the GAF would have no difficulty in providing substantial reinforcements for close support for the Army. It had learned from Sigint by the middle of October that the GAF's close-support forces, which had been virtually eliminated during the fighting in France, had been restored 'on a scale that could hardly have been foreseen two months ago'.[48] At the beginning of October AI had estimated that the production of single-engined fighters had reached a higher level than at any previous date, and it had believed that the upward trend would continue in view of the fact that the GAF had clearly decided to concentrate maximum resources on the expansion of the fighter arm and the development of jet and rocket aircraft, both for the defence of the Reich and the provision of close support for the Army, at the expense of long-range bombers. It had estimated that the GAF had 2,000 single-engined fighters on that date and that an increase to 2,500 was not impossible over the next six months.[49]

AI's appreciation of 28 October was all the more noteworthy, however, in that it was also made in the knowledge that as between defence of the Reich and close-support operations, the GAF was still giving priority to the former. The Enigma had shown that following a considerable ground-attack effort during Operation *Market Garden* and the German counter-attacks on the Nijmegen salient,[50] the balance had been shifted back in favour of defence of the Reich on 3 October in a re-organisation which left some 475 single-engined fighters available to JK II for close support.[51]* A

---

* In September, as disclosed by Enigma, the GAF Commands in the west had been re-organised. Supreme command was invested in Luftflotte Reich. Luftflotte 3 was down-graded to GAF Command West controlling Fliegerkorps IX (long-range bombers) and JK II (close-support fighters). JK II's forces were divided between 5th Jagd Division in the

46. WO 219/1925, No 31 of 22 October.
47. Air Sunset 252 of 28 October.
48. Air Sunset 248 of 12 October.
49. WO 208/4314, MI 14 Appreciations File, Serial 177a, A13(b) Note on the fighting value of the GAF, 1 October.
50. Air Sunsets 238, 239 and 245 of 19 and 22 September, 3 October.
51. DEFE 3/233, HP 2226 of 5 October.

few days later Sigint had disclosed that Göring had ordered a further shift of resources in favour of strategic defence, reducing the close-support forces to some 300 fighters at short notice.[53] A message of 18 October, decrypted on 26 October, had stated that defence of the Reich was unambiguously the GAF's main task; further withdrawals of close-support fighters were to be made accordingly, though the substantial increase in fighter strength would soon allow better close support.[54] A message of 17 October, decrypted on 18 October, had disclosed Luftflotte Reich's orders regarding the use of the close-support forces; their main task was to engage the Allied air forces in the rear of the operational area and over the population working on the West Wall, and direct support of operations at the front would be undertaken only in especially critical situations.[55] In the second half of October further decrypts established that, except during the German surprise offensive which captured Meijel, this policy of conserving effort was being strictly applied.[56] Moreover, from a message from C-in-C West of 25 October, decrypted on 27 October, it might well have been concluded that the close-support forces would be increased only to meet the threat from the Allied offensives. This had stated that OKL planned to bring up very strong fighter forces for close-support operations in the event of large-scale Allied attacks – but not before.[57] There can be no doubt that it was in the light of the decrypt references to the GAF's 'lightning blow' and its 'operational attack' that the Air Ministry set this interpretation aside on 28 October and came down in favour of the view that the enemy was planning a spoiling offensive.

MI 14 and SHAEF reacted somewhat differently to AI's appreciation. On 29 October MI 14, noting that the Enigma had now provided some indication that the GAF was preparing for an attack early in November, believed there was no evidence from army sources that an attack was intended. 'Moreover, any major German offensive operations would seriously interfere with the refitting programme of Panzer divisions', and although the enemy might have to use them in an emergency before they were fully refitted, it was too early to judge whether he considered that such

---

south and 4th JD between Main and Krefeld. JK I, commanding 3rd JD, was subordinated directly to Luftflotte Reich.[52]

52. Air Sunset 240 of 24 September.
53. DEFE 3/235, HP 2737 of 9 October.
54. DEFE 3/243, HP 4627 of 26 October.
55. DEFE 3/239, HP 3733 of 18 October.
56. eg DEFE 3/242, HPs 4256, 4422 and 4455 of 23, 24 and 25 October; DEFE 3/243, HPs 4623 and 4748 of 26 and 27 October; DEFE 3/300, HP 5059 of 30 October.
57. DEFE 3/243, HP 4689 of 27 October.

an emergency had arisen.[58] Also on 29 October SHAEF commented that the enemy was doing his utmost to collect a striking force of at least four refitted Panzer divisions, with 400 tanks, and went on to say that: 'Assuming it all remains at the disposal of C-in-C West, there is a doubt whether it is to be used for counter-attack when the expected Allied offensive against the Reich has developed, or whether the intention is, before that time, to launch an ambitious spoiling attack. The latter course is no doubt over-ambitious and considerably the less likely of the two, but it would be very tempting to try to put the Allies off until the winter is really here and so until next spring, by which time some miracle may have happened'. It believed that if the Germans chose to make a spoiling attack, it would scarcely be made except in the sector between Arnhem and Roermond, where the Ruhr was most directly threatened and the parachute infantry assembled.[59] On 31 October it observed that 'the recent reorganisation of the fighter force and project for first few days of November might signify intention to carry out offensive in the near future, and presumably current operations by XLVII Pz Corps might develop into large scale operations. To recapture Nijmegen would be considerable achievement, and successful spoiling attack might settle the campaign in the North for the winter months. Must be an important factor in enemy's appreciation to undertake such an operation before port of Antwerp fully developed. ... No evidence yet about Sixth Pz Army crossing the Rhine. Forecast during November continuation of Pz refit. Part of Sixth Pz Army might be called to other fronts, but is probably wanted for use in West. No reason to suppose oil situation could not support intensive offensive fighting for, say, one week'.[60]

AI then complicated the situation by having second thoughts. On 1 November it admitted that the GAF preparations which had led it to favour the intention to carry out a spoiling attack might be defensive, not offensive.[61] But further references to the GAF's special project were obtained from the decrypts in the first week of November. They included an order by Göring that provision must be made for fitting out all fighters as fighter-bombers at 24 hours' notice; reports about the equipment of 24 day-fighter Gruppen belonging to JG 1, 3, 4, 11, 27, 77 and 300 (almost the entire fighter force available for defence of the Reich) and of the movement forward of some of their advance detachments; a warning from Luftgau VI to Kassel and Düsseldorf that advance

---

58. WO 208/4317 of 29 October.
59. WO 219/1925, No 32 of 29 October.
60. RUBY/SH 88 of 31 October.
61. AWL 3255 of 1 November.

detachments of fighter squadrons would arrive at short notice; detailed messages about the units involved; and a message indicating that 12 November was the last date for making preparations to receive the fighter reinforcements.[62]

The Air Ministry summed up this information on 7, 9 and 12 November. On 7 November it appreciated that 'German plans for rapid, secret, build-up of close-support forces on Western Front in connection with a still undefined "project" appear to be nearing maturity'. It went on to say that the latest Sigint not only bore out the view it had expressed in the appreciation of 28 October to the effect that the Germans were planning a spoiling attack but also gave more details about their intentions. The further details available were that the enemy planned to transfer up to 400 single-engined fighters; envisaged ground-attack operations by day and night on a scale in excess of anything he had yet attempted on the western front; and that the main focus of the air concentration was Aachen–Düsseldorf, a sector over which the GAF had been providing fighter cover for the unloading of troops. AI remained uncertain, however, as to whether the objective of the German 'blow' was to be more sustained attacks on Allied ground forces or attacks to neutralise Allied tactical air forces by destroying airfields. On 9 November it raised its estimate of the fighters the Germans planned to have available to between 600 and 700 in 24 to 25 Gruppen, adding that although airfields in northern Holland and the Darmstadt area were now involved, this was probably due to pressure on accommodation and did not invalidate the conclusion that the focus of the concentration was to be Aachen–Düsseldorf. On 12 November it again raised its estimate of the scale of the concentration – to between 800 and 850 single-engined fighters in 28 to 30 Gruppen.* On 6 and 11 November further decrypts had disclosed that II and III Gruppen of SG 4, a specialised ground-attack Geschwader, were being transferred to Germany from the Russian front for training in bad weather ground attack and with new anti-tank weapons for operations in the west, and that Fliegerkorps III, which had been directing ground-support operations on the Baltic front, had been assigned to co-operate with the two northern Army Groups in the west.[63] The Air Ministry's appreciation of 7 November calculated

---

* For the texts of all three of these Air Ministry appreciations see Appendix 24.

62. DEFE 3/300, HP 5214 of 1 November; DEFE 3/302, HPs 5683 of 5 November, 5718, 5748, 5749, 5750 of 6 November; DEFE 3/303, HPs 5834, 5965 of 7 November, 5987, 5996 of 8 November; DEFE 3/304, HPs 6054 of 9 November, 6187 of 10 November.

63. DEFE 3/302, HPs 5683, 5718, 5748, 5750 of 6 November; DEFE 3/305, HP 6345 of 11 November.

that Fliegerkorps III had some 100–150 ground-attack aircraft and regarded its involvement as further evidence that although there was still no sign that the planned reinforcements had begun to arrive, large-scale air operations in close support of the Army were imminent, the main thrust being in the northern sector – a conclusion reinforced by the limited GAF reaction to Third US Army's offensive in the Saar.

Once again, the responses of the other intelligence authorities to this evidence varied in emphasis. On 5 November MI 14 argued that while the Germans might attempt a spoiling attack to throw the Allies off balance, the GAF preparations now appeared to be related to the defence of the Reich against Allied bombing, and that the Panzer divisions were 'more likely to be retained as a mobile reserve than to be used for a spoiling attack. . . . German policy appears to be, therefore, to prepare to meet the Allied offensive'.[64] In an exchange of views on 8 and 9 November between the DMI and SHAEF, however, the DMI said that the recent Sigint had increased 'my hunch' that a German offensive against the flanks of the Aachen salient was planned for the near future[65] while SHAEF, though agreeing that a spoiling attack in the Aachen sector was not excluded, felt that a counter-attack was more likely once it was clear where the Allies were to concentrate their efforts. The use of Sixth Panzer Army for a large counter-offensive was improbable at present; it was much more likely to be dragged in piecemeal with 'bits' going to other fronts.[66] On 10 November, noting that Sixth Panzer Army was so disposed that it was within easy reach of any part of the front north of Aachen, 21st Army Group doubted whether the enemy had either the will or the ability to commit it as a unit; it was more likely that its divisions would be used for plugging gaps, as in Normandy.[67] On 12 November with reference to Army Group B's requests for air cover, MI 14 commented that the enemy clearly appreciated that an Allied offensive was coming and was bringing up reserves to meet it.[68] Decrypts of appreciations and reconnaissance orders had indeed made it plain by then that he expected to be attacked both in the Aachen sector and in the Saar.[69] Also on 12 November SHAEF's intelligence summary concluded that, though Sixth

---

64.   WO 208/4317 of 5 November.
65.   AWL 3296 of 8 November.
66.   RUBY/SH 108 of 9 November.
67.   WO 171/134, No 166 of 10 November.
68.   WO 208/4317 of 12 November.
69.   DEFE 3/301, HP 5441 of 3 November; DEFE 3/302, HP 5742 of 6 November; DEFE 3/303, HPs 5821 and 5886 of 7 November; DEFE 3/304, HP 6134 of 9 November; DEFE 3/305, HP 6355 of 12 November.

Panzer Army was formidable, it was incapable of staging a 'true counter-offensive' for lack of size and adequate fuel supplies; the most obvious use for it was in 'counter-attack if and when and wherever a determined Allied attack towards the Ruhr develops'. On the other hand, it would soon be capable of a 'spoiling attack of considerable power', and SHAEF repeated what it had said on 29 October: if an opportunity offered, the risks involved in making a spoiling attack might be taken.[70] SHAEF's appreciation of 12 November may have been influenced by the Sigint bearing on the GAF's preparations which had come in since MI 14's appreciation of 5 November. In its section devoted to air operations, the appreciation contained a discreetly worded warning that the forthcoming Allied offensive might lead to a re-disposition of the German fighter force which would double the existing close-support strength of about 350 aircraft.

Meanwhile, the JIC had been drawing up its own appreciation. Dated 11 November and entitled 'Recent Intelligence on German Intentions in the West', the JIC report drew attention to the refitting of the five Panzer divisions under Sixth Panzer Army, the possible move to the front of two and later of all three divisions of First Parachute Army, the wireless silence ordered by First Parachute Army and the fact that important troop movements had taken place on 3, 4 and 6 November in the Cologne–Trier area. It recapitulated the intelligence on which the Air Ministry had concluded that the Germans planned to bring forward a large proportion of the air forces in Germany to the Aachen–Düsseldorf area for close support of the Army in the west, with 12 November as the date for the completion of preparations. It did not refer to the Japanese diplomatic decrypts of August and September to which the Air Ministry had given some weight in its appreciation of 28 October.* Whether this was an oversight, or whether the JIC felt that these decrypts had ceased to be significant with the passage of time, it is now impossible to say. It should be noted, however, that so far from mentioning German plans for an autumn offensive, Japanese decrypts since September had been speculating on the possibility of German peace negotiations and of Germany's collapse, and that one recent appreciation from the Japanese Naval Mission in Berlin had even gone some way towards discounting the earlier reports. Dated 30 October and decrypted on 6 November, it had said that the Germans were making frantic efforts to put their defences in order but would not

---

* See above, pp 402–403.

70. WO 219/1926, No 34 of 12 November.

be ready for a general counter-offensive for several months; they believed that their mobilisation, their aircraft production, their development of new weapons and their oil supplies would all begin to tell from November and December 1944, and they had great expectations of staging a counter-offensive about April 1945, but the Mission believed that in face of the expected Allied offensives on the whole front the Germans would be in a very bad way and would probably have to make a second step-by-step withdrawal.*

Before turning to the enemy's intentions the JIC's report observed that whatever Germany's intentions might be, the scale and the fighting efficiency of the air operations would be limited. Shortage of fuel would prevent close-support operations for more than two to three days; most fighter-pilots were ill-trained; most of the airfields were in poor condition, few having concrete runways; and over and above these considerations, the enemy's effort would be severely hampered by Allied air attacks. It nevertheless accepted that the evidence pointed either to a 'limited spoiling attack' aimed at putting off the Allied offensive, possibly even till the spring, or to the decision to use the rested and refitted divisions against the Allied offensive, which the Germans knew to be imminent. But it preferred the latter interpretation on the following grounds. The enemy must realise that 'only by bringing up all possible land and air reinforcements could the Germans hope to have available sufficient striking power for a major counter-attack'. On the other hand, a spoiling attack would be a dangerous gamble; if it failed it would substantially reduce not only the prospects of holding a subsequent Allied offensive but also the strength of Germany's strategic air defence.

This conclusion was given in paragraph 11 of the report:

'We do not think that the evidence . . . warrants the conclusion that the Germans are planning a spoiling offensive. It seems to us that this evidence is consistent with the movement forward of land and air forces to meet the expected Allied offensive. The Germans must realise that the failure to hold this offensive would involve decisive defeat in the field'.

At the same time the JIC added a final paragraph 12, which was not wholly consistent with its own conclusion and which was put in, we may suspect, at the insistence of AI:

---

* In a commentary written at the request of the DMI not long after the German offensive had faltered GC and CS remarked that the 'Japanese are less critical than some in believing what they are told' and added later, with particular reference to the decrypt of 10 September, that the long delay since its receipt had made the Ambassador's information seem to be out-dated.

'We conclude that the enemy are planning to spring a surprise which would almost certainly include attacks on Allied airfields'.[71]

The Chiefs of Staff considered this report on 13 November and decided to discuss paragraph 12 with the Directors of Intelligence on the following day. On 14 November they approved the JIC appreciation subject to the deletion of paragraph 12 and the insertion of an additional sentence ('Attacks on Allied airfields are likely to be included.') in paragraph 11, as the penultimate sentence.[72] Presumably the COS deleted the JIC's remark that the Germans were planning to spring a surprise because they wished to emphasise the main conclusion, which represented their own point of view. A copy of the final version was sent to the Prime Minister, and SHAEF, which had as usual received the original version, was informed of the amendment made by the COS.[73]

The JIC's conclusion, especially as modified by the Chiefs of Staff, was the wrong one. Under Hitler's direction preparations had been going forward since August for launching a major offensive, deceptively code-named *Die Wacht am Rhein*, in November.

□

Hitler had announced at a staff conference at the end of July that the west was the crucial front and that he himself would eventually take responsibility for planning and command there, assisted by a small OKW staff which Jodl was to set up. At a staff conference on 19 August he had announced that he proposed to take the initiative in the west at the beginning of November, when the Allied air forces would be unable to fly. On 2 September he had reaffirmed a recent decision to give priority to the western front in tank production, extended it to all new production of artillery and assault weapons, and ordered the creation of an operational reserve of 25 new divisions; and on 13 September he had ordered the SS Panzer divisions in the west out of the line for refitting and re-constitution under the new Sixth Panzer Army. On 16 September he had told a select staff conference that the counter-offensive would be delivered in the Ardennes, with Antwerp as the objective.[74]

On 25 September he had ordered Jodl to begin detailed

---

71. JIC(44)463(o) of 11 November. A copy of the final version is filed in CAB 121/413, SIC file D/Germany/1 Vol 2.
72. CAB 121/413, COS (44) 368th (o) Meeting, 14 November.
73. AWLs 3314 of 11 November, 3341 of 14 November.
74. Cole, *The Ardennes: Battle of the Bulge* (Washington DC 1965), pp 10–11, 14–17. See also MacDonald, *The Battle of the Bulge* (1984), Chapter 1.

planning for an attack in the Monschau–Echternach sector between 20 and 30 November, the initial objective to be the seizure of bridgeheads on the Meuse between Liège and Namur and the ultimate objective the annihilation of the Allied armies in a battle fought north of the line Antwerp–Liège–Bastogne. Not less than 30 divisions were to be available, ten of them armoured, under four Armies, Fifth and Sixth Panzer Armies abreast in the lead, Seventh and Fifteenth Armies, mainly infantry, covering the flanks. On 11 October, after the discussion of several alternative plans, he had approved an attack in two prongs, far apart, the main one striking north-westwards through the Eifel and the Ardennes before turning due north to meet the secondary thrust from north-west of Aachen. Under this plan (*Die Wacht am Rhein*), which was revealed to the Chiefs of Staff of C-in-C West and Army Group B only on 22 October, Army Group B was to have three Armies, Fifth and Sixth Panzer Armies in the van, Seventh Army in the rear to cover the exposed southern flank. C-in-C West and Army Group B were to hold their front in the west, if necessary at the cost of giving ground, without committing any of the earmarked formations. GAF support was promised on the scale of 1,500 fighters, 100 of them being new jet aircraft, though the scale of support was later reduced. Preparations were to be completed by 20 November and the attack was to begin on 25 November.[75]*

Von Rundstedt (C-in-C West) and Model (Army Group B) had regarded this plan as over-ambitious. By the end of October they had drawn up a more modest one with the GOCs of Fifth and Sixth Panzer Armies and Seventh Army, and Jodl had tried to persuade Hitler to accept a compromise by which the offensive was limited to the seizure of Liège and the envelopment of the Allied forces east of the Meuse. Hitler had refused and had signed the directive for *Die Wacht am Rhein* on 1 November. Von Rundstedt had accepted the directive on 3 November, thinking it futile to appeal against it in person.[77]

From the middle of November the Allied offensives necessitated postponement of *Die Wacht am Rhein* and prompted von Rundstedt and Model to press again for a less ambitious operation.† To no avail. On 26 November the start of the attack was put back to 10

---

* Fifteenth Army – on the northern flank – did not figure in the conference of 22 October. It did feature in later developments of the over-all plan but was not to be employed until the Allies had reacted to the main attack.[76]

† See below, pp 418, 425–426 and Appendix 25 for the course of the Allied offensives and the intelligence about the German reaction to them.

75. Cole, op cit, pp 34–35.
76. ibid, pp 19–22.
77. ibid, pp 23–29.

December, but Jodl informed them 'that there will be absolutely no change in the present plan'. That date had to be abandoned because the fuel dumps were not full and some of the assault divisions were still en route to the concentration zone. On 11 December Hitler set the date as 15 December. On 12 December he altered the attack order to read the 16th. But otherwise he remained obdurate.[78]

Preparations for the attack, which involved the transfer of HQ Fifteenth Army to relieve Fifth Panzer Army and, at the last possible moment, the shift southwards of HQ Seventh Army and the assumption of control in their allotted sectors between Fifteenth and Seventh Armies by Fifth and Sixth Panzer Armies, went forward under strict security precautions and accompanied by extensive deceptive measures. HQ Fifteenth Army left Holland to relieve Fifth Panzer Army in the middle of November and was itself relieved in Army Group H by HQ Armed Forces Command Netherlands (GOC General Christiansen). Christiansen's Command took over the name Fifteenth Army while Fifteenth Army itself was re-named Gruppe von Manteuffel and Fifth Panzer Army was re-named Feldjäger Kommando zbV. HQ Sixth Panzer Army, which was moving from Westphalia, was given the cover-name Rest and Refitting Staff 16. No special effort was made to conceal the concentration of forces in the Cologne area, which was represented as being in preparation for a counter-attack north-west of Cologne. But it was put about that in the Eifel, where the attack was to come, a relatively small force of battered divisions was preparing to contain the right flank of the Allied advance, and the deception was accompanied in that sector by severe security measures.[79]

□

It stands out clearly enough after the event that on the one hand the German generals and, on the other, the British Chiefs of Staff and the JIC were in close accord in emphasising the limitations on Germany's military capabilities, the former using them to urge that Germany should not undertake too ambitious an offensive and the latter relying on them for the conclusion that she would not do so. At the time the Allied authorities had no evidence that Hitler and his generals were at odds on this issue; but in view of Hitler's well-known control of German strategy and his past preferences for the offensive, and given the existence of positive

---

78. ibid, pp 30–32, 69.
79. ibid, pp 49–51; MacDonald, op cit, pp 40–41, 46–48; Pogue, *The Supreme Command* (Washington DC, 1954), pp 360–361.

evidence from Sigint about the formation of Sixth Panzer Army and the movement forward of the German fighter force, it is not a misuse of hindsight to hazard the judgment that the British COS and the JIC made a fundamental mistake in mid-November in failing to allow that he might ignore the limitations on which they themselves set great store. The alternatives of a spoiling attack or preparations for holding, and if necessary counter-attacking, the Allied offensives should both have been kept open.

Once committed, the mistake went uncorrected as we shall now see, and again no misuse of hindsight is involved if that is chiefly explained by the influence on Allied perceptions of the course and the outcome of the Allied offensives. From the middle of November von Rundstedt conducted a skilful resistance. He gave much ground in the south, and was driven back behind the Roer in the north, but he inflicted on the Allies what Montgomery fairly called 'a strategic defeat'.[80] As we now know, the force of the offensives and their success in delaying Hitler's plan encouraged von Rundstedt and Model to redouble their efforts to get the plan reduced. For the Allies, the German difficulties in holding the offensives, coupled with the withholding of Sixth Panzer Army and their own failure to reach the Roer, reinforced the appreciation of Germany's intentions endorsed by the Chiefs of Staff and coloured their interpretation of such further intelligence as was received about the German preparations.

Before reviewing the intelligence obtained from the most productive source – high-grade military Sigint – we may note what little information was obtained from the others. The SIS and SOE supplied no reports on the German preparations or intentions. Neither, according to its post-war history, did the OSS, and it is recorded that in its efforts to penetrate Germany it did not succeed in placing any agents in the Eifel area before the German attack.[81] The Dutch Resistance gave some information about the transfer of HQ Fifteenth Army and about movements of the Parachute divisions.[82] An unidentified POW stated early in December that SS divisions in reserve were to counter-attack as soon as the Allies crossed the Roer, and on an unspecified date another POW, the Commanding Officer of 553rd VG Division, stated that a meeting of divisional commanders had been told early in November that a large-scale counter-attack would be made through Metz and Paris to the Channel by an army under Dietrich at the end of December. The US histories find that the evidence

80. Cole, op cit, pp 35–39, 47; Ellis, op cit, Vol II, pp 166, 178.
81. US War Department, *War Report of the OSS* (1976), pp 285, 305–308, 311; MacDonald, op cit, p 56; Pogue, op cit, p 361.
82. WO 171/134, No 168 of 3 December.

from POW and deserters was otherwise unremarkable until First
US Army obtained at the last minute statements from POW that a
large offensive was coming, probably on 16 or 17 December and
certainly before Christmas, and, on 16 December itself, a report
from a refugee that troops had been massing in woods near
Bitburg on 14 December.[83] Y was all but totally unproductive, its
other problems* being no doubt compounded by the wireless
silence imposed on the German formations.[84] As for PR, although
flying was hampered by bad weather, it was impossible on only one
day in the month before the attack – 13 December – and the
Tactical Reconnaissance Group supporting First US Army flew
361 sorties in that period over the build-up area. Together with
those obtained by fighter-bombers on armed reconnaissance, the
results disclosed increasing road and rail activity, including the
movement of hospital trains and tank-carrying rolling stock. But
priority was given to photographing the Roer and Saar fronts;
between 10 and 15 December only three sorties, all on 14
December, were flown over the Eifel sector. And the interpretation put on the photographs was that the Germans were
reinforcing their reserve formations behind the Roer, such activity
as was detected in the Eifel being regarded as routine
movements.[85]

Insofar as attention was paid to the Japanese diplomatic
decrypts received after the middle of November they can have
done nothing to correct this generally-held presumption. In a
telegram of 16 November, decrypted and sent to the Commands
on 23 November, the Japanese Ambassador reported on an
interview with Ribbentrop. In reply to the question whether
defence might not be Germany's best policy – a strategy of
endurance aimed at beating off all attacks – Ribbentrop had
indeed insisted that Hitler was convinced that the war could not be
won merely by a defensive policy, and in reply to yet another
question he had assured the Ambassador that it would not be long
before Germany had sufficient oil for large-scale operations.
Questioned on the prospects of the German counter-offensive to
which Hitler had referred, Ribbentrop had said, however, that
although a counter-offensive was planned, it was impossible to say
when Germany would be ready for it; moreover, although she

---

* See Appendix 15.

83. Cole, op cit, pp 59–60; Pogue, op cit, p 370; MacDonald, op cit, pp 76,
    93–94.
84. *History of Sigint in the Field*, p 205; MacDonald, op cit, p 57.
85. AIR 41/68, *The Liberation of North-West Europe*, Vol V, p 66; Cole, op cit, pp
    61–62.

intended to deliver the offensive primarily against the west, a situation might arise which compelled her to concentrate considerable forces in the east.[86] In a further telegram of 22 November, decrypted on 27 November, the Ambassador informed Tokyo that he accepted Germany's assurance that, though she could not say when, she intended to carry out an offensive; it was not beyond her power to strike at some point, possibly in the west, and the opportunity to do so would arise when she had broken the present Allied offensive.[87]

Decrypts of high-grade German military messages ensured that the preparations for the transfer of Fifteenth Army to relieve Fifth Panzer Army and for the subsequent deployment of Fifth and Sixth Panzer Armies were not wholly concealed from the Allies. But as a result of the German deception and security measures* the decrypts gave a confused and confusing account of what was taking place. Decrypts of 18 and 19 November referring to the sector known to be held by Fifth Panzer Army spoke of Gruppe von Manteuffel[88] (the cover-name for Fifteenth Army), from which SHAEF had concluded by 26 November – naturally but wrongly – that Fifth Panzer was now being referred to by the name of its old GOC.[89] Further decrypt references to the Gruppe on 1, 4 and 8 December appeared to confirm this assumption.[90] A decrypt of 19 November disclosed that HQ GOC Armed Forces Netherlands had been renamed Armee Abteilung Christiansen, and a decrypt of 27 November indicated that, together with First Parachute Army, it was subordinated to Army Group H.[91] On 1 December SHAEF was speculating that Fifteenth Army was going south or that Fifth Panzer Army was going south and its sector being taken over by Fifteenth Army.[92] On 3 December 21st Army Group believed that Armee Abteilung Christiansen was on the right of First Parachute Army, and, noting that the role and location of HQ Fifteenth Army were therefore unclear, speculated that HQ Fifteenth Army might have gone back to Germany or might reappear between First Parachute Army and Fifth Panzer

---

* The measures were taken to distort gossip, and to prevent the facts from reaching the Allies through PR, POW, deserters, refugees and agents. There is no reason to think that the Germans believed that their cyphers were unsafe.

86. BAY/HP 113 of 23 November.
87. BAY/HP 118 of 27 November.
88. DEFE 3/308, HPs 7029 of 18 November, 7105, 7155 of 19 November.
89. WO 219/1926, No 36 of 26 November.
90. DEFE 3/313, HP 8329 of 1 December; DEFE 3/314, HP 8566 of 4 December; DEFE 3/315, HP 8911 of 8 December.
91. DEFE 3/308, HP 7060 of 19 November; DEFE 3/312, HP 8001 of 27 November.
92. RUBY/SH 151 of 1 December.

Army; it thought it 'disquieting in the fifth year of the war to find an Army HQ disappearing from the map'.[93] This uncertainty was not cleared up by decrypts signalled on 4 and 8 December disclosing that Army Group H's front was held by Fifteenth Army on the right and First Parachute Army on the left;[94] the fact that HQ Armed Forces Netherlands/Armee Abteilung Christiansen had also assumed the name Fifteenth Army went unsuspected.

Decrypts yielded considerable information about the forces known to belong to Sixth Panzer Army but divulged no clues as to the role it was to play. By 19 November air reconnaissance had indicated that SS Panzer divisions were moving to the Cologne–Düsseldorf area and POW had reported that three divisions known to be associated with Sixth Panzer Army were behind the front in the Aachen sector: 1st, 9th and 12th SS Panzer.[95] Late on 19 November a decrypt showed that Sixth Panzer Army and I SS Panzer Corps had been addressed via Army Group B.[96] Between 22 and 25 November further decrypts disclosed that II SS Panzer Corps (from First Parachute Army) with 2nd SS Panzer Division in the München-Gladbach area, with an unspecified Panzer division in the Bonn area, and with 3rd Parachute Division also under command for training purposes, had been subordinated to Sixth Panzer Army for a brief period of rest and refitting before fresh employment.[97] Decrypts signalled on 25 November located 1st SS Panzer Division west of Bonn and 9th SS Panzer Division south of Bonn.[98] SHAEF's intelligence summary of 26 November concluded that Sixth Panzer Army, complete except for Panzer Lehr Division, was deployed west of the Rhine and forward of Cologne; SHAEF believed that its centre of gravity might be south of Cologne, behind Seventh Army rather than behind Fifth Panzer Army.[99] More evidence followed from Flivo signals. On 27 November the decrypt of a message of the previous day contained orders to a Flivo detachment to join I SS Panzer Corps twenty kilometres south-west of Cologne and report on the locations of Panzer Lehr Division and 1st, 2nd, 9th, 10th and 12th SS Panzer Divisions; the Flivo provided the locations of 2nd and 9th SS Panzer Divisions in a message that was decrypted on 28

93. WO 171/134, No 168 of 3 December.
94. DEFE 3/314, HP 8566 of 4 December; DEFE 3/315, HP 8976 of 8 December.
95. WO 219/1926, No 35 of 19 November; WO 208/4317 of 19 November.
96. DEFE 3/308, HP 7157 of 20 November.
97. DEFE 3/310, HPs 7549 of 23 November, 7587 of 24 November, 7706, 7735, 7740 of 25 November.
98. ibid, HPs 7735, 7740 of 25 November.
99. WO 219/1926, No 36 of 26 November.

November.[100] The Flivo attached to II SS Panzer Corps reported in a message decrypted on 1 December that W/T silence had been imposed from 0730 on 30 November.[101] SHAEF summed up the evidence on 3 December: the whereabouts of Sixth Panzer Army were still not wholly clear, but 2nd, 12th and 1st SS Panzer Divisions were in a line from Grevenbroich to Zülpich and 9th and 10th SS Panzer might be further north, perhaps under II SS Panzer Corps.[102]

As for the Panzer and PG divisions under Army Group B, these were satisfactorily accounted for. On 27 November a decrypt disclosed that 10th SS Panzer Division, which had been in the line facing Ninth US Army, was being relieved by 9th Panzer Division.[103] 116th Panzer Division was no longer at the front, but was believed to be refitting close at hand,[104] as was confirmed later in the decrypt of a message of 1 December disclosing that tanks for the division were to be delivered in Bergisch-Gladbach.[105] 3rd PG Division had been in the Roer battle under LXXXI Corps from the start, but was relieved in the line at the beginning of December.[106] 15th PG Division had been committed in the Geronsweiler section in mid-November[107] and was still facing Ninth US Army.[108]

On the whereabouts of the Parachute divisions there was similarly no lack of information, but equally no indication that they were being prepared for offensive action. A decrypt of 12 November having confirmed the existence of 8th Parachute Division, the Allies were satisfied that there were six in all (2nd, 3rd, 5th, 6th, 7th and 8th) in Holland and north Germany.[109] Thereafter, decrypts disclosed on 23 November that 6th Parachute Division had entered the line in the Arnhem area,[110] and on 5 and 6 December that 2nd Parachute Division was at Oldenburg.[111] There was ground for thinking that 5th Parachute

---

100. DEFE 3/311, HP 7925 of 27 November; DEFE 3/312, HP 8095 of 28 November.
101. DEFE 3/313, HP 8297 of 1 December.
102. WO 219/1927, No 37 of 3 December.
103. DEFE 3/311, HP 7954 of 27 November.
104. MacDonald, *The Siegfried Line Campaign* (Washington DC, 1963), p 465; Cole, op cit, p 69.
105. DEFE 3/315, HP 8880 of 8 December.
106. WO 219/1927, No 38 of 10 December.
107. DEFE 3/309, HP 6912 of 17 December.
108. WO 219/1927, No 37 of 3 December.
109. DEFE 3/305, HP 6396 of 12 November; WO 171/134, No 168 of 3 December.
110. DEFE 3/310, HP 7549 of 23 November.
111. DEFE 3/314, HPs 8633 of 5 December, 8740 of 6 December; DEFE 3/315, HP 8810 of 7 December.

Division was at Leyden but might be moving.[112] Meanwhile 3rd Parachute Division had appeared in the Düren sector on 27 November.

Many decrypts disclosed information about train movements. From the middle of November Army Group B issued almost daily requests for fighter cover at first light for trains that were bringing up troops and supplies to specified areas behind the front in the Aachen sector and as far south as Trier.[113] On 3 December decrypts listed train movements which included that of 326th VG to Gerolstein-Bitburg; that of 62nd VG to Wittlich-Kochem; that of 560th VG* to Densborn-Speicher; that of the Führer Begleit Brigade and Assault Gun Brigade 200 to Traben Trabach-Kirn; and of Army Engineer Brigade 47 to Münster-Eifel.[115]†

The GAF decrypts gave unmistakable signs that preparations for some contingency were still going forward. On 14 and 16 November they included references to special security precautions to be adopted by fighter units arriving in the west,[117] and on 20 November disclosed the arrival of the first of the planned GAF reinforcements.[118] Also on that day the decrypt was received of a message of 16 November which called for a daily report on the serviceability of the airfields earmarked for the *Jägeraufmarsch*.[119]‡ By 26 November AI had detected no urgency, but it knew that

---

* 560th VG Division had been in Norway. The completion of its move to Denmark by 30 November was disclosed in a decrypt of 5 December.[114]

† A decrypt of 22 November referred to an order from Hitler for transport to be sent to Grafenwöhr for Panzer Brigade 150. Grafenwöhr was known from decrypts received earlier in November to be the destination for volunteers for a special force which Hitler had set up under Skorzeny. It was to comprise about two battalions of men from throughout the armed forces who had first class training in single combat and knowledge of English and American idiom.[116]

‡ When despatching this signal to the Commands GC and CS noted that *Aufmarsch* denoted the assembly of forces in an area from which operations were to be launched.

112. DEFE 3/315, HP 8810 of 7 December.
113. DEFE 3/307, HP 6792 of 16 November; DEFE 3/308, HP 7221 of 20 November; DEFE 3/309, HPs 7291, 7436 of 21 November; DEFE 3/310, HPs 7516 of 23 November, 8614 of 24 November; DEFE 3/311, HP 7875 of 26 November; DEFE 3/312, HP 8216 of 29 November; DEFE 3/313, HPs 8324 of 1 December, 8427 of 2 December, 8480 of 3 December; DEFE 3/314, HPs 8519 of 3 December, 8609 of 5 December, 8707 of 6 December.
114. DEFE 3/314, HP 8628 of 5 December.
115. DEFE 3/313, HPs 8449, 8459 of 3 December.
116. DEFE 3/301, HPs 5274 of 1 November, 5461 of 3 November; DEFE 3/309, HP 7548 of 22 November.
117. DEFE 3/306, HP 6607 of 14 November; DEFE 3/307, HP 6778 of 16 November.
118. Air Sunset 257 of 23 November.
119. DEFE 3/308, HP 7224 of 20 November; Air Sunset 257 of 23 November.

eleven Gruppen (some 500 aircraft) had already arrived;[120] and several decrypts disclosed that although some of this considerable force was committed in close support of the hard-pressed German front in Alsace, it was so committed only on a day-to-day basis.[121] A decrypt of 1 December contained Model's complaint of 30 November that the Allied air forces were exploiting their mastery in continuous and almost unopposed attacks; he requested counter-action by the GAF as being essential and decisive for the course of the fighting.[122] But subsequent decrypts made it clear that the GAF responded to this appeal only by switching effort from the southern front, and that close support in the Aachen sector remained far from commensurate with the resources available.[123] Between 25 November and 5 December Sigint revealed that the GAF command structure in the west was undergoing another re-organisation. GAF Command West (the successor to Luftflotte 3) was losing direct control of all but long-distance reconnaissance operations. JK II was to be a close-support command in control of the bulk of the fighter force, including units formerly under JK I, and all bombing, ground-attack and night ground-attack forces. Control of the fighters was being shared between two subordinate commands, 3rd Jagd Division and Jagdfliegerführer Mittelrhein, the latter having previously been in control only of night-fighters and subordinated to 3rd JD.[124] Other decrypts in the first few days of December disclosed that the GAF was insisting on especially stringent precautions and emphasising the importance of equipping fighters to operate in a ground-attack role.[125]

This intelligence was being received while the Allied offensives were in full swing. In the south Third US Army's advance against First Army captured Metz on 22 November, and by 3 December it had reached the river Saar on a ten-mile front round Merzig. In

---

120. DEFE 3/309, HPs 7374, 7379 of 21 November; 7411 of 22 November; DEFE 3/310, HPs 7666 of 24 November, 7704 of 25 November; DEFE 3/311, HPs 7759 of 25 November, 7950 of 27 November; Air Sunset 258 of 26 November.

121. DEFE 3/309, HP 7489 of 22 November; DEFE 3/310, HP 7592 of 24 November; DEFE 3/311, HPs 7820, 7891 of 26 November, 7911 of 27 November; DEFE 3/312, HPs 8020 of 28 November, 8128, 8236 of 29 November.

122. DEFE 3/313, HP 8333 of 1 December.

123. Air Sunset 260 of 6 December.

124. DEFE 3/311, HPs 7837, 7921 of 26 and 27 November; DEFE 3/312, HP 8245 of 30 November; DEFE 3/314, HPs 8624 of 5 December, 8711 and 8731 of 6 December.

125. DEFE 3/313, HPs 8272 of 30 November, 8426 of 2 December; DEFE 3/314, HPs 8620 of 5 December, 8689, 8734 of 6 December.

Nineteenth Army's sector First French Army took Belfort on 19 November and reached the Rhine through Mulhouse the following day, while Seventh US Army took Strasbourg on 23 November and then pressed forward to the *Siegfried* line between the Saar and the Rhine. In the north the main offensive by Ninth and First US Armies on the Aachen front made slower progress. Ninth Army took Geilenkirchen on 19 November, but was then held up by counter-attacks; it was not up to the river Roer on most of its front till 9 December. On Ninth Army's right, First Army was also delayed; it did not gain the Roer from Bergstein to Düren till mid-December.[126] Apart from assisting in the attack on Geilenkirchen, 21st Army Group confined itself to clearing the enemy from his salient west of the Meuse. Its operations did not prevent the Germans withdrawing forces southwards to meet the Aachen attack.

High-grade Sigint was plentiful during the fighting. Though none of it was of spectacular interest, and little of it of tactical value to the Allies, it kept them abreast of the changes brought about to the German order of battle by reliefs and reinforcements; and by thus informing their understanding of the enemy's conduct of the battle it influenced their assessment of his wider intentions.*

SHAEF's interpretation of the Sigint evidence on 15 November was that it contained 'every indication' of a supreme defence effort in expectation of the Allied offensives.[127] On 23 November it felt that the enemy's intentions were 'quite clear': to blunt the Allied offensive in the Aachen sector without if possible using Sixth Panzer Army but, if necessary, to commit Sixth Panzer Army in heavy defensive fighting on the Roer line, counter-attacking any bridgehead that was formed.[128] Its intelligence summary of 26 November more or less repeated this conclusion: possibly because Hitler was unwell, Germany was conducting the battle sensibly; she was maintaining a reasonably satisfactory position in the north with her infantry and the armour of Fifth Panzer Army, and was keeping Sixth Panzer Army behind the Roer either to prevent the Allies from seizing bridgeheads or to counter-attack if a favourable opportunity arose.[129] On 19 November MI 14 felt that it was too early to say what form the German reaction to the Allied

---

* See Appendix 25 for a survey of the Sigint received between 8 November and 7 December.

126. Ellis, op cit, Vol II, pp 163, 164, 165; MacDonald, *The Siegfried Line Campaign* (Washington DC 1963), Chapters XVIII to XXIV: Cole, *The Lorraine Campaign* (Washington DC 1950), pp 464, 465 and passim.
127. RUBY/SH 121 of 15 November.
128. RUBY/SH 131 of 23 November.
129. WO 219/1926, No 36 of 26 November.

offensive would take but that it was likely that Sixth Panzer Army would be retained as a mobile reserve and be thrown in when the German High Command had decided that the psychological moment had arrived.[130] On 26 November, however, it believed that German policy was to exhaust the Allies before they reached the Roer, using local reserves but trying to avoid committing Sixth Panzer Army.[131]

In their next intelligence summaries on 3 December SHAEF had nothing new to say about the enemy's intentions and MI 14, though mainly concerned to emphasise that Germany had incurred very severe permanent casualties since 8 November, reported that Sigint had shown that three VG divisions were going to 'the quiet Eifel sector',* which, it noted, had become the usual destination for divisions going north or south to other sectors, and that Sixth Panzer Army was still uncommitted, the enemy apparently being prepared to yield as far as the Roer without bringing them in.[132]

21st Army Group's summary of 3 December rehearsed at considerable length its reasons for discounting a German 'counter-stroke'. The summary concluded that von Rundstedt was fighting the battle intelligently, 'obviously without higher intuition', and that if he continued to conduct it unimpeded, it 'seemed more probable that he will wait to smash our bridgeheads over the Roer, then hold his hand. He is 69'. It noted that although the battle had sucked in almost all the enemy's tactical reserves, it had not yet, with the one exception of Panzer Lehr Division which had been committed on the Saar front, involved his strategic reserve; but it believed that von Rundstedt was unlikely to risk this 'precious guard over the Rhine' until the Allied advance had crossed the Roer and could no longer be blunted by the tactical reserves, or unless an opportunity offered for a counter-stroke which would disrupt the Allied advance for the winter. It recognised that the disruption of the Allied winter campaign would justify many risks. But on the one hand, the loss of Sixth Panzer Army might be an irreparable disaster and, on the other, the pre-conditions for an effective stroke hardly existed. The enemy needed bad weather for it, but that would clog his own movements. He needed guaranteed fuel supplies and more and better infantry than he possessed, and he would have to be sure that the Allies were tired and unbalanced. Moreover, he needed vital ground, but 'there is

---

* These were 62nd, 326th and 560th VG Divisions.

130. WO 208/4317 of 19 November.
131. ibid, of 26 November.
132. ibid, of 3 December.

nowhere obvious for him to go which would hurt us deeply. The bruited drive on Antwerp . . . is just not within his potential'.[133]

In the remaining archives of the time we have found no reference to the source of this report or rumour that the Germans planned a drive on Antwerp, the receipt of which had obviously prompted 21st Army Group to reconsider the previous assessment of their intentions. From the fact that the rumour is not repeated in the intelligence summaries issued by other Commands we may deduce that like 21st Army Group they detected in the other intelligence no grounds for revising the current assessment of the German plans. That this was equally the case in Whitehall is clear not only from the MI 14 appreciations, already quoted, but from the fact that when the Prime Minister called for an up-dated version of the JIC appreciation of 14 November on 3 December he was told that there was 'very little new material to add'.[134] But it was in the development of AI's views that the influence of the JIC's appreciation of 14 November, of Germany's success in delaying the Allied offensive and of the successive postponements of the German initiative was most clearly reflected.

On 12 November, the date which Sigint had given for the completion of arrangements for the concentration of the German fighters, AI had no evidence to suggest that the GAF had changed its plans.* On 18 November it was puzzled that nothing had yet happened; it could see no reason except the weather for the delay, but it still expected the fighters to arrive at any time.[135] But when it issued its next appreciation on 23 November the US offensives were exerting their effect; it still remained puzzled as to why the timetable for the transfer of the fighters was behind schedule, but felt that this might be partly explained by the fact that, with the initiative firmly in Allied hands, the GAF was being compelled to devote an increasing proportion of its fighter effort to defence, particularly to support of the Army and to defence of vulnerable lines of communication against Allied ground-strafing. 'There is thus reason to think that Allied pressure, if maintained as at present, may prevent the consistent development of GAF plans and lead instead to a series of short-term expedients which may prevent the GAF from using to full advantage the large forces which they are still preparing to switch to the west'. It did not believe that the plan for the redistribution of the GAF – the largest to take place since the invasion of Russia in 1941 – could be

---

* See above, p 411 and Appendix 24(iii).

133. WO 171/134, No 168 of 3 December.
134. CAB 121/413, PM Minute D/294/4 of 3 December and exchange between Hollis and JIC Secretary, 4 and 5 December.
135. Air Sunset 256 of 18 November; AWL 3367 of 19 November.

reversed; and it did not exclude the possibility that the GAF still hoped to execute an all-out operation in conjunction with a counter-offensive after the arrival of the main army reserves. But it noted that against the Allied raid on the Leuna oil plants on 21 November* the fighters had been reinforced by fighter units already deployed for 'the project'; and it wondered whether the redistribution might have been intended to give the fighter force greater flexibility to switch between operations in support of the Army and operations against the Allied bombing of the Reich.[136]

In its next two appreciations, issued on 26 and 28 November, AI noted that the fighter movement to the west was still continuing, but without any sign of urgency, and that although the main fighter effort was still being made in defence of the Reich despite the Army's need for close support, 'the intention . . . not to commit strong fighter forces to tactical operations until a German counter-attack can be launched must be envisaged . . .'. The further reinforcement that was known to be intended was probably being held back till the last moment to preserve secrecy and avoid the bombing of the airfields. Unless the plans were upset by the Allied advances, therefore, it would probably be timed to coincide with the major Army counter-attack. But the fuel and airfield situation was probably such that only one major effort over 5 to 6 days could now be assured, and further deterioration might jeopardise all possibility of offensive close support.[137]

AI's next appreciation followed on 6 December. The GAF had made no serious attempt to meet the demands of the Army for air support. The need for such support in the Aachen sector had been met by switching units from the southern sector. Otherwise, except occasionally and in limited numbers, the fighters were still being held back for the defence of the Reich. Its conclusion was that:

'Increased emphasis over the past fortnight on defence of Reich suggests that, whatever intentions GAF may have for further reinforcement of western front, the original plan for "lightning blow" and sudden attack in the west may with some certainty be said to have lapsed. . . . It appears that GAF is after all committing its fighters piecemeal on western front . . . and is also clearly thrown back on the defensive'.[138]

□

---

* See below, pp 525–526 fn†.

136. Air Sunset 257 of 23 November.
137. Air Sunsets 258 and 259 of 26 and 28 November.
138. Air Sunset 260 of 6 December.

After the event GC and CS described AI's appreciation of 6 December as 'a disaster'. There is indeed a cruel irony in the fact that instead of prompting a review of the conclusion reached by the JIC and the Chiefs of Staff in the middle of November – and perhaps a readiness to listen to the contrary warnings which AI had issued earlier – the intelligence received by 6 December had precisely the opposite effect of persuading AI that its warnings had ceased to be valid. But it scarcely needs to be said that the outcome would have been different if any of the intelligence received since mid-November had explicitly contradicted, or at least strongly conflicted with, the assumptions that were being made about how Germany would respond to the Allied offensives. Plainly none of it had done so: and it is on this account that, in the several enquiries they were soon to make into the failure to divine Germany's intention to attack, the Allied authorities were inclined to dwell on the limitations of their sources.

GC and CS's enquiry pointed to the risks of relying too much on the high-grade Sigint. It was dangerous to assume that it was ever complete, for 'it is not always possible to decrypt everything', and dangerous to assume that its evidence would always be explicit – that 'the decrypts will tell us . . .' GC and CS observed in this context that it would be 'interesting, for example, to know how much reconnaissance was flown over the Eifel sector on the US First Army front'. Thus prompted, the DMI stressed the neglect of the other sources, presuming that there had been 'poor air reconnaissance and general patrolling and [lack of] general inquisitiveness'.[139] The DDMI and ACAS(I) agreed that 'tactical reconnaissance, active patrolling, capture for interrogation of prisoners of war and the like must in spite of Ultra still remain the sure guide to enemy intentions for commanders in the field' – but believed that 'in this case weather and the *Siegfried* line and NOT the lack of effort were presumably to blame'.[140] The VCIGS, summing up after considering these enquiries, accepted that 'there is a tendency to place too much value on this source [Ultra] and therefore to neglect (or not to pursue with determination) all the other sources available to us – and this has been, and I think is, the greatest weakness in our I organisation'.[141]

It is true, as we have seen, that the other sources in fact produced very little.* But even if they had been pursued with

---

* See above, pp 418–419.

139.   Cabinet Office file AL 1183B, DMI Minute to V/CIGS, 5 January 1945.
140.   AL 1183A, JIC Secretary's letter to DMI, 6 January, DDMI Minute to DMI, 8 January, draft telegram to Washington, 10 January.
141.   AL 1183B, Memo of 2 February, para 4.

greater determination it is inconceivable that they would have added anything significant to the voluminous Sigint that was available; and the essential question, as GC and CS insisted, is why the prospect that Germany intended to attack was so firmly excluded when the Sigint, even though it was not explicit, was so suggestive as a whole.* GC and CS argued that the high-grade Sigint gave clear warning that a counter-offensive was coming and some warning, though at short notice, of when it was coming, even if it did not give clear indications of where it was coming; and it suggested that the warnings were ignored because of the 'besetting tendency in intelligence . . . to become too wedded to one view of enemy intentions' – in this case to the belief that 'the Germans would counter-attack, head on, when they had been pushed hard enough, probably in the Roer sector . . .'. To this charge the VCIGS made the following reply in his summing up:

'A good case can, of course, be made to show that the evidence was available from Ultra sources only, if we had had sufficient clear-sightedness to see it. A charge easy to make and impossible to disprove. On balance I should say that while it was *possible* from this evidence to draw the correct deduction from it, the odds were very much against doing so . . .'.[143]

These conflicting conclusions might be left to stand as differences of judgment. But it seems reasonable at this distance from the debate to believe that in the course of reviewing the intelligence received in the whole of the period before the attack on 16 December, they paid insufficient attention to chronology. The intelligence received up to 6 December, which we have now considered, provides more support for the reservation of the VCIGS than it does for GC and CS's claim. This is all the more the case in that GC and CS recognised the perils of hindsight, admitting 'how difficult it was then to find the way' and conceding that, had the Germans attacked in the Aachen sector, the

---

* As an example of the significance of Sigint that was overlooked, it may be noted that on 2 December the U-boats in the North Atlantic were told that 'weather reports are of the greatest importance for the war on land and in the air' and that on 3 December they were told that 'all means must be used to get the messages through'. After these signals the number of weather reports from U-boats in the Atlantic began to increase from two or three a day to some 15 a day on 15 December. On 19 December the U-boat Command advised the U-boats that their recent weather reports had 'contributed decisively to determining the beginning of our great offensive in the West'.[142] See further below, p 489.

142. D Synett, 'German meteorological intelligence from the Arctic and North Atlantic' in *Mariners Mirror* August 1985 and US Department of Defense, *Allied Communications Intelligence and the Battle of the Atlantic*, Vol IV. The second publication has been referred to in previous volumes of this history as the Op-20-G History.

143. AL 1183B, Memo of 2 February, para 2.

intelligence would have been quite compatible with that outcome.* After 6 December, on the other hand, GC and CS's charge that the intelligence authorities had become too wedded to one view of enemy intentions is wholly vindicated, even if Sigint was perhaps less clear than it claimed as to when the attack would come. The possibility that the Allied offensives would breach the Roer was fading rapidly. The Sigint evidence that the Germans were continuing and indeed intensifying their build-up further to the south was unmistakable. And yet, as we shall now see, the appreciation of the enemy's intentions made in the middle of November and reiterated in the first week of December was not reviewed again before the start of the German offensive.

Not least on account of the German deception measures, it was by no means the case that the Sigint received after 6 December was unambiguous or conclusive. It provided further indications that Fifteenth Army was moving but no firm evidence as to its whereabouts. A signal decrypted on 8 December suggested that it was transferring to Army Group B: although its contents were insignificant, it was addressed, as GC and CS pointed out when sending it to the Commands, to Fifteenth Army and Army Group B but not to Army Group H.[145] On 10 December MI 14 surmised on this evidence that Fifteenth Army was perhaps moving to release Fifth Panzer Army or Seventh Army for Army Group G.[146] Not till 14 December, however, did Sigint justify a firmer conclusion. A message of 5 December, signalled by GC and CS on 14 December, was signed by General von Zangen (last known as GOC, Fifteenth Army) as acting GOC, Gruppe von Manteuffel; GC and CS deduced from this that Fifteenth Army was in the process of relieving Fifth Panzer Army.[147] In fact the relief had taken place nearly a month earlier.

Several decrypts referred to the Corps subordinated to Gruppe von Manteuffel (in reality Fifteenth Army) and Seventh Army. Orders from C-in-C West of 4 December, decrypted on 11 December, disclosed that LXVII Corps and its Corps troops were to be withdrawn from Army Group H to Army Group B, and be

---

* We may note, for example, that GC and CS did not signal to the Commands a decrypt of 1 December which disclosed that courses for Nazi leaders in Luftgau VI to be held from 3 to 16 December had been cancelled on 30 November owing to 'impending special operation' and that it noted afterwards that the context was comparatively trivial and that the reference to 'special operation' 'no doubt failed to ring a bell'.[144]

144. CX/MSS/384 para A 84 of 1 December.
145. DEFE 3/315, HP 8976 of 8 December.
146. WO 208/4317 of 10 December.
147. DEFE 3/317, HP 9408 of 14 December; AWL 3531 of 16 December.

replaced by Corps Feldt.[148]* A situation report of 4 December, decrypted on 12 December, listed LXVII, XII SS, XLVII Panzer and LXXXI Corps under Gruppe von Manteuffel and LXXIV, LXVI and LXXX Corps under Seventh Army.[150] Another decrypt signalled on 12 December indicated that LXXIV Corps had been subordinated to Gruppe von Manteuffel from 10 December.[151] On 7 December a decrypt gave the state of the divisions in the three Corps that were later listed under Seventh Army. An unspecified Corps (clearly LXXIV) had 353rd Infantry (category II), 344th Infantry (IV), 89th Infantry (IV), 272nd VG (III) and 277th VG (III). LXVI Corps had 26th VG (III) and 18th VG (III). A third Corps, clearly LXXX, had 352nd VG (III) and 212nd VG (category not available).[152]†

There was no new information about Sixth Panzer Army, the explanation being that the enemy had now resorted to the use of Sixth Panzer Army's cover-name (Rest and Refitting Staff 16) in his messages. The first Sigint references to this Staff were decrypted on 8 and 9 December from messages which informed it that tanks had been despatched for 116th Panzer Division‡ and that trains were carrying heavy anti-tank units to Saarbrücken.[153] In a signal decrypted on 12 December it was listed together with Jäger Kommando zbV (the first reference to the cover-name for HQ Fifth Panzer Army) as being under Seventh Army.[154] On 16 December the decrypt of a message of 15 December gave the boundary between Rest and Refitting Staff 16 and Gruppe von Manteuffel (the cover-name for HQ Fifteenth Army). As GC and CS observed when sending it to the Commands, this decrypt provided the first direct evidence that the Staff controlled a front-line sector.[155]

These decrypts provided no grounds for associating Rest and Refitting Staff 16 with Sixth Panzer Army, or Jäger Kommando

---

* Decrypts of 22 and 24 November had shown that LXVII Corps had been withdrawn from the front to become Army Group H Reserve under First Parachute Army.[149]

† The Corps involved at the start of *Die Wacht am Rhein* were LXVII, I SS Panzer, LXVI, XLVII Panzer, LVIII Panzer, LXXXV and LXXX. No intelligence was received about the location of LVIII Panzer and LXXXV, both of which had been withdrawn from First Army early in November.

‡ This division had left the front line, but its precise whereabouts were unknown.

148. DEFE 3/316, HP 9171 of 11 December.
149. DEFE 3/309, HP 7426 of 22 November; DEFE 3/310, HP 7607 of 24 November.
150. DEFE 3/316, HP 9189 of 12 December.
151. ibid, HP 9202 of 12 December.
152. DEFE 3/315, HPs 8794, 8798 of 7 December.
153. ibid, HPs 8880 and 8981 of 8 and 9 December.
154. DEFE 3/316, HP 9189 of 12 December.
155. DEFE 3/318, HP 9551 of 16 December.

zbV with Fifth Panzer Army. But decrypts of 12 and 13 December referred to Sixth Panzer Army's formations without mentioning the Rest and Refitting Staff. One reported that on 10 December all SS units were keeping W/T silence, and gave the designations of Flivo Truppen attached to II SS Panzer Corps and 2nd SS Panzer Division.[156] Others listed the designations of the Flivo Truppen that had been or were to be attached from 14 December to I SS Panzer Corps and 1st, 9th and 12th SS Panzer Divisions.[157]* With hindsight, it is easy to attach significance to these decrypts, but it was obviously more difficult to do so at the time. And the same applies to the changes in the order of battle of the Panzer and PG divisions which were taking place and to the intelligence which became available in the second week of December about two of the Parachute divisions.

Decrypts on 8 and 11 December contained references to 116th Panzer Division which left doubt whether the division was under Fifth Panzer Army or Seventh Army.[159] The first of these also indicated that 2nd Panzer Division, which had been missing from Allied order of battle maps throughout the autumn, was under Army Group B. SHAEF's intelligence summary of 10 December,[160] the last it issued before the German attack, noted that there was no new information about Sixth Panzer Army, but mentioned the withdrawal of armour for rest and refitting as the most notable feature of the past week: 10th SS Panzer, 3rd PG and 116th Panzer Divisions had been taken out of the line in the Aachen sector† and Panzer Lehr in the Saar.‡ Second Army's

---

* Yet other decrypts dealt with new signals instructions that were to come into force from 0300 on 14 December for II Parachute Corps, I and II SS Panzer Corps, XII SS Corps, LXVII, XXX, LXVI, LXXIV, LXXX, LXXXI, LXXVI and LXXXVIII Corps, and 1st, 2nd, 9th and 12th SS Panzer Divisions. SHAEF later argued that these decrypts about signals instructions, which had not been forwarded to the Commands, could not have failed to arouse its considerable suspicions.[158] But GC and CS noted in its subsequent inquiry that similar general issues of new instructions had taken place in Italy and borne no operational significance. It might be added that not all these Corps were to be involved in the Ardennes offensive. With reference to the imposition of W/T silence on all SS formations, GC and CS's enquiry noted that this was less significant than it sounded, as such silences had been ordered on previous occasions.

† See above, p 422.

‡ This left two Panzer divisions (11th and 21st) and two PG divisions (17th SS and 25th) on the Saar front. Panzer Lehr, which had been detached from Sixth Panzer Army about 23 November to try to restore the position in the Saverne gap,[161] disappeared from the front

156. DEFE 3/316, HP 9198 of 12 December.
157. DEFE 3/317, HPs 9267, 9269, 9280 of 13 December.
158. AL 1183A, DMI SHAEF to DMI War Office, 26 January 1945.
159. DEFE 3/315, HPs 8911, 8939 of 8 December; DEFE 3/316, HP 9164 of 11 December.
160. WO 219/1927, No 38 of 10 December.
161. DEFE 3/310, HP 7697 of 24 November.

intelligence summary on 11 December referred to the departure from the front line of two, and possibly all three, of the Panzer-type divisions facing Ninth US Army. 9th Panzer Division was thought to have followed 10th SS Panzer Division out of the line. Whether 15th PG Division had gone too was doubtful.[163] The next day Second Army was more confident that the substitution of infantry divisions for armour from the Meuse to north of Düren was continuing.[164] In the event, 9th Panzer and 15th PG Divisions were used as reinforcements in the German offensive.

Messages of 3 and 8 December referring to 5th Parachute Division were decrypted on 12 and 14 December. The first, sent to Seventh Army's Transport Authority, mentioned elements of 5th Parachute Division which were to be 'inserted'.[165] The second was an order by C-in-C West for the urgent transfer of weapons and transport from 6th Parachute to 5th Parachute Division to improve the latter's armament and mobility.[166] Another decrypt on 14 December disclosed that the relief of 3rd Parachute Division in the Düren sector had been in progress two days earlier.[167] Both 3rd and 5th Parachute Divisions would take part in the German offensive.

If it was difficult to make much of these order of battle changes, there was no doubt that large-scale German train movements to the sector between Aachen and Trier continued. Decrypts of 7, 9 and 10 December disclosed requests for cover on 7 December for seven trains in the area Wittlich–Trier, four in the Kyllburg–Bitburg area, six in the area Brühl–Bergheim and eight in the area Dümpelfeld–Hillesheim; on 8 December for five trains in the area Wittlich–Trier and ten in the area Dümpelfeld–Hillesheim; on 9 December for six in the area Wittlich–Trier, six in the area Dümpelfeld–Hillesheim and six in the Zülpich area; on 10 December for eighteen trains in the area Kochem–Wittlich–Trier, ten in the area Dümpelfeld–Hillesheim and ten in the Zülpich area.[168] A message signalled by GC and CS on 8 December ordered Army Group H to send a motor transport company to the Führer Begleit Brigade at Wittlich.[169] No significance appears to

---

line after taking part in a counter-attack on 4 December[162] and was not heard of again before the German offensive.

162. DEFE 3/314, HP 8561 of 4 December.
163. WO 285/4, No 190 of 11 December.
164. ibid, No 191 of 12 Deccember.
165. DEFE 3/316, HP 9216 of 12 December.
166. DEFE 3/317, HP 9371 of 14 December.
167. ibid, HP 9400 of 14 December.
168. DEFE 3/314, HPs 8777, 8816 of 7 December, 8969 of 9 December; DEFE 3/316, HP 9053 of 10 December.
169. DEFE 3/315, HP 8905 of 8 December.

have been attached to the location given for the Führer Begleit Brigade. Had that been an isolated pointer this would be understandable. But it is surprising that not more was made of it when the train movements to the same sector were so considerable. The train movements were not overlooked. The evidence received about them drew the attention of the Allied authorities to the Eifel sector from 7 December, as it had not done earlier. But no thought was given to the possibility that the movements were related to German plans for a counter-attack or a spoiling attack, and this was for the reason that the Allies had made up their minds that the enemy regarded the battle for the Roer as decisive and was reserving his armour for that sector.

In its summary of 10 December SHAEF, as well as commenting on the withdrawal of armour as the notable feature of the week, observed that a lot of movement had been taking place into, and probably also out of, the 'quiet' Eifel sector.[170] MI 14's summary of the same day reported that Sixth Panzer Army remained in reserve with four divisions behind the Aachen sector, where the fighting had become less intense, and that, taking account of casualties and new arrivals, the enemy had managed to maintain his strength over the past month and even to increase it slightly. It noted that in the Merzig–Karlsruhe sector Allied progress had probably been greater than the Germans had expected but that they still had some reserves in 'the quiet sector' north of Trier and that all new arrivals were being sent to this last sector; six infantry divisions were there, some of them probably not battle-worthy, and possibly 2nd Panzer Division, which had not been located recently.[171] SHAEF's final comments on this intelligence were made on 13 December in its exchanges with Whitehall. It believed that the Ardennes was still being used as a training ground for unblooded VG divisions and was very quiet; that the W/T silence ordered for all SS formations did not indicate a large-scale counter-offensive but rather the shifting of formations, some of which might possibly appear in the line for blooding; that the enemy still regarded the battle for the Roer as the decisive one, but that despite the lack of any sign that he intended a counter-offensive, the superfluity of VG divisions in the Ardennes made it necessary to watch whether blooded divisions were moving away to an active front. SHAEF ended with the suggestion that if this last development did not take place soon 'some relieving attack' was possible in the Ardennes. As for Sixth Panzer Army, it was unlikely to attack across the Roer, but heavy attacks were probable

---

170. WO 219/1927, No 38 of 10 December.
171. WO 208/4317 of 10 December.

there if the Allies broke out of the Hürtgen Forest.[172]

These comments may be compared with statements subsequently made by General Strong (AC of S G2 at SHAEF) and General Bedell Smith (Chief of Staff at SHAEF). General Strong claimed that he had believed for at least a fortnight before the attack that a relieving attack through the Ardennes was one of three possible uses for Sixth Panzer Army. General Smith confirmed that General Strong's view that an attack might come in the Ardennes or east of the Vosges persuaded him to send General Strong to see General Bradley (GOC 12th Army Group) in – as General Strong recalled – 'about the first week of December'.[173] From the contemporary appreciations, however, it seems probable that these recollections were referring to discussions which had produced no more than the view expressed by SHAEF on 13 December that developments in the Ardennes needed careful watching. On 26 November SHAEF had been satisfied that, while Sixth Panzer Army might counter-attack if a favourable opportunity arose, it was being kept behind the Roer.* On 13 December it believed that the enemy still regarded the battle for the Roer as the decisive one. But it had found no sign that he intended a counter-offensive; and while it paid due attention to the evidence of increasing train movements to the Eifel sector, its conclusion about them pending further developments was essentially the same as that of the US formations responsible for the sector, 12th Army Group, First Army and VIII Corps. These all took the movements to be evidence of 'a definite pattern for the seasoning of newly-formed divisions in the comparatively quiet sector opposite VIII Corps prior to their despatch to more active fronts'.[174]†

---

* See above, p 425.

† In an article in the American journal *Military History* for June 1985 Colonel Donald B Bussey, Special Intelligence Officer with US Seventh Army in the Strasbourg sector, has claimed that he believed on the evidence of the Sigint sent to him that the Germans were building up for a major counter-offensive through the Ardennes on the Malmédy–Liège axis, and that although the Sigint was not explicit about the enemy's intentions, there was enough non-Sigint intelligence to flesh out his hypothesis. He particularly recalls about 30 decrypts before 16 December referring to train unloadings in the Eifel, the fact that two Panzer Corps had disappeared from the order of battle in his sector, and a captured document which disclosed before 16 December that one of those Corps had appeared in the sector facing Third US Army. He adds that his G2 told him that 'Twelfth Army Group, SHAEF and US First and Third Armies . . . had lots more information than we do, and they are not arriving at this judgment'. He comments that 'we had been spoiled by this time' by the conviction that the Germans were defeated and the belief that in any case they 'would tell us of their intentions through Ultra'.[175]

172.   RUBY/SH 173 of 13 December.
173.   Pogue, op cit, p 365(n).
174.   ibid, p 365.
175.   'Protecting the Ultimate Advantage' in *Military History*, June 1985, pp 47–48.

The GAF decrypts finally provided the evidence that enemy offensive action on a large scale was imminent. But the clues did not emerge, or were not clearly recognised, till 14 December. Messages referring to the provision of night-fighter crews and pilot aircraft for fighter formations in the Frankfurt area, and also for I, II and III/SG 4 at Ziegenhain, Kirtorf and Kirrlach, had been decrypted on 5 and 6 December;[176] but notwithstanding the inclusion of the special close-support unit SG 4, it was assumed that they related to large-scale interception operations against Allied bombers until, on 14 and 15 December, further decrypts established that these measures had been taken to assist large formations of fighters and fighter-bombers to take off and find their targets in bad weather.[177] As for SG 4, it was known early in November that II and III/SG 4 had been brought to Germany to retrain with a new anti-tank weapon in bad weather ground attack;* on 4 December Sigint had shown that they were being joined by I/SG 4 also from Russia;[178] and it then emerged that III/SG 4 was engaged in close-support operations in the south.[179] But an order of 14 December for III/SG 4 to move to Kirtorf as soon as possible, and this at a time when it might have been expected to stay in the south in support of a local offensive in the Colmar area, was decrypted on 15 December.[180] A strength return of 15 December giving the significant news that the whole of SG 4 was concentrated in the Cologne area for operations as a Geschwader was not decrypted till 16 December.[181] Messages signalled by GC and CS on 8 and 11 December had disclosed that a considerable increase had taken place in the number of serviceable aircraft available to Jagdfliegerführer Mittelrhein.[182] But a message of 14 December by 3rd Jagd Division with unusual urgency, ordering other fighters to move up, was not decrypted till 16 December.[183] The news that some night-fighter formations were to take delivery of 'Window' equipment by 9 December had been obtained from a decrypt of 5 December; but it was not till 15 December that another decrypt revealed that they were to carry out intruder operations against Allied bomber airfields.[184] In the

---

* See above, p 411.

176. DEFE 3/314, HPs 8621, 8689 of 5 and 6 December.
177. DEFE 3/317, HPs 9391, 9491 of 14 and 15 December.
178. DEFE 3/314, HP 8689 of 6 December.
179. DEFE 3/315, HP 8783 of 7 December.
180. DEFE 3/317, HP 9449 of 15 December; Air Sunset 264 of 16 December.
181. DEFE 3/318, HP 9520 of 16 December.
182. DEFE 3/315, HP 8837 of 8 December; DEFE 3/316, HP 9138 of 11 December.
183. DEFE 3/318, HP 9534 of 16 December.
184. CX/MSS/T389/7 of 5 December; DEFE 3/317, HP 9456 of 15 December.

early hours of 16 December, the low-grade GAF traffic revealed that a large-scale operation by Ju 52s and Ju 88s associated with Transport Command was about to take place from the Paderborn area. It was clear from this traffic and from a later Enigma decrypt that the undertaking, which was cancelled almost immediately in further low-grade signals, was no ordinary transport operation, but that it was a paratroop drop; AI believed it was bringing up emergency reinforcements to the Aachen area.[185]

All these items of intelligence were conveyed to the Commands and to AI from GC and CS as they were received. But they did not even in the last hours raise the alarm, and it was not until the evening of 16 December that AI issued a considered appreciation of their significance. This concluded that 'the long-standing plans, never suspended, for major German aggressive operations in the west are nearly matured, presumably . . . as a result of developments in the ground situation thought to necessitate and/or favour counter-attack with active air support'.[186] The appreciation was issued at 1944 on 16 December. On the same day, in a directive from Field Marshal Montgomery to 21st Army Group, it was stated that:

'3. The enemy is at present fighting a defensive campaign on all fronts; his situation is such that he cannot stage major offensive operations. Furthermore, at all costs he has to prevent the war from entering on a mobile phase; he has not the transport or the petrol that would be necessary for mobile operations, nor could his tanks compete with ours in the mobile battle.'[187]

Germany had begun her preliminary artillery bombardment and the launching of V 1 over the battle area at 0530.

□

The Germans attacked First US Army's front from north of Monschau to Echternach. Their order of battle from north to south was:

Sixth Panzer Army

LXVII Corps:	246th VG and 326th Divisions
I SS Panzer Corps:	1st and 12th SS Panzer Divisions, 3rd Parachute Division 12th VG and 277th VG Divisions
II SS Panzer Corps:	2nd and 9th SS Panzer Divisions in reserve

---

185. DEFE 3/318, HP 9546 of 16 December.
186. Air Sunset 264 of 16 December.
187. WO 285/2, M 538 of 16 December.

Fifth Panzer Army

LXVI Corps:	18th VG and 62nd VG Divisions
LVIII Panzer Corps:	116th Panzer and 560th VG Divisions
XLVII Panzer Corps:	2nd Panzer and 26th VG Divisions
	Panzer Lehr Division and Führer Begleit
	Brigade in reserve

Seventh Army

LXXXV Corps:	5th Parachute and 352nd VG Divisions
LXXX Corps:	212th VG and 276th VG Divisions.

Sixth Panzer Army was to capture the Meuse bridges between Liège and Huy and advance to the Albert Canal between Maastricht and Antwerp. Fifth Panzer Army was to cross the Meuse north and south of Dinant, and advance to a line Antwerp–Brussels–Namur–Dinant to protect Sixth Panzer Army's rear. Seventh Army was to advance through Arlon to the junction of the Meuse and Semois rivers and guard Fifth Panzer Army's southern flank.[188]

During 16 and 17 December the enemy made only limited progress. LXVII Corps was checked north and south of Monschau, and so was part of I SS Panzer Corps in the Elsenborn area. But 3rd Parachute Division broke through in the Losheim gap and this enabled a battle group of I SS Panzer Corps (Kampfgruppe Peiper) to reach the Amblève river at Stavelot on 17 December. Further south, LVIII Panzer Corps reached Düren on 17 December and XLVII Panzer Corps advanced to Clerf, while LXXXV Corps threatened Wiltz and LXXX Corps dented the defences in the Echternach area.*

Despite the language of an order of the day from C-in-C West which was captured by several US units – it declared that the hour of destiny had arrived in the west and called for more than mortal deeds as a holy duty to Fatherland and Führer – First US Army and 12th US Army Group were slow to recognise that they were facing more than a diversionary attack.[189] Reinforcements, an armoured division from Ninth Army and another from Third Army, were ordered to be brought up after news of the offensive reached SHAEF in the afternoon. In its summary for the week

---

* For a concise account of the operations during the German offensive see Ellis, *Victory in the West*, Vol 2 (1968), Chapter VIII. For more detailed coverage see Cole, *The Ardennes: Battle of the Bulge* (Washington DC 1965) in the series of official histories of the US Army and MacDonald, *The Battle of the Bulge* (1964).

188. Cole, *The Ardennes*, pp 75–77, 174–175, 212–213.

189. Ellis, op cit, Vol II, pp 180–181; Pogue, op cit, p 374; MacDonald, *The Battle of the Bulge*, pp 185–190; Cole, *The Ardennes*, pp 80–101.

ending 17 December SHAEF appreciated that it faced a 'diversionary attack on a fair scale' probably involving most of Sixth Panzer Army, the main objective of which was 'without doubt' to relieve Allied pressure in the Cologne–Düsseldorf and Saar sectors. But SHAEF added that 'a real success would mean a lot. ... We should not underestimate the attack's potentialities'.[190] MI 14 agreed that relieving pressure was an objective, and it surmised that von Rundstedt might hope to occupy Liège to force the Allies to withdraw and so eliminate the threat to the Ruhr for some time to come.[191] On the evening of 17 December General Eisenhower ordered 82nd US and 101st US Airborne Divisions from SHAEF Reserve to the Ardennes.[192]

The offensive gained dangerous momentum during 18 and 19 December. Although First US Army maintained a firm shoulder against LXVII Corps and parts of I SS Panzer Corps at Monschau and on the Elsenborn ridge, Kampfgruppe Peiper reached La Gleize and Stoumont; LXVI Corps reinforced by the Führer Begleit Brigade closed in on St Vith; LVIII Panzer Corps took Houffalize; and 2nd Panzer Division, breaking out from Clerf, reached the Houffalize–Bastogne road. A wide gap had opened up between St Vith and Bastogne in which there was little to oppose the advance of 2nd Panzer and 116th Panzer Divisions towards the Meuse. Bastogne itself was threatened by Panzer Lehr and 5th Parachute Divisions, and LXXX Corps on the German left wing had taken Echternach and Waldbillig.

On 18 December SHAEF ordered up further reinforcements, armoured and airborne, from Normandy and the United Kingdom, and General Bradley stopped Third US Army's Saar offensive and ordered it to make a relieving attack against the German left wing in the Ardennes. On 19 December General Eisenhower ordered Sixth US Army to go on to the defensive in Alsace and take over a sector of the Saar front to enable Third Army to increase the scale of its relieving attack; and on 20 December, recognising that Bradley could no longer effectively control First and Ninth US Armies from his HQ at Luxembourg, he placed all Allied forces north of the line Givet–Prüm under the operational control of Field Marshal Montgomery.

21st Army Group's intelligence appreciation of 20 December, the first it had issued since the beginning of the offensive, recognised the inaccuracy of its earlier assessments: the enemy had after all undertaken a spoiling attack in which he was evidently prepared to gamble everything in an effort to reach the

---

190. WO 219/1927, No 39 of 17 December.
191. WO 208/4317 of 17 December.
192. Ellis, op cit, Vol II, p 181; MacDonald, *The Battle of the Bulge*, p 262.

vital crossings of the Meuse. It added that while the situation was clearly dangerous, the next 48 hours should show whether, as it had believed all along, his potential was too limited to give him success in a battle which would affect the whole course of the war.[193] The issue was to remain in the balance for somewhat longer than this. On 22 December the JIC appreciated that von Rundstedt was at least intent on damaging the Allied administrative machine and delaying the next offensive, and might be hoping to seize command of the Meuse crossings, thus eliminating the threat to the Ruhr. It believed that he would be careful not to jeopardise his forces, but warned that if Germany gained major successes he might be over-ruled by Hitler, who, it was now clear, had planned a great offensive to stabilise the front approximately from Antwerp to the West Wall and thence along it.[194] On 24 December SHAEF's intelligence summary said there was no shadow of doubt that the enemy would press his offensive to the limit.[195] In fact he reached his limit, and the battle reached its turning point, during 25 and 26 December.

Between 20 and 23 December Sixth Panzer Army failed in its efforts to penetrate the American defence line of Monschau, on the Elsenborn ridge and in the Bütgenbach sector, and 1st SS Panzer Division, hard pressed at Stavelot, was unable to reach its spearhead (Kampfgruppe Peiper) which was ordered to withdraw on 23 December. C-in-C West accordingly shifted the axis of Sixth Panzer Army's advance, ordering II SS Panzer Corps to swing round by way of St Vith, cross the Salm and attack north-west to Liège. In the centre, however, the offensive continued to prosper. On 22 December it took Rodt and forced the abandonment of St Vith. On 23 December it took Salmchâteau, and while 2nd SS Panzer Division advanced north-west from Baraque de Fraiture, LVIII Panzer Corps took Samrée, reached the Hotton-Soy road and extended eastward towards 2nd SS Panzer Division and westward towards Marche and XLVII Panzer Corps while 2nd Panzer Division of XLVII Panzer Corps took Ortheuville and had a spearhead in Foy Notre Dame – some four miles from Dinant and the most westerly point reached by the offensive – by the evening. Further south Panzer Lehr Division by-passed Bastogne, which was surrounded and attacked on 22 December. The Americans holding out in Bastogne were attacked throughout 23 and 24 December, 26th VG Division being reinforced there by a battle group of 15th PG Division which, with 9th Panzer Division, had been released from OKW Reserve. On Fifth Panzer Army's

---

193. WO 171/134, No 169 of 20 December.
194. JIC(44)590(o) of 22 December.
195. WO 219/1927, No 40 of 24 December.

left flank, where Seventh Army sought to establish a defensive front against the relieving attack from Third US Army, the Germans brought in LIII Corps between XLVII Panzer Corps and LXXXV Corps to control operations by 5th Parachute Division and Führer Grenadier Brigade* to block the roads south and south-west of Bastogne.

On 24 December 2nd SS Panzer Division attacked north-west astride the Liège road; Manhay was taken that night and Grandménil on Christmas morning. 116th Panzer Division attacked in the Marche sector and 2nd Panzer Division tried to reach its spearhead at Foy Notre Dame while Panzer Lehr protected its left flank. But 116th Panzer Division made no progress, and 2nd Panzer's efforts failed in the face of massive Allied air attacks and an Allied armoured thrust in the Celles area. 21st Army Group appreciated on 26 December that the counter-attacks on 2nd Panzer Division and the failure of 116th Panzer Division to take Marche meant that the Germans had been denied the communications centres of Marche and Ciney which were essential for their modified plan for Sixth Panzer Army to reach the Meuse south of Liège while Fifth Panzer Army conformed in a north-west curl.[197] The Allies recaptured Grandménil on 26 December and Manhay on 27 December, and in the afternoon of 26 December American troops broke through from the south and raised the siege of Bastogne.

From 27 December until 3 January, when 21st Army Group's forces attacked south-eastward towards Houffalize and the Bulge came under attack from both sides, the Germans re-grouped for another attempt to capture Bastogne and tried to establish start-lines for a renewed attack to the north-west while the Allies sought to strengthen the corridors to Bastogne and maintained pressure against the tip of the Bulge in the Rochefort sector. Except that the GAF achieved surprise in a major attack on Allied airfields on 1 January – in which it destroyed 150 Allied aircraft and damaged 111, but itself lost 270 aircraft with a further 40 damaged –[198]† there was no marked development in the situation.

---

* The Führer Grenadier Brigade, to be distinguished from the Führer Begleit (Escort) Brigade, was not of high combat value and had suffered severely in East Prussia during its only commitment, so far, as a unit. It had not been fully refitted when ordered to the west into OKW Reserve. It again suffered severely while fighting under Seventh Army, but proved tenacious in a defensive role. For a time, because its numbering and unit names were so similar to the *Grossdeutschland* Panzer Division on the eastern front, it was the cause of some confusion among Allied intelligence authorities who at first identified it as the Division.[196]

† The Germans had intended to carry out this attack in the early stages of *Die Wacht am*

196. Cole, *The Ardennes*, pp 401, 533–534, 545.
197. WO 171/134, No 171 of 26 December.
198. Ellis, op cit, Vol II, p 190.

But it became increasingly clear that the enemy would not regain the initiative. On 29 December 21st Army Group appreciated that II SS Panzer Corps and LVIII Panzer Corps had failed to secure start-lines for a further push to Liège and that the enemy was being forced to switch important reinforcements against the threat to the south.[201] On 31 December MI 14 advised the CIGS that the enemy was making every effort to capture Bastogne, which was vital to his communications, and that if he succeeded he might make another attack on the northern flank of the Bulge; but it doubted whether von Rundstedt would favour this course in view of the strength of the Allied reserves.[202] On 31 December SHAEF was confident that, although he had not yet abandoned his offensive, his major plan had been frustrated; he would soon have to decide whether to make another armoured thrust or to go on to the defensive, or even withdraw, and with his communications becoming daily more difficult, time was not on his side.[203]

□

Although these appreciations, like those issued at the height of the fighting, were made in the light of copious high-grade Sigint, their general character makes them a poor guide to the precise effect of the Sigint on the orders and dispositions of the Allies. This went unrecorded at the time and it cannot now be reconstituted. But the fact that the Allies received Sigint not only in large amounts, but also with little delay, must have given them an enormous advantage, even if it was not decisive for the outcome of the battle. PR also made a contribution by keeping watch on the marshalling yards and railways behind the front, reporting on the progress of the German spearheads and looking out for any activity in Holland which might indicate a diversionary

---

Rhein, but it was postponed on account of the unfavourable weather. Sigint had disclosed on 14 and 15 December that the GAF had made preparations for pilot aircraft to guide fighter and ground level formations, in low level flights starting in darkness (see above, p 437). A decrypt of 22 December had reported that eight Gruppen had been carrying out approach flights and low level attacks on practice targets which, at least at one airfield, had included dummy aircraft.[199] But Sigint provided no further warning until two obviously urgent but unintelligible signals were decrypted in the early hours of 1 January. The first was a circular signed at 2230 on 31 December to all Flivos and announcing Keyword *Goldregen* from 0400; the second a circular issued at 1730 on 31 December to '[strong indications JG 1, 6, 26 and an unidentified unit from 3 JD]' announcing *Hermann* X-ray time 0820. GC and CS sent these decrypts out at 0308 on 1 January, but could provide no details.[200]

199. DEFE 3/320, BT 65 of 22 December.
200. DEFE 3/323, BT 878 of 1 January 1945.
201. WO 171/134, No 171 of 26 December.
202. WO 208/4317 of 31 December.
203. WO 219/1927, No 41 of 31 December.

attack on the weakly held British–Canadian sector along the lower Maas.[204]

The flow of decrypts began on the evening of 16 December. Those sent to the Commands that night reported that every Corps had started according to plan at 0745; disclosed that II SS Panzer Corps was at Schmidtheim at 1230 with 1st and 12th SS Panzer Divisions, 277th and 12th VG Divisions and 3rd Parachute Division; showed that LXVII, LXVI and LXXX Corps were involved; and gave notice that JK II's intentions for 17 December were to support Fifth and Sixth Panzer Armies 'particularly by attacking raids by four-engined bombers'.[205]* During 17 December decrypts disclosed that Panzer Lehr Division had joined the attack, that LXXXV Corps was advancing on Panzer Lehr's left and that JK II was to give continuous fighter cover for I SS Panzer Corps's spearheads.[207] A situation report decrypted by midmorning on 18 December gave the positions reached at 2000 the previous evening by I SS Panzer, LXVI, LXVII, LVIII Panzer, LXXXV and LXXX Corps.[208] GAF West's reconnaissance orders for 17 December, decrypted early the same day, gave priority to the Meuse crossings between Liège and Namur.[209] Other decrypts revealed that the weather had foiled plans for a major flying-bomb operation against London and for GAF intruder operations against Bomber Command during the night of 16–17 December.[210] JK II's intentions for the night of 17–18 and for 18 December were decrypted early on 18 December; throughout the night it was to make continuous attacks to delay the move of Allied reinforcements from the Aachen sector, and during the day it was to give fighter cover against fighter-bombers and heavy bombers to the Army's spearheads, with the main effort in the area St Vith–Manderfeld–Monschau.[211] Its intentions for 19 December, decrypted early that day, were to protect the spearheads of Sixth Panzer Army and the bringing up of II SS Panzer Corps.[212] By 19

---

* Model's appreciation of the Allied reaction to the attack made on the evening of 16 December was not, however, decrypted till much later on 8 January 1945. He said that it had achieved surprise, but he expected at the latest early on 17 December the despatch of reserves from Aachen to Eupen – with an effect on the Ruhr offensive that was as yet unassessable.[206]

204. AIR 41/68, pp 87–88.
205. DEFE 3/318, HPs 9588, 9600, 9606, 9612 of 16 December.
206. DEFE 3/326, BT 1635 of 8 January.
207. DEFE 3/318, HPs 9642, 9656, 9671 of 17 December.
208. ibid, HP 9734 of 18 December.
209. ibid, HP 9631 of 17 December.
210. Air Sunset 265 of 17 December.
211. DEFE 3/318, HPs 9707, 9708, 9719 of 18 December.
212. DEFE 3/319, HP 9790 of 19 December.

December Sigint had established that all the GAF units earmarked for the operations in early November were operating except JG 1, whose arrival was reported the following day.[213] Other decrypts of 19 December disclosed that the Führer Begleit Brigade had been ordered to Vielsalm, west of St Vith, late on 18 December; that Panzer Lehr had crossed the river Clerf on the afternoon of 18 December and was threatening Eschweiler on the road to Bastogne; that at 0830 on 19 December LXXXV Corps had intended to thrust towards Harlange; that at 1330 XLVII Panzer Corps had requested air reconnaissance of the Bastogne area and the approach roads from the south; and that 62nd VG Division had been making for Beho.[214]

On 20 December the location of 1st SS Panzer Divisions's spearhead (Kampfgruppe Peiper) at 1400 and the news that it was short of fuel and ammunition were signalled to the Commands within three hours.[215] The location of II SS Panzer Corps HQ at Schmidtheim in the morning, with LXVII Corps on its right and I SS Panzer Corps on its left, was issued at 1729.[216] On Fifth Panzer Army's front decrypts later in the evening reported unsuccessful attacks on St Vith by 18th VG Division on 19 December and by Führer Begleit Brigade on the afternoon of 20 December, and gave the position of Panzer Lehr Division some four miles east of Bastogne that morning.[217] On Seventh Army's front the intended movements of LXXXV Corps battle HQ during the morning were signalled to the Commands in the afternoon.[218] Seventh Army's situation report for 19 December was also decrypted in the afternoon; it appreciated that because of the threat that Allied troops, which on the evidence of German field Sigint had been withdrawn opposite Army Group G, might push to the Bastogne area, Seventh Army must get south of the town to block the roads as soon as possible.[219]*

An order of 20 December forbidding air attacks on road, rail or improvised bridges west of a line Hasselt–Verviers–Bastogne, 'even when Allied troops were crossing', was decrypted early on 21

---

* Another decrypt available on 20 December reported that 11th Panzer Division had been taken out of the line and sent to Fifth Panzer Army; this intelligence proved to be incorrect, but it persuaded SHAEF and 21st Army Group that the division was in the battle area.[220]

213.   Air Sunsets 266 and 267 of 19 and 21 December.
214.   DEFE 3/319, HPs 9791, 9800, 9826, 9828, 9857 of 19 December.
215.   ibid, HP 9926 of 20 December.
216.   ibid, HP 9929 of 20 December.
217.   ibid, HPs 9930, 9938 of 20 December.
218.   ibid, HPs 9915, 9921 of 20 December.
219.   ibid, HP 9913 of 20 December.
220.   ibid, HP 9927 of 20 December; WO 171/134, No 170 of 24 December; WO 219/1927, No 40 of 24 December.

December.[221] Other decrypts available during 21 December disclosed with little delay that 1st SS Panzer Division was asking urgently for air attacks on all roads to Stoumont and La Gleize, the location of Kampfgruppe Peiper; that later attempts to drop supplies there by air had been abandoned on account of the weather; that II SS Panzer Corps with 12th SS Panzer Division was controlling operations in the Elsenborn sector; that Panzer Lehr Division had by-passed Bastogne to the south and checked Allied attempts to break out.[222] JK II's operational intentions for the following day were decrypted in the evening; it was to clear the air over Sixth and Fifth Panzer Armies and carry out ground attacks in support of the German spearheads.[223] In the early hours of 22 December the decrypt of a GAF signal of the previous evening disclosed Army Group B's intentions. It would continue the thrust to the Meuse with the main body of Sixth Panzer Army and seek to capture St Vith and thrust on Marche with Fifth Panzer Army. Sixth Panzer Army was also to thrust north-west via Elsenborn. Seventh Army, thrusting through Arlon, was to continue attacking south-west.[224]

Army Group B's situation report of the evening of 21 December, giving a comprehensive summary of the substantial progress made by Fifth Panzer and Seventh Armies, was signalled to the Commands by GC and CS the following morning.[225] Later decrypts of 22 December reported that LXXXV and LXXX Corps were making for the line Redingen–Mersch–Grevenmacher; that LIII Corps (a new arrival) was taking over 5th Parachute Division and Führer Grenadier Brigade was coming into the line on the right of LXXXV Corps; that Panzer Lehr was successfully enclosing Bastogne and planned to advance to St Hubert; that LXVI Corps with all its formations had been transferred from Fifth to Sixth Panzer Army, the left-hand boundary of the Corps, which was specified in detail, becoming the Army boundary.[226] In messages intercepted late on 22 December and decrypted early on 23 December an unspecified division was reported to be advancing on La Roche to make a bridgehead at Hotton, Panzer Lehr Division reported that the Bastogne garrison had rejected an ultimatum and was attempting to break out, the GAF displayed some anxiety about the northward movement of Allied forces against Seventh Army, and GAF West ordered JK II to be ready to

---

221. DEFE 3/319, HP 9982 of 21 December.
222. DEFE 3/320, BTs 20, 31, 33, 39, 42 of 21 December.
223. ibid, BT 38 of 21 December.
224. ibid, BT 70 of 22 December.
225. ibid, BT 72 of 22 December.
226. ibid, BTs 85, 87, 115, 116, 120 of 22 December.

engage in a major air battle in the afternoon with Allied four-engined bombers, which were the greatest danger to the Army.[227] In a decrypt available in the evening JK II reported that it was engaging the bombers with strong forces over the lines of communications and with weak elements over the battle-field and that it had suffered heavy losses.[228]

By midday on 23 December Army Group B's intentions for the day were signalled to the Allied Commands by GC and CS: while Fifth Panzer and Seventh Armies continued attacking west and north-west over the Ourthe to extend bridgeheads, Sixth Panzer Army was to make a concentric attack to destroy Allied forces in the area of St Vith.[229] A report on Sixth Panzer Army's attack intercepted in the afternoon and decrypted in the evening disclosed that advance elements of 2nd SS Panzer Division were attacking Salmchâteau and Baraque de Fraiture, 2nd SS Panzer having 9th SS Panzer Division on its right and 560th VG Division (under LVIII Panzer Corps) on its left.[230] Army Group B's intentions for 24 December were decrypted in the early hours. They stated that 'whatever happened' the armour under Sixth Panzer Army was to break through via the Salm sector to the Ourthe, that Fifth Panzer Army was to break through between Durbuy (on the Ourthe) and Dinant to reach the Meuse, with its main attack on its left wing, and that Seventh Army was to continue its attack towards the ordered defence line.[231] It was no doubt on this evidence that on 24 December SHAEF appreciated that the enemy would press his offensive to the limit and that SHAEF and 21st Army Group recognised that while the check in the north had led him to switch Sixth Panzer Army's axis of advance, his objectives remained the same and he would try to take Liège from the south.[232]

Decrypts reflecting the attempt to carry out these intentions followed from the late afternoon of 24 December. LVIII Panzer Corps had reported at midday; the Allies were thickening up in the Marche area and pressing south-west and south-east, German spearheads advancing on Dinant were in front of Conneux and south of Foy Notre Dame and there was street fighting in Rochefort.[233] A report made at 1100 had stated that 2nd SS

227.　ibid, BTs 137, 141, 146, 147, 150 of 23 December.
228.　ibid, BT 196 of 23 December.
229.　ibid, BT 158 of 23 December.
230.　ibid, BT 195 of 23 December.
231.　ibid, BT 208 of 24 December.
232.　WO 219/1927, No 40 of 24 December; WO 171/134, No 170 of 24 December.
233.　DEFE 3/320, BT 249 of 24 December.

Panzer Division was making a concentrated attack towards the Ourthe, that Salmchâteau, the crossroads at Baraque de Fraiture and Odeigne were in German hands and that German tanks were on the southern edge of Fraiture, which was still held by the Allies.[234] A decrypt obtained on the evening of 24 December disclosed that 79th VG and 15th PG Divisions had joined the battle during 23 December, the former subordinated to LXXXV Corps.[235]

A message from Dietrich of 24 December, signalled by GC and CS in the early hours of 25 December, reported that the motorised 2nd Flak Division was taking over the air defence of I and II SS Panzer Corps, and that for the crossing of the Ourthe its main effort would be switched from I to II SS Panzer Corps.[236] In other messages decrypted late on 24 December and early on 25 December it was reported that JK II envisaged ground-attack operations at Bastogne, Soy, Erezée and Vielsalm; that XLVII Panzer Corps had requested that Marche be substituted for Bastogne in this list and that a fighter screen be provided for 2nd Panzer Division's spearhead east of Dinant; that 2nd SS Panzer Division had urgently requested fighter protection for its spearheads, which were being hampered by mass fighter-bomber attacks; and that II SS Panzer Corps and an unspecified formation had also complained about the lack of fighter support.[237] Decrypts later in the day included a report from 2nd SS Panzer Division that it had captured Malempré by 0500 and intended to thrust across the Ourthe; a report that 9th Panzer, 16th PG and 27th VG Divisions were in the Bastogne area at 1430 and that Panzer Lehr Division was moving its battle HQ to Gruport (between Rochefort and St Hubert); Army Group B's day report for 24 December, which drew attention to attacks developing against Seventh Army south of Bastogne, where elements of 352nd VG Division had been surrounded; and a GAF situation report issued early on 25 December which added further details about Third US Army's attack from the south and noted that the Allies were reinforcing the Marche area and thrusting on Celles and Conneux.[238]

Situation reports issued on 25 December and decrypted on 26 December described a static situation in the northern sector, hard and fluctuating fighting in the centre, where some progress had been made and a reconnaissance unit had reached the Meuse near

234. DEFE 3/321, BT 259 of 24 December.
235. ibid, BTs 268, 290 of 24 December.
236. ibid, BT 300 of 25 December.
237. ibid, BTs 273, 277 of 24 December, 305, 333, 367 of 25 December.
238. ibid, BTs 335, 338, 359 of 25 December.

Dinant, and increasing pressure on Seventh Army's front.[239] GAF West's reconnaissance orders for 26 December, decrypted early in the day, gave priority to the movement of Allied reinforcements.[240] Its orders to JK II, decrypted by mid-day, suspended the policy of engaging heavy bombers in favour of protecting the German spearheads and thrust lines against fighter-bomber attacks and called for the concentration of the fighters in an effort to strike a decisive blow.[241] AI had concluded on 24 December from its analysis of the operational Sigint that the GAF's support had reached its peak and that it had incurred heavy losses whenever the weather permitted major operations; it had committed all available forces for an all-out effort over a short period, and its effort might decline rapidly if this was exceeded.[242] On 27 December it commented that although JK II was straining every nerve to keep up the scale of its support, the decline in its strength and serviceability was such that it would be unable to carry on unless a break in the weather allowed it a period for recuperation.[243]

The gradual turning of the tide was also reflected in messages issued on 26 December and signalled to the Commands on that day and on 27 December. One reported that there was no way through St Vith, whose importance as a communications centre had been emphasised in a previous decrypt, following a heavy raid by Allied bombers.[244] Panzer Lehr Division reported increasing pressure on its left flank.[245] 2nd Panzer Division urgently requested air protection for columns moving towards Celles, and XLVII Panzer Corps reported that 2nd Panzer Division was fighting its way back to Rochefort under heavy pressure, that 15th PG Division was developing a defence line in Panzer Lehr's sector and that Allied forces from the south had made contact with the garrison encircled in Bastogne.[246]

Messages issued on 27 December and early on 28 December, and decrypted during 28 December, disclosed that 2nd Panzer had failed to relieve its spearhead and had withdrawn to a defence line at Rochefort, that Kampfgruppe Peiper had withdrawn to Stavelot, that elements of 116th Panzer Division had been cut off by strong Allied attacks in the Hotton–Marche area, and that Allied armoured attacks from north and south had forced the

---

239. ibid, BTs 391, 400, 408 of 26 December.
240. ibid, BT 397 of 26 December.
241. ibid, BT 403 of 26 December.
242. Air Sunset 268 of 24 December.
243. Air Sunset 269 of 27 December.
244. DEFE 3/321, BTs 411 of 26 December, 475 of 27 December.
245. ibid, BT 481 of 27 December.
246. ibid, BT 491 of 27 December; DEFE 3/322, BT 504 of 27 December.

Germans to pull back from Dinant.[247] A situation report of the evening of 27 December, decrypted the following evening, gave the lines on which the attacks of Sixth and Fifth Panzer Armies had finally stalled and on which Seventh Army was trying to stem the Allied advance from the south.[248]

On 28 and 30 December several decrypts reflected the enemy's unsuccessful attempts to establish a start-line for another thrust to the north-west.[249] Decrypts of 29 and 30 referring to Allied pressure in the Rochefort sector included a report from Fifth Panzer Army on the evening of 29 December to the effect that LVIII Panzer Corps was taking over from XLVII Panzer Corps responsibility for 2nd Panzer Division's sector at the tip of the Bulge; it had been ordered to withdraw behind the river L'Homme if compelled to do so, but to hold on to its bridgeheads at all costs.[250] 2nd Panzer Division's withdrawal to the east bank was reported in a decrypt of 31 December.[251]

On the southern flank a decrypt signalled just after midnight on 27–28 December disclosed that in agreement with Dietrich and Manteuffel JK II was to operate that day with the strongest possible force of day-fighters, ground-attack aircraft and jet aircraft against a wooded area north of Bastogne.[252] Later decrypts of 28 December reported the intention to use 167th VG Division (a new arrival) and 3rd PG Division in an effort to capture Bastogne.[253] Decrypts of 30 December added that 1st SS Panzer Division, now subordinated under Fifth Panzer Army to XXXIX Panzer Corps (another new arrival), intended to attack in a westerly direction south of Bastogne to re-establish the encirclement of the town.[254] The decrypt of a report giving the location of 1st SS Panzer Division's battle HQ at midday on 31 December was available in the afternoon, and a decrypt of 1 January gave the line taken up by 1st SS Panzer and 167th VG Divisions south of Bastogne.[255] Later decrypts disclosed that their attack had been thwarted by the arrival of a new American Division, that I SS Panzer Corps with 12th SS Panzer Division was taking over a sector south-west of Bastogne, and that 15th PG Division had been relieved by 3rd PG Division.[256]

---

247. ibid, BTs 525, 598 of 28 December.
248. ibid, BT 589 of 28 December.
249. ibid, BTs 599, 613, 614 of 28 December, 727, 738 of 30 December.
250. ibid, BTs 616 of 29 December, 727 of 30 December; DEFE 3/323, BT 763 of 30 December.
251. ibid, BT 811 of 31 December.
252. DEFE 3/322, BT 526 of 28 December.
253. ibid, BT 578 of 28 December.
254. DEFE 3/323, BTs 752, 764, 772 of 30 December.
255. ibid, BTs 839 of 31 December, 898 of 1 January.
256. ibid, BTs 923, 940, 952, 956 of 1 January.

PART XV

The Other Fronts in the Second Half of 1944

CHAPTER 53

The War at Sea

D URING THE second half of 1944 – indeed until April
1945 – the E-boats kept up their torpedo and mining
operations against the Allied supply lines to the Continent.
They did so against great odds, from bases which gradually moved
eastwards from Le Havre from August onwards, and with small
results. As early as 14 July the JIC dismissed them as being 'of no
more than nuisance value';[1] on 22 July the decrypt of a Japanese
signal disclosed that the German Admiralty had admitted that they
were overwhelmed by superior Allied naval and air forces.[2] But
they displayed enormous persistence, and as they were now
equipped with the *Gnat* acoustic torpedo and an entirely novel
torpedo (the *Dackel*)* as well as *Oyster* mines, they would have
caused much greater disruption if it had not been for the
intelligence the Allies derived from Sigint.

The Enigma decrypts regularly disclosed not merely the
number of E-boats present at the various bases, but how many
were leaving for what kind of operation, in what area and (if the
operation was minelaying) with how many mines;† and frequently,
if not invariably, they did so a few hours before the stated time of
departure. The OIC telephoned this intelligence to the operational Commands; and since the Admiralty's Ultra signals followed
behind the telephone discussions – since, indeed, the flow of
intelligence was now so large that 'it became a physical impossibility to confirm every telephone message by signal' – it would be no
easy task to establish in detail the use they made of it.[4] But it is
reasonable to assume that the Sigint played a significant part in
enabling their operations – particularly those carried out by the
night-flying aircraft of Coastal Command and the Fleet Air Arm,

---

* See below pp 455.

† Decrypts supplied the same information regularly about the mines laid by the GAF, but
whereas the E-boats continued the campaign, the last GAF minelaying operation in the
invasion area recorded by Sigint took place on the night of 20–21 August.[3]

1. JIC(44) 302 of 14 July.
2. SJA 571 of 22 July 1944.
3. ADM 223/202, Ultra signal 1202/21 August 1944.
4. ADM 223/209, 'Receipt of Special Intelligence in the Admiralty and its
   dissemination in the German Surface Units Section [of the OIC]', p 8.

by MTBs under the control of frigates especially trained and equipped for the work, and by Bomber Command in its repeated attacks on the enemy bases – to counter the superior speed and manoeuvrability of the E-boats and restrict their attacks on shipping.[5] It may be noted that the Germans themselves attributed the effectiveness of the Allied defences to Allied intelligence. Decrypts in August disclosed that the E-boat Command believed that the destroyers in the Seine Bay were operating with foreknowledge of German movements derived from Allied exploitation of the E-boat VHF/RT traffic.[6]* It was learned after the war that the U-boat Command had deduced from captured Allied documents in July 1944 that the Allies had 'a clear picture of our U-boat, E-boat and air activity'.[8]

Reinforced after the losses inflicted by the raid on Le Havre on 14 June, the Channel E-boats based on Le Havre, Dieppe and Boulogne numbered 20 from early in July. In that month they operated on 19 nights. Towards the end of the month, frustrated in their efforts to get at the cross-Channel supply shipping, they made attacks on convoys off the English coast. They sank two ships in a convoy off Dungeness on the night of 26–27 July and damaged four ships and sank another in a convoy off Beachy Head on the night of 30–31 July. On these occasions they achieved surprise: the decrypts announcing their departure and intentions were not received in time to help the Allied Commands.[9]

Although two E-boats were sunk and five damaged in Bomber Command raids on Le Havre on the nights of 31 July and 2 August, the Channel flotillas were reinforced from the Dutch ports and there was no decline in their activity. And although they again had little success in their attacks on the Allied supply lines despite the withdrawal to Arctic convoy duties of a large part of the Allied force of surface escorts, and less success than in July in their attempts on south coast convoys, the enemy continued to spring surprises. By 21 August Sigint had disclosed that E-boats from Dutch bases had laid *Oyster* mines for the first time in the Thames estuary, off Margate. This development was so serious a

---

* In fact, although the frigates carried 'Headache' operators the evidence suggests that ship-borne Y made little contribution to the anti-E-boat operations at this stage of the war.[7]

5.   AIR 41/74, *The RAF in Maritime War*, Vol V, pp 23–26; Roskill, *The War at Sea*, Vol III Part 2, (1961), pp 123–124.

6.   ADM 223/267 'Use of Special Intelligence during Operation *Neptune*' (USION), p 166.

7.   *A History of the R/T Y Organisation Ashore and Afloat, July 1940–May 1945*, Section II.

8.   ADM 234/68, BR 305(3), p 72.

9.   ADM 223/200, Ultra signals 0038/27 July, 1718/31 July.

threat to the supply shipping that Bomber Command was ordered to attack the E-boat pens at Ijmuiden; in a raid with eight Tallboy bombs on 24 August it did considerable damage to the pens, but there was no evidence of damage to E-boats.[10] And from the second week of August the E-boats in Le Havre were largely diverted from their normal operations to attacks against the Allied anchorages with a new weapon, the *Dackel*. Fired by the E-boats, this was a long-range pattern-running torpedo having a speed of only 9 knots which could be set to run straight for 16 miles and then either a circular or zig-zag course for a further 18 miles. With this capability it could reach the Allied disembarkation beaches and naval bombardment anchorages from a firing position off the entrance to Le Havre.[11]

The *Dackel* was first referred to in naval decrypts of 9 August which reported that the E-boats would operate with it on the nights of 6–7, 8–9 and 9–10 August from Le Havre. It had not been mentioned previously by any other source and at that point the OIC could only say that it was some sort of self-propelled weapon.[12] If it was used before 9–10 August, the Allies did not notice the fact; but on that night without further warning and on the night of 10–11 August without any warning the enemy scored several hits with the weapons.[13] Decrypts of 11 August gave notice that a further attack would be made that night, and also revealed that the E-boats were firing them from near the Le Havre approach buoy, and thus from so great a distance as to make detection and interception impossible.[14] As early as 14 August, however, an indoctrinated inspection team had established the characteristics of the weapon, with assistance from part of a *Dackel* embedded in one of the damaged ships, and measures had been put in hand for the protection of the anchorage with nets.

The next *Dackel* operations took place on some if not all of the nights of 14–15, 16–17, and 17–18 August. Decrypts revealed that they were planned for all three nights and carried out on at least the last of them, when they sank HMS *Fratton*.[15] But this appears to be the last time they were used, and by 30 August Sigint had disclosed that E-boat and *Dackel* operations from Le Havre had been discontinued.[16]

Following the German withdrawal from the Channel in August

---

10. AIR 41/56, *The RAF in the Bombing Offensive against Germany*, Vol VI, p 103.
11. AIR 41/74, p 31 fn 1.
12. ADM 223/201, Ultra signal 2018/9 August.
13. AIR 41/74, p 31 fn 3.
14. ADM 223/201, Ultra signal 1404/11 August.
15. ADM 223/202, Ultra signals 1635 and 1749/15 August, 1435/16 August, 1227, 1637 and 1730/17 August; AIR 41/74, p 48.
16. Naval Headlines of 30 August.

the E-boats did not abandon offensive operations. On 11 September Sigint disclosed that those based on Ijmuiden and Rotterdam, estimated at 20 by the OIC, were to carry out a combined torpedo and minelaying operation off the English south-east coast on the night of 12–13 September. An RAF strike mounted on the basis of this intelligence frustrated this plan, but the operation was carried out on the night of 16–17 September when decrypts revealed that the location was the Cromer area but gave inadequate notice.[17]

Sigint gave good warning, however, of the next E-boat undertaking. Decrypts disclosed by 15 September that with Calais, Boulogne and Dunkirk surrounded, the enemy had decided that only Dunkirk should be kept supplied and that E-boats had been detailed to take supplies in. During 17 September decrypts added that they would do so on the night of 17–18 September and then that the operation had been postponed for 24 hours. Overnight on 18–19 September four E-boats delivered cargo and evacuated von Kluge, but destroyers of the Nore Command sank three E-boats that were providing cover.[18] In later decrypts the E-boat Command reported that these losses had reduced its operational strength to nine boats and refused to take part in further supply operations, the more so because limited fuel stocks were also reducing its effectiveness.[19]*

By the middle of October reinforcements from Germany had restored the number of E-boats in Dutch ports to about twenty. From then till the end of 1944, with never less than this number, they concentrated mainly on mining in the approaches to the Scheldt, and such was their nuisance value to the Antwerp-Thames shipping route that Bomber Command was called in to bomb their bases in December. Their shelters at Ijmuiden were bombed on 15 December and those at Den Helder, Ijmuiden and Rotterdam on 29 December. But no great damage was done and decrypts showed that two additional flotillas had been brought forward from Wilhelmshafen and Heligoland during 18 and 19 December. The number of E-boats operating from the Dutch bases was between 35 and 40 at the end of the year and it had risen to 48 by early January 1945.[20]

□

---

* It also emerged from these decrypts that at the news of the Allied attack on Arnhem (*Market Garden*) on 17 September OKW had ordered the immediate destruction of the ports of Rotterdam, Ijmuiden and Amsterdam, but that these orders were postponed till further notice after strong objections from the E-boat Command.

17. ADM 223/204, Ultra signal 1805/11 September; AIR 41/74, p 113.
18. ADM 223/205, Ultra signal 1013/17 September; Naval Headlines of 15, 18, 19 and 20 September; AIR 41/74, p 113.
19. Naval Headlines of 19, 20, 23, 25 and 29 September.
20. ibid of 4 October and 20 December; AIR 41/74, p 122.

The KdK Command had meanwhile been operating in the Channel with frogmen, the one-man torpedoes which had been used against Anzio (*Marder*)* and an explosive motor-boat steered by radio control from a command speed-boat (*Linse*) which had been developed more recently. The Germans had planned to use these weapons and also a new one-man submarine (*Biber*) immediately and on a large scale against the Allied invasion. In the event they were unable to bring them to bear until the end of June, and then, as a result of inadequate training and the premature use of the weapon whilst it was still technically under-developed, they used up their small stocks of *Linse* without effect. As a result of transportation difficulties, moreover, they were unable to deploy *Biber* until the end of August.†

Sigint had given no indication that the Germans were developing *Linse* and *Biber* and constructing them in large quantities. But the Allies expected attacks with *Marder* and frogmen – if only because Traffic Analysis had revealed by 29 May that a KdK signals unit had been set up at Le Havre.[22]‡ The first attacks, using *Linse* and frogmen, took place on two occasions at the end of June and again on the night of 3 July without result; these were reported after the event by POW and delayed decrypts.[23] The first to come to the knowledge of the Allies was made on the night of 5–6 July, when *Marder* were discovered penetrating the anchorage defences and two fleet minesweepers were sunk. POW taken during the engagement said that 27 of these craft had taken part and it appeared that four of them had been destroyed; decrypts later revealed that only 16 out of 26 had returned to base near Le Havre but that each of them had claimed to have sunk a destroyer or a cruiser and a considerable tonnage of shipping.[24] In a second attack on the night of 7–8 July *Marder*, estimated to number 22, sank another fleet minesweeper and two MTBs and severely damaged the light cruiser *Dragon* for an estimated loss of five certainly and nine probably destroyed.[25] POW taken in this attack

---

* A decrypt of 21 July disclosed that this cover-name had just replaced an earlier one, *Neger*, for security reasons.[21]

† The Germans also intended to use another type of one-man submarine (*Molch*). This was not mentioned in decrypts until 29 August by which time POW had provided information about it, and it was not used in the western theatre till the end of 1944 (see below pp 460, 461).

‡ See above, p 101.

21. ADM 223/287, USION, p 195.
22. ADM 223/196, Ultra signal 1218/9 June.
23. AIR 41/74, p 30; ADM 223/267, USION, p 193.
24. ADM 223/198, Ultra signal 0124/7 July; ADM 223/287, USION, p 197; Naval Headlines, 15 July; Ellis, *Victory in the West*, Vol 1 (1962), p 300.
25. ADM 123/287, USION, p 195; Roskill, op cit, Vol III Part 2, p 125.

disclosed that the two attacks had exhausted the local stock of *Marder* and that while another flotilla of 30 men was training near Kiel, it would probably not arrive in France before the beginning of August. They also provided the first information about the *Linse* weapon.

The next attack, the biggest so far, followed on the night of 2–3 August. Sigint gave good general warning but no precise notice.* On 27 July decrypts disclosed that from that day, and probably on some day after the arrival of essential equipment on 31 July, the Germans planned to carry out a combined operation with *Marder* and *Linse* in the Seine Bay, probably in the eastern part of it, and that Dönitz was interested in it. Decrypts of 31 July indicated that the operation was imminent – they ordered W/T watch to be set on a special frequency from 1200 on 30 July – and added that the *Marder* and *Linse* were to be launched from the same place and that more than one attack would be made on the same night.[26] Although no more precise information was obtained as to the time and scale of the raid, this intelligence no doubt contributed to the fact that the enemy incurred heavy losses. The Allies lost the destroyer *Quorn* and two small warships, and another destroyer, *Blencathra*, and two 7,000-ton transports were damaged, but decrypts obtained on 8 August reported that the Germans had lost 41 of the 58 *Marder* employed, between 7 and 11 of the 20 *Linse* and between 3 and 5 of the 12 motor boats used to control the *Linse*.† It was subsequently learned from captured documents that the Germans had planned to intensify the attack by firing *Dackel* to cover the retreat of the KdK units, but that a Bomber Command raid on Le Havre on the night of 2 August had frustrated this part of the programme.[27]

In the signals decrypted on 8 August the KdK reported that – as, in the light of this outcome, only mass operations by *Linse* were likely to yield successes – it was considering what use to make of its

---

* This was to be the case for several, though not all, of the subsequent operations. The main source of decrypts was the KdK's Enigma key (Bonito) which was read with some delay. The first decrypts relating to the Channel operations dealt with the attacks of 5 and 7 July and were obtained on 15 July. Thereafter, delays in reading the signals varied between two days and a fortnight. In addition, the decrypts never gave the exact time or destination of an attack or other last-minute details since in the nature of the operations decisions on such questions were left to the men on the spot. Thus general notice that an attack was coming was sometimes obtained but not a precise warning.

† These figures corrected the estimates of the operational authorities, who had claimed the destruction of 30 out of 60 *Marder* and 20 out of 30 *Linse*.

26. ADM 223/200, Ultra signals 2146/27 July, 1250 and 1859/31 July; ADM 223/287, USION, pp 195–196.

27. ADM 223/201, Ultra signal 0923/9 August; ADM 223/172, OIC SI 100 of 9 August; Naval Headlines of 9 August; ADM 223/287, USION, pp 196–197; AIR 41/74, p 31; Roskill, op cit, Vol III Part 2, p 125.

limited remaining forces.[28] A decrypt obtained on 9 August added that it had estimated on 6 August that 16 *Linse* and 12 control boats would be available for its next operation.[29] Its next attack in the Seine Bay had by then taken place on the night of 8–9 August without further warning and in it the cruiser *Frobisher* was damaged. The Allies estimated that they had destroyed 40 *Linse* that night. Decrypts of 10 August showed that the number launched had been 16, and that all had been lost together with four control boats; they also showed that the Germans were claiming to have sunk or damaged eight Allied ships, whereas, apart from the *Frobisher*, the Allies had suffered no casualties.[30]

By 10 August Sigint had disclosed that a further operation was planned to take place from Cabourg in the next few days, and by 14 August decrypts had indicated that two attacks from Cabourg were under discussion. One involving frogmen was against an undisclosed W/T station with the object of capturing cypher material. In the other, carried out at the request of the Army, the object was to destroy the locks at Ouistreham; *Linse* control boats were to transport explosive charges to the target and frogmen were to manipulate them over the last 80 yards. The intelligence picture was complicated on 16 August when decrypts disclosed on the one hand that the explosive charges had not arrived in time from Paris and, on the other, that as, on account of the weather, only 11 out of 53 unspecified weapons had started on the previous night in an operation west of the Orne in which the GAF had been asked to co-operate, the remaining 42 weapons would operate on the nights of 16–17 August with GAF support. This further operation, of which the OIC issued good warning, did take place that night. It turned out to be an anti-shipping attack by *Marder* from which, as Sigint later disclosed, 26 *Marder* failed to return after sinking one small landing craft and torpedoing an old blockship and a merchant vessel. Nothing further was learned about the projected attack on a W/T station. Decrypts obtained on 23 August disclosed that after a preliminary reconnaissance on the night of 18–19 August the attack on Ouistreham had been attempted on the night of 19–20 August, without further warning and without coming to the notice of the Allies; the decrypts reported that the mines had sunk prematurely and added that the prospects of using frogmen effectively in the assault area were now poor.

By 26 August Sigint had reported the arrival from Germany at

28. ADM 223/201, Ultra signal 0923/9 August.
29. ibid, 2340/9 August.
30. ADM 223/287, USION, p 198; AIR 41/74, p 31; Roskill, op cit, Vol III Part 2, p 125.

Fécamp of 28 *Biber*, now referred to in decrypts for the first time
but already known on the evidence of POW to be one-man
submarines, in preparation for an attack in the Seine Bay. Good
notice of the attack followed early on 30 August when a decrypt
disclosed that it had been postponed for 24 hours from the night
of 29 August. From further decrypts it emerged that, partly on
account of being disturbed by an air attack which had been
planned to take place as they left the harbour, 10 out of 24 of the
craft had failed to start on the night of 30 August, and that
following the operation, which did no damage, the *Biber* were
being sent back to Germany; plans to operate with *Biber* and *Linse*
from Calais and Boulogne had been frustrated by the decision to
evacuate naval forces from these ports.[31] By 27 August decrypts
had also disclosed that there were to be no more *Marder* operations
in the Channel and that a new flotilla of 60 *Marder*, which was then
in Tournai, had been ordered to prepare to move to the
Mediterranean.[32]

On 2 September decrypts disclosed that a flotilla of *Linse*, which
had been modified to give them a greater range and had recently
been halted at Brussels, had been ordered to Verona.[33] On 29
August decrypts reported that two flotillas of a new KdK weapon
(code-name *Molch*), hitherto unmentioned by Sigint but known
from recent POW evidence to be another type of one-man midget
submarine, were shortly to be sent by rail from Germany to
Fécamp.[34] But by 2 September Sigint had disclosed that these, too,
had been directed to the Mediterranean on the grounds that they
would be unable to operate from Calais or Boulogne.[35]

During September and October Sigint showed that the KdK had
carried out attacks with frogmen, *Marder* and *Linse* against docks
at Antwerp, shipping in the Scheldt, the Nijmegen bridges and the
Allied disembarkation berths on South Beveland without great
success, though also almost invariably without advance warning.[36]
A *Linse* flotilla operating from Flushing was used to supply

---

31. ADM 223/203, Ultra signals 2215/25 August, 1708/28 August, 1330/30
    August, 1021/31 August; Naval Headlines of 26, 30 and 31 August.
32. ADM 223/203, Ultra signal 0710/27 August; ADM 223/287, USION, p 202.
33. ADM 223/203, Ultra signals 1854/29 August, 0020/31 August; ADM
    223/204, Ultra signal 1722/2 September; ADM 223/287, USION, pp
    203–205.
34. ADM 223/203, Ultra signal 1854/29 August; ADM 223/287, USION, pp
    203–204.
35. ADM 223/203, Ultra signals 1630/30 August, 1000/31 August; ADM
    223/204, Ultra signal 1722/2 September.
36. Naval Headlines of 17 and 23 September, 13 and 27 October, 11
    November; ADM 223/312, OIC S 1039 of 17 September; DEFE 3/239, HP
    3746 of 18 October.

Dunkirk and take supplies to Cadzand for the German Army until, as decrypts revealed, these attempts were abandoned with the Army's withdrawal at the end of October.[37] In November, having previously reversed the decision to withdraw *Marder* from the western theatre, the Germans reinforced the KdK with *Biber*; the arrival of these craft at bases in Holland was disclosed by Sigint from 8 November.[38]* In December they made plans for a concentrated assault with torpedoes and mines against the Scheldt shipping as soon as the weather permitted. *Linse* and *Marder* were to be used, together with *Molch* and *Dackel* and a new two-man midget submarine – *Seehund* – and the operations were to be supported by the E-boat Command. At the end of December Dönitz ordered that the KdK was to have priority over all other commands and that the production of *Seehund* was to have priority over all other coastal defence commitments.[40] Sigint did not yet mention *Seehund* – which was to be the most successful of the KdK weapons – and it did not refer directly to these preparations, but it was clear from decrypts and POW evidence that an effort was being made to build up the strength of the KdK's forces. At the beginning of December the OIC calculated that there were 90 midget submarines (*Biber*) and 120 explosive motor-boats (*Linse*) in Holland and 90 *Biber* and 60 *Linse* in the Bight, out of a total strength in north-west Europe of 270 midget submarines (*Biber*, *Molch* and another named *Hecht*, of which nothing was known), 180 *Linse* and 60 one-man torpedoes (*Marder*), and it believed that 240 more midget submarines, 360 more explosive motor boats and 420 one-man torpedoes would soon be operational.[41] On 24 December, by which time decrypts had still made no mention of *Seehund* but had disclosed that 40 *Molch* and 60 *Marder* had moved forward to Dutch bases, it raised its estimate of the potential strength of the KdK forces: some 600 midget submarines and 660 explosive motor-boats might soon be available.[42]

□

---

* Decrypts showed after the event that *Biber* first operated in the Scheldt on the night of 22–23 December. They sank one ship but all the *Biber* were destroyed by Allied MTBs.[39]

37. Naval Headlines of 29 and 30 October; ADM 223/312, OIC S 1081 and 1082 of 29 and 30 October.
38. Naval Headlines, 23 October, 6 and 7 November; ADM 223/312, OIC S 1078 of 24 October, 1089 of 6 November, 1092 of 9 November.
39. ADM 223/313, OIC S 1136–1138 of 23–25 December; Roskill, op cit, Vol III Part 2, p 153.
40. Naval Historical Branch, FDS 65/54, *German Small Battle Unit Operations 1943–1945*, pp 11–15.
41. ADM 223/315, OIC SI 1139 of 2 December.
42. ibid, OIC SI 1168 of 24 December.

At the beginning of July the enemy ordered the five *Schnorchel* U-boats that had been longest on patrol in the Channel to return to Brest and called to Brest five others that were heading for the Channel. The decrypts revealing these decisions clearly indicated his anxiety about continuing to operate in the Channel and the OIC hoped that his effort would not be sustained.[43] But he reversed these decisions when U-984 reported on her experiences. Although she was the only one of the five withdrawn from the Channel that had not been sunk or badly damaged, she had sunk a frigate on 25 June and torpedoed four large American transports on 29 June. By 7 July Sigint had disclosed that four U-boats from Biscay were sailing to the Channel,[44] and while it emerged from later decrypts that inexperienced boats from the Baltic were no longer being sent there, Biscay boats continued to sail in groups of two or three at intervals of about 10 days till the last week of August.[45]

The U-boat Command was no doubt encouraged by further operational reports from U-boats returning from patrol; several were decrypted during July and early August making large claims and asserting that Allied anti-submarine measures were not being pressed home,[46]* and, unlike the OIC, the enemy was not to know that the claims were greatly exaggerated. But the OIC itself was unable to keep a correct tally of the actual successes of the U-boats: it was often uncertain whether Allied casualties had been caused by torpedoes or mines, for while the decrypts disclosed the sailings of U-boats and their return to port, they rarely gave details of their patrol areas before the U-boats reported at the end of their cruises.† And not least because the OIC could not be sure whether

---

* On 8 July, on seeing some of these decrypts, the Prime Minister drew the First Sea Lord's attention to their allegations of inexperience and unpersevering anti-submarine measures in the beachhead.[47]

† One such message from U-763, decrypted on 17 and 18 July, disclosed that she had been hunted for 30 hours after sinking a small merchant ship on 5 July and had unwittingly drifted into the heavily protected waters of Spithead, where she had surfaced near Nab Tower on 7 July. On the strength of her report the U-boat Command planned to lay *Oyster* mines in Spithead. There were many postponements and it was not until the eve of the German evacuation of the Channel on 21 August that Sigint disclosed that this project was finally cancelled.[48]

43. ADM 223/198, Ultra signals 1418/3 July, 0603/4 July; ADM 223/172, OIC SI 991 of 3 July; AIR 41/74, pp 32–33.
44. ADM 223/198, Ultra signals 0158/5 July, 1426/6 July, 0011 and 1356/7 July.
45. ADM 223/172, OIC SI 1019 of 24 July; Naval Headlines of 21 and 27 July; ADM 223/200, Ultra signal 1230/3 August.
46. ADM 223/198, Ultra signals 2055/8 July, 2107/11 July; Naval Headlines of 13 and 20 July, 3 August.
47. Naval Headlines of 8 July; Dir/C Archive, 7204 of 8 July.
48. ADM 223/199, Ultra signals 1230/17 July, 1252/18 July; ADM 223/172, OIC SI 1049 of 22 August; AIR 41/74, p 35; Roskill, op cit, Vol III Part 2, p 127.

a U-boat had been sunk, it could usually only guess at the number on patrol in the Spout at any one time. It was obvious enough, however, that although the estimated number on patrol rose from four or five on 17 July to six on 14 August,[49] their successes remained limited and their losses high. The Admiralty estimated on 27 August that since D-day 44 U-boats had taken part in the Channel battle, of which 25 had been sunk and 3 probably sunk, and that they had sunk 10 merchant ships, 4 escorts and 3 other commissioned ships and damaged 7 merchant ships and 6 naval vessels.

These figures were given to the Prime Minister on 28 August in a memorandum in which the First Sea Lord informed him that the U-boat Command had abandoned the Channel operation: it had 'ordered all U-boats in the Spout to leave for Norway and directed that all U-boats still in Biscay ports should be sailed when ready for the North Atlantic (west coast of England)'.[50] These decisions, announced on 26 and 27 August in messages decrypted on 27 and 28 August, had clearly been delayed for as long as possible. On 2 August U-boats in the Atlantic had been advised that they might have to make their return passage to Norway if the military situation in France changed; on 3 August U-boats in the Channel had been told to estimate their fuel position on the assumption that they might have to make their return passage to Bordeaux, and U-boats in the bases in Brittany had been told to be ready to move down to Bordeaux and La Pallice from 5 September; and on 15 August U-boats in the Channel had been ordered to return to Norway on completion of their cruises.[51] As late as 24 August, on the other hand, decrypts had revealed that U-247 was sailing from Brest for the Channel and that several other boats were being held in readiness to follow.[52] It may be added that, ironically enough, the Channel U-boats had had their most profitable week of the entire campaign between 19 and 26 August, sinking five merchant ships and two flotilla vessels and damaging one merchant ship.[53]

□

When the U-boats were withdrawn from the Channel the

---

49. ADM 223/199, Ultra signal 1333/17 July; ADM 223/17, OIC SI 1040 of 14 August.
50. ADM 223/172, OIC SI 1063 of 28 August; Cabinet Office file 82/43/1(II), First Sea Lord to the Prime Minister, 28 August.
51. ADM 223/200, Ultra signals 2300/2 August, 1305/4 August, 1611/4 August; ADM 223/202, Ultra signal 1517/15 August; Naval Headlines of 3 August.
52. ADM 223/203, Ultra signal 2011/24 August; ADM 223/172, OIC SI 1054 of 24 August.
53. AIR 41/74, p 46.

evacuation of the Brittany bases was in full swing and the Germans had completed their preparations for the evacuation of the entire Biscay coast.

From the end of July, in anticipation of the evacuation and with the object of destroying shipping and U-boats and preventing a break-out from Biscay, the anti-submarine escort groups and the Coastal Command patrols had been reinforced and a special force including two small cruisers as well as destroyers had been set up under CS 10, this indoctrinated Admiral from the Home Fleet being appointed to ensure that maximum use was made of the available Sigint. During July the escort group EG 12 had obtained some successes with the help of Sigint; on the night of 5–6 July it sank two escorts off Brest, having in all probability been placed there on the news that 10 U-boats had been recalled to the base,* and a week later it sank two more escorts off Lorient after decrypts had disclosed that U-boats returning from the Channel had been ordered to make for Lorient in order to avoid the Allied patrols off Brest.[54] On 20–21 July the GAF had made two attacks on this force with Hs 293 glider bombs, but it had since suffered no further interruption.[55]

Early in August, with the approach of the US Armies, the decrypts showed that the evacuation of the Brittany bases was imminent. On 2 August the bases were warned that all but absolutely essential officers and men would man fortresses or return to Germany, and four homeward-bound U-boats were directed from Lorient to Bordeaux. Messages of 5 and 6 August, decrypted on 6 and 7 August, disclosed that of a total of 43 U-boats, 31 were at 24 hours sailing notice with sufficient crews to reach the south Biscay ports; that Captain U-boats West had moved his HQ from Angers to La Rochelle to avoid being overrun by the Americans; and that Dönitz had stressed the importance of continuing the equipment of U-boats with *Schnorchel* at Lorient even though the Americans had reached the outskirts.[56] The exodus of the U-boats began with the sailing of three from Lorient on 7 August; by 14 August, over and above those still sailing for operations in the Channel or for distant patrols, 15 had left Brest, Lorient and St Nazaire for Bordeaux and La Pallice.[57] The flood

---

* See above, p 462.

54. ADM 223/198, Ultra signals 1426 and 1743/7 July, 1210/13 July; Roskill, op cit, Vol III Part 2, p 129.
55. ADM 234/68, p 76.
56. ADM 223/200, Ultra signals 1712/2 August, 1719/6 August; Naval Headlines of 2, 7 and 8 August.
57. ADM 223/172, OIC SI 1033 and 1040 of 7 and 14 August.

of decrypts also covered the movement southwards of escorts, minesweepers and transports from minor ports as well as from the main bases, the movement of stores, equipment and personnel by sea being all the greater because of the impossibility of evacuation overland.

CS 10's force, sailing from Plymouth on 4 August, scored its first success on the night of 5–6 August, entirely destroying a convoy of four ships and four escorts. In the next three weeks, operating much of the time in coastal waters, it participated with the escort groups, Coastal Command and bombers from Bomber Command and US Eighth Air Force – which carried out a dozen raids on the bases between Brest and Bordeaux, over half of them attacks with Tallboy bombs on the U-boat pens – in the destruction of 12 U-boats, 11 large ships, 53 minor war vessels, many of them minesweepers, and two destroyers.[58] The destroyers, T24 and Z24, were sunk in the Gironde by air attack on 24 August after the receipt of a decrypt about their movements.[59] The relationship between the other enemy losses and the many decrypts about the enemy's movements is difficult to establish, but it may safely be assumed that it was considerable. The decrypts also provided detailed accounts of the German losses and casualties, particularly of the heavy damage done to shipping and dockyard equipment in the bombing raids.*

By 16 August, when American forces had reached the outskirts of Brest, Lorient and St Nazaire, the Allies had also cut the sea communications between the Brittany bases and the southern Biscay ports, and on the following day Sigint gave the news that after the Allied landings in southern France Hitler had decided to evacuate south and south-west France except for some fortresses.[61] Sigint disclosed, also on 17 August, that U-boats were finally leaving Biscay for Norway.[62] By the end of the month a steady stream of decrypts was reporting further departures for Norway, Sigint having disclosed by 19 August that the Germans had given up plans to hold Bordeaux, Bayonne, Biarritz and St Jean de Luz as fortresses, while keeping La Rochelle and points on the Gironde, that Bordeaux would be abandoned by 5 September,

---

* Sigint established, however, that no U-boats were damaged by the bombers even when, as at Brest, the roof of the U-boat pens was penetrated three times.[60]

58. Roskill, op cit, Vol III Part 2, p 131.
59. ADM 223/203, Ultra signal 1112/23 August.
60. ADM 223/202, Ultra signals 1959/13 August, 1711/15 August, 1808/19 August; Naval Headlines of 6 and 7 August.
61. DEFE 3/121, XL 6753 of 1408/17 August; also issued as ADM 223/202, Ultra signal 1853/17 August.
62. ADM 223/202, Ultra signal 1539/17 August.

and that all serviceable vessels were to leave and all non-operational vessels were to be destroyed by that date. A decrypt of 21 August revealed that the date had been brought forward to 31 August.[63] In the event, the last U-boats to leave Bordeaux left on 25 August, three of them being of 1,200-tons which sailed with cargo for Penang and Japan, and on 26 August the U-boat base was destroyed and the harbour rendered useless. The last U-boat left from Brest on 3 September, from Lorient on 9 September, from La Pallice on 10 September and from St Nazaire on 23 September.

The U-boats that had sailed for Norway began to arrive there on 18 September, as Sigint disclosed.[64] A total of 26 had sailed, of which four appear to have failed to clear Biscay. The remaining 22, together with nine which returned to Norway from the Channel, reached Norway or a port in Germany without incident, thanks to their use of *Schnorchel* and of avoiding tactics, and not least to the fact that the Allied anti-submarine forces were heavily occupied by the campaign which the U-boat Command had launched in British inshore waters.[65]

□

The memorandum of 28 August in which the First Sea Lord informed the Prime Minister that the U-boats had abandoned the Channel operation,* ended by saying: 'We now pass to the Battle of the Inshore Routes'. The grounds for this conclusion had been provided by decrypts of signals of 26 and 27 August ordering that U-boats in the Channel should leave for Norway while some of those in the Biscay ports should prepare to sail for the 'North Atlantic (west coast of England)'; they had added that the latter were to embark on 'operations in coastal areas and to head . . . in the first place for the area south-west of Land's End and the Scillies'.[66] By 28 August, moreover, other decrypts had revealed that nine U-boats had sailed from Norway to patrol areas in the North Channel, North Minch, the Moray Firth and off Reykjavik and that an unknown number – Sigint later disclosed that it was only three – had left Biscay for the Bristol Channel and areas off

---

* See above, p 463.

63. ibid, 1443 and 1813/19 August, 1954/20 August, 1929/21 August.
64. ADM 223/172, OIC SI 1082 of 18 September.
65. AIR 41/74, p 44.
66. Naval Headlines of 27 August; ADM 223/203, Ultra signals 1405/27 August, 1029/28 August.

southern Ireland.[67] As we now know, the U-boat Command's first objective was to draw Allied anti-submarine resources away from the U-boats that were leaving Biscay for Norway by routes well west of Ireland.[68]

The inshore campaign was unforeseen by the OIC, which had expected the resumption of attacks on the Atlantic routes.* It was indeed a bold move, and one that would have been impractical but for the determination with which the U-boat Command had pressed on with the programme of equipping its existing fleet of Type VII and Type IX boats with *Schnorchel*. Sigint had shown that a sizeable number of them had already been equipped before June 1944.† It had then established that every U-boat leaving the Baltic after July had been converted, and that strenuous efforts to convert those in Biscay as fast as supply and administrative difficulties allowed had continued right up to the evacuation of the bases there. It has also shown that the U-boats were acquiring growing confidence from their experience with the *Schnorchel*; they regularly reported on this on returning from their cruises and their reports were regularly decrypted. The effects of *Schnorchel* had been reflected, moreover, in the fact that there had been a gradual decline since July in the frequency of Allied sightings and the number of U-boats destroyed.

This decline was most noticeable in the northern transit area, where it became more marked from the middle of August. By the end of that month Sigint had shown that eight outward-bound U-boats had cleared the area in the past two weeks and that 14 others had been on passage in it, including three which returned to port with defects, but Coastal Command had made only four sightings and only two attacks.‡ It was on this evidence that the

---

* See below, p 474ff.

† See Volume III Part 1, p 240.

‡ This trend continued in the northern transit area for the rest of the year. During September Coastal Command reduced its patrols in favour of a bigger effort in the inshore waters, and although 17 U-boats were outward-bound and 38 inward bound from Biscay only five attacks were made at sea and one in the Norwegian Leads; these sank two U-boats and damaged a third.[69] In October 42 out of 49 U-boats passed through undetected and only one U-boat (U-1006) was sunk, and that by surface ship.[70] Four were, however, sunk in a Bomber Command raid on Bergen on 4 October. From the beginning of November air patrols in the area were again reduced in view of the poor prospects for sightings, and in order to increase patrols in inshore waters, and the number of U-boats on passage there

67. ADM 223/172, OIC SI 1062 of 28 August; ADM 223/204, Ultra signal 1940/6 September.

68. AIR 41/74, p 61.

69. ADM 223/172, OIC SI 1087 of 25 September, 1095 of 8 October; AIR 41/74, pp 91–92.

70. AIR 41/74, p 97.

OIC issued on 28 August, at the outset of the battle, the warning that *Schnorchel* 'will be found to have affected profoundly the balance of power between the hunter and the hunted in . . . [coastal waters]. The U-boat will be able to remain submerged for up to 10 days without presenting any target detectable by radar or visually except at short range'.[73]

The warning proved to be well-founded. The Allied air patrols had made one sighting on 27 August in the Minches, but found no further trace of U-boats in the period in which the enemy administered the enormous shock of sinking a large tanker in convoy in the North Channel on 30 August, a frigate escort in the same area on 1 September, a 4,000-ton freighter north of Ireland on 3 September and one more freighter and a large tanker on 8 September.[74] It was no consolation to learn from the decrypt of her patrol report, made a week later, that all but one of these sinkings had been achieved by U-482.[75]

In August, in the expectation that with the loss of Biscay all U-boats would be operating from Norwegian ports, the anti-submarine air patrols over the northern transit route between Norway and the Atlantic had been reinforced. Early in July, for the same reason, preparations had been made for routeing the Atlantic convoys to the south of Ireland instead of to the north; but the first big Atlantic convoy did not arrive via the south-west approaches till 27 August and most Atlantic trade was still converging off Northern Ireland at the beginning of September. On 11 September, following U-482's successes, the bulk of Coastal Command's effort was switched from the northern transit route to the inshore patrol areas which had been disclosed by Sigint, and on 17 September the Admiralty ordered that outward and inward-bound convoys should pass south of Ireland whenever possible.[76] On 12 September, following the receipt of a decrypt disclosing that six further U-boats had been allotted patrol areas in the North Channel area, bringing the number there to nine, the Admiralty had also urgently requested C-in-C Mediterranean to sail ten fast escorts to the United Kingdom as early as practicable

---

decreased to 34 following the completion of the exodus from Biscay; only two sightings were made and only one U-boat sunk.[71] In December not one of the 50 boats on passage in or out was sighted.[72]

71.   ADM 223/315, OIC SI 1157 of 15 December; AIR 41/74, p 108.
72.   Roskill, op cit, Vol III Part 2, p 178.
73.   ADM 223/172, OIC SI 1062 of 28 August.
74.   AIR 41/74, pp 62, 83.
75.   ADM 223/204, Ultra signals 1234/11 September, 1850/12 September; ADM 223/172, OIC SI 1082 of 18 September.
76.   AIR 41/74, p 81; Roskill, op cit, Vol III Part 2, p 176.

to reinforce those in Home Waters.[77]

Sigint showed that the total number of U-boats in inshore waters, 13 on 11 September, dropped to nine by 25 September, to five by 2 October and to between two and three in the second half of October,[78] and they achieved no further successes during these weeks. On the other hand, although there was a large increase in alleged sightings of U-boats, no U-boat was sunk in this period. It was apparent that, just as most of the sightings were mistaking water-spouts and whales for periscopes and *Schnorchel*, so most of the U-boats were choosing to lie stopped at periscope depth away from the busiest shipping lanes, waiting for chance targets, in order to avoid the intense anti-submarine patrols. Their lack of zeal was reflected in the decrypts of the reports they made at the end of their cruises, which often stated that no traffic had been seen, as was the dissatisfaction of the U-boat Command, which frequently exhorted them to patrol closer inshore and insisted that rich pickings were to be had if they were bold.[79]

On 9 October Sigint indicated a new departure by disclosing that six U-boats were leaving south Norway for an eleven-week cruise. The decrypt of a message from the German Intelligence Service had disclosed on 21 September that agents in Lisbon had been asked in August to find out the extent to which Allied shipping had been re-routed south of Ireland, and in an end-of-patrol report decrypted on 1 October a U-boat had suggested that the fact that she had seen very little traffic in the North Channel might be due to the diversion of Allied shipping to the south-west approaches. Moreover, in a decrypt of 1 October, the head of the Japanese Naval Mission reported that Dönitz had told him that 'the improved U-boats' which were already operating round Britain, would soon do so in the Channel. On these indications, and in view of the length of the cruise, the OIC inferred that the new destination might be the south-west approaches, including the St George's and the English Channels.[80] The U-boats in fact headed for the English Channel, and it was in this area that the U-boat Command deployed its main effort and achieved most of its limited successes during November and December 1944.

---

77. ADM 223/204, Ultra signals 1654 and 2357/12 September; Naval Headlines of 13 September.
78. ADM 223/172, OIC SI 1078 of 11 September, 1091 of 2 October; ADM 223/315, OIC SI 1106 of 23 October.
79. ADM 223/172, OIC SI 1091 of 2 October, 1097 of 9 October; AIR 41/74, pp 88, 97–100; Roskill, op cit, Vol III Part 2, p 179.
80. ADM 223/205, Ultra signals 1130/1 October, 2022/9 October; ADM 223/172, OIC SI 1091 of 2 October, 1097 of 9 October; SJA 942 of 1 October.

Decrypts had confirmed the intermediate destination of the six U-boats by 15 October, by which time, however, they had disclosed that one had turned back with defects and another had been diverted to patrol off Islay; the remaining four were ordered to make for Cape Clear, the south-west tip of Ireland. One of these – U-1006 – was sunk between the Shetlands and the Faroes on 16 October, and the Allies then turned to good account the knowledge that the remainder were making for Cape Clear. Unaware of the loss of U-1006, the U-boat Command on 24 October ordered three of the four to the central Channel; but on 29 October U-246, one of the three, reported that she had been damaged by air attack off Cape Clear on 25 October and forced to return to Norway. An additional boat – U-991 – was brought in to take her place in the Channel on 7 November; but another one of the group – U-1200 – was sunk of Cape Clear by surface forces on 11 November. U-991 entered the Channel on 12 November and patrolled without success till the end of the month. The sole survivor of the original four – U-978 – sank a merchantman off Barfleur on 23 November and then returned to Norway.[81]

The decrypt of a long situation report from the U-boat Command had meanwhile, on 30 October, provided further evidence of its growing interest in the south-western approaches. The report noted that some of the shipping previously routed exclusively to the North Channel was now using this area; listed the positions along the south Irish coast and on the Land's End and Bristol Channel routes that were probably being followed by convoys; and gave details of the prohibited area which the British authorities had declared early in the war, but which was believed to be no longer dangerous to U-boats in that its minefields had probably not been renewed, and of a swept channel through the area.[82] It was no doubt on the strength of this intelligence that on 31 October Coastal Command arranged to supplement its inshore patrols with close escort sweeps ahead of convoys and that the Admiralty intensified in November the laying of minefields between southern Ireland and the north coast of Devon and Cornwall, work which had been started early in October.[83]*

---

* In order to discourage the U-boats, the Admiralty also took steps to bring this activity to the attention of the Germans, using the double agent *Tate* to report that mines were being laid here and in the North Channel and that U-1006 had been sunk by mine south of Ireland. His reports had the desired effect: a decrypt of 18 November disclosed that U-boats had been warned that mines had been laid and ordered to enter St George's Channel and the Irish Sea

81. Naval Headlines of 16, 24 and 30 October, 9 November, 5 December.
82. ADM 223/315, OIC SI 1111 of 30 October; ADM 223/207, Ultra signal 2317/31 October.
83. AIR 41/74, p 94; Roskill, op cit, Vol III Part 2, pp 81–82.

In the event no U-boat was sunk by mine in the south-west approaches in 1944. As a result, indeed, of the priority the U-boat Command was giving to the English Channel, only two patrolled there during November and December. But this was not known at the time. The accuracy of the OIC's U-boat Tracking Room, which had already suffered during the battle in the Channel up to the end of August, continued to decline thereafter as the tactical conditions of the offensive in inshore waters and other developments brought about changes in the enemy's wireless habits which added to the difficulties produced by his increasing experience of operating *Schnorchel*. At the end of August the OIC had foreseen that *Schnorchel* would enable U-boats to remain submerged for up to 10 days; from the beginning of October decrypts of reports from U-boats and appreciations of *Schnorchel* issued to U-boats were mentioning that periods of 50 and even 70 days had been spent submerged.[85] As well as moving to and from their patrol areas in a state of total submergence, thus greatly reducing the number of Allied sightings, the U-boats were doing so at differing speeds; and this made it impossible for the Tracking Room to judge their current whereabouts by extrapolating from such sightings as were made or from such intelligence as the decrypts had provided. On 30 October the OIC gave this as the main reason why its plot, which was relied on for all convoy escort flying and much of the patrol flying carried out by the Allies, 'did not succeed at all closely in reproducing the reality'.[86] To make matters worse, the volume of Sigint about U-boat movements was itself declining. For a number of reasons – the fact that the U-boats were now normally operating singly; the fact that they were so often submerged; the loss of so many shore W/T stations in Germany's retreat; perhaps, also the consideration that precautions were necessary against the possible compromise by capture of cypher material – the U-boat Command discontinued its long-established practice of signalling sailing orders and patrol instructions to U-boats while they were at sea. Increasingly, the signals sent to them merely supplemented or modified orders given in advance and known only to the U-boat concerned; and

---

only along known shipping routes. A German account confirms that such reports were received from *Tate* on 15 and 24 November and adds that, although none of the intelligence supplied by *Tate* had ever been substantiated, these precautions had to be taken.[84]

84. ADM 223/315, OIC SI 1132 of 20 November; ADM 234/68, p 95. See also E Montagu, *Beyond Top Secret U* (1977), pp 173–177, but this is a garbled account.

85. US Department of Defense, *Allied Communication Intelligence and the Battle of the Atlantic*, Vol II, pp 211, 215, 216; ADM 223/208, Ultra signal 1346/14 November.

86. ADM 223/315, OIC SI 1111 of 30 October; AIR 41/74, p 193.

from early in December, in a further refinement of this process, the signals were increasingly encyphered in Sonderschlüssel – keys restricted to a single U-boat and unreadable by the Allies – instead of in the general U-boat Enigma key. And this was at a time when the Admiralty feared that at any minute the Germans would bring into force a new system (Kurier) for off-frequency high-speed transmissions from the U-boats.[87]*

But if the OIC had repeatedly to report that 'the situation in coastal waters remains obscure',[88] the uncertainty applied only to the whereabouts of individual U-boats and their distribution among the inshore areas.† Not least because W/T communication using the general U-boat key was continuous between Captain U-boats Norway and the U-boat Command, Sigint still provided a good guide to the scale of the enemy's effort and some indication – if not always advance notice – of his intentions. It showed that the number of U-boats committed to the inshore campaign rose steadily during the last two months of 1944, from 6 on 30 October, to 11 on 27 November, to 17 during most of December and to 20 on 1 January 1945,[90] and that while at least one U-boat was always on patrol in the North Channel, the Minches and the Irish Sea, the majority were being sent to the English Channel and, from early in December, to the Scapa area.

On 29 November decrypts disclosed that three U-boats – U-322, U-400 and U-772 – were leaving for an intermediate position west of Shannon and that three other boats were sailing to undisclosed destinations. By 13 December the OIC had concluded that the first group had been ordered into the English Channel; but U-332 had by then been sunk on passage by surface forces and U-400 was sunk, also by surface forces, off Cape Clear on 17 December.

---

* See Appendix 15(iv) for Sonderschlüssel and Kurier.

† Thus, of the U-boats intended for the Irish Sea, a decrypt of 12 November disclosed that U-1202 had been ordered to Milford Haven and a decrypt of 24 November disclosed that U-680 had been ordered to the Bristol Channel. But no more was learned about U-1202, which unsuccessfully attacked the liner *Caernarvon Castle* off Holyhead on 8 December and sank a merchant vessel off Milford Haven on 10 December, and Sigint did not disclose that U-680 was re-directed to the English Channel; presumably her orders were sent in her special key. U-773 patrolled off Cork towards the end of December; but no doubt for the same reason Sigint, which revealed on 12 November that she had been sent on a supply mission to St Nazaire with U-772, did not mention that she had subsequently been ordered to Cork.[89]

87. ADM 223/315, OIC SI 1150 and 1158 of 11 and 18 December; P Beesly, *Very Special Intelligence* (1977), pp 248–249.
88. ADM 223/315, OIC SI 1132 of 20 November, 1137 of 27 November.
89. ibid, OIC SI 1127 of 13 November, 1150 of 11 December; Naval Headlines of 12 and 24 November.
90. ADM 223/315, OIC SI 1111, 1137, 1143, 1166 and 1174 of 30 October, 27 November, 4 and 24 December 1944 and 1 January 1945.

U-772 sank two ships on 23 December and one on 28 December off the Isle of Wight before being sunk by air attack – now a rare event – off Portland on 30 December. A decrypt disclosed on 19 December that the second group – U-1209, U-486 and U-484 – would soon be in the Cherbourg area; nothing had previously been heard of them since their departure on 29 November. Of this group U-486 sank two large merchant ships and a frigate and damaged a second frigate between 18 and 26 December; but U-1209 collided with Wolf Rock and became a total loss and U-484 remained in the Channel till the end of the year without achieving anything.[91]

The first indication that U-boats were operating off Scapa was received on 16 December, when a decrypt revealed that U-297 and U-1020 had been ordered on 14 December to 'get right up to the entrances' in an attempt to intercept an Allied carrier force. The fact had not been disclosed that the U-boat Command had sent them to the area early in the month in the hope of disrupting Allied carrier-borne attacks on the German supply convoys off the Norwegian coast, and U-297 had already been sunk by frigates searching for two other U-boats which Sigint had reported to be en route to Cape Wrath and the North Channel on 26 November. A signal decrypted on 17 December ordered U-278 and U-312, two *Schnorchel* boats from the Arctic force, to the same area and informed them that U-297 and U-1020 were already there. A decrypt of 28 December ordered a fifth boat, U-313, to Scapa and advised her that U-297 and U-312 were still there. No further Sigint was received about any of these U-boats. As we now know, U-312 arrived on 23 December and left on 26 December after damaging herself in attempting to enter the flow through Hoxa Sound, and U-1020 was lost in unknown circumstances. They achieved no successes. But it was a disturbing thought that, like Prien in October 1939, U-boats might now operate in such a sensitive area without warning from Sigint.[92]

During November and December the U-boats in Home Waters sank eight merchantmen and damaged two, while four warships were sunk and two damaged beyond repair. This was a small return for the loss of six of their number and in relation to the large number of U-boats employed – and all the more a testimony to the severe restrictions imposed on the U-boats by their dependence on *Schnorchel* in that, as was clear from Sigint, most of

91. ibid, OIC SI 1143 of 4 December, 1150 of 11 December; Naval Headlines of 11 December; AIR 41/74, p 103; Roskill, op cit, Vol III Part 2, p 185.
92. Naval Headlines of 26 November, 17, 18 and 29 December; ADM 223/315, OIC SI 1150 and 1158 of 11 and 18 December; ADM 234/68, p 90; Roskill, op cit, Vol III Part 2, p 164.

the successes were achieved by three U-boats with determined commanding officers, U-478, U-462 and U-722. On the other hand, the effectiveness of *Schnorchel* as a defence measure was shown by its success in neutralising the Allied anti-submarine air patrols. In an astronomical number of flying hours they made few sightings and even fewer attacks, and sank only one U-boat in these two months. This development threw an enormous burden on the naval anti-submarine forces, and one that was all the greater in that the Admiralty was deriving less assistance from Sigint in deciding when and where to concentrate their patrols. It was obvious as 1944 drew to a close that if the offensive continued, and if the problems presented by *Schnorchel* continued to be accentuated by a decline in the volume of operationally valuable Sigint, a still greater concentration of surface and air defences in and near the inshore areas would be called for. And it was no less obvious that should Germany also renew the offensive against the Atlantic convoys with the new-type U-boats, as Sigint had shown her to be striving to do since the previous autumn, the Allies would be in serious straits. Their anti-submarine and escort forces were already fully stretched in dealing with the inshore campaign and they would be hard put to find the extra forces required for meeting this further threat.

□

The return of the U-boats to the Atlantic convoy routes in the autumn was expected from the end of July. In a memorandum to the First Sea Lord on 20 July the NID warned that 'the Germans are now implementing a plan . . . to be in a position to resume the U-boat offensive in the autumn with a re-trained and reconstituted U-boat fleet'. The bulk of the fleet would consist of the existing types of U-boat fitted with *Schnorchel* and probably with improved search receivers, but a few of each of the new types XXI and XXIII might be operational by August–September and some 20 of each by the end of the year.[93]* On 28 July the JIC repeated the prediction: the enemy would have not only the advantage of the new type U-boats but a retrained older fleet with *Schnorchel*

---

* It was perhaps this memorandum which prompted the First Sea Lord on 29 July to send ANCXF an Ultra signal pointing out that the U-boats in the Channel were still tying down a large force of surface escorts when that was needed both for the impending resumption of Arctic convoys by the Allies and the expected resumption by the enemy of the offensive against Atlantic shipping; ANCXF was urged to strike at the Channel U-boats in every possible way.[94]

93. ADM 223/320, NID 0835 of 20 July 1944.
94. ADM 223/200, Ultra signal 1836/29 July.

and a new search receiver against Allied centimetric radar *when* he resumed Atlantic warfare in the autumn.[95]

There was no precise intelligence to support these warnings. They were issued in a precautionary vein in the expectation that the U-boat effort in the Channel would be over before the autumn, and the possibility that the Germans would first switch their offensive to the inshore waters, as they did from the beginning of September, was not foreseen.* As for the threat from the new types of U-boat, such intelligence as there was was reassuring. A signal from the Japanese Naval Mission in Berlin, decrypted in the middle of June, disclosed that the new U-boats 'would be unable to be in service in the autumn as had been hoped'.† But this provided no grounds for thinking that an offensive resting mainly on the older types would be delayed: the older types still constituted a formidable force. In July the OIC estimated that they totalled 356, 168 at sea or in operational bases and 188 working up or refitting, many with *Schnorchel*, in the Baltic. By the end of July, moreover, it was known from PR that the Germans were pressing forward the completion of U-boat shelters at Bergen and Trondheim, and, from POW, that U-boats were training with a new search receiver (*Samos*) capable of intercepting centimetric radar.[96]‡

Until October, by which time the inshore waters battle was in full swing but the predicted Atlantic offensive had still not materialised, the new types of U-boats continued to be only a subordinate source of anxiety. The closest watch was kept on the rate at which they were being assembled, for which the main source of intelligence was PR, and on the numbers that had been commissioned, which were disclosed by naval Enigma decrypts, but the results were not alarming. The number of Type XXI detected under construction on the assembly slips or lying alongside was 31 on 7 August, 46 on 5 September and 61 on 18 September. As for those commissioned, Sigint had reported the first two by the end of July and the number identified then rose to 4 by 28 August, 9 by 11 September, 11 by 2 October and 15 by 16 October.[97]§ In one

---

* See above, p 467.

† See Volume III Part 1, p 245.

‡ It was soon to emerge that the U-boats used the new receiver, which was attached to the *Schnorchel* mast, for two purposes: to detect approaching aircraft when the U-boat was surfaced and also, when using *Schnorchel*, to get sufficient warning of aircraft to enable them to retract the mast before the aircraft could get a good fix.

§ For Type XXIII see below p 485ff. Uncertainty about the characteristics of this type was

95. JIC (44) 316 of 28 July.

96. ADM 223/172, OIC SI 1019 of 24 July.

97. ibid, OIC SI 1019 of 24 July, 1061 of 28 August, 1077 of 11 September, 1091 of 2 October, 1102 of 16 October.

of the few observations made on these figures up to mid-October NID's U-boat construction section (NID I(d)) commented on 11 September on the length of time the new types were taking to work up and be commissioned, and speculated, in fact correctly, that the delay might be explained by faults incurred during the assembly process.

Estimates of the rates of new-type construction provided by the Germans to the Japanese authorities in Berlin, and obtained from decrypts of Japanese telegrams which were themselves somewhat sceptical, were similarly treated with reserve in London. In a telegram of 12 August, decrypted on 17 August, the Japanese Ambassador reported remarks by Speer, who was in charge of the new-type U-boat construction programme. The monthly output would be more than 18,000 tons [about 20 boats] by October but – this in reply to the question whether the U-boat war would be resumed in that month – Dönitz would wait till a sufficient number of the new U-boats were available to enable him to strike suddenly and in great strength. NID commented that Speer might be exaggerating the output figure, and the JIC doubted on 7 September whether the figure could be achieved. On 16 September – but expectations were then high that the Germans would collapse before the end of the year –* the JIC expressed the view that 'the new type U-boats are unlikely to have any important influence on the course of the war'.[98]

On 27 September the decrypt of a lengthy signal made by the head of the Japanese Naval Mission disclosed that at the end of August, when new-type production was beginning to accelerate, the planned period of 12–15 weeks from the construction of sections to commissioning had not been achieved in practice; that the planned monthly output of the three yards carrying out the final assembly of the boats was 30 boats; that while this output ought to be achieved 'before very long', the methods of construction by which individual plants produced in series single key components made the programme vulnerable to air attack; but that Speer had said that a production rate of 58,000 tons was planned for December 1944. On this NID commented that the Germans might have given exaggerated figures; on the evidence

---

cleared up by mid-July when Sigint indicated that it was intended for use in short-range operations (the North Sea, the Channel or the Mediterranean) by establishing that it was a boat of about 200 tons with torpedo armament, and PR had by then detected U-boats 110 feet long and clearly different from Type XXI. But in its returns of the new-type boats among the total of commissioned non-operational U-boats the OIC did not distinguish between Type XXI and Type XXIII until 28 August.

* See above, pp 367–369.

98. JIC(44) 397 and 407 of 7 and 16 September.

from PR the probable monthly output would be about 16 boats (23,500 tons) in December.[99]

At the same time, it warned that the PR evidence now suggested that about 60 Type XXI might be ready to operate by December 1944, rather than the figure of about 20 that had been offered in July. Though this estimate was soon reduced, it no doubt reflected the fact that euphoria about Germany's imminent collapse had come to an end and it marked the point at which the Admiralty, recognising that Germany had delayed her expected return to the Atlantic in the autumn, focused its anxiety on the prospect that she would resume the offensive against convoys with the Type XXI at the end of the year. On 16 October NID I, which had commented on 25 September on the lack of evidence on the operational readiness of the new types, as distinct from their completion and commissioning, offered its first assessment of the cumulative totals of completed boats (those that had finished the fitting out stage) and of operational boats (those that had finished working up and training in the Baltic). It conceded that the estimates took no account of the delays that might be imposed by Allied bombing and mining, but returned, even so, to the July estimate for operational boats:

	Cumulative total of completed boats	Cumulative total of operational boats
October 1944	15	—
November	25	9
December	40	15
January 1945	65	25
February	95	40
March	125	65
April	155	95

Already on 9 October, however, it had drawn the conclusion from recent Sigint and other sources that Germany 'planned to renew her U-boat offensive with new type U-boats at the end of the year'.

The recent Sigint had begun with the receipt on 1 October of the decrypts of two more signals from the head of the Japanese Naval Mission. In interviews he had recently had with Dönitz and Admiral Meisel (Chief of the Naval Operational Staff) Meisel had claimed that the Germans intended to 'distribute [the new boats] to the front line in October'. Dönitz had said that Germany was resolved to continue the U-boat war to the end; the new boats had three times the endurance of the old and would be able to operate from Kiel, Hamburg, Bremen, Trondheim and Bergen, at all of which bases 'bunkers' existed, and the fact that they would be

---

99. SJA 923 of 27 September.

exposed to threat from British minelaying was a problem that could be overcome.[100]*

Further Sigint had added to the growing anxiety by the end of October. The decrypt of a message from the German Intelligence Service disclosed on 4 October that its Madrid office had been advised that reports of convoy sailings from north America were 'most urgently desired from December'. By 9 October naval Enigma decrypts had revealed that swingeing demands had been made for the release of personnel for U-boat training from the German surface fleet. On 14 October the decrypt of a signal sent by the Japanese Naval Attaché at the end of September revealed that the Germans had assigned a long-range version of the Do 335 aircraft to 'co-operate with the new type U-boats in open sea operations due to begin shortly'.[102] In an earlier signal, the decrypt of which was circulated by NID to the DNI on 23 October, the Attaché had reported that air reconnaissance would be essential for the total underwater operations of the new U-boats in the open ocean, though not for those off focal traffic points and anchorages.

The effect of these decrypts was soon registered in the Allied appreciations. On 9 October NID believed that the decrypts strengthened the previous indications that 'Germany planned to renew her U-boat offensive with the new type U-boats at the end of the year'. On 16 October the JIC also concluded that Germany planned such an offensive with considerable numbers of the new types from the protected bases she was now rapidly constructing in Norway, and on 18 October the Chiefs of Staff requested the JIC to report on whether the enemy would have sufficient fuel for a new U-boat offensive. On 19 October the US naval authorities advised the US Air Forces, which had recently declined a request to bomb the U-boat pens in Norway, that as many as 300 new-type U-boats might soon be operating.[103] And the fear that an offensive was imminent was redoubled when on 23 October Dönitz issued and the Allies decrypted a special address to 'the Atlantic U-boat

---

* This was the first indication that the German ports would be used as operational bases. But on 2 October PR detected the first signs that a U-boat bunker was being built at Farge near Bremen. In reply to the Prime Minister's request for comments on the decrypts the First Sea Lord stated that plans were being made to exploit the U-boat vulnerability to mining.[101]

100. SJA 942 of 1 October. Sent to the Prime Minister as Dir/C Archive, 7723 of 3 October. The First Sea Lord's reply to the PM's request for comments is in a memorandum in the Dir/C Archive dated 6 October.
101. Dir/C Archive, 7723 of 3 and 6 October.
102. SJA 991 of 14 October.
103. JIC(44) 437 and 443 of 16 and 18 October; Craven and Cate, *The Army Air Forces in World War II*, Vol III (1951), p 720.

services'. This address, entitled 'Why U-boat War?' began by announcing that 'the front against the Western Powers had again become the decisive front of the war'. After insisting that imports into the United Kingdom had been reduced to the minimum required to avoid starvation and maintain armaments production, it insisted that 'the new U-boat war must be, and would be, the most important German aim in the war against the Western Powers'; that the prospects for it were wholly favourable; and that 'its effects must make themselves felt before the end of the present year'. 'The final issue of the war might, after all, be decided by the U-boat war that is now gathering way'.[104]

The response to this decrypt was immediate and profound. The OIC's Tracking Room produced on the same day a special unnumbered appreciation to the effect that 'reliable evidence over a period of some months indicates that Dönitz intends launching an all-out U-boat campaign in the near future, and in full confidence that improved radar devices, the SNORT [*Schnorchel*] and the new types of U-boat ... will regain the ascendancy the U-boats enjoyed in 1942'. It believed that the campaign would start sometime between mid-November and mid-December. It considered that 'partial success will hamper the maintenance of our Forces in Europe and a major success might halt our offensive indefinitely and certainly prolong the war as well as acting as a violent stimulant to German morale'. The appreciation was sent by the First Sea Lord to the Prime Minister with a covering note, also dated 23 October, which said that 'the introduction of the SNORT ... and the new type U-boats ... may provide us with a tough proposition'.[105] The main points in the appreciation were repeated in another appreciation drawn up on 23 October by ACNS (U-boats and Trade) for non-Ultra recipients; they included the estimate that the enemy had designed his building programme to maintain an operational strength of 200 U-boats, comprising old types and new types, which would permit him to keep 140 at sea at any one time.

The alarm raised by the intelligence which culminated in the Dönitz decrypt was no doubt kept up by receipt at the end of October of the decrypt of another message from the German Intelligence Service; dated 20 October, this had reminded the station in Madrid of the urgency of the earlier request for information about Atlantic convoy sailings; it had also asked for information about which parts of the Atlantic were not effectively covered by air patrols and had added that the German naval

---

104. DEFE 3/737, ZTPGU 32796 of 23 October.
105. Cabinet Office file 82/43/1 (II).

authorities also wanted information about all convoy traffic along the east coast of north America. At all events, as soon as the Allied air commands had completed on 1 November the bombing operations they had carried out in preparation for the landings on Walcheren, the Admiralty requested high priority for bombing attacks on U-boat construction in Germany and U-boat facilities in Norway in the belief that a new and dangerous U-boat offensive was imminent.[106]*

As we now know, Dönitz's address, which in fact avoided any specific reference to the new-type U-boats, was partly prompted by his embarrassment at the delay in bringing them forward after so much hope had been placed in them; he was continually having to explain to Hitler at this time why he had not started the U-boat offensive.[108]† At the time the suspicion that this might be so – like similar suspicions which earlier decrypts had aroused in the NID – was perhaps revived by the decrypt on 4 November of the signal covering another interview between the Japanese Naval Mission and Admiral Meisel on 30 October. Meisel had said that although it had been intended to operate the new U-boats from October, they were not yet, on account of air raid damage to parts under construction and in transit, numerous enough to have much effect.[110] But even before this decrypt was received the alarm was being checked by the intelligence that was coming in about the rate at which the new U-boats were being commissioned.

The weekly Tracking Room summary issued on 23 October, which had recapitulated the text of the Dönitz address, had added that there was still no evidence that any new-type U-boat was yet in operational service or likely to be in the immediate future. The summary of 30 October repeated this, though adding that 10 Type XXIs had been working up for over 50 days. That for 6

---

* The Air Ministry resisted any further diversion away from the offensive against the oil targets and the matter was referred to the Cabinet's anti-submarine committee. At that committee the Prime Minister ruled against the Admiralty for the time being. At a special sub-committee set up to continue the debate the Air Ministry, sceptical of the supposed increased threat from U-boats, continued to oppose any diversion from existing bombing priorities at least until the threat materialised. At the same time the sub-committee, representing the Air Staff, US Eighth Air Force, the Admiralty and MEW, was unanimous in thinking that bombing of U-boat targets would have to start inflicting major damage before mid-January 1945 if it was to produce any serious effect before May.[107]

† But he had told Hitler on 12 October that the first of Type XXIII and 40 of Type XXI would be operating in the Atlantic in January and February 1945 respectively.[109]

106. AIR 41/74, pp 162–163.
107. ibid.
108. Webster and Frankland, *The Strategic Air Offensive against Germany*, Vol III (1961), p 274.
109. ADM 234/68, p 94.
110. SJA 1102 of 4 November.

November confessed that 'the enemy's new U-boat offensive is still in a very early stage of development and no serious threat can be produced in the immediate future', and it went on to say that 'there is a striking disproportion between the meagreness of the force so far deployed and the magnitude of the fleet of U-boats which should by now have had ample time to complete their working up and which must on any prudent view be considered to be in a state of operational readiness for operations'. In this summary, moreover, the number of U-boats estimated to be in a state of readiness by 1 January – 205 including 19 Type XXI and 14 Type XXIII – did not greatly differ from the estimate made as long ago as July.[111] And the summary for 13 November made no reference to the new U-boats or to the impending offensive beyond the comment that 'no major strategic development or change has manifested itself during the week'.[112]

From the middle of November the Japanese decrypts testified unambiguously to the deferment of the planned U-boat offensive. A decrypt of 20 November disclosed that on 15 November the Naval Attaché had been told by the German Naval Operational Staff that 'the date when the new classes of U-boat will become operational will vary according to the extent of any damage sustained from future air attacks, but they should begin operations in December or January or thereabouts'.[113] A decrypt of 8 December disclosed that on 3 December the Attaché was told that although 'from the Führer downwards the whole Navy and the Ministry of Munitions have seriously set about preparing these U-boats . . . they will probably not start operating till about March of next year'; they had been due to start in November 1944, but construction had been delayed by Allied bombing, and there had also been a gradual postponement on account of the need to make alterations and improvements to the various parts.[114] At the same time, however, PR and the naval Enigma decrypts showed that although construction and completion of the new U-boats were not increasing at the rate the Germans had intended, they were nevertheless improving steadily.

By 6 November the number of Type XXIs known to be under construction, that is on the assembly slips or fitting out alongside, was 75 (as compared with 46 on 5 September) and the number commissioned and working up was 17 (as compared with six). By 18 December these figures had increased to 95 and 35. It was

111. ADM 223/315, OIC SI 1106 of 23 October, 1111 of 30 October, 1119 of 6 November.
112. ibid, OIC SI 1127 of 13 November.
113. SJA 1163 of 20 November.
114. SJA 1259 of 8 December.

clear, moreover, that of the 95 under construction, 15 were near completion; that an average completion rate of 15 a month had been achieved, 7 or 8 of them at Danzig, which had so far escaped the consequences of bombing; that of the 35 commissioned, 12 had been working up for two months; and that the number which had worked up for two months would rise to 20 by the end of December.* By the same date PR had indicated that of the shelters at Hamburg, Kiel, Bremen and Farge, which protected the assembly and fitting out, those at Hamburg and Bremen might also be intended as operational bases additional to those being developed at Trondheim and Bergen for Type XXI and Heligoland for Type XXIII.† And the OIC's analysis of the naval decrypts which disclosed the names of the commanding officers being appointed to Type XXI boats had shown that the majority were experienced and well above average ability.[116]

These indications that the plan to use the new U-boats in a new offensive were still going forward, and particularly the evidence that the new boats were being completed and commissioned in increasing numbers, gradually outweighed the testimony of those decrypts which plainly showed that, on account of delays in output and in working up to operational readiness, the plan was being repeatedly deferred. This was all the more the case because of the alarming experience that, in the battle with the U-boats in the inshore waters, the Enigma was at last failing to provide reliable intelligence on the operations of the U-boats and the intentions of the U-boat Command, and with fears about the introduction of Kurier.‡ On 9 December, though still refusing to bomb the U-boat shelters in Norway, Spaatz gave the Eighth Air Force permission to devote marginal effort to U-boat targets in Germany.[117] And Bomber Command began to attack such targets before the Cabinet's anti-submarine committee, modifying its earlier decision

---

* The German archives, though incomplete, show that the actual rate of completion was between 15 and 20 a month from November 1944. As for the rate of commissioning, the following table compares the Admiralty cumulative estimates with the German figures:[115]

	Admiralty Estimate	German figure
End of October	17	32
End of November	28	45
End of December	42	67

    † See below p 485ff for Type XXIII.

    ‡ See above, p 472 and Appendix 15(iv).

115. ADM 234/68, p 85; ADM 223/315, OIC SI 1112 of 30 October, 1137 of 27 November 1944, 1175 of 1 January 1945; AIR 41/74, pp 160, 165.
116. ADM 223/315, OIC SI 1144 of 4 December, 1158 and 1159 both of 18 December.
117. Craven and Cate, op cit, Vol III, p 720.

and over-riding continuing opposition from the Air Ministry, decided on 19 December that, though only incidental to their major objectives so as not to affect the priority given to oil and communications targets, the heavy bomber forces should attack the new-type U-boat assembly plants, slipways and berths.* A first list of specific targets, issued on 29 December, added the E-boat operational bases at Ijmuiden, Rotterdam and Den Helder to the U-boat slipways at Hamburg, Bremen and Gdynia/Danzig and the U-boat assembly plants at Vegesack, which had been identified as one of the sectional assembly plants in the Japanese decrypts,† and at Kiel.[118]

From 31 December, when Allied strategic bombers carried out the first of their attacks by raiding the slipways at Hamburg,[119] the new policy was to succeed in keeping the completion of new-type U-boats well below the planned level.‡ Even more important, the RAF's minelaying in the Baltic had already greatly prolonged the time taken by completed U-boats to carry out their working up.

Bomber Command had intensified its minelaying in the Baltic with operations off Kiel and Swinemünde on 16–17 August and in the Gulf of Danzig at the end of the month. Over and above their other consequences, these and subsequent minelayings, which had kept the U-boat training and trial areas closed for long periods, finally forced the Germans to begin the transfer of exercises and acceptance trials from the Gulf of Danzig to Lübeck Bay, a greatly inferior location, at the beginning of January 1945.[121] As in earlier periods the naval Enigma decrypts had been invaluable in enabling Bomber Command to carry out the minelaying with

---

* Bomber Command raided Horten in Oslofjord, known from Sigint to be in use for U-boat trials, on the nights of 13 and 29 December and Gdynia on the night of 18 December (not in July, as stated by Roskill, op cit, Vol III Part 2, p 182), as well as Ijmuiden and Rotterdam on the nights of 15 and 29 December.

† See Volume III Part 1, Appendix 11, p 522.

‡ Even before December delays in new-type construction had been imposed by damage done in the area bombing programme from July 1944 and the offensive against transport targets from September. On 29 July a bombing raid on Bremen directed against jet aircraft production destroyed the vital 100-ton crane used for lifting prefabricated sections on the assembly slip. The transportation offensive often closed the north German canals including the Dortmund-Ems Canal; POW disclosed on 11 December that the Dortmund-Ems Canal was being used for the transport of U-boat sections. A raid in August on the electric motor factory in Mannheim reduced the production of Type XXI at Bremen and Hamburg. In September and October Bomber Command's attacks on the Ruhr destroyed storage battery production. Three heavy raids by US Eighth Air Force on Hamburg's oil targets damaged the assembly slipways in November, as was confirmed by Sigint.[120]

118. AIR 41/74, pp 107, 162–163; Roskill, op cit, Vol III Part 2, p 294.
119. AIR 41/74, p 164.
120. ibid, pp 107, 134–135, 155, 166; ADM 233/208, Ultra signal 1310/14 November.
121. AIR 41/74, pp 112, 128, 136.

maximum economy of effort by disclosing the extent and the location of the disruption caused by each operation and the whereabouts of the minesweeping vessels brought in to deal with it. They had also illustrated how greatly the enemy's difficulties were compounded by the shortage of minesweepers. They did not explicitly refer to the effects on the operational readiness of U-boats until early in January 1945. But in a signal of 23 December, decrypted on 5 January, the Baltic Naval Command reported that the mining had 'jeopardised to the utmost the testing and training of new U-boats', that U-boat acceptance trials were 'at a complete standstill' and that the C-in-C Navy had ordered all available measures, including the transfer of a minesweeping flotilla from Norway, to remedy the situation.[122] In response to this intelligence Bomber Command laid another 234 mines in Danzig Bay on the night of 6–7 January.

The Allies did not know that, at least in part as a result of their minelaying, the Germans calculated at the end of January that only one or two Type XXI – instead of 40 – would become available during the next two months and that no increase could be expected before April.[123] But they were soon to obtain from Sigint further evidence that the enemy was recognising that, for such effort as the U-boats could bring to bear against Allied shipping, he would have to rely in the foreseeable future on the old-type U-boats. In a signal sent to the German Naval Attaché in Tokyo early in January, decrypted by 21 January 1945, Dönitz attempted to explain away the many references made in recent months to the impending renewal of the U-boat offensive.[124] The OIC summarized his statement thus: 'It is erroneous to speak of a new U-boat war being suddenly begun; in truth there has been a new campaign ever since the adoption of *Schnorchel* made totally submerged warfare possible . . . Sinkings are expected to go on rising gradually in proportion to the output of new boats, provided they justify the hopes placed in them. The main danger to this development is not the loss of boats while operating, but the effect of heavy air attacks on yards and bases and of the mining of exercise areas and departure routes'.[125]

□

---

122. DEFE 3/498, ZTPG 322431 of 5 January; Naval Headlines of 5 January 1945.
123. ADM 234/68, p 95.
124. Naval Headlines of 21 January.
125. ADM 223/315, OIC SI 1199 of 22 January 1945; US Department of Defense, op cit, Vol II, p 218.

Intelligence on the production of Type XXIII U-boats had no bearing on Allied anxiety about the resumption of the offensive in the Atlantic. Sigint and PR had established by the middle of July that Type XXIII displaced about 200 tons and was 110 feet in length, and was thus intended for short-range operations.* But its technical characteristics, of which full details were obtained by the end of September,† left no doubt that its appearance would constitute a serious threat to Allied shipping off the Scheldt and in British waters in the North Sea and the Channel. Nor could it be overlooked that whereas other considerations than delay in producing operational Type XXI in sufficient numbers – the inability to provide essential air reconnaissance, for example – might defer the despatch of the larger U-boats to 'the open ocean', such considerations need not prevent the despatch of Type XXIII to patrol off ports and focal shipping points in small numbers as and when they became operational.[126]

Until the middle of October the numbers of Type XXIII detected by PR as under construction or completed (8 on 7 August, 13 on 5 September) and the numbers identified by Sigint as commissioned and working up (4 on 7 August, 6 on 5 September) were, indeed, small. On 16 October, on this evidence, NID I rested its first forecast of the cumulative totals of completed and operational boats on the assumption that the planned production rate was 4 a month:

	Cumulative total of completed boats	Cumulative total of operational boats
October 1944	10	—
November	14	7
December	18	10
January 1945	22	14
February	26	18
March	30	22
April	34	26

From 23 October, however, it raised the estimated completion rate to 10 a month; it had realised that concrete shelters now detected by PR over the assembly slips at Hamburg had partly concealed the higher assembly rate to which reference had been made in the Japanese decrypts. And it again raised the estimated number of boats under construction from the end of November, when PR established that Type XXIII were being turned out at Kiel as well

---

* See above, p 476 fn*.

† These were obtained from the decrypts of reports from the Japanese in Berlin (see Volume III, Part 1, Appendix 11) and from documents and photographs acquired in Toulon, where two had been building.

126. ADM 223/315, OIC SI 1111 of 30 October.

as at Hamburg. The number believed to be completed, including those identified by the naval decrypts as having been commissioned, rose less sharply. The number commissioned was thought to be 10 in October, 12 on 6 November and 18 at the end of December, and at that date it was believed that in addition 13 out of the 47 under construction might be completed. If these are added to the 18 commissioned boats, the number of boats thought to be completed was 31 by the end of the year.[127]* Estimates of the number of Type XXIII that had probably reached the state of operational readiness, on the other hand, did not rise above NID's October forecast of 'operational boats'. The OIC believed that 10 of those commissioned had been working up for two months or longer by 1 December and that this number would rise to 14 by the end of the month.[128]

On 18 December the OIC appreciated that 'none of the pre-fab boats is yet operational'. It was referring not to the state of operational readiness, but to the fact that there was still no evidence from the naval decrypts that any had left on an operational cruise.[129] But by that date it was expecting to receive such evidence for Type XXIII at any time. Thus on 24 December, when Sigint reported the movement of a 'protected object' under escort along the Dutch coast, it speculated that this might be a Type XXIII boat and allowed for the possibility of 'a U-boat thrust towards the east coast, possibly in the Humber neighbourhood'.[130]

The anxiety was fully justified. In the last week of 1944 Allied shipping losses in the Channel alone at the hands of the U-boats were already greater than U-boats had achieved in all coastal waters since the beginning of the inshore campaign.[131] Since the beginning of December it had been evident from Sigint and PR

---

* The German records show that it had been hoped to produce at Hamburg and Kiel together at a rate of 10 a month from the end of August and to 'deliver' 55 by the end of December, but Germania Werft at Kiel did not begin production till November, and only 44 were 'delivered', of which 31 were commissioned, by the end of the year. Presumably the number delivered included boats completed but not yet commissioned. The NID's cumulative estimated figures for the number commissioned compared with the German figures are as follows:

	Admiralty estimate	German figure
October	10	18
November	16	25
December	18	31

127. ADM 223/315, OIC SI 1112 of 30 October, 1119 of 6 November, 1137 of 27 November, 1159 of 18 December 1944, 1175 of 1 January 1945; ADM 234/68, p 85.
128. ADM 223/315, OIC SI 1142 of 4 December.
129. ibid, OIC SI 1159 of 18 December.
130. ibid, OIC SI 1166 of 24 December.

that the German Navy was determined to intensify the inshore battle by increasing the scale of operations carried out by the E-boat and KdK Commands.* The appearance of Type XXIII was indeed imminent; the first was to be operating in the North Sea in February 1945 and two more were soon to follow.

□

The old-type U-boats continued to operate in much reduced numbers in distant waters during the second half of 1944. Sigint disclosed their departures and returns from patrol and, usually, the general areas in which they were to operate. Since they operated individually, and not in groups, it revealed their positions on passage or within their operational areas only if they received new orders after sailing; but when this occurred decrypts still contributed to the sinking of some U-boats.

From the Sigint evidence, and from occasional sightings and the facts of their occasional successes, it was known that in June–July there were one or two off the north American coast, two off west Africa, three in the Caribbean and 12 or 13 on passage, including five or six for the Indian Ocean and the large cargo-carrying Japanese submarine I-52 for Bordeaux from the Far East. Thereafter, an average of two were off the north American coast.† They sank half a dozen merchant ships and a similar number of escorts by the end of the year in areas as close in as the St Lawrence estuary, and in December, when it emerged that 2 or 3 were heading there, it was expected that their number would rise.[133] But no U-boats were sent to the Caribbean and West Africa after the end of August; after the loss of the Biscay bases, Type IX U-boats could no longer operate in these areas without being supplied at sea, and the last of the U-boat tankers (U-490) had been sunk in June en route to the Far East.[134] One U-boat (U-1227) operated off Gibraltar from early in October, warning of her arrival being given by the decrypt of a signal advising her that her surprise appearance might offer chances for success; and though she succeeded only in damaging an escort in an attack on a

---

* See above, pp 456, 461.

† One of these, U-1229, was detailed to land spies in Maine, but she was sunk with the assistance of intelligence from decrypts on 20 August. In November decrypts disclosed that U-1230 was attempting to land spies; she succeeded.[132]

131. Roskill, op cit, Vol III Part 2, p 185.
132. ADM 223/315, OIC SI 1174 of 1 January.
133. Department of Defense, op cit, Vol II, Appendix 1; ADM 223/208, Ultra signal 1342/12 November; ADM 234/68, p 90.
134. Roskill, op cit, Vol III Part 2, pp 174–175.

convoy before she was relieved by U-870 at the end of November,
U-870 torpedoed four ships off the Azores and the Straits of
Gibraltar before withdrawing early in January 1945.[135]

Of the U-boats on passage to the Indian Ocean in June and July,
U-490 and U-860 were sunk by US carrier groups in June in the
south Atlantic with the aid of Sigint, as was I-52. The remainder
sank several ships in the south Atlantic before operating in the
Indian Ocean. From June to mid-September five U-boats operated there with two Japanese submarines; between them they sank
17 ships, the highest level of U-boat successes in any theatre
during that period. But U-198 was sunk on 10 August by a British
carrier group after she had scored successes in the Mozambique
Channel, and in September U-859 was sunk by a British
submarine in the approaches to Penang, decrypts having given
advance notice of her date of arrival and her approach route.[136]

Two of the U-boats in the Far East were ordered to Australian
waters in September. One of them was sunk by a US submarine as
it left port, decrypts having again provided advance notice.[137] The
other carried out her patrol, sinking two ships. But the campaign
in the Indian Ocean was not resumed. The reasons were that
several considerations were making Penang untenable as a base,
that torpedoes and spares were running low and that two out of
four further U-boats sent to the Far East were sunk during
September. They had reported their successful passage of the
Denmark Straits and were tracked by dead-reckoning until one
(U-871) was sunk by aircraft from the Azores on 26 September
and the other (U-863) by US aircraft from Brazil on 29
September.[138] Another two (U-195 and U-219) had left Bordeaux
with freight on 21–23 August. In September decrypts disclosed
that U-219 was to refuel U-1062, which was bringing valuable
cargo back from Japan, and this intelligence led to the sinking of
U-1062 by a US carrier group on 30 September; but U-219
survived to reach the Far East, as did U-195.[139]

By the end of September decrypts had revealed that although
the Japanese were pressing for an increase of U-boat operations in
the Far East, the Germans had decided to bring back at least two

---

135. ADM 223/172, OIC SI 1091 of 2 October; ADM 223/315, OIC SI 1166 of 24
      December 1944.
136. ADM 223/172, OIC SI 1074 of 4 September; Naval Headlines of 21
      September; Roskill, op cit, Vol III Part 2, pp 204–205.
137. ADM 223/172, OIC SI 1082 of 18 September; Department of Defense, op
      cit, Vol II, p 230.
138. ADM 223/172, OIC SI 1047 of 21 August, 1090 of 1 October, 1095 of 8
      October.
139. ibid, 1095 of 8 October; ADM 223/315, OIC SI 1156 of 17 December.

U-boats to Europe. Although their departure was deferred, Sigint established by 23 October that the Germans were resisting the Japanese pressure; one U-boat had sailed and three others were expecting to follow. By mid-January five had left for Europe in all, of which one was forced to return with engine defects, as Sigint revealed, and another was lost in unknown circumstances.[140]

Apart from those operating against shipping or carrying cargo, one or two U-boats were always on weather-reporting patrol in the central northern Atlantic; and in November it emerged from Sigint that additional measures were being taken to improve the weather service. A decrypt of 4 November announced that weather reports from U-boats 'were urgently required to assist the assessment of prospects of both German and Allied air operations and the possibility of landings', and ordered six U-boats to make reports: we now know that reports from the Atlantic had ceased on 28 October following the foundering of a U-boat. But after the normal weather patrols had been restored – and increasd to three U-boats from early in December – reports continued to be requested from several U-boats on passage up to mid-December.[141] In a signal decrypted by 22 November a U-boat taking up a weather patrol was informed of the urgency of the need for her reports.[142] From 2 until 15 December the daily number of weather reports made by U-boats greatly exceeded the previously normal level.[143] It is now clear that this unusual activity was part of the preparations for the Ardennes offensive, but the naval intelligence authorities in the OIC and Washington did not regard it as especially significant before the event.*

□

---

* See above, p 430 fn*. Nor was any unusual importance attached to the disclosure by Sigint at the end of November that the weather ship *Wuppertal* was being sent under U-boat escort to take up position 15 miles south of Spitzbergen.[144] But this is not surprising in view of the continual German efforts to improve their weather reporting and of the fact that another weather ship, the *Kehdingen*, had been sunk by the Allies at the end of August, on her arrival after being escorted by U-boat to the Greenland area.[145] For the *Kehdingen* see Volume III, Part 1, Appendix 12.

140. ADM 223/172, OIC SI 1082 of 18 September; ADM 223/315, OIC SI 1106 of 23 October, 1137 of 27 November; Roskill, op cit, Vol III Part 2, p 205(n).
141. Naval Headlines of 6 November; AIR 41/74, p 76; Department of Defense, op cit, Vol II, p 229.
142. Naval Headlines of 22 November.
143. Department of Defense, op cit, Vol II, pp 229, 230.
144. Naval Headlines of 24 and 28 November.
145. ibid, 30 August and 2 September.

In Arctic waters U-boat operations of the accustomed type, with the U-boats adopting patrol lines and acting in groups, continued from the resumption of the Allied convoys to Russia in the middle of August until the end of the year, and indeed to the end of the war. Four large convoys reached Russia by the end of 1944 with the loss of only one escort vessel, and the four return convoys suffered only damage to two escorts and the sinking of two merchant ships, while the escorts sank six U-boats. For Germany this was a poor return for the fact that, though hampered by the withdrawal of the advanced U-boat base from Hammerfest to Harstadt at the end of October and the abandonment of Altenfjord in mid-November,[146]* and though depleted by recent losses,† the Arctic force still numbered 25 to 30 U-boats, of which between six and 19 operated against each convoy.

Despite the fact that a four-wheel Enigma key (Narwhal) replaced the Home Waters' key in the Arctic U-boat Command in September, the naval decrypts continued to provide comprehensive intelligence about the strength and location of the U-boat patrol lines and to disclose the orders issued to them when convoys were sighted; Narwhal presented GC and CS with few difficulties as a result of its long experience with the Shark key. Moreover, the indoctrinated Admiral in command of the escorts now flew his flag in one of the escort carriers instead of in a cruiser, and the much better location, display and communications facilities of that class of vessel enabled him to make prompter and more effective use of the Sigint dispatched to him.

This arrangement went hand in hand with the decision to continue the policy of getting convoys through by taking the

---

* But U-boats also sank seven merchant ships and eight warships in attacks on Soviet coastal traffic and torpedoed a British frigate and an escort carrier in a Fleet operation in the approaches to Altenfjord in August.

† On 17 July the Arctic U-boats had been ordered to form a patrol line across the path of a Home Fleet carrier force returning from one of its attacks on the *Tirpitz*. On the strength of this intelligence aircraft of Coastal Command, operating 600 miles from base, engaged them in a running battle over several days in which three were sunk and four damaged. Decrypts reported the loss of only two of them.[147]

The U-boats were also hampered by the loss, after chance sightings, of two torpedo-transporter U-boats (Type VIIF). U-1060 was driven ashore in a carrier sweep off Norway on 27 October and subsequently destroyed by Coastal Command aircraft. Her sister ship U-1061 was badly damaged by aircraft of Coastal Command between Bergen and Trondheim on 30 October.[148] U-1062, a third U-boat of this type, of which only four were built, was sunk by a US carrier group on her way back from Penang to Europe (see above, p 488). The fourth had been sunk earlier in the war.

146.   ADM 223/207, Ultra signal 1630/29 October; Naval Headlines of 16 November.

147.   ADM 223/172, OIC SI 1019 and 1022 of 24 and 30 July; AIR 41/74, p 58; Roskill, op cit, Vol III Part 22, p 157.

148.   ADM 223/207, Ultra signals 1058/28 October, 2233/30 October.

offensive against the U-boats. Although evasion of their patrol lines was still attempted when circumstances were favourable, the escorting ships and aircraft were commonly sent ahead to attack the U-boats in their known waiting positions while carrier aircraft kept GAF reconnaissance at a distance. Deprived of advance sightings of the convoys and themselves having to approach or get ahead on the surface, since they were not equipped with *Schnorchel*,* the U-boats were at a great disadvantage against these tactics. Two were sunk in the attack on the first Russia-bound convoy (JW 59) for the loss of the escort vessel HMS *Kite*.[150] One was sunk by the escort of the first returning convoy (RA 59), which was not itself sighted. JW 60 reached Kola undetected, though nine U-boats were deployed against it; the decrypt of a signal from Captain U-boats Norway disclosed that he attributed the failure to 'defective data'.[151] Seventeen U-boats operated against RA 60 but sank only two merchant vessels; decrypts showed that Captain U-boats had asked his commanders not to be shaken by this further failure and promised to make as many U-boats as possible effective in time for the next convoy.[152]

The sailing of the next convoy (JW 61) on 20 October was accompanied by several new developments. Allied W/T deception exploiting the enemy's lack of intelligence, and relying on false sightings by the GAF and the known propensity of U-boats to mistake single ships or doubtful hydrophone effects for convoys, led the enemy – 19 U-boats – to pursue a ghost convoy for several days with all the procedure of a genuine convoy operation, and eventually report its arrival in Murmansk.[153] The escort forces for the actual convoy were reinforced by two additional escort groups and a third escort carrier, as they were for subsequent convoys, with the intention of turning any encounter into an all-out offensive against the U-boats.[154] In the third place, Y and Enigma

---

* Sigint disclosed that the first *Schnorchel* boat joined the force in the second week of September; she had been equipped in Bergen. Later in September the decrypt of a signal from the head of the Japanese Naval Mission in Berlin revealed that no merchant ships had been sunk since the convoys had re-started and that the Germans attributed this to the vulnerability of non-*Schnorchel* U-boats to Allied aircraft.[149]

149. ADM 223/172, OIC SI 1078 of 11 September.
150. ADM 223/172, OIC SI 1065 of 29 August; ADM 234/369, BR 1736(44), p 118.
151. ADM 223/172, OIC SI 1082 of 18 September, 1087 of 25 September.
152. Naval Headlines of 28 and 30 September and 4 October.
153. ADM 223/315, OIC SI 1106 of 23 October; ADM 223/206, Ultra signal 1721/19 October; ADM 223/207, Ultra signal 1152/22 October; Naval Headlines of 18 October; ADM 223/88, Colpoys, *Admiralty Use of Special Intelligence in Naval Operations*, p 131.
154. Roskill, op cit, Vol III Part 2, p 167.

disclosed on 21 and 22 October that two Ju 88 torpedo Gruppen (about 40 aircraft) had been transferred to north Norway – the first to be based there since 1942.[155] But although the escorts moved ahead to clear a way through the U-boats, 15 of which lay in the path of the convoy, no U-boat was sunk on account of bad Asdic conditions, and none made an attack; and although the decrypts of several reconnaissance and readiness signals indicated that the GAF intended to attack on 29 October, no aircraft appeared.[156]

Just as JW 61 arrived without loss or incident, so did the return convoy RA 61, and although one escort was damaged, the escorts again found none of the U-boats. As decrypts had shown that a patrol line of 17 U-boats lay in wait for the convoy off Kola, the OIC found this 'inexplicable';[157] presumably the U-boats were avoiding contact. Nor did the GAF make any attempt to attack. Two large liners which sailed as convoy JW 61A to Russia early in November carrying 11,000 Russians (Osttruppen) taken prisoner during the fighting in Europe, and a token Norwegian force which was to accompany the Russian advance into north Norway, similarly arrived and made the return journey without incident.[158] Against the last outward-bound convoy of the year, JW 62, Sigint showed that the original patrol line of 13 U-boats was increased to 17, which all eventually concentrated off Kola to wait for it, but again it suffered no loss and no U-boat was sunk.[159] The GAF did not operate.

Returning as RA 62, the convoy was contacted by four or five U-boats, one of which damaged a destroyer, and while the remainder could not catch up with it, nine Ju 88s also attacked it on 13 December. The convoy sustained no further damage, and one U-boat was sunk and several damaged. A decrypt of 14 December disclosed that Captain U-boats had decided to break off the operation that morning since 'boats without *Schnorchel* cannot carry out worthwhile operations in an area with strong forces of shore-based aircraft', and it emerged from the GAF Enigma that 40 Ju 88s were being diverted to attack a Home Fleet carrier force off Trondheim.[160] But the experience with RA 62 nevertheless set

---

155. ADM 223/206, Ultra signal 2344/20 October; ADM 223/207, Ultra signal 1754/22 October.
156. ADM 223/207, Ultra signals 0440/25 October, 1236/25 October, 1126/29 October; ADM 223/315, OIC SI 1115 of 4 November; ADM 234/369, p 119; Roskill, op cit, Vol III Part 2, p 167.
157. ADM 223/315, OIC SI 1111 of 30 October, 1127 of 13 November.
158. ibid, OIC SI 1119 of 6 November, 1127 of 13 November.
159. ibid, OIC SI 1137 of 27 November, 1143 of 4 December.
160. ibid, OIC SI 1150 of 11 December; Naval Headlines of 12, 14, 15 and 16 December; ADM 234/369, p 119.

a new pattern that was to persist for the rest of the war. Four pairs of convoys were to sail in 1945, all against opposition from U-boats which slowly grew in numbers and which, as more of them came to be fitted with *Schnorchel*, displayed greater persistence and scored more successes. They sank three merchant ships and four escorts, and seriously damaged one escort, and few U-boats were lost. As they also adopted the tactics of concentrating off the approaches to Kola, each convoy involved the escort in a straight battle with them, and Sigint was of little operational value. But since they continued to operate as a group, it was unaffected by the changes that were reducing its value against U-boats in other areas. It thus provided the Allies with the assurance that they would have good notice if any change took place in the operational pattern or the scale of the German effort.

□

Naval and air offensives against German shipping along the Norwegian coast and in the Bight between Kiel and the Hook of Holland were resumed as soon as the progress of *Overlord* allowed. In the Bight attacks became unprofitable from September; Ultra showed that the enemy began to protect his convoys more heavily and to sail them only by night and that they became less frequent on account of Bomber Command's mining of the area. On the Norwegian coast the attacks intensified steadily from the beginning of that month at a time when Germany's shipping situation throughout northern Europe, already severely strained by the summer of 1944, was rapidly deteriorating under the impact of such disastrous set-backs as the loss of all Swedish and Finnish ships and ports,* of such exceptional demands for shipping as those created by her withdrawal in the eastern Baltic and her decision to withdraw troops from Norway, and of the dislocation caused by Bomber Command's minelaying. From September the minelaying in the Baltic was extended to the Kattegat and southern Norway, where it was repeated as often as weather allowed till the end of the year.

The Allied attacks were carried out by submarine, by the Home Fleet with the carriers *Indefatigable* and *Implacable* and with escort carriers, by the Norwegians MTB flotilla based on Lerwick and the

---

* In August the Swedish authorities ceased insuring Swedish ships trading to German ports – a decision which deprived Germany of 25 per cent of the shipping hitherto available for imports – and on 27 September they closed all their Baltic ports to Axis shipping – a decision which forced Germany to move all her iron ore imports to Narvik and thence by sea in German bottoms. The Russian-Finnish armistice of 19 September deprived her of Finnish ships and ports, and also forced her to move parts of Twentieth Mountain Army to north Norway for evacuation to Germany.

small craft of the SOE unit based on the Shetlands, and by the Strike Wings of Coastal Command. All these forces were assisted by static intelligence on the enemy's defences and convoy routes obtained from PR, SIS and SOE. The carrier forces and the planning staff at HQ No 18 Group Coastal Command were also supplied with Sigint. Because of weather conditions and the great distances involved, Sigint reports of the movements of shipping were rarely of direct value during their operations. They relied heavily, however, on analyses carried out in the OIC and at GC and CS of the evidence derived from decrypts over many months about the enemy's shipping routes and routines, convoy policy, minefields and other defences, and about German reactions to various types of Allied attack, along the whole length of the Norwegian coast.[161]

As a result of Allied successes during September – seven ships sunk by submarines, two by carriers, eleven by Coastal Command – the German convoys moved only by night on the 400-mile stretch from Lindesnes to Aalesund from the end of that month.[162] The attacks were stepped up in October and again in November, when they included a sweep by a Home Fleet cruiser and destroyers along the coast between Stavanger and the Naze which sank two merchant ships and four escorts out of a convoy of four ships and six escorts. These losses and the fact that the remainder of the convoy was damaged were disclosed in decrypts, which also disclosed that the attack had intensified German fears of an Allied descent on Norway or Denmark and led the enemy to move E-boats to this area for the first time.[163] He also reinforced his weak fighter strength in the area in spite of the pressing need for fighter forces over Germany; from GAF Enigma decrypts it was learned that between the end of November and mid-December the fighter defences in south Norway were made stronger than they had been at any time since 1940, and that they included night-fighters brought in to combat the night-time anti-shipping sweeps that were being introduced by Coastal Command.[164] A further German measure was the despatch of U-boats to patrol off Scapa in December in an effort to counter raids by carriers of the Home Fleet.* Despite these measures another Home Fleet cruiser incursion into the area was made in January 1945 with equal success.

---

* See above, p 473.

161. ADM 223/315, OIC SI 1123 of 11 November, 1154 of 16 December.
162. Roskill, op cit, Vol III Part 2, p 165; AIR 41/74, p 117.
163. Naval Headlines of 18 and 22 November.
164. ADM 223/315, OIC SI 1135 of 25 November, 1155 of 16 December; Naval Headlines of 20 and 29 November.

We now know that Dönitz told Hitler on 1 December that because of 'constant heavy attacks . . . off the Norwegian coast . . . the time is not far off when ship movements in this region will come to a complete standstill'.[165] In a post-war statement Admiral Ciliax, C-in-C in Norway, also recorded that he viewed the Home Fleet's incursion as a most serious threat: 'of the measures Great Britain took . . . in Norway the most effective were the air attacks . . . against convoys . . . The enemy appears to have obtained news . . . from agents and a very efficient communications system. The same applied to MTB attacks which, based on a good knowledge of local conditions, were carried out with great bravery and skill. At one time the situation along the open stretch of coastline between Kristiansand and Stavanger (after British surface vessels had succeeded in breaking through for the first time) was extremely critical'.[166] Up to that time the attacks had not interfered with the movement of troops out of Norway, most of which took place through Oslo, or prevented the flow of immediately essential supplies to and from Norway.* But despite the German measures and the worsening weather, Allied successes were 22 ships sunk and 19 damaged in November and 13 sunk and 13 damaged in December. This reflected the fact that by December the OIC was passing the Sigint by telephone to the combined naval and air HQ at Rosyth, as it had done for some time to the Commands at Dover, Portsmouth and the Nore. By February 1945 it had inaugurated a running plot of shipping movements based on all the intelligence sources[167] and this was to play its part in the still higher level of successes obtained in the last phase of these operations.

---

* The NID estimated that shipments of ore from Narvik had been reduced from 40,000 tons in October 1943 to 27,000 in October 1944 and 12,000 in November.

165. Führer Conference on Naval Affairs, 11 December 1944.
166. Roskill, op cit, Vol III Part 2, p 167n.
167. AIR 41/74, p 277; Roskill, op cit, Vol III Part 2, p 252.

CHAPTER 54

The Allied Strategic Bombing Offensives

THE MAIN feature in the development of the Allied strategic air offensive in the second half of 1944 was that, by the end of June, 'for the first time in the war a vital target system had been chosen [at a time] when the force and skill necessary to destroy it were available.'[1] The system was German oil production. As an obvious target for Allied attack, it had beckoned at intervals since the beginning of the war, but had been dismissed for a succession of good reasons. Operational factors entered into the slow process by which, in the summer of 1944, the decision was at last taken to give priority to it, but the influence of intelligence was not less important. It was the operational situation which made the Allied strategic air forces freer than ever before to concentrate their efforts, and abler than ever before to deploy them with devastating effect. But if they chose to deploy them against oil, it was because Sigint provided, at just this juncture, testimony to the crucial strategic significance of the state of the enemy's fuel supply. The testimony was positive and unambiguous evidence of the kind Sigint did not supply for any other target system; in GC and CS's view this 'may have been the outstanding service rendered by Special Intelligence to the strategic air war in Europe.' The same may be said of PR, the other main source. Its accuracy in locating the German refineries and synthetic oil plants, and in identifying the damage they sustained once the offensive against them had begun, perfectly complemented the Sigint.

German oil had been regarded as an important target at the beginning of the war, but attacks on it had been abandoned after the early months for a number of strategic and operational reasons such as the expectation that Germany would acquire the Caucasian oilfields, the inaccessibility of the Ploesti plants, which were correctly regarded as fundamental to German supplies, and the operational limitations of night bombing.*

---

* See Volume I pp 240–243, 305 and Volume II, pp 134–137, 258–259, and its Appendix 12.

1. Webster and Frankland, *The Strategic Air Offensive against Germany* (1961), Vol III, p 229.

Consideration of attacks on oil was resumed in June 1943, when the *Pointblank* directive named it as a primary target 'if Ploesti could be bombed'.[2] Ploesti was bombed by US heavy bombers from north African bases in August in a single raid in which, lacking long-range fighter protection, they suffered heavy casualties and achieved results which, though severe enough seriously to alarm the Germans, were seemingly negligible at the time.[3] The Hartley Sub-Committee on Axis Oil, reporting through the JIC,* nonetheless kept up the pressure for an all-out offensive. In November 1943 it reported on the one hand that in consequence of the shortening of her lines in Russia and the Mediterranean, Germany's oil resources would increase considerably if her oil industry was not attacked and, on the other hand, that the movement of US Fifteenth Air Force to bases in Italy was now making her refineries and synthetic oil plants more vulnerable to bombing: 'The insufficiency of oil stocks is still causing Germany grave anxiety and any substantial interference with her oil supplies would seriously weaken her ability to continue the war'.[4] By then, however, the Allied strategic air forces were fully engaged against the *Pointblank* targets and had not yet developed the means of subduing the enemy's day-fighters.† In January 1944 the Combined Chiefs of Staff reaffirmed in a discussion of the use of strategic air power in support of *Overlord* that the destruction of Germany's air combat strength was a primary objective and that the progressive dislocation of Germany's military industrial and economic systems remained the over-all mission. This conclusion did not exclude attacks on oil; no doubt in the light of the JIC's pressure, the Combined Chiefs did indeed go on to say that 'in consideration of recent intelligence reports immediate attack upon oil refineries might be well worth while'. But the CAS, supported by Bomber Command and HQ US Strategic Air Forces (USSTAF), at once opposed giving priority to refineries; they insisted that recent examination of the enemy's oil situation by economic experts provided 'no justification for diverting our effort from the GAF fighter industry . . .'[5]

There followed a considerable change of mind on the part of US Eighth Air Force. On 5 March General Spaatz completed a 'Plan

---

* See Volume II pp 6, 46.
† See Volume III Part 1, Chapter 37.

2. Webster and Frankland, op cit, Vol III, p 46; Ehrman, *Grand Strategy*, Vol V (1956), pp 287–290.
3. Webster and Frankland, op cit, Vol III, pp 46, 227 fn 3.
4. JIC(43) 477 of 22 November; CAB 121/418, SIC file D/Germany/3, JIC(43) 480 of 26 November.
5. AIR 41/66, *The Liberation of North-West Europe*, Vol 1, p 122.

for the Completion of the Combined Bomber Offensive' which recommended the inclusion of oil targets as a primary objective. It argued that 90 per cent of Germany's total output was produced by 54 crude oil refineries and synthetic oil plants, of which the 27 most important were situated in three groups in Silesia, the Ruhr and Ploesti that were well within the range of heavy bombers based in the United Kingdom and Italy; and it claimed that Germany's supplies might be halved if these 27 were destroyed and that, if all 54 were successfully attacked, her production might fall to zero by September 1944. It also made the estimate that 80 per cent of Germany's synthetic oil was produced by 14 of the synthetic oil plants. The case for attacking these targets was presented as only a continuation of existing policy. The campaign against the GAF was entering a stage at which the German fighters had to be forced to accept combat; they would be bound to do so in defence of the oil plants, and if they were defeated in their attempt to do so the German High Command might be forced to conclude that it could not oppose *Overlord* or even continue the war.[6]

There need be no doubt that the fact that the attack on the GAF had made great progress during February, and that the fighters had then begun to avoid combat, played a part in the formulation of the Plan. But it is clear that the decision to press for priority for the oil targets also reflected the anxiety of those who opposed the Allied Expeditionary Air Force's Transportation Plan to find some alternative to it. As well as USSTAF itself, they included the Enemy Objectives Unit of the Economic Warfare Division of the US embassy and the JIC, and it is known that the Enemy Objectives Unit was urging that the time was ripe for an oil offensive,[7] and that US Eighth Air Force had received a similar opinion from the JIC by 24 February.[8]* It was in fact in opposition to the Transportation Plan that at a meeting of the *Overlord* Commanders on 25 March General Spaatz presented the proposal for using his forces to bomb the chief oil plants in 15 days of good weather before directing them to tactical support of *Overlord*.†

This meeting opted for the Transportation Plan after the MEW representative had insisted that German oil stocks in western Europe were such that an offensive against oil production would

---

* This must have been an informal representation as the JIC had not issued any report on Axis oil since those of November 1943, for which see above, p 498.

† See above, pp 109–110.

6. AIR 41/56, *The RAF in the Bombing Offensive against Germany*, Vol VI, p 12; Craven and Cate, *The USAAF in World War II*, Vol III (1951), p 174.

7. Rostow, *Pre-Invasion Bombing Strategy* (Texas 1981), pp 37–38.

8. Craven and Cate, op cit, Vol III, p 173.

be of no assistance in the initial phase of *Overlord*. But on 19 April General Eisenhower gave Spaatz verbal permission to bomb oil targets on the next two days of good weather with a view to seeing whether the attacks succeeded in drawing German fighters into battle. By that date, moreover, Spaatz had been notified by General Arnold of the Combined Chiefs of Staff that there would be no objection if he ordered attacks on Ploesti under the general directive which had called for attacks on the transport system of the German forces who were resisting the Russian advance into south-east Europe; and US Fifteenth Air Force had already bombed Ploesti on 5 and 15 April.[9]

While Fifteenth Air Force continued to attack Ploesti and other oil targets in eastern Europe, US Eighth Air Force, hitherto held up by unsuitable weather, made its first attack on selected synthetic plants with more than 800 bombers on 12 May. It was strongly opposed, losing 46 aircraft and claiming to have shot down nearly 200 fighters (in fact, the Germans lost between 30 and 50), but PR showed that all the targets had been damaged and that three were damaged so seriously that they were temporarily shut down. Eighth Air Force returned to the attack with 400 aircraft on 28 May, bombing five of the plants that had been damaged in the first raid, and on 29 May with a raid on 'the vast and distant' oil plant at Pölitz, in Silesia near Stettin.[10]

The offensive was clearly being effective in continuing the battle with the GAF, all the raids meeting formidable opposition. The more so because Eighth and Fifteenth Air Forces flew diversionary missions to distract the German fighters away from the oil plants, the threat it posed to the enemy's oil supplies was no less effective in tying down fighters that might otherwise have moved to Normandy on and after D-day. At the same time PR was reporting that, like those on Ploesti, the raids had achieved good results, and it was on this account, with a view to accelerating Germany's collapse by destroying her oil production, that Spaatz at last formally directed on 8 June that the oil plants were to be first-priority targets for the US Strategic Air Forces.[11] Since early in May, moreover, high-grade Sigint had provided confirmation of Germany's grave disquiet at the raids and of the threat they posed to her supplies.

Hitherto, while a great deal had been known about the location of her oil plants from the German Press and other overt sources and from PR, which had kept a close watch on the development

---

9. ibid, pp 174–176.
10. ibid, pp 177–178.
11. ibid, p 281.

and expansion of every branch of the industry since 1941,[12] intelligence about her fuel situation in terms of the scale of production and the rate of consumption had remained highly inconclusive.* In particular, Sigint evidence had been sparse and indirect, and almost entirely confined to references to temporary and local fuel shortages.[14] On 30 March, however, in a signal decrypted on 3 May, the Japanese Military Attaché in Berlin, commenting on the alarming situation that would arise if the discrepancy between German and Allied air power were to grow, had noted that while attacks on such industries as coal and aluminium were having no effect on aircraft production, synthetic oil, an obvious target, had not yet been attacked, perhaps because the plants were widely distributed.[15] And from soon after the first raid on the plants by Eighth Air Force on 12 May the Enigma decrypts took up the tale. On 14 May, in a message decrypted on 16 May, OKL told Luftflotte 3 that five heavy and four light/medium Flak batteries which were being sent to France from the eastern front were to be diverted to protect the Tröglitz hydrogenation plant and that other batteries were being diverted from aircraft factories to Pölitz and Blechhammer.[16] As these refineries had not yet been attacked this intelligence strongly pointed to German apprehensions. A decrypt of 21 May disclosed that OKM had advised Naval Gruppe West on 19 May that in consequence of Allied action against Romanian oil and German hydrogenation plants, extensive failures in mineral oil production were to be expected, and considerable reductions in the June allocation of 'furnace oil, diesel etc.'[17] A later decrypt disclosed that Admiral Black Sea had been informed that he would receive no fuel allocation for June.[18]

The thrust of this intelligence was reflected in a report by the JIC on 27 May: 'Although . . . it is impossible to be precise on the time factor, we feel convinced that there is now sufficient evidence to justify the conclusion that a concerted and successful attack on German sources of oil production would, within a period of from 3–6 months, produce a shortage of oil so serious that it would

---

* See Appendix 26. It is interesting that the existence of the new synthetic oil complex built at Brüx in the Sudetenland, so as to be out of range of Allied air attack, was learned from a Press advertisement for a specialist engineer.[13]

12. AIR 41/7, *Photographic Reconnaissance*, Vol II, p 162.
13. ibid, p 163.
14. eg CX/MSS/3046/T30, 3135/T16.
15. BAY/KV 80 of 3 May 1944.
16. CAB 121/418, JIC(44) 218(o) of 27 May; DEFE 3/156, KV 4021 of 16 May.
17. DEFE 3/159, KV 4762 of 21 May.
18. DEFE 3/657, ZTPGM 74141.

render it impossible for her to carry out full operations on three major fronts . . . Both on the short and on the long-term, oil has therefore become a vital factor in German resistance'.[19] It is safe to assume that as well as encouraging Eighth Air Force to persist with its raids, this appreciation prompted the British Air Staff to ask Bomber Command on 3 June to consider attacking ten synthetic oil plants in the Ruhr as soon as its commitments to *Overlord* allowed. AOC-in-C Bomber Command replied that he had already agreed with SHAEF 'to take on oil plants with his marginal effort'.[20] Nor was this the end of Sigint's contribution to the adoption of the attack on oil as an objective of the strategic air offensive.

On 7 June the decrypt of an Enigma message disclosed that on 5 June OKL had advised First Parachute Army, which was based at Nancy, that as a result of renewed Allied interference with the production of aircraft fuel, the most essential requirements for training and 'production plans' could scarcely be met. During June allocations of general purpose aviation fuel could be made only to trainer, bomber, fighter and ground-attack units and to the Director General of Supply. At least until the beginning of July units would have to arrange their entire operations so as to manage with their present stocks or with the small allocations that might be possible. The date of arrival and the size of the July quotas were still undecided and 'in no circumstances could greater allocations be made'. In order to ensure the defence of the Reich and to prevent the collapse of the GAF's readiness for defence in the east it had been necessary to break into the OKW strategic reserve.[21]

In a minute on this decrypt for the Prime Minister the CAS commented on 8 June:

'I regard this as one of the most important pieces of information we have yet received. On the strength of it the Chiefs of Staff have asked for a completely up-to-date appreciation from the JIC and the oil experts. I think that there is little doubt that in the light of this appreciation the strategic bombers should be turned over to synthetic oil plants as soon as *Overlord* can spare them. You will remember that this was our intention but it will need American agreement. I think it would be wrong to attack these targets piecemeal with small forces over a long period. The enemy would then doubtless start organising very efficient smoke screens and would greatly increase his Flak defences. I shall suggest that we should wait a little and then choose a period of fair weather to concentrate the whole force on these targets. Most of the targets are suitable only for

---

19. CAB 121/418, JIC(44) 218(0) of 27 May.
20. Webster and Frankland, op cit, Vol III, p 47.
21. DEFE 3/166, KV 6673 of 7 June.

American daylight bombers but there are a number in the Ruhr which Bomber Command think they can destroy with OBOE and they will set to work on this as soon as they can be spared from *Overlord*. Of course the smoke screens would give little or no protection to these targets'.[22]*

On the same day, 8 June, Spaatz made the oil plants first priority targets for the USSTAF, as already noted.

The terms of the Chiefs of Staff instructions to the JIC were for an immediate 'closer estimate' of the date by which the enemy's shortage of oil would have a decisive effect on the war.[23] The JIC replied cautiously to this impossible question on 12 June: it could add nothing to its appreciation of 27 May,† but was confident that any further reduction of the enemy's production capacity would hasten the gradual run-down of Germany's operational efficiency.[24] On 20 June the Chiefs of Staff ordered the JIC to produce a fortnightly appreciation of the German fuel situation.[25] On 3 July the JIC issued the first such report after reviewing the effects of the bombing of oil targets in June.

Although Bomber Command and US Eighth Air Force were still heavily occupied in support of the land forces in Normandy and in attacks on the V-weapon sites, aircraft factories and rail centres, these effects had nevertheless been considerable. US Fifteenth Air Force had raided Ploesti and oil installations in Austria and Yugoslavia; Eighth Air Force had attacked the important refineries near Hamburg and five major synthetic plants in eastern and central Germany; Bomber Command, unable as yet to operate by day over Germany or to attack distant targets there by night, had nevertheless made its first large-scale raids against synthetic plants in the Ruhr on 12–13 June.[26] In its assessment of the effects the JIC reported that 10 out of 14 known Bergius-type hydrogenation plants and 3 out of 9 Fischer-Tropsch plants had been damaged,‡ but that some of them were back in partial production. Adding to this damage the estimated damage to refineries, including Ploesti, the JIC believed that the total output of oil products in German-controlled Europe had been reduced by the end of June from the previously normal level of 1,200,000 tons a month to about 670,000 tons, and it compared this with the current requirement for operational efficiency of about 1,000,000

---

* On 11 June the Prime Minister replied 'Good'.
† See above, pp 501–502.
‡ For details about the Bergius and Fischer-Tropsch processes, see Appendix 26.

22. Dir/C Archive, 6715 of 8 June.
23. CAB 121/418, COS(44) 184th(o) Meeting, 7 June.
24. ibid, JIC(44) 247 of 12 June.
25. ibid, COS(44) 201st(o) Meeting, 20 June.
26. Craven and Cate, op cit, Vol III, pp 283–284.

tons. In a reference to the decrypt of 7 June,* it added that recent intelligence had confirmed its view that Germany had no free reserve which would absorb the impact of a sudden drop in production. Its conclusion was that 'assuming that Allied air attacks can keep the total output of refined oil products . . . down to its present level of about 670,000 tons per month and that the Germans are forced to fight intensively on three fronts, current supplies would fall short by some 35 per cent of the minimum needed to avoid hampering military operations. This is, however, taking an average for all products; the deficiency in certain products, especially petrol and lubricating oil, will be even more pronounced'.[27]

This report relied for its evidence mainly on PR. This had established, for example, that Bomber Command had done great damage at Gelsenkirchen and that the synthetic plants at Pölitz and Magdeburg had ceased production on 20 June.[28] A decrypt had disclosed that in Bomber Command's raid on the installation at Gelsenkirchen on the night of 12–13 June plant of the 'highest priority' had been put out of action for several months and that some 5,000 tons of stored oil had been destroyed.† But Sigint had produced no other evidence on the damage done by the bombing, and no evidence for its effect on the German oil shortages, since the decrypt of 7 June.

The JIC's assessment was nevertheless sufficiently encouraging, and steps were taken early in July with a view to increasing the effectiveness of the oil offensive. In order to improve photographic reconnaissance and interpretation, on the quality of which the offensive so largely depended, oil experts were attached to the oil division of the Allied CIU, new photographic machinery and processes were introduced and the Spitfire XIX was brought into service for high-speed and high-altitude reconnaissance – this last step being necessary to counter the fear that the Mosquito and the

---

* See above, p 502.

† This information was obtained, exceptionally, from a decrypt in the medium-grade police cypher. Traffic in this cypher (for which see Volume II, Appendix 5) had been intercepted from Germany regularly since May 1944, and it was read currently till September, when the introduction of a new cypher produced some delay in decryption. The traffic was voluminous, as the cypher was now used also by the fire services, ARP authorities and *ad hoc* administrations set up to deal with breakdowns in war production. It supplied much information about damage to factories, breakdowns in water, gas and electricity supplies, emergency movements of coal and other supplies, evacuations of civil population on the eastern front, and the drafting of manpower from industry to the armed forces. But most of the information relating to the air offensive was concerned with the effects of raids on the cities, and it did not produce any further decrypts bearing on the effects of the oil offensive.

27. CAB 121/418, JIC(44) 285(o) of 3 July.
28. AIR 41/7, p 148.

earlier marks of Spitfire were proving to be no match for the new German jet fighters that were now coming into service in small numbers.* And on 7 July the Air Staff and USSTAF set up a new working committee, the Joint Anglo-American Oil Targets Committee. Superseding the existing organisation by which, in association with the US Enemy Objectives Unit, the Hartley Committee had been responsible for assessing the nature and location of targets and the results of the attacks, and the oil section of MEW had contributed calculations of enemy consumption and production, the Committee's task was to supervise the oil campaign 'more scientifically' by reaching quicker decisions on the priority with which the individual oil targets were to be attacked and re-attacked. It had representatives from Bomber Command, USSTAF, A13(c), MI 10, the Enemy Objectives Unit and SHAEF. One of its first decisions was to give priority to attacks on the Bergius plants (eg Pölitz, Leuna, Brüx).[29]

□

US Eighth and Fifteenth Air Forces prosecuted the oil offensive throughout July to the limit that visual conditions and their other commitments allowed. Fifteenth Air Force devoted most of its effort to it, making five attacks on Ploesti and others on refineries and synthetic plants in Silesia, Austria, Hungary and Yugoslavia.† Though still heavily engaged in army support operations and

---

* See Volume III, Part 1, p 332 et seq, and below, p 595 et seq.

† Speer was later to testify that the mining of the Danube with the object of preventing oil shipments to the Reich had even more serious effects than the bombing of Ploesti. The mining was carried out by No 205 Group RAF, operating under US Fifteenth Air Force, during July and August and continued for a few weeks on the stretch west of Belgrade after it had ceased further east with the Soviet occupation of Romania at the end of August. Two raids early in July almost brought the river traffic to a halt, forcing the German mining authorities to take the risk of heavy casualties and order the opening up of the whole length of the river. As a result considerable movement was achieved up to the time of a third raid on 30–31 July. Thereafter shipping casualties mounted from 18 in July to 32 in August. Between July and October a total of 74 ships were sunk and 28 damaged.[30]

The offensive was reflected in Sigint less extensively than in the earlier operations in the spring of 1944 (see Volume III Part 1, pp 41–42). The orders to open up the river were not decrypted, but the decrypt of 2 August of a message of 26 July disclosed an urgent need for oil tankers on the Romanian sector.[31] Another decrypt of 2 August disclosed that on 26 July the Germans were increasing the daily pipeline capacity from Ploesti in order to circumvent the Danube bottle-neck.[32] A decrypt of 5 August contained arrangements of 28 July for the

29. Webster and Frankland, op cit, Vol III, pp 209–210; Craven and Cate, op cit, Vol III, p 286; AIR 41/56, p 58, n 1.

30. Jackson, *The Mediterranean and Middle East*, Vol VI Part 2 (1987), pp 215–216; BR 1736(56)(1), *British Mining Operations 1939–1945*, pp 656–657, 661, 663; AIR 41/56, p 100 fn.

31. DEFE 3/65, XL 4445 of 2 August.

32. ibid.

attacks against V-weapon sites, Eighth Air Force attacked several refineries, including the great complex near Hamburg, and several synthetic plants in central and eastern Germany, including the Bergius plant at Leuna near Leipzig; Leuna, the only plant apart from Pölitz that was capable of producing over 100,000 tons a year, was attacked three times. Bomber Command, which also had to meet many calls for battlefield support and attacks on V-weapon sites, attacked five synthetic plants in the Ruhr towards the end of the month in its first operation against oil targets since that of 12–13 June; but the bulk of its effort over Germany was still devoted to area bombing, including three huge raids on Stuttgart, one on Hamburg and one on Kiel. In its June raids on oil targets Bomber Command's losses had been higher than the average casualties incurred during the battle of Berlin; 93 bombers lost out of 832, 65 of them to night-fighters.[37] In the July raids losses were low; Bomber Command was now using the 'Mandrel' screen over Germany and deploying 'Long Window' against SN2, the existence of which had recently come to light.[38]* In June PR had shown that except at Gelsenkirchen the results of the raids were disappointing. After the July raids PR revealed considerable damage at all five plants and Sigint confirmed that production had been interrupted at two of them.[39]

Several decrypts in July testified to Germany's continued anxiety about the effects of the raids. It was known from a message decrypted on 8 July that on 26 June Luftflotte 3 had reported that 'Allied attacks had caused considerable reduction in fuel supplies' and that June allocation would have to last into July.[40] A decrypt of 11 July disclosed that on 5 July Göring had banned all non-essential flying on account of deep inroads into fuel supplies.[41]† On 10 July, in a signal decrypted on 13 July, the

---

carriage of cargo to the eastern front by Romanian and Greek barges because no German shipping was available for long distance traffic.[33] There were occasional decrypts of messages reporting shipping losses.[34] A few others disclosed the enemy's difficulties in combating the offensive: one of 1 August referred to the use of three Ju 88s as night-fighters;[35] another of 13 October to limitations on the use of mine-detecting aircraft owing to the fuel situation.[36]

* See Volume III Part 1, Appendix 20 for SN2.

† See above, p 224.

33. DEFE 3/113, XL 4869 of 5 August.
34. DEFE 3/230, HP 1364 of 27 September; DEFE 3/237, HP 3182 of 13 October.
35. DEFE 3/65, XL 4349 of 1 August.
36. DEFE 3/237, HP 3182 of 13 October.
37. Webster and Frankland, op cit, Vol III, pp 161–162.
38. ibid, p 174.
39. DEFE 3/61, XL 3485 of 25 July; DEFE 3/62, XL 3530 of 26 July.
40. DEFE 3/53, XL 1260 of 8 July.
41. DEFE 3/54, XL 1671 of 11 July.

Japanese Naval Mission in Berlin informed Tokyo that recent attacks on oil targets in the Balkans had caused considerable damage and that although the state of German synthetic production was 'not too serious', further developments would 'require watchfulness'.[42] In message decrypted on 19 and 20 July the Japanese Ambassador reported that the Allied attacks on the synthetic oil plants were 'a source of very great concern'; the damage being done was so extensive that 'the question arises whether large-scale operations by the German Army may not be affected'.[43] On 27 July another decrypt of a signal from the Naval Mission disclosed that in an interview on 22 July General Korten, the German Chief of Air Staff, had said that while there had been scarcely any damage to the oil depots of the armed forces, which were mostly underground, damage to the synthetic oil plants had been considerable; Germany was therefore abandoning the policy of concentrating production in large plants and embarking on dispersal to about 3,000 self-contained plants.[44]

Korten's reference to plans for dispersal was not the first indication from Sigint that the Germans were now attaching highest priority to counter-measures against the offensive. In the infrequent decrypts reporting on individual raids there had been references to the improvement of the defences at the targets. The decrypt of a message of 22 July, reporting an attack on Brüx on 21 July, gave unusually precise details of the damage done but added that most of the bombs had fallen wide.[45] A decrypt of 29 July commented on a raid on Ploesti on 15 July. It said that seven of the eight refineries attacked had suffered only indirect damage to their railways and storage; the eighth had been hit and would be out of action for about ten days, and production from the whole complex would be 12,300 tons daily from 21 July. Smoke from 1,500 canisters had caused most of the bombs to fall wide. The decrypt also described the Allied methods of attack and analysed ways in which they could be countered.[46] In a telegram of 10 July, decrypted on 19 July, the Japanese Consul in Vienna reported that as a result of raids in June on two oil plants near Vienna, all refining would come to an end from 10 July for four weeks, perhaps for longer, and that as the raids had destroyed all petrol stored above ground – several hundred thousand tons – supply was now dependent on available underground stores until repairs had been carried out; Hitler was exerting the highest pressure for

---

42. SJA 517 of 13 July.
43. BAY/XLs 49 and 53 of 19 and 20 July.
44. BAY/XL 64 of 28 July.
45. DEFE 3/60, XL 3161 of 23 July.
46. DEFE 3/63, XL 3926 of 29 July.

a repairs programme and had sent Speer to Vienna on 4 July.[47]

This information in no way qualified the enthusiasm of the intelligence authorities for the oil offensive. In a paper of 14 July, on Germany's capacity to resist, the JIC found it hard to see how she could put off collapse beyond the end of 1944 in view of her dwindling supplies of oil and non-ferrous metals, and in another paper of 20 July on this subject it insisted that her chief weakness was the seriousness of the overall oil shortage.[48] On 24 July, in its second fortnightly report on the oil situation, it calculated in the light of the damage done to synthetic plants and refineries in July that the rate of production of all finished products in German-controlled Europe had been reduced to 573,000 tons a month as compared with consumption required by the intensive fighting on all fronts of 932,000 tons; and it repeated that 'Germany will be unable to continue the struggle beyond December given intensive fighting on all three fronts and the continued success of Allied air attacks'.[49] In its next report on the oil situation, dated 7 August, it put the monthly rate of production in July at 550,000 tons, 42 per cent of the production level in the previous April (now thought to be 1,360,000 tons); estimated that the military petrol consumption in July had exceeded the production of 233,000 tons by nearly 50 per cent, and that total production in the months of May, June and July had been 2,584,000 tons as against total consumption of 3,166,000 tons; and concluded that at this rate of depletion German reserves would soon be exhausted.[50]

In the paper of 20 July, however, the JIC drew attention to the fact that German fighter production was again recovering as a result of the dispersal of the aircraft industry; and it recognised that there was increasing evidence that next to oil, the chief weakness of the German Army was shortage of tanks, MT and ammunition, and that this was due in no small measure to damage done to communications in the course of Allied bombing in the Ruhr and western Germany. As we shall see, aircraft production and transportation would soon be rivalling oil for priority in the Allied bombing programme. And in the paper of 7 August the JIC gave two warnings. The first was that in the absence of continued bombing of oil, the enemy might achieve a total production of one million tons in August, 75 per cent of the April level. The second was that the Germans had resorted to exceptional measures for

47. BAY/XL 53 of 20 July.
48. CAB 121/413, SIC file D/Germany/1, JIC(44) 302(o) of 14 July; CAB 121/419, SIC file D/Germany/4, JIC(44) 301(o) of 20 July.
49. CAB 121/418, JIC(44) 320(o) of 24 July.
50. ibid, JIC(44) 344(o) of 7 August.

restoring production. A special commission had been appointed to oversee repairs to production plants;* these had been given priority for labour and materials even over armaments producton; and PR had shown that intensive repairs were already in train at plants throughout Germany, Austria and Hungary. Immediately after the completion of this report a telegram drafted by the JIC was sent by the CAS to the Mediterranean air commanders advising them that 'the speed with which the Germans are now repairing oil producing plants' threw the emphasis in Allied bombing operations on to the prevention of any recovery in oil production.[52]

The emergency organisation for the repair of oil installations was to be the enemy's most effective counter-measure; dispersal of the highly complex installations was soon found to be impracticable, as was the attempt to put some of them underground. It need not be doubted, moreover, that the discovery that the organisation had been deployed was one of the considerations which led the USSTAF to intensify its campaign against oil targets in August. It carried out about 60 raids on oil targets throughout Germany and south-eastern Europe, half against storage, a quarter against synthetic oil plants and a quarter against refineries. The targets included (on 9, 17, 18, and 19 August) the refineries at Ploesti, where production was completely stopped before the Russians occupied it at the end of the month,† and the synthetic plants at Blechhammer (on 7 and 22 August) and Pölitz (on 25 August, just when it was recovering from the June attack).[53] But Bomber Command's effort in the oil campaign slackened appreciably in August: the twelve major night raids it made over Germany took in two attacks on the MT plant at Rüsselsheim and only one against a synthetic oil plant – that at Sterkrade which had been slightly damaged in June – and of the tonnage dropped on Germany the greater part was directed against the cities.[54]

---

* The fact that Geilenberg, one of Speer's deputies, had been appointed as a commissioner with special powers for high priority tasks had just been disclosed by the decrypt of a telegram dated 10 July 1944 from the Japanese Consul General in Vienna. After describing the destruction of refineries round Vienna he reported that Geilenberg had been given virtually supreme powers for reconstruction of bombed oil installations and was pressing, among other measures, for the death penalty for individuals obstructing him in this task.[51]

† The Russians allowed a USAAF inspection of Ploesti within a few days of their occupation. The inspection confirmed that the key to the reduction of oil output was that repeated bombing made repairs impossible.

51. FO 837/20, MEW Intelligence Weekly No 132 of 17 August.
52. JIC(44) 346(o) of 7 August.
53. Craven and Cate, op cit, Vol III, pp 296–300.
54. Webster and Frankland, op cit, Vol III, p 176.

Although it also carried out on 27 August a daylight raid on the synthetic oil plant at Homberg, the first in which Bomber Command had ever penetrated beyond the Rhine by day with fighter cover,* the AOC-in-C was complaining that the diversion of his force to oil targets and other tasks was harming the area bombing offensive.

It has been said that in thus largely ignoring the wishes of the Air Staff, Harris and his HQ staff, with their inclination 'to confuse advice with interference, criticism with sabotage and evidence with propaganda', dismissed not only the advice of leading oil technologists, but also the extent to which that advice rested on what the CAS was later to call the irrefutable intelligence of Sigint.[55] In fact there was a long period from the beginning of August during which, the improvements made for PR being off-set by bad weather and the increase of smoke and camouflage at the targets, Sigint evidence became crucial as damage-assessment was hampered by the lack of photographs. It is also true that decrypts reporting on the effects of individual raids were few and far between after 4 August, when a decrypt confirmed PR indications of extensive damage by disclosing that the raid on Leuna on 28 July, the last of three raids on that target in July, had been the 'heaviest so far' and that the plant was 'provisionally entirely out of action'.[56] But references in high-grade Sigint to the existence and the effects of the growing fuel shortage were becoming increasingly frequent.

Between 1 and 14 August several decrypts reported a serious shortage in LXXXIV and XLVII Corps in Normandy; they culminated in von Kluge's request on 16 August for permission to withdraw from Falaise in view of tank deficiency and shortage of fuel, which was 'the decisive factor'.† Decrypts of 4 and 5 August disclosed that fuel shortage was hampering the GAF in the Lyons area and on the eastern front.[57] In a message of 10 August, decrypted on 12 August, OKL ordered a general curtailment of operational activity because of further damage to fuel production by Allied air attacks: reconnaissance was to be flown only when it was essential; four-engined aircraft were to operate only after application to OKL; all other aircraft were to operate only in cases where action would be decisive or when chances of success were good.[58] This was the first reference to restrictions on operational

---

* See below, p 515.
† See above p 265.

55. ibid, p 80; AIR 41/56, p 156.
56. DEFE 3/112, XL 4668 of 4 August.
57. CX/MSS/T266/13 of 4 August; DEFE 3/112, XL 4724 of 5 August.
58. DEFE 3/117, XL 5773 of 12 August.

activity, as distinct from non-essential flying. In another message decrypted on 12 August GAF units withdrawing from western France were ordered on 10 August to evacuate fuel stocks 'down to the last drop'.[59] Messages from Berlin on 13 August, decrypted on 21 August, ordered that all convertible motorised vehicles in German Army supply units on all fronts were to be converted to producer gas by 1 October.[60] In a message not decrypted until 27 August OKL warned Luftflotte 3 on 15 August either that operations must be further curtailed, so as to release fuel for training 120 crews a month for the west, or that the present very low allocation to training for the west be accepted, in which case only one-third of replacement requirements could be met.[61]

The Japanese diplomatic decrypts also testified to the extent of the German anxiety about the effects of the oil offensive. On 7 August, in a signal decrypted on 12 August, the head of the Japanese Naval Mission in Berlin, more emphatic than he had been in July, stated that 'oil is Germany's problem'.[62] In a telegram decrypted on 18 August the Ambassador in Berlin reported that Speer had told him that oil production had been badly hit, especially by the daylight raids, and that although some oil plants were being put underground, they were not yet in production. Speer said that up to the time when the daylight raids on Germany's oil industry had begun Allied air attacks on the German economy had been unco-ordinated, but that since then it could be said for the first time that the Allied air offensive 'might deal a fatal blow to Germany'.* A signal from the head of the Naval Mission on 14 August, decrypted on 21 August, stated that there had been heavy damage in 12 raids in July and that if such raids continued, 'Germany's capacity to prosecute the war will be seriously affected;' he considered that production had dropped to about 50 per cent and said that 'if things continue as at present, stocks of oil will not last more than six months[63]. . .

Relying mainly on the Sigint evidence, which was all the more valuable in view of the all but total lack of PR during August, the JIC's fortnightly report for the first half of August, issued on 21 August, concluded that 'the Allied policy of attacking German oil production, stocks etc is for the first time threatening her with a potentially fatal situation . . .' It stressed once again, however, that the enemy had embarked on an emergency repairs programme

---

* For the signal sent to the Commands based on this decrypt see Appendix 27.

59. DEFE 3/117, XL 5773 of 12 August.
60. DEFE 3/123, XL 7367 of 21 August.
61. DEFE 3/126, XL 8202 of 27 August.
62. BAY/XL 95 of 12 August.
63. BAY/XL 117 of 23 August.

and that production would soon rise if there was no further damage.[64] In its next report on 4 September it estimated that total German output for the whole of August had been only 40 per cent of normal (that is, of the April 1944 level) and that on 1 September the rate of production was under 25 per cent of normal at 300,000 tons, of which only 90,000 tons was motor spirit and none was suitable for normal fighter aircraft. These estimates depended on the Sigint references, but also on the evidence of PR, which had been resumed on 1 September after a long gap and which indicated that all Bergius plants, the primary source of aircraft fuel, were out of action, and on the news of the Russian capture of Ploesti. The report believed that even in the absence of further attacks, total output in September was unlikely to exceed 43 per cent of normal but added that production from the synthetic oil plants would rise in September from 20 per cent to 54 per cent of normal as a consequence of the vigorous German repair programme unless the plants already out of action were kept out of action.[65]

During September, while PR coverage of the effects of the raids remained patchy, Sigint references to the fuel situation were less frequent. On 7 September a decrypt disclosed that in order to avoid the expenditure of fuel on training, all branches of the GAF had been asked to call for volunteers for the fighter arm.[66] A decrypt of 11 September showed that Göring had issued new orders for fuel economy in the GAF on 1 September: flights were to be restricted to the bare essentials 'so that every drop goes to operational training,' and all infringements were to be reported.[67] A message of 12 September, decrypted on 15 September, disclosed that Hitler had taken the quite exceptional step of ordering all bunker fuel to be removed from sea-going vessels and coasters in the eastern Baltic, and the order was relayed in a police decrypt to the port authorities in Emden.[68] But if it was limited, the intelligence remained encouraging, and the tone of the JIC's assessments underwent no change.

Its report of 18 September on the oil situation noted that the Germans had doubled the Flak defences at Pölitz, Leuna, Brüx and Zeitz, and had obviously reduced consumption to conform to output. But it also noted that there had been heavy attacks on 23 synthetic plants since its last report on 4 September, and it did not doubt that although assessment of the results had been hampered

---

64. CAB 121/418, JIC(44) 365(o) of 21 August.
65. ibid, JIC(44) 390(o) of 4 September.
66. CX/MSS/T299/23 of 7 September.
67. DEFE 3/224, XL 9805 of 11 September.
68. DEFE 3/459, ZTPG 283825; GPD 2970DD2.

by bad weather, enemy production, especially of petrol, had been further reduced.[69] The Combined Intelligence Committee believed that the shortage of oil and aircrew would prevent any revival of GAF activity,[70] and on 20 September it stated that: 'provided Allied air attacks on oil targets, particularly on synthetic oil plants, continue on a heavy scale, the GAF will be reduced to a nullity by the middle of November 1944'.[71] By the end of September PR had indicated that German production had suffered a further marked decline, as the JIC stated in its report on the whole month. Issued on 2 October, this estimated that total German oil production had been reduced in that month to 330,000 tons, or 25 per cent of the April 1944 norm. The JIC stressed that this took no account of three attacks on Brüx by Fifteenth and of two on Böhlen, near Leipzig, by Eighth Air Force, for which PR was not yet available.[72]* It was presumably after receiving this further intelligence that on 3 October the Joint Oil Targets Committee assessed total output for September at the lower figure of 304,000 tons (23 per cent of norm).[74] Both estimates added that more than half of total output (175,000 tons) had been produced by other sources than the synthetic plants and the refineries, and mainly by benzol plants.† On the other hand, both attached the warning that while the evidence suggested that of the 91 synthetic plants and refineries still in German hands only 3 were in full production and 28 in partial production, a substantial number would shortly be back in operation if no further damage was inflicted.

We need not doubt that these estimates had sustained the USSTAF in the still more intensive attacks which it directed

---

* The JIC's report recapitulated the estimates made since April. They are here compared with the figures later compiled by the US Strategic Bombing Survey.[73]:

	JIC	USSBS
April	1,344,000 (100%)	810,000
May	1,082,000 (80%)	734,000
June	800,000 (59%)	511,000
July	671,000 (50%)	438,000
August	526,000 (39%)	345,000
September	330,000 (25%)	281,000

† These plants had not previously been thought to be worthwhile targets; there were some 80 of them throughout the Reich, many in the Ruhr close to the coal.[75] See also below, p 518 fn*.

69. CAB 121/418, JIC(44)403(o) of 18 September.
70. JIC(44) 407 of 16 September.
71. JIC(44) 410 of 20 September.
72. CAB 121/418, JIC(44) 423(o) of 2 October.
73. Webster and Frankland, op cit, Vol IV, p 516.
74. ibid, p 515.
75. Craven and Cate, op cit, Vol III, p 841; AIR 41/56, p 127.

against oil targets in September in the face of increasing day-fighter opposition.* After a week of bad weather Eighth Air Force carried out a series of concentrated raids, attacking seven major synthetic plants on 11 September, six on 12 September and three on 13 September, while Fifteenth Air Force made large-scale raids on synthetic plants and refineries in Silesia and Austria.[76] The intelligence had produced no change, on the other hand, in Bomber Command's programme. In September Bomber Command made further daylight atacks on three synthetic oil plants in the Ruhr; PR indicated that heavy damage was done to two of them and that the third raid, a renewed attack on the plant at Gelsenkirchen, was moderately successful.[77]† It was in this month heavily occupied with attacks on French Atlantic ports, V2 sites and targets relating to the battle of Arnhem. But its major operations over Germany were area bombing attacks by night on old targets including Frankfurt, Kiel and Stuttgart and new targets including Darmstadt and Karlsruhe.

☐

It was in these circumstances that on 25 September the Combined Chiefs of Staff took over from SHAEF the control of the strategic air forces. The CAS had obtained approval for the transfer at the 'Octagon' conference earlier in the month on two grounds. The Air Staff, who would exercise their control through the DCAS (Bottomley) and General Spaatz, were better placed than the operational HQs to ensure that the expertise and the intelligence available to the Joint Oil Targets Committee were utilised in a concentrated offensive against enemy oil before the approach of poorer weather reduced bombing accuracy; and they alone were in a position to direct other bombing in such a way as to give maximum help to the Russian advance. The CAS had not stated his more particular reasons for wanting the transfer. The Air Staff knew that proposals were being framed at SHAEF for a bombing campaign against German transportation similar to that which had been carried out in western Europe before *Overlord*,

---

* See below, p 523 ff.

† It also carried out on 23 September a night precision raid with Tallboy bombs which cut the Dortmund-Ems Canal near Münster. This was the first of several such attacks made on the Dortmund-Ems and other canals, on which the increasingly dispersed German armaments industry heavily depended, when transportation bombing started systematically in October.[78]

76. Craven and Cate, op cit, Vol III, pp 301–303.
77. Webster and Frankland, op cit, Vol III, p 171.
78. ibid, pp 181–182.

and feared that SHAEF would give this priority over the offensive against oil. Above all, it was looking for some means of asserting its authority over the direction of Bomber Command's operations.[79]

By September 1944 Bomber Command had become a truly formidable force. The huge building programmes which had started in the winter of 1941–1942, and which had absorbed as much manpower as that devoted to production for the entire British Army, were coming to fruition. The German retreat in the west was reducing the onerous commitment of the heavy bombers to attacks on the V-weapon sites and the French transport system. In the last nine months of the war the weight of bombs Bomber Command dropped on Germany was to exceed by far the total dropped in the first five years. With its acquired skills and the powerful assistance of improved devices for navigation, bomb-aiming and marking, it was at last capable of bombing with accuracy, even in bad weather, by night and by day, and could now do so anywhere in Germany, except in the most difficult conditions. Daylight bombing had become feasible since the US air forces had established day-time air superiority. As late as the end of August the enemy night-fighters had remained a fearsome opponent, the more so as with the contraction of Germany's front they were increasingly concentrated in the Reich; AI reported their final withdrawal from France and the Low Countries on 27 August, and on the previous day the JIC noted that their performance was still improving with the transfer of pilots from bomber units and the increased production of twin-engined fighters.[80] But their withdrawal deprived them of their early warning installations at French and Belgian bases and thus of their capacity for instant response to Bomber Command's raids, as AI recognised on 5 September;[81] on this account, as much as in consequence of fuel shortage, their performance dropped markedly from the beginning of that month except on rare occasions. By then, moreover, the Allies had at last uncovered the secrets of the SN2 and other night-fighter plotting and location devices, while Bomber Command was provided with new jamming devices and well served by improved and largely successful techniques of feint and diversion.* Though they still jumped on

---

* See Volume III, Part 1, Appendices 20 and 21. The mystery surrounding SN2, Naxos and Korfu had finally been solved in July, but Bomber Command, which had from then on kept its H_2S switched off during the approach to the German borders, still found it indispensable for navigation and target finding over the Reich.

79. ibid, pp 57–60; Craven and Cate, op cit, Vol III, p 320.
80. Air Sunset 227 of 27 August; CAB 121/419, JIC(44) 371(o) of 26 August; Webster and Frankland, op cit, Vol III, p 199.
81. Air Sunset 233 of 5 September.

occasions to 5 or even 10 per cent, Bomber Command's casualties averaged only one per cent after September 1944.[82]

Bomber Command nevertheless continued to make only token gestures to the oil offensive, a strategy by which the Air Staff now set great store, and to devote the bulk of its effort to the attack on German cities, a strategy in which the Air Staff had had little faith since the battle of Berlin, and the Air Staff's frustration on this account was all the greater in that the intelligence sources were still providing no grounds for supposing that the effects of area bombing on civilian morale would contribute to Germany's collapse. On 20 July the JIC had made this point emphatically: 'the majority . . now accept Allied bombing with a measure of hopeless resignation . . . the Gestapo is strong and will keep order'.[83] On 26 August it had repeated it. The Allied bombing was probably 'playing a relatively much less important part in determining civilian morale than it did up to a few months ago; it was most unlikely to foment such opposition or produce such chaos as might lead to a collapse of the home front'.[84] Like all earlier judgments on the subject, these assertions rested either on negative evidence,* or on the indirect testimony of many Japanese decrypts, like that of 30 July in which Admiral Abe noted that while the bombing of the cities was having no military effect, the Allied oil offensive was achieving 'catastrophic results',† and on the interrogation, for what that was worth, of German POW.‡ But if they were weakened by the lack of support from direct and explicit evidence, they still stood in sharp contrast to the JIC's assessments of the effects of the oil offensive, for which there was abundant positive evidence.§

The directive issued to Bomber Command on the transfer of control of the strategic air forces reflected the Air Staff's concern

---

* The police cypher (see above, p 504 fn†) was however an important new source of negative evidence. In view of the contents of the messages sent in this cypher, it may be presumed that they would have revealed the existence of any civil unrest, but the only reference to the subject related to a revolt of foreign workers after a raid on the marshalling yards at Saarbrücken in July 1944.

† See above, p 366.

‡ On 27 May 1944 CSDIC issued a survey of POW opinion on morale in the forces and on the home front. This was found to be high despite the area bombing under which 'morale seems to stiffen rather than decline'.[85]

§ As did the occasional positive statement in the German messages. After the devastation of Karlsruhe the decrypt of a long SS Enigma message stated that the morale of the inhabitants under the 'overwhelming assault' had been 'exemplary'.[86]

82.   Webster and Frankland, op cit, Vol III, pp 182, 198–199.
83.   CAB 121/419, JIC(44) 301(o) of 20 July.
84.   Ibid, JIC(44) 371(o) of 26 August.
85.   AIR 40/2392.
86.   DEFE 3/231, HP 1725 of 3 October.

in uncompromising terms. Policy during the next phase of the strategic offensive had been settled on 13 September at a meeting of the DCAS and General Spaatz with Tedder from SHAEF. The bombing should be directed firstly against oil, secondly against transportation and thirdly, 'in certain circumstances', against the GAF. By 'in certain circumstances' they had meant that action would be taken against aircraft production and air facilities only if the German fighters failed to offer themselves for destruction in sufficient numbers during Allied attacks on oil and communications.[87] In the Air Staff's directive to Bomber Command, issued on 25 September, Harris was instructed to give first priority to oil targets including storage, with special emphasis on petrol, and second priority equally to transportation targets and to tank and MT production plants and depots.* He was informed that attacks should be delivered on important industrial areas only 'when weather or tactical conditions are unsuitable for operations against specific primary objectives'. The only other qualification was that support of land and naval operations was 'a continuing commitment'.[88]

□

Bomber Command had hitherto ignored the wishes of the Air Staff. It now flouted the Air Staff's instructions. The official history of the strategic air offensive has commented as follows on the directive of 25 September. 'It was difficult to see how, if the Air Staff's viewpoint endured and prevailed, the main offensive effort of Bomber Command could in the future, as it had in the past, be largely devoted to the general area bombing campaign. Nevertheless, in the final offensive the principal effort of Bomber Command was devoted not only to a resumption, but to a vast expansion of the general area campaign'.[89]

In October Bomber Command dropped more bombs than in any previous month in the war. Seventy-four per cent of them (over 42,000 tons) were dropped on towns, most of them during the so-called 'third battle of the Ruhr' in eight major raids against the main Ruhr centres, and 16 per cent (over 12,000 tons) in operations in support of the armies. Only six per cent (3,653 tons: a smaller tonnage than it had dropped on oil in June, when so much of Bomber Command's effort had been diverted to support

---

* See below, p 520 ff.

87.   Webster and Frankland, op cit, Vol III, pp 60–63.
88.   ibid, p 63, Vol IV, pp 172(n), 173.
89.   ibid, Vol III, p 57.

Overlord) were used against oil targets, most of them in daylight raids towards the end of the month against six synthetic oil plants in the Ruhr which had been damaged earlier and were being re-built, and only 0.9 per cent (522 tons) against transportation targets which included marshalling yards and, in a second attack on it, the Dortmund-Ems Canal.[90]* The Air Ministry's history of Bomber Command's operations comments that 'the enemy thus had a chance to repair the refineries which had been so battered in the second week of September'.[92]

The performance of the US air forces stood out in sharp contrast. Spurred on by the knowledge that the approaching winter would reduce the efficiency of their bombing, and by evidence from PR that the Germans were making desperate efforts to restore the tremendous damage done to the oil installations during September and had begun to disperse the oil industry, and undeterred by the fact that the Germans were increasing the defences at the oil targets with heavy Flak, smoke and camouflage, the USSTAF again devoted to the oil offensive all the effort its other commitments allowed. But it was unable to maintain the level of effort it had achieved in September. Eighth Air Force attacked ten synthetic plants and three other installations, including three in the Ruhr (normally Bomber Command's preserve), the Hamburg refineries and Pölitz, which was again immobilised, and Fifteenth Air Force bombed four major synthetic plants in eastern Germany including Brüx, which was seen to be recovering. There was some anxiety, moreover, that they were not achieving the earlier degree of accuracy in their bombing as a result of cloud and the increase of smoke and camouflage.[93]† For the same reasons, on the other hand, PR was less efficient than before in disclosing the extent of the damage done. As early as 6 October the Combined Strategic Targets Committee‡ was accor-

---

* But it should be remembered that much damage was done to transportation during Bomber Command's area attacks. And this was also true of benzol plants (see above, p 513) which were mainly in industrial cities. Bomber Command's area attacks from October included cities containing these plants and greatly reduced benzol production.[91]

† Many of the synthetic oil plants were situated in isolated areas and were therefore good targets for instrumental bombing through cloud. The US air forces were less proficient than Bomber Command in this form of attack.

‡ At the beginning of October, to assist Bottomley and Spaatz in carrying out their policy, the Air Staff set up a co-ordinating body, the Combined Strategic Targets Committee (CSTC) to advise on priorities between the target systems and on target selection within them in the light of all available intelligence. It was fed by working committees on oil (the existing Joint Oil Targets Committee) on aircraft production (the former Jockey Committee), on tank and

90. ibid, Vol III, p 59; AIR 41/56, pp 114, 127, 142.
91. Craven and Cate, op cit, Vol III, pp 642, 645.
92. AIR 41/56, p 127.
93. Craven and Cate, op cit, Vol III, p 642.

dingly recommending that plants should be re-attacked even by blind bombing and without waiting for PR evidence that they had resumed production:[95] and by mid-October it had become the settled policy of the US air forces 'to attack and re-attack regardless of the reconnaissance data'.[96] Nor was this development the only cause for disquiet. In the first week of October, when the CSTC was also recommending that the weight and density of the raids should be increased, Sigint disclosed that the GAF was carrying out a massive reinforcement of its day-fighters in the Reich.

Although this last development was largely unforeseen by AI, Sigint had given good advance notice of it; as we shall see, its consequences in terms of stiffened opposition to the Allied raids did not materialise till the beginning of November.* But there need be no doubt that the prospect of increasing fighter resistance added to the anxiety with which the Allied operational authorities contemplated the wavering of the oil offensive in October, when the confidence of the intelligence authorities was in any case beginning to wane. As early as 6 October the CSTC was noting that several refineries were in action again and warning that output might double unless the recovery was checked.[97] In its fortnightly report of 16 October on the offensive the JIC put on a brave face. Despite the fact that the decline of PR as a guide to the results of the bombing was aggravated by a decline in the number of Sigint references to its consequences, and that it was therefore impossible to offer any estimate of German output for the first half of the month, it quoted as evidence of the existence of the oil shortage the fact that air and motor fuel was being shipped from Norway to Germany, that town trams were being used to move freight and that lack of fuel was holding up the Todt organisation's programme for putting oil production underground.[98] In its report of the same date on Germany's capacity to resist, the JIC repeated this evidence in support of the view that many factors, but mainly the Allied bombing, were bringing about a condition of under-equipment that was incommensurate with her minimum defensive requirements. But it now conceded that this condition

---

MT production plants and depots and, at Tedder's insistence, on transportation (which brought together again the experts who had advised SHAEF on the transportation offensive before D-day.)[94]

* See below, p 523ff.

94. Webster and Frankland, op cit, Vol III, pp 68, 213.
95. AIR 41/56, p 118.
96. Craven and Cate, op cit, Vol III, p 643.
97. AIR 41/56, p 118.
98. CAB 121/418, JIC(44) 436(o) of 16 October.

would not be brought about for the German Army for about six months and that the GAF might secure such degree of ascendancy over central and eastern Germany as to enable it to protect some vital elements of war production during the coming winter.[99] And its next report on the oil situation, dated 30 October and surveying the offensive during the whole of the month, was still more gloomy.

The report noted that because of incomplete PR the results of some of the Allied raids – a total of 32 against 26 targets – were not known, but accepted that 'total production in October was almost certainly more than in September as the effects of repairs outstripped destruction'. It guessed that total output might have been 430,000 tons (32 per cent of norm) as compared with 316,000 (23½ per cent) for September.* In a special section entitled 'Recovery of Output' it reiterated that 'the enemy's repair effort has, for the time being at least, overtaken the downward trend of production since the attacks . . . began' and described in detail the methods used by the Geilenberg organisation. As another indication of the scale of the German defensive effort, it added that Pölitz was now protected by 310 heavy guns, as compared with 325 in Berlin. In quoting evidence for the effects of the offensive, which was taken from Enigma decrypts, the JIC stressed that the 'effects of the sharp fall in production in September are now becoming apparent'; essential GAF operations were being restricted and fuel allocations to the armies in the west for 10-day periods in October–November were apparently to be only one-sixth of normal requirements. Its conclusion was that the repair programme would raise the output to nearly double that of September if Allied attacks ceased and that, in view of the virtual lack of reserves and the low level of current allocations, any substantial increase in production would probably be reflected in the increased operational efficiency of the armed forces within a few weeks.[101]

□

Among the operational authorities Tedder was the first to respond to these developments. On 25 October he criticised not only Bomber Command's area bombing but the basis of the entire

---

* The USSBS estimate for October was 316,000 tons, by coincidence the same as the JIC's estimate for September.[100]

99. CAB 121/419, JIC(44) 437(o) of 16 October.
100. Webster and Frankland, op cit, Vol IV, p 516.
101. CAB 121/418, JIC(44) 450(o) of 30 October.

strategic offensive: it was a patchwork directed at no single aim. In its place he proposed that the strategic air forces should co-ordinate their attacks with those of the tactical air forces, which were already largely occupied with attacks on rail, road and waterway communications between the fronts and the Ruhr, and devote them mainly to the target system whose destruction would, he insisted, affect all the German armed forces and the German economy and German civilian morale – to the transportation system. Their attacks on oil should be limited to 'policing' – to keeping production down to the September level – and the policing could be confined to the Ruhr. If only reluctantly, and only because the Combined Chiefs of Staff had ruled that the armies must have the support of the heavy bombers when they needed it, the Air Staff fell in with this proposal to the extent of agreeing that transportation should remain the second priority in the strategic offensive when it would have preferred to insist that the strategic air forces should make an all-out effort against the oil targets.[102] But it fully shared Tedder's impatience with the obstinacy of Bomber Command, and it made this plain in a new directive issued on 1 November.

In this directive oil and transportation remained the first and second priorities and they were the only target systems listed: attacks on tank and MT production and depots, which in the September directive had been equal second priority with transportation, were abandoned.* As sent to Bomber Command, the directive further reduced Harris's room for evasion by laying it down that if tactical considerations and weather forced it to undertake area bombing, the areas selected should be those in which attacks would make the maximum contribution to the destruction of oil and of lines of communication. In forcefulness of expression and care to avoid ambiguity the directive was without precedent.[105] But if its effect was to force AOC-in-C Bomber Command out of his stance of silent obstruction into a pained and voluble defence of his bombing policy, it largely failed to change that policy.

---

* The attack on tank and MT targets was included in September both because tank and MT shortage were known to be affecting German operations and in order to prevent the Germans from re-equipping their forces,[103] (see above, Chapter 51). But its inclusion had been opposed by some air authorities and the effect of including it had been that the number of attacks on these targets in October, by Eighth Air Force more than by Bomber Command, had been sufficient to persuade the Air Staff that they were a distraction that was contributing to the weakening of the oil offensive.[104] After October the attack on these targets was not resumed till February 1945.

102.   Webster and Frankland, op cit, Vol III, p 71.
103.   Craven and Cate, op cit, Vol III, pp 647–648; JIC(44) 407 of 16 September.
104.   Webster and Frankland, op cit, Vol III, pp 65–66.
105.   ibid, p 73.

On 1 November he had already written to the CAS to justify area bombing against Tedder's criticism. He insisted that area bombing was succeeding; the Germans had long admitted that it was their biggest headache, they had nearly collapsed more than once under its impact, and it was idiotic to throw over a policy that 'was seven-tenths complete in favour of another attempt to seek a quick, clever, easy and cheap way out'.* In addition, area bombing was incurring low casualties, and he had resisted precision bombing from the need to keep casualties low. His letter started a correspondence in which, from November 1944 to January 1945, the CAS tried, but failed, to win his willing support for the oil offensive. The correspondence ended with Harris's offer to resign, which Portal felt unable to accept for fear of the harm that would follow for the morale of Bomber Command.

The CAS pressed his argument with reference to 'the soundness of the intelligence' which supported it. Thus on 5 November he wrote that 'in the light of all the available intelligence I feel that the whole war situation is poised on oil as on a knife edge, and that by a real concentration of effort at this time we might push it over on the right side'. The oil campaign was a battle between Allied destruction and German repair, and failure to win it might 'prolong the war by several months at least'. Harris eventually fell back on expressions of distrust for the reliability of the intelligence and on gibes in particular at MEW. The MEW experts, he wrote on 12 December, 'have never failed to overstate their case for "panaceas" eg ball-bearings, molybdenum, locomotives etc. insofar as after the battle had been joined . . . more and more sources of supply and other factors unpredicted by MEW have become revealed. The oil plan has already displayed similar symptoms. The benzol plants were an afterthought'. He felt that the Allies should be content with depriving the enemy of 'adequate supplies of aviation fuel'.[106]

It was on these grounds that Bomber Command rejected a particular request from the Air Staff on 3 November that it should attack Leuna and Pölitz. The CSTC had advised that the maximum damage should be inflicted on these distant plants even if they had not resumed production, as there was otherwise a danger that they would recover during the winter months when the limited hours of daylight would rule out attack by the US air forces. Even after the DCAS had emphasised on 13 November that the attacks were essential and that losses would be no greater

---

* The remaining three-tenths comprised (though these lists were frequently changed) the destruction of Magdeburg, Leipzig, Chemnitz, Dresden, Breslau, Posen, Halle, Erfurt, Gotha, Weimar, Eisenach and the rest of Berlin.

106. See ibid, pp 81–94 for a full account of the correspondence.

than in raids on Berlin or Stettin,[107] Bomber Command insisted that it could not attack them by day and that night attacks would entail prohibitive losses. In November, while still devoting over half its effort (28,000 tons) to area bombing, it gave priority in the area bombing to benzol plants and, late in the month, it at last increased its attacks on oil targets; but it still confined its attacks on oil plants to those in the Ruhr and to the Hamburg refineries, leaving those in central and eastern Germany to the USSTAF. But Fifteenth Air Force was practically unable to cross the Alps in November on account of bad weather, and while Eighth Air Force did its utmost against the distant targets it also attacked the Ruhr plants and the Hamburg refineries – they were probably over-bombed.[108] Moreover it took the decision not to revisit Pölitz on a calculation of the probable scale of GAF opposition, and its repeated raids on Leuna and other plants were not sufficient to prevent what the JIC described in its reports on the oil campaign during the month as 'a remarkable recovery' in production.

□

Although the casualties incurred by Bomber Command in the night operations in fact remained low, not least because fuel shortage was beginning to add to the other weaknesses of the German night-fighters, it was in November that the recovery of the enemy's day-fighter effort finally materialised as a threat sufficient to influence the operations of the USSTAF.

In August, with the first reports that they had been encountered in small numbers during USSTAF raids, there had been a brief alarm over the threat to the Allied bombing offensive from jet and rocket aircraft; this had receded by early September, when analysis of the Sigint and PR evidence had enabled AI to give the assurance that the new high performance aircraft would not produce any radical change in the effectiveness of the GAF before the end of 1944.* But a month later Sigint had disclosed a sudden increase in the strength of the enemy's conventional day-fighters in the Reich. Messages decrypted early in October reported that a large force of single-engined fighters – some 400 in ten Gruppen – was transferring to Germany from the close-support force in the west. By 9 October further decrypts had disclosed that, following a major attack by Eighth Air Force on synthetic oil plants on 7 October, the reinforcement was being increased; AI estimated

---

* See Volume III Part 1, Chapter 39 and below, p 596.

107. AIR 41/56, pp 152–154.
108. Webster and Frankland, op cit, Vol III, p 232.

that the number of fighters had risen to 1,330, as compared with 690 in mid-September, and believed that sorties of up to 700 aircraft were not out of the question.[109]*

This development was as unexpected as it was sudden. By the middle of August AI had concluded on the evidence of Sigint and POW that, although the production of single-engined fighters was increasing sufficiently to meet the heavy wastage and permit the formations of new units, shortage of fuel was creating a lack of pilots for new aircraft and a lack of training for new pilots; it was clear, moreover, that any hope of increasing day-fighter strength in the Reich was being frustrated by the demands for close-support on the eastern front.[110] On 5 September it had appreciated that the numerical strength of day-fighters was being kept up, but had insisted that this was 'no longer any criterion of fighting value'.[111] The scale of the enemy's opposition to the USSTAF raids had borne out these conclusions. He had flown some 400 sorties against the early heavy attacks on oil targets in May and June and 300 on two occasions in July; but fighter intervention approaching this scale was not again encountered till the raids of 11, 12 and 13 September.[112] The CIC had then believed that the recovery would be temporary: it had attributed it to the stabilisation of the western front and the reorganisation of the fighter defences, and had stated on 16 September that in view of shortage of oil and aircrew 'no revival . . . on an intensive or sustained scale is possible'.[113] And it was indeed the case that resistance on this scale was not offered again until a month after the receipt of the intelligence about reinforcements at the beginning of October.

AI quickly revised its calculations in the light of the intelligence. On 13 October it believed that day-fighter strength would rise to between 2,000 and 2,500 in the next six months, and it accepted that an increase in operational activity had been made possible not only by continuing increase in aircraft production, but also by the fact that after showing serious weakness in July and August, 'the pilot position was now healthy'. It recognised in fact what it had noticed but failed to emphasise during the summer:† the position had been transformed by the disbandment of 20 long-range bomber Gruppen since July and the transfer of pilots from them

---

* See above, p 408 ff for further details of AI's appreciations of the significance of the fighter build-up.

† See above, p 515.

109. Air Sunsets 246 and 247 of 5 and 9 October.
110. Air Sunsets 216, 222, 225 of 6, 15, 19 August.
111. Air Sunset 233 of 5 September.
112. Craven and Cate, op cit, Vol III, pp 289, 291, 301–302.
113. JIC(44) 407 of 16 September.

and from meteorological, reconnaissance and transport units.[114]*
By 16 October it had informed the JIC that, while there had been
no long-range bomber sorties for two months and almost no
close-support operations in the west, the Germans had enough
fuel for advanced fighter training and maximum deployment for
the defence of the Reich, that first-line fighter strength had risen
by 25 per cent since 1 August and was still rising, and that in view
of this, and with its novel types of aircraft, the GAF might secure
some degree of ascendancy over the Reich, and thus be able to
protect vital war production during the coming winter.[115]

Soon afterwards, a signal from the Japanese Naval Mission in
Berlin on 13 September was decrypted. It said that although
fighter and rocket aircraft production was progressing despite
Allied bombing, the oil shortage, which had been one reason for
the defeat of the Army in France, would prevent the GAF from
displaying its full fighting strength and 'attaining the anticipated
objective of regaining control of the air'. It was now 'questionable
whether the GAF was in fact rallying' and difficult 'to observe any
symptoms of recovery in the war situation as a whole'.[116] And, in
the event, although the day-fighters intervened with unexpected
skill, but still in small numbers, as early as 6 October, their
recovery was not fully reflected in operations until 21 November,
when an Eighth Air Force raid on Leuna was opposed by 400
fighters, the largest number since the early summer.[117] And
although this led Eighth Air Force temporarily to doubt whether it
could continue to give first priority to attacks on the oil targets,[118]
it was to turn out that AI had over-reacted; although the fighters
reappeared in strength against several of the oil raids during
November and December, it was soon apparent that their skill and
persistence were again declining.[119]†

□

---

* AI had known that the bomber force was being disbanded as a result of fuel and
manpower shortage, and that, as well as permitting the release of pilots, this had released
manpower from the very large ground staffs into the army and industry. A few bomber units
were being retained for airborne V 1 launchings and such operations as mining the Scheldt, a
threat which fortunately did not materialise.

† Against these raids, the GAF mustered some 400 day-fighters on 21 November, 500 on
26 November and 750 on 27 November. But except on 27 November, when an entire US
squadron was lost, American casualties were light (5 bombers on 21 November and 11 on 27

114. Air Sunset 248 of 13 October.
115. CAB 121/418, JIC(44) 436(o) of 16 October; CAB 121/419, JIC(44) 437(o)
     of 16 October.
116. BAY/HP 62 of 21 October.
117. Craven and Cate, op cit, Vol III, p 660.
118. ibid, p 661.
119. ibid, p 664.

Transportation bombing had meanwhile come to be a serious rival to the oil offensive since the beginning of November. It had been granted second priority after oil in the directive of 25 September. In the directive of 1 November it retained second priority, but it was also accorded enhanced relative importance, and from that date attacks by the strategic air forces on transportation at last exceeded their attacks on oil.

It was impossible to deny, and there was no lack of evidence to prove, that the vulnerability of German transport to air attack was a source of weakness. The JIC had noted in July that the bombing then taking place on communications in the Ruhr and west Germany, and behind the Allied front, was already partly responsible for the decline in the enemy's war production, and that Germany was already having to divert even essential war freight to the canals because of strain on the railways.[121] In August it had repeated that Allied bombing was producing a perceptible weakening of the German transport system; freight was being diverted from rail to waterways, and the movement of raw materials for war production was being delayed.[122] In October, moreover, the effects of the increase in the Allied bombing of transportation targets were reflected in high-grade decrypts. In a signal of 2 October, decrypted on 10 October, the Japanese Naval Attaché in Berlin reported that the havoc on the lines of communication inside Germany was gradually increasing, the transportation of coal and munitions from the Rhineland being already in considerable confusion.[123] In a message of 20 October, decrypted on 24 October, OKW quoted Speer as saying that between 30 and 35 per cent of all armaments factories were at a standstill because of the destruction of traffic installations and the lack of power.[124] On 29 October another decrypt had disclosed that on 22 October the confusion had been deepened by the destruction of the Mühlheim bridge over the Rhine at Cologne.[125]

From the end of October, when the full programme of transportation bombing was inaugurated, such decrypts multi-

---

November, and on 30 November one of the biggest multiple raids on the oil targets of the whole war met only sporadic resistance) and German losses were high. Signs of poor training were observed in the fighters during the encounters; AI drew attention to this and also appreciated that fuel for operations on this scale would only be available from time to time, not on a sustained basis.[126]

120. Air Sunset 254 of 28 November; CAB 121/418, JIC(44) 488(o) of 1 December.
121. CAB 121/419, JIC(44) 301(o) of 20 July.
122. ibid, JIC(44) 371(o) of 26 August.
123. BAY/HP 44 of 10 October.
124. DEFE 3/242, HP 4397 of 24 October.
125. DEFE 3/244, HP 4921 of 29 October.

plied. In part this reflected the increase in bombing and in part the process by which damage to land lines and telephones was forcing the enemy authorities to resort to radio for their communications. Two railway Enigma keys (Rocket II and Stevenson)* being used in Germany and the west were being read by GC and CS, and some Fish traffic was decrypted from such authorities as the Armaments HQs (Rüstungskommandos) which had been set up to increase and co-ordinate the output of armaments production factories. The many references in the armed forces Enigma keys to supply difficulties were thus supplemented by Sigint testifying in more general terms to the mounting dislocation. An order of 2 November, decrypted on 8 November, called for the greater use of canals and other inland waterways to relieve the railways.[126] A decrypt of 30 November disclosed that by 25 November the damage to communications in the Ruhr had become so bad that despite the catastrophic shortage of MT throughout Germany and in particular in the armed forces, an emergency mobilisation of lorries had been ordered to overcome the difficulties besetting the German forces on the western front as a result of railways destruction; the Italian theatre was to surrender 500 lorries despite the known shortage of MT there.[127] A message decrypted on 19 December indicated that on 18 December greater Flak protection for traffic installations in south Germany and Austria was needed in view of the rising scale of attacks.[128] On 1 January a decrypt disclosed a complaint on 29 December that fighter-bomber attacks in the area between the Moselle and Saarland had destroyed traffic installations on an extreme scale, undoing weeks of laborious repair work, eliminating telephone facilities and making it impossible to re-route trains.[129]

Like the advocates of the continuation of area bombing, which increasingly if also incidentally wrought immense damage to the German railways and other communications especially in the Ruhr, the advocates of the transportation bombing programme did not need this intelligence to encourage them. They believed that Sigint and PR revealed only a tithe of the dislocation the bombing was inflicting and were no guide to its cumulative effects. The transportation bombing was not unlike the area bombing, moreover, in that it depended for target selection less on current intelligence than on the familiarity with Germany's rail and waterways network which was based on pre-war knowledge and

---

* They were re-named Blunderbuss and Culverin respectively.

126. DEFE 3/304, HP 6003 of 8 November.
127. DEFE 3/312, HP 8243 of 30 November.
128. DEFE 3/319, HP 9803 of 19 December.
129. DEFE 3/323, BT 913 of 1 January 1945.

information subsequently obtained from overt sources. But these networks were so extensive that there was much room for divergent opinions as to which targets should be attacked and this problem was accentuated by the fact that the objectives of the transportation bombing were too general to guide the selection of specific target priorities. For these reasons, and also because of the difficulty of co-ordinating the operations of several Allied air forces, the offensive up to the end of 1944 was spread too widely against too many targets.[130]

The Air Staff and the CSTC were concerned from the beginning of November that although the oil offensive nominally enjoyed first priority, SHAEF's enthusiasm for the transportation programme, together with its overriding power to divert the heavy bombers to army support, was in effect relegating oil to second or third place.[131] Their anxiety was not unjustified. It has been argued that the transportation bombing programme was complementary to the oil offensive in that both target-systems could be attacked in the same missions and that both enterprises contributed to the progressive weakening of Germany. In these respects, however, it may equally be said that area bombing was complementary to the oil and the transportation offensives; all three undoubtedly made a decisive contribution to Allied victory. But the Allied failure to prevent the German counter-offensive in the Ardennes was soon to show that while all bombing was contributing to the enemy's eventual collapse, his collapse might well be delayed unless target priorities were carefully observed.

☐

In its report, dated 1 December, on the oil offensive in November the JIC recognised that shortage of fuel was still restricting the enemy's activities on all fronts: it had hampered the movements of Sixth Panzer Army and the deployment of armour on the Baltic front and had reduced the airborne launchings of the V 1 to a half of what would otherwise have been possible, and aviation spirit was still being brought back from Norway. But the JIC drew attention to the fact that since most of the recent Allied attacks had been on the plants in the Ruhr, 10 out of 11 of which were now inactive, repairs to the 11 synthetic plants in central and eastern Germany had been 'relatively little interrupted' and had achieved 'a remarkable recovery.'* Total enemy production in

---

* The JIC was perhaps influenced by the absence of Sigint references to German anxiety, and by the occasional positive reference in decrypts, like that of 23 November in which, in

130.   Craven and Cate, op cit, Vol III, p 657.
131.   AIR 41/56, pp 159, 163, 175.

November had thus risen to 425,000 – 450,000 tons as compared with 375,000 – 400,000 in October.* Of this total the distant plants had produced 175,000 compared with 30,000 in September. In December these plants might, if they remained undisturbed, produce 240,000 tons, of which 185,000 would be petrol, including aviation spirit. 'These plants are, therefore, now the mainstay of Germany's oil position, and successful attacks on them in the next few weeks would lead to a production position as bad or worse than that in September.'[134]†

But it was to prove impossible to sustain the oil offensive at its previous level during December. Even before operations by Eighth Air Force and Bomber Command against oil targets were all but eliminated by the vast demands for ground support and transportation bombing that followed the opening of the enemy's Ardennes offensive, their attacks on oil were reduced by the intensification of the transportation bombing that formed part of the preparations for the planned Allied advance into Germany. Bomber Command nevertheless devoted 11 per cent of its total effort – a small increase – to oil targets. More important, it made a heavy night attack on Leuna, at long last, on 6 December; the raid did great damage, PR indicating that production had practically stopped, and incurred only light casualties.‡ In its attacks on transportation targets and its area raids before the Ardennes offensive it continued to give priority to areas with benzol plants. During the Ardennes offensive it delivered a night attack on Pölitz on 22 December; casualties were again light but the damage done was not extensive. Eighth Air Force attacked Leuna twice before the Ardennes offensive, but was otherwise occupied in ground

---

answer to a question from the Japanese Ambassador, Ribbentrop said that it would not be long before Germany had enough oil for large-scale operations.[132]

* The USSBS figures are 316,000 for October and 337,000 for November.[133] The JIC was thus continuing to over-estimate production though appreciating the trend correctly.

† An annex to this report printed a statement by the former head of the German oil administration in Bucharest, who was now in Russian hands. He disclosed that stocks had dwindled fast from May, that in July Berlin had feared there would be no reserves by August, and that in June, when Hitler had appointed the emergency commission for repairs, with priority over U-boats and aircraft production, Berlin had feared that the war would be lost if the rebuilding of synthetic plants and refineries did not keep up with the damage done. The Germans had decided against the construction of big new plants, including underground plants, for lack of time and materials, but some small plants had been built in forested areas as a stop-gap.

‡ Speer subsequently testified that Bomber Command's night attacks were 'considerably more effective than the daylight attacks [of USSTAF] since heavier bombs are used and an extraordinary accuracy . . . is reported.'[135]

132. BAY/HP 113 of 23 November.
133. Webster and Frankland, op cit, Vol IV, p 516.
134. CAB 121/418, JIC(44) 488(o) of 1 December.
135. Webster and Frankland, op cit, Vol III, pp 234–235.

support and unable to raid the distant targets on account of bad weather. Fifteenth Air Force was less distracted by the transportation programme and calls for army support; it concentrated most of its bombing against the oil plants in Silesia, where it had virtually immobilised Blechhammer before the Russians occupied the area.[136]

The JIC's report on the oil offensive in December was not discouraging. It estimated that total production had fallen to 410,000 tons, from 430,000 in November, and that petrol production had fallen from 170,000 to 145,000 tons. On the evidence of good recent PR, however, it observed that this was due in part to the fact that the enemy had found that repairs became more difficult after each attack; whereas in October repairs had been outstripping destruction, this had ceased to be so. Total production might rise to 530,000 tons in January if attacks were to cease, though the declining rate of recovery of the plants after attacks might keep the output below this level. It would probably decline to the September level if the few remaining active synthetic plants were damaged in the next few weeks.[137]

Some encouragement could be obtained from two Japanese diplomatic decrypts available during the month. A signal from the Naval Attaché in Berlin of 3 December decrypted on 8 December, reported that the transfer of oil plants to underground locations was 'very much behind schedule' despite strenuous effort, and that although aircraft production was good, the fighter aircrew were losing many opportunities for combat on account of oil shortage. From the decrypt on 14 December of a telegram from the Japanese Ambassador dated 6 December it was known that the oil repair squads employed 72,000 workers, and that oil production underground was unlikely to start before March; he estimated that total German output was running at only 300,000 tons a month and commented that oil was 'clearly Germany's greatest worry'.[138]

In Whitehall the Chief of the Air Staff continued to take this view. As late as 22 December, in the correspondence with AOC-in-C Bomber Command which had begun on 1 November, he was still insisting on the merits of the oil offensive. It was not 'another panacea'; if the Allies could 'put out and keep out of action eleven synthetic plants in central Germany' they would achieve 'an early decision in the German war'. He persisted in his advocacy on 3 January 1945, rebutting Harris's argument that attacks on the plants would produce excessive casualties by pointing out that the oil offensive had cost only 1 per cent

136. ibid, p 234; AIR 41/56, pp 173, 174.
137. CAB 121/418, JIC(44) 513(o) of 1 January 1945.
138. SJA 1259 of 8 December; BAY/HP 135 of 14 December.

casualties in the past three months; criticising him for not having sent three times as many bombers to Pölitz on 22 December; and insisting that far from resting solely on appreciations from MEW, the oil plan had been adopted on the advice of the JIC, which had itself relied on the output of the special joint intelligence bodies.[139]

From the middle of January 1945 the CAS's pleas were finally answered, Bomber Command embarking on a series of heavy and accurate attacks on the oil plants deep in Germany. Between then and the middle of February the proportion of its total bombing effort devoted to oil was raised to 26 per cent; and although it still devoted 36 per cent to the bombing of cities, it succeeded in reducing German oil production to a trickle – with immediate consequences on all the fighting fronts, and not least on the Soviet fronts.[140]

In the light of this outcome it is not possible to doubt that, effected in July or August and maintained into the autumn, comparable marginal diversion of its effort from area bombing to the oil offensive would have brought forward to an earlier date the reduction of German production to the low level it reached in September and would at least have prevented it from recovering. In the light of what was known at the time about the enemy's situation it is not reasonable to accept that the threat from the German night-fighter defences constituted a good ground for resisting such a diversion. Nor was there a sufficient argument against it in the fact that Bomber Command was required to direct its effort from area bombing to other targets than oil – to the V-weapon sites, the French Atlantic ports and operations in support of the land fighting. At any rate from the end of September, Bomber Command was explicitly instructed to attack oil and other targets at the expense of area bombing. It is frequently argued that tactical considerations kept down the proportion of the effort Harris devoted to oil, and they certainly have to be taken into account; but on 12 November the CAS – himself a former AOC-in-C Bomber Command – wondered whether it was not 'the magnetism of the remaining German cities, rather than considerations of weather and tactics', that had caused Harris 'to deflect our bombers from their primary objectives'.[141] There is much force in this remark, for Harris did not attempt to conceal his belief that the oil targets were of less strategic value than area bombing or his disregard for the intelligence which conflicted with it.

---

139. Webster and Frankland, op cit, Vol III, pp 86, 88–89.
140. ibid, pp 237–243.
141. ibid, p 84.

No one can say for certain that, given greater resolution in the prosecution of the oil offensive or less obduracy on the part of Bomber Command Germany would have collapsed before the end of 1944. The official history of the offensive accepted that, if the attacks that were made in December and January had been made in October and November, she might still have carried out an Ardennes offensive, using her final stocks for this purpose, and that in any case her resistance would have been prolonged by the stubborn fighting of the infantry, as it was to be in the final stages of the war. It added, however, that it is 'hardly possible not to agree with the judgment which Sir Charles Portal [had made] at the time that neglect of the opportunities provided by the oil offensive might prolong the war for several months'. What can be said, as the official history concluded, is that 'if it had been possible to press home the attack earlier, there can be little doubt that the collapse of Germany would have come sooner'.[142]

---

142. ibid, pp 242–243.

CHAPTER 55

The Flying Bomb Offensive

INTELLIGENCE ABOUT the characteristics and performance of the V 1 flying bomb of course leapt forward from the
start of the German offensive on 12 June 1944. The first
observations of the V 1 in flight established that it normally flew at
between 2,000 and 3,000 feet, and that speeds up to about 300
miles an hour were usual, these heights and speeds being both
lower than had been foreseen.[1] To the preliminary findings from
the inspection of V 1 wreckage in Sweden,* the Air Intelligence
Branch was as early as 16 June able to add the results of the
examination of impacts by, and wreckage from, 70 flying bombs
and to show from the damage done that the warhead was
comparable to the German SB 1,000 kg bomb.[2] By 20 June, after
examining more wreckage, including a reasonably intact missile,
AI had built up a virtually complete scientific and technical
understanding of the weapon and its propulsion system.[3] By 26
June, as a result of the over-running of some of the launching sites
in the Cherbourg peninsula, it had also learned a good deal about
the catapult system used for launching the missile.[4]

The intelligence acquired about the propulsion and launching
of the weapon had little bearing on defence measures. Their
preparation had not been held up by earlier lack of information
on these subjects, and the planned deployment of the defences –
fighters, guns and balloons – was begun on 16 June and was all but
complete by 22 June.[5]† The fact that the weapon's heights and
speeds were lower than had been expected hampered the guns, so
that most of the interceptions were carried out by the fighters. By
25 June, when intelligence could estimate that the reliability and
accuracy of the flying bomb were such that 65 per cent of those

---

* See Volume III Part 1, p 429.
† For the defence plans see Volume III Part 1, pp 415 fn†, 420 fn*.

1. Collier, *The Defence of the United Kingdom* (1957), pp 374–375; CAB 121/213,
   SIC file B/Defence/2, Vol 3, COS(44)196th (o) Meeting, 16 June.
2. AIR 40/1773, AI 2(h) Report No 2243 of 16 June 1944.
3. ibid, Report No 2245 of 20 June.
4. CAB 121/213, COS(44)573 of 26 June.
5. ibid, *Crossbow* Committee, CBC (44) 2nd Meeting, 22nd June, Section 3; AIR
   41/55, *The Air Defence of Great Britain*, Vol VI, pp 88–89.

fired would otherwise have reached the Greater London area, the defences had reduced to 40 per cent the actual proportion impacting.[6] By that date radar had estimated that 1,263 missiles had been launched, of which over 300 had been destroyed by the defences and 450 had landed in the Greater London area.[7] Thereafter, the new *Crossbow* Committee* set up by the Cabinet on 19 June to supervise the development and deployment of counter-measures, both defensive and offensive, found that operational research and technical analysis based on observation of the weapon's performance were adequate for defence decisions. It was this type of intelligence which helped in the development and deployment of better equipment for radar detection, fire control and gun performance, and which pointed to the need to raise the speed of the British fighters in case the Germans introduced a new flying bomb with a better performance. There were reports from agents that a bigger flying bomb existed,[8] but they carried less weight than a theoretical study which showed that the speed of the missile might be increased without difficulty by between 30 and 50 miles an hour and thus be placed beyond the reach of current fighter aircraft.

In the event, this danger did not materialise and the performance of the defences continued to improve. Their improvement was especially marked after 13 July, when at the height of the offensive the bold decision was taken to move the anti-aircraft guns away from the Downs to the coast. During the first week after that re-deployment the defences destroyed half the flying bombs observed, as compared with less than 43 per cent in the previous five weeks. Thereafter the arrival of American equipment – radars and proximity fuses – further improved the operation of the guns, and the proportion of missiles destroyed by the defences as a whole rose to 74 per cent in the third week of August. It was 62 per cent in the last week of the month but had risen to 83 per cent in the last few days before the main offensive ended on 5 September. On 28 August the defences destroyed 90 of the 97 flying bombs which reached the country, and only four missiles reached London.[9]

Another defensive measure, the need to limit the information which reached the enemy about the results of his attack, was taken by the Chiefs of Staff on 30 June when they approved instructions

---

* See Volume III Part 1, p 440.

6. CAB 121/213, COS(44)573 of 26 June, paras 3, 4, 5; Collier, op cit, pp 364–365, 374–375.
7. CAB 121/213, COS(44)574(o) of 26 June, paras 1, 2, 3.
8. ibid, COS(44)611(o) of 9 July, COS(44)654(o) of 22 July.
9. Collier, op cit, p 381 et seq.

to the censorship authorities and the Press and called for a study of ways and means of ensuring that such information as reached the enemy was distorted.[10] One such method which the COS had under consideration in July was a proposal which had been discussed by ADI(Sc), the Ministry of Home Security and the Home Defence Executive soon after the beginning of the offensive. The proposal rested on the Air Ministry's observation that by the end of June most weapons were falling in the south-eastern suburbs, short of what was presumed to be their aiming point in central London. It involved using German agents under British control to send in reports which might dissuade the Germans from correcting their aim and, if possible, induce them to shorten it further. To guard against the danger that the Germans would detect the deception from the radio plotting devices known to be built into 5 per cent of the weapons, from air reconnaissance or from British plot reports, which the Enigma had shown them to be interested in, care would be taken to choose correct points of impact of bombs which flew further than usual but to couple them with the time of impact of bombs which had fallen short. In the event, though the double agents passed a few reports of this sort from the end of June while the deception authorities sought approval for the plan, the Minister of Home Security and the Minister of Production were unwilling to accept responsibility for the deliberate attraction of V 1 fire to any part of London, even to the less heavily built-up areas of the south-east. A more modest scheme, aimed at convincing the Germans that there was no need to lengthen the weapon's range was adopted in the middle of August, too late for it to have much effect; on 18 August the Germans began to close down the launching sites in northern France.[11]*

---

* It was learned from German documents after the war that Flak Regiment 155 (W) – the unit responsible for launching the flying bombs – was perfectly satisfied with what it thought it was achieving. But the source of the most influential of the reports which led the regiment to reach this conclusion was not so much the double agents as a free-lance agent operating from Madrid and basing his information on gossip, imagination and whatever he could find in the newspapers. Such was the reliance that the regiment placed on this agent that it ignored the evidence from the radio DF indicator (FuGe 23) fitted to some of the V 1s, which was the subject of a careful analysis of the weapon's performance written at the end of June. This showed categorically that the bombs were indeed falling short. It has been suggested that the regiment was complacent because it regarded the V 1 offensive as a terror campaign in which the point of impact of the bombs was of little importance.[12]

10. CAB 121/213, Civil Defence Committee, CDC(44) 7th Meeting, 19 June, CBC(44) 2nd Meeting, 22 June, COS(44) 211th and 216th (o) Meetings, 27 and 30 June, COS(44)588(o) of 30 June.
11. ibid, COS(44) 218th and 226th (o) Meetings, 1 and 7 July, COS(44)588(o) of 30 June, 601(o) of 5 July; R V Jones, *Most Secret War* (1978), p 421; Howard, *Strategic Deception* (forthcoming), Chapter 8.
12. Howard, op cit, Chapter 8.

During June and July it was learned from Japanese diplomatic decrypts that the Germans were disappointed with the performance of the V 1 and had abandoned (if they had ever entertained it) the thought that the weapon might enable them to retrieve the situation in Normandy. On 19 June the Japanese Ambassador in Berlin reported that they were hoping to use the weapon against the south coast ports; but on 20 June the Naval Attaché added that unless it was concentrated in the near future against the crack Allied divisions that were waiting on the south-east coast, it was unlikely to have any effect in turning the second front in Germany's favour.[13] On 5 July a decrypt of a telegram from the Japanese Ambassador in Vichy disclosed that Abetz, the military governor in France, had admitted at the end of June that the new weapon would not have a decisive effect on developments in Normandy,[14] and on 22 July the Naval Attaché in Berlin reported that the Air Force authorities had told him that it would not be possible to use the V 1 against Allied landings.[15] A further telegram from the Ambassador followed on 25 July: Ribbentrop had told him that although the V 1 had proved to be inaccurate and could produce no revolutionary change in the situation, great hopes were being pinned on the much more accurate V 2.[16]

□

The main V 1 offensive against the United Kingdom was brought to a close early in September by the Allied advance in France. By the middle of August firings had practically ceased from the launching sites south of the Somme, and the V-weapons organisation had begun to withdraw its equipment to the Low Countries and Germany. Such was its flexibility that the scale of the offensive was not greatly reduced for another fortnight, but the last V 1s to be launched against England from French sites were fired in the early hours of 1 September.

Meanwhile, except for the advance of the Allied armies, offensive counter-measures had been far less effective than the defensive counter-measures. Air attacks on the launching sites and the supply system that served them and on plants engaged in the production of the weapon and of hydrogen peroxide were the only available means of attack or retaliation, others which were considered – landings in the Pas de Calais and the Dieppe area; the destruction by bombing of selected German towns; the use of

---

13. BAY/KVs 230, 233 of 22 and 24 June.
14. BAY/XL 15 of 5 July.
15. BAY/XL 67 of 27 July.
16. BAY/XL 74 of 30 July.

gas – having been rejected by the beginning of July.[17]* But the bombing effort against the production plants and against the launching sites and their supply system was handicapped by a shortage of intelligence.

Intelligence about production, which had always been negligible, remained so after the enemy had opened the campaign. From the examination of wreckage MEW had estimated by 26 June that the production of a flying bomb required 800 man hours, one-sixteenth of the effort that went into producing a Spitfire, but there was little or no evidence about the rate of production. Serial numbers had been obtained from only 2 per cent of the missiles examined; this was too small a base for reliable deductions. A report obtained by the SIS from a neutral engineer with the Siemens firm had said that the rate of production was 1,200 a month, and that stocks stood at 8,500; there was no reason to think that it over-estimated the position, but its reliability could not be assessed. The Air Ministry could only conclude that 'there is no reason to believe that it [production] is not considerable'.[18] There was still no firm intelligence about flying bomb production on 30 June.[19] Nor could the Air Ministry and MEW estimates improve on the SIS report during July and August. On 6 July the Air Ministry noted that the figures given in the account would have enabled the enemy to fire 4,000 a month, a rate which accorded well enough with the firing rate of 3,780 a month detected by the defences.[20] The few works numbers found on flying bomb fuselages by 22 July did not disagree with the SIS's figures.[21] On 27 July, after reconstructing the evidence, such as it was, AI still could not improve on the estimate, but pointed out that it was no guide to the future production rate.[22] On 17 August it suggested that on the evidence of works numbers the monthly production might have risen to nearly 7,000, but it admitted that works numbers were a totally unreliable guide.[23] These estimates may be compared with Germany's actual production figures during 1944 and the first three months of 1945; they averaged

---

* For intelligence on gas warfare, see below, p 573ff.

17. CAB 121/213, WP(44)343 of 26 June and 348 of 27 June, WM(44)82 of 27 June, COS(44) 219th, 220th and 222nd (o) Meetings, 3, 4 and 5 July, JP(44) 177 of 5 July.
18. ibid CBC(44)4 of 26 June, Annex II.
19. ibid CBC(44)8 of 30 June.
20. ibid CBC(44)15 of 6 July, paras 2 and 3.
21. ibid COS(44)645(o) of 22 July.
22. AIR 40/1779, *Crossbow* paper of 27 July 1944, Section 6, Enclosure III.
23. CAB 121/214, SIC file B/Defence/2, Vol 4, CBC(44)56 of 17 August, Annex I.

2,000 missiles a month, with a maximum of 3,419 in September 1944.[24]

There was similarly no improvement in the information available about the places and methods used in the production. Reports from agents, the only source of current reporting on the subject, continued to show that the final assembly of the flying bomb was undertaken at or near the launching sites, the manufacture of the parts having been dispersed and sub-contracted to an unprecedented degree among factories, some of them probably underground, in Germany and the occupied countries. By 6 July the Air Ministry had listed some of the factories that might be involved. One of these, the Volkswagen-werk at Fallersleben, had been attacked twice in June and the damage inflicted led the Germans to transfer its flying bomb assembly plant to safer quarters. Although the list rested only on a general knowledge of German industry, and although the factor-ies were so widely dispersed, the remainder were then accepted as first priority targets. But it was recognised that the production programme could not be seriously disrupted by Allied bombing.[25] Reconsidering the evidence on 27 July, AI noted that, though now abundant, it suffered from an almost universal failure to disting-uish the exact function or stage of manufacture performed, and a failure even to define the exact weapon under construction; only one plant, Fallersleben, had been firmly associated with the assembly of flying bomb fuselages. AI recommended that this alone should be accorded the highest priority and that 17 other plants believed to be associated with other stages of V 1 produc-tion should be treated as low priority targets.[26] And on 17 August it remained sceptical about attempts to reduce the enemy's production programme: stores and production were, it thought, sufficient to maintain the current scale of the German attack indefinitely.[27]

In view of the lack of information about production plants, highest priority for the counter-bombing was first given to the supposed supply sites. On 13 June, in response to the opening of the V 1 offensive, Whitehall decided to mount heavy raids against four supply sites in the Pas de Calais even though it recognised that no connection between them and the launching sites had been definitely established.[28]* Since the Germans were not using these

---

* See Volume III Part 1, p 427.

24. AIR 40/1772.
25. CAB 121/213, CBC(44)15 of 6 July, para 5, CBC(44) 4th Meeting, 7 July, para 3, COS(44)645(o) of 22 July.
26. AIR 40/1779, Section 6, Enclosure III.
27. CAB 121/214, CBC(44)56 of 17 August, Annex I.
28. CAB 121/213, COS(44) 191st (o) Meeting, 13 June, WM(44)77 of 13 June, WP(44)320 of 13 June.

supply sites for the flying bombs, they were able 'to complete their preparations for the start of heavy attacks [on the night of 15 June] without interference from bombing',[29] but the bombing of them continued to have highest priority after the heavy V 1 attacks had begun.[30] Not until the end of June did the suspicion that they were not being used become strong.[31]

Meanwhile, since Whitehall was also unaware that the Germans were making no use of the ski sites,* second priority in the bombing programme had been given to them until 22 June, by which time PR had photographed 71 of the 88 sites since 12 June. It was then concluded that 'there is no proof that any of the ski sites is at present being used'.[32] By then, on the other hand, modified sites† were being identified in increasing numbers. Up to 16 June, when the modified sites were given third place among the bombing priorities, the PRU had been handicapped by bad weather, and only twelve were listed as being operational. By 22 June, however, the PRU had located 44 in the Calais–Somme area, 24 of which were believed to be operational,[33] and the number reported by agents but not yet confirmed by reconnaissance brought the total to over 120. A large proportion of the agents' reports came from the Polish network, which was instructed at the beginning of the German offensive to give priority to locating launching sites. By September 1944, in signals locating them by reference to Michelin road maps or landmarks which would be visible to PR, it had reported about 100 sites to the Poles in London for communication to SOE.[34]

Bombing attacks against modified sites, which had begun by then, increased as attacks on the ski sites were suspended. In the week ending 27 June they absorbed over 40 per cent of the Allied bombing effort; and by 26 June 46 had been raided, of which twelve were known to have sustained severe damage.[35] But if it had been obvious from the outset that the scale of the enemy's

---

* For the ski sites see Volume III Part 1, Chapter 41.
† For the modified sites see Volume III Part 1, p 420 n.

29.   AIR 41/55, p 85; Collier, op cit, p 371.
30.   AIR 41/55, p 89; CAB 121/213, COS(44)196th and 197th(o) Meetings, both of 16 June, WM(44)79 of 1 June.
31.   CAB 121/213, COS(44)211th (o) Meeting, 27 June.
32.   ibid, CBC(44) 2nd Meeting, 22 June, Section 5; AIR 40/1772, Enclosure 95a, Minute of 22 June 1944; AIR 41/55, p 89.
33.   CAB 121/213, CBC(44)2nd Meeting, 22 June; AIR 40/1772, Enclosure 95a, Minute of 22 June 1944.
34.   Garlinski, *Hitler's Last Weapons* (1978; Magnum ed 1979), pp 132, 136–137, 218.
35.   CAB 121/213, COS(44)574(o) of 26 June, paras 5, 7 and 11, CBC(44)9 of 30 June, paras 24–29.

offensive would be governed by the number of firing sites he could keep available, rather than by the V 1 production programme, it now became clear that the Germans could bring modified sites into service at least as quickly as the Allies could eliminate them by bombing.[36] The number of sites identified continued to rise as the location of firings by radar implemented the findings of continuing air reconnaissance.[37] Excluding the 20 sites located in the Cherbourg peninsula, which had now been overrun or evacuated, it was 63 by 30 June, 76 on 2 July, and by the end of July it had increased to 94.[38] As the new *Crossbow* Committee noted on 30 June and 3 July, moreover, radar tracks of V 1s had established that a substantial number of new sites were coming into action before they were detected from the air. Apart from the impossibility of keeping an area of 5,000 square miles under constant photographic surveillance, the Committee also noted that improved German camouflage methods were making it difficult to identify sites from the PR photographs, and that the layout of the sites overrun in the Cherbourg peninsula was so simple that the enemy could probably make good the heaviest bomb damage in about ten days.[39]

From the last week of June an increasing amount of the bombing effort was directed against a new target. The first evidence that the Germans, having brought the components from the factories by rail, were assembling the V 1s at underground depots (to be distinguished from the old supply sites) in the Paris–Rheims area, and then moving them by road to the firing points, had been obtained from Enigma decrypts.* In May these had shown that the German V-weapons organisation, LXV Corps, was interested in a cavern at a place called Nucourt. On 10 June it had mentioned three supply dumps in connection with components for *Maikäfer*, a code-name previously used for the Hs 293, but on 17 and 19 June further decrypts had confirmed the suspicion that the dumps were nevertheless associated with the V 1 and had stated that they were at Nucourt, St Leu d'Esserent and Rilly la Montagne in the Oise valley.[40] At about the same time the SIS began to receive from the Polish network and other

---

* There had been a SOE report in March to the effect that the Germans had a large underground flying bomb depot in St Leu (see Volume III Part 1, p 423 (n)) but it seems obvious that the significance of this report had gone unnoticed at the time.

36. ibid, CBC(44)2 of 24 June, paras 1–14.
37. ibid, COS(44)574(o) of 26 June, paras 12–15.
38. ibid, CBC(44)8 of 30 June; AIR 40/1778, Appendix M.
39. CAB 121/213, CBC(44)9 of 30 June, paras 18–23, CBC(44)11 of 3 July, paras 23–27.
40. CX/MSS/J 109, 115 and 118 of 10, 17 and 19 June.

sources reports of assembly depots in this area from which the flying bombs were transported to the firing points by road.[41] On the strength of this intelligence the US Eighth Air Force had attacked Nucourt and St Leu during the last week of June. Early in July a set of supply returns for the period 9 June to 2 July was decrypted from the Enigma giving the numbers of flying bombs and accessories received and issued by St Leu. From a comparison of these returns with the numbers of V 1s launched it could be deduced that St Leu was the principal supply depot.[42] Bomber Command accordingly attacked St Leu on 4 and 7 July. As a result of these raids there was a sharp, though temporary, decline in the V 1 firing rate.[43] This was quickly confirmed in the Enigma, which made it clear that there had been no falls inside the cavern but that the approach roads had been blocked and that missiles which were arriving were being sent instead to Nucourt.[44] Nucourt was bombed again on 10 July and twice during the night of 15–16 July, the decrypts showing that in the third of these attacks the roof had subsided and a large number of flying bombs had been buried.[45] On 17 July the bomber forces attacked Rilly la Montagne, where repair work was observed in progress after the raid.[46]

Except for a decrypt which, following another raid on St Leu on 3 August, contained a report that one of the dumps of the complex had been badly hit and would probably be out of action for some time,[47] there were no further references to the supply dumps in the Enigma. But agents were reporting depots elsewhere and claiming that flying bombs were being forwarded from them by road to the sites at an average rate of 90 each night.[48] These reports led to bombing raids on Bois de Cassan, Forêt de l'Isle d'Adam and Mery-sur-Oise by 17 July.[49] From 17 July the PRU, following up the agents' reports, reconnoitred some fifty locations, together with the railway routes from Germany to France, in an attempt to identify further depots. Within a few days sixteen sites, over and above Nucourt, St Leu and Rilly, were judged to be suspicious and five of them were thought to be depots. But only one of them (Bois de Cassan) was added to St Leu and Rilly (and Nucourt in the event that it was seen to be under repair) on the list

---

41.   CAB 121/213,CBC(44)4 of 26 June, Annex III, COS(44)573(0) of 26 June.
42.   CX/MSS/J 113/3.
43.   AIR 41/55, p 121–122; Collier, op cit, p 378.
44.   CAB 121/213, CBC(44)12 of 6 July; DEFE 3/51, XL 905 of 5 July.
45.   CX/MSS/J 144/7, 149/7 and 8.
46.   AIR 40/1777, AI 2(h) *Crossbow* Report of 23 October 1944, p 24.
47.   CX/MSS/J 171/8; CX/MSS/T266/3.
48.   CAB 121/213, CBC(44)10 of 3 July, Annex III.
49.   ibid, CBC(44)16 of 10 July.

of first priority targets; in the case of the others there was insufficient evidence that they were yet in use.[50]

At the same time, however, seven V 1 production targets in Germany were placed on the list, and bombing attacks on other targets were being considered. In the second week of July the SOE had reported that the telecommunications HQ for the flying bomb organisation was at Amiens and that a depot near Belfort contained 400 flying bombs in transit from Germany, and plans were made for sabotage against these targets with weapons and explosives dropped by parachute.[51] Bombing attacks against Amiens and other HQs were also contemplated, as were bombing raids agains trains, stations and bridges on the railways from Germany.[52]

While raids on the original supply sites had finally been abandoned in the middle of July, raids on the modified firing sites continued to absorb the bulk of the Allied bombing effort against *Crossbow* targets until bombing priorities were overhauled in the last week of the month.[53]* The overhaul was carried out for the Joint Anglo-American *Crossbow* Target Priorities Committee, set up as a result of the dissatisfaction of the US Strategic Air Forces in Europe with the Air Ministry's choice of targets, which instructed a joint working group to reappraise the available intelligence and make recommendations.[54] The Joint Committee accepted the group's recommendations at the end of July. They gave first priority to the supply depots, listing six of them (Rilly, St Leu, Mery-sur-Oise, Trossy St Maximin, Bois de Cassan and the Forêt de Nieppe, a site from which suspicious activity connected

---

* Table for the week ending 0600/26 July 1944:

	Number of Aircraft	Tons	Number of Targets	% of total Tonnage
Launching Sites	778	2,723	18	64
Supply Depots	100	545	1	13
Large Sites	125	677	2	16
H₂O₂ Hollriegelskreuth	106	240	1	7
Total	1,109	4,185	22	100

50. CAB 121/213, CBC(44)29 of 20 July, Annex III; AIR 40/1777, AI 2(h) *Crossbow* Report, pp 24, 25; AIR 40/1779, Section 6, Enclosure I.
51. CAB 121/213, COS(44)230th (o) Meeting, 11 July, CBC(44) 6th Meeting, 14 July, CBC(44)22 of 15 July, CBC(44)29 of 30 July, Annex V; AIR 41/55, p 146 fn.
52. AIR 40/1779, Section 6, Ecnlosure IV.
53. ibid, Section 6, Enclosure IX.
54. Collier, op cit, p 397; Craven and Cate, *The USAAF in World War II*, Vol III (1951), p 535.

with 'torpedoes' had been reported for some months), arranging that Nucourt should be added to the list at the first sign of repair or other activity there, and instructed AI to make every effort to enlarge the list 'within the limits of intelligence'. The recommendations also gave first priority to two suspected special fuel depots at Dugny and Pacy and to five industrial and production centres in Germany that were thought to be associated with the flying bombs. They decided against attacks on the administrative and operational HQs of the V 1 Command, of which several had been mentioned by agents, and on the Command's transport system. As for the modified launching sites, the recommendation was that, as the offensive against them had had a negligible effect, further heavy attacks were not justified, but the Joint Committee listed 58 of them (out of 92 so far discovered) as second priority targets for harassing attacks.[55]

On 1 August the Joint Committee approved a plan, drawn up at SHAEF, by which the six listed assembly depots and other high priority *Crossbow* targets should all be attacked at once within a period of 24 hours. On account of weather conditions and the fact that the strategic air forces were heavily involved in the land battle and in raids against Germany, this concentrated attack was not carried out. Instead, Bomber Command raided Forêt de Nieppe and six modified sites on 1 August, and Trossy, Bois de Cassan, Forêt de Nieppe and more modified sites on 2 August; and between 3 and 9 August, while US Eighth Air Force attacked Mery-sur-Oise and *Crossbow* targets other than the depots, Bomber Command carried out 12 further raids against Trossy, Bois de Cassan and Forêt de Nieppe and one against St Leu.[56] Apart from a raid on Nieppe on 9 August and one on the suspected depot at the Forêt d l'Isle d'Adam on 18 August, the attacks on depots were then suspended on the advice of the working committee of the Joint *Crossbow* Target Committee, which had meanwhile revised the target priorities at weekly intervals. On 5 August a third fuel dump and three airfields in Holland* were added to the list of first priority targets, and attacks on the launching sites were suspended. A week later the supply depots at Nieppe, Trossy and St Leu were removed from the list, it having been judged that they had been sufficiently damaged, and the launching sites were restored as low priority targets. From the middle of August few

---

* See below, p 545 et seq, for the significance of these.

55. AIR 40/1779, Section 3, Committee minutes of 27 July, item I; Section 4, Schedule 32 of 29 July; Section 5, JCC 2nd Meeting, 28 July; Collier, op cit, p 386.
56. AIR 41/55, pp 149–152.

V 1 targets were kept in the higher priorities: in a process which began on 5 August with the inclusion of liquid oxygen plants among the first priority targets, they were increasingly being replaced by V 2 targets.[57]*

On 4 September the CAS recommended that bombing against all V 1 targets should cease, other than those associated with airborne launching,† and that the active flying bomb defences should be redisposed on the assumption that the only remaining threat was from airborne launches. He also recommended that all attacks on the V 2 organisation should be stopped.‡ These recommendations arose from the belief that the whole of the launching area would soon be in Allied hands. The Vice-Chiefs of Staff accepted them on the following day.[58] In relation to the V 2 this decision has been severely criticised.§ In relation to the V 1 it was not untimely. Except for the air-launched attacks, to which it did not apply, the V 1 offensive against England was virtually over by early September, though the V 1 was soon to be used against targets in the Low Countries; and it has to be remembered that, as the official history has concluded, the offensive counter-measures had 'brought no direct return commensurate with the great effort devoted to them'.[59]

The official history noted that 'of attacks made between 13 June and 1 September those on the storage depots were the most successful', and suggested that when 'a bolder investment in that class of operation might have achieved much', the Allies, 'hampered by their failure to make a clear-cut choice between the various courses open to them, never achieved the singleness of purpose which might have helped them to stake successfully on information that fell short of certainty . . . '[60] There can be no quarrel with this as a general verdict. Even when allowance has been made for the fact that at the time intelligence did not enable the Allies to measure the effect on the weight of the enemy's offensive of attacks on the different targets within the V 1 system, so that it was 'impossible to say how far the irregular scale of the offensive was the result of German tactics and how far it was due

---

* See Chapter 56.
† See below, p 545ff.
‡ See Chapter 56.
§ See Chapter 56, pp 563–564.

57. AIR 40/1779, JCC(25) of 2 August, JCC 3rd Meeting, 5 August, with attached Schedule No 33 of 6 August.
58. CAB 121/214, COS(44)806(o) of 4 September, COS(44)298th (o) Meeting, 5 September.
59. Collier, op cit, p 388.
60. ibid, pp 388–389.

to Allied counter-measures',[61] it may be accepted that the vast expenditure of effort against targets other than the depots, and especially against the firing sites, continued for much longer than was justified by the observable results. The intelligence record indicates, however, that the verdict is perhaps too severe, or too sanguine, in its remarks about the assembly/storage depots.

There was no undue delay in singling out the depots at Nucourt, St Leu and Rilly as most important targets once the Enigma had indicated their function and established their locations, and they were attacked from the last week of June. As for what might have been achieved if the Allies had thereafter confined the bombing effort to depots, it has to be emphasised that while the intelligence was accurate in relation to the three which were identified in the Enigma, that which pointed to the existence of others was unreliable. Captured documents later established that the V1 offensive employed only the three depots at Nucourt, St Leu and Rilly.[62] The four other depots that were placed on the list of first priority targets from mid-July on the strength of reports from Allied agents, and that were heavily attacked from the beginning of August, either did not exist or were not brought into service.

☐

In the course of July the *Crossbow* authorities encountered a further problem—their inability to identify the origin of an increasing number of firings. Beginning on 9 July radar had plotted some tracks from the east which, following the Thames estuary, avoided most of the deployed defences.[63] On 18 July no less than 20 to 25 per cent of all the firings were from this direction, and yet by 27 July PR of an area in Belgium and Holland from which missiles might have been launched had failed to locate a single launching site.[64] By 3 August, however, and despite receiving a report from SOE that four launching sites had been tracked down in Belgium, AI had concluded that these launchings were being made by He 111s based on Dutch airfields,[65] the mystery having prompted ADI (Sc) to re-examine earlier evidence.

Part of this evidence had come in a series of almost daily Enigma decrypts, beginning on 11 July, relating to III/KG 3. In the first of

61. AIR 41/55, p 111.
62. AIR 40/1777, AI 2(h) *Crossbow* Report, pp 25, 26.
63. AIR 20/1661, ASI Report No 151 of 11 December 1944, paras 2.3, 2.4.
64. CAB 121/213, COS(44)654(o) of 22 July; CAB 121/214, CBC(44)36 of 27 July, CBC(44) 10th Meeting, 28 July.
65. CAB 121/214, CBC(44)45 of 3 August and Annex II.

these Fliegerkorps IX ordered a reconnaissance of London and announced that if 'X-time had to be postponed because of V 1 operations' III/KG 3 was to be informed. A few days later a similar decrypt was available in which Fliegerkorps IX's intentions were passed to LXV Army Corps for III/KG 3 and another referred to the fact that three aircraft 'without load' were carrying out reconnaissance in the Portsmouth–Southampton area.[66] By 17 July GC and CS had suggested that III/KG 3 might be a new cover-name for Flak Regiment 155(W),[67] and it was not suspected that the decrypted messages were associated with the launching of the V 1 from aircraft until the end of July. At that point, when the PRU and the CIU had failed to find any launching sites that could account for the radar tracks that were coming from the Belgian area, ADI(Sc) collated the tracks with the Enigma information and thereafter he and GC and CS re-examined earlier transmissions from Peenemünde and Zempin and discovered in them what had previously been missed* – evidence that a training programme for launching the V 1 from the air had started in April and slackened off after being intense from mid-May to mid-June.[69]

Once the re-examination of the evidence had indicated that III/KG 3 had completed its training in June there was no difficulty in concluding that a new unit was undergoing training when, between early September and 11 October, the Baltic plots showed that the test firing of air-launched missiles had returned to the level of May and June.[70] Later in October, in addition to Enigma evidence that III/KG 3 had been re-named I/KG 53, the activities on the Baltic range pointed to the probability that two more Gruppen had been training and AI considered that an increase in air-launched V 1 missiles must be expected.[71]

On 19 September, after a temporary suspension since 4 September during which III/KG 3 moved its bases from Holland to north-west Germany, the air-launched V 1 offensive was

---

* At the end of April it had briefly been suspected that missiles reported in some of the Baltic plots might have been launched from aircraft. But as some of the suspicious plots were quickly associated with experiments with the BV 246 glider bomb, the suspicion had not persisted. In view of the difficulty of distinguishing the tracks of air-launched from those of ground-launched missiles in the decrypts, this is understandable, particularly when there was so much evidence that the Germans were preparing to launch the V 1 from ramps.[68]

66.   CX/MSS/J 139, 144 and 148 of 11, 14 and 17 July.
67.   CX/MSS/J 148 of 17 July.
68.   AIR 20/1661; CAB 121/212, SIC file B/Defence/2, Vol 2, COS(44)375(0) of 28 April.
69.   CX/MSS/SJ 12 of 11 September 1944; AIR 20/1661.
70.   AIR 20/1661; CAB 121/214, COS(44)864(0) of 30 September.
71.   CX/MSS/SJ 16 of 2 October and 22 of 6 November; AIR 20/1661, para 3.1, Figure 2 and para 3.2.

resumed; and by early in October decrypts had indicated that III/KG 3 would soon be joined by a second Gruppe of up to 40 aircraft.[72] Thereafter decrypts gave good notice of III/KG 3's reinforcement. It was known by 22 October not only that the employment of a second Gruppe was imminent but also that a third would probably be operational within a month.[73] The second Gruppe was duly identified in action from the beginning of November and the third on 4 December.[74] With only brief periods of uncertainty the Enigma and low-grade GAF messages also identified the airfields from which I/KG 53 was operating, and from the same sources it was possible to monitor the level of activity and – by comparing the number of sorties flown with the number of missiles reaching England – to measure the efficiency of the weapon system.[75] Low-grade Sigint gave further assistance against the air-launched offensive by exploiting the fact that the movements of German aircraft were now being notified by W/T or R/T to German anti-aircraft sites in or near their flight paths. By interpreting these signals Cheadle was able to give Fighter Command advance warning of the areas from which the airborne V 1s were to be launched, and this was invaluable because the launching aircraft usually flew too low to appear on the radar. In the period September–December 1944 73 per cent of the occasions on which aircraft-launched flying bombs were forecast to Fighter Command. On 53 per cent of the sorties Cheadle gave an average of 70 minutes warning before the radar tracks were received.

In these ways intelligence was of direct assistance to those who planned and carried out the counter-measures, consisting of intruder and interception patrols by fighters. During December high-grade Sigint also showed that German fuel shortage was reducing the offensive; on 22 December ADI(Sc) informed the Prime Minister that on this account the number of sorties over London had recently been kept down to 20 per night.[76] But intelligence gave no warning when on 23 December, for the first time since the resumption of the campaign in September, V 1s were air-launched against a target other than London, falling in

---

72. CAB 121/214, COS(44)864(o) of 30 September, COS(44)888(o) of 8 October.

73. CAb 121/215, SIC file B/Defence/2, Vol 5, COS(44)911(o) of 22 October.

74. ibid, COS(44)984(o) of 21 November; AIR 20/1661.

75. CAB 121/214, COS(44)840(o) of 17 September, CBC(44) 18th Meeting, 23 September, COS(44)888(o) of 8 October; CAB 121/215, COS(44)905(o) of 15 October, 911(o) of 22 October, 951(o) of 6 November, 1038(o) of 18 December, COS(45)36(o) of 13 January.

76. Dir/C Archive, 8270 of 25 December 1944, para 8.

the Manchester area.[77]* Nor did it help to reduce the other problems facing the defences, of which the most important was the need to deploy radar that was capable of detecting the low-flying He 111s and of tracking their V 1s after launch.

The air-launched flying bomb offensive came to an end on 13 January 1945.† In its first phase up to 5 September 1944 the He 111s, operating from Dutch airfields, had released some 200 missiles against London, of which 50 per cent had made landfall and 35 per cent had hit within 15 miles of Charing Cross; and they had also aimed about 90 against Southampton. Between 15 September 1944 and 13 January 1945 a larger number of aircraft operating from Germany fired a total of some 1,200 missiles, almost all against London, but only just over 50 per cent of them crossed the British coast and, as the defences destroyed over 60 per cent of those they observed, only 66 reached the London area.

□

The end of the air-launched offensive did not mark the end of the V 1 campaign. In October 1944 the Germans had begun a ground-launched offensive against Antwerp, Liège and Brussels; it lasted until the end of March 1945. And during March 1945 they carried out a final offensive against London from launching sites in Holland.‡ Intelligence provided good notice of the opening of these two offensives, together with some estimate of their probable scale.

By 30 September 1944 it was known from the Enigma that Flak Regiment 155 (W) was surveying areas south-west and east of Cologne and Bonn and preparing to establish some 30 sites for launchings against Brussels and Antwerp, and there were signs that sites might be set up north of the Ruhr for use against Rotterdam and Amsterdam should they be captured by the Allies.[80] AI's assessment at that time was that the regiment might be able to fire about 100 flying bombs a day against Brussels and Antwerp by the end of October and that launchings might begin

---

* Decrypts obtained on 24 November and 6 December referred to preparations for Operation *Martha*, but it was not possible to associate *Martha* with Manchester before the attacks began.[78]

† The Enigma disclosed at the end of March that KG 53 was being disbanded, and that 58 of its crews had volunteered for service with Me 262s.[79]

‡ For this offensive see below, p 621ff.

77. CAB 121/215, COS(45)36(o) of 13 January.
78. DEFE 3/310, HP 7606 of 24 November; DEFE 3/314, HP 8731 of 6 December; DEFE 3/321, BT 358 of 6 December.
79. DEFE 3/600, BT 8687 of 28 March; DEFE 3/562 BT 9285 of 3 April.
80. CX/MSS/J 249/2 and 4.

on a smaller scale a week or two earlier.[81]* The flying bomb offensive against continental targets did indeed begin on 21 October, with Antwerp as the main target and occasional attacks on Brussels.[83] The rate of firings averaged only 100 a week until the last week in November.[84] It then rose quickly to 350 a week directed mainly at Antwerp and Liège, and from the pattern of the impact of the bombs that fell outside these target areas it became clear that the sites lay in an area between Trier and Koblenz.[85] After a brief lull the offensive was resumed on 11 December, but on 16 December, to coincide with the opening of the German counter-offensive in the Ardennes, it was intensified until it reached the rate of 500 a week in the first few days of 1945. Sixty per cent of the effort was directed at Antwerp, the remainder at Liège, and while some of the firings still came from the Trier-Koblenz area, the bulk of them now came from an area in Holland, to the east of the river Ijssel.[86]

---

* This intelligence prompted SHAEF to request that control of all aspects of *Crossbow* intelligence and operations on the Continent be transferred to it. The COS approved the request on 24 October, but it was not until 15 December, after a series of conferences and committees, that SHAEF established its Continental *Crossbow* Collation and *Crossbow* Intelligence (Interpretations and Operational Recommendations) Section.[82]

81. CAB 121/214, COS(44)864(o) of 30 September.
82. Craven and Cate, op cit, Vol III, p 545.
83. CAB 121/215, COS(44)951(o) of 6 November.
84. ibid, COS(44)983(o) of 21 November.
85. ibid, COS(44)1038(o) of 18 December.
86. ibid, COS(44)1038(o) of 18 December, COS(45)36(o) of 13 January.

CHAPTER 56

The V 2 Rocket Offensive

FROM THE middle of July 1944, when the V 1 offensive was at its height, the authorities in Whitehall, shaken by the sudden realisation that the V 2 rocket was designed to be launched from a simple firing platform, by the news that a large organisation under LXV Corps had been preparing the firing sites under a programme due to be completed by that month, and by the calculation that the Germans had produced about 1,000 rockets, feared that the V 2 offensive might be imminent.* In its regular report to the Chiefs of Staff on 23 July the Air Intelligence Branch argued that 'if more than a few [rockets] were available in the launching area with proper organisation and facilities for launching, we ought to have heard of them'; but it conceded that 'a few could be launched against this country at any time without further notice'.[1] At the meeting of the Cabinet's *Crossbow* Committee on 25 July ADI(Sc) repeated that there was as yet no sign of a movement westward of men and stores on the scale required for a big offensive;† he was confident, moreover, that the intelligence sources would disclose a large-scale movement without delay – when it did take place.[3] But Mr Duncan Sandys, the chairman of the Committee, was not prepared to accept this argument. He thought 'it would be unwise to assume from this negative evidence that a rocket attack is not imminent'; the enemy might well have produced considerably more than 1,000 rockets, and given that the few firing sites in Normandy were well camouflaged and had underground storage facilities, it must be supposed that many existed which had not been located.[4]‡

* See Volume III Part 1, p 445 et seq.

† Since 30 May, when an agent had reported that six 15-ton torpedoes had passed by train into northern France, there had been no evidence of movements until 18 July; PR had then located a train carrying cylindrical shaped loads near Dijon.[2]

‡ As yet, apart from those overrun by the Allies in Normandy, and identified with the help of POW, only one site had been located by agents, at Nieppe on 15 July. PR had been intensified and had paid particular attention to the roads within 5 miles of known storage depots, but had failed to identify any.[5]

1. CAB 121/213, SIC file B/Defence/2, Vol 3, COS(44)645(o) of 22 July.
2. CAB 121/214, SIC file B/Defence/2, Vol 4, COS(44)750(o) of 19 August.
3. CAB 121/213, CBC(44) 9th Meeting, 25 July.
4. ibid, CBC(44)32(o) of 24 July.
5. AIR 34/80, History of PI Investigation (Crossbow), para B 17.

On 26 July the Minister of Home Security called for an urgent re-examination of existing defence arrangements, pointing out that if a rocket attack on the scale then being allowed for were to be superimposed on the flying bomb offensive, the civil defence resources would be exhausted in three or four days. The War Cabinet approved new contingency measures on the following day; they included preparations for the evacuation of 2 million people and of factories and hospitals from London, and for the provision of protected buildings for government staff which had to remain behind.[6] At the same time, anxious about the damage being done by the V 1 as well as about the V 2 threat, the Chiefs of Staff asked the Joint Planners to look again at the feasibility of carrying out operations to occupy the launching areas. Such operations had been considered in June and found to be impracticable.* In their further report, issued on 30 July, the Planners again concluded that amphibious or airborne landings in the Pas de Calais were ruled out by the strength of the enemy's forces there. They could only recommend that SHAEF be urged to steer the US offensive that was about to start in Normandy (Operation *Cobra*) in the Pas de Calais direction. With particular reference to the V 2, moreover, they advised that as it would be a greater threat than the V 1, and could be fired from sites as far north as Ijmuiden, it was strategically vital that the Allies should occupy Holland as quickly as possible after capturing the Pas de Calais. They thus recommended that SHAEF should also be urged to give priority in the coming Allied advance towards Germany to the northern prong of the attack.[7]

By the end of July intelligence pointed somewhat more positively against an imminent V 2 offensive. In telegrams decrypted on 26 July and 3 August the Japanese Naval Attaché in Berlin stated that the 'Army's new torpedo' would be operational in two or three months' time and the Japanese Ambassador reported that improvements were still being made to the weapon.[8] A reliable agent had reported on 3 July that the offensive would begin within two months, and a report was received that Goebbels had remarked on 26 July that the weapon 'has partly entered upon the process of manufacture'. ADI(Sc) drew the attention of the Air Staff, Lord Cherwell and 'C' to this evidence on 30 July,[9]

---

* See above, pp 536–537.

6. CAB 121/214, WP(44)412 of 26 July, WM(44)97 Confidential Annex, 27 July.
7. CAB 121/390, SIC file B/France/6/11 Vol 1, JP(44)191 of 30 July.
8. BAY/XL 67 of 28 July.
9. AIR 20/1711, *Crossbow* Intelligence Weekly Summary No 1 of 30 July.

and on 31 July the JIC relied on it when replying to a request from the Chiefs of Staff for its own assessment of the imminence of a rocket attack. On the strength of it, and also as a result of the absence of evidence that the enemy had made preparations for a considerable attack, the JIC concluded that a heavy and sustained offensive was unlikely to develop during August. It admitted, however, that the evidence was 'fragmentary and inconclusive', and recognised that the military situation might compel 'an earlier, perhaps an immediate, use of the weapon on a small scale'.[10] This assessment was submitted on 2 August to the War Cabinet.[11] It had by then received some further support. Another reliable agent had reported that in Helsinki in the middle of July Ribbentrop had said that, unlike the V 1 attack, the rocket offensive would not be launched prematurely.[12]

□

At the end of July estimates of the probable scale of the German attack rested on two assumptions. The first, that about 1,000 rockets were operational, was derived, as already noted, from intelligence. The second was that the weight of the warhead was probably 7 tons; it represented the best guess of the *Crossbow* scientists, who had concluded by 24 July that the rocket, thought to be 40 feet long and 6 feet in diameter, would have an overall weight of between 30 and 40 tons and a warhead weighing between 5 and 10 tons for a range of 150 miles.[13] When these specifications were considered at a Chiefs of Staff meeting on 25 July Lord Cherwell found it difficult to reconcile the dimensions given for the rocket with the estimate given for its weight, and the Chief of the Air Staff asked whether the intelligence authorities in the Air Ministry had been asked their opinion. Mr Duncan Sandys replied that the intelligence representative on the *Crossbow* Committee had as yet been unable to supply the scientists with any information bearing on the weight.[14] Later on the same day, at a meeting of the *Crossbow* Committee, the chief *Crossbow* scientist assured the Prime Minister that the scientists' calculations about the rocket fitted quite well with intelligence which had subsequently become available. The minutes of the meeting do not record that, as he has related, ADI(Sc) disputed this statement.[15] The

---

10. CAB 121/214, JIC(44)336(o) of 31 July.
11. ibid, WP(44)427 of 2 August.
12. Dir/C Archive, 7283, No 256 of 1 August.
13. CAB 121/213, CBC(44)32(o) of 24 July.
14. ibid, COS(44)247th(o) Meeting, 25 July.
15. ibid, CBC(44) 9th Meeting, 25 July; Jones, *Most Secret War* (1978) p 440.

most recent statement about the rocket from the Air Intelligence Branch, ACAS(I)'s fortnightly report dated 22 July, had made no reference to the size of the weapon or the weight of the warhead.[16]

On 30 July ADI(Sc), in the first of a new series of reports to the Secretary of State for Air, the Air Staff, Lord Cherwell and 'C', drew attention to intelligence which suggested that the rocket was lighter than the scientists believed. The evidence had come from the preliminary examination in the Bois de Baugy, at one of the rocket sites located with the help of POW, of a rocket store, a light railway and trolleys designed to carry cylindrical objects.[17] ADI(Sc) did not in this report attempt an estimate of the weights. As early as 14 July he had also received the decrypt of an Enigma message from Blizna to Peenemünde referring to the despatch of fifty 1,000 kg (1 ton) 'Elephants' and to an order for extra-heavy 'Elephants', but he had perhaps not yet firmly decided that, as turned out to be the case, 'Elephants' stood for warheads.[18]

The *Crossbow* Committee considered the Bois de Baugy evidence on 4 August, by which time closer examination of a trolley at the Royal Aircraft Establishment had indicated a rocket weighing only 12 tons overall. By then, however, closer examination at the RAE of the remains of the rocket that had crashed in Sweden* had suggested that it weighed 24 tons, including 6 tons of fuel and a warhead of 4 tons, and the scientists hesitated to accept the lower specification. They agreed to devote further study to the possibility that the rocket weighed 12 tons, with a warhead of one ton, but argued that there was no sign that more than one type of rocket was being developed and that the trolleys might have been designed for an earlier rocket, since abandoned. They found it difficult, moreover, to see why the Germans should have gone to so much trouble and expense to develop a rocket that, with a warhead of only one ton, would be scarcely more effective than the flying bomb.[19]

On 6 August, in the second of his new weekly reports, ADI(Sc) noted that 'expert opinion is gradually coming into line with the intelligence evidence that the rocket weighs twenty tons or less'. He now quoted the Enigma reference to 'Elephants' normally weighing one ton and suggested that they could be warheads, and revealed that another decrypt had mentioned a consignment of

---

* See Volume III Part 1, pp 445, 447–448, 453–454.

16.   CAB 121/213, COS(44)645(o) of 22 July.
17.   AIR 20/1711, No 1 of 30 July 1944.
18.   CX/MSS/J 145 of 14 July 1944.
19.   CAB 121/214, CBC(44)44 of 2 August, CBC(44) 11th Meeting, 4 August.

4.3 tons of A-Stoff.[20]* This prompted him to suggest that if A-Stoff was liquid oxygen, which was known to be one of the two main fuels,† and if the other main fuel was alcohol, as some sources had claimed, the total weight of the rocket would be about 8 tons. He thought it perhaps significant that those intelligence reports which had claimed that liquid oxygen and alcohol were the main fuels – there had been five since February 1944, three from agents and two from POW – had all also said that the warhead weighed 1, 1½ or 2 tons.

The figure of 8 tons for the total weight had recently been mentioned by a POW electrician who had worked at Peenemünde for four years up to August 1943. Among other information about the rocket development programme that was clearly reliable, he had said that alcohol and liquid oxygen were the main fuels, that the liquid oxygen was fed into the rocket as late as possible before take-off, to avoid the icing of the valves and other moving parts, and that the rocket weighed 8 tons overall and had a warhead of only one ton.[22]

Further intelligence reached London by 7 August in the form of documents captured at Villers-Bocage from the HQ of an organisation in charge of V 2 sites.[23] They included the drawing of a launching site; it showed a lorry with two trailers carrying one fuel, assumed to be liquid oxygen, a lorry containing B-Stoff,‡ which was thought to be the second main fuel, probably alcohol, and a lorry containing T-Stoff,§ which was known to be hydrogen peroxide and to be used for driving the fuel pump. This added nothing to what had already been pieced together, somewhat inconclusively, about the rocket's fuelling system. A second drawing showed a rocket resting on two trolleys and gave its dimensions as 45 feet 10 inches long and 5 feet 7 inches in diameter, with a tail fin diameter of 11 feet 8 inches. This established that the rocket was somewhat longer and slightly smaller in diameter than had been assumed. When the documents were discussed by the *Crossbow* Committee on 10 August the scientists were inclined to accept that it weighed less than they had believed. They were perhaps influenced less by the documents

---

* This decrypt was available on 12 July.[21]

† See Volume III Part 1, p 454.

‡ See Volume III Part 1, p 443.

§ See Volume III Part 1, pp 428–429.

20. AIR 20/1711, No 2 of 6 August 1944.
21. CX/MSS/J 142 of 12 July 1944.
22. AIR 20/3437, ADI(K)409A/1944 of 3 August 1944.
23. AIR 20/4236, AI 2(g) Report No 2259 of 9 August 1944; CAB 121/214, CBC(44)52 of 10 August.

than by the evidence provided by ADI(Sc). He informed the meeting that in 'secret correspondence between Blizna and Peenemünde' there had been the reference to 'Elephants' which almost certainly meant that the warhead weighed one ton, and he quoted the intelligence reports which had coupled a rocket fuelled by liquid oxygen and alcohol with warhead weights of 1, 1½ and 2 tons. He gave 12 tons as his own estimate of the overall weight – the figure arrived at after examination of the trolley by the RAE. Feeling that this was too small, and still puzzled as to why the Germans should have expended so much effort in building a rocket that carried hardly more explosive than the flying bomb, the scientists provisionally set the total weight at 15–18 tons and the warhead at one ton for a range of 200 miles or two tons for a range of 140 miles.[24]

No further intelligence had been received by 19 August, when ACAS(I) summarised in his most recent regular report to the Chiefs of Staff the conclusions AI had reached about the warhead, the fuels and some of the rocket's other characteristics. The RAE was by then convinced that the Swedish rocket had the same external dimensions as those given in the Villers–Bocage documents, and (as ADI(Sc) reported separately on 20 August) was coming to the conclusion that it weighed between 13 and 14 tons overall and had a warhead weighing 2,000 lbs (c. 1 ton) and containing between 1,200 and 1,500 lbs of explosive. Nothing had occurred to cast doubt on the 'secret intelligence' which had indicated that the warhead normally weighed one ton but that heavier ones existed. Other sources had mentioned weights of 1½ to 2 tons, as well as of one ton, and these had also reported that liquid oxygen and alcohol were the two main fuels. One of the fuels was certainly liquid oxygen, but it had not been definitely established that the second was alcohol – though alcohol was its main constituent. An element of uncertainty about the weight of the warhead arose when range was taken into account. All the evidence pointed to a normal range of at least 160 miles with a one-ton warhead, but the warhead could weigh 1½ tons with a range of up to 150 miles, or 2 tons up to 120 miles. Little had been learned recently about the launching process, but it was clear that the rocket was towed to the launching point, where it was fuelled and erected on the firing point and then launched vertically or nearly vertically. It was radio-controlled, but there was no evidence that it was controlled beyond the initial burning phase, a matter of about one and a half minutes. It was obviously intended to be a weapon of considerable precision, but there was some

---

24.   CAB 121/214, CBC(44) 12th Meeting, 10 August.

evidence that the Germans had not yet achieved a great degree of accuracy with it.[25]

In a long account of the development of intelligence about the rocket, issued on 26 August, ADI(Sc) described in greater detail how these conclusions had been arrived at. So far as the weights of the rocket and its warhead were concerned, the first important step had been the supposition towards the end of July that one of the main fuels was liquid oxygen, and that hydrogen peroxide was used only in an auxiliary turbine to work the pumps. This had directed attention to the fact that those agents and POW who had referred to liquid oxygen had claimed that the other main fuel was alcohol; they had also said that the warhead weighed one or 1½ or 2 tons. Another significant item had been the reference in the Blizna–Peenemünde correspondence to 4.3 tons of A-Stoff; this had indicated that if A-Stoff was liquid oxygen the total weight of the rocket was between 9 and 14 tons, but it might be as much as 20 tons if A-Stoff was alcohol.[26] The Villers–Bocage documents with their evidence for B-Stoff had failed to clear up this uncertainty. The identification of A-Stoff as liquid oxygen and B-Stoff as alcohol, or some compound including alcohol, was still tentative. Those same documents, however, had given the dimensions of the rocket, and on this evidence, and after further examination of the rocket from Sweden and the trolley from the Bois de Baugy, the RAE had independently estimated the overall weight at 13½ tons and the weight of the warhead as about 2,000 lbs (1 ton).[27] And there was further evidence (the references to 'Elephants') that the warhead normally weighed one ton, and that an extra-heavy warhead weighing 1½ or 2 tons existed. This chain of evidence led to the conclusion that the rocket weighed between 11½ and 14 tons (including a carcass weight of 2.6 to 3 tons and a fuel weight of between 8 and 9½ tons) and that its performance was 200 miles with a one-ton warhead, 150 miles with a warhead of 1½ tons and 120 miles with a warhead of 2 tons.[28]

In the same exhaustive report ADI(Sc) scrutinised, with results that were far more tentative, the intelligence bearing on other features of the weapon. Nothing was known about the explosive it used.[29] Little was known about its accuracy; several agents had claimed that the intended accuracy was 1 kilometre over a range of 200 km, but information about the firings at Blizna had indicated that the accuracy was not yet impressive, and there had been many

25.   ibid, COS(44)750(o) of 19 August; AIR 20/1711, No 4 of 20 August 1944.
26.   AIR 20/1688 of 26 August 1944, Part II, paras 11, 12.
27.   ibid, paras 14, 15, 16.
28.   ibid, Part III, paras 5, 6.
29.   ibid, para 6.

reports of control troubles. As for its control system or systems, there had been references both to jet-rudders, indicating that the rocket was turned on to a pre-set trajectory by gyroscope, and to elaborate coding arrangements for a radio receiver, while the equipment found on the Swedish rocket also pointed to radio control. But the functioning of the rudders and the receiver was not understood and examination of the Swedish rocket had failed to throw any light on the problem. There had also been puzzling references to dive brakes, but no trace of these had been found among the Swedish fragments. All that could be said for certain was that the missile started vertically with slow acceleration and reached the ground 150 to 200 miles away in 250 to 350 seconds.[30]

On 28 August, in a report to the Chiefs of Staff on the probable scale and time of a V 2 offensive, the *Crossbow* Committee concurred in AI's assessment of the weight of the warhead: the rocket appeared to have an operational range of up to 200 miles; at this range its warhead was about one ton, of which about 80 per cent was high explosive, but at ranges of up to 140 miles it would be technically possible for it to carry a warhead of about 2 tons. The report went on to say that such evidence as was available on the production of the rocket suggested that Germany had stocks sufficient to sustain an offensive for one month at the rate of between 30 and 60 launchings a day. The great speed and high trajectory of the weapon would defeat existing defence measures, and no counter-measures were yet possible, but from what was known about its present accuracy it might be expected that perhaps between a half and two-thirds of those launched would fall in the intended target area. If it were assumed that London would be the sole target, and that an average of 20 flying bombs a day were also landing there during the rocket offensive, up to 80 tons a day would fall within 15 miles of Charing Cross, as compared with 48 tons during the worst week of the flying bomb attacks. The report pointed out that these estimates took no account of the rapid advance of the Allied armies or Allied bombing of the enemy's communications and his rocket storage depots and fuel plants, which might force the enemy to abandon the bombardment. Little was known about the extent to which he had prepared and manned firing sites, or about the locations of the sites, but the start of the attack must be expected at any time.[31]

□

30. ibid, para 6.
31. CAB 121/214, *Crossbow* Committee, 14th Report by the Chairman, 28 August 1944.

After the JIC's report of 31 July to the effect that a rocket offensive on a large scale was unlikely to begin in August* no intelligence bearing on the timing of the offensive had been received from any source until 14 August. On that day the decrypt of a telegram from the Japanese Ambassador in Venice disclosed that Ribbentrop had told the Italian Vice-Minister of Foreign Affairs on 20 July that the V 2 would shortly be brought into use on the western front. On the same day PR detected near Dijon a train of twenty wagons carrying cylindrical objects similar to those seen there on 18 July.† ACAS(I) advised the Chiefs of Staff on 19 August that while this was the sole reliable indication of possible movement into the operational area, it might well mean that the German preparations were far advanced.[32]

In the same report he summarised what had been discovered about launching sites and storage depots. Three sites had been found in Normandy with the help of POW; all had three firing platforms of simple construction which had been well camouflaged, those at Château de Molny consisting only of concrete slabs let into the road surface. It would have been extremely difficult, if not impossible, to locate them from the air. As for the depots examined, the one in the Bois de Baugy was also well camouflaged and POW had reported that the Germans planned to put it below ground. The documents captured at Villers–Bocage had revealed that three depots in Normandy, at La Meauffe, Hautmesnil and in the Bois de Baugy, were to have been completed, with a capacity for 120 rockets, by early in May; and the map included among the documents had shown six other installations the function of which, though clearly associated with the rocket, remained obscure.[33]

On 25 August the *Crossbow* Committee was informed that a POW, a General, had recently stated that the rocket offensive was to begin in mid-September, possibly with earlier attacks on a small scale, and that the High Command had ordered that the firing area was to be held at all costs.[34] In his long report of 26 August analysing the contribution intelligence had made to the under-standing of the rocket programme ADI(Sc) noted that this information tallied with the forecasts that had been made at the end of July, but was no longer confident that the Allies would be

---

* See above p 553.

† See above p 551.

32. CAB 121/214, COS(44)750(o) of 19 August.

33. ibid. See also CAB 121/214, COS(44)691(o) of 5 August, CBC(44)50 of 9 August, CBC(44)52 of 10 August; AIR 40/1219, AI 2(g) Reports No 4/X of 9 August, 5/X of 16 August 1944.

34. CAB 121/214, CBC(44)15th Meeting, 25 August.

alerted by intelligence to the westward movement of German personnel and stores. Although there was no other intelligence to indicate when the offensive would begin, he concluded that 'the Germans will launch the rocket against us as soon as they can amass sufficient effort; this may be soon. . . .' As for the scale of the offensive, he suggested that the threat might never develop in view of the Allied advance; in any case, 'the still existing defects, the relatively small warhead, the increasing difficulties of supply, and our threat to the operational area, all lead us to believe that the magnitude of the menace is small'.[35]

This conclusion rounded off an attempt to assess the scale of the offensive in the light of what was known about the production of the rocket, the storage capacity of the forward depots, the number and rate of fire of the launching sites and the size of the enemy's field organisation. The report emphasised that on all these issues intelligence was scanty. About the numbers of firing sites and the size of the V 2 organisation, and about their location and deployment, next to nothing was known.[36] Production was believed to be widely dispersed, with a few main assembly points; but the factories had not been located, and all that was available was 'weak evidence' from the works numbers in the Blizna–Peenemünde correspondence for a current stock of 2,000 and a production rate of perhaps 500 a month.[37] The capacity of the storage depots was estimated by means of a 'somewhat tenuous argument' from the Villers–Bocage documents. They indicated that the Germans had built three depots in November with a capacity for holding about 120 rockets, and they marked six other installations in that area, numbered from 15 to 20, of which the purpose was obscure. If these installations, which had been photographed by PR, were assumed to be dummy depots, and if the first 14 of them lay east of the Seine, where PR had detected some that were similar, the ratio of dummies to depots would suggest that the Germans had planned storage depots for a total of some 400 rockets. Assuming, again, that this represented a fortnight's supply in the forward area, which was what the Germans were known to have tried to maintain in the flying bomb offensive, the planned rate of fire might be 800 rockets a month. Another possible approach was to compare the rates of launching in the trials of the V 2 with those in the trials of the V 1. The level of activity with the V 2 had been about a third of the V 1, and this again suggested that operational launchings of the rocket might be less than 1,000 a month. The figure of 800 a month could only be

---

35. AIR 20/1688, Part II, para 17 and Part VIII, para 2.
36. ibid, Parts VI and VII.
37. ibid, Part IV, paras 5 and 6, Part VIII, para 2.

a rough guide, for different interpretations of the data could yield rates as low as 500 or as high as 1,500 firings a month. The planned rate of fire would, however, be reduced by the advance of the Allied armies and the effects of Allied bombing.[38]

ADI(Sc)'s assessment of the scale of the offensive was adopted, with little modification, by the *Crossbow* Committee in its appreciation submitted to the Chiefs of Staff on 28 August.* And it may be noted that, though based very largely on conjecture, it corresponded remarkably closely to the facts, as did his estimates of the weight of the rocket and its warhead. The following comparison with the facts, as provided by German records, was later made by ADI(Sc) (Professor R V Jones):[39]

	ADI(Sc) Estimate	*German Statement*
Total Weight	11½–14 tons probably 12–13	12.65 (experimentally down to 11.2 tons)
Warhead Weight	1 ton nominal	1 ton (down to 0.97 tons sometimes)
Liquid Oxygen Weight	4.5 tons	4.9 tons
Alcohol Weight	3.5 tons	3.8 tons
Carcass Weight	2.6–3 tons	2.87 tons
Maximum Range	200–210 miles	207 miles
Total Stocks	perhaps 2,000 (on 26.8.44)	1,800
Monthly Production	About 500 (on 26.8.44)	300 in May 1944 (Average); 618 (Sept 1944– March 1945)
Total Forward Storage	About 400	320
Intended Monthly Rate of Fire	About 800	900 as 'target figure'

On 31 August Mr Duncan Sandys incorporated ADI(Sc)'s estimates in a report to the Minister of Home Security which recapitulated the *Crossbow* Committee's appreciation of 28 August but made two additions to it. The first stressed that the state of production and the state of stocks would be sufficient to sustain a rate of launching of some 30 to 60 rockets a day for a period of *at*

---

* See above p 558.

38.   ibid, Part VIII, para 1.
39.   Jones, op cit, p 453; Churchill, *The Second World War* Vol VI (1954), pp 45–46.

least one month (italics supplied). The other offered an estimate of the duration, as well as of the start, of the offensive: 'The attack may start at any time from now onwards. It will not continue on an appreciable scale after 15 October'. This was prefaced by the statement that the Supreme Allied Commander had made 'a reasonably informed guess' that the Allies would reach the Franco-Belgian frontier sometime between 25 September and 15 October; it was thought that rockets could not be launched against London on any appreciable scale from beyond this line and also that attacks by flying bombs, which had a shorter range than the rocket, should by the second of these dates have ceased altogether, apart from small-scale launchings from aircraft.[40] The Chiefs of Staff recorded their agreement with this appreciation on 1 September.[41] On the same day Sandys told the *Crossbow* Committee that Ministers had decided that the long-term civil defence contingency plans should not yet be implemented, though he hoped that offensive counter-measures against the rocket would not be relaxed prematurely.[42]

In the Air Ministry the question of what to do about counter-measures was then being considered. As ACAS(I) advised the Chiefs of Staff in his report of 2 September, the difficulty of locating V 2 firing sites was still causing grave anxiety; three more had been found by ground reconnaissance in Normandy of which one, differing from others in the size and siting of its concrete slabs, suggested that there was no fixed design to help to reduce the formidable problem of detecting by PR those that lay further north. On the other hand, there was no evidence connecting the rocket with those installations which, according to an earlier conjecture, might have been dummy forward supply depots; and this, as the report announced, meant that no depots of the kind associated with the rocket had been identified east of the Franco-Belgian frontier.[43] It was presumably on the strength of this assurance that on 4 September the CAS advised the Chiefs of Staff Committee that, considering the progress of the Allied ground forces, offensive counter-measures could be suspended forthwith because 'so far as the rocket attack is concerned, I feel it safe to assume that the area within 200 miles of London may already be regarded as neutralised'.[44]

His note supporting this conclusion argued that it was reasonably certain that the maximum range of the V 2 was 200 miles;

40. CAB 121/214, CBC(44)74 of 31 August, paras 7, 9, 22.
41. ibid, COS(44)295th(o) Meeting, 1 September.
42. ibid, CBC(44)16th Meeting, 1 September.
43. ibid, COS(44)795(o) of 2 September.
44. ibid, COS(44)806(o) of 4 September.

that all known preparations for its use were confined to much the same area as the flying bomb sites, apparently with London as the sole target; and that the whole of this area was already in Allied hands, or likely to be so before long. He admitted that the Germans could launch the rocket from Belgium and Holland, but thought this extremely unlikely: there was no evidence that they had made the necessary preparations. On these grounds he proposed that all bombing of the rocket organisation should be stopped, on the understanding that it could be resumed at short notice if targets outside London were attacked; and he also suggested that all radio counter-measures, other than those thought necessary for experimental purposes or as an insurance against the possibility of rocket attacks outside London, might be cancelled.

With some reservations, notably that the gun defences and special radar watches should be maintained against the rocket threat for the time being, the Vice-Chiefs of Staff approved the CAS's proposals on 5 September. They did so with every confidence that the threat would not materialise, as is clear from the fact that they also agreed that periodic reports were no longer required from ACAS(I) or from the chairman of the *Crossbow* Committee, who might prepare his final report at his leisure, and from the terms of the paper they submitted to the War Cabinet on 6 September. In this they declared: 'All those areas from which either the flying bomb or the rocket might be launched against London have been, or are about to be, occupied by Allied troops. There should thus shortly be no further damage to this country from either of these causes, except for the possibility of the airborne launching of flying bombs. . . .'[45] On 7 September, at a Press conference held with the approval of the Chiefs of Staff, Sandys confined his remarks to the flying bomb – the existence of the rocket had not been made public – but announced that 'except possibly for a few last shots, the Battle of London is over'.[46]

These proceedings were severely criticised after the war in the Air Historical Branch's Narrative History. It took issue particularly with the CAS's statement that, because 'they would have to make certain preparations of which we have no evidence and which in present circumstances are extremely unlikely', the Germans would not launch a V 2 offensive from Holland and Belgium:

'This is a surprising statement for two reasons: first, it was well-known that the rocket firing points and storage depots could only be detected with great difficulty – such evidence of preparations for firing as had

---

45.   ibid, COS(44)298th(o) Meeting, 5 September, COS(44)811(o) of 6 September (WP(44)501).

46.   AIR 40/1773, Press statement of 7 September 1944.

been discovered in northern France amounted to little more than half a dozen concrete slabs and two or three storage depots of which there was little or no information until they were actually occupied; second, Holland had not been covered for signs of German preparations to anything like the same extent as Northern France. In short, the argument from silence was a dangerous one; and events were soon to prove it so'.[47]

The argument was certainly incautious, not to say euphoric, when compared with Sandys's more sober appraisal of 31 August, but its consequences were hardly as serious as these remarks suggest. It was shown to be false when on the evening of 8 September, a week after the Allied advance into Belgium had put an end to the heaviest V 1 operations against the United Kingdom, the first V 2s landed in the London area – the first of 27 to reach England out of 35 launched from the suburbs of The Hague and the Island of Walcheren before the rocket offensive was briefly halted on 18 September by the Allied thrust into Holland. By 8 September, however, the decision to suspend Allied bombing and radio counter-measures had hardly come into force. And what is more to the point, just as they had done nothing to delay the offensive, so they proved to be quite ineffective, when resumed, in mitigating its effects. Intelligence about the location of the firing points, the depots, the factories and the fuel plants associated with the V 2, as about the performance and the control of the weapon during its flight, was virtually non-existent when the offensive began, and it was long to remain insufficient for all practical purposes.

□

On 9 September the Chiefs of Staff still took the view that, as the firings from Holland must have been hastily improvised, the offensive would not last long. They advised the War Cabinet to make no public statement and to defer a decision as to whether or not the emergency evacuation measures should be implemented.[48]

By 12 September sound-ranging equipment and flash-spotting on the Continent had traced the firings to the vicinity of Rotterdam and Amsterdam; radar tracks and the examination of recovered fragments had established that the trajectory, speed, size and warhead of the missile were close to what had been estimated; and the SOE, instructed to get the Dutch Resistance movement to report whatever could be discovered, had heard that

47. AIR 41/55, *The Air Defence of Great Britain*, Vol VI, p 228.
48. CAB 121/214, COS(44)303rd(o) Meeting, 9 September, WM(44)119 of 9 September.

there were firing points and a storage depot near The Hague.[49] But no firm operational intelligence on movements had yet been obtained and intensive PR had failed to detect either firing points or other installations. At the same time, the results of the radar watch did not suggest that it would be possible to provide early warning of the arrival of missiles, and although preparations had been made for ground and airborne radio jamming, No 80 Wing RAF, with ground stations controlled from Beachy Head and a continuous patrol of aircraft fitted with interception equipment, had failed to establish that the missile was radio-controlled.[50]* Nor could the Air Ministry add much further information when it next reported on 17 September.

Sixteen rockets had landed by then and three had fallen into the sea. This constituted about 75 per cent of the total number, between three and four a day, that had been launched. Good intelligence on the number launched had come from sound-ranging and radar observations and visual reports of firings from ground agents; all these sources had agreed in narrowing down the launching area to a wooded belt of country in the Wassenaar suburb of The Hague, though two rockets on 16 September appeared to have been fired from Walcheren. Nothing had been learned about the enemy's supply, storage and transport arrangements, or about the production programme. The accuracy of the rocket was not good – only eight had fallen within 12 miles of the centre of London – and in four cases the missile had burst in the air, probably as a result of explosion in the fuel tanks. Examination of the debris indicated that the rocket's radio equipment was simpler than that found in the missile that had been recovered in Sweden, and there was still no clear evidence that it was radio-controlled.[51]

On 18 September, the day after the Allies started the airborne landings near Arnhem in the hope of getting a footing across the lower Rhine, Sandys issued an assessment of the V 2 threat. He noted that the operational range of the rocket, not much more than 200 miles, left the enemy with a very restricted area from which to launch it against London, and that 'having regard to this fact and to the latest Allied thrust into Holland, it would seem that the rocket bombardment cannot be long maintained and that the

---

* From 15 September an intercept unit operated in the Brussels–Eindhoven–Liège area, as close as possible to the V 2 firing sites; its intercepts failed to establish any firm evidence of radio control.

49. ibid, SOE letters to the War Cabinet, 11 and 12 September 1944.
50. ibid, WM(44)122 of 11 September, COS(44)825(o) of 11 September, CBC(44)17th Meeting, 12 September.
51. ibid, COS(44)840(o) of 17 September.

scale of the attack is not likely to reach serious proportions'.[52] Rocket launchings did indeed cease after 18 September, and reliable reports indicated that the Germans had on 17 September ordered the withdrawal of rocket supplies from The Hague.[53] On 23 September, however, the Deputy Chief of the Air Staff advised that launchings against London could not be ruled out until the Allies had overrun the whole of Holland west of Eindhoven, the more so as the missile's range could be increased to perhaps 240 miles without a change of design.[54] The War Cabinet, considering these two assessments on 25 September, accepted the advice of the Chiefs of Staff that no public reference to the rocket should be made for at least another week.[55]

On 25 September, after a lull of six days, a rocket landed near Norwich. By 30 September nine launchings had been detected, of which six had landed in the Norwich area and two elsewhere in East Anglia, and the firing point had been located near Apeldoorn, just under 200 miles from Norwich and just over 250 from London.[56] Another 21 firings had been detected by 8 October; eighteen had apparently been aimed at Norwich and three against London, where one rocket had landed. Ground reports had indicated that they came from three sites, Apeldorn and two in Friesland; but it had also been reported that launching crews and rockets were returning to the area of The Hague, and this would account for the rockets aimed at London.[57] There had meanwhile been no lull in the rocket attack on targets in Belgium and northern France. Following an isolated hit on the outskirts of Paris on 8 September, the offensive had been extended to Lille and the Lille-Liège area by the end of September and to Paris in the first week of October.[58]

The brief campaign against Norwich ended on 12 October, by which date 32 rockets had landed in East Anglia out of a total of 44 fired.[59] Thereafter, the stabilisation of the land front having enabled the Germans to set up firing points in western Holland, all firings were concentrated against the London area and Antwerp, and the Allies resigned themselves to a prolonged offensive

---

52. ibid, CBC(44)75 of 18 September.
53. AIR 41/55, pp 236–237; Collier, *The Defence of the United Kingdom* (1957), p 408.
54. CAB 121/214, COS(44)849(0) of 23 September.
55. ibid, WM(44)127 of 25 September.
56. ibid, COS(44)864(0) of 30 September.
57. ibid, COS(44)868(0) of 8 October.
58. ibid, COS(44)849(0) of 23 September, 864(0) of 30 September; CAB 121/215, SIC file B/Defence/2, Vol 5, COS(44)911(0) of 22 October.
59. Collier, op cit, p 409.

against these targets. In the period 21 October–4 November, when the number of successful firings had reached an average of 14 a day, some two-thirds were directed against Antwerp and the rest against London.[60] On 8 November the German High Command announced in a communiqué that the V 1 bombardment of London had been intensified by the use of a more formidable weapon, and on 10 November the Prime Minister informed the British public that long-range rockets had been fired against the United Kingdom.[61]

A good deal of additional technical intelligence about the rocket had been obtained by then, but the performance of the weapon prevented the development of defensive counter-measures. By 21 November AI had compiled from the examination of debris a comprehensive reconstruction of the design and performance of the missile that was accurate in all but a few details, and was of the opinion that the Germans were unlikely, either by firing a larger rocket or by reducing the range of the existing rocket, to introduce a heavier warhead.[62] On the other hand, continuous airborne and ground watch on the appropriate frequencies had still found no evidence that the rocket was controlled or tracked by radio, and in the middle of November the recovery from some rockets of an integrating accelerometer – an instrument incorporating a gyroscope which measured velocity and controlled the trajectory and the period of the jet thrust – made it clear that, even if that instrument was not yet in series production, radio control was unlikely to be introduced. In December the arrangements made for jamming the rocket's radio were suspended.[63]* It had also been established at an early stage that radar detection of the rocket's flight, though useful in locating the whereabouts of launching points, was unable to give enough notice of a rocket's arrival to make it possible either to establish a public warning

---

* On 12 December the decrypt of a recent telegram from the Japanese Ambassador in Berlin contained information on this subject. The Ambassador admitted that he had been unable to obtain any firm details about the V 2 but went on to say that he had gathered from Speer that the weapon was radio-controlled on entering the stratosphere and for a short time thereafter. On 22 December, asked by 'C' to comment on the signal for the Prime Minister, ADI(Sc) reported that except in the first few days of the bombardment of London, control of the V 2s had been entirely internal, no use being made of radio.[64] Early in 1945 some of the missiles used against Antwerp were suspected of having radio equipment but the evidence was inconclusive.[65]

60. CAB 121/215, COS(44)951 of 6 November.
61. Collier, op cit, p 413.
62. AIR 20/3437, AI 2(g) Report No 1684 of 21 November 1944.
63. CAB 121/215, COS(44)983(o) of 21 November, 1038(o) of 18 December.
64. Dir/C Archive, 8720 of 22 December.
65. CAB 121/215, COS(45)36(o) of 13 January, 122(o) of 21 February.

system or to take active defence measures.[66]*

Until the V 2 organisation was driven out of Holland by the Allied armies in March 1945, the only available counter-measure, therefore, was the bombing of V 2 operational sites. Intelligence on these increased from September; little of it could be turned to account, however, and the bombing had little effect on the enemy's campaign. Much of the intelligence was obtained from the Corncrake Enigma traffic which, temporarily suspended at the end of July when Blizna was evacuated, had been resumed on 16 August. It first threw light on the V 2 organisation on 19 and 21 September, when GC and CS decrypted signals transmitted between 14 and 16 September. They referred to a visit by SS General Kammler to Walcheren and reported that the Walcheren battery had fired its first rockets on 16 September and that the battery at The Hague and the Gruppe Süd battery had each fired three. At the end of September further decrypts mentioned Gruppe Süd, Gruppe Nord, Batteries 485 and 836 and SS Werfer Battery 500, all having connections with General Kammler, and during October the traffic located Gruppe Nord at Baumholder, near Trier, and Battery 836 at Rheinfeld. The decrypts also disclosed that V 2 trials had been transferred to a new site: they located it at Tuchel, north of Bromberg (Bydgoszcz) in October.[68]†

A document captured in Holland in October gave details which, together with reports from agents, enabled AI to say early in November that the organisation comprised three batteries with

---

* Against the danger that rocket damage might produce flooding of the London Underground, a system for warning the London Passenger Transport Board was instituted early in January 1945; but the notice given rarely exceeded 1½ minutes and the system was not reliable enough for general use. The search for a tolerably effective public warning system continued, but without success, until the end of the offensive. The hope that prediction would improve sufficiently to make it practicable to engage the rockets with anti-aircraft guns never materialised.[67]

† See Volume III Part 1, pp 438, 443, 485 for Corncrake and General Kammler. By the end of October the Enigma showed that Kammler had been placed in command of the V-weapons organisation with the title of Reichsführer SS Sonderbevollmächtigter 2 and in February 1945 a decrypt revealed that his title had been changed to GOC Armee Korps ZV (AKZV).[69] In April 1945 he was also put in charge of the administration and production of jet aircraft, see below p 619.

66. CAB 121/214, COS(44)840(o) of 17 September, 849(o) of 23 September; CAB 121/215, COS(44)918(o) of 23 October.
67. CAB 121/215, COS(44)1046(o) of 23 December, COS(45)122(o) of 21 February, 218(o) of 26 March, 262(o) of 12 April, CBC(45) 1 of 8 January, 7 of 22 March, CBC(45) 1st Meeting, 15 January, 2nd Meeting, 26 March; Collier, op cit, pp 415, 417.
68. CX/MSS/J 299 of 19 September 1944 et seq.
69. CX/MSS/J 326/1 and 2; DEFE 3/509, BT 5347 of 21 February 1945.

Gruppe Nord, of which two were operating from The Hague against London and one from Friesland against Antwerp, and two or three with Gruppe Süd which were thought to be operating against Antwerp.[70] Later in November evidence from documents and POW, which was coming in at an increasing rate, left little doubt that there were six batteries in all and indicated that the total manpower involved was between 10,752 and 13,812, including 2,620–2,740 men in the firing units and 1,160–1,270 in technical units.[71] In November Allied Y units in Belgium began to intercept low-grade wireless traffic between the HQs and the sub-formations of the V 2 organisation. This provided more precise intelligence about the German order of battle, and established that the scale of the German effort was not being greatly expanded. Although there were then three more in reserve, in February 1945 the number of batteries operating was still two against England from the neighbourhood of The Hague, one of them with a detachment near The Hook, and four against Antwerp from Zwolle, Enschede and an area near Koblenz.[72]

These low-grade decrypts were obtained so promptly that it was initially hoped that fighters and fighter-bombers might be able to carry out attacks against individual launching points when rockets were about to be fired. But further analysis quickly showed that while they often gave an hour's warning of the intention to fire, they were useless for operational purposes because they rarely gave advance notice of which sites within a battery would be firing.[73]

Some intelligence about the V 2 production programme was obtained in October, when the Allies captured a factory in Luxembourg and found it to be one of five that were producing a rocket component. Its documents showed that the Germans had planned to produce 12,360 rockets by October 1944 with a production rate of 1,000 a month. They also showed that by July 1944 the Luxembourg firm had delivered only 10 per cent of its contract, but it had to be assumed that stocks of the rocket could not have been less than 2,000 by the beginning of October and that, even if the Germans had not yet approached the planned production rate, production would be more than adequate to sustain the existing rate of firings unless it could be interrupted by

70. CAB 121/215, COS(44)905(o) of 15 October, 951(o) of 6 November; Collier, op cit, p 410.

71. AIR 20/4236, AI 3(e) Report of 16 November 1944.

72. CAB 121/215, COS(44)1038(o) of 18 December, COS(45)122(o) of 21 February; AWL 4033 of 20 February.

73. AIR 41/55, p 273.

Allied bombing.[74]* Nothing was learned, however, about the whereabouts of other production plants; the documents did not identify the other four firms, although they gave some support to POW claims that the most important component assembly plant was an underground factory near Nordhausen. And little was known about the arrangements for the distribution and storage of rockets. Reliance had thus to be put on the Allied bombing offensive against the enemy's general transportation network rather than on attacks against specific *Crossbow* targets.

The bombing had been steadily increased since the beginning of the offensive, particular attention being paid to the launching areas near The Hague and the approaches to them. If it did anything to impede the offensive there was no evidence to that effect by the beginning of December. In December the Allies raised the restrictions they had previously placed on bombing out of consideration for Dutch civilians, and concentrated their bombing effort more closely against targets, many of them in built-up areas, which were suspected of being directly associated with the storage and transport of rockets and with the production of liquid oxygen. But there was no certainty that the targets were important for the V 2 offensive, and it remained impossible to judge whether the attack on them was having any serious effect.[76]

Intelligence improved only in relation to two targets, locating the launching areas more precisely and establishing the importance of the Nordhausen factory, and these were targets that it was not practicable to attack. As already noted, the actual firing points within launching areas were difficult to pin-point and were changed so frequently that it was not profitable to subject them to precision bombing. At the end of December the Chiefs of Staff considered and rejected a proposal from the Minister of Home Security that the heavy bombers of Bomber Command should be used for mass attacks on the launching areas near The Hague: they estimated that the operation would divert 1,200 to 1,500 Lancasters from urgent tasks in support of the land campaign, that it would achieve only a temporary interruption of the V 2 offensive, and that it would achieve this only at the expense of heavy loss of life and property among the Dutch.[77] On 26 January

---

* It has been reported since the war that 5,789 rockets were produced by March 1945 and that from September 1944 production was maintained at just over 600 a month.[75]

74.   CAB 121/215, COS(44)951(o) of 6 November.
75.   Irving, *The Mare's Nest* (1964), pp 298, 306.
76.   CAB 121/215, COS(45)47(o) of 16 January, 51(o) of 18 January, COS(45) 17th Meeting, 17 January; AIR 41/55, pp 265–266, 269–270, 275–278.
77.   CAB 121/215, COS(44)410th(o) Meeting of 23 December, Annex II, COS(44)1046(o) of 27 December; Collier, op cit, pp 414–415.

the proposal was reconsidered by the Defence Committee and again rejected on these grounds.[78] By then it had long been plain from the evidence of POW that the most important, perhaps the sole, assembly point for the V 2 was the underground plant near Nordhausen; and there were reports in November that it was turning out thirty rockets a day and had the capacity to turn out forty. By 4 December, however, a close examination from the air had revealed that the factory, housed in two parallel tunnels about a mile long, was protected by up to 300 feet of gypsum. No existing bombs were likely to penetrate this and on 22 December the Chiefs of Staff accepted that the target was not a practicable one.[79] In January 1945, though still far from confident that it would be seriously damaged, they relented, recommending to the Defence Committee that the strategic air forces should be asked to plan an attack. Intelligence had established by then that the plant was also producing the Jumo jet engine, and the V 2 offensive was becoming heavier.[80]

78. CAB 121/215, DO(45) 1st Meeting, 26 January.
79. ibid, COS(44)984 of 21 November, COS(45)36 of 13 January, COS(44)389th and 409th(o) Meetings, 4 and 22 December.
80. ibid, COS(45)47(o) of 16 January, 51(o) of 18 January, COS(45)17th Meeting, 17 January.

CHAPTER 57

The Threat from Other Unconventional Weapons

THE POSSIBILITY that the Germans would resort to chemical warfare continued to worry the Allied political and military authorities until the end of 1944, if only in particularly anxious times like the approach of D-day in Normandy and towards the end of the Ardennes offensive. In the view of the intelligence bodies, the threat was becoming increasingly remote, and the possibility that the enemy would resort to biological warfare, which was the subject of diplomatic rumours and agents' reports from the end of 1943, was even less likely to materialise. For these conclusions they had substantial evidence, both positive and negative, from Sigint; but in the nature of the case they could not give absolute assurances.

The possible use of gas by the Germans had been discussed by the Allies, for the first time since the spring of that year, in August 1943 at the Quebec conference, the Italians having reported during the armistice negotiations that Ribbentrop had threatened to use gas against them. The Combined Chiefs of Staff had decided against issuing a declaration of their determination to retaliate until the armistice was concluded, though authorising General Eisenhower to make such a declaration then, if he thought appropriate.[1]

There is no evidence that the JIC was consulted over these decisions; nor did the voluminous Sigint from Italy contain, either then or later, any suggestion that the Germans contemplated the use of gas there.* But during September 1943 the JIC was involved in the revision of the paper of April 1943 in which the Anglo-American Combined Intelligence Committee had concluded that Germany and Japan were unlikely to initiate gas

---

* See below pp 577, 578, 579, 581.

1. CAB 121/100, SIC file A/Policy/Chemical Warfare/1, Vol I, COS(Q) 42 of 22 August and note to the Prime Minister, 24 August 1943, NAF 344 of 30 August; CAB 121/101, A/Policy/Chemical Warfare/1, Vol 2, COS(43) 206th (o) Meeting, 2 September, WM(43)123 of 6 September, FAN 221 of 8 September 1943.

warfare in the near future.* In the course of the discussions on the subject with the JIC in Washington the London JIC noted that, since the spring, in the context of the Soviet advances and the expectation of an invasion of western Europe, 'a considerable number of reports' had suggested that Germany would resort to gas. But it could find no convincing support for them, and it believed on general grounds that 'the likelihood of Germany using gas [had become] more remote'. As well as being deterred by Allied air superiority, she must surely realise that in the event of her defeat, 'a possibility now widely appreciated', such action would incur increased Allied retribution; and as for the contingency of a wild decision by Hitler, the General Staff was now more likely than before to obstruct its execution.[2] The new edition of the CIC's paper, issued on 9 October, adopted these conclusions.[3]

The JIC returned to the subject in November 1943 when it was asked for its views on the suggestion that the Allies should threaten to use gas in retaliation for Germany's resort to V-weapons against the United Kingdom.† It advised against the suggestion for several reasons. The use of gas would appreciably lower German morale, but morale was 'already very low', and gas attacks were not likely to produce unconditional surrender. Russia, who would expect to be consulted, would probably object to the Allies initiating gas warfare if she was waging a successful war of movement at the time. Germany's preparations for civilian defence against gas were 'fairly complete' and Hitler would certainly retaliate, perhaps by using the V-weapons for chemical warfare.[4] On the strength of these arguments the Chiefs of Staff advised the Defence Committee on 8 December against announcing that gas warfare would be initiated in retaliation for the V-weapons. At the same time, they accepted the conclusion of the Joint Planners that, 'so far as is known', Germany had no new gas against which British defences would be inadequate. This conclusion, as we now know, was inaccurate;‡ but it perhaps strengthened the Chiefs of Staff in the view, which was itself correct, that they could safely ignore rumours to the effect that Germany planned to initiate the use of gas with the V-weapons.[5]

These rumours, which were coming in from agents and Allied and neutral embassies, were referring to the threat of biological as

---

* See Volume II, p 121.
† See Volume III, Part 1, pp 399, 415 fn.
‡ See Volume II, p 119 (n).

2. JIC(43)373(o) of 9 September, 386(o) of 21 September.
3. CAB 121/101, JIC(43)423(o) of 9 October.
4. JIC(43)499(o) of 11 November.
5. CAB 121/101, COS(43)754(o) of 8 December.

well as chemical warfare. They were taken somewhat more seriously in the United States.* The OSS, while recognising that they were inconclusive, brought them to the attention of the US Chiefs of Staff in December 1943; and in January 1944 the US authorities stepped up their own biological warfare research.[6] They also advocated that anti-biological warfare precautions should be taken by the troops to be landed in Normandy, a post-war report on their activities noting that 'prior to the invasion of Europe in June 1944 it was generally considered by most of the intelligence agencies that our enemies had made considerable preparations for biological warfare and were using it in a war of nerves as a threatened secret weapon'. This report conceded, however, that 'on several occasions British intelligence could not see eye to eye with our efforts ... Their experts ... had not construed intelligence reports as we evidently had and did not foresee any danger from this agent'.[7] This was certainly the JIC's view when it reported on the eve of D-day at the request of SHAEF. It pointed out that it could not give an absolutely conclusive answer because there was no evidence from reliable sources – biological warfare had not been mentioned in Sigint – but it was confident that it would have received firm evidence that Germany was engaged in defence training and an immunisation programme if she had reached a stage at which she was able to resort to biological warfare.[8]

The British assessment of the threat from gas underwent no change in the six months before D-day. In February 1944 the *Overlord* Executive Planning Committee, making no reference to biological warfare, asked the JIC whether the Germans would use gas against the United Kingdom before and during the Normandy landings. The JIC replied that the possibility that she would use gas before D-day was 'so remote as to be negligible', and it felt she was unlikely to do so after D-day unless she had first used it in military operations and the Allies had retaliated by using gas against her civilian population; in that event she would not use gas on a scale that would seriously interfere with *Overlord*.[9] A month

---

* See Volume III, Part 1, p 48.

6. Report to the Secretary of War by Mr George W Merck, printed with Hearings before the sub-committee on Health and Scientific Research of the Committee on Human Resources, US Senate, Ninety-fifth Congress (Washington, 1977), p 67.

7. Raymond C Cochrane, *Biological Warfare Research in the United States* (History of the Chemical Warfare Service in World War II) November 1947. Regraded unclassified per 743184, pp 136–138.

8. JIC(44)231(o) of 5 June, in reply to SHAEF's request in JIC(44)225(o) of 31 May.

9. JIC(44)44(o) of 3 February.

later the JIC replied in similar terms when asked whether Germany might be emboldened to resort to gas if she felt that a decisive defeat of *Overlord* would enable her to obtain an early end to the war: it was unlikely that she would conclude that any advantage to be derived from using gas could be decisive before the Allies had retaliated.[10]

On 14 March the Chiefs of Staff accepted the JIC's conclusions.[11] Though the CAS then thought it remained possible that Germany would use gas in defence of the beaches as distinct from resorting to it in a wholesale attack, SHAEF made no such qualification when it issued on 25 March a statement of its views about Allied policy with regard to retaliation; this began by saying that 'there is at present no evidence that the Germans intended to begin chemical warfare'.[12] The question under discussion was whether the Allies should announce in advance that they would retaliate if Germany resorted to chemical warfare on the beaches. On 28 April the Chiefs of Staff, on the advice of the Joint Planners, decided against issuing such a warning unless they received 'firm intelligence' of her intention to do so.[13]

On 9 April, commenting on the draft of a new periodical report by the Inter-Services Committee on Chemical Warfare, the JIC had meanwhile repeated that it was 'still improbable' that Germany would initiate the use of gas.[14] It did not dispute the evidence in the Inter-Services Committee's report to the effect that the German armed forces were equipped for and against chemical warfare, and that Germany maintained the production of gas at a high level and was engaged in unremitting research for new materials and methods.* But it insisted that such evidence was of no value in determining whether she intended to initiate gas warfare or had the capacity to do so at short notice – which the JIC doubted on the strength of the general considerations that were likely to influence her decisions.

The JIC made it plain when delivering its judgments that it had no positive evidence for them, and was unlikely to receive any. But

---

* The report was circulated on 17 May.[15] Its evidence, which included indications that Germany had introduced two new types of gas containers, FE 41 and FE 42, in two successive years, had come mainly from captured documents and equipment. But a single naval Enigma decrypt of 8 February had mentioned that FE 42 was to be stored under special safeguards.[16]

10.   CAB 121/101, JIC(44)89(o) of 9 March.
11.   ibid, COS(44) 85th (o) Meeting, 14 March.
12.   ibid, COS(44)304(o) of 30 March (SHAEF Operation Memorandum No 15 of 25 March).
13.   ibid, JP(44)91 of 26 April, COS(44) 138th (o) Meeting, 28 April.
14.   JIC(44)142 of 9 April.
15.   CAB 121/101, COS(44)420(o) of 17 May.
16.   DEFE 3/137, VL 5795 of 8 February 1944.

it was no doubt fortified by the indications, mostly negative, that were being provided by Sigint. It mentioned in the March report that it had information on Germany's arrangements for the removal of gas stocks from Italy and from dumps in France which might support the inference that she was anxious not to provoke gas warfare. This information was in part derived from a high-grade decrypt of October 1943 which had given instructions for the transport of Italian gas stocks to Germany; the decrypt had added that if safe transport was in doubt the material was to be destroyed in such a way as to avoid arousing suspicions that Germany was initiating the use of gas.[17] There was another decrypt in December 1943 about the safe custody in Italy of Italian gas stocks for which there was no storage capacity in Germany.[18] In February 1944 a decrypt from Fliegerführer North-West expressed some anxiety about the possible use of gas by the Allies.[19]

The intelligence situation did not change in the few weeks before *Overlord* was launched. The only references to the subject in the German decrypts in April and May were an incomplete report about the distribution of new filters in the Mediterranean, an order from OKH to the effect that gas ammunition stored in Rome was to be sunk at sea at least six miles from the coast and instructions from the Sea Defence Commandant in western Greece on 26 May for the testing of anti-gas preparations.[20] Two signals on the subject from the Japanese naval authorities in Berlin were also decrypted. The first, obtained on 6 May, was to the effect that Germany would not initiate gas warfare but would not hesitate to use gas in reprisal.[21] The second, decrypted on 18 May, reported that the Germans believed it unlikely that the Allies would resort to gas when they opened the second front; gas warfare would be disadvantageous to them and there was a complete lack of evidence of preparations for it in the equipment of aircraft and in other directions.[22]

On 22 May the Chiefs of Staff reiterated their advice that the Allies should not issue an advance warning that they would retaliate if Germany initiated gas warfare.[23] A few days later, while making it plain that he did not believe that Germany would use gas

---

17. CX/MSS/3305/T35.
18. CX/MSS/T37/23.
19. DEFE 3/136, VL 5712 of 7 February 1944.
20. DEFE 3/652, ZTPGM 69283; DEFE 3/153, KV 3293 of 9 May; CX/MSS/T200/89, DEFE 3/164, KV 6132 of 2 June.
21. JMA 6193 of 6 May.
22. SJA 184 of 18 May.
23. CAB 121/101, COS(44)450(o) of 22 May.

tactically, the Prime Minister nevertheless asked them to reconsider their opposition to an advance warning of retaliation; they stuck to their view and he accepted it.[24] But he could not contain his true feelings when on 11 June he saw the first decrypt obtained on the subject of gas after D-day. A message from OKW of 2 June, decrypted and sent out to the Allied Commands from GC and CS on 10 June, it asked C-in-C South-West (Kesselring) to 'report by return whether the English, American and French troops are carrying their respirators or whether they are carried with the baggage trains'.[25] On 11 June the Prime Minister wrote a letter to Eisenhower and requested in a minute marked 'Action this day' that it be sent at once by special messenger. It said:

> This telegram seems to me to be of the greatest importance, and may portend action on the part of the enemy. I presume you will have it conveyed to General Montgomery. It is quite possible that Hitler will use this weapon. I have already asked for consideration whether we should not give a full warning beforehand of what the consequences would be to them.

'C' forwarded the letter with a covering note pointing out that the message had been sent to Kesselring in Italy, though it might have been repeated to Rundstedt and other commanders, and suggesting that if Eisenhower had any comment he should send it on the SCU/SLU link.[26]

There is no record of any response to the Prime Minister from Eisenhower or Montgomery. It is clear, however, that although the number of Sigint references to gas increased after D-day, none of them called for any revision of the JIC's long-standing assessment of the danger. A decrypt of 12 June disclosed that OKH had refused Kesselring's request for a medical officer with gas training.[27] Signals decrypted on 10 and 21 June reported the despatch of anti-gas equipment to Cherbourg and Brest.[28] Another decrypt of 21 June indicated that the FE 42 gas container was being distributed in north-west France.[29] It was not inconceivable that such a measure was in preparation for the first use of gas, but in the absence of more telling evidence this seemed highly unlikely. Among the Japanese diplomatic telegrams, moreover, one from the Consul-General in Vienna, decrypted on 22 June, reported that Germany had refrained from chemical warfare in

---

24. ibid, COS(44) 169th and 173rd (o) Meetings, 25 and 26 May.
25. DEFE 3/169, KV 7277 of 10 June.
26. Dir/C Archive, 6764 of 11 June.
27. DEFE 3/170, KV 7726 of 12 June.
28. DEFE 3/169, KV 7332 of 10 June; DEFE 3/176, KV 9057 of 21 June.
29. DEFE 3/176, KV 9057 of 21 June.

the knowledge that the British possessed a superior liquid gas.[30] On 28 June the JIC advised the Inter-Services Committee on Chemical Warfare that as Germany had not used gas during the initial phase of Operation *Overlord*, her resort to it had become even more improbable.[31]

Such information as was obtained in July bore out the accuracy of the JIC's conclusion. There were further references in the Enigma to the disposal of gas stores by sinking off the Italian coast.[32] By 17 July examination of captured material had established that the Germans had undertaken no preparations for the use of gas in the Cherbourg area, and under interrogation the Sea Defence Commandant, Normandy had insisted that Germany had no intention of initiating gas warfare. Other decrypts disclosed unambiguously that the Germans were anxious lest the Allies might initiate it. A decrypt of 12 July warned that their use of smoke shells in Normandy might develop into gas attacks.[33] Another of 30 July contained an order of 29 July to 5th Jagd Division: it was not to use practice gas ammunition-pouring bottles, gas candles and tear and nose gas generators – lest this enabled the Allies to assert that Germany had initiated gas warfare.[34]

At the insistence of the Prime Minister, the pros and cons of first use of gas, as also of biological warfare, by the Allies had nevertheless been under examination in Whitehall since the first week of July. On 5 July, in consultation with the JIC, the Joint Planners had completed another enquiry into the merits of using gas in retaliation against the V-weapons. They had recommended, once again, that the Allies should not initiate gas warfare; against the V-weapons sites gas would have only a harrassing effect, and its use against them might unleash chemical warfare in Normandy.[35] The Chiefs of Staff had accepted the recommendation on 6 July.[36] On the same day, however, declaring that he would not use it unless it was a matter of life and death, or would shorten the war by a year, the Prime Minister had asked them for a 'cold-blooded calculation' of the case for using gas. His motive was not only the possibility that the bombardment of London by the V-weapons might become 'a serious nuisance' but also the need to gain more ground in Normandy 'so as not to be cooped up in a

---

30. BAY/KV 231 of 23 June.
31. JIC(44)278(o) of 28 June.
32. DEFE 3/55, XL 1938 of 14 July; DEFE 3/64, XL 4104 of 30 July.
33. DEFE 3/54, XL 1687 of 12 July.
34. DEFE 3/64, XL 4052 of 30 July.
35. CAB 121/101, JP(44)177 of 5 July.
36. ibid, COS(44) 222nd (o) Meeting, 5 July.

small area'; and he felt it was 'absurd to consider morality on this topic when everybody used it in the last war without a word of complaint from the moralists or the Church'.[37]

The Chiefs of Staff completed their review on 28 July, the Prime Minister having expressed impatience at the delay.[38] The JIC advised them that the Germans would at once retaliate and that, although the immediate effect of a gas attack would be to lower morale in Germany, morale would recover as protective measures improved.[39] The Joint Planners advised them that gas warfare would seriously interrupt war production in Germany and England, but that the advantage would lie with the Allies as they could deliver a heavier scale of attack.[40] The Chiefs of Staff's advice to the Prime Minister was that the first use of gas or biological warfare by the Allies would have no decisive effect on the duration or the result of the war.[41] In accepting their advice the Prime Minister commented: 'But clearly I cannot make head against the parsons and warriors at the same time'.[42]

In the middle of August the Inter-Services Committee on Chemical Warfare put it to the JIC that, following the July plot and the subsequent purge of army officers, the General Staff might be less able to restrain Hitler from resorting to the use of gas.[43]* The JIC conceded in its reply of 24 August that the only contingency in which Hitler might order the use of gas had arisen, in that he now faced 'imminent military disaster'. But it noted that it had still received no evidence of preparations to resort to gas or of any acceleration in anti-gas precautions; and it insisted that because the German Army and Air Force were no longer in a position to initiate gas warfare even if they were ordered to do so, and because it was obvious that Germany would suffer most from any attempt to resort to gas, even this danger had receded.[45] As it happened, the only intelligence item of any consequence since the

---

* This anxiety was not wholly unfounded. Speer later testified that pressure for use of nerve gas was at this stage growing in a limited circle of Hitler's entourage, mostly from Goebbels, Bormann and Ley. He added, however, that, although Hitler toyed with the idea of using it on the eastern front, he was deterred by the risk of Allied retaliation in view of Allied air superiority.[44]

37.   ibid, PM Personal Minute to the COS D 217/4 of 6 July.
38.   ibid, PM Minute D 234/4 of 25 July.
39.   JIC(44)311(o) of 18 July, 328(o) of 26 July.
40.   CAB 121/101, COS(44)661(o) of 26 July.
41.   ibid, COS(44) 251st (o) Meeting, 28 July, Annex I.
42.   ibid, PM Minute D 238/4 of 29 July.
43.   ibid, Minute to the JIC, 18 August.
44.   Stockholm International Peace Research Institute (SIPRI), *The Problems of Chemical and Biological Warfare*, Vol I (1971), pp 301–302, 314.
45.   JIC(44)376(o) of 24 August.

end of July had been received on 17 August: the decrypt of a telegram in which the Japanese Ambassador in Berlin reported that Speer had told him that 'the present war gas' was superior to the hydrocyanic gas or anything similar, but had added that Germany did not intend to use gas unless driven to it.[46] The NID commented that this remark left it uncertain whether she would use gas only in retaliation or would do so if driven by military necessity. The JIC was clearly unimpressed; its paper did not mention this item.

On 14 September SHAEF announced that 'the most likely period for the use of gas' in Normandy was over, and ordered a reduction in the scale of provision of anti-gas equipment.[47] In the middle of November, however, and again at the end of December, prompted by the fear that Hitler might be tempted to use gas in the field if the Ardennes offensive succeeded in breaking through to the Meuse, SHAEF asked the JIC whether its views had changed.[48] The JIC replied reassuringly on both occasions, though it admitted in the December reply that the development feared by SHAEF could not be absolutely excluded.[49] There had by then been little new intelligence since August. At the Tolstoy conference in Moscow in October the Russian General Staff had reported references by POW to a new secret weapon; the Russians wondered whether this might be gas, but had added that they had no firm evidence to support the suggestion.[50] An Enigma decrypt had disclosed that the Germans were still sinking gas ammunition at sea off the Italian coast.[51] Early in November, however, the British and American Military Attachés in Ankara had received a report to the effect that Germany was producing a heavy odourless gas for use against towns. And on 11 December the Enigma had referred for the first time to gas stocks in Germany; a decrypt of that date reported the distribution of 'Sondermunition K', mostly to north and central Germany, from depots at Lübbecke and Krugau (near Berlin).[52] The JIC commented on this decrypt in its reply to SHAEF at the end of December; as the distribution was taking place inside Germany, away from the fighting fronts, it pointed to the dispersal of stocks rather than to

---

46. BAY/XL 107 of 18 August.
47. CAB 121/102, SIC file A Policy/Chemical Warfare/1, Vol 3, SHAEF Operation Memorandum No 15 of 14 September 1944.
48. JIC(44)475(o) of 18 November: *Possibility of the Germans using Gas on the Western Front*, Strong telegram to JIC S72801 of 29 December.
49. JIC(44)475(o) of 18 November, 515(o) of 31 December.
50. CAB 121/160, SIC file A/Strategy/15, COS(44)915(o) of 26 October, p 3.
51. DEFE 3/231, HP 1523 of 29 September.
52. DEFE 3/316, HP 9136 of 11 December.

preparations for initiating gas warfare.[53] But SHAEF's anxiety was not allayed. On 7 January 1945, when it was clear that the Germans were abandoning the Ardennes offensive, it informed the JIC that it was disturbed by the recent increase in the frequency with which Sigint was referring to gas.[54]

Decrypts on the subject had indeed increased in number from the end of December. Some had referred to anti-gas equipment in depots or with military units.[55] One had requested all fortresses in the west to confirm that all details about Germany's war gases had been destroyed.[56] Another had disclosed that the GAF was enquiring about the manufacture and storage of war gases in the Nuremberg area.[57] In a message dated 20 December, signalled by GC and CS to the Commands on 26 December, OKH had emphasised to C-in-C West the importance of capturing American gas mask filters in the condition in which they had left the factory.[58] This last decrypt had particularly alarmed SHAEF; in its signal of 7 January to the JIC it suggested that Germany's decision as to whether or not to initiate gas warfare might depend on her discovering whether she had gases against which the American respirator was ineffective.[59]

Replying to SHAEF on 8 January the JIC conceded that some of these references, unlike earlier ones, might indicate that Germany was preparing to initiate gas warfare, and that it would carry out an urgent review.[60]* Two days later the Washington JIC took the view that while there was still no firm evidence of the intention to do so, Germany's fanatical leadership might well employ gas at any time.[61] On 18 January the Prime Minister made a statement in the House of Commons to the effect that the Allies would instantly retaliate if the Germans resorted to gas warfare.

Intelligence appreciations on Germany's preparations for biological warfare had meanwhile remained unchanged since the JIC's pronouncement of June 1944.† In July, when the Chiefs of Staff were considering the circumstances in which the Allies might

---

* For the report made as a result of this review see Appendix 28.
† See above, p 575.

53. JIC(44)515(o) of 31 December.
54. GAD/SH 209 of 7 January 1945.
55. DEFE 3/323, BT 770 of 30 December; DEFE 3/325, BT 1448 of 6 January.
56. DEFE 3/325, BT 1460 of 6 January.
57. ibid, BT 1326 of 5 January.
58. DEFE 3/321, BT 414 of 26 December.
59. GAD/SH 209 of 7 January.
60. *Possibility of the Germans using gas on the Western Front,* JIC (London) telegram to JIC (SHAEF) of 8 January; JIC(45)11(o) of 8 January.
61. *Possibility of the Germans using gas on the Western Front,* 'C' to JIC (London) with JIC(W) telegram of 10 January.

initiate the use of gas,* the JIC had extended its share of the enquiry to biological warfare, and had repeated its earlier assurance: there was still no good evidence that Germany was in a position to initiate it, and there would be if she were.[62] This was still the case at the end of September; the JIC's conclusion was then endorsed by the Sub-Committee on Biological Warfare, which the Chiefs of Staff had set up in June to advise on Allied preparations for and against the use of biological weapons.[63] The Sub-Committee could not exclude the possibility that Germany would authorise the use of the weapons on a limited scale by saboteurs or resort to them in a final act of desperation; but it noted that there was no reliable evidence for this conjecture and that the Italian authorities had reported that when they had given up work on biological warfare in 1940 the Germans had also abandoned it.[64] In October the Sub-Committee circulated an analysis by MI 10 of the reports that had been received on the subject up to the beginning of September; most of them had given 'chiefly imaginative' information which could be 'dismissed summarily on technical grounds', and none of them had mentioned such essential precautions as the inoculation of troops.[65] In November it thought the danger that Germany would use biological warfare was remote.[66]†

□

That this was also true of the threat of atomic weapons had

---

* See above, p 580.

† This was the last pronouncement on the subject. In February 1945 the Sub-Committee learned that the authorities in the United States remained unconvinced that there was no danger, but it did not pursue the suggestion that, because of the American doubts, another review of the evidence was called for.[67] The post-war Cochrane Report on biological warfare research in the United States (see above, p 575) records that 'not until early 1945 was it generally agreed to be too late for Germany to use biological warfare as a tactical weapon', and that 'the findings of the *Alsos* mission were the first indication that the truth about enemy activities was considerably at variance with the intelligence reports'. The provisional findings of the *Alsos* mission were reported to the Chiefs of Staff in June; they included the news that Hitler had apparently forbidden all work on offensive biological warfare and the fact that, although this order had not been obeyed to the letter, the German work had been inferior to that of the Allies in the quality of the personnel employed and the scope of the research.[68]

62. JIC(44)311(o) of 18 July.
63. CAB 121/103, SIC file A/Policy/Chemical Warfare/2, COS(44)514(o) of 12 June, BW(44) 1st Meeting of 8 July.
64. ibid, BW(44) 20 of 29 September, COS(44)892(o) (Restricted) of 10 October (BW(44)21).
65. ibid, BW (44) 24 of 19 October.
66. ibid, BW (44) 28 of 24 November.
67. ibid, BW (45) 1 of 1 February, COS(45)160(o) of 9 March (BW(45)3), COS (45) 68th Meeting, 14 March.
68. ibid, BW (45) 10 of 4 June.

become the settled opinion of the British scientists attached to the Directorate of Tube Alloys (DTA) since the summer of 1943, when they concluded that, while the Germans were researching on atomic energy, their primary objective was not the production of a weapon but the development of power, and that the danger that they would acquire an atomic weapon before they were defeated could be discounted.[69]* The intelligence committee set up by the US TA organisation early in 1943, with which the exchange of intelligence and assessment was complete from the summer of 1943,[70]† did not accept this conclusion without reservations until its accuracy was established beyond all doubt by the capture of German scientists and documents in the closing months of the war. But none of the intelligence received after the summer of 1943 persuaded the authorities in London to revise their views.

The correctness of their 1943 assessment and their success in thereafter building upon it 'an almost uncannily accurate picture of the German effort'[71] were remarkable in view of the fact that TA was a subject on which it was difficult to obtain reliable intelligence. Sigint threw no light on it since the German work, which was in any case shrouded in secrecy, did not get beyond the research stage. On account of the need for preserving secrecy about the Allied interest in the work, the Allied intelligence-gathering agencies could not be briefed in detail, only instructed generally to search for information on new weapons, unusual new materials and new scientific activity.‡ But the SIS was able to set these precautions aside in its contacts with scientists in neutral countries and, through them, with well-disposed scientists in Germany; it was these contacts, to the development of which the SIS attached the highest priority, which provided the bulk of the evidence in the period before the Allied occupation forces were able to seize documents and interrogate scientists on the continent.

In October 1943 Niels Bohr – urged to do so by Lord Cherwell – escaped from Copenhagen to London. In messages sent to London in the previous June he had implied that he did not think it possible that Germany would produce an atomic bomb; but he had added that although it would 'hardly be responsible to rely on

---

* See Volume II, pp 122–128.

   † For full details about the DTA and the US TA organisation see Gowing, *Britain and Atomic Energy 1939–1945* (1964) and R G Hewlett and O E Anderson, *The New World 1939–1946* (Pennsylvania State UP 1962).

   ‡ See Appendix 29.

69. Gowing, *Britain and Atomic Energy 1939–1945* (1964), p 367.
70. ibid, p 149; information from Sir Michael Perrin.
71. Gowing, op cit, p 368.

the effects of a single bomb . . . procurable only with an enormous effort, the situation would of course be quite different if it were true that enough heavy water could be made to manufacture a large number of atomic bombs'. After his arrival in London different people derived slightly different impressions from his statements on the views he had formed from meeting German physicists regularly in Copenhagen. ADI (Sc) gathered from him that Heisenberg had at least implied that Germany was working on an atomic bomb.[72] The recollection of Sir Michael Perrin (of the DTA) is that Bohr believed that the Germans had concluded that the project was impracticable in the timescale of the war; their research programme was slackening off and the greater part of their effort was probably being devoted to the use of heavy water for ordinary uranium bombs, which would do no more damage than a heavy conventional bombing raid.[73]*

The DTA's appreciation that 'the Germans were not tackling atomic energy in a big way and that the Allies need fear the use neither of atomic bombs nor of radioactive fission products by the Germans' was strengthened by further evidence by the end of 1943.[75] By then a report had been obtained of a talk between a Swiss scientist and the German Professor Clusius.. Clusius had said that he had abandoned work on uranium at Munich, that the separation of uranium isotopes by diffusion had been given up as hopeless and that though a method based on the solubility of isotopes in the form of salts in alcohols was being attempted in Berlin, nothing of any practical value had yet emerged. It was known that Professor Hahn, an anti-Nazi who had been in the forefront of uranium experiments in 1938, had gone to Sweden to lecture on uranium fission. The DTA felt that if any large-scale work was going on in Germany the Germans would not have allowed this, as they would have had to assume that however secret the work was, Hahn would know about it. The US authorities had received reports to the effect that 700 tons of sodium uranate were still at the Union Minière refinery at Oolen in Belgium; if true,

---

* In the spring and summer of 1944 Bohr was to be more emphatic that 'from all information available to us', Germany had never in the initial stages of the war deemed it worthwhile to attempt to produce a bomb. He was commenting on rumours that a large increase was taking place in Germany's nuclear activity, which he thought might be attributable to the fact that Germany had got wind of the progress of the Allies. He was by then pressing the US and British governments to accept international control of atomic weapons, and he added that 'one must be prepared that a competition in the near future may become a serious reality'.[74]

72. Jones, *Most Secret War* (1978), p 473.
73. Information from Sir Michael Perrin.
74. CAB 126/39, Memoranda of 18 April, 19 and 30 May, 3 July 1944.
75. Gowing, op cit, p 367.

they were in the DTA's view 'the strongest possible proof' that Germany was not doing any large-scale TA work. In fact, the SIS had information that these reports referred to part of the stock of uranium oxide at Oolen which had been sent to Duisburg at the end of 1942, but which had been returned to Oolen for conversion to ammonium uranate; but the DTA was still unable to connect interest in ammonium uranate with work on a TA project.[76] Documents received from the Norwegian underground at the end of the year had established that the USAAF raid in November 1943 had virtually put an end to the production of heavy water at Vemork.[77]* The DTA summed up the evidence in a report on 5 January 1944:

'All the evidence available to us leads us to the conclusion that the Germans are not in fact carrying out large-scale work on any aspect of TA. We believe that after an initial serious examination of the project, the German work is now confined to academic and small-scale research, much of which is being published in current issues of their scientific journals'.[78]

The chief subject of this report was the question whether, accepting that Germany was not working on a bomb, she might still be developing radio-active fission products for military use. Washington had raised this matter in the summer of 1942† and again in August and September 1943. On the second of these occasions, US experts had suggested, not on the basis of any evidence but in the course of a feasibility study, that the Germans might be able in the course of the next year to use heavy water to produce radio-active solids for use in bombs, and to do so on a scale sufficient to make it necessary to evacuate parts of London.[79] In September 1943 the DTA had discounted 'any imminent danger of this weapon being used against us'; there was no evidence that Germany had the requisite power machine, and if she had, she would be much more likely to use it to separate plutonium for the development of a weapon which would be much more effective than fission products. It had allowed, however, that, as fission products would probably be produced more quickly, she might turn to them in an attempt to avert

---

* See Volume II, p 127.
† See Volume II, p 126.

76. CAB 126/177, 'Possible use of fission products as a military weapon', 5 January 1944.
77. ibid, ADI(K) 511A/1943 of 22 December, 2/1944 of 2 January.
78. ibid, 'Possible use of fission products as a military weapon', 5 January.
79. UK Atomic Energy Archive, TA (43) 1st Meeting, 20 August; TA (43) 1 of 8 September. (Copies in CAB 126/47).

defeat; and the TA Consultative Council had authorised work to start on the design and development of a simple detector.[80] In December 1943 Washington had returned to the subject, this time because reference in the neutral Press to the existence of a decisive German secret weapon had led the US experts to speculate that the enemy might be planning to use TA as a radio-active powder in the V-weapons.[81]

The DTA's report of 5 January 1944 again dismissed this speculation. It also expressed the view that any decision by the Allies to embark on large-scale precautionary measures might, by alerting the enemy, increase the difficulty of obtaining reliable intelligence about Germany's actual TA work.[82] In view of this second consideration, and also because it believed that 'we should receive information in sufficient time if the Germans were really engaged on a large-scale programme which involved, as it would have to do, an industrial effort comparable to . . . any one of the different parts of the American TA programme', it recommended in a separate report on the same day that no serious effort should be devoted to the development of detectors.[83] These conclusions were conveyed to General Ismay for the Chiefs of Staff and to General Groves, the head of the US TA organisation.[84] General Groves replied later in January:

'We agree that the use of TA weapon is unlikely. The indirect and negative evidence developed by your agencies to date is in support of this conclusion. But we also feel that as long as definite possibilities exist which question the correctness of this opinion in its entirety or in part, we cannot afford to accept it as a final conclusion'.[85]

No further information came to hand in the first half of 1944 except that in March a US mission, which had been interviewing Italian scientists to find out whether they knew anything about a German TA programme, reported that it had come across no evidence pointing to experimental activity with explosives based on nuclear energy. This persuaded General Groves's Military Committee that the German effort was still in the research

---

80. ibid, TA (43) 1 of 8 September; 2nd Meeting, 13 September; CAB 126/177, DTA letter of 2 September 1943.

81. CAB 126/177, Extract from Akers letter of 9 December 1943, ANCAM telegrams from Washington Nos 3 and 5 of 1 January 1944.

82. ibid, 'Possible use of fission products as a military weapon', 5 January.

83. ibid, 'Detectors for radioactive fission products', 5 January 1944.

84. ibid, CANAM telegram to Washington No 3 of 6 January; Anderson to Ismay, 7 January 1944.

85. ibid, ANCAM No 13 of 20 January. See also Groves, *Now it can be told* (1963), pp 186–187.

stage.[86]* But the Committee's reservations, however slight they had become, still caused a brief alarm a month before *Overlord*. On 11 May General Eisenhower informed General Marshall and the British Chiefs of Staff that he had been advised by General Groves that the possibility that the Germans would resort to radio-active fission weapons against the Normandy landings was 'infinitesimal and very remote'; he had passed the advice unofficially to a very limited number of people, but he was assuming that, since he had heard nothing officially from the Combined Chiefs of Staff, the enemy would not use radio-active fission products, a threat against which he had taken no adequate precautions.[88] This startled General Ismay into a request that the DTA should advise the Chiefs of Staff on this threat; they had either to tell General Eisenhower that it could be discounted or to put in hand urgent defensive measures.[89]

General Ismay was presumably informed that the DTA had reaffirmed on 11 May, when discussing the programme for the manufacture of detectors, that it was 'extremely unlikely' that Germany would resort to the military use of fission products.[90] On 19 May, following a discussion by the Chiefs of Staff at which they reduced the priority given to the detector programme and decided that there was no need for Service training in the use of detectors, he told General Eisenhower that they believed the threat was unlikely to arise and approved the limited action he had taken.[91]

In June 1944, when any lingering anxiety was being reduced by the non-appearance of radio-active fission products in the Normandy fighting and the V-weapons offensive, it was once more revived by a German scientist who disclosed that Auer Gesellschaft in Berlin was producing metallic uranium in large quantities. In view of the fact that there was no obvious commercial use for uranium metal, this report, which was followed by others to the effect that Auer Gesellschaft was receiving ammonium and sodium uranate from Oolen, prompted the DTA to suggest in September that the Auer Gesellschaft should be bombed; and the

---

* The report could not cover those scientists who were in Rome, but they had nothing to add when they were eventually interviewed.[87]

86. Groves, op cit, pp 189–194.
87. ibid, pp 208–210.
88. CAB 126/177, Eisenhower to Marshall and the COS, 11 May 1944.
89. ibid, Ismay minute of 13 May.
90. ibid, minutes of 11 May.
91. ibid, minutes of 18 May, letter to Eisenhower of 19 May, minute to DTA 20 May 1944.

the suggestion was still being discussed in October.[92] In October, however, Oolen was occupied by the Allies. Documents taken there showed that while its stocks had been removed to Germany in 1942, 80 tons had been sent back for conversion to ammonium uranate and return to Germany between October 1943 and March 1944, and that not all of this had yet been returned.* The DTA's comment on these transactions was that it was 'inconceivable' that the Germans were returning TA processed materials to Oolen for conversion to ammonium salt.[93] But Auer was destroyed by the US Eighth Air Force in March 1945 after documents found at Strasbourg had confirmed that it was involved in the manufacture of uranium metals for atomic energy.[94]

Apart from the interrogation of scientists in Italy, the seizure and examination of the Oolen plant was the second TA project carried out by the *Alsos* Mission. Set up under US Army control to investigate scientific targets in liberated Europe and Germany when they came under Allied occupation, the Mission had a TA section which had planned its programme in close liaison with the DTA through a Manhattan Project office in London since January 1944, but which did not originally intend to execute the programme jointly with the DTA.[95] The first instalment of the programme – separate interrogations of Professor Joliot in Paris by *Alsos* and the DTA – was completed in September 1944. Joliot's contacts with German scientists had not been close. But he had the 'very definite opinion' that those he knew whose reputation might have involved them had not been engaged on TA work. He had himself been ordered to resume TA research by Vichy in August 1943, but had not been pressed when he refused; he thought it possible that the initiative might have come from Germany, either because she had a secret project or because she had heard rumours of the work going on in the USA.[96] A DTA report in October on developments in Germany since 1942 noted that Joliot's judgment agreed with Bohr's, with what Italian scientists had said and with a recent report from one of Bohr's colleagues in Copenhagen. As for what he had said about the Vichy initiative – his sole factual evidence – the DTA thought that it fitted in with

---

* See p 938.

92. CAB 126/179, DTA to Anderson, 5 September 1944.
93. CAB 126/179, SAWTA telegram No 30 of 12 October.
94. CAB 126/244, TAIC 4th Meeting, 28 February 1945; Groves, op cit, pp 230–231.
95. Groves, op cit, pp 194–198, 207–208.
96. CAB 126/37, Report of 19 September 1944 on interviews with Joliot, by *Alsos* 28 and 30 August, by the DTA 5 and 7 September. See also Goudsmit, *Alsos; the Failure in German Science* (1947), pp 34–36.

the view that Germany had increased her research towards the end of 1943 as a result of rumours of the US programme, rather than in the belief that she could develop plants before the end of the war.[97]

The DTA report was followed by a joint Anglo-American report dated 28 November.* It concluded as follows:

'The information which has been obtained can only justify the conclusion that German work on TA has not yet reached a stage where the construction of large plants has started, and that there is no likelihood of the use by the Germans of a TA bomb, or of a TA power unit or the fission products which would be obtained from such a unit, for many months at least'.

It went on to recommend that in order to keep German curiosity to the minimum, further Allied investigations should be concentrated in the two areas of Berlin and Bisingen and be carried out jointly, DTA representatives being added to the *Alsos* forces and a joint Anglo–US Intelligence Committee being set up to assess their findings. The two governments accepted these recommendations in January 1945 and the TA Intelligence Committee's regular meetings began at the end of that month.[98]†

The decision to concentrate further investigations on Berlin and Bisingen arose in the first case from what had been learned about Auer Gesellschaft and, in the second, from reports that had been received about the whereabouts of Heisenberg. In the spring of 1944 the OSS and SIS had both heard that his Kaiser Wilhelm Institute had moved from Berlin to Bisingen, near Hechingen, towards the end of 1943, and in September it was reported to be at Hechingen.[100]‡ In October it was reported that Heisenberg was working on a bomb but not expecting success before the end of the war. British PR of the Hechingen area, begun in July, produced

---

* See Appendix 29.

† When the recommendations were being discussed in Whitehall 'C' argued that in the light of the difficulties experienced in the assessment of intelligence on the beams and the V-weapons (see, respectively, Volume I and Volume III Part 1), it was imperative to avoid confusion between the duties and responsibilities of scientific experts and intelligence officers by appointing two intelligence officers, ADI(Sc) and a representative of the SIS, to join Michael Perrin as the British members of the Intelligence Committee and by making them directly responsible to the Chiefs of Staff and not to the JIC.[99] The DTA offered no objection to 'C's proposal.

‡ After the raids on Stuttgart in July 1944 a police decrypt revealed that Heisenberg urgently needed coke for 'work of the utmost importance' at the Conselmann Physics Institute at Hechingen.

97.   CAB 126/184, DTA report of 5 October 1944, para 5.
98.   CAB 126/244, CANAM telegram No 179 of 1 January 1945, Minutes of
        meeting 23 January, TAIC First Meeting, 30 January.
99.   ibid, CANAM 8190 of 15 December 1944, Minute of 20 December.
100. Groves, op cit, pp 216–217.

no good results until November; it then showed that buildings at Bisingen which had been taken to be possibly associated with TA work were in fact producing shale oil.[101] At the end of November, however, the *Alsos* Mission reached the University of Strasbourg and, as well as obtaining confirmation that Auer Gesellschaft was manufacturing uranium metals, discovered that von Weizsäcker, who was known to be a colleague of Heisenberg, had left for Hechingen some months previously.

The documents captured in von Weizsäcker's office in Strasbourg and the interrogation of his staff left no doubt, on the other hand, that Germany's TA work had not developed beyond the experimental stage. They showed that although Hitler had been advised of the possibility of an atomic weapon in 1942, the Germans had failed to separate U 235 and that, while they had apparently started separation on a small scale by means of a centrifuge and were constructing a uranium pile, they had only recently succeeded in manufacturing uranium metal at Auer Gesellschaft and had not by August 1944 taken their experiments to the point at which they were aware of the difficulties they would have to overcome before the pile could function.[102] The assessment later provided by the US director of *Alsos* was that:

'In short, they were about as far as we were in 1940, before we had begun any large-scale efforts on the atom bomb at all. Although it was evident from the papers that the work had a high priority and that the Army was taking part in it, nowhere did we find evidence of a large effort. As far as the German scientists were concerned, the whole thing was still on an academic scale'.[103]

A British assessment of the Strasbourg evidence, as given at the time by ADI(Sc) to the Prime Minister, was that:

'Scientific research is proceeding on a fairly wide scale under the patronage of Goering, and a new way of effecting the vital refining may have been discovered; but there is no sign yet of any large production effort; and so a German TA weapon could probably not be made for some time. The work at present has a priority below oil repairs and fighter production'.[104]

There followed up to March 1945 several rumours to the effect that Germany had an atomic bomb.[105] It was possibly on account

---

101. Jones, op cit, pp 476–479; Groves, op cit, pp 216–217. See also Appendix 29.
102. Groves, op cit, pp 221–223; Goudsmit, op cit, pp 65–70. Samples of the Strasbourg documents appear in a preliminary report by Goudsmit of 8 December 1944 in the US National Archives, Records Group No 227 Folder 6 S-I Intelligence.
103. Goudsmit, op cit, pp 70–71.
104. Dir/C Archive, 8192 of 12 December 1944.
105. For example BAY/BT 140 of 29 March 1945.

of these rumours that some of the US military authorities remained sufficiently apprehensive as to be inclined to bomb Hechingen, where the exact location of the Kaiser Wilhelm Institute was fixed by PR at the end of February.[106] But they were finally convinced that Germany had not developed atomic weapons by information collected by *Alsos* when it entered Heidelberg towards the end of March.*

☐

In August 1944 the JIC listed, for the first time in a single consolidated analysis, all the new weapons with which intelligence had shown that – in contrast to the nuclear development – the Germans had made 'notable recent advances'.[113]

As for sea weapons, in addition to the new-type U-boats, *Schnorchel* and the KdK small craft, the paper listed the suction-armed mine (*Oyster*) and the anti-invasion mine (KMA or *Katie*), the acoustic homing torpedo (*Gnat*) and the zig-zag torpedo (*Curly* or *Lut*), deep-firing torpedoes, an infra-red search receiver and an infra-red searchlight, and a thermal DF set (*Donaugerät*), parts of which the JIC report said had been captured in France.†

---

* The Heidelberg evidence confirmed that the German work had not gone beyond the laboratory stage, and that it was related to the use of TA as a source of power, not to the development of a bomb. It was concerned with the development of uranium piles, with no sign of interest in plutonium or thorium. The development was being carried out by two competing groups, each with a small heavy water pile, one at Berlin, which had recently been evacuated to Stadtilm near Erfurt, and the other at Hechingen under Heisenberg.[107] *Alsos* captured the Stadtilm pile, partially dismantled, on 12 April.[108] On 17 April it located at Celle a new centrifuge laboratory, recently evacuated from Heidelberg, and found that 'the one centrifuge that would have been in working order would have taken 100 years to produce any useful results ...'[109] On 23 April it reached the Hechingen area where it located the second uranium pile, which was found to lack any kind of radiation protection, took charge of its stocks of heavy water and uranium oxide, captured Hahn and von Weizsacker, obtained from Weizsäcker further records about the German research programme, and eventually, on 3 May, captured Heisenberg.[110] The small scale of the German effort at the end of the war was finally confirmed by the examination of the installations at Stadtilm and Hechingen and the interrogation of the scientists. The interrogation showed, moreover, that 'the Germans knew practically nothing about the American and British effort: they believed they themselves were ahead of the Allies'.[111] At the news of Hiroshima, which reached them in their captivity, they could hardly believe that Allied scientists had solved a problem they had written off as insoluble within the expected time-scale of the war.[112]

† For *Oyster* and the KMA mine see above, pp 93–94, 165–167; for *Gnat* see Volume III

106. Goudsmit, op cit, p 75; CAB 126/244, TAIC 4th Meeting, 28 February 1945.
107. CAB 126/244, TAIC 6th Meeting, 9 April 1945; Groves, op cit, pp 231–233.
108. Goudsmit, op cit, pp 88–91.
109. ibid, pp 92–94.
110. CAB 126/244, TAIC 9 April; Groves, op cit, pp 241–244.
111. Gowing, op cit, p 368.
112. Groves, op cit, Chapter 24.
113. JIC(44)359(o) of 24 August.

The land weapons listed were high performance light anti-tank weapons for infantry; a new heavy tank (67 tons) armed with 8.8 cm guns which appeared to be superior to any Allied tank; heavy self-propelled 8.8 cm and 12.8 cm anti-tank guns, the former on Panther chassis, the latter on Tiger chassis; possibly a new heavy rocket which might carry a 1,500 lb warhead to a range of 25 miles; and new anti-handling devices for fitting to standard mines.

In addition to the V-weapons, Hs 293 and jet and rocket-propelled aircraft (He 280, Me 262, Me 163, Ar 234, Do 335 and He 219 were listed) the air weapons in the list were BV 246, the *Mistel* composite aircraft,* and liquid explosives and proximity fuses, for which, however, the evidence was only tentative.

The intelligence sources mentioned a few more developments by the end of 1944. POW referred to Hs 294 and 295, advances on Hs 293 which appeared to be associated with experiments with underwater explosions for sinking ships, and to experiments with a homing or steered projectile for the Flak defences, which was probably the *Wasserfall*, and other ground-to-air missiles.† They also reported the development of a new torpedo engine using hydrogen peroxide and other chemicals and running at 45 knots up to 25,000 yards; this was probably related to the Walter torpedo, which had been mentioned by Sigint. Sigint disclosed the intention to introduce another jet fighter, the He 162.‡ ADI(Sc) listed these developments in a memorandum in December in which he also analysed decrypts of signals from the Japanese Naval Attaché reporting at length on a demonstration of new naval, army and air weapons that had recently taken place at the armaments research establishment at Rechlin. Analysis of these decrypts established that nearly all the weapons shown to the Japanese had been included in the JIC's August report. The exceptions were two new army mortars which had not yet gone into production, a new anti-aircraft shell fitted with incendiary pellets which ignited on striking the target aircraft, and an air-to-air guided missile (the X–4) for launching from fighters against bombers.[114]

ADI(Sc)'s conclusions in this memorandum were that the Germans had been consistently fertile in producing new weapons; and that while the most notable were the new U-boats, new fuels

---

Part 1, p 220 et seq; for the zig-zag torpedo see above, p 455 and for the search receiver and searchlight see Volume III Part 1, pp 516 (n) and 702 (n 2).

* See above, p 168 for the use of *Mistel* off Normandy.

† See Volume III Part 1, p 51 (n).

‡ See below, pp 616–617.

114. SJA 1287 of 13 December; Dir/C Archive, Memo from ADI (Sci) of 22 December; Jones, op cit, p 464.

and rocket and jet propulsion, several others were now coming into production which, if available in sufficient numbers, would have a pronounced influence on operations if Germany could overcome the difficulties in producing them. In the event, if we leave aside the V-weapons, the new-type U-boats and the jet and rocket-propelled aircraft, together with *Schnorchel* and the KdK craft, there was to be little additional intelligence about the new weapons before the end of the war. In January 1945 Sigint was to reveal that the Germans had persisted with the development of *Mistel* after withdrawing it from the Channel; a decrypt then reported that an additional 40 had been commissioned urgently, and subsequent decrypts showed that some of the last GAF attacks of the war used *Mistel* against Russian bridges and power stations.[115] What were presumably references to the X–4 were to appear in decrypts in March and April 1945 which mentioned that Me 262 fighters were equipped with a new long-range air-to-air missile named R-4-M.[116] With these further exceptions, the other weapons did not come into service, or, like the new U-boats themselves, did not do so in time to affect the course of the war. After the end of 1944, moreover, the intelligence sources did not reveal the existence of new developments to which they had not already referred – with the single but disturbing exception that Sigint disclosed that work was proceeding on new U-boats (Types XVI B and XXVI W) which were to be still more revolutionary than Types XXI and XXIII.*

Sigint did indicate, on the other hand, that some earlier projects had been abandoned. Japanese signals decrypted in March 1945 reported that the Germans had given up the idea of producing a conventional four-engined bomber, which was presumably a reference to the Me 264 and the He 227.[117]† And in terms which appeared to spell the abandonment of the Ju 287, the six-engined jet-propelled bomber incorporating the principle of swept-forward wings to which POW had referred in the summer of 1943,‡ Japanese decrypts in April 1945 quoted the German Chief of Air Staff as saying that far from being able to drop bombs on the American mainland, Germany would not be in a position to launch even a V 2 attack there for another two years.[118] This

---

* See Volume III Part 1, p 239.

† See Volume III Part 1, p 347

‡ See Volume III Part 1, p 335.

115. DEFE 3/326, BT 1529 of 7 January 1945; ADM 223/317, OIC SI 1320 of 30 April.
116. eg DEFE 3/563, BT 9640 of 6 April.
117. SJAs 1685 and 1688 of 19 March.
118. SJA 1755 of 6 April.

aircraft, which made a test flight in the summer of 1944, was identified by PR at Rechlin in July 1944 and at Brandis in February 1945, and confirmed as being jet-propelled by a POW who had seen it early in 1945.[119]

□

Next only to the V 2, with which the Germans opened their offensive in September, and the new U-boats which, as we have seen, were causing the Allies grave anxiety by that time, the most serious of the new weapons were the jet and rocket aircraft, which seemed likely in the summer of 1944 to become operational at any time.

Despite their failure to make an appearance during the *Overlord* battles, uneasiness about the effect they might soon have on the Allied strategic bombing offensives continued to mount from the end of June. The evidence which the Enigma had by then provided to the effect that the new types were on the verge of entering squadron service was followed at the end of July by a Japanese decrypt containing a disturbing estimate of the progress of the production programme.* It was followed a few days later by the first encounter of the new types with the US bombers; during a raid on Leuna on 28 July seven Me 163 were sighted which did not attack but manoeuvred menacingly as though to demonstrate their superiority.[120] The bombing of jet and rocket manufacturing plants and testing establishments by the US Air Forces, which had begun in April, was increased in July and again in August.[121]

The identification of these targets by POW and PR had been confirmed by the Enigma, but neither Sigint nor any other source reported on the outcome of the attacks. Scattered references in decrypts did indicate, however, that if not as a result of the attacks, then for other reasons, the production and the movement towards operational readiness of the new types were proceeding less fast than had been expected. On 6 August AI calculated on the basis of order of battle intelligence and its experience of GAF training procedures that not more than a total of 100 jet and rocket-propelled aircraft would be operational by September.[122] Later in August the decrypts carried the disturbing news that the first front-line Me 262 unit, formed out of a disbanded bomber

---

* See Volume III Part 1, pp 350–352.

119. *Air Ministry Intelligence*, pp 374–375; Irving, *The Rise and Fall of the Luftwaffe* (1974), pp 253, 280.

120. Craven and Cate, *The Army Air Forces in World War II*, Vol III (Chicago 1951), p 295.

121. ibid, p 288.

122. Air Sunset 216 of 6 August 1944.

Gruppe from I/KG 51, had been set up in France; but by 2 September they had disclosed that it had been forced to withdraw to Holland, that it was an experimental unit designed to gain front-line experience in the ground-attack role, and that it was having teething troubles partly on account of the difficulty of obtaining adequately trained crews.[123] In August a decrypt carried a directive from Hitler forbidding all discussion of the employment and operational possibilities of the Me 262, 'which is still in its experimental stage and available only in small numbers,' and early in September another disclosed that two more disbanded bomber Gruppen known to be converting to Me 262 'would not be operational for some time'.[124] It may be added that except on 16 August, when one Me 163 made 'passes' during a bombing raid, US bombers did not encounter the new types after 28 July until the second week of September.[125]*

On 5 September, in the light of these indications, AI appreciated that 'the appearance of the Me 262 in considerable numbers by 1st October is not anticipated. There is no reason at present to suppose that the development of jet and rocket-propelled aircraft is proceeding quickly enough to produce any radical alteration in the effectiveness of the GAF in 1944'.[127] It repeated this conclusion in a report issued by the JIC on 8 September which said that while 100 Me 262 were expected to be in service by the end of October, they were unlikely materially to affect the position 'unless the war goes on through the winter'.[128] And the JIC itself concluded on 16 September that in view of the shortage of aircrew 'no revival [of the GAF] on a sustained or intensive scale is possible' and that 'jets are unlikely to produce any change'.[129]

Neither these appreciations, which were in any case produced at the point when the hope that the war would be over by the end of 1944 was about to subside, nor the fact that Sigint produced no further significant references to the development of the jet programme before the end of September did much to reduce the uneasiness felt at SHAEF and the US air commands. Early in

---

* But in the three weeks following the first interception of a Mosquito PR flight in the Munich area at the end of July, (see Volume III Part 1, p 351), Me 262 intercepted four out of 13 of these aircraft and shot down one of them. This produced the demand for the use of Type XIX Spitfires for the PR flights. Mosquito losses rose from 0.6% to 2.95% by October.[126]

123. Air Sunsets 216 and 227 of 6 and 27 August, 232 of 2 September.
124. CX/MSS/T287/98, T296/10.
125. Craven and Cate, op cit, Vol III, p 300, 302–303.
126. AIR 41/7, *Photographic Reconnaissance*, Vol II, pp 148, 156.
127. Air Sunset 233 of 5 September.
128. JIC(44) 395 of 8 September.
129. JIC(44) 407 of 16 September.

September Spaatz temporarily gave jet and rocket installations priority second only to oil plants for the operations of the US strategic bombers. In the next three weeks heavy attacks were made on several of these targets including Kiel, where Sigint had disclosed that the Walterwerke were producing the power unit of the Me 163, and Sigint also reported that Me 262 production had been set back by damage to the Jumo factory at Dessau.[130] But it was realised by the end of September that production was too dispersed and too well-concealed to justify a sustained bombing programme.

From the beginning of October Sigint reported the entrance of Me 262 into front-line service both in the fighter and the ground-attack roles. It gave advance notice of the movement on 5 October of 13 Me 262s from the experimental unit at Lechfeld to a base in Holland under fighter Gruppe III/JG 6. During the rest of the month observation and US airborne Y showed them appearing from time to time against the US bomber raids but still using the unaggressive tactics of recent months either from the desire to conserve their strength until a sufficient number of aircraft had been built up for a decisive attack or from the need to acquire further training. But on 1 November between four and six Me 262s and two Me 163 attempted an attack, and on 2 November the Enigma disclosed that the unit had been re-named Gruppe Nowotny after a GAF fighter ace.[131] Meanwhile the day-time ground-attack unit in Holland had become a front-line unit under the name I/KG 5. It operated from time to time against airfields and bridges (including the Nijmegen bridge) and the decrypts showed that while it still had teething troubles, its strength had slowly been increased to 29 aircraft by the end of the month.[132]

Other sources of disquiet in October were on the one hand the receipt of intelligence to the effect that the Ar 234 had entered service and, on the other, the continued absence of accurate intelligence about the Do 335. Sigint had made no reference to the Ar 234 since the previous February* and there had been no PR sightings; but POW had reported that it was being manufactured at Brandenburg/Havel and assembled at the Arado base at Alt Lönnewitz, and the GAF Enigma disclosed that a special aircraft had made a successful reconnaissance of the Normandy beaches on 2 August. On 14 October the decrypt of a signal from the

---

* See Volume III Part 1, p 350.

130.   AIR 40/2393, AI 2(a) Report of 29 September 1944.
131.   DEFE 3/301, HP 5346 of 2 November; *Use of Ultra by the US War Department*, pp 64, 67–68.
132.   Air Sunset 245 of 3 October; *Use of Ultra by the US War Department*, pp 59, 63.

Japanese Naval Attaché reported that the Germans had carried out a successful reconnaissance of south-east England at the end of September; the Attaché believed the aircraft had been an Me 262, but AI correctly surmised that this and the August flight had been made by the Ar 234.[133] Later in the month, as well as reporting other reconnaissance flights, in none of which was the aircraft sighted, the GAF Enigma disclosed that the Ar 234 was also to be used as a fighter-bomber with KG 76, one of the disbanded bomber units which had become associated with jet aircraft.[134] And on 10 November the decrypt of a signal from the Japanese Naval Mission, sent on 31 October, provided a lengthy account of the Ar 234's impressive characteristics.[135] As for the Do 335, AI, which had been misled by intelligence received in the spring into assuming that it was a jet or rocket aircraft, remained under that impression until towards the end of October; and far from being aware that its production had been severely set back by the destruction of Dornier plant in Allied air raids, it was in October misled into expecting it to come into squadron service by decrypts listing the Do 335 among the few aircraft for which dummies were to be produced for deception purposes* and referring to its projected use in the forthcoming U-boat offensive.†

From early in October, as an indication of the continuing concern, the intelligence authorities were reassessing their earlier conclusions. On 3 October AI noted that with the 'emergence' of the 'rocket-propelled' Do 335, Germany had four rocket or jet aircraft under development (the others being Me 262, Me 163 and Ar 234) and that while only the Me 262 had yet progressed beyond the trial stage, it was 'nevertheless clear that the GAF . . . may build up a sizeable rocket and jet-propelled force by spring 1945 failing active interference with production, training and re-equipment programme'.[136] On 13 October it appreciated that the operational strength of the new types was now between 75 and 80 aircraft and that, unless development could be interrupted by Allied bombing, the figure could double by the end of 1944 and reach 300 by April 1945.[137] And on 16 October, by which time intelligence was pointing to a rapid recovery of Germany's single-engined convent-

---

* See Volume III Part 1, pp 345–346.

† See above, p 478.

133. SJA 995 of 14 October.
134. DEFE 3/243, HP 4588 of 26 October; DEFE 3/304, HP 5736 of 6 November.
135. SJA 1118 of 10 November.
136. Air Sunset 245 of 3 October.
137. Air Sunset 248 of 13 October.

ional fighter force,* the JIC added the warning that with the help of the jet aircraft the GAF might gain some degree of ascendancy over the areas of vital war production in the Reich during the coming winter.[138]

The chief development disclosed by Sigint in November and early December was the conversion of Me 262s from the ground-attack to the fighter role. The Me 262 fighter unit that had been operating from Holland was withdrawn to north Germany after a US air attack on its base in mid-November, and early in December the Enigma showed that it was operating there as a front-line unit (III/JG 7)[139] By the same date decrypts had revealed that half of all the Staffeln of I/KG 51 were being converted into fighters, thus forming another Gruppe of Me 262 fighters which was soon to be designated I/JG 7, and that they were under orders to break up Allied bomber formations without engaging in combat. AI pointed out that this, the 'first regular jet-propelled fighter unit to appear under the normal system of numerals', was the first step towards the creation of a fighter Geschwader equipped wholly with Me 262 which would have three Gruppen of four Staffeln each, but that only two Gruppen as yet existed with, probably, only a total of six to seven Staffeln. It added that the conversion and training even for two Gruppen was not likely to be completed in the near future, but that these developments 'may portend the greater allocation of Me 262 to the fighter arm at the expense of ground attack'.[140] These developments did, indeed, mark the beginning of the GAF's departure from Hitler's previous insistence on using the Me 262 in the ground-attack role; and some indication that the process of conversion would be slow was provided by the decrypt of a signal issued to all German military attachés on 10 November. It stated that Allied propaganda was minimising the importance of the new German weapon, the jet-fighter, and was claiming that the Me 262 did not give battle, and went on to say that the jet-fighter was still in the experimental stage and to explain that the Allied claim was 'in part accounted for by the fact that those encountered by the enemy were bomber aircraft of the jet type which do not [perform] the task of getting involved in combat.[141]

Sigint also disclosed during November that the Me 262 was to be used for reconnaissance as well as in the fighter and ground-attack

---

* See above, pp 408, 523ff.

138. JIC(44)437 of 16 October.
139. DEFE 3/310, HP 7669 of 24 November; DEFE 3/310, HP 8119 of 28 November; DEFE 3/312, HP 8560 of 4 December.
140. DEFE 3/314, HP 8560 of 4 December; Air Sunset 261 of 7 December.
141. *Use of Ultra by the US War Department*, pp 54–55.

roles; some tactical reconnaissance units equipped with the aircraft had already been formed, whereas the Ar 234 reconnaissance unit had shown no sign of expanding. As for the state of the jet ground-attack units, there was no evidence that the Gruppe under KG 51 had developed; nor that, of the other two disbanded bomber units known to be converting to jets under Fliegerkorps IX, KG 54 had moved towards operational readiness; nor that an operational detachment of the other, KG 76, which had been reported in November as due to be equipped with Ar 234, had yet materialised. There was also no evidence of marked progress with the Me 163; crew training was still continuing, but the Me 163 Geschwader, JG 400, had made no move towards operational readiness and AI doubted whether more than one Gruppe had been formed.[142]

AI summarised this evidence on 7 December. It believed that while it was too soon to conclude that the Me 163 programme had been scrapped,* it was clear that the Me 262 was to be the mainstay of the GAF's plans for recovery. It also believed that while the fact that the Me 262 was assuming so many roles suggested that its production was proceeding well, Sigint left 'little doubt that the crew supply and training constitute a bottleneck holding up the expansion of the Me 262 force'. It estimated that the total of jet and rocket types in first-line units would be between 175 and 200 aircraft by 1 January 1945 and between 300 and 400 by the end of April.[143] This estimate, which was not much higher than that offered in mid-October and which was based on close scrutiny of decrypts related to the order of battle of the jet units and the activity at jet training establishments, was offered after taking account of a signal sent by the Japanese Naval Attaché at the end of November after meetings with Speer, Milch, Dr Heinkel and senior GAF officers, which was decrypted on 2 December. He said that, although his figures were estimates and might be exaggerated, production of Me 262 was expected to be 300 in November, 500 in December and 1,000 in January 1945, and that production of Me 163 would be 100 a month by the end of 1944, when a total of 500 would be available.[144]

Early in December the jets of JG 7 made occasional attacks on the US bombers; a decrypt of 4 December revealed that on the previous day I/KG 51 had claimed that three Me 262s had broken

---

* It was not yet known that the Me 163 was being superseded by the He 162, to which Sigint had first referred at the end of October. See below, p 616.

142. Air Sunset 261 of 7 December.
143. ibid.
144. SJA 1233 of 2 December.

up a force of 30 bombers and shot down one Liberator.[145] But there were to be no further attempts to intercept the bombers until 2 February 1945.[146] The interruption was no doubt due to preparations for the Ardennes offensive, and during that offensive Sigint was plentiful on the employment of the ground-attack jet units. By 21 December decrypts had disclosed that those of I/KG 51 were about to be joined by other ground-attack jet units – a further Gruppe of Me 262s, II/KG 1, and the Ar 234 Gruppe of III/KG 76 – and also by jet-fighter Gruppe III/JG 7. AI estimated on 21 December that when these units had been brought up, the total number of jets committed would be 130 (80 ground-attack, 40 fighters and 10 reconnaissance aircraft).[147] This force was no larger than might have been expected from AI's predictions of the front-line jet strength that would be available by the end of 1944. But in combination with the shock administered by the Ardennes offensive, and by the failure of intelligence to give advance notice of the massive GAF attack on Allied air bases that took place on 1 January 1945,* the size of the force and the skill and determination with which it was used produced a wave of pessimism in London and Washington and throughout the Allied Commands as to the probable duration of the war and as to the serious consequences that could follow from the recuperative power of German industry – and above all from the entry into service of jet and rocket aircraft and the new U-boats alongside the V-weapons – if the war was prolonged.[148]

These fears found expression in a new strategic bombing directive. Issued on 15 January, it was markedly ambiguous, retaining oil targets as the first priority and communications as the second priority, but stating that jet production, training and operational establishments had 'now become primary objectives' and specifying that 'certain objectives in the enemy's U-boat organisation' should receive marginal or incidental attention.[149] It was no doubt the outcome of a compromise between the Air Staff and General Spaatz. The Air Staff did not believe that the jet aircraft constituted an immediate threat, and although it agreed that they might create a dangerous situation if their development was not checked, it also felt that their development would be more effectively checked by maintaining the offensive against oil and

---

* See above, p 442–443.

145. DEFE 3/314, HP 8585 of 4 December.
146. Craven and Cate, op cit, Vol III, p 729.
147. Air Sunset 267 of 21 December.
148. Craven and Cate, op cit, Vol III, pp 715–717; Webster and Frankland, *The Strategic Air Offensive*, Vol III (1961), pp 95–96.
149. Webster and Frankland, op cit, Vol III, pp 181–182.

communications targets than by direct attack on jet targets.[150] Spaatz was no longer prepared to rely mainly on the offensive against oil and communications. According to the British official account, he forwarded the directive to US Eighth and Fifteenth Air Forces with the statement that jet targets had been made 'a principal objective for attack' because 'unless adequate measures were taken, the Germans would have between 400 and 500 jet aircraft available for operations against us by early summer', and according to the official US account he had already on 9 January, in agreement with SHAEF, decided to 'elevate jet production to first priority, co-equal with oil'.[151]

---

150. ibid, p 96.
151. ibid, p 97; Craven and Cate, op cit, Vol III, p 719.

PART XVI

The Defeat of Germany

CHAPTER 58

The Final Allied Bombing Offensives and the End of the War in the Air

B Y THE beginning of 1945 the cumulative effects of the Allied air offensive against the oil targets, as against communications targets, were mounting steadily, and any relaxation that might have followed the bombing directive of 15 January, which retained first priority for those targets but accepted that jet targets were also a primary objective, was off-set by Bomber Command's greater participation in the oil offensive from the same date. In the first four months of 1945 Bomber Command dropped 181,000 tons of bombs over Germany, one-fifth of the total dropped in the whole war, and while the proportion directed against cities fell to 35 per cent, as compared with 53 per cent in the last quarter of 1944, the proportion dropped on oil targets rose from 14 to 26.2 per cent.[1]

In its reports on the results of the oil offensive during January the JIC estimated that, in conjunction with Russian seizures of plants, it had reduced total production of all types to between 345,000 and 375,000 tons and that no fighter aircraft petrol was being produced by the end of the month. It predicted that within six weeks of mid-March the German ground and air forces would be completely immobilised and noted that while the Navy might be in less severe straits, there was evidence that supplies were insufficient for the full U-boat training programme and that bulk reserves of heavy diesel were exhausted. It also noted that the shortage of oil was now being aggravated by a shortage of coal resulting from the bombing of communications and the over-running of Silesia by the Soviet advances.[2]

Early in February the lack of heavy diesel reserves was confirmed by a decrypt in which OKM announced that supplies were now available only from current production. By 8 February decrypts had reported that German troop movements on 21st Army Group's front were being slowed down by lack of fuel. On 21 February a decrypt disclosed that GAF personnel immobilised in the west through fuel shortage were to be drafted into army

---

1. Webster and Frankland, *The Strategic Air Offensive*, Vol III (1961), p 110; Terraine, *The Right of the Line* (1985), p 675.
2. JIC(45) 29(o) of 23 January, JIC(45) 40(o) of 3 February.

units on the eastern front. In a decrypt of 22 February the Japanese Naval Attaché reported that reconnaissance and attacks against the Arctic convoys by the GAF in north Norway had been limited by lack of fuel.[3] The JIC's review early in March of the effects of the oil offensive in February estimated that total German production had been 'the lowest it has ever been', 280,000 tons or 21 per cent of the production norm of the spring of 1944, and that the low output of MT fuel and diesel had hampered the distribution of other oil products.[4]

The last of the monthly JIC reports on the offensive, issued on 3 April, concluded that 'the final stage in the destruction of Germany's oil resources had been reached by the third week of March'. Production had fallen by then to a monthly rate of 30,000 tons, 6 per cent of the norm, and with the disintegration of the German transport system, the distribution of even that small output had become impossible.[5]

Bomber Command increased its contribution to the attack on transportation targets only marginally, from 13 to 14.4 per cent of its bomb load, but the increased weight of the total Allied offensive against those targets was having consequences no less devastating than the attack on oil from the beginning of the year. On 19 March the JIC reported that Germany's war production had fallen steeply during the past two months due to loss of territory and air attack, particularly on transport,[6] and by that date the offensive was bringing about in a final concentrated phase the complete sealing-off of the Ruhr.

Pressure for this more concentrated objective, as against SHAEF's preference for attacks on widespread targets, mounted from the middle of January, when high-grade Sigint began to provide evidence of the general disruption of the railways and, in particular, of its effect in producing a serious shortage of ammunition and coal. A shortage of ammunition had begun in the autumn of 1944 in part because of bombing of synthetic oil plants, which were the principal source of the supply of nitrogen to the explosives industry. It appears that MEW was unaware of this.[7] But the intelligence authorities were at any rate aware of the ammunition shortage. A message of 10 January decrypted on 18 January disclosed that 'in view of the raw material, production and transport situation, supplies of ammunition for large-scale

---

3. DEFE 3/531, ZTPG 334949; DEFE 3/505, BT 4359 of 8 February 1945; DEFE 3/509, BT 5307 of 21 February; SJA 1562 of 22 February.
4. JIC(45) 74 of 4 March.
5. JIC(45) 110 of 3 April.
6. JIC(45) 90(o) of 19 March.
7. Webster and Frankland, op cit, Vol III, pp 236–237.

fighting can only be met if consumption is restricted to operations of strategic importance'.[8] A decrypt of 20 January added that 'in certain cases even the engagement of worthwhile targets must be foregone'.[9] On 2 March a decrypt revealed that 88 mm Flak ammunition was to be used against Allied bombers only exceptionally, on account of serious deficiencies.[10]

The decrypt of a situation report addressed to Army Group G on 16 January disclosed that the rail system was 'very strained' in the Mainz area, 'strained' at Cologne, 'extremely strained' in the Saarbrücken district, 'unsatisfactory' in the Karlsruhe district, and that the Rhine bridge at Maxau would probably be impassable for a fortnight.[11] In a message of 28 January the Armaments Ministry complained that factories were closing owing to lack of coal.[12] In a signal decrypted on 3 February the Japanese Naval Attaché reported that the inability of the Germans to move commodities such as coal from the places where they were produced was having an adverse effect on various war supplies.[13] And by that date AI had compiled a mass of evidence on coal shortages from decrypts of signals sent by the local armaments production Kommandos. On 8 February, prompted by MEW, the JIC used this evidence in support of the argument that the interruption of coal supplies from the Ruhr could halt all rail transport and have 'effects as important as oil'.[14]

A plan for bringing about 'the interdiction of the Ruhr' was under discussion at SHAEF and the CSTC by 10 February.[15] It was not implemented until early in March, but between then and 24 March when the Ruhr had been completely sealed off, concentrated bombing of the area paralysed the railways and created a coal crisis throughout Germany, and brought about a further precipitate fall in all forms of war production. On 19 March the JIC calculated that in the past two months tank production had dropped by 40 per cent and ammunition and armaments production by between 30 and 35 per cent.[16]

□

8.   DEFE 3/330, BT 2635 of 18 January.
9.   DEFE 3/331, BT 2879 of 20 January.
10. DEFE 3/512, BT 6076 of 2 March.
11. DEFE 3/330, BT 2725 of 19 January.
12. CX/MSS/T445/56.
13. SJA 1472 of 3 February; BAY/BT 65 of 9 February.
14. JIC(45) 50 of 8 February.
15. Webster and Frankland, op cit, Vol III, pp 254–255.
16. JIC(45) 90(o) of 19 March.

The implementation of the plan to seal off the Ruhr had been held up by, on the one hand, the anxiety of the CSTC that it would divert some effort from the oil offensive and, on the other hand, by the lingering belief of both the British and American air authorities that by some dramatic use of their air superiority they might precipitate a German surrender.[17] Beginning on 3 February they embarked on the blitz in eastern Germany which culminated in the bombing of Dresden. In the last week of February the US Air Force insisted on carrying out a plan drawn up in the autumn of 1944 (Operation *Clarion*) for attacks on small hitherto unscathed communications centres in western and central Germany with the aim of bringing about a quick end to the war through the demoralisation of the population and the final disruption of the economy.[18]

Like the plan for Operation *Clarion*, the origin of the decision to bomb Dresden – 'the title deed of that controversial operation', in the words of the official history of the Strategic Air Offensive[19] – went back to July 1944. In a minute to the Prime Minister the Chiefs of Staff observed in the first week of July 1944 that 'the time might well come in the not too distant future when an all-out attack by every means at our disposal on German civilian morale might be decisive . . .'. They were not contemplating an intensification of area bombing of towns; the Air Staff no longer had faith in this strategy as a means of bringing about the defeat of Germany by its effects on either civilian morale or industrial production. On the contrary, they were beginning to think that at a time when the war had been all but won by a combination of all arms, a catastrophic single blow from the air might push Germany over the brink of surrender and avoid a final protracted phase of desperate resistance and guerrilla war. This was made clear in a memorandum drawn up by the Chief of the Air Staff at the beginning of August after consultation with the Foreign Office, the Political Warfare Executive and MEW. The plan he outlined would be put into effect 'once the issue of the war is clear beyond doubt', and its object was to persuade the German political and military authorities that they 'must accept the necessity of organised surrender . . . or be replaced by an alternative Command which does so'.[20]

In this memorandum the preferred operation was a shattering attack of 'catastrophic force' on Berlin, though similar blows against large towns such as Hamburg and Munich were mentioned

---

17. Webster and Frankland, op cit, Vol III, pp 255–257.
18. ibid, p 255.
19. ibid, p 55.
20. ibid, pp 52–53.

as alternatives; and yet another suggestion was that 'immense devastation could be produced if the entire attack was concentrated on a single big town other than Berlin and the effect would be especially great if the town was one hitherto relatively undamaged'. Approving the memorandum on 5 August, the Chiefs of Staff chose the Berlin proposal and invited Eisenhower, to prepare plans for 'an attack on Berlin on the lines suggested'.[21] It was in this form, also, that the project reached the JIC and the Joint Planners. At a meeting on 8 August the JIC noted that Operation *Braddock* – distribution of sabotage materials throughout Germany by SOE – might be used in the proposed attack on 'the German government machine', and it recorded at its meeting of 22 August that the Chiefs of Staff had requested it to take all steps to improve target intelligence for 'the attack on the German government machine' and to advise when the conditions had arisen in which the attack might appropriately be made.[22] This request had been made on the recommendation of the Joint Planners, who had, however, reported on 17 August that they did not believe the plan was 'likely to achieve any worth while degree of success'.[23]

In the event, appropriate conditions did not arise during the remaining months of 1944, which saw a steady waning of Allied confidence in the prospects of bringing Germany to the brink of defeat before the end of the year, and it was in different circumstances that the plan (now called Operation *Thunderclap*) was revived at the beginning of 1945. On 16 January, following the start of the new Russian offensive, the JIC asked the JIS to assess how much of the German military and civil administrative machine was still located in Berlin, and to report on the effect on the Germans of a concentrated attack carried out on 'the heart of the Government quarter in Berlin' in conjunction with the Russian offensive.[24] By 22 January the Director of Bomber Operations in the Air Ministry had also suggested that 'if the operations were launched at a time when there was still no obvious slackening in the momentum of the Russian drive, it might well have the appearance of a close co-ordination in planning between the Russians and ourselves. Such a deduction on the part of the enemy would greatly increase the moral effect of both operations'.[25]

On 25 January the JIC issued two reports. The first, entitled 'Bombing of Berlin', referred to the fact that the JIC had been instructed in August 1944 to advise when conditions had arisen

21. ibid, pp 54–55.
22. JIC(44) 38th Meeting of 8 August, 42nd Meeting of 22 August.
23. Webster and Frankland, op cit, Vol III, pp 98–99.
24. JIC(45) 4th (o) Meeting of 16 January; JIC(45) 27(o) of 22 January.
25. Webster and Frankland, op cit, Vol III, p 99.

which could justify air attack on the German government machine. It pointed out that the value of such attacks must now be judged by reference to their effects on the eastern front, and would depend on the care with which they were timed to coincide with developments there, but went on to state:

'(e)   We do not believe that, even so timed, the devastation of Berlin would of itself break Germany's will to resist, shatter the control of the Nazi regime or lead to a plea for an armistice.

(f)   No benefit to be derived from the bombing of Berlin would justify any diversion whatever from the task of putting out of action oil plants and tank factories,* which remains of paramount importance . . .'

It conceded, however, that as raids on Berlin carried out without prejudice to this paramount task would, even if intermittent and on a smaller scale than evisaged for Operation *Thunderclap*, materially assist the Russians, and might even have a political value in demonstrating to the Russians a desire on the part of the British and Americans to assist them, they would justify temporary diversion from any targets other than oil plants and tank factories. In the second report of 25 January, which was entitled 'Strategic Bombing in relation to the present Russian Offensive', the JIC stated that the Russian offensive was likely to have a decisive effect on the length of the war and explored the various ways in which the Strategic Air Forces might assist it in the next few weeks. It repeated that, even for the purpose of assisting the Russians,†

---

* Tanks had just been added to the priority targets, without the issuing of a new directive,[26] in the light of recent evidence that the German armoured divisions were re-fitting. On 16 January the JIC had estimated that production had been reduced to 450 a month by the bombing of factories, but a few days later it believed that this figure had risen to 550.[27] On 25 January it recommended that tank factories should be bombed with priority second only to oil after receiving intelligence from Sigint that tanks were being delivered direct from the factories to front-line units.[28]

† As distinct from any effect they might have on German morale. On 16 January the JIC believed there was little prospect that civilian morale, boosted by the Ardennes offensive, would collapse.[29] On 21 January it reported that home morale remained unaffected by Allied bombing.[30] On 27 February, in a paper on Operation *Clarion*, it commented that there was no intelligence as to its effects but that 'it is perhaps significant that, a week after the event there is still no information from our most reliable intelligence source'.[31] On 19 March, the first reference to the subject since January, it stated that 'the disturbances, which have already flared up amid the confusion of violent air bombing and the movement of masses of refugees, have been quite unorganised and purely local in scope. There is no evidence yet

26.   ibid, pp 104–105.
27.   JIC(45) 19 (Draft) of 16 January; JIC(45) 22(o) of 21 January.
28.   JIC(45) 31(o) of 25 January.
29.   JIC(45) 19 (Draft) of 16 January.
30.   JIC(45) 22(o) of 21 January.
31.   JIC(45) 72(o) of 25 February.

attacks on oil targets and tank factories merited the highest priority, but it again suggested that a series of raids on Berlin would justify temporary diversion from other targets before going on to recommend that sea-mining in the Skagerrak and the Baltic to delay the reinforcement of the eastern front from Norway and Latvia, attacks on rail bottlenecks to delay its reinforcement from Italy and Hungary and attacks on rail communications in Germany, to delay its reinforcement from the western front, also deserved consideration.[33]

When the DCAS told Bomber Command on 25 January that the full *Thunderclap* plan was now under consideration, and Harris proposed that the main attack on Berlin should be supplemented by attacks on Chemnitz, Leipzig and Dresden, these JIC reports had not been circulated. The CAS had clearly seen them when he told the DCAS on 26 January that he thought attacks on Berlin on the *Thunderclap* scale would not be decisive, and should not be attempted 'in the near future' at the expense of the absolute priority for attacks on oil targets and the need to deal with jet factories and submarine yards. But the long-standing interest in delivering a 'single catastrophic blow' had now been submerged in the wish to demonstrate that the strategic air forces could contribute to the Soviet offensives, and so much so that the CAS agreed that, subject to observing those priorities, 'we should use available effort in one big attack on Berlin and attacks on Dresden, Leipzig, Chemnitz, or any other cities where a severe blitz will not only cause confusion in the evacuation from the East but will also hamper the movement of troops from the West'. And if any doubt remained as to whether this programme should be carried out, it was dissipated by the intervention of the Prime Minister. Answering an enquiry from him on 26 January as to whether Berlin and other large cities in east Germany should not now be 'considered especially attractive targets', the Secretary of State for Air advised him that such a programme was under examination and received the following reply: '... I am glad that this is "under examination". Pray report to me tomorrow what is going to be done'.[34]

On the following day the DCAS sent Harris the two JIC reports, explained that the CAS had doubts about the full-scale *Thunderclap* plan, but requested him, subject to the over-riding claims of oil and other approved targets within the current directive, to carry

---

that the feeling of defiance of authority will so increase as to lead to mass violence, panic or hysteria beyond the powers of repression and control by the SS'.[32]

32.   JIC(45) 90(o) of 19 March.
33.   JIC(45) 31(o) and 34(o) of 25 January.
34.   Webster and Frankland, op cit, pp 100–103.

out as soon as conditions allowed one big attack on Berlin and related operations against Dresden, Leipzig, Chemnitz and 'any other cities where a severe blitz will not only cause confusion in the evacuation from the East but will also hamper the movement of troops from the West'. In discussions with General Spaatz and at SHAEF in the next few days these attacks were granted second priority after synthetic oil plants for the strategic air forces operating from the United Kingdom, and on 3 February the US Eighth Air Force carried out a massive daylight attack on Berlin.[35]

These decisions were made independently of any consultation with the Russians, with whom the subject was first discussed at the Yalta conference on 4 February. On that day the Russians submitted a memorandum on the progress of their offensive which included, among other suggestions as to how the Western Allies might assist it, the suggestion that the Germans should be prevented from moving troops to the east from the western front, Norway and Italy by air attacks against communications, and in particular that the bombers should 'paralyze the centres: Berlin and Leipzig'. In the remaining discussions at Yalta, however, which centred on the wish of the Russians to establish a bombline to the east of which the western air forces would not operate, they seem to have been anxious to discourage attacks by the western air forces in eastern Germany, and agreement on a bombline proved impossible.[36]

Bomber Command's attack on Dresden with just over 800 bombers took place on the night of 13 February. As part of the concentrated attack that had been authorised at the end of January, which continued with heavy daylight raids by US Eighth Air Force on Dresden on 14 and 15 February and 2 March and on Berlin on 24 February and a heavy night raid by Bomber Command on Chemnitz on 14 February, we should not expect it to have been influenced by the receipt of last-minute intelligence any more than it depended on Russian requests for support. But this point is confirmed by the fact that the only references in the intelligence archives relating to the raid occur in a last-minute exchange of signals between the air intelligence authorities. In the afternoon of 12 February AI informed HQ US Strategic Air Force that General Spaatz had just told the DCAS that there was evidence of troop concentrations in the Dresden area; it added that it had no confirmation of this from Ultra or PR, asked for the source of General Spaatz's statement and was told that it was HQ

---

35.   ibid, pp 103–104, 107.
36.   ibid, pp 105–106; CAB 80/92, COS (45) 114(o) of 22 February (Annex to 2nd Military Meeting, Yalta, 4 February).

Eighth Air Force. On the afternoon of 13 February another signal from AI to Spaatz's HQ reported that as far as could be established Eighth Air Force had 'no evidence for the assertion about Dresden. Apparently the information came from SHAEF Rear but they disown it and have nothing to support it.' To this signal HQ USSTAF replied in the early hours of 14 February that it had found no evidence to substantiate the statement and that SHAEF (Main) had no knowledge of any such movements.[37]

□

In the defence of the Reich against Allied bombing, as in support of the German Army, the GAF made no significant impact on operations in the west after the beginning of 1945. By the end of January the Enigma had disclosed that some 800 single-engined fighters had been switched to the eastern front since the beginning of the Russian offensives and that the roughly similar number that remained in the west were severely restricted by exhaustion, the loss of skilled aircrew and the lack of adequate training of aircrew that followed from the mounting fuel shortage.[38] Even before the completion of this massive transfer – ever since the GAF had wound up its contribution to the Ardennes battles with the great attack on Allied bases on 1 January* – these restrictions had been so apparent and the GAF had already been so vastly outnumbered that Allied operations were being carried out without considering the intelligence that still flowed in from Sigint about the enemy's order of battle and tactical intentions which AI continued to send regularly to the Commands. From early in February, when Sigint had established that the GAF had made no move to reinforce its strength in the west as the Allies crossed the Rhine, the Air Ministry ceased to issue the regular Sunset commentaries by which the Commands had for so long been kept informed about Sigint's coverage of the general state of the GAF and the main developments that were taking place in it.

Sigint remained useful in that it assured the Allies that they would not be surprised by unexpected recovery on the enemy's part or by unannounced decisions, either strategic or tactical. It showed that no withdrawals from the east were made when the Russian offensive paused from the end of February. From the beginning of the year the Enigma decrypts confirmed POW

---

* See above, p 442–443.

37. AWLs 3941 of 1725/12 February, 3952 of 1331/13 February; GAD/STA 3 of 0202/14 February.

38. Air Sunset 277 of 27 January.

reports and indications from Y to the effect that the GAF, unable to offer more than token opposition to the Allied bombers over Germany, was preparing to carry out intruder operations by night-fighters over Bomber Command's bases – a tactic which it had contemplated at the beginning of the Ardennes offensive but which had then been foiled by bad weather, and which it finally abandoned, as Sigint disclosed, in March.[39]* Decrypts giving warning that the GAF had ordered suicide attacks against the Remagen bridge in mid-March gave the Allied Commands time to strengthen the AA defences there and to mount attacks on the enemy's airfields.†

Above all, however, the decrypts were valuable for the evidence they provided about the extent to which the GAF was transferring production and training from conventional to jet aircraft and succeeding in bringing jet aircraft into the front line. Still a source of considerable Allied anxiety in mid-January 1945, when Spaatz gave jet aircraft targets equal priority with the oil targets, the jet aircraft continued to alarm the Allies for brief periods from time to time down to the end of hostilities, and Sigint, the main source of intelligence about them, was sometimes the cause of the alarms.‡ But its over-all effect was to keep the Allied anxiety in check.

The decision to give high priority to jet targets was to no avail in January, weather preventing any attacks on them. In February there were some attacks, but the targets were no longer given priority.[42] The speed and scale of the Russian advances, and the

---

* High-grade Sigint gave warning on 20 February that intruder operations were imminent and on the night of 3–4 March, without further warning, four Gruppen (140) of night-fighters attacked Bomber Command's bases from Northumberland to Oxford. On this night and in similar attacks on a smaller scale on three subsequent nights 22 bombers were shot down for the loss of 20 German fighters. Bomber Command's losses might have been more severe if the Sigint warning had not led to the strengthening of the anti-aircraft defences and the introduction of dawn patrols.[40]

† See below, p 681.

‡ For example, the JIC warned on 16 January that the Germans might use jet aircraft as night-fighters. Sigint contained evidence that Me 262s were used for the first time as night-fighters against Mosquitoes on 21 February and also mentioned the intention to use the Ar 234 as a night-fighter. But there were no further references to this development until Ar 234s operated at night for the first time on 30 March.[41]

39. Air Sunset 264 of 16 December 1944; DEFE 3/327, BT 1925 of 11 January 1945; DEFE 3/328, BT 2234 of 14 January; DEFE 3/329, BT 2388 of 15 January; *Air Ministry Intelligence*, p 173.

40. DEFE 3/508, BT 5232 of 20 February; DEFE 3/509, BT 5388 of 22 February; AWL 4049 of 22 February; DEFE 3/513, BTs 6429, 6442 and 6448 of 6 March; AIR 41/10, *The Rise and Fall of the German Air Force*, p 383; Collier, *The Defence of the United Kingdom* (1957), p 421.

41. JIC(45) 19(0) (Draft) of 16 January.

42. Craven and Cate, *The Army Air Forces in World War II*, Vol III (Chicago, 1951), p 719.

hope that they would lead to a quick end of hostilities, had generated renewed confidence that the new aircraft could not decisively influence the course of the war. Moreover, the jets had made no attempt to interfere with Allied bombers since early December, and though the 20–30 available ground-attack Me 262s had been used to support the Army in northern Alsace, they had operated to little effect. Two papers by the JIC reflected the changing context in which the threat from the new aircraft was being assessed. On 22 January it still predicted that monthly production of jet and rocket aircraft would rise from the present figure of 200 to about 300 in April to between 500 and 700 in August.[43] But on 23 January, in a review of the combined effects of the Russian advance and of the Allied air offensive against oil targets, it predicted that the German ground and air forces would be completely immobilised within six weeks of the middle of March.[44]

During February the more relaxed assessment of the threat appeared to be vindicated. Me 262s opposed the US bombers on 9 February in small numbers, but were not again encountered until the end of the month, when they appeared in small numbers and evaded combat.[45] Enigma decrypts of 6 and 21 February threw some light on their continued inactivity; they disclosed that jet fuel had become so scarce that the restrictions which already applied to conventional aircraft must in future be observed by jet aircraft.[46] The latter also suffered a serious setback on 16 February in a US raid on the jet airfield near Regensburg in which 23 Me 262s were destroyed and 19 damaged on the ground.[47] The decrypts of signals from the Japanese Naval Attaché testified, however, to the high hopes the Germans were still placing in the Me 262. In one of 3 February, referring to the inability of the GAF to offer any defence against the US bombers on account of the superiority of the US fighters to the FW 190, he reported that they hoped to bring the Me 262 into service on a large scale; and in a signal of 22 February, decrypted on 28 February, he disclosed that over and above the jet ground-attack aircraft already active on the western front, the Germans were forming a corps of about 500 Me 262s and reserving the necessary fuel for their 'trump card'.[48]

There was much conjecture as to whether the trump card referred to an Army counter-attack in the east or the offensive by

---

43. JIC(45) 22(o) of 21 January.
44. JIC(45) 29(o) of 23 January.
45. Craven and Cate, op cit, Vol III, pp 729, 734.
46. DEFE 3/504, BT 4224 of 6 February; DEFE 3/509, BT 5321 of 21 February.
47. Craven and Cate, op cit, Vol III, p 730.
48. BAY/BTs 65 of 9 February, 112 of 4 March.

the new U-boats or plans for the final defence of Germany, but to
AI it was obvious that it referred to the corps of 500 Me 262s and
was associated with the fact that, as Sigint had revealed, six
disbanded long-range bomber Geschwader had been reforming
under Fliegerkorps IX since the previous August. At the same
time, AI was confident that such a corps would not become
operational in 1945. On the basis of a wealth of Sigint references.
AI believed that largely as a result of fuel shortage the training
organisation for the jet units would be unable to supply crew both
to Fliegerkorps IX and to the Me 262 Geschwader (JG 7) with
which it would be in competition. In the same assessment AI
pointed to another source of reassurance. It noted that the
Attaché had not mentioned in connection with the corps the
rocket-propelled Me 163, and drew attention to the fact that in his
signal of 22 February, decrypted on 28 February, he had reported
that only one-tenth of the special fuel required for this aircraft was
available.[49]*

Little had been heard of the Me 163 since the beginning of the
year. It is now known that its development had been held back not
only by fuel shortage, but by the fact that it was being superseded
by the He 162. The single-engined jet-propelled He 162 was
developed under such stringent security conditions and with such
rapidity that Sigint was for some months the sole source of
information about it.† The first reference to it had been provided
by the decrypt of a signal by the Japanese Naval Attaché on a visit
he had made to Dr Heinkel on 11 and 12 October 1944. He
referred to it as a rocket‡ aircraft with a speed of 530 mph and a
flight duration of about 30 minutes; it was expected to reach the
test stage in December 1944 and, as it was easy and economical to
make, as many as 1,000 might be produced by the spring, Hitler
having recently approved manufacture by other large companies
as well as Heinkel.[51] The next evidence had come in the decrypt of

---

* The fuel was now referred to as hydrazine instead of bromacetone (see Volume III Part
1, p 352.

† The He 162 was designed, tried out and approved for large-scale production in less than
four months. In September 1944 a programme was drawn up for an output of 1,000 by April
1945, and this figure was stepped up in December following the decision to abandon the Me
163. Mass production began in December in Vienna before the prototype had been fully
tested. In the event, the disruption of communications limited the production of this aircraft
before the advance of the Allied armies necessitated the removal of the plant.[50]

‡ The Japanese normally referred both to jet and rocket aircraft as rocket aircraft. While
realising that this was a jet aircraft, GC and CS and AI appear, however, to have thought it
was the He 280.

49.   JIC(45) 79 (Draft) of 5 March; eg DEFE 3/509, BT 5321 of 21 February;
      BAY/BT 112 of 4 March.
50.   AIR 41/10, p 314; Webster and Frankland, op cit, Vol III, p 273.
51.   SJA 1038 of 24 October 1944; *Use of Ultra by the US War Department*, p 85.

another signal from the Attaché early in December. He called it the Volksjäger (People's Fighter) and explained that it was a single-engined jet with the engine mounted on top of the fuselage.[52] Later in December, after a visit with Speer to an experimental establishment, the Japanese Ambassador had referred to it as 'the 162, a plane with a rocket engine like the Me'.[53] In January 1945 the He 162 at last figured in a GAF Enigma decrypt, which referred to the 162 as being 'of the greatest importance for breaking the enemy's air terror'. In February another Enigma decrypt confirmed that it was a Heinkel model and yet another disclosed that five Me 262s taxi-ing for five minutes consumed enough fuel for one He 162 sortie. In the same month the decrypt of a signal from 7th Jagd Division indicated that the He 162 programme was progressing rapidly and enabled AI to establish that an aircraft seen by PR at the Heinkel works at Vienna/Schwechat in December was an He 162.[54]

At the end of February there was anxiety not only on account of the uncertainty about the He 162, but also as a result of references in Sigint to mounting production of jet aircraft. The decrypt of a long report at that time from the Japanese Naval Attaché estimated that Germany's total monthly production of front-line aircraft, which had been expected to double from 3,000 to 6,000 during 1944, was between 2,800 and 3,000, and went on to give current monthly rates of production by types of aircraft to the end of January 1945. AI commented on the figure for total output that although it was markedly lower than those previously provided by the Attaché for July and December 1944 (4,500 and 4,000) it was still considerably above that derived by AI from other intelligence sources. The other sources indicated that production had failed to reach 3,000 by the beginning of 1944 and that it had been falling steadily for the last three months from a lower starting point than that given by the Japanese – that it had been 2,035 in November, 1,900 in December and 1,600 in January.* As for current monthly production by types of aircraft, AI compared the Japanese

---

* But AI agreed with the reasons given by the Japanese for the failure of the Germans to reach their targets. These were the direct effects of bombing, the dispersal of the industry, the large-scale change-over from conventional to jet engines, interruption to the even supply of components caused by the systematic bombing of communications, modifications in aircraft types, the survival of faults in the jet and rocket power units, shortage of aluminium, and the loss of the occupied territories. It noted, however, that the supply of components had been interrupted more by the area bombing than by the bombing of communications.

52. *Ultra Material as a Source of Technical Intelligence*, p 6; SJA 1233 of 2 December 1944; BAY/HP 121 of 5 December.
53. *Ultra Material as a Source of Technical Intelligence*, p 6.
54. ibid, p 6; DEFE 3/325, BT 1424 of 6 January 1945; DEFE 3/509, BT 5266 of 20 February; DEFE 3/511, BT 5956 of 28 February.

estimates with its own as follows:–

	Japanese figures	AI's figures
Me 163	100	15
Me 262	500	150–200*
Ar 234	40	35*
Ta 152† and FW 190	1,000	Peak of 750 in November 1944
Me 109	800	Peak of 850 in October 1944
Ju 388	100	10
Do 335	30 or more	Still in experimental stage
Other types produced in small amounts or undergoing alteration	Several hundred	250 Ju 88s and less than 100 other types

The Japanese decrypt also gave cumulative output to the end of January 1945 for the Me 163 (400–500 aircraft) and the Me 262 (about 1,000). AI's estimates were about 135 for the Me 163 and 750–800 for the Me 262.[56]

In March AI's assurances had to compete with a marked increase in jet-fighter activity. During the first three weeks of the month a force of 80 Me 262 and Ar 234, formed as Sigint had disclosed from detachments of KG 51 and KG 76, operated at the rate of 50 sorties a day against the Remagen bridge and Allied preparations for crossing the Rhine. Their operations were not highly effective, and they were brought to an end from 21 March by intensive Allied strikes against their airfields.[57] These strikes, which continued after decrypts had disclosed that 26 jets had been destroyed and 29 damaged, put a stop to ground-attack operations, but they only temporarily reduced the GAF's capacity to offer jet opposition to the Allied bomber raids. Following the resumption of this opposition on a small scale at the end of February, the largest number of new-type fighters yet encoun-

---

   * A Japanese decrypt of 19 March[55] quoted Köller, the German Chief of Air Staff, as giving the following figures for actual and planned production in February:

Me 262	actual 296	planned 450
Ar 234	actual 19	planned 13
He 162	actual 46	planned 100

   † Ta 152 was a FW aircraft of exceptionally high performance planned as a replacement for the FW 190.

55. BAY/BT 129 of 23 March; SJA 1688 of 19 March.
56. SJA 1573 of 28 February; JIC(45) 79(Draft) of 5 March.
57. eg DEFE 3/512, BT 6100 of 2 March; CX/MSS/487 para A 9.

tered – 50 Me 262 and Me 163 – had operated against US attacks on oil targets on 2 March. There had been no further opposition from jets till 15 March, when a few appeared but made no organised efforts at interception. On 18 March, however, during a raid on Berlin, US Eighth Air Force lost 24 bombers and 5 fighters, mainly to jet aircraft which attacked in formations as large as 36 aircraft and displayed a greater variety of tactics than had been expected.[58] Although the jet opposition met with on several days during the rest of March was smaller and less determined, it was on a scale sufficient to make the Allies think in terms of 'a new phase in the air war' and of 'a new GAF'.[59]

From the middle of March Sigint left no doubt that the Germans were making further efforts to expand the Me 262 fighter force by every available means. Night-fighter units were being called on to surrender crews for emergency training on Me 262, and by the end of the month the call had been extended to other arms of the GAF including day-fighter units, V 1 launchers and even jet ground-attack units.[60] And this evidence that they were making a supreme effort to accelerate the programme culminated in the disclosure in a Fish decrypt of 5 April that Hitler had on 27 March appointed SS Engineer General Kammler, the plenipotentiary for V-weapons, as plenipotentiary for jet aircraft in charge of every aspect of the jet programme except tactical control of the units themselves.[61] But a signal from the Japanese Naval Attaché decrypted on 19 March had reported that in an interview on 13 March the German Chief of Air Staff had confessed that Allied bombing, technical problems and 'ceaseless modifications' were giving rise to 'disappointments and vexations' in the production of the new types, and that in spite of every effort it would take time to raise the GAF from the 'regrettably low ebb' to which it had been reduced mainly by shortage of fuel due to bombing and transport problems.[62]

From the end of March, with the western Allies across the Rhine in strength and the Russians advancing into Germany, the effort to maintain jet production rapidly collapsed as the western Allies, and (in the case of Ar 234) the Russians, over-ran the jet factories. The small operational jet force disintegrated no less rapidly as the Allied air attacks on its operational airfields developed into an all but continuous offensive. From the end of March Sigint revealed that, while conventional units were being disbanded, it was still

---

58.   Craven and Cate, op cit, Vol III, pp 739–743.
59.   ibid, pp 744–745.
60.   eg DEFE 3/517, BT 7313 of 15 March; CX/MSS/T498/75, T501/3, 31.
61.   AWL 4498 of 9 April; CX/MSS/T511/87.
62.   SJA 1685 of 19 March.

hoped that the equivalent of two Geschwader of Me 262 fighters could be rushed into service.[63] But from mid-April a series of decrypts ordered the disbandment first of all jet training units other than those for Me 262 fighters, then of front-line jet ground-attack units, and eventually of front-line fighter units.[64] The first few operational He 162 were caught up in the collapse. In March the decrypt of a signal from the Japanese Naval Attaché had reported that 46 He 162 had been produced in February and that 100 were expected in March.[65] GAF Enigma decrypts showed that on 12 April five He 162 were with units of JG 1, and on 19 April that OKL had ordered JGs 1 and 301 to operate with He 162 and such Ta 152 as were available. But by that date other signals were being decrypted which showed that these units were to be disbanded once their aircraft stocks were exhausted.[66]

□

In the V-weapon offensives the Allies obtained little relief until, in the last days of March, the Germans were driven from launching areas within range of worthwhile targets. From early in March, moreover, the Germans, having at last increased the range of the flying bomb, were briefly able to resume ground-based attacks with it on the United Kingdom for the first time since September 1944.

During January flying bomb attacks against Belgian targets continued on a reduced scale, at the rate of 150 a week, and from 19 January Antwerp was the only target. It became clear, however, that new launching sites were being prepared; one was identified in the Rotterdam-Dordrecht area. And from the beginning of February, carried out more and more from the Rotterdam area and other sites in Holland and less and less from the German sites, the attack on Antwerp again intensified, rising to over 500 in the week ending 17 February and to about 600 in the following week.[67] This last figure proved to be the peak: 420 missiles landed in the week ending 9 March, 300 in the next fortnight, and on 29 March firings against Antwerp came to an end.[68] AI, which had predicted on 13 January that Flak Regiment 155 (W) would have

---

63. CX/MSS/T513/36; DEFE 3/566, KOs 336 and 379 of 13 and 14 April; DEFE 3/569, KO 1012 of 21 April.

64. DEFE 3/569, KO 1080 of 22 April; DEFE 3/570, KO 1257 of 24 April; DEFE 3/571, KOs 1592, 1635 and 1723 of 28, 29 and 30 April.

65. BAY/BT 129 of 23 March.

66. CX/MSS/T521/20; DEFE 3/568, KO 954 of 21 April.

67. CAB 121/215, SIC file B/Defence/2, Vol 5, COS(45) 122(0) of 21 February.

68. ibid, COS(45) 262(0) of 16 April.

the capacity to fire at the rate of 700 a week during February,[69] got evidence soon afterwards that the offensive might not go beyond that level. There had been evidence from Enigma decrypts in the previous August that the enemy was forming a second flying bomb regiment, Flak Regiment 255 (W),[70] but later in January the same source disclosed that this plan had been abandoned.[71]

In February intelligence had provided firm evidence that the Germans were increasing the range of the flying bomb. This possibility had exercised the counter-measures authorities since the start of the V 1 campaign,* and their suspicions had been borne out in September and October 1944 by the decrypts of signals from the Japanese Naval Attaché in Berlin. He had then reported that although the campaign had been suspended following the Allied capture of the firing sites, the Germans hoped after some unavoidable delay to resume it with V 1s of longer range from bases in the rear of their front line and from Germany itself.[72] No further evidence was obtained until February 1945. The wreckage of flying bombs landing in Belgium then indicated that in recent models of the missile the weight of the wings and of the warhead had been reduced.[73] And on 21 February the Enigma, which had already at the end of January disclosed that the V 1 activities on the Baltic test ranges had been moved to the Nordholz-Cuxhafen area and that firings northwards along the coast of Jutland had started on 27 January with the normal V 1 range of about 150 miles, disclosed that from 24 February the range would be increased to about 230 miles. In two other decrypts of 21 February, moreover, Himmler's adjutant reported that Himmler had approved a V 1 programme submitted to him on 8 February and General Kammler advised Naval Command West on 18 February that because he was interested for tactical reasons in the air situation between The Hague and the English coast, he wanted to establish within ten days an observation post at Dunkirk.[74]

Commenting on these developments on 22 February, AI noted that with its new range the V 1 could be used against London from bases in western Holland and that in normal circumstances it

---

* See above, p 534..

69. ibid, COS (45) 36(0) of 13 January.
70. CX/MSS/T273/22, T276/64.
71. CAB 121/215, COS(45) 122(0) of 21 February; AWL 3809 of 23 January 1945.
72. SJAs 918 of 20 September, 1006 of 17 October.
73. AIR 41/55, *Air Defence of Great Britain*, Vol VI, p 299.
74. AWL 3851 of 30 January 1945; DEFE 3/509, BTs 5347 and 5348 of 21 February.

would be ready about a month after the beginning of the trials, that is from the middle of March. It suspected, however, that since the greater range would be obtained by the simplest possible modification, probably a reduction in the weight of the warhead, the attack might begin earlier, and that if the Dunkirk observation post was associated with it, it might have been timed for 1 March.[75] The Chiefs of Staff were so informed on 25 February; the attack might begin about the end of February and within one or two weeks of the initial launchings it might be possible for the Germans to sustain a rate of 30 to 50 launchings a day over a considerable period. They were also advised that, although extensive reconnaissance was being flown, no launching sites had yet been detected in south-west Holland despite ground reports of suspicious activity in two particular areas.[76] These conclusions, and a summary of the intelligence underlying them, were sent to the Prime Minister by General Ismay in a minute on 26 February.[77]

Later the same day – on an unused airfield near The Hague and in a factory district at Vlaardingen, six miles west of Rotterdam – the PRU and the CIU detected two launching sites with ramps oriented on London; so far as could be judged from the evidence of earlier PR sorties, they had been completed in about ten days. A third site, near Delft, was discovered after the end of the campaign.[78]

Ground-launched flying bombs hit London on 3 March, for the first time since the beginning of the previous September. Examination of wreckage showed that no major changes of design had occurred, and it was noted that although the enemy had achieved a range of 200 miles and that 250 miles might be possible, accuracy was poor. The weight of the attack proved to be much lighter than AI had estimated. Twenty-one missiles were fired between 0300 on 3 March and 1100 on 5 March; ten of them were shot down and seven reached the London area. Thereafter, the rate of attack slackened and the defences in the United Kingdom surpassed the best rate of success achieved in 1944. Up to 29 March 1945, when this final phase of the V 1 campaign came to an end, 125 flying bombs had been detected over England, perhaps as little as half of the number actually fired; 91 of these had been shot down, 86 by Anti-Aircraft Command, and only 13

75.　AWL 4061 of 24 February.

76.　CAB 121/215, COS(45) 51st (o) Meeting, 25 February.

77.　ibid, Annex to Ismay minute to the Prime Minister, 26 February.

78.　ibid, COS(45) 191(o) of 20 March; AWLs 4155 and 4295 of 6 and 20 March; AIR 41/55, p 300.

had reached the London area.[79]

In a message decrypted on 9 March the V-weapons authorities had reported that, in view of the increased range, launching sites for the V 1 were no longer to be confined to Holland; surveys were to be made of suitable locations in Germany. By 20 March it was known from decrypts that ten places were to be surveyed between Bremen and Emden, roughly as far from Antwerp as the sites in Holland were from London.[80] But the attacks on Antwerp ceased on 29 March. A week after the end of the campaign a decrypt disclosed that on 7 April Kammler had agreed to a further reduction in the weight of the warhead of the V 1 if that would enable it to reach without delay a range of 500 km (about 350 miles); he attached the greatest importance to the rapid development of a new version, which should be operational by mid-April.[81] On 13 April, however, what appears to have been the last Enigma decrypt to refer to the flying bomb revealed that on 11 April, on Kammler's orders, the experimental V-weapon unit at Cuxhafen, and its detachments at Wesermünde and in Denmark, were closing down.[82]

At the end of February the Prime Minister and the Minister of Home Security had meanwhile questioned the adequacy of the bombing effort against the V 2 sites; anxiety was growing about the state of morale in London, and some critics may also have been encouraged by the fact that, following the intensification of precision attacks on the launching areas near The Hague, no rockets had been fired against London during 24 and 25 February. On 3 March there was a still heavier attack on the Haagssche Bosch near The Hague, thought to be the forward storage area for the rockets fired against the United Kingdom, by the medium bombers of the 2nd Tactical Air Force. The raid caused severe civilian damage and loss of life in a densely populated area, an outcome which reinforced the reply the Chiefs of Staff gave on 7 March to representations from the Minister of Home Security. They explained that the bombing policy of harassing all profitable targets associated with the launching areas was already achieving all that could be expected from air action alone and that, although heavy air attacks against the Nordhausen factory were still being considered, it was clear that no serious

79. AIR 41/55, pp 300, 302, 303; CAB 121/215, COS(45) 191(o) of 20 March; Collier, op cit, p 395.
80. DEFE 3/514, BT 6743 of 9 March; AWL 4201 of 10 March; DEFE 3/519, BT 7829 of 20 March.
81. DEFE 3/564, BT 9804 of 8 April; AWL 4498 of 9 April.
82. CX/MSS/T518/16 of 13 April; AWL 4556 of 16 April.

direct damage could be inflicted on it.[83] By 20 March there was some evidence that the Germans had abandoned the Haagssche Bosch, but they were still firing from the launching area south of The Hague, from eastern Holland and from the Koblenz area, and the number of rockets fired only slightly declined.

Firings against the United Kingdom stopped abruptly on 27 March, by which time 1,054 rockets had landed in England and 61 close offshore, killing over 2,500 people and seriously injuring 6,500. Those against Antwerp came to an end on the following day, by which time eleven rockets had also been fired, somewhat inaccurately, against the Rhine crossing at Remagen. Fighter-bomber attacks on targets associated with the launchings against the United Kingdom continued till 3 April, there being no evidence that the Germans had withdrawn from The Hague. But a decrypt of 30 March had disclosed that a unit engaged in the attacks on Antwerp had been withdrawing since 26 March, and the low-grade wireless traffic of the V 2 organisation then disclosed that the V 2 units which had operated against Antwerp from eastern Holland had withdrawn into Germany at the end of March, with orders to proceed to Nordhausen, and that those located near Koblenz had moved 50 miles to the east.[84] Between 6 and 9 April Enigma decrypts disclosed that on orders from OKW the Army was to defend the Nordhausen area at all costs, so as to secure the production of V-weapons and jet fighters 'until the last moment', that a veto had been placed on the use of Kammler's troops for any other purpose, but also that some of those troops had been subordinated to Army Group Student for defence tasks.[85] The last Enigma messages containing references to V 2 were decrypted on 9, 10 and 13 April; they called for the destruction of a V 2 on three trucks in Bromskirchen railway station, to prevent its capture by the Allies.[86] In the absence of any firm evidence after the middle of April, speculation continued as to the whereabouts of the V 2 units,[87] but no further rockets were launched up to the time of Germany's unconditional surrender.

□

---

83. CAB 121/215, Minutes from the PM, General Ismay and Mr Morrison, 26 February and 1 March 1945, COS(45) 62nd Meeting CA of 7 March; AIR 41/55, pp 289–290, 293–294.

84. CAB 121/215, COS(45) 191(o) of 20 March, 262(o) of 16 April; DEFE 3/601, BT 8888 of 30 March; AWL 4432 of 3 April; AIR 41/55, pp 305–306; Collier, op cit, p 420 and Appendix XLIX.

85. CX/MSS/T510/103 of 6 April; DEFE 3/563, BT 9713 of 7 April; DEFE 3/564, BT 9991 of 9 April, amended in DEFE 3/565, KO 130 of 11 April; AWLs 4498 of 9 April, 4521 of 11 April.

86. DEFE 3/564, BT 9931 of 9 April; DEFE 3/565, KO 15 of 10 April; DEFE 3/566, KOs 315, 369 of 13 April.

87. AWLs 4556 and 4618 of 16 and 23 April, 4671 of 1 May.

CHAPTER 59

The End of the War at Sea

I N THE last four months of the war the efforts of the U-boat Command were no less unrelenting than those of the V-weapons authorities. Between 1 January and 7 May the Allies lost 398,000 tons of merchant shipping. U-boats accounted for 263,000 tons of it, a quarterly rate of sinkings that was higher than that for any quarter in 1944.[1] In the last weeks of the war, moreover, Allied losses were still on an upward trend – 30 ships sunk or damaged between mid-March and 1 May – and U-boats were still leaving Bergen on war cruises on 4 May, when the enemy surrender in north Germany had led to the order for their recall.

Almost all the losses were the work of the conventional U-boats. The number of old-type U-boats operating with *Schnorchel* from Norwegian ports increased steadily from the beginning of the year. Sigint showed that on 1 January it was 75, of which 32 were on patrol: on 5 March it was 90 (49 at sea); and by 1 April it was 110 of which 55 were operating.[2] Although approximately 50 U-boats were sunk over this period, the number transferred to the Atlantic Command from refits and the diminishing programme of conventional U-boat construction – over 100 – more than made up for the losses. Against this outflow from the Baltic the air-mining of the Kattegat and south Norwegian waters was intensified in February, but while this delayed the outflow, it did not come near to stopping it before the German minesweeping organisation finally collapsed at the end of March.

The majority of these U-boats continued to operate in the British inshore waters. Between three and four a month sailed for patrol areas in the Irish Sea and a still larger number operated in the English Channel. Despite the enormous concentration of anti-submarine forces against them, their successes showed no tendency to decline. By the end of March, however, their own casualties had risen to such a pitch that the enemy withdrew them from the English Channel and the North Channel and deployed a number of them, for the first time for many months, on the

---

1. Ehrman, *Grand Strategy*, Vol VI (1956), p 17.
2. ADM 233/315, 316, OIC SI 1174 of 1 January, 1212 of 5 February, 1241 of 5 March and 1280 of 2 April 1945.

convoy route well to the south of Ireland. No orders for
withdrawal were decrypted, but signals allotting patrol positions in
this area to seven U-boats were decrypted on 1 and 2 April. They
sank or damaged four ships in the next few days but five of them
had been sunk by 10 April.[3]

It was, as we now know, in an effort to distract the anti-
submarine defences and provide relief to the U-boats in the
coastal waters that the U-boat Command also attempted to resume
pack tactics in mid-Atlantic early in April. On 26 March, knowing
that about 20 Type IX boats were at sea and that eight of them
were on passage to an area north of the Azores, the OIC foresaw
that this might happen; and on 2 April six of these U-boats were
ordered in Offizier signals to form a reconnaissance line in the
area 49° 30′N, 25°W and sweep WSW along the convoy lanes. In a
signal decrypted on 3 April they were encouraged to attack
ruthlessly and reminded that the Allies, having experienced no
surface attacks on convoys for one and a half years, were prepared
only for underwater attacks. Signals decrypted on 9 April
addressed them as Gruppe *Seewolf* and gave them twelve successive patrol lines to be adopted in the course of their sweep. Two
US escort carriers and 20 destroyers were being moved to the area
by 16 April, and by 24 April they had sunk four of the U-boats.
The U-boat Command dispersed the group on 24 April, by which
time it had made no contact with convoys, and ordered it to
operate off Halifax and south of New York.[4]

The two survivors from Gruppe *Seewolf* were sunk soon after
arriving off the American coast. In all, ten of the 16 U-boats sent
to this area in 1945 had been sunk by the end of the war, virtually
all of them with the help of decrypts.[5] They achieved few successes
after the middle of January.[6]

Apart from maintaining the Arctic force of some 20 U-boats,*
the U-boat Command made no sustained effort in other areas. An
occasional single U-boat operated off Reykjavik and the Straits of
Gibraltar. Three U-boats sailed from Norway to the Far East, but
the first was sunk off Norway by a British submarine in February
and in April the second was damaged in an air attack and forced to
return. The third, U-234, sailed on 16 April with General Kessler,

---

* See above, p 490ff.

3. Naval Headlines of 1 and 2 April; Roskill, *The War at Sea*, Vol III Part 2
    (1961), pp 467–469.
4. ADM 223/316, 317, OIC SI 1270 of 26 March, 1319 of 30 April; Naval
    Headlines of 4 and 11 April.
5. US Department of Defense, *Allied Communication Intelligence and the Battle of
    the Atlantic*, Vol II, Appendix 1.
6. ADM 234/68, BR 305(3), p 97; Roskill, op cit, Vol III Part 2, p 297.

the newly appointed Air Attaché to Tokyo on board; she surrendered to the US Navy in mid-Atlantic on 12 May. Four U-boats from the Far East were recalled to Norway in December 1944 and January 1945; their arrival was reported on different dates in April. Two others were on passage to Europe when Germany surrendered, and six, including two ex-Italian cargo-carrying submarines, remained in Japan or Japanese-occupied ports.[7]

□

For all the efforts of the old-type U-boats, the over-riding concern of the U-boat Command was to bring forward the day when the new types could join them; and the over-riding fear of the Allied authorities from the beginning of the year was that this day might arrive at any time. Their anxiety about the effect it would have in terms of an increase in the U-boat offensive did not decline following the decision in December 1944 to divert part of the strategic bombing effort against the new-type U-boats – a decision incorporated in the new strategic bombing directive of 15 January 1945.* On 6 January the First Sea Lord had warned the Chiefs of Staff that a major offensive was likely to start in February or March, one in which the combination of Type XXI U-boats in the Atlantic, Type XXIII and Type VIIC with *Schnorchel* in coastal waters and the longer range old-type boats in the eastern Atlantic and the Indian Ocean might increase the number of U-boats on patrol to 70 in the spring and 90 in the summer, putting an intolerable strain on the anti-submarine resources and raising Allied shipping losses to half as much again as in the spring of 1943.[8] His representations not only produced the new bombing directive but also led to the decision to half the planned despatch of 41 destroyers and 260 escort vessels to the Far East and a request for a large reinforcement of Coastal Command.[9] At the Anglo-American staff talks at Malta on 2 February the Combined Chiefs of Staff confirmed this decision and, being advised by the Joint Planners that it might not by itself be sufficient to guarantee early success against *Schnorchel* and the new U-boats, sanctioned further measures: to maintain and if possible increase the marginal bomber effort against assembly yards and ·operating

---

* See above, p 601.

7. US Department of Defense, op cit, Vol II, Chapter XII.
8. CAB 80/90, COS(45)14(0) of 6 January.
9. Roskill, op cit, Vol III Part 2, p 286; AIR 41/74, *The RAF in Maritime War*, Vol V, p 280.

bases; to double if possible the air-mining effort against the U-boats including the training areas; to intensify attacks on enemy minesweepers and shipping used to supply the Norwegian bases.[10]

These measures were at once put into effect, though without being incorporated in a new bombing directive, and they succeeded in substantially delaying the operational readiness of the new-type U-boat fleet. But the extent to which the completion and working up of the new U-boats was being held up by the bombing of their yards and bases and disruption in their training areas, as also by the fact that they continued to encounter numerous technical faults which had to be rectified, could not be accurately estimated by the intelligence authorities. PR and Sigint continued to provide a reliable check on the numbers completed and the numbers commissioned, but neither source threw light on their rates of progress towards operational readiness. When this was the case and when, on the other hand, so much was known about the increase in their numbers and the absolute priority that the enemy was giving to bringing them forward, the OIC had little choice but to err on the side of caution in its appreciations. And this was all the more the case because of its anxiety about the continuing decline in the amount of Sigint available about U-boats at sea that was resulting from changes in German cypher and signals procedures.* On 22 January the OIC reported that the effects of Sonderschlüssel on the Tracking Room's plot were becoming 'gravely adverse'. A month later it expressed serious anxiety that Kurier, which it feared would be in operational use by the end of March, would make ship-borne interception and DF of U-boat signals impossible if and when the new-type U-boats resumed pack attacks.[11]

On 16 January the JIC noted that Types XXI and XXIII were now being completed at the rate of 16 and 9 a month, that there was evidence that the planned output of Type XXI was 30 a month, and that it was probable that Germany had 'other types of even higher capabilities in the design stage'.† It believed that the expected Atlantic offensive would materialise in or before March, and would be supplemented by intensified operations by Type

---

* See Appendix 15(v) for Sonderschlüssel and Kurier.

† This was a reference to what were now known to be called the Type XVIIB U-boats (see Volume III Part 1, p 239). At the end of April the OIC reported that four were under construction, of which two might be completed. In fact two had been undergoing trials for some months.[12]

10.   AIR 41/74, pp 198–202.
11.   ADM 223/315, 316, OIC SI 1199 of 22 January, 1231 of 23 February.
12.   ADM 234/68, p 87; ADM 223/317, OIC SI 1318 of 30 April.

XXIII U-boats and the KdK craft in the coastal waters.[13] On 21 January it repeated the warning that the offensive would start within four to six weeks, and 'almost certainly not later than the end of March'. The Germans had postponed it only until they could launch it with a large number of U-boats, and they had now accumulated a considerable force of old and new types; its present strength of 200, including new-type U-boats working up, might rise to 275 in April and 430 in August.[14] Early in February the OIC estimated that the number of operational U-boats of all types had risen to 168 from 137 on 1 October 1944 and 157 on 1 December.[15] In the event, while its later estimates of the numbers of U-boats working up continued to grow, its estimates of the numbers that were operational showed no significant increase:[16]

	Number working up	*Number Operational*
29 Jan.	172 (54 XXIs and 23 XXIIIs)	159 (2 XXIIIs)
26 March	201 (95 XXIs and 44 XXIIIs)	168 (1 XXI and 3 XXIIIs)
30 April	196 (94 XXIs and 43 XXIIIs)	174 (6 XXIs and 14 XXIIIs)

If it had not been for the steady increase in the monthly rate of sinkings of the conventional U-boats at sea throughout those months, the delays to working up (of the new types especially) and the destruction of new types in bombing raids on the yards, its fears about the expansion of the operational fleet would have been fully vindicated.

By early in February the Enigma had disclosed that the U-boat training organisation had moved westward, two flotillas to Kiel and one to Wilhelmshafen.* The OIC recognised that the transfer might result in a slowing-down of the training of the new U-boats, but feared that it might equally have the effect of shortening the training time and accelerating the expected U-boat offensive since other decrypts had shown that two school flotillas had been ordered to transfer all sea-worthy boats to active operations immediately. It estimated, moreover, that the number of newly

---

* The OIC believed the move was brought about by the Russian advances, which did lead to the decision to stop U-boat construction at Danzig and Gdynia at this time, but it was in fact Bomber Command's mining of the eastern Baltic which necessitated the transfer of training (see pp 483–484). The Enigma showed that U-boat training and repairs still continued in Danzig Bay until the middle of March. The OIC reported on 19 March that the area had been finally abandoned.[17]

13. JIC(45)19(o) (Draft) of 16 January.
14. JIC(45)22(o) of 21 January.
15. ADM 223/316, OIC SI 1212 of 5 February.
16. ADM 223/316, 317, OIC SI 1207 of 29 January, 1271 of 26 March, 1318 of 30 April.
17. ADM 223/316, OIC SI 1235 of 26 February, 1251 of 12 March, 1261 of 19 March.

commissioned Type XXI had risen from 54 on 29 January to 63 on 3 February, the largest weekly increase so far.[18] On 12 February the OIC estimated that some 94 Type XXI were under construction, of which six might be completed, and that 67 were commissioned and working up; and for the first time it hazarded an estimate of the number that might be ready to operate—34 of the 67 that had been commissioned.[19] In fact, by mid-February 107 Type XXI had been delivered to the Navy, of which eight had been destroyed or damaged, seven were practically ready for operations, 27 were under final training, 30 were still undergoing acceptance trials and 34 were less advanced.[20] On 19 February the OIC noted that despite the fact that a very large number of U-boats were ready or nearly ready for operations, there was 'still no sign of the major U-boat offensive'.[21] But it did not revise its earlier appreciations to the effect that the offensive would materialise in or before March.

Its caution appeared to be justified when, in signals dated 17 February, decrypted on 21 February, the head of the Japanese Naval Mission in Berlin reported interviews held with Dönitz and Wagner, his Chief of Staff. Dönitz had said that large-scale U-boat operations would begin at an early date using Type XXI in a total front-line force that was increasing 'in a steep curve'; Wagner had been confident that large-scale operations would start 'very soon'.[22] The OIC commented on 26 February that there was no indication that a full-scale offensive had been launched.[23] On 5 March it reported that there was 'still no light on the mystery of the non-appearance of the Type XXI U-boats', of which 41 were now thought to be fit for operations.[24]

It may be concluded from the language of this appreciation that the OIC was beginning to suspect that its worst fears could be laid aside, and this was certainly its response to a further Japanese decrypt in which the 'mystery' was cleared up. In signals decrypted on 12 March 1945 the head of the Japanese Naval Mission reported on another interview with Dönitz's Chief of Staff held on 5 March. Wagner had said that losses of U-boats round the United Kingdom had risen but that when the new high-speed U-boats began operations they would not run the risk of heavy losses at sea; although air raid damage to the U-boats and plant at their

---

18.   ADM 223/316, OIC SI 1202 and 1206 of 29 January, 1212 of 5 February.
19.   ibid, OIC SI 1221 of 12 February.
20.   AIR 41/74, p 174.
21.   ADM 223/316, OIC SI 1227 of 19 February.
22.   SJAs 1560 and 1561 of 21 February.
23.   ADM 223/316, OIC SI 1235 of 26 February.
24.   ibid, 1241 of 5 March.

bases and risks from mines when leaving or returning to port were and would remain serious problems. He had added that although it was hoped to sail a few Type XXI U-boats in March, they were still developing faults from having been put into mass production before experiments with them had been completed; for this reason, and also because great care was being taken in crew training, they were not likely to start operations on a larger scale till May or, at a really conservative estimate, till June.[25] In the light of this decrypt the JIC was able on 19 March to give the assurance that no serious threat would arise from the U-boats 'unless and until ocean operations can be mounted simultaneously with inshore patrols', and that operations on any scale by the new-type U-boats were unlikely to begin until late in April at the earliest. It was no doubt confident that Germany would by then be defeated or on the verge of defeat, since it added that U-boat operations might be maintained from Norway 'for an appreciable time after the *de facto* surrender of Northern Germany'.[26]

On the same day an Enigma decrypt disclosed that U-2511, the first Type XXI to leave the Baltic, had left Kiel for Norway on 18 March. The OIC's records showed that she had been the eleventh to commission and had been working up for five months, and that her captain, Schnee, was an experienced U-boat commander. Subsequent decrypts disclosed that a periscope defect delayed the beginning of his operational patrol from 26 March, that he sailed from Bergen on 17 April only to be forced back with diesel defects on 21 April, and that he did not finally get away for his first and last cruise till 3 May.[27] No signals relating to U-2511's time at sea were decrypted.*

If the intelligence about U-2511 underlined the narrowness of the margin by which the Allies escaped the threat from the new-type U-boats, so did other Sigint which, from the middle of April, supported the possibility that Germany might continue to operate U-boats from Norway even after the Baltic ports had been occupied. Decrypts showed from that date that she was preparing to transfer to Norway U-boats which still lacked equipment and training; 22 such U-boats were mentioned, of which six or seven had already sailed. By 23 April the OIC noted that of the 35 that had left since the beginning of the month, 25 had recently

---

* She carried out a dummy attack on a British cruiser before returning to Norway in accordance with the surrender decree.[28]

25. SJAs 1654 and 1655 of 12 March.
26. JIC(45)90(0) of 19 March.
27. ADM 223/316, 317, OIC SI 1261 and 1270 of 19 and 26 March, 1310 of 23 April; Naval Headlines of 4 May.
28. ADM 234/68, p 98.

completed working up. It estimated by 30 April that 48 had left, most of them barely worked up; they included five Type XXI and 10 Type XXIII, raising the numbers of these types outside the Baltic to six and 14 respectively. By the same date the Enigma had disclosed that 30 school U-boats were to move into the operational category, and that plans were laid for establishing the W/T control centre at Bergen.[29] From the beginning of May, however, in intense Allied air attacks on the continuing exodus, 23 U-boats were sunk out of a total of 28 lost in these last few days of the war.[30]

On 30 April the OIC estimated that six Type XXI were operational, 94 working up and 19 still under construction; and on 7 May it believed that a total of 21 were available for operations.[31] In fact, 13, including U-2511, had completed their working up and 91 were completing their acceptance trials.[32]

□

The progress of the Type XXIII U-boats and the probability that they would become operational at any time had meanwhile been a source of continuing alarm since the end of January, when the Enigma revealed that two of them had arrived at Horten in south Norway, the first of the new-type U-boats to leave the Baltic.[33] On 12 February, after a decrypt had disclosed that one of them, U-2322, had been told to set watch on the frequency used by U-boats in the coastal waters of the United Kingdom, the OIC believed that she might have been at sea for a week and guessed that she had probably headed for the Scapa-Firth of Forth area; it was known that at least one Type VII *Schnorchel* boat was already in that area.[34] Decrypts available on 25 and 26 February disclosed the return of another Type XXIII, U-2324, to Kristiansand and gave her patrol report: she had operated off Newcastle, had made an unsuccessful attack on 18 February but had otherwise made no contacts.[35] A signal decrypted by 28 February warning U-2322 of minefields off the Firth of Forth confirmed that she was still on patrol, and there was still no evidence that she had returned to port by 5 March.[36]

---

29.   ADM 223/316, 317, OIC SI 1298, 1310 and 1319 of 16, 23 and 30 April.
30.   Roskill, op cit, Vol III Part 2, p 469.
31.   ADM 223/317, OIC SI 1318 of 30 April, 1329 of 7 May.
32.   Roskill, op cit, Vol III Part 2, p 302.
33.   ADM 223/316, OIC SI 1206 of 29 January.
34.   ibid, 1220 of 12 February.
35.   Naval Headlines of 25 and 26 February; ADM 223/316, OIC SI 1235 of 26 February.
36.   Naval Headlines of 28 February; ADM 223/316, OIC SI 1241 of 5 March.

The fact that these U-boats had sailed 'without any mention of it in W/T', as the OIC emphasised, led to great uncertaintly as to whether others might be on patrol. As it happened, in each case when a Type XXIII was at sea the Enigma disclosed the fact; but it did not give details of the patrol area, and the Admiralty was unable to decide in relation to Allied casualties whether to attribute them to a Type XXIII or to a conventional U-boat. A situation report of 3 May, decrypted on 4 May, stated that Type XXIIIs had made a total of six cruises and sunk one ship in each of four of them; and that none of the U-boats had been sunk.[37]*

On 30 April the OIC estimated that 14 Type XXIII were operational, 43 working up and 15 still under construction.[39] In fact out of a total of 63 delivered to the Navy by that date, six were fully operational, 17 had moved to Norway but were not yet fully operational, two had been destroyed in air attacks and 38 were still working up.[40]

For all that they caused so much legitimate anxiety from the autumn of 1944, the Type XXIIIs thus made a negligible contribution to the last stage of the U-boat campaign in the coastal waters around the United Kingdom. And this was also the case with the operations of the battle groups of the KdK Command in relation to the E-boat campaign against the Allied supply routes to the continent. The E-boats maintained their minelaying operations and their attacks on the East Coast and Thames-Scheldt convoys till they were forced by fuel shortage and the steady erosion of the facilities at their Dutch bases by Allied air attacks to discontinue them at the end of April.[41] They suffered only occasional losses – the force still numbered about 40 boats at the end of April – and despite the fact that the Enigma continued to provide nearly current intelligence about their operations, often depriving them of the advantage of surprise, their successes were considerably higher than those obtained by the small battle-units.†

Till a week before the end of hostilities the KdK persisted in mounting operations, but the scale of their operations fell far

---

* In all, six Type XXIII made eight cruises. Following U-2324 and U-2322, U-2321 operated off the Firth of Forth in March and U-2329 and U-2326 in April. U-2322 and U-2324 also operated off the Thames estuary in April. On the last night of the war a sixth Type XXIII, U-2336, sank two ships in the Firth of Forth, having missed the order to all U-boats to cease operations and return to base.[38]

† See table at p 638 below.

37. Naval Headlines of 4 May.
38. ADM 223/64, pp 98–99.
39. ADM 223/317, OIC SI 1318 of 30 April.
40. AIR 41/74, p 176.
41. ADM 223/316, 317, OIC SI 1285 and 1315 of 9 and 30 April.

short of the enormous effort expended on the production of these weapons. On 19 March the NID estimated from Sigint and other sources that stocks of the weapons still amounted to between 500 and 600 midget U-boats, 300 explosive motor boats (*Linse*) and 300 one-man torpedoes (*Marder*) despite the heavy losses that had been incurred. At the end of April it estimated that some 300 midget U-boats, 300 *Linse* and 100 *Marder* were still available in Holland and Denmark.[42] But operational front-line strength remained low and barely kept pace with casualties. According to the German records the front-line strength in Holland, a half to a third of which might be operational at any one time, was 86 midget U-boats and 87 *Linse* in January and 70 midget U-boats and 17 *Linse* early in April.[43] Even in proportion to the scale of operational activity, moreover, the results achieved were unimpressive.

Such operations as were carried out in the rivers inland in support of the Army, for which the KdK used the smaller midget U-boats (*Biber and Molch*) and *Linse* in addition to frogmen, were without exception fruitless. Sigint gave no warning when 17 Biber made a final attack on the Nijmegen bridge on 13 January, but it disclosed that the attack had been abortive and that the 'Nijmegen Special Force' had then been disbanded.[44] Attacks by frogmen against the Remagen bridges on 16 and 17 March were beaten off; decrypts disclosing that the attacks were planned and that attempts to carry them out on 9, 11 and 12 March had been cancelled had been despatched to the Allied Commands since 9 March.[45] Decrypts disclosed on 16 and 20 March that the KdK intended to make a final mass attack at Remagen despite the deterioration of the situation there and the consequent loss of suitable launching bases; but Sigint had reported by 22 March that the operation had been abandoned and by 24 March that the KdK force had been withdrawn.[46] Decrypts had meanwhile disclosed since 12 March that frogmen and *Linse* were being mobilised to

---

42. ADM 223/317, OIC SI 1321 of 30 April, 1323 of 2 May.

43. Roskill, op cit, Vol III Part 2, p 270 n; Naval Historical Branch, FDS 65/54, *German Small Battle Unit Operations 1943–1945*, pp 25–26.

44. FDS 65/54, p 51; DEFE 3/329, BT 2428 of 15 January; DEFE 3/330, BT 2665 of 18 January.

45. FDS 65/54, pp 53–54; DEFE 3/314, BT 6687 of 9 March; DEFE 3/515, BTs 6837 and 6922 of 10 March; DEFE 3/516, BTs 7122 of 13 March, 7196 and 7204 of 14 March; DEFE 3/517, BT 7373 of 16 March; Naval Headlines of 11, 14 and 16 March; ADM 223/316, OIC SI 1259 of 18 March.

46. FDS 65/54, p 54; DEFE 3/517, BTs 7363, 7374 and 7388 of 16 March; DEFE 3/518, BT 7739 of 20 March; DEFE 3/519, BT 7794 of 20 March; DEFE 3/520, BTs 8042 and 8054 of 23 March, 8174 of 24 March; Naval Headlines of 17, 20, 21, 23 and 24 March.

combat Allied crossings at various other points along the Rhine.[47] But Sigint pointed to no successful operations up to the end of March, referring only to cancellations and to failed attempts.[48] From the end of March it referred to KdK preparations for resistance to Allied advances in the Ems estuary and Schleswig Holstein, but did not report any operations.[49]

The KdK operations against Allied shipping were more sustained. It used *Biber*, *Molch* and *Linse* for torpedo attacks and minelaying in the Scheldt estuary and a new longer-range midget U-boat (*Seehund*)* in operations off the English coast between Yarmouth and Dungeness to supplement the E-boat attacks on the Thames–Antwerp convoy route. Only with *Seehund*, however, did it obtain any substantial success.

Sigint had given no warning that *Seehund* was being developed. When the Japanese Naval Mission in Berlin reported in a signal decrypted at the end of December 1944 that 'small-type U-boats' were ready for operations to prevent the Allied use of Antwerp the OIC was uncertain whether the reference was to a new weapon, to *Biber* or indeed to Type XXIII.[50] By the end of January 1945 it knew that *Seehund* was a new weapon, but had concluded that it was quite unsuited to operations off the English coast: POW taken during its first use in an operation off the Scheldt at the beginning of the month had indicated that the Germans were regarding it as expendable after use, that its navigation system was simple in the extreme and that like the *Hecht*, which had been abandoned and which it had replaced, it constituted no great advance on *Biber*.[51] This conclusion was soon disproved. Between 30 January and 5 February decrypts relating to an operation by 12 *Seehund* off the east coast disclosed that although only five had reached the operational area and only one had carried out an attack – without success – all had returned to base, and that the KdK was encouraged by the outcome.[52]

---

* See above, p 461.

47. DEFE 3/515, BT 6986 of 12 March; DEFE 3/516, BTs 7122 of 13 March, 7196 and 7204 of 14 March; DEFE 3/517, BTs 7265, 7286 and 7314 of 15 March, 7373 of 16 March; DEFE 3/518, BT 7530 of 18 March; Naval Headlines of 13 to 16 March, 18 March.

48. eg DEFE 3/520, BTs 8166, 8197 and 8209 of 24 March; DEFE 3/600, BTs 8502 and 8511 of 27 March; DEFE 3/601, BTs 8647 of 28 March, 8866 of 30 March; Naval Headlines of 25, 27 and 28 March.

49. Naval Headlines of 27 March, 12 and 22 April.

50. SJA 1328 of 26 December 1944.

51. AIR 41/74, p 251; Roskill, op cit, Vol III Part 2, p 271; ADM 223/315, 316, OIC SI 1183, 1188 and 1204 of 8, 15 and 29 January 1945.

52. ADM 223/304, Ultra signal 1124/30 January; Naval Headlines of 31 January and 4 February; ADM 223/316, OIC SI 1215 of 5 February.

From the second week of February, when a decrypt disclosed that *Seehund* was classified as the Type XXVIIB U-boat,[53] it operated regularly off the English east coast and Sigint showed that the Germans were determined to increase the scale and range of its operations. On 1 March a decrypt disclosed that no *Seehund* would be sent to the Mediterranean until, perhaps by the end of March, the strength at Ijmuiden had been built up to 80 boats, the number required for attacks on the Thames-Scheldt shipping route in view of the fact that only 30 per cent could be operationally ready at any one time.[54]* In decrypts of 17 and 18 March it was reported that the *Seehund's* range was being increased from 320 to 450 miles by using the compensating tank for fuel, and that while the Yarmouth area would remain the most favourable area for operations, operations west of the line Dover-Calais were being considered.[56]†

A decrypt at the end of March revealed that the largest possible number of *Seehund* would be sent to operate off Dungeness as soon as the weather improved, and a decrypt of 5 April added that nine *Seehund* equipped for the increased range were ready for operations in this new area.[58] Notice of their intention to sail on the afternoon of 7 April was decrypted that night; on 9 and 11 April they sank one merchant ship and damaged two others, but five out of 13 *Seehund* failed to return.[59] Decrypts later disclosed

---

* This build-up, which perhaps did not allow for losses, was apparently not achieved. In an analysis issued on 1 May the OIC reported that in eight PR sorties during April an average of 30 *Seehund* had been located in Ijmuiden at any one time and that Sigint indicated that this figure represented about 75 per cent of those in port. The OIC's estimate of the number of *Seehund* in Holland and the Bight at the end of April was 75.[55]

† From 25 March *Seehund* were also used in small numbers on sailings from Ijmuiden with supplies for Dunkirk. Preparations for this, involving the use of special containers, were disclosed by Sigint from early in March and decrypts reported their arrival at and departure from Dunkirk on several occasions between 25 March and the beginning of May.[57]

53. ADM 223/304, Ultra signal 1211/12 February; ADM 223/316, OIC SI 1222 of 12 February.
54. DEFE 3/542, ZTPG 346455; ADM 223/305, Ultra signal of 2104/1, March; ADM 223/305, OIC S 1205 of 2 March.
55. ADM 223/317, OIC SI 1321, 1322 and 1323 of 30 April, 1 and 2 May.
56. DEFE 3/549, ZTPG 352155; ADM 223/306 Ultra signals 1710/17 March, 1902/17 March, 1750/18 March; Naval Headlines of 18 March; ADM 223/317, OIC SI 1262 of 19 March.
57. Roskill, op cit, Vol III Part 2, p 279; Naval Headlines of 11 and 19 March, 6 and 29 April, 1 May.
58. DEFE 3/555, ZTPG 358454; ADM 223/307, Ultra signals 1122/1 April, 1301/5 April; Naval Headlines of 1 and 7 April.
59. ADM 223/307, Ultra signal 0006/8 April; ADM 223/316, 317, OIC SI 1287 and 1308 of 9 and 23 April.

that three *Seehund* were to carry out a further attack off Dungeness on the night of 22 April and that two more had sailed for the area on the evening of 23 April.[60] As late as 30 April a decrypt reported the intention to send a *Seehund* to Spithead, where it might arrive that night.[61]

As with other KdK operations, Sigint rarely gave advance warning of the *Seehund* sorties,* but after the event it usually, if by no means invariably, reported the objectives of the operation, the number of craft engaged and the German estimates of the results achieved and the casualties suffered. On this evidence, after correlating it with Allied operational reports, the OIC estimated that in the months of February and March 74 *Seehund* operated, of which between 44 and 52 reached the operational area, and sank five ships, possibly six, for the loss of 28, possibly 29, *Seehund*. On the basis of attacks claimed in 26 out of something between 44 and 52 arrivals in the operational area, it estimated that the probable level of hits was 16 to 20 per cent of attacks made and, on the assumption that the attacks were made with two torpedoes, 10 per cent of torpedoes fired. A tentative comparison with the results achieved by the *Schnorchel* U-boats in inshore waters indicated that, in terms of crew lost per casualty inflicted, the two arms were yielding much the same return – a 'comparatively low performance' which in the case of the *Seehund* was due to its low serviceability as well as poor torpedo performance.[63]

Performance improved in April; in the week 9–16 April alone the OIC credited *Seehund* with sinking one merchant ship and damaging two others – these off Dungeness – and sinking one tanker.[64] But post-war analysis has confirmed that the effectiveness of *Seehund* in the home theatre over the whole period from January to May 1945 was as much below that of the E-boats as it

---

* It did, however, give warning early in February that a landing was to be carried out at Granville by a raiding party from the Channel Islands – not by the KdK – when moon and tide were next favourable, in about four weeks' time. The Admiralty issued this warning, but the landing, carried out on the night of 8–9 March, achieved surprise, doing considerable damage.[62]

60. ADM 223/308, Ultra signals 2222/20 April, 1602/21 April, 1000/23 April, 0522/25 April, 1222/25 April.
61. ADM 223/309, Ultra signal 2244/30 April.
62. ADM 223/304, Ultra signals 0350/8 February, 1508/9 February; Roskill, op cit, Vol III Part 2, p 276.
63. ADM 223/317, OIC SI 1312 of 25 April.
64. ibid, 1300 of 16 April.

was higher than that of the other KdK weapons.[65]* These other weapons – *Biber*, *Molch* and *Linse* – contributed to the high nuisance value of the KdK in necessitating increases in Allied patrols and static defences, but they caused no Allied shipping losses in January and February[66] and their activities were severely restricted thereafter, as Sigint disclosed.

At the end of February a decrypt revealed that *Molch* flotillas were being withdrawn from Holland, design faults having so far prevented them from operating.[67] A decrypt of 19 March disclosed that on account of the depletion of equipment and the poor prospects for obtaining replacements all five *Biber* flotillas in the west were being combined into one flotilla with one base organisation and that the two flotillas of *Linse* were also being amalgamated.[68] Unlike *Seehund* reinforcements, which reached the Dutch bases by sea, these other craft could only be brought in overland.

Sigint had reported no claims to successes in *Biber* or *Linse* operations by 17 March when a signal from the KdK, decrypted on 21 March, advised that *Biber* and *Seehund* should always fire two torpedoes to increase 'the slender prospects of hits', and also announced that *Biber* would in future be used for minelaying as well as for torpedo operations.[69] In the next month there was still

---

*
The German E-boat and Small Battle Unit Coastal
Offensive in the Home Theatre
January–May, 1945

Type of Craft	Total Sorties	Losses	Allied ships sunk by:		Allied ships damaged by:	
			Torpedo	Mine	Torpedo	Mine
E-boat	351	10	6–12,972	25–75,999	1–1,345	7–26,408
Seehund	142	35	9–18,451	Nil	3–18,384	Nil
Biber and Molch	102	70	Nil	7–491	Nil	2–15,516
Linse	171	54	Nil	Nil	Nil	Nil
Totals	766	169	15–31,423	32–76,490	4–19,729	9–41,924

65. Roskill, op cit, Vol III Part 2, p 279.
66. ibid, p 272.
67. ADM 223/305, Ultra signals 1302/23 February, 1817/25 February, 1035/26 February; ADM 223/316, OIC SI 1237 of 26 February.
68. DEFE 3/549, ZTPG 352616; ADM 223/306, Ultra signal 1033/19 March; Naval Headlines of 19 March.
69. ADM 223/306, Ultra signal 1751/21 March; ADM 223/316, OIC SI 1269 of 26 March.

no evidence of operational successes by *Biber* and *Linse*.* But in a signal decrypted on 18 April Admiral Commanding Netherlands insisted that, in any curtailment of operations necessitated by lack of fuel, offensive operations by the E-boat Command and the KdK were to have priority over defensive operations in support of the Army; only when the fuel situation forced the cessation of offensive operations were their boats to be used defensively as floating batteries or, if that was not feasible, their crews enlisted in the land forces.[71] And in a signal decrypted as late as 25 April Dönitz, though agreeing to the release of limited stocks of naval fuel to the Army in Holland, still insisted on the continuing importance of offensive E-boat and KdK operations for the course of the war.[72]

Offensive operations with *Biber* and *Linse*, as with *Seehund*, were at least being attempted up to that date and even beyond it. Decrypts received between 20 and 22 April had shown that *Linse* had sailed on the nights of 17, 19 and 20 April for a new type of operation – attacks on the Allied convoys to Ostend in which they used Dunkirk for refuelling and as an advanced base. But a signal of 24 April decrypted on 26 April added that, in view of the loss on passage of 12 of the best boats without any apparent success, the operation would not be repeated.[73] Decrypts of 22 April had disclosed that of six *Biber* which tried to mine the Scheldt on 21 April, four had returned prematurely and two had been lost; and a decrypt of 28 April disclosed that another minelaying sortie by *Biber* on 26 April had failed to reach the target area.[74] On 26 April, however, the decrypt of a directive issued to all the KdK units on 23 April disclosed that the scope and frequency of all operations other than those by *Seehund* were to be cut back and superfluous maintenance and operational personnel trained for land fighting.[75]

The KdK eventually ordered the cessation of resistance to the

---

* At the end of March, however, and again in mid-April decrypts indicated that *Linse* had transported agents to points on the coast in northern France and Belgium.[70]

70.   ADM 223/307, Ultra signals 1143/25 March, 1816/27 March; ADM 223/308, Ultra signals 0219/13 April, 1749/15 April; ADM 223/317, OIC SI 1300 of 16 April.

71.   ADM 223/308, Ultra signal 1243/18 April; ADM 223/314, OIC S 1252 of 18 April.

72.   ADM 223/308, Ultra signal 1305/25 April.

73.   ibid, Ultra signals 2236/20 April, 1841/22 April, 2200/26 April; Naval Headlines of 21 April.

74.   ADM 223/308, Ultra signal 1841/22 April; ADM 223/309, Ultra signals 1554/28 April, 2015/28 April.

75.   ADM 223/308, Ultra signal 2200/26 April.

Allies on 3 May, and on 4 May it recalled all craft still at sea. On 5 May, following the receipt of OKM's order for the ending of hostilities, it informed OKM in a signal decrypted on 6 May that nine *Seehund* still at sea were expected back at Ijmuiden on 10 May.[76]

□

Naval and air attacks against German shipping off the Norwegian coast continued unabated from the beginning of the year, and there was a steady increase in the level of Allied successes in part as a result of the inauguration in the OIC of a running plot of shipping movements based on all intelligence sources.* By the middle of April shipping movements were so reduced on this account and because ships had been withdrawn to take part in the evacuation of troops and refugees from Germany's eastern provinces that the JIC advised that the attacks should cease; it noted that, together with the minelaying in the Kattegat and south Norway, they had succeeded in delaying the evacuation to Germany of the eleven German divisions still in Norway.[77]

It still remained the case that decrypts were rarely received in time to assist in individual operations, but an exception arose in relation to the movement to Germany of three of the Z-class destroyers that had remained in northern Norway. Decrypts of signals reporting that they had moved south as far as Tromsö were available on 26 January, and another signal disclosing that they had left Narvik at 1900 on 26 January was decrypted early the following day. On this evidence the C-in-C Home Fleet sent two cruisers to intercept them. The cruisers encountered the destroyers and damaged two of them with long-range gunfire but close engagement was impossible in the absence of destroyers, which had been retained in a carrier operation against coastal shipping.[78] The Enigma showed that two of the destroyers reached the Baltic on 1 February.[79]

The Home Fleet continued to be on guard against a possible breakout from the Baltic by enemy main units which had been kept under constant observation by PR and through Sigint. No such move was made, but on 27 March the JIC was asked by the

---

* See above, p 495.

76. ADM 223/309, Ultra signals 1909/5 May, 1230/6 May; Naval Headlines of 7 May.
77. JIC(45) 121 of 13 April.
78. Naval Headlines of 26 and 27 January and 1 February; Roskill, op cit, Vol III Part 2, pp 253–254.
79. Naval Headlines of 1 and 4 February.

Chiefs of Staff about the possibility that Germany's imminent defeat on land might prompt her into a desperate last fling with her Fleet as in 1918. It replied on 2 April that such action was improbable and that it expected to receive notice in the form of preliminary movements if any action was contemplated.[80]* In spite of this assurance the Admiralty recalled HMS *Renown* from the Eastern Fleet and laid plans against an attempt by the Germans to break into the Channel or the Atlantic.[81]

---

* For the fate of the German main units in the Baltic see below p 743 fn*.

80.   JIC(45)106(0) of 27 March, 107(0) of 2 April.
81.   Roskill, op cit, Vol III Part 2, p 260.

CHAPTER 60

The Soviet Offensives, December 1944 to the Spring of 1945

BY THE last week of December it was known from high-grade Sigint that the Germans expected the Russians to resume the attack in Latvia and deliver successive blows against the whole of the central sector as soon as stable winter conditions permitted.[1] Assessments issued by Fremde Heere West, by the Japanese Naval Mission in Berlin and by Third Panzer Army on the northern wing of Army Group Centre had recently been decrypted; they had all concluded that attacks in Latvia and against East Prussia would be co-ordinated with a major offensive in Poland.[2] But the weather remained bad, and in Whitehall the anxiety caused by Germany's unexpected attack in the Ardennes* was compounded by lack of direct information about Russia's intentions or about her strengths on the different sectors of the front.[3]

In the hope of removing this uncertainty, and of ensuring if possible that Russia did not postpone her offensive, Air Chief Marshal Tedder was sent to Moscow at the end of December – only to be held up by the weather en route. On 6 January, therefore, the Prime Minister addressed an enquiry to Stalin, who immediately replied by promising an offensive along the whole of the central front 'not later than the second half of January'.[4] Stalin did more than he promised. The date for the Soviet offensive had already been set provisionally for between 15 and 20 January, but on 8 January, in consideration of the difficulties the western Allies had encountered in the Ardennes, he ordered the attack towards Breslau to begin on 12 January and that across the Vistula on 14 January. The attack towards Königsberg was set for 13 January and that on Danzig for 14 January.[5]

---

* See above, Chapter 52.

1. WO 208/4317, MI 14 Weekly Summaries for the CIGS, 24 and 31 December 1944; CX/MSS/ROB 23 of 23 December, 24 of 28 December.
2. DEFE 3/320, BT 237 of 23 December; CX/MSS/ROB 22 of 19 December, 23 of 23 December, 24 of 28 December (item 15); SJA 1259 of 8 December.
3. CAB 121/464, SIC file D/Russia/4, Vol 1, JIC(44)479(0) of 27 November.
4. Ehrman, *Grand Strategy*, Vol VI (1956), pp 80–81.
5. Seaton, *The Russo-German War 1941–45* (1971), pp 530, 532, 533; Erickson, *The Road to Berlin* (1983), pp 449, 455.

In the few days that remained before the beginning of the Russian offensive London's information about the eastern front was confined to what could be learned from the decrypts of German messages. These reported that Russian preparations for a major offensive were continuing in the Narev sector – where, however, there was no sign that action was imminent – and in East Prussia – where the preparations were particularly advanced in the Insterburg area.[6]

When the Russians went on to the offensive their forces between Latvia and the Carpathians were disposed in six main groups of armies (Fronts). One contained the German forces in Courland and around Memel. The 3rd Belorussian Front lay along the borders of East Prussia. The 2nd Belorussian lay along the Vistula to the north of Warsaw and the 1st on the west bank of the river to the south. From there to the Carpathians the line was held by the 1st and 4th Ukrainian Fronts. The main thrust was to be made by the 1st Belorussian and the 1st Ukrainian Fronts, with a joint strength of some 163 divisions, 6,400 tanks and 4,700 aircraft, in two parallel offensives, 1st Belorussian's towards Bromberg (Bydgoszcz), Poznan and Radom and 1st Ukrainian's towards Cracow and Breslau. 3rd Belorussian was to operate towards Königsberg while 2nd Belorussian attacked to the north-west against Danzig to seal off East Prussia from the rest of Germany and protect the right flank of 1st Belorussian's advance.[7]

The Russians were opposed on these fronts by three German Army Groups. Army Group North (Sixteenth and Eighteenth Armies) was encircled in Courland. Army Group Centre (Third Panzer Army and Fourth and Second Armies) held East Prussia and northern Poland to the junction of the Narev and the Vistula north of Warsaw. Army Group A (Ninth, Fourth Panzer, Seventeenth and First Panzer Armies) held a line along the Vistula from north of Warsaw to the Carpathians in Czechoslovakia. Army Group Centre and Army Group A faced the main offensive with, between them, 70 divisions; only five of them were Panzer Divisions.[8]*

---

* Beginning on 24 January Hitler re-designated the Commands and carried out wholesale dismissals of the commanders. Army Group North was renamed Army Group Courland. Army Group Centre was renamed Army Group North (Third Panzer and Fourth Armies). Army Group A was renamed Army Group Centre (Fourth Panzer, Seventeenth and First Panzer Armies). As Army Groups Courland (with 26 divisions) and North (with 27 divisions) were by then both cut off from the Reich, a new Army Group Vistula was formed under

6. DEFE 3/326, BT 1599 of 7 January 1945; CX/MSS/T426/26 and 29, T430/10; CX/MSS/ROB 27 of 28 January.

7. Seaton, op cit, pp 531, 532; Erickson, op cit, pp 447–448; Ehrman, op cit, Vol VI, pp 81–82.

8. Seaton, op cit, pp 529–530.

Beginning their advance on 12 January, 1st Ukrainian's forces were across the Warthe by 17 January, having penetrated 100 miles on a 160–mile front in six days, and Cracow fell to them on 19 January. They entered Germany between 20 and 23 January. 1st Belorussian's advance took Radom on 16 January, Warsaw on 17 January, Lodz on 19 January and Bromberg on 23 January, and began to cross the German frontier on 26 January. By the end of the month both thrusts were across the Oder. 3rd Belorussian's attack had meanwhile made slower progress, capturing Tilsit on 18 January but failing to break Third Army; but 2nd Belorussian's offensive had entered East Prussia on 19 January and captured Tannenberg on 21 January, and by 26 January, having reached the Baltic at Elbing from 23 January, it had cut off Third Panzer and Fourth Armies and part of the disintegrating Second Army in East Prussia. A counter-attack by Fourth Army, which temporarily threatened the Soviet position around Elbing and a German breakthrough to the Vistula, had failed by the end of the month. In two weeks of fighting the Soviet armies had come to within 40 miles of Berlin and 100 miles of Dresden.[10]

The western Allies had the news of the Russian advance on the central front in a German message of 15 January, decrypted on the following day, which reported the formidable artillery bombardment that had preceded the attack from the Vistula bridgehead at Sandomierz on 12 January.[11] A message of 16 January, decrypted on 18 January, reported the capture of Radom.[12] Subsequent decrypts made it clear that although the German forces were making a fighting withdrawal, they were gravely handicapped by fuel shortage, by the lack of defence preparations in areas surprised by the speed of the Russian advance, and by the receipt of impossible orders from higher HQs. On 20 January, in a message decrypted on 22 January, Wehrkreis authorities in the Polish corridor and north-west Poland were instructed to construct tank barriers and field works in towns that were in Russian hands by 23 January.[13] Army Group A's situation report for 20 January disclosed that Cracow had fallen, that the Russians had forced their way to within 3 miles of Breslau on Fourth Panzer

---

Himmler's command with Second and Ninth Armies to cover Danzig and Pomerania. These changes were disclosed by Fish and Japanese diplomatic decrypts between 27 January and 5 February.[9]

9. WO 208/4317 of 28 January (Annex) and 4 February; DEFE 3/502, BTs 3584 and 3592 of 28 January; BAY/BTs 49 of 1 February, 57 of 5 February.
10. Seaton, op cit, pp 534–538, 548, 550; Erickson, op cit, pp 456–472.
11. CX/MSS/T431/32; CX/MSS/ROB 27 (item 6).
12. CX/MSS/T433/13.
13. CX/MSS/T437/5.

Army's front and that Ninth Army had broken out from the Lodz area after heavy fighting.[14] From orders and reconnaissance reports issued by the GAF it was clear that advanced Russian elements were across the Oder at Steinau on 26 January, and that Russian infantry was then pressing forward eleven miles west of the river.[15] On 28 January, in the light of other decrypts indicating that infantry in considerable strength had been brought up to the Russian forward troops, MI concluded that the Russians should be able to continue the offensive or at least to hold any German counter-attacks, of which there was as yet no sign.[16]

On the Russian advances into East Prussia there was little or no Sigint till the end of January. The decrypt of a message issued by Army Group North on 26 January then disclosed that the Russian armies were massing for a breakthrough and that the situation at Königsberg was critical.[17] Messages of 28 and 31 January, decrypted on 30 January and 3 February, reported Fourth Army's counter-attack in the Elbing area and OKH's refusal to meet Fourth Army's request for reinforcements from outside East Prussia.[18] By 31 January the decrypts had shown that Königsberg was surrounded, though it could still be supplied from Pillau,[19] and that at the request of Third Panzer Army the *Prinz Eugen* had since 29 January been carrying out bombardments near Cranz in an attempt to delay the Russian spearheads while part of the Memel garrison got away down the Kurische Nehrung.[20]

Hitler had ordered the evacuation of Memel on 22 January. Together with the decision of C-in-C Fleet to withdraw warships from Königsberg,[21] the order was decrypted on 24 January; it specified that removal of the civilian population by sea was not to be allowed to interfere with the evacuation of Service personnel or with the shipping needed for the withdrawal of divisions from Courland.[22] The removal of divisions from Courland to Swinemünde and Stettin had begun in the middle of the month. Between 18 and 22 January arrangements for the transfer of 31st, 32nd and 227th Infantry Divisions and 4th Panzer Division produced a large number of decrypts, many of them from the Navy which was using the *Scheer*, the *Lützow*, the *Prinz Eugen* and

---

14. CX/MSS/T443/1.
15. CX/MSS/T445/16.
16. Wo 208/4317 of 28 January.
17. CX/MSS/ROB 28 (item 11).
18. CX/MSS/T444/52, T448/48.
19. CX/MSS/T443/54, T445/3.
20. DEFE 3/502, BT 3614 of 28 January.
21. DEFE 3/500, BT 3246 of 24 January; Naval Headlines of 25 January.
22. DEFE 3/500, BT 3243 of 24 January; Naval Headlines of 25 January.

U-boat target ships in the evacuation.[23] Decrypts of 24 January and 1 February disclosed that the operation had been interrupted by the decision to transfer III SS Panzer Corps with three divisions from Courland to Danzig, with all possible speed.[24] By 31 January decrypts reported Hitler's decision to withdraw two further divisions – 201st and 389th Infantry – as soon as possible in view of the critical need to reinforce Army Group Vistula.[25] The decrypts had established by then that the Germans were not carrying out a general evacuation from Courland and that the divisions they were withdrawing could not possibly be assembled for a counter-offensive in East Prussia or Poland: the shipping available would move only one division with equipment in a week, and the divisions were not being moved without their equipment because they were being put into the front immediately they disembarked.[26] Subsequent decrypts disclosed that the transfer of III SS Panzer Corps and of 32nd Infantry Division and 4th Panzer Division (without its tanks) was not completed till 20 February,[27] and that 389th Infantry Division was still in transit in mid-March.[28]*

---

* By 11 March it was known from Sigint that eight nominal divisions had been withdrawn from Courland since the middle of January, two of which had been committed in the Stettin area and five to the west of Danzig.[29] A decrypt of 24 March disclosed that the transfer of the remainder of the divisions that were to be withdrawn was being given second priority after that of cadres from East Prussia and Danzig.[30] 215th Infantry, 12th GAF Field and 389th Infantry Divisions were then en route from Libau.[31] They brought the number withdrawn to eleven by mid-April, when the transfers ceased; all but one had gone to Pomerania and West Prussia and most of them had gone into action at once and been destroyed in the Danzig Bay bridgeheads. 22 divisions then remained in Courland.[32]

23. DEFE 3/330, BT 2621 of 18 January; DEFE 3/331, BT 2883 of 20 January; DEFE 3/500, BT 3170 of 23 January; CX/MSS/T435/91; Naval Headlines of 21 January.

24. DEFE 3/501, BT 3286 of 24 January; DEFE 3/503, BT 3929 of 1 February, amended in DEFE 3/504, BT 4185 of 5 February.

25. Naval Headlines of 31 January.

26. WO 208/4317 of 21 and 28 January.

27. DEFE 3/511, BT 5926 of 28 February; DEFE 3/512, BT 6096 of 2 March.

28. DEFE 3/519, BT 7800 of 20 March.

29. WO 208/4317 of 25 February; WO 208/4318, MI 14 Weekly Summary for the CIGS, 11 March,

30. DEFE 3/520, BT 8207 of 24 March.

31. DEFE 3/508, BT 5207 of 20 February; DEFE 3/509, BT 5340 of 21 February; DEFE 3/512, BT 6170 of 3 March; DEFE 3/514, BT 6686 of 9 March; DEFE 3/516, BT 7029 of 12 March; DEFE 3/519, BT 7800 of 20 March.

32. CX/MSS/467 para C1, T478/42, 484 para D3, 491 para A31, 497 para D23, T498/24, 502 para D10, T504/2, 505 para D11, T505/83, 514 para D6, 516 para D12, 520 paras D1, 11, 12, 21, 524 para D8, 527 para D1, 528 paras D14, 16, T528/16, T531/37, 532 para D32, 533 para D10, 535 paras D27, 30, 539 para B1.

On 31 January a sudden thaw on all sectors of the front threatened to bring operations to a standstill. The Russians estimated, as they reported at the Yalta conference on 4 February, that 45 German divisions had by then been routed; that up to a further 15, surrounded in Poland, would soon be eliminated; and that while 26 remained isolated at Courland, up to 27 more were cut off in East Prussia.[33] The western Allies were assuming that in view of the thaw, of her growing logistical problems and of the prospect of increasing German resistance, Russia would now pause on the Oder; but in judging how long she would pause there and whether and when she would strike elsewhere they were, as the JIC stated on 6 February, 'severely handicapped' by lack of information about her intentions and capabilities no less than by uncertainty as to Germany's ability to extricate her divisions and bring up reinforcements from other fronts.[34]

Decrypts between 1 and 5 February disclosed that the Japanese authorities in Berlin regarded Germany's prospects as 'exceedingly unfavourable'. In their view, 'the question whether the Germans can . . . establish and consolidate a strong new line unfortunately remains . . . very much unanswered'. But they added that rather than use reserves in driblets, Hitler had decided to accept a temporary loss of territory and resources and assemble his forces for a big offensive 'in another week or two'.[35] In the situation report they tabled at the Yalta conference on 4 February the Russians estimated that the Germans had already transferred 16 divisions to the east from Germany, the west and Italy and that for the defence of Berlin and the approaches to Vienna they might transfer a further 40 divisions from those theatres and from Norway; and they expressed the hope that the western Allies would take advantage of this, for them, favourable development to launch an offensive in the west in the first half of February and also do all they could to prevent the German withdrawals, particularly from Italy.[36] As for their own intentions, however, they would only say that they would continue the present offensive for as long as the weather allowed and that, pending the opening of their summer offensive, they would do all in their power to carry out local operations to prevent the transfer of German forces from east to west. As for the western Allies, they could give no firm assurance that they would be able to prevent German reinforcements reaching the east or, as the Russians particularly desired, that they would stage an advance from Italy to assist a

---

33. CAB 121/464, JASON telegrams 128 and 239 of 4 and 8 February.
34. JIC(45)42(0) of 6 February.
35. BAY/BTs 49 of 1 February, 58 of 5 February.
36. CAB 121/464, JASON 128 of 4 February.

Soviet offensive towards Vienna.[37] At the end of the conference, however, at the suggestion of General Marshall, they decided to resume the supply to the Russians, under the previous safeguards, of Sigint about German intentions and order of battle.*

Notwithstanding the weather and their other difficulties – which included the fact that following the fall of Budapest in mid-February the Germans counter-attacked north and south of the Danube† – the Russians pushed on with their offensive. The 2nd Belorussian Front attacked in Pomerania towards Neustettin on 10 February. It was brought to a standstill after ten days, but on 24 February it resumed its advance into eastern and central Pomerania, while part of the 1st Belorussian Front prepared to attack in western Pomerania on 1 March and 3rd Belorussian Front moved its left wing towards the Gulf of Danzig to cut off a German retreat from the Frische Nehrung. On 5 March 2nd Belorussian forces reached Koslin, cutting off Army Group Vistula's Second Army, and 1st Belorussian Front took Kolberg and Stargard and threatened Stettin. Both Fronts then closed in on Danzig and Gdynia while 3rd Belorussian's final attack on Königsberg, which had been delayed by a German counter-attack, was prepared for 13 March; Königsberg was taken after heavy fighting on 10 April. By that time 1st Belorussian on its southern front had taken Poznan on 22 February and Küstrin on 29 March, while 1st Ukrainian Front had encircled Glogau on 11 February, Breslau on 15 February and Oppeln on 19 March, and had completed the conquest of Upper Silesia by taking Ratibor on 30 March.[39]

At the time of 2nd Belorussian's attack on 10 February high-grade Sigint disclosed that the Germans were strengthening the chain of command on that front and bringing in reinforcements. The gap between Second Army in the Polish corridor and Ninth Army in Brandenburg was being taken over by HQ Third

---

* For the earlier supply of Sigint to Moscow see Volume II, p 59 et seq. The resumed service was carried out, as before, in telegrams sent via 'C' to the British Military Mission in Moscow. SHAEF was already sending daily situation reports on the western front to the British Military Mission and by 28 February the War Office was supplying a weekly summary of the German Army's order of battle to the Soviet Military Mission in London.[38]

† See below p 657ff.

37. Ehrman, op cit, Vol VI, pp 103–104, based on the conference record in COS(45)114(o), 1st and 2nd Military Meetings, 4 February, 1st and 2nd Tripartite Military Meetings, 5 and 6 February. (A copy of the record is in CAB 121/161, SIC file A/Strategy/16).

38. CAB 121/464, COS(45)114(o), COS (Argonaut) 9th Meeting, 9 February; Dir/C Archive, 8704 of 28 February; Papers of Air Marshall Robb, Minutes of Meeting at SHAEF, 22 January (held in RAF Museum, Hendon).

39. Seaton, op cit, pp 540–543, 550–552; Erickson, op cit, pp 517–526, 542–543.

Army, withdrawn from East Prussia; what had been HQ Upper Rhine was appearing near Stettin as Eleventh Army; an SS Belgien Division had arrived from the west and 4th SS Police PG Division from Hungary; and the divisions coming from Latvia were apparently destined for Pomerania.[40] It was clear during the first week of the renewed offensive that the Germans were holding firm in the approaches to Danzig from the east and the south; but their messages were being decrypted with up to a week's delay, and little was learned about the fighting near Stettin beyond the fact that 4th SS Police PG Division had been put into the battle immediately on its arrival.[41] In a message of 20 February, decrypted on 24 February, Army Group Vistula reported that it was expecting an immediate attack on Ninth Army and an attack towards Konitz which Second Army with its 'badly battered armoured forces' was unlikely to be able to hold.[42] On 21 February, when his military advisers were calling for withdrawals from East Prussia and Pomerania, Hitler sealed the fate of the German divisions there by insisting that the Oder-Neisse line must be defended and the railway from Stettin to Danzig held at all costs.[43] These orders were not decrypted. By 25 February, however, decrypts had disclosed that HQ Third Panzer Army had replaced the inexperienced Eleventh Army in the Stargard area,* that further reinforcements were being sent to Stettin in the shape of 10th SS Panzer Division, withdrawn from the west, and that the Germans were anxious that a Russian attack between Stargard and the lower Oder might prevent the execution of some plan of their own.[45]

The fact that the Russians had broken through at Neustettin on 28 February was disclosed in an army decrypt of 7 March,[46] when naval decrypts added that the situation was becoming critical at Stettin and Swinemünde on 6 March and that Admiral Eastern

---

* Beginning with a message of 5 March, decrypted on 13 March, Sigint referred to Eleventh Army as Eleventh SS Panzer Army and indicated that it was carrying out for Himmler some special task associated with the comb-out of SS personnel for the fighting fronts. At the beginning of April a decrypt located it at Kassel, subordinated to C-in-C West.[44] For its operations in the west see below, pp 719, 723, 725.

40. WO 208/4317 of 11 February; DEFE 3/505, BT 4330 of 8 February; DEFE 3/506, BTs 4503 and 4533 of 10 February, 4600 of 11 February.
41. WO 208/4317 of 18 February.
42. DEFE 3/510, BT 5593 of 24 February.
43. Seaton, op cit, pp 540–541; Erickson, op cit, p 518.
44. DEFE 3/516, BTs 7124 of 13 March, 7206 of 14 March; DEFE 3/601, BT 8873 of 30 March; DEFE 3/563, BT 9540 of 6 April.
45. WO 208/4317 of 25 February; WO 208/4318 of 4 March.
46. CX/MSS/481 para D8.

Baltic was preparing to evacuate Rügenwalde and Stolpemünde.[47] Decrypts on 9 and 10 March revealed that by 5 March 32nd Infantry, 4th SS Police PG and 7th Panzer Divisions had been badly mauled by the Russian advance and that Second Army in the Danzig-Stolp area, lacking fuel and transport, had had grave doubts about its power to continue resisting.[48] On 11 March in the light of this and other Sigint MI 14 calculated that at least seventeen divisions had been cut off at Danzig and Gdynia.[49] On 12 March decrypts of messages issued by Second Army on 10 and 11 March disclosed that it was still holding a shortened front line but expected fresh attacks by strongly superior Soviet forces; that lack of fuel was still jeopardising the conduct of operations and causing heavy losses; and that its divisions were in a serious plight. 7th Panzer Division had twelve tanks (six serviceable) and 28 assault guns (18 serviceable); 4th Panzer Division had 36 (11) tanks and 6 (4) guns; 4th SS Police PG Division had 2 (1) tanks and 42 (13) guns; infantry divisions had an average 3 assault guns; in some divisions battalion strengths were down to 100–130 men.[50] Another decrypt of 12 March gave directions issued the previous day for the future conduct of operations. Second Army was to defend Danzig and Gdynia, which were of decisive importance for the supply of Courland and Army Group North; Army Group North was to keep open communications with Second Army across the Frische Nehrung.[51]

In East Prussia, meanwhile, the Sigint had shown that although the Germans were not completely cut off, but had an escape route along the Frische Nehrung, they were not contemplating a large-scale evacuation.[52] Decrypts of 8 and 11 February had contained the arrangements for the transport of Third Panzer Army HQ to Danzig,[53] but there were no reports of withdrawal of divisions until the first week of March, when a decrypt disclosed that 549th VG Division was leaving East Prussia for Gdynia.[54] On 24 February, moreover, a decrypt had reported that 5th Panzer Division had made a counter-attack from Königsberg and succeeded in making contact with the German forces in the Samland

---

47. DEFE 3/514, BTs 6529 and 6610 of 7 March; Naval Headlines of 8 March.
48. DEFE 3/514, BT 6686 of 9 March; DEFE 3/515, BTs 6778, 6812 and 6836 of 10 March.
49. WO 208/4318 of 11 March.
50. DEFE 3/515, BTs 6954 and 6992 of 12 March; DEFE 3/516, BT 7033 of 12 March.
51. DEFE 3/516, BT 7038 of 12 March.
52. DEFE 3/506, BT 4716 of 13 February; DEFE 3/509, BT 5389 of 22 February.
53. DEFE 3/505, BT 4393 of 8 February; DEFE 3/506, BT 4600 of 11 February.
54. DEFE 3/514, BT 6744 of 9 March.

peninsula.[55] A decrypt of 5 March, which exhorted the troops in East Prussia to fight on to the end, had claimed that Army Group North was proving the soundness of the bridgehead policy by tying down 100 Soviet divisions.[56] Before the Russians resumed their attack on 13 March, on the other hand, several decrypts had revealed that the German forces in the bridgehead were in desperate straits. A decrypt from the railway Enigma disclosed a report of 5 March from Army Group North on the supply situation, which was complicated by the fact that Pillau, the main supply route, had been iced up since early February; this carried the complaint that no ammunition had been delivered since 2 March.[57] A decrypt of 9 March contained the Army Group's statement that it had lost 35,000 killed or wounded between 19 and 28 February and received only 5,000 replacements; on 2 March alone Fourth Army had suffered 4,300 casualties as compared with a daily average of 3,000.[58] A report of 12 March from Parachute Panzer Corps Hermann Göring in the Königsberg pocket, decrypted on 14 March, said that its four divisions confronted 22 Russian divisions; it had 41 tanks against 4 Russian tank brigades and 2 tank regiments, 68 assault guns against 700, and 68 artillery brigades against 230. The report added that 2nd Parachute Panzer Division had lost 10,326 men, including 306 officers, between 13 January and 8 March, that 45 of its 106 Grenadier Companies were commanded by NCOs, and that between 7 and 10 March the daily allocation of ammunition for the entire Corps had been 525 rounds.[59]

On 10 March Army Group North reported that the Russians had completed their preparations for a large-scale attack in Fourth Army's area.[60] This report was decrypted on 12 March, as were messages of 11 March in which the Army Group expected simultaneous attacks on its entire front, including Königsberg, and OKH noted the fact that the 3rd Belorussian and 1st Baltic Fronts had been combined under the command of Vasilevskii as an indication of the importance the Russians were attaching to the rapid elimination of Army Group North.[61]* Subsequent decrypts

---

* Sigint had disclosed in mid-February that the Germans had learned that 1st Baltic Front was being relieved by 2nd Baltic and moving to East Prussia.[62] The decrypt of an Enigma

55. DEFE 3/510, BT 5593 of 24 February.
56. CX/MSS/T476/53 of 5 March.
57. SR/287/31.
58. DEFE 3/514, BT 6747 of 9 March.
59. DEFE 3/516, BT 7137 of 14 March.
60. DEFE 3/515, BT 6956 of 12 March; see also CX/MSS/ROB 37 of 19 March.
61. CX/MSS/T486/46 and 66.
62. CX/MSS/ROB 33 of 21 February, 34 of 28 February.

disclosed the speed of the Russian offensive, which had split Fourth Army into two by 18 March.[64] An order from Hitler on 23 March to the effect that all possible measures must be taken to supply Fortress Königsberg was decrypted on 27 March.[65] In another message of 23 March, decrypted on 31 March, OKL reported that it was doing all in its power to provide the aircraft fuel without which GAF East Prussia could not supply the Prussian fortress, but that there was a shortage of fuel on all fronts.[66] By 1 April a decrypt disclosed that the whole of the Königsberg sea canal had come under Russian gunfire on 29 March.[67] Hitler had refused to sanction the evacuation of the city and the Samland peninsula till 26 March, by which time it was too late to save most of the troops and their equipment.[68]

In the Danzig area Sigint showed that the Russians were steadily closing in on Second Army's depleted forces.[69] A return issued by Second Army on 17 March, decrypted on 23 March, reported that 14 out of 15 divisions were suitable only for limited defensive employment (category IV).[70] By 25 March the Army could no longer keep open the land communications with East Prussia,[71]* and the naval Enigma had disclosed that the Russians had reached the inner defence belt at Danzig on 23 March and that Captain U-boats Baltic was withdrawing from Danzig and Admiral Eastern Baltic from Gdynia.[73] A report from Captain U-boats of 26 March, decrypted by 28 March, added that all U-boats and other vessels of the U-boat Command, including new construction 'up to U–3534,' were leaving Danzig.[74] Earlier naval decrypts had revealed that Dönitz had ordered the immediate transfer of 800 U-boat technicians to Hamburg in mid-March and that they had suffered

---

message of 12 March disclosed that they had learned from POW that Vasilevskii had assumed command of both 3rd Belorussian and 1st Baltic Fronts.[63]

   * On 21 March, as the naval Enigma disclosed on the following day, the German surface fleet had been sent back from the western Baltic to carry out bombardments in the Gulf of Danzig in support of the Army. Led by the *Prinz Eugen*, the *Leipzig*, and the *Lützow*, it kept up this activity till early April in what proved to be its last large operation.[72]

63. CX/MSS/ROB 37 of 19 March.
64. WO 208/4318 of 18 March.
65. DEFE 3/600, BT 8622 of 27 March.
66. DEFE 3/561, BT 9035 of 31 March.
67. Naval Headlines of 1 April.
68. Seaton, op cit, pp 551–552; Erickson, op cit, pp 542–543.
69. WO 208/4318 of 18 March.
70. DEFE 3/520, BT 8090 of 23 March.
71. WO 208/4318 of 25 March.
72. DEFE 3/519, BT 7968 of 22 March; DEFE 3/520, BT 8036 of 23 March; Naval Headlines of 22 March, 25 March, 2 April.
73. Naval Headlines of 25 March.
74. ibid, of 28 March.

casualties when their ship was mined on 18 and 19 March.[75] Orders for demolition and for mining and blocking measures in the east Baltic ports were issued on 27 March and decrypted by 31 March.[76] Among these measures, the *Gneisenau* was blown up to block the harbour basins at Gdynia.[77]

□

The suggestion that the Germans planned a counter-offensive, first made by the Japanese at the beginning of February,* was repeated by them with less and less conviction throughout the month and in the first half of March. A Japanese diplomatic decrypt of 5 February reported that large forces were being assembled east of Stettin and behind the Oder at Sagan for a major attack aimed at recovering Upper Silesia and East Prussia.[78] In the next fortnight several decrypts from the Japanese embassy in Berlin carried the assurance that the attack would begin soon,[79] but two decrypts in the last week of February expressed anxiety at Germany's delay, and pessimism as to her prospects of success.[80] Early in March a decrypt disclosed that the Japanese Ambassador had been told on 28 February that a counter-attack was to be delivered against the Russian advance to the Baltic in eastern Pomerania. When the Russians reached Koslin early in March Hitler did indeed call for the reconquest of Pomerania and ordered five armoured divisions from Army Group Centre to the Stettin area; they arrived too late and were swallowed up by the Soviet advance.[81] On 7 March, in a telegram decrypted on 11 March, the Ambassador reported that the long-planned counter-offensive had been switched to the area south-east of Berlin and would be launched in two or three weeks.[82] In the middle of March the Japanese were doubting that it would ever take place.[83] In fact, on 16 January Hitler had decided to commit Sixth Panzer Army to Hungary despite the protests of OKH that it was

---

* See above, p 648.

75. DEFE 3/516, BT 7199 of 14 March; DEFE 3/519, BT 7860 of 21 March; Naval Headlines of 15 March.
76. Naval Headlines of 31 March.
77. ibid, of 3 April.
78. BAY/BT 58 of 5 February.
79. BAY/BTs 62 of 8 February, 68 of 9 February, 71 of 10 February, 91 of 21 February.
80. BAY/BTs 106 of 26 February, 108 of 28 February.
81. Seaton, op cit, pp 541–542; Erickson, op cit, p 522.
82. BAY/BT 117 of 12 March.
83. BAY/BT 126 of 21 March.

desperately needed on the Oder,[84] and on 5 and 6 March a major German offensive had been launched there.

The first indication of the intention to attack in Hungary came from decrypts available from the middle of January referring to the transfer of Sixth Panzer Army from the western front. The decrypts did not specify its destination but it seemed at the time that some or all of its divisions must be being sent to stem the increasingly rapid Soviet advance on the northern fronts.*As late as 11 February, by which date there was firm Sigint evidence that 2nd and 9th SS Panzer Divisions were moving to Hungary, MI still believed that I SS Panzer Corps with 1st and 12th SS Panzer Divisions might be going to Himmler's command in Pomerania, and so advised the Soviet authorities through the Military Mission in Moscow.[85]† By 13 February, however, MI 14 was able to inform the Mission that the probable destination of the whole of Sixth Panzer Army was southern Slovakia or northern Hungary and that it was being transferred under strict security precautions similar to those which had been adopted before the Ardennes offensive.[86] The precautions were referred to in a message decrypted on 13 February which required that all concerned in the move of a 'Rest and Refitting Group' should give 'a written pledge of absolute secrecy on pain of death' and insisted that the move should not be shown in situation maps.[87] There were few further decrypts about the move between then and 6 March, but air reconnaissance of the Hungarian railways by AFHQ provided further evidence of the arrival of armour in western Hungary which was passed to the Russian General Staff. By 6 March it was clear from decrypts that the rest and refitting group was associated with Sixth Panzer Army and that other cover-names were being used for the Army and its individual divisions.[88] But a message decrypted on 12 February had already confirmed that 1st SS Panzer Division was among the divisions moving to Hungary and a decrypt of 22 February disclosed that they also included the fourth of Sixth Panzer Army's divisions, 12th SS Panzer

---

* For the details see below, p 668

† For the resumption of the despatch of Intelligence to the British Military Mission, see above p 649.

84. Seaton, op cit, p 536; Erickson, op cit, p 508; Ziemke, *Stalingrad to Berlin* (Washington DC 1968), p 422.
85. Dir/C Archive, 8704 of 28 February, MI 14/285 of 11 February.
86. ibid, MI 14/286 of 13 February. See also AWL 3984 of 17 February.
87. DEFE 3/506, BT 4744 of 13 February.
88. AWL 3990 of 17 February; WO 208/4318 of 4 March; DEFE 3/513, BTs 6363 of 5 March, 6486 of 6 March.

Division.[89] A message of 28 February requiring the transfer of the remaining units of II SS Panzer Corps from Army Group B to be accelerated by all available means was not decrypted till 7 March, when the Russians were informed that Sixth Panzer Army was in the Danube area east of Bratislava.[90]

Sigint provided no intelligence about the purpose of Sixth Panzer Army's counter-attack. On 18 February MI 14 thought it 'difficult to find an objective which would pay a reasonable dividend. The concentration area which is believed to be the Vienna-Gyor area seems too far south for operations through the Moravska-Ostrava gap.'[91] On 20 February, on the other hand, General Marshall advised the Soviet authorities that the Germans were preparing to counter-attack from Vienna through Moravska-Ostrava to Lodz, as well as in Pomerania.[92]* By the end of February, however, the Soviet commanders had concluded, following a brief attack by I SS Panzer Corps between 17 and 24 February which drove the Russians out of their bridgehead on the river Hron (Gran), that Sixth Panzer Army's offensive would be made on the Third Ukrainian Front in the Lake Balaton area.[93]

Despite the uncertainty of Sixth Panzer Army's destination, there was evidence from Sigint as early as the middle of February that the Germans were planning some action in Hungary. On 14 February decrypts had disclosed that OKW also planned to evacuate the Mostar-Sarajevo-Visegrad salient in Yugoslavia with a view to releasing five infantry divisions for an operation in southern Hungary.[94]† And on 21 February MI 14 was able to send to Moscow an appreciation based on several other Sigint references to this operation.[95] Named *Waldteufel* by the Germans and Operation *South Hungary* by GC and CS, the operation was to be carried out by 7th SS Mountain, 11th GAF Field, 104th Jäger, 297th Infantry and 1st Mountain Divisions from Yugoslavia and perhaps by other divisions in Hungary. There was no firm evidence as to where the attack would be made; it might come south of the river Drava, from the Barcs area or Osijek (Esseg), or

---

* For the intelligence on the preparations in Pomerania see above p 650.
† See also below, p 659 et seq.

89. DEFE 3/506, BT 4694 of 12 February; DEFE 3/509, BT 5402 of 22 February; WO 208/4317 of 25 February.
90. DEFE 3/514, BT 6545 of 7 March; AWL 4178 of 7 March.
91. WO 208/4317 of 18 February.
92. Erickson, op cit, pp 511, 528.
93. ibid, pp 509–511; Seaton, op cit, p 554.
94. DEFE 3/507, BTs 4789 and 4830 of 14 February; WO 208/4317 of 18 February.
95. Dir/C Archive, 8704 of 28 February, MI 14/290 of 21 February.

north of the river, eastwards to Nagykanisza and then northwards. A decrypt had associated this attack with another Operation *Frühlingserwachen*,* but MI 14 was uncertain whether *Waldteufel* would be accompanied by a thrust to the south-east from Lake Balaton or whether, if there were to be such a thrust, it would be made by Sixth Panzer Army; that Army might alternatively be used to widen the scope of the operation by attacking eastward in the sector north of the Danube bend. MI 14 remained puzzled as to the purpose of the offensive; it suggested that as it would do little to serve the needs of the German economy, the objectives must lie in the propaganda effect of a victory over the Russians and the removal of the threat to Vienna.[96]

On 24 February the decrypt of 'an urgent and most secret' message from OKW to C-in-C South-East disclosed that concentration for the operation was to be completed by 25 February.[97] By 4 March a report that two of the divisions from Yugoslavia were crossing the Drava south of Nagykanisza and some indications of a concentration of German armour north of Lake Balaton provided 'slight evidence' that the offensive would be made north of the river and be co-ordinated with a thrust from the lake to the south-east.[98] As we now know, the Russians had much more advance information, having learned from Hungarian deserters the dates and localities of the attacks and, from the Yugoslavs, something of its objectives.[99]

The offensive began on the night of 5 March, Army Group E attacking across the Drava with 104th Jäger, 297th Infantry, 11th GAF Field and 1st Cossack Divisions† in an attempt to seize bridgeheads and Army Group South's Second Panzer Army – Panzer in name only – attacking south of Lake Balaton with four infantry divisions. Army Group South's main attack followed on 6 March against the Russian 3rd Ukrainian Front between Lakes Balaton and Velencze; using the Army Group's Sixth Army on the left and Sixth Panzer Army on the right – in all, ten Panzer and five infantry divisions – its objective was to envelop 3rd Ukrainian Front between the Danube and the Drava and, by establishing bridgeheads across the Danube, to recover Budapest and eastern Hungary.[100] The Panzer thrust briefly gave the Russians some

---

* In fact *Frühlingserwachen* was the German name for the operation over-all; *Waldteufel* related only to that part of it carried out by forces of Army Group E.

† See below p 660, for the substitution of 1st Cossack for 7th SS Mountain Division.

96. WO 208/4315, MI 14K Appreciation/7/45 of 22 February.
97. CX/MSS/T469/77; WO 208/4317 of 25 February.
98. WO 208/4318 of 4 March.
99. Erickson, op cit, p 513.
100. ibid, pp 508–509, 510; Seaton, op cit, p 554.

cause for anxiety but the offensive was short-lived; on 14 March Army Group South threw in its last Panzer reserves in a vain attempt to push to the Danube. Second Panzer Army's attack had meanwhile been held by the weight of the Russian artillery and Army Group E had been unable to retain its bridgeheads.[101] Sigint provided little information during the offensive, the decrypts being available only with some delay. Not until 12 March did they reveal that the offensive had begun, and not until 17 March that Sixth Panzer Army was taking part.[102] On 18 March, however, MI 14 knew from decrypts that the Russians had gone over to the offensive in Hungary.[103]

The Soviet offensive opened on 16 March with an attack by 3rd Ukrainian Front against the German Sixth Army north-west of Lake Velencze. This thrust, which struck south-west to seize the area between the two lakes and to cut off part of Sixth Army and the whole of Sixth Panzer Army, was followed on 17 March by an attack from 2nd Ukrainian Front's left wing towards Gyor. By 22 March the two Fronts had converged and had all but encircled Sixth Panzer Army south of Szekesfehervar. Sixth Panzer Army fought its way out; but its escape developed into a disorderly rout, and the Russian advance swept on until, by early April, it had cleared the Germans out of Hungary.[104] Fish and Enigma decrypts of situation reports from Army Group South, Sixth Army, Sixth Panzer Army and Second Panzer Army confirmed the speed of the advance; but they were being received with delays of between three and seven days, and they by no means provided a detailed account of the fighting. On 25 March MI 14 deduced that the Germans north-east and north of Balaton had avoided encirclement from the north-east by a 'timely disengagement'.[105] On 2 April the speed of the Russian advance suggested to MI 14 that 'for once the Germans may have cut their losses and disengaged in an endeavour to concentrate their forces for the defence of the Bratislava gap.'[106] But on 8 April the decrypt of a report from Army Group South on 4 April, the day on which Bratislava fell, disclosed that its stock of ammunition and fuel had sunk so low that the continuance of operations could no longer be guaranteed; for two days, moreover, the Army Group had had no

---

101. Erickson, op cit, pp 513–514; Seaton, op cit, pp 554–555.
102. DEFE 3/515, BT 6998 of 12 March; DEFE 3/516, BTs 7032 and 7079 of 13 March; DEFE 3/517, BT 7430 of 17 March; WO 208/4318 of 18 March.
103. WO 208/4318 of 18 March.
104. Seaton, op cit, pp 555–557; Erickson, op cit, pp 515–517.
105. WO 208/4318 of 25 March. Fish (Gurnard) decrypts between 17 and 20 March are in CX/MSS/ROB 38 of 29 March (II, item 35), 39 of 6 April (II, items 21 and 24).
106. WO 208/4318 of 2 April.

wireless communication with OKH or with its Armies or even with its own advance battle HQ.[107]

□

In the light of developments in Hungary, the JIC assumed in January 1945 that the German forces in central and southern Yugoslavia – 9 German, 3 Croat and one Cossack divisions – would be withdrawn into the north-west corner; the four non-German divisions were likely to disintegrate and one of the German divisions would probably be disbanded in the withdrawal, and the eight remaining divisions would be used either to defend the Bratislava gap or to preserve a wedge between the Italian and the Hungarian fronts.[108] The Germans did indeed carry out such a withdrawal in the next three months, but not to the exclusion of two limited offensives.

The first was carried out from early in January in the Barcs area of the river Drava, to eliminate Russian bridgeheads threatening Second Panzer Army in southern Hungary; it continued with inconclusive results, as Sigint showed, till towards the end of February.[109] Early in February, in order to safeguard his vulnerable communications, C-in-C South-East wished also to go on to the offensive against the Partisans with elements of 104th Jäger Division in the Bihac area and two other divisions in the Tuzla area (north-west of Zvornik across the Drina), but was thwarted by OKW, which had already advised him that he must contract his front and be ready to use four of his divisions for a counter-offensive in southern Hungary (Operation *Waldteufel*).

The first hint of this was given in a message decrypted on 7 February which reported that Hitler had agreed that elements of 104th Jäger Division could be used in a limited attack towards Tuzla, but only if their timely arrival in the assembly area for 'the large-scale undertaking' was 'unconditionally assured'.[110] That the large-scale undertaking was an operation in southern Hungary emerged on 14 February from the decrypt of a message of 10 February in which OKW warned the C-in-C that after that

---

107. DEFE 3/564, BT 9870 of 8 April.
108. JIC(45)19(o) of 16 January, Annex A para 27; JIC(45)22(o) of 21 January, p 6 para 26.
109. WO 208/4317 of 7 January and 21 February; as examples of the Sigint, DEFE 3/325, BT 1435 of 6 January; DEFE 3/330, BT 2728 of 19 January; DEFE 3/500, BT 3009 of 22 January; DEFE 3/502, BT 3573 of 28 January; DEFE 3/507, BTs 4982 of 16 February, 4997 of 17 February; CX/MSS/ROB 26 of 15 January (II, item 7). See also EDS/Apprec/20, Chapter 2, pp 22–23.
110. DEFE 3/505, BT 4272 of 7 February.

operation 297th Infantry, 104th Jäger and 11th GAF Divisions would remain with Second Panzer Army, though 7th SS Mountain and 1st Mountain Divisions might return to him if the situation permitted, and instructed him to redistribute his forces for the revised assignment of protecting the flanks of Army Group South and of the forces under C-in-C South-West in Italy by defending the line Senj-Bihac-Banja Luka-Doboj-Syrmia.[111] Hitler then vetoed the contraction of the front, permitting only the abandonment of the Visegrad bridgehead, and the C-in-C was informed that, although he must hold Sarajevo, the forces required from him for southern Hungary must be ready by the completion date for their assembly. These developments were not covered by Sigint, but the C-in-C's reactions, sent on 16 February, were decrypted on 21 February. He doubted whether he could hold Sarajevo, to the south of which his forces were in full flight and Mostar had already fallen, and he was contemplating an immediate withdrawal to the Senj-Syrmia line. He also doubted whether from that line he could assure the protection of the armies on his flanks with the forces conditionally promised to him after Operation *Waldteufel*; the task might be accomplished if his withdrawal succeeded without great losses, and if large-scale operations were not undertaken by the Partisans or the western Allies.[112]

In response to these warnings, as we now know, the C-in-C was permitted on 23 February to substitute 1st Cossack Division for 7th SS Mountain Division in the *Waldteufel* force, and it was partly as a result of his representations that Operation *Waldteufel* was postponed till early in March.[113] As the decrypts disclosed, the need to use 104th Jäger Division to assist the transfer of 22nd Infantry Division from Visegrad to the Drina front had been prolonged by severe Partisan opposition,[114] and on the Sarajevo front the Germans remained anxious about the growing numerical superiority of the Partisans and the very thin distribution of their own forces.[115]

The pressure from the Partisans temporarily declined at the end

---

111. DEFE 3/507, BTs 4789 and 4830 of 14 February.
112. DEFE 3/509, BT 5338 of 21 February, WO 208/4315, MI 14K Appreciation/8/45 of 23 February; WO 208/4317 of 25 February.
113. EDS/Apprec/20, Chapter 1, pp 2–3, 10, 23, 29–30; Chapter 2, pp 11–12, 22–25, 26.
114. As examples, DEFE 3/500, BT 3009 of 22 January; DEFE 3/503, BT 3832 of 31 January; DEFE 3/507, BTs 4801 of 14 February, 4878 of 15 February; DEFE 3/508, BTs 5063 and 5113 of 18 February; DEFE 3/509, BT 5492 of 23 February; DEFE 3/510, BT 5745 of 26 February; DEFE 3/512, BT 6064 of 1 March.
115. DEFE 3/508, BT 5148 of 19 February.

of February, as was confirmed by a German appreciation decrypted on 8 March,[116] but on 12 March OKW instructed the C-in-C South-East to put it about that the divisions he had released for *Waldteufel* would return to him at the conclusion of that operation.[117] The OKW message, decrypted on 17 March, was a response to a long appreciation from the C-in-C on 9 March, decrypted on 15 and 16 March, in which he had pointed out that although he had so far contented himself with the promise of 1st Mountain Division at the end of *Waldteufel*, if a rapid success in south Hungary was not forthcoming he might have to be given another division sooner than intended; it might otherwise be too late to save the situation in the Bihac area.[118] In the event, while three of the divisions released for *Waldteufel* were retained in Hungary, 104th Jäger Division was sent to reinforce XV Mountain Corps in the Bihac area, the Partisans having launched an offensive from there towards Trieste on 20 March.[119]

The Germans then held a line of communication from Sarajevo through Brod to Zagreb, and were protecting its flanks sufficiently to ensure the eventual retreat of their garrisons to prepared defence lines from which, as the JIC believed, they still hoped to maintain a wedge between the German armies in Italy and Hungary.[120] But with Hitler at last sanctioning withdrawal from Sarajevo – also on 20 March – the first stage of the retreat coincided with the Partisan offensive. British forces assisted the offensive with supplies and air support, and with naval and artillery operations along the coast and raids by the Special Boat Squadron on the islands, in accordance with arrangements agreed between Tito and Alexander at a meeting in Belgrade; they included the stationing of No 281 Wing RAF at Zara from 22 March.[121]* The Partisan advance was held up temporarily by the arrival of 104th Jäger Division; but it took Bihac on 4 April, and early in April the German retreat from Sarajevo to a defence line running from Karlovac through Zagreb and Varazdin to link with Second Panzer Army was further threatened by a Partisan offensive on its eastern flank.

---

* At this meeting it was agreed that Allied and Yugoslav officers should meet regularly for the exchange of order of battle intelligence and that the Yugoslavs should receive a weekly British intelligence summary.[122]

116. DEFE 3/514, BT 6647 of 8 March.
117. DEFE 3/517, BT 7445 of 17 March.
118. ibid, BTs 7241 of 15 March, 7405 of 16 March.
119. EDS/Apprec/20, Chapter 3, p 36.
120. JIC(45)90(o) of 19 March, para 19.
121. CAB 101/228, pp 76–77, 88, 92; CAB 80/93, COS(45)187(o) of 20 March for the record of the conference.
122. CAB 80/95, COS(45)187(o), pp 7, 12.

The Partisan offensives were accompanied by the customary large volume of high-grade Sigint. But the decrypts were being obtained with some delay, usually three days in the case of naval messages from the coast and up to a week in the case of the Army's messages; and on this account, and in view of the rapidly changing situation, there was some difficulty in assessing the enemy's intentions. On 5 April AFHQ believed that even though the German forces were now cut off from the Austria-Hungary theatre by the Russian advance towards Vienna, they would still try to secure escape routes into Italy or south Germany by holding a line in the north-west, and that 'local surrender within Yugoslavia is improbable'.[123] By 7 April, when the Partisans had advanced up the coast to Jablanac, opposite the island of Rab, it appeared that the German withdrawal was so disorganised that the Yugoslav Army would meet little resistance until it came up to the garrisons at Karlovac and Fiume.[124] On 8 April, the day before the Allies began their final offensive on the Italian front, MI 14 thought the Germans envisaged holding an intermediate line in Yugoslavia running north and south through Brod; but it also wondered whether Tito would present the western Allies, and particularly the Italians, with an unpleasant *fait accompli* by pushing into the Istrian peninsula.[125]

In the event, XXI Mountain Corps did not get back to the river Sava at Brod till mid-April, by which time it was too late for the Germans to make a stand there. As they fell back on Zagreb a decrypt of 20 April disclosed that they had been anxious on 16 April that the Bulgarians would attack across the Drava towards Zagreb in conjunction with an offensive by Tito from south of the town,[126] and in a message of 19 April, decrypted on 21 April, they gave details of another defence position that was to run from east of Novska to east of Barcs.[127] In a message of 20 April, decrypted on 21 April, OKW informed Army Group E that any withdrawal westward beyond this position would require Hitler's approval.[128]

123. JIC(45)125(0) of 12 April (JIC(AF)/4/45 of 5 April).
124. CAB 101/126, pp 151–152; CAB 101/228, p 94.
125. WO 208/4318 of 8 April.
126. DEFE 3/568, KO 912 of 20 April.
127. ibid, KO 943 of 21 April; WO 208/4318 of 22 April.
128. DEFE 3/568, KO 990 of 21 April; WO 208/4318 of 22 April.

CHAPTER 61

The Gaining of the Rhine

AT THE beginning of January 1945 the Germans attacked in the Saar and the Colmar pocket in what proved to be their last offensive in the west, and achieved some initial success. Meanwhile the Allies were counter-attacking in the Ardennes. In mid-January First and Third US Armies met at Houffalize, eliminating the Bulge; Second British Army began Operation *Blackcock* to drive the enemy from the triangle of territory between the rivers Wurm (just north of Geilenkirchen), Roer and the Maas (from Maeseyck to Roermond); and Hitler withdrew Sixth Panzer Army from Army Group B. In the next fortnight the Germans abandoned the Saar offensive and the Allies counter-attacked in the Colmar pocket; 12th US Army Group drove the enemy back to his starting line for the Ardennes offensive; and Second British Army completed Operation *Blackcock*.

On 1 January Army Group G's First Army made a three-pronged attack in the Saar on a front from west of Saarbrücken to east of Pirmasens. West and east of Saarbrücken the attack made little impression, but in the Hardt Forest, in the area of Bitche, it almost reached the Hagenau-Saarguemines road. On 5 January Nineteenth Army, under Army Group Upper Rhine, joined the offensive, establishing a bridgehead over the Rhine at Gambs-heim, north of Strasbourg, and on 6 January First Army launched a new attack south-east of Wissembourg using 21st Panzer Division and 25th PG Division. On 7 January Nineteenth Army attacked northwards in the Colmar pocket. During the second week of January the penetration in the Bitche area was gradually reduced, but the Germans brought in XXXIX Panzer Corps HQ from the Ardennes, 6th SS Mountain Division from Norway, 7th Parachute Division from Holland and 10th SS Panzer Division from C-in-C West Reserve, and First Army continued its thrust south-east of Wissembourg while Nineteenth Army enlarged the Gambsheim bridgehead and pressed on in the Colmar pocket, threatening Strasbourg from the south. On 18 January the enemy succeeded in opening up a narrow corridor between the Gambsheim bridgehead and the thrust from Wissembourg, and on 22 January the Allies withdrew behind the river Moder.

The Germans re-grouped and attacked the new front on 24 January. Three bridgeheads were gained, but two had to be abandoned immediately and the Germans were forced to go over to the defensive. Meanwhile, the attack in the Colmar pocket had been suspended; one of the divisions engaged in it had been withdrawn for transfer to the eastern front; and the Allies had counter-attacked from north and south.[1]

There was no explicit warning of the enemy offensives in Alsace from high-grade Sigint or any other source, but the possibility that they would be attempted had been foreseen by General Eisenhower on 19 December when he decided that Seventh US Army should take over some of Third US Army's front so that more weight could be put into the latter's drive against the enemy's southern flank in the Ardennes.[2] In the last week of December high-grade Sigint provided information about changes in First Army's order of battle[3] which prompted a comment by MI 14, late on 31 December, that the order of battle needed careful watching 'in view of the number of Divisions apparently not in the line'.[4]* In its summary of the same date for the CIGS MI 14 remarked that the provision by the enemy of reinforcements for the Ardennes depended in part on whether he decided to make diversionary attacks elsewhere. There had been signs of such intentions in Holland, the Saar (particularly in the area of Saarguemines and Bitche) and even in the Colmar pocket.[6]

A decrypt signalled to the Commands by GC and CS very early on 5 January reported the intention of an unspecified authority to form a bridgehead in the neighbourhood of Gambsheim just as the operation began.[7] Another decrypt signalled at 0346, disclosed that on that day Army Group G intended to open an exit for the mobile divisions and make a strong reconnaissance thrust from Wissembourg towards Hagenau.[8] Decrypts available on 6 and 7 January showed that 21st Panzer Division was involved; that its

---

* They included 21st Panzer Division and 25th PG Division.[5]

1. Ellis, *Victory in the West*, Vol II (1968), pp 247–249; WO 219/1928, SHAEF Intelligence Summaries Nos 42–45; WO 208/4317, MI 14 Weekly Summaries for the CIGS, 7, 14, 21 and 28 January 1945.
2. Ellis, op cit, Vol II, p 181.
3. DEFE 3/321, BTs 436, 437 of 26 December 1944; DEFE 3/322, BTs 575, 622, 688 of 29 December, 715 of 30 December; DEFE 3/323, BTs 785 of 30 December, 828, 844 of 31 December.
4. DEFE 3/323, BT 844 of 31 December.
5. DEFE 3/321, BT 288 of 24 December; DEFE 3/323, BTs 782, 785 of 30 December, 844 of 31 December.
6. WO 208/4317 of 31 December.
7. DEFE 3/325, BT 1272 of 5 January.
8. ibid, BT 1275 of 5 January.

objectives were Hagenau and Zabern; and that when it was temporarily checked late on 6 January 25th PG Division had been brought up in support.[9] A decrypt signalled at 1900 on 8 January disclosed the intention of the two Divisions to continue the thrust the next day[10] and their operations were reflected in decrypts available between 10 and 14 January.[11]

Meanwhile high-grade Sigint was showing that the enemy was bringing up major reinforcements.* A reference apparently associating XXXIX Panzer Corps, which had been in the Ardennes, with the Saar was contained in a decrypt of 7 January.[13] Decrypts of 9 January confirmed the Corps's presence on First Army's front.[14] Decrypts on 10 January disclosed that it was in charge of the armoured thrust south-east from Wissembourg,[15] and another available the next day showed that, in response to Hitler's demand for quicker information about developments at critical points, XXXIX Panzer Corps (and two other Corps engaged in the Saar offensive, LXXXIX and XC) had been told to make special reports direct to OKW.[16] A decrypt signalled on 12 January indicated that XXXIX Panzer Corps might be directly subordinated to Army Group G.[17]

It had been known since mid-November that 6th SS Mountain Division and 2nd Mountain Division were likely to move soon to Denmark from Norway.[18] On 31 December MI 14 told the CIGS that the destination of 6th SS Mountain Division, which had started to leave Norway early in December, was still uncertain.[19] A decrypt of 4 January reported that the last elements of the Division had cleared Norway a week earlier.[20] A decrypt available on 6 January, of a message on 28 December, referred to large movements by rail to Army Group G,[21] and MI 14's surmise that

---

* It also disclosed that General Blaskowitz – dismissed by Hitler after the reverses suffered in the Moselle area in September – was back in command of Army Group G vice General Balck.[12]

9. ibid, BT 1438 of 6 January; DEFE 3/326, BTs 1504, 1528 of 7 January.
10. DEFE 3/326, BT 1693 of 8 January.
11. DEFE 3/327, BTs 1826, 1865 of 10 January; DEFE 3/328, BTs 2003, 2036 of 11 January, 2091 of 12 January, 2164 of 13 January, 2245 of 14 January.
12. DEFE 3/327, BT 1851 of 10 January.
13. DEFE 3/326, BT 1591 of 7 January.
14. ibid, BT 1716 of 9 January; DEFE 3/327, BT 1791 of 9 January.
15. DEFE 3/327, BTs 1811, 1813 of 10 January.
16. DEFE 3/328, BT 2017 of 11 January.
17. ibid, BT 2161 of 12 January.
18. WO 208/4317 of 19 November.
19. ibid, 31 December.
20. DEFE 3/324, BT 1119 of 4 January.
21. DEFE 3/325, BT 1385 of 6 January.

these comprised 6th SS Mountain Division was confirmed the next day when a decrypt disclosed that the Division was at Kaiserslautern on 5 January.[22] A decrypt of 10 January showed that it was in the front line under LXXXIX Corps.[23]

A C-in-C West report about railway movements on 5 January, decrypted on 9 January, included 10th SS Panzer Division and 7th Parachute Division, but did not give their destinations.[24] However, decrypts on 10 January disclosed that 7th Parachute Division was being brought up east of Bitche,[25] and decrypts on 11 January disclosed Army Group H's intention the previous evening to use both 7th Parachute Division and 10th SS Panzer Division in the drive from Wissembourg, the latter's task being to establish a bridgehead over the river Moder in the neighbourhood of Bischwiller (south-east of Hagenau).[26]

Decrypts signalled on 9 January showed that 2nd Mountain Division was becoming available for C-in-C West. GOC Denmark had reported on 5 January that all units of the Division were ready for operations, except those which were still in Norway but expected to arrive the next day, and some elements which were going direct to C-in-C West.[27] A decrypt of 10 January disclosed an order by OKW on 6 January to GOC Denmark to send a regimental group of 2nd Mountain Division to C-in-C West by 12 January without fail.[28] A decrypt of 14 January showed that the Division was going to Alsace to replace 269th VG Division, which had been ordered to move at once to the eastern front from the Colmar pocket where it was taking part in the offensive.[29]

Decrypts signalled on 22 and 23 January reported the enemy's intention to follow the Allies to the Moder, thrust over the river and attack with armour to the high ground north-east of Brumath.[30] Decrypts of 23 and 24 January partly revealed the German re-grouping. 25th PG Division was to attack Schweighausen, just west of Hagenau. 10th SS Panzer Division was moving into the area of Bischwiller on the left of 7th Parachute Division. The latter's battle HQ at noon on 24 January was disclosed with an indication of the right-hand boundary of its

---

22.　DEFE 3/326, BT 1535 of 7 January.
23.　DEFE 3/327, BT 1811 of 10 January.
24.　ibid, BTs 1756, 1759 of 9 January.
25.　ibid, BTs 1811, 1813 of 10 January.
26.　ibid, BTs 1916, 1917, 1960 of 11 January.
27.　DEFE 3/326, BTs 1721, 1723 of 9 January; DEFE 3/327, BT 1766 of 9 January.
28.　DEFE 3/327, BT 1885 of 10 January.
29.　DEFE 3/329, BT 2263 of 14 January.
30.　DEFE 3/500, BTs 3062 of 22 January, 3120 of 23 January.

sector.[31] 21st Panzer Division's sector in the afternoon of 23 January was also reported.[32] Decrypts on 26 and 27 January reported the successful formation of bridgeheads, followed almost immediately by the abandonment of two of them.[33] On 28 January MI 14 was confident that the enemy had gone over to the defensive in face of superior Allied pressure on the whole front.[34] By then MI 14 knew from decrypts of 27 and 28 January that 7th Parachute Division was to transfer to an unspecified destination outside Army Group G,[35] and that there were indications from Army Y and high-grade Sigint that 21st Panzer Division and 25th PG Division were withdrawing into reserve.[36]

On 4 January, when the Bulge was being attacked on three sides, 21st Army Group appreciated that the Germans were not in a position to renew their offensive towards Liège.[37] On 7 January SHAEF was still of the opinion that they had not yet given up in the Ardennes,[38] but in the ensuing week it became clear that they had decided to withdraw and were doing so in good order, helped by the weather.[39] From high-grade Sigint and battlefield information MI 14 concluded on 14 January that three Corps HQs (I and II SS Panzer and LXXXV), four Panzer Divisions (1st, 2nd, 12th SS, 9th) and 3rd PG Division were out of contact.[40] On 17 January GC and CS decrypted a message of 10 January from Army Group B to the effect that Hitler had ordered it to give up all its SS Panzer Divisions 'for employment elsewhere'. SS Panzer Divisions not currently employed, and scattered elements, could only be used on Army Group B's express order if a breakthrough threatened.[41] Decrypts on 21 January disclosed that Sixth Panzer Army with I and II SS Panzer Corps, and 1st, 2nd and 12th SS Panzer Divisions were to be pulled out from the morning of 22 January, and to be followed by 9th SS Panzer Division and the two Führer Brigades.

---

31. ibid, BTs 3119, 3167, 3174 of 23 January; DEFE 3/501, BT 3275 of 24 January.
32. DEFE 3/500, BT 3182 of 23 January.
33. DEFE 3/501, BTs 3378, 3469 of 26 January, 3486 of 27 January.
34. WO 208/4317 of 28 January.
35. DEFE 3/502, BTs 3519 of 27 January, 3578 of 28 January.
36. WO 285/6, Second Army Intelligence Summary No 239 of 28 January; DEFE 3/520, BT 3519 of 27 January.
37. WO 171/3838A, 21st Army Group Intelligence Summary No 173 of 4 January.
38. WO 219/1928, SHAEF Intelligence Summary No 42 of 7 January.
39. ibid, No 43 of 14 January.
40. WO 208/4317 of 14 January; DEFE 3/326, BT 1534 of 7 January; DEFE 3/327, BTs 1776 of 9 January, 1898 and 1903 of 10 January, 1979 of 11 January; DEFE 3/328, BTs 2198, 2205, 2209, 2212 of 13 January, 2226 of 14 January.
41. DEFE 3/330, BT 2597 of 17 January.

Fifth Panzer Army was to take over Sixth Panzer Army's sector with the latter's formations and Army troops other than the SS formations.[42]

As for the destination of Sixth Panzer Army, SHAEF on 19 January thought it likely to be going east but unlikely to be 'thrown into the avalanche in Poland'; it might be retained for defence of the German frontier.[43] MI 14 on 21 January thought that 'elsewhere' meant either the eastern front, where the Russian winter offensive, which had begun on 12 January, was carrying all before it, or the Saar.[44] By 26 January the Allies had captured a document indicating that I SS Panzer Corps was to go to Army Group H in Holland on 22–23 January and II SS Panzer Corps to Army Group G in Alsace on 24–25 January. The circumstances were, however, consistent with this being a plant,[45]* while decrypts available on 26, 27 and 28 January gave significant pointers to an eastward movement.[47] On 28 January MI 14 judged (correctly as it proved) that these decrypts clinched the matter,[48] and SHAEF thought that even if the document was genuine it had been overtaken by the logic of events.[49] On 1 February, as we shall see, General Eisenhower was satisfied that Sixth Panzer Army was going to the east.

Despite the departure of Sixth Panzer Army the Germans continued to resist stubbornly in the Ardennes. According to a message on 24 January, decrypted on 25 January and evidently referring to Seventh Army, the Army's plan was to make a slow withdrawal to the West Wall.[50] In an appreciation on 23 January (not decrypted for a week) C-in-C West noted that Allied pressure was delaying the release of German formations.[51] Nevertheless, on 28 January MI accepted that seven divisions had been withdrawn from the line in the past week[52] and SHAEF appreciated that a

---

* A much later decrypt of a message from Army Group B of 24 January disclosed orders for full exploitation of the movement of Sixth Panzer Army as a large-scale deception. Transport of I SS Panzer Corps and its subordinate forces to the Dutch area and of II SS Panzer Corps to Alsace was to be simulated.[46]

42. DEFE 3/331, BT 2998 of 21 January.
43. Notes of Meeting at SHAEF 19 January (Robb Papers held at RAF Museum, Hendon).
44. WO 208/4317 of 21 January.
45. WO 285/6, No 237 of 26 January.
46. DEFE 3/572, KO 1945 of 3 May 1945.
47. DEFE 3/500, BTs 3463, 3470 of 27 January; DEFE 3/501, BTs 3561, 3571, 3596, 3608 of 28 January. See also AWL 3828 of 27 January.
48. WO 208/4317 of 28 January.
49. WO 219/1928, No 45 of 28 January.
50. DEFE 3/501, BT 3318 of 25 January.
51. DEFE 3/503, BT 3752 of 30 January.
52. WO 208/4317 of 28 January.

quota of armour and infantry was going north to the Cologne sector.[53] A decrypt of 25 January showed that 12th VG Division was arriving north of Erkelenz.[54] Army Y had indications from 24 January that 116th Panzer Division was moving and on 27 January that parts of it were behind the Roer.[55] Decrypts available on 28 January disclosed that XLVII Panzer Corps HQ (without its subordinated divisions) was moving north from the Ardennes front to Fifteenth Army,[56] and a decrypt of 31 January showed that 116th Panzer Division would be subordinated to it.[57]

A message decrypted on 27 January, reporting the withdrawal of battle outposts to the east bank of the Roer the previous evening,[58] marked the end of Operation *Blackcock*. During the battle, reports made by XII SS Corps commanding the German divisions in the triangle were decrypted regularly without much delay.[59] But they yielded no important insights and gave no indication of any special anxiety on the part of the Germans, who brought in minimal reinforcements. MI 14's view on 28 January was that they had been content to delay Second British Army's advance.[60] By contrast numerous decrypts in the second half of the month showed that the enemy was anxious about his vulnerability around Orscholz in the Moselle valley.[61]

The opening of the Saar offensive was accompanied by attacks on Allied airfields. A notable feature was the strict wireless silence observed by the formations involved.[62] 5th Jagd Division was reinforced by three fighter Geschwader and on 4 January AI estimated that the enemy was putting up some 130 single-engined sorties per day on the Saar front from a strength of 400 aircraft.[63] Here and in the Ardennes bad weather was the dominating factor

---

53. WO 219/1928, No 45 of 28 January.
54. DEFE 3/501, BT 3316 of 25 January.
55. WO 285/6, Nos 235 of 24 January, 238 of 27 January.
56. DEFE 3/502, BTs 3547, 3552 of 28 January.
57. DEFE 3/503, BT 3840 of 31 January.
58. DEFE 3/501, BT 3481 of 27 January.
59. DEFE 3/329, BT 2387 of 15 January; DEFE 3/330, BTs 2572, 2575 of 17 January, 2703 of 18 January; DEFE 3/331, BTs 2759, 2805 of 19 January, 2855 of 20 January, 2890 of 21 January; DEFE 3/500, BTs 3055 of 22 January, 3154 of 23 January; DEFE 3/501, BTs 3277 of 24 January, 3293, 3316, 3324, 3350 of 25 January, 3443 of 26 January, 3487, 3494 of 27 January.
60. WO 208/4317, MI 14 Weekly Summary for the CIGS, 28 January.
61. DEFE 3/329, BTs 2299 of 14 January, 2314, 2376 of 15 January; 2469 of 16 January; DEFE 3/330, BTs 2546, 2560 of 17 January; DEFE 3/331, BT 2920 of 21 January; DEFE 3/502, BTs 3623, 3643, 3688 of 29 January; DEFE 3/503, BT 3839 of 30 January.
62. Air Sunset 271 of 2 January.
63. Air Sunset 272 of 4 January.

during the next ten days. On 13 January AI thought that there was no clear evidence about the GAF's intentions on the western front, but there were signs of increasing emphasis on the Saar sector.[64] On 16 January AI reported that a fairly large re-disposition of forces to meet the Russian winter offensive was in progress comprising (so far) two fighter Geschwader, with some 250 aircraft, and a Geschwader with 100 fighter-bombers. All these had been withdrawn from the northern parts of the western front, which probably pointed to the intention to maintain the air effort in support of the Saar offensive.[65] Two more fighter Geschwader had been ordered east by 21 January, but the southern sector was still immune from withdrawals.[66] Reviewing the situation on 27 January, when the western front had lost two more fighter Geschwader, AI estimated that fighter strength in the west had fallen to 600 aircraft and fighter-bomber strength to 50 aircraft. This was comparable with the position before the build-up for the Ardennes offensive.[67] In a message to his Command on 24 January, decrypted the next day, the AOC Jagdkorps II emphasised the importance of supporting the Army despite the drastic reduction in strength because of the demands of the eastern front: 'Germany was at stake'.[68] But on 1 February AI appreciated that, apart from the protection of troop transports leaving for the east, the only positive commitments being undertaken in the west (all on a minor scale) were the reconnais-sance of Allied preparations for the expected offensive, harassing raids on Antwerp and occasional minelaying in the Scheldt estuary. Otherwise the GAF was likely to remain a negligible factor.[69]

□

At the beginning of February the Allies were poised to start the operations, planned by Eisenhower and approved at the 'Argo-naut' conference at Malta, for the last campaign. The destruction of the German forces west of the Rhine would be followed by the seizure of bridgeheads over the river and the advance into Germany. The major effort would be made north of the Ruhr by 21st Army Group (First Canadian, Second Army and Ninth US Army); it would be supported by a subsidiary attack south of the

---

64. Air Sunset 274 of 13 January.
65. Air Sunset 275 of 16 January.
66. Air Sunset 276 of 21 January.
67. Air Sunset 277 of 27 January.
68. DEFE 3/501, BT 3333 of 25 January.
69. Air Sunset 278 of 1 February.

Ruhr from the Frankfurt area. The Ruhr itself would be contained. In a directive on 1 February Eisenhower said that the success of the Russian winter offensive, which had compelled the enemy to withdraw forces from the western front, made it important to close to the Ruhr north of Düsseldorf as speedily as possible. Accordingly, 21st Army Group was to attack on 8 February from Nijmegen (Operation *Veritable*) and on 10 February from the Roer (Operation *Grenade*). Montgomery's directives for the operations stated his intention to destroy all enemy forces in the area west of the Rhine from Nijmegen as far south as the general line Jülich-Düsseldorf, as a preliminary to crossing the Rhine and engaging the enemy in mobile warfare to the north of the Ruhr. First Canadian Army, keeping its left on the Rhine, was to attack south-east to gain the general line Xanten-Geldern; Ninth US Army, supported in the early stages by the left wing of 12th US Army Group, was to attack north-east with its right on the line Jülich-Düsseldorf.[70]

In the first ten days of February the Allies overran the Colmar pocket; the town was captured on 3 February and the Germans destroyed the last bridge (at Chalempré) on 9 February. Third US Army attacked towards Prüm. First US Army advanced on the Roer dams. Schmidt was captured on 7 February and the main dam on 10 February, whereupon the Germans opened the discharge valves of the reservoirs with results which compelled the postponement of *Grenade* for nearly a fortnight. *Veritable* duly opened on 8 February.[71]

The reference in General Eisenhower's directive of 1 February to the withdrawal of German forces to the eastern front no doubt had Sixth Panzer Army prominently in view, but other divisions from the west were already known to have been transferred and more would follow in February. Decrypts on 8 and 9 January of messages sent on 2 and 6 January had shown that 711th Infantry Division was moving from Holland to Hungary,[72] and, as we have seen, the departure of 269th VG Division to the eastern front had been disclosed by a decrypt on 14 January.* MI 14 surmised on 21 January that 712th Infantry Division, known from a decrypt of 13 January to have left Army Group B,[73] might be in Russia.[74] This had been confirmed by 28 January.[75] In the closing days of the

---

* Above, p 666.

70. Ellis, op cit, Vol II, pp 197, 204–212, 250.
71. ibid, pp 249, 250, 264.
72. DEFE 3/326, BT 1673 of 8 January; DEFE 3/327, BT 1762 of 9 January.
73. DEFE 3/328, BT 2186 of 13 January.
74. WO 208/4317 of 21 January.
75. ibid, 28 January; WO 219/1928, No 45 of 28 January.

month there had been indications that 21st Panzer Division and 25th PG Division were being withdrawn from the Saar front into reserve.* In a message on 5 February, decrypted on 8 February, Army Group G reported that 36 trains of 21st Panzer Division and 13 trains of 10th SS Panzer Division (last reported by high-grade Sigint on 28 January as subordinated to XXXIX Panzer Corps)[76] had 'departed'.[77] A message on 8 February stating that all 21st Panzer Division's transports were to be sent to an area east of Berlin was decrypted on 12 February,[78] when a report was received from the Russians that they had taken prisoners from the Division.[79] By 7 February 26 trains of 10th SS Panzer Division had left Army Group G according to a decrypt of 9 February.[80] Decrypts available on 10 and 12 February pointed to an eastward move,[81] and a message on 17 February, decrypted on 19 February, gave Stettin as the Division's destination.[82] Meanwhile the departure from Army Group G of the battle and operations echelons of 25th PG Division had been reported in a decrypt of 4 February.[83] SHAEF knew a week later that the Russians had identified the Division at Küstrin.[84]†

In the first ten days of February high-grade Sigint provided copious evidence that the Germans expected a major Allied offensive designed to reach the Rhine in the north, but were uncertain where it would strike. Army Group H's day report for 27 January, and a situation report on the same day by First Parachute Army, were decrypted on 1 and 2 February. Army Group H (which was responsible from the North Sea to Roermond) suggested that ranging fire by the Allies west and south-west of the Reichswald pointed to preparations to attack north of the Maas,[85] while First Parachute Army (in command from Nijmegen to Roermond) thought that preparations were in hand fron Venlo southwards.[86] Appreciations issued on 28 January by Fremde Heere West and by C-in-C West on 29 January

---

* Above, p 667.

† After these transfers the Panzer and PG Divisions left with C-in-C West were: 2nd, 9th, 11th, 116th Panzer and Panzer Lehr, 3rd and 15th PG and 17th SS PG.

76. DEFE 3/502, BT 3581 of 28 January.
77. DEFE 3/505, BT 4358 of 8 February.
78. DEFE 3/506, BT 4698 of 12 February.
79. WO 219/1929, No 48 of 18 February.
80. DEFE 3/505, BT 4455 of 9 February.
81. DEFE 3/506, BTs 4537 of 10 February, 4688 of 12 February.
82. DEFE 3/508, BT 5175 of 19 February.
83. DEFE 3/504, BT 4094 of 4 February.
84. WO 219/1929, No 47 of 11 February.
85. DEFE 3/503, BT 3938 of 1 February.
86. ibid, BT 3993 of 2 February.

were also decrypted on 2 February. The former had no clue to Montgomery's intentions now that he had reached the Roer south of Roermond, but thought that the offensive would be continued in conjunction with the Americans and referred to a report by a 'usually reliable agent' that a new large-scale offensive from the Aachen bulge to north of Venlo was being mounted.[87] C-in-C West surmised that thinning out in progress on Second British Army's southern wing was part of preparations for a large-scale attack on the Maas bend north of Roermond.[88] But in a message of 2 February, decrypted on 3 February, C-in-C West told Army Group B and Army Group G that as there was no West Wall north of Monschau it was essential to shift reserves into the area behind Fifteenth Army, which was in command from south of Roermond to approximately the Urft dam and Schleiden.[89]

A GAF message on 4 February, decrypted on 5 February, reported that Army Group H was aware of continual movement between the Reichswald, Venlo and Roermond and that Army Group B had reported increasing artillery fire between Jülich and Düren.[90] Decrypts available on 6 February reported heavy artillery concentrations between Venlo and Roermond which suggested reinforcements, 'strikingly strong' Allied movements at 'sHertogenbosch and heavy vehicle traffic over Nijmegen bridge in both directions.[91] Decrypts of 7 February included an appreciation of 4 February in which FHW again acknowledged that it lacked intelligence about 21st Army Group's intentions,[92] and a report late on 5 February in which Fifteenth Army said that it expected local reconnaissance thrusts between Jülich and Düren, but not an imminent large-scale attack.[93] In its day report for 5 February, decrypted on 8 February, Army Group B referred to continued 'strategic concentration' by the Allies in the Aachen sector: large-scale attacks aimed at occupying the Ruhr must be expected any day. The movement of German forces north was therefore of decisive importance but was only progressing slowly because the fuel required had been released to the forces given up 'to the East'.[94]

Suspicion that 21st Army Group's main thrust would be in the sector between Venlo and Roermond persisted after *Veritable* had

87. ibid, BT 3949 of 2 February.
88. ibid, BT 3990 of 2 February.
89. DEFE 3/504, BT 4026 of 3 February.
90. ibid, BT 4150 of 5 February.
91. ibid, BTs 4209, 4247 of 6 February.
92. DEFE 3/505, BT 4265 of 7 February.
93. ibid, BT 4263 of 7 February.
94. ibid, BT 4359 of 8 February.

begun on 8 February. It was the basis of a GAF operations order that evening, which also admitted that the Allied situation on the entire front from Roermond to Schleiden was not yet clear. The decrypt of the order was signalled to the Commands on 10 February.[95] In his day report for 8 February (issued on 9 February and decrypted on 11 February) C-in-C West said that 21st Army Group's attack must be looked at in the framework of the overall Allied plan as preliminary to, and linked with, the main attack on the Maas bend.[96]

Regarding the move of German forces to the north, high-grade Sigint had disclosed by the end of January that XLVII Panzer Corps HQ and 116th Panzer Division were moving to Fifteenth Army.* A decrypt of 1 February showed that 15th PG Division was also going north from the Ardennes.[97] From a decrypt on 5 February the Flivo with XLVII Panzer Corps was placed at Krefeld,[98] and a decrypt of 7 February reported that the Corps had been subordinated to First Parachute Army in tactical reserve, with 116th Panzer Division and 15th PG Division, which were both at München Gladbach, under command.[99] Decrypts of 2 and 7 February established that 7th Parachute Division, earlier reported to be leaving Army Group G,† was detraining in the area between the Maas and the Rhine which was the objective of *Veritable*.[100]

It was also learnt that Army Group B was endeavouring to move forces from the Ardennes to resist First US Army's drive towards the Roer dams. Decrypts signalled on 5 and 6 February disclosed that 3rd PG Division had taken over a sector from Schleiden to Schmidt,[101] and SHAEF appreciated on 11 February that both 9th Panzer Division and Panzer Lehr appeared to be struggling northward towards the Cologne sector.[102] Decrypts signalled on 2 and 4 February revealed that Fifth Panzer Army had side-stepped north and was holding a sector from Schleiden to Prüm between Fifteenth and Seventh Armies.[103]

The withdrawal from the Saar front of 21st Panzer, 10th SS Panzer, 25th PG and 7th Parachute Divisions left no room for doubt that the offensive had been abandoned. There were,

---

* Above, p 669.
† See above, p 667.

95. DEFE 3/506, BT 4508 of 10 February.
96. ibid, BT 4603 of 11 February.
97. DEFE 3/503, BT 3914 of 1 February.
98. DEFE 3/504, BT 4179 of 5 February.
99. DEFE 3/505, BT 4269 of 7 February.
100. DEFE 3/503, BT 3986 of 2 February; DEFE 3/505, BT 4279 of 7 February.
101. DEFE 3/504, BTs 4164 of 5 February, 4170 of 6 February.
102. WO 219/1929, No 47 of 11 February.
103. DEFE 3/503, BT 3959 of 2 February; DEFE 3/504, BT 4135 of 4 February.

moreover, indications that XXXIX Panzer Corps HQ and 256th Infantry Division were also leaving.[104] A decrypt on 4 February pointed to the latter's destination as being the Moselle valley,[105] where, as we have seen,* the Germans feared an Allied attack. The arrival in the sector of 256th Division's forward elements was learnt from a decrypt of 9 February.[106]

A decrypt available on 28 January, which referred to Himmler as commanding in the Poznan area on the eastern front, was followed by other indications that the Army Group Upper Rhine was no longer operational.[107] This possibility was confirmed by Army Group G's situation report for 3 February, decrypted the next day.[108]

When *Veritable* began on 8 February the German front south of Nijmegen between the Rhine and the Maas was held by First Parachute Army's LXXXVI Corps with 84th and 180th Infantry Divisions, elements of 7th Parachute Division and a regiment of 2nd Parachute Division. In the first two days the offensive made excellent progress. By 10 February advanced elements of First Canadian Army were fighting in Cleve and threatening the Cleve-Gennep highway through the Reichswald. The Germans reinforced, first with the rest of 7th Parachute Division and a regiment of 6th Parachute Division from Arnhem and late on 10 February, when flooding had clearly made an assault crossing of the Roer impracticable for some time, with XLVII Panzer Corps. Cleve was taken on 11 February, but by the middle of the month the Germans had established a check line running from the Rhine through Moyland and Goch to the Maas. This was held from the Rhine to Goch by XLVII Panzer Corps with 116th Panzer Division, 15th PG Division, elements of 346th Division, which were being brought in with the rest of 6th Parachute Division from Holland, and elements of 7th Parachute Division, and from Goch to the Maas by LXXXVI Corps with the now battered 84th and 180th Divisions and assorted Parachute elements.[109]

On 17 February First Canadian Army cut the Calcar–Goch road and entered Goch two days later. The Germans brought in II Parachute Corps with 7th Parachute Division both sides of Goch

---

* See above, p 669.

104. DEFE 3/502, BT 3634 of 29 January; DEFE 3/503, BTs 3851 of 31 January, 3986 of 2 February; DEFE 3/504, BT 4031 of 2 February.
105. DEFE 3/504, BT 4092 of 4 February.
106. DEFE 3/505, BT 4455 of 9 February.
107. DEFE 3/502, BT 3592 of 28 January; DEFE 3/503, BTs 3917 and 3942 of 1 February.
108. DEFE 3/504, BTs 4092, 4094 of 4 February.
109. Ellis, op cit, Vol II, pp 254–265.

and made a vigorous, but finally unsuccessful, counter-attack along the Calcar–Goch road with XLVII Panzer Corps reinforced by Panzer Lehr Division. When First Canadian Army took Moyland from 6th Parachute Division on 22 February it had broadened the six-mile front between the Rhine and the Maas from which it had started to twenty miles, but the Germans were still holding a coherent defence line, which was further reinforced by 8th Parachute Division.[110]

Grenade began on 23 February when Ninth US Army crossed the Roer and quickly established bridgeheads. The enemy sought to contain the Americans with elements of 9th and 11th Panzer Divisions, 338th Division (diverted on its way from the Colmar pocket to Calcar) and Panzer Lehr, which was switched from First Canadian Army's front. On 28 February Ninth US Army broke out. By 1 March it was in Neuss, opposite Düsseldorf, and München Gladbach, was approaching Kempen and had taken Roermond and Venlo. Meanwhile First Canadian Army had continued its stubbornly contested advance. On 1 March contact was made by its right wing with elements of Ninth US Army and no effective German forces remained west of Geldern. But in several more days of hard fighting, against resistance which was often fanatical, the Allies were unable to prevent the Germans making an orderly withdrawal across the Rhine, blowing the bridges as they went. The last bridgehead at Wesel, held by rearguards from the Parachute divisions, was evacuated on 10 March.[111]

The movement of enemy armour during *Veritable* and *Grenade* was comprehensively reported in high-grade Sigint, but with some delay. The subordination of XLVII Panzer Corps to First Parachute Army had been disclosed on 7 February,* but a message on 12 February indicating that it was being committed in the Cleve area was not available for four days.[112] A decrypt of 17 February reported that 11th Panzer Division was leaving the Moselle valley for an unknown destination,[113] and another of 18 February that Panzer Lehr was moving from Schleiden to locations south and east of Düren.[114] C-in-C West's day report for 18 February, decrypted on 22 February, disclosed that Panzer Lehr was moving from Army Group B to Army Group H; that 11th Panzer Division was to assemble in the Wickrath–

---

* See above, p 674.

110. ibid, pp 267–270.
111. ibid, pp 272–277.
112. DEFE 3/507, BT 4963 of 16 February.
113. DEFE 3/508, BT 5024 of 17 February.
114. ibid, BT 5064 of 18 February.

Grevenbroich area under Fifteenth Army as Army Group B Reserve; and that 9th Panzer Division, also now under Fifteenth Army, was moving to a location south-east of Düren.[115] C-in-C West's day report for 19 February was not decrypted until 26 February; it showed that Panzer Lehr, less a regimental group in Army Reserve, had been subordinated to XLVII Panzer Corps, and that six trains with 11th Panzer Division had reached Fifteenth Army.[116] Decrypts available on 27 and 28 February disclosed that elements of both 9th Panzer and 11th Panzer (the latter 'small in number') were being thrown in against *Grenade*, but were nowhere near redressing the weakness between Linnich and Jülich, and that Army Group B wanted the move of 11th Panzer Division expedited and a mobile formation of Panzer Lehr to come quickly from Army Group H to prevent a further Allied thrust between München Gladbach and Rheydt.[117]

The main sources of tactical intelligence were air reconnaissance, Army Y and battlefield identifications. The air plan for *Veritable/Grenade* included a big artillery reconnaissance effort between D-day and D+2. In the event, bad weather forced the abandonment of this effort during the opening stages of *Veritable*, though tactical reconnaissance was able to observe the movement of enemy troops on D-day and later. A sortie on D-day, which located concentrations of rolling stock on the west bank of the Rhine near Krefeld, provided a target for the Allied Strategic Air Force to give direct support to the land battle, though the results of its bombing were reported to have been 'rather scattered'. In the later stages of the ground fighting reconnaissance aircraft kept a sharp watch day and night for signs of a general enemy withdrawal. On 2–3 March reconnaissance discovered a large concentration of motor transport between Mors and Krefeld and at the approaches to the Orsoy ferry which became the target of US fighter-bombers. Another PR sortie the following night revealed similar concentrations in the Duisburg area but the weather was too bad for bombing attacks.[118]

Y enjoyed a marked revival. VHF links, especially those of the Parachute divisions, supplied a steady flow of information, mostly in plain language, to forward Sigint units whose main problem was to get the information to Corps intelligence staffs in good time.[119] Second Army's intelligence summaries provide some examples.

---

115. DEFE 3/509, BT 5369 of 22 February.
116. DEFE 3/511, BT 5777 of 26 February.
117. ibid, BTs 5865 of 27 February, 5971 of 28 February.
118. AIR 41/68, *The Liberation of North-West Europe*, Vol V, pp 143, 148–151, 160–161.
119. *History of Sigint in the Field*, pp 209–210.

The likely commitment of elements of 8th Parachute Division from Roermond was reported on 14 February; the concentration of parachutists on First Canadian Army's front on 26 February; a contretemps between II Parachute Corps and civilians who wanted to show white flags on 1 March; the provision of the bulk of the rearguard by the parachutists on 2 March.[120] On 8 March Y reported that the enemy appreciated the danger of lingering in the Wesel bridgehead and planned to evacuate three batteries of artillery, the remnants of a Werfer regiment and eighty 88mm guns during the evening.[121] The complete layout of 116th Panzer Division for 18, 19, 26 and 27 February was obtained by DF.[122]

As for battlefield identifications, the presence of a regiment of 6th Parachute Division in Cleve was known on 10 February and the arrival of 116th Panzer and 15th PG Divisions on 12 February.[123] Prisoners taken on 14 and 15 February disclosed the arrival of 346th Division[124] and on 20 February of Panzer Lehr.[125] 11th Panzer Division's reconnaissance battalion was recognised on Ninth US Army's front on 25 February and prisoners were taken that day from 9th Panzer Division.[126] On 26 February Ninth US Army identified 338th Infantry Division, which had come from the Upper Rhine, at Erkelenz,[127] and on 27 February Panzer Lehr, returning from the Canadian front, yielded prisoners at Rheindahlen.[128]

□

When Ninth US Army began *Grenade* on 23 February First US Army attacked across the Roer to guard its flank and clear the triangle between Jülich, Cologne and the confluence of the Erft and the Rhine south of Düsseldorf. On 1 March First US Army crossed the Erft and was astride the roads from Jülich and Düren to Cologne. Meanwhile Third US Army had captured Prüm and Trier and advanced to the Prüm and Kyll rivers, and had established bridgeheads over the Saar below its junction with the Moselle and across the Moselle at Trier. The US Armies had been opposed by Model's Army Group B with Fifteenth Army from north of Cologne to south of Düren, Fifth Panzer Army from

---

120.   WO 285/6, Nos 256, 267, 271, 272 of 14 and 25 February, 1 and 2 March.
121.   ibid, No 279 of 9 March.
122.   *History of Sigint in the Field*, p 210.
123.   WO 285/6, Nos 252, 254 of 10 and 12 February.
124.   ibid, Nos 256, 257 of 14 and 15 February.
125.   ibid, No 262 of 20 February.
126.   ibid, No 267 of 25 February.
127.   ibid, No 268 of 26 February.
128.   ibid, No 269 of 27 February.

south of Düren to Prüm (exclusive) and Seventh Army from Prüm to the Moselle. Early in March Seventh Army was subordinated to Army Group G, and the staff at Fifteenth Army and Fifth Panzer Army exchanged sectors.[129]

First US Army's VII Corps reached the Rhine north of Cologne on 4 March, attacked the city the next day and captured it on 7 March. The Army's other two Corps attacked south-eastwards, from the area of Euskirchen, to meet Third US Army, driving north-east, at Ahrweiler. Both US Armies broke through the enemy's front. On 7 March First US Army reached the Rhine at Remagen, capturing the railway bridge intact, and Third US Army reached the river at Andernach. Much of the German Fifteenth Army was surrounded and destroyed. Seventh Army was severely battered and retreated southwards across the Moselle. By 10 March the Allies had virtually closed up to the Rhine between Sinzig and Wesel.[130]

The Germans reacted with desperation to the Remagen catastrophe, but were unable to prevent the Allies consolidating and extending their bridgehead. After a week it was eight miles long and five miles deep and by 25 March it had reached the river Sieg in the north, was over the Autobahn to the east on a 15-mile stretch, and across the river Wied in the south.[131]

On 8 March Eisenhower confirmed that the major assault across the Rhine would be made by 21st Army Group on 24 March. Meanwhile 6th US Army Group was to begin an offensive in the Saar with the object of keeping German forces away from the main effort in the north by defeating them west of the Rhine, closing up to the river from the Moselle southwards and establishing bridgeheads between Mainz and Mannheim. 12th US Army Group's Third Army was to assist these operations by striking south-east across the Moselle in the rear of the German front in the Saar. This front was defended by the German First Army under Army Group G, and the Moselle by Seventh Army, also now subordinated to Army Group G.[132]

At first Seventh US Army, attacking between Hagenau and Saarbrücken, made slow progress through the West Wall defences, but Third US Army crossed the Moselle in force between Treis and Traben Trabach and took Bad Kreuznach on 16 March with intact bridges over the river Nahe. On 20 March Third US

---

129. Ellis, op cit, Vol II, pp 279–281; MacDonald, *The Last Offensive* (Washington DC 1973), Chapter X.
130. Ellis, op cit, Vol II, p 282; MacDonald, op cit, Chapter X; WO 219/1930, No 51 of 11 March.
131. WO 219/1930, Nos 52 and 53 of 18 and 25 March.
132. Ellis, op cit, Vol II, p 282.

Army was about five miles from Mainz and in the outskirts of
Worms, and Seventh US Army broke through the West Wall
capturing Saarbrücken and Zweibrücken. By 22 March the US
Armies had advanced beyond Pirmasens, clearing a 20-mile
stretch of the West Wall, and had closed up to the Rhine from just
south of Mainz to just south of Ludwigshafen. On 23 March Third
US Army made a bridgehead south of Mainz in the neighbourhood of Oppenheim and entered Speyer. The only bridge still
available for evacuation, at Germersheim, was destroyed the next
day, and by 25 March the Allies were well on the way to
Darmstadt. First and Seventh German Armies had been cut to
pieces in this débacle.[133]

The subordination of the German Seventh Army to Army
Group G and the exchange of sectors between the staffs at
Fifteenth Army and Fifth Panzer Army were reported in
high-grade Sigint on 4 and 7 March.[134] Changes in the German
High Command were also reported. A decrypt of 1 March
disclosed that Blaskowitz from Army Group G had taken over
Army Group H in the north from Student.[135] The replacement as
C-in-C West of von Rundstedt by Kesselring from Italy, and the
latter's order that the change was not to be announced for the time
being for security reasons, were revealed by a decrypt on 11
March.[136]*

After the exchange of sectors, General von Zangen, commanding Fifteenth Army, prompted von Rundstedt to seek permission
to withdraw part of his Army's front to a line from Münstereifel to
Daun.[138] This proposal was rejected by Hitler, as a decrypt
disclosed on 8 March[139] when the situation of Fifteenth Army was
already beyond repair. Other decrypts revealed that on 6 and 7
March 11th Panzer Division and elements of Panzer Lehr, which
had been opposing the Allied advance north of Cologne, had been
ordered south to the Bonn area;[140] at 1130 on 7 March 11th
Panzer Division was to cross the Bonn bridge, with precedence
over all other traffic, and prepare to counter-attack southwards,[141]

---

* The announcement was not made until 1 April in an order of the day. This was
decrypted on 3 April.[137] See also p 702 below.

133. ibid, p 283; WO 219/1930, Nos 52 and 53 of 18 and 25 March.
134. DEFE 3/512, BTs 6210, 6241 of 4 March; DEFE 3/514, BT 6517 of 7
      March.
135. DEFE 3/512, BT 6034 of 1 March.
136. DEFE 3/515, BT 6913 of 11 March.
137. DEFE 3/562, BT 9340 of 3 April.
138. MacDonald, op cit, p 195.
139. DEFE 3/514, BT 6673 of 8 March.
140. ibid, BTs 6543 of 7 March, 6639 of 8 March.
141. ibid, BT 6655 of 8 March.

but by 2100 that evening employment of the division in the Bonn bridgehead was 'no longer expedient'.[142] The catastrophe at Remagen had become of paramount importance and this was reflected by high-grade Sigint in the days that followed. In an order at 2240 on 7 March, decrypted on 9 March, C-in-C West declared that it was of decisive importance that the situation at Remagen 'be thoroughly cleaned up' during the night 7–8 March and the bridge immediately and lastingly destroyed. All available elements of 11th Panzer Division were to be used and Army Group B was to liaise immediately with GAF West.[143] Orders for swimming saboteurs of the KdK to be brought from Army Group G were also given that evening and decrypted on 9 March.[144]* Decrypts available on 10 March included a statement by C-in-C West at 1130 the previous day that the Remagen situation demanded the concentration of all forces in any way available;[147] Army Group B orders on 8 March for reinforcements to be brought up urgently to 11th Panzer Division;[148] and a message sent at 0115 on 10 March by 15th Flieger Division stating that the utter destruction of the bridge was of decisive importance for the defence of the Rhine and must be accomplished that day, if necessary by suicide attacks for which three volunteers were to be selected.[149]† In a message early on 11 March, decrypted the next day, C-in-C West passed on an OKW order putting officers on a junior commanders course temporarily at Army Group B's disposal to remedy the situation at Remagen.[151] A mass of decrypts bore witness to the GAF's continuing attempts to destroy the railway bridge and, after it had finally collapsed, the pontoon

---

* There were further KdK decrypts on 10, 11 and 12 March.[145] KdK attacks planned for 9, 11 and 12 March had to be cancelled for various reasons. Attacks made on 16 and 17 March were frustrated by the precautions taken by the Allies.[146] See also above, pp 634–635.

† A decrypt of 11 March reported that one aircraft had failed to attack because its ailerons jammed, one had attacked through thick cloud and missed the target, and the third might have scored a hit near the eastern bank.[150]

142. ibid, BT 6673 of 8 March.
143. ibid, BT 6689 of 9 March.
144. ibid, BT 6687 of 9 March.
145. DEFE 3/515, BTs 6837 of 10 March, 6922 of 11 March, 6986 of 12 March.
146. Naval Historical Branch, FDS 54/54, *German Small Battle Unit Operations 1943–1945* pp 52–54; MacDonald, op cit, pp 228–229.
147. DEFE 3/515, BT 6779 of 10 March.
148. ibid, BT 6816 of 10 March.
149. ibid, BT 6795 of 10 March.
150. ibid, BT 6884 of 11 March.
151. ibid, BT 6976 of 12 March.

bridges which had been quickly constructed to supplement it.[152]* Towards the end of March the enemy also fired 11 V 2 rockets somewhat unsuccessfully against the Remagen bridgehead.[154]

In its intelligence summary on 11 March SHAEF commented that the Germans would try to eliminate the bridgehead, but it was extremely doubtful whether they would succeed.[155] It was not long before signs that the Germans were of much the same opinion appeared in high-grade Sigint. In a situation report made early on 12 March, and decrypted the same day, Army Group B spoke of the 'ruthless' conduct of Allied operations to reinforce and widen the bridgehead, and to repair bridges after their 'repeated destruction' by artillery and air bombardment.[156] GAF orders for 14 March, decrypted on that day, noted that the Allies had four bridges in operation and were bringing up strong reinforcements.[157] In a message on the same day, decrypted on 18 March, C-in-C West told Model that an allotment of tanks and assault guns could be expected soon, but that he could not have any battle-worthy formations from other Commands to wipe out the bridgehead. He must concentrate on preventing its extension at all costs.[158] Another decrypt available on 18 March reported Hitler's view that only counter-attacks on the flanks offered any prospect of success. There was no future in attacking the eastern face where the Allies held dominating heights.[159] By 17 March OKW was referring to the bridgehead as a 'strategic menace'.[160] The SHAEF intelligence summary for 18 March agreed that 'Remagen' had developed for the enemy from an unfortunate incident into a major threat. He had failed to prevent its expansion even though he had brought up four Panzer/PG Divisions (11th Panzer, Panzer Lehr, 9th Panzer, 3rd PG), a Panzer Brigade (106) and six Infantry/VG divisions (62nd, 272nd, 277th, 26th, 3rd Parachute, 340th.)[161] At the end of the following

---

* Between 8 and 20 March the GAF flew about 640 sorties against the Remagen bridgehead, using Ju 87s, Me 109s, and FW 190s as well as jet fighter-bombers.[153]

152. WO 208/4318, MI 14 Weekly Summary for the CIGS, 18 March; and, as examples of the decrypts, DEFE 3/515, BT 6946 of 12 March; DEFE 3/516, BTs 7023, 7036 of 12 March, 7083, 7111, 7113 of 13 March, 7235, 7236 of 14 March; DEFE 3/517, BTs 7302 of 15 March, 7396 of 16 March, 7494 of 17 March; DEFE 3/518, BT 7566 of 18 March.
153. AIR 41/68, p 172.
154. CAB 121/215, SIC file B/Defence/2 Vol 5, COS(45)262(o) of 16 April.
155. WO 219/1930, No 51 of 11 March.
156. DEFE 3/515, BT 6938 of 12 March.
157. DEFE 3/516, BT 7138 of 14 March.
158. DEFE 3/518, BT 7535 of 18 March.
159. ibid, BT 7599 of 18 March.
160. ibid, BTs 7544, 7584 of 18 March.
161. WO 219/1930, No 52 of 18 March.

week, during which the bridgehead had expanded steadily, SHAEF noted that two more divisions (353rd, 363rd) had arrived, but all were so weak* that opposition to the constant Allied pressure round the whole perimeter had never been more than moderate. Nervousness about other parts of the front had led to the withdrawal of Panzer Lehr and an unsuccessful attempt to withdraw 3rd PG Division.[163]

Concerning the conquest of the Palatinate high-grade Sigint offered only a few, often belated, contributions. It could be inferred from a decrypt on 8 March that Seventh Army was being reinforced by 159th VG Division from Nineteenth Army on the upper Rhine and 6th SS Mountain Division from First Army in the Saar.[164] In a message on 11 March, which was not decrypted until 16 March, C-in-C West's Chief of Staff stated categorically that Seventh Army was 'to remain where it is and defend itself'. Two more divisions, 198th VG from Nineteenth Army and 559th VG from First Army, were to be brought up to it very urgently.[165]† A message of 11 March, which was not decrypted until 17 March, said that because of low fighting strength and daily losses the Moselle could only be defended by a series of strongpoints.[167] In a message on 16 March, decrypted the next day, C-in-C West emphasized that the withdrawal of Seventh Army's left wing would have catastrophic consequences and must be strictly limited.[168] C-in-C West's approval on 21 March for Army Group G's main battle HQ to withdraw to the east bank of the Rhine so that it could exercise firm control of the general defence of the river was disclosed in a decrypt of 22 March.[169] The disaster suffered by First Army was reflected in a message early on 22 March, decrypted the next day. This reported that all planned movements were made impossible by complete Allied air superiority, the destruction of roads and lack of fuel. Three of the Army's Corps HQs, LXXXII, LXXXV and XIII SS, had been over-run by

---

* A decrypt sent out late on 6 March disclosed that because of infantry losses Hitler had authorised the ruthless employment in battle by Infantry/VG divisions of all specialists, except anti-tank personnel, as soon as their weapons or equipment were out of action or not required.[162]

† Decrypts of 18 March reported that on 14 March 198th VG Division was arriving south of Bingen as C-in-C West Reserve and that on 17 March it was under orders to push to the river Nahe north of Bad Kreuznach.[166]

162. DEFE 3/514, BT 6509 of 6 March.
163. WO 219/1930, No 53 of 25 March.
164. DEFE 3/514, BT 6773 of 8 March.
165. DEFE 3/517, BTs 7375, 7381 of 16 March.
166. DEFE 3/518, BTs 7541, 7605 of 18 March.
167. ibid, BT 7510 of 17 March.
168. DEFE 3/517, BT 7426 of 17 March.
169. DEFE 3/519, BT 7947 of 22 March.

tanks, were without signals or motor transport, and had ceased to represent operational staffs.[170]

In its intelligence summary of 11 March SHAEF described the previous week as a black one for the enemy. The Rhineland had been lost with the flower of three Armies. Some 120,000 prisoners had been taken and there were more to come.[171] On 18 March MI 14 considered that the enemy's forces were now so inadequate that he could do no more than attempt to meet each threat as it arose.[172] On the same day SHAEF judged that the Saar was as good as lost to the enemy and it was the turn of First and Seventh Armies to be decimated, while the Remagen bridgehead had developed into a major threat, forcing the enemy to commit much of his slender Panzer resources to prevent its expansion.[173] A week later, when the Germans had suffered what MI called 'a crippling blow' in the Palatinate,[174] SHAEF estimated that, between them, First and Seventh Armies had lost some twelve divisions since the Allies crossed the Moselle. The German Armies in the west had suffered 'a veritable trouncing' during their most disastrous 30 days since the pursuit across France, and their situation was 'catastrophic'.[175]

□

After the successful conclusion of *Veritable* and *Grenade*, when the last rearguards of First Parachute Army withdrew to the east bank of the Rhine on 10 March, 21st Army Group prepared to launch an assault crossing of the river on 24 March. 21st Army Group's crossing was to be made between (inclusive) Rheinberg and Rees by Ninth US Army on the right and Second British Army on the left. The assault crossing was to be quickly followed by an airborne landing close ahead. The communications centre at Wesel was to be captured and the bridgehead expanded southwards, eastwards and northwards to provide a base for future operations deeper into Germany by the three Armies of 21st Army Group.[176]

21st Army Group quickly established a firm footing on the east bank against opposition of varying quality from First Parachute Army. By midnight 27–28 March Ninth US Army had closed in to

170. DEFE 3/520, BT 8146 of 23 March.
171. WO 219/1930, No 51 of 11 March.
172. WO 208/4318 of 18 March.
173. WO 219/1930, No 52 of 18 March.
174. WO 208/4318 of 25 March.
175. WO 219/1930, No 53 of 25 March.
176. Ellis, op cit, Vol II, p 285.

the outskirts of the Ruhr between the Rhine and Sterkrade. Second British Army's right was some 10 miles east of Wesel; its centre was across the river Issel; and its left was threatening Emmerich. The enemy had committed his armoured reserve in widely separated areas: 15th PG Division against Second Army's centre and left; XLVII Panzer Corps HQ with 116th Panzer Division south of the Lippe in Ninth US Army's sector.[177]

Meanwhile, beginning on 25 March, First US Army had broken out of the Remagen bridgehead. On 28 March its armoured spearheads reached Marburg. Ninth US Army advanced east rapidly along the northern outskirts of the Ruhr, and on 1 April the two US Armies met at Lippstadt near Paderborn. The Ruhr was surrounded, with Army Group B's Fifteenth Army and Fifth Panzer Army and part of Army Group H's First Parachute Army inside the pocket.[178]

On 24 March the German front from the Dutch coast to the Ruhr was the responsibility of Army Group H with Twenty-fifth Army and First Parachute Army under command. Between the coast and Emmerich Twenty-fifth Army had LXXXVIII Corps with four divisions (331st, 34th SS, 361st, 346th). From Emmerich to south of Haffen First Parachute Army had 6th, 8th and 7th Parachute Divisions under II Parachute Corps; next, southward to Dinslaken, came LXXXVI Corps with 84th and 180th Divisions; and then LXIII Corps with 2nd Parachute Division and some scratch units holding some 20 miles of front. XLVII Panzer Corps with 116th Panzer and 15th PG Divisions was in reserve behind First Parachute Army. Orders had been given for the formation in Holland of two new Parachute divisions. The employment of Flak units in a ground role in support of the Army was being organised,* and Hitler had ordered the transfer of all training units and schools into rearward positions so as to create a strategic

---

* A directive on 5 March to Flak Korps III (operating with Army Group B) and Flak Korps VI (with Army Group H), decrypted on 6 March, laid down that support of the Army in the bridgeheads, protection of crossing places, employment of artillery where there was a shortage and the provision of mobile forces to engage air landings were to have priority over the anti-aircraft protection of troops and the lines of communication.[179] Decrypts of orders issued by Army Group B and Army Group H in accordance with this directive were decrypted on 17 March.[180] PR paid particular attention to the location of Flak (and ground artillery) positions prior to the assault and was helped by some good weather. A special sortie provided the Airborne Corps with photographs of the dropping zones only 24 hours old.[181]

177. ibid, pp 289–294.
178. ibid, pp 296, 304.
179. DEFE 3/513, BT 6465 of 6 March.
180. DEFE 3/518, BTs 7507, 7526 of 17 March.
181. AIR 41/68, pp 178, 190–191, 199.

zone in depth behind both eastern and western fronts.[182]*

After the withdrawal of First Parachute Army across the Rhine both Army Y (mainly through DF) and high-grade Sigint had helped to locate its new dispositions.[183] A decrypt on 16 March disclosed the boundaries of 6th and 8th Parachute Divisions and the take-over by 180th Division of a sector held by a scratch Division Hamburg.[184] The latter's absorption into 84th and 180th Divisions was reported in a decrypt of 20 March.[185] The presence of LXIII Corps on First Parachute Army's left wing, with 2nd Parachute Division under command, was disclosed by decrypts available on 21 and 22 March.[186] A decrypt of 14 March revealed that an unspecified Corps (clearly XLVII Panzer) was in First Parachute Army Reserve on 11 March with 116th Panzer and 15th PG Divisions, against an expected crossing in the Wesel area.[187] Decrypts on 16 and 17 March located 116th Panzer at Halle and 15th PG at Dülmen.[188] A decrypt of 14 March referred to proposals for equipping Parachute divisions with assault guns.[189] Another of 22 March disclosed that C-in-C West had been promised 1,100 AFVs from the March output in addition to 200 already allotted.[190]† Second Army's estimate on 22 March was that there might be 100–150 AFVs in First Parachute Army's sector.[192] The intention to form two new Parachute divisions on cadres drawn from the divisions in Italy was reported in a decrypt of 4 March. Decrypts of 24 March disclosed that they were to be set up in Holland in the neighbourhood of Groningen.[193]‡ Hitler's order

---

* See below, p 717.

† A later decrypt of 7 April contained C-in-C West's warning to Army Groups that only 75 per cent of promised tank allocations could be expected.[191]

‡ A decrypt of 31 March showed that the Wiener Neustadt–Graz area had been substituted.[194] For further details of the move from Italy see below, pp 698–699.

182. WO 285/6, No 289 of 19 March; WO 219/1930, Nos 52, 53 of 18 and 25 March.
183. WO 285/6, Nos 285–287, 289 of 15, 16 and 19 March; *History of Sigint in the Field*, pp 217.
184. DEFE 3/517, BT 7390 of 16 March.
185. DEFE 3/519, BT 7784 of 20 March.
186. DEFE 3/519, BTs 7855, 7957 of 21 and 22 March; DEFE 3/520, BT 8016 of 22 March.
187. DEFE 3/516, BT 7143 of 14 March.
188. DEFE 3/517, BTs 7390, 7439 of 16 and 17 March.
189. DEFE 3/516, BT 7183 of 14 March.
190. DEFE 3/519, BT 7964 of 22 March.
191. DEFE 3/563, BT 9704 of 7 April.
192. WO 285/6, No 292 of 22 March.
193. DEFE 3/513, BT 6276 of 4 March; DEFE 3/520, BTs 8148, 8181 of 24 March.
194. DEFE 3/600, BT 8978 of 31 March.

for the transfer of training units into rearward positions to support the fronts was disclosed by a decrypt on 25 March.[195]

In the run-up to the assault it was clear from high-grade Sigint that the enemy was in no doubt that 21st Army Group would launch a large-scale attack across the lower Rhine and that he thought it would probably be made in the sector which the Allies had in fact chosen, but was not entirely sure. A decrypt of 21 March revealed that on 16 March Army Group H was told to expect Second Army to make its main attack between Emmerich and Wesel with First Canadian Army screening its left flank.[196] A GAF situation report of 18 March – decrypted on 20 March – concluded that large-scale operations from the Waal bridgehead were unlikely because the water was too high.[197] On 22 March another decrypt disclosed that on 19 March Army Group H was worried because the fact that it had been forced to concentrate its strength on First Parachute Army's northern wing had produced weakness in other sectors, particularly that of LXIII Corps where a front of 33 km was held by 2nd Parachute Division and emergency units; for the time being it did not expect the Allies to make a major attack on the Ruhr, but its forces there were so thin that the Allies could force a crossing at any time.[198] In a message on 20 March – decrypted the next day – OKW emphasised the importance of getting a clear picture of Allied preparations for attack between the coast and Arnhem.[199] Army Group H's day report for 21 March, decrypted on 22 March, spoke of heavy MT traffic in front of the left wing of Twenty-fifth Army and the right and centre sectors of First Parachute Army. Air attacks on Twenty-fifth Army's battle HQ and other BHQs might indicate that a large-scale Anglo-US attack was imminent. Patrols were being sent out all along the fronts held by the two Armies to establish Allied intentions.[200] On 22 March First Parachute Army expected the main attack between Grieth (opposite Emmerich) and Orsoy (north of Duisburg), with a secondary attack south of Duisburg.[201] (This message was not decrypted until 25 March). In a message early on 23 March, decrypted that evening, Army Group H thought that the continuous use of smoke screens and attacks on airfields showed that the Allies were ready for large-scale attacks over the Rhine between Arnhem and Rees with

---

195. DEFE 3/599, BT 8330 of 25 March.
196. DEFE 3/519, BT 7931 of 21 March.
197. DEFE 3/518, BT 7710 of 20 March.
198. DEFE 3/520, BT 8016 of 22 March.
199. DEFE 3/519, BT 7853 of 21 March.
200. ibid, BT 7957 of 22 March.
201. DEFE 3/520, BT 8283 of 25 March.

all the British formations and after most thorough preparations.[202]

21st Army Group's attack created considerable confusion in which communications security considerations were often disregarded. On 24 March one unit reported that it had suffered unprecedented casualties. A battalion of 15th PG Division intervened, but 116th Panzer Division was not committed and Army Y located its main body in the Halle–Zehlen area in mid-afternoon. The next day the collapse of 180th Division compelled the commitment of 116th Panzer south of the Lippe, as its reconnaissance battalion disclosed through Army Y.[203] After the Allied break-out on 29 March the Division was brushed aside into the Ruhr and Y was able to give a positive assurance that it was not in the way of the Allied advance. The Division continued to compromise its activities until the pocket was liquidated. 15th PG Division was less indiscreet, but it was heard ordering a counterattack with tanks on 26 March, and its artillery regiment gave away a good deal of information. 6th, 7th and 8th Parachute Divisions provided a stream of information on VHF until the pace of retreat became too fast for regular communications to be maintained.[204]

From 29 March high-grade decrypts left no doubt that Army Group H was in dire straits. On 27 March it had no forces to close a gap between II Parachute Corps and LXXXVI Corps and no more resources for the defensive battle except five battalions taken from Twenty-fifth Army, 'ruthlessly weakening it'.[205] On 28 March it acknowledged that because of the ever widening front, heavy casualties, and the decline of its fighting strength, the Allies could break through wherever they concentrated.[206] On 29 March Blaskowitz had no forces available to mop up an Allied breakthrough at Haltern.[207] On 30 March he told C-in-C West that the infantry strength of 7th and 8th Parachute Divisions was about 200 each; 13 assault guns with II Parachute Corps were serviceable, but no tanks; ammunition was almost exhausted and it was doubtful if any more could be brought up. Only limited local attacks were possible.[208] A message from C-in-C West on 3 April, decrypted on 5 April, showed that the splitting of First Parachute Army had been recognised by the transfer of XLVII Panzer and

---

202. ibid, BT 8141 of 23 March.
203. WO 285/6, Nos 294 and 295 of 24 and 25 March; *History of Sigint in the Field*, pp 216–217.
204. *History of Sigint in the Field*, p 217.
205. DEFE 3/561, BT 9070 of 1 April.
206. DEFE 3/601, BT 8970 of 31 March.
207. ibid, BT 8826 of 29 March.
208. DEFE 3/561, BT 9002 of 31 March.

LXIII Corps to Army Group B.[209]*

As in the case of 21st Army Group's Rhine crossing, the enemy expected a major offensive from the Remagen bridgehead. In an appreciation on 19 March, decrypted on 22 March, C-in-C West forecast that First US Army's main effort would be made north and east from the bridgehead.[210] German forces were disposed accordingly under Fifteenth Army with three Corps HQs, LIII, LXXIV, and LXVII.[211]† SHAEF's intelligence summary of 25 March showed the enemy's order of battle round the bridgehead as comprising eleven divisional formations and a Panzer Brigade (353rd, 62nd, 3rd PG, 3rd Parachute, Panzer Brigade 106, 9th Panzer, 340th, 11th Panzer, 326th, 272nd, 26th).[215] In fact Panzer Lehr was there too, having returned after a short absence, while 11th Panzer was being withdrawn during the night 24–25 March and sent to Frankfurt to be at Army Group G's disposal. Decrypts available on 25 March disclosed Panzer Lehr's return.[216] The message about 11th Panzer's transfer was not decrypted until 28 March.[217]

The direction of the American thrusts came as a surprise and achieved an immediate breakthrough.[218] Decrypts in the next few days left no doubt that Army Group B, like Army Group H on its right, was in dire straits. Late on 25 March Panzer Lehr reported that it had suffered considerable losses in heavy fighting and from artillery and air attack. 62nd VG Division, which was relieving it, was 'very weak'. The divisional staffs of 363rd Infantry and 3rd PG had apparently been overrun.[219] In its report for 25 March, issued on 26 March and decrypted on 28 March, Fifteenth Army spoke of considerable losses. There were no more reserves. 26th VG Division's fighting strength had fallen to 300 while 326th VG Division was an even worse case.[220] A decrypt of 29 March

---

* See further below, p 722 and fn†.

† On 25 March C-in-C West transferred LXXXIX Corps at the southern tip of the bridgehead from Army Group G to Army Group B. (The order was decrypted the next day).[212] Confusion resulted,[213] and a message on 26 March, decrypted on 29 March, disclosed that the transfer had been cancelled.[214]

209. DEFE 3/562, BT 9492 of 5 April.
210. DEFE 3/519, BT 7952 of 22 March.
211. MacDonald, op cit, p 344.
212. DEFE 3/599, BT 8451 of 26 March.
213. MacDonald, op cit, p 349.
214. DEFE 3/600, BTs 8738, 8739 of 29 March.
215. WO 219/1930, No 53 of 25 March.
216. DEFE 3/599, BTs 8344, 8356 of 25 March; WO 208/4318 of 25 March.
217. DEFE 3/600, BT 8631 of 28 March.
218. WO 208/4318 of 2 April; MacDonald, op cit, pp 344, 345.
219. DEFE 3/600, BTs 8542, 8548 of 25 March.
220. ibid, BT 8697 of 28 March.

reported that Panzer Lehr had blown up 12 tanks because of lack of fuel and had only two serviceable, while 3rd PG had three serviceable.[221] Army Group B's evening report on 29 March, which was decrypted on 31 March, included references to Fifteenth Army's Staff being surrounded, and to battle groups of 272nd VG and 9th Panzer Divisions, each of which numbered fewer than 100 men.[222] A message of 30 March, decrypted on 2 April, reported that the Army Group's situation was becoming critical because of the state of its forces, the extremely strained position regarding fuel and ammunition and the impossibility of moving troops and supplies by rail. It had insufficient strength to have a decisive influence on the intentions of the Allies.[223]

The striking evidence from high-grade Sigint of the parlous state of Army Group B and Army Group H, following hard upon Army Group G's disaster in the Palatinate, together with recent evidence, also from high-grade Sigint, of some decline in German morale and discipline,[224] must have given the Allied High Command confidence that bold offensives could be undertaken without running undue risks.

---

221. DEFE 3/601, BT 8824 of 29 March.
222. ibid, BT 8959 of 31 March.
223. DEFE 3/561, BT 9182 of 2 April.
224. DEFE 3/513, BT 6438 of 6 March; CX/MSS/482 para A 36; DEFE 3/514, BTs 6642, 6652, 6664 of 6 March; CX/MSS/484 para C 46; DEFE 3/515, BT 6978 of 12 March; DEFE 3/516, BT 7126 of 13 March; DEFE 3/599, BTs 8263, 8336 of 25 March; DEFE 3/601, BT 8863 of 30 March; CX/MSS/506 para C 43; CX/MSS/516 para A 44.

CHAPTER 62

The Winter Stalemate and the Last Battle in Italy

A LTHOUGH THE Allied air offensive against communications between Italy and the Reich continued with mounting intensity throughout the winter, the land front went quiet after 8 January 1945. And while planning went ahead for a spring offensive, it did so within restraints imposed by the Allied strategy of seeking the final decision on the western front. On 2 February the Combined Chiefs of Staff informed Field-Marshal Alexander, now SACMED, that up to five Canadian and British divisions would be withdrawn from his theatre to the western front – three from Italy forthwith and two from Greece as soon as they could be released – and that he must do his utmost with his reduced forces to prevent the withdrawal of German divisions from Italy by limited offensive action and reliance on deception plans. The withdrawal of the Canadian Corps from the Italian front began in the second week in February.[1]

The Allies were largely disappointed in their hope of preventing German troop withdrawals. In January Army Group C ceded ten Mountain Jäger companies to the western front and 356th Infantry Division to Hungary.[2] 16th SS PG Division was moved to Hungary early in February and on 20 February 715th Infantry Division was ordered to the Reich. On 22 March two of C-in-C South-West's crack formations, 1st and 4th Parachute Divisions, were required to find 6,000 men as cadres for new Parachute divisions, and on 5 April 710th Infantry Division was ordered to the eastern front.[3] At the same time Germany made no change in her strategy of yielding no ground in Italy and Hitler maintained his grip on the conduct of operations there. On 21 January he issued a directive making all Commanders-in-Chief, GOCs and divisional commanders personally responsible for reporting all significant decisions in time for him to countermand them.[4] Kesselring, who had resumed command of Army Group C in January, was not exempted from this order. He suggested on 15

---

1. Ehrman, *Grand Strategy*, Vol VI (1956), pp 83–87, 93, 94; CAB 106/750, SACMED report to CCS, (HMSO 1951), pp 24, 30, 31.
2. Cabinet Office Historical Section, EDS/Appreciation/20, Chapter 1, p 34.
3. ibid, Chapter 2, p 31, Chapter 3, p 13.
4. ibid, Chapter 1, p 3.

February that the left wing of Army Group C should be withdrawn to the *Genghis Khan* line, but was smartly rebuffed; the Führer's instruction of 15 December* forbidding any further withdrawal remained in force.[5]

Supply shortages, aggravated by the Allied air offensive against his lines of communication and by poor weather, had prompted Kesselring to make this recommendation. On 21 February he told OKW that Army Group C's stocks of fuel and of ammunition for light and medium howitzers were sufficient only for ten days of battle, and requested larger quotas. OKW replied that there could be no improvement of his 'admittedly difficult' supply position in the foreseeable future. On 6 March he again complained that the air strikes and a Swiss ban on the transit of coal since early February had reduced supplies to his theatre below a tolerable level. The Brenner route was by then almost permanently disrupted, though it was used at the end of March for the withdrawal of the cadres for the new Parachute divisions, and alternative routes were subject to massive interference.[6]

The German order of battle had meanwhile been modified by the switch between XIV Panzer Corps and I Parachute Corps, which had begun early in January†, by the withdrawal from Italy in January and February of 356th Infantry, 16th SS PG and 715th Infantry Divisions (the last being replaced in I Parachute Corps by 278th Infantry)[7] and by changes made at the end of February. XIV Panzer Corps was then transferred from Tenth Army to Fourteenth Army in order to achieve unity of command west of Bologna; Fourteenth Army reverted from the Army of Liguria to the direct tactical control of C-in-C South-West; Tenth Army's front was extended to take in XCVII Corps, covering the Adriatic coast, as well as LXXIII Corps, whose sector was from north of Lake Comacchio to Venice.[8] In addition, in response to operations undertaken by Fifth US Army between 18 and 21 February to establish a new start-line for an offensive that would by-pass Bologna to the west, the Germans brought 114th Jäger Division (then en route from their left wing to the Franco–Italian frontier) into the line in LI Mountain Corps's sector.[9] At the end of

---

* See above, p 352.
† See above, p 360.

5. ibid, Chapter 2, pp 7, 31.
6. ibid, Chapter 2, pp 34, 37, 38, Chapter 3, p 14.
7. ibid, Chapter 2, p 31, Tactical Appendix, p 5.
8. ibid, Chapter 2, p 32, Tactical Appendix, p 8.
9. ibid, Chapter 2, pp 30, 31.

February, following these changes, the order of battle (from left to right) was as follows:[10]

Tenth Army

XCVII Corps:	188th Reserve Mountain, 237th Infantry, 710th Infantry.
LXXIII Corps:	Miscellaneous units.
LXXVI Panzer Corps:	162nd (Turcoman), 42nd Jäger, 362nd Infantry, 98th Infantry, 26th Panzer.
I Parachute Corps:	4th Parachute, 278th Infantry, 334th Infantry, 1st Parachute. In rear 90th PG.

Fourteenth Army

XIV Panzer Corps:	305th Infantry, 65th Infantry, 157th Mountain, 94th Infantry. In rear 29th PG.
LI Mountain Corps:	232nd Infantry, 114th Jäger, 148th Infantry, Italia.

Army of Liguria

LXXV Corps:	(Franco–Italian frontier) 34th Infantry, 5th Mountain, Littorio and elements of Monte Rosa.
Corps Lombardy:	San Marco, Fortress Brigade 135, most of Monte Rosa.

Further small changes were made in the next few weeks. At the beginning of March, to counter a second phase of Fifth US Army's preparatory movements, 29th PG was brought in from reserve to support 232nd Infantry and 114th Jäger Divisions.[11] On 22 March 334th Infantry from I Parachute Corps relieved 29th PG, which was withdrawn into reserve near Modena,[12] and 305th Infantry Division was transferred from XIV Panzer Corps to I Parachute Corps – as was learned from a decrypt available on 27 March.[13] At the beginning of April 29th PG and 90th PG were switched, the former being located in the Treviso area as a precaution against an amphibious operation at the top of the Adriatic, and 710th Infantry Division was ordered to transfer from the Adriatic coast to the eastern front.[14]

☐

---

10. ibid, Chapter 1, Tactical Appendix, p 13, Chapter 2, Tactical Appendix, p 12.
11. ibid, Chapter 3, p 5.
12. ibid, Chapter 3, pp 6, 14.
13. DEFE 3/600, BT 8517 of 27 March.
14. EDS/Appreciation/20, Chapter 4.

The extensive re-grouping of the enemy's line went largely unnoticed by Army Y, the German VHF links having fallen silent at the end of active operations.[15] The agent networks developed by the SIS in 1944, in some cases in collaboration with SIM, the Italian Secret Service, provided some information on the enemy's movements and order of battle; this prompted frequent PR flights and had the additional value that it offered cover for the use of high-grade Sigint in air attacks on sensitive targets. As a source of intelligence on the development of Germany's defence lines and the state of her lines of communication PR was 'invaluable', as Alexander was later to tell the Combined Chiefs of Staff.[16] Maps of the Adige defence line from the eastern shore of Lake Garda to Chioggia on the Adriatic, which accompanied AFHQ's intelligence summary for the week ending 6 March, are a good illustration of its achievement.[17] The very detailed information in these maps was derived solely from PR, which also regularly provided thorough coverage of the damage inflicted on the German lines of communication.[18] But the Allies continued to obtain the bulk of their intelligence from high-grade Sigint; and though this was still reduced in volume as a result of the security precautions adopted by the enemy in the previous autumn, it kept them fully informed about his order of battle, his policy, his supply problems and his withdrawal of formations to other theatres.

His policy emerged from the decrypt, signalled to the Commands by GC and CS on 19 January, of Hitler's reply of 5 January to New Year greetings from von Vietinghoff, which declared that 'in these decisive days everything depends on no foot of ground being given up',[19] and from his order of 21 January, which was decrypted on 20 February.[20] This was the order making all Cs-in-C, GOCs and divisional commanders personally responsible for reporting every decision on an operational movement, every intended attack by formations from division upwards which was outside the scope of general directives from higher command, every offensive scheme on a quiet front calculated to attract attention to that front, every disengaging or withdrawal movement, and every intended abandonment of a position, local strongpoint or fortress – and for doing so early enough to enable Hitler to intervene and have any possible counter-order reach

---

15. *History of Sigint in the Field*, pp 149–153.
16. CAB 106/750, p 20.
17. WO 204/971, No 9 of 6 March.
18. AIR 41/58, *The Italian Campaign*, Vol II, p 175.
19. DEFE 3/331, BT 2769 of 19 January.
20. DEFE 3/509, BT 5274 of 20 February.

advanced troops in good time.* It was not solely on the evidence of these decrypts, however, that Allied intelligence remained confident that the enemy was not contemplating a major change of strategy.[21] On the eve of the final offensive the JIC (AF) appreciated that if the enemy showed no intention of withdrawing to more economical lines except when compelled, this was only partly due to Hitler's reluctance to yield ground. He needed north Italy for victualling and his mobility was so straitened that he could not afford to expend his fuel stocks in making a major withdrawal. He had to trust that he could repulse the Allied offensive in his existing very strong positions, where he clearly intended to accept battle. He had doubtless weighed up the risks to his armies if, in the event, the Allies broke through.[22]

In a decrypt available on 19 January Lemelsen, acting GOC Tenth Army, reported that the fuel situation made an effective distribution of forces impossible for the time being and was considerably reducing tactical movements, with army stocks of fuel currently totalling 0.7 consumption units.[23] The acute coal shortage was referred to in decrypts of 29 and 30 January in which Kesselring told OKW that he was introducing an emergency production programme which should be sustainable until the beginning of March.[24] In a message of 13 February, signalled to the Commands on 23 February, Kesselring appealed for an emergency supply of coal to keep the railways running and asked that the situation should be brought to the Führer's attention.[25] In another on 23 February, reporting divisional moves, Kesselring remarked that 26th Panzer Division was not employable as a strategic reserve because of the fuel shortage.[26] A miscellaneous collection of supply returns by C-in-C South-West's and Tenth Army's Quartermasters covering ammunition (following a proforma which MI 14 and GC and CS had unravelled early in January), fuel and rations was decrypted during the month,[27] as

---

* See above, p 691.

21. WO 204/971, AFHQ Intelligence Summaries Nos 4 of 30 January, 8 of 27 February and 10 of 13 March 1945.
22. JIC(45)125(0) of 12 April (JIC(AF)/4/45 of 5 April).
23. DEFE 3/330, BT 2747 of 19 January.
24. DEFE 3/502, BTs 3642 and 3750 of 29 and 30 January.
25. DEFE 3/509, BT 5448 of 23 February.
26. ibid, BT 5451 of 23 February.
27. DEFE 3/327; BT 1882 of 10 January; DEFE 3/503, BT 3992 of 2 February; DEFE 3/507, BTs 4753 of 13 February, 4971 and 4973 of 16 February; DEFE 3/508, BTs 5053 and 5106 of 17 and 18 February; DEFE 3/509, BTs 5259 and 5341 of 20 and 21 February; DEFE 3/510, BT 5676 of 25 February.

was a message from Jodl to the Cs-in-C South-West, West, South-East and Norway calling for the ruthless limitation of all air operations because of the crisis in the supply of aviation fuel.[28]

The messages exchanged between C-in-C South-West and OKW about the supply situation in the last ten days of February were decrypted early in March. In one of these Jodl told Kesselring on 23 February that he must not expect any amelioration of his 'admittedly difficult' fuel and ammunition situation in the foreseeable future. Ammunition, particularly light and medium howitzer ammunition, must be saved for the large-scale battle; as for fuel, he must build up the necessary reserve from allocations which on average per day exceeded his consumption.[29] Replying to this message (which seems to have nettled him) Kesselring reported that he had ordered the establishment of blocked fuel stocks as a minimum reserve for tactical movements, but these could only be formed if supplies came through and rigorous economy was practiced. Normal supplies were not coming through and fuel used for moving divisions away was not being replaced. He asked Jodl to look at the problem again and make it possible for Army Group C to face the approaching campaign with the essential minimum stocks.[30] In another of the decrypts Kesselring's Chief of Staff explained the short-fall in the arrival of supply trains, declared that the throttling of supplies in order to move troops was not tolerable and doubted whether the transfer of 715th Infantry Division could be carried out at the rate envisaged.[31] Reporting that the Allied air offensive had reached a peak on 28 February in extremely heavy attacks on the Brenner, the C-in-C said that damage to this vital traffic artery was not only delaying the movement of 715th Infantry Division, but also decisively crippling supply and thus the conservation of stocks for the expected offensive.[32] On 6 March an incomplete message of 1 March was decrypted which was thought to refer to Army Group C; mobility was being 'limited to a degree hardly endurable'.[33]

The state of the railway frontier routes had by then reached an exceedingly low ebb, as AFHQ noted on 6 March,[34] and in the second half of March and the first ten days of April high-grade Sigint yielded many references to the 'very difficult' traffic

---

28. DEFE 3/510, BT 5510 of 23 February.
29. DEFE 3/513, BT 6351 of 4 March.
30. DEFE 3/512, BT 6125 of 2 March.
31. DEFE 3/513, BT 6253 of 4 March.
32. ibid, BT 6402 of 5 March.
33. ibid, BT 6495 of 6 March.
34. WO 204/971, No 9 of 6 March.

situation and the interruption of the Brenner line.[35] On 20 March the C-in-C's QM appealed for two technical battalions to maintain power supplies and coal production, described as 'life and death tasks'.[36] Several supply returns by both armies and by the C-in-C's QM were also decrypted,[37] including on 2 April Tenth Army's fuel return for 22 March.[38] Naval decrypts drew attention to the restrictions which shortage of fuel imposed on the operations of the Small Battle Units Command (KdK).[39]*

If it was clear that the enemy's ability to maintain protracted heavy fighting, and especially to withdraw to more economical positions, was extremely limited on the eve of the Allied offensive, as AFHQ appreciated,[40] high-grade Sigint had meanwhile provided full details of the withdrawal of formations from Army Group C to other theatres. Information of 3 January that ten Mountain Jäger companies were leaving was available on 13 January,[41] and the fact that they had gone to 2nd Mountain Division (in the Colmar pocket) on 25 January.[42] In a message of 19 January, decrypted on 27 January, C-in-C South-West reported that the movement of 356th Infantry Division had been delayed by ice and snow; it would leave from the Verona–Treviso area probably on 26 January, part of it travelling via the Brenner and part via Tarvisio.[43]† The decrypt of a message of 3 February

---

* For the intelligence available about these operations see Appendix 21.

† A decrypt of 1 February said that 31 trains carrying the division were en route on 28 January, of which 20 had been handed over on the Brenner.[44] By 29 January another train had been handed over on the Brenner and four in Tarvisio.[45] A report by C-in-C South-West on 2 February that the movement of the battle echelon of the division had been completed, and that four out of another 16 trains had been handed over, was available on 5 February.[46]

35. DEFE 3/517, BT 7398 of 16 March; DEFE 3/519, BT 7933 of 22 March; DEFE 3/520, BT 8114 of 23 March; DEFE 3/599, BTs 8324 and 8416 of 23 and 25 March; DEFE 3/600, BT 8573 of 27 March; DEFE 3/601, BT 8965 of 31 March; DEFE 3/561, BT 9170 of 1 April; DEFE 3/564, BT 9930 of 9 April.
36. DEFE 3/601, BT 8799 of 29 March.
37. DEFE 3/600, BTs 8706 and 8712 of 28 March; DEFE 3/601, BTs 8791 and 8926 of 29 and 30 March; DEFE 3/561, BTs 9148 and 9234 of 1 and 2 April; DEFE 3/562, BTs 9421 and 9439 of 4 April; DEFE 3/563, BT 9672 of 6 April.
38. DEFE 3/562, BT 9258 of 2 April.
39. DEFE 3/516, BT 7162 of 14 March; DEFE 3/518, BTs 7468 and 7548 of 17 and 18 March; DEFE 3/520, BT 8076 of 23 March; DEFE 3/562, BT 9500 of 5 April.
40. WO 204/971, No 14 of 10 April.
41. DEFE 3/328, BT 2200 of 13 January.
42. DEFE 3/501, BT 3371 of 25 January.
43. ibid, BT 3468 of 27 January.
44. DEFE 3/503, BT 3868 of 1 February.
45. ibid, BT 3997 of 2 February.
46. DEFE 3/504, BT 4176 of 5 February.

from the naval liaison officer with Tenth Army reporting that 16th SS PG was being withdrawn from the line for transfer to Germany was signalled on 4 February.[47]* A decrypt on 23 February of a message from the C-in-C of 18 February included the information that 715th Infantry Division was being relieved in the line.[52] The fact that it was leaving the theatre was revealed by high-grade Sigint on 27 February.[53] In messages of 28 February, signalled on 4 and 5 March, the C-in-C and his Chief of Staff warned that the movement would be delayed by the damage to the railways.[54]† A message warning I Parachute Corps that 10th and 11th Parachute Divisions were to be set up from 1st and 4th Parachute Divisions was signalled on 4 March.[57] The executive order given by Keitel on 19 March was available on 24 March; it said that Hitler had ordered the formation of 10th and 11th Parachute Divisions in Holland,‡ that in view of the withdrawal of Allied forces from Italy I Parachute Corps was to supply 6,000 cadre personnel without waiting for replacements, and that C-in-C South-West was to arrange the immediate despatch of complete battalions or sub-units.[58]§ A message from Jodl of 5 April telling the C-in-C that the Führer had ordered 710th Infantry Division to

---

* Further references to its move, which took it to Hungary, were made in decrypts on 8 and 12 February.[48] A report by C-in-C South-West on 10 February that 28 trains had left, an unknown number of which had been handed over on the Brenner, was decrypted on 17 February,[49] but four trains were still en route on 26 February.[50] The C-in-C South-West reported on 28 February that all trains carrying the Division had been handed over.[51]

† Four trains out of 54 had left by 1 March[55] and the progress of the move was chronicled in further decrypts on 16, 22, 23 and 27 March, the last of which showed that the division had finally cleared Italy on 22 March.[56]

‡ Later changed to the Wiener Neustadt-Graz area, see above, p 568.

§ In messages decrypted on 29 March[59] Army Group C was told that so far as possible cadres should bring their basic equipment with them as none was available in the Reich; 10th Parachute Division would be given 715th Division's arms and equipment, which would be replaced from Italian production, and 11th Parachute Division would be equipped from Italian production. The movement of the cadre units, which travelled via the Brenner, was

47.   ibid, BT 4136 of 4 February.
48.   DEFE 3/505, BT 4388 of 8 February; DEFE 3/506, BT 4632 of 12 February.
49.   DEFE 3/508, BT 5004 of 17 February.
50.   DEFE 3/512, BT 6157 of 3 March.
51.   DEFE 3/514, BT 6671 of 8 March.
52.   DEFE 3/509, BT 5451 of 23 February.
53.   DEFE 3/511, BT 5862 of 27 February.
54.   DEFE 3/513, BTs 6263 and 6402 of 4 and 5 March.
55.   DEFE 3/514, BT 6654 of 8 March.
56.   DEFE 3/517, BT 7398 of 16 March; DEFE 3/519, BT 7933 of 22 March; DEFE 3/520, BTs 8046 and 8108 of 23 March; DEFE 3/600, BT 8528 of 27 March.
57.   DEFE 3/513, BT 6276 of 4 March.
58.   DEFE 3/520, BT 8181 of 24 March.
59.   DEFE 3/600, BT 8747 of 29 March; DEFE 3/601, BT 8781 of 29 March.

the eastern front was decrypted on 8 April; for coast defence between the Tagliamento and the Isonzo it was to be replaced by a regimental group formed from police units and placed under XCVII Corps.[61] A further decrypt, signalled on 11 April, showed that this movement was well under way by 7 April.[62]

High-grade decrypts similarly provided a comprehensive account of the changes made in the order of battle on the Italian front. The fact that XIV Panzer Corps and I Parachute Corps had changed places and that LXXIII Corps was north of Lake Comacchio was disclosed early in January.* Further changes made in the second half of February were reported as they occurred – the move of 114th Jäger Division from Tenth Army's left wing, where it was to be replaced north of Lake Comacchio by 162nd (Turcoman) Division, and its diversion to LI Mountain Corps's sector, in decrypts signalled on 15 and 23 February;[65] the transfer of XIV Panzer Corps from Tenth to Fourteenth Army, and the subordination of XCVII Corps to Tenth Army, in decrypts of 4 and 5 March.[66] Decrypts available on 16, 24 and 27 March established that 29th PG Division, identified in the line at the beginning of the month, was being relieved by 334th Infantry Division and sent back into reserve, and that 305th Infantry Division was being transferred from XIV Panzer Corps to I Parachute Corps.[67] Decrypts of 5 and 7 April revealed that the two mobile divisions in Army Group Reserve, 29th PG behind Fourteenth Army and 90th PG behind Tenth Army, were changing places.[68]

The two Armies had continued to issue weekly reports on the

---

reported in decrypts of 4 and 9 April.[60] By 30 March five trains had left and by 4 April six out of nine had been handed over.

* See above, pp 360, 692. But this information was not included in AFHQ's battle maps till the second half of February.[63] In view of the dearth of Army Y during the lull in the fighting, and the fact that few prisoners were being taken, the promulgation of intelligence derived from high-grade Sigint was no doubt delayed by the need for security. The important readjustment that took place between Tenth and Fourteenth Armies in the second half of February was not shown on the order of battle map issued by AFHQ until 3 April.[64]

60. DEFE 3/562, BTs 9402 and 9436 of 4 April; DEFE 3/565, BT 9930 of 9 April.
61. DEFE 3/564, BT 9793 of 8 April.
62. DEFE 3/565, KO 109 of 11 April.
63. WO 204/971, Nos 6 and 7 of 13 and 20 February.
64. ibid, No 13 of 3 April.
65. DEFE 3/507, BT 4870 of 15 February; DEFE 3/509, BT 5862 of 23 February.
66. DEFE 3/513, BTs 6290 and 6392 of 4 and 5 March.
67. DEFE 3/517, BT 7397 of 16 March; DEFE 3/520, BT 8241 of 24 March; DEFE 3/600, BT 8517 of 27 March.
68. DEFE 3/563, BTs 9543 of 5 April, 9676 of 7 April.

state of their divisions, and since the beginning of January they had incorporated as an additional item the divisional day strengths. Most of the reports had been decrypted.[69] Those issued by Fourteenth Army for 24 March and by Tenth Army for 26 March, the last to be decrypted before the Allied offensive, were available at the end of March.[70] They gave the following efficiency ratings.*

Tenth Army

I Parachute Corps:	1st Parachute = II, 26th Panzer = II, 278th and 305th Infantry = III, 4th Parachute = II.
LXXVI Panzer Corps:	98th Infantry = II, 42nd Jäger = III, 362nd Infantry = III, 162nd (Turcoman) = IV.
XCVII Corps:	710th Infantry = III–IV, 237th Infantry = III, 188th Mountain = (not given).†
Army Group Reserve:	90th PG = II.

Fourteenth Army

LI Mountain Corps:	148th Infantry = IV, 232nd Infantry = IV, 114th Jäger = IV,‡ 334th Infantry = III, Italia = Fit for anti-guerrilla operations.
XIV Panzer Corps:	94th Infantry = III, 8th Mountain = II–III, 65th Infantry = III.
Army Group Reserve:	29th PG = II.

---

* See above, p 259 fn*, for the definition of these ratings.

† A decrypt of 2 April disclosed that 188th Reserve Mountain had been up-graded.[71]

‡ An indent by C-in-C South-West for 14 Company and 29 platoon commanders for refitting 114th Jäger Division was decrypted early in April.[72]

69. For Tenth Army, DEFE 3/328, BT 2248 of 14 January; DEFE 3/329, BTs 2337 and 2338 of 15 January; DEFE 3/330, BTs 2667 and 2734 of 18 and 19 January; DEFE 3/503, BTs 3966 and 3972 of 2 February; DEFE 3/504, BTs 4003 and 4004 of 3 February; DEFE 3/512, BT 6152 of 3 March; DEFE 3/513, BTs 6317 of 4 March; 6475 of 6 March; DEFE 3/517, BTs 7347 and 7350 of 16 March, 7432 of 17 March; DEFE 3/520, BTs 8103, 8106, 8112 and 8126 of 23 March; DEFE 3/601, BTs 8786 of 29 March, 8954 and 8986 of 31 March. For Fourteenth Army, DEFE 3/329, BTs 2481 and 2564 of 16 January; DEFE 3/504, BT 4001 of 3 February; DEFE 3/506, BT 4715 of 13 February; DEFE 3/509, BT 5486 of 23 February; DEFE 3/512, BTs 6073 and 6169 of 2 and 3 March; DEFE 3/513, BT 6262 of 4 March; DEFE 3/513, BTs 6833 and 6877 of 10 and 11 March; DEFE 3/520, BT 8167 of 24 March; DEFE 3/601, BT 8789 of 29 March.

70. DEFE 3/601, BTs 8786 and 8789 of 29 March.

71. DEFE 3/561, BT 9235 of 2 April.

72. DEFE 3/562, BT 9251 of 2 April.

Two German divisions – 5th Mountain and 34th Infantry – were on the Franco–Italian frontier under LXXV Corps: both had been categorised II in mid-February.[73]

There were decrypts of AFV returns for 10 January (incomplete), 10 February and 25 February.[74] On 25 February C-in-C South-West had 252 tanks (222 serviceable), 294 assault guns (263 serviceable), 530 anti-tank guns (486 serviceable); and 151 Italian assault guns (138 serviceable). The state of division reports for 26 March (Tenth Army) and 24 March (Fourteenth Army) showed divisional holdings of tanks, assault guns and anti-tank guns and also those of subordinated army units equipped with AFVs.

The same two reports confirmed in detail the German order of battle. When the Allies went over to the offensive in the second week of April they were fully informed of the order of battle of Army Group C, which was from east to west:[75]

Tenth Army (General Herr)

XCVII Corps:	(Adriatic coast and Istria): 188th and 237th Infantry Divisions.*
LXXIII Corps:	(Coast defence between Venice and the Po): minor units only.
LXXVI Panzer Corps:	(Lake Comacchio to Route 9): 162nd (Turcoman) Infantry, 42nd Jäger, 362nd Infantry, and 98th VG† divisions.
Corps Reserve:	15th Regiment from 29th PG Division.
I Parachute Corps:	(Route 9 to Monte Grande): 26th Panzer, 4th Parachute, 278th VG, 1st Parachute and 305th Infantry Divisions.
Army Reserve:	29th PG and 155th Field Training Divisions in the Treviso area.

Fourteenth Army (General Lemelsen)

XIV Panzer Corps:	(Monte Grande to Route 65): 65th Infantry, 8th Mountain and 94th Infantry Divisions.

---

* Decrypts of 9, 11 and 12 April disclosed that this Corps with its subordinate divisions was to be transferred from Army Group C to Army Group E under C-in-C South-East; the Isonzo river became the boundary between the two Commands and C-in-C South-West's zone was extended northwards to include parts of Austria.[76]

† On 6 April 278th, 98th and 334th Infantry Divisions were renamed Volksgrenadier divisions as a reward for 'distinguished conduct in the field'.[77]

73. DEFE 3/509, BT 5285 of 20 February.
74. DEFE 3/331, BT 2837 of 10 January; DEFE 3/510, BT 5624 of 24 February; DEFE 3/513, BT 6357 of 5 March.
75. EDS/Appreciation/20, Chapter 4, pp 18–20.
76. DEFE 3/564, BT 9982 of 9 April; DEFE 3/565, KO 158 of 11 April; DEFE 3/566, KO 260 of 12 April.
77. EDS/Appreciation/20, Chapter 4, pp 13–14.

LI Mountain Corps: (Route 65 to coast): 334th VG, 114th Jäger, 232nd Infantry, Italia and 148th Infantry Divisions; battle group of 90th PG Division.

Army Group Reserve: 90th PG Division (less battle group) in the Modena area.

Army of Liguria (Marshal Graziani)

Corps Lombardy: (Gulf of Genoa): San Marco Division and Battle Group Meinhold (Fortress Brigade 135 and elements of Monte Rosa Division).

LXXV Corps: (Franco–Italian frontier): 34th Infantry, Littorio and 5th Mountain Division, and elements of Monte Rosa Division.

□

When the Allies opened the offensive in Italy the Germans were on the verge of collapse on the other fronts. The western Allies were across the Rhine on a wide front between Wesel and Karlsruhe, and in their advance they had almost isolated the Ruhr and had captured Frankfurt and Heidelberg. The Russian offensive had reached the Oder, forty miles from Berlin, and the Silesian industrial basin in the Breslau area, while south of the Carpathians it had taken Budapest and was closing in on Vienna. Within Italy, moreover, the SS Commander, General Karl Wolff, had at the beginning of March made approaches to the Allies with a view to the surrender of the German forces.[78]* But an agreement depended on General von Vietinghoff, who had again succeeded Kesselring as C-in-C South-West† and von Vieting-

---

* Wolff's first approach was in fact made to the SOE wireless operator who had provided the W/T link between Badoglio and the Allies during the negotiations for the Italian armistice (see Volume III Part 1, p 109). Captured by the Italian Police on a mission to the Partisans in the Brescia area in the middle of February, he was taken to see Wolff on 26 February and sent on to Switzerland with a message for Field Marshal Alexander in which Wolff offered to act as an intermediary with Kesselring or any other German authority named by the Allies. On reaching Switzerland, however, he was interned by the Swiss Police and unable to report his mission to SOE until 9 March, the day on which Wolff himself had his first meeting in Switzerland with Allen Dulles of the OSS.[79]

† Kesslering's appointment to succeed von Rundstedt as C-in-C West on 9 March and his replacement as C-in-C South-West by von Vietinghoff had been disclosed by high-grade decrypts on 11 and 26 March.[80] The Japanese Ambassador in Berlin also reported it in a telegram of 15 March, decrypted on 20 March.[81]

78. ibid, Chapter 3, pp 33–35; Ehrman, op cit, Vol VI, pp 122–128.
79. Dulles, *The Secret Surrender* (1967), pp 96–99; Beevor, SOE: *Recollections and Reflections 1940–1945* (1981), pp 91, 143.
80. DEFE 3/515, BT 6913 of 11 March; DEFE 3/599, BT 8415 of 26 March.
81. BAY/BT 126 of 21 March.

hoff's attitude was still unknown. On 5 April the JIC (AF) noted that there was 'as yet no sign that the High Command [in Italy] is thinking of an independent surrender' and it felt that the maintenance of strong enemy forces on the Italian front, while partly dictated by the virtual isolation of the Italian theatre, might also be designed for the protection and manning of an Alpine redoubt.[82]*

SACMED's plan for the offensive was that, after preliminary operations to improve its positions at the east and south-east corners of Lake Comacchio, Eighth Army's V Corps would attack northwards from Lugo and II Polish Corps simultaneously westwards towards Castel San Pietro, Medicina and Bologna. It was hoped that these attacks, and the fear that they would be supported by an amphibious operation north of the Po, would draw the enemy reserves to his left wing. After preliminary operations on the west coast towards Massa, Fifth Army would launch its main attack a few days after Eighth Army, aiming to cut Route 9 west of Bologna, and would then advance west of the Reno to the Po. Meanwhile Eighth Army would seek to break through the narrow corridor between Argenta and Lake Comacchio and advance on Ferrara. If all went well Eighth Army would exploit along Route 16 on the Ferrara–Rovigo–Padua axis, and Fifth Army along Route 12 on the axis Modena–Ostiglia–Verona. At the opening of its main assault each Army in turn would have the support of the vastly preponderant Allied air forces.[83]

Eighth Army's preliminary operations were sufficiently threatening for PG Regiment 15 to be ordered south to join LXXVI Panzer Corps, where it arrived about 7 April.[84] The main offensive on 9 April hit 362nd and 98th Divisions and the left wing of 26th Panzer Division, which were driven back to the river Santerno and by 12 April to the river Sillaro. Tenth Army decided to withdraw I Parachute Corps from the salient south of Imola, thus shortening its front and enabling 278th VG Division to be extracted and to relieve 98th VG Division. Meanwhile 42nd Jäger Division came under pressure on the western shore of Lake Comacchio, where PG Regiment 15 was brought into action, and the remainder of 29th PG Division was ordered south. A threat was developing to the Argenta gap; if Eighth Army could force the gap, and thereafter break through the *Genghis Khan* position

---

* For the Alpine redoubt see below Chapter 63.

82. JIC(45)125(o) of 12 April (JIC(AF)/4/45 of 5 April).
83. Ehrman, op cit, Vol VI, p 120; CAB 106/750, pp 33–36.
84. EDS/Appreciation/20, Chapter 4, pp 13–14.

on the Reno, it would be able to exploit towards the Po and to encircle the right wing of Tenth Army.[85]

In the first days of April von Vietinghoff had asked permission to withdraw Tenth Army and the left wing of Fourteenth Army into the *Genghis Khan* position but this was refused.[86] He now returned to the charge in a long appreciation submitted early on 14 April (before Fifth US Army launched its main offensive at 0900 that day), which was supported by a report from his Chief of Staff on the state of the Army Group's supplies. The Allies, he said, had launched an all-out offensive with a superiority in material which was on a scale not hitherto experienced and which could not be counterbalanced by the fortitude of his troops. 98th VG Division was exhausted; 26th Panzer, 362nd Infantry and 42nd Jäger Divisions were hard hit. All local reserves had been committed. The Allies could maintain their offensive in its present scope and an attack by Fifth Army west of Bologna must be expected any day. The reinforcements required to sustain Tenth Army's left flank could only be provided from I Parachute Corps, which must make a fighting withdrawal from its salient. Since it seemed that neither new formations nor replacements and supplies, particularly of fuel, could be brought up, the *Genghis Khan* position could not be held for long. If OKW intended to keep the Allies as far and as long as possible from the Reich fortress, the Army Group must be withdrawn to the Ticino–Po line so as to thwart the Allied intention to destroy it. The decision to withdraw must be taken in good time since Tenth Army would have to hold its front for at least two weeks while the forces in the west withdrew. The supply of ammunition, fuel and rations was such that the conduct of operations was more or less assured for the next 14 days. Thereafter lack of fuel would decisively influence the Army Group's fighting strength and hence its conduct of operations.[87]

Hitler's reply, despatched by Jodl on 17 April, was a flat negative. Commanders and staff officers were to be informed that by order of the Führer all proposals for a change of strategy were to be discontinued. C-in-C South-West's task of defending every foot of ground must be fulfilled with the utmost steadfastness.[88]

Meanwhile, following preliminary operations directed at Massa and Carrara on the Ligurian coast, which began on 5 April, Fifth US Army had opened its main offensive on 14 April. IV US Corps, attacking the Roffeno massif at the junction between XIV

---

85. ibid, pp 31–35.
86. ibid, p 16.
87. ibid, pp 38, 39–40.
88. ibid, p 40.

Panzer and LI Mountain Corps, had taken 1,000 prisoners in two days from 94th and 334th Divisions and captured Vergato. On 16 April II US Corps had attacked between Routes 64 and 65. By 18 April 94th Infantry and 8th Mountain Divisions were collapsing and 90th PG Division had been committed in support of 94th Division. On Eighth Army's front Bastia had fallen on 15 April. Tenth Army had intended to bring 26th Panzer Division across to assist in holding the Argenta gap, but its move was delayed by Allied pressure on I Parachute Corps, and Argenta, bravely defended by 29th PG Division, was taken on 17 April. AFHQ's intelligence summary issued on 18 April recorded the capture of 10,000 prisoners since the start of the battle. On 20 April IV US Corps cut Route 9 at Ponte Samoggia, north-west of Bologna, and Eighth Army took Budrio and forced a crossing of the Reno in the sector held by 362nd Division. Von Vietinghoff ordered the Army of Liguria to begin Operation *Herbstnebel** and informed Hitler that only in a 'mobile strategy' did he see any chance of preventing the splitting and subsequent crushing of his front, adding dutifully that he awaited the Führer's orders. The reply on 21 April, ordering him to defend his present position with fanatical grimness as the only means of breaking the Allied offensive, was the Führer's last intervention in the operations on the Italian front.[89]

The disaster to which Hitler's obduracy had condemned Army Group C now impended. Bologna was captured on 21 April, Fifth Army entering from the west and Eighth Army from the east. LXXVI Panzer Corps was withdrawing to form a bridgehead over the Po in the area of Ferrara, maintaining tenuous touch with I Parachute Corps on its right in the Cento area. During 21 April the Allies broke through in the sector held by 362nd Infantry Division, on the right of LXXVI Panzer Corps, which lost touch with 278th VG Division on the left of I Parachute Corps. On 22 April 362nd, 98th and the remnants of 42nd Jäger Divisions were making for the Po. Defence of the Ferrara bridgehead devolved almost entirely on 29th PG and 26th Panzer Divisions. Fourteenth Army no longer had a connected front. Two of XIV Panzer Corps's divisions, 65th Infantry and 305th Infantry (the latter had been transferred from I Parachute Corps on 18 April), were withdrawing east of Bologna to the Panaro river in reasonably good order. 8th Mountain and 94th Infantry Divisions were

---

* See above, p 342ff.

89. WO 204/971, No 15; EDS/Appreciation/20, Chapter 4, pp 41–52; CAB 106/750, pp 42–45; Fisher, *Cassino to the Alps* (Washington DC, 1977), pp 473–482.

struggling back towards the Po west of Bologna. Contact had been lost with LI Mountain Corps whose withdrawal was being gravely hampered by the Partisans.[90]

On 22–23 April I Parachute Corps (1st and 4th Parachute and 278th VG Divisions) and 305th and 65th Infantry Divisions on XIV Panzer Corps's left wing were brought to bay on the Panaro. All the formations suffered heavy losses in men and equipment, particularly 278th VG and 65th Infantry Divisions at Finale. The latter was virtually destroyed and its commander was killed. On the morning of 23 April von Senger, commanding XIV Panzer Corps, disbanded his headquarters and ordered it to re-assemble at Legnago on the Adige whither he proceeded on foot with his operational staff.[91]

On 24 April the survivors from the Panaro crossed the Po from a bridgehead at Sermide after destroying 31 Tiger tanks, 11 assault guns and the artillery of I Parachute Corps and GHQ units. The GOC of 305th Infantry Division was among the prisoners of war. The Ferrara bridgehead, defended with great resolution by 29th PG and 26th Panzer Divisions, was evacuated during the night 24–25 April. Prisoners included the Corps commander. West of Bologna Fifth US Army had reached the Po at San Benedetto on 22 April. Handfuls of 334th VG, 232nd Infantry and 114th Jäger Divisions managed to cross at Cremona and straggled on northwards towards Milan and Bergamo protected by survivors of 90th PG Division. 148th Infantry and the Italia Divisions were trapped south of Parma and surrendered to Fifth Army.[92]

The Po was the watershed between defeat and rout. The skeletal forces of LXXVI Panzer, I Parachute and XIV Panzer Corps were left with nothing with which to fight and LI Mountain Corps had ceased to exist. On 25 April the Committee of National Liberation of Northern Italy (CLN) proclaimed a general uprising. On 27 April the last enemy forces in Genoa surrendered and on 28 April Graziani's German Chief of Staff formally surrendered the Army of Liguria, although LXXV Corps assembled north of Turin and refused to lay down its arms until 2 May. Mussolini was captured by the CLN on 27 April and shot the next day. As Eighth Army raced for Trieste and Fifth Army for the Alps they encountered only a few bursts of last ditch defiance.[93]

□

---

90. EDS/Appreciation/20, Chapter 4, pp 52–56.
91. ibid, pp 56–59.
92. ibid, pp 59–62.
93. ibid, pp 63–69.

Throughout the last battle, as throughout the campaign in Italy, the Allies received a flood of Sigint about the tactical situation of the German forces and the assessments and decisions of the German higher commands. With the renewal of active operations the enemy's VHF links sprang back into life, and their interception enabled the Army Y organisation to provide a comprehensive tactical picture.[94] It is true that, on account of the improvements in German communications security,* the intelligence from Army Y was less precise, and was received less promptly, than formerly. It is also true that during the opening phase of the offensive – Eighth Army's assault on LXXVI Panzer Corps – high-grade Sigint provided little tactical intelligence because of the inability of GC and CS to break the Flivo Enigma key (Puma) since November 1944.† After mid-April, however, GC and CS read regularly the Enigma key used by Tenth Army (Albatross); decrypts from Tenth Army's front were plentiful from 17 April.

On that day they disclosed that 26th Panzer Division, under I Parachute Corps for the past 24 hours, was to be put into the front south-east of Budrio, and that it and other formations under I Parachute Corps were having difficulties with fuel.[95] From decrypts of 19 April it was learned that I Parachute Corps had carried out a withdrawal of its divisions the previous evening and regrouped them so as to release 26th Panzer Division from the Budrio area.[96] Decrypts dealing with further withdrawals by I Parachute Corps during the night of 20–21 April followed on 21 April; they included orders to 1st Parachute Division to leave patrols in the *Genghis Khan* line in an effort to persuade the Allies that the line was still occupied.[97] Other decrypts of 21 April disclosed that Tenth Army had ordered the dissolution of divisional battle schools and the incorporation of fit men from replacement units into fighting units, and had issued code-names for the Po position.[98] Messages reporting that the infantry fighting strength of 26th Panzer Division was down to 23 men on the morning of 21 April, and that its left wing was being penetrated, were signalled on 22 April, as was a warning that all the Reno bridges had been destroyed by Allied air attack and the information that LXXVI Panzer Corps had moved its battle headquarters to the east of Ferrara because of guerrilla attacks.[99]

---

* See Appendix 15.
† See above, p 352fn† and Appendix 15(ii).

94. *History of Sigint in the Field*, pp 149–153.
95. DEFE 3/567, KOs 616 and 622 of 17 April.
96. DEFE 3/568, KOs 824 and 834 of 19 April.
97. ibid, KOs 960 and 983 of 21 April; DEFE 3/569, KO 1015 of 21 April.
98. DEFE 3/569, KO 1016 of 21 April.
99. ibid, KOs 1041, 1044 and 1068 of 22 April.

Although GC and CS signalled it to the Commands with highest priority, this operational intelligence must frequently have been overtaken by events. But C-in-C South-West's lengthy appreciation of the morning of 14 April, with his warning that his Army Group would be destroyed if it was not withdrawn to the Ticino–Po line, was decrypted between the afternoon of 15 April and the early morning of 16 April.[100] A supporting assessment of Army Group C's supply position by his Chief of Staff was decrypted on 16 and 17 April.[101] Hitler's reply to the effect that the Army Group must defend its present positions with fanatical zeal as the only means of breaking the Allied offensive, which was despatched by Jodl on 21 April, was for the most part decrypted the following afternoon.[102]* A message from the C-in-C of 20 April, reporting that there had been heavy losses of personnel and armour in the sectors held by 94th Infantry, 8th Mountain, 42nd Jäger and 29th PG Divisions, was also decrypted on 22 April.[104]

On 23 April decrypts reflected the rapid worsening of the German position. Elements of 26th Panzer and 29th PG Divisions had been crossing the Po during 21 and 22 April.[105] The front near Gallo had been shattered by the destruction or defection on 278th VG Division's left wing of 362nd Infantry Division during the night of 21–22 April, and 278th Division was yielding ground on both sides of the Reno.[106] On the evening of 23 April GC and CS signalled the decrypt of orders issued by Tenth Army at 1030 on the previous day for withdrawal to the general line from a position on the Panaro river to the Po bridgehead; this line must be held long enough to permit an orderly retreat over the Po; those elements not needed in its defence were to cross the Po on 22–23 April and organise defences at key points on the Po defence line in collaboration with LXXIII Corps.[107] A message from C-in-C South-West at 1100 on 22 April reporting that the situation was extremely critical, and that a rallying point was being built up on the Po, was signalled in the early hours of 24 April.[108]

---

* See above p 704 for these exchanges. Part of the reply, saying that the large-scale withdrawals would lead to certain destruction owing to Allied air superiority, and that the C-in-C's resources were still greater than those on any other front, was not decrypted till 23 April.[103]

100.   DEFE 3/566, KO 496 of 15 April; DEFE 3/567, KO 519 of 16 April.
101.   DEFE 3/567, KOs 555 of 16 April, 586 and 588 of 17 April.
102.   DEFE 3/569, KO 1071 of 22 April.
103.   ibid, KO 1156 of 23 April.
104.   ibid, KOs 1072, 1076 and 1094 of 22 April.
105.   ibid, KOs 1126, 1130 and 1151 of 23 April.
106.   ibid, KOs 1137, 1160 and 1183 of 23 April.
107.   ibid, KO 1188 of 23 April.
108.   ibid, KO 1219 of 24 April.

Messages from the main front on 23 April giving routes by which various divisions were to withdraw or fight their way back to the Po and instructions for crossing the river and constructing a defence line, were available during 24, 25 and 26 April.[109] Others, available on 25 April, reflected the disintegration of the Army of Liguria: on 23 April the Naval Chief Command South had reported that orders had been given for the evacuation of the whole Ligurian coast; naval personnel were to be incorporated into the Army after carrying out minelaying and other crippling measures;[110] and on 24 April Corps Lombardy had reported an uprising in Genoa.[111] A further message from C-in-C South-West reported on 24 April that there had been very heavy losses of arms and ammunition and that by exhausting the last reserves from industry sufficient fuel could be obtained for a few more days. This was not decrypted until 28 April.[112]

From 29 April most of the decrypts related to evacuation from the Ligurian and the Adriatic coasts. Detachment commanders in the Genoa area had been ordered to fight their way north on 26 April;[113] a message of 27 April had reported that some of the detachments had been surrounded and that most of the Italian Navy had joined the Allies.[114] A message of 29 April, signalled on 1 May, gave an assembly area north of Turin for LXXV Corps, and added that all the towns were in revolt.[115] Decrypts available during 29 April disclosed orders of 28 April that preparations for the evacuation of Venice should be completed by the evening of 29 April, and that LXXIII Corps was, as ordered by the Führer, subordinating all naval personnel to the Army to form a battle group in the *Blue* line, which ran from Chioggia along the Adige to Verona and Lake Garda.[116] The arrangements made by LXXIII Corps on 28 April for thinning out on the coast in order to occupy the mountain approaches to the *Blue* line, and keep them open for the withdrawal of the main body, were signalled on 30 April.[117] A message of 29 April, signalled on 1 May, reported that the *Blue* line had been broken in two places and that, in order to maintain contact with Fourteenth Army, Tenth Army had begun a further withdrawal.[118]

---

109. DEFE 3/570, KOs 1275, 1300 and 1312 of 24 April, 1403 and 1404 of 25 April, 1419 of 26 April.
110. ibid, KO 1379 of 25 April.
111. ibid, KO 1364 of 25 April.
112. DEFE 3/571, KO 1613 of 28 April.
113. ibid, KO 1690 of 29 April.
114. DEFE 3/572, KO 1754 of 30 April.
115. ibid, KO 1839 of 1 May.
116. DEFE 3/571, KOs 1651 and 1697 of 29 April.
117. DEFE 3/572, KO 1763 of 30 April.
118. ibid, KO 1832 of 1 May.

CHAPTER 63

The Land Fronts Meet

THROUGHOUT the winter of 1944–1945, as they prepared for the final advances into Germany, the western Allies were exercised by the problem of assessing rumours and reports to the effect that the Nazi authorities intended to hold out in a last-ditch stronghold or National Redoubt in the Alps.

We now know that the reports were the product of a deception plan mounted by the Sicherheitsdienst from November 1944, when it was alerted to the fact that the American authorities were making enquiries about the possible existence of such a project. The purpose of the plan, which was supported by Goebbels in a propaganda campaign from early in 1945, was to deflect the western Allies from insisting on the total defeat of Germany by exaggerating the scale of the resistance she would put up behind the protected lines of an Alpine fortress. In retrospect we can also see that several circumstances lent credibility to the story. In the first place C-in-C South-West was in fact building defences in the southern foothills of the Alps to protect the lines of communication between Germany and the armies in Italy and, eventually, as Kesselring hoped, to enable those armies to hold out while German troops escaped from the Soviet fronts into the Anglo–American zones. In the second place, it was towards the Alps that, as Sigint disclosed, many government departments and military HQs retreated in stages from Berlin from early in February 1945. Thirdly, some German authorities including Hofer, the Gauleiter of the Tyrol, were pressing for the construction of an Alpine fortress from November 1944; and in the end, though not until April 1945 when it was far too late, Hitler did authorise the necessary preparations.[1]

SHAEF first gave serious attention to the possibility that Germany had plans for a National Redoubt in its intelligence summary for 10 December 1944. This mentioned that since August a number of reports had referred to new activity in the old defence lines built in south Germany in the 1930s, and that others had claimed that the whole of western Austria and some frontier districts in Upper Bavaria and Italy had been declared an 'Alpine

---

1. Cabinet Office Historical Section, EDS/Appreciation/19, Chapter 4, pp 46–48; EDS/Appreciation/20, Chapter 1, pp 44–46, Chapter 4 p 11; Minott, *The Fortress that never was* (1965), p 25, using a SD source.

Defence Zone'. SHAEF noted that the reports had not been supported by such PR sorties as had been flown. But it believed that the story might have 'some basis in fact', and that in view of its large area the zone might have 'nothing to do with normal defence activity'. Some reports had suggested that it was to be a stronghold in which the Nazis would fight a last-ditch organised battle, others that it was the base from which they would direct guerrilla warfare throughout Europe after the collapse of organised resistance; the latter seemed more plausible.[2] At the end of December SHAEF concluded on the strength of reports indicating that headquarters, offices and factories were being constructed underground, and that men had been called up in the Vorarlberg for training in guerrilla warfare, that the Nazis were definitely preparing such a base.[3]

By then Whitehall had received rumours from Switzerland about a 'redoubt' area in the Bavarian Alps and of the presence of groups of 'partisans' in the Austrian Alps and the Vorarlberg. But no evidence pointing to plans for a redoubt had been obtained from decrypts of German messages. Since the middle of 1944 Sigint had from time to time provided details about the plans of the German Command in Italy for a final defence line in the foothills of the Alps – the Alpenvorland line or the *Blue* line – to block the approaches into Austria through the Tyrol.[4] But Whitehall did not doubt that the construction of this line was what SHAEF had called 'normal defence activity'. The same was true of the plans disclosed by Sigint in November and December for defence lines which continued the *Blue* line north and north-east of the Istrian peninsula and for a defence line from northern Yugoslavia to Lake Balaton.[5] In January 1945 MI 14 issued an appreciation to this effect; even in the Alpenvorland, where the use of rock caverns and emplacements made the line stronger than it was in the plain, these defences consisted only of field works dug by local labour and containing practically no concrete.[6]

On 4 February 1945 MI 14 circulated two appreciations, the

2. WO 219/1927, SHAEF Weekly Intelligence Summary No 38 for the week ending 10 December 1944, para 2(a) and (b).
3. ibid, No 41 of 31 December.
4. DEFE 3/156, KV 4145 of 17 May 1944; DEFE 3/116, XL 5638 of 11 August; DEFE 3/326, BT 1686 of 8 January 1945; CX/MSS/238 para B 14, T380/135; CX/MSS/S 141, 162, 166.
5. DEFE 3/303, HP 5966 of 8 November; DEFE 3/314, HPs 8528 and 8539 of 4 December, 8678 of 5 December; DEFE 3/318, HP 9668 of 17 December 1944.
6. WO 208/4315, MI 14 Appreciation of 4 January 1945.

first of which referred to a dubious SIS report of 'continued preparations' for a final stronghold in Austria and Bavaria. In the second, however, it emphasised that there was no further evidence that Germany was building inner defence lines; if she had plans for such defences, a possibility which could not be ruled out, they would take account of areas that 'would appeal to German romanticism', like the Rhine, the Black Forest, Nuremberg and Munich, as well as of the existence of natural obstacles, of the proximity of industrial and food-producing areas and of accessibility to the Mediterranean.[7] Thereafter MI 14 and the JIC reviewed the matter at regular intervals, but always sceptically. On 18 February the JIC concluded that although there might be last-ditch resistance in south Germany and the Alpine province of Austria if Hitler and Himmler remained free agents, there was no firm evidence yet that Nazi leaders planned to establish an HQ there; in any case the resistance would not be prolonged against an organised attack.[8] Reports referring to plans for an Alpine redoubt were still being received, including information from Switzerland to the effect that it included Thuringia and that Himmler was involved in it. On 16 March the decrypt of a Japanese diplomatic telegram from Berne reported that considerable stocks of war material were being accumulated in 'two last battlegrounds', or 'redoubts', one comprising Wilhelmshafen, Hamburg and Kiel, and the other Munich, Salzburg, Vienna and the north of Italy. On 18 March, however, MI 14 circulated a report from the British Military Attaché in Berne based on interviews with deserters and others: 90 per cent of the deserters had heard nothing of a National Redoubt and the other informants had indicated that such fortifications as were being built were so inefficient as to suggest that their sole purpose was to keep up the morale of the local population.[9]

In contrast to the lack of Sigint evidence for the organisation of a redoubt many decrypts disclosed from early in February that HQs and government departments were being evacuated from Berlin. Although Dönitz remained there for the present, OKM's Operations Department and Intelligence Division were sent to Wilhelmshafen early in February.[10] There were indications by 11 February that OKW's less operational staffs were being transfer-

---

7. ibid, MI 14 Notes on Germany's Last Stand, 4 February; WO 208/4319, MI 14/10/5/45 of 4 February.
8. JIC(45)55 of 18 February.
9. WO 208/4319, MI 14/10/12/45 of 18 March.
10. Naval Headlines of 6–8 February, 20 February; BAY/BT 96 (SJA 1560) of 24 February.

red to central and south-western Germany;[11] and by 3 March it was known that its Directorate of Signals had been authorised to survey the Weimar district of Thuringia for accommodation for 250 civilians.[12] By 5 March decrypts had located elements of OKH HQ and of SS Operations HQ in Thuringia and had referred to the transfer of some OKL staff to the same area,[13] and by 11 March they had disclosed that control of police wireless networks had been moved from Berlin to Weimar.[14] In the next week they revealed that OKH's Directorates of Signals and of Legal Affairs were in Thuringia, that a department of the SS's Economics and Administrative Office was at Coburg, and that Abwehr and SD wireless stations had been set up at Nuremberg.[15]

By 11 March, on the other hand, it was known that the Foreign Ministry had informed the diplomatic corps that the government was staying in Berlin and that there was no plan to move the foreign missions to the Salzburg area; and MI 14 accepted that this information might be interpreted in one or two ways: either the government did not intend to go south when it did move, or it was making 'secret preparations for the final stand' in the south and would not welcome the presence of foreign diplomatic missions there.[16] On 18 March, however, commenting on the transfers of the military, police and Abwehr departments, it noted that they were moving as might be expected to a fairly central area where they would be reasonably safe from being overrun from east or west, and that this implied that they would withdraw to the mountain fortress of southern Bavaria and Austria only at the last moment, 'if at all'.[17]

As we have already seen, the reports reaching London about the National Redoubt were but a small over-flow from the large amount of false information, including blue-prints of fortifications, that the SD was feeding to the OSS through its contacts in Switzerland and Austria. Moreover, from early in March Wolff, the SS General in Italy, used the threat that Germany intended to make a last stand in an Alpine redoubt as a bargaining counter in his negotiations for a surrender in Italy with Dulles, the chief OSS

11. WO 208/4317, MI 14 Weekly Summary for the CIGS, 11 February.
12. DEFE 3/512, BT 6180 of 3 March; WO 208/4319, MI 14/10/10/45 of 5 March.
13. WO 208/4319, MI 14/10/10/45 of 5 March; CX/MSS/T470/40, T473/46, T474/4, T477/3, 40.
14. WO 208/4319, MI 14/10/11/45 of 11 March.
15. ibid, MI 14/10/12/45 of 18 March; CX/MSS/490 paras A54, B 6 and 8, 491 para A 43, T491/42, 55.
16. WO 208/4319, MI 14/10/11/45 of 11 March.
17. ibid, MI 14/10/12/45 of 18 March.

representative in Switzerland.[18] Dulles subsequently insisted that the OSS was not alarmed by the threat, and the US official military history has claimed that it had no serious influence on the operational decisions taken at SHAEF.[19] It seems clear, however, that SHAEF accepted that the evidence must be taken to be a reliable guide to German intentions. On 10 March the JIC at SHAEF considered that the prolific evidence about the setting up of a redoubt in western Austria did not mean that large-scale preparations had yet been made for organised resistance there; but it advised that, if not quickly overrun, the area could become a base for guerrilla activities.[20] And on 11 March SHAEF's weekly intelligence summary announced that 'accumulated ground information and a limited amount of photographic evidence now make it possible to give a rather more definite estimate of the progress of plans for the "last-ditch stand" of the Nazi Party'.[21]

This summary noted that the ground reports all pointed to the existence of plans for a last stronghold in an Alpine block, covering western Austria and stretching from the lakes below Munich in the north to the Italian lakes in the south, where, 'defended both by nature and by the most secret weapons yet invented, the powers that have hitherto guided Germany will survive to organise her resurrection' – her liberation from the occupying forces by an underground army trained in guerrilla warfare. It noted that while the Allies were thrusting towards the heart of north Germany, both from the east and from the west, the main trend of German defence policy 'does seem directed primarily to the safeguarding of the Alpine zone'. Kesselring was holding on desperately in Italy while defence lines were built in the Alpine foothills, and defences in depth were being constructed through the Black Forest to Lake Constance and from west of Graz to the Hungarian frontier. Air cover had disclosed activity at about twenty sites where ground sources had reported underground accommodation for stores and men and underground factories. 'It thus appears that ground reports of extensive preparations for the accommodation of the German Maquis-to-be are not unfounded.' The summary admitted that only ground information was available on the amount of troops, stores and weapons already in the redoubt, but it noted that this information suggested that considerable numbers of SS and specially chosen

---

18. Dulles, *The Secret Surrender* (1967), pp 98, 119–120, 152, 160; Minott, op cit, p 25.
19. Minott, op cit, pp 89–90, using correspondence with Dulles; MacDonald, *The Last Offensive* (Washington DC 1973), p 431.
20. JIC(45)87(o) of 13 March (JIC SHAEF(45)3 of 10 March).
21. WO 219/1930, No 51 of 11 March.

units were being systematically withdrawn to Austria and that some of the most important ministries and personalities of the Nazi regime were already established in the area.

On 20 March the Prime Minister asked the JIC to review the evidence as a matter of urgency. He had on 16 March underlined the reference to a southern 'redoubt' in his copy of the Japanese diplomatic decrypt from Berne,[22]* and he had since then received in a letter from the Austrian Archduke Otto a warning that the Germans were preparing a last-ditch stand.† Passing this on to the JIC, he remarked that he was puzzled by Germany's 'strange resistance' at Budapest and Lake Balaton and by the retention of Kesselring's army in Italy, but added that as Hitler was 'so foolishly obstinate about everything . . . there may be no meaning behind these moves'.[24] In its reply on 24 March the JIC fully agreed with this last point: the existence of a plan for a National Redoubt was not needed to explain Germany's strategy in Hungary and Italy, which reflected Hitler's dislike of abandoning territory, the wish to keep the Russians out of Austria and to keep Italy nominally in the war, and the hope of retaining the Hungarian oil and bauxite and the useful economic resources of northern Italy. The JIC also distrusted the agents' reports of the construction of underground buildings and the stocking of underground dumps. It knew that some of the excavation work was part of a wider programme for the dispersal of industry, and it described the reports as being 'mainly from Swiss sources and none of a high grade of reliability', and observed that the colour of many of them suggested that they were part of a German attempt to convince the Allies that the total defeat of Germany would be unprofitable, if not impossible. It accepted, however, that the confirmation by PR of underground activity at some 20 sites in the area, as reported in SHAEF's summary, constituted sufficient evidence to support the assumption that the Germans at least had theoretical or notional plans for a National Redoubt. But it off-set the concession by emphasising that they would not be able to muster forces sufficient for successful resistance beyond a redoubt of narrow geographical limits in the Voralberg and the Tyrol between the Swiss frontier and Salzburg.[25]

---

* See above, p 713.

† This was not confirmed by SOE sources who had been 'in and out' of Austria and seen no trace of organised resistance.[23]

22. Dir/C Archive, 8840 of 16 March.
23. CAB 121/419, SIC file D/Germany/4, COS(45)210(o) of 26 March.
24. JIC(45)93(o) of 20 March. For the full text of the Archduke's letter see CAB 121/419, COS(45)195(o) of 21 March, 210(o) of 26 March.
25. CAB 121/419, JIC(45)97(o) of 24 March.

MI 14, which had remained highly suspicious of all items of evidence other than those provided or supported by Sigint, noted on 25 March the receipt, at last, of one such item: the decrypt of a Führer Directive of 20 March which, excluding 'pure German' units, had ordered that all other training units of the Home (Ersatz) Army were to be put into rearward positions to create a strategic defence zone in depth on the eastern and western fronts.[26] MI 14 surmised that the 'pure German' units might be being retained for a National Redoubt and, emboldened by the Sigint, it selected as being more reliable than most a ground report which had claimed that 16 divisions were to garrison the redoubt, that food and ammunition for two years were to be stocked and that food supplies were planned for 600,000 people including hostages. With this sole exception, however, the Sigint was still referring only to the transfer of Abwehr, SS, OKW, OKL and OKH staffs to Thuringia.[27] On 1 April MI 14 commented that an increasing number of the ground reports suggested that no special preparations were being made for a last-ditch stand further south, and added that its belief that Thuringia was to be a 'brain centre' of the enemy's war effort had been confirmed by documents handed over by a German officer deserter who had been adjutant to OKH's Director of Signals.[28]

General Eisenhower and his staff had meanwhile concluded, as he subsequently stated, that 'the evidence was clear that the Nazis intended to make the attempt [to set up a stronghold in the south] ... and had decided to give him (sic) no opportunity to carry it out'.[29] They had received an appreciation from Seventh US Army, dated 25 March, which fully accepted the ground reports which continued to urge that Germany was planning a final stand in the Alps,[30] and on 27 March they had learned that General Marshall was impressed by their own appreciation of 11 March.[31] It was on this account – if also in the light of the fact that the Russians were on the Oder within forty miles of Berlin, whereas nearly 200 miles of difficult country lay between the capital and the western Allies in the north – that on 28 March, the Russians having proffered no information as to their intentions, Eisenhower advised Stalin in a

26. DEFE 3/520, BT 8059 of 23 March.
27. DEFE 3/519, BT 7796 of 20 March; DEFE 3/599, BTs 8308 of 25 March, 8465 of 26 March; DEFE 3/600, BT 8569 of 27 March; DEFE 3/601, BT 8788 of 29 March; CX/MSS/495 para A 2, 3 and 40, T495/9, 499 para A 73, T504/5; AWL 4423 of 2 April.
28. WO 208/4319, MI 14/10/14/45 of 1 April; WO 208/4318, MI 14 Weekly Summary for the CIGS, 2 April.
29. Ehrman, *Grand Strategy*, Vol VI (1956), pp 132–134.
30. MacDonald, op cit, pp 407, 409; Minott, op cit, pp 54–55.
31. Pogue, *The Supreme Command* (Washington DC 1954), p 435.

personal message that after completing the isolation of the Ruhr he proposed to effect a junction with the Soviet forces by driving along the axis Erfurt–Leipzig–Dresden, 'this being the area to which the main German Governmental Departments are being moved', and that he further proposed to make a secondary advance to the Regensburg–Linz area with a view to joining up with the Russians in the Danube valley and 'preventing the consolidation of German resistance in Redoubt in southern Germany'.[32]

The British authorities no longer disputed that Germany might have plans to establish a redoubt; but they objected to Eisenhower's proposals as a departure from an agreement made by the Combined Chiefs of Staff at the Malta conference, held before going on to Yalta, that the western Allies would carry out their main thrust north of the Ruhr, and they pressed for the earliest possible entry into Berlin. But when Stalin accepted the proposals on 1 April Eisenhower ordered 21st Army Group to limit its advance in the north to the line of the Elbe while the American armies swept to the Elbe across central Germany. In a directive on 2 April he ordered that Ninth US Army should revert to the command of 12th US Army Group; that after mopping up the enemy in the Ruhr 12th Army Group should thrust along the axis Kassel–Leipzig with 6th US Army Group protecting its right flank and preparing a thrust on the axis Nuremberg–Regensburg–Linz; and that 21st Army Group on its left should advance to the river Leine, capture Bremen and then advance to the line of the Elbe.[33]

□

A period of spectacular advances by the western Allies now began. By 9 April First US Army in the centre of 12th Army Group had crossed the Weser and Leine rivers and was approaching the Harz mountains, while Third US Army on its right had secured Gotha and much of the Thuringian Forest and Ninth US Army on the left was across the Leine and approaching Hildesheim. In 21st Army Group Second British Army had one Corps across the Leine north of Hanover and another close to Verden on the Weser south of Bremen.[34]

Meanwhile Army Group B had been making unsuccessful attempts to break out eastward from the Ruhr to meet scratch forces attacking westward to relieve it. To command these forces, and to fill the gap in the front created by the encirclement of Army

32. Ehrman, op cit, Vol VI, pp 132–133.
33. ibid, pp 134–146, 301.
34. Ellis, *Victory in the West*, Vol II (1968), pp 304–306.

Group B, the Germans had brought in HQ Eleventh Army from the eastern front, placing it between Paderborn and Mühlhausen under the direct command of C-in-C West. Army Group G had shifted northwards with Seventh Army between Mühlhausen and Meiningen and First Army from Meiningen to Heilbronn. The sector between Heilbronn and Basel was defended by Nineteenth Army, also directly subordinate to C-in-C West. It being no longer possible for C-in-C West to control the whole front from his HQ in the south, a new HQ North-West had been formed under Field Marshal Busch. Yet another army, Twelfth Army, had been ordered to concentrate in the Harz mountains.[35]

By midnight on 12–13 April Ninth US Army's armoured spearheads had reached the Elbe both sides of Magdeburg. On 15 April First US Army's armour, by-passing relatively strong opposition in the Harz mountains and from some towns – Dessau, Halle, Leipzig – reached the Molde river, capturing bridges intact. Advancing through Erfurt and Coburg, Third US Army was by 15 April also close to the stop-line for the advance which Eisenhower had set at Bayreuth–Chemnitz–east of Leipzig–along the Molde to its junction with the Elbe at Dessau–northwards down the Elbe. Its right flank was protected by Seventh US Army which had reached Bamberg. Further south 6th US Army Group had been held up north of Stuttgart and was still west of the Black Forest at Kehl. On 21st Army Group's front Second Army, taking Celle on 12 April, reached the Elbe on 17 April and by 19 April was a few miles short of Hamburg. But it made only slow progress towards Bremen, while First Canadian Army, which had the task of clearing Holland and German Friesland, also met some determined opposition. In north Holland Groningen was cleared on 16 April and by 19 April the Germans held only a small area round Delfzijl on the Ems estuary. South of the Zuyder Zee, Arnhem held out until 14 April and Apeldoorn until 18 April. For once Hitler authorised a withdrawal and the Germans retired to the Grebbe river.[36]

The Ruhr pocket was split in two at Hagen on 14 April and by 18 April all resistance had ceased. On the other fronts, however, the Germans fought on. Ninth US Army's bridgeheads over the Elbe were counter-attacked and Eleventh Army was ordered to mount harassing operations against Allied flanks and communications from its pocket in the Harz mountains created by the Allied advance. An attempt to relieve the pocket by a thrust with an improvised Panzer division failed. On 24 April Twelfth Army,

---

35. ibid, pp 309, 324; WO 208/4318 of 8 and 15 April.
36. Ellis, op cit, Vol II, pp 304–306, 310–311, 323–325.

which had been brought in to hold the sector between Magdeburg and Leipzig with orders similar to those given to Eleventh Army, was ordered to turn about and counter-attack from the south-west to relieve Berlin.[37]

By 25 April, when the first contact was made with the Russians on the Elbe, both Ninth and First US Armies had completed the mopping-up of their sectors. On 26 April Third US Army was across the Danube both sides of Regensburg and at the end of the month it was into Austria, with spearheads nearing Linz. Seventh US Army had shattered the Nuremberg–Stuttgart–Black Forest line and had captured Augsburg and Munich. First French Army was moving along the northern shore of Lake Constance.[38] In the north Bremen was finally cleared on 27 April. Second British Army crossed the Elbe during the night 27–28 April, met the Russians at Wismar on 2 May, took the formal surrender of Hamburg on 3 May and reached Lübeck on 5 May.[39]

Throughout the final weeks in the west the Allies were well supplied with tactical intelligence.* Army Y again became a prolific source, for though the German formations ceased to use VHF in the confusion, they also abandoned the use of their medium-grade cypher, resorting to plain language and simple codes on their MF communications. Artillery units in particular provided much precise information about HQ locations and gun positions.[41] High-grade Sigint also yielded a very large volume of intelligence. The speed of events and the overwhelming superiority of the Allies on the ground and in the air combined with the wealth of Army Y to render much of it superfluous or irrelevant for operational purposes, but it gave a clear picture of the enemy's last desperate efforts to hold a line.

On 21st Army Group's front a decrypt on the evening of 31 March carrying orders from Hitler for an attack, under Student's command, into the west flank of Second Army's breakthrough to the north-east by all available forces from First Parachute Army, Twenty-fifth Army and scratch units was followed on 1 April by decrypts of orders from Kesselring and Jodl. Kesselring ordered Army Group H to assemble a strong battle group for a deep thrust

---

* In order to be nearer targets and take advantage of short periods of good weather a PR Wing was moved in from England, but by the time it was operational at the end of March there was little left for it to do and even the PR squadrons of 2nd Tactical Air Force were being used on 'odd jobs'.[40]

37. MacDonald, op cit, pp 402–406.
38. Ellis, op cit, Vol II, p 326 et seq.
39. ibid, pp 316, 337–338.
40. AIR 41/7, *Photographic Reconnaissance*, Vol II, pp 165–166, 168.
41. *History of Sigint in the Field*, p 217.

from north of Bocholt towards Haltern and Dülmen. Jodl subordinated LXXXVIII Corps (from Twenty-fifth Army) and II Parachute Corps to Student.[42] A message containing Student's intentions, issued late on 1 April and decrypted early on 2 April, disclosed that ammunition and fuel were insufficient for an attack.[43] On 3 April the decrypts of further messages from him showed that he had issued orders for preliminary operations to get the Allies out of Odenzaal but could not undertake them unless he received fuel, ammunition and reinforcements.[44] A message from C-in-C West of 3 April, decrypted on 5 April, disclosed that the attack had been abandoned and that Student had been ordered to carry out mobile operations in defence of the northern Holland–Emden area.[45] Messages from Blaskowitz and Kesselring on 5 April were signalled to the Commands on 7 and 8 April. Blaskowitz reported that Student was being outflanked and pressed back to the Ijssel, that First Parachute Army was already by-passed by the Allied threat to the Weser and that Army Group H could defend the area south of Emden and prevent an Allied advance into the north German plain only if it received reinforcements. Kesselring replied that Army Group H's task was to stop the Allied advance to the Ems, Jade and Weser estuaries, and the ports of Emden, Wilhelmshafen and Bremen, and that it must if necessary be given priority over the maintenance of contact with the German forces in Holland.[46] A message from Army Group H of 7 April, decrypted on 8 April, disclosed that Student's sector was being taken over by First Parachute Army and that he was assuming command of Wehrkreis units, a new 2nd Naval Infantry Division* and other formations under an unspecified Army Corps. The order of battle was then Twenty-fifth Army on the Ijssel, First Parachute Army from the Ijssel to the Weser and Gruppe Student from the Weser to a line running east from the river just south of Paderborn.[48]

On the Remagen front the enemy's attempts to establish new defence lines, organise counter-attacks and prevent the threatened encirclement of Army Group B, were reflected in

---

* By 6 April four naval infantry divisions had been identified from decrypts. In a message of 5 April, decrypted on 6 April, Blaskowitz described 2nd Naval Infantry Division as unfit for offensive employment.[47]

42. DEFE 3/516, BTs 9068 of 31 March, 9081, 9111 of 1 April.
43. ibid, BT 9189 of 2 April.
44. DEFE 3/562, BTs 9279, 9302 of 3 April.
45. ibid, BT 9492 of 5 April.
46. DEFE 3/563, BT 9737 of 7 April; DEFE 3/564, BT 9801 of 8 April.
47. ibid, BTs 9591, 9631 of 6 April, 9686 of 7 April.
48. DEFE 3/564, BT 9816 of 8 April; WO 208/4318 of 8 April.

decrypts available on 28, 29 and 30 March.[49] A decrypt of 30 March indicated that Hitler was issuing orders for remedial action himself.[50] There followed on 1 April decrypts of messages exchanged the previous day between Kesselring and Model, who was mounting an attack by a Corps group under Bayerlein to break through the encirclement. At 1600 on 31 March Kesselring urged Model to strengthen the attack by withdrawing forces from the Rhine and the Sieg (where the Germans were establishing a defensive front): Model's reply two hours later gave a succinct appreciation of Army Group B's predicament. He intended Bayerlein's attack to restore communications to the east. If necessary, Bayerlein would be given additional forces, but the scope for this was limited by the need to hold firm on the Rhine and the Sieg. A firm 'eastern flank' (ie a firm front against the Allies driving eastwards) was essential, and Army Group B was unable to provide this itself. If a firm eastern flank could not be established the Rhine and Sieg fronts would have to be withdrawn in good time. If Army Group B had to hold its existing positions without opening up communications the most important supplies would last, without re-supply by air, for about 2 to 3 weeks, but the stocks of fuel and ammunition had not been assessed.* Army Group B's mobility was so low that a breakthrough (to the east) would only be possible without the bulk of the heavy equipment. He therefore recommended establishing a firm front under independent command on Army Group B's eastern flank, whence an attack could be launched with sufficient forces to cut off the enemy and restore communications. And he requested that XLVII Panzer Corps and LXIII Corps (which were being cut off from Army Group H by Ninth US Army's advance) should be subordinated to Army Group B to protect its northern flank on the Lippe and the Ruhr rivers.[52]†

Hard on the heels of this exchange GC and CS, at 1821 on 1 April, signalled the decrypt of another message from Kesselring,

---

* In a message on 30 March, which was not decrypted until 5 April, Army Group B's QM reported up to 14 days' supply with most rigid rationing.[51]

† In a message on 1 April, decrypted on 4 April, Model reported that the situation had obliged him to order these two Corps to form a defence front on the Lippe in contact with Army Group B.[53] C-in-C West's order transferring them to Army Group B was issued on 3 April and decrypted two days later.[54]

49. DEFE 3/600, BTs 8718 of 28 March, 8798, 8813, 8821 of 29 March; DEFE 3/601, BT 8937 of 30 March.
50. DEFE 3/601, BT 8935 of 30 March.
51. DEFE 3/563, BT 9549 of 5 April.
52. DEFE 3/561, BT 9082 of 1 April.
53. ibid, BT 9247 of 4 April.
54. DEFE 3/562, BT 9492 of 5 April.

sent late on 31 March, telling Model that Hitler had ordered an attack west of Kassel, 'concentrically from west and east' in the general direction of Korbach.[55] Decrypts signalled in the next few days showed that Model was finding it difficult to exercise effective control of the operation and find forces to maintain its momentum, and revealed that HQ Eleventh Army, from the eastern front, had been brought in to control the attack from the east and made directly subordinate to C-in-C West.[56] In a message on 3 April, signalled on 5 April, Kesselring said that Eleventh Army's task was to assemble all available forces west of the Weser for an attack towards Korbach to re-establish contact with Army Group B.[57] The failure of the operation was not surprising in view of the inadequacy of Eleventh Army's attacking force as listed in a message decrypted on 7 April.[58]* A GAF message on 5 April, decrypted the next day, reported that Eleventh Army's attack had been abandoned,[59] and a decrypt available on 8 April disclosed that C-in-C West had ordered the Army to make the Allied advance costly and slow by using the Harz mountains for skilfully planned blocking positions defended by small parties of determined men, thus gaining time for new measures.[60]

Decrypts of 31 March and 1 April disclosed enquiries by Army Group B about the feasibility of air supply.[61] Over the next fortnight GC and CS provided a steady flow of decrypts on this subject. On 1 April C-in-C West and OKL ruled out the possibility of air supply on an adequate scale.[62] On 5 April C-in-C West told Army Group B that it could expect 32 tons daily,[63] and Army Group B asked for rifle and machine pistol ammunition 'for the defence of the [Model's] fortress', which had plans to produce its own ammunition but needed filling apparatus.[64] On 6 and 7 April Army Group B was suggesting the use of seaplanes which could land on reservoirs; its Flivo was reporting on the serviceability of airfields for night landings; and Model was urging OKW to accept

---

* It consisted of SS Panzer Brigade Westphalia reinforced by Tiger Abteilung 507, one shadow division and elements of two more, elements of the reinforced Panzer Training Unit Franconia, the reinforced Army Engineer Brigade 688 (Panzer Jäger Abteilung Lammers) Battle Group Grotsan, (static) Panzer Company Döberitz and 'all available troops and units in area north of Kassel or being brought up'.

55. DEFE 3/561, BT 9143 of 1 April.
56. DEFE 3/562, BTs 9375, 9417 of 4 April, 9481 of 5 April.
57. DEFE 3/563, BT 9534 of 5 April.
58. ibid, BT 9745 of 7 April.
59. ibid, BT 9607 of 6 April.
60. DEFE 3/564, BT 9894 of 8 April.
61. DEFE 3/561, BTs 9030, 9082 of 31 March, 1 April.
62. DEFE 3/562, BT 9373 of 4 April.
63. DEFE 3/563, BT 9662 of 6 April.
64. ibid, BT 9678 of 7 April.

the risk of losing aircraft because of inadequate landing grounds in view of the decisive importance of air supply.[65] On 13 April Model reported that, with extreme economy, ammunition would last another three days, fuel another week and rations indefinitely. The supply of weapons was so bad that only some 20 per cent of the troops in the fortress were properly equipped, while another 20 per cent had pistols only.[66]

By then the fortress was almost at its last gasp. In its day report for 11 April, decrypted on 14 April, Army Group B described the Allies as poised for the decisive blow.[67] In a message on 13 April, decrypted two days later, Model said that the 'unexpected' intervention of eight new Allied formations had produced a radical change in the situation, which was extremely critical. It was decisively conditioned by air supply, which had failed to match needs, the absence of long-range anti-tank guns, and the lack of mobility, which prevented the effective use of the numerous Flak guns for anti-tank defence. Army Group B would fight to the last cartridge.[68] After resistance finally ceased on 19 April MI believed that 350,000 prisoners had been taken and seventeen divisions liquidated.[69]

On 6 April GC and CS signalled to the Commands the decrypt of a message of 2 April from Hitler to Kesselring. The Führer complained that the Allies were conducting operations as though German resistance had already collapsed. He himself would give all strategic directions and sanction every unavoidable withdrawal. C-in-C West's task was to force the wavering front to hold, compel obedience to the Führer's orders and replace every commander who failed to stand firm.[70] As we have seen, Hitler intervened personally with directives for Army Group H and Army Group B. Decrypts available between 6 and 8 April showed that it was also on his instructions that orders were issued for the Thuringian Forest to be held as a main defence zone by Seventh Army and First Army under Army Group G.[71] On 8 April MI commented that there was coherent enemy resistance only on the northern and southern flanks. In the centre the issue of orders for holding positions already lost and for counter-attacks which never materialised showed that the enemy had lost control of the battle.[72]

---

65. ibid, BTs 9692, 9712 of 7 April; DEFE 3/564, BT 9812 of 8 April.
66. DEFE 3/567, KO 503 of 15 April.
67. DEFE 3/566, KO 377 of 14 April.
68. DEFE 3/567, KO 513 of 15 April.
69. WO 208/4318 of 22 April.
70. DEFE 3/563, BT 9588 of 6 April.
71. ibid, BTs 9590, 9627, 9632, 9643 of 6 April, 9687, 9713 of 7 April; DEFE 3/564, BTs 9806, 9836 of 8 April.
72. WO 208/4318 of 8 April.

Decrypts of 10 and 12 April disclosed Hitler's orders on 7 April for the re-organisation of the High Command necessitated by the deep Allied penetration in the centre. Field Marshal Busch* became C-in-C North-West with C-in-C Netherlands, First Parachute Army and Army Group Blumentritt (formerly Student) subordinated. As C-in-C Netherlands, General Blaskowitz commanded Twenty-fifth Army and the GAF and naval forces, and was personally responsible to Hitler for the defence of Fortress Holland. Army Group B, with Fifth Panzer Army and Fifteenth Army, was subordinated directly to OKW. C-in-C West was left with Army Group G (First and Seventh Armies) and Eleventh and Nineteenth Armies. The boundary between C-in-C North-West and C-in-C West ran eastwards through Paderborn, Holzminden and Salzgitter.[74]

As we have seen, when the attempt to relieve Army Group B failed, Eleventh Army was ordered to use the Harz mountains to block the Allied advance and gain time for new measures. A decrypt available on 10 April disclosed that these included assembling another Army, Twelfth Army.[75] The Allied advance to the Elbe created a pocket in the Harz mountains in which Eleventh Army was trapped with four divisions.[76] An exhortation to Eleventh Army from Hitler on 17 April to attack the weakest points on the Allied flanks and supply lines, using detached groups of battle-worthy troops, living off the country as the Russians had done in 1942–1943, was decrypted on 18 April.[77] In a message that day, decrypted on 21 April, Kesselring urged the Army to make a stand on the Brocken and, if this was impossible, to fight to the last in separate groups.[78] The abortive attempt by the improvised Panzer Division Clausewitz† to break through to Eleventh Army, by a thrust from the area Ulzen–Salzwedel towards Brunswick, was disclosed in a decrypt on 19 April.[81] Resistance finally ceased on 22 April when MI 14 told the CIGS

---

* The appointment of Busch to be C-in-C North Coast had been disclosed by decrypts on 22 March.[73]

† References to the setting up of this division appeared in high-grade Sigint from 6 April.[79] A decrypt on 15 April located it at Heisterberg under XXXIX Panzer Corps.[80]

73. DEFE 3/520, BTs 8030, 8032 of 22 March.
74. DEFE 3/565, KOs 38 of 10 April, 218 of 12 April.
75. ibid, KO 62 of 10 April.
76. WO 208/4318 of 22 April.
77. DEFE 3/568, KO 758 of 18 April.
78. ibid, KO 946 of 21 April.
79. DEFE 3/563, BTs 9586, 9639 of 6 April; DEFE 3/565, KO 77 of 15 April; DEFE 3/568, KO 773 of 19 April.
80. DEFE 3/566, KO 471 of 15 April.
81. DEFE 3/568, KO 829 of 19 April.

that some 60,000 prisoners had been taken in the pocket, including part of the Army HQ and three Corps commanders.[82]

By 15 April high-grade Sigint had disclosed that Twelfth Army controlled three Corps; XLI Panzer and XX Corps from East Prussia and XLVIII Panzer Corps from west of Breslau.[83] On the demise of Eleventh Army, Twelfth Army took over the sector from Magdeburg to Leipzig.[84] In operational instructions issued on 21 April, and decrypted on 23 April, Twelfth Army was told that in the area between Salzwedel and Brunswick there were widely scattered elements of Ninth and First US Armies, which were probably having supply difficulties. Its task was to smash these scattered groups and bring the Allied advance up to and across the Elbe to a standstill by attacking flanks and communications. After that, the Allied forces which had thrust east on both sides of the Harz mountains were to be annihilated.[85] With the Russians now closing in on Berlin all this was merely wishful thinking, rapidly overtaken by events. Messages of 22 and 23 April, decrypted on 24 April, disclosed that Twelfth Army's sector had been extended north-west where XXXIX Panzer Corps had been subordinated to it, and that on 23 April Twelfth Army had ordered XXXIX Panzer Corps to move by the quickest route to the north bank of the Elbe in the area Wittstock–Pritzwalk.[86] A decrypt of 25 April contained Kesselring's orders to Twelfth Army on the previous day to hold strong forces to thrust north-eastwards towards Berlin.[87] In MI 14's words, the Army thereby achieved the distinction, 'probably unique and certainly unenviable', of fighting on two fronts at the same time.[88]*

While the Allies were carrying all before them in the centre they continued to meet obstinate resistance on the northern and southern wings. On 15 April MI 14 noted that the virtual cutting off of Holland had left Twenty-fifth Army with six divisions and a considerable number of fortress troops to hold the country. The Allied advance on Oldenburg had been delayed by First Parachute Army which included three good, but weak, divisions.[89] These were 7th and 8th Parachute Divisions and 15th PG Division. In a message on 13 April, decrypted the next day, C-in-C North-West

---

* See further below, pp 731–732.

82. WO 208/4318 of 22 April.
83. CX/MSS/T515/38, 54 and para A 29; DEFE 3/569, KO 1216 of 24 April.
84. WO 208/4318 of 22 April.
85. DEFE 3/569, KO 1201 of 23 April.
86. ibid, KO 1216 of 24 April.
87. DEFE 3/570, KO 1327 of 25 April.
88. WO 208/4318 of 29 April.
89. ibid, of 15 April.

ordered ruthless use of flooding for the defence of Fortress Holland.[90] A decrypt of 18 April disclosed that Hitler had authorised withdrawal from the Ijssel position to the Grebbe line the previous day,[91] and another of 20 April that Blaskowitz had enough men for the defence of the fortress but not enough weapons.[92] A message from the SS and Police Commander to Himmler on 24 April, decrypted on 26 April, reported daily deterioration of the internal situation in the fortress and poor German morale.[93] Another message decrypted on 26 April estimated that food for the civilian population would not last beyond 10 May.[94] Further decrypts followed on this subject. Negotiations for the relief of the civilian population were opened with the Allies and in a decrypt available late on 1 May Blaskowitz informed Busch that the negotiations had just been successfully completed. The Allied 'Chief Negotiator' (Eisenhower's Chief of Staff) had tried to extend the discussion to military operations in Blaskowitz's sphere of command. This had been rejected, but it could serve as a basis for further contact if OKW thought this was necessary.[95]

During the second half of April First Parachute Army continued its stubborn defence. On 22 April MI reported that little progress had been made except towards Bremen and on 29 April that the resistance put up by the two Parachute Divisions, 15th PG Division and a large number of naval units had remained strong.* The enemy had retired only slowly to the northern side of the Ems estuary and towards Oldenburg.[98] In a message on 29 April, decrypted on 1 May, C-in-C North-West spoke of an elastic conduct of operations in First Parachute Army's sector after the release of forces to Army Group Blumentritt (on First Parachute Army's left) for employment as required against the Russians or the British. The coastal fortresses would be held.[99] In an appreciation late on 1 May, decrypted the next day, C-in-C

---

* Orders for drafting GAF personnel into First Parachute Army were decrypted on 10 and 14 April.[96] Decrypts of 11 April disclosed orders by C-in-C North-West for the incorporation into 15th PG Division of available elements of the PG training formation *Grossdeutschland* and 'the NCO school'.[97]

90. DEFE 3/566, KO 430 of 14 April.
91. DEFE 3/567, KO 725 of 18 April.
92. DEFE 3/568, KO 864 of 20 April.
93. DEFE 3/570, KO 1453 of 26 April.
94. ibid, KO 1465 of 26 April.
95. DEFE 3/572, KO 1844 of 2 May.
96. DEFE 3/565, KO 80 of 10 April; DEFE 3/566, KO 379 of 14 April.
97. DEFE 3/565, KO 127 of 11 April.
98. WO 208/4318 of 22 and 29 April.
99. DEFE 3/572, KO 1797 of 1 May.

North-West said that, after the switching of First Parachute Army's fittest formations, withdrawal in the Weser–Ems area and the encirclement of the fortresses Emden, Wilhelmshafen and Wesermünde and, soon afterwards, of Bremerhafen and Cuxhafen were to be expected. On the Elbe front German forces, including the reinforcements, were sufficient to delay the Allied advance but not to stop it.[100] In a message sent early on 3 May and decrypted the same day, Busch's Chief of Staff reported that since it became known that the Führer had fallen and the struggle was primarily one against Bolshevism, the will to fight had declined to such an extent that no further resistance worth speaking of could be expected.[101]

Regarding the southern wing MI 14 reported on 15 April that the Germans had prevented any large scale breakthrough between Coburg and Nuremberg. Further south-west comparatively strong forces (under Nineteenth Army) had also held the Allies successfully in difficult country.[102] Decrypts available on 14 April of messages late the previous evening disclosed that Army Group G needed all available forces in the battle north-west of Nuremberg and was considerably weakening its left flank by withdrawing 2nd Mountain and 17th SS PG Divisions from Heilbronn. Nineteenth Army must therefore be prepared to seal off penetrations and maintain contact with First Army.[103] As MI reported on 22 April, the withdrawal of these two divisions caused a fatal weakening of the enemy's front which resulted in the loss of Stuttgart.[104] Decrypts of 21 and 22 April reflected the enemy's critical situation in the sector.[105]

As the Allied threat developed to the Austrian frontier north-east of Passau, high-grade Sigint disclosed that futile efforts, beginning on 21 April, were being made to build up an armoured force, comprising 11th Panzer Division (described as 'by far the prime unit'), 2nd Panzer and 2nd SS Panzer Divisions, to attack the Allied flank.[106]

On 2 and 3 May GC and CS decrypted a message from Kesselring on 29 April on the state of his forces. The fighting

---

100. ibid, KO 1878 of 2 May.
101. ibid, KO 1938 of 3 May.
102. WO 208/4318 of 15 April.
103. DEFE 3/566, KO 407 of 14 April.
104. WO 208/4318 of 22 April.
105. DEFE 3/568, KOs 971, 976 of 21 April; DEFE 3/569, KOs 1034, 1087 of 22 April.
106. DEFE 3/569, KOs 1134 of 23 April, 1215, 1230 of 24 April; DEFE 3/570, KOs 1291, 1329, 1334, 1337, 1339, 1371 of 25 April, 1457, 1461, 1475 of 26 April; DEFE 3/571, KOs 1501, 1503, 1542, of 27 April, 1610 of 28 April, 1653 of 29 April.

strength of Seventh Army was equivalent to 17 infantry battalions and it had 24 tanks. First Army had four divisional formations and one Panzer Division, with a fighting value of 14 battalions and 80 tanks, facing 11 Allied infantry and 5 armoured divisions with 1,000 tanks, plus reserves. Nineteenth Army faced 8 Allied infantry and 4 armoured divisions (850 tanks), plus reserves, with 14 divisional formations, 12 of which were encircled or outflanked and without communications; Nineteenth Army's fighting value, including Volkssturm, was 10 battalions with 16 tanks and there was fuel for 4 to 5 days. The space for GAF operations was becoming narrower and narrower. Kesselring's conclusion was that the situation required delaying operations to defend the north Alpine front and maintain contact with the German forces in Czechoslovakia. Political collapse was ever more apparent and must be opposed by all imaginable means.[107]

□

When accepting Eisenhower's proposal on 1 April,* Stalin had gone out of his way to add that he was allotting only secondary forces to an attack on Berlin: 'Berlin has lost its former strategic importance', and the main Soviet advance in that direction would probably be resumed in the second half of May following the clearance of Austria. But on 1 April the Soviet armies were ordered to begin a major offensive against Berlin on 16 April. First Belorussian Front (Zhukov) was to make the main advance from its bridgehead on the Oder. First Ukrainian Front (Koniev) was to give support and to undertake a subsidiary offensive against Dresden and Leipzig. Second Belorussian Front was meanwhile to attack around Stettin and drive west and north-west into Mecklenburg. It has been said that these orders were issued because the Soviet authorities had grounds for believing that the western Allies planned to take Berlin before the Russian forces reached it.[108]

However that may be, the western Allies were learning from Sigint that the Germans expected a Soviet thrust against Berlin. In a signal of 24 March, decrypted on 29 March, the Japanese Naval Attaché in Berlin reported that Russian transfers from Pomerania indicated that the next major offensive would be delivered on the Oder and Neisse fronts with the object of taking Berlin and

---

* Above, pp 717–718.

107. DEFE 3/572, KOs 1866, 1944 of 2 and 3 May.
108. Seaton, *The Russo–German War 1941–45* (1971), p 365; Erickson, *The Road to Berlin* (1983), p 531.

moving up to the Elbe.[109] In the first week of April a Fish decrypt disclosed that on 30 March Army Group Vistula expected this offensive to start before all the reinforcements had arrived from Pomerania.[110] On 8 April, on the strength of recent information about Soviet Command changes, and of German reports that the Russians had established bridgeheads on the west bank of the Oder, MI 14 concluded that 'whether or not the Russians contemplate a frontal attack or the envelopment of Berlin . . . the only factor against a resumption of the offensive in this sector in the immediate future seems to be the possibility that the Russians have not yet been able to complete the troop transfers they have planned'.[111] In telegrams decrypted on 12 and 15 April the Japanese reported that on 6 and 9 April the Germans were uncertain only as to when the attack on Berlin would begin.[112] There followed on 15 April, when other decrypts had disclosed the continued transfer of forces from the Second Belorussian Front to the Oder sector,[113] the decrypt of an appreciation issued by OKW on 9 April: a Soviet offensive on the Oder between Frankfurt and Schwedt was 'immediately imminent', though bad weather might force a delay.[114]

It was in these circumstances that on 15 April the US Ambassador in Moscow asked Stalin for news of Russia's intentions on the central sector. Stalin replied that she was about to renew the offensive there but that the main thrust would be towards Dresden, with a subsidiary attack on Berlin.[115]

Sigint provided no further information about the offensive until 21 April, when the decrypt of a German Army message disclosed that it had begun on 16 April[116] and the decrypt of a telegram from the Japanese embassy in Berlin reported that the Germans believed that parallel attacks would be made across the Oder and the Neisse and would develop into a single offensive against Berlin.[117]* In its first assessment of what was happening, issued on

---

* From this point the Japanese diplomatic decrypts ceased to be a valuable source. They had already revealed that the Ambassador had left Berlin for the south at the request of the German Foreign Ministry on 14 April, and they subsequently revealed that Admiral Abe had

109. BAY/BT 147 of 1 April 1945 (SJA 1731 of 29 March).
110. CX/MSS/ROB 40, circulated on 8 April (IV, item 5). Reported to the Foreign Office in Boniface summary of 9 April (Dir/C Archive, 8981).
111. WO 208/4318 of 8 April.
112. BAY/KO 4 of 12 April; BAY/KO 8 of 18 April.
113. CX/MSS/ROB 41, circulated 20 April (II, item 20); CX/MSS/T519/4, of 15 April.
114. CX/MSS/ROB 41, circulated 20 April (II, item 20); CX/MSS/T520/19 of 15 April; WO 208/4318 of 15 April.
115. Seaton, op cit, p 565.
116. DEFE 3/568, KO 977 of 21 April.
117. BAY/KO 10 of 21 April.

22 April, MI 14 noted that the Russians were maintaining total silence, but conjectured 'from knowledge of Russian order of battle and German unofficial reports' that Zhukov was using two tank armies to outflank Berlin from the north while Koniev closed in with at least two more tank armies to outflank the city from the south-west.[119] Thereafter – though frequently with a delay of up to three days – decrypts disclosed the advance of the two Russian Fronts as they made contact south-east of Berlin on 23 April and completed its encirclement to the west two days later. The situation on the evening of 24 April was disclosed on 26 April by the decrypt of an appreciation from Army Group Vistula; it reported that Russian spearheads were south of Potsdam, and in Teltow, with others wheeling north out of Brandenburg, and that in the north one army was on the edge of the city and two armies advancing eastwards from both sides of Oranienburg.[120] Another message of 24 April, decrypted by 27 April, reported that the inner ring of the city had been penetrated in places.[121] On 25 April Koniev's subsidiary offensive towards Dresden and Leipzig met patrols of First US Army near Torgau on the Elbe, some fifty miles below Dresden.

Two days earlier, Hitler having refused to join the other Nazi leaders in leaving Berlin and his unrealistic orders for counter-attacks having produced no results, Keitel and Jodl tried to organise a relief operation by Twelfth Army. As we have seen, Twelfth Army had been forming in the Harz mountains against the American advance since the middle of April.* A decrypt, signalled to the Commands by GC and CS early on 25 April contained the order for it to turn east. Other decrypts of 25 April included one of a message from Jodl approving its plan for a counter-attack towards Beelitz.[122] On 29 April its main force surprised the Russians near Belzig, broke through to the lake at Potsdam and succeeded in evacuating the Potsdam garrison; but on 1 May, its strength exhausted, it was preparing to fall back on

---

left Berlin for Hamburg on 20 April and that the Air Attaché had moved to Salzburg with OKL by 21 April. The final decrypts were obtained on 7 May; they were telegrams from the Ambassador reporting on his enquiries to the Foreign Ministry about the whereabouts of German 'notables'.[118]

  * Above, pp 725, 726.

118. BAY/KO 11 of 22 April (SJA 1815 of 18 April); BAY/KO 13 of 23 April (SJA 1818 of 21 April); BAY/KO 16 of 27 April; BAY/KO 26 of 7 May. See also BAY/KO 17 of 27 April and BAY/KO 25 of 7 May for Abe's later wanderings and eventual escape to Sweden.
119. WO 208/4318 of 22 April.
120. DEFE 3/570, KO 1449 of 26 April.
121. CX/MSS/ROB 43, circulated 27 April (II, item 22).
122. DEFE 3/570, KOs 1346, 1355, 1386 and 1392 of 25 April.

the Elbe.[123] Decrypts of messages reporting the progress of its 'attacking spearhead' on 27 and 28 April were not available until 29 and 30 April.[124] A message from Twelfth Army's XX Corps of 29 April stating that it was not possible to continue the attack towards Berlin, especially because support from battle-worthy elements of Ninth Army could no longer be expected to arrive, was decrypted on 3 May.[125]

Sigint had disclosed on 29 April that Ninth Army, encircled to the south-east of Berlin, had been ordered by OKH on 27 April to break out and join Twelfth Army's attack.[126] On 1 May, in a message decrypted on 3 May, Twelfth Army had reported that GOC Ninth Army had arrived and that he expected up to 20,000 of his men to fight their way through.[127] In the event, only small forces managed to escape before Twelfth Army began its withdrawal.[128] A report issued by GOC Twelfth Army on 4 May was decrypted on 6 May; his troops were in desperate straits in a narrow pocket east of the Elbe, but after fighting 'the Bolshevists' to the last round he would try to get them to the west bank 'for the reconstruction of the Fatherland'.[129]

The decrypts of messages from Berlin had meanwhile included, on 26 April, Hitler's orders for the division of OKW into Operations Staff A under Dönitz in the north and Operations Staff B under General Winter with its HQ in the south[130] and, on 27 April, an exhortation issued by Jodl following the news that the Soviet and US forces had made contact on the Elbe. The latter advised the commanders under Operations Staff B that 'the fight is to be conducted with final determination against Bolshevism. Every available force is therefore to be put in against the Bolshevik arch enemy. In contrast to this the loss of large areas of territory to Anglo–American forces fades into the background.' It also stressed that any transfers of forces from west to east remained subject to the permission of OKW, which remained directly responsible to Hitler.[131] A message of 28 April, decrypted on 29 April, repeated that 'Army Group intentions of a basic nature' must be submitted to the Führer, but conceded that Cs-in-C could make their own decisions if the circumstances were pressing.[132]

123. Seaton, op cit, p 597; Erickson, op cit, pp 591–592, 594, 601, 621.
124. DEFE 3/571, KOs 1633 of 29 April, 1709 of 30 April.
125. DEFE 3/572, KO 1905 of 3 May.
126. DEFE 3/571, KO 1654 of 29 April.
127. DEFE 3/572, KO 1899 of 3 May.
128. Seaton, op cit, pp 579–580; Erickson, op cit, pp 592–594, 621.
129. DEFE 3/571, KO 2063 of 6 May.
130. DEFE 3/570, KO 1444 of 26 April.
131. DEFE 3/571, KO 1558 of 27 April.
132. ibid, KO 1695 of 29 April.

But the last messages issued by Hitler or on his behalf – queries about the whereabouts of the armies – were intercepted late on 29 April and decrypted on 1 May.[133] As we now know, he committed suicide on the evening of 30 April, and the Chief of the General Staff at once sought a truce with the Russians. At 0300 on 1 May, a plain language intercept announced with 'Führer Priority' that negotiations had begun with the Russians for a cease-fire in Berlin. On 2 May the city was surrendered.[134]

☐

Meanwhile the American advance through central Germany had been so rapid as to destroy any remaining belief that Germany could succeed in organising resistance in a southern redoubt on any large scale, but the prospect could not be excluded that elements of the German leadership would still escape to the mountains and make a final stand there.

As early as 31 March US Sixth Army Group had concluded that 'the turn of military events is effectively destroying the National Redoubt for want of territory and personnel' – but it had added that 'any retreat into the mountains of south-east Germany will hardly be voluntary on the part of the German leaders'.[135] On 10 April the JIC SHAEF had reported that the progress of Allied operations would not permit an organised retreat into the redoubt from the north – but it had noted that the redoubt could be occupied by enemy forces from Italy, Yugoslavia and Army Group South, and that they might be joined by some elements from Germany.[136] Similar conclusions were reached by the British authorities. On 15 April MI 14 believed that 'whatever German plans may be – and evidence tends to show that no large-scale developments of defence lines have taken place – the ultimate boundaries of the redoubt area must be defined by the speed and direction of the Allied advance . . . Allied superiority . . . will probably enable the Allies to over-run the outlying areas of the redoubt with considerable speed and will force the German desperadoes back into the hard core of the mountains, from which they may be difficult to dislodge'.[137] On 17 April, after discussing the appreciation from JIC SHAEF of 10 April, the London JIC accepted that as the Germans would be able to take only a few

133. DEFE 3/572, KO 1846 of 1 May.
134. AWL 4687.
135. MacDonald, op cit, pp 407–408, quoting 6th Army Group Weekly Intelligence Summary No 28 of 31 March.
136. JIC(45)134(o) of 15 April (JIC SHAEF(45)13 of 10 April).
137. WO 208/4319, MI 14/10/16/45 of 15 April.

POW into the redoubt, they would probably choose certain important prisoners as hostages.[138] And in Italy on 18 April 15th Army Group issued a detailed study which discounted prolonged German defence of a redoubt on a continuous front, but thought it possible that small forces of fanatical Nazis would attempt to conduct guerrilla warfare in some of the redoubt area.[139]

General Eisenhower took these appreciations into account on 14 April when he decided that his forces would make their next advance through Regensburg to effect a junction with the Russians in the Danube valley; he noted that 'even then the National Redoubt could remain in being, and it must be our aim to break into it rapidly before the enemy has an opportunity to man it and fully organise its defences', and he accordingly also ordered an advance on Salzburg.[140] These advances made rapid progress from 20 April. The thrust into the Danube valley took Regensburg on 24 April and crossed into Austria at the end of the month, while the thrust to the south, taking Augsburg on 24 April and Munich on 30 April, and meeting little resistance on its approach to the inner redoubt area, reached Innsbruck on 3 May and Berchtesgaden and Salzburg on 4 May.[141]

As the southern thrust neared the inner area of the supposed redoubt the prospect finally receded that Germany would be able to offer serious resistance there. SHAEF's intelligence summary of 29 April noted that preparations for active defences were 'relatively undeveloped'. However, PR and ground reports had revealed widespread tunnelling works, which pointed to preparations for massive defence, and government departments and service HQs had moved into the area.[142] The evidence for the move of the departments and HQs from Thuringia to the Salzburg area, as also of that of the foreign missions to Bad Gastein, had come from high-grade Sigint during the second week of April.[143] By 29 April decrypts had established that OKH's battle HQ and its Directorate of Signals were near Reichenhall and that

---

138. JIC(45) 27th(o) Meeting, 17 April.
139. CAB 106/448 Part IV, Section G Appendix A (G2 15th Army Group report of 18 April 1945).
140. Ehrman, op cit, Vol VI, pp 147–148.
141. ibid, pp 158–159. For an extended treatment see MacDonald, op cit, Chapter XVIII.
142. WO 219/1931, No 58 of 29 April.
143. WO 208/4319, MI 14/10/15/45 of 8 April, 10/16/45 of 15 April, 10/17/45 of 22 April; WO 208/4318 of 8, 15 and 22 April; see also as examples of the Ultra messages DEFE 3/600, BT 8569 of 27 March; DEFE 3/562, BT 9458 of 4 April; DEFE 3/564, BTs 9843, 9871 of 8 April; DEFE 3/566, KO 495 of 15 April; DEFE 3/569, KOs 1078 and 1106 of 22 April; AWLs 4491 and 4533 of 9 and 13 April.

Himmler's field HQ was at Glasenbach.[144] By the same date, moreover, the assumption that some elements would try to hold out in the area – if only war criminals and Nazis who refused to accept defeat – had at last been supported by Sigint: decrypts had begun to refer to 'the Alpine Fortress'.

We now know that these references were prompted by a directive from Hitler. Counter-signed by Winter before his departure for Berchtesgaden on 20 April, and issued on 24 April, this directive, which was not decrypted, had ordered that an inner fortress should be prepared in the Alps as 'a last bulwark of fanatical resistance'. The preparations, for which OKW was to issue detailed instructions, had included the closure of the area to civilians and the removal of superfluous foreign workers, the provision of accommodation for British, American and French POW, the stockpiling of supplies and the construction of emergency factories for the production of munitions and explosives. As we also know from the German records of the time, Winter recognised on his arrival in Berchtesgaden that these measures could not be carried out at so late a stage.[145] But decrypts available on 1 and 2 May indicated that he was making every effort to carry them out or to appear to be doing so. In messages of 29 April, decrypted on 1 May, he informed Jodl that the final requirements for the Army's attempt to relieve Berlin would considerably delay the last possibility of bringing food into the Alpine fortress from Czechoslovakia, and he advised Kesselring that Brunico, Lienz, Kitzbühel and St Johann were to be made available for HQs.[146] A message to Hitler of 28 April, decrypted on 2 May, reported that the Allies were approaching Munich and that an attempt to make a fighting withdrawal would involve the loss of the troops intended for the front line of the Alpine fortress.[147] Another decrypt of 2 May disclosed that on 27 April Winter had appointed General Jaschke as GOC North of the Fortress with instructions to block the entrances to the area Wolfgangsee–Salzburg–Tegernsee–Füssen and prepare for its defence in collaboration with Gauleiter Hofer, newly designated by Hitler as Reich Defence Commissar for the Alpine front.[148]

---

144. WO 208/4319, MI 14/10/19/45 of 29 April. And for examples of decrypts on the continued move of German military and SS staffs into the south, as used by MI 14 see DEFE 3/570, KOs 1338 and 1380 of 25 April, 1498 of 27 April; DEFE 3/571, KOs 1562 of 27 April, 1750 of 30 April; DEFE 3/572, KO 1776 of 30 April; AWLs 4637 and 4653 of 26 and 27 April.
145. Ellis, op cit, Vol II Appendix X.
146. DEFE 3/572, KOs 1814 and 1829 of 1 May.
147. ibid, KO 1856 of 2 May.
148. ibid, KO 1858 of 2 May.

Meanwhile, the decrypts of SS Enigma messages had disclosed Himmler's last-minute involvement in efforts to organise a stronghold in the south. On 22 April he had submitted a peace offer to the Allies via Count Bernadotte. But in a message sent on 25 April and decrypted on 27 April Obergruppenführer Berger, his recently appointed deputy in Bavaria, had cautioned the Chief of Staff of Himmler's Field HQ against some unspecified plan for action in the south by referring to strong hostility to Himmler in the area; the reply, decrypted on 29 April, had shown that the plan had been cancelled.[149] On 28 April, however, the day after the Allies rejected his peace offer, Himmler had himself sent a message calling on Berger to collect together all the SS forces in the south.[150] Berger's reply, decrypted on 1 May, stated that the disintegration taking place was on a scale reminiscent of 1918, and insisted on the need to concentrate all German forces in the south under one command.[151] It was followed by another message from Himmler, decrypted on 2 May; this pleaded with Berger to 'collect the SS units militarily under your command and head them yourself. Defend the entrance to the Alps for me'.[152]* On 3 May a

---

* Apart from the SS decrypts and others referred to in our text, four in the last weeks of the war referred to concentration camps. The first contained orders of 16 April for the transfer to Dachau at all costs of Jewish prisoners at Flossenberg in Bavaria.[153] The next was the decrypt of a report to Himmler of 1 May about the 'most monstrous statements' about Dachau made to the International Red Cross by SS and Security Service officers in flagrant disobedience of orders.[154] On the same day Frank informed Himmler that the International Red Cross was taking over responsibility for the camp at Theresienstadt because of the 'extraordinary role in world opinion' played by the camp and of the risk of disorders there.[155] That message was signalled to the Commands on 3 May as was the fourth decrypt, in which the Reich Administration in the area commanded by C-in-C North-West had been told on 30 April that Himmler was going to issue special orders about the treatment of concentration camp prisoners.[156] In addition, there were two Police decrypts in April 1945 which showed that Himmler had ordered the inclusion of prisoners at Mauthausen in the general German withdrawal and that some action was contemplated in which Germans as well as foreigners were to be subjected to 'special treatment'.[157]

Apart from a few Police decrypts in the second half of 1944 and early in 1945 about the movement into concentration camps of Jews from France, Hungary and the Baltic States and about the use of camp inmates as forced labour,[158] the above decrypts were the first Sigint references to concentration camps since the cessation in February 1943 of the daily returns referred to in Volume II, p 675. There were no Sigint references to the extermination camps.

149. CX/MSS/SC 1 and 2 of 30 April and 2 May.
150. DEFE 3/571, KO 1698 of 29 April.
151. DEFE 3/573, CX/MSS/C 515 of 1 May.
152. DEFE 3/572, KO 1852 of 2 May.
153. DEFE 3/573, CX/MSS/C 476 of 19 April, sent to the Commands as DEFE 3/568, KO 794 of 19 April.
154. DEFE 3/573, CX/MSS/C 515 of 2 May.
155. DEFE 3/572, KO 1911 of 3 May.
156. DEFE 3/573, CX/MSS/C 519 of 3 May, sent to the Commands as DEFE 3/572, KO 1934 of 3 May.
157. GPD 4068/10, 4085/221.
158. eg GPD 2719/8, 3029/24, 4059/15, 4085/203.

decrypt disclosed that on 1 May Kaltenbrunner had emphasised to Himmler the suitability of the Tyrol as a place for lasting resistance: 'There various interests of Allies or neutrals come into conflict. Conflicts could be made more acute by skilful political game and military energy in Tito manner and German resistance be preserved'.[159]

Messages decrypted on 3 and 4 May gave details of Jaschke's defence measures.[160] But a decrypt of 6 May revealed that he had been dismissed on 2 May and his command split up between a GOC North-West and a GOC North-East.[161] By then, moreover, in a message issued on 2 May and decrypted on 3 May, Winter had reported to Jodl that C-in-C South-West was negotiating an armistice in Italy and that 'the southern front of the Alpine fortress is thus open'.[162]

□

Wolff, the SS General in Italy, had arrived in Switzerland with a plenipotentiary from General von Vietinghoff to arrange further negotiations with the Allies on 23 April, when the defeated German armies in Italy were escaping across the Po.* The negotiations had begun at Caserta on 28 April and the instrument of surrender had been signed on the following day; ceasefire was to be at 1400 on 2 May.[163]

While these exchanges were going on it was learnt from an SS Enigma decrypt of 25 April that Himmler told Wolff on 23 April that it was imperative to hold the front in Italy intact; in an SS message of 26 April, decrypted on 28 April, Himmler was informed by Kaltenbrunner that the situation at the front was critical and that Wolff was suspected of favouring armistice negotiations.[164] These two decrypts were followed by another, on 30 April, of a message to Hitler of 29 April in which Kaltenbrunner gave details of the armistice terms and reported that Kesselring probably favoured capitulation.[165] Another decrypt available on 30 April disclosed that Kesselring had recently been appointed C-in-C South and that the Cs-in-C South-East and South-West has been subordinated to him.[166]

---

* For Wolff's earlier approach to the Allies see above, p 702.

159. DEFE 3/572, KO 1886 of 3 May.
160. ibid, KOs 1951 of 3 May, 1971 of 4 May.
161. ibid, KO 2070 of 6 May.
162. ibid, KO 1914 of 3 May.
163. Ehrman, op cit, Vol VI, p 128; EDS/Appreciation/20, Chapter 4, p 79 et seq.
164. CX/MSS/529 para B 8 of 25 April; DEFE 3/573, CX/MSS/C 499 of 28 April.
165. DEFE 3/573, CX/MSS/C 507 of 30 April.
166. ibid, CX/MSS/C 505 of 30 April.

In the event, Kesselring's attitude remained uncertain until after the cease-fire orders were issued on 1 May. He had been well aware that contact had been made with the Allies and had agreed to his name being used; but he had insisted that he would not make a binding agreement while Hitler lived, and he did not know that plenipotentiaries had been despatched to Allied Headquarters to negotiate. On 29 April, on hearing from the Gauleiter of the Tyrol and Operations Staff B that Army Group C was about to surrender, he decided to replace von Vietinghoff by Schulz from Army Group G and ordered all his subordinates to have no contact with the enemy without his explicit and prior sanction. On 1 May, when the envoys returned from Caserta with the surrender document, they placed Schulz under arrest. But later that day Wolff, von Vietinghoff's Chief of Staff, Schulz, Lemelsen and Herr (the Commanders of Fourteenth and Tenth Armies respectively), von Pohl (the GAF) and Löwisch (the Navy) met in conference and agreed to urge Kesselring to ratify the surrender; and when he could not be reached they issued the cease-fire orders and informed SACMED accordingly. News of Hitler's death was broadcast just before midnight. But fearful of the effect of the surrender on the other Army Groups, and anxious to gain time for as many Germans as possible to surrender to the western Allies, Kesselring at first withheld his consent and ordered the arrest of von Vietinghoff and Wolff. Persuaded at last by Wolff and Schulz to accept the *fait accompli*, he withdrew this order and on 2 May informed Dönitz, Keitel and Winter that a ceasefire had been concluded without his knowledge but that, as the ceasefire orders had been issued to Army Group C, he felt compelled to cover the surrender with his name.[167]

From decrypts of messages issued by Kesselring on 29 April the Allies learned of his initial opposition to the surrender agreement. In one of them, available on 1 May, he notified Seventh Army, Army Group G, Nineteenth Army and First Army that reports of Allied negotiations with Army Group C were aimed at crippling the German will to resist, and insisted that there must be no parleying without his express permission.[168] In another, available on 3 May, he called on Army Group C to continue delaying operations in Italy with the object of assisting the defence of the northern Alpine front and maintaining communications with Czechoslovakia.[169] But apart from the decrypt of Winter's message to Jodl of 3 May, announcing that 'the southern front of the Alpine Fortress is thus open', Sigint provided no further informa-

---

167. Ehrman, op cit, Vol VI, p 128; EDS/Appreciation/20, Chapter 4, p 79 et seq.
168. DEFE 3/572, KO 1794 of 1 May.
169. ibid, KO 1944 of 3 May.

tion. Messages of 3 May disclosing that Dönitz had authorised Kesselring to sign the armistice were decrypted on 4 May.[170]

□

A proclamation of 1 May announcing that Hitler had appointed Dönitz to succeed him in place of Göring, his legal deputy, had been decrypted very early on 2 May.[171] The news did not come as a total surprise to the Allies. On 22 April, when submitting his peace offer via Count Bernadotte, Himmler had represented himself as being in a position to implement an instrument of surrender because Hitler was ill and was unlikely to live for more than a few days. On 26 April Sigint had revealed that Göring had been arrested by the SS. In SS Enigma messages decrypted early that day Göring had notified Himmler on 22 April that he had arrived at Obersalzburg, had advised Himmler on 23 April that he had asked Hitler for instructions, as his deputy, on learning that the Führer could no longer carry on the government of the Reich, and had issued on the morning of 24 April an appeal to Hitler, expressing his loyalty and his bewilderment at being arrested.[172] Later on 26 April the decrypt of a message sent from SS HQ Berchtesgaden to Himmler on the evening of 23 April had confirmed that Göring had been arrested.[173] Although, as we now know, his arrest had been ordered by Hitler, these decrypts had suggested that it might have been made on the initiative of the SS. On 27 April, however, another decrypt had shown otherwise. This had contained a message from Kaltenbrunner to Himmler on the evening of 25 April from which it was clear that, as well as having no prior knowledge of the affair, Himmler had sent Kaltenbrunner to Obersalzburg to find out the facts; Kaltenbrunner reported that he did not know what to do with Göring and was worried that the Allies might make air landings in an attempt to seize him.[174] At the end of April, in the last telegram he sent to Tokyo, the Japanese Ambassador reported that the Foreign Ministry had told him that Göring had been 'retired' by the unanimous decision of the military authorities; this telegram was decrypted on 7 May.

Sigint said no more about Göring's fate before 9 May, when he fell into US hands. As for Himmler's intentions and whereabouts, his fruitless appeals to the SS for the defence of the Alps* were

---

* See above, pp 736–737.

170. DEFE 3/573, CX/MSS/C 523 of 4 May.
171. DEFE 3/572, KO 1847 of 2 May.
172. CX/MSS/SC 1 of 30 April; DEFE 3/573, CX/MSS/C 489, 490, both of 26 April.
173. CX/MSS/SC 1 of 30 April; DEFE 3/573, CX/MSS/C 491 of 26 April.
174. CX/MSS/SC 1 of 30 April; DEFE 3/573, CX/MSS/C 494 of 27 April.

followed by a message of 2 May, decrypted on 5 May, in which he informed Kesselring and Rendulic (C-in-C Army Group South) that he was in the north with Dönitz, to whom he had submitted himself 'faithfully and loyally'.[175]

Other messages issued on 5 May, and decrypted the same day, registered the end of German resistance in the west. One of them authorised C-in-C North-West to surrender.[176] Another contained OKM's order that action against the British and American forces should cease forthwith.[177] The first German delegates arrived at SHAEF HQ the same day and an instrument of surrender was signed on 7 May.

□

Together with the surrender of Trieste to 2nd New Zealand Division of Eighth Army, also on 2 May, the surrender in Italy completed the exposure of the western flank of Army Group E in Yugoslavia. This had been threatened since Tito's forces, after clearing the Germans from the coast and the islands in the northern Adriatic with British naval and artillery support, had reached the outskirts of Fiume on 20 April. Crossing from Cherso island into Istria on 23 April, they had surrounded Fiume and continued their advance to Trieste, thus precipitating the Allied decision to despatch the New Zealand Division to establish military government in Venezia Giulia, including those parts of it that were already occupied by the Partisans.[178]

On 23 April the German force holding Trieste, Fiume and the Istrian peninsula – XCVII Corps with 188th Mountain and 237th Infantry Divisions and other miscellaneous formations – had reported that Fiume was threatened with encirclement and requested that its orders to hold the position should be reconsidered. C-in-C South-East had refused; he hoped to relieve the Corps with forces from Pola and the Ljubljana area and thus gain time to extricate the divisions of Army Group E from Yugoslavia to positions on the Austro–Hungarian border and make contact with the southern flank of Army Group South.[179] These forces comprised five field divisions (7th SS Mountain, 22nd, 41st and 181st Infantry and 104th Jäger) and six others (1st and 2nd Cossack, 11th GAF Field and three Croat divisions).[180] By 22 April

---

175. DEFE 3/573, CX/MSS/C 524 of 5 May.
176. DEFE 3/572, KO 2027 of 5 May.
177. ibid, KO 2028 of 5 May.
178. Ehrman, op cit, Vol VI, pp 129–131; CAB 101/228, p 94.
179. EDS/Appreciation/20, Chapter 4, pp 93, 94.
180. WO 208/4318 of 29 April.

they had already pulled back on their eastern flank to the line running from Novska to Barcs from which the C-in-C had been ordered not to withdraw further without Hitler's permission.* In a message of 22 April, however, which was decrypted on 27 April, he had reported that he would not be able to hold the line (the *Gishelher* position) for long; it was already threatened by Yugoslav forces, which had pushed across the Danube and the Drava in the middle of the month, and in view of the situation at Fiume and the fact that he was unable to form a firm front in the south, where he was protected only by a series of strongpoints, he feared that he would soon have to apply for freedom of action to withdraw to Zvonomir.[181]

By 30 April he was making a fighting retreat in good order to Zvonomir, but he had been unable to extricate reinforcements for Fiume from the south and XCVII Corps's position had collapsed. Messages of 28 April reporting that it could no longer hold out at Fiume were decrypted on 30 April and 1 May.[182] An order of 28 April from C-in-C South-East to XCVII Corps, Sea Defence Commandant Istria and the Naval Chief Command South was decrypted on 2 May; on the receipt of a code-word they were to try to fight their way out, evacuating war material, particularly artillery, but otherwise destroying their weapons and fighting equipment as well as harbour installations.[183] The order went into effect on 1 May. But the German forces were by then hemmed in by 13 Yugoslav divisions and they surrendered to the Yugoslavs on 7 May.[184]

After bowing to the inevitable and accepting the surrender in Italy on 2 May, Kesselring suggested to Dönitz that similar armistice terms for C-in-C South-East should be sought from the western Allies, and the C-in-C South-East, fearing that rapid British and Yugoslav advances would leave the bulk of his forces cut off in Yugoslav territory at the mercy of the Partisans, made the same request. Their pleas were rejected on 4 May, when Dönitz insisted that the Army Groups in the east represented the last bulwark against Bolshevism and must fight on to ensure that as many Germans as possible were saved from slavery.[185] This was reflected in a message decrypted on 5 May in which Army Group Centre, Army Group South and Army Group E were told that

---

* See above, p 662.

181. DEFE 3/571, KO 1540 of 27 April.
182. DEFE 3/572, KOs 1768 of 30 April, 1833 of 1 May.
183. ibid, KO 1852 of 2 May.
184. EDS/Appreciation/20, Chapter 4, p 95.
185. ibid, pp 11, 12, 87–88, 95–97.

their task was to secure the junction of their fronts in such a way as to save as large an area as possible from Bolshevism.[186] Other exhortations for the continuation of the war against Bolshevism appearing in decrypts of 5 May were an order from AOC Luftflotte 4 that the fight against 'the Bolshevik chaos and utter destruction' must continue,[187] and a declaration from Keitel to the Wehrmacht to the effect that continued fighting presented 'the only possibility of saving millions of German soldiers from certain destruction by Bolshevist despotism'.[188] In another directive of 5 May, decrypted on 7 May, Keitel ordered formations in contact with the forces of the western Allies to lay down their arms; 'the battle against the Western Powers has lost its meaning, but the struggle against the East continues'.[189] On 6 May, however, C-in-C South-East was advised by Kesselring that his forces must lay down their arms where they stood on 9 May in accordance with the terms for Germany's unconditional surrender; he was by then moving back from the Zvonomir position into Carinthia, but one-third of Army Group E was still in Yugoslavia with no hope of crossing into Austria before the deadline.[190] Besides many disclosing the desperate situation in the Fiume area, the last decrypts referring to Yugoslavia included a situation report of 4 May from the C-in-C, decrypted on 6 May, which spoke of increasing pressure from strong forces on the other fighting fronts and a request from OKW to General Winter on 5 May, also decrypted on 6 May, for a report on the extent to which Army Group Ostmark (the new name for Army Group South) could assist C-in-C South-East to fight his way back to the line Klagenfurt–Radkersburg.[191]

□

Resistance to the Russians was in fact virtually confined after 2 May to Army Group Centre's front between Dresden and Brno. To the north of Berlin the Russians had captured Königsberg on 9 April and Pillau on 25 April. German resistance east of Danzig had then collapsed. In a message of 27 April, decrypted on 2 May, Army East Prussia (the former Army Group North) had announced that its forces were helplessly exposed to air attack and could no longer resist the Russian advance to Danzig;[192] and in

---

186. CX/MSS/T540/1.
187. CX/MSS/T539/20.
188. CX/MSS/T539/19.
189. DEFE 3/572, KO 2083 of 7 May.
190. EDS/Appreciation/20, pp 97–98.
191. DEFE 3/572, KOs 2031, 2037 of 6 May.
192. ibid, KO 1881 of 2 May.

messages of 3 and 5 May, decrypted on 4 and 6 May, it had reported that they had been evacuated to Bornholm with special instructions as to how to behave to the western Allies.[193]* West of Danzig the Russian offensive across the Oder from south-west of Stettin, begun on 20 April, had at first been contained by Third Panzer Army. But in a message of 27 April, decrypted on 30 April, Army Group Vistula had reported that Third Panzer Army's fighting morale had collapsed.[196] On 2 May decrypts were available of messages ordering demolition in all ports west of Swinemünde; they prescribed different measures according to whether a port was threatened by Soviet or British forces.[197] On the same day the Russian advance met British troops at Wismar on the Baltic. On Army Group South's front the Soviet advance to Vienna, ordered on 1 April, had meanwhile made rapid progress. By 8 April Sigint had shown that the city was all but surrounded.[198] It had fallen on 13 April, and within 48 hours the Russians were threatening the defences which Army Group South was hastily preparing on a line from Maribor and Graz to Brno.[199]

On 15 April the Russians had switched their main effort in the south to the front north of Brno, which was held with some sixty divisions by Army Group Centre. The Russian offensive towards Moravska Ostrava, begun on 15 April, had met heavy resistance – Moravska Ostrava did not fall until 30 April – but in a separate offensive beginning on 24 April Soviet forces had taken Brno on 26 April. On 24 April they had informed General Eisenhower of their intention to clean out the Germans not only up to the east bank of the Elbe but also from the valley of the Vltava (Moldau) river, thus indicating that they planned to take Prague. On 30 April, resisting British pressure for an advance to Prague, he had

---

* Among a large volume of decrypts from this sector a naval message of 25 April, decrypted on 3 May, disclosed that 130,000 wounded and 137,000 refugees had been evacuated from the Danzig Bay pockets since the beginning of the month.[194] The main units of the German Fleet had not taken part in the operations. The *Scheer* had been sunk by air attack on 10 April in Kiel, where the *Hipper* had been damaged earlier and the *Emden* beached. The *Köln* had been sunk at Wilhelmshafen. The *Lützow* was partially submerged in Swinemünde after an air attack on 16 April. The *Prinz Eugen*, the *Leipzig* and the *Nürnberg* were laid up in Danish ports. The last message from the Fleet was intercepted on 8 May following Germany's capitulation; it was a plain language message from the *Prinz Eugen* saying 'Long live Germany and the undefeated Navy'.[195]

193. ibid, KOs 1990 of 4 May, 2045 of 6 May.
194. ibid, KO 1918 of 3 May.
195. DEFE 3/568, KO 890 of 20 April; Naval Headlines of 20 April, 9 May.
196. DEFE 3/571, KO 1701 of 30 April.
197. DEFE/572, KO 1870 of 2 May; Naval Headlines of 2 May.
198. WO 208/4318 of 8 April, based on DEFE 3/561, BT 9200 of 2 April and DEFE 3/563, BT 9726 of 7 April.
199. Seaton, op cit, pp 557–558; Erickson, op cit, pp 549–552.

replied that his armies would halt on a line some sixty miles west of the city.[200]

By the end of April Sigint had disclosed that, having detected that the Russians had moved their only two mobile armies in the south to the Brno area, the Germans expected an early advance on Prague.[201] It had also disclosed that they were taking all possible steps to resist it. On 26 April, in a message decrypted the following day, Hitler had entrusted C-in-C Army Group Centre, General Schörner, with full powers in the Protectorate and instructed him to ensure that in the event of internal unrest he had sufficient forces to suppress a rising and protect the industrial base that was crucial for the future conduct of operations.[202]* Between 26 and 29 April decrypts were available of messages ordering the transfer of divisions to Army Group Centre from Army Group South's front west of Vienna;[204] and on 29 April, in a message decrypted on 1 May, Operations Staff B announced that these transfers were to have unlimited priority over all other transport even though this would delay the last possibilities of sending food from the Protectorate to the 'Alpine fortress'.[205]

On 3 May, as well as confirming that Moravska Ostrava had fallen,[206] the decrypts carried Schörner's appreciation of the situation on 2 May. He foresaw that as the powers of resistance of his formations were declining, the Russians would cut off his salient at Moravska Ostrava and force him back to the Brno–Olomouc–Freudenthal road, and he conceded that this loss of territory would reduce the economic base that was required for the continuation of the war. But he still had strong defence forces of highly seasoned troops and was confident that, provided deliveries of fuel and ammunition were assured, he could hold Bohemia and Moravia.[207] On 4 May, in a message decrypted the

---

* A decrypt of 30 April revealed that Operations Staff B had confirmed Schörner's powers on 27 April following complaints of resistance to them by Frank, the 'Reich Protector', and the SS authorities. It emerged from subsequent decrypts that Frank continued to intrigue in the hope of being granted complete freedom of action in Bohemia and Moravia, with a view to seeking a separate peace with the western Allies and stirring up distrust between them and Russia.[203]

200. Ehrman, op cit, Vol VI, pp 157–161; Erickson, op cit, pp 622–625.
201. WO 208/4318 of 29 April.
202. DEFE 3/571, KO 1559 of 27 April.
203. ibid, KO 1716 of 30 April; DEFE 3/573, CX/MSS/C 501, 505, 514, 518, 521.
204. DEFE 3/570, KO 1432 of 26 April; DEFE 3/571, KOs 1647 of 29 April, 1711 of 30 April; DEFE 3/572, KOs 1757 of 30 April, 1815 of 1 May; DEFE 3/572, KO 1880 of 2 May.
205. DEFE 3/572, KO 1814 of 1 May.
206. ibid, KOs 1925 and 1949 of 3 May.
207. ibid, KO 1902 of 3 May.

same day, he reported that his First Panzer Army was withdrawing to the Brno–Olomouc line.[208]

The American armies were then near Linz and Pilsen, within sight of the line sixty miles west of Prague where General Eisenhower had agreed on 30 April that they would halt. On 4 May he advised the Russians, whose forces were still over 100 miles from the city, that if the situation so required he was ready to advance to the western banks of the Elbe and the Vltava 'in conjunction with the Soviet move to clear the east banks'. The Soviet authorities declined the suggestion, explaining that their announcement of 24 April had meant that they intended to clear both banks of the Vltava and requesting that, as they had already re-grouped their forces accordingly, he should not move his forces east of the line Budejovic–Pilsen–Karlsbad. Eisenhower accepted this request, issuing the necessary orders on 6 May.[209]

The Russians had been planning to complete the encirclement of Army Group Centre's forces east of Prague by delivering two powerful offensives on its flanks from 7 May, one from north-west of Dresden by First Ukrainian Front, the other by Second Ukrainian Front from south of Brno. On 4 May, however, their plans were upset by the Prague uprising, a popular demonstration prompted by the news that American troops had entered Bohemia. As a result of this development they brought forward the start of their offensives to 6 May and re-cast their operations; First Ukrainian Front would now advance along the west banks of the Elbe and the Vltava and encircle Prague from the west and the south-west while Second Ukrainian Front, strengthened by an additional army, drove against Pilsen.[210] The Prague uprising had also surprised the Czech resistance organisation which was deferring action pending the receipt by air of arms from the west. On 5 May, however, it decided to take control of the rising, and on 8 May, the day after the German government signed the unconditional surrender terms, its National Council was able to announce that it had negotiated the unconditional surrender of the German forces in the city.[211] High-grade decrypts available during the rising had included orders from Schörner of 5 May to the effect that 'the incipient disturbances' were to be put down with 'most brutal violence' and SS reports on the evening of 6 May to the effect that ruthless repression was bringing about the

---

208. ibid, KO 1997 of 4 May.
209. Ehrman, op cit, Vol VI, pp 157–161.
210. Erickson, op cit, pp 617, 632, 638.
211. ibid, pp 634–636.

restoration of law and order.[212]*

Schörner issued a further message to his troops on 7 May. It denied that peace terms involving capitulation to the Soviet forces were being accepted; 'there will never be a question of capitulation to the Bolsheviks. . . . The unconquered troops of Army Group Centre will fight on bravely and steadfastly. . . .'[214] This was decrypted on 8 May after Germany had signed the unconditional surrender terms. On the same day the western Allies intercepted a plain language message from Kesselring ordering Army Group Centre and Army Group South to offer no resistance to the American troops advancing into the Protectorate and further south.[215] Late in the evening of 8 May, having received no reply to his ultimatum from General Schörner, Marshal Koniev ordered his armies to resume operations; in the early hours of 9 May his tanks reached Prague, where they were joined by the leading elements of Second Ukrainian Front's advance at about noon.[216] Moving forwards, the Russians joined forces with the Americans on the agreed line, east of Chemnitz and north-east of Pilsen, on 11 May. They claimed that Schörner had violated the peace terms by trying to withdraw to the westward, but as MI 14 noted on 13 May, there was no evidence from Sigint that he had issued any orders for the continuation of operations after the armistice terms had come into effect.[217]

---

* The SS reports added that units under the Russian General Vlasov were attacking Waffen SS troops on their way into Prague. Vlasov's anti-Soviet movement, formed in November 1944, had deployed a division (the 1st Division, known as 600th Infantry Division by the Germans) on the Oder, where it had suffered heavy casualties in April. Decrypts available at the end of that month had disclosed that the Germans intended to send it to Moravska Ostrava, but also that they were preparing to disarm it in the event of trouble. The division had in fact moved to the Prague area to join up with a second Vlasov division that was arriving from Austria and southern Germany. At the news of the uprising it turned on the SS troops; but on 8 May, when it realised that the western Allies were not advancing beyond Pilsen, it rejoined the Germans. Vlasov's second division had meanwhile moved west and surrendered to the American forces.[213]

212. DEFE 3/572, KOs 2064 of 6 May, 2071 of 7 May.
213. DEFE 3/568, KO 988 of 21 April; DEFE 3/570, KO 1500 of 27 April; DEFE 3/572, KOs 1777 of 30 April, 2073 of 7 May.
214. DEFE 3/572, KO 2083 of 8 May.
215. CX/MSS/T543/8.
216. Erickson, op cit, pp 638–640.
217. WO 208/4318 of 13 May.

APPENDICES

APPENDIX 1

The Intelligence Branch at COSSAC and SHAEF

COSSAC originally intended that his staff, which was to be developed into an executive HQ of the Supreme Commander of the Allied Expeditionary Force (SHAEF) while also acting as the planning staff for the cross-Channel invasion, should be a compact co-ordinating body. It would delegate as much as possible to its subordinate commands as and when they were formed, and would obtain from them and from existing intelligence bodies in the UK the intelligence appreciations it needed.[1] The head of his intelligence branch, the British Major-General Whitefoord, was determined to avoid the duplication that would result if it undertook the collection and appreciation of intelligence for itself. He also feared that delays would result if, later on, the HQ of the Supreme Allied Commander was responsible for appreciating intelligence and disseminating it to his subordinate commanders. Whitefoord had personally experienced those difficulties while with the British Expeditionary Force in France in 1940, and he felt that while they might have been unavoidable in the case of an overseas HQ like AFHQ in the Mediterranean, they should be avoided by an HQ that was based in the United Kingdom during the planning stages and in close touch with it thereafter.

In the spring of 1943, when it was suggested that the Combined Intelligence Section (CIS) should be transferred to COSSAC, the British Chiefs of Staff upheld Whitefoord's view. At the end of May, with the agreement of the US Joint Chiefs of Staff, they laid it down that COSSAC's staff should 'collect from the three Services and other Government Departments and Agencies the type of information required for the planning of the invasion and prepare the intelligence data in a form suitable for operational planning', while for general appreciations it would normally call on those prepared by the JIC for the Chiefs of Staff.[2] In July 1943

---

1. CAB 106/969, *History of COSSAC*, pp 6, 10–11; Harrison, *Cross-Channel Attack*, (Washington 1951), pp 49–51.
2. Mockler-Ferryman, *Military Intelligence Organisation*, p 134; CAB 121/380, SIC File D/France/6/6, COS(43)63rd(o) Meeting of 1 April, 111th and 112th (o) Meetings of 25 and 26 May; JIC(43)181(o) of 21 April, JIC(43)217 of 20 May.

the CIS accordingly became part of 21st Army Group when that evolved out of GHQ Home Forces.[3]

In September 1943 the CIS was nevertheless detached from 21st Army Group and, re-named the Theatre Intelligence Section (TIS), placed under COSSAC. This transfer was made for reasons of administrative convenience and it long remained nominal; although calling itself TIS SHAEF from January 1944, the Theatre Intelligence Section was not amalgamated into SHAEF's intelligence division until May of that year.[4] COSSAC acquired three further organisations. In September 1943 a Theatre Documents Section (TDS), with staff trained by MIRS,* was formed for the purpose of collecting and making immediate operational appreciations from documents captured in the field.[5] In December the Army Photographic Interpretation Section (APIS) previously attached to GHQ Home Forces was transferred to TIS COSSAC.[6] Towards the end of 1943, when responsibility for co-ordinating all raids and reconnaissance ventures carried out in north-west Europe was transferred from Combined Operations HQ to COSSAC, some of the intelligence staff of Combined Operations HQ was merged with COSSAC's intelligence branch.[7] Like the TIS, however, this staff was primarily engaged in collating, assessing and disseminating to Commands intelligence on topography and defences which it received from other agencies. The principle that COSSAC should neither procure intelligence for itself nor attempt to appreciate operational intelligence was to this extent breached even before his staff evolved into a full executive HQ for SHAEF. The principle was nevertheless reaffirmed at the end of 1943, when the British and US authorities also agreed, with particular reference to Ultra, that it should continue to apply when operations began. In order 'to prevent delays detrimental to the conduct of operations which would result from any attempt to canalise information through Supreme HQ', the Supreme Allied Commander would receive intelligence direct from London and Washington, as would the major HQs in the field, and the main task of his intelligence staff would be to digest that intelligence, together with the field intelligence sent in by the subordinate HQs, for his benefit. It

---

* For the formation of the Military Intelligence Research Section in 1943 see Volume 3 Part 1, p 471 and above, p 28.

3. Mockler-Ferryman, op cit, p 146.
4. Pogue, *The Supreme Command*, (Washington 1954), p 72.
5. Mockler-Ferryman, op cit, pp 67, 70, 134, 137.
6. AIR 41/7, *Photographic Reconnaissance*, Vol II, p 142.
7. Harrison, op cit, p 52; CAB 106/969, pp 33–34. CAB 106/3, *History of the Combined Operations Organisation 1940–45*, pp 71–72, 74.

would not itself procure field intelligence or duplicate the work of the other intelligence agencies by attempting appreciations of the intelligence it received.[8]

In spite of this decision and in spite of the fact that the detailed force-planning of Operation *Overlord* had been delegated to the Army, Navy and Air Commanders of the Allied Expeditionary Force, the Supreme Commander's intelligence staff steadily grew in size from the end of 1943, as American officers from the US and British and American officers from AFHQ took up their allotted posts. Having previously consisted of some 35 officers (20 British and 15 American), by May 1944 it numbered 160, including some 50 in the TIS. By April 1945 the number had increased to 209. In this process the intention that it should be limited in its functions was gradually set aside. As G2 SHAEF, under the British Major-General Whiteley from AFHQ, it developed from January 1944 alongside the Whitehall machinery into 'a rival intelligence system',[9] supplying the Supreme Allied Commander with appreciations of current intelligence, and with notes and studies bearing on future operations, and preparing for the procurement of intelligence on its own account once operations had begun. The extent of the resulting duplication may be seen in the fact that by March 1944 the SHAEF Intelligence Branch was producing operational memoranda and directives on such varied subjects as the procedure for co-ordination and control and for the provision of intelligence from air reconnaissance (including PR), on POW interrogation,* on how to write intelligence summaries, how to deal with captured documents and how to handle technical intelligence.[11]

The natural consequence of these developments was the creation of a joint intelligence staff at SHAEF (later to be called the Combined Intelligence Staff) in February 1944, and of a JIC SHAEF in July. In February the JIC London accepted SHAEF's claim that there would be no clash with the JIC's own organisation because the new staff's work would be largely tactical.[12] But by

---

* In dealing with enemy POW SHAEF had no responsibility other than to co-ordinate policy, brief interrogation agencies in the field on SHAEF requirements and disseminate information obtained from this source.[10]

8. Mockler-Ferryman, op cit, pp 125, 134; CAB 121/380, JIC(43)403 of 28 September, COS(W)947 of 12 November, FACS 3 of 3 February 1944 for the final Joint Directive.

9. Webster and Frankland, *The Strategic Air Offensive against Germany*, Vol III (1961), p 303.

10. Mockler-Ferryman, op cit, pp 137, 147.

11. See directives and memoranda in CAB 121/380, 25 March–22 May 1944.

12. JIC(44)8th(o) Meeting, 22 February.

April the SHAEF staff was trespassing on the JIC's preserves in a wide-ranging assessment of how the battle after *Overlord* might develop.[13]* The plan for a JIC SHAEF was put to General Bedell Smith, Eisenhower's Chief of Staff, on 30 June by the new ACOS G2 SHAEF, the British Major-General Kenneth Strong, also from AFHQ, who was appointed only a fortnight before D-day. Bedell Smith approved it with some reluctance on 4 July: 'I have approved the attached directive to "the JIC SHAEF" because you want it and because you know your business better than I. However my personal feeling is that it is unnecessary and even a mistake to set up in our HQ a JIC when this body should be a section of your Staff Division. In other words it tends towards a recognition of the principle of "Command by Committee", a system which the SHAEF Command is trying, with some success, to get away from'.[14] But General Strong had made some attempt to avoid duplication and conflict with the JIC organisation in Whitehall by accepting the latter's invitation for a SHAEF representative to attend meetings of the JIC's own Joint Intelligence Staff when papers affecting SHAEF were being discussed.[15]

---

* See above, p 377.

13. JIC(44)19th and 21st(o) Meetings, 2 and 16 May.
14. WO 219/1667, Box A 141. See also Mockler-Ferryman, op cit, p 43; Pogue, op cit, p 72.
15. JIC(44)23rd Meeting, 30 May, 24th (o) Meeting, 6 June.

APPENDIX 2

The Martian Reports

The lay-out of the Martian reports, which remained unchanged for over two years from the spring of 1942, was as follows:

PART I – STRATEGIC SURVEY

PART II – ENEMY FORCES

This incorporated CIS's own work on German fixed defences (batteries, strongpoints, observation posts, wire, minefields, AA guns, searchlights, mobile gun positions) and related it to intelligence about the German Army's order of battle and chain of command which CIS obtained from MI 14.

PARTS III AND IV – TOPOGRAPHY AND MAPS

Since topography did not call for a weekly summary, these confined themselves to reporting on such important enemy developments as inundations in France and the Low Countries and to keeping recipients informed of the progress being made with the production of GSGS's special map series of France. CIS issued separate reports on the topographic information required. for planning purposes and battle briefing.

PART V – TRANSPORT AND INDUSTRY

This concentrated on such information about transport and communications as might affect the crucial battle for the bridge-head, but also included information about the ports, communications, fuel, power, water, food and industry that would supply the Allied armies after they had broken out of the bridgehead.

PART VI – POLICE AND CIVILIANS

This covered the French administrative and political structure and its relations with the German occupying authorities. It included information on a great variety of subjects, from the personalities of politicians to the addresses of local sewage authorities, that Allied military commanders might need for their dealings with the

753

French authorities. (Of his account of the civil and military situation in France the official historian noted that although it 'has been clarified here and there in the light of after-knowledge, most of its important features and a great many additional details were known to the Allied commanders when *Overlord* was being planned).[1]

PARTS VII AND VIII – AIR AND NAVAL

These gave the latest information, as obtained from the Admiralty and the Air Ministry, about such enemy dispositions and activities as might affect the Allied crossing and the initial battle.

Each Martian report was illustrated by air photographs, by reproductions of documents taken from POW and of plans of coastal defence work supplied by agents, and by maps and diagrams; and each contained several annexures. To take an example, the report of 18 November 1942[2] contained:

Annexure   I   German Railway Artillery
             II   German Navigational Beam Installations
           III Notes on Defences near Zeebrugge
           IV The French Trades Union Movement
           V   SS General (name withheld)
           VI Divisional Emblems in the German Army

By the middle of 1942 the variety and scale of the German coastal defences increased so fast that CIS had to devise new methods for presenting the latest state of information about them in a form that permitted easy updating and rapid dissemination in additional consolidated reports. The old system of recording the intelligence on ordinary charts was replaced by one using gridded charts overlaid by traces on which, with different symbols representing each element (heavy, medium and light coast batteries, railway guns, AA guns, radar stations, searchlights), the defences were plotted. At the same time, the strength of the defences on each stretch of coast was calculated by a battery calibre–miles formula, which multiplied the number of guns by the calibre in inches and divided it by the length of the coast, and represented it on a trace in different colours according to the ratio revealed. On yet another trace the relative suitability of the beaches and beach exits in each sector was recorded, to meet any demand for the latest information. These traces were photostated and distributed, for use with the gridded charts, together with a textual report listing for each known battery its position, the

---

1. Ellis, *Victory in the West*, Vol 1, (1962), p 45.
2. WO 219/1934, Martian Report No 25 of 18 November 1942.

number and calibre of its guns and such other details as its arc of fire, its rate of fire and the nature of its emplacement.

From the spring of 1943, in addition to the work of evaluating and updating this intelligence, CIS was involved in preparing for its dissemination in final form to the forces that would take part in the invasion. Plans had to be made for printing all that was known about the defences and other military installations on novel 'chart-maps',* which now replaced the gridded charts, before they were distributed; they would be used by all forces engaged, down to the inshore craft and the craft giving close-range fire-support. The Inter-Service Information Series topographic handbooks for the *Overlord* area had to be prepared. For earlier operations these handbooks, which contained all essential information about beaches, ports, terrain, local resources, hygiene, meteorology and related subjects, had been produced by the ISTD; partly, no doubt, for reasons of security those produced for *Overlord* forces were drawn up by the CIS from the voluminous material provided by ISTD. CIS also supplied details for inclusion in the new map series (1:50,000 and 1:12,000) that GSGS was producing for *Overlord*. Existing maps were based on an out-dated and partly inaccurate French survey. PR provided most of the data for the new series but the CIS was responsible for checking details.

---

* NID took the initiative in urging the need for these in 1941, the object being to produce a standardised inter-Service base for plotting enemy defences which combined the features found on normal charts with the map details required by forces fighting over beaches and up to 10 miles inland. Chart-maps (scale 1:50,000) were available for the area from the Scheldt to Brest by May 1944.[3]

3. ADM 223/287, Gonin report on *Overlord*, p 5.

APPENDIX 3

MI 14 Appreciations on the German Order of Battle October 1942

(i) MI 14b/3/251 of 2 October 1942

The formation of Armoured Divisions in France

1. Since the departure of 25 Panzer Division for the Eastern Front in late May 1942, the Germans have temporarily stopped forming new armoured divisions in France, and have been using the French tank-training areas for the very similar purpose of refitting armoured divisions that had suffered heavily in Russia. Thus, until recently, the three main tank-training areas of France were occupied by divisions in need of refit, as under:

Area	Formation	Date arrived	Date left
MAILLY	10 Pz Div	Late April 42	Mid June 42
COETQUIDAM	6 Pz Div	Mid July 42	–
NIORT–PARTHENAY	7 Pz Div	Late May 42	Mid August 42

It will be seen, therefore, that two of the French tank-training areas are empty owing to the departure of the formations previously occupying them, though the moves were only local. The departure of 7 Pz Div from the NIORT–PARTHENAY area is of such recent date, that there has hardly been time for us to hear of its having a successor; the MAILLY area, on the other hand, has now been empty for a long time, and we have not heard of any formation taking the place vacated by 10 Panzer Division, except that the bulk of 337 Infantry Division moved into the area in mid July, and, for lack of satisfactory information, must still be considered as being there. It is most improbable, however, that the Germans would allow the presence of an infantry division to interfere with the formation or refit of an armoured division, so it must be considered that the Germans now have two tank-training areas in France available for the formation or refit of armoured units; it is only reasonable to expect to see both these areas put to their normal use shortly, and, indeed, there are indications that the formation of new armoured divisions in France has already begun.

2. Reports, as inevitable as the truth they were anticipating, that a new armoured division, to be known as 26 Panzer Division was being, or about to be, formed were received as early as late June

1942 (Serials 1, 2, 3)* and were confirmed about a month later (Serials 4, 5). 23 Infantry Division, the division selected for conversion, was reported to be in the YPRES area on 11 September 1942 (Serial 6), though a report from a good source, received at a later date, appears to indicate that it actually arrived towards the end of July, which seems to be very likely, in view of the little time that now remains before the date scheduled for the completion of the conversion (Serial 4).

3. At about the same time, reports began to be received that another armoured division, which it has not yet been possible to connect with 26 Panzer Division, was in process of formation in Western France (Serial 7). These reports have become much more numerous recently, and, although they have made no attempt to identify the new 'division', they have mostly been remarkable for their explicitness and their abundance of circumstantial detail, for which reasons they deserve serious consideration (Serials 8, 9, 10, 11, 12, 13, 14, 15). It is noticeable that all these more recent reports concur in locating the new 'division' in the tank-training area of RENNES–COETQUIDAM, but without entirely breaking the connection with NIORT shown in Serial 7, as will be shown in paragraph 4 below.

4. All reports received appear to agree that the new 'division' is being formed by the normal process of converting an infantry division or of duplicating an armoured division; reports stating, or suggesting, the duplication of 6 Panzer Division are shown at Serials 8, 9, 13, 14, 16 and those concerning the duplication of 7 Panzer Division (hence, probably the connection with NIORT in Serial 7) at Serials 7, 8, 9, 14. The infantry division reported as having been selected for conversion is 17 Infantry Division (Serials 3, 8, 17, 18); this suggestion was no more than was to be expected, since 17 Infantry Division has been in the LOUDEAC area (ie in close proximity to 6 Panzer Division) since it returned from Russia to refit in late June 1942, and indeed that may be the reason why a potentially first class field-force division was sent to that particular area. The fact that it has been accepted as having moved recently to the QUIMPER–LORIENT area, and so become responsible for the defence of a coastal sector (Serials 19, 20) does not exclude the possibility of its conversion, since it is still very close to the tank-training area at COETQUIDAM and the two roles are not incompatible.

5. The possibilities that the new 'division' in the RENNES area is either part of 6 Panzer Division which is NOT in process of duplication, or the nucleus of the new 26 Panzer Division, cannot

---

* See Annexure for serials.

be excluded, and are discussed separately in the two following paragraphs.

6.   *6 Panzer Division*. The evidence of the new emblem (Serials 10, 13) would suggest that 6 Panzer Division has had allotted to it a tank regiment that has been formed, or refitted, independently in Germany, and there is ample evidence to suggest that a tank regiment has at least started to arrive in Brittany, but the fact that tanks have been reported bearing the normal divisional emblem makes this easy prima facie explanation of the new emblem appear unacceptable. Furthermore, nearly all reports, especially those shown at Serials 8–15, have identified this new 'division' *in addition* to 6 Panzer Division (the independent reference to 6 Panzer Division is not always shown in the extract given in the Annexure), so that there is no possibility of a confusion of the two, and two reports, (Serials 10, 11) have actually given the exact location of the Headquarters of the new 'division' in such a way as to prevent any possibility of taking the Headquarters in question for that of 6 Panzer Division; since the simultaneous existence of two Headquarters with different emblems rules out the possibility that 6 Panzer Division is changing its emblem (Serial 13).

7.   *26 Panzer Division*. The only sources that connect the 'division' in Brittany with the new 26 Panzer Division are those shown at Serials 2 and 3; the source shown at Serial 3 cannot be considered reliable as far as events and localities in France are concerned, and that shown at Serial 2 is thought to have been anticipating the event. Furthermore, it appears very unlikely that 26 Panzer Division would be formed in the COETQUIDAM area, which is already occupied, when the other two tank-training areas are apparently empty, as shown in paragraph 1 above, and one, the MAILLY area, has been free of armoured troops at least for nearly four months.

8.   Finally it appears difficult to avoid the conclusion that two armoured divisions are in the process of formation in France, 26 Panzer Division, by the conversion of 23 Infantry Division, which may be expected to appear at either NIORT or MAILLY in due course, and a second division in the COETQUIDAM area. This division cannot be identified yet, (though current German practice would indicate that '27 Panzer Division' might be its eventual title), nor can the process by which its formation is being achieved yet be determined though geographical considerations favour the duplication of 6 Panzer Division, possibly with the help of 301 Tank Regiment (Serial 13), or the conversion of 17 Infantry Division; the conversion of 17 Infantry Division seems, at present to be the most likely alternative.

It should be added that, if the above conclusion is correct, the new 'division' in Brittany, increases the number of German divisions now in the West, except in the case of the conversion of 17 Infantry Division, *but in no way increases the enemy strength*, since, if any of the tanks that are known to have been sent to France from Germany have been allotted to it, the conclusion becomes unavoidable that 6 Panzer Division cannot have reached as advanced a stage as would otherwise appear probable – and has been accepted – from the fact that it has now been in France for five months.

9. A list of relevant reports received is given in the Annexure, to which constant reference is made throughout the foregoing paper.

Annexure

Date	Report	Source
21 Jun 42	26 Pz Div probably forming in France	US MA Berne 21 Jun 42
24 Jun 42	26 Pz Div probably forming at COETQUIDAM	Raphael 7242
7 Aug 42	Indications that a 26 Pz Div is in process of formation in Brittany in same area as 17 Inf Div. This division may be in process of conversion	MEF Intelligence Summary 791
16 Jul 42	23 Inf Div will be transformed into an armoured division on 1 Nov 42	Ilex 7391
1 Aug 42	23 Inf Div will be transformed into 26 Pz Div	Ilex 7850
11 Sep 42	HQ 23 Inf Div YPRES	Ilex 8959
Jun 42	7 Pz Div at NIORT. May be expanding into two divisions. There are two 'motorised divisional staffs' here	Carlyon 2014
25 Jul 42	Elements of 7 Pz Div possibly being formed into new armoured division. 17 Inf Div possibly being converted into an armoured division. 6 Pz Div or division which has emblem: 'Yellow circle' at COETQUIDAM	Raphael 8170
10 Aug 42	7 Pz Div probable that another armoured division will be formed from it Unidentified Pz Div possibly part of 6 Pz Div, possibly new, at COETQUIDAM	Raphael 9060
13 Aug 42	Unguarded Div HQ with emblem – Quai Châteaubriant, RENNES	New on trial 9189
15 Aug 42	Quai Châteaubriant, RENNES. Div HQ well guarded by sentry in black tank troop uniform. The emblem of this division is the yellow circle with round yellow central dot	New on trial 9271
17 Aug 42	At the moment there are units of two divisions at the Camp of COETQUIDAM	
22 Aug 42	6 Pz Div RENNES–COETQUIDAM. In addition other elements of an armoured unit with the emblem – (yellow) are also in this area. It is possible that they belong either to 6 Pz Div, which is changing its emblem, or to a new armoured division in formation by doubling the 6th or through the 301st Panzer Regiment. (New source contradicted this later).	New on trial 8495 Also AX 7747 1 Jul 42

Date	Report	Source
18 Sep 42	RENNES. Armoured division with emblem: 'Yellow circle with yellow point in centre'. Probably a new armoured division being formed from 6 or 7 Pz Div	Raphael 9374
20 Sep 42	Unidentified Pz Div RENNES	BAS Washington 1/1712
14 Sep 42	6 Pz Div to be split to form a new division	BAS Washington 1/1694
7 Aug 42	17 Inf Div probably in course of being motorised	AX 8808
21 Sep 42?	17 Inf Div motorised. Unconfirmed information says it is to be reorganised into an armoured division	JZ/Darek 9330
18 Sep 42	QUIMPER–LORIENT. 17 Inf Div	Raphael 9374
21 Aug 42	HQ Inf Regt and Inf Bn, (17 Inf Div) QUIMPER	Medard 9358

(ii) MI 14b/3/258 of 26 October 1942

The formation of Armoured Divisions in France

1. In our paper M.I.14b/3/251 dated 2 Oct 42, an attempt was made to give a picture of German armour in France in general and of the formation of new armoured divisions in particular. The conclusion reached was that, in addition to the established presence of three armoured divisions (6, 7 and 10 Panzer Divisions) in France for the purpose of a refit that must be considered to be more or less complete, the following divisions were in process of formation:

(a) 26 Panzer Division, by conversion of 23 Infantry Division, in the AMIENS–ACHEUX–DOULLENS area, the armoured element being supplied by duplication of 10 Panzer Division. (The conversion of 23 Infantry Division is an established fact (Serial 1);* the participation of 10 Panzer Division was conjectured from the study of reports).

(b) An unidentified armoured division in the RENNES area, which we tentatively suggested might become 27 Panzer Division, all reports leading to the conclusion that it was probably being formed by conversion of 17 Infantry Division, while the armoured element was being supplied by duplication of 6 and/or 7 Panzer Divisions.

A summary of the reports leading to this conclusion was attached as an annexure to the above paper; none of them are recapitulated here except those which, though necessarily rejected at the time of writing, appear, in the light of information more recently received, to acquire a new significance.

2. At the time of writing our last paper on this subject, 23

---

* See Annexure for serials.

Infantry Division was known to have been withdrawn from Russia, and to have its Headquarters at YPRES (serial 2); we suggested that this location was probably only a temporary one, and that 23 Infantry Division (or 26 Panzer Division) might be expected to move in due course to one of the normal tank training areas, of which that at MAILLY and that in the area NIORT–PARTHENAY had been unoccupied for some time and apparently still are. It should be borne in mind throughout the course of this paper that this move has NOT yet been reported; 23 Infantry Division has been consistently reported as being in the YPRES area, the report of most recent date being shown at Serial 3.

3. In addition to this we have had ample encouragement to maintain the two conclusions shown in para. 1 above, in various reports received since writing our last paper. Those referring to the duplication of 10 Panzer Division are shown at serials 4–10, while the report shown at Serial 11, in addition to providing an obvious connecting link between 26 Panzer Division and the unidentified armoured 'division' in the AMIENS area, indicated that 26 Panzer Division was well on the way to completing its formation, which was borne out by the appointment of a commander, (Serial 12). Reports showing the continuance of an unidentified armoured 'division' at RENNES are shown at serials 13 and 14, the latter having sufficient detail to be worthy of more than usually serious attention, while the report shown at serial 15 actually referred to 27 Panzer Division.

4. There was, in fact, no reason to suppose that the formation of these two new armoured divisions was not proceeding along the lines we had predicted and in the areas in which we had located them until the recent receipt of the report shown at Serial 16, the result of which is to make it very difficult to believe that 23 Infantry Division is still in the YPRES area, since it could hardly come under LE MANS for railway purposes unless it were in the West of France, and the report of a railway movement, shown at Serial 17, seems to bear out the fact that a large part of the division (*without* equipment) may have been moved away from the YPRES area to an unknown destination between 17 and 19 Aug 42, after being relieved by troops from the MONS–CHARLEROI area between 3 and 5 Aug 42. This move, if it were established, would not be in complete contradiction to the report shown at serial 2, since this report only mentions the Headquarters of the division, which may well have moved wholly or in part at a later date, the move not having been reported to us; in fact, divisional Headquarters may not have moved at all, for the reason shown in para. 6(c) below.

5. The report shown at serial 16 is not, as it stands, sufficient to enable us to determine whether 23 Infantry Division has moved to

the North-West of France (i.e. the NIORT–PARTHENAY area), both of which would depend on LE MANS as a railway distributing centre. A long questionnaire arising from the report under discussion has been sent to M.I.6 and an answer has been urgently requested; until it is received the problem is not likely to be solved, but in the meantime it is as well to show what arguments we have in favour of the division's having moved to either area:
(a) COETQUIDAM. The reports shown at Serials 18, 19, 20 and 21 definitely connect 26 Panzer Division with this area. The connection with 17 Infantry Division shown in Serials 19, 20 and 21 cannot be entertained for one moment, but it is possible that this unsound conclusion may have been drawn from sound geographical premises.
(b) NIORT–PARTHENAY. 7 Panzer Division has recently moved to the NANTES–ANGERS area, leaving the tank training area of NIORT–PARTHENAY empty, while that at COET-QUIDAM appears to be rather more than full.

It will be remembered that 6 and 7 Panzer Divisions have *both* been reported as duplicating to form a new armoured division.
6.   It remains to consider what the 'division' being formed by the duplication of 10 Panzer Division in the AMIENS area can be, and the following possibilities suggest themselves:
(a)   29 Panzer Division is being formed (Serial 4). It is not possible to entertain this alternative as our information stands at present, for the Germans have hitherto numbered all their armoured divisions serially from 1 upwards, and the formation of a 29 Panzer Division would necessarily presuppose the formation of a 27 Panzer Division, which, it must be remembered, has by no means yet been established, and of a 28 Panzer Division, which has not yet been reported at all.
(b)   The new 'division' is motorised, and NOT armoured; the report shown at Serial 9 is undecided, while those shown at Serials 22 and 23 definitely state that it is to be motorised.
(c)   10 Panzer Division is being duplicated to form the armoured element of 26 Panzer Division. This possibility cannot yet be excluded, for the move of 23 Infantry Division from YPRES has not yet been specifically reported, and, in any case, past experience shows that the Germans do not think it necessary for a tank regiment to join the division to which it will be allotted until training has reached a very advanced stage.
7.   There is, therefore, no reason yet for departing from our earlier conclusion that, in addition to the three armoured divisions already in France, one more is certainly in process of formation, 26 Panzer Division, in an area yet to be established and possibly one other, 27 Panzer Division, in the area RENNES–COETQUIDAM. The possibility does however now arise that 26

Panzer Division and the second armoured 'division' at COET-
QUIDAM may be one and the same, a possibility which could not
be entertained at the time of writing our earlier paper; if this is so,
it must be presumed that the second 'division' in the AMIENS area
is to be motorised, unless it is established by irrefutable evidence
that two armoured divisions are actually in process of formation in
France. This paper is purposely left inconclusive, its object being
to pave the way for the adoption of either of the above
conclusions, as soon as the evidence permits.

8. As regards the quantity of armour these divisions represent,
an interesting report recently received is shown at Serial 24, which
if true, may be the explanation of the many so far unfulfilled
prophecies we have received that 10 Panzer Division is on the
point of leaving France; there is no confirmation of this report
beyond that shown at Serial 25, which at least indicates that, if 10
Panzer Division reached as advanced a stage of refit as we had
reason to believe two or three months ago, it must have lost many
of its tanks since that date for one reason or another.

9. A summary of relevant reports is given in the Annexure, to
which constant reference is made throughout the foregoing
paper.

Annexure

Date	Report	Source
1 Aug 42	23 Inf Div will be transformed into 26 Pz Div on 1 Nov 42	Ilex 7391 and 7850
11 Sep 42	HQ, 23 Inf Div, YPRES	Ilex 8959
5 Oct 42	23 Inf Div, ENGHIEN–RENAIX area	BAS Washington I/1758
24 Sep 42	10 Pz Div being doubled to form 29 Pz Div	Carlyon 9839
8 Sep 42	Elements of 10 Pz Div forming a new armoured division at AUX(AUXI?)	JX/Darek 9493
8 Sep 42	Unidentified armoured division as ACHEUX	JX/Darek 9520
8 Sep 42	HQ, unidentified armoured division, ACHEUX	Carlyon 9534
18 Sep 42	ACHEUX – HQ unidentified division with emblems 'yellow diagonal stroke'. Probably new armoured division being formed by extension of 10 Pz Div	Raphael 9374
5 Sep 42	AMIENS area. Unidentified armoured or motorised division with emblem: 'Yellow diagonal stroke'	Raphael 9162.
31 Aug 42	Armoured troops with emblem in yellow seen. Either 10 Pz Div with new emblem, or newly formed division. (AMIENS area)	AX 8681
13–18 Jul 42	Four trains transporting tanks passed through VALENCIENNES en route for DOUAI and LILLE	Bosanquet 9937
13 Oct 42	Appointment of Oberst Freiherr von LUTTWITZ as GOC 26 Pz Div with promotion to Major-General	CX/MSS 1521/ T.1
8 Sep 42	Unidentified armoured division at RENNES	JX/Darek 9520
8 Sep 42	11 Tank Regiment, of 6 Pz Div, RENNES, being detached to form a new division with emblem: 'Yellow circle with dot in centre', in Brittany	JX/Darek 9493

Date	Report	Source
29 Sep 42	27 Pz Div on Western Front	New on trial 9358
15 Oct 42	The following divisions are on the Western front and, from point of view of rolling stock, appear to depend on an HQ or service established at LE MANS: 15, 320, 17, 333, 23, 335 and 337	Ilex 77
3 Aug 42	(i) 38 *full* troop trains starting from various places in MONS–CHARLEROI area detrained in the following places: (a) 26 trains in area YPRES–ROULERS; (b) 12 trains (presumably) just over the frontier from YPRES	New 9567 Jethro 9729
17–19 Aug 42	(ii) 27 *empty* trains came to YPRES–GHENT area to *pick up* troops, 14 of them to the same destinations as the 26 trains shown in (i)a above	
7 Jun 42	26 Pz Div probably forming at COETQUIDAM	Raphael 7242
7 Aug 42	Indications that a 26 Pz Div is in process of formation in Brittany, in same area as 17 Inf Div. This Division may be in process of conversion	MEF Intelligence Summary 791
Early Sep 42	17 Inf Div 'Débris' brought to France to be transformed into 26 Pz Div	2e Section, 22 Sep 42
15 Sep 42	17 Inf Div LOUDEAC, possibly being transformed into 26 Pz Div	Etat-Major de Gaulle
29 Sep 42	New division being formed from 10 Pz Div to be motorised rather than armoured	BAS Washington I/1741
19 Aug 42	AMIENS–DOULLENS. Motorised division with emblem: 'Yellow diagonal stroke'	Raphael 9690
26 Sep 42	6, 7, 10, 26 Pz Divs in area of Heeresgruppe von Rundstedt. 35% of their personnel and material has been taken to supplement armoured divisions in Russia and Libya. Transports of men and tanks have left France	Paradox 9660
7 Oct 42	10 Pz Div HQ AMIENS. Receiving daily supply of new tanks from Germany	New on trial 9892

APPENDIX 4

Comparison of MI 14 Estimate of German Order of Battle in France with Actual German Locations September 1942 and February 1943

(i)   On 28 September 1942 MI 14 listed the following formations in France:

Panzer Divisions:	6th, 7th and 10th
SS Divisions:	Adolf Hitler, Das Reich
Infantry Divisions:	15th, 17th, 23rd, 106th, 170th, 246th, 302nd, 304th, 306th, 319th, 320th, 321st, 327th, 332nd, 333rd, 335th, 337th, 708th, 709th, 711th, 712th, 715th, 716th plus two divisions not identified
Training Divisions:	Four

*The actual list was as follows:**

Panzer Divisions:	6th, 7th, 10th
SS Panzer Divisions:	1st (recently converted from Adolf Hitler), 2nd (recently converted from Das Reich)
Infantry Divisions:	The list is identical with that of MI 14 except that it includes 167th and 257th Divisions and does not give 170th and 246th Divisions
Newly created Divisions:	38th, 39th and 65th Infantry Divisions, and 325th Sicherungsdivision
Training Divisions:	Not specified

---

* Compiled from Müller-Hillebrand, *Das Heer 1933–45*, Vol III (1969), p 212.

(ii) *On 21 February 1943 MI 14 produced a table of movements from and to France between September 1942 and mid-February 1943.* Except where otherwise stated in the remarks column MI 14's assessments were correct. Ten of the movements listed by MI 14 were disclosed or confirmed by high-grade Sigint and five were accepted on the basis of information received from the Russian General Staff*

Formation	Left for	Arrived from	Remarks
1st Panzer		Russia (Jan)	
6th Panzer	Russia (Nov)		
7th Panzer	Russia (Dec)		
10th Panzer	Tunisia (Dec)		
27th Panzer	Russia (Jan)		Movement reported by Russian General Staff. In fact 27th Panzer was formed in Russia in September 1942 from elements of 22nd Panzer, newly arrived from the west, and from GHQ troops. (Müller-Hillebrand, op cit, Vol III, p 311)
SS Hermann Göring	Tunisia (Dec)		
SS Leibstandarte Adolf Hitler	Russia (Jan)		
SS Reich	Russia (Jan)		
SS Totenkompf	Russia (Jan)		
17th Infantry	Russia (Dec)		17th Infantry did not arrive in Russia till April 1943 (Müller-Hillebrand, op cit, Vol III, p 286). MI 14 may have received early intelligence of the move
167th Infantry	Russia	Russia	Reported by Russian General Staff
275th Infantry	Russia		
302nd Infantry	Russia (Jan)		
304th Infantry	Russia (Dec)		
306th Infantry	Russia (Nov)		
320th Infantry	Russia (Jan)		
321st Infantry	Russia (Jan)		
326th Infantry		Germany (Nov)	In fact set up in the west December 1942 (Müller-Hillebrand, op cit, Vol III, p 296)
327th Infantry	Russia (Jan)		

* Reproduced from WO 208/4308.

Formation	Left for	Arrived from	Remarks
328th Infantry		Russia (Oct)	According to Müller-Hillebrand (op cit, Vol III, p 296), 328th Infantry arrived in the west Jan 1943. MI 14's information may have been more accurate.
332nd Infantry	About to leave for Russia		332nd Infantry left the west for Russia shortly before March 1943 (Müller-Hillebrand, op cit, Vol III, p 297)
333rd Infantry	Russia (Jan)		
335th Infantry	Russia (Dec)		
344th Infantry		Germany (Nov)	In fact set up in the west autumn 1942 as a static division (Müller-Hillebrand, op cit, Vol III, p 298)
347th Infantry		Germany (Nov)	In fact set up in the autumn of 1942 as a static division and posted to the west Nov 1942. (Müller-Hillebrand, op cit, Vol III, p 298).

APPENDIX 5

MI 14 Report on the Visit of the Japanese Ambassador in Berlin to the German Defences in France*

October 1943

The following has been received from a MOST SECRET source and reports the impressions of a highly placed observer who visited PARIS and the Atlantic Coast from BREST southwards in the last weeks of October. Much of his information was derived from senior German officers.

A.   GERMAN ORDER OF BATTLE AND STRENGTHS

1.   Field Marshal RUNDSTEDT has a dual role. As Commander in Chief of Army Group D he controls the forces in the NETHERLANDS (under Gen. CHRISTIANSEN), the 15th Army (Gen. SALMUTH), the 7th Army (Gen. DOLLMANN), the 1st Army (Gen. BLASKOWITZ) and the 19th Army (Gen. von BODENSTERN). At the same time as Supreme Commander of the Armies in the WEST (Militäroberbefehlshaber WEST) he controls the forces commanded by the Chief of the Military Administration in BELGIUM and FRANCE (respectively Gen. FALKENHAUSEN and Gen. STUELPNAGEL), 3rd Air Fleet (Marshal SPERRLE) and Naval Group West.

2.   Between BREST and NANTES Gen. FAHRMBACHER, G.O.C. (? XXV Corps) is responsible for defences. Gen. GALLEN-CAMP, Commander of LXXX Corps, is responsible for the defence of LA ROCHELLE area.

3.   'Coastal defence' divisions are distributed as follows:

a.   NETHERLANDS Army (covering the NETHERLANDS down to the mouth of the RHINE) – 4 divisions.

b.   15th Army (from mouth of RHINE to WEST of LE HAVRE) – 9 divisions.

c.   7th Army (thence to Southern banks of Loire) – 8 divisions.

d.   1st Army (thence to Spanish frontier) – 4 divisions.

e.   19th Army (French Mediterranean Coast) – 6 divisions.

---

* The Appreciation is reproduced from WO 208/4311.

4. One-third of these divisions have three regiments each and remaining two-thirds two regiments each but these latter are being greatly reinforced up to the strength of three regiments.

5. The 'Coast defence' divisions have a static role but 'mechanised' divisions which constitute the general reserve are shared by other fronts, eg two divisions from the general reserve were recently sent to RUSSIA. The size of this general reserve varies according to circumstances but it is made up at present as follows: six infantry divisions, four panzer divisions, five motorised divisions. In addition three reserve panzer divisions were being sent from Germany, two Air-borne divisions from ITALY and a number of infantry divisions from other fronts. These infantry divisions had, however, suffered heavily and would have to rest and refit on arrival in FRANCE. The 'mechanised' divisions are under the direct control of the Army Group and are distributed along the lines of communication in such a way that they can be rushed anywhere at short notice. The forces under the Chief of Military Administration in BELGIUM and FRANCE are garrison troops and consist respectively of 25 Battalions and 17 Regiments.

5A. Recruit training schools for various branches of the Army forces had been moved from Germany to France. There is a cadre unit which maintains a constant flow of tank troops for twelve independent Tank Battalions (TIGER and PANTHERS). There were also ten depot divisions training recruits sent to France and several Field divisions which are now being formed from these recruits. These were not, however, under RUNDSTEDT's command but are under Gen. FROMM in Germany.

The total number of German forces under 'the supreme Commander of the Armies in the WEST' was 1,400,000. This figure does not include the training units and depot divisions mentioned above.

MI 14 Comments

1. The observer did not visit the whole of the French coast and his O of B information was probably supplied by German Chief of Staff in Paris.

The following is a comparison between the observer's report and our picture at date of visit.

Divisions	Observer		M.I. 14	
	'Mechanised'	15	Offensive	10
	'Coastal'	31	Defensive	28
			Unidentified	2
		46		40
	Depot	10	Depot	5

	Observer	*M.I. 14*
Landeschützen	17 Regts (50–60 Bns) in FRANCE	129 Bns in *all* have been identified. Many
	25 Bns in NE FRANCE and BELGIUM	of these may have left or been disbanded

It is not clear whether (a) offensive divisions in the coastal sectors (b) Res Pz divs similarly employed are included in the term 'mechanised' or 'coastal'. The observer possibly counted a few divisions twice and the Germans would not undeceive him.
2. We believe that 15 out of a total of 40 divs are 3-regts. There is some indication that personnel are being provided to form the third regt.
3. The immediate transfer of two airborne divs from ITALY is unlikely.

B. DEFENCES

6. The Germans attach importance to sectors in the following order:
a. Straits area.
b. Normandy, and Brittany Peninsula.
c. The remainder which are regarded as only secondary fronts. The possibility of invasion across the PYRENEES after an Allied landing on the IBERIAN Peninsula is not altogether ruled out of consideration but no special defences have been constructed for this contingency and mobile forces held in reserve at NAR-BONNE and other strategic points are prepared to hold the passes in the PYRENEES if necessary.
7. The fortified zones surrounding naval bases conform for the most part to established principles of fortification. The important feature of the defence lines is that they are not arranged in one continuous and connected line but are arranged to operate independently down to the smallest unit. In other areas, strong points (Widerstandsneste) have been constructed in large numbers all along the coast, the gaps between these strongpoints being closed by obstacles (mainly land mines). Each strongpoint is equipped with various types of arms and normally has 3-weeks supply of food so that it can conduct an independent defence. Running all the way behind the permanent line of fortifications field works are being constructed as support positions.
8. In the area from the harbour and naval bases (viz BREST, LORIENT, ST NAZAIRE, LA ROCHELLE and BORDEAUX in the area visited by the observer) defence works have been specially

strengthened and fortified zones have been established to meet attack by land, sea or air. Each of these zones is under a fortress commander (Kommandeur der Verteidigungszone) with unified control over all three services.

9. German defences on the French coast are very close to the beach and the German plan is evidently to smash Allied landing operations as far as possible at the water's edge. However, forts surrounding naval bases are protected on the landward side and this applies even to the smallest strongpoints. All forces from Army Group down to detachments charged with the permanent defence of the coastal area are provided with a large mobile reserve force so that even were the Allies to effect a partial landing an attempt could be made to smash them by flanking fire from the strongpoints close at hand and by a sortie of the mobile force. To avoid unnecessary casualties and loss of material by Allied bombardment and bombing, reinforced concrete has been used without stint even for single machine gun emplacements.

10. In view of the extent of the coast and of the inferiority of the GAF it might not be possible to prevent an Allied landing at some point but it would not be easy for an Allied landing force to drive off a counter-attack by a powerful German reserve force which could be assembled quickly. It should therefore be difficult for the Allies, even if they formed a bridgehead for a short period, to form a real second front in France. (The observer realised that the area which he had visited was generally speaking only a secondary front but nevertheless felt confirmed in his opinion by the completeness of the preparations and the fact that the defences were being still further strengthened).

11. Heavy naval guns in use in the areas inspected by the observer range from 36 cms to 17 cms. There are also 15 and 12 cm 8 barrelled mortars; 12, 10.5 and 8 cm AA guns; and A/Tk guns of various calibres. Although the small arms include a large number of captured weapons (FRENCH, BELGIAN, CZECH, RUSSIAN and DUTCH) most of the weapons are of new design. The strongpoints are equipped with weapons of the latest design including automatic hand grenade throwers (with a rate of 120 to the minute) and flame-throwers installed in casemates. Guns are sited so that fire can be concentrated on one object whether at sea or on land.

Note by MI 14
We have no knowledge of an automatic grenade thrower with a rate of 120 r.p.m.

C. GERMAN ARMY MORALE

12. The observer was impressed by the excellent morale of all troops and the strictness of their military discipline. There is a complete solidarity between the fighting men and they are possessed of a loyal sense of responsibility.

D. EFFECT OF AIR RAIDS

13. The observer visited only a limited area but considered he had seen hardly any substantial air-raid damage except to house property, 90 per cent of which had been destroyed at LORIENT and ST NAZAIRE. There has been a certain amount of damage to harbour installations as well as to urban areas at other important ports. The destruction of the locks at ST NAZAIRE in the March raid last year caused only temporary inconvenience and powerful concrete lock gates have now been fitted.

E. ATTITUDE OF THE FRENCH

14. The observer formed the following impressions after conversations with Army and SS leaders. The French have recently been encouraged by events to engage in a more active opposition, stimulated mainly by Communists and British agents. In general, however, the French are still apathetic and, while they are co-operating only reluctantly in the German war effort are unlikely to do much to hamper German military operations in the event of an Allied landing.

F. GENERAL COMMENT BY M.I. 14

Although German senior officers were clearly out to impress the observer his report, while exaggerating factual information, is a reasoned and well considered document.

APPENDIX 6

Sigint Preparations for D-Day

(i) Arrangements made for the Production of Sigint

A programme for expanding the resources available for Sigint had been devised by GC and CS and approved by the Chiefs of Staff and the Foreign Office early in 1943. Implemented as a matter of priority in the next twelve months, it had by the spring of 1944 raised the staff at GC and CS from 3,800 to 5,600* and had greatly increased the number of tactical Sigint units that would be ready to take to the field on D-day by training 5,000 additional people for Army Y units and bringing about a comparable increase in the number of RAF Y staff. At the same time, the number of Army and Air Force intercept sets rose from 264 in August 1942 to 357 in August 1943 and 609 in June 1944. Much of the increase in the Royal Navy's intercept resources, from 200 people manning some 50 sets in 1939 to 5,000 people manning some 350 shore-based sets and several hundred sets at sea in 1945, occurred between the spring of 1943 and D-day.

By the beginning of 1944, for the first time in the war, the resources available for Sigint were temporarily in excess of what was necessary for current purposes. But as well as ensuring that the great increase in traffic that was expected from D-day could be handled without interruption to the coverage of the Italian and the Russian fronts, this enabled the Sigint authorities to carry out essential research on the wireless networks that might appear when D-day arrived and the codes and cyphers they were likely to carry. The German Navy had made daily use of wireless in Home Waters and its normal Enigma keys were regularly broken; but it would undoubtedly resort to additional frequencies and might introduce new keys when France was invaded; indeed, there had been hints in the Enigma decrypts that it intended to resort to a new form of communication – called Kurier by the Germans and Squash by the British† – and also to extend the use of four-wheel

---

* Some of this additional staff was in fact used up in the struggle to keep abreast of the improvements the Germans made from September 1943 to the security of their high-grade cyphers (See Volume III Part I, pp 51–52), so that a further 130 WRNS had to be drafted to GC and CS in the spring of 1944 to ensure that it could handle the expansion of traffic from D-day.

† See Appendix 15 (iv).

keys and issue individual keys (Sonderschlüssel) to U-boats operating in the Channel.* Unlike the Navy, the Air Force and the Army in the west had hitherto made no regular use of wireless; but they had used it in periodic anti-invasion exercises from the time of the Dieppe raid and, particularly in the Army, W/T exercises were now taking place on a larger scale. Only by keeping an exhaustive watch for exercise traffic and other new wireless traffic could GC and CS and the Y units identify its frequencies, call-signs and keys and thus acquire the knowledge which would determine the interception and cryptanalytic priorities to be accorded to the networks when they became operational – and which, before then, would enable the Sigint authorities to estimate the scale on which W/T traffic was likely to be intercepted from D-day, and thus make adequate arrangements for processing it and forwarding the results to the Commands.

Against the networks of the GAF, whose signals procedures were well known and whose general key (Red) had been read daily since 1940, the research produced results with little delay. The function of new frequencies was identified as they appeared and, more than that, new Enigma keys were now broken. Before the beginning of 1944 only one key in use in the west apart from the Red had been broken for more than the occasional day – that of Luftgau Western France (Snowdrop). But GC and CS broke the key of Luftflotte 3, the GAF Command in the west, (Jaguar) in February, the general practice key (Blue) in March and the key of the chief fighter authority under Luftflotte 3 (Jagdkorps II; Cricket) in April. Wasp, the key of Fliegerkorps IX which had returned to be Luftflotte 3's bomber arm by April, had been read since January 1942. In February, moreover, Fliegerkorps II, whose key (Locust) had long been read in Italy, moved to France, and from April Snowdrop was at last read regularly. None of these keys yet carried much traffic of operational importance, but all except Locust and Wasp were broken almost daily from these dates.

With assistance from the order of battle identifications supplied by agents and the Resistance via the SIS and the SOE, and by the decrypts of medium and low-grade Army signals,† considerable progress was also made against the much more complex communications network of the Army in the west, where each separate Army had a normal key and a staff key and there were keys for C-in-C West, for OKH and for Army supply. Most of the keys and

---

* It was as a result of these threats that as already noted (Volume II, Appendix 19) GC and CS requested the US Navy authorities in July 1942 to increase their manufacture of four-wheel Bombes.

† See below, p 780.

their associated frequencies and call-signs had been identified by the spring of 1944, but the cryptanalytic attack on the keys met with little success. The Army's cypher security and W/T discipline were far stricter than the GAF's, and as it had no general key for use in all theatres, no Army key in use in the west had been broken by the autumn of 1943 if we exclude the SS keys (Quince and Orange) which had yielded valuable intelligence about the SS divisions since 1942.* From the autumn of 1943 GC and CS read a Wehrkreis key (Falcon) intermittently but no other key until March 1944. Practice traffic in C-in-C West's key (Bantam) was then broken during W/T exercises and was read thereafter from time to time. The key of the military occupation authorities in France (Nightjar), which was useful for its reports on sabotage and air raids against German communications and on the German measures to keep communications open, was also broken in March and read regularly from April. It remained uncertain whether GC and CS would be more successful against Army keys from D-day, when the traffic load would increase; and it was not impossible that Enigma intelligence about the Army would be confined to what could be obtained from the GAF keys, particularly the general key, which was already disclosing information about the parachute divisions, and the GAF liaison (Flivo) keys, which were expected to make their appearance and to prove as valuable as they had been in other theatres.

In the event, as we shall see, GC and CS succeeded in breaking several of the most important Army keys within two or three days of the landings, as well as important new Flivo keys. And in the meantime the shortage of Army Enigma decrypts was offset by two other developments. In the first place C-in-C West's Fish link with Berlin (Jellyfish), first intercepted in January 1944, was broken in March, following the entry into service of Colossus Mark I early in 1944.† Its decrypts between March and D-day were not numerous but they included valuable detailed returns for individual divisions in the C-in-C's Command as well as strategic appreciations, the first of which was an appreciation obtained on 6 April.‡ Similar appreciations had previously been decrypted on the Fish link between Berlin and the Commands in Italy (Bream), and this source continued to provide general appreciations and order of battle intelligence.§ In the second place, Army signals

---

* A big effort to break a major Wehrkreis key (Greenshank) during 1943 had failed except on one or two days, nor was it broken again, and then only for one day, until May 1944.

† See Volume III Part I, pp 479–482. In May an attempt was made to break the GAF Fish link between Luftflotte 3 and Berlin (Anchovy), but without success.

‡ See p 53.

§ Another important addition to the high-grade Sigint sources made at this time was the

using low-grade codes and a medium-grade cypher were being intercepted and decrypted in increasing amounts by the expanded Y Service units in England from the end of 1943. The medium-grade cypher had been solved in April 1943. The low-grade codes, which included tank codes, did not appear in any large quantity till the end of that year, but GC and CS then established that components of sixty per cent of them had already been used and solved in the Mediterranean. From the beginning of 1944 they, together with the medium-grade cypher, provided many order of battle identifications below the divisional level.

(ii)   Arrangements made for the Dissemination of Sigint to the Commands

During the early stages of operation *Torch,** and still more so during the raid on Dieppe,† such preparations as had been made to ensure that the operational authorities derived the maxium benefit from Sigint proved inadequate, primarily for two reasons. GC and CS, the producers of high-grade Sigint, and the SCU/SLU organisation, which provided the channels for its distribution, had been given too little notice of Allied plans and few details about them. In relation to low-grade Sigint, too little attention had been paid to the training and the communications of the Y units, and scarcely any to the need to co-ordinate the work of the British and US units. Before the invasion of Sicily and the landings in Italy better provision had been made in each of these directions and still more thorough measures were adopted at an earlier stage in the preparations for the larger and far more hazardous cross-Channel invasion.

As early as May 1943 the Y Board proposed that the Sigint and Y authorities should be represented on COSSAC's planning staff. The proposal was not adopted – it was decided, indeed, that for security reasons COSSAC's HQ should not receive Sigint in undisguised form until much later.[1] But at the end of 1943 COSSAC was authorised to establish a Special Intelligence Board

---

breaking of the cypher used by the Japanese Naval Mission and Naval Attaché in Berlin. As already noted (Volume III Part I, p 244) this cypher was solved at GC and CS early in 1944. To be precise, it was solved in March; and we should add that GC and CS and the US authorities collaborated in solving it.

* See Volume II, Appendix 18.

† See Volume II, Appendix 13.

1.   Mockler-Ferryman, *Military Intelligence Organisation*, p 135.

to be responsible for co-ordinating the *Overlord* plans of the British and US Y units and for holding discussions with the central Sigint and Y authorities. Such discussions, the first comprehensive discussions to take place at a high level between operational and Sigint authorities since the beginning of the war, began with four meetings at GC and CS in January 1944, when COSSAC HQ was being merged into SHAEF. At these meetings DMI COSSAC/ SHAEF, the chairman of the Special Intelligence Board, outlined the *Overlord* plan and the proposed organisation and chain of command of the *Overlord* operational staffs which would receive high-grade Sigint from Bletchley on SCU/SLU links.* Other visitors, who included representatives from the US Army/Air Y organisation, explored the ways in which GC and CS could assist 21st Army Group's Y organisation and the US Army/Air Y Service in exploiting the medium and low-grade communications of the German Army and the Police, and, as we have seen, made arrangements for the deception staffs to receive all relevant Service, Abwehr and Axis diplomatic decrypts.†

The contacts thus established between GC and CS and the intelligence staffs at the *Overlord* HQs, particularly 21st Army Group, continued without a break until *Overlord* was launched; they culminated in May in a visit to GC and CS by a member of 21st Army Group's intelligence staff to display the maps drawn up for the operation and demonstrate the day-to-day objectives set for the invasion forces. They were invaluable to GC and CS, enabling it to ensure that every section understood the ways in which it might contribute, to make appropriate changes in interception and cryptanalytic priorities in the period before D-day and prepare for the still greater changes that would be called for when the assault began, and to estimate and make

---

* GC and CS, which had Americans on its staff, was to service SHAEF and the American Commands, as well as the British and Canadian, in accordance with the agreement with the US War Department which had operated in the Mediterranean theatre. At SHAEF and the British and Canadian Commands the handling and the security of the GC and CS product was the responsibility of the SCU/SLU organisation, but a system had by now been developed by which it was collated with intelligence from other sources. The US Commands followed a different system. US intelligence officers trained at GC and CS were responsible for the security of high-grade Sigint and for interpreting it for the indoctrinated members of the staff, but they handled it in isolation from other intelligence and were themselves kept separate from the remainder of the staff. After the war, the US officers who had been involved concluded that on balance the British had been the better system; one of their arguments was that 'Ultra must never become a neatly packaged replacement for tedious work with other evidence'.[2]

† See p 45 above.

2. US Special Research History, *Synthesis of Experiences in the Use of Ultra Intelligence by US Army Field Commands in the European Theater of Operations*, (SRH–006), p 16 (Declassified 1978).

provision for the weight of signals that might then have to be carried on its direct links to the *Overlord* Commands.*

Three of the links in the new SCU/SLU network – those to SHAEF, 21st Army Group and the HQ of the US Strategic and Tactical Air Forces – were opened on 26 January. By April, as trained staff became available, the network had been extended to the HQs of the Allied Expeditionary Air Forces, 2nd Tactical Air Force, US Eighth Air Force, First US Army and ANCXF.† In May three mobile SCU/SLU stations were established – for Second British Army and its air component, No 83 Group, for First Canadian Army and its air component, No 84 Group, and for Third US Army. Some time before D-day advanced parties from SHAEF and HQ 21st Army Group joined ANCXF at Portsmouth, and made use of his SCU/SLU facilities. The complete network, as it operated on D-day, was as follows:

Station	Location	Authority
ST/SH	Bushy Park	USSTAF and SHAEF
EF/AD	Stanmore	AEAF and ADGB
TA	Uxbridge	2nd Tactical Air Force
FU	Bryanston Square	First US Army Group (FUSAG)
DL	Wycombe Abbey	Eighth USAF
MI	Wycombe Abbey	Bomber Command
XF/SHA	Portsmouth	ANCXF and SHAEF (Advanced)
AG	Portsmouth	21st Army Group
ON	Portsmouth	Second British Army and No 83 Group
CR	Leatherhead	First Canadian Army and No 84 Group
ZE	Knutsford	Third US Army
YK	Bristol	First US Army[4]

During the crossing the SCU/SLU service was confined to the Command ship, which circulated the intelligence to other HQs until their forward stations got ashore. Second British Army's station landed in France on D-day; from 8 June it provided a service to General Montgomery's advanced HQ at Banville,

---

* The close relations established before D-day were maintained afterwards, especially with 21st Army Group, which sent a daily telegram to GC and CS outlining the operational situation and setting down the principal problems in the solution of which Ultra might be of use.

† In a departure from the long-standing procedure by which Ultra, together with all other intelligence, was sent to the naval commands in Home Waters and the Atlantic from the Admiralty by the OIC, ANCXF's SCU/SLU link at first carried the naval as well as other high-grade Sigint: it was extended to the Cs-in-C Nore, Portsmouth, Plymouth and Dover on 15 May. But the OIC disliked the direct service from GC and CS for naval intelligence, and it was abandoned at the end of May. ANCXF continued to receive a wide selection of non-naval Sigint on his SCU/SLU link.[3]

3. History of the SLUs, p 55; ADM 223/286, Denning report, pp 11–12.
4. History of the SLUs, pp 43–45.

General Dempsey personally selecting what should be sent. First US Army's station landed on *Omaha* beach on 10 June. In the next five weeks the service had to be maintained in duplicate for forward and rear stations until the Rear HQs of Second British Army, First US Army, First Canadian Army, 2nd Tactical Air Force, 21st Army Group, 1st (now 12th) US Army Group and Third US Army had joined the advanced HQs. Thereafter the network continued to expand; it was eventually carrying GC and CS's output to no less than fifty recipients.[5]*

From the outset, and throughout its expansion, the system operated without any serious hitch – an impressive feat of organisation and a tribute to the meticulous planning which had brought it into existence by stages from an early date, in order to give the *Overlord* intelligence staffs and the SCU/SLU personnel and their US counterparts experience in using it, and which had called for careful calculations in advance of the load of traffic it would have to bear. As an illustration of the experience that had to be acquired, the rule was laid down that after their arrival in France recipients below the level of Army Groups were each to receive from GC and CS only such Ultra as was immediately essential to them and were not to retain Ultra signals for more than 24 hours, the senior commands being responsible for providing them with digests on the wider background. As for the traffic load, GC and CS had estimated in January 1944 that the link to SHAEF, which would receive the entire output, would have to handle 16,000 signal groups a day. In the event it carried an average 18,000 groups a day during the first three weeks after D-day without congestion; only in the first few days, when traffic greatly exceeded the estimate, was it severely taxed. These calculations in their turn had rested on an estimate of the number of German signals that were likely to be decrypted from D-day onwards and of what proportion of them would have to be summarised for transmission to the Commands. GC and CS had calculated that the proportion of priority Army and Air Force decrypts would amount to 2,000 a day from D-day. In fact for some weeks after D-day, out of an average daily intercept load of 4,840 signals, it processed for the Commands a daily average of 2,500 Army and Air Force decrypts obtained from about 30 Enigma keys, together with a smaller selection from the naval Enigma decrypts, of which the total rose from 1,500 to 2,000 daily over this period. It kept its output within the planned capacity of the SCU/SLU links only by adopting a more rigorous standard of

---

* See lists, p 975ff.

5.   ibid, pp 46, 48.

selection and summarising than it had used in its signals to the
Mediterranean Commands – a demanding as well as a highly
skilled exercise when all decrypts had still to be scanned, but one
that was performed without any observable decline in the quality
of its service.

Other measures to ensure the efficiency of the service concerned the intercept stations. Since all the enemy's high-grade
frequencies could be intercepted in the United Kingdom, it was
unnecessary to consider the forward decryption of Enigma, which
had been conceded temporarily to Cairo during the campaign in
the Western Desert,* nor was it necessary to make arrangements
for the forward interception of Enigma traffic on MF low power.
By increases of staff and land-lines, however, everything possible
was done to prepare for the expected increase in the volume of
intercepts, to reduce the time it took to forward intercepts from
the intercept stations to Bletchley and to avoid delay in sorting and
routeing them within GC and CS. And in the case of the naval
Enigma keys in the Channel area, which unlike those of the GAF
used few frequencies and unlike those of the Army were being
broken daily before *Overlord* was launched,† arrangements were
made for the first and last time in the war to intercept the traffic at
Bletchley Park itself. This step was taken with some hesitation in
view of the risk to security involved in having GC and CS
associated with masts and aerials. But Mr Frank Birch, the head of
the Naval Section, secured approval for it, and it was fully justified
by the exceptional speed with which the naval Enigma was
decrypted during the crucial days in which the assault forces were
crossing the Channel and getting ashore.

The arrangements made for exploiting the enemy's medium
and low-grade communications during and after the invasion
were necessarily more complicated and more various.

Until September 1943 21st Army Group and ETOUSA shared
in the United Kingdom the interception and exploitation of the
medium and low-grade Army traffic while GC and CS undertook
the training of the new staff, both US and British, that would man
the large number of Y stations that would be needed in France.
From September 21st Army Group and ETOUSA became
separately responsible for training the British and American Y
units and controlling them once they had gone into the field. But
their discussions with GC and CS in January 1944 led to
agreements by which they exchanged all their important medium-
grade decrypts – the exchange to be carried out by teleprinter

---

* See Volume II, p 375.

† On and before D-day GC and CS was reading the 12 most important of the 17 German
naval keys.

transmission via GC and CS once the two Y HQs had moved to France – and by which GC and CS duplicated the work undertaken in the field. This second arrangement was made in order to ensure that GC and CS's cryptanalytic and intelligence follow-up support was always available as a safeguard against breakdowns and communications difficulties of the kind the field units had encountered in Tunisia. In addition, GC and CS was made solely responsible for intercepting and exploiting all traffic on the flanks of the invasion area until the Allies had broken out of the bridgehead.

For RAF Y, as for that of the Army, a large increase in the number of field stations, both W/T and R/T, was effected in time for D-day, and every important warship in the D-day armada and the bombarding force was provided with a 'Headache' unit for the interception and interpretation of the enemy's air and naval R/T communications on VHF.* As these stations and units would depend for their effectiveness on the back-up they received from the Cheadle Broadcast against tactical W/T traffic and from the Kingsdown Hook-up in the case of R/T,† additional staff was also trained for Cheadle and the Kingsdown HDUs,‡ and an effort was made to improve the means by which Cheadle. and Kingsdown received back-up from the Air Section at GC and CS.

By September 1943, thanks to the efforts of Mr J E S Cooper the head of the Air Section, the work of solving the low-grade codes and medium cyphers of the GAF had been centralised at GC and CS, which relayed the solutions to Cheadle – and via Cheadle to RAF Y units – and GC and CS had been authorised to transmit direct to the main air Commands tactical air intelligence from sources not available to Cheadle and Kingsdown. In April 1944 it was agreed that from D-day GC and CS should also transmit this intelligence to Cheadle and Kingsdown, which would collate it with their own decrypts and relay it at their discretion on their existing broadcast channels to all the Commands and on newly introduced channels to the ships, formations and Y units in the invasion area. This agreement constituted a considerable concession on the part of the Y authorities in the Air Ministry, who had long resisted what they regarded as undue centralisation of tactical air intelligence at GC and CS, and it undoubtedly contributed to

---

* See Volume II, pp 194–195 for 'Headache'. 50 warships in all were fitted with 'Headache'. In addition, the early warning coastal radar screen on the south coast was extended by stationing frigates in the Channel – in the hope of making it impossible for E-boats to leave bases within range of the convoys without being detected.[6]

† See Volume III Part 1, pp 320–321.

‡ See Volume I, p 180.

6. ADM 234/366, BR 1736(42)(1), p 44.

the fact that the RAF Y units did valuable work in Normandy. But the arrangements it produced were inevitably a compromise: it was impossible to reconcile the need to exploit the tactical traffic of the GAF at the stations which intercepted it and, on the other hand, the inexorable process by which GC and CS had become the chief repository of Sigint expertise on the GAF. Partly for this reason, partly on account of congestion on the communications links at Cheadle and Kingsdown, and partly because of the disorganisation and low level of activity of the GAF, which itself encountered great delays in sending its signals, they proved to be the least effective of all the measures adopted before *Overlord* with the object of maximising the value of Sigint during the invasion.

The naval coastal Y stations were strengthened to deal with the expected increase in the VHF traffic of the German light surface craft and the heavy coast defence batteries on the French coast. Just before D-day the code used by the batteries, which had for some time been producing useful intelligence on their order of battle, began to carry intelligence about the coastal divisions and, occasionally, other Army formations, and arrangements were made to send this from GC and CS to HQ 21st Army Group and ANCXF by teleprinter. But they sent very few signals after the beginning of the Allied bombardment.

APPENDIX 7

Decrypts of Signals Reporting the Tour of the Military Defences of Northern France by the Japanese Naval Attaché in Berlin, 4 and 5 May 1944

(Reproduced from BAY/KVs 97, 103 and 123
of 8, 9 and 13 May 1944)

BAY/KV 97: TOO 1906/8/5/1944

A *Chain of Command* v. Rundstedt in Supreme Command Army, Speer (Comment. presumably Sperrle) of Air, Krancke of Navy. Rommel specially appointed by Hitler to lead an assault army when France invaded. If Allies invade several places at same time their divided forces will be destroyed by Rommel in northern France and v. Rundstedt in southern France or elsewhere. (From information Military Attaché Berlin it appears that very recently decided to place Rommel in command Channel area and v. Rundstedt southern France with Geyr (Comment: suggest Geyr v. Schweppenburg commanding assault army under Supreme Command v. Rundstedt.) Navy in command fighting while Allies on seas. Command transferred to Army without further instructions if Allies reach coast.

B *Allied Plans* Main blow expected northern France and Channel area.

C *German Operational Policy* Since his inspection autumn 1943 Rommel's policy has been to destroy Allies near coast, most of all on beaches, without allowing penetration inland. Thorough fortification coastal areas where possibility attack is great and main strength deployed near coast. As defence against airborne operations planned to cut communications between seaborne and airborne troops and to destroy them individually. Germans will be aided by excellent road network and airborne troops will everywhere speedily be encircled.

D *Army Dispositions* 15th Army under Salmuth defending Channel area. Operational area in Channel region from Caen to Belgian-Dutch frontier. HQ in suburbs Lille. Consists of four corps and 18 divisions. 11 divisions in line along 350 km. coastline. 3 concentrated at mouth of Seine. HQs these front line divisions in towns and villages 20 to 30 miles from coast. As general rule each division had two regiments on coastline and one in vicinity HQ. Remaining divisions distributed among small towns and villages about 50 km. from coast as precautions against Allied air raids and airborne landings between Rouen and Ghent. These second line divisions could be rushed to coast and concentrated in average time of 1 to 1½ hours.

E *Air Force* Unable to obtain much information during tour but information from Berlin shows Luftflotte 3 under Speer (sic – see above) in Channel area and Luftflotte 5 under Kammhuber in Norwegian coastal area. Their total strength about 3000 aircraft (including 1200 bombers and 1500 fighters). Although can temporarily divert forces from defence of Germany in event Allied penetration, in position great numerical inferiority to Allied force of over 10,000 aircraft.

F *Naval Forces* Naval Channel forces (Comment: presumably forces under Admiral Commanding Channel Coast) under Liebe (Comment: presumably Rieve). HQ at Rouen. Area reaches from St. Malo to Belgian-Dutch frontier. Four base forces (Comment: Sea Defence Commandants); Calais Force east of Somme; Seine-Somme Force; Normandy Force; and the former British (Comment; information incomplete but presumably Channel Islands.) Also two guard forces with HQs at Boulogne and Brest (Comment: presumably respectively 2nd and 3rd Defence Divisions). Shelters each accommodating 8 to 16 torpedo boats (Comment: presumably E-boats), minesweepers etc. in all harbours. Roofing 2 metres and sidewalls 1.8 metres.

G *Coastal Batteries* I. Harbours very strongly defended by naval garrison forces. Between Ostende and Boulogne, counting naval batteries alone, 28 batteries and garrison force of 16,000. 24 batteries between Boulogne and Le Havre. Principal batteries: 1 battery of 3 guns (40 cm.), 1 battery of 3 guns (38 cm.) and 1 battery of 4 guns (28 cm.) at Calais. 1 battery of 3 guns (38cm.) at Le Havre. 1 railway battery of 4 guns (28cm.) at Ostende 'and so on'. At Ostende for seaward defence 4 guns of 28 cm. (Comment: not stated whether same or additional battery), 2 guns of 15 cm., 12 guns 10.5 cm., 4 anti-tank guns of 5 cm., 8 high angle guns of 7.7 cm and 20 machine guns. Two thirds have angle of fire of 120° and remainder can fire in any direction. Other harbours much the same and Allies must be prepared for fierce concentrations of fire in any part. II. Army batteries and air force high angle batteries in intervals between these naval fortifications. 5 or 6 naval batteries attached to each front line division. Where great possibility Allied landings batteries of 7.7 to 28 cm. guns situated at intervals of 3 to 5 km. III. Most important of front line batteries and magazines in underground air raid shelters with 3.5 m. concrete roofing while other batteries and supply establishments have 2 m. roof (Comment: following applies also to boat shelters discussed para. F above). Most of shelters quickly constructed since autumn 1943 on special orders Hitler. All skilfully camouflaged and provide considerable security against air raids. Good food provided and morale excellent. IV. Other (Comment: not clear what category excluded) batteries all equipped with individual radar and can fire at night with accuracy. Radar sets of 1940 type, mostly *Riese*, but some of D-type. Air Force has separate sets at all strategic positions. Thus not only Channel shipping but number and movement Allied aircraft immediately known.

H   *Other Fortifications and Defences* I. Various kinds mines in waters and harbours where landing craft might be expected. Harbours so mined that may be detonated from shore. Numerous obstructions constructed with ferro-concrete piles so as to ground landing craft at high water. II. (Slight indications piles of wood and felled trees) have been scattered and extensive minefields laid up to 50 km. behind stretches of coast on which landings feared as protection against air landings. Land mines most effective defence against airborne invasion and laid on a large scale. Standard practice to lay 50 kg. at each corner 1 square meter. Minefield 200 to 500 m. wide. III. As result battle experience anti-tank ditches now increased to depth 3 m. and width 20 m. (Comment: then follows incomplete passage mentioning 'roads leading to coast' and also 'blocked with concrete walls'). All inhabitants houses facing coast evacuated and placing demolition charges completed. Also full use in every suitable place of flame-throwers, depth-charge throwers, anti-submarine nets, searchlights etc.

I   *Effect of Allied Air Raids* Repeated attacks on Channel fortifications commenced in April after two year lull. Attaché watched day precision bombing with fair degree accuracy by formations of some 50 aircraft against Le Havre, Le Touquet and Calais batteries. Expected that such attacks will continue. But even when direct hit is sustained small scale attacks with bombs of two tons or less on fortress batteries inside a shelter cause comparatively little damage.

J   *German Retaliatory Measures* Weapons (slight indications in the hands of) 65 Corps commanded by General Haiman (Comment agreed with MI 14 suggest Heinemann) and under direct control Hitler. Each in a separate shelter. Appears that number being continually increased.

BAY/KV 103: TOO 1847/9/5/1944 – continuation of BAY/KV 97

A *GERMAN STRATEGY ACCORDING Liaison Officer 15 Army* Heavy losses first to be inflicted on landing forces and then main force inland to be surrounded and annihilated. Consequently since Rommel took command strengthening coastal defences and movement of troops to coastal sector particularly noticeable (Comment: in context this follows Paragraph C. of BAY/KV 97 and presumably is amplification not qualification thereof).

B *Expected Time of Landing* Ordinarily weather and sea conditions French side of Channel bad from middle October to middle March, calm from early April to late September, and particularly good May to end August. Tidal range about 4.5 metres Ostende, 8 to 9 Le Havre, and 10 to 12 Cherbourg and further West. So Allies likely to commence landing when high water occurs before dawn. Age of moon very important factor and German Command (especially Navy) of view time chosen will be when moon seven-eighths full, that is early May or early June.

C *Place of Landing* Coastline west of Somme generally consists of 50 to 100 metre cliffs except for sandy beach extending for about 50 km. between Seine and Orne. Unless Allies have some novel plan most difficult land large forces in this area and even small forces will need harbour facilities of Cherbourg, Fécamp, Dieppe etc. On other hand coast east of Somme is unbroken sandy beach especially south of Boulogne and between Calais and Ostende, and should be possible to land forces anywhere. Also suitable for operations after landings. However country low-lying and troop movements easily hampered by flooding. German Command (especially Navy) accordingly of view landing will centre on Boulogne with main force to east and small part to west. Strenuously reinforcing defences this area. They also appreciate that beachheads and diversionary landings with detached forces are quite probable in Le Havre-Cherbourg area, Dutch coast north of the Hague, west coast of Denmark etc.

D *German Army* 15th, 7th, 1st and 19th Armies also the assault army under direct command Rommel (Comment: compare end

Paragraph A BAY/KV 97) total about 65 divisions, all the pick of German Army. In addition 65 Corps for special retaliatory action under direct command Hitler.

BAY/KV 123: TOO 2018/13/5/1944 – continuation of BAY/KV 103

A   German defences precisely planned and thoroughly executed. Morale front line forces extremely high. Allies will have great difficulty in breaking through the fierce opposition which will be offered by pick of German forces. Wrong however to be complacent. Allies possess absolute command of sea and great air superiority and have additional advantage of year's lead in Radar. Hamburg, for example, had air defences sufficient to make air attack very hazardous but was notwithstanding destroyed by unforeseen method of attack. But in this area Allies must expect heavy losses in any landing operations which follow familiar pattern and chances of success considered very slight indeed.

B   Attaché agrees in general with estimate German Command in North France (Comment: see BAY/KV 103) that if landing attempted north France main force will probably land between Boulogne and Ostende, with a part of force south of Boulogne and perhaps diversionary landings Le Havre – Cherbourg region and Dutch coast. But if Allies want swift landing operations which could be carried out with most confidence seems probable will choose Biscay and Mediterranean coast of France. Here German defences still weak in comparison with Channel while Allies would have effective air support from north Africa, Italy and Britain. But must have political control Iberian Peninsula as necessary preliminary to this and Spain must at least be absolutely neutral and Portugal must join the war or allow use of airfields.

C   GAF and particularly fighter force still full of fight. All the power of Channel defences can be brought to bear, and moreover German forces in spite partial disruption land and sea transport network can very easily be concentrated Channel area. There is, therefore, as German Command north France also considers, small likelihood of landings first ten days May. If north France in fact the target Allies must at least intensify present air assault and smash German capacity to fight over long period and on extensive scale. For this another month or more required. If moon and tide be taken into account landings first ten days June at earliest.

D   Allied intelligence network throughout France and conjecture

Allies informed to certain extent of defence policy, state of defences, results air atttacks etc. Germans on other hand find it difficult to obtain information from England not beyond bounds of possibility that German forces may be caught off guard.

E   In recent exercises carried out by Germans in Paris reported that Allies though they succeeded in landing (strong indications 90 divisions) were finally routed.*

---

* When the first of these decrypts was shown to the Prime Minister he marked it 'Important'. (Dir/C Archive, 6439 of 7 May). The importance of all three messages lay not so much in the accuracy of the factual information they gave, for most of this information had been reconstructed from the whole gamut of intelligence sources. The importance lay in the spreading out of the whole picture just as though a JIC delegation had itself been able to travel in Fifteenth Army's area – it is significant that the Attaché seems not to have toured that of Seventh Army – and to check the available intelligence at first hand.

APPENDIX 8

Decrypt of the Appreciation by C-in-C West of 8 May 1944

Despatched to the Commands between 0412 and 0513 on 14 May 1944, as KV 3763.

(Reproduced from DEFE 3/155)

Appreciation by CHARLIE in CHARLIE West eighth May. Distribution: CHARLIE in CHARLIE South West, OKW, OKH, Chief Engineer HEERESGRUPPE BAKER, ARMEEGRUPPE VON ZANGEN, five eight reserve Panzer corps for planning staff ARMEEGRUPPE GEORGE (comment, HEERESGRUPPE in KV three two nought five and three three eight six). (One) Allies. (Able) West Coast front. From first to seventh, in predominantly favourable operational conditions, Allied air activity very strong, at times less towards end of week owing weather. Targets: railway installations, including attacks, usually without lasting effect, on pinpoint targets (railway bridges, viaducts and dams). Further attacks on airfields, with, on average, medium or slight damage, and on factories and supply organisations with sometimes heavy damage. Attacks on construction sites had on average only slight effect, on fairly small scale and, for present, without recognisable unity of plan, the fortress installations of the coastal defence in the channel were attacked with relatively slight damage and losses. Heaviest attack was on troop camp MAILLY LE CAMP, heavy casualties (about four hundred) and heavy damage to buildings. Damage to materials relatively small owing dispersal. Flights to supply agents considerably increased in bright moonlight compared with previous week. Nothing new from photo recce and visual recce. Normal convoy traffic round ENGLAND. Yoke established as from fourth May revival of BRITISH and USA army W/T traffic to normal strength. Yoke picked up Anglo-American landing exercise FABIUS in area ISLE OF WIGHT and provided evidence for conjecture that Allies, in view of outer beach obstacles known to them, were attempting to achieve a modified landing and battle technique for foremost landing wave. Activity of light Allied naval craft in general somewhat weaker than previous week. During MTB attack on German convoy GRANVILLE to GUERNSEY night seventh eight steamship of seven five nought tons sunk by torpedo. Allied mining from the air remained lively with SCHWERPUNKT off submarine bases, LEZARDRIEUX and against CHANNEL ISLAND narrows. NO special information from agents apart from plethora of landing dates, mainly pointing to first half May. Appreciation: Anglo-American invasion preparations in ENGLAND completed. Although visual and photo recce had NOT yet been able to include whole English south coast, it was clear from the observed concentrations of landing shipping space, especially in area north of ISLE OF WIGHT (PORTSMOUTH – SOUTHAMPTON), that a special SCHWERPUNKT was being formed in that area. Observed tonnage of landing shipping space could be taken as sufficient for one two to one three divisions (less heavy equipment and rear elements) for fairly short sea routes. In all (estimating the capacity of the other English south coast harbours NOT so far covered by visual and photo recce) probable employment of at least two nought and probably more divisions in first wave must be expected. To these must certainly be added strong air-landing forces, for which (in addition to local parachute operations behind German main defence line) NORMANDY and perhaps also BRITTANY were suitable for operations on a large scale with the object of forming a bridgehead. The SCHWERPUNKT within the whole threatened channel front stretching from (strong indications SCHELDT) to northern tip of BRITTANY, appeared to be roughly from BOULOGNE as far as NORMANDY inclusive. For this it was essential for the Allies to capture large harbours with good performance. Of primary importance as such: LE HAVRE and CHERBOURG. Of secondary importance (also in performance): BOULOGNE and BREST. Systematic destruction of railways continued. Allies were already effectively hampering supply and troop movements, and in the event of active operations would hamper latter in particular. Latterly Allies had also been attacking important railway bridges on the lower SEINE. Supplying by air of agents and of resistance movements had been stepped up very greatly and acts of sabotage, especially on railways, had increased. As soon as favourable weather for combined landing operations (a series of days continuous fine weather) set in, the Allied attack might begin. It was bound to be heralded and preceded by ceaseless air-attacks increased to utmost strength against coastal fortifications and all rearward communications, headquarters and selected targets. This stage could as yet NOT be recognised. In future it could not be expected with certainty that the Allied landing would be made only on an incoming tide before the beginning of dawn. The most recent Allied landing exercise indicated that the Allies attached special importance to recognising and clearing the outer beach obstacles at low water. A readjustment of Allied landing tactics to meet this factor might

entail a delay in the beginning of the attack. (Baker)
MEDITERRANEAN coast front. Lively Allied submarine activity
off RIVIERA coast, with bombardment on two occasions. Air
attacks on SPANISH International Red Cross ship near SETE.
French troops established by Yoke for first time in LA MAD-
DALENA and northern SARDINIA. Commando undertakings
and raids against southern French coast a constant possibility.
Necessary conditions for a major attack did NOT yet appear to be
completely fulfilled. (Two) development of coastal defence. (Able)
West coast front. Development of field works, outer-beach
obstacles and staking of ground against air landings had been
driven forward with all available labour. Similarly with mining. In
area of GOC Armed Forces NETHERLANDS defensive capacity
had been further increased by employment of two naval manning
Abteilungen sanctioned by OKW to man the forward water
position and the new land front south of the river barrier.
Flooding in area GOC Armed Forces NETHERLANDS had been
completed except for small places. Lack of building materials for
defensive positions, due to transport difficulties, had NOT yet
been overcome. Expedients such as fetching material from
stations in the rear had been initiated but without adequate
results. Three five permanent installations were brought into
service from twenty-third to thirtieth April. Total these now one
one two seven one. Considerable increase in mining. Personnel
evacuated first to seventh May: area GOC Armed Forces
NETHERLANDS five two including two nought males aged one
five to six nought. Area Military Commander BELGIUM six
nought seven including one five one males one five to six nought.
Area Military Commander FRANCE from West coast battle zone
one two eight two including one nought eight males one five to six
nought. Readiness for defence behind the SCHWERPUNKT
front increased by the bringing up of two Parachute Division and
seven Werfer Brigade and by the elements which had already
arrived of nine one Air Landing Division and of PANZER LEHR
Division. NORMANDY was being further strengthened, also in
the interior, against air landings by special measures taken by
CHARLIE in CHARLIE West. (Baker) MEDITERRANEAN
coast front. Good progress in development of field works,
minelaying on country open to air landings and laying of
minefields. Number of permanent installations unchanged at
seven nought two. Eight five eight five persons, including seven
eight one males one five to six nought, evacuated by Military
Commander in FRANCE from the battle zone first to seventh
May. The defensive capacity of the CANAL DU MIDI depression
increased by arrival of three four one Assault Gun Brigade in area
west of NARBONNE. (Three) situation in the interior. Operations

to put down terrorist and resistance groups continued with success. During April five six nine terrorists were killed, four four six three captured, five two eight persons rounded up for labour. Increased sabotage against railways and armament production. Generally speaking NO important changes. First May was quiet apart from few partial strikes which were immediately stopped. The population in a state of expectancy for the invasion. People with property were concerned for personal safety. Flight of this class from town to country had begun.

APPENDIX 9

Intelligence on Germany's Reinforcement of the Cotentin Peninsula and its Effect on First US Army's Operational Plans, 24 to 27 May 1944

As the Allies were aware, the position in the Cotentin before the reinforcement took place was that 709th Infantry Division held an extended front on the eastern and northern coasts of the peninsula and 243rd Infantry Division was astride the base of the peninsula, protecting the west coast south of Le Haye-du-Puits. The decrypts of 24–27 May showed that 243rd had moved northwards and was holding the coast north of Le Haye, that 91st Infantry Division, newly arrived from Germany, occupied the centre between 709th and 243rd Divisions and that Parachute Regiment 6, which had arrived with 91st, lay further south in 243rd's former area. In addition, and primarily to provide protection against airborne attacks, several non-divisional formations had been brought into the peninsula from Germany, not from other parts of France: 101 Werfer Regiment, 206 Panzer Battalion, 70 Army Assault (Sturm) Battalion, 17 Machine Gun Battalion, 100 Panzer Training Battalion.[1]

In the light of this intelligence the plans for US air-drops in the Cotentin and for the landing on the *Utah* beach were hastily revised. It had been intended to drop 82nd US Airborne Division at a point near Le Haye-du-Puits from which it could dominate the corridor through which Germany was expected to send reinforcements after D-day, and to drop 101st US Airborne Division on the east coast in order to seize the causeways across the flooded strip behind the *Utah* beach. But 82nd's dropping area was now strongly held by German troops, and while it was less important and also impracticable to block the corridor, the threat to the *Utah* landings from German counter-attack had greatly increased. At HQ First US Army (General Bradley) on the evening of 27 May it

---

1. WO 205/532, Weekly *Neptune* Report of 21 May 1944; DEFE 3/160, KVs 5081, 5158 of 24 and 25 May; DEFE 3/161, KV 5416 of 27 May; WO 208/3573, Weekly Summary for the CIGS, 29 May.

was accordingly decided that both airborne divisions should drop
behind the *Utah* beach, to operate in close contact with each other
and the seaborne assault force, that landing schedules should be
changed to secure the earlier landing at *Utah* of combatant troops,
and that the follow-up at *Utah* by 79th US Division should be
advanced by over a month to D+8. At the same time, the date set
for the capture of Cherbourg was put back over a week, to D+15.[2]

---

2. CAB 44/245, Operation 'Overlord', Chapter II, Book III, p 362; Harrison,
    Cross-Channel Attack (Washington DC 1951), pp 185–188.

APPENDIX 10

Allied Intelligence on German Divisions on the Eve of D-Day

(i) Intelligence on the Composition, Strength, Equipment and State of the German Divisions

Until the end of April 1944 MI 14's assessments of the quality of divisions rested mainly on what it knew of the battle experience of a given unit or formation and its performance. For the many units and formations in the west which had never been in battle, however, MI 14 was forced back on the more generalised approach of estimating from fragments of intelligence how long it was taking on average to bring different types of division to operational state. The fragments related to a variety of matters – the date on which the unit had been set up; the quality of the cadre; the conscription class of the recruits and the proportions of over-age or medically sub-standard men; types and amounts of weapons and equipment; state of training – and they were obtained from the whole range of sources. Battle reports from Italy, POW, agents, captured documents, censorship, Press and radio all contributed; and they were supplemented by high-grade decrypts from Italy and the eastern front and, occasionally, by decrypts referring to formations in the western theatre.

The situation was improved from the end of April by the receipt of a series of long Fish decrypts which not only provided detailed returns of men and equipment for a number of divisions, but were invaluable in correcting and extending the general conclusions previously reached about the capabilities of several categories of division.

The following Fish decrypts dealt with infantry divisions:

Date and Reference	Formation	Summary of Contents
25 April (KV 2002 and 2234 in DEFE 3/43)	363rd Infantry, known to belong to the 21st conscription class and located in Denmark.	A 'striking deficiency' of NCOs, an almost total lack of MT; infection among its 8,000 horses had severely affected artillery training. Classified as Category IV (fit only for defence).
28 April (KV 2272 in DEFE 3/44)	92nd and 278th Infantry in C-in-C West's command.	Grave deficiencies in NCOs and MT.

799

Date and Reference	Formation	Summary of Contents
8 May (KV 3185 in DEFE 3/47)	77th Infantry recently arrived in France, a small division of 25th conscription class.	Up to the strength laid down for the 1944-type small division, at 8,000 including foreigners, but fit only for defence.
24 May* (KV 5050 in DEFE 3/160)	2nd and 3rd Parachute of which only 3rd Parachute was in France.	Full details of 3rd Parachute, showing personnel up to strength. Deficiencies in infantry weapons.
27 May (KV 5373 in DEFE 3/161)	276th and 277th Infantry with Nineteenth Army.	Full details of manpower and state of readiness. 276th described as 'immobile'.

The armoured divisions appeared together in general returns of 20 April and 19 May and in tank and gun returns of 25 May and 11 June. The return of 20 April was only partially decrypted, on 28 April.[1] Parts of the return of 19 May were decrypted on 25 May[2] and others on 11 June.[3] The tank and gun return of 25 May was not available till 7 June.[4] The return of 11 June was decrypted on 13 June.[5] It will be seen from these dates that by no means all of the following intelligence was available during the anxious discussion that preceded D-day. Because the decrypts were incomplete, some of the divisions were not covered. Although some information was extracted from them, the tank and gun returns used an unfamiliar pro forma which was not fully solved till the autumn with the help of a captured document, so that the intelligence was not complete for any division. It is here summarised division by division:

12th SS Panzer. The return of 20 April, decrypted on 28 April,† showed that the division then contained 484 officers, 2,004 NCOs and 19,920 men, and listed its deficiencies as 182 officers, 2,500 NCOs – a striking deficiency – and no men. This suggested that

---

* But this was a GAF Enigma decrypt, not Fish.

† Only the returns for 2nd and 12th SS Panzer Divisions were decrypted. The Prime Minister asked for a summary of the decrypt on one sheet of paper. It was sent to him on 4 May, with comments signed by the CIGS which stressed that 2nd SS Panzer was still much below strength and that the MT deficiency was particularly noteworthy, and pointed out that although 12th SS Panzer was well up to war establishment, it was suffering from a lack of fuel for training.[6]

1. DEFE 3/44, KV 2295 of 28 April 1944.
2. DEFE 3/160, KVs 5097 and 5129 of 25 May.
3. DEFE 3/170, KV 7584 of 11 June.
4. DEFE 3/166, KV 6705 of 7 June.
5. DEFE 3/171. KV 7853 of 13 June.
6. Dir/C Archive, 6386 and 6408 of 1 and 4 May.

establishment strength was 25,170, and that the division was over twice as large as most infantry divisions and 10,000 men larger than the average of Army infantry divisions, thus confirming the suspicion that SS divisions were receiving preferential treatment. Another notable deficiency was 231 trucks out of a total of 2,000 and there was a serious shortfall in tractors. The tank return of 25 May from C-in-C West, available on 7 June, indicated that the division would have 88 Pzkw IV, 29 Pzkw V (Panthers) and 30 x 75 mm anti-tank guns. The further return of 11 June stated that the division had 42 serviceable IVs and 32 serviceable Vs.

2nd SS Panzer. Statistics about this division were given both in the return of 20 April and in the return of 19 May. This latter return was not issued until 11 June but that turned out to be before 2nd SS Panzer was committed. It thus showed its rate of growth, the only division for which this was learned. Its armoured strength was shown only in the later return which disclosed that it had 55 Pzkw IV (with a deficiency of 46), 37 Pzkw V (with a deficiency of 62), and 42 assault guns (with no deficiency). In the April return the manpower strength was 17,025 and this rose to 18,930 in May, when there was still a deficiency of 1,582. The return of 19 May showed that a shortage of motor cycles, cars, lorries and tractors remained acute. Details of other units in 2nd SS Panzer, down to SS Butchery Company 2, were given in full in the April return, of which the report on the division's rate of training was an important feature. A battle group of the division was conditionally available for offensive tasks but the bulk of the division was not ready, the chief deficiencies being then a lack of NCOs, men, signals and engineering equipment – as well as transport. The return of 25 May reported that it had 23 Pzkw V, but the number of Pzkw IV was corrupt in the text.

17th SS PG. Details were given in C-in-C West's return of 19 May which was available on 25 May. Its most important disclosure was that the division had no tanks and apparently did not expect to receive any; its chief armoured strength resided in its 42 assault guns. The return showed that two-thirds of the men were in their twenty-third week of training, the rest in their twentieth. The division's battle groups were conditionally suitable for offensive tasks, and the remaining elements for local defence. Special difficulties were shortages of officers, NCOs, MT and vehicle spares. The return showed that the division's transport included horses and bicycles. A fragmentary message dated 4 June showed that the division still had no tanks, but this was not decrypted until 20 June.[7]

---

7. DEFE 3/175, KV 8866 of 20 June.

11th Panzer. It was evident that full details of the division were given in C-in-C West's return of 19 May. But much of this message was garbled and all that emerged from it about 11th Panzer was that its serviceability was hampered by a shortage of infantry, guns and MT.

116th Panzer. Some indication of the length of time the Germans thought it would take to fuse 179th Reserve Panzer Division with the remains of 116th Panzer Division from Russia was given in a decrypt of a message of 2 May when OKH thought that its Flak battalion would have to operate as a static unit until it could be motorised in September 1944.[8] Fairly full details were, however, included in the C-in-C's report of 19 May and were issued to the Commands on 25 May. As well as the usual statistics the report stated that 'the state of training of the division has improved since 1 May, but is still insufficient. During the last week training has been seriously impeded by preparation for and execution of the transfer . . . Owing to the shortage of MT and equipment, the division is only fit for limited offensive tasks with weak elements . . . Only very slow progress is being made with the repair of the few tractors brought with the division from the East . . .' The report showed that the division had an actual strength of 13,414 men and a deficiency of 1,457. It had received 68 out of its complement of 78 Pzkw IV, none of its complement of 73 Pzkw V and 21 self-propelled (SP) anti-tank guns, and only 6 of its expected 12 assault guns. Only about half its motor cycles, cars and lorries had arrived.

1st SS Panzer. According to the return of 19 May the division had an actual strength of 17,257 with a deficiency of 4,143 (mostly NCOs), a tank strength of 41 Pzkw V and 45 Pzkw IV, and 42 assault guns. The division was better outfitted than 2nd Panzer SS but was short of heavy weapons and wheeled vehicles. The return added: 'Inspection of the main body of the replacement personnel . . . and the training capabilities of commanders and subordinate commanders show that 6 weeks training time must be demanded for the division . . . The division is not ready for operations . . . There are deficiencies in small arms, light infantry weapons, entrenching tools and camouflage suits . . . training is thereby rendered particularly difficult . . . Increased activity of the air war has interfered with the bringing up of fresh material and caused a drop in performance at MT parks. 1,685 members of the division are at present on courses . . . in the Reich'. This information was not issued until 11 June.[9] The return of 25 May showed the

---

8. DEFE 3/47, KV 3070 of 7 May.
9. DEFE 3/170, KVs 7584 of 11 June, 7612 of 12 June.

division as having 45 Pzkw IV and 41 Pzkw V, with the expectation of a dozen more of each.

9th Panzer. The return of 25 May gave it as having 48 Pzkw IV.

(ii) MI 14's Table of Equivalent Strengths prepared for the Chiefs of Staff

(Reproduced from WO 208/3573, MI 14 Weekly Notes of 22 May 1944, Appendix A)

Statement as to the Panzer, Panzer Grenadier and Field Divisions in the West in Terms of Full-Strength, First-Quality Divisions.

Divisions	Remarks	Estimate in terms of full-strength, 1st quality
2nd and 21st Panzer 12th SS Panzer 17th SS PG 352nd and 353rd Infantry	All good class divs which should be complete at Y-date (ie D-day)	6–7
Panzer Lehr	Formed in 1944 from demonstration units for service in Hungary. Recently returned to the West and nearly up to strength; lacks training as a division	
1st SS Panzer	Recently arrived from Russia and appears to be weak	1–2
2nd SS Panzer	Bulk of division not ready for operations	
3rd Parachute	Nearly up to strength but requires further training	2–3
331st Infantry	Arrived from Russia in March 44 much under strength. Is getting small reinforcements	
84th Infantry	Lacks training	
? Division	Another division may appear in West	

Divisions	*Remarks*	*Estimate in terms of full-strength, 1st quality*
9th Panzer ⎫ 11th Panzer ⎬ 116th Panzer ⎭	In process of formation out of battered and Reserve Panzer Divisions	1–2
5th Parachute ⎫ 85th and 91st ⎬ Infantry ⎭	All class C divisions with no battle experience*	
6th Parachute	Now forming. The necessity for finding replacements for 1st Parachute (Italy) will probably retard its progress	2
? Division	Another offensive division may appear in the West.	

Total 21 divs of which only 18 accepted in the West   12–16

NOTE: It should be noted that of the ten Panzer and PG divisions and fourteen Field divisions at present accepted in the west the undermentioned have not been dealt with in the preceding paragraph, namely: 77th, 271st, 272nd, 275th, 276th and 277th Infantry Divisions.

The reason for excluding them is that they are holding coastal sectors and were as a type specifically excluded by COSSAC.

(iii) DMO's Brief for the Chiefs of Staff, 22 May 1944

(Reproduced from WO 106/4154)

OPPOSITION TO 'OVERLORD'

The bare comparison in paragraph 9 of this Paper [JIC(44) 210(o) of 20 May†] between the rate of German build-up originally considered acceptable by COSSAC and the rate which the JIC now consider the Germans are likely to achieve is misleading.

Two factors make the position less gloomy than this bare comparison suggests –

---

* MI 14 classified divisions as A, B or C according to their adjudged battle worthiness.

† This paper contained the first draft of the Chiefs of Staff minute to the Prime Minister of 23 May – see Appendix (iv) below.

First, the 'OVERLORD' plan has been revised since COSSAC's original estimate was prepared. In result, the assault has been increased from 3 to 5 seaborne divisions with an additional 2⅔ airborne divisions. It is planned also to achieve a quicker rate of build-up of our forces.

A table showing comparative figures is at the Annex to this brief.*

Second, the rate of reinforcement of German divisions in the first two months after 'OVERLORD' D Day is now estimated to amount to a maximum of only 13 divisions as against 15 which COSSAC, making his estimate when our rate of build-up was slower than is now planned, considered acceptable.

I suggest, therefore that the following paragraph should be added as paragraph 10 –

'10. It should be noted, however, that since COSSAC laid down his conditions in his appreciation of 30 July 1943, the "OVERLORD" plan has been revised with the object of increasing the breadth and weight of the initial assault, ensuring the earlier capture of a deep water port, and improving the rate of our build-up. These factors, together with the reduction in the likely rate of German reinforcements against "OVERLORD" in the first two months of the operation, should in some measure compensate for the present increase in German opposition during the initial phases of the operation.'

I recommend, therefore, that you should approve this draft minute to the Prime Minister, subject to the addition of the new paragraph 10 above.

---

* See p 806.

ANNEX

Day	COSSAC's original estimate of 30 July 1943 for acceptable rate of build-up of German divisions (a)	Present estimate of rate of German build-up in JIC (44) 210 (o) Final of 20 May 1944 (b)	Estimate of own build-up at time of COSSAC's estimate in column (a) (c)			Present Estimate of own build-up (See Note) (d)		
			Seaborne equivalent Divisions	Airborne equivalent Divisions	Effective Divisions	Seaborne equivalent Divisions	Airborne equivalent Divisions	Effective Divisions
D	3	3	$4\frac{1}{3}$	$1\frac{1}{3}$	$5\frac{2}{3}$	6	$2\frac{2}{3}$	$8\frac{2}{3}$
D+2	5	6–7	8	$1\frac{1}{3}$	$9\frac{1}{2}$	$7\frac{2}{3}$	$2\frac{2}{3}$	$10\frac{1}{2}$
D+8	9	11–14	$14\frac{2}{3}$	–	$14\frac{2}{3}$	$15\frac{2}{3}$	–	$15\frac{2}{3}$

Note: The figures given in column (d) have NOT been published officially by 21 Army Group, but we understand are those which have been used in detailed planning.

(iv) COS Minute to the Prime Minister, 23 May 1944

(Reproduced from CAB 121/394, COS (44) 167th (o) Meeting, 23 May)

PRIME MINISTER

Opposition to OVERLORD

1.   COSSAC, in his appreciation of the 30th July, 1943, laid down two major conditions concerning the scale of enemy opposition to OVERLORD. These conditions were –
(i) 'It is essential that there should be an overall reduction in the German fighter force between now and the time of the surface assault.'
(ii) 'The number of German offensive divisions in reserve must not exceed a certain figure on the target date, if the operation is to have a reasonable chance of success. The German reserves in France and the Low Countries as a whole, excluding divisions holding the coast, GAF divisions, and training divisions, should not exceed, on the day of the assault, twelve full-strength, first-quality divisions. In addition, the Germans should not be able to transfer more than fifteen first-quality divisions from Russia, during the first two months. Moreover, on the target date, the divisions in reserve should be so located that the number of first-quality divisions which the Germans could deploy in the OVERLORD area, to support the divisions holding the coast, should not exceed three divisions on D Day, five divisions by D+2, or nine divisions by D+8'.
2.   During the military discussions of the Moscow Conference of last year, General Ismay, at a meeting on the 20th October, informed the Russians of these conditions. At a subsequent meeting, Marshal Voroshilov, referring to the statement that German reserves in France and the Low Countries as a whole must not be more than about twelve full-strength, first-quality divisions on the day of the assault, enquired what action would be taken if there were thirteen or fourteen good divisions in this area and if the other conditions were favourable. General Ismay explained that the estimate of twelve divisions was an approximation, and that if there were thirteen or fourteen divisions present, it might still be thought that the invasion had a reasonable prospect of success.

3. In view of the above, and of Marshal Voroshilov's interest in this question, you may like to compare the conditions laid down by COSSAC with our up-to-date estimate of the opposition we are likely to encounter.

Air Forces

4. On the basis of our most recent evidence of production, wastage and strength, we estimate that the overall first-line strength of the German Air Force, at the time of OVERLORD, will be about 5,250 aircraft, of which some 2,700 will be fighters. This compares with an overall first-line strength, as at 30th July, 1943, of some 4,870 aircraft, of which 2,175 were fighters.

5. So far as the OVERLORD area of operations is concerned, it is thought that, in the light of the risks which the German High Command is taking in other theatres of war in order to defeat OVERLORD, up to 1,600 first-line aircraft (including reinforcements brought in after D Day) may become engaged in the course of operations. Of this total some 650 might be fighters. This compares with an estimate made in July, 1943, of a total of some 1,175 first-line aircraft, including some 500 fighters.

6. Although the first-line strength of the GAF has increased, this increase has been achieved in part at the expense of reserves and the GAF is today severely handicapped by lack of depth and reduced production. This, together with its qualitative decline, renders the GAF incapable of sustaining a scale of effort such as would normally be expected of an air force with a first-line strength of this size.

Land Forces

7. We estimate that, on the target date of OVERLORD, the Germans will have six to seven full-strength, first-quality divisions in reserve in France and the Low Countries. They will also have in reserve some eleven to fourteen offensive divisions of rather lower quality, roughly equivalent to some six to nine full-strength, first-quality divisions. Instead of twelve full-strength, first-quality divisions in reserve, as stipulated by COSSAC there will thus be a total of seventeen to twenty-one offensive divisions which will be the equivalent of some twelve to sixteen full-strength first-quality divisions.

8. During the first two months it is unlikely that the Germans will be able to transfer any divisions from the Russian front to the West, but they may make available, from elsewhere, for use against OVERLORD, some five to seven divisions of varying strength and quality. Dependent on the course of events on the Russian and Italian fronts, and at the cost of major withdrawals in the Mediterranean theatre, a further six divisions, at the most,

might also be brought against OVERLORD. This represents a maximum of thirteen divisions which might be brought against OVERLORD, as compared with the maximum of fifteen which COSSAC considered acceptable.

9. In the following table we compare the build-up in equivalent full-strength, first-quality divisions, which, according to COSSAC's conditions, should not be exceeded, with that which we now believe the Germans might achieve. Our estimate makes no allowance for interference by air or airborne attack or by sabotage.

German build-up

Time	Maximum build-up acceptable to COSSAC	Present Estimate
By D Day	3	3
D+2	5	6–7
D+8	9	11–14

10. It should be noted, however, that since COSSAC laid down his conditions in his appreciation of the 30th July, 1943, the OVERLORD plan has been revised with the object of increasing the breadth and weight of the initial assault, ensuring the earlier capture of a deep water port, and improving the rate of our build-up. These factors, together with the reduction in the likely rate of German reinforcements against OVERLORD in the first two months of the operation, should in some measure compensate for the present increase in German opposition during the initial phases of the operation.

Signed A F BROOKE
C PORTAL
ANDREW CUNNINGHAM

23rd May 1944

(v) *Divisions not at present identified in France and the Low Countries, but whose Transfer to the West is possible before OVERLORD Y Date.*

Reproduced from JIC (44) 215 (0) of 25 May, Appendix.

Formation	W.E.	State of Training	Remarks	Evaluation within Categories
1	2	3	4	5
'X' Panzer Division	15,500	Experienced combat division	This division was formed during the winter of 1941–42 and has recently been engaged in very heavy fighting on the southern half of the Russian Front and may, therefore, be expected to be well below strength.	
'Y' Panzer Grenadier Division	15,000	Experienced combat division, but probably contains drafts of inexperienced troops	On the Eastern Front since the beginning of the Russian campaign and was heavily engaged in March–April 1944 in South Russia. If already in the West, this division must have just arrived and probably in a battered state.	B
60 Pz. Grenadier Division	15,000	Experienced combat division	This division, which used to be in France, has recently been transferred from the Russian Front to Germany, to refit. It is probably depleted in strength.	B
2 Parachute Division	12,000	Experienced combat division	This division has suffered heavy casualties in Russia. It is at present being pulled out of the line to refit in Germany, preparatory to being transferred to the West. It might possibly have re-incorporated 6 Para. Regt., which formed part of it when it operated in Italy last year, but which has since been sent to France from Germany.	B

Formation	W.E.	State of Training	Remarks	Evaluation within Categories
1	2	3	4	5
6 Parachute Division	12,000	1 month to 6 weeks	Only just identified. Might possibly be forming in Central France.	C
'Z' Infantry Division	13,000	Experienced combat division, but probably contains drafts of inexperienced troops	On the Eastern Front since the beginning of the Russian campaign. Probably suffered heavily in the fighting on the Central Russian Front in winter 1943–1944. If in the West this division is probably newly arrived and below strength.	B
363 Infantry Division	13,000	Part field training, part basic only	Formed Oct.–Nov. 1943 on a W.E. of three infantry regiments each of two battalions and one artillery regiment of three or four batteries. Probably contains a stiffening of seasoned troops and is numerically fairly strong but training is known to be very incomplete. Known to be 55 per cent below establishment in M.T. At present in Denmark. Its transfer to the West now seems less likely than was once thought.	C

Our commentry on this table follows on next page.

The seven divisions mentioned are listed here with the reasons for their inclusion.

'Y' PG and 'Z' Infantry: These were 18th PG and 296th Infantry; they had been mentioned together with identified western divisions in signals decrypted during a C-in-C West W/T exercise on 18 and 19 May,[1] but were otherwise thought to be in Russia. By 5 June the Russians had reported that they were still on the eastern front.[2]

'X' Panzer Division: This was probably 23rd Panzer, last heard of in Russia; by 5 June MI 14 was satisfied that it was not in the west.[3]

60th PG Division: This was no doubt included because a decrypt had recently mentioned that it had been withdrawn from Russia to Germany.[4]

2nd Parachute Division: In a decrypt of 14 May this had been listed with other formations including 91st Infantry Division as being brought up to strengthen C-in-C West's defences, and on 23 and 24 May other decrypts had associated it with II Parachute Corps, which had recently been brought up[5] and with 3rd Parachute Division, which was in France.[6] On 5 June, however, a decrypt of 2 June having disclosed that it was still in the Ukraine on 21 May, MI 14 noted that nothing since 24 May had suggested the presence of it or any elements of it in the west.[7] In making this comment MI 14 presumably meant to exclude Parachute Regiment 6, which was known to have formed part of the division when it operated in Italy in 1943, since it had just learned that the regiment had arrived in the Cotentin (see above, p 797); but it is not clear whether MI 14 realised that what had escaped it during May was the fact that the decrypts mentioning 2nd Parachute Division had been referring only to Parachute Regiment 6.

6th Parachute Division: This had been identified by Sigint on 13 May[8] and it seemed possible that it was forming in central France.

363rd Infantry Division: The decrypts had located this in Denmark, but had pointed to some association with C-in-C West by giving him as the addressee of a signal about the division at the end of

---

1. DEFE 3/157, KVs 4371 and 4494 of 18 and 19 May 1944.
2. WO 208/3573, MI 14 Weekly Summary for the CIGS, 5 June.
3. ibid.
4. AWL 2038 of 18 May.
5. DEFE 3/155, KV 3763 of 14 May; DEFE 3/159, KV 4917 of 23 May; DEFE 3/160, KV 5017 of 24 May.
6. DEFE 3/160, KV 5050 of 24 May.
7. DEFE 3/164, KV 6151 of 2 June; AWL 2178 of 5 June.
8. DEFE 3/154, KV 3689 of 13 May.

April.[9] It was no more than a conjecture that it might move south, but it was one of the first to be transferred to Normandy from outside France and the Low Countries.

---

9. DEFE 3/43, KV 2002 of 25 April; DEFE 3/45, KV 2649 of 2 May; AWL 1948 of 2 May.

(vi) Forecast of the strength and quality of divisions on 'Overlord' Y date.

Reproduced from JIC (44) 215 (o) of 25 May, Appendix A.

Formation	W.E.	State of Training	Remarks	Evaluation within Categories
1	2	3	4	5
1 Panzer and Panzer Grenadier Divisions				
2 Panzer	15,500	Experienced	Reforming in France since the beginning of 1944 after sustaining heavy losses in Russia. Majority of personnel have had battle experience, remainder being new recruits. No evidence of tank and vehicle strength.	?A
21 Panzer	15,500	Field training	Original 21 Pz Div. destroyed in Tunisia, May 1943. Reconstituted July–Aug. and is believed to be well equipped and at full strength. Personnel include cadres from experienced divisions and recruits from training units who should be thoroughly trained. Slight evidence that the division contains two tank regiments. Probably up to establishment in men, tanks and vehicles.	A
(a) Panzer Divisions				
9 Panzer	15,500	Part field training, part basic only	The first and last divisions were formed as reserve panzer divisions in Summer 1943, and the second in Oct.–Nov. 1943. They are reorganising to operate as full-scale panzer divisions, a process which would normally take at least three months, but will probably take considerably less since they are each absorbing the remnants of	C
11 Panzer	15,500	"		C
116 Panzer	15,500	"		C

Formation	W.E.	State of Training	Remarks	Evaluation within Categories
1	2	3	4	5
			battle-tried, though shattered, mechanised divisions which are due to arrive in the West from Russia. Part of each division will, therefore, consist of battle-tried personnel, though the bulk of the original personnel were probably new recruits in Jan. 1944. Evidence in the case of one of these divisions shows major deficiencies in vehicles and complete lack of Mark V (Panther) tanks which are known to be on their W.E. Owing to these deficiencies elements only of the divisions are at present capable of employment in an offensive role.	
Panzer Lehr Division		Field training	Organisation and exact strength unknown but appears to be comparable in size to normal panzer division since on its recent arrival in the West from Hungary, it occupied 84 trains. Formed early in 1944 from demonstration units. Has not yet engaged as a division in operations but probably contains personnel with battle experience.	A–B
(b) SS Panzer Divisions 1 SS Pz (Leibstandarte Adolf Hitler)	23,000	Experienced combat division	This division is now arriving in the West. A first-class SS Panzer Division but it has been heavily engaged on the Eastern Front since autumn 1943 and when it does arrive will probably be in a battered state.	B

Formation	W.E.	State of Training	Remarks	Evaluation within Categories
1	2	3	4	5
2 SS Pz (Das Reich)	23,000	Experienced combat division still reforming	Transferred in Feb. 1944 to France from Russia. The division was more than 50 per cent below strength on arrival. Some of the deficiencies have already been made good but many of the new recruits have only had a few weeks' training with the division and at present it is unlikely that the division as a whole will be fully operational by "Overlord" Y date. No evidence of tank strength but known to be seriously below establishment in M.T.	B
12 SS Pz (Hitlerjugend)	23,000	Field training	Started forming in July 1943. Cadres were provided by 1 SS Pz Div. Leibstandarte Adolf Hitler. Non-German personnel amount to about 25 per cent. Must be considered one of the best divisions in the West. No evidence of tank strength but up to establishment in M.T.	A
(c) SS Panzer Grenadier Divisions				
17 SS PG (Götz von Berlichingen)	19,000	Six–seven months	Started forming Oct.–Nov. 1943. Includes cadres of men with battle experience. Its G.O.C. served as Chief of Staff to General Hausser, by far the ablest SS general and should therefore make a competent commander. Proportion of non-German personnel probably 50 per cent. At mid-May was still considerably below strength in M.T. and suffered from important deficiencies in officers and n.c.o's. Bulk of division capable of	A–B

Formation	W.E.	State of Training	Remarks	Evaluation within Categories
1	2	3	4	5
			operating in offensive rôle but subject to restricted mobility.	
2 *Field Divisions*				
3 Para.	12,000	Five months	Probably started forming early in 1944. Recent evidence suggests that it is well up to strength as regards personnel but it still requires further training before it can be reckoned as a first-class division.	B
(a) Parachute Divisions				
5 Para. Div.	12,000	About five months	Probably started forming early in 1944. It is still below strength. Recent evidence suggests that it is much weaker than 3 Para. Div. as regards both personnel and equipment, and is fit at present for defensive employment only.	C
(b) 3 Regiment Infantry Divisions (2 Battalion)	13,000	Part field training, part basic only	Divisions formed Dec. 1943–Jan. 1944. Organised on W.E. of three infantry regiments of two battalions and artillery regiment of three or four batteries. Include drafts from divisions on Eastern Front and new recruits, including large proportion of non-Germans. These divisions at present occupy coastal sectors, they are completing formation and training. Unlikely to be fully operational by "Overlord" Y date.	C
271 Inf.				
272 Inf.	"	"		C
275 Inf.	"	"		C
276 Inf.	"	"		C
277 Inf.	"	"		C

Formation	W.E.	State of Training	Remarks	Evaluation within Categories
1	2	3	4	5
331 Inf. Div.	"	"	Formed late in 1941 and transferred to West at end of March after two years' service on Eastern Front. Under strength at time of arrival but has probably received reinforcement since. Will contain a considerable nucleus of personnel with battle experience. Just possible it might be operational by Y date	B
352 Inf.	13,000	Field training	These divisions were formed in Oct.–Nov. 1943 and are organised on a W.E. similar to the divisions in the 270-series. They consist of cadres of battle-experienced personnel and new recruits including many non-Germans of which a high proportion are of Russian origin. The divisions are now fully operational.	A
353 Inf.	13,000	"		A
(c) 2 Regiment Infantry Divisions				
77 Inf.	13,000	Part field training, part basic only	New divisions which started forming in Feb.–Mar. 1944. Consist of cadres from battle-tried divisions and new recruits including many non-Germans. Probably organised on W.E. of two infantry regiments, each of three battalions with artillery regiment of three batteries. 84 Infantry Division is unlikely to become fully operational until a month after "Overlord" Y date. 77 Inf. Div., which is known to be 35 per cent below establishment in vehicles, and 85 Inf. Div. are not in as advanced a stage of formation.	C
84 Inf.	13,000	"		B
85 Inf.	13,000	"		C

Formation	W.E.	State of Training	Remarks	Evaluation within Categories
1	2	3	4	5
91 Inf. Div.	13,000	Part field training, part basic only	This division has just arrived in the West from Germany. Originally intended as an Air Landing Division but now appears to have become a normal 2-regiment infantry division.	C
3 L.E. Divisions				
242 Inf.	14,000	Trained in coast defence	Formed in the summer of 1943 as 'bodenständig' divisions, *i.e.*, for a mainly defensive role. At present hold coastal sectors; are probably able to provide one mobile regimental group for local counter-attack. Have under command several units of the "Ostlegion". Some indication that these divisions now only have two regiments.	B
(a) 3 Regiment Infantry Divisions				
243 Inf.	„	„		B
244 Inf.	„	„		B
245 Inf.	„	„		B
265 Inf.	14,000	Trained in coast defence	Formed in the late spring of 1943. Similar in employment and capabilities to the divisions of the 240-series. Have provided drafts for divisions in Russia and Italy, thus losing some of their best personnel. The latter probably replaced by units of the "R.O.A." and "Ostlegion".	B
266 Inf.	„	„		B
319 Inf.	17,000	Trained in coast defence	Although not positively located for several months there is no evidence for its departure from the Channel Islands where it has been stationed for over a year. It was formed in autumn 1940 as a field division but its subsequent employment suggests that it has been downgraded to the status of an L.E. division. Some evidence for its reorganisation on a two-regiment (six battalion) W.E.	B

Formation	W.E.	State of Training	Remarks	Evaluation within Categories
1	2	3	4	5
326 Inf.	14,000	Trained in coast defence	Formed autumn 1942 as a "bodenständig" division and held a coastal sector for a year. Best men drafted to Russia but these are believed to have been replaced partly by new recruits and partly by "Ostlegion" troops. Present location in Pas de Calais possibly suggests reorganisation as a field division.	B
338 Inf.	14,000	Trained in coast defence	"Bodenständig" division which has held present coastal sector for more than eighteen months. Includes many foreign elements. Capable of providing one mobile regimental group for local counter-attack out of own transport resources.	B
343 Inf.	12,000	Trained in coast defence	This group of Lower Establishment divisions, organised on a W.E. of two infantry regiments and one artillery regiment, were formed late in 1942. Shortly after completion they were sent from Germany to occupy coastal sectors in the West. Their personnel consists mainly of men from older age groups with a fair proportion of foreigners. The foreign element is believed to have been increased by the allocation of one or	B
344 Inf.	„	„		B
346 Inf.	„	„		B
347 Inf.	„	„		B
348 Inf.	„	„		B

(b) 2 Regiment Infantry Divisions

Formation	W.E.	State of Training	Remarks	Evaluation within Categories
1	2	3	4	5
			two "Ostlegion" battalions to each division during the latter half of 1943. These divisions surrendered many of their best personnel to divisions in Russia and Italy. Their present transport resources would enable each division to provide only one mobile regimental group for local counter-attack. There are, however, indications that 348 Inf. Div. which was transferred from the coast to an inland sector has undergone some form of reorganisation.	
708 Inf.	12,000	Trained in coast defence	Lower Establishment divisions. Many of their personnel have been drafted to field divisions.	B
709 Inf.	"	"		B
711 Inf.	"	"	Have held coastal sectors in the West since early 1942. Originally organised on a W.E. of two infantry regiments and one battery of artillery.	B
712 Inf.	"	"	There is some evidence for the expansion of the latter into a regiment, and unconfirmed reports suggest the addition of a third infantry regiment composed of non-German personnel. There is no evidence for the up-grading of any of these divisions on lines similar to the recently converted 715 Inf. Div.	B
716 Inf.	"	"		B
719 Inf.	"	"		B

Formation	W.E.	State of Training	Remarks	Evaluation within Categories
1	2	3	4	5
(c) Reserve Divisions				?
148 Res.	15,000	See under Remarks	The Reserve divisions are essentially training and draft-finding organisations. Their strength in personnel at any given time depends on the extent to which the influx of new recruits from the depots in Germany keeps pace with the outgoing drafts for the Field Army. The bulk of their personnel remains with the divisions for three months' training before being despatched to the field formations. The main influx of recruits takes place at the beginning of Jan., April, July and Oct., and the main exodus at the end of Mar., June, Sept. and Dec. It is, therefore, possible to calculate when the Reserve Divisions are likely to be at their lowest ebb.	
156 Res.	,,			
157 Res.	,,			
158 Res.	,,			
159 Res.	,,			
165 Res.	,,			
171 Res.	,,			
182 Res.	,,			
189 Res.	,,			
191 Res.	,,		These divisions contain a nucleus of trained personnel generally with battle experience, who are responsible for the training of recruits. Their fighting value depends mainly on the position which it occupies. A Reserve division in a coastal sector, where it disposes of static coastal artillery in addition to its own allocation of field artillery and anti-tank guns, is probably equal in value to a 700-class division, while one occupying an area in the interior of France probably has a relatively	

Formation	W.E.	State of Training	Remarks	Evaluation within Categories
1	2	3	4	5
			small fighting value, particularly in a counter-attack role. 157 Res. Div., however, which has had considerable experience in anti-partisan operations, possesses many of the characteristics of a partly-trained mountain division. There are indications that the Reserve divisions at present stationed in Belgium and N.E. France (*i.e.* 156, 165, 171, 182, 191 Res. Divs.) may be undergoing some form of reorganisation to convert them to Field Divisions. This possible reorganisation is NOT believed to affect Reserve division in the rest of France.	
(d) G.A.F. Infantry Divisions				
16 G.A.F. Inf.	10,000	Trained in coast defence	Organised on a W.E. of two infantry regiments, one regiment of artillery, and services on coy scale. Have surrendered many of their best personnel to field divisions and parachute formations. There are indications that they are passing under Army control and that they are being reorganised on a W.E. similar to that of the 270- and 350-classes of divisions. In view of their continued employment in coastal sectors, it is unlikely, however (with the exception 19 G.A.F.), that they are intended to achieve the mobility of the field divisions.	B
17 G.A.F. Inf.	"	"		B
18 G.A.F. Inf.	"	"		B
19 G.A.F. Inf.	"	"		B

Formation	W.E.	State of Training	Remarks	Evaluation within Categories
1	2	3	4	5
One unidentified division			Consistently reported in the area of Dieppe. Evidence tends to suggest that this may be Limited Employment division, although it may be only a fortress organisation and on receipt of further evidence be classed as a static division.	C
One unidentified division			This division has just been located in the Toulouse area. We have so far no evidence as to its W.E. strength or category, but it appears likely to be a field division.	C

APPENDIX 11

Extracts from the First Sea Lord's Minute of 25 May 1944 to the Prime Minister about Measures against U-Boat Dispositions

(Reproduced from Dir/C Archive, 6594 of 25 May; it was initialled by the Prime Minister on 25 May).

GERMAN PLAN . . .

'It will be noticed that the plan is designed to provide for boats which have not sailed on D-day, and it is not clear to what extent it may be modified or by what stages it may be implemented before D-day. Four U-boats have already sailed and are now believed to be in the W Channel, possibly in the area off N Coast of France . . .

COUNTER MEASURES

'Constant night air patrols have been flown in the Channel and two attacks have already been made. In the day time air patrols are covering our Channel convoy routes.

'A/S sweeps by surface forces take place each night; eg. a special support group operated, during the whole of the night of the 23rd – 24th May, N of the Brest Peninsula between 15 and 30 miles from the French coast. The hunt was continued until noon on the 24th. Fighter protection was provided but there were no enemy air reactions and no contact was made with the U-boats.

'Four support groups are being held in immediate readiness in the Western Approaches Cmd. completing their final training and equipping. These Groups are sailing for Plymouth Cmd. in the next four days, but can sail earlier if need be.

'We are watching the Assembly Area W. of Brest and we do not intend to attack it until we are sure the enemy is committed. It is most important that he should not be able to alter his plan without making signals.

'There are another four support groups in W Approaches at short notice to attack the enemy assembly area, or to move into the mouth of the Channel if we feel the enemy is forestalling D-day or acting on an assumed D-day which is earlier than the real one'.

APPENDIX 12

Allied Estimates of the German Air Situation at D-Day

(Extracted from JIC (44) 215(o) of 25 May)

Total Strength of the G.A.F. at "Overlord" Y Date.

1. In the last edition of this paper, in view of many factors which could not at the time be accurately assessed, we based our estimate of the scale of air opposition to "Overlord" on a total strength of 4,500 aircraft. This represented the mean between the extreme strengths then considered likely at "Overlord" Y date. It is now estimated that at the 1st May the total first-line strength of the G.A.F. was 5,190 aircraft and, in view of current trends, this figure is likely to be slightly exceeded by "Overlord" Y date. This situation has been brought about by a policy of conservation affecting the G.A.F. as a whole, which the Germans are likely to continue up to "Overlord" D Day in order to build up the greatest possible strength to meet the invasion in the West and a renewal of the offensive in the East. There has, moreover, recently been some recovery in the total intake from new production and repair of L.R. Bomber and S.E. Fighter types which may lead to an increase in the operational strength of these categories. On the basis, therefore, of our most recent evidence, we now estimate that the total strength of the G.A.F. at "Overlord" Y date will be about 5,250 first-line aircraft, disposed as follows:—

Western Front (including Germany N of 49°)	...	2,350
South Germany and Austria	... ...	300
Mediterranean	... ...	750
Russian Front	... ...	1,450
Non-operational	... ...	400
Total	... ...	5,250

Fighting Value.

2. The above estimate of strength and the estimated scales of effort given in paragraphs 19, 20, and 21 are misleading unless account is also taken of the low fighting value and operational inefficiency of the G.A.F. of to-day. This results from the virtual disappearance of the G.A.F.'s stored reserves of aircraft and the

fact that Germany's inadequate output of new aircraft would make it almost impossible for the G.A.F. to sustain its present first-line strength over a protracted period of intensive operations. This weakness has coincided with a correspondingly far greater increase in the strength and quality of the G.A.F.s opponents, and has prevented the employment of the G.A.F. on a scale commensurate with its actual first-line strength. Moreover, the G.A.F. is seriously short of formation leaders and of thoroughly trained and experienced crews. This weakness in the personnel of the G.A.F. has resulted in an increasing lack of efficiency among both the bomber and the fighter units. Therefore, if the G.A.F. attempts to fight hard over a prolonged period, the Germans will find it impossible to make good their losses of aircraft and crews and the first-line strength of the G.A.F. could not be maintained.

Disposition of the G.A.F. in the West immediately before "Overlord" Y Date.

3. The increasing weight of the Allied day and night bombing of targets in France and other occupied territory in the West may lead to some increases in the day and night fighter defences of these areas; nevertheless, the bulk of the G.A.F. fighter strength will, we feel, continue to be based in Germany and Austria to meet the day and night strategic bombing of Germany. Some increase in L.R. Bomber strength is likely in N.E. and Western France for attacks on targets along the South coast of England. The disposition of the G.A.F. on the Western Front on "Overlord" Y date may therefore be as follows:—

	L.R.B.	F.B.	S.E.F.	T.E.F.	L.R.R.	T.R.	Coastal	Total
S.W. France (S. of 46°)	60	...	...	20	15	...	...	95
France (W. of Seine to 46°)	175	35	90	60	35	20	...	415
France (E. of Seine) and Belgium	100	35	120	130	5	25	...	415
Holland	30	...	40	75	10	...	...	155
Germany (N. of 49°)	175	...	600	350	...	...	...	1,125
Denmark and Holland	10	...	50	15	30	...	40	145
Total	550	70	900	650	95	45	40	2,350

Forces Immediately Available.

4.   Of the above forces about 900 aircraft would be immediately available for employment as a *Close Support Force* on D Day. These might consist of:–

		First-line
L.R. Bombers	... ...	500*
Fighter Bombers	... ...	70
S.E. Fighters	... ...	220
T.E. Fighters	... ...	75
Tac. Recce.	... ...	35
	Total ...	900

*Including anti-shipping units.

Immediate Reinforcements.

5.   The following reinforcements will probably be made available, mainly from Germany and the Mediterranean, in order to oppose the landing:–

	L.R.B.	F.B.	S.E.F.	T.E.F.	Total
D Day to D + 1	110	...	90	30	230
D + 1 to D + 4	90	50	140	20	300
Total	200*	50	230	50	530

*Mainly anti-shipping units.

Further Reinforcements.

6.   Any further aircraft which might be made available for "Overlord" would probably represent replacements rather than reinforcements as such. The total of 450 S.E. Fighters (including reinforcements) represents 50 per cent. of the total S.E. fighter force of 900 aircraft likely to be available in Northern Germany and the West. The S.E. night fighter force, amounting at 1st May to 250 aircraft, included in the latter total would probably be reserved for defence in depth, together with the remainder of the S.E. day fighters which would also be required to provide cover not only for the whole Western front coast line but also for at least Western Germany. Similarly the bulk of the T.E. fighter force would probably be reserved for defence in depth against both day and night attacks on Germany and targets in France outside the immediate "Overlord" area.

7.   Up to 100 S.E. fighters, however, would probably be drawn

from the defences in depth for a short-term reinforcement of the Close Support Force for a major counter-attack. It is assumed that the Allied bombing from Italy of S. Germany, Austria and S.E. Europe will continue, and will succeed in tying down the fighter defences of those areas; should this not occur, up to a further 70 S.E. fighters might be made available.

8. *Second-line Units.*–In addition, 110 second-line aircraft comprising 30 long-range bombers, 10 fighter-bombers, 50 S.E. fighters and 20 T.E. fighters, might be made available, although it is more probable that these second-line units would be reserved for the defence of South or South-Western France against the possibility of subsidiary Allied landings.

Summary.

9. Thus the total first-line strength likely to be engaged *directly against "Overlord"* may comprise:–

					Aircraft
Forces immediately available	...	...	...	...	900
Reinforcements D + 1 to D + 4		...	...	...	530
Further reinforcements:–					
From defence in depth	...	...	...	100	
From S. Germany and Austria		...	...	70	
					170
			Total	...	1,600
Second-line Units	...	...	...	...	...	110

Scale of Effort before Assault.

10. Now that the Germans appreciate that preparations for the Allied invasion have been completed, the night bomber effort against any particular embarkation targets may reach a maximum of 275–300 sorties on any one night. Against such targets an effort of 175–200 sorties per night may be developed for three or four nights running. Such activity prior to the assault is likely and may extend to targets inland, only scattered attacks, however, are likely to develop north of the line Bristol Channel-Wash. South of this line it is unlikely that a concentration of more than 50 per cent. of the attacking force will be achieved. Such operations would, however, reduce the potential scale of L.R. Bomber effort against "Overlord" on and after D day, and if heavy losses were incurred such raids would probably be discontinued. This effort may be backed up by occasional daylight sneak raids by bombers or fighter-bombers against the South and South-East Coast. Intruder operations against Allied bomber bases by up to 10 L.R. Bombers a night will probably be continued.

11. A part of the L.R. Bomber force may be used before "Overlord" for sea-mining operations off the South and South-East coasts of England, possibly extending to the Bristol Channel. This would, however, be at the expense of the L.R. Bomber effort against targets in the United Kingdom, and is unlikely to exceed the following scale of effort:–

					Sorties
Maximum any one night	...	...	...	...	100–150
Intensive 3–4 nights per week		...	...	...	50–75
Sustained per night	...	...	...	...	25

Scale of Effort During and After Assault.
12. *L.R. Bombers.*–The total L.R. Bomber Force of 700 aircraft (including anti-shipping units) which may be built up by D+4 will constitute the main striking power of the G.A.F. during the initial stages of "Overlord". Recent evidence indicates that, as a result of training which has been carried out during the past two months, the Germans may attempt to operate the L.R. Bomber force by day as well as by night. The force is likely to suffer from lack of experience of daylight bombing under operational conditions. Moreover, the fighter escort which would be essential will have had virtually no recent experience of escorting bombers by day.

13. Nevertheless, every effort will be made to employ the L.R. Bomber force to the maximum extent both by day and by night in order to bring the heaviest possible weight of air attack against the assault forces before they are firmly established ashore. Daylight operations by Long Range as well as by fighter bombers are likely to include attacks on troop concentrations with anti-personnel bombs. In the event of heavy losses being sustained daylight operations by L.R. Bombers would probably not continue after the first 48 hours. Units as a whole are well crewed-up, but there is still a shortage of experienced crews and the standard of efficiency is not high except in a few specialised units.

14. If the L.R. Bomber force has not suffered substantial losses in daylight operations and has not been effectively attacked at its bases, a strong sustained effort (including that of anti-shipping units) might be achieved during the first week, averaging 200 sorties per 24 hours with a maximum for one 24-hour period of 450 sorties, in operations against follow-up convoys at sea and against the bridgehead area. This effort is likely to include mine-laying operations off the beach-heads which might account for up to 75 sorties per night with a maximum of 100.

Anti-Shipping Operations.
15. The L.R. Bomber force of 700 is likely to include 250

anti-shipping aircraft. These will be divided approximately equally between torpedo units (equipped mainly with Ju. 88s and a few He. 111s and Ju. 188s) and units operating with radio-controlled bombs (equipped with Do 217s, He. 177s, FW 200s). These units may for the most part remain based in S.W. France, using advanced landing grounds in N.W. France, if necessary, rather than move to bases nearer the "Overlord" landing area, which might be more exposed to bombing. In addition, to these anti-shipping units normal L.R. bomber units may use circling torpedoes to attack shipping concentrations. These have, however, not hitherto proved very effective weapons.

16.   The anti-shipping scale of attack might reach a maximum of 150 sorties on one night during the early stages of the assault, and initially radio-control bombers may be predominant. All recent experience has shown that G.A.F. anti-shipping units, particularly torpedo-bombers, incur heavy losses in attacks on convoys; in the face of strong defences they are unlikely to be capable of sustained effort on a big scale, having regard to the lack of aircraft reserves and to the shortage of trained and experienced crews. This effort is, therefore, likely to decline to an average sustained effort of 50–75 sorties per night by the end of the first week. Operations will take place mainly at dusk or dawn or in favourable moonlight conditions; torpedo bombers may operate by day if there is suitable cloud cover.

17.   *Ground Attack Forces.*–The G.A.F. offensive effort by day will be mainly by ground-attack units (FW. 190s) supplemented by aircraft from S.E. and T.E. Fighter units (FW. 190s, Me. 109s and Me. 110s, Me. 410s, Ju. 88s) operating with small and medium H.E. and anti-personnel bombs, and 21-cm. rocket mortars. During the initial stages of the assault these attacks are likely to be directed against landing craft, shipping and the immediate bridgehead area. At a later stage, and in support of a counter-attack, the principal objectives would include strong points, artillery and A.F.Vs. in the sector against which the main weight of the German counter-attack would be thrown; attacks would also be made against Allied forces concentrating preparatory to counter-attacking a German thrust. A considerable proportion of fighters and fighter bombers are likely to be inexperienced in Close Support operations by daylight. The total ground-attack effort is unlikely to exceed 400 sorties in any one 24-hour period. The sustained effort during the first few days is unlikely to exceed 200 sorties per 24-hour period.

18.   The bulk of the S.E. Fighters, however, will be employed defensively, mainly on escort duties covering ground attack and

other daylight operations, and on defensive scrambles over airfields and other vital points in rear areas.

Total Scale of Effort.

19. Immediately the Germans appreciate that "Overlord" has been launched, they will begin to redispose their air forces in France and the Low Countries and to bring up their reinforcements from elsewhere. These movements are likely to be delayed and disorganised by Allied air attack on airfields and communications. Meanwhile, however, the immediately available L.R. Bomber and close support forces must be expected to put up the maximum possible scale of effort from dawn D Day to dawn D+1. This might amount to a total of 1,100/1,250 sorties inclusive of anti-shipping operations. Once the Allies are established on shore, the G.A.F. will attempt to conserve its effort for some days in order to build up the greatest possible strength with which to support the first major counter-attacks by the land forces. During this period the effort against the bridgehead (except in the case of Long-range Bombers) is unlikely to exceed 60–75 per cent. of the maximum scale of effort which may be attained in the counter-attack. Allowing for the arrival of all reinforcements, this maximum effort, in respect of the bridgehead area only, might for one 24-hour period, rise to—

	Sorties	
L.R. Bombers ...	350–400	(including anti-shipping operations)
Ground Attack ...	200–220 *	
S.E. Fighters ...	950–1,000	
T.E. Fighters ...	80–100	(Operating with bombs and/or rocket mortars)
Tac. Recce.	20–30	
Total	1,600–1,750	

* The employment of fighters as ground attack aircraft might lead to an increase of 75–100 sorties in the ground attack effort with at least a corresponding decline in fighter sorties.

20. Such fighter effort as might at the same time be put up against strategic day and night bombing or other Allied air operations, together with long-range reconnaissance sorties, is excluded from the above estimate; the latter might amount to 30–40 sorties outside the bridgehead area, some aircraft carrying bombs on armed reconnaissance.

21. If Allied interference with G.A.F. bases and ground organisation is particularly effective, this total effort would not be

achieved, and in any event it would probably quickly decline to some 600–700 sorties per 24 hours. Assuming that serious losses were incurred, the lack of reserves would result in a wasting force. The average scale of effort might again rise for one or two days, in support of a further major counter-attack by ground forces, to 1,000–1,250 sorties for 24 hours.

Operational Efficiency.
22. The above scales of effort are those of which the G.A.F. should be capable. In view of the low fighting value and operational inefficiency of the G.A.F., however, these scales of effort may not be reached in face of Allied air superiority.

Operations subsequent to "Overlord".
23. By D+20 there would probably be no air forces on the West coast of France other than the anti-shipping units based in South-West France and a few L.R. reconnaissance aircraft. Assuming that the Allies are continuing to make good progress, the Germans to oppose a landing in Western France would not be able to divert from "Overlord" more than 50 per cent. of the then effective serviceable strength of the L.R. Bomber Force, including the greater part of the surviving anti-shipping forces. S.E. and T.E. Fighters would probably be drawn from the forces defending rear areas in Germany and the West rather than from "Overlord", and some of these would operate as Fighter-bombers and with mortars. It is estimated that the serviceable strength of the forces which would oppose such a landing would consist of–

L.R. Bombers (including anti-shipping aircraft) ...	125
S.E. Fighters	75
T.E. Fighters	20
Reconnaissance	5
Total	225

These forces might be supplemented by a further 110 second-line aircraft, as indicated in paragraph 7.

24. By D+20 the demands of "Overlord" will probably have reduced the strength of the G.A.F. in South France not engaged against "Overlord" to 25 torpedo Bombers and 25 S.E. Fighters. The anti-shipping units in South-West France would by this time be seriously reduced in strength and heavily engaged against "Overlord". A similar diversion of effort to that given in paragraph 23 might be expected against a landing on the French Mediterranean coast.

Sigint issued to the Assault Forces during their Passage on 6 June 1944

In the following list of signals those marked AUM (Admiralty Ultra Message) were issued by the OIC to Naval Commanders, and those marked KV were issued by GC and CS to SCU/SLU recipients. The originals are to be found in ADM 223/195 and DEFE 3/166 respectively.

All times B (British Double Summer Time).

(i) Intelligence about German reactions to the assault

Time of despatch to Allied Commands	Reference	Contents
0132	KV 6546	Sea Defence Commandant, Normandy, aware at 2355/5 June that some reported parachutists were dummies.
0146	KV 6547	SDC Normandy reported that some parachutists had been captured and that landings were continuing.
0155	KV 6548	At 2321/5 June 319th Infantry Division ordered an alert for the area Caen–Mont St Michel.
0219	KV 6549	SDC Channel Islands informed at 0032/6 June of airborne landing on south-east coast of the Cotentin.
0242	AUM	(a) At 0139 a minesweeper between Guernsey and Cherbourg was warned that Allied MTBs were north of the Cotentin.* (b) At 0152 all naval units between Flushing and Cherbourg were ordered to immediate readiness.

---

* This was probably a reference to the deception Operation *Big Drum* off Cap Barfleur.

Time of despatch to Allied Commands	*Reference*	*Contents*
0338	AUM	At 0210 all harbour defence vessels between Flushing and Cherbourg ordered to reinforce patrol positions immediately.
0420	AUM	At 0348 5th TB Flotilla ordered to attack landing boats off Port-en-Bassin and Grandcamp.
0427	AUM	At 0352 armed trawlers from Le Havre ordered to attack landing boats off Ouistreham and Cabourg.
0435	AUM	At 0402 Naval Gruppe West broadcast news of landing in Seine Bay between Cabourg and Marcouf.
0509	AUM	U-boats in Norwegian waters ordered to immediate readiness against indications of invasion.
0516	AUM	LCT III from Port-en-Bassin and St Vaast ordered to attack landing craft off Grandcamp.
0523	AUM	5th E-boat Flotilla had left Cherbourg by 0420.
0535	KV 6573	At 0221 SDC Normandy reported no locations to the north-eastward owing to radar failure.
0544	AUM	At 0350 six U-boats bound north-about for the Atlantic ordered to mark time.
0728	AUM	At 0621 8th Destroyer Flotilla in the Gironde ordered to prepare to move to Brest.
0741	KV 6582	GAF informed no Axis ships at sea at 0530 between Cherbourg and Zeebrugge.
0807	AUM	At 0513 all U-boats informed of Allied landing in Seine Bay.
0849	KV 6585	At 0100 an unknown Army authority reported parachute drops in the areas Caen, Cotentin and Le Havre.*

---

* The reference to Le Havre was to the Allied deception Operation *Titanic*, which involved dummy paratroop drops in that area.

Time of despatch to Allied Commands	Reference	Contents
0910	KV 6586	SDC Normandy reported at 0630 Marcouf battery under heavy fire, enemy tanks ashore between Vire and Orne, Pointe du Hoe climbed.

(ii) AUMs reporting instructions to U-boats

Time of despatch to Allied Commands	
0533/6 June	Six U-boats which had recently left the Baltic via south Norway ordered to halt and stay in positions.
0807/6	At 0513 all U-boats informed that the Allies were landing in Seine Bay.
0919/6	Five U-boats which had recently entered the Atlantic from Norway ordered to Biscay at highest speed, but submerged by day.
1402/6	Seven U-boats on hand in the Arctic ordered to return to Narvik and remain at immediate readiness, leaving nine on patrol off Jan Mayen.
1945 and 2123/6	A total of 18 U-boats had sailed from the three bases south of Brest.
2057/6	a. One U-boat, probably non-*Schnorchel*, ordered to operate between the Scillies and the Lizard. b. Unknown number of *Schnorchel* U-boats ordered at noon to leave (probably) Brest via a given position between Ushant and Lands End to the area between Cherbourg and Portland.
0109/7	Seven of the 18 U-boats from bases south of Brest had been ordered to occupy an area 150 miles west of the Gironde.
0110/7	The six U-boats off south Norway ordered to a patrol line 30 miles from the coast between Trondheim and Bergen.
0212/7	One *Schnorchel* U-boat from La Pallice ordered to the area Cherbourg–Portland by route given in 2057/6 (b).

APPENDIX 14

Intelligence Relating to 21st Panzer Division and 352nd Infantry Division up to D-Day

(i) 21st Panzer

The Sigint which confirmed in mid-May that 21st Panzer had moved to the Caen area provided no details as to its make-up or the location of its constituent elements.* But the intelligence staff at 21st Army Group at once appreciated that 'we shall on D-day make contact with 716th, 709th, 243rd, the fringe of 711th, and, within a very short time, with 352nd Infantry and 21st Panzer';[1] and if only because its move brought it so close to the invasion area, every effort was made to acquire further information.

The results of the investigation into its make-up, which had to be based on PR and ground reports of train movements and tank sightings, were summed up by 21st Army Group on 28 May. 'The likeliest conclusion' was that the division had a Panther battalion, a Pzkw IV battalion, a third battalion presumably of Pzkw IVs but conceivably of Tigers, and presumably an assault gun battalion formed the fourth battalion calling for a Brigade HQ. It might therefore have as many as 240 tanks and 40 assault guns, as compared with the 160 tanks and 40 assault guns of a normal Panzer army division.[2] In fact, as was discovered by 9 June from a captured document, the division had only two Panzer battalions, one of Pzkw IVs and one of French tanks, and 40 assault guns, and it went into battle with only 127 tanks and no assault guns.[3]

With regard to its location, the division had been extensively deployed and allotted a variety of offensive and defensive tasks. Its armour was disposed north-east of Falaise, from which position it carried out practice swoops up to the coast and back; hence the tank tracks which Allied intelligence detected north of the Caen–Bayeux lateral. One battalion from each of its Panzer Grenadier Regiments (lorried infantry) had been sited north of

---

* See above, pp 80–81.

1. WO 205/532, Weekly *Neptune* Review of 14 May 1944.
2. ibid, 28 May.
3. WO 171/129, 21st Army Group Intelligence Summary of 9 June.

Caen, one on each side of the Orne, 125 PG Regiment to the east
and 192 PG Regiment to the west. The other battalion of 192 PG
Regiment was deployed with twenty-four 88 mm anti-tank guns
on the Périers ridge, halfway between Caen and Bayeux and three
miles south of *Sword* beach. The rest of its artillery was south of the
Périers ridge and on the high ground south-east of Caen. The Flak
units were deployed around Caen.[4]

The Allies failed to unearth any firm evidence on these
dispositions before D-day. It was known that 21st Panzer had been
stationed over a wide area while it was at Rennes, and it was soon
suspected that it had detrained at Bayeux, and possibly as far east
as Lisieux, as well as at Caen.[5] 21st Army Group noted on 21 May
that 'air recce has not yet revealed precisely where 21 Pz is
harbouring, but photography of railway stations indicates detraining activity over a wider area than earlier reports suggested, from
Bayeux to . . . Lisieux. Slight signs of mechanised transport are
reported in the Forêt de Cinglais [south of Caen] and it may be
that . . . the woods are concealing from the air the concentration of
armoured vehicles. . . . In the existing slimness of our evidence it
seems most reasonable to accept the view that, however dispersed
the divisional area, the tanks of 21 Pz leaguer just south of Caen.'[6]
In the next two weeks Sigint made no reference to the division, but
12,000 PR prints of the landing area were made for the Army
authorities.[7] Neither PR nor any other source had provided clues
to 21st Panzer's precise deployment by 4 June, as 21st Army
Group confessed in its last report before D-day. This said 'nothing
more has come to light about 21 Pz; but there is slowly growing
evidence in the photographs of tank tracks north of Caen–Bayeux
lateral'. It added that the location of the division was among 'the
chief gaps in our knowledge of the enemy in the *Neptune* area'.[8]
Nor did the situation change between then and D-day. Extensive
final air reconnaissance over north-west France, begun on D−2,
had detected no new evidence about the location of the enemy's
armoured formations by the evening of D−1.[9] It is true that late
on the evening of D−1 the first ground report relating to 21st
Panzer since its move to Caen was received in London. It stated,
correctly, that 2nd Battalion of the Division's 125 PG Regiment
had its HQ at Colombelles, an eastern suburb of Caen. The

4. Ellis, *Victory in the West*, Vol I, (1962), p 201; D'Este, *Decision in Normandy*
    (1983), pp 125, 126, 134.
5. WO 219/1942, Martian Report No 97 of 24 May.
6. WO 205/532, of 21 May.
7. AIR 41/24, *The Liberation of North-West Europe*, Vol III, p 35.
8. WO 171/129, of 4 June.
9. Ellis, op cit, Vol I, p 130.

intelligence authorities noted that it was unsupported by other evidence.[10]* It was in any case received too late for action; 6th Airborne Division's parachute brigades were already en route.

It will be obvious from the foregoing that although the intelligence authorities were primarily concerned to locate 21st Panzer's tanks, they did not exclude the possibility that the division was dispersed; and it has been argued that they should in these circumstances have made special efforts to determine the precise whereabouts of its units.[12] Given that Sigint was silent and that 21st Panzer succeeded in concealing its dispositions from air observations, it is difficult to envisage what more they could have done. As distinct from reports of rail movements in the coastal zone, which were still received from agents outside the zone, ground reports from agents operating in the zone, the only other possible source, were virtually unobtainable once the Germans had evacuated most of the civilians; as already noted, only one was received on 21st Panzer, and that at the last minute.

It remains to ask whether there was an intelligence failure in the sense that the intelligence authorities did not ensure that I Corps and its commanders were fully aware of their final conclusions. As summarised by the JIC on 25 May, the final conclusions were to the effect that elements of 21st Panzer, as of 352nd Infantry, would be encountered in the forenoon of D-day and be joined by the whole Panzer Division by last light.[13] As we have seen, on the other hand, the contemporary orders and the later testimony of I Corps's commanders indicate that they continued down to D-day to believe that all or most of 21st Panzer lay 20 to 30 miles south-east of Caen with the tanks, that it would counter-attack as a whole division, and that they would not meet it before they reached Caen.† It is far from clear that they had good grounds for this belief. Although 21st Army Group's summary of 4 June may not have reached them, they received its summary of 21 May – the War Diary of 2 Canadian Armoured Brigade referred to it on 23 May[14] – and on 22 May an appreciation by Second Army not only advised I Corps that there might be up to 540 German tanks in its D-day area but also specifically warned it to expect immediate local

---

* This report is perhaps the basis of the claim that it was known before D-day that 21st Panzer PG battalions had been placed astride the Orne.[11] The claim is unsupported by any other evidence.

  † See above, p 136.

10. CAB 44/244, Chapter II, Book II, p 167.
11. Hastings, *Overlord: D-day and the Battle for Normandy* (1984) p 116.
12. D'Este, op cit, p 127.
13. JIC(44)215(o) of 25 May.
14. D'Este, op cit, p 124(n).

counter-attacks by reserves and tanks of 21st Panzer and 352nd Infantry near the coast and an armoured attack on its left flank by 12th SS Panzer in the evening.[15]

(ii) 352nd Infantry

The other gaps singled out by 21st Army Group on 4 June were 'the location of 352nd Infantry and whether 245th Infantry is in the area'. 245th Infantry had in fact gone to Dieppe.* But Rommel had moved 352nd forward from St Lo in March: two of its regiments joined the two regiments of 716th Infantry behind *Gold* beach and along the cliffs behind *Omaha* beach and its third regiment went into reserve at Bayeux.† During April intelligence disclosed that such a process of reinforcement was taking place in several sectors.[17] By 14 May it was known from PR that the process had taken place in 716th's sector between Isigny and the river Dives, but in the absence of any reference to 352nd, 21st Army Group found it 'a most unsatisfactory state of affairs that we cannot specifically identify all the elements which go to make up the sector. . . . This much is evident – that we shall on D-day make contact immediately with 716th, 709th, 243rd, the fringe of 711th and, within a very short time, 352nd Infantry and 21st Panzer'.[18]

On 4 June the intelligence picture remained essentially unchanged, but 21st Army Group came close to divining the truth. 'For some time now in other areas coastal divisions have been narrowing their sectors, while divisions the role of which has hitherto been read as lay-back have nosed forward into the gaps provided by the reduced responsibility of the coastal divisions. . . . The evidence that the same has happened on the left in the case of 716th Division is slender indeed . . . ; yet it should not be surprising if we discovered that it has two regiments in the line and one in reserve, while on its left 352nd has one regiment up and two to play. . . .'[19]

---

* See above, p 87 fn*.

† There is no foundation for the claim that 352nd was only on the coast on D-day because it happened to be holding an anti-invasion exercise.[16]

15. WO 285/3, Planning and Intelligence Summary No 23 of 22 May.
16. Haswell, *The Intelligence and Deception of the D-day Landings* (1979), p 181; D'Este, op cit, p 113(n).
17. WO 205/532 of 23 April.
18. ibid, 14 May.
19. ibid, 4 June.

The truth was that 716th had only two regiments, both of which were on the coast, though it also had one of its battalions or a unit of foreigners in reserve,[20] and that, as we have seen, 352nd had two regiments in the line and one in reserve. It would nevertheless seem harsh in the light of 21st Army Group's conclusion to speak of a failure of intelligence were it not for the probability that 21st Army Group's intelligence summary of 4 June did not reach the Commands before the assault sailed.* As it was, the troops landing on *Gold* and *Omaha* beaches believed that the coast was held by one regiment of 716th Division, a static division which was over-extended along a stretch of 53 miles from the Vire estuary to the Orne–Dives area, thought to be low in morale and composed to the extent of over 50 per cent of Poles and Russians, and expected no serious counter-attack until the Germans had brought up mobile reserves – the nearest of which, 352nd Infantry, a Field Division comprising some experienced elements from Russia and Africa that was known to be partly mobile and rated as offensive, was thought to be twenty miles inland in the St Lo–Caumont area.[23]

---

* This undoubtedly accounts for the claim that 21st Army Group discovered 352nd's presence on the coast 'just before the invasion . . . but was unable to inform the troops'.[21] This claim has given rise to the rumour that firmer intelligence about the whereabouts of the division was obtained after 21st Army Group had issued the appreciation of 4 June, but before the landings took place.[22] Such subsequent information would *a fortiori* have been too late, but there is no record that any was received.

20. Harrison, *Cross-Channel Attack* (Washington DC, 1951), p 257; CAB 44/245, Chapter II, Book III, p 397.
21. Harrison, op cit, p 319(n).
22. D'Este, op cit, p 135(n); Hastings, op cit, p 67.
23. Harrison, op cit, p 319; CAB 44/243, Chapter II, Book I, pp 73–74; CAB 44/245, p 397.

The Sources of High-Grade Sigint after D-Day

By the summer of 1944 the Germans had already embarked on a programme for improving the security of the Enigma, Fish and the medium-grade cyphers. The threat to GC and CS was to become increasingly serious from that date. By the spring of 1945, despite the re-organisation of its methods and the development of new machinery to counter the enemy's innovations, the cumulative effect of the programme had rendered its hold on the Enigma precarious, uncertain from week to week; and it had ceased to be able to read the medium-grade hand cyphers of the Army, the Air Force and the Police in stages from August 1944 to February 1945.* As luck would have it, however, the programme did not gather momentum until a month after the invasion of Normandy. Moreover, thanks to Germany's inability to bring her various measures into force without further delays or to apply all of them to all keys simultaneously, GC and CS in fact succeeded down to the end of the war in breaking with only brief interruptions, if also with some decline in the speed of decryption, a large proportion of such Enigma and Fish keys as remained in use.

(i) The Western Front

Although further German cypher precautions had already been foreshadowed in decrypts, none of them was brought into force before the Normandy landings. The preparations made at GC and CS for the exploitation and dissemination from D-day of a greatly increased volume of high-grade Sigint were thus amply rewarded.†

The naval Enigma keys in use in the west, most of which continued to be read currently, carried an enormous volume of traffic in the first few days after the invasion, and the situation

---

* The German Army in France made much less use of its medium-grade cypher than had been expected, and from February 1945 it adopted a new one which was practically unbreakable; it had been used by the Army in Italy and by the GAF since August 1944 and by the Police since September 1944.

† See Appendix 6.

reports encyphered in these keys provided valuable intelligence about the Army and the GAF throughout the fighting in Normandy. At first the volume of decrypts on the western GAF keys, no less than 15 of which were being read with little delay by D-day,* was even heavier. Although it soon subsided, most of these keys continued to be read regularly till towards the end of the year. The traffic in them dealt mainly with GAF reinforcements and operations, and provided only indirect intelligence about the ground fighting; but direct intelligence of great value on order of battle, the movements and the intentions of the German Army was obtained, as GC and CS had foreseen, from the new GAF Flivo key (Ocelot). Broken on 31 May, almost as soon as it was identified, Ocelot was read currently from 8 June, when the traffic of 7 June became available, till the end of August, and it was read regularly if not always currently for the rest of 1944. Intelligence about the ground fighting in Normandy was also obtained from two other new GAF keys, that of Flak Korps III (Platypus), which was broken intermittently from 16 June, and that of the Parachute Army (Firefly), broken frequently from the end of June.

In the first phase of the fighting in Normandy the volume of Army Enigma decrypts was not large. The key of C-in-C South-West in Italy (Puffin) and the SS keys (Orange and Quince), which were being read regularly, yielded some decrypts relating to the western front, but the keys belonging to the formations in France largely resisted GC and CS's attack. The Army Y Service key (Pullet) was broken occasionally from 8 June, and that of C-in-C West (Bantam) was read for only one day (9 June) and those of Seventh Army (Duck I and Duck II) for only two days (10 and 11 June) before 17 June. From that date, however, GC and CS's research on the Army keys began to produce results. Bantam and Duck were read regularly from 17 June to 26 June, and then from time to time until the end of July; 12th SS Panzer Division's key (Penguin) was read from mid-June from time to time;† and the Army supply key (Peewit) was broken frequently from 19 June. And from the beginning of August, when the Allied break-out from Normandy and the landings in the south of France led to a spectacular increase in German W/T traffic, these keys were all read almost daily. The volume of decrypts obtained

---

* They included the General (Red), Luftflotte 3 (Jaguar), Luftflotte Reich (Hyena), Jagdkorps I (Cockroach), Jagdkorps II (Cricket), Fliegerkorps II (Locust), Fliegerkorps IX (Wasp), Fliegerkorps X (Gnat), Luftgau West France (Snowdrop), Luftgau Belgium and North France (Lily), Luftgau West Germany (Daffodil).

† Very few divisional keys were identified and only one other was broken – Diver, the key of 319th Infantry Division in the Channel Islands, which was read occasionally from 16 October.

in August from Army keys, including that of the occupation authorities in France (Nightjar) and the first western railway key to be broken (Blunderbuss), was not to be surpassed in any other month until March 1945. Volume declined steadily from September with the return of static warfare, but other keys were now broken for the first time – notably a Wehrkreis staff key (Falcon II) and a second western railway key (Culverin), which were read from early in October.

From the beginning of September 1944 there was a further decline in the volume of GAF traffic with the reduction in the scale of the enemy's air operations. And from the same date GC and CS lived with the constant anxiety that the GAF Enigma keys would become unreadable as a result of the steady extension to them of two new German security measures. The first (Enigma Uhr) was applied to two western keys in July and eventually extended to about 15 GAF keys in all. The second came into force for ten GAF keys, including some of the principal western keys, in August and was extended to a further 14 keys by the end of February 1945. In the event these threats were overcome with little if any decline in the proportion of total GAF traffic read at GC and CS, though with some reduction in the speed of decryption, by improvements in the Allied machinery and methods and with help from the fact that, with the shrinking of the German fronts, the GAF progressively relied on a smaller number of separate operational keys. As a result of this last process, by which only two of the original western keys (Jaguar and Ocelot) were still in use by the beginning of December, the Enigma in fact produced during the last three months of 1944 a more complete picture of the GAF's activities on all fronts than at any previous period in the war.

The extension of the new security measures to the Army keys caused anxiety from September, and particularly from November, when the Army adopted additional security measures. Though it produced some decline in the speed of decryption, this development was also overcome with only a short-lived reduction in the proportion of traffic decrypted, and by the beginning of 1945, thanks again to the fact that the Army was increasingly concentrating its traffic on to a small number of general keys, notably Puffin and Falcon, as it withdrew into Germany, the proportion of traffic decrypted surpassed all earlier levels. From February 1945 GC and CS's output of Army decrypts exceeded its output of GAF decrypts for the first time in the war.

This was the result in part of GC and CS's continuing success against the important Army keys, in part of the fact that the dislocation of communications was forcing more Army traffic on to the air and in part of the decline in the activity of the GAF, but it was also due to the introduction of improved security measures

for the GAF's traffic from 1 February 1945. This step administered a greater setback to GC and CS than any it had yet
encountered. To begin with it cut the daily average of GAF
message-parts decrypted from 1,800 to 1,000, and its effects were
not fully overcome until mid-March.

Although the proportion of GAF traffic decrypted had recovered by then, and although GC and CS had continued to break
new GAF and Army keys, of which several made their appearance
with individual units or for localised purposes from February in
the growing disintegration, there was a sharp fall from the
beginning of April in the volume of GAF and Army Enigma traffic
intercepted, and thus in the volume of decrypts, which lasted till
the end of hostilities.

From the same date the volume of Fish decrypts from the
western theatre also underwent a decline, the first since the
autumn of 1944. GC and CS's success against Fish had suffered a
serious setback a few days after D-day; improved security was
introduced on C-in-C West's link with Berlin (Jellyfish), which
ceased to be readable. The link between Berlin and C-in-C
South-West (Bream) had continued to provide valuable intelligence about the fighting in Normandy till July, but it and other
links then adopted the new security procedures. In October 1944,
however, GC and CS had begun to produce solutions again and
from that date, as delays in decryption decreased and as additional
Fish links made their appearance in the west,* there was a steady
increase in the volume of decrypts which did not fall off till the
end of March 1945. The volume was higher in March 1945 than in
any other month of the war.

(ii) The Italian Front

Although the Enigma keys in use in Italy took second place to the
western keys in GC and CS's priorities from D-day in Normandy,
they continued to provide a reasonably comprehensive assessment
of the enemy, and until the autumn of 1944 they did so with little
or no delay.

Of the GAF keys the General (Red) key was less used in Italy
than elsewhere, but it continued to be read currently till the end of

---

* The most important new links were Army Group B to Berlin (Grilse; first broken in June
1944), Army Group H to Berlin (Bleak; first broken in August 1944); Army Group H to
Berlin (Lumpsucker; first broken in November 1944), the link between Army Group B North
and Army Group B South (Toadfish; first broken in December 1944), the link between Army
Group B and Army Group H (Triggerfish; first broken in December 1944).

the war. A Command key, that used first by Luftflotte 2 and then by the succession of GAF HQs in Italy (Leopard), was also read till the end of the war, frequently if not absolutely regularly, and with a fair degree of currency. The Flivo key (Puma), which had long been the most important source of operational intelligence, invaluable for both Army and GAF order of battle and intentions, continued to be read regularly and almost always currently till mid-November 1944, when it adopted new security measures. From that date, given the relatively low degree of priority that could be allotted to it, it was read only occasionally.

This was a serious setback, and all the more so because only one Army Enigma key in Italy was still being read regularly – that which carried traffic between C-in-C South-West and Berlin (Puffin) – and this was little used for communications relating to the Italian front after the invasion of Normandy. The keys of Fourteenth Army (Kingfisher) and Tenth Army (Albatross), which had rarely yielded decrypts of great operational import- ance, had ceased to be read regularly in August for lack of priority. But the situation was saved by the recovery of C-in-C South-West's Fish link (Bream). Bream had been lost following its adoption of improved security measures in July 1944; but GC and CS began to produce solutions in October. From then until the end of the war Bream decrypts regularly supplied a large volume of intelligence which, consisting as it did of the signals exchanged between enemy Commands at the highest level, lost little of its value from the fact that the decrypts were now obtained with delays of a week or even more.

From the autumn of 1944, moreover, the Fish decrypts were supplemented by the fact that despite the resort by the German Army to improved security measures, GC and CS recovered some Army Enigma keys. The Y key in Italy (Sparrow) was broken again from November after a gap since July, and read regularly until February 1945. Albatross was again read regularly from the beginning of November, and in the last two months of the war it was heavily used and carried for the first time decrypts of great operational value. Another key in use in northern Italy (Shrike) still yielded from time to time important intelligence about the movements of German reinforcements and reserves.

The main naval key in the Mediterranean (Porpoise), which was read currently throughout, increasingly provided additional in- formation about the ground fighting as the German Armies retreated.

(iii) The Soviet Fronts and the Balkans

Although it remained considerable, the volume of Enigma decrypts from these theatres declined substantially after the summer of 1944. The consequence at first of the fact that work on the western keys was making so great a demand on the resources of GC and CS, the reduction was prolonged from the autumn, when the extension of the German cypher security measures progressively increased the effort required for success against the eastern keys, and the drastic disorganisation produced by the Russian advances led to the closing down of Commands and frequent changes of W/T networks and keys.

By the end of June GC and CS was reading regularly only one GAF Command key, that of Fliegerkorps I (Ermine), outside the Balkans, and work on the main Balkans GAF key (Gadfly) became unprofitable because the contents declined in importance from September. Thereafter, most of the subordinate Balkan keys disappeared as Germany withdrew the bulk of her air forces – though a new key for the GAF Y service in the area (Mustard II) produced a large yield of decrypts from June till the end of 1944 and that of Fliegerführer Croatia (Yak) continued to be read with profit into 1945 – and most of the six or seven Fliegerkorps and Luftflotte keys in use on the other fronts were read only for short periods, the value of the intelligence they yielded being barely commensurate with the effort applied to them. The main exception was the new key (Gorilla) introduced in September for Luftflotte 4, in command in Hungary and all areas to the south; this was read regularly till the end of the war. The General (Red) key remained in use and was also read regularly, but its contents declined in value.

Of the Army keys, that which was in use between OKH and Army Group North, between Army Groups North and Centre and between both Army Groups and their subordinate armies (Avocet, formerly Vulture) was broken regularly until August 1944, but then only occasionally until the beginning of 1945; but from that date, when it progressively became the key used by most of the remaining active units on the eastern front, it was again broken regularly and provided increasingly comprehensive coverage of the fighting. On the main Russian fronts a few other keys were broken, and then for brief periods only; thus Third Panzer Army's key (Flamingo) was read for several days in August 1944. In the Balkans, Army Group E's old key (Raven) was read regularly till April 1945, but its ambit steadily shrank until it was in use only in the Aegean. The keys of Second Panzer Army (Wryneck I and II) were read frequently until Second Panzer

Army was moved to Army Group South; thereafter they were broken only occasionally and traffic in these keys had virtually disappeared by the end of 1944. A new Balkan key (Quail), introduced for Army Group E's remaining formations in September 1944, was broken with increasing frequency till the end of the war.

On these fronts, as in Italy, the decline in the volume and scope of the Enigma decrypts was more than off-set by GC and CS's success against the Fish links. Most of the links between Berlin and the eastern Army Commands had been broken before the middle of 1944, but new ones were broken for Army Group E (Gurnard) from June, for Army Group Courland (Whiting) from June, for Army Group Vistula (Crooner) from February 1945. They all carried an enormous load of signals throughout the German retreat, and though there was some falling off in the number of links and the volume of traffic after March 1945, the decrypts kept the western Allies well informed about the main developments, if not about the day-to-day fighting, on every front.

(iv) Naval Sigint

GC and CS had been alerted by decrypts before the summer of 1944 to the fact that the German Navy had plans for increasing the security of its Enigma communications by methods which differed from those of the GAF and the Army, but its ability to read the main naval keys regularly and currently was scarcely affected until November 1944. From September 1944 the extra security measures and improvised individual keys, the latter brought into force in the various fortresses formed by the Germans round the western European ports, added to its labours, but most of the new keys were read without great difficulty, and the fortress keys, of which some 30 were solved, were in any case of no great importance.

As a result, indeed, of the increased use of W/T by the enemy which accompanied his withdrawals in the eastern Baltic, in western Europe and from Norway, and which was accentuated by the disruption of his other communications by Allied air attacks, the volume of decrypts continued to grow.* The number of naval messages decrypted, which averaged 10,000 a week at the time of

---

* The breakdown of land-lines and telephones between Berlin and Paris and between Paris and the naval commands on the French coast yielded a large volume of decrypts about the administration, the supply structure and the operational problems of the U-boat Command.

the Normandy landings, was 15,320 in the week ending 18 August, and while that figure was not reached again in 1944, it was exceeded in March 1945; the peak figure for the whole war was 19,902 decrypts in the week from 11 to 17 March. Between November 1944 and February 1945, however, the Allies gradually lost the ability to decrypt the most important part of the traffic of the U-boat Command. And from the beginning of April 1945, when it first encountered problems in breaking the main Baltic key, GC and CS was aware that it would inevitably lose its long-held grip on the naval Enigma if hostilities lasted much longer.

The first of the German innovations to cause anxiety was not a cryptographic precaution, but a new communications procedure named Kurier by the Germans (Squash by the Allies) which used a special communications apparatus. The first mention of it was obtained in June 1944 from a document captured from U-505,* which, however, referred to it only as a new procedure, and from decrypts announcing that trials were to take place, which described it as 'important for the war'. The trials took place in August, when decrypts disclosed details about the procedures, including the deviations from basic frequencies which the U-boats used, established that the Germans had found that the system was not yet reliable, but also produced the disturbing news that since the German control had picked up some of the U-boat transmissions, whereas British stations had failed to intercept any of them, specialised equipment was involved.

The Germans did not resume the trials until 18 November, and in the interval British wireless and intercept experts developed a means of receiving the signals by cathode ray tube and photographing them. With experimental equipment of this nature a sufficient number of Kurier transmissions were obtained by mid-December to give a complete understanding of the system and enable the authorities to put in hand the production in quantity of the required apparatus. At this point the Germans introduced a further complication. Hitherto the deviations from

---

* The seizure of U-505 – she was captured and towed into Bermuda – had an interesting sequel. To avoid German suspicions that her cyphers had been taken the Allies took special steps – initiated by the First Sea Lord personally – to ensure complete secrecy by all concerned and to keep her crew in strict isolation, and the Germans remained unaware of her fate till early in 1945. But one of her officers then managed to pass a message back to Germany to the effect that her signal and cypher equipment had been captured. The Admiralty's history of the U-boat war based on German war records (ADM 234/68, BR 305(3), p 81) states that the U-boat Command thereupon concluded that this explained why in the summer of 1944 Allied forces had 'contrived to turn up at pre-arranged rendezvous times with the same punctuality as the U-boat themselves'. The news can have had little influence, however, on the German Navy's programme for improved cypher security, which was well advanced by the time it was received.

basic frequencies to be used by the U-boats had been announced daily in an Enigma signal which was invariably decrypted. On 9 December a new procedure came into force by which the deviations were announced using tables carried by the U-boats. Even though the announcement was decrypted, the fact that the tables were not available prevented the interception of any further signals while the German trials lasted – they lasted till the beginning of February 1945 – and necessitated the development and production of machinery designed to pick up any deviations within 200 kilocycles either side of a basic frequency and to measure them to within an accuracy of one kilocycle. This difficult feat was completed by the beginning of April 1945.

Although decrypts had recently reported that trials were to be re-started with some of the new-type U-boats, no further trials were carried out and Kurier never became operational. Had it done so, it is probable that, as the standard practice for the German shore stations was to repeat in full those signals they received from ships at sea, the Allies would have suffered no serious loss of intelligence so long as they continued to break the U-boat Enigma. But their ability to do this was undermined by the introduction of individual Enigma keys. Soon after D-day in Normandy Sigint disclosed that such keys (Sonderschlüssel) had been issued to some of the U-boats that were sent into the Channel. Those U-boats did not make use of them, but inde-cypherable signals obviously based on special keys began to be transmitted to and from U-boats in November 1944, and by February 1945 special keys were carrying practically all the operational traffic of the U-boat Command. In January two of the keys were broken for brief periods, but with such difficulty as to show that further success was unlikely; only one other was solved, in April 1945, and this result confirmed that further progress would be impossible without the development of new methods of attack.

While the special keys thus brought about the long-term, and probably the permanent, loss of the most important part of the U-boat Sigint, the regular decryption of other naval Enigma keys, of which about a dozen were of major importance, remained unaffected – but only until 1 April 1945. On that day an additional new precaution, an improved setting procedure, was brought into force for the Baltic key. GC and CS had reconstructed the settings by the end of the month. But it had experienced the loss of some decrypts, and considerable delays in the decryption of the rest; and in addition to knowing that these problems would be encountered regularly, it had by then been confronted by the disclosure that the new procedure was to be extended from 1 May to the main western key. It had to be assumed that the system would eventually be extended to all naval keys; and although GC and CS nevertheless believed that it would probably have been able to restore the earlier level of decryption in time if the war had not come to an end, it knew that this would have been impossible without a huge increase in staff and in the existing types of machinery.

(v) Enigma Keys Attacked by GC and CS between June 1944 and May 1945

Part 1   The German Air Force

GC and CS Name	Date Broken	Date Identified by GC and CS and Duration	Remarks
Armadillo	9.4.44 (By capture)	May 1944 (to August)	Flugsicherungs Regt West.
Raccoon	11.6.44	June 1944	Kampfgeschwader 66.
Cress	13.6.44	May 1944 (to August)	Y Service Western Europe
Platypus	16.6.44	May 1944 (to January 1945)	Flak Korps III.
Opossum	?	June 1944 (to August)	Kampfgeschwader 100.
Firefly	End of June	January 1942 (to December 1944)	First Parachute Army.
Gibbon	?	July 1944 (to August)	Geschwader key.
Jerboa	5.7.44	July 1944 (to February 1945)	Special key for V 1 sites; Flak Regt 155.
Glowworm	16.7.44	June 1944 (to September)	Fallschirm AOK 1 (First Army) (used by Italian units only).
Chipmunk	2.8.44	January 1944 (to March 1945)	Versuchsverband OBdL. Broken only once.
Gorilla	5.9.44	September 1944 (to end of war)	Luftflotte 4 (Hungary and southwards).
Wallflower	1.12.44	December 1944 (to March 1945)	Luftgau VI.
Gentian	2.12.44	September 1943 (to end of war)	Luftgau III.
Violet	10.12.44	March 1945 (to April)	Luftgau VIII. Not the same Violet as the general Luftgau key 1940–41 (see Vol II, p 660).
Chimpanzee	15.12.44	November 1944 (to end of war)	Luftflotte 10 (a training organisation).
Chamois	?	March 1945 (to end of war)	Flak Korps V.
Termite	?	March 1945 (to April)	Fliegerdivision 9.
Marmoset	1.3.45	September 1944 (to April 1945)	Flak Korps V.
Otter	?	April 1945	Kampfgeschwader 200.
Monkey	23.3.45	February 1945 (to April)	Flak Korps II.
Moth	11.4.45	March 1945 (to May)	Fliegerkorps II (later Luftwaffe Kdo Nord Ost).
Goat	28.4.45	April 1945 (to end of war)	Flak Korps VI.

Part 2   *The German Army*

GC and CS Name	Date Broken	Date Identified by GC and CS and Duration	Remarks
Avocet	?	June 1944 (to May 1945)	OKH/Army Group North; Army Group North/Army Group Centre and their subordinate armies. Re-name of Vulture (see Vol II, p 662).
Penguin	15.6.44	June 1944 (to July/August)	12th SS Panzer Division.
Peewit	19.6.44	June 1944 (to May 1945)	Supply key, Western Front.
Nightjar II	7.7.44	February 1944 (to August)	Military occupation authorities, France. See Vol III Part 1, p 485 for Nightjar I.
Swan	August 1944 (By capture)	May 1943 (to April 1945)	First Army. Only spasmodically broken.
Emu I and II	1.8.44	August 1944 (to May 1945)	Inter-Armies key Italy/South-east Europe.
Flamingo	3.8.44	June 1944 (to May 1945)	Third Panzer Army.
Dodo II	10.8.44	November 1942 (to April 1945)	Fifth Panzer Army. See also Vol II, p 666.
Gosling	8.9.44	May 1943 (to April 1945)	Nineteenth Army.
Quail	12.9.44	October 1944 (to May 1945)	Re-name of Vulture (see Vol II, p 662). Army Group E and subordinate Corps.
Quail II	2.11.44		
Guillemot	?	October 1944 (to November)	Kdr des Festungsbereiches West.
Wheatear	?	October 1944 (to November)	OBW special key.
Lorient	2.10.44	September 1944 (to April 1945)	Lorient to OBW and Army Group B.
Falcon II	5.10.44	? (to March/April 1945)	Used as Staff key for general Wehrkreis key Greenshank (see Vol II, p 662).
Falcon I	November 1944	Autumn 1943 (to March 1945)	Chiefly used for communications within Wehrkreis VI (Münster).
Pigeon	10.10.44	August 1944 (to March 1945)	Y key Western Front.
Diver	16.10.44	June 1944 (to April 1945)	319th Infantry Division, Channel Islands.
Tomtit	?	November 1944 (to February 1945)	South-east Germany.
Egret	8.11.44	August 1944 (to October)	Special Western Front key, OKH?
Flycatcher	21.11.44	October 1944 (to April 1945)	OKH/Crete
Ibis	28.11.44	October 1944 (to April 1945)	Used by V 2 formations, Holland.
Bunting	?	December 1944 (to January 1945)	Supply key Army Groups E and F?
Cassowary	?	January 1945 (to April)	General Plenipotentiary Hungary?
Oriole	1.1.45	October 1944 (to April 1945)	Y key OKH/Army Group G. Broken only once.
Whimbrel	15.1.45	January 1945 (to February)	Sixth Panzer Army.

Part 3   The German Navy

GC and CS Name	Period of Use by German Navy	Date Broken	Remarks
Bounce	28.8.44 to 5.5.45	At intervals from December 1944	Used between operational commands of KdK and its flotillas. Called Kleist by Germans.
Fortress keys			See p 851.
Catfish	August 1944 to ?	?	Used in Aegean. Called Athena by Germans.
Atlantik	20.10.44 to ? / October 1944 to ?	Read, but ? date	Used by stations on Atlantic coast and in Boulogne area. Built up from settings for September of Dolphin (see Vol II, pp 663–664).
Barbara	23.11.44 to ? end of war	?	Bight area.
Hackle	15.3.45 to 8.5.45	18.4.45	Netherlands area. Called Gefion by Germans. Keys previously issued as Barbara.
Albanien	5.2.45 to 2.5.45	5.2.45	Southern Adriatic.
Aegaeis	First reference 21.2.45 to ?	Never read	Aegean.
Fischreiher	17.3.45 to ?	Never read	Used by U-boat authorities in western areas for service messages (Betriebsfunksprüche).

Part 4   Non-Service Keys

GC and CS Name	Date Broken	Date Identified by GC and CS and Duration	Remarks
Blunderbuss	6.8.44	September 1942 (to May 1945)	Railway key Western Europe. At first named Rocket II. (For Rocket see Vol II, p 668).
Culverin	2.10.44	October 1944 (to November)	Railway key Western Europe. At first named Stevenson.
Roulette III	16.2.45	February 1944 (to May 1945)	Senior police officers, occupied Europe. (See also Vol III, p 487).
Plum	14.3.45	March 1945 (to April)	SS key.

APPENDIX 16

OIC Note on some Enemy Reactions to Operation *Neptune*

(OIC SI 980 of 21 June 1944)*

First Fortnight

1. In the first fortnight of Operation Neptune, we suffered a total of 105 shipping casualties due to enemy action. About 40% of these vessels were sunk, and the remainder damaged. Table I classifies these casualties according to class.

Table 1

Class	Number of Allied Ships		
	Sunk	Damaged	Total
Cruisers and above	0	2	2
Destroyers, Frigates, Corvettes	10	7	17
Minesweepers	3	7	10
Light coastal forces	2	3	5
Landing ships	7	18	25
Landing craft	13	9	22
Merchant vessels	9	15	24
Total	44	61	105

Notes 1 The casualties listed are those inflicted by enemy action at sea. Thus losses of landing craft due to beach mines are excluded. (The necessary data for such losses are not yet available.)

2 The figures may require modification in the light of later information.

2. *Comparison of First two weeks' Casualties*

Table 2 summarises broadly the casualties suffered in the first and second weeks.

Table 2

	Number of Allied Ships		
	Sunk	Damaged	Total
First week	36	38	74
Second week	8	23	31
First two weeks	44	61	105

* Reproduced from ADM 223/172.

3. *Cause of Allied Casualties*

The following table details our shipping casualties according to cause.

Table 3

Cause of Casualty	Number of Allied Ships sunk or Damaged in		
	1st Week	2nd Week	1st 2 Weeks
E boat attack	18	0	18
Mining	31	13	44
Shore batteries	7	6	13
Aircraft Attack	8	6	14
U boat attack	0	2	2
Destroyer & T/B actions	2	0	2
Actions with minor enemy surface craft (M/S etc)	0	3	3
Uncertain	8	1	9
Total	74	31	105

The drop in casualties from E boat attack and from mining is thus mainly responsible for the reduced scale of loss in the second week. As regards mining, the reduction was to be expected, since wider searched channels were created in the second period, initial lays had been largely located and swept etc. It is a reasonable prediction that henceforth losses should remain well below those incurred in the first period.

4. *Enemy E boat Effort*

The sharp reduction in the scale of E boat activity is illustrated in Table 3.

Table 4   *E boat Effort and Results*

	1st Week	2nd Week	Both Weeks
Average number on strength	31	25	28
Number of operations carried out	20	14	34
Number of sorties carried out	170	84	254
Number of casualties inflicted –			
Allied ships sunk	12	0	12
Allied ships damaged	6	0	6
Number of E boats destroyed	5	10	15
Average number of sorties per week per E boat on strength	5.5	3.5	4.5

Notes 1 E boats considered are those based on Cherbourg, Havre, Boulogne, and Ostend.

2 The 18 Allied casualties noted were due to torpedoes. It is not yet known how many of the mining casualties were caused by E boat lays.

The reduction in the scale of effort (as shown by the number of sorties per week per boat on strength) was due partly to

1. Natural diminution of serviceability in consequence of the abnormally high activity of the first week – which was some 6 times greater than their pre-Neptune rate of activity and partly to

2. Damage to boats and disorganisation caused by the bombing of Havre and Boulogne in the second week.

It is unlikely that weather had any influence on the level of activity. Though the wind was on the average higher in the second week, only one intended operation is known to have been cancelled for this cause. Further, the full-moon period, in which operations do not normally occur, fell in the first week.

4(1) *Nature of Operations*

In the first seven days, nearly all E boat operations consisted of minelaying or torpedo-carrying sorties. During the second period, they were less directly offensive; boats carried out a few diversionary sweeps (to cover the movements of M/S and other craft) and, in the last few days, some were engaged in transporting material from Cherbourg to the projected new base of St. Malo.

4(2) *E boats Lost*

The following are the causes whereby E boats were destroyed:

Table 5

Probable Cause	No. of E boats destroyed
Air attack on Havre	10
Air attack on E boats at sea	2
Mines	2
Surface craft (Destroyer & M.G.B.s)	1
	15

4(3) *Exchange Rate*

The enemy sank 12 of our ships by torpedo for the loss of 5 E boats in action, and of another 10 in port. Thus they sank less than 1 allied ship per E boat destroyed, in the operations of the first fortnight. Ignoring the heavy losses inflicted in the air raid on Havre, the exchange rate was about 2½ Allied ships sunk per E-boat lost in action. This compares with about 6 ships sunk per E boat lost in Channel operations in Jan.–May 1944.

Though details are somewhat confused, it is probable that our surface forces made contact with at least some E-boats, on about ⅓ to ½ of the occasions when the latter operated in the first two weeks. Of the total of 254 sorties, about 200 (very approximately) were on torpedo or combined torpedo-minelaying operations. These sorties resulted in the sinking of 12 vessels, and the damaging of 6 more – i.e. on the average, 1 ship was sunk for every 17 sorties, and 1 ship was sunk or damaged for every 11 sorties.

5. *Casualties due to Aircraft*

Table 6 summarises the means by which aircraft inflicted casualties on our shipping.

Table 6

Class		Number of Allied Ships	
	Sunk	Damaged	Total
Aerial Torpedo	2	3	5
Bombing	2	7	9
Total	4	10	14

Notes 1 It is possible that 1 ship was sunk and 1 damaged by FX bombs. These are included in the second line of the Table.

2 The number of casualties due to aircraft-laid mines is unknown.

3 Data on the scale of G.A.F. effort is still fragmentary.

APPENDIX 17

The Capture of Cherbourg: the Sigint Evidence

Decrypts on 17 and 18 June 1944 reflected a worsening situation in the Cotentin peninsula. At 0300 on 17 June Naval Gruppe West prohibited any more land transport to Cherbourg.[1] The immediate withdrawal into the Fortress of naval and air elements had been ordered.[2] At 2230 on 17 June the Commander of Fortress Cherbourg complained to Seventh Army that General von Schlieben had declined to reinforce the Fortress on the grounds that he was under orders to carry out a fighting withdrawal. This would further deplete forces which were already badly mauled. The western half of the peninsula had been completely opened by the withdrawal of 77th Infantry Division, and a thrust to the Fortress was expected at any moment.[3] On 18 June concentrated air attacks to screen the Army were to be made at 0850, 1320, and 1740 at the foot of the peninsula on the west coast.[4] Just before midnight on 18 June GC and CS signalled that LXXXIV Corps's situation report that morning had stated that General Hellmich had been killed and the fighting strength of formations in the Cotentin further reduced.[5]

A message on the afternoon of 18 June, signalled to Commands by GC and CS at 0703 the next morning, disclosed that forces of all branches of the armed services outside and inside the Fortress had, by Hitler's order, been subordinated to General von Schlieben who would himself be directly under Seventh Army. So long as possible without imperilling the Fortress, he was to hold large parts of the coast, including the north-west corner of the peninsula and Cap de la Hague.[6] This information was amplified in the afternoon by a signal from GC and CS containing a decrypt to which Fahrmbacher, the acting GOC LXXXIV Corps, Rommel and Seventh Army all contributed. Fahrmbacher said that Hitler had ordered that the Fortress was to be held without fail: every day counted for the conduct of the war as a whole. Rommel said

---

1. DEFE 3/173, KV 8481 of 17 June.
2. DEFE 3/174, KV 8504 of 17 June.
3. ibid, KV 8618 of 18 June.
4. ibid, KV 8659 of 18 June.
5. ibid, KV 8721 of 18 June.
6. DEFE 3/175, KV 8760 of 19 June.

that von Schlieben was to withdraw only when hard pressed: mining and every sort of trap must be used. Seventh Army specified a line from Vauville to St Vaast de la Hague, which was to be defended, adding that Rommel expected that it would be a point of honour for everyone from General to private to hold the Fortress.[7]

Two signals decrypted on 19 June reflected the disastrous results of the delay caused by Hitler's interference over the move of 77th Infantry Division south from the Montebourg sector to join Gruppe Hellmich on a defence line along the Prairie Marécageuses.* The first, despatched from GC and CS at 0344, told Commands that the division had intended to reach the area of La Haye du Puits by midday 18 June, but that according to a Flivo message that evening its rearguards had been unable to get through and had been subordinated to 709th Division (in von Schlieben's northern Gruppe).[8] The second, sent in the afternoon, disclosed that Seventh Army had been told early that day that contact had been established by reconnaissance elements with 77th Division, which had suffered heavy losses on the way south and had not got through. Its General had been severely wounded. The acting Commander was said to intend to break through to the south during the night 18–19 June.[9] A Flivo message on 20 June reporting that 1,200 men had joined the southern defence line, bringing 80 prisoners of war with them, was signalled by GC and CS on 22 June.[10]

A report at 0800 on 20 June that the main body of Gruppe von Schlieben had reached the Fortress area was signalled by GC and CS around midday.[11] At 2059 GC and CS signalled that the Fortress Commander had been told at 1600 that there would be a supply drop at about 0001–0115 by 31 aircraft south or west of Cherbourg.[12] The reply, at 2100, that the drop should be made on the west, not the south because of the proximity of the Allies, was not available until 0048 on 21 June.[13] The drop was not wholly successful. A message available on 22 June reported that containers, probably intended for Cherbourg, had been dropped in Jersey and Guernsey.[14]

---

* See above, p 175.

7. ibid, KV 8790 of 19 June.
8. DEFE 3/174, KV 8734 of 19 June.
9. DEFE 3/175, KV 8803 of 19 June.
10. DEFE 3/176, KV 9097 of 22 June.
11. DEFE 3/175, KV 8913 of 20 June.
12. ibid, KV 8951 of 20 June.
13. ibid, KV 8968 of 21 June.
14. DEFE 3/176, KV 9119 of 22 June.

Hitler's request to know what elements of 243rd, 77th and 91st Divisions were in the Fortress received the reply that it was impossible to say as they were still all mixed up.[15]

At 0722 on 21 June GC and CS signalled a situation report from von Schlieben very early that morning. The bulk of the very exhausted 709th Division had been incorporated in the land front and was being reinforced by sailors and the crews of static Flak batteries which had been put out of action. Staffs were being combed out. There had been heavy officer casualties and the morale of troops who had not yet been in action was bad. The good treatment of prisoners of war by the Allies was dangerous.[16] At 2158 GC and CS signalled information of a supply drop between 2300 and 0100 that night; visual signs were to be laid out at a dropping zone west of Cherbourg.[17] At 2217 GC and CS sent out information from the Fortress that, as the W/T and radio beacon had been destroyed by artillery and the airfield was unserviceable, white Verey-lights and recognition signals would be fired as the aircraft approached.[18] Some of these supplies, too, fell in Jersey and Guernsey.[19]

Decrypts on 22 June revealed messages passed the previous day between Hitler and von Schlieben. Hitler had exhorted him to defend Cherbourg as Gneisenau had defended Kolberg (in the Napoleonic wars). The German people and the whole world were watching and the honour of the German armed forces, and his own honour, were at stake.[20] Von Schlieben had replied that he would do his duty, but late that night he addressed a lament to Rommel: 709th Division was spiritually and numerically exhausted; the Fortress garrison was over age, untrained and pill-box minded; numbers gave a misleading picture;* the high officer casualties caused serious misgiving; leaderless groups of 77th and 243rd Divisions were a handicap, not a support, and two weak battalions of Russians were of very doubtful value; reinforcements were urgently needed for the task which Hitler had said was decisive.[22]

Information that there was to be a low-level supply drop by 20 aircraft between 2230 and 0200 on the night of 22–23 June was

---

* A message of 22 June but not available until 23 June gave a ration strength of 25,000.[21]

15. DEFE 3/175, KVs 8952 and 8980 of 20 and 21 June.
16. DEFE 3/176, KV 9001 of 21 June.
17. ibid, KV 9070 of 21 June.
18. ibid, KV 9080 of 21 June.
19. ibid, KV 9208 of 22 June.
20. ibid, KV 9173 of 22 June.
21. DEFE 3/177, KV 9319 of 23 June.
22. DEFE 3/176, KV 9167 of 22 June.

complained that no supplies arrived on the dropping zone; thirteen containers were recovered elsewhere.[24]

Notification of a supply drop during the night 23–24 June was contained in GC and CS's signal at 2102 on 23 June.[25] The decrypt of a message from the Fortress late on 23 June naming an area suitable for landing by freight-carrying gliders was signalled by GC and CS at 0410 on 24 June.[26] This was followed at 0952 by a message despatched at mid-day on 23 June to Army Group B naming suitable dropping zones for parachutists, and stating that landing from the sea was still possible in the arsenal area,[27] and at 1058 by an Army Group B message sent at 1100 on 23 June envisaging the reinforcement of Cherbourg by a Parachute Regiment, dropped and landed by air, and a Grenadier Regiment transported by sea.[28] By the evening it was known that the reinforcement of Cherbourg by sea and air had been cancelled by OKW decision. The harbour and kernel of the Fortress were to be defended to the last with all available forces, and isolated strong points were to fight to the last round. The Allies were to be tied down and hindered from making the harbour serviceable for as long as possible.[29]

Information that a supply drop was to take place between 2300 and 0130 on the night of 24–25 June was signalled by GC and CS at 2029 on 24 June[30], followed at 2146 by the decrypt of a message from von Schlieben to the effect that the garrison, which had been compressed into a narrow space, would hardly survive an attack (on 25 June).[31] During the afternoon of 24 June JK II told Panzer Lehr Division that its main effort was being transferred to Cherbourg at the request of Seventh Army,[32] but the Air Ministry commented on that day that, apart from small-scale and partly ineffective nightly supply drops, there had been no serious attempt to provide air support for the Cherbourg garrison.[33] On 25 June Army Group B wanted the whole GAF effort in the Caen area; none was available for von Schlieben.[34]

---

23.   ibid, KV 9216 of 22 June.
24.   DEFE 3/177, KV 9256 of 23 June.
25.   ibid, KV 9318 of 23 June.
26.   ibid, KV 9359 of 24 June.
27.   ibid, KV 9375 of 24 June.
28.   ibid, KV 9382 of 24 June.
29.   ibid, KV 9409 of 24 June.
30.   ibid, KV 9430 of 24 June.
31.   ibid, KV 9443 of 24 June.
32.   ibid, KV 9422 of 24 June.
33.   Air Sunset 196 of 24 June.
34.   DEFE 3/178, KV 9563 of 25 June.

At midday on 25 June GC and CS informed the Commands that in a message at 0930 that morning von Schlieben had told Seventh Army and Army Group B that the harbour and other installations had been thoroughly destroyed. The loss of the town within a very short time was inevitable since the Allies had already penetrated the perimeter. There was no chance of getting his 3,000 wounded away. The annihilation of the remaining troops must be expected. He asked whether the general situation required this.[35]

As mentioned above,* fighting continued after von Schlieben's surrender on 26 June. A message sent at 1040 on 28 June reporting that the central mole was still in German hands, and that no new attempts to force the harbour for mine-sweeping had been made so far, was signalled by GC and CS that afternoon.[36]

---

* See pp 188–189.

35. ibid, KV 9501 of 25 June.
36. DEFE 3/179, KV 9943 of 28 June.

APPENDIX 18

Intelligence about the German Defences before Operation *Goodwood*

It has been said that Ultra gave 'no warning of the multiple defence lines south-east of Caen . . . which brought *Goodwood* to a halt so quickly';[1] and that claim has subsequently been repeated with great emphasis.[2] In fact, Allied intelligence about the German infantry and armour in line and in reserve east of the Orne was very nearly correct. Ultra had reported the move of 12th SS Panzer Division to the Lisieux area, and the fact that 272nd Infantry Division had relieved 1st SS Panzer Division, which would stay close behind the front in I SS Panzer Corps Reserve.[3] Although Heavy Panzer Abteilung 503 in LXXXVI Corps Reserve 'had slipped under our guard', as 21st Army Group's intelligence summary for 20 July acknowledged,[4] its presence did not seriously diminish the immense Allied numerical superiority in tanks, while the bombing of its assembly area on 18 July left it with only nine of its Tiger tanks in action.[5]

Commander Royal Artillery VIII Corps estimated that the Germans disposed of some 300 guns. This figure was later accepted as reasonably correct, but it was noted that no mention was made of a similar number of heavy mortars.[6] In his appreciation the CRA drew particular attention to the large number of enemy guns west, north and east of Garcelles Secqueville, where he expected that the armour would meet considerable gun opposition which it would be difficult to neutralise by counter battery fire at extreme range. This information was probably based mainly on aerial reconnaissance[8] complemented, and perhaps prompted, by two important Ultra decrypts of 10 and 14 July reporting the deployment of units of Flak Korps III in this area.[9] The decrypt of 10 July disclosed that

---

1. Bennett, *Ultra in the West* (1979), p 108.
2. D'Este, *Decision in Normandy* (1983), pp 376–377.
3. DEFE 3/53, XL 1437 of 9 July; DEFE 3/56, XL 2161 of 15 July.
4. WO 171/131, No 147 of 20 July.
5. Cabinet Office Historical Section, EDS II 4/iii, s 103.
6. Ellis, *Victory in the West*, Vol 1 (1962), p 336.
7. CAB 44/249, *D-day*, Chapter IV Book II, pp 27, 28.
8. AIR 41/7, *Photographic Reconnaissance*, Vol II, p 164; AIR 41/67, *The Liberation of North-West Europe*, Vol IV, pp 42, 43.
9. DEFE 3/53, XL 1484 of 10 July; DEFE 3/55, XL 1953 of 14 July.

Assault Regiment 2 had Mixed Abteilung II/52 in the area Bourguébus–Garcelles Secqueville–St Aignan and Mixed Abteilung 266 in the area Bretteville–Rocquancourt–Hubert Folie. The decrypt of 14 July reported that there was a battle group with four Flak battle groups in the area Bretteville–Rocquancourt–Garcelles Secqueville on 12 July. The delayed decryption on 18 July of two reports giving some additional information about Flak Korps III's order of battle on and behind the Bourguébus ridge, where VIII Corps's attack was brought to a standstill, was therefore not crucial.[10]*

The strength and depth of the German positions in the *Goodwood* sector is emphasised by several sources. Both the official British publications note that, while the ground appeared inviting to armour, there were important features favouring anti-tank defence of which the Germans had taken full advantage. No evidence is offered, however, that the attack was handicapped by ignorance of the actual lay-out of the defences. One of them considers that from 'the overprint maps of the enemy defences, the air photographs provided in quantity to the formations taking part, and the detailed information on the enemy forces, particularly armour, contained in all formation intelligence summaries very full knowledge of the enemy should have obtained at all levels.' It adds – and this is not a criticism of intelligence – 'whether the strength of the German positions, especially the gun area round Bourguébus ridge, was fully appreciated by all commanders, is open to question.'[11]

Neither O'Connor, who commanded VIII Corps, reflecting on the battle in the autumn of 1944, nor Dempsey in 1951, criticised the intelligence available about the enemy. O'Connor said that, although a very material amount of tactical surprise had been achieved, the enemy knew that the best tank country was south of Caen: he was naturally alive to the threat of an armoured breakthrough in the sector, where he concentrated a large amount of anti-tank artillery. The first gun line had been overcome with

---

* According to the decrypts signalled by GC and CS on 18 July Assault Regiment 2 had Mixed Abteilung I/20 with five batteries in the Frénouville area, Mixed Abteilung II/52 with five batteries around St Aignan, and Mixed Abteilung 266 with six batteries in the area Tilly la Campagne–Garcelles Secqueville–Rocquancourt on 10 July, and on 15 July Assault Regiment 2 had one SS Flak Abteilung with three heavy batteries in the area Rocquancourt–Caillouet–Laise la Ville, and another with two heavy batteries and one medium battery in the area Bourguébus–St Aignan–Fontenay.

10. DEFE 3/58, XLs 2574 and 2595 of 18 July.
11. CAB 44/249, p 16; Ellis, op cit, Vol I, pp 332, 335, 336. See also Bennett, op cit, p 108; D'Este, op cit, pp 376, 377.

the help of the air bombardment, but it proved impossible to penetrate the second gun line.[12] As we have seen above, the existence of this gun line was well known.*

---

* But 21st Army Group's intelligence summary for 20 July claimed that the enemy's anti-tank weapons enabled him to convert a series of isolated strongpoints into 'an improvised gun line which stopped our armour.'[13] In the light of the CRA's appreciation of this seems rather disingenuous.

12.   CAB 44/249, pp 159, 160.
13.   WO 171/131, No 147 of 20 July.

APPENDIX 19

Decrypts Covering the Escape of XXI Mountain Corps

It was on 19 October, from the decrypt of Army Group E's orders of the previous day, that the Allied intelligence authorities knew of the 'decisive importance' attached to keeping open the road northwards from Scutari via Podgorica–Niksic–Trebinje–Mostar: the road was needed for the withdrawal of XXI Mountain Corps.[1] The location of Corps HQ at Scutari and the movements of 181st Infantry Division were known from a message of 26 October which was decyphered and sent to the Commands the same evening.[2] Thereafter – not always quite so promptly – the decrypts kept up a flow of detailed information about the progress of the Corps and its subordinate divisions, and the attacks on them by Partisans and Allied aircraft, those originating with the naval authorities in the south Adriatic often being the most recent in date. One naval message, sent on 3 November and decrypted on 5 November, set the main defence line as Elbasan–Durazzo–Kotor and expected further movement northwards in about eight days.[3] Another decrypt of 5 November contained not such up-to-date news. This was of an incomplete message of 27 October on the Gurnard link from the Abwehr representative with Army Group E, and revealed the plans of the Army Group Commander ultimately to bring together XXI and XXII Mountain Corps. XXI Mountain Corps was then aiming at reaching Trebinje, north of Kotor, but its journey thence to Mostar was being jeopardised by the actions in that area of Second Panzer Army's V SS Mountain Corps which, contrary to orders, was withdrawing its southern wing. As a result the road from Trebinje would have to be fought for against 'enemy forces who, completely uncontrolled, were streaming through one hundred kilometres gap in front between XXI and V SS Corps'. The Commander was worried about the difficulty of this operation 'having regard also to Allied landing now reported at Dubrovnik'.[4] On 7 November a decrypt contained information sent to Second Panzer Army on 2 November about the movement, to start about 7 November, of elements of 181st

---

1. DEFE 3/240, HP 3852 of 19 October 1944.
2. DEFE 3/243, HP 4641 of 26 October.
3. DEFE 3/302, HP 5585 of 5 November.
4. ibid, HP 5682 of 5 November.

Infantry towards Trebinje; another on 10 November indicated that on 7 November Second Panzer Army was also expecting the arrival there of 297th Infantry Division in the next few days.[5] On 12 November – the day on which the attempt at the coastal route came to a standstill –* MI 14 appreciated that the Germans were faced with a drive from Podgorica through Partisan-held territory either via Mostar–Sarajevo or, more centrally, via Andrijevica to Visegrad.[7] A week later MI 14 summarised the decrypts that had become available in noting the large concentration of forces still in the Podgorica area and northern Albania, their preparations for a breakthrough via Niksic and Mostar delayed by Partisan activities.[8] And on 26 November it observed that no appreciable progress in fighting a way out had been achieved.[9] Among the messages decrypted between the compilation of these two MI 14 summaries was one of 19 November – decrypted on 20 November – from the Sea Defence Commandant South Adriatic describing the forces attacking 181st Infantry Division in the Danilovgrad area as 'apparently well-armed and well-led regular troops'.[10]

By 3 December MI 14 knew from Sigint of the planned relief operation of the Corps by 22nd Infantry Division.[11] The decrypt disclosing this move was dated 30 November – a week after the decision was taken. It is a long report from C-in-C South-East of 26 November; 22nd Infantry Division was assembling in the Prijepolje area in order, after repairing the bridge over the Lim, to push as far as the road fork south of Bijelopolje to meet an unspecified Mountain Corps. GC and CS commented: 'Doubtless XXI Corps since XXII Corps moving NW from Pristina via Kraljevo and Uzice from 16th'.[12] On 10 December MI 14 reported that no contact had yet been made between the two forces and that the relief force in its turn had met stiff Partisan resistance and was threatened with encirclement, 'though it probably will succeed in forcing its way out northwards'.[13] The decrypts on which this summary was based included one of 5 December of a message

---

* Though the Corps's intention to thrust along this route after 12 November continued to appear in the decrypts.[6]

5. DEFE 3/303, HP 5890 of 7 November; DEFE 3/304, HP 6154 of 10 November.
6. eg DEFE 3/306, HP 6748 of 15 November.
7. WO 208/4317, MI 14 Weekly Summary for the CIGS, 12 November.
8. ibid, 19 November.
9. ibid, 26 November.
10. DEFE 3/308, HP 7198 of 20 November.
11. WO 208/4317, MI 14 Weekly Summary for the CIGS, 3 December.
12. DEFE 3/313, HP 8254 of 30 November.
13. WO 208/4317, MI 14 Weekly Summary for the CIGS, 10 December.

from the Sea Defence Commandant Albania of 4 December complaining of 'complete' enemy mastery of the air which made withdrawals in territory affording only poor cover much more difficult. The result was considerable losses through continuous attacks by multi-engined aircraft and fighter-bombers.[14] Several decrypts covered the German problems in dealing with the attacks on the Bioce bridge over the Tara.[15] Even the weather could be traced in the decrypts.[16]

On 17 December MI 14 expected the link between XXI Mountain Corps and 22nd Infantry Division to take place in a few days.[17] As well as situation reports on the progress being made towards the link-up, MI 14 had received on 13 December the decrypt of Army Group E's orders of 7 December making arrangements against the time when the link-up had been achieved. Decisive measures were to be taken for the rapid continuation of the march in such ways as closing up from Bioce northwards to avoid further mishaps to the bridge and by deploying 297th Infantry Division against Sahovici, north-west of Bijelopolje, for which 'maximum march performance' was demanded; as a hint of what it expected Army Group E observed that through Macedonia and Serbia German withdrawing forces had achieved marches of up to 50 km. After 297th Division had reached Mojkovac (which is south-west of Bijelopolje) it was to be subordinated to XCI Corps (to which 22nd Infantry belonged): XCI Corps would be responsible for the accelerated passage of all remaining elements of XXI Mountain Corps via Visegrad to Sarajevo. Elements of 297th Division were destined for the Drina position.[18] Other decrypts showed more effects of Allied air attacks. One of 19 December contained a report by XXI Mountain Corps on 16 December showing that bombers and fighters had been active on the entire road of advance (sic) from 1000 to 1700 hours, dropping leaflets to disrupt morale and causing considerable losses in men and material.[19] Another of 20 December, which was shown to the Prime Minister, reported that Allied air attacks on 17 December were having an almost crippling effect; it was also in this decrypt that the strong artillery fire of Floydforce at Danilovgrad was noted.[20] Also on 20 December a message with the news that the spearheads of XXI Mountain Corps and 22nd

---

14. DEFE 3/314, HP 8636 of 5 December.
15. DEFE 3/314, HP 8733 of 6 December; DEFE 3/315, HP 8910 of 8 December; DEFE 3/316, HP 9052 of 10 December.
16. DEFE 3/313, HP 9225 of 12 December.
17. WO 208/4317, MI 14 Weekly Summary for the CIGS, 17 December.
18. DEFE 3/317, HP 9340 of 13 December.
19. DEFE 3/319, HP 9781 of 19 December.
20. ibid, HP 9876 of 20 December.

Infantry Division had met on 18 December was decrypted.[21] Reproducing this in its summary for the CIGS of 24 December MI 14 commented 'There is likely to be little delay in the enemy's subsequent withdrawal westwards over R Drina'.[22] On 22 January C-in-C South-East's report of 14 January was decrypted: vanguards of Army Group E were through the defences of the extended Visegrad bridgehead and 'the great disengagement movement in the South East area' was concluded.[23]

---

21. DEFE 3/319, HP 9988 of 20 December.
22. WO 208/4317, MI 14 Weekly Summary for the CIGS, 24 December.
23. DEFE 3/500, BT 3009 of 22 January 1945.

APPENDIX 20

KdK Operations in the Mediterranean, 1944–45

The development of the Small Battle Units Command (Kommando der Kleinkampfverbände – KdK) began when the 10th Italian MAS Flotilla went over to the Germans at the Italian surrender, but it was not formally established until April 1944. It was then subordinated directly to OKM and given its own Enigma key (Bonito). The key was broken in May and was thereafter read with some delay, but without difficulty except for a brief period in September–October 1944. Its initial operations were directed primarily against the Anzio bridgehead.*

It was learnt from decrypts that after the loss of its base near Anzio the KdK contemplated limiting itself to defensive operations from its Mediterranean bases and to making plans for sabotage when La Spezia, Genoa and other ports were captured by the Allies.[1] In a message of 4 August, signalled to the Commands by GC and CS on 7 August, the local KdK authorities recommended that, as there was no prospect of successful offensive operations in Italy, the assault craft should be transferred to northern France or some other more promising theatre.[2] From 15 August, however, as decrypts showed, they were called on to operate against the Allied landings in the south of France, and the KdK was persuaded that operations could still be carried out profitably in the Mediterranean if its command arrangements were reorganised and strengthened.[3]

In fact the KdK's activities against the Allied bridgehead in the south of France met with no success. Enigma decrypts disclosed on 16 August that three German-manned Italian MAS boats were to attack the landings as soon as possible;[4] they did so on the night of

---

* See Volume III Part 1, pp 194–195.

1. For examples see Naval Headlines of 16 and 26 June, 1, 7 and 21 July 1944; DEFE 3/178, KVs 9542 and 9650 of 25 and 26 June; DEFE 3/49, XL 343 of 1 July; DEFE 3/52, XLs 1009 and 1033 of 7 July; DEFE 3/57, XL 2442 of 17 July; DEFE 3/59, XL 2818 of 20 July; DEFE 3/62, XLs 3549 and 3971 of 26 and 29 July; DEFE 3/63, XL 3971 of 29 July.
2. DEFE 3/114, XL 5121 of 7 August.
3. DEFE 3/123, XLs 7357 and 7365 of 21 August; DEFE 3/126, XLs 8141 and 8229 of 27 and 28 August; Naval Headlines of 28 and 29 August.
4. DEFE 3/119, XL 6496 of 16 August; DEFE 3/120, XL 6516 of 18 August; Naval Headlines of 16 and 17 August.

17–18 August to no effect, though the Enigma message reporting their departure from Imperia was not signalled to the Commands till the afternoon of 18 August.[5] On the night of 18–19 August the three boats were all sunk in an attack on St Tropez; the decrypt announcing their intentions was sent to the Allied Commands at 1609 on 18 August.[6] On 20 and 21 August the Enigma gave warning that a German assault boat flotilla and some Italian assault boats were being moved to Villefranche and that they would be operating on the nights of 22 and 23 August.[7] It gave no advance warnings of the sorties they made on the nights of 24 to 29 August inclusive before being forced back to San Remo,[8] but their reports on their operations were decrypted and the successes they claimed were not substantiated.[9]

By the end of August the KdK had created an operational command for the Adriatic–Aegean area (Operations Staff Haun) and one for the western Mediterranean at San Remo (Operations Staff Hartmann).* In September, soon after its arrival at San Remo, Operations Staff Hartmann under a new commander (Böhme) was renamed K-Staff Italy. In December Haun's staff at Trieste was subordinated to K-Staff Italy and renamed 6th K-Division. In January 1945, when the German Naval Command Italy was re-named Naval Chief Command South, K-Staff Italy became K-Staff South and moved its HQ to Vigo di Fassa.[11] The Allies knew of these command arrangements from the Bonito

---

* At this point the Italian midget submarine (CB) organisation was absorbed into the KdK. The Enigma showed that the Germans had discussed the use of CBs in December 1943, that they had assembled some at Trieste in June 1944, and that a flotilla of them arrived at Pola in November.[10]

5. DEFE 3/121, XL 6933 of 18 August.
6. Roskill, *The War at Sea* (Vol III Part 2 (1961)), p 100 and fn 1; Naval Historical Branch, FDS 65/54, *German Small Battle Unit Operations 1943–45*, p 39; DEFE 3/121, XL 6933 of 1609/18 August.
7. Naval Headlines of 21 August; DEFE 3/122, XL 7177 of 20 August; DEFE 3/123, XLs 7309 and 7328 of 21 August.
8. Naval Headlines of 27, 29 to 31 August, 1 and 2 September; DEFE 3/125, XLs 7977 and 7993 of 26 August; DEFE 3/126, XLs 8020 of 26 August, 8261 and 8321 of 28 August, 8468 of 29 August; DEFE 3/128, XLs 8573 and 8630 of 30 August, 8693 of 31 August; DEFE 3/220, XLs 8762 of 31 August, 8886 of 1 September.
9. Roskill, op cit, Vol III Part 2, pp 101–102: FDS 65/54, pp 39–40.
10. DEFE 3/694, ZTPGR 4251 of 28 December 1943; Naval Headlines of 2 July 1944; DEFE 3/49, XL 321 of 1 July; DEFE 3/302, HP 5734 of 6 November; DEFE 3/304, HP 6031 of 8 November; DEFE 3/312, HP 8032 of 28 November.
11. DEFE 3/669, ZTPGMs 86584, 86595; DEFE 3/670. ZTPGM 87404; DEFE 3/680, ZTPGM 97938; DEFE 3/472, ZTPG 206715; DEFE 3/324, BT 1186 of 4 January 1945; DEFE 3/325, BT 1342 of 5 January. See also FDS 65/54, pp 38–40.

decrypts, which also provided a comprehensive running account of the numbers, types and fortunes of the craft under the two Commands.

In the western Mediterranean there was one flotilla of assault boats: 1st Assault Boat Flotilla (later K-Flotilla 611). This was based initially at Villefranche, then at San Remo and finally, from March 1945, at Genoa. From San Remo it made only one offensive sortie in September. Between then and the end of 1944 Enigma decrypts reported its losses in two sorties but gave no advance warning of them. By January 1945 it had suffered such severe casualties in its operations and from Allied shelling of the port, that it could operate only in the immediate vicinity of San Remo against Allied patrols. Between then and the end of April, when San Remo was evacuated, it made some ten sorties with only one success – damage to a French destroyer on 17 April.[12] A decrypt available on 17 March disclosed that K-Staff South was opposing the formation of a new K-Division at La Spezia because its existing forces were 'already feeble and inactive'.[13] There were also two flotillas of *Marder* (one-man torpedoes): K-Flotilla 363, which lost 12 out of 16 craft in its first sortie in December and did not operate again, and 364, which suffered heavy losses in two sorties in September but continued to operate occasionally from San Remo. From decrypts it was shown that it had incurred serious casualties in two sorties in December.[14] From decrypts there was also information about two other K-Flotillas: K-Flotilla 411 which, using the *Molch*-type of one-man midget submarine, lost ten out of eleven submarines in its first and last operation on 20 September; and K-Flotilla 213, equipped with the *Linse* (radio-controlled explosive motor-boat), which although then based at Ravenna, may have supplied the craft which operated off the south of France in the first half of September 1944. In October a detachment from it lost all its craft to Allied shell-fire soon after

---

12. Roskill, op cit, Vol III Part 2, pp 111, 243; FDS 65/54, pp 41–43; Naval Headlines of 17 September, 27 and 28 October 1944, 16 January 1945, 10 February and 19 April; DEFE 3/675, ZTPGMs 89897, 89898, 92335; DEFE 3/681, ZTPGM 98798; DEFE 3/243, HPs 4503 and 4679 of 25 and 27 October; DEFE 3/317, HPs 9286 and 9343 of 13 December; DEFE 3/318, HP 9587 of 16 December; DEFE 3/319, HP 9941 of 20 December; DEFE 3/505, BT 4491 of 10 February; DEFE 3/508. BT 5238 of 20 February; DEFE 3/518, BT 7690 of 19 March; DEFE 3/519, BTs 7767 and 7815 of 20 and 21 March; DEFE 3/567, KO 688 of 18 April.

13. DEFE 3/517, BT 7468 of 17 March.

14. Roskill, op cit, Vol III Part 2, pp 101, 111; FDS 65/54, p 40; DEFE 3/220, XL 8878 of 1 September; DEFE 3/223, XL 9592 of 9 September; DEFE 3/225, HP 122 of 14 September; DEFE 3/320, BTs 90 and 121 of 22 December; DEFE 3/322, BT 647 of 29 December.

arriving in San Remo. This detachment operated briefly against Leghorn from Genoa in January 1945.[15]*

In the Adriatic, in addition to K-Flotilla 213, the KdK had 2nd Assault Boat Flotilla (later K-Flotilla 612) from November 1944; Enigma decrypts showed that its arrival had been delayed by the demands of other theatres, particularly Normandy, and the difficulty of finding suitable bases.[18] From Pola it carried out small raids and landed agents during the winter of 1944–1945, and from November a detachment from it operated with the 3rd E-boat Flotilla from Lussino. Allied raids drove this detachment in February 1945 to Brioni; it operated from there till the end of April.[19] Enigma decrypts usually gave general warning of its intentions and disclosed the frequent postponements of its plans, but rarely gave tactical warning of the attacks. For example, before the most successful of its raids – that on Split on the night of 11 February in which HMS *Delhi* was slightly damaged and a landing craft severely damaged – the decrypts disclosed on 2 February that the attack was planned for the next good weather after 9 February, but provided no precise alert.[20] The Third Assault Boat

---

* Germany built 690 *Marder*, of which 150 operated in the Mediterranean, 400 *Molch*, of which 30 operated in the Mediterranean, and 1,080 *Linse*, of which 120 operated in the Mediterranean.[16] In the spring of 1945 decrypts disclosed that she contemplated sending *Seehund* (two-man midget submarines) to Italy, but none appear to have arrived.[17]

15. Roskill, op cit, Vol III Part 2, p 101; FDS 65/54, pp 41–42, 44; Naval Headlines of 29 September, 3 and 27 October, 2 March; DEFE 3/681, ZTPGMs 98257, 98528; DEFE 3/682, ZTPGM 99716; DEFE 3/122, XL 7217 of 20 August; DEFE 3/126, XL 8060 of 26 August; DEFE 3/220, XL 8878 of 1 September; DEFE 3/226, HP 337 of 16 September; DEFE 3/230, HP 1482 of 28 September; DEFE 3/232, HP 1925 of 2 October; DEFE 3/243, HP 4503 of 25 October; DEFE 3/301, HP 5431 of 2 November; DEFE 3/305, HP 6287 of 11 November; DEFE 3/310, HP 7628 of 24 November; DEFE 3/503, BT 2975 of 2 February 1945; DEFE 3/519, BT 7789 of 20 March; DEFE 3/570, KOs 1268 and 1442 of 24 and 26 April.
16. Roskill, op cit, Vol III Part 2, Appendix W.
17. DEFE 3/508, BT 5086 of 18 February; DEFE 3/512, BT 6088 of 2 March; DEFE 3/562, BT 9405 of 4 April; DEFE 3/565, KO 241 of 12 April.
18. DEFE 3/112, XL 4562 of 3 August 1944; DEFE 3/226, HP 354 of 16 September; DEFE 3/301, HP 5431 of 2 November; DEFE 3/318, HP 9587 of 16 December.
19. FDS 65/54, p 46; Naval Headlines of 8 December 1944, 1 March 1945; DEFE 3/311, HPs 7894 and 7968 of 26 and 27 November; DEFE 3/312, HP 8032 of 28 November; DEFE 3/313, HPs 8367 and 8497 of 1 and 3 December; DEFE 3/315, HP 8814 of 7 December; DEFE 3/320, BT 105 of 22 December; DEFE 3/323, BT 892 of 31 December; DEFE 3/572, KO 1863 of 2 May 1945.
20. Roskill, op cit, Vol III Part 2, pp 111–112; FDS 65/54, pp 45–46; Naval Headlines of 4 February; DEFE 3/503, BT 4000 of 2 February; DEFE 3/506, BTs 4517 and 4568 of 10 and 11 February; DEFE 3/507, BTs 4829 and 4951 of 14 and 16 February; DEFE 3/508, BTs 5013 and 5228 of 17 and 20 February.

Flotilla (later K-Flotilla 613) was formed at Fiume in December 1944, but it saw virtually no action.[21]

The KdK authorities also shared with the Mediterranean naval commands the control of four Special Operations Units (MEKs) which were used mainly in sabotage operations against harbour installations, shipping in ports, and radar installations. Decrypts showed that MEK 80, operating from San Remo from December 1944, made unsuccessful attempts to capture Allied troops for interrogation and landed a few agents behind the Allied lines before being over-run by the Partisans in April 1945.[22] MEK 71 operated from Pola against the Adriatic coast from November 1944 until the end of February. Decrypts then disclosed that C-in-C South-West had ordered the KdK to improve German intelligence on the threat of Allied landings, which was seriously hampered by the lack of air reconnaissance, by devoting more effort to landing agents behind the Allied lines, and that MEK 71 was to take on this work. It was divided for the purpose into three detachments operating from Pola, Venice and La Spezia. It was driven out of Pola by Allied air raids in March; but it left behind a small rearguard which operated against Ancona till mid-April.[23] MEK 90, at Dubrovnik until October 1944, was then withdrawn to

---

21. DEFE 3/682, ZTPGM 99289.
22. Naval Headlines of 15 and 22 December 1944; DEFE 3/664, ZTPGMs 81836, 81840, 81863, 81891; DEFE 3/665, ZTPGM 82213; DEFE 3/312, HP 8032 of 28 November; DEFE 3/317, HP 9451 of 15 December; DEFE 3/319, HPs 8934 and 9925 of 19 and 20 December; DEFE 3/320, BT 12 of 21 December; DEFE 3/506, BT 4585 of 11 February 1945; DEFE 3/570, KO 1442 of 26 April; DEFE 3/571, KO 1533 of 27 April.
23. FDS 65/54, pp 45–46; Naval Headlines of 27 to 29 November 1944, 1 to 3 March and 8 March 1945; DEFE 3/678, ZTPGMs 95149, 95676; DEFE 3/685, ZTPGMs 102332, 102514; DEFE 3/242, HP 4459 of 25 October; DEFE 3/243, HPs 4598 of 26 October, 4653 and 4713 of 27 October; DEFE 3/302, HPs 5699 and 5734 of 6 November; DEFE 3/303, HP 5793 of 6 November; DEFE 3/304, HPs 6010 and 6031 of 8 November, 6119 and 6124 of 9 November, 6171 and 6180 of 10 November; DEFE 3/305, HPs 6383 and 6462 of 12 November; DEFE 3/306, HPs 6605 and 6715 of 14 and 15 November; DEFE 3/309, HPs 7438, 7450 and 7464 of 22 November; DEFE 3/311, HPs 7767 of 25 November, 7893, 7894, 7922 and 7968 of 27 November; DEFE 3/312, HPs 8021, 8032 and 8034 of 28 November; DEFE 3/313, HPs 8367 and 8497 of 1 and 3 December; DEFE 3/316, HP 9135 of 11 December; DEFE 3/318, HP 9682 of 17 December; DEFE 3/319, HPs 9759 and 9771 of 18 December; DEFE 3/320, BTs 105 and 121 of 22 December; DEFE 3/509, BT 5404 of 22 February 1945; DEFE 3/511, BTs 5944, 5961 and 5962 of 28 February, 5985 of 1 March; DEFE 3/512, BTs 6002, 6088 and 6248 of 1, 2 and 4 March; DEFE 3/514, BT 6622 of 8 March; DEFE 3/520, BTs 8076 and 8187 of 23 and 24 March.

Germany and sent to Norway in April 1945.[24] MEK 20, which was in the Aegean, had been withdrawn to Germany in August 1944.

Apart from the diversion of its craft to the work of transporting agents, KdK activities were hampered from the beginning of March 1945 not only by the shortening of the coastline held by the Germans and the lengthening of the hours of daylight, but also, as decrypts disclosed, by the shortage of fuel and the withdrawal of men and equipment from the Mediterranean. In the first week of March C-in-C South-West ruled out the reinforcement of the K-Flotillas because he could not guarantee allocations of fuel even to the existing units, and ten days later K-Staff South was ordered to send to Germany all the craft and equipment produced in northern Italy in January and February.[25] In April it was known from decrypts that K-Staff South, which had recently complained that its operations were coming to a standstill, including the landing of agents, had been ordered to send to Germany all one-man submarines held at its production centre at Sesto Calende, and that KdK in Berlin had warned that its forces in Italy would be useless for coastal defence unless fuel was provided.[26] In March, however, a decrypt had disclosed that the KdK had resisted a plan by which the special SD organisation under Skorzeny would take over its Mediterranean units,[27] and those units remained indefatigable in the use of their limited resources.

In the Ligurian Sea they virtually confined themselves to landing agents and saboteurs until the German Army withdrew beyond the Po; however, decrypts reported frequent sorties for this purpose. Five agents were arrested at Leghorn on 27 March after decrypts had disclosed that a party had been landed there from La Spezia on 18 March;[28] other agents, who were shown in a decrypt of 20 April to have been landed at Viareggio, were captured on 25 April.[29] A message signalled by GC and CS on 26 April disclosed that 28 agents had been landed in the south of

---

24.   DEFE 3/664, ZTPGM 81879; DEFE 3/677, ZTPGM 94816; DEFE 3/112, XL 4562 of 3 August 1944; DEFE 3/232, HP 2135 of 4 October; DEFE 3/235, HP 2520 of 7 October; DEFE 3/305, HP 6475 of 13 November; DEFE 3/506, BT 4660 of 12 February 1945.

25.   Naval Headlines of 5 and 6 March, 6 April; DEFE 3/512, BT 6246 of 4 March; DEFE 3/513, BT 6373 of 5 March; DEFE 3/515, BT 6837 of 11 March; DEFE 3/517, BTs 7336 and 7358 of 16 March, 7468 of 17 March; DEFE 3/562, BTs 9405 and 9500 of 4 and 5 April.

26.   DEFE 3/565, KO 241 of 12 April; DEFE 3/568, KO 802 of 19 April.

27.   DEFE 3/517, BT 7461 of 17 March.

28.   DEFE 3/518, BT 7546 of 18 March; Naval Headlines of 18 March; WO 204/971, AFHQ Intelligence Summary No 12 of 27 March.

29.   DEFE 3/568, KO 883 of 20 April; WO 204/971, No 16 Part IV of 25 April.

France, 5 on the west coast of Italy and 28 on the Adriatic coast.[30]

In the Adriatic most of the effort in March went into a combined operation with E-boats against Ancona, to attack shipping in the port, raid the airfield and pipe-line and to land agents. Between 3 and 13 March, when they disclosed that the operation had been ordered for that day, the decrypts also disclosed its preparation and its objectives in considerable detail. On 14 March they showed that it had been postponed for 24 hours, and on 15 March that it had been broken off following Allied sightings of the E-boats. Decrypts of further messages reported that eight agents had been landed and that the attack on the airfield and the pipe-line, repeated on the night of 19 March, had failed.[31] On 27 March AFHQ reported that four agents had been captured and that the attempt to sabotage the pipe-line had been frustrated.[32] The planning, the execution and, in many cases, the failure of a series of similar but smaller operations were disclosed in Enigma decrypts in April and early May; several attempts to land agents and saboteurs near Cattolica and between Ravenna and Ancona, a raid by swimming saboteurs against Zara and a final all-out sabotage effort against targets in the Ancona area that was ordered on 28 and 29 April on the eve of the German surrender.[33]

This last project was no doubt planned in response to orders issued by the KdK Command on 24 April that its units were to go on fighting to the end, as the Nazi party's political division of OKM had insisted in a decrypt available on 8 April.[34] It was accompanied by last-ditch acts of defiance in the western Mediterranean. Decrypts signalled on 23 and 24 April disclosed the intention to

---

30. Naval Headlines of 27 April; DEFE 3/570, KO 1430 of 26 April.
31. Naval Headlines of 4 and 5 March, 13 to 17 March, 19 March, 21 March; DEFE 3/512, BTs 6153 and 6176 of 3 March, 6249 of 4 March; DEFE 3/513, BTs 6277 and 6454 of 4 and 6 March; DEFE 3/515, BTs 6764 and 6786 of 9 and 10 March; DEFE 3/516, BTs 7094 of 13 March, 7162 and 7185 of 14 March; DEFE 3/517, BTs 7289 and 7454 of 15 and 17 March; DEFE 3/518, BTs 7553 and 7583 of 18 March, 7733 of 20 March.
32. WO 204/971, No 12 of 27 March.
33. Naval Headlines of 24 and 31 March, 2 to 4 April, 10 April, 18 April, 20 April, 22 April; WO 204/971, No 16 Part IV of 25 April; DEFE 3/520, BT 8186 of 24 March; DEFE 3/601, BTs 8773 of 29 March, 8810, 8868 and 8885 of 30 March; DEFE 3/561, BTs 9065, 9084 and 9123 of 1 April, 9190 of 2 April (amended in DEFE 3/563, BT 9612 of 6 April); DEFE 3/562, BT 9409 of 4 April; DEFE 3/563, BT 9612 of 6 April; DEFE 3/564, BTs 9825 and 9945 of 8 and 9 April; DEFE 3/565, KOs 121 of 11 April, 205, 219 and 224 of 12 April; DEFE 3/566, KOs 252 of 12 April, 355, 357 and 358 of 13 April, 398 and 475 of 14 and 15 April; DEFE 3/567, KOs 547 of 16 April, 595, 607, 646 and 656 of 17 April; DEFE 3/568, KOs 800 and 833 of 19 April, 975 and 984 of 21 April; DEFE 3/572, KO 1863 of 2 May.
34. Naval Headlines of 8 April, 25 April; DEFE 3/570, KO 1268 of 24 April.

operate against Allied patrols and carry out *Marder* attacks in the harbours of Nice, Monaco and Toulon.[35] Others available on 26 and 27 April disclosed that 17 small craft had made a suicide attack on Leghorn on 24 April;[36] only two of the craft survived the attack, at least eight being destroyed by Allied action.[37]

35. DEFE 3/569, KOs 1185 and 1250 of 23 and 24 April.
36. DEFE 3/570, KOs 1431 and 1467 of 26 April; DEFE 3/571, KO 1513 of 27 April.
37. Roskill, op cit, Vol III Part 2, pp 243–244; FDS 65/54, p 44; WO 204/971, No 17 of 2 May.

APPENDIX 21

Sigint on the Activities of the Italian Partisans, June 1944–April 1945

Partisan operations in Italy, hitherto a comparatively minor threat to the enemy's lines of communication, became a source of serious anxiety to the Germans from 7 June 1944, when General Alexander called on the Partisans to rise against the Germans and sabotage their communications, and they remained so until, on 14 November, he ordered the Partisans to halt large-scale activity and lie low for the winter.[1]

Analysis of the voluminous information reaching the Allies about these operations from their contacts with the Partisans is beyond the scope of an account of Allied intelligence, but we here summarise what was learned about them at the time from the high-grade German and Japanese decrypts. These provided reliable evidence of the German assessment of, and response to, the threat.

In a message on 3 June 1944, signalled by GC and CS three days later, C-in-C South-West asked the Supreme SS and Police Commander in Italy to take counter-measures against numerous guerrilla bands reported to be assembling between Siena and Lake Trasimeno.[2] From a decrypt of 17 June it was learned that on 13 June Armee Abteilung von Zangen reported Partisan activities in northern Italy which included cutting the road between La Spezia and Reggio Emilia in several places by blowing up bridges.[3] Decrypts available on 18 June contained the information that on 17 June guerrillas were making surprise attacks in part of LI Mountain Corps's sector and that early on 18 June 3rd PG Division had captured Roccastrada (which was behind the line held by XIV Panzer Corps) but that the clearing up of the rearward areas was expected to take a considerable time.[4] Flivo messages on 19 June, signalled to the Commands on 20 June, reported that 90th PG Division was heavily engaged with Partisans and with the French, while in 15th PG Division's sector Italian

---

1. D Stafford, *Britain and European Resistance 1940–1945* (1980), pp 193–194.
2. DEFE 3/166, KV 6612 of 6 June 1944.
3. DEFE 3/173, KV 8423 of 17 June.
4. ibid, KV 8685 of 18 June.

civilians had reportedly betrayed German positions in the previous few days thereby causing losses.[5]

How seriously the Germans now viewed the Partisan threat was shown by the decrypt on 20 June of an order issued the previous day by Kesselring for dissemination down to the smallest units.[6] This said that the guerrilla situation in the Italian area, particularly in central Italy, had grown sufficiently acute to constitute a serious danger for the fighting troops and their supply, as well as for the armaments industry. Accordingly the fight against guerrillas was to be carried out with the utmost rigour and all available means. Any commander who in choice and severity of method went beyond the restraint usually practised by the Germans would be protected. Immediate severe intervention was the only deterrent that would nip large-scale transgressions in the bud. On 21 June this decrypt was sent to the Prime Minister with two others which reported that 90th PG Division was engaged in heavy fighting with guerrillas west of the road to Siena.[7]

On 21 June GC and CS signalled a message of 17 June informing OKW that increasing Partisan activity in north Italy had made it necessary to reinforce the protection of several stretches of railway line. Marsch battalions could no longer be used for this purpose since replacements were urgently needed for fighting formations.[8] On 25 June a decrypt contained a message of 24 June from the Flivo with 3rd PG Division reporting fighting with guerrillas in the line of communications area.[9] A Luftflotte 2 report on 26 June, decrypted on 27 June, said that despatch riders were being fired on near Arezzo while Partisan activity on the Reggio–La Spezia road was increasing daily and was better organised.[10] In a message of 27 June, decrypted on the following day, the Flivo with 15th PG Division (under LXXVI Panzer Corps) defined an area around Poppi which was considered to be Partisan territory. In one sector there were four guerrilla groups with 1,000 men.[11] Also on 28 June GC and CS signalled a report of 25 June by C-in-C South-West on the Partisan situation. There had been two surprise guerrilla attacks south-east of Radicondoli (near Siena) in Fourteenth Army's sector. In one engagement, in which the Partisans had been in radio contact with the British, many had been killed and a village had been burned down. In an operation

---

5.   DEFE 3/175, KV 8921 of 20 June.
6.   ibid, KV 8925 of 20 June.
7.   Dir/C Archive, 6853 of 21 June; CX/MSS/T221/20 and 21.
8.   DEFE 3/176, KV 9004 of 21 June.
9.   DEFE 3/177, KV 9483 of 25 June.
10.   DEFE 3/178, KV 9745 of 27 June.
11.   DEFE 3/179, KV 9952 of 28 June.

near Camerino (in LI Mountain Corps's sector) 70 guerrillas had been killed and 18 German soldiers freed. In north Italy a munitions factory west of Turin and railway repair shops in Milan had been attacked; railway tracks had been blown up south-west of Gorizia; and there had been a battle between police and guerrillas east of Postumia.[12] A message of 22 June, signalled on 29 June, ordered the arrest of all males between the ages of 18 and 45 in the area between the main defence line and the line Cecina–Siena–Cettadi–Cassetto–Ancona, and stated that all arrested in anti-guerrilla operations were to be sent to the Reich.[13]

An order issued by Kesselring on 1 July to the effect that his warning of severest measures against guerrillas must not be an empty threat, was decrypted on 2 July: where guerrillas were present in large numbers a percentage of the male population was to be arrested and, in the event of violence occurring, shot; villages in which Germans were fired on were to be burned down and culprits publicly hanged; neighbourhoods were to be held responsible for all acts of sabotage.[14] The decrypt of a message from Luftlotte 2 containing the information that in an operation in the west Apennines no resistance worth mentioning had been encountered and that 50 guerrillas had been killed and 700 taken prisoner was signalled on 4 July.[15] Another GAF message reporting that 240 guerrillas had been killed and 250 captured in an operation south of Fidenza (between Parma and Piacenza) was signalled on 7 July.[16] A report by the Flivo with 42nd Jäger Division (in Liguria) on an operation against a Garibaldi Brigade of guerrillas by four battalions between 2 and 7 July was signalled on 12 July.[17] The guerrillas, organised on Bolshevik lines, had been some 500 strong and well-armed; the higher command was good with a well-developed signals network. The lower chain of command was bad and unenterprising. Fighting value had been slight. The German casualties were 4 dead and 17 wounded. 104 guerrillas had been killed and the booty included four 7.5 centimetre guns and some motor transport. A decrypt of 15 July disclosed an attack by guerrillas on barracks in Pinerolo following an air raid.[18] Another of 19 July disclosed that in an operation south-west of Parma 22 guerrillas had been killed and 81 German soldiers liberated by 18 July.[19] Decrypts available on 22 July

---

12. ibid, KV 9949 of 28 June.
13. DEFE 3/48, XL 43 of 29 June.
14. DEFE 3/49, XL 451 of 2 July.
15. DEFE 3/50, XL 674 of 4 July.
16. DEFE 3/52, XL 1068 of 7 July.
17. DEFE 3/54, XL 1722 of 12 July.
18. DEFE 3/56, XL 2114 of 15 July.
19. DEFE 3/58, XL 2706 of 19 July.

mentioned that the Assault Boat School at Stresa had been attacked by guerrillas on successive nights, and that on the night 19–20 July guerrillas wearing German uniforms had released 60 prisoners from the gaol at Imperia.[20] On 24 July it was known from a decrypt that only isolated and weak contact was made in an anti-guerrilla operation south of the Via Emilia on 23 July.[21] A GAF message of 24 July, decrypted on 25 July, reported that a railway protection battalion had deserted to the guerrillas; that a steel works had been occupied by guerrillas; and that 34 guerrillas had been killed and 150 taken prisoner in an operation under Luftflotte 2.[22] Another decrypt, available on 31 July, contained a message of 30 July about another anti-guerrilla operation; in this Luftflotte 2 claimed 337 killed, 1,438 prisoners and 82 Germans freed.[23] In a message dated 26 July, signalled to the Commands on 5 August, C-in-C South-West reported guerrilla attacks on railways, bridges, cable lines and persons; 447 guerrillas had been killed and 280 shot or hanged.[24] In a telegram of 21 July, decrypted on 16 August, the Japanese embassy to the Italian government reported from Venice that guerrilla activity had increased throughout northern Italy since the fall of Rome despite Axis counter-measures; it estimated the number of guerrillas at between 400,000 and 500,000.

During August and September 1944 Enigma decrypts contained little about the Partisans. But in a telegram of 6 September, decrypted on 23 September, the Japanese embassy in Venice reported that although the Germans and the Italians had had considerable success in their large-scale punitive operations, guerrilla activity was still increasing particularly around Turin and along the Franco–Italian frontier, where severe German reprisals were having little effect.[25] On 27 September decrypts of further Japanese telegrams dated 10 and 16 September reported that in the Turin area the guerrillas had rallied since the Allied landings in the south of France.[26]

On 1 October the decrypt of a GAF message of the previous day reported 400 guerrillas killed, 800 prisoners taken and large quantities of booty captured in an operation in the Apennines.[27] According to the decrypt of a message available on 7 November

---

20. DEFE 3/60, XL 3073 of 22 July.
21. DEFE 3/61, XL 3361 of 24 July.
22. ibid, XL 3414 of 25 July.
23. DEFE 3/64, XL 4155 of 31 July.
24. DEFE 3/113, XL 4757 of 5 August.
25. BAY/HP 10 of 23 September.
26. BAY/HP 32 of 4 October.
27. DEFE 3/232, HP 1790 of 1 October.

3,633 Partisans had been killed and 8,421 taken prisoner, 336 Germans and Italians had been freed, and 24 mortars and large quantities of small arms had been captured in anti-guerrilla operations between 8 and 19 October.[28] On 20 October, in a telegram from Venice decrypted on 17 November, the Japanese gave the following Italian estimates: the total number of guerrillas was 94,000, of which 30,000 were 'formidable'; there were 30,000 in Piedmont, 27,000 in eastern Italy, and a large number on the frontier with France.[29] On 30 October, in a signal decrypted on 3 November, the Japanese Naval Attaché in Berlin, reporting on a recent visit to Italy, said that the Germans were succeeding in the vigorous measures to put down the guerrillas.[30]

Attempts to quell the Partisans were reflected in several Enigma decrypts in November. In a decrypt available on 10 November Corps Lombardy reported that the (newly arrived) Littorio Division had made its first contact with guerrillas south-west of Piacenza; its task was to annihilate them from there to the coast and the Corps named several bombing targets in the area.[31] From another, signalled on 15 November, it was known that the GAF Command had told LXXV Corps that it was unable to support an anti-guerrilla operation because of fuel shortage.[32] A decrypt of 18 November disclosed that Corps Lombardy had asked for reconnaissance of a suspected guerrilla airfield which was alleged to handle fairly strong air traffic at night.[33] GAF orders for 21 and 22 November (signalled on 23 November) included PR of a guerrilla airfield.[34] It was known from a decrypt available at the end of December that Corps Lombardy was still being troubled by guerrillas in the third week of December; its Flivo reported clashes south-west of Acqui and north of Bobbio, and German casualties in guerrilla ambushes at Sestri Levante.[35] And on 19 December LXXV Corps carried out a successful anti-guerrilla operation north-east of Turin, according to a decrypt signalled on 29 December.[36]

On 28 November the Japanese embassy, by then in Brescia, reported (in a telegram decrypted on 13 December) that as a result of positive measures, amnesty and the cold weather, 20,000

---

28. DEFE 3/303, HP 5803 of 7 November.
29. BAY HP 99 of 17 November.
30. SJA 1091 of 3 November.
31. DEFE 3/304, HP 6177 of 10 November.
32. DEFE 3/306, HP 6725 of 15 November.
33. DEFE 3/308, HP 7048 of 18 November.
34. DEFE 3/310, HP 7509 of 23 November.
35. DEFE 3/322, BT 698 of 29 December.
36. ibid, BT 697 of 29 December.

guerrillas in northern Italy had surrendered.[37] And on 29 December the decrypt of a circular issued by the German Ministry of Foreign Affairs on 22 December was available; it stated that 50,000 guerrillas had surrendered, and attributed the Axis success to the fact that the stabilisation of the Apennines front, unexpected by the Partisans, had faced them with the prospect of 'another winter with the Germans'.

During the winter 1944–1945 the Partisans were indeed hard-pressed by the Germans, who were able to give them attention as Allied military pressure on the main front relaxed. They also faced vigorous police activity in the towns. As a result the active strength of the Partisans dwindled rapidly, as was reported in further Japanese diplomatic decrypts. In January the Naval Attaché in Berlin reported that guerrillas had been instructed to disperse because they could not be supplied with arms and ammunitions for the present.[38] And the Ambassador in Brescia gave the total number of 'bandits' who had surrendered as 74,000. The remainder he described as 'pretty tough', chiefly Communists and mainly in the Piedmont and Emilia districts.[39] In February a telegram from the same Ambassador reported that the activities of the 'bandits' had been much diminished by winter and punitive measures except in eastern Udine and western Piedmont.[40] In March decrypts disclosed that by the third week of February Partisan activity in the Ossola region was restricted to the lower Ossola valley and that even there only a few units were effective.

In mid-March, however, it was known from a decrypt that on 3 March 40,000 Partisans and 2,000 ex-Carabinieri were ready to rise, and another – not available till 24 April – showed that at the end of March Partisans in the Val d'Aosta were re-organising and gaining strength. On 11 April the decrypt of a message from C-in-C South-West of 2 April provided evidence of increasing guerrilla activity in northern Italy and Istria.[41] Another decrypt contained a message that a police undertaking in the Gorizia area in the third week of April had ended with over 170 guerrillas killed and 350 taken prisoner.[42]

It was arranged that the Partisans would resume their activities on a large scale when the Allies returned to the offensive, with a

---

37. BAY/HP 136 of 15 December.
38. BAY/BT 33 of 19 January 1945, (SJA 1407 of 17 January, with TOO 12 January).
39. BAY/BT 40 of 25 January.
40. BAY/BT 95 of 24 February.
41. DEFE 3/565, KO 98 of 11 April.
42. DEFE 3/571, KO 1644 of 29 April.

view to preventing the destruction of Italian resources and to maintaining order as the Germans retreated. During the last phase, however, which began when the final Allied offensive opened on 19 April, the only decrypt worthy of mention was that of a telegram sent by the Japanese Ambassador from Brescia. Forwarded for him by his colleague in Berne, the telegram, dated 25 April and decrypted on 30 April, reported in general terms increasing guerrilla activity in organised attacks.

APPENDIX 22

The July Plot

The attempt to assassinate Hitler on 20 July 1944 took place against the background of intelligence reports to the effect that civilian and Service morale had declined so sharply since the Normandy landings and the opening of the Russian offensives that the regime was threatened. In the decrypts of Japanese telegrams the Ambassador in Berlin was reporting that the spirit of the people remained as resolute as ever and that the leaders were not considering any compromise,[1] but another revealed that the Japanese Consul-General in Vienna had learned indirectly from German government authorities by 22 June that in view of the success of the landings 'anti-Prussian and anti-Nazi elements may have an effect which would be by no means negligible'.[2] The SIS received similar reports in July: the rapid Soviet advances and the quite unexpected progress of the western invasion had produced 'a very noticeable deterioration' in civilian morale and rumours that opposition to the regime was being organised by workers and in 'certain military circles'.[3] From a reliable intermediary in a neutral capital, moreover, the SIS had learned that the success of the landings had dealt a serious blow to German prestige in Japanese circles in Berlin, which were inclined to believe that a change of regime, carried out with the approval of the Army and the Party, was 'extremely probable'.[4] There is no firm evidence, however, that, as distinct from generalised surmises, Whitehall received any specific advance notice of the actual assassination attempt.

In January 1944 the JIC had reported that 'there is at present no evidence that any faction exists within the Army or within the Party, or still less among the people as a whole, which is likely to overthrow the present regime within the foreseeable future'.[5] It had repeated in February that 'direct revolutionary action is highly improbable. ... There is no subversive organisation'.[6] On 23 March it had mentioned that there was some 'slight evidence' that

---

1. BAY/XL 44 of 15 July 1944.
2. BAY/KV 231 of 23 June.
3. Dir/C Archive, Nos 213 of 1 July, 235 of 17 July.
4. Dir/C Archive, No 227 of 17 July.
5. JIC(44)12(0) of 11 January.
6. JIC(44)42 of 18 February, paras 161, 162.

an opposition movement existed, but in April and again on 3 June it had still been of the view that opposition was not organised.[7] In March an approach was made to the British Mission in Stockholm by Trott zu Solz, one of the leaders of the German underground, who offered to provide information about 'an anti-Nazi organisation in which certain high German military officers were interested'. In May the SIS got reports from Lisbon to the effect that the opposition in Germany was planning to dispose of Hitler and that its preparations were under way. On 1 June, however, a meeting, called together by the Foreign Office to consider whether it would serve any purpose to make contact with the German underground movements, had reached the same conclusion as the JIC. The meeting had divided the known opposition into two main groups: Christian Socialists concerned with the future of Germany, who were of no immediate consequence, and high military officers who might collaborate if offered better terms than unconditional surrender. With regard to the latter, there was some evidence that some Generals were now anti-Nazi, but nothing to suggest that they were organised or that they had reached agreement with civilian groups. They were unlikely to take 'isolated action'; if they did 'they could not succeed'.[8] On 18 June MI 14 drew the attention of the CIGS to recent Enigma evidence that the Abwehr was being fused with the SD under Himmler's control and commented that 'the possibility of a *coup d'état* against Hitler (unless one sponsored by Himmler himself – and this is an unlikely event) is more remote than ever'.[9]

Towards the end of June Trott zu Solz was seen in Stockholm by a representative of SIS in an attempt to obtain further intelligence. He reported that Trott had provided a statement on the aims of the organisation he claimed to represent, had requested some form of recognition of its existence and some qualification of the term 'unconditional surrender' and had said that another emissary would later visit Stockholm to learn the British government's reply; and he asked for instructions as to further dealings with such people, 'seeing that from an intelligence point of view their only value is confined to a general survey of the anti-Nazi group of which they are members'. He was told to insist that there would be no departure from the Allied insistence on unconditional surrender, the Foreign Office taking the view on 6 July that 'these people . . . won't act without our backing, which, if given, might gravely embarrass us later'.

---

7.   JIC(44)109(o) of 23 March, 127(o) of 3 April, 228(o) of 3 June.
8.   Woodward, *British Foreign Policy in the Second World War*, Vol V (1976), p 362.
9.   WO 208/3573, MI 14 Weekly Summary for the CIGS 18 June.

As late as 14 July the JIC believed that the vigilance of the Gestapo and the recent promotion of Nazis to the highest rank in the Services made it unlikely that the military leaders would seek an armistice.[10] But on 18 July it instructed the JIS to reconsider this last assessment and to find out what evidence there was on the form a German collapse might take.[11] We do not know whether Whitehall received a last-minute warning from the US authorities.

Unlike the SIS, the OSS had maintained contact with the German underground since before January 1943 through its representative in Berne, Mr Allen Dulles. In despatches dated 13 and 14 July he advised Washington that an attempt to assassinate Hitler, on the preparations for which he had reported somewhat sceptically following meetings with the plotters in April and May, might take place at any time.[12]

On 22 July the OSS reported that it had been obvious by the first week of July that the German government was aware of 'impending revolt in high military circles' and was preparing to place the military establishment under Nazi control.[13] It was obvious by then that the plot had failed. An announcement on the German radio that Hitler was alive, the first indication that the *coup* had been attempted, was heard by the BBC at 1740 on 20 July, and Hitler broadcast to the nation about midnight.[14] The first Sigint evidence, a naval Enigma signal from Dönitz reporting the attempt on Hitler's life, naming the Generals involved, announcing that Himmler was replacing General Fromm as GOC Home Army and ordering an immediate 'state of alarm readiness' was intercepted late on 20 July and decrypted about 0900 on 21 July. It stated that orders from Army authorities were not to be obeyed, but that requests and instructions from Himmler 'were to be complied with'.[15]* Signals from the GAF authorities and from Keitel ordering that only instructions from Himmler himself were to be obeyed were decrypted on 21 July.[17] A signal from OKM of 21 July, decrypted on 22 July, ordered the Navy to exercise the

---

* The proclamation issued by the conspirators on 20 July, giving their instructions, was not decrypted till 22 and 23 July. It was intercepted in two separate Enigma signals, the second of which broke off before the end.[16]

10. JIC(44)302(o) of 14 July.
11. JIC(44)314 of 18 July.
12. Dulles, *Germany's Underground* (1978 reprint), pp 135–140; Hoffmann, *The History of the German Resistance 1933–1945* (English edn 1977), pp 225, 235–239, and its appendix I (Nos 3 and 4).
13. Hoffmann, op cit, Appendix I, No 5.
14. Hoffmann, op cit, p 439; Dulles, op cit, p 1.
15. DEFE 3/441, ZTPG 265561 of 2345/20 July; DEFE 3/573, CX/MSS/C 280 of 0935/21 July.
16. DEFE 3/573, CX/MSS/C 286 of 1504/22 July, C 289 of 2034/23 July.
17. ibid, CX/MSS/C 281 and 282 of 1120 and 2120/21 July.

sharpest watch on the source of all instructions. But on 21 July another naval Enigma signal cancelled Dönitz's state of alarm message; this was also decrypted on 22 July.[18] On 25 July the decrypt of a GAF Enigma signal issued early on 21 July confirmed Himmler's new appointment and carried his orders for extreme vigilance by the SS and the Police, who were authorised to call on GAF supply authorities for assistance.[19]

The first of a stream of diplomatic decrypts was available on 22 July; it was a circular issued by the German Ministry of Foreign Affairs at 0800 on 21 July giving guidance on how to play down the significance of the plot. The remainder were of no importance apart from two Japanese messages sent from Berlin on 21 July and decrypted on 24 and 25 July – the first reporting that 'the city had returned to normal', the second that 'repercussions on the general situation have been small'[20] – and a signal from the Japanese Naval Attaché decrypted on 28 July; this advised Tokyo that it was 'quite impossible to regard the incident as an enemy-instigated plot with no deeper significance. . . . The possibility cannot . . . be excluded that the counter-measures taken hereafter may be such that . . . the underlying conditions will . . . deteriorate still further'.[21]

---

18.   DEFE 3/441, ZTPG 265901.
19.   CX/MSS/T255/53.
20.   SJA 584 of 25 July.
21.   SJA 599 of 28 July.

Tactical Intelligence during Operation *Market Garden*, 17 to 25 September 1944

Early on 17 September Army Y indicated that elements of 9th and 10th SS Panzer Divisions, operating as two battle groups of battalion strength under the command of a third battle group called 10th SS Panzer Frundsberg, were among the forces delaying XXX Corps's advance from the Escaut canal.[1] By 18 September, however, the Dutch Resistance had reported that some elements of 9th SS Panzer were on the Ijssel river.[2] On 17 and 18 September Y was plentiful in the Best–Zon sector, but at Nijmegen the only intelligence came from 'civilian sources', and there was none about the situation at Arnhem.[3] On 20 September Second Army could still only guess that the opposition at Arnhem included SS personnel and some tanks under 9th SS Panzer.[4] By 21 September Y and POW had identified Corps Feldt in the Nijmegen sector with 6th Parachute Division, said to consist of only two regiments of one-battalion strength, several other GAF units and Division Scherbening from Wehrkreis VI (this was 406th Landesschützen Division) under command. Further south, the composition of the combined 9th–10th SS Panzer force remained unclear until 23 September, when POW established that Panzer Brigade 107, Battle Group Frundsberg and a third group in the Nijmegen area were operating as independent formations, though all containing elements from SS PG Regiment 21 of 10th SS Panzer Division, and that 10th SS Panzer was not itself operating.[5] On 21 September POW gave warning that elements of 59th Infantry Division were approaching from the west with orders to attack, and 245th Infantry (also from Fifteenth Army) and Panzer Brigade 107 were identified on XXX Corps's eastern flank.[6]

---

1. WO 285/4, Second Army Intelligence Summary No 105 of 17 September 1944.
2. ibid, No 106 of 18 September; WO 171/133, 21st Army Group Intelligence Summary No 160 of 18 September.
3. WO 285/4, Nos 105 of 17 September, 106 of 18 September.
4. ibid, No 108 of 20 September.
5. ibid, No 111 of 23 September.
6. ibid, No 109 of 21 September.

During 22 September Y followed the Panzer Brigade's activities in the German offensive at Veghel.[7]

High-grade Sigint yielded a good deal of tactical information, but it was decrypted with some delay and added little to what had been learned from the sources in the field. The GAF decrypts were the exception. From them the first indication of the GAF's reaction to the landings was available in the early hours of 18 September; JK II was to be reinforced from 3rd Jagd Division, hitherto reserved for the defence of the Reich and itself allotted two more Gruppen of FW 190.[8] Signalled to the Commands at 1038 on 18 September, another decrypt disclosed orders of 1430 on 17 September for the diversion of aircraft of 5th Jagd Division to the area of the landings.[9] Later in the day other decrypts showed the problems of 5th JD in operating its aircraft remote from its usual bases south of the Main.[10] At 1812 on 18 September the decrypt of orders issued by Luftflotte 3 at 0430 on that day was signalled to the Commands. These made it clear that the main effort was being transferred into the landings areas, with defence of the Reich temporarily taking second place; Fliegerkorps IX was being put at two hours' readiness; JK II was to act principally against any airborne reinforcements but also to operate against bombers and fighters supporting the landings.[11] From 13 September the GAF decrypts also frequently gave advance notice of orders and intentions, mainly relating to JK II and 5th JD, but they were of little value in view of the Allied control of the air.[12]* Requests from the German Army for air support were usually decrypted too late to be of much operational use.[14] The decrypts of the situation reports of the ground fighting issued by the enemy

---

* The Allied fighter screen was so powerful that the German fighters rarely got through. As it became known later, only 75 were sent to the Arnhem–Nijmegen area on the first day. The effort briefly increased thereafter, but the Allied escorting force numbered 586 US and 193 British fighters.[13]

7. ibid, No 110 of 22 September.
8. DEFE 3/266, HPs 486 and 494 of 18 September.
9. DEFE 3/227, HP 510 of 18 September.
10. ibid, HP 547 of 18 September; CX/MSS/T311/6.
11. DEFE 3/227, HP 541 of 18 September.
12. eg DEFE 3/227, HPs 565 of 18 September, 618 of 19 September, 734 of 21 September; DEFE 3/228, HPs 805 of 21 September, 837, 841 and 898 of 22 September.
13. AIR 41/67, The *Liberation of North-West Europe*, Vol IV, pp 150, 151, 152–153, 164; CAB 106/972, I Airborne Corps Report on Allied Operations in Holland September–October 1944, para 76.
14. eg DEFE 3/228, HPs 920 and 927 of 23 September; DEFE 3/229, HPs 1024, 1035, 1106 of 24 September, 1152, 1176, 1191, 1209, of 25 September, 1224 of 26 September.

added little to those received from the Allied formations.[15]

This was also true of the order of battle intelligence. A decrypt of 18 September disclosed that 406th Division was being brought in, but the news that it had been in action that evening in the Nijmegen area with four battle groups (27,000 men) and a GAF field battalion was not decrypted till 21 September.[16] References on 19 September to the arrival of 59th Infantry and on 20 September to the fact that Panzer Brigade 107 had been diverted from Aachen were decrypted after those formations had been identified in the field.[17] References to the German intention to make the counter-attack at Veghel, which was called off on 23 September, were not received until late on 24 and early on 25 September.[18]* Decrypts of 21 September located II SS Panzer Corps at Doetinchem and disclosed that Wehrkreis VI had assembled 4,763 men for it (Division Bohlmann) on 17 and 18 September.[19]

---

* According to the US official history, Dutch sources gave warning of the German preparations for this operation (see above, p 389).

15. eg DEFE 3/227, HPs 516, 518 of 18 September, 578 of 19 September, 643, 660, 661, 668 of 20 September; DEFE 3/228, HPs 813 of 22 September, 904 of 23 September; DEFE 3/229, HPs 1004, 1010, 1019 of 24 September, 1211 of 25 September.

16. DEFE 3/227, HPs 501, 522 of 18 September, 729 of 21 September.

17. ibid, HPs 584, 619 of 19 September, 669 of 20 September; Ellis, *Victory in the West* Vol II (1968), p 35; MacDonald, *The Siegfried Line Campaign* (1963), p 153.

18. DEFE 3/229, HPs 1019 of 24 September, 1119, 1127 of 25 September.

19. DEFE 3/227, HP 729 of 21 September; DEFE 3/228, HP 803 of 21 September.

APPENDIX 24

Air Ministry Appreciations on the Build-up of the German Fighter Force in the West November 1944

(i) Air Sunset 253 of 7 November 1944

GERMAN AIR FORCE

Western Front

1. German plans for rapid, secret build up of close support forces on western front in connection with a still undefined 'project' appear to be nearing maturity: further information not only bears out conclusions in Air Sunset 252, but also fills out picture of German intentions.

2. On 6/11 Luftgau VI area Enschede–Bonn–Erfurt–Hildesheim ordered subordinate airfields to prepare for arrival at short notice of SEF units from central and eastern Germany as follows:

(A) 6 airfields in Ruhr for JG 77 (probably 3 Gruppen from Berlin area, perhaps 100 serviceable aircraft).
(B) 5 airfields in Kassel area for JG 300 (probably Gruppen from Berlin area, perhaps 75 serviceable a/c).
(C) 1 airfield in Paderborn area for JG 301 (probably 1 Gruppe, perhaps 25 serviceable aircraft).

3. These dispositions, covering reinforcements comprising up to 200/A serviceable aircraft, are almost certainly only part of the planned reinforcement of the west. In addition to Luftgau VI, which requires stocking up of 11 airfields, on 26/10 Luftgau XI (the northern neighbour of Luftgau VI) on same day asked for data covering 9 airfields. Hence similar reinforcement in area between Bremen and Osnabrueck must be expected: in this connection it should be noted that JG 27 in NW Germany has made preparations to join signals network of the close-support command on the western front.

4. Above information, indicating transfer for operations on the western front of up to 400 serviceable aircraft from strategic defence, confirms Air Sunset 252. In addition, however, it now seems clear that, as well as greatly increased fighter cover, GAF plans envisage ground-attack operations both by night and by day on a scale in excess of anything yet attempted on the western

front, and it is possible that some part of SEF reinforcements may be used as fighter-bombers. Such a possibility is indicated by repeated mentions of preparation to fit bomb-racks to SE fighters in the west (including whole of JG 26), but similar use of SE fighters has been projected more than once in the past with small effect. Apart, however, from this extemporisation, there is evidence that night ground-attack units will be employed as part of close-support forces: thus:

A. Battle unit Hallensleben controlling the Ju 87 units (now comprising some 100 aircraft) and the FW 190 fighter-bombers of 111/KG 511 has been added to Jagdkorps II Signals list.

B. There are strong indications that NSG 2 (in Cologne area) is preparing to join NSG 1 in the Ruhr. This may give added concentration, but there is no indication to date that Ju 87s operating against ground targets have been very effective.

5. Above preparations point with considerable certainty to Area U/Duesseldorf–Aachen as main area of air concentration and probable Schwerpunkt of operations, and it is perhaps not fortuitous that, since 3/11, GAF has provided daily fighter cover for 'important' troop transports unloading in this sector. Growing emphasis on ground-attack, as well as SEF reinforcements from further east, indicates that German intention is not simply to contest allied air superiority by increasing own defensive fighter forces, but rather to strike an offensive blow. Objective of this blow is still uncertain, but following two possibilities should be entertained:

A. More sustained attacks on Allied ground forces, following example of Allied tactical air forces in battle of France.

B. Attacks on Allied airfields with a view to neutralising Allied tactical air forces.

6. In favour of latter alternative are references to 'three' intended operations, arguing an operation of short endurance: also phrase 'lightning blow' used on 26/10 in connection with German 'project'. Such attacks might be contemplated whether major ground operations begin on allied or on German initiative. However, the transfer to the west of 3 FW 190 fighter-bomber units, released by the German evacuation of Latvia, argues a programme of stiffening air opposition to Allied ground forces in the west, although units concerned are unlikely to become available in time for operations at present in preparation. These units are now refitting and preparing for W Front operations, including training with anti-tank rocket launchers; intention is therefore clearly to employ them primarily against Allied ground forces.

(ii) Air Sunset 254 of 9 November 1944

GERMAN AIR FORCE

Western Front

1. Preparations for German 'project' discussed in Air Sunset 252 and 253 are to be completed by 12/11, indicating that operation is timed to start about middle of month.

The spoof wireless traffic arranged on 27/10 was ordered to begin from midnight 8/11.

2. There is still no clear indication of nature of project, but it is evidently on an even larger scale than envisaged in Air Sunset 253, most recent evidence indicating that no less than 600–700 serviceable SE fighters may be brought in from strategic defence. Reinforcements amount to 24–25 Gruppen, comprising JG 1, JG 3, JG 4 and JG 11 in addition to Geschwader previously listed (JG 27, JG 77, JG 300 and JG 301) as well as unknown number of Me 163 apparently going to Twente and Deelen. Extension of preparations to cover airfields in N Holland and also (JG 11) in Darmstadt area probably reflects difficulty in accommodating large numbers of aircraft and should not be regarded as invalidating previous indications that main concentration is to be expected in area Aachen/Duesseldorf.

3. Orders late on 8/11 for transfer of flying elements only of JG 26 to Darmstadt area are not thought to be part of German plans, but are rather immediate reaction to 3rd Army offensive, pending arrival of further forces. Whether JG 26 will continue to operate in this area will depend on degree of Allied pressure maintained. If pressure is severe, it may dislocate German plans for reinforcement and even lead to their radical revision. There is, however, no indication so far pointing in this direction, and until further notice maintenance of planned GAF programme should be expected.

4. Appearance of Fliegerdivision 3 (formerly operating in Latvia) on western front falls into line with preparation to employ fighter-bomber units from Baltic front in the west, and will probably take effect when these units become operational. It is unlikely to affect impending operations.

(iii) Air Sunset 255 of 12 November 1944

GERMAN AIR FORCE

Western front

1. In reaction to 3rd Army offensive beginning 8/11, GAF carried out following moves:

A. SE fighters under Jagdkorps II (JG 2 and JG 26) were tactically subordinated to Jagddivision 5: there were therefore no Jagdkorps II operations on 10/11 and none proposed for 11/11. However, moves of JG 26 to Darmstadt area, ordered on 8/11, proved impracticable, and it therefore covered rear army area in small-scale operations on 11/11. Move was still projected, if possible on 12/11.

B. All available Ju 87 night harassing bombers (NSG 1 and NSG 2) and FW 190 fighter bombers (111/KG 51) were transferred south probably to airfields in area between Mannheim and Karlsruhe.

C. 1 or 2 AR 234s from Rheine moved to Biblis to provide better recce cover.

2. Limited nature of reaction is obvious and, together with small scale of effort in Nancy–Metz area, averaging not more than 100–150 sorties per day since 8/11, indicates that Germans are unwilling to commit major forces in this theatre or to dislocate planned reinforcement to Cologne/Aachen area by utilising in south those SEF units now preparing to move westwards from central Germany. The fact that units under 1(B) above were described on 11/11 as temporarily in southern sector, and were then scheduled for operations further north, suggests that GAF appreciates imminence of further Allied offensives on 1st and/or 2nd Army fronts.

3. Thus, so far as can be seen, GAF intentions as set out in Air Sunset No 254 remain unchanged, although delays in preparation of airfields may make it difficult to complete preparations by 12/11, as planned. There is so far no indication of move of aircraft or flying elements to the west, but SEF dispositions envisaged appear to be as follows:

A. Quakenbrueck, Bissel: 2 Gruppen (JG 6)

B. Twente, Steenwijk, Nordhorn: 3 Gruppen (JG 1)

C. Greven, Fuerstenau, Plantluenne: 3 Gruppen (JG 26)

D. Kirchellen, Boenninghardt, Hilden: 3 Gruppen (JG 27)

E. Cologne area, including Lippe: 4–5 Gruppen (JG 27)

F. Nidda, Merzhausen, Altenstadt: 3 Gruppen (JG 2)

G. Babenhausen, Biblis, Griesheim: 3 Gruppen (JG 11)

H. Donau–Eschingen, Rottweil, Deckenpfronn: 3 Gruppen (JG 53)

I. Kassel area, including Hessisch–Lichtenau, Ziegenhain, Bracht and Schachten: 4–5 Gruppen (JG 300 and JG 301)

4. There has been no confirmation of suggested move of JG 3 and JG 4 (with 8 Gruppen in all), and it is suggested that these units, both particularly experienced in strategic defence, may on reconsideration be held back against deep penetration raids, their place on western front being taken by JG 1 and JG 6. Hence SE fighter force on western front is likely, if planned dispositions are completed, to amount to 28–30 Gruppen, or probably as a maximum 800–850 serviceable aircraft, the operational capacity of which will, however, be limited by fuel supply, airfield serviceability and maintenance problems.

5. In addition to above SE fighter forces, the Germans probably plan to make immediately available a ground-attack force comprising 80–90 Ju 87s (NSG 1 and NSG 2), 25–30 Me 262s (1/KG 51), 15 AR 234 (KG 760) and 35 FW 190 fighter-bombers (111/KG 51). In addition it is thought that up to 50 FW 190s of SG 4 (at present retraining after withdrawal from Latvia) might become available within 7–10 days in an emergency. These ground-attack forces, it is now clear, will be controlled by Fliegerdivision 3, which has experience of close-support operations on the Baltic front, and which has been specifically assigned to the area of the two northern German army groups in the west. The establishment of this new chain of command on 11/11 may perhaps be regarded as further evidence both of German preparation for imminent large-scale close-support operations, involving close collaboration between the army and the GAF, and also as indicating that the northern section is regarded as the area of main effort.

APPENDIX 25

Sigint during the Allied Offensives, 8 November to 7 December 1944

In the south, where in mid-November the front was held under Army Group G by First Army with LXXXII Corps, XIII SS Corps and LXXXIX Corps from south-west of Trier to south of Lunéville and by Nineteenth Army with LXIV Corps, IV GAF Field Corps and a temporary HQ from south of Lunéville to the Swiss frontier,[1]* the Germans made do against the Allied offensive with modest reinforcements, most of which went to First Army, at the cost of a large sacrifice of ground. Third US Army's advance against First Army captured Metz on 22 November, and by 3 December it had reached the Saar river on a ten-mile front around Merzig. On Nineteenth Army's front the First French Army took Belfort on 19 November and reached the Rhine through Mulhouse on 20 November, while Seventh US Army reached Strasbourg on 23 November and then pressed forward against the *Siegfried* line between the Saar and the Rhine. By mid-December the US Armies held a front running from Saarlautern through Bitche, Lauterbourg and Strasbourg to Sélestat, though further south Nineteenth Army (now subordinated to Himmler as C-in-C Upper Rhine) still held a bridgehead over the Rhine which included Colmar and extended to the Vosges.[3]

Though none of it was of spectacular interest, and little of it of tactical value, the Sigint received during this fighting kept the Allies abreast of the changes to the enemy's order of battle that were brought about by reliefs and reinforcements. A message decrypted on 17 November established that 25th PG Division, a new arrival, had a battle group on the Thionville area which was being reinforced.[4] Decrypts signalled to the Commands between 20 November and 4 December showed that 256th, 245th and

---

* Decrypts showed at the end of November that IV GAF Field Corps had been renamed XC Corps and that the improvised HQ had been replaced by LXII Corps.[2]

1. Cole, *The Lorraine Campaign* (Washington DC 1950), pp 309, 311, 312.
2. DEFE 3/313, HPs 8211 and 8239 of 30 November 1944.
3. Cole, op cit, pp 464, 465 and passim; Ellis, *Victory in the West*, Vol II (1968), p 165.
4. DEFE 3/307, HP 6911 of 17 November.

719th Infantry Divisions, last located in Holland, were joining Army Group G.[5] On 25 November a decrypt indicated that Panzer Lehr Division had been brought up from Sixth Panzer Army to restore the position on Nineteenth Army's left wing.[6] On 27 November a decrypt disclosed that Panzer Lehr's counter-attack had been taken in the flank on 25 November, and another of 29 November revealed that Panzer Lehr was being relieved by 245th Infantry on 27 November.[7] Messages sent on 4 December, one of which was decrypted on the same day, reported that a counter-attack delivered by Panzer Lehr and 11th Panzer Divisions was meeting strong resistance.[8] Sigint, which had shown that 11th Panzer Division had been committed from Army Group Reserve at the beginning of Third US Army's attack, established that it remained continuously in the line till mid-December,[9] but there was no later information about Panzer Lehr in the decrypts before the German offensive. A series of decrypts about 21st Panzer Division showed that it was transferred from Nineteenth Army to First Army on 11 November and was in and out of the line between then and 3 December, when it was again relieved; there was nothing to suggest that it was then moving out of the battle, and later decrypts disclosed that it was re-committed by 10 December and was being relieved once again, this time by 719th Infantry, on 14 December.[10]

Decrypts giving details of the state of Army Group G's formations were available between 3 and 6 December. Of First Army's divisions only 11th Panzer was placed in category II. 21st Panzer, Panzer Lehr and 17th SS PG were in category III together

---

5. DEFE 3/308, HP 7246 of 20 November; DEFE 3/311, HP 7757 of 26 November; DEFE 3/312, HPs 8101 and 8181 of 29 November; DEFE 3/314, HP 8546 of 4 December.

6. DEFE 3/310, HP 7697 of 25 November.

7. DEFE 3/311, HP 7940 of 27 November; DEFE 3/312, HP 8181 of 29 November.

8. DEFE 3/314, HP 8561 of 4 December; DEFE 3/316, HP 9189 of 9 December.

9. DEFE 3/303, HP 5956 of 8 November; DEFE 3/304, HP 6087 of 9 November; DEFE 3/305, HP 6293 of 11 November; DEFE 3/306, HPs 6627 and 6732 of 14 and 15 November; DEFE 3/308, HP 7205 of 20 November; DEFE 3/309, HP 7343 of 21 November; DEFE 3/312, HP 8069 of 28 November; DEFE 3/313, HP 8326 of 1 December; DEFE 3/314, HP 8541 of 4 December; DEFE 3/315, HP 8942 of 8 December; DEFE 3/316, HP 9192 of 12 December; DEFE 3/317, HP 9364 of 14 December; DEFE 3/318, HP 9522 of 16 December.

10. DEFE 3/305, HP 6417 of 12 November; DEFE 3/308, HP 7218 of 20 November; DEFE 3/310, HP 7512 of 23 November; DEFE 3/311, HP 7757 of 25 November; DEFE 3/312, HP 8175 and 8188 of 29 November; DEFE 3/313, HPs 8326 and 8478 of 1 and 3 December; DEFE 3/314, HP 8542 of 4 December; DEFE 3/316, HP 9197 of 12 December; DEFE 3/317, HP 9411 of 14 December.

with 25th PG, 36th VG and such elements of 256th Infantry as had arrived. Its remaining effective divisions (416th Infantry, 19th VG, 347th VG, 361st VG and a battle group comprising 555th VG and the remnants of 48th Infantry) were in category IV. 462nd VG was encircled in Metz. A battle group was being formed from the remnants of 562nd VG which had been smashed in the fighting round Saverne.[11] Nineteenth Army, in a message of 28 November signalled by GC and CS on 3 December, reported that its strength had been so depleted that it could maintain the Alsace bridgehead only if reinforced at once by entire powerful formations.[12] Decrypts of 6 December disclosed that Nineteenth Army was losing XC Corps HQ and was itself being removed from Army Group G and subordinated to the Reichsführer SS, who was setting up a new HQ as C-in-C Upper Rhine.[13]

As for the effort of the GAF on the southern front, Sigint revealed that its responses to the opening of Third US Army's offensive, though prompt, was limited.[14] On 12 November AI believed that the enemy was unwilling to dislocate the planned concentration of his air forces in the Aachen–Cologne sector.[15] Decrypts of 16 and 17 November did indeed disclose that the forces sent against Third US Army had been recalled.[16] On 23 November, when First and Nineteenth Armies were in grave difficulties, a decrypt disclosed that 5th Jagd Division had ordered an all-out effort in the Saarebourg–Saverne area.[17] In the next two weeks orders for close-support operations in the south were decrypted almost daily.[18] These showed that 5th JD was reinforced on a day-to-day basis by JG 2 and JG 4 in the last week of November and by JG 2 in the first few days of December; and that from 6 December III/SG 4, a specialist ground-attack unit, was placed at 5th JD's disposal.[19] But these efforts were clearly not being allowed to disturb the plans for reinforcing the GAF in the north.

---

11. DEFE 3/313, HPs 8464 and 8465 of 3 December; DEFE 3/314, HPs 8597 and 8736 of 5 and 6 December.
12. DEFE 3/313, HP 8451 of 3 December.
13. DEFE 3/315, HPs 8754 and 8758 of 6 December.
14. Air Sunsets 254 of 9 November, 255 of 12 November. See Appendix 24 (ii and iii).
15. Air Sunset 255 of 12 November. See Appendix 24 (iii).
16. DEFE 3/307, HPs 6873, 6875 and 6878 of 16 and 17 November.
17. DEFE 3/309, HP 7489 of 23 November.
18. DEFE 3/310, HPs 7575 and 7703 of 23 and 25 November; DEFE 3/311, HPs 7813, 7820, 7891 and 7911 of 25, 26 and 27 November; DEFE 3/312, HPs 8016, 8020, 8125 and 8236 of 28, 29 and 30 November.
19. DEFE 3/313, HP 8431 of 2 December; DEFE 3/314, HPs 8525 and 8618 of 4 and 5 December; DEFE 3/315, HPs 8783 and 8838 of 7 December; DEFE 3/316, HPs 9032 and 9193 of 10 and 12 December.

On the Aachen front, held by Army Group B with XII SS Corps
and LXXXI Corps under Fifth Panzer Army from Geilenkirchen
to Schevenhutte and LXXIV Corps and 116th Panzer Division
under Seventh Army from Schevenhutte to Vossenack, the major
offensive by Ninth and First US Armies made slower progress.
Ninth Army took Geilenkirchen on 19 November despite meeting
an early counter-attack from Army Group B's Reserve – XLVII
Panzer Corps with 9th Panzer and 15th PG Divisions – but was
then held up by further counter-attacks; it was not up to the Roer
on most of its front till 9 December. On its right, First Army was
also delayed. It did not gain the banks of the Roer from Bergstein
to Düren till mid-December.[20]

In messages decrypted on 10, 12 and 16 November before the
American advance started, Army Group B reported that it
expected an offensive on both sides of Aachen, that it could not
yet release 116th Panzer on account of its weak fighting strength
in the Hürtgen sector and that the line south-west of Düren was
inadequately manned.[21] Decrypts of 17 and 18 November disclosed that XII SS Corps had been ordered to use XLVII Panzer
Corps for a counter-attack to recover its defence line south of
Geilenkirchen, but in messages decrypted on 18 and 19 November
it reported that the counter-attack had been called off.[22] In its day
report for 17 November, decrypted on 19 November, Army
Group B stated that 9th Panzer's counter-attack had failed and
that the situation was especially tense on 275th Infantry Division's
sector west of Eschweiler; but it added that by employing all its
resources it had beaten off nearly all attacks along the 70-mile
front and that it would be able to prevent a breakthrough
provided it received reinforcements, fighter support and adequate
artillery ammunition and fuel.[23]

From 21 November Sigint disclosed that more reinforcements
were arriving. Decrypts of that day revealed that XII SS Corps was
expecting 10th SS Panzer Division from Holland and would
resume its counter-attack when this reinforcement arrived; that
183rd VG Division had been relieved by 15th PG; and that 344th
Infantry Division, last located on Second British Army's front, was
also moving in.[24] A message of 25 November decrypted on 27

---

20. MacDonald, *The Siegfried Line Campaign* (Washington DC 1963), Chapters
    XVIII–XXIV: Ellis, op cit, Vol II, pp 163, 164.
21. DEFE 3/304, HP 6190 of 10 November; DEFE 3/305, HP 6398 of 12
    November; DEFE 3/307, HP 6811 of 16 November.
22. DEFE 3/307, HPs 6912 and 6993 of 17 and 18 November; DEFE 3/308, HPs
    7030 and 7134 of 18 and 19 November.
23. DEFE 3/308, HPs 7098 and 7105 of 19 November.
24. DEFE 3/309, HPs 7278, 7315 and 7369 of 21 November.

November, reported that Army Group B was expecting further arrivals to relieve the pressure on the sector west of Düren;[25] these proved to be 3rd Parachute Division, which took over there on 27 November, and 353rd Infantry, which a decrypt of 2 December located south-west of Düren.[26] On 28 November a decrypt reported that 363rd VG, also from Holland, was relieving 340th VG under Fifth Panzer Army.[27] Requests for further reinforcements and complaints about the lack of GAF support were decrypted from the end of November. In a message decrypted on 30 November Seventh Army reported that 89th and 344th Infantry Divisions had been depleted in costly fighting in the Hürtgen Forest and required early relief, and that 353rd Infantry would soon be in the same state unless reinforcements arrived.[28] On the same day the decrypt of a report from Model complained that the Allies were exploiting their mastery of the air to an increasing extent; troops and civilians were under continuous and unopposed attack and counter-action by the GAF was essential and decisive for the course of the fighting.[29] Messages decrypted on 4 December complained of the lack of air support in the sectors held by 9th Panzer and 15th PG and requested reinforcements to meet the continuing decline in the fighting strength of LXXIV Corps.[30] An urgent personal request from GOC 3rd Parachute Division to AOC JK II for air support was decrypted on 5 December, and a similar request from LXXXI Corps on 8 December.[31]

---

25.   DEFE 3/311, HP 7954 of 27 November.
26.   DEFE 3/313, HP 8383 of 2 December.
27.   DEFE 3/312, HP 8088 of 28 November.
28.   DEFE 3/313, HP 8375 of 30 November.
29.   ibid, HP 8333 of 30 November.
30.   DEFE 3/314, HPs 8535 and 8548 of 4 December.
31.   ibid, HP 8622 of 5 December; DEFE 3/315, HP 8911 of 8 December.

APPENDIX 26

Intelligence on the Axis Oil Situation up to the Summer of 1944

1. ORGANISATION

The Hartley Committee (the Technical Sub-Committee on Axis Oil, to give it its formal title) took over from the Lloyd Committee, itself a sub-committee of the Hankey Committee, in April 1942.* It was chaired by Sir Harold Hartley and consisted of representatives from the Admiralty, the War Office, the Air Ministry, the Ministry of Economic Warfare, the Ministry of Fuel and Power, the Prime Minister's Statistical Branch, the US embassy, the Petroleum Board and Shell Petroleum Company Ltd. Its responsibilities were to report through and under the guidance of the JIC on (a) the quantity of oil produced and consumed by the enemy and of the stocks at his disposal, and (b) trends in these three quantities, with a view to estimating whether and when the enemy might run short of oil.

It had two sub-committees, one for the technical examination of captured oil products and the other for studying the evidence on the enemy's production. For estimates of the enemy's consumption it relied on the MEW (for civilian consumption) and (for consumption by the Axis armed forces) on the three Service departments – NID 7 in the Admiralty, MI 10(c) in the War Office and AI 3(c) in the Air Ministry.

Efforts to exchange assessments with the Soviet authorities were spasmodic and unproductive. Russian estimates of the German oil position were sent to London in October 1941 by the Lloyd Committee's representative in Moscow.[1] In February 1942 a representative of the Lloyd Committee discussed British estimates in Moscow and the Russian experts had agreed with them.[2] No further contact appears to have been made until December 1943, when the exhaustive JIC report of 26 November was forwarded to Moscow.[3] There is no record of any Soviet response to it. Liaison

---

* See Volume I, pp 102–103; Volume II, pp 7, 46, 134–135.

1. CAB 121/418, SIC file D/Germany/3, JP(41)853 of 15 October.
2. ibid, POG(42)5 of 21 February.
3. ibid, JIC(43)480 of 26 November, COS(43)292nd (o) Meeting, 30 November, JIC 2010/43 to No 30 Military Mission, 13 December 1943.

with the US authorities, on the other hand, was close. After the
Anglo–American talks in London in the summer of 1943* the
assessments issued by the Hartley Committee and the JIC were,
essentially, agreed combined assessments. British, American and
combined agencies were all represented on the Joint Anglo-
American Oil Targets Committee when that was set up in July
1944.†

2. THE INTELLIGENCE SOURCES AND THE STATE OF INTELLIGENCE

The starting point for wartime estimates was the work done before
the war by the Industrial Intelligence Centre towards locating the
German oil plants and assessing the quantity of German stocks.‡
In the first two years of the war the sources available were such
that it was impossible to keep abreast of changes in the situation.
In June 1941 Lord Hankey told the Defence Committee that 'the
estimate of German shortages in oil was largely conjectural'.[4] In
July 1941 the Lloyd sub-committee listed its sources (official
statistics obtained from neutral countries; escapees; decrees
published in Axis Europe; reports from the SIS and other secret
sources indicating general trends; intercepts) but confessed that it
was relying mainly on estimates of the enemy's oil consumption
which the Service departments derived largely from comparable
United Kingdom statistics and on estimates of oil production
arrived at in discussion with the oil companies.[5] A report in
January 1942 admitted that estimates were still 'built up mainly by
statistical methods'; it described the state of intelligence as
'inadequate' and noted that there were 'unfortunately many
aspects of the German oil situation on which we have no direct
information at all'.[6]

1942 saw the beginning of the build-up of systematic information about the location of Germany's oil plants, notably as a result
of the expansion of PR.[7] But there was little or no improvement in
intelligence about the scale of production, consumption and

---

* See Volume II, pp 136–137.
† See p 505.
‡ See Volume I, p 65.

4. ibid, DO(41)1st Meeting, 16 June.
5. CAB 66/17, WP(41)162 (POG(41)9) of 11 July 1941).
6. CAB 121/418, 'Report on Sources of Oil Intelligence by the Hartley
   Committee' dated January 1942.
7. AIR 41/7, *Photographic Reconnaissance*, Vol II, p 162.

stocks. In May 1942 the Chiefs of Staff were informed that 'conjecture must play a large part in any estimate [made]'.[8] In June 1943 the JIC noted that of 179 secret reports received between November 1942 and April 1943, only 40 had been graded as reliable and that these, though valuable, had been of little assistance in the preparation of statistical calculations in the enemy's oil position.[9] These reports were from agents and diplomatic sources; references to the oil situation in the high-grade Sigint were few and far between until May 1944. From that date the amount of high-grade Sigint evidence on oil became substantial* and although it still gave no basis for precise estimates of the levels of production, consumption and stocks, it enabled the Allies, in conjunction with PR, to arrive at consistent appreciations of the German oil position.

Difficult as it was to produce precise calculations, it was still more difficult before the summer of 1944 to forecast the likely effects of oil shortage on the enemy's strategy or his ability to continue the war. The intelligence authorities rarely hazarded such forecasts, and then only in cautious language and in general terms. This was the case in November 1943 when, for the first time since the early months of the war, they suggested that the air offensive might give priority to oil targets. As late as May 1944, when strongly supporting the oil offensive, the JIC conceded that 'the difficulty is to assess on even an approximate basis how soon oil shortage will have a direct and appreciable effect on Germany's military strategy and operations in the field'.[10]†

3. INTELLIGENCE ESTIMATES OF THE AXIS OIL POSITION 1940–1944

A. Over-all Estimates

The trends of British annual approximate estimates during the war can be tabulated as follows:–

---

* See above, Chapter 54.
† See below, p 501.

8. CAB 121/418, COS(42)125(o) of 6 May.
9. CAB 77/20, AO(43)25 and 30, also circulated as JIC(43)253 and 257 of 25 June and 19 June.
10. CAB 121/418, JIC(44)218(o) of 27 May (covering AO(44)41).

Appendix 26

Table I

Intelligence Annual Estimates of the Axis Oil Position 1940–44
(in 000 tons)

1940[1]			1941[1]			1942[1]			1943			1944		
Stock at 1.1.40 Supplies	Current Supplies	Consumption	Stock at 1.1.41 Supplies	Current Supplies	Consumption	Stock at 1.1.42 Supplies	Current Supplies	Consumption	Stock at 1.1.43 Supplies	Current Supplies	Consumption	Stock at 1.1.44 Supplies	Current Supplies	Consumption
4100	16300	13800	6600	14500	17700	3400	15810	16640	4000[2]	15965[3]	16263[3]	3702	10692[4]	14394[5]

Notes

1. Stock, Current Supplies and Consumption are given in MEW Intelligence Weekly No 72A of 3 July 1943, Statistical Appendix Table I (Filed in FO 837/17).
2. JIC(43)480 of 26.11.43. Stock of 4,000,000 agreed with the Americans in July 1943 (See Volume II pp 136 and 137).
3. JIC(44)218(o) of 27.5.44.
4. JIC(44)218(0) of 27.5.44 estimated current supplies for *the first six months* of 1944 at 7,979,000 tons. From July to December 1944 the JIC reported the current supply of oil for *each month*. (JIC(44)320(0) of 24.7.44; JIC(44)390(o) of 4.9.44; JIC(44)423(o) of 2.10.44; JIC(44)450(o) of 30.10.44; JIC(44)488(o) of 1.12.44; JIC(44)513(o) of 1.1.45). Total supply for the *second six months* of 1944 derived from the monthly estimates amounted to 2,713,000. Estimated supplies for the whole year 1944 amounted to 10,692,000 tons.
5. No JIC estimates of consumption in 1944 published, but JIC (44)390(o) of 4.9.44 reported that fuel reserves had been exhausted by then.

B. Supply. The Production of Oil.

Current Supplies for each year of the war set out in Table I above were composed of estimates of the output of crude and shale oil, synthetic oil, tar oil and substitute and mined oil by *all* the Axis European Countries. In 1943, taken as an example, the composition of the estimated 15,965,000 tons can be broken down into:[11]

Table II

Estimated 1943 Current Supplies

Crude and Shale Oil:

Germany	685,000	
Austria	1,038,000	
Hungary	720,000	
Romania	5,135,000	
All other countries	662,000	
Total		8,240,000

Synthetic Oil:

Bergius plants and Fischer-Tropsch oils	
Total	5,425,000

Tar and substitute and mined oils:

Total	2,300,000

Grand Total	15,965,000

11. CAB 121/418, JIC (44)218(o) of 27 May, Appendix Table I.

These figures for Axis production do not reveal the fact that by 1943 Germany herself was still obtaining much less crude oil from foreign sources than before the Allied blockade began in September 1939.

Before the war Germany was importing nearly 60% of her total supply from countries outside the continent of Europe.* When the blockade cut off these overseas sources Germany sought to substitute for them oil imported overland, the main potential source being Romania. In 1939 Romania had exported 451,000 tons to Germany and 1,680,000 tons to other countries. By 1941, now dominated by Germany, Romania was exporting 2,114,000 tons to the Reich and 226,000 tons to non-Axis countries. Even so oil from Romania did not fully replace the imports from overseas lost by Germany as the result of the blockade.†

Despite heavy political pressure from Germany Romania continued to retain a substantial quantity of her own production, arguing that her economy and army depended more completely on fuel oil than did any other European country. For this reason, while Romanian production continued to be very large, German total oil imports fell below 3m. tons in 1940 and so remained until the end of the war.

To off-set lost overseas imports Germany, apart from political pressure on Romania, made a major effort to increase her domestic output of crude oil by opening new wells. Aware of the German effort and somewhat under-estimating German domestic output in 1940, British Intelligence calculated statistics which compare well with German official statistics.

Table III
Production of Crude Oil in Greater Germany
(000 tons)

	Actual (a)	Intelligence Estimate (b)	Remarks
1940	1454	1026 (1)	
1941	1612	1210 (2)	See next
1942	1729	1480 (3)	page for
1943	1933	1723 (4)	notes
1944	1654	[2390](c)	

---

* British intelligence authorities believed that during the five years before the outbreak of war Germany added to her reserves by secretly importing more than 1 million tons from overseas sources (German Basic Handbook, Economic Survey Section D, p 4 dated December 1944).

† German imports of oil products (in 000 tons) (including those from Romania):

1938	4957
1939	5165
1940	2075
1941	2807
1942	2359
1943	2766

(USSBS Table 37, p 75).

(a) Webster and Frankland, Vol IV p 509: derived from 'Oil as a Factor in the German War Effort 1933–1945' (AO(46)1 of 8 March 1946).
(b) Derived from JIC reports: (1) JIC(42)309 of 15.8.42, Appendix Table II. (2) JIC(42)309 of 15.8.42, Appendix Table III. (3) JIC(43)340 of 18.8.43, Appendix A. (4) JIC(44)218(o) of 27.5.44, Appendix Table I.
(c) Estimate for 1944 published in JIC(44)218(o) of 27.5.44. This estimate had not taken into account the effect on the enemy of *Overlord* and it had to be withdrawn. It is of interest that the intelligence authorities expected so considerable an expansion of output in 1944.

For the British intelligence authorities synthetic production rather than the supply of crude oil was the outstanding feature of the German oil economy, but it was shrouded in a cloak of secrecy.[12]

Two processes of deriving synthetic oil from coal were used in Germany. The Bergius process rested on liquifying coal by forcibly combining it with hydrogen under great pressure. The Fischer-Tropsch process depended on deriving a gas mixture of hydrogen and carbon monoxide from coal and coke, the gas passed over a catalyst, usually cobalt, to remove sulphur from the gas before it was liquified in condensers.[13]*

Throughout the war intelligence estimates of the production of oil by the two processes were somewhat high, chiefly because production by the Fischer-Tropsch process was over-estimated.

Table IV[14]
Intelligence Estimates of the Production of Synthetic Oil
(ooo tons)

	Bergius	Fischer-Tropsch	Total
1938	935	321	1256
1939	1350	710	2060
1940	1950	800	2750
1941	2350	950	3300
1942	2800	1090	3890
1943	3690	1350	5040
1944	?	?	[3433]

---

* Separate estimates for the two processes for the whole of 1944 are not available but a tótal estimate for 1944 can be derived from the JIC reports used in compiling Table I on p 916 above. JIC(44)218(o) of 27 May estimated the total output for January–June 1944 at 2,552,000 tons. From July to December 1944 the JIC published each month an estimate of the monthly output of synthetic oil. In July, August and September the estimates were broken down into production by the Bergius and Fischer-Tropsch processes but in October, November and December the JIC published only the estimated output of the two processes combined.

12. FO and MEW Economic Advisory Branch, German Basic Handbook, Economic Survey of December 1944, Section D, p 6.
13. ibid, pp 6–7.
14. ibid, p 7.

Table V
Actual Production of Synthetic Oil[15]
(ooo metric tons)

	Hydrogenation (ie Bergius process)	Fischer-Tropsch	Total
1940	1504	449	1953
1941	2107	474	2581
1942	2772	446	3218
1943	3431	484	3915
1944	1875	306	2181

C. Consumption

Estimated consumption of oil by all Axis countries in 1943 was put by British Intelligence at 16,263,000 tons (see Table I) and broken down as follows:[16]

Table VI
Estimated 1943 Consumption

1. Armed Forces		
(a) Armies	4,217,000	
(b) Naval	1,731,000	
(c) Air Force	2,423,000	
(d) Todt	320,000	8,691,000
2. Civil, including exports to neutrals		7,147,000
Losses in retreats and by air attack	325,000	
Losses by tanker sinkings	100,000	425,000
		16,263,000

Consumption by the Axis armed forces was calculated by the British Service departments using, as their base, knowledge of the strength and employment of the Axis forces, information from

---

15. CAB 121/418, AO(46)1 of 8 March, p 159, Table 1.
16. ibid, JIC(44)218(0) of 27 May, Annexes I and II.

British oil companies experienced in British consumption and such references to enemy consumption as were obtained from reliable intelligence sources, for example Sigint on the enemy's fuel situation in the Middle East.

Estimating the consumption of non-military users was largely in the hands of MEW who estimated the quantities used by motor cycles, private cars, buses, trucks, railways, inland shipping, bunkers, commercial aviation, agriculture, industry and households in Germany and added to the total estimated consumption of Germany the estimated consumption of oil by Czechoslavakia, Poland, Finland, Norway, Denmark, Belgium and Holland, France, Hungary, Italy, Romania, the Balkans and the Baltic states.[17]

D. Stocks

The 'stock' of oil comprised:

(a) the amount required by the oil industry itself in order to produce synthetic oil and refined crude oil and to carry fuel oil to the ultimate users;

(b) the amount of oil, above that required by the oil industry itself, which was immediately available to the armed forces, the economy and the governmental administration.

In the examination of the German 'position' or 'situation' the lowest quantity needed for the production and distribution of oil itself was defined as the 'distributional minimum'. The difference between the total stock of oil and the distributional minimum was defined as the 'margin' or 'free reserve'.

Before the German victories in western Europe in June 1940 the Lloyd Committee put the German distributional minimum at 1 m tons.[18] After the German victories the Lloyd Committee calculated that the distributional minimum for 'German Europe' amounted to 2.5 m tons,[19] a figure more or less adhered to by the British intelligence authorities after July 1940 and during 1941 and 1942. In August 1943 the JIC raised it to 3 m tons[20] and in November 1943 to 4 m tons.[21]* In its last major general review of

---

* The figure was originally considered to be c.3 m tons, but had been amended to 4 m tons as a result of the American/British discussions (see Volume II pp 136–137).

17. ibid, Annex II.
18. CAB 66/8, WP(40)191 of 4 June (Third Report of the Lloyd Committee).
19. CAB 66/9, WP(40)267 of 14 July (Fourth Report of the Lloyd Committee).
20. CAB 121/418, JIC(43)340 of 18 August.
21. ibid, JIC(43)480 of 26 November.

the German oil position in May 1944 the JIC added that the German armed forces themselves held strategic reserves of about 1 m tons on the threatened battle fronts.[22] In effect therefore the total stock was estimated to be 5 m tons just before D-day.

In British intelligence terminology the enemy was to a greater or less degree 'short of oil' and in a 'critical situation' if the German European stock of oil fell below the 'distributional minimum'. By this test the intelligence authorities firmly identified the beginning of a prolonged crisis in July 1941, following the invasion of Russia.

Table VII
Estimates of the Axis Position April 1941 – March 1943
(000 tons)

	Total Stock*	Distributional Minimum†
April 1941	6300	4000
July 1941	5550	4000
October 1941	4200	4000
January 1942	3250	4000
April 1942	3000	4000
July 1942	2450	4000
October 1942	2450	4000
January 1943	2700	4000
April 1943	3100	4000

In February 1942 the Lloyd Committee, reflecting on the estimates of the total stock of oil, came to the conclusion that the Axis reserve of oil had been 'reduced to the irreducible minimum necessary to allow distribution', and that from now on the Axis no longer held a margin of stocks and would be 'obliged to balance its expenditure against income'.[23] In May 1942 the COS were told that the only course now open to the Germans was to reduce civilian consumption.[24] This course was adopted in Germany and the estimates of stocks circulated by the JIC began to increase from early in 1943. In November 1943 the stock was estimated to be 4,031,000 tons, equal to that of January 1943.[25] On 26 April 1944 the JIC reported that Germany had accumulated since the beginning of 1944 a 'marginal reserve' of between 250,000 and 500,000 tons above the distributional minimum and that if she retained her production resources, the surplus of production would amount to 450,000–525,000 tons during the three months

---

* Approximates obtained from graphs in JIC(43)340 of 18.8.43 Annex VII.
† As adopted by the Anglo–American agreement July 1943.

22. ibid, JIC(44)218(o) of 27 May.
23. CAB 77/18, POG(L)(42)2 of 21 February.
24. CAB 121/418, COS(42)125(o) of 6 May.
25. ibid, JIC(43)480 of 26 November.

April–June 1944.[26] The intelligence authorities realised that in the spring of 1944 the German stock of oil was notably increasing. On 27 May 1944[27] the JIC put the stock at:–

1 January 1943	4,000,000 tons
31 December 1943	3,702,000 tons
30 June 1944	4,083,000 tons

The assessment of the position just before D-day held that:

1. Excluding military strategic reserves the total Axis stocks of oil were no more than the distributional minimum;
2. The German armed forces held strategic reserves amounting to about 1,000,000 tons;
3. If simultaneous Allied offensives were to be launched on the east and west fronts stocks would be largely governed by 'local supply difficulties'.*

It was forecast that under those circumstances an operational oil shortage would develop in about two months.[28]

4. INTELLIGENCE APPRECIATIONS OF THE EFFECTS OF THE OIL SITUATION.

The Lloyd Committee's conclusion in October 1939, to the effect that 'it would appear that in the spring of 1940 Germany's oil position will be critical', was quickly modified.† In January 1941 the Committee agreed that there was no evidence to show that the military effort of Germany or Italy was restricted by a shortage of oil[29] and in May 1941 it forecast that the German position was likely to improve by April 1942.[30] The attack on Russia was not foreseen.

The German invasion of Russia in June 1941 inevitably led the British intelligence authorities to the conclusion that German stocks would fall below the distributional minimum, affecting the armed forces, the economy or the enemy's administration. A sub-committee under Sir Harold Hartley studied the situation and its report was examined by the Lloyd Committee in December

---

* On the eastern front the supply of oil depended wholly upon synthetic oil plants.
† See Volume I, pp 233–234.

26. ibid, JIC(44)175(o) of 26 April.
27. ibid, JIC(44)218(o) of 27 May.
28. ibid.
29. CAB 66/41, WP(41)2 of 2 January (Fifth Report of the Lloyd Committee).
30. CAB 121/418, WP(41)85 of 23 May (Sixth Report of the Lloyd Committee).

1941.[31] The findings were that although there was evidence of German oil shortages, there were as yet no indications of a level of stocks 'inadequate for strategic needs'. To forecast the oil position was impossible. It would depend on the military operations in the coming winter, the effect of a forced reduction of consumption by the German essential war industries and the steady increase in the output of synthetic oil; moreover much depended on German efforts to capture the Russian oilfields and on the extent and effectiveness of Allied interference in German operations.

In May 1942, with the opening of the second German offensive in Russia, the COS were informed that the Germans might be able to maintain their Russian campaign at peak intensity for no more than a maximum of six months.[32] This, the first major intelligence forecast of the effect of oil shortage on military operations, was modified by December 1942. In August the Hartley Committee reported that the stock position was 'exceedingly low' and that 'it may be that civil supplies in Germany have been reduced below the fuel efficiency level during the winter' of 1941–1942.[33] In December 1942 it concluded that further cuts in civil consumption would be more harmful to the German war effort than restricting Service consumption. The German oil situation would be 'at its most critical stage' between December 1942 and mid-1943. Increased production of oil in 1943 might enable another campaign against the Caucasus but if it required a rate of consumption equivalent to that of the winter 1941–1942 Germany might be compelled to shorten her eastern front or further restrict civil consumption.[34]

Between December 1942 and mid-1943 the German oil situation was indeed critical but the authorities could not assess the effects on German strategy. By April 1943 the JIC saw that the enemy oil position had been strengthened by rising production of synthetic oil and reduction of consumption following the destruction of the Sixth Army at Stalingrad and the shortening of the eastern front, but it believed that although the oil position was now stronger than it was at the beginning of 1942, 'Germany will be unable for a considerable time to meet in full both the requirements of the armed forces and civilian needs essential to the war effort'.[35]

In November 1943 the JIC appreciated that German plans to provide adequate supplies of oil in 1943 had failed to reach the

---

31. CAB 66/20, WP(41)300 of 15 December (Ninth Report of the Lloyd Committee).
32. CAB 121/418, COS(42)125(0) of 6 May.
33. ibid, JIC(42)309 of 15 August.
34. ibid, JIC(42)487 of 12 December.
35. ibid, JIC(43)151 of 5 April.

objective and that the refining capacity of SE Europe was barely sufficient to meet requirements, and it pointed out that Allied advances had brought all enemy sources of oil within the range of Allied air attack.[36] How this argument, with its implication that an attack on oil production would lead to early German defeat, influenced Allied bombing priorities has already been analysed in Chapter 54.

---

36. ibid, JIC(43)480 of 26 November.

APPENDIX 27

The Report by the Japanese Ambassador in Berlin on his Interview with Speer on 9 August 1944

(Reproduced from BAY/XL 111 of 19 August 1944)

According to Japanese Ambassador Berlin on Twelfth; Minister of Munitions Speer told him on Ninth: (Able) After big raid on Hamburg last summer Germany had been anxious for future but Allies had not carried out raids on unified plan. Allied raids had been like attacks upon delta in lower reaches instead of upon source of the river and however much one attacked at such divergent points it was impossible to achieve a fatal blow. For instance, where the destruction of one factory, 'a', automatically involved a stoppage of work in another factory, 'b', the Allies had many times raided 'b' in addition to 'a', the result from the German point of view being same as if only 'a' had been destroyed, while during time 'a' being restored it had been possible to get 'b' going again. (Baker) Fundamental errors in Allied claims that raids had brought about a falling off of 20 or 30 per cent in production of munitions. Actually Germans had planned for normal rise and had carried out their plans. Steepness of upward curve only affected. Since Hamburg raid Germans had reduced percentage of damage in proportion to quantity of bombs dropped by 60 or 70 per cent. Munitions production at Hamburg now 140 per cent of what it had been before the bombing. (Charlie) Change however when daylight raids with long distance American fighters became main feature of raids, particularly against oil. Then for first time really scientific raiding began which might deal a fatal blow to Germany. Problem of oil was the greatest now confronting them. (Dog) Air raids might become danger to munitions production if systematically carried out. Only way to overcome danger is to regain air superiority. There was no intention of allowing German production of fighters and 'Zerstoerers' to fall behind production of twin-engined planes however big American production might become. If Germany's man-power and oil were not wiped out (and there is no expectation of that) they would be able to free themselves from

925

danger now existing and thereafter increase production of oil and stocks. (Easy) By February this year production of fighters and 'Zerstoerers' had fallen to 1250 per month but by July production had reached 4500 and he proposed to bring figure to 6500 or seven thousand by end of year. (Fox) Underground factories at present amount to 800,000 square metres and would soon reach one million square metres. When that is reached monthly production in underground factories alone would be one thousand and by end of year planned to have three million square metres underground. (George) As to effects of raids, some industries were relatively vulnerable and others not. Aircraft production came under latter category and there were many instances of factories which Allies claimed had been totally destroyed having been got going again in two days and restored to 50 per cent of normal efficiency in two weeks. (How) The proportion of fighters and 'Zerstoerers' to all other types, including bombers, recce, transport and training planes etc had risen to 70 or 80 per cent since the beginning of this year, (previously it had been proportionally equal). Taking one hundred as figure at beginning of war, figure for middle of 1944 was 360 (Comment. All types). Production of 'engineless planes' would next year be 2000 a month. (Item) Finally, (Comment. Japanese summing up) articles the production of which had definitely been impaired are ball bearings and oil, and an increase in car production had been hampered.

Note: It is difficult to know what exactly the Japanese Ambassador meant by 'Zerstoerers', which normally stood for twin-engined fighters.

APPENDIX 28

Intelligence on the Threat from Chemical Warfare in 1945

The JIC's review of the possibility that Germany was preparing to initiate gas warfare,* which was carried out by a sub-committee, produced six reports between 17 January and 23 April 1945. The first of these[1] found in the decrypts received before and during the Ardennes offensive no convincing evidence of the intention to use gas to extend or exploit the success of that operation.† As for subsequent Sigint references to gas, it believed that all but one denoted anxiety about the possibility that the Allies would resort to it, rather than German preparations for its use. The exception was a decrypt which had recently referred to the introduction on the Italian front of practice reports at times when weather conditions were suitable for gas warfare; this might be more than a precautionary measure. But the CIGS separately advised the Prime Minister that such reports would be equally necessary for defensive preparations and for offensive operations.[3]

The second JIC report, dated 29 January,[4] noted that POW interrogations had produced no suggestion that Germany planned to use gas, and no evidence even of any increase in anti-gas training. It believed that the latest Sigint references to gas, though remaining more numerous than in the past, were also associated only with precautionary measures. Those received since the middle of January had dealt with the movement of anti-gas equipment in Italy and the west, with the urgent allocation of such equipment to divisions presumably destined for the eastern front and to 6th VG Division at Poznan, and with anti-gas training for

---

* For the instigation of this review see above, p 582.

† In a decrypt of 10 January, on which the JIC report did not comment, OKM had instructed the German Naval Attaché in Tokyo to issue a categorical denial of reports from American POW and other quarters that there had been a gas alarm during the Ardennes battle.[2]

1. CAB 121/102, SIC file A/Policy/Chemical Warfare/1, Vol 3, JIC(45) 18(o) of 17 January.
2. DEFE 3/521, ZTPG 324998.
3. DEFE 3/330, BT 2730 of 19 January 1945; Dir/C Archive, 8458 and 8463 of 19 and 24 January.
4. CAB 121/102, JIC(45) 36(o) of 29 January.

civilians in factories and on digging parties.[5] On one of these decrypts however – it had reported on 23 January that volatile war gas (Luftkampfstoff) was being transported to Army Group North – MI 14 had previously commented that it was 'the most positive indication to date of a possible offensive use of gas'.[6]

In its third and fourth reports, of 12 and 28 February,[7] the JIC had nothing new to offer by way of comment. On 12 February it noted that as the Russians were now on the Oder, the time when Germany could profitably have resorted to gas on the eastern front had probably passed.* On 28 February it noted that the latest Sigint references had almost all emanated from the eastern front and had virtually confirmed that Germany had no plan to initiate gas warfare; they had related to the dispersal of anti-gas stocks and the evacuation of gas factories and depots from areas threatened by the Russian advances.[9] On 2 March Whitehall received comments from the Russian General Staff on the subject.† They provided much detailed evidence to the effect that the Germans were increasing the provision of anti-gas equipment and intensifying anti-gas training and discipline, all of it pointing to anxiety to improve their defence against gas, but nevertheless suggested that the Allies should also step up their precautions.[10]

Between the end of February and the date of the JIC's next report, 28 March, Sigint references to gas were confined to the diplomatic decrypts. In one of these the Japanese Naval Attaché in Stockholm summarised a Swiss newspaper article which had claimed that German preparations for the use of gas included the distribution of containers marked to be opened only on orders

---

* But a Japanese signal from the Military Attaché in Berlin – decrypted on 5 February – showed German anxiety lest the Russians might use gas. Tokyo had been asked to provide information on the nature of Soviet gas equipment, 'especially in Siberia', and on the location of potential factories producing it.[8]

† All but the first of the reports by the JIC's sub-committee were sent to the BMM Moscow, for discussion with the Russians, as well as to the overseas commands of the western Allies.

5. As examples of individual decrypts, DEFE 3/328, BT 2188 of 13 January; DEFE 3/329, BTs 2292 of 14 January, 2379 of 15 January, 2426 of 15 January; AWL 3769; DEFE 3/500, BTs 3176 and 3241 of 23 and 24 January; DEFE 3/501, BT 3442 of 26 January; DEFE 3/502, BT 3522 of 27 January; Dir/C Archive, 8522, Boniface summary for the Foreign Office, 29 January.
6. DEFE 3/500, BT 3180 of 23 January.
7. CAB 121/102, JIC(45) 52(0) of 12 February, 70(0) of 28 February.
8. BAY/BT 60 of 5 February.
9. CAB 121/102, JIC(45) 70(0) of 28 February. The decrypts relating to movement on the eastern front included: DEFE 3/507, BTs 4755 of 13 February, 4912 of 15 February; DEFE 3/508, BTs 5176 of 19 February, 5209 of 20 February; DEFE 3/509, BT 5473 of 23 February; DEFE 3/510, BT 5670 of 25 February.
10. CAB 121/102, BMM telegram MIL 2426 of 2 March.

from the Führer.[11] In another telegram, however, the Japanese Ambassador in Berlin reported that the 'well-informed' were denying 'tendentious' Soviet propaganda to the effect that Germany might resort to gas.[12] The JIC report of 28 March noted the lack of evidence for offensive preparations and observed that the fact that the Germans had not used gas against the Allied crossing of the Rhine strengthened the conclusion that – except, possibly, on desperate orders from Hitler, in the final stages – they would not resort to it.[13]

In April a series of Enigma decrypts referred to the difficulties incurred in loading gas at Passau on the Danube, announced that the sinking of gas stocks in the North Sea had been forbidden and disclosed that remaining stocks of a special type of K ammunition (Spitzen K) were not to be destroyed or specially marked in any way.[14] They were followed on 21 April by the decrypt of a message of 16 April which disclosed that Hitler had reserved to himself the right to order the sinking of gases, including Spitzen K; OKW accordingly cancelled its own previous orders for the sinking of barges loaded with gas stocks, though it still required the removal from barges and their berths, as distinct from the ammunition stocks themselves, of all gas ammunition markings.[15]* Further orders were decrypted on 23 and 24 April: Nineteenth Army was informed that other gas ammunition should not be evacuated until all Spitzen GN 3 had been dispersed into barges and got away; and Army Group G in south Germany insisted that, in order to avoid the 'far-reaching consequences' that would follow if they were fired or destroyed in error, gas ammunition stocks must be carefully marked.[17] Perhaps as a result of the solitary reference to Hitler among these decrypts relating to the enemy's efforts to evacuate gas stocks, the final JIC report, issued on 23 April, did not entirely rule out the possibility that he might still give a reckless last-minute order for the use of gas. But it was confident

---

* This intervention by Hitler was presumably the basis for the story which, based on documents released in East Berlin, appeared in the British Press in 1981 to the effect that he had ordered stocks of the Tabun and Sarin gases to be loaded on to barges on the Elbe and the Danube, the barges to be moved away from towns, not sunk, if Allied air attacks prevented them from being sent away downstream. It claimed that Hitler's interest in the gases was associated with plans for a last-ditch stand in the Southern Redoubt.[16]

11. SJA 1533 of 8 March.
12. BAY/BT 126 of 21 March.
13. CAB 121/102, JIC(45) 104(0) of 28 March.
14. DEFE 3/562, BTs 9283 and 9353 of 3 April; DEFE 3/568, KOs 810 of 19 April, 869 and 872 of 20 April.
15. DEFE 3/569, KO 1004 of 21 April.
16. *Sunday Times* of 22 February 1981, 'Hitler's Deadly Secrets' by Gwynne Roberts.
17. DEFE 3/569, KO 1168 of 23 April; DEFE 3/570, KO 1284 of 24 April.

that few of the commanders in the field would now obey such an order, and that Germany's capacity to wage chemical warfare was, in any case, so reduced that Allied operations would not be seriously affected.[18]

A further report on Germany's preparations for chemical warfare followed in the middle of June, after the end of the war in Europe, when the Chemical Warfare Committee informed the Chiefs of Staff of the provisional result of the investigations carried out on the continent by the *Alsos* mission. The mission had found that stocks and equipment were in larger quantities than had been expected, but that every item was nevertheless of high quality; that in some respects the provisions made seemed to have been unnecessarily elaborate; and that while the effectiveness of some of the weapons was doubtful, others – the nerve gases Tabun, Sarin and Soman – might have 'outstanding merits'.[19]

18.   CAB 121/102, JIC(45) 137(o) of 23 April.
19.   ibid, COS (45) 401(o) of 16 June.

APPENDIX 29

TA Project: Enemy Intelligence

Excerpts from the joint Anglo–US Report to the Chancellor of the
Exchequer and Major General L R Groves
28 November 1944
(Reproduced from CAB 126/244)

1. INTRODUCTION.

The war has reached a stage at which the rapid collapse of
Germany is possible and it is therefore advisable to put forward
now the plan to be followed for the investigation, on the spot, of
T.A. work which is in progress. By agreement between the British
and Americans this subject has been excluded from the activities
of the various organisations which have been set up to examine
other scientific and technical work being done in Germany ...
[The present report has been written after full discussion with the
British and US authorities responsible for T.A. Intelligence work.]
Recommendations are made for the strengthening of the joint
British and American T.A. Intelligence organisation during the
period before the defeat of Germany, and for the action and
organisation which will be needed for investigation in Germany at
the earliest possible moment.

Although neither confirmed positive or negative intelligence is
available in the information accumulated to date it appears most
probable, from the indirect evidence thus far reported, that no
large military programme is under way for the employment of
T.A. products in the immediate future. But the possibilities
inherent in a successful application of the scientific research on the
fission of uranium are fully appreciated in Germany and research
certainly, and pilot scale work probably, is being carried out at an
accelerated rate.

Investigation of the position in Germany should therefore be
made with care and the action taken should be designed, as far as
may be possible, to find out what ideas are in the minds of those
responsible for the work as much as to collect purely factual
information on its present state. Efforts should be made to
prevent the driving underground of those scientists and technicians who could contribute novel ideas to the work and whose

interest in its long-term applications might only be increased by a widespread investigation.

This position makes it advisable, before setting out the recommendations referred to above, to summarise the information now available to us on the position of T.A. work in Germany and to state the conclusions which can, in our opinion, be drawn therefrom.

2. T.A. WORK IN GERMANY.

No serious effort was made to find out what work was being done in Germany on the T.A. project until the Directorate of Tube Alloys was set up at the end of 1941. It was then agreed that the nature of the work would make it impracticable to get information from Germany by sending agents into the country with this specific objective in view. No such agent would be likely to be able to get accurate information, at first hand, on such a complex technical problem and it would, in any case, be necessary to provide him with a dangerously detailed picture of the state of knowledge and the ideas current in Britain and the U.S.A.

It was also impossible to make any use of photographic reconnaissance until such time as evidence had accumulated as to the whereabouts of any constructional activities which would indicate the probability of the presence of large-scale or pilot plants.

The best method of attack seemed to be the investigation through neutral or occupied countries, of the whereabouts and activities of those German scientists who would be expected to be closely associated with any work on T.A. The problems to be solved before any large-scale applications of the project could be made were so novel that they could no more be tackled in Germany than in the U.K. or U.S.A. without full co-operation with academic scientists.

In addition, efforts have been made to follow any abnormal German interest in materials, such as uranium and heavy water, whose use would be specifically connected with the T.A. project and to find traces of any official organisation responsible for the work in Germany.

(a) Scientific Research.

Professor *W. Heisenberg* is the most obvious German physicist to be associated with this work and his name has, in fact, been connected with it in many reports. Before the war he held the chair of Theoretical Physics at Leipzig University. Those who know him personally are of the opinion that he is a patriotic German who, if his country was involved in war, would do all he could to help. Opinions are not so certain as to his enthusiasm for the Nazi party. He is not a Jew but, before the war, was attacked in the German press as a "White Jew" because of his support for Jewish scientists.

From information obtained from various sources it seems certain that Heisenberg left Leipzig and was working in Berlin from the beginning of 1942 till the end of 1943. He was Director of the Kaiser Wilhelm Institut für Physik and also Professor of Theoretical Physics at Berlin University. Research in connection with T.A. was carried out at the K.W.I. für Physik (Boltzmann-strasse 10, Berlin-Dahlem) during this period, which came to an end when the laboratory was damaged by bombing at the end of 1943.

Since then very reliable reports indicate that one or more research institutes have been set up in the neighbourhood of Hechingen and Bisingen. Heisenberg is known to be working there, as also are von Laue and other physicists who might reasonably be supposed to be concerned with T.A. These two places are in Hohenzollern, about 30 miles south of Stuttgart, and we suspect that these new research institutes are the present centre of T.A. research work.

Aerial reconnaissance has shown that, between July 1944 and November very active constructional work has been undertaken at three sites near Bisingen, Engstlatt and Dussingen. The latter two villages are about 2 miles S.W. and 12 miles N.E. of Bisingen respectively. The plants being built at all three sites are similar in character and, in the present early stage of construction, show no resemblance to any known plants though they are clearly of a chemical rather than of an engineering type. It is equally impossible to connect them definitely with any T.A. activity but this must be seriously considered in view of the reports of Heisenberg's activities in this area.

Information has also been received that Hechingen and the neighbouring district are 'prohibited areas' under military control.

In the summer of 1942 a report was received that Heisenberg was in charge of experimental work on the production of a U.235 bomb and on the use of the fission reaction as a source of power. He was said to be doubtful about the practicability of the former but confident of the latter application and to be satisfied with the progress of the work. It appeared from this report that Heisenberg's work involved systems containing uranium and some heavy hydrogen (deuterium) compound and he was stated to have had ½ ton of heavy water and to be due to receive a further ton.

Professor Planck, during a visit to Rome in the spring of 1943, said that Heisenberg claimed, 'in his usual optimistic way', that uranium could be employed for the generation of power in three or four years.

Although Heisenberg would seem to have been primarily concerned with T.A. work during the war there is evidence that he has been associated with other war projects and he has certainly published papers which show that he has also done an appreciable amount of detached scientific research.

Professor *O. Hahn* is particularly qualified to contribute to T.A. research and was responsible for the original work in Germany on the fission of uranium and thorium. He was and has remained throughout the war, Director of the Kaiser Wilhelm Institut für Chemie (Altensteinerstrasse 48, Berlin-Dahlem). He is, however, well-known for his strongly anti-Nazi views and it seems unlikely that he would be admitted to any knowledge of T.A. work being carried out in Germany under the auspices of an official organisation. It is of great interest to note that, throughout the war, Hahn and his co-workers at the K.W.I. für Chemie have published a large number of papers dealing with the isolation and properties of the fission products of uranium and also with the formation and properties of element 93. These papers, however, do not refer to element 94 though the nature of the relationship between elements 93 and 94 and the scientific qualifications of Hahn and his co-workers would make it quite certain that they are aware of the formation of 94 from 93 and of the greater interest in, and importance of, its properties.

Hahn visited Rome in 1941 and Stockholm in October 1943 to give lectures on the phenomenon of fission. In Stockholm he told Dr. Lise Meitner and Swedish physicists that there seemed no chance of the practical utilisation of fission chain reactions in uranium for many years to come.

Hahn also visited Paris after the fall of France but refused to go, as a member of the victorious country, to see Joliot in his laboratory there.

Prof. *W. Bothe* who, as a nuclear physicist, might be expected to be working on the T.A. project has spent some time in Joliot's laboratory in Paris where he was particularly concerned with the operation of the cyclotron. He has also built a cyclotron in his own laboratory in Heidelberg (Kaiser Wilhelm Institut für Medizinische Forschung) but the work he did in Paris and that published from Heidelberg, with all of which Dr. *Gentner* has been associated, seems to have been concerned with academic studies in nuclear physical problems and to have had no direct application to the T.A. project.

Professor *K. Clusius* of Munich University, who discovered the 'thermal diffusion' method for the separation of isotopes, was reported to have been working on the separation of the uranium isotopes during 1942 but to have had no success by the beginning of 1943. He appears to have dropped this work but said that another method, depending on differential solubility of the isotopes and using uranium salts in alcohol, was being studied in Berlin. He also sent Dr. *Grothe* from his laboratory to Professor T. Svedberg in Uppsala to study the technique of the ultra-centrifuge with which he has worked for many years.

It has been reported that Prof. Kuhn worked on the separation of isotopes by the centrifuge method at Kiel. This work was however abandoned and Kuhn left Germany for Switzerland where he is now living.

A very detailed report on the theory of the thermal diffusion method of isotope separation was published by R. Fleischmann and H. Jensen in Ergebnisse der Exakten Naturwissenschaften for 1942. This contains a reference to the possibility of separating the uranium isotopes by the use of the volatile compound UF_6.

Clusius and Dr. *L. Waldmann* of his laboratory have also published papers on the theory of the methods of isotope separation involving thermal diffusion and exchange reactions.

Prof. *P. Harteck* is known to have been occupied, during 1942 and 1943, with work on the separation of heavy water. Both he, and Drs. H. Jensen and Suess, have paid several visits to the Norsk-Hydro plant at Vemork and were principally interested in attempts to increase the rate of production of heavy water there by the addition of the catalytic exchange process to the normal electrolytic concentration plant.

Harteck is believed to have been continuing his work on heavy water at Freiburg in the early part of 1944.

Several papers have been published, by him and his collaborators, which disclose their interest in isotope separation, with special reference to heavy water, and in the nuclear physics of the uranium fission reaction.

There have also been some very interesting publications from the private laboratory of *M. von Ardenne* (Berlin-Lichterfelde Ost), who made money from radio patents and has, for some years, been working on the technical applications of electronics. Since 1939 he has been active in work on the development of electron microscopes. At the end of 1941 *F.G. Houtermans* published, from his laboratory, a long paper discussing, from a theoretical point of view, the energy consumption in the separation of isotopes and comparing the advantages of different methods with a view to 'a possible future isotope separation for technical purposes'. The investigation does not seem, however, to have any practical value and no attempt is made to extend the calculations to cover the problems that would be involved in a large-scale plant.

Since the appearance of this paper he has published others on nuclear physics with particular reference to fission and there are indications that von Ardenne has installed a high-voltage generator in his laboratory for use in connection with this work.

In papers describing this apparatus von Ardenne expresses his thanks to the Research Department of the Reichspost (Director Dr. Pose) for their help. This organisation seems, from other reports, to have been specially interested during the war in the design and operation of cyclotrons and an official from it visited Prof. Bohr's research institute at Copenhagen immediately after the fall of Denmark to examine the cyclotron there. Other officials have visited Siegbahn's laboratory in Sweden, where Lise Meitner is now working, to see the cyclotron there.

Reports have also been received that the Reichspost have laboratories in which high tension apparatus has been installed and that the work carried out there is under the direction of von Ardenne and Dr. Flugge.

This connection between von Ardenne and the Reichspost is confirmed by a recent paper in Zt. f. Physik (1944. *122*, 740) by von Ardenne and F. Bernhard, on a nuclear physical method for the determination of small amounts of carbon in iron, written from the 'Kernphysikalischen Institut des Reichspostministeriums, Berlin-Lichterfelde-Ost'.

Information from physicsts in Sweden and Switzerland who have corresponded with, and had visits from, German scientists all confirms the fact that research on the T.A. project has been carried out in Germany throughout the war but it is extremely difficult to form a definite opinion as to the urgency and purpose of this work. Heisenberg most clearly stands out as being associated with T.A. research work directed to practical applications, on a bomb or as a source of energy, and being carried out as a secret project and with official support. The number of papers published on the subject, however, is surprisingly large and the information in some of them would have been expected to be regarded as of practical importance and to have been kept secret. For example, a paper by Gehlen in Zeit. für Physik (1943, *121*, 268) gives values for the capture cross-section of commercial aluminium. The work was carried out in Leipzig in 1942 at Heisenberg's suggestion. Also there are German scientists who could certainly make important contributions to the subject but are not engaged on this work. In particular, *von Weizsäcker*, who has been Heisenberg's leading collaborator, was appointed to the chair of Physics at Strasbourg at the end of 1942 apparently for prestige purposes. *Reddemann* and *Euler* were reported as having been killed on the Eastern front at the end of 1941.

On the other hand there have been delays between the submission of papers to scientific journals and their publication of varying extent and, in many cases, of much greater than average length. This, and the remarkable omission of reference to 94 in the many papers by Hahn and his co-workers, suggests that there is some official censorship of papers on T.A.

The safest explanation seems to be that German scientists who have undoubtedly appreciated the potential importance of T.A. from the beginning, have continued to do as much work on the subject as has been possible. In the early stages of the war they probably had effective support from the German Wehrmacht or Nazi Party authorities and the project was accorded high priority and regarded as being of practical importance. From the end of 1942 or beginning of 1943 the conclusion seems to have been drawn that large-scale plants could not be built in time to produce a weapon for use in the war and the priority attached to T.A. was lowered in favour of work on other 'secret weapons' such as V.1 and V.2. Research, nevertheless, has continued and from the end of 1943 has even increased in intensity. There is no positive evidence that this is due to a successful solution of the various technical problems or is associated with the final design or construction of large-scale plants, though the new plants in the Bisingen area might be connected with T.A. It may well be due to a renewal of official interest through the acquisition of information in Germany about the scale of the T.A. work which is being carried out in the U.S.A. It must certainly be assumed, and there is some supporting evidence, that the Germans know of the American programme in general terms if not in considerable detail.

We believe that this increase in T.A. research activity in Germany is the psychological result of their knowledge of the great progress which has been made by the Allies and is not due to any real hope that they can build plants themselves to be of use in the war. It may be directed to finding out as much as possible about the scientific aspects of the project before the war ends, in order to strengthen the German position as much as may be possible for post-war development of the project.

(b) Essential Materials.

No large-scale effort on T.A. is possible unless supplies of uranium are available in amounts much in excess of the normal industrial requirements and an effort has therefore been made to find whether the Germans have tried to produce or acquire large amounts of uranium.

The mines at Joachimstal were acquired by Germany when Czecho-slovakia was overrun in 1939 and the refining of their products was taken over by the Auer Gesellschaft. A report in

1942 stated that Clusius, in his research work on the separation of the uranium isotopes, was using material from Joachimstal and in 1944 a very reliable report from Lise Meitner in Stockholm stated that the Auer Gesellschaft was making metal 'in large quantities'.

Before the war, however, the output of uranium from Joachimstal was small and expert geological opinion suggests that it would not, under any circumstances, be possible to get more than 30 tons per year from this source.

Aerial reconnaissance photographs of the mines in June 1944 showed no indications of abnormal working and it seems safe to conclude that the Germans could not get the quantity of uranium that would be needed for large-scale T.A. plants from Joachimstal and have, indeed, made no great effort to do so.

Since the fall of Belgium and France in 1940 much the largest stock of uranium in Europe has been available to them from the refinery of the Union Minière at Oolen.

Until the end of 1943 no accurate information was available as to the amount of material which could have been captured by the Germans but, thereafter, reports were received which indicated that several hundred tons of crude concentrates had been removed from Belgium and that some 60 tons of this had been returned in order that it should be converted to pure ammonium uranate.

The whole history of these Union Minière stocks has been made clear by a special investigation carried out by the *Alsos* Mission as soon as Belgium was liberated.

From the beginning of the war till May 1940 no abnormal deliveries of uranium compounds were made to Germany but, when Le Havre was captured in June 1940, a stock of 380 tons of crude concentrates (containing about 50% U_3O_8) was seized. Between this date and August 1941 some 60 tons of refined oxide was also delivered from Oolen to the Auer Gesellschaft. Finally in the spring of 1942 the remaining Union Minière stock of about 600 tons of crude concentrates and 120 tons of refined products was acquired by the Germans. This last transaction was carried out by Rohstoff Handels Gesellschaft m.b.h. (ROGES) though the presence in Brussels of the Auer representative who had shown great interest in uranium makes it possible that ROGES were only acting on behalf of this firm.

As far as the direct evidence shows, however, the material acquired by ROGES was stored at Stassfurt and it was some 80 tons of this material that was returned to Oolen in October 1943 and March 1944 for conversion to ammonium uranate. Although this refined product was ready for return to Germany between December 1943 and June 1944 no effort was made to get it back until two days before the Allies re-entered Oolen and, in fact, it was captured by them.

The general inference from these facts would seem to be that the German handling of the uranium supplies from Belgium does not warrant any assumption that large-scale T.A. plants are in operation or are shortly due to start. Nor does it suggest the existence, in Germany, of an efficient organisation to deal with T.A. work with executive authority and at high priority.

The Germans have, however, taken steps to acquire all available stocks of uranium. This may only be a question of normal commercial interest but is perhaps more likely to be due to a realisation of the inherent importance of the T.A. project and a conviction of its ultimate successful application together with an appreciation of the importance which would then attach to the possession of uranium supplies.

But Auer Gesellschaft have certainly obtained abnormally large amounts of uranium compounds during the war. This fact, taken with the reports of their activity in the preparation of metal, makes it safe to assume that they have been carrying out work, which may well have reached a pilot scale, in connection with T.A. research programmes in the country.

Another material which, in large quantities, can only be of interest to T.A. work is heavy water. It is not, however, an essential material in the same sense as is uranium.

Immediately after the German occupation of Norway the Norsk Hydro electrolytic plant at Vemork (near Rjukan) was put to the production of heavy water at the maximum rate and other Norsk Hydro plants were equipped to produce it in smaller amounts. The Vemork plant was severely damaged by sabotage in February 1943 and the Germans then ordered its repair as a matter of high priority. It was again damaged by bombing in October 1943. After this second attack the Germans agreed that no more heavy water should be made by Norsk Hydro. They attempted to take the remaining stocks to Germany but these were sabotaged en route. The plant which was used for the final stages of the concentration of heavy water was dismantled and stored at the Norsk Hydro factory until September 1944, when it was removed by the Germans without warning or discussion with Norsk Hydro staff.

About 2½ tons of heavy water have, in all, been sent from Norway to Germany since 1940.

During the last few months there have been indications of a sudden and abnormal interest by the Germans in thorium. This element, and its compounds, may well have many applications other than T.A. work but it is, perhaps, significant to note that in May 1944 the Germans took steps to acquire all thorium stocks in France of which the existence had been known to them since the occupation in 1940. At the same time they instituted enquiries in

Sweden as to the possibility of obtaining there supplies of both uranium and thorium.

A recent report has also stated that Auer Gesellschaft are now making thorium metal though nothing is yet known of the scale of this work and there is no conclusive proof that it has direct connection with the T.A. project.

(c) German Organisation for T.A. work.

In the early part of the war it seems likely that T.A. research in Germany was regarded as being of high importance and that some official support and priority was given to the work. This official interest would appear to have declined and may have been based on a conclusion that the project could not be realised in time to be of use during the war.

It has not, however, been possible to find any detailed evidence as to the nature and responsibility of any official German organisation in charge of the T.A. programme.

After the fall of Paris in 1940 a German physicist, Dr. *K. Diebner*, visited Prof. Joliot's laboratory and cross-examined him in great detail on the work which he had been doing on uranium. Diebner is a very active Nazi, though an indifferent physicist, and was in military uniform. He was again present at a meeting in Berlin in January 1942 when one of the Norsk Hydro engineers was summoned to discuss the possibility of increasing the rate of production of heavy water. This meeting was held in Forschungs-abteilung I, Hardenbergstrasse 10, which was one of the O.K.W. offices. Other army officers were also present.

Diebner's publications in the scientific literature since 1931 have been connected with various aspects of nuclear physics. From 1936 onwards he has published no original work but, from the P.T.R. in Berlin, has written an annual survey of work on artificial radioactivity. These surveys have been continued at any rate up to 1942.

The activity of the Reichspost research department, which has already been noted, may, of course, imply that this Government department has a connection with the official organisation of T.A. work but there is no proof of this as yet. There is, on the other hand, a considerable amount of evidence showing that nuclear physics, not necessarily connected with the specific problems of T.A., is a 'fashionable' subject in Germany and that many laboratories are devoting their work to this subject.

3. ORGANISATION OF T.A. INTELLIGENCE WORK.

Until very recently the information which has been available on the nature and scale of T.A. work in Germany has been meagre and it has not been practicable, owing to the inaccessibility of Europe, to follow up the majority of the reports which have been received. This has been explicable because of the very unusual nature of the problems which must everywhere be faced in the early stages of research on the T.A. project and we have been satisfied that the type of reports which have been received, as well as their detailed contents, justify the conclusion that work on the project in Germany had not reached a production scale and was not being regarded as of direct military importance during the war.

In addition to all other considerations the prime importance of security has limited the framework and intensity of investigations in this field. Separate channels were considered necessary for the handling of subject matter to be circulated among the few who, by direction, were permitted to participate in the project work. This prevented the normal use of existing organisations in the two countries.

Since the beginning of 1942 summary reports of the information available in the U.K. and the conclusions drawn from it were sent to the American T.A. Authorities and, at the end of 1943, very close liaison was established . . . as a result of an exchange of cables between the Chancellor of the Exchequer and General Groves.

Since this close liaison was established, the information obtained by independent British and American investigations has been made fully available to all parties interested. Co-ordination has been successful and investigations have been jointly considered before any action has been proposed to the executive authorities. Similar sources of information have been used by both sides. . . .

The policy for conducting investigations has been based on the use of existing organisations, both economic and military for getting information on general subjects such as secret weapons, uses of unusual materials and new scientific developments. Information of specific interest to the T.A. project is likely to be included in such general terms. This plan was followed instead of setting up a separate organisation, staffed with specialists familiar with T.A. work, to be in conformity with the general arrangements for security which have been referred to above.

When the liberation of Europe was started with the Italian campaign many scientists became available for interrogation. The Americans set up a small mission of scientists which was sent to this theatre to undertake an investigation of sources not normally approached by the military and beyond their appreciation unless previously briefed in the subject matter. This could not be done because of the security rules previously mentioned.

This American mission, known as *Alsos*, was reorganised for the invasion of Western Europe and went with the Armed Forces to France and Belgium.

The Service organisations of the American Army and Navy and the various divisions of O.S.R.D. participate in the mission, which is now engaged in interrogating all informants having scientific intelligence on new developments for the war.

Professor S.A. Goudsmit is the Scientific Chief of the Alsos Mission and he handles directly the investigations on the T.A. project with suitable expert consultants to assist him.

Up to the present all T.A. targets of any value in France and Belgium have been successfully approached and have been submitted to both the British and American officers interested.

Military Supreme Headquarters Command are cognisant of and are supporting the activities of the Alsos Mission and are giving the investigations for T.A. the highest priority.

The arrangements for liaison on T.A., though they have been somewhat informal in character, have so far worked well. Now, however, the increasingly large number of reports bearing on T.A. activities that are being collected and the impending investigations in Germany itself make it desirable that the organisation be more clearly defined to ensure that all reports are made available to those concerned, and that the necessary examination and cross-checking of them is efficiently carried out.

With this end in view it is recommended that a joint Anglo–American T.A. Intelligence Committee be formally set up which should meet at regular, and frequent, intervals to pool and discuss all reports concerning German T.A. activities and make the best arrangements possible for the further examination of any of them, as may be desirable, by the appropriate organisations in Britain and the U.S.A. . . .

It is recommended that the proposed Committee should report, jointly, to the Chancellor of the Exchequer and to General Groves.

4. INVESTIGATION OF T.A. ACTIVITIES IN GERMANY.

The occupation and defeat of Germany may involve a slow advance into the country against organised resistance to the end, or there may be a sudden collapse which would be followed by a rapid over-running of the whole country by the Allied forces.

In the former case targets of possible interest for the T.A. project will be uncovered one by one and arrangements for their investigation can probably be made as the occasion arises and according to their nature. But if the state of T.A. work in Germany is, in fact, what we believe it to be it seems very unlikely that important information would be available or could be obtained in this way and it is more probable that a lengthy programme of investigation in Germany would have to be organised after the final defeat.

Should there be a rapid collapse of organised resistance, however, there is a very much better chance that information could be obtained which would give a clear picture of the German ideas and plans for the development of the T.A. project.

Such information could probably only be obtained as a result of quick action and it is thought to be desirable to concentrate this in such a way as not to spread, further than may be inevitable, in Germany, any curiosity about the present status and potentialities of T.A. Until a policy has been agreed for the post-war control of T.A. in Germany and, indeed in the rest of Europe, it would seem very unwise to arouse German interest in the project any further than is absolutely necessary to enable us to get confirmation or otherwise of our present opinions on the state of the work there.

It is recommended that, in the first instance, detailed investigation of the T.A. project in Germany be concentrated in two areas, Berlin and Bisingen and the surrounding country.

In Berlin it should be possible to find traces of any official Wehrmacht or Nazi Party organisation responsible for the project; to examine the various laboratories of the Kaiser Wilhelm Institut, of the Reichspost and the private laboratory of von Ardenne; and to investigate the activities of the Auer Gesellschaft. In Bisingen and the neighbourhood it might be possible to study the activities of the research institutes which are believed to have been set up there and to capture, and hold for examination, Heisenberg and other German scientists working in them.

These two preliminary investigations are likely, if conditions are favourable, to provide an accurate picture of the position of T.A. work in Germany. If this should confirm our present ideas it would be possible to check any details, without arousing special curiosity, by subsequent investigation at secondary centres such as Government, university or industrial laboratories elsewhere in Germany. These latter investigations might well be carried out by members of other organisations, who would include them in their normal activities and make no special point of their interest in T.A.

Arrangements are being made in advance by the American Alsos Mission to secure the two special T.A. target areas in Germany as soon as the military situation permits. It is recommended that this be a joint undertaking with the British contributing to the present American organisation as may be necessary to ensure a successful investigation. Suggestions are put forward, in an Appendix to this report,* for the organisation and technical facilities which are required for this purpose. . . .

---

* Not reproduced.

The Polish, French and British Contributions to the Breaking of the Enigma: A Revised Account

Since the publication of Volume I of this History in 1979 a great deal of new information has come to light on the Polish and French contributions to the breaking of the Enigma. We here summarise those parts of it which are essential to an understanding of British work on the Enigma, a subject on which this account supersedes Appendix I of Volume I. Records traced in the GC and CS archives since 1979 show that some errors were introduced in that Appendix from a secondary account, written in 1945, which relied on the memories of the participants when it was dealing with the initial breakthrough into the Enigma. Subsequent Polish and French publications show that other errors arose from a Mayer memorandum, written in 1974, which apart from various interviews recorded in British newspapers in the early 1970s was the only Polish source used in compiling the Appendix to Volume I.

The new Polish publications are heavily dependent on material supplied by Marian Rejewski, who achieved the original recovery of Enigma wirings. Accounts by him of his work, written in 1967 but based on a report he wrote in France in 1942, appeared as appendices in W Kozaczuk, *Enigma: How the German Machine was broken, and how it was read by the Allies in World War Two* (London, 1984), which is the English language edition, with editorial notes, of *W Kregu Enigmy* (Warsaw, 1979). The appendices are:

Appendix B, 'A Conversation with Marian Rejewski', by R A Woytak.

Appendix C, 'Summary of Our Methods for Reconstructing Enigma and Reconstructing Daily Keys and of German Efforts to Frustrate those Methods'.

Appendix D, 'How the Polish Mathematicians Broke Enigma'.

Appendix E, 'The Mathematical Solution of the Enigma Cypher'.*

---

* Appendices D and E were originally published in Poland in 1980 and 1979 respectively. Appendices B and E were also published in *Cryptologia*, Volume 6, No 1, January 1982, together with Rejewski's 'Remarks on Appendix I to British Intelligence in the Second World War' which is quoted in Kozaczuk's book as Rejewski, 'Uwagi do Appendix I'. Another translation of Appendix D, with comments by Cy Deavours and Jack Good, was published in

On the French contribution, the important publications that have appeared since Bertrand's book of 1973 are P Paillole, *Notre Espion chez Hitler* (Paris, 1985) and Gilbert Bloch, 'La Contribution française à la Reconstruction et au Décryptement de l'Enigma militaire Allemande en 1931–1932', in *Revue Historique des Armées*, No 4, December 1985.*

We begin by noting some amendments to what was said in Volume I Appendix I about the Enigma, the electro-mechanical encyphering machine which was put on the commercial market in the early 1920s. It was adopted with modifications and improvements by the German Navy in 1926, the German Army in 1928 and the German Air Force in 1935. A plugboard version was introduced by the Army in 1930 and by the Navy in 1934.† By the outbreak of war in 1939, by which time additional wheels had been introduced and the procedure for using the machine had been improved, the German authorities judged that they had rendered it secure even in the event of capture; and they had indeed made of it a cypher which presented formidable obstacles to the cryptanalyst. Even if one possessed the machine and its wheels, the arrangement of the components, including the wheels and the inter-connecting plugs, allowed 0.269×10^{24} possible settings for each key.‡ Different keys were in use not only in the Navy, the Army and the Air Force, but also for different purposes or in different areas within each of the Services. Most elements of each key changed regularly, while wheel-order changes, initially made only once a quarter, became increasingly more frequent.

For some years after the outbreak of war the Germans made no further fundamental changes to the Enigma machine, and as the changes that were then made came into operation piece-meal, the machine in essentially the form it had acquired by 1939 remained the principal cypher of the German armed forces until 1945 for communications other than those between the highest commands. We need not doubt that this outcome reflected the practical

---

Annals of the History of Computing, Volume 3, No 3, July 1981. J Garlinski, *Intercept: Secrets of the Enigma War* (London 1979), has an appendix by Colonel Lisicki which is fuller on some minor details than Rejewski's accounts, but less informative on the mathematical solution.

* Gilbert Bloch has also written *Enigma avant Ultra*, an exhaustive analysis of all the literature so far published on the breaking of the Enigma. This has not yet been published and we are grateful to him for placing it at our disposal.

† This Appendix deals almost exclusively with this version, which was designated Enigma I by the Army during the few years when Enigma II, a large machine with the same cryptographic principles, was also being used.

‡ Different figures have been quoted, partly because of variation in the number of plugs used in the calculation. Rejewski's figure of 5×1092 allows for the number of possible wirings of three wheels and the reflector.

difficulties involved in replacing or modifying the many machines in use throughout the greatly extended wartime commands, and the delays resulting from manufacturing difficulties in the wartime economy, and was not solely due to the confidence of the Germans in the security of the cypher. But to the extent that their confidence played a part, the grounds for it had been undermined long before 1939. As early as the end of 1932, with the assistance of material provided by the French, the Poles had reconstituted the Service version of the Enigma, and from 1933 to the end of 1938 they had solved the Army settings regularly, and several of those in use by the other Services.

The latest French and Polish publications confirm that the French contribution began when the then Captain Bertrand, head of Section D of the Service de Renseignement, acquired several documents, which included two manuals giving operating and keying instructions for Enigma I, from Asché (Hans-Thilo Schmidt), a German employed in the cypher branch of the German Army. They establish that, as was previously indicated on the evidence of the GC and CS archives, copies of these documents were given to the Poles and the British at the end of 1931.* On the British lack of interest in the documents, GC and CS's archives add nothing except that it did not think them sufficiently valuable to justify helping Bertrand to meet the costs. It would seem that its initial study of the manuals was fairly perfunctory since it was not until 1936 that it considered undertaking a theoretical study of the Enigma indicator system with a view to discovering whether the machine might be reconstituted from the indicators if enough messages were available.

The Poles, who received the documents on 7 December 1931, expressed greater interest – so much so that Bertrand provided them in May and September 1932 with further documents from Asché which included some monthly lists giving the daily settings of the Enigma machine for the Army key.† But their initial enthusiasm was short-lived; it of course turned out that without full knowledge of the machine, and particularly of the internal wiring of its wheels, not even the possession of the daily settings was of any assistance.

This was the problem which Marian Rejewski, one of three young mathematicians then employed in the Warsaw cryptologic office after a training in cryptanalysis which had begun in 1929, started to attack in October or November 1932. He was armed

---

* Volume I, p 488.

† By September 1932, on the evidence of Colonel Paillole's book, Asché had supplied the monthly lists for December 1931 and May, September and October 1932.

with German Army Enigma intercepts, an example of the commercial Enigma, the two manuals supplied by Bertrand in 1931 and (though he apparently received these after some delay) two of the monthly sheets of daily settings which Bertrand had supplied in 1932. By the end of the year, or by early in January 1933, he had solved the wheel wirings by exploiting the indicator system; up to the autumn of 1938 (for the Army) the Enigma indicators consisted of the result of encyphering, twice in succession, the chosen three-letter setting of each message using the machine at the basic setting for that day. It was a brilliant achievement even though the lists of daily settings received from the French were essential to this quick success. Rejewski's own assessment that the lists were decisive adds that although he devised an attack on the indicators which would not need prior knowledge of the plug connections, this would have required so much labour over a long period that he was uncertain whether the Polish Cypher Bureau would have agreed to it. (Kozaczuk, op cit, Appendix E, p 279, and Appendix D, p 258.)

On this basis the Poles decrypted Enigma traffic from 1933 to December 1938 despite the changes made to the machine or to the procedure for its use, and they apparently did so without further assistance from the French. The French continued to receive documents from Asché, and to pass them to the Poles, until August 1938; according to Colonel Paillole, the documents included lists of daily settings for 34 months within the period from November 1932 to September 1938 which Asché provided on 17 separate occasions between October 1932 and August 1938. On Rejewski's evidence, however, the Poles did not pass any of this material to their Enigma specialists, presumably because the specialists were in any case being successful against the Army keys. As for the extent of their success, the Polish evidence now available clarifies and corrects what was said in Volume I.* Initially only Army traffic was decrypted regularly since after 1934, when the Navy and the Air Force began to use the same plugboard version of the machine as the Army, there were too few Navy and Air Force messages to make regular reading possible; the solution of the daily setting of any key depended on receiving some 60 or 80 intercepts using the setting.† Following a change of indicator

---

* Volume 1, pp 490–491.

† Rejewski (see 'Remarks on Appendix I', *Cryptologia*, January 1982, p 79; Kozaczuk, op cit Appendix B, p 237, and Appendix D, p 246) also rebuts what was said in Volume I (pp 490–491) to the effect that the Poles made their original break into the Enigma by reading, with some help from stolen settings, the traffic on a pre-1931 version of the machine that was used by the Navy. This statement was based on a secondary GC and CS account of the meeting with the Poles in July 1939. A contemporary account of that meeting has now been

procedure for the naval machine, on 1 May 1937, the methods used by the Poles for the other Enigma keys became inapplicable to the naval Enigma. Towards the end of the period a Sicherheits-dienst key was also decrypted regularly.

Having solved the wirings of the wheels, the Poles constructed replicas of the machine, about a dozen being completed by mid-1934, and later they developed methods which so speeded up the recovery of the daily settings that only about ten to twenty minutes' work was needed, given enough traffic. A change of reflector, in November 1937, was soon overcome, and a two weeks' test in January 1938 showed that about 75 per cent of the material was then decyphered. Changes made towards the end of 1938 had a more serious effect. The first was an alteration in the indicator procedure for the Army (and presumably the Air Force). Instead of using a basic setting for the day the operator now each time chose his own setting, and he transmitted this in clear, followed by the encypherment, still twice in succession, of the message setting. The Poles overcame the difficulties caused by this change, with only a partial interruption to their success, by constructing six Bombes (by November 1938) and developing the use of perfor-ated sheets, both methods being specialised to the new indicator procedure. From 15 December 1938, however, two additional wheels (IV and V) were brought into operation so that the three wheels in use could then be selected in sixty ways instead of six. Thanks to the fact that the SD used the new wheels with the old indicator procedure, the Poles quickly found the wiring of the new wheels but the work of finding daily SD settings theoretically increased ten-fold; in practice by considerably more, since there was no time to make the extra 54 catalogues of the type which had provided a speedy solution for the original six possible wheel orders. For the Army key the position was worse, since solution of the 90 per cent of settings which included either of the new wheels was impossible without the production of further perforated sheets on a large scale or else of more Bombes, or at least without the provision of additional wheels and extra operating staff for the existing Bombes. The Poles did not have sufficient resources to

---

found. It makes only one specific reference to naval keys – to the effect that the Poles had not read any of them since May 1937 – but it speaks of the Poles 'getting in at the start', and this may have misled the compilers of the secondary account. It appears that the wartime cryptanalysts at GC and CS, who had only a general knowledge of the origins of the Polish success and no information about what the Poles had obtained from Bertrand, believed that the Poles had broken the machine used by the Navy from 1926–1934, which was without a plugboard. It is evident, moreover, that the Poles provided GC and CS with some details about that machine, perhaps early in 1940. But this by no means implies that they had broken it, and even if they had, it is certain that the pre-1934 naval machine was quite irrelevant to Rejewski's solution of the wiring of the Army plugboard Enigma.

enable them to overcome this set-back. They also experienced greater difficulties from 1 January 1939, when the Germans slightly increased the number of plug connections used.

This was the situation when Bertrand called the meeting with the British and the Poles which took place in Paris on 9–10 January 1939. The Polish representatives said little there about the Enigma, since they had not been authorised to disclose their achievements, but in view of the deteriorating international situation the Poles called a second meeting at which, near Warsaw late in July, they provided details of their success and of the methods they had developed, and promised to supply Britain and France with a replica of the Enigma machine. The British representatives (Denniston and Knox from GC and CS and the head of DSD9, in charge of the Admiralty's Interception Service) undertook to supply certain tables (of the effect of the Enigma with various wheel orders) and some particular intercepts. Bertrand delivered a replica of the machine in London on 16 August. Paillole adds that various documents on the Polish methods were sent to GC and CS via Paris somewhat earlier. (Paillole, op cit, p 167.)

Turning to the British position at that time, we can now amplify and correct the earlier account.* In all probability the fact that GC and CS had shown little interest in the documents received from Bertrand in 1931 is partly explained by the small quantity of its Enigma intercepts; until well into the 1930s traffic in central Europe, transmitted on medium frequencies at low power, was difficult to intercept in the United Kingdom. It is noteworthy that when GC and CS made a follow-up approach to Bertrand in 1936 the sole outcome was an agreement to exchange intercepts, and in November 1938 GC and CS was still waiting to receive intercepts for a period up to September 1938. During the Spanish Civil War a considerable quantity of Enigma traffic had become available as a result of the involvement of German naval units in the Spanish area. No progress had been made with this traffic, which was different from traffic on an Italian machine that was also in use in Spain,† but its interception may 'have prompted the further exchanges with Bertrand in 1938 in which he provided the plain and cypher texts of four Army Enigma messages with the

---

* See Volume I, pp 488, 491.

† It was wrongly stated in Volume I (pp 54 and 491) on the basis of the secondary report compiled in 1945 that in 1937 GC and CS recovered the wirings of the machine used by the German, Italian and Franco forces in Spain. In fact the machine it broke had been bought for the Italian forces some time earlier and was also used to a minor extent by Franco's forces; there is no evidence of German use of this machine. It proved to have one minor improvement over the commercial model which had been available at GC and CS for over ten years. For GC and CS's exploitation of this machine in the war see Volume I, p 210.

plugboard connections and settings used (the wheels were I, II and III).*

By 1938, however, GC and. CS had developed methods of attacking the Enigma which included under the name *Saga* that which Rejewski had used in his solution of the first three wheels and the reflector. At the Paris meeting in January 1939 Knox outlined a more complicated version of this method and asked Bertrand to try to obtain 16 alphabets at specified positions if he could not obtain the wirings themselves.† British accounts of that meeting also mention that Major Ciezki, the only Polish crypt-analyst present, explained the Polish method of obtaining the message settings from the indicator system used by the German Army up to 15 September 1938, and state that it was the same as the method used at GC and CS to find message settings. A British account of the Warsaw meeting shows that Knox had by then seen the possibilities of obtaining key solutions from the new indicating system introduced by the Germans in September 1938 by using 'females' (that is, cases of the same letter occurring at distance three when the three-letter message setting was enciphered twice in succession); he was proposing, once the wirings were known, to record the female positions on film until he learned of the Polish perforated sheets, which he recognised as being cheaper to make and perhaps easier to align. The account goes on to say that, apart from the Bombes themselves, only one of the ideas underlying the Polish exploitation methods was 'new', namely that of taking three females (involving the same letters) from the indicators as data for the Bombes.

It is now clear that, as Rejewski correctly surmised, (Kocaczuk, op cit, Appendix D, p 257) where the GC and CS cryptanalysts had failed was in guessing the fundamental connections between the keyboard and the entry drum, that is, those before modification by the plugging and were therefore unable to find the wiring of the wheels and the reflector. If they had thought of using the straight alphabet instead of the keyboard order known from the commer-cial Enigma, and also used by the Italians, they would have solved the wirings (except for an equivalence) from the 'crib' provided by

---

* The only other Asché material known to have been received by GC and CS was the encypherment of the 26 letters in keyboard order, likewise with settings, which are referred to in Bertrand's book (p 32). According to Paillole, Bertrand supplied sheets of settings early in 1938, or even earlier. If he did, they did not reach the people most concerned; a memorandum drawn up at GC and CS as late as September 1938 referred to the 1931 documents as if no other details had been received since, and it requested that the French be asked to give information about the Army Enigma which would have been known already if recent sheets of settings had been studied.

† In May Bertrand reported that he had had no opportunity to do this.

the texts of the four messages obtained from Bertrand in 1938.* But in view of the theoretical advances they had made and of the practical success they had obtained against the Italian Enigma, it is not surprising that, as the Poles recognised, Knox quickly grasped the significance of what he learned at the Warsaw meeting (ibid, Appendix B, p 236). As soon as the wirings were received, GC and CS adapted some British Typex machines to work like the Enigma and started the necessary preparations for exploitation with the Polish perforated sheets for which, the Poles having described the method as 'Netzverfahren' (net procedure), it used the name 'Netz'.

The punching of the first copy of the Netz, which took about a month, did not start till mid-November 1939. It had awaited the design and completion of an adequately fast machine which gave a printed record of the positions of the females, in gauge with the squared paper used. The second copy, for only 24 out of the 60 possible wheel orders, was despatched. to France (to 'Bruno' centre, at Gretz-Armainvillers) with a covering note dated 28 December, together with copies of 'Jeffreys sheets' which were a novel form of catalogue of the effect of any two wheels and the reflector. By 7 January 1940 the second copy of the remaining Netz was ready but had not been despatched. The date supplied by the Polish sources, 17 January 1940, for the first solution of any wartime Enigma setting, that for Green of 28 October 1939, is thus correct; our dating of the solution in the second half of December 1939† was based on the 1945 account.†

What would otherwise be the curious failure of the GC and CS cryptanalysts to secure an earlier solution with their complete set of Netz is largely explained by the work they did in an effort to reduce the number of wheel orders to try. Such analysis had to concentrate on the different 'turnover' positions, and in some cases it gave wrong results because the positions given for the 'turnover' notches on wheels IV and V in the data received from the Poles had unfortunately been interchanged. It is apparent, indeed, that it was this delay which engendered the suspicion that the Germans had made a serious change in the machine at the outbreak of war, presumably involving new wheels or a new reflector. On the other hand, it may well be that once this confusion had been cleared up, the British work facilitated the first Polish solution. Following the Polish success three solutions were made at GC and CS before 23 January 1940 – those for 25 October 1939 (Green), for 17 January 1940 (probably Red) and 6

---

* It is, however, uncertain whether GC and CS had the Sicherheitsdienst intercepts which enabled the Poles to solve the new wheels IV and V.

† see Volume I, p 493.

January 1940 (Red). According to a GC and CS memorandum dated 25 January the first two were simplified by a new method for reducing the wheel orders.

By the end of March 1940 some 50 wartime settings had been solved by the Netz method for three keys – the Green (Army administrative), the Blue (GAF practice) and the Red (GAF general operations) – but generally with considerable delay. Between mid-April and mid-May, however, there were continuous and almost current solutions, also by the Netz method, of the setting for the Yellow key, which had been introduced for operations in Norway. The main reasons for the improved results were the volume of Yellow traffic (several times the 100 message parts that were needed for a successful Netz attack) and the increasing numbers and experience of the Enigma party at GC and CS, which had begun to work three full shifts just before the invasion of Norway. These developments gave GC and CS considerable advantages over the Enigma party at Bruno, where the small Polish team which had escaped to France worked practically alone and with fewer intercepts: it is not surprising that, as noted in Volume I, the Polish records credited GC and CS with 83 per cent of the solutions exchanged between the two centres in the period to mid-June 1940.

On 1 May 1940 the Germans brought into force another modification of the indicator system for all Army and GAF keys except the Yellow; thenceforward the three-letter setting of each message was encyphered once only.* The change made the Netz system unusable, but despite this considerable set-back the Red setting for 20 May was solved on the following day, and was thereafter solved daily with little delay for the rest of the war. In Volume I it was inferred that this breakthrough was attributable to the arrival at GC and CS in May of the first British Bombe. Further research has shown that this explanation was incorrect. The breakthrough was achieved by a new hand method which exploited the habits of some of the German cypher operators, known as 'Cillies' at GC and CS. Two features of this new method may be mentioned for the major contributions they made to its effectiveness. One was the 'Herivel tip' for the position of the numbered rings on the wheels, the other being a system of reducing the number of wheel orders to be tried (of two such

---

* Gordon Welchman, *The Hut Six Story* (London 1982), and J Stengers, 'Enigma, the French, the Poles and the British, 1931–1940' in *The Missing Dimension* (Christopher Andrew and David Dilks eds London 1984), did not accept this date on the ground that a Polish list of solutions shows a gap of only five days in mid-May. But that list does not distinguish between the keys, and all the solutions recorded for the first 14 days of May were for the Yellow key. That 1 May is the correct date is established by a copy of the German manual in the GC and CS archives, where the description of the new indicator system is marked 'Gültig ab 1.5.1940'.

systems invented by Knox, this one, which dated from January 1940, remained valid after the indicator change of 1 May 1940).*

The first British Bombe had in fact been installed at GC and CS at an earlier date – on 18 March 1940. It was designed to do a different job from that for which the Polish machines had been developed. Before leaving Warsaw Knox had commented that the Polish methods all depended on the machine encypherment of the German indicators 'which may at any moment be cancelled'. After the Warsaw meeting he and Turing saw the possibility of developing a Bombe method for situations in which routine beginnings of messages could be applied to cypher text, and the first specification for British Bombes, drawn up by Turing, was intended to serve this function while also being available for use against the indicators in the Polish manner.† By early October 1939 it was being studied by Keen, of the British Tabulating Machine Company. But his design was delayed by difficulty in meeting the requirement to test 26 hypotheses at each position of the wheels, and at some stage the decision was taken to produce prototypes without this facility.

This decision was then overtaken by the discovery that the diagonal board would provide a simpler method of 'simultaneous scanning' to test all 26 hypotheses for the plugging of the input letter. According to the 1945 account, this 'great advance in

---

* These methods were developed at GC and CS (see Kozaczuk, op cit, p 107, additional note; and Welchman, op cit, Chapter 6, and 'From Polish Bomba to British Bombe: The Birth of Ultra', in *Intelligence and National Security*, Volume 1, No 1, January 1986. Welchman's account of Cillies, which includes an explanation of the 'Herivel tip' is however incomplete). Kozaczuk (op cit, pp 87–88) also mentions that the Poles had discovered that Enigma plugging instructions for the GAF key were used by the Germans to encrypt a code used by the GAF for meteorological and other messages between aircraft and ground stations. He says the Poles found this practice useful for arriving at Enigma solutions (Kozaczuk, op cit, p 117). There is nothing in the GC and CS archives to suggest that it knew of a connection between such a code and Enigma plugging, although one document has been found which might conceivably be referring to it, and it did not influence GC and CS's work. If the Poles derived any help from the connection it was presumably short-lived, since Rejewski did not refer to it when he named Knox's reduction method, Cillies and the 'Herivel tip' as the methods used by the cryptanalysts at 'Cadix', near Uzès, to read some Enigma from October 1940 to November 1942.

We may add that Rejewski had earlier stated (Kozaczuk, op cit, Appendix D, p 270) that the Poles did not work on (German) Enigma at Cadix. This is probably correct since it is known that the Poles at Cadix read Enigma with solutions supplied by GC and CS. Although Rejewski believed that GC and CS sent no Enigma keys to Cadix its records show that, despite the risks involved, it was carrying out its agreement with Bertrand to the extent of still sending settings 'of a minor character' in April 1942 after earlier providing a fuller service, if not the complete service for which Bertrand had pressed.

† Its greater speed and size gave the first British Bombe the power of at least twelve Polish Bombes in this second role, for which, however, it was apparently never used, presumably because the Netz method was working well. The first recorded success of this Bombe was in contributing in June to the few solutions of naval settings for days in April that were obtained on the basis of the material taken from VP2623 (See Volume I, p 163).

Bombe theory' took place in the spring of 1940.* In the summer of 1940 Turing recorded that the idea arose when it became clear that the Bombes would be required to use less favourable material than had been envisaged; this evidence also suggests a date in May 1940 when the Netz method had ceased to be usable. It was certainly in June or July that Turing devised a method of testing that provided the full benefits available from the diagonal board. These developments produced a machine that was so radically different from the Polish Bombe that it was at first, but only briefly, given the new name 'Spider'. The first new machine was installed on 8 August.

Although this Bombe and the original Bombe, which returned to GC and CS in September 1940 after being converted, sometimes provided faster solutions of the Brown key (the key used by the GAF unit involved in the development of navigational beams) from September 1940, they could not at once replace the hand methods. For some months after that it was the hand methods which chiefly ensured GC and CS's continued success against the Red key and the extension of that success to other GAF keys, even though the growing number of Bombes and the fact that study of decrypts greatly facilitated the identification of routine features in the German messages were beginning to produce faster solutions and thus to reduce the labour of attacking the increasing number of keys.

It remains to offer a revised assessment of the Polish contribution to the Allied success against the wartime Enigma. Any assessment of the time it saved at GC and CS must be conjectural and subjective, but we ought to correct the errors contained in our earlier account in the light of the evidence that has since become available.

The most important part of the Polish contribution was their provision of the wirings of wheels I to V. As previously stated, the first wartime capture of Enigma wheels was from U-33 in February 1940. But those wheels, only three altogether, included VI and VII, which were special to the Navy, and it is unlikely that the knowledge of their wirings would have enabled GC and CS to recover the wirings of wheels I to V. This would have been particularly true if the presence and function of the plugboard had remained unknown, as would have been the case if no material had been received from Asché. At least three Army Enigma machines were captured intact in Norway, however, and were in use at GC and CS by 17 May. In addition to the fact that,

---

* Writing from memory, Welchman (*Hut 6 Story*, p 77) gives a much earlier date for his idea of the diagonal board for using the reciprocal property of the plugging.

even if no assistance had been received from the Poles, these would have allowed the reading of the Yellow key for the day or days covered by the captures, they provided wheels I to V.

It is certain that, with only the above advances, the Red key would not have been read currently before the fall of France without the Polish assistance; but it is not impossible that some progress would have begun against it by then. The discovery of the type of Cilli which proved so valuable for the near-current solution of the Red key from May 1940 was in fact made about January 1940 with assistance from the decrypts for one or two earlier days that then became available as a result of the Polish contribution. But there was enough external evidence to have made the discovery feasible by that date in any case, and solution of indicators in the traffic intercepted before the indicator change of 15 September 1938* had already provided an insight into the types of message setting preferred by the German operators. As with the 'Herivel tip', which was also vital for the hand methods using the Cillies, and which was also derived from the study of operator behaviour, these advances might have been made much later in the absence of the Polish assistance than they were made in fact. But when it is remembered that many of the key people in GC and CS's attack on the Enigma were either pre-war staff or had started this work at the very beginning of the war after receiving a brief training at various dates in the first half of 1939 it does not seem unreasonable to assume that they would have produced some results against the Red not long after the fall of France.

In what has been said so far it has been assumed that just as GC and CS had seen the possibilities of hand methods of exploitation comparable to the Polish Netz independently of the Poles, so it would in any case have discovered, not much later than it did in fact, the hand methods which were applied when the Netz procedure became useless. But what, without the contribution of the Poles, would it have achieved in the development of the Bombe, which was crucial to its longer term success? In Volume I we stated that it is also 'virtually certain that the GC and CS Enigma team would in any case have realised the need to develop analogue machinery for recovering the daily keys'.† This statement was supported by the knowledge that Turing had an interest in machine computation. It may now be added that he had already designed machines to assist his work on two mathematical problems, one being an electrical binary multiplier and the other using special gear wheels. (A Hodges, *Alan Turing: The Enigma*

---

* See above, p 951.
† p 494.

(1983), pp 138–140, 155–158). Further support for the statement may be found in the fact that the German cryptographic researchers had put forward the idea of a Polish-type Bombe as constituting a threat to the security of the indicating system which was superseded on 1 May 1940. But it is still the case that the Polish Bombes came as a surprise to GC and CS in 1939: as already noted, its report on the Warsaw meeting recorded that only one idea was new 'apart from the machines themselves . . .' And on the evidence now available it seems probable that without the benefit of the Polish contribution British work on Bombe design, let alone production, would otherwise have begun ten months to a year later than was in fact the case rather than seven months later as was suggested in Volume 1.

The most important consideration in this calculation is not the gift of the idea of the Bombe nor the receipt of technical drawings of it,* but the fact that GC and CS would not have contemplated Bombe-type methods for an Enigma without a plugboard, and probably not before the exact function of the plugboard had been proved. Without the Polish success this would not have been until the receipt in May 1940 of the machines captured in Norway, which also supplied a full set of the Army and GAF wheels.†

In the event GC and CS did not recover the wirings of any of the eight normal wheels by cryptanalysis, though it was successful in recovering the components of the split reflectors of the later naval version of the Enigma. It obtained those for wheels I to V from the Poles in August 1939 (and later from the Norway captures in May 1940), those for VI and VII from U-33 in February 1940, those for VIII – the existence of which was previously unknown – from a naval capture in August 1940.‡ But it could have recovered those for three or more wheels, including at least one of those special to the Navy, from the documents taken from the German patrol boat VP2623 in April 1940;§ these included a large quantity of matched plain and cypher text, with message settings, for two days, and by the summer GC and CS had successfully tested a method of recovering wirings from such material.

---

* It is in fact uncertain whether any drawings were received – the GC and CS archives record the receipt of such details only for the Cyclometer, which was designed for preparing the Netz – but it is also doubtful whether they would have been valuable.

† The Asché material supplied to GC and CS by the French had indeed shown the existence of plugging, and its function had been correctly interpreted, but other interpretations of its effect on the logic of the machines were perhaps possible.

‡ Some writers (Rohwer and Jäckel, *Die Funkaufklärung und ihre Rolle im Zweiten Weltkrieg*, pp 84–86; Kozaczuk, op cit, p 14) have wrongly assumed that the naval wheels were not obtained until they were captured from the *München* and the *Lauenburg* in May and June 1941. They also appear to believe that all the naval wheels were different from those of the Army and the GAF, whereas wheels I to V were common to all three Services.

§ See Volume I, pp 163, 336.

It is impossible to estimate for how long and to what extent the delay in the start of GC and CS's Bombe programme from August 1939 to a date somewhat later than May 1940 would have been reflected in the construction of fewer Bombes than were produced, and thus in a long-term reduction in the readability of Enigma keys.* It seems reasonable, however, to repeat, with additional comments, the earlier conclusion that as distinct from that of the GAF keys, 'the regular solution of the German naval and army keys began so much later . . . that it is unlikely that the Polish contribution made any difference to the dates from which they were mastered'.†

In the case of the Army this statement refers only to the period after the indicator change on 1 May 1940 and also excludes the Yellow key, which was classified as being supplied by the Army. The main reasons for the delay in making progress against Army keys other than the Yellow after that date were in the first instance lack of intercept resources and subsequently lack of intercepted material. During the invasion of France the volume and the importance of the GAF Red traffic were so great that the intercept stations and the GC and CS cryptanalysts, fully stretched in dealing with it, were unable to devote any attention to Army operational traffic. Thereafter Army operational keys were rarely active before the arrival of German forces in north Africa and the German invasion of Russia. The Green key continued for some time to carry a large volume of traffic, but external features showed that it was non-operational, and particular difficulties in intercepting the traffic also contributed to lack of progress against this key. In fact the first north African Army key was broken once in March 1941 and once in April 1941 with the use of Cillies and then not again until September when there was an average of at least one break every two days until November.

The reasons for the delay in reading the naval Enigma regularly were different. In December 1939, using material provided by the Poles, Turing determined the new naval indicating procedure.‡ It was more secure than the procedures used by the GAF and the

---

* As an example of the imponderables involved here it should be noted that, as things were, there might have been less delay in producing the first satisfactory Bombe if the first specification had been able to take account of experience gained with the hand methods against the Red key after the indicator changes of 1 May 1940. In that case it might have incorporated the improved logic based on the reciprocal property of the plugging which enabled later Bombes to trace a chain of implications at speed for all settings.

† Volume I, p 495.

‡ At the Warsaw meeting it was arranged that the Poles should receive the British intercepts of naval Enigma for May 1937, the period immediately following the change of the naval indicating procedure. It was presumably after this, but before the Polish cryptanalytic data had arrived at GC and CS, that the Poles read about 100 messages for the first eight days of May 1937.

Army, but he realised that it allowed a method of eliminating some wheel orders (known as Banburismus) if tables used for the second stage of the encypherment of the message settings could be captured or laboriously constructed. The importance of Banburismus was emphasised by the early wartime captures which showed that the Navy was using extra wheels.

The documents taken from VP2623 in April 1940, which would have been sufficient to establish the indicator system and develop Banburismus if that work had not already been done with the help of the Poles, made it possible not only to read the few April days they covered but also to solve a few other days with the Banburismus method. Although the first such purely cryptanalytic success was not obtained till November 1940, others soon followed. Their main importance was to demonstrate that, in view of the greater volume of traffic that was becoming available, regular solution would be possible if the crucial tables, which had been changed in July, could be obtained. They were obtained through the planned captures of the trawler *Krebs* and the weather ships *München* and *Lauenburg* in March, May and June 1941,* which provided lists of daily settings. These captures made possible through daily reading of the traffic the development of that familiarity with its content which ensured that regular solution could continue with Banburismus and a modest use of Bombes. If Bombe development had started later than it did in fact, Banburismus would have sufficed to read the traffic but it would have been read less currently in proportion to the smaller number of Bombes available. In the event the situation in which there were enough Bombes for use against all 336 naval wheel orders, so that Banburismus could be dispensed with and a generally quicker solution of the daily setting achieved, was not reached until mid-1943.

In conclusion, we should reiterate that, thanks to the discretion of the Polish and French authorities and the loyalty of those among them who were interrogated by the Germans, no hint ever reached the enemy's ears of the Allied success against the Enigma to which they had so greatly contributed.

---

* See Volume 1, pp 337–338.

Bibliography

A. UNPUBLISHED OFFICIAL PAPERS

(i) Papers which have received PRO reference numbers

Cabinet Office		
Committee of Imperial Defence: Meetings	CAB	2
Committee of Imperial Defence: Memoranda	CAB	4
Committee of Imperial Defence *ad hoc* Sub-Committees of Enquiry: Proceedings and Memoranda	CAB	16
Cabinet Registered Files	CAB	21
Cabinet Minutes to September 1939	CAB	23
Cabinet Memoranda to September 1939	CAB	24
Cabinet Committees to 1939: General Series, Meetings and Memoranda	CAB	27
International Conferences: Meetings and Memoranda	CAB	29
Historical Section: Military Narratives	CAB	44
Committee of Imperial Defence: Advisory Committee on Trade Questions in time of war, Meetings and Memoranda	CAB	47
Committee of Imperial Defence: Industrial Intelligence in Foreign Countries, Meetings and Memoranda of its Standing Committee	CAB	48
Committee of Imperial Defence: Chiefs of Staff Committee to September 1939, Meetings and Memoranda	CAB	53
Committee of Imperial Defence: Deputy Chiefs of Staff Sub-Committee to September 1939, Meetings and Memoranda	CAB	54
Committee of Imperial Defence: Joint Planning Sub-Committee to September 1939	CAB	55
War Cabinet: Minutes	CAB	65
War Cabinet: Memoranda, WP series	CAB	66
WP(G) series	CAB	67
WP(R) series	CAB	68
War Cabinet: Defence Committee (Operations), Meetings and Memoranda	CAB	69
War Cabinet: Committees on Oil Policy, Meetings and Memoranda	CAB	77

War Cabinet: Chiefs of Staff Committee
  Meetings   CAB 79
War Cabinet: Chiefs of Staff Committee
  Memoranda   CAB 80
War Cabinet: Chiefs of Staff Sub-Committees:
  Inter-Services Committee on Chemical
  Warfare; Future Operations (Enemy)
  Planning Section   CAB 81
War Cabinet: Deputy Chiefs of Staff Committee,
  Meetings and Memoranda   CAB 82
War Cabinet: Ministerial Committee on Military
  Co-ordination, Meetings and Memoranda   CAB 83
War Cabinet: Joint Planning Committee,
  Meetings and Memoranda   CAB 84
War Cabinet: Anglo–French Committees:
  Meetings and Memoranda of Anglo–French
  Liaison Committee and of Foreign (Allied)
  Resistance Committee   CAB 85
War Cabinet: Committee on Anti-U-boat
  Warfare, Meetings and Memoranda   CAB 86
War Cabinet: Combined Chiefs of Staff
  Committees and Sub-Committees, Meetings
  and Memoranda   CAB 88
War Cabinet: Ministerial Committee on Military
  Policy in the Middle East   CAB 95
War Cabinet: Miscellaneous Committees;
  Combined Report on the Dieppe Raid   CAB 98
War Cabinet: International Conferences:
  British–United States Staff Conversations   CAB 99
Official War Histories: Military   CAB 101
                 Civil   CAB 102
War Cabinet: Telegrams   CAB 105
Historical Section: Files   CAB 106
Minister of Defence: Secretariat Files   CAB 120
Special Secret Information Centre Files   CAB 121
British Joint Staff Mission Washington File   CAB 122
Atomic Energy Files   CAB 126

Admiralty

Admiralty and Secretariat Papers   ADM 1
Admiralty and Secretariat Cases   ADM 116
Admiralty Historical Section, 1914–1918 War
  Histories   ADM 137
Admiralty Publications   ADM 186, 234
War History Cases and Papers   ADM 199
First Sea Lord's Papers   ADM 205

Naval Intelligence Papers (including Admiralty
   Ultra Signals)   ADM 223

War Office

Directorate of Military Operations and
   Intelligence   WO 106

War of 1939–1945:
   War Diaries, Middle East Forces   WO 169
                 Central Mediterranean Forces   WO 170
                 North-west Europe   WO 171
                 British North Africa Forces   WO 175

Appreciations File   WO 190

Directorate of Military Operations: Collation
   Files   WO 193

War of 1939–1945:
   Military HQ Papers, BEF   WO 197
                 Home Forces   WO 199
                 Middle East Forces   WO 201
                 Military Missions   WO 202
                 AFHQ   WO 204
                 21st Army Group   WO 205

Directorate of Intelligence   WO 208

War Diaries: SHAEF   WO 219

Monographs   WO 277

Papers of General Dempsey   WO 285

Air Ministry

Registered Files   AIR 2

Chief of Air Staff's Papers   AIR 8

Publications   AIR 10

Private Office Papers   AIR 19

Unregistered Files   AIR 20

War of 1939–1945: Periodical Returns,
   Summaries and Bulletins   AIR 22

Overseas Commands   AIR 23

Allied Central Interpretation Unit   AIR 34

Directorate of Intelligence and other
   Intelligence Papers   AIR 40

RAF Monographs and Narratives   AIR 41

Ministry of Defence

War of 1939–1945 Intelligence from enemy
   radio communications: SCU/SLU signals to Allied
   Commands conveying special intelligence
   reports based on intelligence from German
   Army and Air Force traffic;
   Teleprinted translations of decrypted
   German and Italian naval radio messages   DEFE 3

Foreign Office

General Correspondence after 1906, Political — FO 371
Ministry of Economic Warfare Papers — FO 837
Papers on Psychological Warfare — FO 898
Private Collections of various Ministers and
    officials — FO 800

(ii) Papers which have not received PRO reference numbers

The following lists include papers which have not yet been, and may never be, released to the public domain. The reader is reminded that the preface to each of the volumes of this history sets out the procedure under which the historians have been permitted to use the domestic files of the intelligence-collecting bodies from which some papers in this section of the bibliography come.

High-Grade Decrypts

Germany Army and Air Force traffic — CX/JQ, CX/MSS
German Police traffic — GPD
Japanese Military Attaché traffic — JMA
Japanese Naval Attaché traffic — SJA
Daily selections of decrypts for the
    Prime Minister — Dir/C Archive

Sigint Reports and Signals based on High-Grade Decrypts

Series containing information on the
    GAF — CX/JQ/A1, CX/MSS/A1
Series containing information on the
    German Army — CX/JQ/M1, CX/MSS/M1
Series containing information on the
    German Navy — CX/JQ/N1, CX/MSS/N1
Reports of general interest concerning
    the German Army, Air Force, Police
    and Y Service — CX/JQ/S, CX/MSS/S
Series of special German radar plot
    reports — CX/MSS/J
Reports on German secret weapons,
    signals regiments — CX/MSS/SJ
Account of the German RDF
    reporting system — CX/MSS/RDF
Reports on German railways — CX/MSS/SR

German reports on Russian unit
  locations, installations and orders of
  battle   CX/MSS/ROB

GC and CS Naval Section reports   Z, ZG

GC and CS Naval Section daily reports
  containing excerpts from decrypts   Naval Headlines

Appreciations concerning the GAF for
  inclusion in signals to Commands   Air Sunsets

Signals to Commands with political
  content   BAY series; CX/MSS/SC

Signals between Service Ministries and
  Commands relevant to Sigint   CXG and AWL series
       (outgoing)
       GAD (incoming)
       RUBY/SH (from
       SHAEF)

Historical Accounts

Admiralty Reports: BR 1736(51)(A and B), *Defeat of the Enemy
  Attack on Shipping 1939–45*
  BR 1736(56)(1), *British Mining Operations*
  FDS 65/54, *German Small Battle Units 1943–1945*

C Morgan, *NID History 1939–1942*

Brigadier L E Mockler-Ferryman, *Military Intelligence Organisation*

Air Ministry Intelligence (in two volumes)

Air Historical Branch Narrative, *The RAF in the Middle East
  Campaigns*, Vol XI

Air Vice Marshal Sir V Goddard, *Epic Violet*

Handling of Naval Special Intelligence

History of the R/T organisation ashore and afloat

History of Sigint in the Field

History of the Special Liaison Units

AI 2(g), Ultra Material as a Source of Technical Intelligence
  Technical Intelligence Sources

AI 3(b), Use of Ultra
  Work of AI 3(b)

AI 3(e), Use of Ultra

Bomber Command Counter-Measures

Use of Ultra by the US War Department

Possibility of the Germans using Gas on the Western Front

Records of Government Departments and Establishments

Cabinet Office: Private Office
  Historical Section
  Enemy Documents Section

JIC: Meetings and Memoranda

UK Atomic Energy Agency

B. UNPUBLISHED PRIVATE PAPERS

G Bloch, Enigma avant Ultra

Sir A Cadogan, Diaries and Papers 1909–66
(Archives of Churchill College, Cambridge)

N Chamberlain, Papers
(Library of Birmingham University)

Group-Captain M G Christie, Correspondence and Reports
(Archives of Churchill College, Cambridge)

Hugh Dalton, Diary
(Library of the London School of Economics)

Major-General F H N Davidson, Papers
(King's College, London)

Captain H M Denham RN, Memoirs, papers, correspondence re his time
as Naval Attaché Stockholm 1940–45
(Archives of Churchill College, Cambridge)

Vice-Admiral Denning, Account of the PQ 17 Convoy
(Archives of Churchill College, Cambridge under ref ROSK 5/72)

A G Denniston, Papers on codebreaking in World War I and World War
II 1914–79
(Archives of Churchill College, Cambridge)

Admiral J H Godfrey, Memoirs
(Archives of Churchill College, Cambridge and National Maritime
Museum, Greenwich)

Lord Hankey, Official and personal papers 1890–1963
(Archives of Churchill College, Cambridge)

D McLachlan and P Beesly, Material for works on Naval Intelligence
(Archives of Churchill College, Cambridge)

Lt Gen Sir H R Pownall, Diaries
(Archives of Churchill College, Cambridge)

Air Chief Marshal Sir J Robb, Papers
(RAF Museum, Hendon)

Lord Templewood, Papers
(Library of the University of Cambridge)

Lord Vansittart, Papers 1930–45
(Archives of Churchill College, Cambridge)

C. PUBLICATIONS

(i) Official Histories

British

J R M Butler, *Grand Strategy* Vol II (1957)

B Collier, *The Defence of the United Kingdom* (1957)

T K Derry, *The Campaign in Norway* (1952)

J Ehrman, *Grand Strategy* Vol V (1956), Vol VI (1956)

L F Ellis, *The War in France and Flanders 1939–40* (1954)
      Victory in the West Vol I (1962), Vol II (1968)

M R D Foot, *SOE in France* (1966)

M Gowing, *Britain and Atomic Energy* (1964)

J M A Gwyer and J R M Butler, *Grand Strategy* Vol III, Parts 1 and 2
      (1964)

F H H Hinsley and CAG Simkins, *Security and Counter-Intelligence* (forth-
      coming)

M Howard, *Grand Strategy* Vol IV (1972)
      Strategic Deception (forthcoming)

General Sir W Jackson, *The Mediterranean and Middle East*, Vol VI Part 2
      (1987), Part 3 (forthcoming)

W N Medlicott, *The Economic Blockade*, Vol I (1952), Vol II (1959)

Brigadier C J C Molony, *The Mediterranean and Middle East*, Vol V (1973),
      Vol VI part 1 (1984)

Major-General I S O Playfair, *The Mediterranean and Middle East*, Vol I
      (1954), Vol II (1956), Vol III (1960), Vol IV (1966)

M M Postan, D Hay and J D Scott, *Design and Development of Weapons*
      (1964)

Captain S W Roskill RN, *The War at Sea* Vol I (1954), Vol II (1957), Vol
      III Part 1 (1960), Part 2 (1961)

Sir C Webster and N Frankland, *The Strategic Air Offensive* 4 volumes
      (1961)

Sir L Woodward, *British Foreign Policy in the Second World War* Vol I
      (1970), Vol II (1971), Vol III (1971), Vol IV (1976)

American

M Blumenson, *Breakout and Pursuit* (Washington DC, 1961)
      Salerno to Cassino (Washington DC, 1969)

R C Cochrane, *Biological Warfare Research in the United States* (History of
      the Chemical Warfare Service in World War II, November 1947)

H M Cole, *The Lorraine Campaign* (Washington DC, 1950)
      The Ardennes: Battle of the Bulge (Washington DC, 1965)

W F Craven and J L Cate, *The Army Air Forces in World War II* Vol II
      (Chicago, 1949), Vol III (Chicago, 1951)

E J Fisher, *Cassino to the Alps* (Washington DC, 1977)

A Garland and H Smyth, *Sicily and the Surrender of Italy* (Washington DC,
      1965)

G A Harrison, *Cross Channel Attack* (Washington DC, 1951)

R G Hewlett and O E Anderson, *The New World 1939–1946* (Vol I of A
      History of the US Atomic Energy Commission (Pennsylvania State
      University Press, 1962))

G F Howe, *North-West Africa: Seizing the Initiative in the West* (Washington
      DC, 1957)

C B MacDonald, *The Siegfried Line Campaign* (Washington DC, 1965)
     The Last Offensive (Washington DC, 1973)

M Matloff and E M Snell, *Strategic Planning for Coalition Warfare 1941–1942* (Washington DC, 1953)

M Matloff, ibid, *1943–1944* (1959)

F C Pogue, *The Supreme Command* (Washington DC, 1954)

US Department of the Army, *The German Campaign in Russia; Planning and Operations* (1955)

US Department of Defense, *Allied Communication Intelligence and the Battle of the Atlantic* (Op-20-G History)

US Special Research History, *Synthesis of Experiences in the Use of Ultra Intelligence by US Army Field Commands in the European Theater of Operations* (SRH-006, declassified 1978)

US Strategic Bombing Survey, *The Effects of Strategic Bombing on the German War Economy* (Synoptic Volume issued by the Overall Economic Effects Division, October 1945)

US War Department History Project, Strategic Services Unit, *War Report of the OSS* (New York, 1976)

Canadian

C P Stacey, *Six Years of War* (Ottawa, 1955)
     The Victory Campaign (Ottawa, 1960)

Australian

G Long, *Australia in the War of 1939–45*
     Series I, Vol 1 *To Benghazi* (Canberra, 1952)
          Vol 2 *Greece, Crete and Syria* (Canberra, 1953)

New Zealand

D M Davin, *History of New Zealand in the Second World War: Crete* (Wellington, 1953)

W G McClymont, ibid: *To Greece* (Wellington, 1959)

(ii) Other Publications

The following list does not aim to be complete. It includes all the items cited in the text except that those of ephemeral interest have been excluded. Items which have appeared since the earlier volumes of the history were published, and which are therefore not cited in the text, have been included but once again only if they are of continuing value.

More comprehensive lists may be found in other bibliographies, for which see Section D below.

Unless otherwise stated all the works listed here are published in the United Kingdom.

G Aders, *History of the German Nightfighter Force* (1979)

C Amort and I M Jedlica, *The Canaris File* (1970)

C M Andrew, 'The British Secret Service and Anglo–Soviet Relations in the 1920s' in *The Historical Journal*, Vol XX (1977), No 3
'More on the Zinoviev Letter' in *The Historical Journal*, Vol XXII (1979)
'British Intelligence and the Breach with Russia in 1927' in *The Historical Journal*, Vol XXV (1982), No 4
Secret Service: The making of the British Intelligence Community (1985)

C M Andrew and D Dilks (eds) *The Missing Dimension: Governments and Intelligence Communities in the Twentieth Century* (1984)

Annals of the History of Computing (Vol 3, No 3 of July 1981)

S Aster, *1939: The Making of the Second World War* (1973)

P Auty and R Clogg (eds), *British Policy towards Wartime Resistance in Yugoslavia* (1975)

C Babington Smith, *Evidence in Camera* (1958)

E Barker, *British Policy in south-east Europe in the Second World War* (1976)

R Barker, *Aviator Extraordinary: The Sidney Cotton Story* (1969)

P Beesly, *Very Special Intelligence* (1977)

J Beevor, *SOE: Recollections and Reflections 1940–1945* (1981)

H-O Behrendt, *Rommels Kenntnis vom Feind in Afrikafeldzug* (Freiburg, 1980) English translation, *Rommel's Intelligence in the Desert Campaign* (1985)

R Bennett, *Ultra in the West* (1979)

G Bertrand, *Enigma ou la plus grande Enigme de la Guerre* (Paris, 1973)

G Bloch, 'La Contribution française à la Reconstruction et au Décryptement de l'Enigma militaire allemande en 1931–1932' in *Revue Historique des Armées*, No 4, December 1985

D G Boadle, Dissertation on Sir Robert Vansittart (Library of the University of Cambridge)

C Bohlen, *Witness to History 1929–1969* (1973)

H Bonatz, *Seekrieg in Äther* (Herford, 1981)

B Bond (ed), *Chief of Staff: The Pownall Diaries* Vol 1 (1972)

O Bradley, *A Soldier's Story* (1951)

D Brown, *Tirpitz: the Floating Fortress* (1977)

D B Bussey, 'Protecting the Ultimate Advantage' in *Military History* (Herndon, Va), June 1985

H C Butcher, *Three Years with Eisenhower* (1946)

P Calvocoressi, *Top Secret Ultra* (1980)

B A Carroll, *Design for Total War* (Mouton 1968)

M Carver, *El Alamein* (1962)
        Tobruk (1964)

W S Churchill, *The Second World War* (6 vols 1948–1954)

E Clayton, *The Enemy is Listening* (1980)

I Colvin, *Vansittart in Office* (1965)

T P Conwell-Evans, *None so Blind* (1957)

M van Creveld, *Hitler's Strategy: The Balkan Clue 1940–41* (1974)

C G Cruickshank, *The Fourth Arm: Psychological Warfare 1938–45* (1977)
    Deception in World War II (1979)

Cryptologia, Vol 6 (1982), No 1 (Terre Haute, Indiana)

Admiral Lord Cunningham, *A Sailor's Odyssey* (1951)

A G Denniston, 'The Government Code and Cypher School between the
  Wars' in *Intelligence and National Security*, Vol 1, (1986) No 1

C D'Este, *Decision in Normandy* (1983)

H Deutsch, *The Conspiracy against Hitler in the Twilight War* (1968)

D Dilks (ed), *The Diaries of Sir Alexander Cadogan* (1971)

W Dornberger, *V2* (English edn 1954)

A W Dulles, *The Secret Surrender* (1967)
    Germany's Underground (1978 reprint)

General D D Eisenhower, *Crusade in Europe* (1946)

J Erickson, *The Road to Stalingrad* (1975)
    The Road to Berlin (1983)

N E Evans, 'Air Intelligence and the Coventry Raid' in *RUSI Journal*,
  September 1976

J Ferris, 'Whitehall's Black Chamber: British Cryptology and the
  Government Code and Cypher School 1919–1929' in *Intelligence
  and National Security*, Vol II (1987) No 1.

M R D Foot, *Resistance: an Analysis of European Resistance to Nazism
  1940–45* (1976)

M R D Foot and J M Langley, *MI 9: Escape and Evasion* (1979)

J Garlinski, *Hitler's Last Weapons* (1978)
    Intercept: Secrets of the Enigma War (1979)

M Gauché, *Le Deuxième Bureau au Travail* (Paris, 1953)

M Gilbert, *Winston S Churchill* Vol V (1976), Vol VI (1983), Vol VII (1986)

I J Good, 'Pioneering work on computers at Bletchley' in N Metropolis
  (ed), *A history of computing in the 20th century* (New York, 1980)

G O Gorodetsky, *Stafford Cripps' Mission to Moscow 1940–42* (1984)

S A Goudsmit, *Alsos: the Failure in German Science* (1947)

L R Groves, *Now it can be told* (1963)

F de Guingand, *Operation Victory* (1964)
    From Brasshat to Bowler (1979)

J Harvey (ed), *The Harvey Diaries* (1970)

M Hastings, *Overlord: D-day and the Battle for Normandy* (1984)

J Haswell, *The Intelligence and Deception of the D-day Landings* (1979)

A Hodges, *Alan Turing: the Enigma* (1983)

P Hoffmann, *The History of the German Resistance 1933–1945* (English edn
1977)

D Hunt, *A Don at War* (1966)

D Irving, *The Mare's Nest* (1964)
    The Virus House (1967)
    The Rise and Fall of the Luftwaffe (1974)

B Johnson, *The Secret War* (1978)

R V Jones, *Most Secret War* (1978)

D Kahn, *The Codebreakers: the Story of Secret Writing* (1967)
'Codebreaking in World War I and II' in *The Historical Journal,* Vol XXIII (1980) No 3

B H Klein, *Germany's Economic Preparations for War* (Harvard, 1959)

W Kozaczuk, *Bitwa o tajemnice. Sluzby wywiadowcze Polski i Rzeszy Niemieckiej 1922–1939 (The Battle of Secrets. The Intelligence Services of Poland and the German Reich 1922–1939)* (Warsaw, 1967)
'The Key to the Secrets of the Third Reich' in *Poland* Nos 6 and 7 (Warsaw, 1975)
Enigma: How the German machine cipher was broken, and how it was read by the Allies in World War Two (Polish edn 1979; transl. University Publications of America, 1984)

R Langhorne (ed), *Diplomacy and Intelligence during the Second World War: Essays in honour of F H Hinsley* (1985)

B Leach, *German Strategy against Russia 1939–1941* (1973)

R Lewin, *Ultra goes to War* (1978)
The American Magic (1982)

B H Liddell Hart, *History of the Second World War* (1970)

General U Liss, *Westfront 1939–40* (Neckargemund, 1959)

N Longmate, *The Doodlebugs* (1980)
Hitler's Rockets (1985)

C B MacDonald, *The Battle of the Bulge* (1984)

R Manvell and H Fränkel, *The Canaris Conspiracy* (1969)

A J Marder, *From the Dardanelles to Oran* (1974)
Operation Menace (1976)

G Martelli, *Agent Extraordinary* (1966)

J C Masterman, *The Double Cross System* (1968)

D McLachlan, *Room 39* (1968)

M Middlebrook, *The Nuremberg Raid* (1975)
Convoy (1976)

K Middlemass, *Diplomacy of Illusion* (1972)

P S Milner-Barry, 'Action This Day: The letter from Bletchley Park cryptanalysts to the Prime Minister, 21 October 1941' in *Intelligence and National Security*, Vol 1, (1986), No 2

A S Milward, *The German Economy at War* (1965)
War, Economy and Society 1939–1945 (1977)

R G Minott, *The Fortress that never was* (1965)

E Montagu, *Beyond Top Secret U* (1977)

Field Marshal Lord Montgomery, *El Alamein to the River Sangro* (1949)
Memoirs (1958)

F Moravec, *Master of Spies* (1975)

F Morgan, *Overture to Overlord* (1950)

General B H Müller-Hillebrand, *Das Heer 1933–1945*, Vol I (Darmstadt, 1954) Vols II and III (Frankfurt/Main, 1956, 1969)

P Paillole, *Services Spéciaux* (Paris, 1975)
   Notre Espion chez Hitler (Paris, 1985)

B A H Parritt, *The Intelligencers* (privately printed)

A Price, *Instruments of Darkness* (1977)
   Luftwaffe Handbook (1977)

B Randell, 'The Colossus' in N Metropolis (ed), *A history of computing in the 20th century* (New York, 1980)

M Rejewski, 'A Conversation', 'Summary of our Methods for reconstructing Enigma and reconstructing daily keys and of German efforts to frustrate those methods', 'How the Polish Mathematicians broke Enigma', and 'The mathematical Solution of the Enigma Cypher' in Kozaczuk, *Enigma: How the German machine cypher was broken and how it was read by the Allies in World War II* (transl. 1984) Appendices B to E.

D Richards and H Saunders, *The Royal Air Force 1939–1945* (3 vols 1953–1954)

G Ritter, *The German Resistance* (1958)

J Rohwer, *The Critical Convoy Battles of March 1943* (1977)
   ' "Special Intelligence" und die Geleitzugsteuering in Herbst 1941' in *Marine Rundschau*, November 1978
   'Die Einfluss der allierten Funkaufklärung auf den Verlauf des Zweiten Weltkrieges' in *Vierteljahrshefte für Zeitgeschichte*, Heft 3 1979

J Rohwer and P Beesly, ' "Special Intelligence" und die Vernichtung der "Scharnhorst" ' in *Marine Rundschau*, October 1977

J Rohwer and E Jäckel, *Die Funkauflkärung und ihre Rolle im Zweiten Weltkrieg* (Stuttgart, 1979)

W W Rostow, *Pre-Invasion Bombing Strategy* (Texas, 1981)

C Ryan, *A Bridge Too Far* (1974)

A Seaton, *The Russo–German War 1941–45* (1971)

B F Smith, 'Admiral Godfrey's Mission to America, June/July 1941' in *Intelligence and National Security*, Vol 1 (1986), No 3

A Speer, *Inside the Third Reich* (1971)

D Stafford, *Britain and European Resistance 1940–1945* (1981)

J Stengers, 'Enigma, the French, the Poles and the British 1931–1940' in C M Andrew and D Dilks (eds) *The Missing Dimension* (1984)

Stockholm International Peace Research Institute (SIPRI), *The Problems of Chemical and Biological Warfare* Vol 1, (1971)

Major-General K W D Strong, *Intelligence at the Top* (1968)
   Men of Intelligence (1970)

D Synett, 'German Meteorological Intelligence from the Arctic and North Atlantic' in *Mariner's Mirror*, August 1985

J Terraine, *The Right of the Line* (1985)

W K Wark, *The Ultimate Enemy: British Intelligence and Nazi Germany 1933–39* (1985)

G Warner, *Iraq and Syria* (1974)

G Welchman, *The Hut Six Story* (1982)
> 'From Polish Bomba to British Bombe: the Birth of Ultra' in *Intelligence and National Security*, Vol 1 (1986) No 1

A R Wells, *Studies in British Naval Intelligence 1880–1945* (University of London Dissertation) 1972

B Whaley, *Codeword Barbarossa* (1973)

M Wheeler, *Britain and the War for Yugoslavia* (1980)

Field Marshal Lord Wilson, *Eight Years Overseas* (1948)

F W Winterbotham, *Secret and Personal* (1969)
> *The Ultra Secret* (1974)

R Wohlstetter, *Pearl Harbor: Warning and Decision* (1962)

H Wynn and S Young, *Prelude to Overlord* (1983)

A P Young, *The 'X' Documents* (1974)

D. BIBLIOGRAPHIES

G C Constantinides, *Intelligence and Espionage: an analytical bibliography* (Boulder, Col 1983)

A G S Enser, *A Subject Bibliography of the Second World War: Books in English 1939–1974* (Deutsch 1977); 1975–1983 (Gower 1985)

W Pforzheimer (ed), *Bibliography of Intelligence Literature* (Eighth edn 1985)

Scholar's Guide to Intelligence Literature; Bibliography of the Russell J Bowen Collection in the Joseph Mark Lauinger Memorial Library, Georgetown University (Frederick, Md, University Publications of America, Inc, 1983)

Series Prefixes and Delivery Groups used for SCU/SLU Signals to Commands

Series Prefixes	Date of Currency	DEFE 3 Serial Numbers
OL*	14.3.41 to 19.11.41	DEFE 3/686–690, 892, 894
KOT	March 1941 to 23.4.41	DEFE 3/891
MK	20.11.41 to 23.7.42	DEFE 3/745–764
MKA	23.7.42 to 25.8.42	DEFE 3/766–771
QT	25.8.42 to 31.12.42	DEFE 3/772–791
PK	4.11.42 to 25.11.42	DEFE 3/897
VM	31.12.42 to 21.4.43	DEFE 3/792–811
ML	21.4.43 to 5.8 43	DEFE 3/812–831
JP	5.8.43 to 18.11.43	DEFE 3/871–890
VL	18.11.43 to 1.4.44	DEFE 3/5–19, 129–152, 765
KV	1.4.44 to 28.6.44	DEFE 3/35–47, 153–179
XL	29.6.44 to 13.9.44	DEFE 3/48–65, 112–128, 220–224
HP	13.9.44 to 21.12.44	DEFE 3/225–244, 300–319
BT	21.12.44 to 9.4.45	DEFE 3/320–331, 500–520, 561–564, 599–601
KO	9.4.45 to 15.5.45	DEFE 3/565–572

The above digraphs represent the main series of signals to Commands. Within them, the delivery groups in the following lists denote the individual recipients of Ultra material.

Delivery Groups

1. MEDITERRANEAN COMMANDS

Beginning March 1941:

BA	British Troops Greece (viz General Wilson)
GQ	GHQ (British Military Attaché) Greece (viz Athens)
MB	BMA Belgrade (British Military Attaché)
CO	Cairo†

---

* This digraph was also used for a short period on signals sent to General Freyberg in Crete.

† Initially for Director CBME for passing to Navy, Army and RAF HQs, as appropriate. Later supplemented by such delivery groups as AL and WD.

By autumn 1941:

AL	Naval HQ Alexandria; later for AFHQ (Allied Force HQ)
MA	Malta for AHQ (Air HQ); later for VAM (Vice Admiral in Charge) and AOC
WD*	C-in-C Eighth Army and for DAF (Desert Air Force) when co-located

March 1942:

NC	Naval Co-operation Wing, Alexandria (service via AL), followed by
NCA	Advanced HQ Naval Co-operation Wing, Benghazi

September 1942:

SM	Captain (Submarines), Beirut

By April 1943:

LM	MAC (Mediterranean Air Command) Tunis, La Marsa
SB	General Alexander (15th Army Group at Tunis, Sidi bou Said, and later (October 1943) at Bari)
BI	AOC Coastal Air Force, Bizerta
ZU	HQ Eighth Army, Zuara (later Sicily)
DB	FOCNA (Flag Officer Commanding North Atlantic) and AOC Gibraltar (from April 1943)

During summer 1943:

OR	HQ Seventh Army (Sicily)
KQ	Fifth Army (Salerno)
TR	242 Group and FOTALI (Flag Officer Taranto, Adriatic and Liaison (Italy)), Taranto
JY	US Fifteenth Air Force, Bari

By the end of 1943 signals were being sent to the following Commands:–

AL (Alexandria)	C-in-C Levant
BI (Bastia)	63 Fighter Wing; Light Coastal Forces; 328 Wing
CO (Cairo)	GHQ ME; AHQ ME
DB (Gibraltar)	FOCNA; AOC

---

* During July 1942 this delivery group also served General Auchinleck's forward tactical HQ. Other Army commanders established similar arrangements for their tactical HQs throughout later campaigns.

JY (Bari)	NASAF (North-West African Strategic Air Force)
LM (La Marsa)	AFHQ Command Post; MAAF (Mediterranean Allied Air Forces)
MA (Malta)	VAM; AOC
NC (Alexandria)	201 Group
NCA (Benghazi)	247 Group
SB (Bari)	15th Army Group; NATAF (North-West African Tactical Air Force)
SM (Beirut)	1st Sub Flotilla
TR (Taranto)	242 Group (Coastal); Light Coastal Forces
ZU, ZUA (Vasto)	Eighth Army HQ: Eighth Army Air Force

2. WESTERN FRONT COMMANDS

From January 1944 the supply of Ultra to Western Commands was arranged to the following recipients:

SH   SHAEF (Supreme HQ Allied Expeditionary Force), Norfolk House
AG* 21st Army Group, St Paul's School
ST   USSAFE (US Strategic Air Forces in Europe), Bushy Park
EF   AEAF (Allied Expeditionary Air Force), Stanmore
TA* 2nd TAF (Tactical Air Force), Uxbridge
XF   ANCXF (Allied Naval Commander Expeditionary Force), Portsmouth, and later in France and Germany

3. By the end of the war the following delivery groups had come into use:

MEDITERRANEAN COMMANDS

AL (Alexandria)	FOLEM (Flag Officer Levant and Eastern Mediterranean); AHQ East Med
CO (Cairo)	RN HQ; GHQ ME; HQ RAF ME; 'A' Force (Deception Authorities)
DB (Gibraltar)	FOGMA (Flag Officer Gibraltar and Mediterranean Approaches); C-in-C; AOC
HS, HSA (Marocco)	Eighth Army; DAF; TAC HQ DAF
JY (Bari)	US Fifteenth Air Force
KQ (Verona)	Fifteenth Army HQ; XXII TAC
LE (Leghorn)	FONAM (Flag Officer North Africa and Mediterranean); 338 Wing

---

* 21st Army Group and 2nd TAF were later served by the single delivery group TG.

NA (Naples)	FONAM
OW (Algiers)	FOWM (Flag Officer Western Mediterranean); 210 Coastal Group
RJ (Bari)	BAF (Balkans Air Force); Special Ops Med; Land Forces Adriatic
SB (Florence)	15th Army Group
TR (Taranto)	FOTALI; 242 Coastal Group
WZ (Ancona)	SNONA (Senior Naval Officer North Adriatic); 287 Wing

WESTERN COMMANDS

AD (Stanmore)	Fighter Command
CR (NE Delden)	First Canadian Army; 84 Group
DL (Wycombe Abbey)	US Eighth Air Force
EFR (Stanmore)	AEAF (Rear)
FZ (Augsburg)	Seventh US Army; XII TAC
GU (Maisons-Laffitte)	First Allied Airborne Army
LF (Heidelberg)	6th US Army Group; 1st TAF: 'A' Force
MI (High Wycombe)	Bomber Command
NX (Wiesbaden)	US Ninth Air Force
ON, ONA (Lüneburg)	Second British Army; 83 Group
QX, QXA (Brunswick)	Ninth US Army; XXIX TAC
SH (Rheims)	SHAEF
SHR (Versailles)	SHAEF (Rear)
ST (St Germain)	USSAFE (Main)
STA (Rheims)	USSAFE (Advanced)
STR (Bryanston Sq)	USSTAF (Rear)
TG (Süchtein)	21st Army Group; 2nd TAF
TGA (S of Lüneburg)	21st Army Group TAC
UC (Bad Neuenahr)	Fifteenth US Army
WA (Washington)	G2 British Missions
WM (Bad Wildungen)	12th US Army Group; 'A' Force
XF (St Germain)	ANCXF
YK, YKA (Weimar)	First US Army; IX TAC
ZE (Regensburg)	Third US Army
ZEA (Erlangen)	XIX TAC

Index